Contents

Acknowledgements 4

Introductions 6

The British Hit Singles 1952—1980:

PART 1 Alphabetically by Artist 9

About 3000 chart acts listed alphabetically with chronological title list showing date disc first hit the chart, title, label, catalogue number, highest position reached, number of weeks on chart. Top ten placings and number ones highlighted.

PART 2 Alphabetically by Title 237

Approximately 9000 hits listed alphabetically by title with artists' names and year of initial chart entry. Different versions of the same song are indicated.

PART 3 Facts and Feats 281

Including:
Most weeks on chart
Most hits
The number one hits
Straight in at number one
Biggest jump to number one
The 'unsuccessful' number two hits
Least successful chart act

INTRODUCTIONS

If You Wanna Be Happy, I Believe, The Best You Can Do is *Keep On*, reading this book.

Do You Remember, Rock 'n' Roll (Parts I & II), Reggae Like It Used To Be, or *Sweet Soul Music, Who Was It* played *Rhythm And Greens* or *The Story Of The Blues*?

Um Um Um Um Um Um. Ain't Got A Clue, Who Put The Bomp in *Our Favourite Melodies*.

The answers are in this book. Between the covers you will meet the Elvises, Presley, Costello and *There's A Guy Works Down The Chip Shop*. There's the Lees, Brenda, Leapy and Hazelwood, the Brothers Doobie, Righteous and Everly and Sisters Kaye, Sledge and Beverley. The Yellow Magic, Electric Light, Tommy Dorsey and Royal Philharmonic Orchestras are all here, along with Roy C, Vicky D, M and Miss X. *Say Hello Wave Goodbye* to *Mother-In-Law, Daddy Cool, Sister Jane, Brother Louie, Cousin Norman* and *Grandad. Don't Forget To Remember Fat Bottomed Girls, Fanlight Fanny* and *Me and Mrs Jones. Take Your Mama For A Ride* to *Pasadena, Baker Street, Rio* and *Nairobi* on *Trains And Boats And Planes, Ships In The Night* or a *Big Yellow Taxi*.

Nevertheless Don't Let Me Be Misunderstood. You See The Trouble With Me, I Want More Money Money Money. Ain't Too Proud To Beg.

So please buy at least two copies of this book.

JO RICE

I first saw 45 r.p.m. records at a neighbour's home two houses down the street. It was rather a daring expedition, almost a 'come up and see my etchings' job, but the prospect of actually seeing two of the songs I had heard on the radio cast fear to the wind. Bobby S., at fourteen twice my age and the street tough, boasted that he had copies of 'Party Doll' by Buddy Knox and 'Gone' by Ferlin Husky. When he showed these precious objects to me, he was no longer full of bravado but rather imbued with the sense of wonder that filled every early rock 'n roll fan. Alas, a couple of years later, when I was old enough to have gotten my own copies of 'Party Doll' and 'Gone', Bobby was doing time for interstate car theft.

There are other singles I treasure as if they were parts of my own body (though I clean them less frequently). 'Lisa' by Ferrante and Teicher wasn't a hit, but it was performed by my childhood piano playing idols. They were having hit instrumentals while I was taking lessons, and this was enough to make me pilgrimage to Barker's discount store on US 1 to get their autographs on their then-new single. This remains the only time I have ever asked a celebrity to sign a record sleeve. Who is there after Ferrante and Teicher? (In this book, Jose Ferrer, and I am certainly not interested in *his* musicianship.)

'Hey Jude' by the Beatles was number one for seven weeks on my first radio station, WDCR in Hanover, New Hampshire. I counted down the brand new Tri-Town Top Twenty-Five every Monday afternoon at three, and grew quite accustomed to putting on 'Hey Jude' at 4:52. One day an engineer named John Russell burst into the studio and blurted out 'They've changed the teaching of mathematics at Hanover High! From now on, instead of having the kids learn to count "one-two-three", they're teaching them " 'Hey Jude'-two-three." ' I could never figure out if this remark was abstruse or obtuse. Regardless, it is the only thing I recall John Russell ever saying.

I still have my original copy of 'Anarchy in the U.K.' by the Sex Pistols in the clear plastic sleeve. I shiver thinking how, caught in the excitement of an emerging major group, I played this platter for my softball team at a party. It temporarily stopped the merrymaking stone dead, and the focus of attention turned to slagging off the record. One would think the children of rock 'n' roll, who encountered their own parents' opposition to new music, might be careful not to make the same antagonistic mistake now they were adults. No way. It is likely that the punk generation, mohican haircuts or no, will deride their offspring's music in 2000.

This is the fourth edition of our biennial *Hit Singles*. We hope we'll still be around in 2000, or, to be more precise with our publishing schedule, 2001. For now, I hope your most fondly remembered singles are included in both this book and your collection. Memories, memories. We all have them. Records, records. If only we had them all!

PAUL GAMBACCINI

In late 1957 I purchased a copy of the Crickets' *That'll Be The Day*. This was not the first single I had bought but it was a deeply significant investment because it was my first forty-five. My previous trips to the St. Albans record shops had always ended with ten inches rather than seven – ever since *Singing The Blues* (the Tommy Steele version) way back at the beginning of '57 I had stuck rigidly to the 78 r.p.m. format.

On the bus home Tony Watkins informed me with great authority that I had wasted my six shillings as the 45 r.p.m. disc would never catch on. I seem to remember that the main thrust of his argument was that the middle bit of these new-fangled platters would fall out after a mere couple of plays. I was not 100 % confident as I attempted to defend my reckless action, but one thought sustained me through those dark hours of doubt – if I had purchased *All Shook Up* as a forty-five that July I would still have an Elvis disc in my collection despite Ian Brown's sister sitting on it in October.

As things turned out of course, Tony was wrong and I was right. He was converted and went on to buy nearly everything the Everly Brothers ever recorded – as forty-fives, but I refused to gloat (after all the man had good taste) and our friendship survived the clash of speeds. Furthermore our middles never came out.

Since 1957 nothing has cured me of my addiction to records, and to singles in particular. I fear now that nothing ever will. Pop music appeals to nearly all adolescents of all generations, but at the age of around eighteen, the sheep and the goats get separated. Some relegate pop music to a background role in their lives but others just carry on wanting – nay, needing – to hear and know all there is to know about records and their insatiable thirst for information by then has extended to much more than the singer and the song. I was one of the latter breed. I knew that my brother was another but little did I know that far away in Connecticut and Walton-on-Thames there were two other goats in Paul Gambaccini and Mike Read (known as Mic to his friends – hi there, Mike) whose passion for records would eventually lead to an inextricable twining of their lives with the Rice brothers.

But there also have been good things to come out of my love for records and I hope that fellow fanatics will agree that the GRRR/Guinness books have been some of them. In the meantime I am still buying singles with manic enthusiasm and even have a standing order with my local record shop in Thame to buy every single that makes the Top 75. (It's not a chart return shop, record companies, but anyway my scorched earth policy of buying everything presumably has no effect on the chart at all, helping every disc equally). And the wheel has come full circle for I am now re-collecting 78 r.p.m. records. I have over 1000 and have even got hold of *All Shook Up* again. I am keeping it away from Ian Brown's sister.

TIM RICE

The Hit Singles Rap

The Singing Dogs, The Nashville Cats,
The Mockingbirds and the Rat Trap Rats.
In Sugar Town and Mexico
They're Lookin' High and Swingin' Low
For Mona Lisa and My Frend Stan,
Robin Hood and Mary Anne.
On Engine Engine Number Nine
You never get Tired Of Toein' The Line.

Sailing, Walking, Drivin' Home.
On Echo Beach Like A Rolling Stone.
When Zorba Danced The Spanish Stroll
And Johnny Reggae'd to Rock 'n' Roll.
Where Emily Played Down Tobacco Road
With The Runaway Boys and the Highway Code.
Every Ruby Tuesday Happy Jack's
In The Hong Kong Garden Sugar Shack.

Here Comes The Judge so Stand By Me.
Through the Green Door with a Brand New Key,
We'll Run For Home for the House of Fun
By The Silvery Moon and The Rising Sun.
No Milk Today just Red, Red Wine
Blowin' In The Windmills Of Your Mind.
From The Milky Way to Planet Earth
The Singles Rap For What It's Worth . . .

MIKE READ

PART 1

The British Hit Singles: Alphabetically by Artist

The information given in this part of the book is as follows: Date disc first hit the chart, title, label, catalogue number, highest position reached on chart, number of weeks on the chart. Number one records are highlighted with a red star, other top ten records by a black dot and a black dagger indicates hits still on chart at 31 December 1982, as follows:

★ **Number one single**

● **Top ten single**

† **Single still on chart at 31 December 1982**

For the purposes of this book, a record is considered a re-issue if it hits the chart for a second time with a new catalogue number. Otherwise the re-appearance of any record is considered a mere re-entry.

Describing a recording act in one sentence is often fraught with danger, but we have attempted to do so above each act's list of hits. Although we are aware that many of the 'vocalists' thus described also play an instrument, we have only mentioned this fact where the artist's instrumental skills were an important factor in the record's success.

ABBA *Sweden, male/female vocal/instrumental group*

Date		Title *Label Number*	Position	Weeks
20 Apr 74	★	**WATERLOO** *Epic EPC 2240*	**1**	9 wks
13 Jul 74		**RING RING** *Epic EPC 2452*	**32**	5 wks
12 Jul 75		**I DO I DO I DO I DO I DO** *Epic EPC 3229*	**38**	6 wks
20 Sep 75	●	**S. O. S.** *Epic EPC 3576*	**6**	10 wks
13 Dec 75	★	**MAMMA MIA** *Epic EPC 3790*	**1**	14 wks
27 Mar 76	★	**FERNANDO** *Epic EPC 4036*	**1**	15 wks
21 Aug 76	★	**DANCING QUEEN** *Epic EPC 4499*	**1**	15 wks
20 Nov 76	●	**MONEY MONEY MONEY** *Epic EPC 4713*	**3**	12 wks
26 Feb 77	★	**KNOWING ME KNOWING YOU** *Epic EPC 4955*	**1**	13 wks
22 Oct 77	★	**THE NAME OF THE GAME** *Epic EPC 5750*	**1**	12 wks
4 Feb 78	★	**TAKE A CHANCE ON ME** *Epic EPC 5950*	**1**	10 wks
16 Sep 78	●	**SUMMER NIGHT CITY** *Epic EPC 6595*	**5**	9 wks
3 Feb 79	●	**CHIQUITITA** *Epic EPC 7030*	**2**	9 wks
5 May 79	●	**DOES YOUR MOTHER KNOW** *Epic EPC 7316*	**4**	9 wks
14 Jul 79	●	**ANGELEYES/VOULEZ-VOUS** *Epic EPC 7499*	**3**	11 wks
20 Oct 79	●	**GIMME GIMME GIMME (A MAN AFTER MIDNIGHT)** *Epic EPC 7914*	**3**	12 wks
15 Dec 79	●	**I HAVE A DREAM** *Epic EPC 8088*	**2**	10 wks
2 Aug 80	★	**THE WINNER TAKES IT ALL** *Epic EPC 8835*	**1**	10 wks
15 Nov 80	★	**SUPER TROUPER** *Epic EPC 9089*	**1**	12 wks
18 Jul 81	●	**LAY ALL YOUR LOVE ON ME** *Epic EPCA 1456*	**7**	7 wks
11 Dec 81	●	**ONE OF US** *Epic EPCA 1740*	**3**	10 wks
20 feb 82		**HEAD OVER HEELS** *Epic EPC A 2037*	**25**	7 wks
23 Oct 82		**THE DAY BEFORE YOU CAME** *Epic EPC A 2847*	**32**	6 wks
11 Dec 82		**UNDER ATTACK** *Epic EPC A 2971*	**26†**	wks

Russ ABBOTT *UK, male vocalist*

Date		Title *Label Number*	Position	Weeks
6 Feb 82		**A DAY IN THE LIFE OF VINCE PRINCE** *EMI 5249*	**61**	1 wk
20 Feb 82		**A DAY IN THE LIFE OF VINCE PRINCE** (re-entry) *EMI 5249*	**75**	1 wk

ABC *UK, male vocal/instrumental group*

Date		Title *Label Number*	Position	Weeks
31 Oct 81		**TEARS ARE NOT ENOUGH** *Neutron NT 101*	**19**	8 wks
20 Feb 82	●	**POISON ARROW** *Neutron/Phonogram NT 102*	**6**	11 wks
15 May 82	●	**THE LOOK OF LOVE** *Neutron/Phonogram NT 103*	**4**	11 wks
4 Sep 82	●	**ALL OF MY HEART** *Neutron/Phonogram NT 104*	**5**	8 wks

Mike D'ABO — See *MANFRED MANN*

Father ABRAHAM and the SMURFS

Holland, male vocalist as himself and Smurfs

Date		Title *Label Number*	Position	Weeks
3 Jun 78	●	**THE SMURF SONG** *Decca F 13759*	**2**	17 wks
30 Sep 78		**DIPPETY DAY** *Decca F 13798*	**13**	12 wks
2 Dec 78		**CHRISTMAS IN SMURFLAND** *Decca F 13819*	**19**	7 wks

Father ABRAPHART and the SMURPS

UK, male vocal group (Jonathan King under an assumed name)

Date		Title *Label Number*	Position	Weeks
16 Dec 78		**LICK A SMURP FOR CHRISTMAS (ALL FALL DOWN)** *Petrol GAS 1*	**58**	4 wks

Hit transferred to Magnet MAG 139 after first week on chart. See also Jonathan King.

AC/DC *Australia/UK, male vocal/instrumental group*

Date		Title *Label Number*	Position	Weeks
10 Jun 78		**ROCK 'N' ROLL DAMNATION** *Atlantic K 11142*	**24**	9 wks
1 Sep 79		**HIGHWAY TO HELL** *Atlantic K 11321*	**56**	4 wks
2 Feb 80		**TOUCH TOO MUCH** *Atlantic K 11435*	**29**	9 wks
28 Jun 80		**DIRTY DEEDS DONE DIRT CHEAP** *Atlantic HM 2*	**47**	3 wks
28 Jun 80		**WHOLE LOTTA ROSIE** *Atlantic HM 4*	**36**	8 wks
28 Jun 80		**HIGH VOLTAGE** (LIVE VERSION) *Atlantic HM 1*	**48**	3 wks
28 Jun 80		**IT'S A LONG WAY TO THE TOP (IF YOU WANNA ROCK'N'ROLL)** *Atlantic HM 3*	**55**	3 wks
13 Sep 80		**YOU SHOOK ME ALL NIGHT LONG** *Atlantic K 11600*	**38**	6 wks
29 Nov 80		**ROCK 'N' ROLL AIN'T NOISE POLLUTION** *Atlantic K 11630*	**15**	8 wks
6 Feb 82		**LET'S GET IT UP** *Atlantic K 11706*	**13**	6 wks
3 Jul 82		**FOR THOSE ABOUT TO ROCK (WE SALUTE YOU)** *Atlantic K 11721*	**15**	6 wks

Group Australia only for first 7 hits.

ACE *UK, male vocal/instrumental group*

Date		Title *Label Number*	Position	Weeks
9 Nov 74		**HOW LONG** *Anchor ANC 1002*	**20**	10 wks

Richard ACE *Jamaica, male vocalist*

Date		Title *Label Number*	Position	Weeks
2 Dec 78		**STAYIN' ALIVE** *Blue Inc. INC 2*	**66**	2 wks

ACES — See *Desmond DEKKER & the ACES*

ACT ONE *US, male/female vocal/instrumental group*

Date		Title *Label Number*	Position	Weeks
18 May 74		**TOM THE PEEPER** *Mercury 6008 005*	**40**	6 wks

ADAM and The ANTS

UK, male vocal/instrumental group

Date		Title *Label Number*	Position	Weeks
2 Aug 80		**KINGS OF THE WILD FRONTIER** *CBS 8877*	**48**	5 wks
11 Oct 80	●	**DOG EAT DOG** *CBS 9039*	**4**	16 wks
6 Dec 80	●	**ANTMUSIC** *CBS 9352*	**2**	wks
27 Dec 80	●	**YOUNG PARISIANS** *Decca F13803*	**9**	wks
24 Jan 81		**ZEROX** *Do It DUN 8*	**45**	9 wks
24 Jan 81		**CAR TROUBLE** *Do It DUN 10*	**33**	9 wks
21 Feb 81	●	**KINGS OF THE WILD FRONTIER** *CBS 8877*	**2**	13 wks
9 May 81	★	**STAND AND DELIVER** (re-entry) *CBS A 1065*	**1**	15 wks
12 Sep 81	★	**PRINCE CHARMING** *CBS A 1408*	**1**	12 wks
12 Dec 81	●	**ANT RAP** *CBS A 1738*	**3**	10 wks
27 Feb 82		**DEUTSCHER GIRLS** *Ego 5*	**13**	6 wks
13 Mar 82		**THE ANTMUSIC EP (THE B-SIDES)** *Do It DUN 20*	**46**	4 wks
22 May 82	★	**GOODY TWO SHOES** *CBS A 2367*	**1**	11 wks
18 Sep 82	●	**FRIEND OR FOE** *CBS A 2736*	**9**	8 wks
27 Nov 82		**DESPERATE BUT NOT SERIOUS** *CBS A 2892*	**33†**	5 wks

Credited as Adam Ant from Goody Two Shoes onwards. Tracks on The Antmusic EP (The B-sides): *Friends, Kick!, Physical.*

Date	Title *Label Number*	Position	

Arthur ADAMS *US, male vocalist*

24 Oct 81	**YOU GOT THE FLOOR** *RCA 146*	**38**	5 wks

Cliff ADAMS *UK, orchestra*

28 Apr 60	**LONELY MAN THEME** *Pye International 7N 25056*	**39**	2 wks

Gayle ADAMS *US, female vocalist*

26 Jul 80	**STRETCHIN' OUT** *Epic EPC 8791*	**64**	1 wk

Marie ADAMS — See *Johnny OTIS Show*

ADDRISI BROTHERS *US, male vocal duo*

6 Oct 79	**GHOST DANCER** *Scotti Brothers K 11361*	**57**	3 wks

ADVERTS *UK, male/female vocal/instrumental group*

27 Aug 77	**GARY GILMORE'S EYES** *Anchor ANC 1043*	**18**	7 wks
4 Feb 78	**NO TIME TO BE 21** *Bright BRI*	**38**	4 wks

AFRICA BAMBAATA and the SOUL SONIC FORCE *US, male instrumental group*

28 Aug 82	**PLANET ROCK** *21/Polydor POSP 497*	**53**	3 wks

AFTER THE FIRE

UK male vocal/instrumental group

9 Jun 79	**ONE RULE FOR YOU** *CBS 7025*	**40**	6 wks
8 Sep 79	**LASER LOVE** *CBS 7769*	**62**	2 wks

AFTERNOON BOYS — See *YOUNG STEVE and the AFTERNOON BOYS*

AIR SUPPLY

Australia, male vocal/instrumental group

27 Sep 80	**ALL OUT OF LOVE** *Arista ARIST 362*	**11**	11 wks
2 Oct 82	**EVEN THE NIGHTS ARE BETTER** *Arista ARIST 474*	**44**	4 wks

Laurel AITKEN and the UNITONE

Jamaica/Cuba, male vocal/instrumental group

17 May 80	**RUDI GOT MARRIED** *I-Spy SEE 6*	**60**	3 wks

Jewel AKENS *US, male vocalist*

25 Mar 65	**THE BIRDS AND THE BEES** *London HLN 9954*	**29**	8 wks

Morris ALBERT *Brazil, male vocalist*

27 Sep 75	● **FEELINGS** *Decca F 13591*	**4**	10 wks

ALBERTO Y LOST TRIOS PARANOIAS

UK, male vocal/instrumental group

23 Sep 78	**HEADS DOWN NO NONSENSE MINDLESS BOOGIE** *Logo GO 323*	**47**	5 wks

ALESSI *US, male vocal duo*

11 Jun 77	● **OH LORI** *A&M AMS 7289*	**8**	11 wks

ALFI and HARRY

US, male, David Seville, under two false names

23 Mar 56	**THE TROUBLE WITH HARRY** *London HLU 8242*	**15**	5 wks

See also David Seville, Chipmunks.

ALL STARS — See *Louis ARMSTRONG*

ALL STARS — See *Junior WALKER and the ALL STARS*

Richard ALLAN *UK, male vocalist*

24 Mar 60	**AS TIME GOES BY** *Parlophone R 4634*	**44**	1 wk

Steve ALLAN *UK, male vocalist*

27 Jan 79	**TOGETHER WE ARE BEAUTIFUL** *Creole CR 164*	**67**	1 wk
10 Feb 79	**TOGETHER WE ARE BEAUTIFUL** (re-entry) *Creole CR 164*	**70**	1 wk

ALLISONS *UK, male vocal duo*

23 Feb 61	● **ARE YOU SURE** *Fontana H 294*	**2**	16 wks
18 May 61	**WORDS** *Fontana H 304*	**34**	5 wks
15 Feb 62	**LESSONS IN LOVE** *Fontana H 362*	**30**	6 wks

ALLNIGHT BAND *UK, male instrumental group*

3 Feb 79	**THE JOKER (THE WIGAN JOKER)** *Casino Classics CC 6*	**50**	3 wks

Herb ALPERT

US, male instrumentalist, trumpet/vocalist

3 Jan 63	**THE LONELY BULL** *Stateside SS 138*	**22**	9 wks
9 Dec 65	● **SPANISH FLEA** *Pye International 7 N 25335*	**3**	20 wks
24 Mar 66	**TIJUANA TAXI** *Pye International 7 N 25352*	**37**	4 wks
27 Apr 67	**CASINO ROYALE** *A & M AMS 700*	**27**	14 wks
3 Jul 68	● **THIS GUY'S IN LOVE WITH YOU** *A & M AMS 727*	**3**	16 wks
26 Mar 69	**THIS GUY'S IN LOVE WITH YOU** (re-entry) *A & M AMS 727*	**47**	1 wk
9 Apr 69	**THIS GUY'S IN LOVE WITH YOU** (2nd re-entry) *A & M AMS 727*	**49**	1 wk
7 May 69	**THIS GUY'S IN LOVE WITH YOU** (3rd re-entry) *A & M AMS 727*	**50**	1 wk
18 Jun 69	**WITHOUT HER** *A & M AMS 755*	**36**	5 wks
12 Dec 70	**JERUSALEM** *A & M AMS 810*	**47**	1 wk

Date	Title *Label Number*	Position	
2 Jan 71	**JERUSALEM** (re-entry) *A & M AMS 810*	**42**	2 wks
13 Oct 79	**RISE** *A & M AMS 7465*	**13**	13 wks
19 Jan 80	**ROTATION** *A & M AMS 7500*	**46**	3 wks

Spanish Flea, Tijuana Taxi, Casino Royale, Without Her *and* Jerusalem *credit Herb Alpert and The Tijuana Brass.* The Lonely Bull *credits only The Tijuana Brass. Alpert vocalises only on* This Guy's in Love with You *and* Without Her.

ALPHABETA — See *Izhar COHEN and ALPHABETA*

ALTERED IMAGES

UK, male/female vocal/instrumental group

Date	Title *Label Number*	Position	
28 Mar 81	**DEAD POP STARS** *Epic EPC A 1023*	**67**	2 wks
26 Sep 81	● **HAPPY BIRTHDAY** *Epic EPC A 1522*	**2**	17 wks
11 Dec 81	● **I COULD BE HAPPY** *Epic EPC A 1834*	**7**	12 wks
27 Mar 82	**SEE THOSE EYES** *Epic EPC A 2198*	**11**	7 wks
22 May 82	**PINKY BLUE** *Epic EPC A 2426*	**35**	6 wks

ALTHIA and DONNA *Jamaica, female vocal duo*

Date	Title *Label Number*	Position	
24 Dec 77	★ **UP TOWN TOP RANKING** *Lightning LIG 506*	**1**	11 wks

AMEN CORNER

UK, male vocal/instrumental group

Date	Title *Label Number*	Position	
26 Jul 67	**GIN HOUSE BLUES** *Deram DM 136*	**12**	10 wks
11 Oct 67	**WORLD OF BROKEN HEARTS** *Deram DM 151*	**26**	6 wks
17 Jan 68	● **BEND ME SHAPE ME** *Deram DM 172*	**3**	12 wks
31 Jul 68	● **HIGH IN THE SKY** *Deram DM 197*	**6**	13 wks
29 Jan 69	★ **(IF PARADISE IS) HALF AS NICE** *Immediate IM 073*	**1**	11 wks
25 Jun 69	● **HELLO SUZIE** *Immediate IM 081*	**4**	10 wks
14 Feb 76	**(IF PARADISE IS) HALF AS NICE** (re-issue) *Immediate IMS 103*	**34**	5 wks

AMERICA *US, male vocal/instrumental group*

Date	Title *Label Number*	Position	
18 Dec 71	**HORSE WITH NO NAME** *Warner Bros. K 16128*	**49**	2 wks
8 Jan 72	● **HORSE WITH NO NAME** (re-entry) *Warner Bros. K 16128*	**3**	11 wks
25 Nov 72	**VENTURA HIGHWAY** *Warner Bros. K 16219*	**43**	4 wks
6 Nov 82	**YOU CAN DO MAGIC** *Capitol CL 264*	**59**	3 wks

AMERICAN BREED

US, male vocal/instrumental group

Date	Title *Label Number*	Position	
7 Feb 68	**BEND ME SHAPE ME** *Stateside SS 2078*	**24**	6 wks

AMES BROTHERS *US, male vocal group*

Date	Title *Label Number*	Position	
4 Feb 55	● **NAUGHTY LADY OF SHADY LANE** *HMV B 10800*	**6**	6 wks

Laurie ANDERSON

US, female vocalist/instrumentalist, keyboards

Date	Title *Label Number*	Position	
17 Oct 81	● **O SUPERMAN** *Warner Bros. K 17870*	**2**	6 wks

Leroy ANDERSON *US, orchestra*

Date	Title *Label Number*	Position	
28 Jun 57	**FORGOTTEN DREAMS** *Brunswick 05485*	**28**	1 wk
12 Jul 57	**FORGOTTEN DREAMS** (re-entry) *Brunswick 05485*	**30**	1 wk
6 Sep 57	**FORGOTTEN DREAMS** (2nd re-entry) *Brunswick 05485*	**24**	2 wks

Lynn ANDERSON *US, female vocalist*

Date	Title *Label Number*	Position	
20 Feb 71	● **ROSE GARDEN** *CBS 5360*	**3**	20 wks

Moira ANDERSON *UK, female vocalist*

Date	Title *Label Number*	Position	
27 Dec 69	**HOLY CITY** *Decca F 12989*	**43**	2 wks

Chris ANDREWS *UK, male vocalist*

Date	Title *Label Number*	Position	
7 Oct 65	● **YESTERDAY MAN** *Decca F 12236*	**3**	15 wks
2 Dec 65	**TO WHOM IT CONCERNS** *Decca F 22285*	**13**	10 wks
14 Apr 66	**SOMETHING ON MY MIND** *Decca F 22365*	**45**	1 wk
28 Apr 66	**SOMETHING ON MY MIND** (re-entry) *Decca F 22365*	**41**	2 wks
2 Jun 66	**WHATCHA GONNA DO NOW** *Decca F 22404*	**40**	4 wks
25 Aug 66	**STOP THAT GIRL** *Decca F 22472*	**36**	4 wks

Eamonn ANDREWS *Ireland, male vocalist*

Date	Title *Label Number*	Position	
20 Jan 56	**SHIFTING WHISPERING SANDS** (PARTS 1 & 2) *Parlophone R 4106*	**18**	3 wks

ANEKA *UK, female vocalist*

Date	Title *Label Number*	Position	
8 Aug 81	★ **JAPANESE BOY** *Hansa HANSA 5*	**1**	12 wks
7 Nov 81	**LITTLE LADY** *Hansa/Ariola HANSA 8*	**50**	4 wks

ANGELETTES *UK, female vocal group*

Date	Title *Label Number*	Position	
13 May 72	**DON'T LET HIM TOUCH YOU** *Decca F 13284*	**35**	5 wks

ANGELIC UPSTARTS

UK, male vocal/instrumental group

Date	Title *Label Number*	Position	
21 Apr 79	**I'M AN UPSTART** *Warner Bros. K 17354*	**31**	8 wks
11 Aug 79	**TEENAGE WARNING** *Warner Bros. K 17426*	**29**	6 wks
3 Nov 79	**NEVER 'AD NOTHIN'** *Warner Bros. K 17476*	**52**	4 wks
9 Feb 80	**OUT OF CONTROL** *Warner Bros. K 17558*	**58**	3 wks
22 Mar 80	**WE GOTTA GET OUT OF THIS PLACE** *Warner Bros. K 17576*	**65**	2 wks
2 Aug 80	**LAST NIGHT ANOTHER SOLDIER** *EMI-Angelic Upstarts Z 7*	**51**	4 wks
7 Feb 81	**KIDS ON THE STREET** *Zonophone Z 16*	**57**	3 wks

Bobby ANGELO and the TUXEDOS

UK, male vocal/instrumental group

Date	Title *Label Number*	Position	
10 Aug 61	**BABY SITTIN'** *HMV POP 892*	**30**	6 wks

ANGELS *US, female vocal group*

Date	Title *Label Number*	Position	
3 Oct 63	**MY BOYFRIEND'S BACK** *Mercury AMT 1211*	**50**	1 wk

Left **ASSOCIATION** Despite a string of classic singles which included 'Windy', 'Cherish', 'Never My Love' and 'Along Comes Mary', their time for chart living was brief *Bottom row left to right* **E. ARNOLD** He made the world go away and followed suit himself the following year **P. P. ARNOLD** Her first cut was the brightest **AIR SUPPLY** All out of love but not out of breath

Date	Title *Label Number*	Position	

Date Title *Label Number* Position

ANGELWITCH *UK, male vocal/instrumental group*

7 Jun 80	**SWEET DANGER** *EMI 5064*	**75**	1 wk

ANIMALS *UK, male vocal/instrumental group*

16 Apr 64	**BABY LET ME TAKE YOU HOME** *Columbia DB 7247*	**21**	8 wks
25 Jun 64	★ **HOUSE OF THE RISING SUN** *Columbia DB 7301*	**1**	12 wks
17 Sep 64	● **I'M CRYING** *Columbia DB 7354*	**8**	10 wks
4 Feb 65	● **DON'T LET ME BE MISUNDERSTOOD** *Columbia DB 7445*	**3**	9 wks
8 Apr 65	● **BRING IT ON HOME TO ME** *Columbia DB 7539*	**7**	11 wks
15 Jul 65	● **WE'VE GOTTA GET OUT OF THIS PLACE** *Columbia DB 7639*	**2**	12 wks
28 Oct 65	● **IT'S MY LIFE** *Columbia DB 7741*	**7**	11 wks
17 Feb 66	**INSIDE - LOOKING OUT** *Decca F12332*	**12**	8 wks
2 Jun 66	● **DON'T BRING ME DOWN** *Decca F 12407*	**6**	8 wks
7 Oct 72	**HOUSE OF THE RISING SUN** (re-issue) *RAK RR 1*	**25**	6 wks
18 Sep 82	**HOUSE OF THE RISING SUN** (re-entry of re-issue) *RAK RR 1*	**11**	10 wks

See also Eric Burdon

Paul ANKA *Canada, male vocalist*

9 Aug 57	★ **DIANA** *Columbia DB 3980*	**1**	25 wks
8 Nov 57	● **I LOVE YOU BABY** *Columbia DB 4022*	**3**	15 wks
8 Nov 57	**TELL ME THAT YOU LOVE ME** *Columbia DB 4022*	**25**	2 wks
31 Jan 58	● **YOU ARE MY DESTINY** *Columbia DB 4063*	**6**	13 wks
30 May 58	**CRAZY LOVE** *Columbia DB 4110*	**26**	1 wk
26 Sep 58	**MIDNIGHT** *Columbia DB 4172*	**26**	1 wk
30 Jan 59	● **(ALL OF A SUDDEN) MY HEART SINGS** *Columbia DB 4241*	**10**	13 wks
10 Jul 59	● **LONELY BOY** *Columbia DB 4324*	**3**	17 wks
30 Oct 59	● **PUT YOUR HEAD ON MY SHOULDER** *Columbia DB 4355*	**7**	12 wks
26 Feb 60	**IT'S TIME TO CRY** *Columbia DB 4390*	**28**	1 wk
31 Mar 60	**PUPPY LOVE** *Columbia DB 4434*	**33**	4 wks
14 Apr 60	**IT'S TIME TO CRY** (re-entry) *Columbia DB 4390*	**47**	1 wk
5 May 60	**PUPPY LOVE** (re-entry) *Columbia DB 4434*	**37**	3 wks
15 Sep 60	**HELLO YOUNG LOVERS** *Columbia DB 4504*	**44**	1 wk
15 Mar 62	**LOVE ME WARM AND TENDER** *RCA 1276*	**19**	11 wks
26 Jul 62	**A STEEL GUITAR AND A GLASS OF WINE** *RCA 1292*	**41**	4 wks
28 Sep 74	● **(YOU'RE) HAVING MY BABY** *United Artists UP 35713*	**6**	10 wks

ANKLEBITERS — See *Fogwell FLAX and the ANKLEBITERS from FREEHOLD JUNIOR SCHOOL*

Billie ANTHONY *UK, female vocalist*

15 Oct 54	● **THIS OLE HOUSE** *Columbia DB 3519*	**4**	16 wks

Miki ANTHONY *UK, male vocalist*

3 Feb 73	**IF IT WASN'T FOR THE REASON THAT I LOVE YOU** *Bell 1275*	**27**	7 wks

Ray ANTHONY *US, orchestra*

4 Dec 53	● **DRAGNET** *Capitol CL 13983*	**7**	1 wk
8 Jan 54	**DRAGNET** (re-entry) *Capitol CL 13983*	**11**	1 wk

Richard ANTHONY *France, male vocalist*

12 Dec 63	**WALKING ALONE** *Columbia DB 7133*	**37**	5 wks
2 Apr 64	**IF I LOVED YOU** *Columbia DB 7235*	**48**	1 wk
23 Apr 64	**IF I LOVED YOU** (re-entry) *Columbia DB 7235*	**18**	9 wks

ANTI-NOWHERE LEAGUE

UK, male vocal/instrumental group

23 Jan 82	**STREETS OF LONDON** *WXYZ ABCD 1*	**48**	5 wks
20 Mar 82	**I HATE ... PEOPLE** *WXYZ ABCD 2*	**46**	3 wks
3 Jul 82	**WOMAN** *WXYZ ABCD 4*	**72**	2 wks

ANTI-PASTI — See *EXPLOITED and ANTI-PASTI*

ANTS — See *ADAM and the ANTS*

APHRODITE'S CHILD

Greece, male vocal/instrumental group

6 Nov 68	**RAIN AND TEARS** *Mercury MF 1039*	**30**	7 wks

APPLEJACKS

UK, male/female vocal/instrumental group

5 Mar 64	● **TELL ME WHEN** *Decca F 11833*	**7**	13 wks
11 Jun 64	**LIKE DREAMERS DO** *Decca F 11916*	**20**	11 wks
15 Oct 64	**THREE LITTLE WORDS** *Decca F 11981*	**23**	5 wks

Charlie APPLEWHITE *US, male vocalist*

23 Sep 55	**BLUE STAR** (THE MEDIC THEME) *Brunswick 05416*	**20**	1 wk

Helen APRIL — See *John DUMMER and Helen APRIL*

APRIL WINE

Canada, male vocal/instrumental group

15 Mar 80	**I LIKE TO ROCK** *Capitol CL 16121*	**41**	5 wks
11 Apr 81	**JUST BETWEEN YOU AND ME** *Capitol CL 16184*	**52**	4 wks

AQUARIAN DREAM

US, male/female vocal/instrumental group

24 Feb 79	**YOU'RE A STAR** *Elektra LV 7*	**67**	1 wk

ARCHIES *US, male/female vocal group*

11 Oct 69	★ **SUGAR SUGAR** *RCA 1872*	**1**	26 wks

ARGENT *UK, male vocal/instrumental group*

4 Mar 72	● **HOLD YOUR HEAD UP** *Epic EPC 7786*	**5**	12 wks
10 Jun 72	**TRAGEDY** *Epic EPC 8115*	**34**	7 wks
24 Mar 73	**GOD GAVE ROCK & ROLL TO YOU** *Epic EPC 1243*	**18**	8 wks

Date	Title *Label Number*	Position	

Date Title *Label Number* Position

Ship's Company and Royal Marine band of H.M.S. ARK ROYAL

UK, male choir and marine band

23 Dec 78	**THE LAST FAREWELL** *BBC RESL 61*	**46**	6 wks

Joan ARMATRADING *UK, female vocalist*

16 Oct 76 ●	**LOVE AND AFFECTION** *A & M AMS 7249*	**10**	9 wks
23 Feb 80	**ROSIE** *A & M AMS 7506*	**49**	5 wks
14 Jun 80	**ME MYSELF I** *A & M AMS 7527*	**21**	11 wks
6 Sep 80	**ALL THE WAY FROM AMERICA** *A & M AMS 7552*	**54**	3 wks
12 Sep 81	**I'M LUCKY** *A & M AMS 8163*	**46**	5 wks
16 Jan 82	**NO LOVE** *A & M AMS 8179*	**50**	5 wks

Louis ARMSTRONG

US, male band leader/trumpet and vocals

19 Dec 52 ●	**TAKES TWO TO TANGO** *Brunswick 04995*	**6**	10 wks
13 Apr 56 ●	**THEME FROM THE THREEPENNY OPERA** *Philips PB 574*	**8**	11 wks
15 Jun 56	**TAKE IT SATCH** (EP) *Philips BBE 12035*	**29**	1 wk
13 Jul 56	**THE FAITHFUL HUSSAR** *Philips PB 604*	**27**	2 wks
6 Nov 59	**MACK THE KNIFE** *Philips PB 967*	**24**	1 wk
4 Jun 64 ●	**HELLO DOLLY** *London HLR 9878*	**4**	14 wks
7 Feb 68 ★	**WHAT A WONDERFUL WORLD/ CABARET** *HMV POP 1615*	**1**	29 wks
26 Jun 68	**SUNSHINE OF LOVE** *Stateside SS 2116*	**41**	7 wks

Take it Satch *tracks: Tiger Rag/ Mack the Knife/ The Faithful Hussar/ Back O'Town Blues.* Mack the Knife *is a re-issue of* Theme From the Threepenny Opera *under a different title.* Cabaret *was not listed with* What a Wonderful World *until 14 Feb 68. The four hits on Philips are all credited to Louis Armstrong with his All Stars.*

Eddy ARNOLD *US, male vocalist*

17 Feb 66 ●	**MAKE THE WORLD GO AWAY** *RCA 1496*	**8**	17 wks
26 May 66	**I WANT TO GO WITH YOU** *RCA 1519*	**49**	1 wk
9 Jun 66	**I WANT TO GO WITH YOU** (re-entry) *RCA 1519*	**46**	2 wks
28 Jul 66	**IF YOU WERE MINE MARY** *RCA 1529*	**49**	1 wk

P. P. ARNOLD *US, female vocalist*

4 May 67	**FIRST CUT IS THE DEEPEST** *Immediate IM 047*	**18**	10 wks
2 Aug 67	**THE TIME HAS COME** *Immediate IM 055*	**47**	2 wks
24 Jan 68	**GROOVY** *Immediate IM 061*	**41**	4 wks
10 Jul 68	**ANGEL OF THE MORNING** *Immediate IM 067*	**29**	11 wks

ARPEGGIO *US, male/female vocal group*

31 Mar 79	**LOVE AND DESIRE** (PART 1) *Polydor POSP 40*	**63**	3 wks

ARRIVAL *UK, male/female vocal/instrumental group*

10 Jan 70 ●	**FRIENDS** *Decca F 12986*	**8**	9 wks
6 Jun 70	**I WILL SURVIVE** *Decca F 13026*	**16**	11 wks

ARROWS *US/UK, male vocal/instrumental group*

25 May 74 ●	**A TOUCH TOO MUCH** *RAK 171*	**8**	9 wks
1 Feb 75	**MY LAST NIGHT WITH YOU** *RAK 189*	**25**	7 wks

ARSENAL F.C. FIRST TEAM SQUAD

UK, male football team vocalists

8 May 71	**GOOD OLD ARSENAL** *Pye 7N 45067*	**16**	7 wks

John ASHER *UK, male vocalist*

15 Nov 75	**LET'S TWIST AGAIN** *Creole CR 112*	**14**	6 wks

ASHFORD and SIMPSON

US, male/female vocal duo

18 Nov 78	**IT SEEMS TO HANG ON** *Warner Bros. K 17237*	**48**	4 wks

ASHTON, GARDNER AND DYKE

UK, male vocal/instrumental group

16 Jan 71 ●	**RESURRECTION SHUFFLE** *Capitol CL 15665*	**3**	14 wks

ASIA *UK, male vocal/instrumental group*

3 Jul 82	**HEAT OF THE MOMENT** *Geffen GEF A2494*	**46**	5 wks
18 Sep 82	**ONLY TIME WILL TELL** *Geffen GEF A2228*	**54**	3 wks

ASSOCIATES *UK, male vocal/instrumental duo*

20 Feb 82 ●	**PARTY FEARS TWO** *Associates ASC 1*	**9**	10 wks
8 May 82	**CLUB COUNTRY** *Associates ASC 2*	**13**	10 wks
7 Aug 82	**18 CARAT LOVE AFFAIR/LOVE HANGOVER** *Associates ASC 3*	**21**	8 wks

18 Carat Love Affair listed until 28 August only.

ASSOCIATION *US, male vocal/instrumental group*

22 May 68	**TIME FOR LIVING** *Warner Bros. WB 7195*	**23**	8 wks

Gali ATARI — See *MILK AND HONEY*

Chet ATKINS *US, male instrumentalist - guitar*

17 Mar 60	**TEENSVILLE** *RCA 1174*	**46**	1 wk
5 May 60	**TEENSVILLE** (re-entry) *RCA 1174*	**49**	1 wk

ATLANTA RHYTHM SECTION

US, male vocal/instrumental group

27 Oct 79	**SPOOKY** *Polydor POSP 74*	**48**	4 wks

ATLANTIC STARR

US, male/female vocal/instrumental group.

9 Sep 78	**GIMME YOUR LOVIN'** *A & M AMS 7380*	**66**	3 wks

ATMOSFEAR *UK, male vocal/instrumental group*

17 Nov 79	**DANCING IN OUTER SPACE** *MCA 543*	**46**	7 wks

Date	Title *Label Number*	Position	

ATOMIC ROOSTER

UK, male vocal/instrumental group

Date	Title *Label Number*	Position	
6 Feb 71	**TOMORROW NIGHT** *B & C CB 131*	**11**	12 wks
10 Jul 71	● **THE DEVIL'S ANSWER** *B & C CB 157*	**4**	13 wks

ATTRACTIONS — See *Elvis COSTELLO*

Winifred ATWELL

UK, female instrumentalist - piano

Date	Title *Label Number*	Position	
12 Dec 52	**BRITANNIA RAG** *Decca F 10015*	**11**	1 wk
9 Jan 53	● **BRITANNIA RAG** (re-entry) *Decca F 10015*	**5**	5 wks
15 May 53	**CORONATION RAG** *Decca F 10110*	**12**	1 wk
29 May 53	● **CORONATION RAG** (re-entry) *Decca F 10110*	**5**	5 wks
25 Sep 53	**FLIRTATION WALTZ** *Decca F 10181*	**12**	1 wk
9 Oct 53	● **FLIRTATION WALTZ** (re-entry) *Decca F 10181*	**10**	1 wk
6 Nov 53	**FLIRTATION WALTZ** (2nd re-entry) *Decca F10181*	**12**	1 wk
4 Dec 53	● **LET'S HAVE A PARTY** *Philips PB 213*	**2**	9 wks
23 Jul 54	● **RACHMANINOFF'S 18TH VARIATION ON A THEME BY PAGANINI** *Philips PB 234*	**9**	7 wks
1 Oct 54	**RACHMANINOFF'S 18TH VARIATION ON A THEME BY PAGANINI** (re-entry) *Philips PB 234*	**19**	2 wks
26 Nov 54	**LET'S HAVE A PARTY** (re-entry) *Philips PB 213*	**14**	6 wks
26 Nov 54	★ **LET'S HAVE ANOTHER PARTY** *Philips PB 268*	**1**	8 wks
4 Nov 55	● **LET'S HAVE A DING DONG** *Decca F 10634*	**3**	10 wks
16 Mar 56	★ **POOR PEOPLE OF PARIS** *Decca F 10681*	**1**	16 wks
18 May 56	**PORT AU PRINCE** *Decca F 10727*	**18**	6 wks
20 Jul 56	**LEFT BANK** *Decca F 10762*	**14**	7 wks
26 Oct 56	● **MAKE IT A PARTY** *Decca F 10796*	**7**	12 wks
22 Feb 57	**LET'S ROCK 'N ROLL** *Decca F 10852*	**28**	2 wks
15 Mar 57	**LET'S ROCK 'N ROLL** (re-entry) *Decca F 10852*	**24**	2 wks
6 Dec 57	● **LET'S HAVE A BALL** *Decca F 10956*	**4**	6 wks
7 Aug 59	**SUMMER OF THE SEVENTEENTH DOLL** *Decca F 11143*	**24**	2 wks
27 Nov 59	● **PIANO PARTY** *Decca F 11183*	**10**	7 wks

Various hits listed above were medleys as follows: Let's Have a Party: *Boomps A Daisy/ Daisy Bell/ If You Knew Suzie/ Knees Up Mother Brown/ The More We Are Together/ She Was One Of The Early Birds/ That's My Weakness Now/ Three O'Clock In The Morning.* Let's Have Another Party: *Another Little Drink/ Broken Doll/ Bye Bye Blackbird/ Honeysuckle And The Bee/ I Wonder Where My Baby Is Tonight/ Lily of Laguna/ Nellie Dean/ Sheik of Araby/ Somebody Stole My Gal/ When The Red Red Robin.* Let's Have a Ding Dong: *Happy Days Are Here Again/ Oh Johnny Oh Johnny Oh/ Oh You Beautiful Doll/ Ain't She Sweet/ Yes We Have No Bananas/ I'm Forever Blowing Bubbles/ I'll Be Your Sweetheart/ If These Lips Could Only Speak/ Who's Taking You Home Tonight.* Make It a Party: *Who Were You With Last Night/ Hello Hello Who's Your Lady Friend/ Yes Sir That's My Baby/ Don't Dilly Dally On The Way/ Beer Barrel Polka/ After The Ball/ Peggy O'Neil/ Meet Me Tonight In Dreamland/ I Belong To Glasgow/ Down At The Old Bull And Bush.* Let's Rock 'n Roll: *Singin' The Blues/ Green Door/ See You Later Alligator/ Shake Rattle And Roll/ Rock Around The Clock/ Razzle Dazzle.* Let's Have a Ball: *Music Music Music/ This Ole House/ Heartbreaker/ Woody Woodpecker/ Last Train To San Fernando/ Bring A Little Water Sylvie/ Puttin' On The Style/ Don't You Rock Me Daddy-O.* Piano Party: *Baby Face/ Comin' Thru' The Rye/ Annie Laurie/ Little Brown Jug/ Let Him Go Let Him Tarry/ Put Your Arms Around Me Honey/ I'll Be With You In Apple Blossom Time/ Shine On Harvest Moon/ Blue Skies/ I'll Never Say Never Again/ I'll See You In My Dreams. See also Various Artists - All Star Hit Parade.*

Brian AUGER — See *Julie DRISCOLL, Brian AUGER and the TRINITY*

AUTUMN *UK, male vocal/instrumental group*

Date	Title *Label Number*	Position	
16 Oct 71	**MY LITTLE GIRL** *Pye 7N 45090*	**37**	6 wks

Frankie AVALON *US, male vocalist*

Date	Title *Label Number*	Position	
10 Oct 58	**GINGERBREAD** *HMV POP 517*	**30**	1 wk
24 Apr 59	**VENUS** *HMV POP 603*	**16**	6 wks
22 Jan 60	**WHY** *HMV POP 688*	**20**	4 wks
28 Apr 60	**DON'T THROW AWAY ALL THOSE TEARDROPS** *HMV POP 727*	**37**	4 wks

AVALON BOYS — See *LAUREL and HARDY with the AVALON BOYS*

AVERAGE WHITE BAND

UK, male vocal/instrumental vocal group

Date	Title *Label Number*	Position	
22 Feb 75	● **PICK UP THE PIECES** *Atlantic K 10489*	**6**	9 wks
26 Apr 75	**CUT THE CAKE** *Atlantic K 10605*	**31**	4 wks
9 Oct 76	**QUEEN OF MY SOUL** *Atlantic K 10825*	**23**	7 wks
28 Apr 79	**WALK ON BY** *RCA XC 1087*	**46**	5 wks
25 Aug 79	**WHEN WILL YOU BE MINE** *RCA XB 1096*	**49**	5 wks
26 Apr 80	**LET'S GO ROUND AGAIN PT.1** *RCA AWB 1*	**12**	11 wks
26 Jul 80	**FOR YOU FOR LOVE** *RCA AWB 2*	**46**	4 wks

AVONS *UK, male/female vocal group*

Date	Title *Label Number*	Position	
13 Nov 59	● **SEVEN LITTLE GIRLS SITTING IN THE BACK SEAT** *Columbia DB 4363*	**3**	13 wks
7 Jul 60	**WE'RE ONLY YOUNG ONCE** *Columbia DB 4461*	**45**	2 wks
27 Oct 60	**FOUR LITTLE HEELS** *Columbia DB 4522*	**45**	3 wks
26 Jan 61	**RUBBER BALL** *Columbia DB 4569*	**30**	4 wks

Hoyt AXTON *US, male vocalist*

Date	Title *Label Number*	Position	
7 Jun 80	**DELLA AND THE DEALER** *Young Blood YB 82*	**48**	4 wks

Roy AYERS *US, male vocalist*

Date	Title *Label Number*	Position	
21 Oct 78	**GET ON UP, GET ON DOWN** *Polydor AYERS 7*	**41**	4 wks
2 Feb 80	**DON'T STOP THE FEELING** *Polydor STEP 6*	**56**	3 wks

See also Roy Ayers and Wayne Henderson.

Roy AYERS and Wayne HENDERSON

US, male duo (Roy Ayers is vocalist and plays vibrophone, Wayne Henderson plays trumpet)

Date	Title *Label Number*	Position	
13 Jan 79	**HEAT OF THE BEAT** *Polydor POSP 16*	**43**	5 wks

See also Roy Ayers.

Charles AZNAVOUR *France, male vocalist*

Date	Title *Label Number*	Position	
22 Sep 73	**THE OLD FASHIONED WAY** *Barclay BAR 20*	**50**	1 wk
20 Oct 73	**THE OLD FASHIONED WAY** (re-entry) *Barclay BAR 20*	**38**	12 wks
22 Jun 74	★ **SHE** *Barclay BAR 26*	**1**	14 wks
27 Jul 74	**THE OLD FASHIONED WAY** (2nd re-entry) *Barclay BAR 20*	**47**	2 wks

AZYMUTH *Brazil, male instrumental group*

Date	Title *Label Number*	Position	
12 Jan 80	**JAZZ CARNIVAL** *Milestone MSP 101*	**19**	8 wks

Bob AZZAM *Egypt, singing orchestra*

Date	Title *Label Number*	Position	
26 May 60	**MUSTAPHA** *Decca F 21235*	**23**	14 wks

B

B, B, and Q BAND

US, male vocal/instrumental group

Date	Title *Label Number*	Position	
18 Jul 81	**ON THE BEAT** *Capitol CL 202*	**41**	5 wks

B. B. S. UNLIMITED — See *Eddie DRENNON and B. B. S. UNLIMITED*

B-52'S *US, male/female vocal/instrumental group*

Date	Title *Label Number*	Position	
11 Aug 79	**ROCK LOBSTER** *Island WIP 6506*	**37**	5 wks
9 Aug 80	**GIVE ME BACK MY MAN** *Island WIP 6579*	**61**	3 wks

B-MOVIE *UK, male vocal/instrumental group*

Date	Title *Label Number*	Position	
18 Apr 81	**REMEMBRANCE DAY** *Deram DM 437*	**61**	3 wks
27 Mar 82	**NOWHERE GIRL** *Some Bizzarre BZZ 8*	**67**	4 wks

B. T. EXPRESS *US, male instrumental/vocal group*

Date	Title *Label Number*	Position	
29 Mar 75	**EXPRESS** *Pye International 7N 25674*	**34**	6 wks
26 Jul 80	**DOES IT FEEL GOOD/GIVE UP THE FUNK (LET'S DANCE)** *Calibre CAB 503*	**52**	4 wks

Alice BABS *Sweden, female vocalist*

Date	Title *Label Number*	Position	
15 Aug 63	**AFTER YOU'VE GONE** *Fontana TF 409*	**43**	1 wk

BABY O *US, male/female vocal/instrumental group*

Date	Title *Label Number*	Position	
26 Jul 80	**IN THE FOREST** *Calibre CAB 505*	**46**	5 wks

BABYS *US/UK, male vocal/instrumental group*

Date	Title *Label Number*	Position	
21 Jan 78	**ISN'T IT TIME** *Chrysalis CHS 2173*	**45**	3 wks

BACCARA *Spain, female vocal duo*

Date	Title *Label Number*	Position	
17 Sep 77	★ **YES SIR I CAN BOOGIE** *RCA PB 5526*	**1**	16 wks
14 Jan 78	● **SORRY I'M A LADY** *RCA PB 5555*	**8**	9 wks

Burt BACHARACH *US, orchestra and chorus*

Date	Title *Label Number*	Position	
20 May 65	● **TRAINS AND BOATS AND PLANES** *London HL 9928*	**4**	11 wks

BACHELORS *Ireland, male vocal group*

Date	Title *Label Number*	Position	
24 Jan 63	● **CHARMAINE** *Decca F 11559*	**6**	19 wks
4 Jul 63	**FARAWAY PLACES** *Decca F 11666*	**36**	3 wks
29 Aug 63	**WHISPERING** *Decca F 11712*	**18**	10 wks
23 Jan 64	★ **DIANE** *Decca F 11799*	**1**	19 wks
19 Mar 64	● **I BELIEVE** *Decca F 11857*	**2**	17 wks
4 Jun 64	● **RAMONA** *Decca F 11910*	**4**	13 wks
13 Aug 64	● **I WOULDN'T TRADE YOU FOR THE WORLD** *Decca F 11949*	**4**	16 wks
3 Dec 64	● **NO ARMS CAN EVER HOLD YOU** *Decca F 12034*	**7**	12 wks
1 Apr 65	**TRUE LOVE FOR EVER MORE** *Decca F 12108*	**34**	6 wks
20 May 65	● **MARIE** *Decca F 12156*	**9**	12 wks
28 Oct 65	**IN THE CHAPEL IN THE MOONLIGHT** *Decca F 12256*	**27**	10 wks
6 Jan 66	**HELLO DOLLY** *Decca F 12309*	**38**	4 wks
17 Mar 66	● **THE SOUND OF SILENCE** *Decca F 12351*	**3**	13 wks
7 Jul 66	**CAN I TRUST YOU** *Decca F 12417*	**26**	7 wks
1 Dec 66	**WALK WITH FAITH IN YOUR HEART** *Decca F 22523*	**22**	9 wks
6 Apr 67	**OH HOW I MISS YOU** *Decca F 22592*	**30**	8 wks
5 Jul 67	**MARTA** *Decca F 22634*	**20**	9 wks

BACHMAN-TURNER OVERDRIVE

Canada, male vocal/instrumental group

Date	Title *Label Number*	Position	
16 Nov 74	● **YOU AIN'T SEEN NOTHIN' YET** *Mercury 6167 025*	**2**	12 wks
1 Feb 75	**ROLL ON DOWN THE HIGHWAY** *Mercury 6167 071*	**22**	6 wks

BAD COMPANY

UK, male vocal/instrumental group

Date	Title *Label Number*	Position	
1 Jun 74	**CAN'T GET ENOUGH** *Island WIP 6191*	**15**	8 wks
22 Mar 75	**GOOD LOVIN' GONE BAD** *Island WIP 6223*	**31**	6 wks
30 Aug 75	**FEEL LIKE MAKIN' LOVE** *Island WIP 6242*	**20**	9 wks

BAD MANNERS

UK, male vocal/instrumental group

Date	Title *Label Number*	Position	
1 Mar 80	**NE-NE NA-NA NA-NA NU-NU** *Magnet MAG 164*	**28**	14 wks
14 Jun 80	**LIP UP FATTY** *Magnet MAG 175*	**15**	14 wks
27 Sep 80	● **SPECIAL BREW** *Magnet MAG 180*	**3**	13 wks
6 Dec 80	**LORRAINE** *Magnet MAG 181*	**21**	12 wks
28 Mar 81	**JUST A FEELING** *Magnet MAG 187*	**13**	9 wks
27 Jun 81	● **CAN CAN** *Magnet MAG 190*	**3**	13 wks
26 Sep 81	● **WALKING IN THE SUNSHINE** *Magnet MAG 197*	**10**	9 wks
21 Nov 81	**BUONA SERA** *Magnet MAG 211*	**34**	9 wks
1 May 82	**GOT NO BRAINS** *Magnet MAG 216*	**44**	5 wks
31 Jul 82	● **MY GIRL LOLLIPOP (MY BOY LOLLIPOP)** *Magnet MAG 232*	**9**	7 wks
30 Oct 82	**SAMSON AND DELILAH** *Magnet MAG 236*	**58**	3 wks

BADFINGER *UK, male vocal/instrumental group*

Date	Title *Label Number*	Position	
10 Jan 70	● **COME AND GET IT** *Apple 20*	**4**	11 wks
9 Jan 71	● **NO MATTER WHAT** *Apple 31*	**5**	12 wks
29 Jan 72	● **DAY AFTER DAY** *Apple 40*	**10**	11 wks

Joan BAEZ *US, female vocalist*

Date	Title *Label Number*	Position	
6 May 65	**WE SHALL OVERCOME** *Fontana TF 564*	**26**	10 wks
8 Jul 65	● **THERE BUT FOR FORTUNE** *Fontana TF 587*	**8**	12 wks
2 Sep 65	**IT'S ALL OVER NOW BABY BLUE** *Fontana TF 604*	**22**	8 wks
23 Dec 65	**FAREWELL ANGELINA** *Fontana TF 639*	**35**	3 wks

Date	Title *Label Number*	Position	
20 Jan 66	**FAREWELL ANGELINA** (re-entry) *Fontana TF 639*	**49**	1 wk
28 Jul 66	**PACK UP YOUR SORROWS** *Fontana TF 727*	**50**	1 wk
9 Oct 71	● **THE NIGHT THEY DROVE OLD DIXIE DOWN** *Vanguard VS 35138*	**6**	12 wks

Adrian BAKER *UK, male vocalist*

19 Jul 75	● **SHERRY** *Magnet MAG 34*	**10**	8 wks

Hilda BAKER and Arthur MULLARD

UK, female/male vocal duo

9 Sep 78	**YOU'RE THE ONE THAT I WANT** *Pye 7N 46121*	**22**	6 wks

George BAKER SELECTION

Holland, male/female vocal/instrumental group

6 Sep 75	● **PALOMA BLANCA** *Warner Bros. K 16541*	**10**	10 wks

Long John BALDRY *UK, male vocalist*

8 Nov 67	★ **LET THE HEARTACHES BEGIN** *Pye 7N 17385*	**1**	13 wks
28 Aug 68	**WHEN THE SUN COMES SHININ' THRU** *Pye 7N 17593*	**29**	7 wks
23 Oct 68	**MEXICO** *Pye 7N 17563*	**15**	8 wks
29 Jan 69	**IT'S TOO LATE NOW** *Pye 7N 17664*	**21**	8 wks

Kenny BALL and his JAZZMEN

UK, male band, Kenny Ball vocals and trumpet

23 Feb 61	**SAMANTHA** *Pye Jazz Today 7NJ 2040*	**13**	15 wks
11 May 61	**I STILL LOVE YOU ALL** *Pye Jazz 7NJ 2042*	**24**	6 wks
31 Aug 61	**SOMEDAY** *Pye Jazz 7NJ 2047*	**28**	6 wks
9 Nov 61	● **MIDNIGHT IN MOSCOW** *Pye Jazz 7NJ 2049*	**2**	21 wks
15 Feb 62	● **MARCH OF THE SIAMESE CHILDREN** *Pye Jazz 7NJ 2051*	**4**	13 wks
17 May 62	● **THE GREEN LEAVES OF SUMMER** *Pye Jazz 7NJ 2054*	**7**	14 wks
23 Aug 62	**SO DO I** *Pye Jazz 7NJ 2056*	**14**	8 wks
18 Oct 62	**THE PAY OFF** *Pye Jazz 7NJ 2061*	**23**	6 wks
17 Jan 63	● **SUKIYAKI** *Pye Jazz 7NJ 2062*	**10**	13 wks
25 Apr 63	**CASABLANCA** *Pye Jazz 7NJ 2064*	**21**	11 wks
13 Jun 63	**RONDO** *Pye Jazz 7NJ 2065*	**24**	8 wks
22 Aug 63	**ACAPULCO 1922** *Pye Jazz 7NJ 2067*	**27**	6 wks
11 Jun 64	**HELLO DOLLY** *Pye Jazz 7NJ 2071*	**30**	7 wks
19 Jul 67	**WHEN I'M 64** *Pye 7N 17348*	**43**	2 wks

BANANARAMA *UK, female vocal group*

10 Apr 82	● **REALLY SAYING SOMETHING** *Deram NANA 1*	**5**	10 wks
3 Jul 82	● **SHY BOY** *London NANA 2*	**4**	11 wks
4 Dec 82	**CHEERS THEN** *London NANA 3*	**45†**	4 wks

Really Saying Something credited to Bananarama with Funboy Three. See also Funboy Three, Funboy Three and Bananarama

BAND *Canada, male vocal/instrumental group*

18 Sep 68	**THE WEIGHT** *Capitol CL 15559*	**21**	9 wks
4 Apr 70	**RAG MAMA RAG** *Capitol CL 15629*	**16**	9 wks

BAND AKA *UK, male vocal/instrumental group*

15 May 82	**GRACE** *Epic EPC A2376*	**41**	5 wks

BANDITS — See *Billy COTTON and his Band*

BANDWAGON — See *Johnny JOHNSON and the BANDWAGON*

Honey BANE *UK, female vocalist*

24 Jan 81	**TURN ME ON TURN ME OFF** *Zonophone Z 15*	**37**	5 wks
18 Apr 81	**BABY LOVE** *Zonophone Z 19*	**58**	3 wks

BANNED *UK, male vocal/instrumental group*

17 Dec 77	**LITTLE GIRL** *Harvest HAR 5145*	**36**	6 wks

BANSHEES — See *SIOUXSIE and the BANSHEES*

Chris BARBER'S JAZZ BAND

UK, male band, Chris Barber trombone

13 Feb 59	● **PETITE FLEUR** *Pye Nixa NJ 2026*	**3**	22 wks
31 Jul 59	**PETITE FLEUR** (re-entry) *Pye Nixa NJ 2026*	**22**	2 wks
9 Oct 59	**LONESOME** *Columbia DB 4333*	**27**	2 wks
4 Jan 62	**REVIVAL** *Columbia SCD 2166*	**50**	2 wks
1 Feb 62	**REVIVAL** (re-entry) *Columbia SCD 2166*	**43**	2 wks

BARBRA and NEIL *US, female/male vocal duo*

25 Nov 78	● **YOU DON'T BRING ME FLOWERS** *CBS 6803*	**5**	12 wks

See also Barbra Streisand, Neil Diamond, Donna Summer and Barbara Streisand.

BARCLAY JAMES HARVEST

UK, male vocal and instrumental group

2 Apr 77	**LIVE** (EP) *Polydor 2229 198*	**49**	1 wk
16 Apr 77	**LIVE** (EP) (re-entry) *Polydor 2229 198*	**49**	1 wk
26 Jan 80	**LOVE ON THE LINE** *Polydor POSP 97*	**63**	2 wks
22 Nov 80	**LIFE IS FOR LIVING** *Polydor POSP 195*	**61**	3 wks

Tracks on Live EP: *Rock'n'Roll Star / Medicine Man (Parts 1 & 2).*

BARDO *UK, male/female vocal duo*

10 Apr 82	● **ONE STEP FURTHER** *Epic EPC A2265*	**2**	8 wks

BAR-KAYS *US, male vocal/instrumental group*

23 Aug 67	**SOUL FINGER** *Stax 601 014*	**33**	7 wks
22 Jan 77	**SHAKE YOUR RUMP TO THE FUNK** *Mercury 6167 417*	**41**	4 wks

Richard BARNES *UK, male vocalist*

23 May 70	**TAKE TO THE MOUNTAINS** *Philips BF 1840*	**35**	6 wks
24 Oct 70	**GO NORTH** *Philips 6006 039*	**49**	1 wk
7 Nov 70	**GO NORTH** (re-entry) *Philips 6006 039*	**38**	3 wks

Left **ADRIAN BAKER** A lifelong Beach Boy fan. Adrian became a member for a couple of American tours

Centre **JOAN BAEZ** Made her debut at the first ever Newport folk festival in 1959

Right **BARDO** Britain's Eurovision entry 1982 – ex Prima Donna singer Sally-Ann Triplett and Stephen Fischer

Bottom picture **BANANARAMA** A big hit – a bunch of fyffes!

Date	Title *Label Number*	Position	

BARRACUDAS

UK/US, male vocal/instrumental group

Date	Title *Label Number*	Position	
16 Aug 80	**SUMMER FUN** *EMI-Wipe Out Z 5*	**37**	6 wks

Wild Willy BARRETT — See *John OTWAY and Wild Willy BARRETT*

J. J. BARRIE *Canada, male vocalist*

Date	Title *Label Number*	Position	
24 Apr 76	★ **NO CHARGE** *Power Exchange PX 209*	**1**	11 wks

Ken BARRIE *UK, male vocalist*

Date	Title *Label Number*	Position	
10 Jul 82	**POSTMAN PAT** *Post Music PP 001*	**44**	8 wks
25 Dec 82	**POSTMAN PAT** (re-entry) *Post Music PP 001*	**70**†	1 wk

BARRON KNIGHTS

UK, male vocal/instrumental group

Date	Title *Label Number*	Position	
9 Jul 64	● **CALL UP THE GROUPS** *Columbia DB 7317*	**3**	13 wks
22 Oct 64	**COME TO THE DANCE** *Columbia DB 7375*	**42**	2 wks
25 Mar 65	● **POP GO THE WORKERS** *Columbia DB 7525*	**5**	13 wks
16 Dec 65	● **MERRY GENTLE POPS** *Columbia DB 7780*	**9**	7 wks
1 Dec 66	**UNDER NEW MANAGEMENT** *Columbia DB 8071*	**15**	9 wks
23 Oct 68	**AN OLYMPIC RECORD** *Columbia DB 8485*	**35**	4 wks
29 Oct 77	● **LIVE IN TROUBLE** *Epic EPC 5752*	**7**	10 wks
2 Dec 78	● **A TASTE OF AGGRO** *Epic EPC 6829*	**3**	10 wks
8 Dec 79	**FOOD FOR THOUGHT** *Epic EPC 8011*	**46**	6 wks
4 Oct 80	**THE SIT SONG** *Epic EPC 8994*	**44**	4 wks
6 Dec 80	**NEVER MIND THE PRESENTS** *Epic EPC 9070*	**17**	wks
5 Dec 81	**BLACKBOARD JUMBLE** *CBS A 1795*	**52**	4 wks

Joe BARRY *US, male vocalist*

Date	Title *Label Number*	Position	
24 Aug 61	**I'M A FOOL TO CARE** *Mercury AMT 1149*	**49**	1 wk

John BARRY

UK, male instrumental group/orchestra

Date	Title *Label Number*	Position	
10 Mar 60	● **HIT AND MISS** *Columbia DB 4414*	**10**	12 wks
28 Apr 60	**BEAT FOR BEATNIKS** *Columbia DB 4446*	**40**	2 wks
9 Jun 60	**HIT AND MISS** (re-entry) *Columbia DB 4414*	**45**	1 wk
14 Jul 60	**NEVER LET GO** *Columbia DB 4480*	**49**	1 wk
18 Aug 60	**BLUEBERRY HILL** *Columbia DB 4480*	**34**	3 wks
8 Sep 60	**WALK DON'T RUN** *Columbia DB 4505*	**49**	1 wk
22 Sep 60	**WALK DON'T RUN** (re-entry) *Columbia DB 4505*	**11**	13 wks
8 Dec 60	**BLACK STOCKINGS** *Columbia DB 4554*	**27**	9 wks
2 Mar 61	**THE MAGNIFICENT SEVEN** *Columbia DB 4598*	**48**	1 wk
16 Mar 61	**THE MAGNIFICENT SEVEN** (re-entry) *Columbia DB 4598*	**45**	2 wks
6 Apr 61	**THE MAGNIFICENT SEVEN** (2nd re-entry) *Columbia DB 4598*	**50**	1 wk
8 Jun 61	**THE MAGNIFICENT SEVEN** (3rd re-entry) *Columbia DB 4598*	**47**	1 wk
26 Apr 62	**CUTTY SARK** *Columbia DB 4816*	**35**	2 wks
1 Nov 62	**JAMES BOND THEME** *Columbia DB 4898*	**13**	11 wks
21 Nov 63	**FROM RUSSIA WITH LOVE** *Ember S 181*	**44**	1 wk
19 Dec 63	**FROM RUSSIA WITH LOVE** (re-entry) *Ember S 181*	**39**	2 wks
11 Dec 71	**THE PERSUADERS** *CBS 7469*	**13**	15 wks

Billed as the John Barry Seven on Hit and Miss, Walk Don't Run, Black Stockings, The Magnificent Seven *and* Cutty Sark. *Others John Barry Orchestra.*

Len BARRY *US, male vocalist*

Date	Title *Label Number*	Position	
4 Nov 65	● **1-2-3** *Brunswick 05942*	**3**	14 wks
13 Jan 66	● **LIKE A BABY** *Brunswick 05949*	**10**	10 wks

Toni BASIL *US, female vocalist*

Date	Title *Label Number*	Position	
6 Feb 82	● **MICKEY** *Radialchoice TIC 4*	**2**	12 wks
1 May 82	**NOBODY** *Radialchoice/Virgin TIC 2*	**52**	4 wks

Alfie BASS — See *Michael MEDWIN, Bernard BRESSLAW, Alfie BASS & Leslie FYSON*

Fontella BASS *US, female vocalist*

Date	Title *Label Number*	Position	
2 Dec 65	**RESCUE ME** *Chess CRS 8023*	**11**	10 wks
20 Jan 66	**RECOVERY** *Chess CRS 8027*	**32**	5 wks

Shirley BASSEY *UK, female vocalist*

Date	Title *Label Number*	Position	
15 Feb 57	● **BANANA BOAT SONG** *Philips PB 668*	**8**	10 wks
23 Aug 57	**FIRE DOWN BELOW** *Philips PB 723*	**30**	1 wk
6 Sep 57	**YOU YOU ROMEO** *Philips PB 723*	**29**	2 wks
19 Dec 58	**AS I LOVE YOU** *Philips PB 845*	**27**	2 wks
26 Dec 58	● **KISS ME HONEY HONEY KISS ME** *Philips PB 860*	**3**	17 wks
9 Jan 59	★ **AS I LOVE YOU** (re-entry) *Philips PB 845*	**1**	17 wks
31 Mar 60	**WITH THESE HANDS** *Columbia DB 4422*	**38**	2 wks
21 Apr 60	**WITH THESE HANDS** (re-entry) *Columbia DB 4422*	**31**	2 wks
12 May 60	**WITH THESE HANDS** (2nd re-entry) *Columbia DB 4422*	**41**	2 wks
4 Aug 60	● **AS LONG AS HE NEEDS ME** *Columbia DB 4490*	**2**	30 wks
11 May 61	● **YOU'LL NEVER KNOW** *Columbia DB 4643*	**6**	17 wks
27 Jul 61	★ **REACH FOR THE STARS/ CLIMB EV'RY MOUNTAIN** *Columbia DB 4685*	**1**	16 wks
23 Nov 61	**REACH FOR THE STARS/ CLIMB EV'RY MOUNTAIN** (re-entry) *Columbia DB 4685*	**40**	2 wks
23 Nov 61	● **I'LL GET BY** *Columbia DB 4737*	**10**	8 wks
15 Feb 62	**TONIGHT** *Columbia DB 4777*	**21**	8 wks
26 Apr 62	**AVE MARIA** *Columbia DB 4816*	**34**	4 wks
31 May 62	**FAR AWAY** *Columbia DB 4836*	**24**	12 wks
30 Aug 62	● **WHAT NOW MY LOVE** *Columbia DB 4882*	**5**	17 wks
28 Feb 63	**WHAT KIND OF FOOL AM I?** *Columbia DB 4974*	**47**	2 wks
26 Sep 63	● **I (WHO HAVE NOTHING)** *Columbia DB 7113*	**6**	20 wks
23 Jan 64	**MY SPECIAL DREAM** *Columbia DB 7185*	**32**	7 wks
9 Apr 64	**GONE** *Columbia DB 7248*	**36**	5 wks
15 Oct 64	**GOLDFINGER** *Columbia DB 7360*	**21**	9 wks
20 May 65	**NO REGRETS** *Columbia DB 7535*	**39**	4 wks
11 Oct 67	**BIG SPENDER** *United Artists UP 1192*	**21**	15 wks
20 Jun 70	● **SOMETHING** *United Artists UP 35125*	**4**	21 wks
2 Jan 71	**THE FOOL ON THE HILL** *United Artists UP 35156*	**48**	1 wk
23 Jan 71	**SOMETHING** (re-entry) *United Artists UP 35125*	**50**	1 wk
27 Mar 71	**(WHERE DO I BEGIN) LOVE STORY** *United Artists UP 35194*	**34**	9 wks
7 Aug 71	**FOR ALL WE KNOW** *United Artists UP 35267*	**46**	1 wk
21 Aug 71	● **FOR ALL WE KNOW** (re-entry) *United Artists UP 35267*	**6**	23 wks
15 Jan 72	**DIAMONDS ARE FOREVER** *United Artists UP 35293*	**38**	6 wks
3 Mar 73	● **NEVER NEVER NEVER** *United Artists UP 35490*	**8**	18 wks
14 Jul 73	**NEVER NEVER NEVER** (re-entry) *United Artists UP 35490*	**48**	1 wk

Mike BATT *UK, male vocalist*

Date	Title *Label Number*	Position	
16 Aug 75	● **SUMMERTIME CITY** *Epic EPC 3460*	**4**	8 wks

Mike Batt is, among other things, the voice behind the Wombles - see Wombles. On this hit, billed as Mike Batt (with the New Edition.)

BAUHAUS *UK, male vocal/instrumental group*

Date	Title *Label Number*	Position	
18 Apr 81	**KICK IN THE EYE** *Beggars Banquet BEG 54*	**59**	3 wks
4 Jul 81	**THE PASSIONS OF LOVERS** *Beggars Banquet BEG 59*	**51**	2 wks
6 Mar 82	**KICK IN THE EYE** (EP) *Beggars Banquet BEG 74*	**45**	4 wks
19 Jun 82	**SPIRIT** *Beggars Banquet BEG 79*	**42**	5 wks
9 Oct 82	**ZIGGY STARDUST** *Beggars Banquet BEG 83*	**15**	7 wks

Tracks on Kick In The Eye EP: *Kick In The Eye (Searching For Satori), Harry, Earwax.*

Les BAXTER *US, orchestra and chorus*

Date	Title *Label Number*	Position	
13 May 55	● **UNCHAINED MELODY** *Capitol CL 14257*	**10**	9 wks

BAY CITY ROLLERS

UK, male vocal/instrumental group

Date	Title *Label Number*	Position	
18 Sep 71	● **KEEP ON DANCING** *Bell 1164*	**9**	13 wks
9 Feb 74	● **REMEMBER (SHA-LA-LA)** *Bell 1338*	**6**	12 wks
27 Apr 74	● **SHANG-A-LANG** *Bell 1355*	**2**	10 wks
27 Jul 74	● **SUMMERLOVE SENSATION** *Bell 1369*	**3**	10 wks
12 Oct 74	● **ALL OF ME LOVES ALL OF YOU** *Bell 1382*	**4**	10 wks
8 Mar 75	★ **BYE BYE BABY** *Bell 1409*	**1**	16 wks
12 Jul 75	★ **GIVE A LITTLE LOVE** *Bell 1425*	**1**	9 wks
22 Nov 75	● **MONEY HONEY** *Bell 1461*	**3**	9 wks
10 Apr 76	● **LOVE ME LIKE I LOVE YOU** *Bell 1477*	**4**	6 wks
11 Sep 76	● **I ONLY WANNA BE WITH YOU** *Bell 1493*	**4**	9 wks
7 May 77	**IT'S A GAME** *Arista 108*	**16**	6 wks
30 Jul 77	**YOU MADE ME BELIEVE IN MAGIC** *Arista 127*	**34**	3 wks

BE BOP DELUXE

UK, male vocal/instrumental group

Date	Title *Label Number*	Position	
21 Feb 76	**SHIPS IN THE NIGHT** *Harvest HAR 5104*	**23**	8 wks
13 Nov 76	**HOT VALVES** (EP) *Harvest HAR 5117*	**36**	5 wks

Hot Valves EP *contains the following tracks: Maid In Heaven/ Blazing Apostles/ Jet Silver And The Dolls Of Venus/ Bring Back The Spark.*

BEACH BOYS *US, male vocal/instrumental group*

Date	Title *Label Number*	Position	
1 Aug 63	**SURFIN' USA** *Capitol CL 15305*	**34**	7 wks
9 Jul 64	● **I GET AROUND** *Capitol CL 15350*	**7**	13 wks
29 Oct 64	**WHEN I GROW UP (TO BE A MAN)** *Capitol CL 15361*	**44**	2 wks
19 Nov 64	**WHEN I GROW UP (TO BE A MAN)** (re-entry) *Capitol CL 15361*	**27**	5 wks
21 Jan 65	**DANCE DANCE DANCE** *Capitol CL 15370*	**24**	6 wks
3 Jun 65	**HELP ME RHONDA** *Capitol CL 15392*	**27**	10 wks
2 Sep 65	**CALIFORNIA GIRLS** *Capitol CL 15409*	**26**	8 wks
17 Feb 66	● **BARBARA ANN** *Capitol CL 15432*	**3**	10 wks
21 Apr 66	● **SLOOP JOHN B** *Capitol CL 15441*	**2**	15 wks
28 Jul 66	● **GOD ONLY KNOWS** *Capitol CL 15459*	**2**	14 wks
3 Nov 66	★ **GOOD VIBRATIONS** *Capitol CL 15475*	**1**	13 wks
4 May 67	● **THEN I KISSED HER** *Capitol CL 15502*	**4**	11 wks
23 Aug 67	● **HEROES AND VILLAINS** *Capitol CL 15510*	**8**	9 wks
22 Nov 67	**WILD HONEY** *Capitol CL 15521*	**29**	6 wks
17 Jan 68	**DARLIN'** *Capitol CL 15527*	**11**	14 wks
8 May 68	**FRIENDS** *Capitol CL 15545*	**25**	7 wks
24 Jul 68	★ **DO IT AGAIN** *Capitol CL 15554*	**1**	14 wks
18 Dec 68	**BLUEBIRDS OVER THE MOUNTAIN** *Capitol CL 15572*	**33**	5 wks
26 Feb 69	● **I CAN HEAR MUSIC** *Capitol CL 15584*	**10**	13 wks
11 Jun 69	● **BREAK AWAY** *Capitol CL 15598*	**6**	11 wks
16 May 70	● **COTTONFIELDS** *Capitol CL 15640*	**5**	17 wks
3 Mar 73	**CALIFORNIA SAGA - CALIFORNIA** *Reprise K 14232*	**37**	5 wks
3 Jul 76	**GOOD VIBRATIONS** (re-issue) *Capitol CL 15875*	**18**	7 wks
10 Jul 76	**ROCK AND ROLL MUSIC** *Reprise K 14440*	**36**	4 wks
31 Mar 79	**HERE COMES THE NIGHT** *Caribou CRB 7204*	**37**	8 wks
16 Jun 79	● **LADY LYNDA** *Caribou CRB 7427*	**6**	11 wks
29 Sep 79	**SUMAHAMA** *Caribou CRB 7846*	**45**	4 wks
29 Aug 81	**BEACH BOYS MEDLEY** *Capitol CL 213*	**47**	4 wks

BEAKY — See *Dave DEE, DOZY, BEAKY, MICK and TICH*

The BEAT *UK, male vocal/instrumental group*

Date	Title *Label Number*	Position	
8 Dec 79	● **TEARS OF A CLOWN/RANKING FULL STOP** *2 TONE CHS TT 6*	**6**	11 wks
23 Feb 80	● **HANDS OFF - SHE'S MINE** *Go Feet FEET 1*	**9**	9 wks
3 May 80	● **MIRROR IN THE BATHROOM** *Go Feet FEET 2*	**4**	9 wks
16 Aug 80	**BEST FRIEND/ STAND DOWN MARGARET** (DUB) *Go Feet FEET 3*	**22**	9 wks
13 Dec 80	● **TOO NICE TO TALK TO** *Go Feet FEET 4*	**7**	wks
18 Apr 81	**DROWNING/ALL OUT TO GET YOU** *Go Feet FEET 6*	**22**	8 wks
20 Jun 81	**DOORS OF YOUR HEART** *Go Feet FEET 9*	**33**	6 wks
4 Dec 81	**HIT IT** *Go Feet FEET 11*	**70**	2 wks
17 Apr 82	**SAVE IT FOR LATER** *Go-Feet FEET 333*	**47**	4 wks
18 Sep 82	**JEANETTE** *Go-Feet FEET 15*	**45**	3 wks
4 Dec 82	**I CONFESS** *Go-Feet FEET 16*	**54**	3 wks

BEATLES *UK, male vocal/instrumental group*

Date	Title *Label Number*	Position	
11 Oct 62	**LOVE ME DO** *Parlophone R 4949*	**17**	18 wks
17 Jan 63	● **PLEASE PLEASE ME** *Parlophone R 4983*	**2**	18 wks
18 Apr 63	★ **FROM ME TO YOU** *Parlophone R 5015*	**1**	21 wks
29 Aug 63	★ **SHE LOVES YOU** *Parlophone R 5055*	**1**	31 wks
5 Dec 63	★ **I WANT TO HOLD YOUR HAND** *Parlophone R 5084*	**1**	21 wks
26 Mar 64	★ **CAN'T BUY ME LOVE** *Parlophone R 5114*	**1**	14 wks
9 Apr 64	**SHE LOVES YOU** (re-entry) *Parlophone R 5055*	**42**	2 wks
14 May 64	**I WANT TO HOLD YOUR HAND** (re-entry) *Parlophone R 5084*	**48**	1 wk
11 Jun 64	**AIN'T SHE SWEET** *Polydor 52 317*	**29**	6 wks
9 Jul 64	**CAN'T BUY ME LOVE** (re-entry) *Parlophone R 5114*	**47**	1 wk
16 Jul 64	★ **A HARD DAY'S NIGHT** *Parlophone R 5160*	**1**	13 wks
3 Dec 64	★ **I FEEL FINE** *Parlophone R 5200*	**1**	14 wks
15 Apr 65	★ **TICKET TO RIDE** *Parlophone R 5265*	**1**	12 wks
29 Jul 65	★ **HELP!** *Parlophone R 5305*	**1**	14 wks
9 Dec 65	★ **DAY TRIPPER/ WE CAN WORK IT OUT** *Parlophone R 5389*	**1**	12 wks
16 Jun 66	★ **PAPERBACK WRITER** *Parlophone R 5452*	**1**	11 wks
11 Aug 66	★ **YELLOW SUBMARINE/ ELEANOR RIGBY** *Parlophone R 5493*	**1**	13 wks
23 Feb 67	● **PENNY LANE/ STRAWBERRY FIELDS FOREVER** *Parlophone R 5570*	**2**	11 wks
12 Jul 67	★ **ALL YOU NEED IS LOVE** *Parlophone R 5620*	**1**	13 wks
29 Nov 67	★ **HELLO GOODBYE** *Parlophone R 5655*	**1**	12 wks
13 Dec 67	● **MAGICAL MYSTERY TOUR** (DOUBLE EP) *Parlophone SMMT/ MMT 1*	**2**	12 wks
20 Mar 68	★ **LADY MADONNA** *Parlophone R 5675*	**1**	8 wks
4 Sep 68	★ **HEY JUDE** *Apple R 5722*	**1**	16 wks
23 Apr 69	★ **GET BACK** *Apple R 5777*	**1**	17 wks
4 Jun 69	★ **BALLAD OF JOHN AND YOKO** *Apple R 5786*	**1**	14 wks
8 Nov 69	● **SOMETHING/ COME TOGETHER** *Apple R 5814*	**4**	12 wks

Date	Title *Label Number*	Position	
14 Mar 70	● **LET IT BE** *Apple R 5833*	**2**	9 wks
24 Oct 70	**LET IT BE** (re-entry) *Apple R 5833*	**43**	1 wk
13 Mar 76	● **YESTERDAY** *Apple R 6013*	**8**	7 wks
27 Mar 76	**HEY JUDE** (re-entry) *Apple R 5722*	**12**	7 wks
27 Mar 76	**PAPERBACK WRITER** (re-entry) *Parlophone R 5452*	**23**	5 wks
3 Apr 76	**STRAWBERRY FIELDS FOREVER** (re-entry) *Parlophone R 5570*	**32**	3 wks
3 Apr 76	**GET BACK** (re-entry) *Apple R 5777*	**28**	5 wks
10 Apr 76	**HELP!** (re-entry) *Parlophone R 5305*	**37**	3 wks
10 Jul 76	**BACK IN THE U. S. S. R.** *Parlophone R 6016*	**19**	6 wks
7 Oct 78	**SGT. PEPPER'S LONELY HEARTS CLUB BAND - WITH A LITTLE HELP FROM MY FRIENDS** *Parlophone R 6022*	**63**	3 wks
5 Jun 82	● **BEATLES MOVIE MEDLEY** *Parlophone R 6055*	**10**	9 wks
16 Oct 82	● **LOVE ME DO** (re-entry) *Parlophone R 4949*	**4**	7 wks

Get Back is "with Billy Preston", see also Billy Preston, Billy Preston and Syreeta. Tracks on Magical Mystery Tour EP: *Magical Mystery Tour/ Your Mother Should Know/ I Am The Walrus/ Fool On The Hill/ Flying/ Blue Jay Way. See also Tony Sheridan and the Beatles.*

Gilbert BECAUD *France, male vocalist*

Date	Title *Label Number*	Position	
29 Mar 75	● **A LITTLE LOVE AND UNDERSTANDING** *Decca F 13537*	**10**	12 wks

Jeff BECK *UK, male vocalist/instrumentalist - guitar*

Date	Title *Label Number*	Position	
23 Mar 67	**HI-HO SILVER LINING** *Columbia DB 8151*	**14**	14 wks
2 Aug 67	**TALLYMAN** *Columbia DB 8227*	**30**	3 wks
28 Feb 68	**LOVE IS BLUE** *Columbia DB 8359*	**23**	7 wks
4 Nov 72	**HI-HO SILVER LINING** (re-issue) *Rak RR 3*	**17**	11 wks
9 Oct 82	**HI-HO SILVER LINING** (re-entry of re-issue) *RAK RR*	**62**	4 wks

See also Jeff Beck and Rod Stewart.

Jeff BECK and Rod STEWART

UK, male vocal/instrumental duo

Date	Title *Label Number*	Position	
5 May 73	**I'VE BEEN DRINKING** *Rak RR 4*	**27**	6 wks

See also Jeff Beck, Rod Stewart, Donovan with Jeff Beck Group.

BEDROCKS *UK, male vocal/instrumental group*

Date	Title *Label Number*	Position	
18 Dec 68	**OB-LA-DI OB-LA-DA** *Columbia DB 8516*	**20**	7 wks

Celi BEE and the BUZZY BUNCH

US, male/female vocal/instrumental group

Date	Title *Label Number*	Position	
17 Jun 78	**HOLD YOUR HORSES BABE** *TK TKR 6032*	**72**	1 wk

BEE GEES *UK, male vocal/instrumental group*

Date	Title *Label Number*	Position	
27 Apr 67	**NEW YORK MINING DISASTER 1941** *Polydor 56 161*	**12**	10 wks
12 Jun 67	**TO LOVE SOMEBODY** *Polydor 56 178*	**50**	1 wk
26 Jun 67	**TO LOVE SOMEBODY** (re-entry) *Polydor 56 178*	**41**	4 wks
20 Sep 67	★ **MASSACHUSETTS** *Polydor 56 192*	**1**	17 wks
22 Nov 67	● **WORLD** *Polydor 56 220*	**9**	16 wks
31 Jan 68	● **WORDS** *Polydor 56 229*	**8**	10 wks
27 Mar 68	**JUMBO/ THE SINGER SANG HIS SONG** *Polydor 56 242*	**25**	7 wks
7 Aug 68	★ **I'VE GOTTA GET A MESSAGE TO YOU** *Polydor 56 273*	**1**	15 wks
19 Feb 69	● **FIRST OF MAY** *Polydor 56 304*	**6**	11 wks
4 Jun 69	**TOMORROW TOMORROW** *Polydor 56 331*	**23**	8 wks
16 Aug 69	● **DON'T FORGET TO REMEMBER** *Polydor 56 343*	**2**	15 wks
28 Mar 70	**I. O. I. O.** *Polydor 56 377*	**49**	1 wk
5 Dec 70	**LONELY DAYS** *Polydor 2001 104*	**33**	9 wks
29 Jan 72	**MY WORLD** *Polydor 2058 185*	**16**	9 wks
22 Jul 72	● **RUN TO ME** *Polydor 2058 255*	**9**	10 wks
28 Jun 75	● **JIVE TALKIN'** *RSO 2090 160*	**5**	11 wks
31 Jul 76	● **YOU SHOULD BE DANCING** *RSO 2090 195*	**5**	10 wks
13 Nov 76	**LOVE SO RIGHT** *RSO 2090 207*	**41**	4 wks
29 Oct 77	● **HOW DEEP IS YOUR LOVE** *RSO 2090 259*	**3**	15 wks
4 Feb 78	● **STAYIN' ALIVE** *RSO 2090 267*	**4**	20 wks
15 Apr 78	★ **NIGHT FEVER** *RSO 002*	**1**	20 wks
25 Nov 78	● **TOO MUCH HEAVEN** *RSO 25*	**3**	13 wks
17 Feb 79	★ **TRAGEDY** *RSO 27*	**1**	10 wks
14 Apr 79	**LOVE YOU INSIDE OUT** *RSO 31*	**13**	9 wks
5 Jan 80	**SPIRITS (HAVING FLOWN)** *RSO 52*	**16**	7 wks

Act was UK/Australia up to and including Tomorrow, Tomorrow.

BEGGAR and CO

UK, male vocal/instrumental group

Date	Title *Label Number*	Position	
7 Feb 81	**(SOMEBODY) HELP ME OUT** *Ensign ENY 201*	**15**	10 wks
12 Sep 81	**MULE (CHANT NO.2)** *RCA 130*	**37**	5 wks

BEGINNING OF THE END

US, male vocal/instrumental group

Date	Title *Label Number*	Position	
23 Feb 74	**FUNKY NASSAU** *Atlantic K 10021*	**31**	6 wks

Harry BELAFONTE *US, male vocalist*

Date	Title *Label Number*	Position	
1 Mar 57	● **BANANA BOAT SONG** *HMV POP 308*	**2**	18 wks
14 Jun 57	● **ISLAND IN THE SUN** *RCA 1007*	**3**	25 wks
6 Sep 57	**SCARLET RIBBONS** *HMV POP 360*	**18**	6 wks
1 Nov 57	★ **MARY'S BOY CHILD** *RCA 1022*	**1**	12 wks
22 Aug 58	**LITTLE BERNADETTE** *RCA 1072*	**16**	7 wks
28 Nov 58	● **MARY'S BOY CHILD** (re-entry) *RCA 1022*	**10**	6 wks
12 Dec 58	**SON OF MARY** *RCA 1084*	**18**	4 wks
11 Dec 59	**MARY'S BOY CHILD** (2nd re-entry) *RCA 1022*	**30**	1 wk

See also Harry Belafonte & Odetta.

Harry BELAFONTE and ODETTA

US, male/female vocal duo

Date	Title *Label Number*	Position	
21 Sep 61	**HOLE IN THE BUCKET** *RCA 1247*	**32**	2 wks
12 Oct 61	**HOLE IN THE BUCKET** (re-entry) *RCA 1247*	**34**	6 wks

See also Harry Belafonte.

BELL and JAMES *US, male vocal duo*

Date	Title *Label Number*	Position	
31 Mar 79	**LIVIN' IT UP (FRIDAY NIGHT)** *A & M AMS 7424*	**68**	1 wk
14 Apr 79	**LIVIN' IT UP (FRIDAY NIGHT)** (re-entry) *A & M AMS 7424*	**59**	2 wks

BEE GEES The Bee Gees are awarded King Arthur's Round Table for selling 2 million copies of Massachusetts. (The United States refused to reciprocate by giving Massachusetts to Richard Harris for his part in *Camelot*)

Left **CLIFF BENNETT** Alone – after his Rousers had rebelled
Bottom left **DAVE BERRY** Dave Berry – poised to shoot up the chart
Below **BEAT** Not a clown, mirror or Prime Minister in sight

Date	Title *Label Number*	Position	

Archie BELL and the DRELLS

US, male vocal group

Date	Title *Label Number*	Pos	Wks
7 Oct 72	**HERE I GO AGAIN** *Atlantic K 10210*	**11**	10 wks
27 Jan 73	**THERE'S GONNA BE A SHOWDOWN** *Atlantic K 10263*	**36**	5 wks
8 May 76	**SOUL CITY WALK** *Philadelphia International PIR 4250*	**13**	10 wks
11 Jun 77	**EVERYBODY HAVE A GOOD TIME** *Philadelphia International PIR 5179*	**43**	4 wks

See also Philadelphia International All-Stars

Freddie BELL and the BELLBOYS

US, male vocal/instrumental group

Date	Title *Label Number*	Pos	Wks
28 Sep 56	● **GIDDY-UP-A-DING-DONG** *Mercury MT 122*	**4**	10 wks

Maggie BELL *UK, female vocalist*

Date	Title *Label Number*	Pos	Wks
15 Apr 78	**HAZELL** *Swan Song SSK 19412*	**37**	5 wks

See also B.A. Robertson and Maggie Bell.

William BELL *US, male vocalist*

Date	Title *Label Number*	Pos	Wks
29 May 68	**TRIBUTE TO A KING** *Stax 601 038*	**31**	7 wks

See also Judy Clay and William Bell.

BELLAMY BROTHERS *US, male vocal duo*

Date	Title *Label Number*	Pos	Wks
17 Apr 76	● **LET YOUR LOVE FLOW** *Warner Bros. K 16690*	**7**	12 wks
21 Aug 76	**SATIN SHEETS** *Warner Bros. K 16775*	**43**	3 wks
11 Aug 79	● **IF I SAID YOU HAVE A BEAUTIFUL BODY WOULD YOU HOLD IT AGAINST ME** *Warner Bros. K 17405*	**3**	14 wks

BELLBOYS — See *Freddie BELL and the BELLBOYS*

La BELLE EPOQUE *France, female vocal duo*

Date	Title *Label Number*	Pos	Wks
27 Aug 77	**BLACK IS BLACK** *Harvest HAR 5133*	**48**	1 wk
10 Sep 77	● **BLACK IS BLACK** (re-entry) *Harvest HAR 5133*	**2**	13 wks

BELLE STARS

UK, female vocal/instrumental group

Date	Title *Label Number*	Pos	Wks
5 Jun 82	**IKO IKO** *Stiff BUY 150*	**35**	6 wks
17 Jul 82	**THE CLAPPING SONG** *Stiff BUY 155*	**11**	9 wks
16 Oct 82	**MOCKINGBIRD** *Stiff BUY 159*	**51**	3 wks

BELMONTS — See *DION and the BELMONTS*

David BENDETH

Canada, male vocalist and multi-instrumentalist

Date	Title *Label Number*	Pos	Wks
8 Sep 79	**FEEL THE REAL** *Sidewalk SID 113*	**44**	5 wks

BENELUX and Nancy DEE

Belgium/Holland/Luxembourg, female vocal group

Date	Title *Label Number*	Pos	Wks
25 Aug 79	**SWITCH** *Scope/Hansa SC 4*	**52**	4 wks

Boyd BENNETT *US, male vocalist*

Date	Title *Label Number*	Pos	Wks
23 Dec 55	**SEVENTEEN** *Parlophone R 4063*	**16**	2 wks

Chris BENNETT — See *MUNICH MACHINE*

Cliff BENNETT and the REBEL ROUSERS *UK, male vocal/instrumental group*

Date	Title *Label Number*	Pos	Wks
1 Oct 64	● **ONE WAY LOVE** *Parlophone R 5713*	**9**	9 wks
4 Feb 65	**I'LL TAKE YOU HOME** *Parlophone R 5229*	**42**	3 wks
11 Aug 66	● **GOT TO GET YOU INTO MY LIFE** *Parlophone R 5489*	**6**	11 wks

Peter E. BENNETT *UK, male vocalist*

Date	Title *Label Number*	Pos	Wks
7 Nov 70	**THE SEAGULL'S NAME WAS NELSON** *RCA 1991*	**45**	1 wk

Tony BENNETT *US, male vocalist*

Date	Title *Label Number*	Pos	Wks
15 Apr 55	★ **STRANGER IN PARADISE** *Philips PB 420*	**1**	16 wks
16 Sep 55	**CLOSE YOUR EYES** *Philips PB 445*	**18**	1 wk
13 Apr 56	**COME NEXT SPRING** *Philips PB 537*	**29**	1 wk
5 Jan 61	**TILL/ SERENATA** *Philips PB 1079*	**35**	2 wks
18 Jul 63	**THE GOOD LIFE** *CBS AAG 153*	**27**	13 wks
6 May 65	**IF I RULED THE WORLD** *CBS 201735*	**40**	5 wks
27 May 65	**I LEFT MY HEART IN SAN FRANCISCO** *CBS 201730*	**46**	2 wks
30 Sep 65	**I LEFT MY HEART IN SAN FRANCISCO** (re-entry) *CBS 201730*	**40**	5 wks
9 Dec 65	**I LEFT MY HEART IN SAN FRANCISCO** (2nd re-entry) *CBS 201730*	**25**	7 wks
23 Dec 65	**THE VERY THOUGHT OF YOU** *CBS 202021*	**21**	9 wks

Gary BENSON *UK, male vocalist*

Date	Title *Label Number*	Pos	Wks
9 Aug 75	**DON'T THROW IT ALL AWAY** *State STAT 10*	**20**	8 wks

George BENSON

US, male vocalist/instrumentalist - guitar

Date	Title *Label Number*	Pos	Wks
25 Oct 75	**SUPERSHIP** *CTI CTSP 002*	**30**	6 wks
4 Jun 77	**NATURE BOY** *Warner Bros. K 16921*	**26**	6 wks
24 Sep 77	**THE GREATEST LOVE OF ALL** *Arista 133*	**27**	7 wks
31 Mar 79	**LOVE BALLAD** *Warner Bros. K 17333*	**29**	9 wks
26 Jul 80	● **GIVE ME THE NIGHT** *Warner Bros. K 17673*	**7**	10 wks
4 Oct 80	● **LOVE X LOVE** *Warner Bros. K 17699*	**10**	8 wks
7 Feb 81	**WHAT'S ON YOUR MIND** *Warner Bros. K 17748*	**45**	5 wks
14 Nov 81	**TURN YOUR LOVE AROUND** *Warner Bros. K 17877*	**29**	11 wks
23 Jan 82	**NEVER GIVE UP ON A GOOD THING** *Warner Bros. K 17902*	**14**	10 wks

Billed as George 'Bad' Benson on first hit. See also Aretha Franklin and George Benson.

Date Title *Label Number* Position

Brook BENTON *US, male vocalist*

Date	Title *Label Number*	Position	
10 Jul 59	**ENDLESSLY** *Mercury AMT 1043*	**28**	2 wks
6 Oct 60	**KIDDIO** *Mercury AMT 1109*	**42**	3 wks
3 Nov 60	**KIDDIO** (re-entry) *Mercury AMT 1109*	**41**	3 wks
16 Feb 61	**FOOLS RUSH IN** *Mercury AMT 1121*	**50**	1 wk
13 Jul 61	**BOLL WEEVIL SONG** *Mercury AMT 1148*	**30**	9 wks

Ingrid BERGMAN — See *Dooley WILSON*

Elmer BERNSTEIN *US, orchestra*

Date	Title *Label Number*	Position	
18 Dec 59	● **STACCATOS THEME** *Capitol CL 15101*	**4**	10 wks
10 Mar 60	**STACCATOS THEME** (re-entry) *Capitol CL 15101*	**40**	1 wk

Chuck BERRY *US, male vocalist/guitarist*

Date	Title *Label Number*	Position	
21 Jun 57	**SCHOOL DAY** *Columbia DB 3951*	**24**	2 wks
12 Jul 57	**SCHOOL DAY** (re-entry) *Columbia DB 3951*	**24**	2 wks
25 Apr 58	**SWEET LITTLE SIXTEEN** *London HLM 8585*	**16**	5 wks
11 Jul 63	**GO GO GO** *Pye International 7N 25209*	**38**	6 wks
10 Oct 63	● **LET IT ROCK/ MEMPHIS TENNESSEE** *Pye International 7N 25218*	**6**	13 wks
19 Dec 63	**RUN RUDOLPH RUN** *Pye International 7N 25228*	**36**	6 wks
13 Feb 64	**NADINE (IS IT YOU)** *Pye International 7N 25236*	**27**	6 wks
2 Apr 64	**NADINE (IS IT YOU)** (re-entry) *Pye International 7N 25236*	**43**	1 wk
7 May 64	● **NO PARTICULAR PLACE TO GO** *Pye International 7N 25242*	**3**	12 wks
20 Aug 64	**YOU NEVER CAN TELL** *Pye International 7N 25257*	**23**	8 wks
14 Jan 65	**PROMISED LAND** *Pye International 7N 25285*	**26**	6 wks
28 Oct 72	★ **MY DING-A-LING** *Chess 6145 019*	**1**	17 wks
3 Feb 73	**REELIN' AND ROCKIN'** *Chess 6145 020*	**18**	7 wks

Dave BERRY *UK, male vocalist*

Date	Title *Label Number*	Position	
19 Sep 63	**MEMPHIS TENNESSEE** *Decca F 11734*	**19**	13 wks
9 Jan 64	**MY BABY LEFT ME** *Decca F 11803*	**41**	1 wk
23 Jan 64	**MY BABY LEFT ME** (re-entry) *Decca F 11803*	**37**	8 wks
30 Apr 64	**BABY IT'S YOU** *Decca F 11888*	**24**	6 wks
6 Aug 64	● **THE CRYING GAME** *Decca F 11937*	**5**	12 wks
26 Nov 64	**ONE HEART BETWEEN TWO** *Decca F 12020*	**41**	2 wks
25 Mar 65	● **LITTLE THINGS** *Decca F 12103*	**5**	12 wks
22 Jul 65	**THIS STRANGE EFFECT** *Decca F 12188*	**37**	6 wks
30 Jun 66	● **MAMA** *Decca F 12435*	**5**	16 wks

Billed as Dave Berry & The Cruisers on the first two hits.

Mike BERRY *UK, male vocal group*

Date	Title *Label Number*	Position	
12 Oct 61	**TRIBUTE TO BUDDY HOLLY** *HMV POP 912*	**24**	6 wks
3 Jan 63	● **DON'T YOU THINK IT'S TIME** *HMV POP 1105*	**6**	12 wks
11 Apr 63	**MY LITTLE BABY** *HMV POP 1142*	**34**	7 wks
2 Aug 80	● **THE SUNSHINE OF YOUR SMILE** *Polydor 2059 261*	**9**	12 wks
29 Nov 80	**IF I COULD ONLY MAKE YOU CARE** *Polydor POSP 202*	**37**	9 wks
5 Sep 81	**MEMORIES** *Polydor POSP 287*	**55**	5 wks

HMV hits creditd to Mike Berry with the Outlaws. See also Outlaws.

BEVERLEY SISTERS *UK, female vocal trio*

Date	Title *Label Number*	Position	
27 Nov 53	**I SAW MOMMY KISSING SANTA CLAUS** *Philips PB 188*	**11**	1 wk
11 Dec 53	● **I SAW MOMMY KISSING SANTA CLAUS** (re-entry) *Philips PB 188*	**6**	4 wks
13 Apr 56	**WILLIE CAN** *Decca F 10705*	**23**	4 wks
1 Feb 57	**I DREAMED** *Decca F 10832*	**24**	2 wks
13 Feb 59	● **LITTLE DRUMMER BOY** *Decca F 11107*	**6**	13 wks
20 Nov 59	**LITTLE DONKEY** *Decca F 11172*	**14**	7 wks
23 Jun 60	**GREEN FIELDS** *Columbia DB 4444*	**48**	1 wk
7 Jul 60	**GREEN FIELDS** (re-entry) *Columbia DB 4444*	**29**	2 wks

See also Various Artists - All Star Hit Parade No. 2.

BIDDU *UK, orchestra*

Date	Title *Label Number*	Position	
2 Aug 75	**SUMMER OF '42** *Epic EPC 3318*	**14**	8 wks
17 Apr 76	**RAIN FOREST** *Epic EPC 4084*	**39**	4 wks
11 Feb 78	**JOURNEY TO THE MOON** *Epic EPC 5910*	**41**	1 wk

BIG APPLE BAND — See *Walter MURPHY and the BIG APPLE BAND*

BIG BEN BANJO BAND *UK, instrumental group*

Date	Title *Label Number*	Position	
10 Dec 54	● **LET'S GET TOGETHER NO. 1** *Columbia DB 3549*	**6**	4 wks
9 Dec 55	**LET'S GET TOGETHER AGAIN** *Columbia DB 3676*	**19**	1 wk
30 Dec 55	**LET'S GET TOGETHER AGAIN** (re-entry) *Columbia DB 3676*	**18**	1 wk

These hits were both medleys as follows: Let's Get Together No. 1 : *I'm Just Wild About Harry/ April Showers/ Rock-a-Bye Your Baby/ Swanee/ Darktown Strutters Ball/ For Me And My Gal/ Oh You Beautiful Doll/ Yes Sir That's My Baby.* Let's Get Together Again: *I'm Looking Over A Four-leafed Clover/ By The Light Of The Silvery Moon/ Oh Susannah/ Baby Face/ I'm Sitting On Top Of The World/ My Mammy/ Dixie's Land/ Margie.*

BIG BOPPER *US, male vocalist*

Date	Title *Label Number*	Position	
26 Dec 58	**CHANTILLY LACE** *Mercury AMT 1002*	**30**	1 wk
9 Jan 59	**CHANTILLY LACE** (re-entry) *Mercury AMT 1002*	**12**	7 wks

BIG ROLL BAND — See *Zoot MONEY and the BIG ROLL BAND*

BIG SOUND — See *Simon DUPREE and the BIG SOUND*

BIG THREE *UK, vocal/instrumental group*

Date	Title *Label Number*	Position	
11 Apr 63	**SOME OTHER GUY** *Decca F 11614*	**37**	7 wks
11 Jul 63	**BY THE WAY** *Decca F 11689*	**22**	10 wks

Barry BIGGS *Jamaica, male vocalist*

Date	Title *Label Number*	Position	
28 Aug 76	**WORK ALL DAY** *Dynamic DYN 101*	**38**	5 wks
4 Dec 76	● **SIDESHOW** *Dynamic DYN 118*	**3**	16 wks
23 Apr 77	**YOU'RE MY LIFE** *Dynamic DYN 127*	**36**	4 wks
9 Jul 77	**THREE RING CIRCUS** *Dynamic DYN 128*	**22**	8 wks
15 Dec 79	**WHAT'S YOUR SIGN GIRL** *Dynamic DYN 150*	**55**	7 wks
20 Jun 81	**WIDE AWAKE IN A DREAM** *Dynamic DYN 10*	**44**	6 wks

Date **Title** *Label Number* **Position**

Ivor BIGGUN *UK, male vocalist*

Date	Title *Label Number*	Position	Weeks
2 Sep 78	**WINKER'S SONG (MISPRINT)** *Beggars Banquet BOP 1*	**22**	12 wks
12 Sep 81	**BRAS ON 45 (FAMILY VERSION)** *Dead Badger BOP 6*	**50**	3 wks

First hit gives minor credit to Ivor's backing group (UK, male), the Red Nosed Burglars. Second hit credited to Ivor Biggun and the D Cups.

BILBO *UK, male vocal/instrumental group*

Date	Title *Label Number*	Position	Weeks
26 Aug 78	**SHE'S GONNA WIN** *Lightning Lig 548*	**42**	7 wks

Mr. Acker BILK

UK, male band leader, vocalist/instrumentalist - clarinet

Date	Title *Label Number*	Position	Weeks
22 Jan 60	● **SUMMER SET** *Columbia DB 4382*	**5**	19 wks
9 Jun 60	**GOODNIGHT SWEET PRINCE** *Melodisc MEL 1547*	**50**	1 wk
18 Aug 60	**WHITE CLIFFS OF DOVER** *Columbia DB 4492*	**30**	9 wks
8 Dec 60	● **BUONA SERA** *Columbia DB 4544*	**7**	18 wks
13 Jul 61	● **THAT'S MY HOME** *Columbia DB 4673*	**7**	17 wks
2 Nov 61	**STARS AND STRIPES FOREVER/ CREOLE JAZZ** *Columbia SCD 2155*	**22**	10 wks
30 Nov 61	● **STRANGER ON THE SHORE** *Columbia DB 4750*	**2**	55 wks
26 Jul 62	**GOTTA SEE BABY TONIGHT** *Columbia SCD 2176*	**24**	9 wks
27 Sep 62	**LONELY** *Columbia DB 4897*	**14**	11 wks
24 Jan 63	**A TASTE OF HONEY** *Columbia DB 4949*	**16**	9 wks
21 Aug 76	● **ARIA** *Pye 7N 45607*	**5**	11 wks

Stranger On The Shore, Lonely *and* A Taste Of Honey *credit Mr Acker Bilk with the Leon Young String Chorale.* Aria *credits Acker Bilk (no 'Mr.') His Clarinet And Strings. All others Mr. Acker Bilk and his Paramount Jazz Band.*

BIMBO JET

France, male/female vocal/instrumental group

Date	Title *Label Number*	Position	Weeks
26 Jul 75	**EL BIMBO** *EMI 2317*	**12**	10 wks

Umberto BINDI *Italy, male vocalist*

Date	Title *Label Number*	Position	Weeks
10 Nov 60	**IL NOSTRO CONCERTO** *Oriole CB 1577*	**47**	1 wk

La BIONDA *Italy, male/female vocal group*

Date	Title *Label Number*	Position	Weeks
7 Oct 78	**ONE FOR YOU ONE FOR ME** *Philips 6198 227*	**54**	4 wks

BIRDS *UK, male vocal/instrumental group*

Date	Title *Label Number*	Position	Weeks
27 May 65	**LEAVING HERE** *Decca F 12140*	**45**	1 wk

Jane BIRKIN and Serge GAINSBOURG

UK/France, female/male vocal duo

Date	Title *Label Number*	Position	Weeks
30 Jul 69	● **JE T'AIME. . . MOI NON PLUS** *Fontana TF 1042*	**2**	11 wks
4 Oct 69	★ **JE T'AIME. . . MOI NON PLUS** (re-issue) *Major Minor MM 645*	**1**	14 wks
7 Dec 74	**JE T'AIME. . . MOI NON PLUS** (2nd re-issue) *Atlantic K 11511*	**31**	9 wks

Elvin BISHOP *US, male instrumentalist - guitar*

Date	Title *Label Number*	Position	Weeks
15 May 76	**FOOLED AROUND AND FELL IN LOVE** *Capricorn 2089 204*	**34**	4 wks

Cilla BLACK *UK, female vocalist*

Date	Title *Label Number*	Position	Weeks
17 Oct 63	**LOVE OF THE LOVED** *Parlophone R 5065*	**35**	6 wks
6 Feb 64	★ **ANYONE WHO HAD A HEART** *Parlophone R 5101*	**1**	17 wks
7 May 64	★ **YOU'RE MY WORLD** *Parlophone R 5133*	**1**	17 wks
6 Aug 64	● **IT'S FOR YOU** *Parlophone R 5162*	**7**	10 wks
14 Jan 65	● **YOU'VE LOST THAT LOVIN' FEELIN'** *Parlophone R 5225*	**2**	9 wks
22 Apr 65	**I'VE BEEN WRONG BEFORE** *Parlophone R 5265*	**17**	8 wks
13 Jan 66	● **LOVE'S JUST A BROKEN HEART** *Parlophone R 5395*	**5**	11 wks
31 Mar 66	● **ALFIE** *Parlophone R 5427*	**9**	12 wks
9 Jun 66	● **DON'T ANSWER ME** *Parlophone R 5463*	**6**	10 wks
20 Oct 66	**A FOOL AM I** *Parlophone R 5515*	**13**	9 wks
8 Jun 67	**WHAT GOOD AM I** *Parlophone R 5608*	**24**	7 wks
29 Nov 67	**I ONLY LIVE TO LOVE YOU** *Parlophone R 5652*	**26**	11 wks
13 Mar 68	● **STEP INSIDE LOVE** *Parlophone R 5674*	**8**	9 wks
12 Jun 68	**WHERE IS TOMORROW** *Parlophone R 5706*	**40**	3 wks
12 Feb 69	● **SURROUND YOURSELF WITH SORROW** *Parlophone R 5759*	**3**	12 wks
9 Jul 69	● **CONVERSATIONS** *Parlophone R 5785*	**7**	12 wks
13 Dec 69	**IF I THOUGHT YOU'D EVER CHANGE YOUR MIND** *Parlophone R 5820*	**20**	9 wks
20 Nov 71	● **SOMETHING TELLS ME (SOMETHING IS GONNA HAPPEN TONIGHT)** *Parlophone R 5924*	**3**	14 wks
2 Feb 74	**BABY WE CAN'T GO WRONG** *EMI 2107*	**36**	6 wks

Jeanne BLACK *US, female vocalist*

Date	Title *Label Number*	Position	Weeks
23 Jun 60	**HE'LL HAVE TO STAY** *Capitol CL 15131*	**41**	4 wks

BLACK GORILLA

UK, male/female vocal/instrumental group

Date	Title *Label Number*	Position	Weeks
27 Aug 77	**GIMME DAT BANANA** *Response SR 502*	**29**	6 wks

BLACK LACE *UK, male vocal/instrumental group*

Date	Title *Label Number*	Position	Weeks
31 Mar 79	**MARY ANN** *EMI 2919*	**42**	4 wks

BLACK SABBATH

UK/US, male vocal/instrumental group

Date	Title *Label Number*	Position	Weeks
29 Aug 70	● **PARANOID** *Vertigo 6059 010*	**4**	18 wks
3 Jun 78	**NEVER SAY DIE** *Vertigo SAB 001*	**21**	8 wks
14 Oct 78	**HARD ROAD** *Vertigo SAB 002*	**33**	4 wks
5 Jul 80	**NEON KNIGHTS** *Vertigo SAB 3*	**22**	9 wks
16 Aug 80	**PARANOID** (re-issue) *Nems BSS 101*	**14**	12 wks
6 Dec 80	**DIE YOUNG** *Vertigo SAB 4*	**41**	7 wks
7 Nov 81	**MOB RULES** *Vertigo SAB 5*	**46**	4 wks
13 Feb 82	**TURN UP THE NIGHT** *Vertigo/Phonogram SAB 6*	**37**	5 wks

Group UK only for first 3 hits and re-issue of Paranoid.

Date	Title *Label Number*	Position	

Date Title *Label Number* Position

BLACK SLATE

UK/Jamaica, male vocal/instrumental group

Date	Title *Label Number*	Position	
20 Sep 80	● **AMIGO** *Ensign ENY 42*	**9**	9 wks
6 Dec 80	**BOOM BOOM** *Ensign ENY 47*	**51**	6 wks

Band of the BLACK WATCH

UK, military band

Date	Title *Label Number*	Position	
30 Aug 75	● **SCOTCH ON THE ROCKS** *Spark SRL 1128*	**8**	14 wks
13 Dec 75	**DANCE OF THE CUCKOOS** *Spark SRL 1135*	**37**	8 wks

Tony BLACKBURN *UK, male vocalist*

Date	Title *Label Number*	Position	
24 Jan 68	**SO MUCH LOVE** *MGM 1375*	**31**	4 wks
26 Mar 69	**IT'S ONLY LOVE** *MGM 1467*	**42**	3 wks

BLACKBYRDS *US, male vocal/instrumental group*

Date	Title *Label Number*	Position	
31 May 75	**WALKING IN RHYTHM** *Fantasy FTC 114*	**23**	6 wks

BLACKFOOT *US, male vocal/instrumental group*

Date	Title *Label Number*	Position	
6 Mar 82	**DRY COUNTY** *Atco K 11686*	**43**	4 wks

BLACKFOOT SUE

UK, male vocal/instrumental group

Date	Title *Label Number*	Position	
12 Aug 72	● **STANDING IN THE ROAD** *Jam 13*	**4**	10 wks
16 Dec 72	**SING DON'T SPEAK** *Jam 29*	**36**	5 wks

BLACKHEARTS — See *Joan JETT and the BLACKHEARTS*

Bill BLACK'S COMBO

US, male instrumental group, Bill Black, bass

Date	Title *Label Number*	Position	
8 Sep 60	**WHITE SILVER SANDS** *London HLU 9090*	**50**	1 wk
3 Nov 60	**DON'T BE CRUEL** *London HLU 9212*	**32**	7 wks

BLACKWELLS *US, male vocal group*

Date	Title *Label Number*	Position	
18 May 61	**LOVE OR MONEY** *London HLW 9334*	**46**	2 wks

Vivian BLAINE *US, female vocalist*

Date	Title *Label Number*	Position	
10 Jul 53	**BUSHEL AND A PECK** *Brunswick 05100*	**12**	1 wk

Joyce BLAIR — See *Miss X*

Peter BLAKE *UK, male vocalist*

Date	Title *Label Number*	Position	
8 Oct 77	**LIPSMACKIN' ROCK 'N' ROLLIN'** *Pepper UP 36295*	**40**	4 wks

BLANCMANGE *UK, male vocal/instrumental group*

Date	Title *Label Number*	Position	
17 Apr 82	**GOD'S KITCHEN/I'VE SEEN THE WORD** *London BLANC 1*	**65**	2 wks
31 Jul 82	**FEEL ME** *London BLANC 2*	**46**	5 wks
30 Oct 82	● **LIVING ON THE CEILING** *London BLANC 3*	**7†**	9 wks

Billy BLAND *US, male vocalist*

Date	Title *Label Number*	Position	
19 May 60	**LET THE LITTLE GIRL DANCE** *London HL 9096*	**15**	10 wks

BLOCKHEADS — See *Ian DURY and the BLOCKHEADS*

BLONDIE

US/UK, female/male vocal/instrumental group

Date	Title *Label Number*	Position	
18 Feb 78	● **DENIS** *Chrysalis CHS 2204*	**2**	14 wks
6 May 78	● **(I'M ALWAYS TOUCHED BY YOUR) PRESENCE DEAR** *Chrysalis CHS 2217*	**10**	9 wks
26 Aug 78	**PICTURE THIS** *Chrysalis CHS 2242*	**12**	11 wks
11 Nov 78	● **HANGING ON THE TELEPHONE** *Chrysalis CHR 2266*	**5**	12 wks
27 Jan 79	★ **HEART OF GLASS** *Chrysalis CHE 2275*	**1**	12 wks
19 May 79	★ **SUNDAY GIRL** *Chrysalis CHS 2320*	**1**	13 wks
29 Sep 79	● **DREAMING** *Chrysalis CHS 2350*	**2**	8 wks
24 Nov 79	**UNION CITY BLUE** *Chrysalis CHS 2400*	**13**	10 wks
23 Feb 80	★ **ATOMIC** *Chrysalis CHS 2410*	**1**	9 wks
12 Apr 80	★ **CALL ME** *Chrysalis CHS 2414*	**1**	9 wks
8 Nov 80	★ **THE TIDE IS HIGH** *Chrysalis CHS 2465*	**1**	12 wks
24 Jan 81	● **RAPTURE** *Chrysalis CHS 2485*	**5**	8 wks
8 May 82	**ISLAND OF LOST SOULS** *Chrysalis CHS 2608*	**11**	9 wks
24 Jul 82	**WAR CHILD** *Chrysalis CHS 2624*	**39**	4 wks

BLOOD SWEAT AND TEARS

US, male vocal/instrumental group

Date	Title *Label Number*	Position	
30 May 69	**YOU'VE MADE ME SO VERY HAPPY** *CBS 4116*	**35**	6 wks

BLOODSTONE *US, male vocal/instrumental group*

Date	Title *Label Number*	Position	
18 Aug 73	**NATURAL HIGH** *Decca F 13382*	**40**	4 wks

Bobby BLOOM *US, male vocalist*

Date	Title *Label Number*	Position	
29 Aug 70	● **MONTEGO BAY** *Polydor 2058 051*	**3**	14 wks
12 Dec 70	**MONTEGO BAY** (re-entry) *Polydor 2058 051*	**42**	3 wks
9 Jan 71	**MONTEGO BAY** (2nd re-entry) *Polydor 2058 051*	**47**	2 wks
9 Jan 71	**HEAVY MAKES YOU HAPPY** *Polydor 2001 122*	**31**	5 wks

Kurtis BLOW *US, male vocalist*

Date	Title *Label Number*	Position	
15 Dec 79	**CHRISTMAS RAPPIN'** *Mercury BLOW 7*	**30**	6 wks
11 Oct 80	**THE BREAKS** *Mercury BLOW 8*	**47**	4 wks

BLUE *UK, male vocal/instrumental group*

Date	Title *Label Number*	Position	
30 Apr 77	**GONNA CAPTURE YOUR HEART** *Rocket ROKN 522*	**18**	8 wks

Babbity BLUE *UK, female vocalist*

Date	Title *Label Number*	Position	Weeks
11 Feb 65	**DON'T MAKE ME** *Decca F 12053*	**48**	2 wks

Barry BLUE *UK, male vocalist*

Date	Title *Label Number*	Position	Weeks
28 Jun 73	● **(DANCING) ON A SATURDAY NIGHT** *Bell 1295*	**2**	15 wks
3 Nov 73	● **DO YOU WANNA DANCE** *Bell 1336*	**7**	12 wks
2 Mar 74	**SCHOOL LOVE** *Bell 1345*	**11**	9 wks
3 Aug 74	**MISS HIT AND RUN** *Bell 1364*	**26**	7 wks
26 Oct 74	**HOT SHOT** *Bell 1379*	**23**	5 wks

BLUE FEATHER

Holland, male vocal/instrumental group

Date	Title *Label Number*	Position	Weeks
3 Jul 82	**LET'S FUNK TONIGHT** *Mercury/Phonogram MER 109*	**50**	4 wks

BLUE FLAMES — See *Georgie FAME*

BLUE GRASS BOYS — See *Johnny DUNCAN and the BLUE GRASS BOYS*

BLUE HAZE *UK, male vocal/instrumental group*

Date	Title *Label Number*	Position	Weeks
18 Mar 72	**SMOKE GETS IN YOUR EYES** *A & M AMS 891*	**32**	6 wks

BLUE JEANS — See *Bob B. SOXX and the BLUE JEANS*

BLUE MINK

UK/US, male/female vocal/instrumental group

Date	Title *Label Number*	Position	Weeks
15 Nov 69	● **MELTING POT** *Philips BF 1818*	**3**	15 wks
28 Mar 70	● **GOOD MORNING FREEDOM** *Philips BF 1838*	**10**	10 wks
19 Sep 70	**OUR WORLD** *Philips 6006 042*	**17**	9 wks
29 May 71	● **BANNER MAN** *Regal Zonophone RZ 3034*	**3**	14 wks
11 Nov 72	**STAY WITH ME** *Regal Zonophone RZ 3064*	**11**	13 wks
17 Feb 73	**STAY WITH ME** (re-entry) *Regal Zonophone RZ 3064*	**43**	2 wks
3 Mar 73	**BY THE DEVIL** *EMI 2007*	**26**	9 wks
23 Jun 73	● **RANDY** *EMI 2028*	**9**	11 wks

BLUE OYSTER CULT

US,male vocal/instrumental group

Date	Title *Label Number*	Position	Weeks
20 May 78	**(DON'T FEAR) THE REAPER** *CBS 6333*	**16**	14 wks

BLUE RONDO a la TURK

UK, male vocal/instrumental group

Date	Title *Label Number*	Position	Weeks
14 Nov 81	**ME AND MR SANCHEZ** *Virgin VS 463*	**40**	4 wks
13 Mar 82	**KLACTOVEESEDSTEIN** *Virgin VS 476*	**50**	5 wks

BLUE ZOO *UK, male vocal/instrumental group*

Date	Title *Label Number*	Position	Weeks
12 Jun 82	**I'M YOUR MAN** *Magnet MAG 224*	**55**	3 wks
16 Oct 82	**CRY BOY CRY** *Magnet MAG 234*	**13**	10 wks

BLUENOTES — See *Harold MELVIN and the BLUENOTES*

BLUES BAND *UK, male vocal/instrumental group*

Date	Title *Label Number*	Position	Weeks
12 Jul 80	**BLUES BAND** (EP) *Arista BOOT 2*	**68**	2 wks

Tracks on Blues Band EP: *Maggie's Farm/ Ain't it Tuff/ Diddy Wah Diddy/ Back Door Man.*

Colin BLUNSTONE *UK, male vocalist*

Date	Title *Label Number*	Position	Weeks
12 Feb 72	**SAY YOU DON'T MIND** *Epic EPC 7765*	**15**	9 wks
11 Nov 72	**I DON'T BELIEVE IN MIRACLES** *Epic EPC 8434*	**31**	6 wks
17 Feb 73	**HOW COULD WE DARE TO BE WRONG** *Epic EPC 1197*	**45**	2 wks
29 May 82	**TRACKS OF MY TEARS** *PRT 7P 236*	**60**	2 wks

See also Neil MacArthur and Dave Stewart with Colin Blunstone.

BOB and EARL *US, male vocal duo*

Date	Title *Label Number*	Position	Weeks
12 Mar 69	● **HARLEM SHUFFLE** *Island WIP 6053*	**7**	13 wks

BOB and MARCIA

Jamaica, male/female vocal duo

Date	Title *Label Number*	Position	Weeks
14 Mar 70	● **YOUNG GIFTED AND BLACK** *Harry J HJ 6605*	**5**	12 wks
5 Jun 71	**PIED PIPER** *Trojan TR 7818*	**11**	13 wks

BODYSNATCHERS

UK, female vocal/instrumental group

Date	Title *Label Number*	Position	Weeks
15 Mar 80	**LET'S DO ROCK STEADY** *2Tone CHS TT 9*	**22**	9 wks
19 Jul 80	**EASY LIFE** *2Tone CHS TT 12*	**50**	3 wks

Humphrey BOGART — See *Dooley WILSON*

Hamilton BOHANNON

US, male vocalist/instrumentalist - drums

Date	Title *Label Number*	Position	Weeks
15 Feb 75	**SOUTH AFRICAN MAN** *Brunswick BR 16*	**22**	8 wks
24 May 75	● **DISCO STOMP** *Brunswick BR 19*	**6**	12 wks
5 Jul 75	**FOOT STOMPIN' MUSIC** *Brunswick BR 21*	**23**	6 wks
6 Sep 75	**HAPPY FEELING** *Brunswick BR 24*	**49**	3 wks
26 Aug 78	**LET'S START THE DANCE** *Mercury 6167 700*	**56**	4 wks
13 Feb 82	**LET'S START TO DANCE AGAIN** *London HL 10582*	**49**	5 wks

BOILING POINT

US, male vocal/instrumental group

Date	Title *Label Number*	Position	Weeks
27 May 78	**LET'S GET FUNKTIFIED** *Bang BANG 1312*	**41**	6 wks

Marc BOLAN *UK, male vocalist*

Date	Title *Label Number*	Position	Weeks
9 May 81	**RETURN OF THE ELECTRIC WARRIOR** (EP) *Rarn MBSF 001*	**50**	4 wks
19 Sep 81	**YOU SCARE ME TO DEATH** *Cherry Red CHERRY 29*	**51**	4 wks

See also T. Rex. Tracks on Return Of The Electric Warrior EP: *Sing Me A Song, Endless Sleep, The Lilac Hand Of Menthol Dan.*

Date	Title *Label Number*	Position	

BOMBERS

US, Male/female vocal/instrumental group

Date	Title *Label Number*	Position	
5 May 79	**(EVERYBODY) GET DANCIN'** *Flamingo FM 1*	**37**	7 wks
18 Aug 79	**LET'S DANCE** *Flamingo FM 4*	**58**	3 wks

Ronnie BOND *UK, male vocalist*

Date	Title *Label Number*	Position	
31 May 80	**IT'S WRITTEN ON YOUR BODY** *Mercury MER 13*	**52**	5 wks

Gary 'U.S.' BONDS *US, male vocalist*

Date	Title *Label Number*	Position	
19 Jan 61	**NEW ORLEANS** *Top Rank JAR 527*	**16**	11 wks
20 Jul 61	● **QUARTER TO THREE** *Top Rank JAR 575*	**7**	13 wks
30 May 81	**THIS LITTLE GIRL** *EMI AMERICA EA 122*	**43**	6 wks
22 Aug 81	**JOLE BLON** *EMI AMERICA EA 127*	**51**	3 wks
31 Oct 81	**IT'S ONLY LOVE** *EMI AMERICA EA 128*	**43**	3 wks
17 Jul 82	**SOUL DEEP** *EMI AMERICA EA 140*	**59**	3 wks

Known as U.S. Bonds on his 1961 hits.

BONEY M

Various West Indian Islands male/female vocal group

Date	Title *Label Number*	Position	
18 Dec 76	● **DADDY COOL** *Atlantic K 10827*	**6**	13 wks
12 Mar 77	● **SUNNY** *Atlantic K 10892*	**3**	10 wks
25 Jun 77	● **MA BAKER** *Atlantic K 10965*	**2**	13 wks
29 Oct 77	● **BELFAST** *Atlantic K 11020*	**8**	13 wks
29 Apr 78	★ **RIVERS OF BABYLON/BROWN GIRL IN THE RING** *Atlantic /Hansa K 11120*	**1**	40 wks
7 Oct 78	● **RASPUTIN** *Atlantic /Hansa K 11192*	**2**	10 wks
2 Dec 78	★ **MARY'S BOY CHILD - OH MY LORD** *Atlantic /Hansa K 11221*	**1**	8 wks
3 Mar 79	● **PAINTER MAN** *Atlantic /Hansa K 11255*	**10**	6 wks
28 Apr 79	● **HOORAY! HOORAY! IT'S A HOLI HOLIDAY** *Atlantic/Hansa K 11279*	**3**	9 wks
11 Aug 79	**GOTTA GO HOME/EL LUTE** *Atlantic/Hansa K 11351*	**12**	11 wks
15 Dec 79	**I'M BORN AGAIN** *Atlantic/Hansa K 11410*	**35**	7 wks
26 Apr 80	**MY FRIEND JACK** *Atlantic/Hansa K 11463*	**57**	5 wks
14 Feb 81	**CHILDREN OF PARADISE** *Atlantic/Hansa K 11637*	**66**	2 wks
21 Nov 81	**WE KILL THE WORLD (DON'T KILL THE WORLD)** *Atlantic/Hansa K 11689*	**39**	5 wks

El Lute *only listed with* Gotta Go Home *from 29 Sep 79.*

Graham BONNET *UK, male vocalist*

Date	Title *Label Number*	Position	
21 Mar 81	● **NIGHT GAMES** *Vertigo VER 1*	**6**	11 wks
13 Jun 81	**LIAR** *Vertigo VER 2*	**51**	4 wks

Graham BONNEY *UK, male vocalist*

Date	Title *Label Number*	Position	
24 Mar 66	**SUPERGIRL** *Columbia DB 7843*	**19**	8 wks

BONNIE — See *DELANEY and BONNIE and FRIENDS*

BONZO DOG DOO-DAH BAND

UK, male vocal/instrumental group

Date	Title *Label Number*	Position	
6 Nov 68	● **I'M THE URBAN SPACEMAN** *Liberty LBF 15144*	**5**	14 wks

BOOKER T. & THE M. G.'S

US, male instrumental group

Date	Title *Label Number*	Position	
11 Dec 68	**SOUL LIMBO** *Stax 102*	**30**	9 wks
7 May 69	● **TIME IS TIGHT** *Stax 119*	**4**	18 wks
30 Aug 69	**SOUL CLAP '69** *Stax 127*	**35**	4 wks
15 Dec 79	● **GREEN ONIONS** *Atlantic K 10109*	**7**	12 wks

BOOMTOWN RATS

Ireland, male vocal/instrumental group

Date	Title *Label Number*	Position	
27 Aug 77	**LOOKING AFTER NO. 1** *Ensign ENY 4*	**11**	9 wks
19 Nov 77	**MARY OF THE FOURTH FORM** *Ensign ENY 9*	**15**	9 wks
15 Apr 78	**SHE'S SO MODERN** *Ensign ENY 13*	**12**	11 wks
17 Jun 78	● **LIKE CLOCKWORK** *Ensign ENY 14*	**6**	13 wks
14 Oct 78	★ **RAT TRAP** *Ensign ENY 16*	**1**	15 wks
21 Jul 79	★ **I DON'T LIKE MONDAYS** *Ensign ENY 30*	**1**	12 wks
17 Nov 79	**DIAMOND SMILES** *Ensign ENY 33*	**13**	10 wks
26 Jan 80	● **SOMEONE'S LOOKING AT YOU** *Ensign EN 34*	**4**	9 wks
22 Nov 80	● **BANANA REPUBLIC** *Ensign BONGO 1*	**3**	11 wks
31 Jan 81	**THE ELEPHANT'S GRAVEYARD (GUILTY)** *Ensign BONGO 2*	**26**	6 wks
11 Dec 81	**NEVER IN A MILLION YEARS** *Mercury MER 87*	**62**	3 wks
20 Mar 82	**HOUSE ON FIRE** *Mercury/Phonogram MER 91*	**24**	8 wks

Daniel BOONE *UK, male vocalist*

Date	Title *Label Number*	Position	
14 Aug 71	**DADDY DON'T YOU WALK SO FAST** *Penny Farthing PEN 764*	**17**	15 wks
1 Apr 72	**BEAUTIFUL SUNDAY** *Penny Farthing PEN 781*	**48**	1 wk
15 Apr 72	**BEAUTIFUL SUNDAY** (re-entry) *Penny Farthing PEN 781*	**21**	9 wks

Debby BOONE *US, female vocalist*

Date	Title *Label Number*	Position	
24 Dec 77	**YOU LIGHT UP MY LIFE** *Warner Bros. K 17043*	**48**	2 wks

Pat BOONE *US, male vocalist*

Date	Title *Label Number*	Position	
18 Nov 55	● **AIN'T THAT A SHAME** *London HLD 8173*	**7**	9 wks
27 Apr 56	★ **I'LL BE HOME** *London HLD 8253*	**1**	22 wks
27 Jul 56	**LONG TALL SALLY** *London HLD 8291*	**27**	3 wks
17 Aug 56	**I ALMOST LOST MY MIND** *London HLD 8303*	**14**	7 wks
24 Aug 56	**LONG TALL SALLY** (re-entry) *London HLD 8291*	**18**	4 wks
7 Dec 56	● **FRIENDLY PERSUASION** *London HLD 8346*	**3**	21 wks
11 Jan 57	**I'LL BE HOME** (re-entry) *London HLD 8253*	**19**	2 wks
11 Jan 57	**AIN'T THAT A SHAME** (re-entry) *London HLD 8173*	**22**	2 wks
1 Feb 57	● **DON'T FORBID ME** *London HLD 8370*	**2**	16 wks
26 Apr 57	**WHY BABY WHY** *London HLD 8404*	**17**	7 wks
5 Jul 57	● **LOVE LETTERS IN THE SAND** *London HLD 8445*	**2**	21 wks
27 Sep 57	● **REMEMBER YOU'RE MINE/THERE'S A GOLDMINE IN THE SKY** *London HLD 8479*	**5**	18 wks
6 Dec 57	● **APRIL LOVE** *London HLD 8512*	**7**	23 wks
13 Dec 57	**WHITE CHRISTMAS** *London HLD 8520*	**29**	1 wk
4 Apr 58	● **A WONDERFUL TIME UP THERE** *London HLD 8574*	**2**	17 wks
11 Apr 58	● **IT'S TOO SOON TO KNOW** *London HLD 8574*	**7**	12 wks
27 Jun 58	● **SUGAR MOON** *London HLD 8640*	**6**	12 wks
29 Aug 58	**IF DREAMS CAME TRUE** *London HLD 8675*	**16**	11 wks
5 Dec 58	**GEE BUT IT'S LONELY** *London HLD 8739*	**30**	1 wk
16 Jan 59	**I'LL REMEMBER TONIGHT** *London HLD 8775*	**28**	1 wk

Date	Title *Label Number*	Position	
6 Feb 59	**I'LL REMEMBER TONIGHT** (re-entry) *London HLD 8775*	**21**	1 wk
20 Feb 59	**I'LL REMEMBER TONIGHT** (2nd re-entry) *London HLD 8775*	**18**	7 wks
10 Apr 59	**WITH THE WIND AND THE RAIN IN YOUR HAIR** *London HLD 8824*	**21**	3 wks
22 May 59	**FOR A PENNY** *London HLD 8855*	**28**	3 wks
26 Jun 59	**FOR A PENNY** (re-entry) *London HLD 8855*	**19**	6 wks
31 Jul 59	**'TWIXT TWELVE AND TWENTY** *London HLD 8910*	**18**	6 wks
18 Sep 59	**'TWIXT TWELVE AND TWENTY** (re-entry) *London HLD 8910*	**26**	1 wk
23 Jun 60	**WALKING THE FLOOR OVER YOU** *London HLD 9138*	**40**	2 wks
14 Jul 60	**WALKING THE FLOOR OVER YOU** (re-entry) *London HLD 9138*	**46**	1 wk
4 Aug 60	**WALKING THE FLOOR OVER YOU** (2nd re-entry) *London HLD 9138*	**39**	2 wks
6 Jul 61	**MOODY RIVER** *London HLD 9350*	**18**	10 wks
7 Dec 61	● **JOHNNY WILL** *London HLD 9461*	**4**	13 wks
15 Feb 62	**I'LL SEE YOU IN MY DREAMS** *London HLD 9504*	**27**	9 wks
24 May 62	**QUANDO QUANDO QUANDO** *London HLD 9543*	**41**	4 wks
12 Jul 62	● **SPEEDY GONZALES** *London HLD 9573*	**2**	19 wks
15 Nov 62	**THE MAIN ATTRACTION** *London HLD 9620*	**12**	11 wks

There's A Goldmine In The Sky *was only credited for the week of 27 Sep 57 with* Remember You're Mine.

Ken BOOTHE *Jamaica, male vocalist*

Date	Title *Label Number*	Position	
21 Sep 74	★ **EVERYTHING I OWN** *Trojan TR 7920*	**1**	12 wks
14 Dec 74	**CRYING OVER YOU** *Trojan TR 7944*	**11**	10 wks

BOOTSY'S RUBBER BAND

US, male vocal/instrumental group

Date	Title *Label Number*	Position	
8 Jul 78	**BOOTZILLA** *Warner Bros. K 17196*	**43**	3 wks

BOSTON *US, male vocal/instrumental group*

Date	Title *Label Number*	Position	
29 Jan 77	**MORE THAN A FEELING** *Epic EPC 4658*	**22**	8 wks
7 Oct 78	**DON'T LOOK BACK** *Epic EPC 6653*	**43**	5 wks

Eve BOSWELL *Hungary, female vocalist*

Date	Title *Label Number*	Position	
30 Dec 55	● **PICKIN' A CHICKEN** *Parlophone R 4082*	**9**	7 wks
2 Mar 56	**PICKIN' A CHICKEN** (re-entry) *Parlophone R 4082*	**16**	3 wks
6 Apr 56	**PICKIN' A CHICKEN** (2nd re-entry) *Parlophone R 4082*	**20**	3 wks

BOW WOW WOW

UK, female/male vocal/instrumental group

Date	Title *Label Number*	Position	
26 Jul 80	**C30, C60, C90, GO** *EMI 5088*	**34**	7 wks
6 Dec 80	**YOUR CASSETTE PET** *EMI Wow 1*	**58**	6 wks
6 Dec 80	**W.O.R.K. (N.O. NAH NO! NO! MY DADDY DON'T)** *EMI 5153*	**62**	3 wks
15 Aug 81	**PRINCE OF DARKNESS** *RCA 100*	**58**	4 wks
7 Nov 81	**CHIHUAHUA** *RCA 144*	**51**	4 wks
30 Jan 82	● **GO WILD IN THE COUNTRY** *RCA 175*	**7**	13 wks
1 May 82	**SEE JUNGLE (JUNGLE BOY) TV SAVAGE** *RCA 220*	**45**	3 wks
5 Jun 82	● **I WANT CANDY** *RCA 238*	**9**	8 wks
31 Jul 82	**LOUIS QUATORZE** *RCA 263*	**66**	2 wks

Your Cassette Pet *listed as* Louis Quatorze *on 6 Dec 80 only. Tracks on* Your Cassette Pet *(available only as a cassette) are: Louis Quatorze; Gold He Said; Umo-Sex-Al Apache; I Want My Baby On Mars; Sexy Eiffel Towers; Giant Sized Baby Thing; Fools Rush In; Radio G String*

David BOWIE *UK, male vocalist*

Date	Title *Label Number*	Position	
6 Sep 69	**SPACE ODDITY** *Philips BF 1801*	**48**	1 wk
20 Sep 69	● **SPACE ODDITY** (re-entry) *Philips BF 1801*	**5**	13 wks
24 Jun 72	● **STARMAN** *RCA 2199*	**10**	11 wks
16 Sep 72	**JOHN I'M ONLY DANCING** *RCA 2263*	**12**	10 wks
9 Dec 72	● **THE JEAN GENIE** *RCA 2302*	**2**	13 wks
14 Apr 73	● **DRIVE-IN SATURDAY** *RCA 2352*	**3**	10 wks
30 Jun 73	● **LIFE ON MARS** *RCA 2316*	**3**	13 wks
15 Sep 73	● **THE LAUGHING GNOME** *Deram DM 123*	**6**	12 wks
20 Oct 73	● **SORROW** *RCA 2424*	**3**	9 wks
5 Jan 74	**SORROW** (re-entry) *RCA 2424*	**30**	4 wks
23 Feb 74	● **REBEL REBEL** *RCA LPBO 5009*	**5**	7 wks
20 Apr 74	**ROCK AND ROLL SUICIDE** *RCA LPBO 5021*	**22**	7 wks
22 Jun 74	**DIAMOND DOGS** *RCA APBO 0293*	**21**	6 wks
28 Sep 74	● **KNOCK ON WOOD** *RCA 2466*	**10**	6 wks
1 Mar 75	**YOUNG AMERICANS** *RCA 2523*	**18**	7 wks
2 Aug 75	**FAME** *RCA 2579*	**17**	8 wks
11 Oct 75	★ **SPACE ODDITY** (re-issue) *RCA 2593*	**1**	10 wks
29 Nov 75	● **GOLDEN YEARS** *RCA 2640*	**8**	10 wks
22 May 76	**TVC 15** *RCA 2682*	**33**	4 wks
19 Feb 77	● **SOUND AND VISION** *RCA PB 0905*	**3**	11 wks
15 Oct 77	**HEROES** *RCA PB 1121*	**24**	8 wks
21 Jan 78	**BEAUTY AND THE BEAST** *RCA PB 1190*	**39**	3 wks
2 Dec 78	**BREAKING GLASS**(EP) *RCA BOW 1*	**54**	7 wks
5 May 79	● **BOYS KEEP SWINGING** *RCA BOW 2*	**7**	10 wks
21 Jul 79	**D.J.** *RCA BOW 3*	**29**	5 wks
15 Dec 79	**JOHN I'M ONLY DANCING (AGAIN) (1975)/ JOHN I'M ONLY DANCING (1972)** *RCA BOW 4*	**12**	8 wks
1 Mar 80	**ALABAMA SONG** *RCA BOW 5*	**23**	5 wks
16 Aug 80	★ **ASHES TO ASHES** *RCA BOW 6*	**1**	10 wks
1 Nov 80	● **FASHION** *RCA BOW 7*	**5**	wks
10 Jan 81	**SCARY MONSTERS (AND SUPER CREEPS)** *RCA BOW 8*	**20**	6 wks
28 Nov 81	**WILD IS THE WIND** *RCA BOW 10*	**24**	10 wks
6 Mar 82	**BAAL'S HYMN (EP)** *RCA BOW 11*	**29**	5 wks
10 Apr 82	**CAT PEOPLE (PUTTING OUT FIRE)** *MCA 770*	**26**	6 wks

Tracks on Breaking Glass EP: *Breaking Glass/ Art Decade/ Ziggy Stardust. All 3 versions of* John I'm Only Dancing *are different versions. Tracks on* Baal's Hymn EP: *Baal's Hymn, The Drowned Girl, Remembering Marie, The Dirty Song, Ballard of the Adventurers. See also Queen and David Bowie, David Bowie and Bing Crosby.*

David BOWIE and Bing CROSBY

UK/US, male vocal duo

Date	Title *Label Number*	Position	
27 Nov 82	● **PEACE ON EARTH - LITTLE DRUMMER BOY** *RCA BOW 12*	**3**†	5 wks

See also David Bowie, Queen and David Bowie, Bing Crosby, Bing Crosby and Grace Kelly, Bing Crosby and Jane Wyman.

BOX TOPS *US, male vocal/instrumental group*

Date	Title *Label Number*	Position	
13 Sep 67	● **THE LETTER** *Stateside SS 2044*	**5**	12 wks
20 Mar 68	**CRY LIKE A BABY** *Bell 1001*	**15**	12 wks
23 Aug 69	**SOUL DEEP** *Bell 1068*	**22**	9 wks

Date	Title *Label Number*	Position	

Jimmy BOYD *US, male vocalist*

27 Nov 53 ● **I SAW MOMMY KISSING SANTA CLAUS** *Columbia DB 3365* — **3** 6 wks

See also Frankie Laine & Jimmy Boyd.

Jacqueline BOYER *France, female vocalist*

28 Apr 60 **TOM PILLIBI** *Columbia DB 4452* — **33** 2 wks

BOYSTOWN GANG *US, male/female vocal group*

22 Aug 81 **AIN'T NO MOUNTAIN HIGH ENOUGH** *WEA DICK 1* — **46** 6 wks
31 Jul 82 ● **CAN'T TAKE MY EYES OFF YOU** *ERC 101* — **4** 11 wks
9 Oct 82 **SIGNED SEALED DELIVERED (I'M YOURS)** *ERC 102* — **50** 3 wks

Wilfred BRAMBELL and Harry H. CORBETT *UK, male vocal duo*

28 Nov 63 **AT THE PALACE** (PARTS 1 & 2) *Pye 7N 15588* — **25** 12 wks

Johnny BRANDON *UK, male vocalist*

11 Mar 55 ● **TOMORROW** *Polygon P 1131* — **8** 6 wks
29 Apr 55 **TOMORROW** (re-entry) *Polygon P 1131* — **16** 2 wks
1 Jul 55 **DON'T WORRY** *Polygon P 1163* — **18** 4 wks

Laura BRANIGAN *US, female vocalist*

18 Dec 82 **GLORIA** *Atlantic K 11759* — **51**† 2 wks

BRASS CONSTRUCTION *US, male vocal/instrumental group*

3 Apr 76 **MOVIN'** *United Artists UP 36090* — **23** 6 wks
5 Feb 77 **HA CHA CHA(FUNKTION)** *United Artists UP 36205* — **37** 5 wks
26 Jan 80 **MUSIC MAKES YOU FEEL LIKE DANCING** *United Artists UP 615* — **39** 6 wks

BRAT *UK, male vocalist*

10 Jul 82 **CHALK DUST - THE UMPIRE STRIKES BACK** *Hansa SMASH 1* — **19** 8 wks

BRAVOS *Spain/Germany, male vocal/instrumental group*

30 Jun 66 ● **BLACK IS BLACK** *Decca F 22419* — **2** 13 wks
8 Sep 66 **I DON'T CARE** *Decca F 13367* — **16** 11 wks

BREAD *US, male vocal/instrumental group*

1 Aug 70 ● **MAKE IT WITH YOU** *Elektra 2101 010* — **5** 14 wks
15 Jan 72 **BABY I'M A WANT YOU** *Elektra K 12033* — **14** 10 wks
29 Apr 72 **EVERYTHING I OWN** *Elektra K 12041* — **32** 6 wks
30 Sep 72 **GUITAR MAN** *Elektra K 12066* — **16** 9 wks
25 Dec 76 **LOST WITHOUT YOUR LOVE** *Elektra K 12241* — **27** 7 wks

Freddy BRECK *Germany, male vocalist*

13 Apr 74 **SO IN LOVE WITH YOU** *Decca F 13481* — **44** 4 wks

BRECKER BROTHERS *US, male vocal/instrumental group*

4 Nov 78 **EAST RIVER** *Arista ARIST 211* — **34** 5 wks

BRENDON *UK, male vocalist*

19 Mar 77 **GIMME SOME** *Magnet MAG 80* — **14** 9 wks

Rose BRENNAN *UK, female vocalist*

7 Dec 61 **TALL DARK STRANGER** *Philips PB 1193* — **31** 9 wks

Walter BRENNAN *US, male vocalist*

28 Jun 62 **OLD RIVERS** *Liberty LIB 55436* — **38** 3 wks

Tony BRENT *UK, male vocalist*

19 Dec 52 ● **WALKIN' TO MISSOURI** *Columbia DB 3147* — **9** 2 wks
2 Jan 53 ● **MAKE IT SOON** *Columbia DB 3187* — **9** 4 wks
9 Jan 53 ● **WALKIN' TO MISSOURI** (re-entry) *Columbia DB 3147* — **7** 5 wks
23 Jan 53 **GOT YOU ON MY MIND** *Columbia DB 3226* — **12** 1 wk
13 Mar 53 ● **MAKE IT SOON** (re-entry) *Columbia DB 3187* — **9** 3 wks
30 Nov 56 **CINDY OH CINDY** *Columbia DB 3844* — **16** 6 wks
8 Feb 57 **CINDY OH CINDY** (re-entry) *Columbia DB 3844* — **30** 1 wk
28 Jun 57 **DARK MOON** *Columbia DB 3950* — **17** 14 wks
28 Feb 58 **THE CLOUDS WILL SOON ROLL BY** *Columbia DB 4066* — **24** 3 wks
9 May 58 **THE CLOUDS WILL SOON ROLL BY** (re-entry) *Columbia DB 4066* — **20** 2 wks
5 Sep 58 **GIRL OF MY DREAMS** *Columbia DB 4177* — **16** 7 wks
24 Jul 59 **WHY SHOULD I BE LONELY** *Columbia DB 4304* — **24** 4 wks

Bernard BRESSLAW *UK, male vocalist*

5 Sep 58 ● **MAD PASSIONATE LOVE** *HMV POP 522* — **6** 11 wks

See also Michael Medwin, Bernard Bresslaw, Alfie Bass and Leslie Fyson.

Teresa BREWER *US, female vocalist*

11 Feb 55 ● **LET ME GO LOVER** *Vogue/ Coral Q 72043* — **9** 10 wks
13 Apr 56 ● **A TEAR FELL** *Vogue/ Coral Q 72146* — **2** 15 wks
13 Jul 56 ● **SWEET OLD-FASHIONED GIRL** *Vogue/ Coral Q 72172* — **3** 15 wks
10 May 57 **NORA MALONE** *Vogue/ Coral Q 72224* — **26** 2 wks
23 Jun 60 **HOW DO YOU KNOW IT'S LOVE** *Coral Q 72396* — **21** 11 wks

Date	Title *Label Number*	Position	

BRIAN AND MICHAEL *UK, male vocal duo*

Date	Title *Label Number*	Position	
25 Feb 78	★ **MATCHSTALK MEN AND MATCHSTALK CATS AND DOGS** *Pye 7N 46035*	1	19 wks

BRICK *US, male vocal/instrumental group*

Date	Title *Label Number*	Position	
5 Feb 77	**DAZZ** *Bang 004*	36	4 wks

Alicia BRIDGES *US, female vocalist*

Date	Title *Label Number*	Position	
11 Nov 78	**I LOVE THE NIGHT LIFE (DISCO'ROUND)** *Polydor 2066 936*	32	10 wks

BRIGHOUSE AND RASTRICK BRASS BAND *UK, male brass band*

Date	Title *Label Number*	Position	
12 Nov 77	● **THE FLORAL DANCE** *Transatlantic BIG 548*	2	13 wks

Bette BRIGHT *UK, female vocalist*

Date	Title *Label Number*	Position	
8 Mar 80	**HELLO I AM YOUR HEART** *Korova KOW 3*	50	5 wks

Sarah BRIGHTMAN *UK, female vocalist*

Date	Title *Label Number*	Position	
11 Nov 78	● **I LOST MY HEART TO A STARSHIP TROOPER** *Ariola/Hansa AHA 527*	6	14 wks
7 Apr 79	**THE ADVENTURES OF THE LOVE CRUSADER** *Ariola/Hansa AHA 538*	53	5 wks

First hit credited to Sarah Brightman and Hot Gossip, second to Sarah Brightman and the Starship Troopers.

Johnny BRISTOL *US, male vocalist*

Date	Title *Label Number*	Position	
24 Aug 74	● **HANG ON IN THERE BABY** *MGM 2006 443*	3	11 wks

See also Amii Stewart and Johnny Bristol.

Jet BRONX and the FORBIDDEN *UK, male vocal/instrumental group*

Date	Title *Label Number*	Position	
17 Dec 77	**AIN'T DOIN' NOTHIN'** *Lightning L1G 507*	49	1 wk

BROOK BROTHERS *UK, male vocal duo*

Date	Title *Label Number*	Position	
30 Mar 61	● **WARPAINT** *Pye 7N 15333*	5	14 wks
24 Aug 61	**AIN'T GONNA WASH FOR A WEEK** *Pye 7N 15369*	13	10 wks
25 Jan 62	**HE'S OLD ENOUGH TO KNOW BETTER** *Pye 7N 15409*	37	1 wk
16 Aug 62	**WELCOME HOME BABY** *Pye 7N 15453*	33	6 wks
21 Feb 63	**TROUBLE IS MY MIDDLE NAME** *Pye 7N 15498*	38	4 wks

Elkie BROOKS *UK, female vocalist*

Date	Title *Label Number*	Position	
2 Apr 77	● **PEARL'S A SINGER** *A & M AMS 7275*	8	9 wks
20 Aug 77	● **SUNSHINE AFTER THE RAIN** *A & M AMS 7306*	10	9 wks
25 Feb 78	**LILAC WINE** *A & M AMS 7333*	16	7 wks
3 Jun 78	**ONLY LOVE CAN BREAK YOUR HEART** *A & M AMS 7353*	43	5 wks
11 Nov 78	**DON'T CRY OUT LOUD** *A & M AMS 7395*	12	11 wks
5 May 79	**THE RUNAWAY** *A & M AMS 7428*	50	5 wks
16 Jan 82	**FOOL IF YOU THINK IT'S OVER** *A & M AMS 8187*	17	10 wks
1 May 82	**OUR LOVE** *A & M AMS 8214*	43	5 wks
17 Jul 82	**NIGHTS IN WHITE SATIN** *A & M AMS 8235*	33	5 wks

Norman BROOKS *US, male vocalist*

Date	Title *Label Number*	Position	
12 Nov 54	**A SKY BLUE SHIRT AND A RAINBOW TIE** *London L 1228*	17	1 wk

BROTHERHOOD OF MAN *UK, male/female vocal group*

Date	Title *Label Number*	Position	
14 Feb 70	● **UNITED WE STAND** *Deram DM 284*	10	9 wks
4 Jul 70	**WHERE ARE YOU GOING TO MY LOVE** *Deram DM 298*	22	10 wks
13 Mar 76	★ **SAVE YOUR KISSES FOR ME** *Pye 7N 45569*	1	16 wks
19 Jun 76	**MY SWEET ROSALIE** *Pye 7N 45602*	30	7 wks
26 Feb 77	● **OH BOY (THE MOOD I'M IN)** *Pye 7N 45656*	8	12 wks
9 Jul 77	★ **ANGELO** *Pye 7N 45699*	1	12 wks
14 Jan 78	★ **FIGARO** *Pye 7N 46037*	1	11 wks
27 May 78	**BEAUTIFUL LOVER** *Pye 7N 46071*	15	12 wks
30 Sep 78	**MIDDLE OF THE NIGHT** *Pye 7N 46117*	41	6 wks
3 Jul 82	**LIGHTNING FLASH** *EMI 5309*	67	2 wks

BROTHERLOVE — See *PRATT and McLAIN with BROTHERLOVE*

BROTHERS *UK, male vocal group*

Date	Title *Label Number*	Position	
29 Jan 77	● **SING ME** *Bus Stop Bus 1054*	8	9 wks

BROTHERS FOUR *US, male vocal group*

Date	Title *Label Number*	Position	
23 Jun 60	**GREENFIELDS** *Philips PB 1009*	49	1 wk
7 Jul 60	**GREENFIELDS** (re-entry) *Philips PB 1009*	40	1 wk

BROTHERS JOHNSON *US, male vocal /instrumental duo*

Date	Title *Label Number*	Position	
9 July 77	**STRAWBERRY LETTER 23** *A & M AMS 7297*	35	5 wks
2 Sep 78	**AIN'T WE FUNKIN' NOW** *A & M AMS 7379*	43	6 wks
4 Nov 78	**RIDE-O-ROCKET** *A & M AMS 7400*	50	4 wks
23 Feb 80	● **STOMP** *A & M AMS 7509*	6	12 wks
31 May 80	**LIGHT UP THE NIGHT** *A&M AMS 7526*	47	4 wks
25 Jul 81	**THE REAL THING** *A & M AMS 8149*	50	3 wks

Edgar BROUGHTON BAND *UK, male vocal/instrumental group*

Date	Title *Label Number*	Position	
18 Apr 70	**OUT DEMONS OUT** *Harvest HAR 5015*	39	5 wks
23 Jan 71	**APACHE DROPOUT** *Harvest HAR 5032*	49	1 wk
6 Feb 71	**APACHE DROPOUT** (re-entry) *Harvest HAR 5032*	35	2 wks
13 Mar 71	**APACHE DROPOUT** (2nd re-entry) *Harvest HAR 5032*	35	1 wk
27 Mar 71	**APACHE DROPOUT** (3rd re-entry) *Harvest HAR 5032*	33	1 wk

Crazy World of Arthur BROWN *UK, male vocal/instrumental group*

Date	Title *Label Number*	Position	
26 Jun 68	★ **FIRE** *Track 604 022*	1	14 wks

Date	Title *Label Number*	Position	

Dennis BROWN *Jamaica, male vocalist*

Date	Title *Label Number*	Position	
3 Mar 79	**MONEY IN MY POCKET** *Lightning LV 5*	**14**	9 wks
3 Jul 82	**LOVE HAS FOUND ITS WAY** *A & M AMS 8226*	**47**	6 wks
11 Sep 82	**HALFWAY UP HALFWAY DOWN** *A & M AMS 8250*	**56**	3 wks

James BROWN *US, male vocalist*

Date	Title *Label Number*	Position	
23 Sep 65	**PAPA'S GOT A BRAND NEW BAG** *London HL 9990*	**25**	7 wks
24 Feb 66	**I GOT YOU** *Pye International 7N 25350*	**29**	6 wks
16 Jun 66	**IT'S A MAN'S MAN'S MAN'S WORLD** *Pye International 7N 25371*	**13**	9 wks
10 Oct 70	**GET UP I FEEL LIKE BEING A SEX MACHINE** *Polydor 2001 071*	**32**	7 wks
27 Nov 71	**HEY AMERICA** *Mojo 2093 006*	**47**	3 wks
18 Sep 76	**GET UP OFFA THAT THING** *Polydor 2066 687*	**22**	6 wks
29 Jan 77	**BODY HEAT** *Polydor 2066 763*	**36**	4 wks
10 Jan 81	**RAPP PLAYBACK (WHERE IZ MOSES?)** *RCA 28*	**39**	5 wks

Billed as James Brown and The Famous Flames on the first three hits.

Joanne BROWN — See *Tony OSBORNE*

Joe BROWN

UK, male vocalist/instrumentalist - guitar

Date	Title *Label Number*	Position	
17 Mar 60	**DARKTOWN STRUTTERS BALL** *Decca F 11207*	**34**	6 wks
26 Jan 61	**SHINE** *Pye 7N 15322*	**33**	6 wks
11 Jan 62	**WHAT A CRAZY WORLD WE'RE LIVING IN** *Piccadilly 7N 35024*	**37**	2 wks
17 May 62	● **A PICTURE OF YOU** *Piccadilly 7N 35047*	**2**	19 wks
13 Sep 62	**YOUR TENDER LOOK** *Piccadilly 7N 35058*	**31**	6 wks
15 Nov 62	● **IT ONLY TOOK A MINUTE** *Piccadilly 7N 35082*	**6**	13 wks
7 Feb 63	● **THAT'S WHAT LOVE WILL DO** *Piccadilly 7N 35106*	**3**	14 wks
21 Feb 63	**IT ONLY TOOK A MINUTE** (re-entry) *Piccadilly 7N 35082*	**50**	1 wk
27 Jun 63	**NATURE'S TIME FOR LOVE** *Piccadilly 7N 35129*	**26**	6 wks
26 Sep 63	**SALLY ANN** *Piccadilly 7N 35138*	**28**	9 wks
29 Jun 67	**WITH A LITTLE HELP FROM MY FRIENDS** *Pye 7N 17339*	**32**	4 wks
14 Apr 73	**HEY MAMA** *Ammo AMO 101*	**33**	6 wks

Joe Brown's male vocal/ instrumental backing group, the Bruvvers, were credited on all his hits except Shine, With A Little Help From My Friends *and* Hey Mama.

Peter BROWN *US, male vocalist*

Date	Title *Label Number*	Position	
11 Feb 78	**DO YA WANNA GET FUNKY WITH ME** *TK TKR 6009*	**43**	4 wks
17 Jun 78	**DANCE WITH ME** *TK TKR 6027*	**57**	5 wks

Polly BROWN *UK, female vocalist*

Date	Title *Label Number*	Position	
14 Sep 74	**UP IN A PUFF OF SMOKE** *GTO GT 2*	**43**	5 wks

Sharon BROWN *UK, female vocalist*

Date	Title *Label Number*	Position	
17 Apr 82	**I SPECIALIZE IN LOVE** *Virgin VS 494*	**38**	9 wks

BROWN SAUCE *UK, male/female vocal group*

Date	Title *Label Number*	Position	
12 Dec 81	**I WANNA BE A WINNER** *BBC RESL 101*	**15**	12 wks

Duncan BROWNE *UK, male vocalist*

Date	Title *Label Number*	Position	
19 Aug 72	**JOURNEY** *RAK 135*	**23**	6 wks

Jackson BROWNE *US, male vocalist*

Date	Title *Label Number*	Position	
1 Jul 78	**STAY** *Asylum K 13128*	**12**	11 wks

Tom BROWNE *US, male vocalist*

Date	Title *Label Number*	Position	
19 Jul 80	● **FUNKIN' FOR JAMAICA (N.Y.)** *Arista ARIST 357*	**10**	11 wks
25 Oct 80	**THIGHS HIGH (GRIP YOUR HIPS AND MOVE)** *Arista ARIST 367*	**45**	5 wks
30 Jan 82	**FUNGI MAMA (BEBOPAFUNKADISCOLYPSO)** *Arista ARIST 450*	**58**	4 wks

BROWNS *US, male/female vocal group*

Date	Title *Label Number*	Position	
18 Sep 59	● **THE THREE BELLS** *RCA 1140*	**6**	13 wks

BROWNSVILLE STATION

US, male vocal/instrumental group

Date	Title *Label Number*	Position	
2 Mar 74	**SMOKIN' IN THE BOY'S ROOM** *Philips 6073 834*	**27**	6 wks

Dave BRUBECK QUARTET

US, male instrumental group

Date	Title *Label Number*	Position	
26 Oct 61	● **TAKE FIVE** *Fontana H 339*	**6**	15 wks
8 Feb 62	**IT'S A RAGGY WALTZ** *Fontana H 352*	**36**	3 wks
17 May 62	**UNSQUARE DANCE** *CBS AAG 102*	**14**	13 wks

Tommy BRUCE *UK, male vocalist*

Date	Title *Label Number*	Position	
26 May 60	● **AIN'T MISBEHAVIN'** *Columbia DB 4453*	**3**	16 wks
8 Sep 60	**BROKEN DOLL** *Columbia DB 4498*	**36**	4 wks
22 Feb 62	**BABETTE** *Columbia DB 4776*	**50**	1 wk

First two hits credit the Bruisers, Tommy's backing group. See also Bruisers.

BRUISERS *UK, male vocal/instrumental group*

Date	Title *Label Number*	Position	
8 Aug 63	**BLUE GIRL** *Parlophone R 5042*	**31**	6 wks
26 Sep 63	**BLUE GIRL** (re-entry) *Parlophone R 5042*	**47**	1 wk

See also Tommy Bruce

Tyrone BRUNSON *US, male instrumentalist-bass.*

Date	Title *Label Number*	Position	
25 Dec 82	**THE SMURF** *Epic EPC A 3024*	**69†**	1 wk

BRUVVERS — See *Joe BROWN*

ARTHUR BROWN Arthur Brown captured in one of his mellower moments – about to bite a chunk out of the microphone

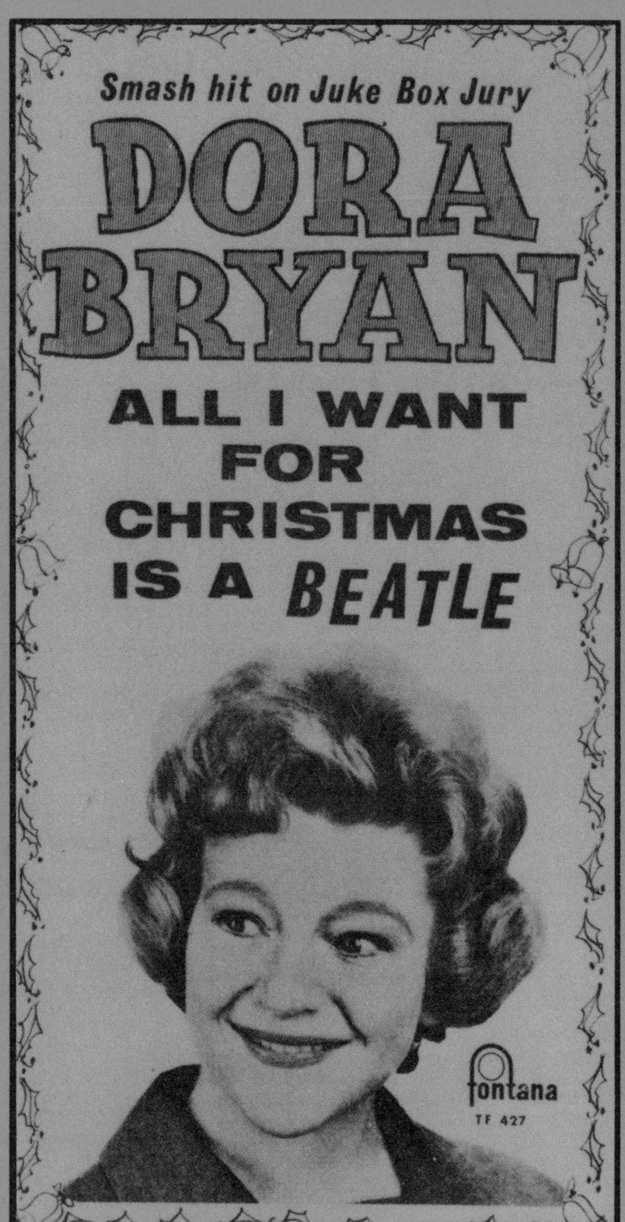

Smash hit on Juke Box Jury
DORA BRYAN
ALL I WANT FOR CHRISTMAS IS A BEATLE
fontana
TF 427

DORA BRYAN There is no record of the Beatles wanting Dora Bryan

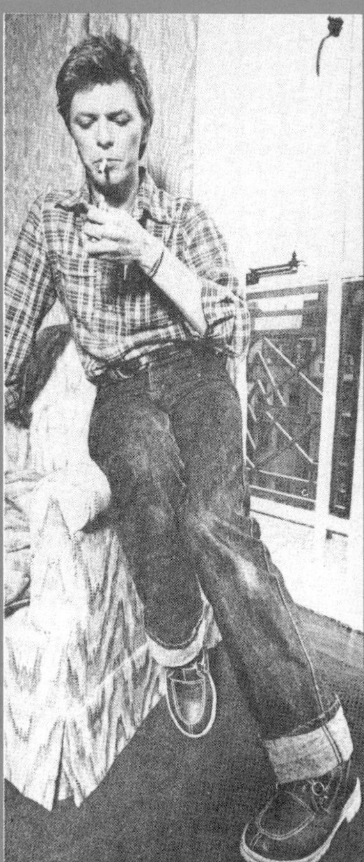

BOWIE Started showbusiness life as David Jones, R & B singer, mime artist and Anthony Newley soundalike

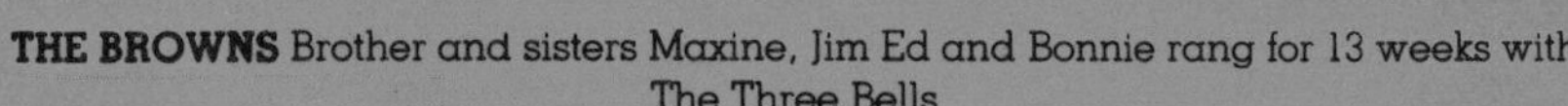

THE BROWNS Brother and sisters Maxine, Jim Ed and Bonnie rang for 13 weeks with The Three Bells

Date	Title *Label Number*	Position		Date	Title *Label Number*	Position	

Dora BRYAN *UK, female vocalist*

Date	Title *Label Number*	Position	Weeks
5 Dec 63	**ALL I WANT FOR CHRISTMAS IS A BEATLE** *Fontana TF 427*	**20**	6 wks

Anita BRYANT *US, female vocalist*

Date	Title *Label Number*	Position	Weeks
26 May 60	**PAPER ROSES** *London HLL 9144*	**49**	1 wk
30 Jun 60	**PAPER ROSES** (re-entry) *London HLL 9144*	**45**	1 wk
14 Jul 60	**PAPER ROSES** (2nd re-entry) *London HLL 9144*	**24**	2 wks
6 Oct 60	**MY LITTLE CORNER OF THE WORLD** *London HLL 9171*	**48**	2 wks

BUBBLEROCK

UK, Jonathan King, male vocalist, under false name

Date	Title *Label Number*	Position	Weeks
26 Jan 74	**(I CAN'T GET NO) SATISFACTION** *UK 53*	**29**	5 wks

See also Jonathan King.

Roy BUCHANAN *US, male instrumentalist, guitar*

Date	Title *Label Number*	Position	Weeks
31 Mar 73	**SWEET DREAMS** *Polydor 2066 307*	**40**	3 wks

Lindsey BUCKINGHAM *US, male vocalist*

Date	Title *Label Number*	Position	Weeks
16 Jan 82	**TROUBLE** *Mercury MER 85*	**31**	7 wks

BUCK'S FIZZ *UK, male/female vocal group*

Date	Title *Label Number*	Position	Weeks
28 Mar 81	★ **MAKING YOUR MIND UP** *RCA 56*	**1**	12 wks
6 Jun 81	**PIECE OF THE ACTION** *RCA 88*	**12**	9 wks
15 Aug 81	**ONE OF THOSE NIGHTS** *RCA 114*	**20**	10 wks
28 Nov 81	★ **THE LAND OF MAKE BELIEVE** *RCA 163*	**1**	16 wks
27 Mar 82	★ **MY CAMERA NEVER LIES** *RCA 202*	**1**	8 wks
19 Jun 82	● **NOW THOSE DAYS ARE GONE** *RCA 241*	**8**	9 wks
27 Nov 82	**IF YOU CAN'T STAND THE HEAT** *RCA 300*	**20**†	5 wks

BUDGIE *UK, male vocal/instrumental group.*

Date	Title *Label Number*	Position	Weeks
3 Oct 81	**KEEPING A RENDEZVOUS** *RCA BUDGIE 3*	**71**	2 wks

BUGGLES *UK, male vocal/instrumental duo*

Date	Title *Label Number*	Position	Weeks
22 Sep 79	★ **VIDEO KILLED THE RADIO STAR** *Island WIP 6524*	**1**	11 wks
26 Jan 80	**THE PLASTIC AGE** *Island WIP 6540*	**16**	8 wks
5 Apr 80	**CLEAN CLEAN** *Island WIP 6584*	**38**	5 wks
8 Nov 80	**ELSTREE** *Island WIP 6624*	**55**	4 wks

B. BUMBLE and the STINGERS

US, male instrumental group

Date	Title *Label Number*	Position	Weeks
19 Apr 62	★ **NUT ROCKER** *Top Rank JAR 611*	**1**	15 wks
3 Jun 72	**NUT ROCKER** (re-issue) *Stateside SS 2203*	**19**	11 wks

BUNNYMEN — See *ECHO and the BUNNEYMEN*

Eric BURDON *UK, male vocalist*

Date	Title *Label Number*	Position	Weeks
27 Oct 66	**HELP ME GIRL** *Decca F 12502*	**14**	10 wks
15 Jun 67	**WHEN I WAS YOUNG** *MGM 1340*	**45**	3 wks
6 Sep 67	**GOOD TIMES** *MGM 1344*	**20**	11 wks
18 Oct 67	● **SAN FRANCISCAN NIGHTS** *MGM 1359*	**7**	10 wks
14 Feb 68	**SKY PILOT** *MGM 1373*	**40**	3 wks
15 Jan 69	**RING OF FIRE** *MGM 1461*	**35**	5 wks

Help Me Girl, When I Was Young, Good Times *and* Ring Of Fire *are credited to Eric Burdon and the Animals. See also the Animals.*

Geoffrey BURGON *UK, orchestra*

Date	Title *Label Number*	Position	Weeks
26 Dec 81	**BRIDESHEAD THEME** *Chrysalis CHS 2562*	**48**	4 wks

Keni BURKE *US, male vocalist*

Date	Title *Label Number*	Position	Weeks
27 Jun 81	**LET SOMEBODY LOVE YOU** *RCA 93*	**59**	3 wks

Hank C. BURNETTE

Sweden, male multi-instrumentalist

Date	Title *Label Number*	Position	Weeks
30 Oct 76	**SPINNING ROCK BOOGIE** *Sonet SON 2094*	**21**	8 wks

Johnny BURNETTE *US, male vocalist*

Date	Title *Label Number*	Position	Weeks
29 Sep 60	● **DREAMIN'** *London HLG 9172*	**5**	16 wks
12 Jan 61	● **YOU'RE SIXTEEN** *London HLG 9254*	**3**	12 wks
13 Apr 61	**LITTLE BOY SAD** *London HLG 9315*	**12**	12 wks
10 Aug 61	**GIRLS** *London HLG 9388*	**37**	5 wks
17 May 62	**CLOWN SHOES** *Liberty LIB 55416*	**35**	3 wks

Rocky BURNETTE *US, male vocalist*

Date	Title *Label Number*	Position	Weeks
17 Nov 79	**TIRED OF TOEIN' THE LINE** *EMI 2992*	**58**	7 wks

Ray BURNS *UK, male vocalist*

Date	Title *Label Number*	Position	Weeks
11 Feb 55	● **MOBILE** *Columbia DB 3563*	**4**	13 wks
26 Aug 55	**THAT'S HOW A LOVE SONG WAS BORN** *Columbia DB 3640*	**14**	6 wks

BURUNDI STEIPHENSON BLACK

Burundi, drummers and chanters with orchestral additions by Mike Steiphenson of France

Date	Title *Label Number*	Position	Weeks
13 Nov 71	**BURUNDI BLACK** *Barclay BAR 3*	**31**	14 wks

Lou BUSCH *US, orchestra*

Date	Title *Label Number*	Position	Weeks
27 Jan 56	● **ZAMBESI** *Capitol CL 14504*	**2**	17 wks

See also Joe 'Fingers' Carr.

Kate BUSH *UK, female vocalist*

Date	Title *Label Number*	Position	Weeks
11 Feb 78	★ **WUTHERING HEIGHTS** *EMI 2719*	**1**	14 wks
10 Jun 78	● **MAN WITH THE CHILD IN HIS EYES** *EMI 2806*	**6**	11 wks
11 Nov 78	**HAMMER HORROR** *EMI 2887*	**44**	6 wks
17 Mar 79	**WOW** *EMI 2911*	**14**	10 wks
15 Sep 79	● **KATE BUSH ON STAGE** (EP) *EMI MIEP 2991*	**10**	9 wks

Date	Title *Label Number*	Position	
26 Apr 80	**BREATHING** *EMI 5058*	**16**	7 wks
5 Jul 80	● **BABOOSHKA** *EMI 5085*	**5**	10 wks
4 Oct 80	**ARMY DREAMERS** *EMI 5106*	**16**	9 wks
6 Dec 80	**DECEMBER WILL BE MAGIC AGAIN** *EMI 5121*	**29**	7 wks
11 Jul 81	**SAT IN YOUR LAP** *EMI 5201*	**11**	7 wks
7 Aug 82	**THE DREAMING** *EMI 5296*	**48**	3 wks

Tracks on On Stage EP: *Them Heavy People/ Don't Push Your Foot on the Heartbrake/ James and the Cold Gun/ L'Amour Looks Something Like You.*

BUSTER *UK, male vocal/instrumental group*

Date	Title *Label Number*	Position	
19 Jun 76	**SUNDAY** *RCA 2678*	**49**	1 wk

Prince BUSTER *Jamaica, male vocalist*

Date	Title *Label Number*	Position	
23 Feb 67	**AL CAPONE** *Blue Beat BB 324*	**18**	13 wks

BUTTERSCOTCH *UK, male vocal group*

Date	Title *Label Number*	Position	
2 May 70	**DON'T YOU KNOW** *RCA 1937*	**17**	11 wks

BUZZCOCKS *UK, male vocal/instrumental group*

Date	Title *Label Number*	Position	
18 Feb 78	**WHAT DO I GET** *United Artists UP 36348*	**37**	3 wks
13 May 78	**I DON'T MIND** *United Artists UP 36386*	**55**	2 wks
15 Jul 78	**LOVE YOU MORE** *United Artists UP 36433*	**34**	6 wks
23 Sep 78	**EVER FALLEN IN LOVE (WITH SOMEONE YOU SHOULDN'T'VE HAVE)** *United Artists UP 36455*	**12**	11 wks
25 Nov 78	**PROMISES** *United Artists UP 36471*	**20**	10 wks
10 Mar 79	**EVERYBODY'S HAPPY NOWADAYS** *United Artists UP 36499*	**29**	6 wks
21 Jul 79	**HARMONY IN MY HEAD** *United Artists UP 36541*	**32**	6 wks
25 Aug 79	**SPIRAL SCRATCH** (EP) *New Hormones ORG 1*	**31**	6 wks
6 Sep 80	**ARE EVERYTHING/WHY SHE'S A GIRL FROM THE CHAINSTORE** *United Artists BP 365*	**61**	3 wks

Tracks on Spiral Scratch EP: *Breakdown/ Time's Up/ Boredom/ Friends Of Mine. Sleeve of EP (not the label) credits "Buzzcocks with Howard Devoto".* Why She's A Girl From The Chainstore *listed from 13 Sep 80.*

BUZZY BUNCH — See *Celi BEE and the BUZZY BUNCH*

Max BYGRAVES *UK, male vocalist*

Date	Title *Label Number*	Position	
14 Nov 52	**COWPUNCHER'S CANTATA** *HMV B 10250*	**11**	1 wk
2 Jan 53	● **COWPUNCHER'S CANTATA** (re-entry) *HMV B 10250*	**8**	1 wk
23 Jan 53	● **COWPUNCHER'S CANTATA** (2nd re-entry) *HMV B 10250*	**6**	5 wks
6 Mar 53	● **COWPUNCHER'S CANTATA** (3rd re-entry) *HMV B 10250*	**10**	1 wk
14 May 54	● **HEART OF MY HEART** *HMV B 10654*	**7**	8 wks
10 Sep 54	● **GILLY GILLY OSSENFEFFER KATZENELLEN BOGEN BY THE SEA** *HMV B 10734*	**7**	7 wks
5 Nov 54	**GILLY GILLY OSSENFEFFER KATZENELLEN BOGEN BY THE SEA** (re-entry) *HMV B 10734*	**20**	1 wk
21 Jan 55	**MR. SANDMAN** *HMV B 10821*	**16**	1 wk
18 Nov 55	● **MEET ME ON THE CORNER** *HMV POP 116*	**2**	11 wks
17 Feb 56	**BALLAD OF DAVY CROCKETT** *HMV POP 153*	**20**	1 wk
25 May 56	**OUT OF TOWN** *HMV POP 164*	**18**	7 wks
5 Apr 57	**HEART** *Decca F 10862*	**14**	8 wks
2 May 58	● **YOU NEED HANDS/ TULIPS FROM AMSTERDAM** *Decca F 11004*	**3**	25 wks
22 Aug 58	**LITTLE TRAIN/ GOTTA HAVE RAIN** *Decca F 11096*	**28**	2 wks
2 Jan 59	**MY UKELELE** *Decca F 11077*	**19**	4 wks
18 Dec 59	● **JINGLE BELL ROCK** *Decca F 11176*	**7**	4 wks
10 Mar 60	● **FINGS AIN'T WOT THEY USED T'BE** *Decca F 11214*	**5**	15 wks
28 Jul 60	**CONSIDER YOURSELF** *Decca F 11251*	**50**	1 wk
1 Jun 61	**BELLS OF AVIGNON** *Decca F 11350*	**36**	5 wks
19 Feb 69	**YOU'RE MY EVERYTHING** *Pye 7N 17705*	**50**	1 wk
5 Mar 69	**YOU'RE MY EVERYTHING** (re-entry) *Pye 7N 17705*	**34**	3 wks
6 Oct 73	**DECK OF CARDS** *Pye 7N 45276*	**13**	15 wks

See also Various Artists - All Star Hit Parade No. 2. Cowpuncher's Cantata *is a medley with the following songs: Cry Of The Wild Goose/ Riders In The Sky/ Mule Train/ Jezebel.* You Need Hands *was listed by itself on 2 May 58.* Tulips From Amsterdam *was first listed on 9 May 58 and both sides continued to be listed until the end of the record's chart run.*

Charlie BYRD — See *Stan GETZ and Charlie BYRD*

Donald BYRD *US, male vocalist/instrumentalist*

Date	Title *Label Number*	Position	
26 Sep 81	**LOVE HAS COME AROUND/LOVING YOU** *Electra K 12559*	**41**	6 wks

BYRDS *US, male vocal/instrumental group*

Date	Title *Label Number*	Position	
17 Jun 65	★ **MR. TAMBOURINE MAN** *CBS 201765*	**1**	14 wks
12 Aug 65	● **ALL I REALLY WANT TO DO** *CBS 201796*	**4**	10 wks
11 Nov 65	**TURN! TURN! TURN!** *CBS 202008*	**26**	8 wks
5 May 66	**EIGHT MILES HIGH** *CBS 202067*	**24**	9 wks
5 Jun 68	**YOU AIN'T GOIN' NOWHERE** *CBS 3411*	**45**	3 wks
13 Feb 71	**CHESTNUT MARE** *CBS 5322*	**19**	8 wks

Edward BYRNES and Connie STEVENS *US, male/female vocal duo*

Date	Title *Label Number*	Position	
5 May 60	**KOOKIE KOOKIE (LEND ME YOUR COMB)** *Warner Bros. WB 5*	**27**	8 wks

See also Connie Stevens.

BYSTANDERS *UK, male vocal/instrumental group*

Date	Title *Label Number*	Position	
9 Feb 67	**98.6** *Piccadilly 7N 35363*	**45**	1 wk

C

C. C. S. *UK, male vocal/instrumental group*

Date	Title *Label Number*	Position	
31 Oct 70	**WHOLE LOTTA LOVE** *RAK 104*	**13**	13 wks
27 Feb 71	● **WALKIN'** *RAK 109*	**7**	16 wks
4 Sep 71	● **TAP TURNS ON THE WATER** *RAK 119*	**5**	13 wks
4 Mar 72	**BROTHER** *RAK 126*	**25**	8 wks
4 Aug 73	**BAND PLAYED THE BOOGIE** *RAK 154*	**36**	5 wks

ÇA VA ÇA VA *UK, male vocal/instrumental group*

Date	Title *Label Number*	Position	
18 Sep 82	**WHERE'S ROMEO?** *Regard RG 103*	**49**	5 wks

CADETS *UK, male/female vocal group*

Date	Title *Label Number*	Position	
3 Jun 65	**JEALOUS HEART** *Pye 7N 15852*	**42**	1 wk

Hit has credit "with Eileen Read lead vocal".

Above **BUCK'S FIZZ** Mike, Cheryl, Jay and Bobby – Eurovision Winners 1981

Left **SUSAN CADOGAN** Hurt so good but still smiling

Right **TONY CAPSTICK** 'Do you know, when I were a lad, you could get a tram down into t'town, buy 3 mens' suits and an overcoat, a pair o' good boots, go and see George Formby at t'Palace Theatre, get blind drunk, have some steak and chips, a bunch of bananas and 3 stone o' monkey nuts . . . and still have change left out of a farthing'

Date	Title *Label Number*	Position	

Susan CADOGAN *UK, female vocalist*

5 Apr 75	● **HURT SO GOOD** *Magnet MAG 23*	**4**	12 wks
19 Jul 75	**LOVE ME BABY** *Magnet MAG 36*	**22**	7 wks

Al CAIOLA *US, orchestra*

15 Jun 61	**THE MAGNIFICENT SEVEN** *HMV POP 889*	**34**	6 wks

CALIBRE CUTS

Montage of 16 other discs, see footnote

17 May 80	**CALIBRE CUTS** *Calibre CAB 502*	**75**	2 wks

Calibre Cuts *is a montage of 13 singles and 3 re-makes of hit titles by session musicians. The titles are :* Big Apple Rock *by Black Ivory,* Don't Hold Back *by Chanson,* The River Drive *by Jupiter Beyond,* Dancing at the Disco *by L.A.X.,* Girls Mellow Right On *by Lowrell,* Pata Pata *by Osibisa,* I Like It *by Players Association,* We Got The Funk *by Positive Force,* Holdin' On *by Tony Rallo and the Midnight Band,* Can You Feel the Force *by Real Thing,* Miami Heatwave *by Seventh Avenue,* Rappers Delight *by Sugarhill Gang,* Que Tal America *by Two Man Sound. The three re-makes by session musicians are* Ain't No Stopping Us Now, Bad Girls *and* We Are Family. *Act descriptions are, of course, various.*

Eddie CALVERT

UK, male instrumentalist - trumpet

18 Dec 53	★ **OH MEIN PAPA** *Columbia DB 3337*	**1**	21 wks
8 Apr 55	★ **CHERRY PINK & APPLE BLOSSOM WHITE** *Columbia DB 3581*	**1**	21 wks
13 May 55	**STRANGER IN PARADISE** *Columbia DB 3594*	**14**	4 wks
29 Jul 55	● **JOHN AND JULIE** *Columbia DB 3624*	**6**	11 wks
2 Mar 56	**ZAMBESI** *Columbia DB 3747*	**18**	1 wk
23 Mar 56	**ZAMBESI** (re-entry) *Columbia DB 3747*	**13**	6 wks
7 Feb 58	● **MANDY** *Columbia DB 3956*	**9**	14 wks
20 Jun 58	**LITTLE SERENADE** *Columbia DB 4139*	**28**	2 wks

Andy CAMERON *UK, male vocalist*

4 Mar 78	● **ALLY'S TARTAN ARMY** *Klub 03*	**6**	8 wks

Tony CAMILLO'S BAZUKA

US, male instrumental/vocal group

31 May 75	**DYNOMITE** PART 1. *A & M AMS 7168*	**28**	5 wks

CAMOUFLAGE featuring MYSTI

UK, male/female vocal/instrumental group

24 Sep 77	**BEE STING** *State STAT 58*	**48**	3 wks

Ethna CAMPBELL *UK, female vocalist*

27 Dec 75	**THE OLD RUGGED CROSS** *Philips 6006 475*	**33**	11 wks

Glen CAMPBELL *US, male vocalist*

29 Jan 69	● **WICHITA LINEMAN** *Ember EMBS 261*	**7**	13 wks
7 May 69	**GALVESTON** *Ember EMBS 263*	**14**	10 wks
7 Feb 70	**TRY A LITTLE KINDNESS** *Capitol CL 15622*	**45**	2 wks
9 May 70	● **HONEY COME BACK** *Capitol CL 15638*	**4**	19 wks
26 Sep 70	**EVERYTHING A MAN COULD EVER NEED** *Capitol CL 15653*	**32**	5 wks
21 Nov 70	● **IT'S ONLY MAKE BELIEVE** *Capitol CL 15663*	**4**	14 wks
27 Mar 71	**DREAM BABY** *Capitol CL 15674*	**39**	3 wks
4 Oct 75	● **RHINESTONE COWBOY** *Capitol CL 15824*	**4**	12 wks
26 Mar 77	**SOUTHERN NIGHTS** *Capitol CL 15907*	**28**	6 wks

See also Bobbie Gentry & Glen Campbell.

Jo-Anne CAMPBELL *US, female vocalist*

8 Jun 61	**MOTORCYCLE MICHAEL** *HMV POP 873*	**41**	3 wks

Junior CAMPBELL *UK, male vocalist*

14 Oct 72	● **HALLELUJAH FREEDOM** *Deram DM 364*	**10**	9 wks
2 Jun 73	**SWEET ILLUSION** *Deram DM 387*	**15**	9 wks

Pat CAMPBELL *Ireland, male vocalist*

15 Nov 69	**THE DEAL** *Major Minor MM 648*	**31**	5 wks

Ian CAMPBELL FOLK GROUP

UK, male vocal/instrumental group

11 Mar 65	**THE TIMES THEY ARE A-CHANGIN'** *Transatlantic SP 5*	**42**	2 wks
1 Apr 65	**THE TIMES THEY ARE A-CHANGIN'** (re-entry) *Transatlantic SP 5*	**47**	1 wk
15 Apr 65	**THE TIMES THEY ARE A-CHANGIN'** (2nd re-entry) *Transatlantic SP 5*	**46**	2 wks

CAN *Germany, male vocal/instrumental group*

28 Aug 76	**I WANT MORE** *Virgin VS 153*	**26**	10 wks

CANDIDO *US, male multi-instrumentalist*

18 Jul 81	**JINGO** *Excaliber EXC 102*	**55**	3 wks

CANDLEWICK GREEN

UK, vocal/instrumental group

23 Feb 74	**WHO DO YOU THINK YOU ARE** *Decca F 13480*	**21**	8 wks

CANNED HEAT *US, vocal/instrumental group*

24 Jul 68	● **ON THE ROAD AGAIN** *Liberty LBS 15090*	**8**	15 wks
1 Jan 69	**GOING UP THE COUNTRY** *Liberty LBF 15169*	**19**	10 wks
17 Jan 70	● **LET'S WORK TOGETHER** *Liberty LBF 15302*	**2**	15 wks
11 Jul 70	**SUGAR BEE** *Liberty LBF 15350*	**49**	1 wk

Freddy CANNON *US, male vocalist*

14 Aug 59	**TALLAHASSEE LASSIE** *Top Rank JAR 135*	**17**	8 wks
1 Jan 60	● **WAY DOWN YONDER IN NEW ORLEANS** *Top Rank JAR 247*	**3**	16 wks
10 Mar 60	**CALIFORNIA HERE I COME** *Top Rank JAR 309*	**33**	1 wk
17 Mar 60	**INDIANA** *Top Rank JAR 309*	**42**	1 wk
24 Mar 60	**CALIFORNIA HERE I COME** (re-entry) *Top Rank JAR 309*	**46**	1 wk
19 May 60	**THE URGE** *Top Rank JAR 369*	**18**	10 wks
20 Apr 61	**MUSKRAT RAMBLE** *Top Rank JAR 548*	**32**	5 wks
28 Jun 62	**PALISADES PARK** *Stateside SS 101*	**20**	8 wks

Date	Title *Label Number*	Position	

Jim CAPALDI *UK, male vocalist*

27 Jul 74	**IT'S ALL UP TO YOU** *Island WIP 6198*	**27**	6 wks
25 Oct 75	● **LOVE HURTS** *Island WIP 6246*	**4**	11 wks

Tony CAPSTICK and the CARLTON MAIN/FRICKLEY COLLIERY BAND

UK, male vocalist and male instrumental band

21 Mar 81	● **THE SHEFFIELD GRINDER/CAPSTICK COMES HOME** *Dingles SID 27*	**3**	8 wks

CAPTAIN and TENNILLE

US, male instrumentalist-keyboards/female vocalist

2 Aug 75	**LOVE WILL KEEP US TOGETHER** *A & M AMS 7165*	**32**	5 wks
24 Jan 76	**THE WAY I WANT TO TOUCH YOU** *A & M AMS 7203*	**28**	6 wks
4 Nov 78	**YOU NEVER DONE IT LIKE THAT** *A & M AMS 7384*	**63**	3 wks
16 Feb 80	● **DO THAT TO ME ONE MORE TIME** *Casablanca CAN 175*	**7**	10 wks

CAPTAIN BEAKY — See *Keith MICHELL, CAPTAIN BEAKY and his BAND*

CAPTAIN SENSIBLE *UK, male vocalist*

26 Jun 82	★ **HAPPY TALK** *A & M CAP 1*	**1**	8 wks
14 Aug 82	**WOT** *A & M CAP 2*	**26**	7 wks

Irene CARA *US, female vocalist*

3 Jul 82	★ **FAME** *RSO 90*	**1**	16 wks
4 Sep 82	**OUT HERE ON MY OWN** *Polydor/RSO 66*	**58**	3 wks

CARAVELLES *UK, female vocal duo*

8 Aug 63	● **YOU DON'T HAVE TO BE A BABY TO CRY** *Decca F 11697*	**6**	13 wks

Carl CARLTON *US, male vocalist*

18 Jul 81	**SHE'S A BAD MAMA JAMA (SHE'S BUILT, SHE'S STACKED)** *20th Century TC 2488*	**34**	8 wks

Larry CARLTON — See *Mike POST featuring Larry CARLTON*

Eric CARMEN *US, male vocalist*

10 Apr 76	**ALL BY MYSELF** *Arista 42*	**12**	7 wks

Kim CARNES *US, female vocalist*

9 May 81	● **BETTE DAVIS EYES** *EMI America EA 121*	**10**	9 wks
8 Aug 81	**DRAW OF THE CARDS** *EMI America EA 125*	**49**	4 wks
9 Oct 82	**VOYEUR** *EMI America EA 143*	**68**	2 wks

Renato CAROSONE and his SEXTET

Italy, male vocalist, instrumental backing group

4 Jul 58	**TORERO - CHA CHA CHA** *Parlophone R 4433*	**25**	1 wk

CARPENTERS

US, male/female vocal/instrumental duo

5 Sep 70	● **(THEY LONG TO BE) CLOSE TO YOU** *A & M AMS 800*	**6**	18 wks
9 Jan 71	**WE'VE ONLY JUST BEGUN** *A & M AMS 813*	**28**	7 wks
18 Sep 71	**SUPERSTAR/ FOR ALL WE KNOW** *A & M AMS 864*	**18**	13 wks
1 Jan 72	**MERRY CHRISTMAS DARLING** *A & M AME 601*	**45**	1 wk
23 Sep 72	● **I WON'T LAST A DAY WITHOUT YOU/ GOODBYE TO LOVE** *A & M AMS 7023*	**9**	16 wks
7 Jul 73	● **YESTERDAY ONCE MORE** *A & M AMS 7073*	**2**	17 wks
20 Oct 73	● **TOP OF THE WORLD** *A & M AMS 7086*	**5**	18 wks
2 Mar 74	**JAMBALAYA (ON THE BAYOU)/ MR. GUDER** *A & M AMS 7098*	**12**	11 wks
8 Jun 74	**I WON'T LAST A DAY WITHOUT YOU** (re-issue) *A & M AMS 7111*	**32**	5 wks
18 Jan 75	● **PLEASE MR. POSTMAN** *A & M AMS 7141*	**2**	12 wks
19 Apr 75	● **ONLY YESTERDAY** *A & M AMS 7159*	**7**	10 wks
30 Aug 75	**SOLITAIRE** *A & M AMS 7187*	**32**	5 wks
20 Dec 75	**SANTA CLAUS IS COMIN' TO TOWN** *A & M AMS 7144*	**37**	4 wks
27 Mar 76	**THERE'S A KIND OF HUSH (ALL OVER THE WORLD)** *A & M AMS 7219*	**22**	6 wks
3 Jul 76	**I NEED TO BE IN LOVE** *A & M AMS 7238*	**36**	5 wks
8 Oct 77	● **CALLING OCCUPANTS OF INTERPLANETARY CRAFT (THE RECOGNIZED ANTHEM OF WORLD CONTACT DAY)** *A & M AMS 7318*	**9**	9 wks
11 Feb 78	**SWEET SWEET SMILE** *A & M AMS 7327*	**40**	4 wks

I Won't Last A Day Without You AMS 7023 listed by itself 23 Sep 72. Goodbye To Love, *the other side, listed by itself from 30 Sep 72 until the end of the record's chart run.* Mr Guder *listed with* Jambalaya *from 16 Mar 74 until end of the record's chart run.*

Joe "Fingers" CARR

US, male instrumentalist - piano, Lou Busch under a false name

29 Jun 56	**PORTUGUESE WASHERWOMAN** *Capitol CL 14587*	**20**	5 wks

See also Lou Busch.

Linda CARR and the LOVE SQUAD

US, female vocalist, female vocal backing group

12 Jul 75	**HIGHWIRE** *Chelsea 2005 025*	**15**	8 wks

See also Linda and the Funky Boys - it's the same Linda.

Pearl CARR and Teddy JOHNSON

UK, female/male vocal duo

20 Mar 59	**SING LITTLE BIRDIE** *Columbia DB 4275*	**12**	8 wks
6 Apr 61	**HOW WONDERFUL TO KNOW** *Columbia DB 4603*	**23**	11 wks

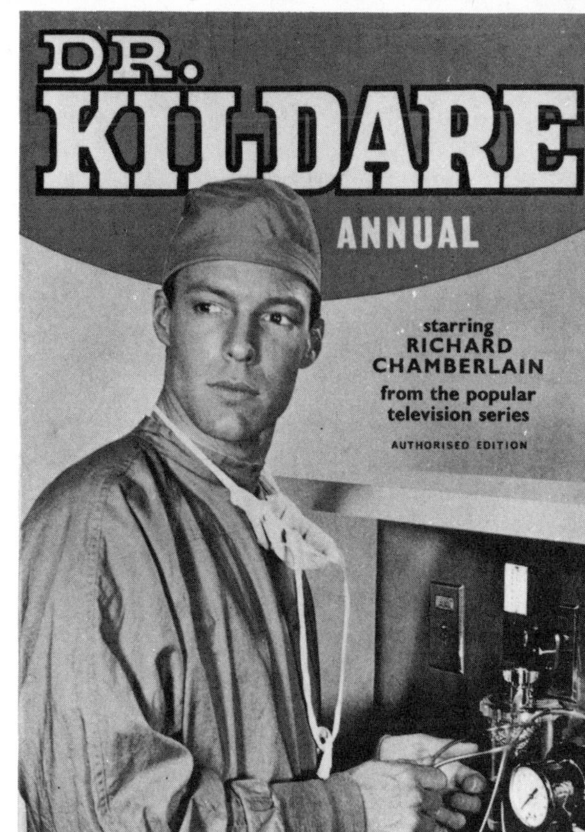

DR.
KILDARE
ANNUAL
starring
RICHARD
CHAMBERLAIN
from the popular
television series
AUTHORISED EDITION

RICHARD CHAMBERLAIN proving beyond doubt that the chart was doctored in 1962

CAPTAIN SENSIBLE Sensible attempts the hokey-cokey

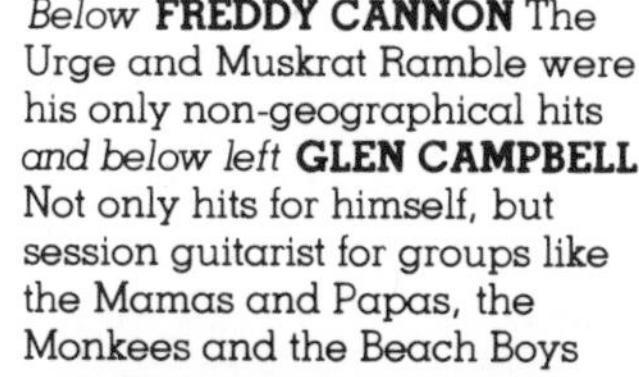

Below **FREDDY CANNON** The Urge and Muskrat Ramble were his only non-geographical hits *and below left* **GLEN CAMPBELL** Not only hits for himself, but session guitarist for groups like the Mamas and Papas, the Monkees and the Beach Boys

Date	Title *Label Number*	Position	

Valerie CARR *UK, female vocalist*

Date	Title *Label Number*	Position	
4 Jul 58	**WHEN THE BOYS TALK ABOUT THE GIRLS** *Columbia DB 4131*	**29**	1 wk
18 Jul 58	**WHEN THE BOYS TALK ABOUT THE GIRLS** (re-entry) *Columbia DB 4131*	**30**	1 wk

Vikki CARR *US, female vocalist*

Date	Title *Label Number*	Position	
1 Jun 67	● **IT MUST BE HIM (SUEL SUR SON ETOILE)** *Liberty LIB 55917*	**2**	20 wks
30 Aug 67	**THERE I GO** *Liberty LBF 15022*	**50**	1 wk
12 Mar 69	**WITH PEN IN HAND** *Liberty LBF 15166*	**43**	1 wk
26 Mar 69	**WITH PEN IN HAND** (re-entry) *Liberty LBF 15166*	**40**	2 wks
30 Apr 69	**WITH PEN IN HAND** (2nd re-entry) *Liberty LBF 15166*	**40**	2 wks

Raffaella CARRA *Italy, female vocalist*

Date	Title *Label Number*	Position	
15 Apr 78	● **DO IT DO IT AGAIN** *Epic EPC 6094*	**9**	12 wks

Ronnie CARROLL *UK, male vocalist*

Date	Title *Label Number*	Position	
27 Jul 56	**WALK HAND IN HAND** *Philips PB 603*	**13**	8 wks
29 Mar 57	**THE WISDOM OF A FOOL** *Philips PB 667*	**20**	2 wks
31 Mar 60	**FOOTSTEPS** *Philips PB 1004*	**36**	3 wks
22 Feb 62	**RING A DING GIRL** *Philips PB 1222*	**46**	3 wks
2 Aug 62	● **ROSES ARE RED** *Philips 326532 BF*	**3**	16 wks
15 Nov 62	**IF ONLY TOMORROW** *Philips 326550 BF*	**33**	4 wks
7 Mar 63	● **SAY WONDERFUL THINGS** *Philips 326574 BF*	**6**	14 wks

Jasper CARROTT *UK, male vocalist*

Date	Title *Label Number*	Position	
16 Aug 75	● **FUNKY MOPED/ MAGIC ROUNDABOUT** *DJM DJS 388*	**5**	15 wks

CARS *US, male vocal/instrumental group*

Date	Title *Label Number*	Position	
11 Nov 78	● **MY BEST FRIEND'S GIRL** *Elektra K 12301*	**3**	10 wks
17 Feb 79	**JUST WHAT I NEEDED** *Elektra K 12312*	**17**	10 wks
28 Jul 79	**LET'S GO** *Elektra K 12371*	**51**	4 wks
5 Jun 82	**SINCE YOU'RE GONE** *Elektra K 13177*	**37**	4 wks

Clarence CARTER *US, male vocalist*

Date	Title *Label Number*	Position	
10 Oct 70	● **PATCHES** *Atlantic 2091 030*	**2**	13 wks

CARVELLS

UK, male vocalist/instrumentalist (Alan Carvell under a group name)

Date	Title *Label Number*	Position	
26 Nov 77	**THE L.A.RUN** *Creole CR 143*	**31**	4 wks

CASCADES *US, male vocal group*

Date	Title *Label Number*	Position	
28 Feb 63	● **RHYTHM OF THE RAIN** *Warner Bros. WB 88*	**5**	16 wks

Johnny CASH *US, male vocalist*

Date	Title *Label Number*	Position	
3 Jun 65	**IT AIN'T ME BABE** *CBS 201760*	**28**	8 wks
6 Sep 69	● **A BOY NAMED SUE** *CBS 4460*	**4**	19 wks
23 May 70	**WHAT IS TRUTH** *CBS 4934*	**21**	11 wks
15 Apr 72	● **A THING CALLED LOVE** *CBS 7797*	**4**	13 wks
22 Jul 72	**A THING CALLED LOVE** (re-entry) *CBS 7797*	**48**	1 wk
3 Jul 76	**ONE PIECE AT A TIME** *CBS 4287*	**32**	7 wks

A Thing Called Love *with the Evangel Temple Choir.* One Piece At A Time *with The Tennessee Three.*

CASINOS *US, male vocal group*

Date	Title *Label Number*	Position	
23 Feb 67	**THEN YOU CAN TELL ME GOODBYE** *President PT 123*	**28**	7 wks

Mama CASS *US, female vocalist*

Date	Title *Label Number*	Position	
14 Aug 68	**DREAM A LITTLE DREAM OF ME** *RCA 1726*	**11**	12 wks
16 Aug 69	● **IT'S GETTING BETTER** *Stateside SS 8021*	**8**	15 wks

See also Mamas and the Papas.

David CASSIDY *US, male vocalist*

Date	Title *Label Number*	Position	
8 Apr 72	● **COULD IT BE FOREVER** *Bell 1224*	**2**	17 wks
16 Sep 72	★ **HOW CAN I BE SURE** *Bell 1258*	**1**	11 wks
25 Nov 72	**ROCK ME BABY** *Bell 1268*	**11**	9 wks
24 Mar 73	● **I'M A CLOWN/ SOME KIND OF A SUMMER** *Bell MABEL 4*	**3**	12 wks
13 Oct 73	★ **DAYDREAMER/ THE PUPPY SONG** *Bell 1334*	**1**	15 wks
11 May 74	● **IF I DIDN'T CARE** *Bell 1350*	**9**	8 wks
27 Jul 74	**PLEASE PLEASE ME** *Bell 1371*	**16**	6 wks
5 Jul 75	**I WRITE THE SONGS/ GET IT UP FOR LOVE** *RCA 2571*	**11**	8 wks
25 Oct 75	**DARLIN'** *RCA 2622*	**16**	8 wks

See also The Partridge Family.

CAST OF IDIOTS — See *Rick DEES and his CAST OF IDIOTS*

Roy CASTLE *UK, male vocalist*

Date	Title *Label Number*	Position	
22 Dec 60	**LITTLE WHITE BERRY** *Philips PB 1087*	**40**	3 wks

CASUALS *UK, male vocal/instrumental group*

Date	Title *Label Number*	Position	
14 Aug 68	● **JESAMINE** *Decca F 22784*	**2**	18 wks
4 Dec 68	**TOY** *Decca F 22852*	**30**	8 wks

CATS *Holland, male instrumental group*

Date	Title *Label Number*	Position	
9 Apr 69	**SWAN LAKE** *BAF 1*	**48**	1 wk
21 May 69	**SWAN LAKE** (re-entry) *BAF 1*	**50**	1 wk

CATS U.K. *UK, female vocal group*

Date	Title *Label Number*	Position	
6 Oct 79	**LUTON AIRPORT** *WEA K 18075*	**22**	8 wks

Date	Title *Label Number*	Position	

CENTRAL LINE

UK, male vocal/instrumental group.

31 Jan 81	**(YOU KNOW) YOU CAN DO IT** *Mercury LINE 7*	**67**	3 wks
15 Aug 81	**WALKING INTO SUNSHINE** *Mercury MER 78*	**42**	10 wks
30 Jan 82	**DON'T TELL ME** *Mercury MER 90*	**55**	3 wks
20 Nov 82	**YOU'VE SAID ENOUGH** *Mercury/Phonogram MER 117*	**58**	3 wks

CERRONE

France, male producer and multi- instrumentalist

5 Mar 77	**LOVE IN C MINOR** *Atlantic K 10895*	**31**	4 wks
29 Jul 78	● **SUPER NATURE** *Atlantic K 11089*	**8**	12 wks
13 Jan 79	**JE SUIS MUSIC** *CBS 6918*	**39**	4 wks

Frank CHACKSFIELD *UK, orchestra*

3 Apr 53	● **LITTLE RED MONKEY** *Parlophone R 3658*	**10**	3 wks
22 May 53	● **LIMELIGHT** *Decca F 10106*	**2**	24 wks
12 Feb 54	● **EBB TIDE** *Decca F 10122*	**9**	2 wks
24 Feb 56	**IN OLD LISBON** *Decca F 10689*	**15**	4 wks
31 Aug 56	**DONKEY CART** *Decca F 10743*	**26**	2 wks

Little Red Monkey *credited to Frank Chacksfield's Tunesmiths.*

CHAIRMEN OF THE BOARD

US, male vocal group

22 Aug 70	● **GIVE ME JUST A LITTLE MORE TIME** *Invictus INV 501*	**3**	13 wks
14 Nov 70	● **YOU'VE GOT ME DANGLING ON A STRING** *Invictus INV 504*	**5**	13 wks
20 Feb 71	**EVERYTHING'S TUESDAY** *Invictus INV 507*	**12**	9 wks
15 May 71	**PAY TO THE PIPER** *Invictus INV 511*	**34**	7 wks
4 Sep 71	**CHAIRMAN OF THE BOARD** *Invictus INV 516*	**48**	2 wks
15 Jul 72	**WORKING ON A BUILDING OF LOVE** *Invictus INV 519*	**20**	8 wks
7 Oct 72	**ELMO JAMES** *Invictus INV 524*	**21**	7 wks
16 Dec 72	**I'M ON MY WAY TO A BETTER PLACE** *Invictus INV 527*	**38**	1 wk
13 Jan 73	**I'M ON MY WAY TO A BETTER PLACE** (re-entry) *Invictus INV 527*	**30**	5 wks
23 Jun 73	**FINDERS KEEPERS** *Invictus INV 530*	**21**	9 wks

CHAKACHAS

Belgium, male vocal/instrumental group

11 Jan 62	**TWIST TWIST** *RCA 1264*	**48**	1 wk
27 May 72	**JUNGLE FEVER** *Polydor 2121 064*	**29**	7 wks

George CHAKIRIS *US, male vocalist*

2 Jun 60	**HEART OF A TEENAGE GIRL** *Triumph RGM 1010*	**49**	1 wk

Richard CHAMBERLAIN *US, male vocalist*

7 Jun 62	**THEME FROM DR. KILDARE (THREE STARS WILL SHINE TONIGHT)** *MGM 1160*	**12**	10 wks
1 Nov 62	**LOVE ME TENDER** *MGM 1173*	**15**	11 wks
21 Feb 63	**HI-LILI HI-LO** *MGM 1189*	**20**	9 wks
18 Jul 63	**TRUE LOVE** *MGM 1205*	**30**	6 wks

CHAMELEONS — See *LORI and the CHAMELEONS*

CHAMPAGNE

US, male/female vocalal/instrumental group

9 May 81	● **HOW 'BOUT US** *CBS A 1046*	**5**	13 wks

CHAMPS *US, male instrumental group*

4 Apr 58	● **TEQUILA** *London HLU 8580*	**5**	9 wks
17 Mar 60	**TOO MUCH TEQUILA** *London HLH 9052*	**49**	1 wk

CHAMPS BOYS *France, male instrumental group*

19 Jun 76	**TUBULAR BELLS** *Philips 6006 519*	**41**	6 wks

Gene CHANDLER *US, male vocalist*

5 Jun 68	**NOTHING CAN STOP ME** *Soul City SC 102*	**41**	4 wks
3 Feb 79	**GET DOWN** *20th Century BTC 1040*	**11**	11 wks
1 Sep 79	**WHEN YOU'RE NUMBER 1** *20th Century TC 2411*	**43**	5 wks
28 Jun 80	**DOES SHE HAVE A FRIEND** *20th Century/Chi-Sound TC 2451*	**28**	9 wks

CHANGE *US, male/female vocal/instrumental group*

28 Jun 80	**A LOVER'S HOLIDAY/GLOW OF LOVE** *WEA K 79141*	**14**	8 wks
6 Sep 80	**SEARCHING** *WEA K 79156*	**11**	10 wks

Bruce CHANNEL *US, male vocalist*

22 Mar 62	● **HEY! BABY** *Mercury AMT 1171*	**2**	12 wks
26 Jun 68	**KEEP ON** *Bell 1010*	**12**	16 wks

CHANSON *US, male/female vocal group*

13 Jan 79	**DON'T HOLD BACK** *Ariola ARO 140*	**33**	7 wks

CHANTAYS *US, male instrumental group*

18 Apr 63	**PIPELINE** *London HLD 9696*	**16**	14 wks

CHANTER SISTERS *UK, female vocal group*

17 Jul 76	**SIDE SHOW** *Polydor 2058 734*	**43**	5 wks

Harry CHAPIN *US, male vocalist*

11 May 74	**W. O. L. D.** *Elektra K 12133*	**34**	5 wks

CHAQUITO

UK, male arranger/conductor Johnny Gregory under false name

Date	Title *Label Number*	Position	Weeks
27 Oct 60	**NEVER ON SUNDAY** *Fontana H 265*	**50**	1 wk

CHARLENE *US, female vocalist*

Date	Title *Label Number*	Position	Weeks
15 May 82	★ **I'VE NEVER BEEN TO ME** *Motown TMG 1260*	**1**	12 wks

Don CHARLES *UK, male vocalist*

Date	Title *Label Number*	Position	Weeks
22 Feb 62	**WALK WITH ME MY ANGEL** *Decca F 11424*	**39**	5 wks

Ray CHARLES *US, male vocalist/instrumentalist,*

Date	Title *Label Number*	Position	Weeks
1 Dec 60	**GEORGIA ON MY MIND** *HMV POP 792*	**47**	1 wk
15 Dec 60	**GEORGIA ON MY MIND** (re-entry) *HMV POP 792*	**24**	7 wks
19 Oct 61	● **HIT THE ROAD JACK** *HMV POP 935*	**6**	12 wks
14 Jun 62	★ **I CAN'T STOP LOVING YOU** *HMV POP 1034*	**1**	17 wks
13 Sep 62	● **YOU DON'T KNOW ME** *HMV POP 1064*	**9**	13 wks
13 Dec 62	**YOUR CHEATING HEART** *HMV POP 1099*	**13**	8 wks
28 Mar 63	**DON'T SET ME FREE** *HMV POP 1133*	**37**	3 wks
16 May 63	● **TAKE THESE CHAINS FROM MY HEART** *HMV POP 1161*	**5**	20 wks
12 Sep 63	**NO ONE** *HMV POP 1202*	**35**	7 wks
31 Oct 63	**BUSTED** *HMV POP 1221*	**21**	10 wks
24 Sep 64	**NO-ONE TO CRY TO** *HMV POP 1333*	**38**	3 wks
21 Jan 65	**MAKIN' WHOOPEE** *HMV POP 1383*	**42**	4 wks
10 Feb 66	**CRYIN' TIME** *HMV POP 1502*	**50**	1 wk
21 Apr 66	**TOGETHER AGAIN** *HMV POP 1519*	**48**	1 wk
5 Jul 67	**HERE WE GO AGAIN** *HMV POP 1595*	**38**	1 wk
19 Jul 67	**HERE WE GO AGAIN** (re-entry) *HMV POP 1595*	**45**	2 wks
20 Dec 67	**YESTERDAY** *Stateside SS 2071*	**44**	4 wks
31 Jul 68	**ELEANOR RIGBY** *Stateside SS 2120*	**36**	9 wks

Tina CHARLES *UK, female vocalist*

Date	Title *Label Number*	Position	Weeks
7 Feb 76	★ **I LOVE TO LOVE (BUT MY BABY LOVES TO DANCE)** *CBS 3937*	**1**	12 wks
1 May 76	**LOVE ME LIKE A LOVER** *CBS 4237*	**28**	7 wks
21 Aug 76	● **DANCE LITTLE LADY DANCE** *CBS 4480*	**6**	13 wks
4 Dec 76	● **DR. LOVE** *CBS 4779*	**4**	10 wks
14 May 77	**RENDEZVOUS** *CBS 5174*	**27**	6 wks
29 Oct 77	**LOVE BUG-SWEETS FOR MY SWEET** (MEDLEY) *CBS 5680*	**26**	4 wks
11 Mar 78	**I'LL GO WHERE YOUR MUSIC TAKES ME** *CBS 6062*	**27**	8 wks

Dick CHARLESWORTH and his CITY GENTS

UK, male instrumental group, Dick Charlesworth clarinet

Date	Title *Label Number*	Position	Weeks
4 May 61	**BILLY BOY** *Top Rank JAR 558*	**43**	1 wk

CHARLEY — See *JOHNNY and CHARLEY*

CHARO and the SALSOUL ORCHESTRA *US, female vocalist and orchestra*

Date	Title *Label Number*	Position	Weeks
29 Apr 78	**DANCE A LITTLE BIT CLOSER** *Salsoul SSOL 101*	**44**	4 wks

CHAS and DAVE

UK, male vocal/instrumental duo

Date	Title *Label Number*	Position	Weeks
11 Nov 78	**STRUMMIN'** *EMI 2874*	**52**	3 wks
26 May 79	**GERTCHA** *EMI 2947*	**20**	8 wks
1 Sep 79	**THE SIDEBOARD SONG (GOT MY BEER IN THE SIDEBOARD HERE)** *EMI 2986*	**55**	3 wks
29 Nov 80	● **RABBIT** *Rockney 9*	**8**	wks
12 Dec 81	**STARS OVER 45** *Rockney KOR 12*	**21**	8 wks
13 Mar 82	● **AIN'T NO PLEASING YOU** *Rockney KOR 14*	**2**	11 wks
17 Jul 82	**MARGATE** *Rockney KOR 15*	**46**	4 wks

See also *Tottenham Hotspur FA Cup Squad.* Strummin' *by Chas and Dave, with Rockney. UK male instrumental backing group.*

CHEAP TRICK *US, male vocal/instrumental group*

Date	Title *Label Number*	Position	Weeks
5 May 79	**I WANT YOU TO WANT ME** *Epic EPC 7258*	**29**	9 wks
2 Feb 80	**WAY OF THE WORLD** *Epic EPC 8114*	**73**	2 wks
31 Jul 82	**IF YOU WANT MY LOVE** *Epic EPC A 2406*	**57**	3 wks

Chubby CHECKER *US, male vocalist*

Date	Title *Label Number*	Position	Weeks
22 Sep 60	**THE TWIST** *Columbia DB 4503*	**49**	1 wk
6 Oct 60	**THE TWIST** (re-entry) *Columbia DB 4503*	**44**	1 wk
30 Mar 61	**PONY TIME** *Columbia DB 4591*	**27**	6 wks
17 Aug 61	**LET'S TWIST AGAIN** *Columbia DB 4691*	**37**	3 wks
28 Dec 61	● **LET'S TWIST AGAIN** (re-entry) *Columbia DB 4691*	**2**	27 wks
11 Jan 62	**THE TWIST** (2nd re-entry) *Columbia DB 4503*	**14**	10 wks
5 Apr 62	**SLOW TWISTIN'** *Columbia DB 4808*	**23**	8 wks
9 Aug 62	**DANCIN' PARTY** *Columbia DB 4876*	**19**	13 wks
23 Aug 62	**LET'S TWIST AGAIN** (2nd re-entry) *Columbia DB 4691*	**46**	1 wk
13 Sep 62	**LET'S TWIST AGAIN** (3rd re-entry) *Columbia DB 4691*	**49**	3 wks
1 Nov 62	**LIMBO ROCK** *Cameo-Parkway P 849*	**32**	10 wks
31 Oct 63	**WHAT DO YA SAY** *Cameo-Parkway P 806*	**37**	4 wks
29 Nov 75	● **LET'S TWIST AGAIN/ THE TWIST** (re-issue) *London HL 10512*	**5**	10 wks

See also Chubby Checker & Bobby Rydell.

Chubby CHECKER and Bobby RYDELL

US, male vocal duo

Date	Title *Label Number*	Position	Weeks
19 Apr 62	**TEACH ME TO TWIST** *Columbia DB 4802*	**45**	1 wk
20 Dec 62	**JINGLE BELL ROCK** *Cameo-Parkway C 205*	**40**	3 wks

See also Chubby Checker, Bobby Rydell.

CHECKMATES — See *Emile FORD and the CHECKMATES*

CHECKMATES LTD.

US, male vocal/instrumental group

Date	Title *Label Number*	Position	Weeks
15 Nov 69	**PROUD MARY** *A & M AMS 769*	**30**	8 wks

Date	Title *Label Number*	Position	

CHEETAHS *UK, male vocal/instrumental group*

1 Oct 64	**MECCA** *Philips BF 1362*	**36**	3 wks
21 Jan 65	**SOLDIER BOY** *Philips BF 1383*	**39**	3 wks

CHELSEA F.C. *UK, male football team vocalists*

26 Feb 72	● **BLUE IS THE COLOUR** *Penny Farthing PEN 782*	**5**	12 wks

CHEQUERS *UK, male vocal/instrumental group*

18 Oct 75	**ROCK ON BROTHER** *Creole CR 111*	**21**	5 wks
28 Feb 76	**HEY MISS PAYNE** *Creole CR 116*	**32**	5 wks

CHER *US, female vocalist*

19 Aug 65	● **ALL I REALLY WANT TO DO** *Liberty LIB 66114*	**9**	10 wks
31 Mar 66	● **BANG BANG (MY BABY SHOT ME DOWN)** *Liberty LIB 66160*	**3**	12 wks
4 Aug 66	**I FEEL SOMETHING IN THE AIR** *Liberty LIB 12034*	**43**	2 wks
22 Sep 66	**SUNNY** *Liberty LIB 12083*	**32**	5 wks
6 Nov 71	● **GYPSIES TRAMPS AND THIEVES** *MCA MU 1142*	**4**	13 wks
16 Feb 74	**DARK LADY** *MCA 101*	**36**	3 wks
16 Mar 74	**DARK LADY** (re-entry) *MCA 101*	**45**	1 wk

See also Sonny & Cher.

CHERI *UK, female vocal duo*

19 Jun 82	**MURPHY'S LAW** *Polydor POSP 459*	**13**	9 wks

CHEROKEES *UK, male vocal/instrumental group*

3 Sep 64	**SEVEN DAFFODILS** *Columbia DB 7341*	**33**	5 wks

Don CHERRY *US, male vocalist*

10 Feb 56	● **BAND OF GOLD** *Philips PB 549*	**6**	11 wks

CHIC *US, male/female vocal/instrumental group*

26 Nov 77	● **DANCE DANCE DANCE (YOWSAH YOWSAH YOWSAH)** *Atlantic K 11038*	**6**	12 wks
1 Apr 78	● **EVERYBODY DANCE** *Atlantic K 11097*	**9**	11 wks
18 Nov 78	● **LE FREAK** *Atlantic K 11209*	**7**	16 wks
24 Feb 79	● **I WANT YOUR LOVE** *Atlantic LV 16*	**4**	11 wks
30 Jun 79	● **GOOD TIMES** *Atlantic K 11310*	**5**	11 wks
13 Oct 79	**MY FORBIDDEN LOVER** *Atlantic K 11385*	**15**	8 wks
8 Dec 79	**MY FEET KEEP DANCING** *Atlantic K 11415*	**21**	9 wks

CHICAGO *US, male vocal/instrumental group*

10 Jan 70	● **I'M A MAN** *CBS 4715*	**8**	11 wks
18 Jul 70	● **25 OR 6 TO 4** *CBS 5076*	**7**	13 wks
9 Oct 76	★ **IF YOU LEAVE ME NOW** *CBS 4603*	**1**	16 wks
5 Nov 77	**BABY WHAT A BIG SURPRISE** *CBS 5672*	**41**	3 wks
21 Aug 82	● **HARD TO SAY I'M SORRY** *Full Moon K 79301*	**4**	15 wks

CHICKEN SHACK *UK, male/female vocal/instrumental group*

7 May 69	**I'D RATHER GO BLIND** *Blue Horizon 57-3153*	**14**	13 wks
6 Sep 69	**TEARS IN THE WIND** *Blue Horizon 57-3160*	**29**	6 wks

CHICORY TIP *UK, male vocal/instrumental group*

29 Jan 72	★ **SON OF MY FATHER** *CBS 7737*	**1**	13 wks
20 May 72	**WHAT'S YOUR NAME** *CBS 8021*	**13**	8 wks
31 Mar 73	**GOOD GRIEF CHRISTINA** *CBS 1258*	**17**	13 wks

CHIFFONS *US, female vocal group*

11 Apr 63	**HE'S SO FINE** *Stateside SS 172*	**16**	12 wks
18 Jul 63	**ONE FINE DAY** *Stateside SS 202*	**29**	6 wks
26 May 66	**SWEET TALKIN' GUY** *Stateside SS 512*	**31**	8 wks
18 Mar 72	● **SWEET TALKIN' GUY** (re-issue) *London HL 10271*	**4**	14 wks

CHILD *UK, male vocal/instrumental group*

29 Apr 78	**WHEN YOU WALK IN THE ROOM** *Ariola Hansa AHA 511*	**38**	5 wks
22 Jul 78	● **IT'S ONLY MAKE BELIEVE** *Ariola Hansa AHA 522*	**10**	12 wks
28 Apr 79	**ONLY YOU (AND YOU ALONE)** *Ariola/Hansa AHA 536*	**33**	5 wks

CHI-LITES *US, male vocal group*

28 Aug 71	**(FOR GOD'S SAKE) GIVE MORE POWER TO THE PEOPLE** *MCA MU 1138*	**32**	6 wks
15 Jan 72	● **HAVE YOU SEEN HER** *MCA MU 1146*	**3**	12 wks
27 May 72	**OH GIRL** *MCA MU 1156*	**14**	9 wks
23 Mar 74	● **HOMELY GIRL** *Brunswick BR 9*	**5**	13 wks
20 Jul 74	**I FOUND SUNSHINE** *Brunswick BR 12*	**35**	5 wks
2 Nov 74	● **TOO GOOD TO BE FORGOTTEN** *Brunswick BR 13*	**10**	11 wks
21 Jun 75	● **HAVE YOU SEEN HER/ OH GIRL** (re-issue) *Brunswick BR 20*	**5**	9 wks
13 Sep 75	● **IT'S TIME FOR LOVE** *Brunswick BR 25*	**5**	10 wks
31 Jul 76	● **YOU DON'T HAVE TO GO** *Brunswick BR 34*	**3**	11 wks

CHINA CRISIS *UK, male vocal/instrumental group*

7 Aug 82	**AFRICAN AND WHITE** *Inevitable/Virgin INEV 011*	**45**	5 wks

CHIPMUNKS *US, male vocalist, David Seville as a chipmunk vocal group*

24 Jul 59	**RAGTIME COWBOY JOE** *London HLU 8916*	**11**	8 wks

See also David Seville, Alfi & Harry.

CHORDETTES *US, female vocal group*

17 Dec 54	**MR. SANDMAN** *Columbia DB 3553*	**11**	8 wks
31 Aug 56	● **BORN TO BE WITH YOU** *London HLA 8302*	**8**	9 wks
18 Apr 58	● **LOLLIPOP** *London HLA 8584*	**6**	8 wks

Above **NEIL CHRISTIAN** His group the Crusaders included Jimmy Page *Top* **CHUBBY CHECKER AND BOBBY RYDELL** Teaching each other to twist *Centre* **GIGLIOLA CINQUETTI** Ten years between hits in which time she learned English

CLASSICS IV As well as scoring themselves, Dennis Yost, James Cobb, Wally Eaton, Kim Venable and Joe Wilson were also a session group, working behind singers like Tommy Roe, The Tams and Billy Joe Royal. James Cobb charted with the same number ('Spooky') in 1979 as a member of the Atlantic Rhythm Section *and below* **CLASSIX NOUVEAUX** Sal Solo perfects his Yul Brynner/Duncan Goodhew impression

Date	Title *Label Number*	Position	

CHORDS *UK, male vocal/instrumental group*

6 Oct 79	**NOW IT'S GONE** *Polydor 2059 141*	**63**	2 wks
2 Feb 80	**MAYBE TOMORROW** *Polydor POSP 101*	**40**	5 wks
26 Apr 80	**SOMETHING'S MISSING** *Polydor POSP 146*	**55**	3 wks
12 Jul 80	**THE BRITISH WAY OF LIFE** *Polydor 2059 258*	**54**	3 wks
18 Oct 80	**IN MY STREET** *Polydor POSP 185*	**50**	4 wks

Neil CHRISTIAN *UK, male vocalist*

7 Apr 66	**THAT'S NICE** *Strike JH 301*	**14**	10 wks

CHRISTIE *UK, male vocal/instrumental group*

2 May 70	★ **YELLOW RIVER** *CBS 4911*	**1**	22 wks
10 Oct 70	**SAN BERNADINO** *CBS 5169*	**49**	1 wk
24 Oct 70	● **SAN BERNADINO** (re-entry) *CBS 5169*	**7**	13 wks
25 Mar 72	**IRON HORSE** *CBS 7747*	**47**	1 wk

David CHRISTIE *France, male vocalist*

14 Aug 82	● **SADDLE UP** *KR KR 9*	**9**	12 wks

John CHRISTIE *Australia, male vocalist*

25 Dec 76	**HERE'S TO LOVE (AULD LANG SYNE)** *EMI 2554*	**24**	6 wks

Lou CHRISTIE *US, male vocalist*

24 Feb 66	**LIGHTNIN' STRIKES** *MGM 1297*	**11**	8 wks
28 Apr 66	**RHAPSODY IN THE RAIN** *MGM 1308*	**37**	2 wks
13 Sep 69	● **I'M GONNA MAKE YOU MINE** *Buddah 201 057*	**2**	17 wks
27 Dec 69	**SHE SOLD ME MAGIC** *Buddah 201 073*	**25**	8 wks

Tony CHRISTIE *UK, male vocalist*

9 Jan 71	**LAS VEGAS** *MCA MK 5058*	**21**	9 wks
8 May 71	● **I DID WHAT I DID FOR MARIA** *MCA MK 5064*	**2**	17 wks
20 Nov 71	**IS THIS THE WAY TO AMARILLO** *MCA MKS 5073*	**18**	13 wks
10 Feb 73	**AVENUES AND ALLEYWAYS** *MCA MKS 5101*	**37**	4 wks
17 Jan 76	**DRIVE SAFELY DARLIN'** *MCA 219*	**35**	4 wks

CHRISTMAS TREES — See *SANTA CLAUS and the CHRISTMAS TREES*

CHUCKS *UK, male/female vocal group*

24 Jan 63	**LOO-BE-LOO** *Decca F 11569*	**22**	7 wks

Gigliola CINQUETTI *Italy, female vocalist*

23 Apr 64	**NON HO L'ETA PER AMARTI** *Decca F 21882*	**17**	17 wks
4 May 74	● **GO (BEFORE YOU BREAK MY HEART)** *CBS 2294*	**8**	10 wks

CIRRUS *UK, disco aggregation*

30 Sep 78	**ROLLIN' ON** *Jet 123*	**62**	1 wk

CITY BOY *UK, male vocal/instrumental group*

8 Jul 78	● **5-7-0-5** *Vertigo 6059 207*	**8**	12 wks
28 Oct 78	**WHAT A NIGHT** *Vertigo 6059 211*	**39**	5 wks
15 Sep 79	**THE DAY THE EARTH CAUGHT FIRE** *Vertigo 6059 238*	**67**	3 wks

CITY GENTS — See *Dick CHARLESWORTH and his CITY GENTS*

C.J.& CO. *US, male vocal/instrumental group*

30 Jul 77	**DEVIL'S GUN** *Atlantic K 10956*	**43**	2 wks

CLANNAD *Ireland, male/female vocal group*

6 Nov 82	● **THEME FROM HARRY'S GAME** *RCA 292*	**5**†	8 wks

Jimmy CLANTON *US, male vocalist*

21 Jul 60	**ANOTHER SLEEPLESS NIGHT** *Top Rank JAR 382*	**50**	1 wk

Eric CLAPTON

UK, male vocalist/instrumentalist-guitar

27 Jul 74	● **I SHOT THE SHERIFF** *RSO 2090 132*	**9**	9 wks
10 May 75	**SWING LOW SWEET CHARIOT** *RSO 2090 158*	**19**	9 wks
16 Aug 75	**KNOCKIN' ON HEAVEN'S DOOR** *RSO 2090 166*	**38**	4 wks
24 Dec 77	**LAY DOWN SALLY** *RSO 2090 264*	**39**	6 wks
21 Oct 78	**PROMISES** *RSO 21*	**37**	7 wks
5 Jun 82	**I SHOT THE SHERIFF** (re-issue) *RSO 88*	**64**	2 wks

See also Derek and Dominos, Dominos. and Delaney and Bonnie and friends featuring Eric Clapton

Dee CLARK *US, male vocalist*

2 Oct 59	**JUST KEEP IT UP** *London HL 8915*	**26**	1 wk
11 Oct 75	**RIDE A WILD HORSE** *Chelsea 2005 037*	**16**	8 wks

Petula CLARK *UK, female vocalist*

11 Jun 54	**THE LITTLE SHOEMAKER** *Polygon P 1117*	**12**	1 wk
25 Jun 54	● **THE LITTLE SHOEMAKER** (re-entry) *Polygon P 1117*	**7**	9 wks
18 Feb 55	**MAJORCA** *Polygon P 1146*	**12**	4 wks
25 Mar 55	**MAJORCA** (re-entry) *Polygon P 1146*	**18**	1 wk
25 Nov 55	● **SUDDENLY THERE'S A VALLEY** *Nixa N 15013*	**7**	10 wks
26 Jul 57	● **WITH ALL MY HEART** *Pye Nixa N 15096*	**4**	18 wks
15 Nov 57	● **ALONE** *Pye Nixa N 15112*	**8**	12 wks
28 Feb 58	**BABY LOVER** *Pye Nixa N 15126*	**12**	7 wks
26 Jan 61	★ **SAILOR** *Pye 7N 15324*	**1**	15 wks
13 Apr 61	**SOMETHING MISSING** *Pye 7N 15337*	**44**	1 wk
13 Jul 61	● **ROMEO** *Pye 7N 15361*	**3**	15 wks
16 Nov 61	● **MY FRIEND THE SEA** *Pye 7N 15387*	**7**	13 wks
8 Feb 62	**I'M COUNTING ON YOU** *Pye 7N 15407*	**41**	2 wks
28 Jun 62	**YA YA TWIST** *Pye 7N 15448*	**14**	11 wks
20 Sep 62	**YA YA TWIST** (re-entry) *Pye 7N 15448*	**45**	2 wks
2 May 63	**CASANOVA/ CHARIOT** *Pye 7N 15522*	**39**	7 wks
12 Nov 64	● **DOWNTOWN** *Pye 7N 15722*	**2**	15 wks
11 Mar 65	**I KNOW A PLACE** *Pye 7N 15772*	**17**	8 wks
12 Aug 65	**YOU BETTER COME HOME** *Pye 7N 15864*	**44**	3 wks
14 Oct 65	**ROUND EVERY CORNER** *Pye 7N 15945*	**43**	3 wks
4 Nov 65	**YOU'RE THE ONE** *Pye 7N 15991*	**23**	9 wks

Date	Title *Label Number*	Position	
10 Feb 66	● **MY LOVE** *Pye 7N 17038*	**4**	9 wks
21 Apr 66	**A SIGN OF THE TIMES** *Pye 7N 17071*	**49**	1 wk
30 Jun 66	● **I COULDN'T LIVE WITHOUT YOUR LOVE** *Pye 7N 17133*	**6**	11 wks
2 Feb 67	★ **THIS IS MY SONG** *Pye 7N 17258*	**1**	14 wks
25 May 67	**DON'T SLEEP IN THE SUBWAY** *Pye 7N 17325*	**12**	11 wks
13 Dec 67	**THE OTHER MAN'S GRASS** *Pye 7N 17416*	**20**	9 wks
6 Mar 68	**KISS ME GOODBYE** *Pye 7N 17466*	**50**	1 wk
30 Jan 71	**THE SONG OF MY LIFE** *Pye 7N 45026*	**41**	1 wk
13 Feb 71	**THE SONG OF MY LIFE** (re-entry) *Pye 7N 45026*	**32**	11 wks
15 Jan 72	**I DON'T KNOW HOW TO LOVE HIM** *Pye 7N 45112*	**47**	1 wk
29 Jan 72	**I DON'T KNOW HOW TO LOVE HIM** (re-entry) *Pye 7N 45112*	**49**	1 wk

Dave CLARK FIVE

UK, male vocal/instrumental group

Date	Title *Label Number*	Position	
3 Oct 63	**DO YOU LOVE ME** *Columbia DB 7112*	**30**	6 wks
21 Nov 63	★ **GLAD ALL OVER** *Columbia DB 7154*	**1**	19 wks
20 Feb 64	● **BITS AND PIECES** *Columbia DB 7210*	**2**	11 wks
28 May 64	● **CAN'T YOU SEE THAT SHE'S MINE** *Columbia DB 7291*	**10**	11 wks
13 Aug 64	**THINKING OF YOU BABY** *Columbia DB 7335*	**26**	4 wks
22 Oct 64	**ANYWAY YOU WANT IT** *Columbia DB 7377*	**25**	5 wks
14 Jan 65	**EVERYBODY KNOWS** *Columbia DB 7453*	**37**	4 wks
11 Mar 65	**REELIN' AND ROCKIN'** *Columbia DB 7503*	**24**	8 wks
27 May 65	**COME HOME** *Columbia DB 7580*	**16**	8 wks
15 Jul 65	● **CATCH US IF YOU CAN** *Columbia DB 7625*	**5**	11 wks
11 Nov 65	**OVER AND OVER** *Columbia DB 7744*	**45**	4 wks
19 May 66	**LOOK BEFORE YOU LEAP** *Columbia DB 7909*	**50**	1 wk
16 Mar 67	**YOU GOT WHAT IT TAKES** *Columbia DB 8152*	**28**	8 wks
1 Nov 67	● **EVERYBODY KNOWS** *Columbia DB 8286*	**2**	14 wks
28 Feb 68	**NO ONE CAN BREAK A HEART LIKE YOU** *Columbia DB 8342*	**28**	7 wks
18 Sep 68	● **RED BALLOON** *Columbia DB 8465*	**7**	11 wks
27 Nov 68	**LIVE IN THE SKY** *Columbia DB 8505*	**39**	6 wks
25 Oct 69	**PUT A LITTLE LOVE IN YOUR HEART** *Columbia DB 8624*	**31**	4 wks
6 Dec 69	● **GOOD OLD ROCK 'N ROLL** *Columbia DB 8638*	**7**	12 wks
7 Mar 70	● **EVERYBODY GET TOGETHER** *Columbia DB 8660*	**8**	8 wks
4 Jul 70	**HERE COMES SUMMER** *Columbia DB 8689*	**44**	3 wks
7 Nov 70	**MORE GOOD OLD ROCK 'N ROLL** *Columbia DB 8724*	**34**	6 wks

(Everybody Knows *on DB 7453 and* Everybody Knows *on DB 8286 are two different songs. The two Rock 'N' Roll titles are medleys as follows:* Good Old Rock 'N' Roll: *Good Old Rock 'N Roll The two Rock 'N' Roll titles are medleys as follows:* Good Old Rock 'N Roll: *Good Old Rock 'N' Roll/ Sweet Little Sixteen/ Long Tall Sally/ Whole Lotta Shakin' Goin' On/ Blue Suede Shoes/ Lucille/ Reelin' and Rockin'/ Memphis Tennessee.* More Good Old Rock 'N Roll: *Rock And Roll Music/ Blueberry Hill/ Good Golly Miss Molly/ My Blue Heaven/ Keep A Knockin'/ Loving You/ One Night/ Lawdy Miss Clawdy.*

John Cooper CLARKE *UK, male vocalist*

Date	Title *Label Number*	Position	
10 Mar 79	**¡GIMMIX! PLAY LOUD** *Epic EPC 7009*	**39**	3 wks

CLASH *UK, male vocal and instrumental group*

Date	Title *Label Number*	Position	
2 Apr 77	**WHITE RIOT** *CBS 5058*	**38**	3 wks
8 Oct 77	**COMPLETE CONTROL** *CBS 5664*	**28**	2 wks
4 Mar 78	**CLASH CITY ROCKERS** *CBS 5834*	**35**	4 wks
24 Jun 78	**(WHITE MAN) IN HAMMERSMITH PALAIS** *CBS 6383*	**32**	7 wks
2 Dec 78	**TOMMY GUN** *CBS 6788*	**19**	10 wks
3 Mar 79	**ENGLISH CIVIL WAR (JOHNNY COMES MARCHING HOME)** *CBS 7082*	**25**	6 wks
19 May 79	**THE COST OF LIVING** (EP) *CBS 7324*	**22**	8 wks
15 Dec 79	**LONDON CALLING** *CBS 8087*	**11**	10 wks
9 Aug 80	**BANKROBBER** *CBS 8323*	**12**	10 wks
6 Dec 80	**THE CALL UP** *CBS 9339*	**40**	6 wks
24 Jan 81	**HITSVILLE UK** *CBS 9480*	**56**	4 wks
25 Apr 81	**THE MAGNIFICENT SEVEN** *CBS 1133*	**34**	5 wks
28 Nov 81	**THIS IS RADIO CLASH** *CBS A 1797*	**47**	5 wks
1 May 82	**KNOW YOUR RIGHTS** *CBS A 2309*	**43**	3 wks
26 Jan 82	**ROCK THE CASBAH** *CBS A 2429*	**30**	10 wks
25 Sep 82	**SHOULD I STAY OR SHOULD I GO/STRAIGHT TO HELL** *CBS A 2645*	**17**	9 wks

Tracks on Cost Of Living EP: *I Fought The Law/Groovy Times/Gates Of The West/Capital Radio.*

CLASSICS IV *US, male vocal/instrumental group*

Date	Title *Label Number*	Position	
28 Feb 68	**SPOOKY** *Liberty LBS 15051*	**46**	1 wk

CLASSIX NOUVEAUX

UK, male vocal/instrumental group

Date	Title *Label Number*	Position	
28 Feb 81	**GUILTY** *Liberty BP 388*	**43**	7 wks
16 May 81	**TOKYO** *Liberty BP 397*	**67**	3 wks
8 Aug 81	**INSIDE OUTSIDE** *Liberty BP 403*	**46**	5 wks
7 Nov 81	**NEVER AGAIN (THE DAYS TIME ERASED)** *Liberty BP 406*	**44**	4 wks
13 Mar 82	**IS IT A DREAM** *Liberty BP409*	**11**	9 wks
29 May 82	**BECAUSE YOU'RE YOUNG** *Liberty BP 411*	**43**	4 wks
30 Oct 82	**THE END ... OR THE BEGINNING** *Liberty BP 414*	**60**	2 wks

Judy CLAY and William BELL

US, male/female vocal duo

Date	Title *Label Number*	Position	
20 Nov 68	● **PRIVATE NUMBER** *Stax 101*	**8**	14 wks

See also William Bell.

Jimmy CLIFF *Jamaica, male vocalist*

Date	Title *Label Number*	Position	
25 Oct 69	● **WONDERFUL WORLD BEAUTIFUL PEOPLE** *Trojan TR 690*	**6**	13 wks
14 Feb 70	**VIETNAM** *Trojan TR 7722*	**47**	1 wk
28 Feb 70	**VIETNAM** (re-entry) *Trojan TR 7722*	**46**	2 wks
8 Aug 70	● **WILD WORLD** *Island WIP 6087*	**8**	12 wks

Buzz CLIFFORD *US, male vocalist*

Date	Title *Label Number*	Position	
2 Mar 61	**BABY SITTIN' BOOGIE** *Fontana H 297*	**17**	13 wks

Linda CLIFFORD *US, female vocalist*

Date	Title *Label Number*	Position	
10 Jun 78	**IF MY FRIENDS COULD SEE ME NOW** *Curtom K 17163*	**50**	5 wks
5 May 79	**BRIDGE OVER TROUBLED WATER** *RSO 30*	**28**	7 wks

CLIMAX BLUES BAND

UK, male vocal/instrumental group

Date	Title *Label Number*	Position	
9 Oct 76	● **COULDN'T GET IT RIGHT** *BTM SBT 105*	**10**	9 wks

Date **Title** *Label Number* **Position**

Date **Title** *Label Number* **Position**

Patsy CLINE *US, female vocalist*

Date	Title *Label Number*	Position	
26 Apr 62	**SHE'S GOT YOU** *Brunswick 05866*	**43**	1 wk
29 Nov 62	**HEARTACHES** *Brunswick 05878*	**31**	5 wks

George CLINTON

US, male vocalist/instrumentalist

Date	Title *Label Number*	Position	
4 Dec 82	**LOOPZILLA** *Capitol CL 271*	**57**†	4 wks

Rosemary CLOONEY *US, female vocalist*

Date	Title *Label Number*	Position	
14 Nov 52	● **HALF AS MUCH** *Columbia DB 3129*	**3**	9 wks
5 Feb 54	● **MAN** *Philips PB 220*	**7**	5 wks
8 Oct 54	★ **THIS OLE HOUSE** *Philips PB 336*	**1**	18 wks
17 Dec 54	★ **MAMBO ITALIANO** *Philips PB 382*	**1**	16 wks
20 May 55	● **WHERE WILL THE BABY'S DIMPLE BE** *Philips PB 428*	**6**	13 wks
30 Sep 55	● **HEY THERE** *Philips PB 494*	**4**	11 wks
29 Mar 57	**MANGOS** *Philips PB 671*	**25**	2 wks
26 Apr 57	**MANGOS** (re-entry) *Philips PB 671*	**17**	7 wks

From 19 Feb 54 other side of Man, Woman *by José Ferrer was also credited. See José Ferrer.*

CLOUD *UK, male instrumental group*

Date	Title *Label Number*	Position	
31 Jan 81	**ALL NIGHT LONG/TAKE IT TO TOPTOP** *UK Champagne FUNK 1*	**72**	1 wk

CLOUT *South Africa, female vocal/instrumental group*

Date	Title *Label Number*	Position	
17 Jun 78	● **SUBSTITUTE** *Carrere EMI 2788*	**2**	15 wks

Jeremy CLYDE — See *Chad STUART and Jeremy CLYDE*

CLYDE VALLEY STOMPERS

UK, male instrumental group

Date	Title *Label Number*	Position	
9 Aug 62	**PETER AND THE WOLF** *Parlophone R 4928*	**25**	8 wks

COAST TO COAST

UK, male vocal/instrumental group

Date	Title *Label Number*	Position	
31 Jan 81	● **(DO) THE HUCKLEBUCK** *Polydor POSP 214*	**5**	15 wks
23 May 81	**LET'S JUMP THE BROOMSTICK** *Polydor POSP 249*	**28**	7 wks

COASTERS *US, male vocal group*

Date	Title *Label Number*	Position	
27 Sep 57	**SEARCHIN'** *London HLE 8450*	**30**	1 wk
15 Aug 58	**YAKETY YAK** *London HLE 8665*	**12**	8 wks
27 Mar 59	● **CHARLIE BROWN** *London HLE 8819*	**6**	12 wks
30 Oct 59	**POISON IVY** *London HLE 8938*	**15**	7 wks

Eddie COCHRAN *US, male vocalist*

Date	Title *Label Number*	Position	
7 Nov 58	**SUMMERTIME BLUES** *London HLU 8702*	**18**	6 wks
13 Mar 59	● **C'MON EVERYBODY** *London HLU 8792*	**6**	13 wks
16 Oct 59	**SOMETHIN' ELSE** *London HLU 8944*	**22**	3 wks
22 Jan 60	**HALLELUJAH I LOVE HER SO** *London HLW 9022*	**28**	1 wk
5 Feb 60	**HALLELUJAH I LOVE HER SO** (re-entry) *London HLW 9022*	**22**	3 wks
12 May 60	★ **THREE STEPS TO HEAVEN** *London HLG 9115*	**1**	15 wks
6 Oct 60	**SWEETIE PIE** *London HLG 9196*	**38**	3 wks
3 Nov 60	**LONELY** *London HLG 9196*	**41**	1 wk
15 Jun 61	**WEEKEND** *London HLG 9362*	**15**	16 wks
30 Nov 61	**JEANNIE, JEANNIE, JEANNIE** *London HLG 9460*	**31**	4 wks
25 Apr 63	**MY WAY** *Liberty LIB 10088*	**23**	10 wks
24 Apr 68	**SUMMERTIME BLUES** (re-issue) *Liberty LBF 15071*	**34** 8	8 wks

Joe COCKER *UK, male vocalist*

Date	Title *Label Number*	Position	
22 May 68	**MARJORINE** *Regal-Zonophone RZ 3006*	**48**	1 wk
2 Oct 68	★ **WITH A LITTLE HELP FROM MY FRIENDS** *Regal-Zonophone RZ 3013*	**1**	13 wks
27 Sep 69	● **DELTA LADY** *Regal-Zonophone RZ 3024*	**10**	11 wks
4 Jul 70	**THE LETTER** *Regal-Zonophone RZ 3027*	**39**	6 wks

COCKEREL CHORUS *UK, male vocal group*

Date	Title *Label Number*	Position	
24 Feb 73	**NICE ONE CYRIL** *Youngblood YB 1017*	**14**	12 wks

COCKNEY REBEL — See *Steve HARLEY*

COCKNEY REJECTS

UK, male vocal/instrumental group

Date	Title *Label Number*	Position	
1 Dec 79	**I'M NOT A FOOL** *EMI 5008*	**65**	2 wks
16 Feb 80	**BADMAN** *EMI 5035*	**65**	3 wks
26 Apr 80	**THE GREATEST COCKNEY RIPOFF** *EMI Z2*	**21**	7 wks
17 May 80	**I'M FOREVER BLOWING BUBBLES** *EMI Z 4*	**35**	5 wks
12 Jul 80	**WE CAN DO ANYTHING** *EMI-Cockney Rejects Z 6*	**65**	2 wks
25 Oct 80	**WE ARE THE FIRM** *EMI-Cockney Rejects Z 10*	**54**	3 wks

CO-CO *UK, male/female vocal/instrumental group*

Date	Title *Label Number*	Position	
22 Apr 78	**BAD OLD DAYS** *Ariola Hansa AHA 513*	**13**	7 wks

El COCO *US, male vocal/instrumental group*

Date	Title *Label Number*	Position	
14 Jan 78	**COCOMOTION** *Pye International 7N 25761*	**31**	4 wks

COCONUTS — See *Kid CREOLE and the COCONUTS*

COFFEE *US, female vocal group*

Date	Title *Label Number*	Position	
27 Sep 80	**CASANOVA** *De-Lite MER 38*	**13**	10 wks
6 Dec 80	**SLIP AND DIP/I WANNA BE WITH YOU** *De-Lite DE 1*	**57**	3 wks

Alma COGAN *UK, female vocalist*

Date	Title *Label Number*	Position	
19 Mar 54	● **BELL BOTTOM BLUES** *HMV B 10653*	**4**	9 wks
27 Aug 54	**LITTLE THINGS MEAN A LOT** *HMV B 10717*	**11**	2 wks
8 Oct 54	**LITTLE THINGS MEAN A LOT** (re-entry) *HMV B 10717*	**19**	1 wk
22 Oct 54	**LITTLE THINGS MEAN A LOT** (2nd re-entry) *HMV B 10717*	**18**	2 wks
3 Dec 54	● **I CAN'T TELL A WALTZ FROM A TANGO** *HMV B 10786*	**6**	11 wks
27 May 55	★ **DREAMBOAT** *HMV B 10872*	**1**	16 wks
23 Sep 55	**BANJO'S BACK IN TOWN** *HMV B 10917*	**17**	1 wk
14 Oct 55	**GO ON BY** *HMV B 10917*	**16**	4 wks

Date	Title *Label Number*	Position	
16 Dec 55	**TWENTY TINY FINGERS** *HMV POP 129*	**17**	1 wk
23 Dec 55	● **NEVER DO A TANGO WITH AN ESKIMO** *HMV POP 129*	**6**	5 wks
30 Mar 56	**WILLIE CAN** *HMV POP 187*	**13**	8 wks
13 Jul 56	**THE BIRDS AND THE BEES** *HMV POP 223*	**25**	4 wks
10 Aug 56	**WHY DO FOOLS FALL IN LOVE** *HMV POP 223*	**22**	3 wks
2 Nov 56	**IN THE MIDDLE OF THE HOUSE** *HMV POP 261*	**26**	1 wk
23 Nov 56	**IN THE MIDDLE OF THE HOUSE** (re-entry) *HMV POP 261*	**20**	3 wks
18 Jan 57	**YOU ME AND US** *HMV POP 284*	**18**	6 wks
29 Mar 57	**WHATEVER LOLA WANTS** *HMV POP 317*	**26**	2 wks
31 Jan 58	**THE STORY OF MY LIFE** *HMV POP 433*	**25**	2 wks
14 Feb 58	**SUGARTIME** *HMV POP 450*	**16**	10 wks
2 May 58	**SUGARTIME** (re-entry) *HMV POP 450*	**30**	1 wk
23 Jan 59	**LAST NIGHT ON THE BACK PORCH** *HMV POP 573*	**27**	2 wks
18 Dec 59	**WE GOT LOVE** *HMV POP 670*	**26**	4 wks
11 Aug 60	**TRAIN OF LOVE** *HMV POP 760*	**27**	5 wks
20 Apr 61	**COWBOY JIMMY JOE** *Columbia DB 4607*	**37**	6 wks

Shaye COGAN *US, female vocalist*

Date	Title *Label Number*	Position	
24 Mar 60	**MEAN TO ME** *MGM 1063*	**43**	1 wk

Izhar COHEN and ALPHABETA

Israel, male/female vocal group

Date	Title *Label Number*	Position	
13 May 78	**A BA NI BI** *Polydor 2001 781*	**20**	7 wks

Cozy COLE *US, male instrumentalist, drums*

Date	Title *Label Number*	Position	
5 Dec 58	**TOPSY** PARTS I AND II *London HL 8750*	**29**	1 wk

Nat "King" COLE *US, male vocalist*

Date	Title *Label Number*	Position	
14 Nov 52	● **SOMEWHERE ALONG THE WAY** *Capitol CL 13774*	**3**	7 wks
19 Dec 52	● **BECAUSE YOU'RE MINE** *Capitol CL 13811*	**6**	2 wks
2 Jan 53	**FAITH CAN MOVE MOUNTAINS** *Capitol CL 13811*	**11**	1 wk
16 Jan 53	**FAITH CAN MOVE MOUNTAINS** (re-entry) *Capitol CL 13811*	**12**	2 wks
23 Jan 53	● **BECAUSE YOU'RE MINE** (re-entry) *Capitol CL 13811*	**10**	1 wk
6 Feb 53	● **FAITH CAN MOVE MOUNTAINS** (2nd re-entry) *Capitol CL 13811*	**10**	1 wk
13 Feb 53	**BECAUSE YOU'RE MINE** (2nd re-entry) *Capitol CL 13811*	**11**	1 wk
24 Apr 53	● **PRETEND** *Capitol CL 13878*	**2**	18 wks
14 Aug 53	● **CAN'T I?** *Capitol CL 13937*	**9**	3 wks
18 Sep 53	● **CAN'T I?** (re-entry) *Capitol CL 13937*	**6**	4 wks
18 Sep 53	● **MOTHER NATURE AND FATHER TIME** *Capitol CL 13912*	**7**	7 wks
30 Oct 53	● **CAN'T I?** (2nd re-entry) *Capitol CL 13937*	**10**	1 wk
16 Apr 54	● **TENDERLY** *Capitol CL 14061*	**10**	1 wk
10 Sep 54	● **SMILE** *Capitol CL 14149*	**2**	14 wks
8 Oct 54	**MAKE HER MINE** *Capitol CL 14149*	**11**	2 wks
25 Feb 55	● **A BLOSSOM FELL** *Capitol CL 14235*	**3**	10 wks
26 Aug 55	**MY ONE SIN** *Capitol CL 14327*	**18**	1 wk
16 Sep 55	**MY ONE SIN** (re-entry) *Capitol CL 14327*	**17**	1 wk
27 Jan 56	● **DREAMS CAN TELL A LIE** *Capitol CL 14513*	**10**	9 wks
11 May 56	● **TOO YOUNG TO GO STEADY** *Capitol CL 14573*	**8**	14 wks
14 Sep 56	**LOVE ME AS IF THERE WERE NO TOMORROW** *Capitol CL 14621*	**24**	2 wks
5 Oct 56	**LOVE ME AS IF THERE WERE NO TOMORROW** (re-entry) *Capitol CL 14621*	**11**	13 wks
19 Apr 57	● **WHEN I FALL IN LOVE** *Capitol CL 14709*	**2**	20 wks
5 Jul 57	**WHEN ROCK 'N ROLL CAME TO TRINIDAD** *Capitol CL 14733*	**28**	1 wk
18 Oct 57	**MY PERSONAL POSSESSION** *Capitol CL 14765*	**21**	2 wks
25 Oct 57	**STARDUST** *Capitol CL 14787*	**24**	2 wks
29 May 59	**YOU MADE ME LOVE YOU** *Capitol CL 15017*	**22**	3 wks
4 Sep 59	**MIDNIGHT FLYER** *Capitol CL 15056*	**27**	1 wk
18 Sep 59	**MIDNIGHT FLYER** (re-entry) *Capitol CL 15056*	**23**	3 wks
12 Feb 60	**TIME AND THE RIVER** *Capitol CL 15111*	**29**	1 wk
26 Feb 60	**TIME AND THE RIVER** (re-entry) *Capitol CL 15111*	**23**	2 wks
31 Mar 60	**TIME AND THE RIVER** (2nd re-entry) *Capitol CL 15111*	**47**	1 wk
26 May 60	● **THAT'S YOU** *Capitol CL 15129*	**10**	8 wks
10 Nov 60	**JUST AS MUCH AS EVER** *Capitol CL 15163*	**18**	10 wks
2 Feb 61	**THE WORLD IN MY ARMS** *Capitol CL 15178*	**36**	10 wks
16 Nov 61	**LET TRUE LOVE BEGIN** *Capitol CL 15224*	**29**	10 wks
22 Mar 62	**BRAZILIAN LOVE SONG** *Capitol CL 15241*	**34**	4 wks
31 May 62	**THE RIGHT THING TO SAY** *Capitol CL 15250*	**42**	4 wks
19 Jul 62	**LET THERE BE LOVE** *Capitol CL 15257*	**11**	14 wks
27 Sep 62	● **RAMBLIN' ROSE** *Capitol CL 15270*	**5**	14 wks
20 Dec 62	**DEAR LONELY HEARTS** *Capitol CL 15280*	**37**	3 wks

Let There Be Love *with George Shearing (UK), male instrumentalist - piano.*

Natalie COLE *US, female vocalist*

Date	Title *Label Number*	Position	
11 Oct 75	**THIS WILL BE** *Capitol CL 15834*	**32**	5 wks

John Ford COLEY — See *ENGLAND DAN and John Ford COLEY*

Dave and Ansil COLLINS

Jamaica, male vocal duo

Date	Title *Label Number*	Position	
27 Mar 71	★ **DOUBLE BARREL** *Technique TE 901*	**1**	15 wks
26 Jun 71	● **MONKEY SPANNER** *Technique TE 914*	**7**	12 wks

Jeff COLLINS *UK, male vocalist*

Date	Title *Label Number*	Position	
18 Nov 72	**ONLY YOU** *Polydor 2058 287*	**40**	8 wks

Judy COLLINS *US, female vocalist*

Date	Title *Label Number*	Position	
17 Jan 70	**BOTH SIDES NOW** *Elektra EKSN 45043*	**14**	11 wks
5 Dec 70	● **AMAZING GRACE** *Elektra 2101 020*	**5**	32 wks
24 Jul 71	**AMAZING GRACE** (re-entry) *Elektra 2101 020*	**48**	1 wk
4 Sep 71	**AMAZING GRACE** (2nd re-entry) *Elektra 2101 020*	**40**	7 wks
20 Nov 71	**AMAZING GRACE** (3rd re-entry) *Elektra 2101 020*	**50**	1 wk
18 Dec 71	**AMAZING GRACE** (4th re-entry) *Elektra 2101 020*	**48**	2 wks
22 Apr 72	**AMAZING GRACE** (5th re-entry) *Elektra 2101 020*	**20**	19 wks
9 Sep 72	**AMAZING GRACE** (6th re-entry) *Elektra 2101 020*	**46**	2 wks
23 Dec 72	**AMAZING GRACE** (7th re-entry) *Elektra 2101 020*	**49**	3 wks
17 May 75	● **SEND IN THE CLOWNS** *Elektra K 12177*	**6**	8 wks

Phil COLLINS *UK, male vocalist/instrumentalist*

Date	Title *Label Number*	Position	
17 Jan 81	● **IN THE AIR TONIGHT** *Virgin VSK 102*	**2**	10 wks
7 Mar 81	**I MISSED AGAIN** *Virgin VS 402*	**14**	8 wks
30 May 81	**IF LEAVING ME IS EASY** *Virgin VS 423*	**17**	8 wks
23 Oct 82	**THRU' THESE WALLS** *Virgin VS 524*	**56**	2 wks
4 Dec 82	● **YOU CAN'T HURRY LOVE** *Virgin VS 531*	**6**†	4 wks

Rodger COLLINS *US, male vocalist*

Date	Title *Label Number*	Position	
3 Apr 76	**YOU SEXY SUGAR PLUM (BUT I LIKE IT)** *Fantasy FTC 132*	**22**	6 wks

COLORADO *UK, female vocal group*

Date	Title *Label Number*	Position	
21 Oct 78	**CALIFORNIA DREAMIN'** *Pinnacle PIN 67*	**45**	3 wks

COMETS — See *Bill HALEY and his COMETS*

COMMODORES

US, male vocal/instrumental group

Date	Title *Label Number*	Position	
24 Aug 74	**MACHINE GUN** *Tamla Motown TMG 902*	**20**	11 wks
23 Nov 74	**THE ZOO (THE HUMAN ZOO)** *Tamla Motown TMG 924*	**44**	2 wks
2 Jul 77	● **EASY** *Motown TMG 1073*	**9**	10 wks
8 Oct 77	**BRICK HOUSE/SWEET LOVE** *Motown TMG 1086*	**32**	6 wks
11 Mar 78	**TOO HOT TO TROT/ZOOM** *Motown TMG 1096*	**38**	4 wks
24 Jun 78	**FLYING HIGH** *Motown TMG 1111*	**37**	7 wks
5 Aug 78	★ **THREE TIMES A LADY** *Motown TMG 1113*	**1**	14 wks
25 Nov 78	**JUST TO BE CLOSE TO YOU** *Motown TMG 1127*	**62**	4 wks
25 Aug 79	● **SAIL ON** *Motown TMG 1155*	**8**	10 wks
3 Nov 79	● **STILL** *Motown TMG 1166*	**4**	11 wks
19 Jan 80	**WONDERLAND** *Motown TMG 1172*	**40**	4 wks
1 Aug 81	**LADY (YOU BRING ME UP)** *Motown TMG 1238*	**56**	5 wks
21 Nov 81	**OH NO** *Motown TMG 1245*	**44**	3 wks

Perry COMO *US, male vocalist*

Date	Title *Label Number*	Position	
16 Jan 53	★ **DON'T LET THE STARS GET IN YOUR EYES** *HMV B 10400*	**1**	15 wks
4 Jun 54	● **WANTED** *HMV B 10691*	**4**	14 wks
25 Jun 54	● **IDLE GOSSIP** *HMV B 10710*	**3**	15 wks
1 Oct 54	**WANTED** (re-entry) *HMV B 10691*	**18**	1 wk
10 Dec 54	**PAPA LOVES MAMBO** *HMV B 10776*	**16**	1 wk
30 Dec 55	**TINA MARIE** *HMV POP 103*	**24**	1 wk
27 Apr 56	**JUKE BOX BABY** *HMV POP 191*	**22**	6 wks
25 May 56	● **HOT DIGGITY** *HMV POP 212*	**4**	13 wks
21 Sep 56	● **MORE** *HMV POP 240*	**10**	11 wks
28 Sep 56	**GLENDORA** *HMV POP 240*	**18**	6 wks
14 Dec 56	**MORE** (re-entry) *HMV POP 240*	**29**	1 wk
7 Feb 58	★ **MAGIC MOMENTS** *RCA 1036*	**1**	17 wks
7 Mar 58	● **CATCH A FALLING STAR** *RCA 1036*	**9**	10 wks
9 May 58	● **KEWPIE DOLL** *RCA 1055*	**9**	7 wks
30 May 58	**I MAY NEVER PASS THIS WAY AGAIN** *RCA 1062*	**15**	8 wks
5 Sep 58	**MOON TALK** *RCA 1071*	**17**	11 wks
7 Nov 58	● **LOVE MAKES THE WORLD GO ROUND** *RCA 1086*	**6**	14 wks
21 Nov 58	**MANDOLINS IN THE MOONLIGHT** *RCA 1086*	**13**	12 wks
27 Feb 59	● **TOMBOY** *RCA 1111*	**10**	12 wks
10 Jul 59	**I KNOW** *RCA 1126*	**13**	16 wks
26 Feb 60	● **DELAWARE** *RCA 1170*	**3**	13 wks
10 May 62	**CATERINA** *RCA 1283*	**37**	4 wks
14 Jun 62	**CATERINA** (re-entry) *RCA 1283*	**45**	2 wks
30 Jan 71	● **IT'S IMPOSSIBLE** *RCA 2043*	**4**	23 wks
15 May 71	**I THINK OF YOU** *RCA 2075*	**14**	11 wks
21 Apr 73	● **AND I LOVE YOU SO** *RCA 2346*	**3**	31 wks
25 Aug 73	● **FOR THE GOOD TIMES** *RCA 2402*	**7**	27 wks
8 Dec 73	**WALK RIGHT BACK** *RCA 2432*	**33**	10 wks
12 Jan 74	**AND I LOVE YOU SO** (re-entry) *RCA 2346*	**40**	4 wks
25 May 74	**I WANT TO GIVE** *RCA LPBO 7518*	**31**	6 wks

COMPAGNONS DE LA CHANSON

France, male vocal group

Date	Title *Label Number*	Position	
9 Oct 59	**THE THREE BELLS** *Columbia DB 4358*	**27**	1 wk
23 Oct 59	**THE THREE BELLS** (re-entry) *Columbia DB 4358*	**21**	2 wks

Song is sub-titled "The Jimmy Brown Song".

CONGREGATION *UK, male/female choir*

Date	Title *Label Number*	Position	
27 Nov 71	● **SOFTLY WHISPERING I LOVE YOU** *Columbia DB 8830*	**4**	14 wks

Arthur CONLEY *US, male vocalist*

Date	Title *Label Number*	Position	
27 Apr 67	● **SWEET SOUL MUSIC** *Atlantic 584 083*	**7**	14 wks
10 Apr 68	**FUNKY STREET** *Atlantic 583 175*	**46**	1 wk

Billy CONNOLLY *UK, male vocalist*

Date	Title *Label Number*	Position	
1 Nov 75	★ **D. I. V. O. R. C. E.** *Polydor 2058 652*	**1**	10 wks
17 Jul 76	**NO CHANCE (NO CHARGE)** *Polydor 2058 748*	**24**	5 wks
25 Aug 79	**IN THE BROWNIES** *Polydor 2059 160*	**38**	7 wks

Jess CONRAD *UK, male vocalist*

Date	Title *Label Number*	Position	
30 Jun 60	**CHERRY PIE** *Decca F 11236*	**39**	1 wk
26 Jan 61	**MYSTERY GIRL** *Decca F 11315*	**44**	1 wk
9 Feb 61	**MYSTERY GIRL** (re-entry) *Decca F 11315*	**18**	9 wks
11 Oct 62	**PRETTY JENNY** *Decca F 11511*	**50**	2 wks

CONSORTIUM *UK, male vocal group*

Date	Title *Label Number*	Position	
12 Feb 69	**ALL THE LOVE IN THE WORLD** *Pye 7N 17635*	**22**	9 wks

CONTOURS *US, male vocal group*

Date	Title *Label Number*	Position	
24 Jan 70	**JUST A LITTLE MISUNDERSTANDING** *Tamla Motown TMG 723*	**31**	6 wks

Russ CONWAY *UK, male instrumentalist, piano*

Date	Title *Label Number*	Position	
29 Nov 57	**PARTY POPS** *Columbia DB 4031*	**24**	5 wks
29 Aug 58	**GOT A MATCH** *Columbia DB 4166*	**30**	1 wk
28 Nov 58	● **MORE PARTY POPS** *Columbia DB 4204*	**10**	7 wks
23 Jan 59	**THE WORLD OUTSIDE** *Columbia DB 4234*	**24**	1 wk
20 Feb 59	★ **SIDE SADDLE** *Columbia DB 4256*	**1**	30 wks
6 Mar 59	**THE WORLD OUTSIDE** (re-entry) *Columbia DB 4234*	**24**	3 wks
15 May 59	★ **ROULETTE** *Columbia DB 4298*	**1**	19 wks
21 Aug 59	● **CHINA TEA** *Columbia DB 4337*	**5**	13 wks
13 Nov 59	● **SNOW COACH** *Columbia DB 4368*	**7**	9 wks

Date	Title *Label Number*	Position	
20 Nov 59	● **MORE AND MORE PARTY POPS** *Columbia DB 4373*	**5**	8 wks
10 Mar 60	**ROYAL EVENT** *Columbia DB 4418*	**15**	7 wks
21 Apr 60	**FINGS AIN'T WOT THEY USED T'BE** *Columbia DB 4422*	**47**	1 wk
19 May 60	**LUCKY FIVE** *Columbia DB 4457*	**14**	9 wks
29 Sep 60	**PASSING BREEZE** *Columbia DB 4508*	**16**	10 wks
24 Nov 60	**EVEN MORE PARTY POPS** *Columbia DB 4535*	**27**	9 wks
19 Jan 61	**PEPE** *Columbia DB 4564*	**19**	9 wks
25 May 61	**PABLO** *Columbia DB 4649*	**45**	2 wks
30 Nov 61	● **TOY BALLOONS** *Columbia DB 4738*	**7**	11 wks
22 Feb 62	**LESSON ONE** *Columbia DB 4784*	**21**	7 wks
29 Nov 62	**ALWAYS YOU AND ME** *Columbia DB 4934*	**33**	4 wks
3 Jan 63	**ALWAYS YOU AND ME** (re-entry) *Columbia DB 4934*	**35**	3 wks

See also Dorothy Squires and Russ Conway. Always You And Me *featured Russ Conway talking as well as playing piano. Several of the discs were medleys as follows:* Party Pops: *When You're Smiling/ I'm Looking Over a Four-Leafed Clover/ When You Wore a Tulip/ Row Row Row/ For Me And My Girl/ Shine On Harvest Moon/ By The Light Of The Silvery Moon/ Side By Side.* More Party Pops: *Music Music Music/ If You Were The Only Girl In The World/ Nobody's Sweetheart/ Yes Sir That's My Baby/ Some Of These Days/ Honeysuckle And The Bee/ Hello Hello Who's Your Lady Friend/ Shanty In Old Shanty Town.* More And More Party Pops: *Sheik of Araby/ Who Were You With Last Night/ Any Old Iron/ Tiptoe Through The Tulips/ If You Were The Only Girl In The World/ When I Leave The World Behind.* Even More Party Pops: *Ain't She Sweet/ I Can't Give You Anything But Love/ Yes We Have No Bananas/ I May Be Wrong/ Happy Days And Lonely Nights/ Glad Rag Doll. He really did feature* If You Were The Only Girl In The World *on two different hits.*

Martin COOK — See *Richard DENTON and Martin COOK*

Peter COOK *UK, male vocalist*

15 Jul 65	**THE BALLAD OF SPOTTY MULDOON** *Decca F 12182*	**34**	5 wks

See also Peter Cook & Dudley Moore.

Peter COOK and Dudley MOORE

UK, male vocal duo, Dudley Moore featured pianist

17 Jun 65	**GOODBYE-EE** *Decca F 12158*	**18**	10 wks

See also Peter Cook.

Sam COOKE *US, male vocalist*

17 Jan 58	**YOU SEND ME** *London HLU 8506*	**29**	1 wk
14 Aug 59	**ONLY SIXTEEN** *HMV POP 642*	**23**	4 wks
7 Jul 60	**WONDERFUL WORLD** *HMV POP 754*	**27**	8 wks
29 Sep 60	● **CHAIN GANG** *RCA 1202*	**9**	11 wks
27 Jul 61	● **CUPID** *RCA 1242*	**7**	14 wks
8 Mar 62	● **TWISTIN' THE NIGHT AWAY** *RCA 1277*	**6**	14 wks
16 May 63	**ANOTHER SATURDAY NIGHT** *RCA 1341*	**23**	12 wks
5 Sep 63	**FRANKIE AND JOHNNY** *RCA 1361*	**30**	6 wks

COOKIES *US, female vocal group*

10 Jan 63	**CHAINS** *London HLU 9634*	**50**	1 wk

Rita COOLIDGE *US, female vocalist*

25 Jun 77	● **WE'RE ALL ALONE** *A&M AMS 7295*	**6**	13 wks
15 Oct 77	**(YOUR LOVE HAS LIFTED ME)HIGHER AND HIGHER** *A&M AMS 7315*	**49**	1 wk
29 Oct 77	**(YOUR LOVE HAS LIFTED ME)HIGHER AND HIGHER** (re-entry) *A&M AMS 7315*	**48**	1 wk
4 Feb 78	**WORDS** *A & M AMS 7330*	**25**	8 wks

Alice COOPER *US, male vocalist*

15 Jul 72	★ **SCHOOL'S OUT** *Warner Bros. K 16188*	**1**	12 wks
7 Oct 72	● **ELECTED** *Warner Bros. K 16214*	**4**	10 wks
10 Feb 73	● **HELLO HURRAY** *Warner Bros. K 16248*	**6**	12 wks
21 Apr 73	● **NO MORE MR. NICE GUY** *Warner Bros. K 16262*	**10**	10 wks
19 Jan 74	**TEENAGE LAMENT '74** *Warner Bros. K 16345*	**12**	7 wks
21 May 77	**(NO MORE) LOVE AT YOUR CONVENIENCE** *Warner Bros. K 16935*	**44**	2 wks
23 Dec 78	**HOW YOU GONNA SEE ME NOW** *Warner Bros. K 17270*	**61**	6 wks
6 Mar 82	**SEVEN AND SEVEN IS (LIVE VERSION)** *Warner Bros. K 17924*	**62**	3 wks
8 May 82	**FOR BRITAIN ONLY/UNDER MY WHEELS** *Warner Bros. K 17940*	**66**	2 wks

For the first 5 hits, 'Alice Cooper' was the name of the entire group not just of the lead vocalist.

Tommy COOPER *UK, male vocalist*

29 Jun 61	**DON'T JUMP OFF THE ROOF DAD** *Palette PG 9019*	**40**	2 wks
20 Jul 61	**DON'T JUMP OFF THE ROOF DAD** (re-entry) *Palette PG 9019*	**50**	1 wk

Harry H. CORBETT — See *Wilfred BRAMBELL and Harry H. CORBETT*

Frank CORDELL *UK, orchestra*

24 Aug 56	**SADIE'S SHAWL** *HMV POP 229*	**29**	2 wks
16 Feb 61	**BLACK BEAR** *HMV POP 824*	**44**	2 wks

Phil CORDELL — See *SPRINGWATER*

Louise CORDET *France, female vocalist*

5 Jul 62	**I'M JUST A BABY** *Decca F 11476*	**13**	13 wks

Don CORNELL *US, male vocalist*

3 Sep 54	★ **HOLD MY HAND** *Vogue Q 2013*	**1**	21 wks
22 Apr 55	**STRANGER IN PARADISE** *Vogue Q 72073*	**19**	2 wks

Lynn CORNELL *UK, female vocalist*

20 Oct 60	**NEVER ON SUNDAY** *Decca F 11277*	**30**	9 wks

Charlotte CORNWELL — See *Julie COVINGTON, Rula LENSKA, Charlotte CORNWELL and Sue JONES-DAVIES*

CORONETS *UK, male/female vocal group*

25 Nov 55	**TWENTY TINY FINGERS** *Columbia DB 3671*	**20**	1 wk

Vladimir COSMA *Hungary, orchestra*

14 Jul 79	**DAVID'S SONG (MAIN THEME FROM "KIDNAPPED")** *Decca FR 13841*	**64**	1 wk

Don COSTA *US, orchestra*

13 Oct 60	**NEVER ON SUNDAY** *London HLT 9195*	**27**	9 wks
22 Dec 60	**NEVER ON SUNDAY** (re-entry) *London HLT 9195*	**41**	1 wk

Right **PHIL COLLINS** Genesis – The last Phil and Testament

Above **ALICE COOPER** Started at the top but from then on the chart positions got progressively lower

Right **NAT 'KING' COLE** Nat's tenth hit warns 'The gypsies say and I know why, a falling blossom only touches lips that lie'

BILLY COTTON His first hit celebrates the coronation of Queen Elizabeth II

Date	Title *Label Number*	Position	Date	Title *Label Number*	Position

Elvis COSTELLO and the ATTRACTIONS

UK, male vocalist/instrumentalist, guitar

5 Nov 77 **WATCHING THE DETECTIVES** *Stiff BUY 20* **15** 11 wks
11 Mar 78 **(I DON'T WANNA GO TO) CHELSEA** *Radar ADA 3* **16** 10 wks
13 May 78 **PUMP IT UP** *Radar ADA 10* **24** 10 wks
28 Oct 78 **RADIO RADIO** *Radar ADA 24* **29** 7 wks
10 Feb 79 ● **OLIVER'S ARMY** *Radar ADA 31* **2** 12 wks
12 May 79 **ACCIDENTS WILL HAPPEN** *Radar ADA 35* **28** 8 wks
16 Feb 80 ● **I CAN'T STAND UP FOR FALLING DOWN** *F. Beat XX1* **4** 8 wks
12 Apr 80 **HI FIDELITY** *F. Beat XX3* **30** 5 wks
7 Jun 80 **NEW AMSTERDAM** *F. Beat XX5* **36** 6 wks
20 Dec 80 **CLUBLAND** *F. Beat XX12* **60** 4 wks
3 Oct 81 ● **A GOOD YEAR FOR THE ROSES** *F. Beat XX 17* **6** 11 wks
11 Dec 81 **SWEET DREAMS** *F. Beat XX 19* **42** 8 wks
10 Apr 82 **I'M YOUR TOY** *F. Beat XX 21* **51** 3 wks
19 Jun 82 **YOU LITTLE FOOL** *F. Beat XX 26* **52** 3 wks
31 Jul 82 **MAN OUT OF TIME** *F. Beat XX 28* **58** 2 wks
25 Sep 82 **FROM HEAD TO TOE** *F. Beat XX 30* **43** 4 wks
11 Dec 82 **PARTY PARTY** *A & M AMS 8267* **48†** 3 wks

Billed as Elvis Costello on hits in 1977 and 1980 with the exception of Clubland. I'm Your Toy *credits Elvis Costello and the Attractions with the Royal Philharmonic Orchestra. See Royal Philharmonic Orchestra.*

COTTAGERS — See *Tony REES and the COTTAGERS*

Billy COTTON and his BAND

UK, male bandleader, vocalist, with band and chorus

1 May 53 ● **IN A GOLDEN COACH** *Decca F 10058* **3** 10 wks
18 Dec 53 **I SAW MOMMY KISSING SANTA CLAUS** *Decca F 10206* **11** 3 wks
30 Apr 54 **FRIENDS AND NEIGHBOURS** *Decca F 10299* **12** 1 wk
14 May 54 ● **FRIENDS AND NEIGHBOURS** (re-entry) *Decca F 10299* **3** 11 wks

In a Golden Coach *has the credit "Vocal by Doreen Stephens" but also featured Billy Cotton as an unbilled narrator,* I Saw Mommy Kissing Santa Claus *has the credits "Vocals by the Mill Girls and the Bandits",* Friends and Neighbours *"Vocal by the Bandits". See also Various Artists - All Star Hit Parade No. 2.*

Mike COTTON'S JAZZMEN

UK, male instrumental band, Mike Cotton trumpet

20 Jun 63 **SWING THAT HAMMER** *Columbia DB 7029* **36** 4 wks

John COUGAR *US, male vocalist*

23 Oct 82 **JACK AND DIANE** *Riva RIVA 37* **25** 8 wks

COUGARS *UK, male instrumental group*

28 Feb 63 **SATURDAY NITE AT THE DUCK POND** *Parlophone R 4989* **33** 8 wks

COUNTRYMEN *UK, male vocal group*

3 May 62 **I KNOW WHERE I'M GOING** *Piccadilly 7N 35029* **45** 2 wks

Don COVAY *US, male vocalist*

7 Sep 74 **IT'S BETTER TO HAVE (AND DON'T NEED)** *Mercury 6052 634* **29** 6 wks

Julie COVINGTON *UK, female vocalist*

25 Dec 76 ★ **DON'T CRY FOR ME ARGENTINA** *MCA 260* **1** 15 wks
3 Dec 77 **ONLY WOMEN BLEED** *Virgin VS 196* **12** 11 wks
15 Jul 78 **DON'T CRY FOR ME ARGENTINA** (re-entry) *MCA 260* **63** 3 wks

See also Julie Covington, Rula Lenska, Charlotte Cornwell and Sue Jones-Davies.

Julie COVINGTON, Rula LENSKA, Charlotte CORNWELL and Sue JONES-DAVIES *UK, female vocal group*

21 May 77 ● **O.K?** *Polydor 2001 714* **10** 6 wks

See also Julie Covington

Warren COVINGTON — See *Tommy DORSEY Orchestra starring Warren COVINGTON*

Patrick COWLEY — See *SYLVESTER with Patrick COWLEY*

Michael COX *UK, male vocalist*

9 Jun 60 ● **ANGELA JONES** *Triumph RGM 1011* **7** 13 wks
20 Oct 60 **ALONG CAME CAROLINE** *HMV POP 789* **41** 2 wks

Floyd CRAMER *US, male instrumentalist, piano*

13 Apr 61 ★ **ON THE REBOUND** *RCA 1231* **1** 14 wks
20 Jul 61 **SAN ANTONIO ROSE** *RCA 1241* **36** 8 wks
23 Aug 62 **HOT PEPPER** *RCA 1301* **46** 2 wks

Les CRANE *US, male vocalist*

19 Feb 72 ● **DESIDERATA** *Warner Bros. K 16119* **7** 14 wks

Jimmy CRAWFORD *UK, male vocalist*

8 Jun 61 **LOVE OR MONEY** *Columbia DB 4633* **49** 1 wk
16 Nov 61 **I LOVE HOW YOU LOVE ME** *Columbia DB 4717* **18** 10 wks

Randy CRAWFORD *US, female vocalist*

21 Jun 80 **LAST NIGHT AT DANCELAND** *Warner Bros. K 17631* **61** 2 wks
30 Aug 80 ● **ONE DAY I'LL FLY AWAY** *Warner Bros. K 17680* **2** 11 wks
30 May 81 **YOU MIGHT NEED SOMEBODY** *Warner Bros. K 17803* **11** 13 wks
8 Aug 81 **RAINY NIGHT IN GEORGIA** *Warner Bros. K 17840* **18** 9 wks
31 Oct 81 **SECRET COMBINATION** *Warner Bros. K 17872* **48** 3 wks
30 Jan 82 **IMAGINE** *Warner Bros. K 17906* **60** 1 wk
13 Feb 82 **IMAGINE** (re-entry) *Warner Bros. K 17906* **75** 1 wk
5 Jun 82 **ONE HELLO** *Warner Bros. K 17948* **48** 4 wks

See also Crusaders

Date	Title *Label Number*	Position	

CRAZY ELEPHANT *US, male vocal group*

Date	Title *Label Number*	Position	
21 May 69	**GIMME GIMME GOOD LOVIN'** *Major Minor MM 609*	**12**	13 wks

CREAM *UK, male vocal/instrumental group*

Date	Title *Label Number*	Position	
20 Oct 66	**WRAPPING PAPER** *Reaction 591 007*	**34**	6 wks
15 Dec 66	**I FEEL FREE** *Reaction 591 011*	**11**	12 wks
8 Jun 67	**STRANGE BREW** *Reaction 591 015*	**17**	9 wks
5 Jun 68	**ANYONE FOR TENNIS (THE SAVAGE SEVEN THEME)** *Polydor 56 258*	**40**	3 wks
9 Oct 68	**SUNSHINE OF YOUR LOVE** *Polydor 56 286*	**25**	5 wks
15 Jan 69	**WHITE ROOM** *Polydor 56 300*	**28**	8 wks
9 Apr 69	**BADGE** *Polydor 56 315*	**18**	10 wks
28 Oct 72	**BADGE** (re-issue) *Polydor 2058 285*	**42**	4 wks

CREATION *UK, male vocal/instrumental group*

Date	Title *Label Number*	Position	
7 Jul 66	**MAKING TIME** *Planet PLF 116*	**49**	1 wk
3 Nov 66	**PAINTER MAN** *Planet PLF 119*	**36**	2 wks

CREATURES

UK, male/female vocal/instrumental group

Date	Title *Label Number*	Position	
3 Oct 81	**MAD EYED SCREAMER** *Polydor POSPD 354*	**24**	7 wks

Creatures are Siouxsie and Budgie who is the Banshee's drummer. See Siouxsie and the Banshees.

CREEDENCE CLEARWATER REVIVAL

US, male vocal/instrumental group

Date	Title *Label Number*	Position	
28 May 69	● **PROUD MARY** *Liberty LBF 15223*	**8**	13 wks
16 Aug 69	★ **BAD MOON RISING** *Liberty LBF 15230*	**1**	15 wks
15 Nov 69	**GREEN RIVER** *Liberty LBF 15250*	**19**	11 wks
14 Feb 70	**DOWN ON THE CORNER** *Liberty LBF 15283*	**31**	6 wks
4 Apr 70	● **TRAVELLIN' BAND** *Liberty LBF 15310*	**8**	12 wks
20 Jun 70	● **UP AROUND THE BEND** *Liberty LBF 15354*	**3**	12 wks
4 Jul 70	**TRAVELLIN' BAND** (re-entry) *Liberty LBF 15310*	**46**	1 wk
5 Sep 70	**LONG AS I CAN SEE THE LIGHT** *Liberty LBF 15384*	**20**	9 wks
20 Mar 71	**HAVE YOU EVER SEEN THE RAIN** *Liberty LBF 15440*	**36**	6 wks
24 Jul 71	**SWEET HITCH-HIKER** *United Artists UP 35261*	**36**	8 wks

Kid CREOLE and the COCONUTS

US, male vocalist with female vocal group.

Date	Title *Label Number*	Position	
13 Jun 81	**ME NO POP I** *Ze/Island WIP 6711*	**40**	7 wks
15 May 82	● **I'M A WONDERFUL THING, BABY** *Ze/Island WIP 6756*	**4**	11 wks
24 Jul 82	● **STOOL PIDGEON** *Ze/Island WIP 6793*	**7**	9 wks
9 Oct 82	● **ANNIE I'M NOT YOUR DADDY** *Ze/Island WIP 6801*	**2**	8 wks
11 Dec 82	**DEAR ADDY** *Ze/Island WIP 6840*	**29**†	3 wks

Me No Pop I *billed as 'Kid Creole and the Coconuts present Coati Mundi'.*

CREW CUTS *Canada, male vocal group*

Date	Title *Label Number*	Position	
1 Oct 54	**SH-BOOM** *Mercury MB 3140*	**12**	9 wks
15 Apr 55	● **EARTH ANGEL** *Mercury MB 3202*	**4**	20 wks

Bernard CRIBBINS *UK, male vocalist*

Date	Title *Label Number*	Position	
15 Feb 62	● **HOLE IN THE GROUND** *Parlophone R 4869*	**9**	13 wks
5 Jul 62	● **RIGHT SAID FRED** *Parlophone R 4923*	**10**	10 wks
13 Dec 62	**GOSSIP CALYPSO** *Parlophone R 4961*	**25**	6 wks

CRICKETS *US, male vocal/instrumental group*

Date	Title *Label Number*	Position	
27 Sep 57	★ **THAT'LL BE THE DAY** *Vogue Coral Q 72279*	**1**	14 wks
27 Dec 57	● **OH BOY** *Coral Q 72298*	**3**	15 wks
10 Jan 58	**THAT'LL BE THE DAY** (re-entry) *Vogue Coral Q 72279*	**29**	1 wk
14 Mar 58	● **MAYBE BABY** *Coral Q 72307*	**4**	10 wks
25 Jul 58	**THINK IT OVER** *Coral Q 72329*	**11**	7 wks
24 Apr 59	**LOVE'S MADE A FOOL OF YOU** *Coral Q 72365*	**26**	1 wk
8 May 59	**LOVE'S MADE A FOOL OF YOU** (re-entry) *Coral Q 72365*	**30**	1 wk
15 Jan 60	**WHEN YOU ASK ABOUT LOVE** *Coral Q 72382*	**27**	1 wk
26 May 60	**BABY MY HEART** *Coral Q 72395*	**33**	4 wks
21 Jun 62	● **DON'T EVER CHANGE** *Liberty LIB 55441*	**5**	13 wks
24 Jan 63	**MY LITTLE GIRL** *Liberty LIB 10067*	**17**	9 wks
6 Jun 63	**DON'T TRY TO CHANGE ME** *Liberty LIB 10092*	**37**	4 wks
2 Jul 64	**(THEY CALL HER) LA BAMBA** *Liberty LIB 55696*	**21**	10 wks

Although not credited on the records, Buddy Holly was featured on the first 4 hits. See also Buddy Holly.

CRISPY AND COMPANY

US, male vocal/instrumental group

Date	Title *Label Number*	Position	
16 Aug 75	**BRAZIL** *Creole CR 109*	**26**	5 wks
27 Dec 75	**GET IT TOGETHER** *Creole CR 114*	**21**	6 wks

CRITTERS *US, male vocal/instrumental group*

Date	Title *Label Number*	Position	
30 Jun 66	**YOUNGER GIRL** *London HL 10047*	**38**	5 wks

Tony CROMBIE and his ROCKETS

UK, male vocal/instrumental group, Tony Crombie drums

Date	Title *Label Number*	Position	
19 Oct 56	**TEACH YOU TO ROCK/ SHORT'NIN' BREAD** *Columbia DB 3822*	**25**	2 wks

Bing CROSBY *US, male vocalist*

Date	Title *Label Number*	Position	
14 Nov 52	● **ISLE OF INNISFREE** *Brunswick 04900*	**3**	12 wks
19 Dec 52	● **SILENT NIGHT** *Brunswick 03929*	**8**	2 wks
19 Mar 54	● **CHANGING PARTNERS** *Brunswick 05244*	**10**	1 wk
2 Apr 54	● **CHANGING PARTNERS** (re-entry) *Brunswick 05244*	**9**	1 wk
23 Apr 54	**CHANGING PARTNERS** (2nd re-entry) *Brunswick 05244*	**11**	1 wk
7 Jan 55	**COUNT YOUR BLESSINGS** *Brunswick 05339*	**18**	1 wk
21 Jan 55	**COUNT YOUR BLESSINGS** (re-entry) *Brunswick 05339*	**11**	2 wks
29 Apr 55	**STRANGER IN PARADISE** *Brunswick 05410*	**17**	2 wks
27 Apr 56	**IN A LITTLE SPANISH TOWN** *Brunswick 05543*	**22**	3 wks

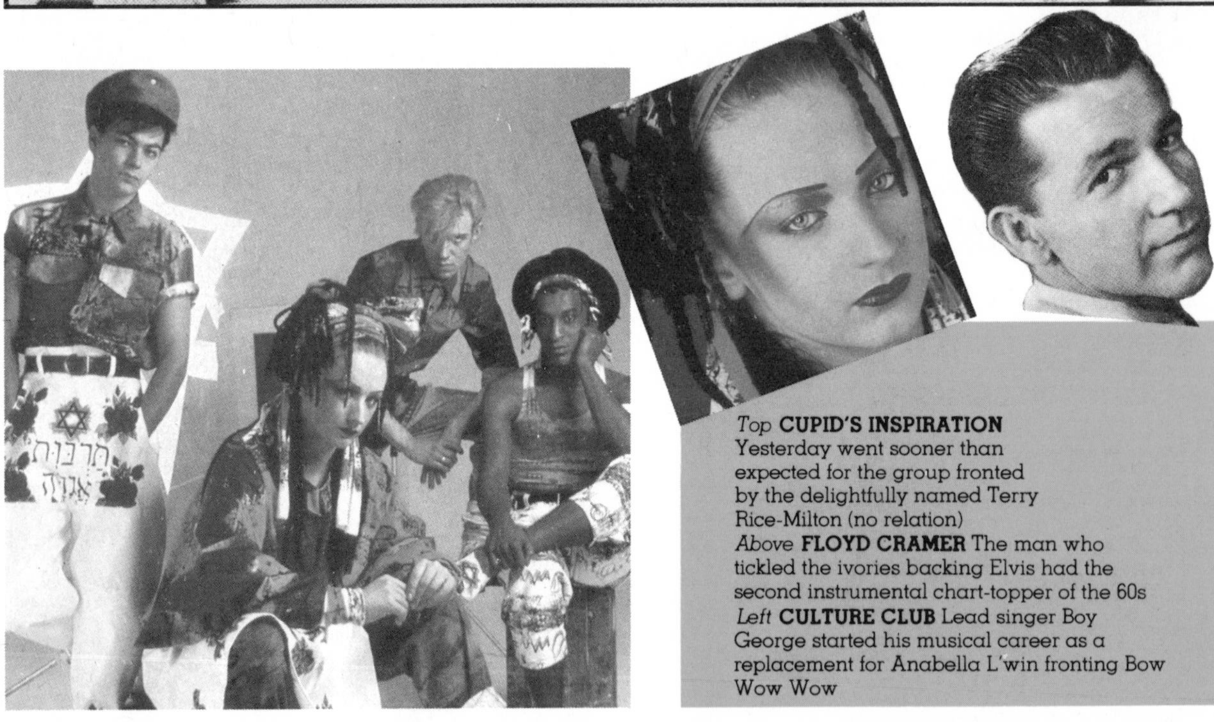

Top **CUPID'S INSPIRATION** Yesterday went sooner than expected for the group fronted by the delightfully named Terry Rice-Milton (no relation)
Above **FLOYD CRAMER** The man who tickled the ivories backing Elvis had the second instrumental chart-topper of the 60s
Left **CULTURE CLUB** Lead singer Boy George started his musical career as a replacement for Anabella L'win fronting Bow Wow Wow

Date	Title *Label Number*	Position	
24 May 57	● **AROUND THE WORLD** *Brunswick 05674*	**5**	15 wks
9 Aug 75	**THAT'S WHAT LIFE IS ALL ABOUT** *United Artists UP 35852*	**41**	4 wks
3 Dec 77	● **WHITE CHRISTMAS** *MCA 111*	**5**	7 wks

See also Bing Crosby and Grace Kelly, Bing Crosby and Jane Wyman, David Bowie and Bing Crosby.

Bing CROSBY and Grace KELLY

US, male/female vocal duo

Date	Title *Label Number*	Position	
23 Nov 56	● **TRUE LOVE** *Capitol CL 14645*	**4**	27 wks

See also Bing Crosby, Bing Crosby and Jane Wyman, David Bowie and Bing Crosby.

Bing CROSBY and Jane WYMAN

US, male/female vocal duo

Date	Title *Label Number*	Position	
5 Dec 52	● **ZING A LITTLE ZONG** *Brunswick 04981*	**10**	2 wks

See also Bing Crosby, Bing Crosby and Grace Kelly, David Bowie and Bing Crosby.

CROSBY, STILLS and NASH

US/UK, male vocal/instrumental group

Date	Title *Label Number*	Position	
16 Aug 69	**MARRAKESH EXPRESS** *Atlantic 584 283*	**17**	9 wks

See also Stephen Stills.

Christopher CROSS *US, male vocalist*

Date	Title *Label Number*	Position	
19 Apr 80	**RIDE LIKE THE WIND** *Warner Bros. K 17582*	**69**	1 wk
14 Feb 81	**SAILING** *Warner Bros. K 17695*	**48**	6 wks
17 Oct 81	**ARTHUR'S THEME (BEST THAT YOU CAN DO)** *Warner Bros. K 17847*	**56**	4 wks
9 Jan 82	● **ARTHUR'S THEME (THE BEST YOU CAN DO)** *Warner Bros. K 17847*	**7**	11 wks

CROWN HEIGHTS AFFAIR

US, Male vocal/instrumental group

Date	Title *Label Number*	Position	
19 Aug 78	**GALAXY OF LOVE** *Philips 6168 801*	**24**	10 wks
11 Nov 78	**I'M GONNA LOVE YOU FOREVER** *Mercury 6188 808*	**47**	4 wks
14 Apr 79	**DANCE LADY DANCE** *Mercury 6168 804*	**44**	4 wks
3 May 80	● **YOU GAVE ME LOVE** *De-Lite MER 9*	**10**	12 wks
9 Aug 80	**YOU'VE BEEN GONE** *De-Lite MER 28*	**44**	4 wks

CRUISERS — See *Dave BERRY*

CRUSADERS *US, male vocal/instrumental group*

Date	Title *Label Number*	Position	
18 Aug 79	● **STREET LIFE** *MCA 513*	**5**	11 wks
26 Sep 81	**I'M SO GLAD I'M STANDING HERE TODAY** *MCA 741*	**61**	3 wks

Vocalist on Street Life *was Randy Crawford, though uncredited - see also Randy Crawford.* I'm So Glad I'm Standing Here Today *credits 'featured vocalist Joe Cocker'. See Joe Cocker.*

Bobby CRUSH *UK, male instrumentalist, piano*

Date	Title *Label Number*	Position	
4 Nov 72	**BORSALINO** *Philips 6006 248*	**37**	4 wks

CRYIN' SHAMES

UK, male vocal/instrumental group

Date	Title *Label Number*	Position	
31 Mar 66	**PLEASE STAY** *Decca F 12340*	**26**	7 wks

CRYPT-KICKERS — See *Bobby 'Boris' PICKETT and the CRYPT-KICKERS*

CRYSTALS *US, female vocal group*

Date	Title *Label Number*	Position	
22 Nov 62	**HE'S A REBEL** *London HLU 9611*	**19**	13 wks
20 Jun 63	● **DA DOO RON RON** *London HLU 9732*	**5**	16 wks
19 Sep 63	● **THEN HE KISSED ME** *London HLU 9773*	**2**	14 wks
5 Mar 64	**I WONDER** *London HLU 9852*	**36**	3 wks
19 Oct 74	**DA DOO RON RON** (re-issue) *Warner Spector K 19010*	**15**	8 wks

CUFF-LINKS *US, male vocal group*

Date	Title *Label Number*	Position	
29 Nov 69	● **TRACY** *MCA MU 1101*	**4**	16 wks
14 Mar 70	● **WHEN JULIE COMES AROUND** *MCA MU 1112*	**10**	14 wks

CULTURE CLUB

UK, male vocal/instrumental group

Date	Title *Label Number*	Position	
18 Sep 82	★ **DO YOU REALLY WANT TO HURT ME** *Virgin VS 518*	**1**†	15 wks
27 Nov 82	● **TIME (CLOCK OF THE HEART)** *Virgin VS 558*	**3**†	5 wks

Larry CUNNINGHAM and the MIGHTY AVONS *Ireland, male vocal/instrumental group*

Date	Title *Label Number*	Position	
10 Dec 64	**TRIBUTE TO JIM REEVES** *King KG 1016*	**40**	8 wks
25 Feb 65	**TRIBUTE TO JIM REEVES** (re-entry) *King KG 1016*	**46**	3 wks

CUPID'S INSPIRATION

UK, male vocal/instrumental group

Date	Title *Label Number*	Position	
19 Jun 68	● **YESTERDAY HAS GONE** *Nems 56 3500*	**4**	11 wks
2 Oct 68	**MY WORLD** *Nems 56 3702*	**33**	8 wks

CURE *UK, male vocal/instrumental group*

Date	Title *Label Number*	Position	
12 Apr 80	**A FOREST** *Fiction FICS 10*	**31**	8 wks
4 Apr 81	**PRIMARY** *Fiction FICS 12*	**43**	6 wks
17 Oct 81	**CHARLOTTE SOMETIMES** *Fiction FICS 14*	**44**	4 wks
24 Jul 82	**HANGING GARDEN** *Fiction FICS 15*	**34**	4 wks
27 Nov 82	**LET'S GO TO BED** *Fiction FICS 17*	**44**	4 wks

CURLS — See *Paul EVANS and the CURLS*

Chantal CURTIS *France, female vocalist*

Date	Title *Label Number*	Position	
14 Jul 79	**GET ANOTHER LOVE** *Pye 7P 5003*	**51**	3 wks

Date	Title *Label Number*	Position	

CURVED AIR

UK, male/female vocal/instrumental group

7 Aug 71	● **BACK STREET LUV** *Warner Bros. K 16092*	**4**	12 wks

Adge CUTLER and the WURZELS

UK, male vocal/instrumental group

2 Feb 67	**DRINK UP THY ZIDER** *Columbia DB 8081*	**45**	1 wk

See also Wurzels.

Johnny CYMBAL *US, male vocalist*

14 Mar 63	**MR. BASS MAN** *London HLR 9682*	**24**	10 wks

D

Vicky D *UK, female vocalist*

13 Mar 82	**THIS BEAT IS MINE** *Virgin VS 486*	**42**	6 wks

D, B, M and T *UK, male vocal/instrumental group*

1 Aug 70	**MR. PRESIDENT** *Fontana 6007 022*	**33**	8 wks

D TRAIN *US, male vocalist/instrumentalist*

6 Feb 82	**YOU'RE THE ONE FOR ME** *Epic EPC A 2016*	**30**	8 wks
8 May 82	**WALK ON BY** *Epic EPC A 2298*	**44**	6 wks

Paul DA VINCI *UK, male vocalist*

20 Jul 74	**YOUR BABY AIN'T YOUR BABY ANYMORE** *Penny Farthing PEN 843*	**20**	8 wks

Terry DACTYL and the DINOSAURS

UK, male vocal/instrumental group

15 Jul 72	● **SEASIDE SHUFFLE** *UK 5*	**2**	12 wks
13 Jan 73	**ON A SATURDAY NIGHT** *UK 21*	**45**	4 wks

DAKOTAS *UK, male instrumental group*

11 Jul 63	**THE CRUEL SEA** *Parlophone R 5044*	**18**	13 wks

See also Billy J. Kramer & the Dakotas.

Jim DALE *UK, male vocalist*

11 Oct 57	● **BE MY GIRL** *Parlophone R 4343*	**2**	16 wks
10 Jan 58	**JUST BORN** *Parlophone R 4376*	**27**	1 wk
17 Jan 58	**CRAZY DREAM** *Parlophone R 4376*	**24**	2 wks
7 Mar 58	**SUGARTIME** *Parlophone R 4402*	**25**	3 wks

DALE AND GRACE *US, male/female vocal duo*

9 Jan 64	**I'M LEAVING IT UP TO YOU** *London HL 9807*	**42**	2 wks

DALE SISTERS *UK, female vocal group*

23 Nov 61	**MY SUNDAY BABY** *Ember S 140*	**36**	6 wks

Roger DALTREY *UK, male vocalist*

14 Apr 73	● **GIVING IT ALL AWAY** *Track 2094 110*	**5**	11 wks
4 Aug 73	**I'M FREE** *Ode ODS 66302*	**13**	10 wks
14 May 77	**WRITTEN ON THE WIND** *Polydor 2121 319*	**46**	2 wks
2 Aug 80	**FREE ME** *Polydor 2001 980*	**39**	6 wks
11 Oct 80	**WITHOUT YOUR LOVE** *Polydor POSP 181*	**55**	4 wks

DAMNED *UK, male vocal/instrumental group*

5 May 79	**LOVE SONG** *Chiswick CHIS 112*	**20**	8 wks
20 Oct 79	**SMASH IT UP** *Chiswick CHIS 116*	**35**	5 wks
1 Dec 79	**I JUST CAN'T BE HAPPY TODAY** *Chiswick CHIS 120*	**46**	5 wks
4 Oct 80	**HISTORY OF THE WORLD (PART 1)** *Chiswick CHIS 135*	**51**	4 wks
28 Nov 81	**FRIDAY 13TH (EP)** *Stale One TRY 1*	**50**	4 wks
10 Jul 82	**LOVELY MONEY** *Bronze BRO 149*	**42**	4 wks

Kenny DAMON *US, male vocalist*

19 May 66	**WHILE I LIVE** *Mercury MF 907*	**48**	1 wk

Vic DAMONE *US, male vocalist*

6 Dec 57	**AN AFFAIR TO REMEMBER** *Philips PB 745*	**29**	1 wk
31 Jan 58	**AN AFFAIR TO REMEMBER** (re-entry) *Philips PB 745*	**30**	1 wk
9 May 58	★ **ON THE STREET WHERE YOU LIVE** *Philips PB 819*	**1**	17 wks
1 Aug 58	**THE ONLY MAN ON THE ISLAND** *Philips PB 837*	**24**	3 wks

DANA *Ireland, female vocalist*

4 Apr 70	★ **ALL KINDS OF EVERYTHING** *Rex R 11054*	**1**	15 wks
25 Jul 70	**ALL KINDS OF EVERYTHING** (re-entry) *Rex R 11054*	**47**	1 wk
13 Feb 71	**WHO PUT THE LIGHTS OUT** *Rex R 11062*	**14**	11 wks
25 Jan 75	● **PLEASE TELL HIM THAT I SAID HELLO** *GTO GT 6*	**8**	14 wks
13 Dec 75	● **IT'S GONNA BE A COLD COLD CHRISTMAS** *GTO GT 45*	**4**	6 wks
6 Mar 76	**NEVER GONNA FALL IN LOVE AGAIN** *GTO GT 55*	**31**	4 wks
16 Oct 76	**FAIRYTALE** *GTO GT 66*	**13**	16 wks
31 Mar 79	**SOMETHING'S COOKIN' IN THE KITCHEN** *GTO GT 243*	**44**	5 wks
15 May 82	**I FEEL LOVE COMIN' ON** *Creole CR 32*	**66**	3 wks

DAN-I *UK, male vocalist*

10 Nov 79	**MONKEY CHOP** *Island WIP 6520*	**30**	9 wks

Date	Title *Label Number*	Position		Date	Title *Label Number*	Position

Charlie DANIELS BAND

US, male vocal/instrumental group

22 Sep 79 **THE DEVIL WENT DOWN TO GEORGIA** *Epic EPC 7737* **14** 10 wks

Johnny DANKWORTH

UK, male orchestral/group leader/instrumentalist, alto sax

22 Jun 56 ● **EXPERIMENTS WITH MICE** *Parlophone R 4185* **7** 12 wks
23 Feb 61 ● **AFRICAN WALTZ** *Columbia DB 4590* **9** 21 wks

DANNY and the JUNIORS

US, male vocal group

17 Jan 58 ● **AT THE HOP** *HMV POP 436* **3** 14 wks
10 Jul 76 **AT THE HOP** (re-issue) *ABC 4123* **39** 5 wks

Bobby DARIN *US, male vocalist*

1 Aug 58 **SPLISH SPLASH** *London HLE 8666* **28** 1 wk
9 Jan 59 **QUEEN OF THE HOP** *London HLE 8737* **24** 2 wks
29 May 59 ★ **DREAM LOVER** *London HLE 8867* **1** 19 wks
25 Sep 59 ★ **MACK THE KNIFE** *London HLE 8939* **1** 16 wks
22 Jan 60 **MACK THE KNIFE** (re-entry) *London HLE 8939* **30** 1 wk
29 Jan 60 ● **LA MER (BEYOND THE SEA)** *London HLE 9034* **8** 10 wks
10 Mar 60 **MACK THE KNIFE** (2nd re-entry) *London HLE 8939* **50** 1 wk
31 Mar 60 ● **CLEMENTINE** *London HLK 9086* **8** 12 wks
21 Apr 60 **LA MER (BEYOND THE SEA)** (re-entry) *London HLE 9034* **40** 2 wks
30 Jun 60 **BILL BAILEY** *London HLK 9142* **36** 1 wk
14 Jul 60 **BILL BAILEY** (re-entry) *London HLK 9142* **34** 1 wk
16 Mar 61 ● **LAZY RIVER** *London HLK 9303* **2** 13 wks
6 Jul 61 **NATURE BOY** *London HLK 9375* **24** 7 wks
12 Oct 61 ● **YOU MUST HAVE BEEN A BEAUTIFUL BABY** *London HLK 9429* **10** 11 wks
26 Oct 61 **COME SEPTEMBER** *London HLK 9407* **50** 1 wk
21 Dec 61 ● **MULTIPLICATION** *London HLK 9474* **5** 13 wks
19 Jul 62 ● **THINGS** *London HLK 9575* **2** 17 wks
4 Oct 62 **IF A MAN ANSWERS** *Capitol CL 15272* **24** 6 wks
29 Nov 62 **BABY FACE** *London HLK 9624* **40** 4 wks
25 Jul 63 **EIGHTEEN YELLOW ROSES** *Capitol CL 15306* **37** 4 wks
13 Oct 66 ● **IF I WERE A CARPENTER** *Atlantic 584 051* **9** 12 wks
14 Apr 79 **DREAM LOVER/MACK THE KNIFE** (re-issue) *Lightning LIG 9017* **64** 1 wk

Come September *is an instrumental credited to the Bobby Darin Orchestra.*

Guy DARRELL *UK, male vocalist*

18 Aug 73 **I'VE BEEN HURT** *Santa Ponsa PNS 4* **12** 13 wks

James DARREN *US, male vocalist*

11 Aug 60 **BECAUSE THEY'RE YOUNG** *Pye International 7N 25059* **29** 7 wks
14 Dec 61 **GOODBYE CRUEL WORLD** *Pye International 7N 25116* **28** 9 wks
29 Mar 62 **HER ROYAL MAJESTY** *Pye International 7N 25125* **36** 3 wks
21 Jun 62 **CONSCIENCE** *Pye International 7N 25138* **30** 6 wks

DARTS *UK, male/female vocal/instrumental group*

5 Nov 77 ● **DADDY COOL - THE GIRL CAN'T HELP IT** *Magnet MAG 100* **6** 13 wks
28 Jan 78 ● **COME BACK MY LOVE** *Magnet MAG 110* **2** 12 wks
6 May 78 ● **BOY FROM NEW YORK CITY** *Magnet MAG 116* **2** 13 wks
5 Aug 78 ● **IT'S RAINING** *Magnet MAG 126* **2** 11 wks
11 Nov 78 **DON'T LET IT FADE AWAY** *Magnet MAG 134* **18** 11 wks
10 Feb 79 ● **GET IT** *Magnet MAG 140* **10** 9 wks
21 Jul 79 ● **DUKE OF EARL** *Magnet MAG 147* **6** 11 wks
20 Oct 79 **CAN'T GET ENOUGH OF YOUR LOVE** *Magnet MAG 156* **43** 6 wks
1 Dec 79 **REET PETITE** *Magnet MAG 160* **51** 7 wks
31 May 80 **LET'S HANG ON** *Magnet MAG 174* **11** 14 wks
6 Sep 80 **PEACHES** *Magnet MAG 179* **66** 3 wks
29 Nov 80 **WHITE CHRISTMAS/SH-BOOM (LIFE COULD BE A DREAM)** *Magnet MAG 184* **48** 7 wks

DAVE — See *SAM and DAVE*

DAVE — See *CHAS and DAVE*

DAVID and JONATHAN *UK, male vocal duo*

13 Jan 66 **MICHELLE** *Columbia DB 7800* **11** 6 wks
7 Jul 66 ● **LOVERS OF THE WORLD UNITE** *Columbia DB 7950* **7** 16 wks

Anne-Marie DAVID *France, female vocalist*

28 Apr 73 **WONDERFUL DREAM** *Epic EPC 1446* **13** 9 wks

Jim DAVIDSON *UK, male vocalist*

27 Dec 80 **WHITE CHRISTMAS/TOO RISKY** *Scratch SCR 001* **52** 4 wks

Paul DAVIDSON *Jamaica, male vocalist*

27 Dec 75 ● **MIDNIGHT RIDER** *Tropical ALO 56* **10** 10 wks

Dave DAVIES *UK, male vocalist*

19 Jul 67 ● **DEATH OF A CLOWN** *Pye 7N 17356* **3** 10 wks
6 Dec 67 **SUSANNAH'S STILL ALIVE** *Pye 7N 17429* **20** 7 wks

Windsor DAVIES and Don ESTELLE

UK, male vocal duo

17 May 75 ★ **WHISPERING GRASS** *EMI 2290* **1** 12 wks
25 Oct 75 **PAPER DOLL** *EMI 2361* **41** 4 wks

Above **VIC DAMONE** His number one was a Lerner and Loewe song from *My Fair Lady*
Far right **SAMMY DAVIS** One of three people sharing the distinction of having charted with Frank Sinatra, the others being Nancy Sinatra and Count Basie
Right **BOBBY DARIN** He had 4 stabs at the chart with Mack the Knife, came home twice with Bill Bailey and slept for 20 years with his Dream Lover

Date	Title *Label Number*	Position	

Billie DAVIS *UK, female vocalist*

7 Feb 63	● **TELL HIM** *Decca F 11572*	**10**	12 wks
30 May 63	**HE'S THE ONE** *Decca F 11658*	**40**	3 wks
9 Oct 68	**I WANT YOU TO BE MY BABY** *Decca F 12823*	**33**	8 wks

See also Mike Sarne.

John DAVIS and the MONSTER ORCHESTRA *US, male vocal/instrumental group*

10 Feb 79	**AIN'T THAT ENOUGH FOR YOU** *Miracle M 2*	**70**	2 wks

Mac DAVIS *US, male vocalist*

4 Nov 72	**BABY DON'T GET HOOKED ON ME** *CBS 8250*	**29**	6 wks
15 Nov 80	**IT'S HARD TO BE HUMBLE** *Casablanca CAN 210*	**27**	wks

Ruth DAVIS — See *Bo KIRKLAND and ruth DAVIS*

Skeeter DAVIS *US, female vocalist*

14 Mar 63	**END OF THE WORLD** *RCA 1328*	**18**	13 wks

Spencer DAVIS GROUP *UK, male vocal/instrumental group*

5 Nov 64	**I CAN'T STAND IT** *Fontana TF 499*	**47**	3 wks
25 Feb 65	**EVERY LITTLE BIT HURTS** *Fontana TF 530*	**43**	2 wks
18 Mar 65	**EVERY LITTLE BIT HURTS** (re-entry) *Fontana TF 530*	**41**	1 wk
10 Jun 65	**STRONG LOVE** *Fontana TF 571*	**50**	1 wk
24 Jun 65	**STRONG LOVE** (re-entry) *Fontana TF 571*	**44**	3 wks
2 Dec 65	★ **KEEP ON RUNNING** *Fontana TF 632*	**1**	14 wks
24 Mar 66	★ **SOMEBODY HELP ME** *Fontana TF 679*	**1**	10 wks
1 Sep 66	**WHEN I COME HOME** *Fontana TF 739*	**12**	9 wks
3 Nov 66	● **GIMME SOME LOVING** *Fontana TF 762*	**2**	12 wks
26 Jan 67	● **I'M A MAN** *Fontana TF 785*	**9**	7 wks
9 Aug 67	**TIME SELLER** *Fontana TF 854*	**30**	5 wks
10 Jan 68	**MR. SECOND CLASS** *United Artists UP 1203*	**35**	4 wks

Billy DAVIS JR. — See *Marilyn McCOO and Billy DAVIS JR.*

Sammy DAVIS JR. *US, male vocalist*

29 Jul 55	**SOMETHING'S GOTTA GIVE** *Brunswick 05428*	**19**	2 wks
19 Aug 55	**SOMETHING'S GOTTA GIVE** (re-entry) *Brunswick 05428*	**11**	5 wks
9 Sep 55	● **LOVE ME OR LEAVE ME** *Brunswick 05428*	**8**	6 wks
30 Sep 55	**THAT OLD BLACK MAGIC** *Brunswick 05450*	**16**	1 wk
7 Oct 55	**HEY THERE** *Brunswick 05469*	**19**	1 wk
4 Nov 55	**LOVE ME OR LEAVE ME** (re-entry) *Brunswick 05428*	**18**	2 wks
20 Apr 56	**IN A PERSIAN MARKET** *Brunswick 05518*	**28**	1 wk
28 Dec 56	**ALL OF YOU** *Brunswick 05629*	**28**	1 wk
22 Mar 62	**WHAT KIND OF FOOL AM I?/ GONNA BUILD A MOUNTAIN** *Reprise R 20048*	**26**	8 wks

See also Sammy Davis Jr. and Carmen McRae, Frank Sinatra and Sammy Davis Jr.

Sammy DAVIS JR. and Carmen McRAE *US, male/female vocal duo*

16 Jun 60	**HAPPY TO MAKE YOUR ACQUAINTANCE** *Brunswick 05830*	**46**	1 wk

See also Sammy Davis Jr., Frank Sinatra and Sammy Davis Jr.

DAWN *US, male/female vocal group*

16 Jan 71	● **CANDIDA** *Bell 1118*	**9**	11 wks
10 Apr 71	★ **KNOCK THREE TIMES** *Bell 1146*	**1**	27 wks
31 Jul 71	● **WHAT ARE YOU DOING SUNDAY** *Bell 1169*	**3**	12 wks
10 Mar 73	★ **TIE A YELLOW RIBBON ROUND THE OLD OAK TREE** *Bell 1287*	**1**	39 wks
4 Aug 73	**SAY, HAS ANYBODY SEEN MY SWEET GYPSY ROSE** *Bell 1322*	**12**	15 wks
5 Jan 74	**TIE A YELLOW RIBBON ROUND THE OLE OAK TREE** (re-entry) *Bell 1287*	**41**	1 wk
9 Mar 74	**WHO'S IN THE STRAWBERRY PATCH WITH SALLY** *Bell 1343*	**37**	4 wks

See also Tony Orlando. First two hits credit Dawn, the next three Dawn featuring Tony Orlando, and the final one Tony Orlando and Dawn.

Bobby DAY *US, male vocalist*

7 Nov 58	**ROCKIN' ROBIN** *London HL 8726*	**29**	2 wks

Doris DAY *US, female vocalist*

21 Nov 52	● **MY LOVE AND DEVOTION** *Columbia DB 3157*	**10**	2 wks
2 Apr 54	★ **SECRET LOVE** *Philips PB 230*	**1**	29 wks
27 Aug 54	● **BLACK HILLS OF DAKOTA** *Philips PB 287*	**7**	8 wks
1 Oct 54	● **IF I GIVE MY HEART TO YOU** *Philips PB 325*	**4**	11 wks
8 Apr 55	● **READY WILLING AND ABLE** *Philips PB 402*	**7**	9 wks
9 Sep 55	**LOVE ME OR LEAVE ME** *Philips PB 479*	**20**	1 wk
21 Oct 55	**I'LL NEVER STOP LOVING YOU** *Philips PB 497*	**17**	2 wks
25 Nov 55	**I'LL NEVER STOP LOVING YOU** (re-entry) *Philips PB 497*	**19**	1 wk
29 Jun 56	★ **WHATEVER WILL BE WILL BE** *Philips PB 586*	**1**	22 wks
13 Jun 58	**A VERY PRECIOUS LOVE** *Philips PB 799*	**16**	11 wks
15 Aug 58	**EVERYBODY LOVES A LOVER** *Philips PB 843*	**25**	3 wks
26 Sep 58	**EVERYBODY LOVES A LOVER** (re-entry) *Philips PB 843*	**27**	1 wk
12 Mar 64	● **MOVE OVER DARLING** *CBS AAG 183*	**8**	16 wks

See also Doris Day and Frankie Laine, Doris Day and Johnnie Ray

Doris DAY and Frankie LAINE *US, female/male vocal duo*

14 Nov 52	● **SUGARBUSH** *Columbia DB 3123*	**8**	2 wks
5 Dec 52	● **SUGARBUSH** (re-entry) *Columbia DB 3123*	**8**	6 wks

See also Doris Day, Frankie Laine, Doris Day and Johnnie Ray, Frankie Laine and Jimmy Boyd, Frankie Laine and Johnnie Ray.

Doris DAY and Johnnie RAY *US, female/male vocal duo*

3 Apr 53	**MA SAYS PA SAYS** *Columbia DB 3242*	**12**	1 wk
17 Apr 53	**FULL TIME JOB** *Columbia DB 3242*	**11**	1 wk
24 Jul 53	● **LET'S WALK THATA-WAY** *Philips PB 157*	**4**	14 wks

See also Doris Day, Johnnie Ray, Doris Day & Frankie Laine, Frankie Laine & Johnnie Ray.

Date **Title** *Label Number* **Position**

D.B.M.

German, male/female vocal/instrumental group

Date	Title *Label Number*	Position	
12 Nov 77	**DISCO BEATLEMANIA** *Atlantic K 11027*	**45**	3 wks

Chris DE BURGH *Ireland, male vocalist*

Date	Title *Label Number*	Position	
23 Oct 82	**DON'T PAY THE FERRYMAN** *A & M AMS 8256*	**48**	5 wks

DE CASTRO SISTERS *US, female vocal group*

Date	Title *Label Number*	Position	
11 Feb 55	**TEACH ME TONIGHT** *London HL 8104*	**20**	1 wk

Lynsey DE PAUL *UK, female vocalist*

Date	Title *Label Number*	Position	
19 Aug 72	● **SUGAR ME** *MAM 81*	**5**	11 wks
2 Dec 72	**GETTING A DRAG** *MAM 88*	**18**	8 wks
27 Oct 73	**WON'T SOMEBODY DANCE WITH ME** *MAM 109*	**14**	7 wks
8 Jun 74	**OOH I DO** *Warner Bros. K 16401*	**25**	6 wks
2 Nov 74	● **NO HONESTLY** *Jet 747*	**7**	11 wks
22 Mar 75	**MY MAN AND ME** *Jet 750*	**40**	4 wks

See also Lynsey De Paul and Mike Moran

Lynsey DE PAUL and Mike MORAN

UK, female/male vocal and instrumental duo, pianos

Date	Title *Label Number*	Position	
26 Mar 77	**ROCK BOTTOM** *Polydor 2058 859*	**19**	7 wks

See also Lynsey De Paul

Stephanie DE SYKES *UK, female vocalist*

Date	Title *Label Number*	Position	
20 Jul 74	● **BORN WITH A SMILE ON MY FACE** *Bradley's BRAD 7409*	**2**	10 wks
19 Apr 75	**WE'LL FIND OUR DAY** *Bradley's BRAD 7509*	**17**	7 wks

Born With A Smile On My Face *credits Stephanie De Sykes With Rain, male vocal group.*

DEAD END KIDS

UK, male vocal and instrumental group

Date	Title *Label Number*	Position	
26 Mar 77	● **HAVE I THE RIGHT** *CBS 4972*	**6**	10 wks

DEAD KENNEDYS

US, male vocal/instrumental group

Date	Title *Label Number*	Position	
1 Nov 80	**KILL THE POOR** *Cherry Red CHERRY 16*	**49**	3 wks
30 May 81	**TOO DRUNK TO FUCK** *Cherry Red CHERRY 24*	**36**	6 wks

DEAN — See *JAN and DEAN*

Jimmy DEAN *US, male vocalist*

Date	Title *Label Number*	Position	
26 Oct 61	● **BIG BAD JOHN** *Philips PB 1187*	**2**	13 wks
8 Nov 62	**LITTLE BLACK BOOK** *CBS AAG 122*	**33**	4 wks

Diana DECKER *US, female vocalist*

Date	Title *Label Number*	Position	
23 Oct 53	● **POPPA PICCOLINO** *Columbia DB 3325*	**2**	8 wks
8 Jan 54	● **POPPA PICCOLINO** (re-entry) *Columbia DB 3325*	**5**	2 wks

Dave DEE *UK, male vocalist*

Date	Title *Label Number*	Position	
14 Mar 70	**MY WOMAN'S MAN** *Fontana TF 1074*	**42**	4 wks

See also Dave Dee, Dozy, Beaky, Mick and Tich.

Dave DEE, DOZY, BEAKY, MICK and TICH *UK, male vocal/instrumental group*

Date	Title *Label Number*	Position	
23 Dec 65	**YOU MAKE IT MOVE** *Fontana TF 630*	**26**	8 wks
3 Mar 66	● **HOLD TIGHT** *Fontana TF 671*	**4**	17 wks
9 Jun 66	● **HIDEAWAY** *Fontana TF 711*	**10**	11 wks
15 Sep 66	● **BEND IT** *Fontana TF 746*	**2**	12 wks
8 Dec 66	● **SAVE ME** *Fontana TF 775*	**4**	10 wks
9 Mar 67	**TOUCH ME TOUCH ME** *Fontana TF 798*	**13**	9 wks
18 May 67	● **OKAY!** *Fontana TF 830*	**4**	11 wks
14 Oct 67	● **ZABADAK!** *Fontana TF 873*	**3**	14 wks
14 Feb 68	★ **LEGEND OF XANADU** *Fontana TF 903*	**1**	12 wks
3 Jul 68	● **LAST NIGHT IN SOHO** *Fontana TF 953*	**8**	11 wks
2 Oct 68	**WRECK OF THE ANTOINETTE** *Fontana TF 971*	**14**	9 wks
5 Mar 69	**DON JUAN** *Fontana TF 1000*	**23**	9 wks
14 May 69	**SNAKE IN THE GRASS** *Fontana TF 1020*	**23**	8 wks

See also Dave Dee, DBM and T.

Joey DEE and the STARLITERS

US, male vocal/instrumental group

Date	Title *Label Number*	Position	
8 Feb 62	**PEPPERMINT TWIST** *Columbia DB 4758*	**33**	8 wks

Kiki DEE *UK, female vocalist*

Date	Title *Label Number*	Position	
10 Nov 73	**AMOUREUSE** *Rocket PIG 4*	**13**	13 wks
7 Sep 74	**I GOT THE MUSIC IN ME** *Rocket PIG 12*	**19**	8 wks
12 Apr 75	**(YOU DONT KNOW) HOW GLAD I AM** *Rocket PIG 16*	**33**	4 wks
11 Sep 76	**LOVING AND FREE/ AMOUREUSE** (RE-ISSUE OF AMOUREUSE) *Rocket ROKN 515*	**13**	8 wks
19 Feb 77	**FIRST THING IN THE MORNING** *Rocket ROKN 520*	**32**	5 wks
11 Jun 77	**CHICAGO** *Rocket ROKN 526*	**28**	4 wks
21 Feb 81	**STAR** *Ariola ARO 251*	**13**	10 wks
23 May 81	**PERFECT TIMING** *Ariola ARO 257*	**66**	3 wks

See also Elton John and Kiki Dee. Amoureuse, *when re-issued on the same record as a new title,* Loving and Free, *was only listed on the charts for 5 weeks of the record's eight-week run. On 18 Sep, 25 Sep and 2 Oct 1976,* Loving And Free *was the only title mentioned.* I Got The Music In Me *and* (You Dont Know) How Glad I Am *credited to The Kiki Dee Band.* Chicago *was one side of a double sided chart entry, the other being* Bite Your Lip (Get Up and Dance) *by Elton John. See also Elton John.*

Nancy DEE — See *BENELUX and Nancy DEE*

DEEDEE — See *DICK and DEEDEE*

Carol DEENE *UK, female vocalist*

Date	Title *Label Number*	Position	
26 Oct 61	**SAD MOVIES** *HMV POP 922*	**44**	3 wks
25 Jan 62	**NORMAN** *HMV POP 973*	**24**	8 wks
5 Jul 62	**JOHNNY GET ANGRY** *HMV POP 1027*	**32**	4 wks
23 Aug 62	**SOME PEOPLE** *HMV POP 1058*	**25**	10 wks

Date Title *Label Number* Position

DEEP FEELING *UK, male vocal/instrumental group*

Date		Title *Label Number*	Position	Weeks
25 Apr 70		**DO YOU LOVE ME** *Page One POF 165*	**45**	1 wk
9 May 70		**DO YOU LOVE ME** (re-entry) *Page One POF 165*	**34**	4 wks

DEEP PURPLE *UK, male vocal/instrumental group*

Date		Title *Label Number*	Position	Weeks
15 Aug 70	●	**BLACK NIGHT** *Harvest HAR 5020*	**2**	21 wks
27 Feb 71	●	**STRANGE KIND OF WOMAN** *Harvest HAR 5033*	**8**	12 wks
13 Nov 71		**FIREBALL** *Harvest HAR 5045*	**15**	13 wks
1 Apr 72		**NEVER BEFORE** *Purple PUR 102*	**35**	6 wks
16 Apr 77		**SMOKE ON THE WATER** *Purple PUR 132*	**21**	7 wks
15 Oct 77		**NEW LIVE AND RARE** *Purple PUR 135*	**31**	4 wks
7 Oct 78		**NEW LIVE AND RARE II** EP *Purple PUR 137*	**45**	3 wks
2 Aug 80		**BLACK NIGHT** (re-issue) *Harvest HAR 5210*	**43**	6 wks
1 Nov 80		**NEW LIVE AND RARE VOLUME 3** *Harvest SHEP 101*	**48**	3 wks

Tracks on New Live And Rare *Black Night (live)/Painted Horse/When A Blind Man Cries.* New Live And Rare Violume 2 EP *Burn (Edited version)/Coronarias Redig/Mistreated (live)/Rock Me Baby.* New Live And Rare Volume 3 EP *Smoke On The Water/Bird Has Flown/Grabsplatter.*

DEEP RIVER BOYS *UK, male vocal group*

Date		Title *Label Number*	Position	Weeks
/ Dec 56		**THAT'S RIGHT** *HMV POP 263*	**29**	1 wk

Rick DEES and his CAST OF IDIOTS

US, male vocalist plus vocal/instrumental support

Date		Title *Label Number*	Position	Weeks
18 Sep 76	●	**DISCO DUCK** *RSO 2090 204*	**6**	9 wks

DEF LEPPARD *UK, male vocal/intrumental group*

Date		Title *Label Number*	Position	Weeks
17 Nov 79		**WASTED** *Vertigo 6059 247*	**61**	3 wks
23 Feb 80		**HELLO AMERICA** *Vertigo LEPP 1*	**45**	4 wks

Desmond DEKKER and the ACES

Jamaica, male vocal/instrumental group

Date		Title *Label Number*	Position	Weeks
12 Jul 67		**007** *Pyramid PYR 6004*	**14**	11 wks
19 Mar 69	★	**ISRAELITES** *Pyramid PYR 6058*	**1**	14 wks
25 Jun 69	●	**IT MIEK** *Pyramid PYR 6068*	**7**	11 wks
2 Jul 69		**ISRAELITES** (re-entry) *Pyramid PYR 6058*	**45**	1 wk
10 Jan 70		**PICKNEY GAL** *Pyramid PYR 6078*	**42**	3 wks
22 Aug 70	●	**YOU CAN GET IT IF YOU REALLY WANT** *Trojan TR 7777*	**2**	15 wks
10 May 75	●	**ISRAELITES** (re-issue) *Cactus CT 57*	**10**	9 wks
30 Aug 75		**SING A LITTLE SONG** *Cactus CT 73*	**16**	7 wks

You Can Get It If You Really Want *credited only to Desmond Dekker.*

DELANEY and BONNIE and FRIENDS featuring Eric CLAPTON

US male/female vocal/instrumental group

Date		Title *Label Number*	Position	Weeks
20 Dec 69		**COMIN' HOME** *Atlantic 584 308*	**16**	9 wks

DELEGATION *UK, male vocal & instrumental group*

Date		Title *Label Number*	Position	Weeks
23 Apr 77		**WHERE IS THE LOVE (WE USED TO KNOW)** *State STAT 40*	**22**	6 wks
20 Aug 77		**YOU'VE BEEN DOING ME WRONG** *State STAT 55*	**49**	1 wk

DELFONICS *US, male vocal group*

Date		Title *Label Number*	Position	Weeks
10 Apr 71		**DIDN'T I (BLOW YOUR MIND THIS TIME)** *Bell 1099*	**43**	1 wk
24 Apr 71		**DIDN'T I (BLOW YOUR MIND THIS TIME)** (re-entry) *Bell 1099*	**22**	8 wks
10 Jul 71		**LA-LA MEANS I LOVE YOU** *Bell 1165*	**19**	10 wks
16 Oct 71		**READY OR NOT HERE I COME** *Bell 1175*	**41**	4 wks

"DELIVERANCE" SOUNDTRACK

US, male instrumental duo, Eric Weissberg and Steve Mandell, banjos

Date		Title *Label Number*	Position	Weeks
31 Mar 73		**DUELLING BANJOS** *Warner Bros. K 16223*	**17**	7 wks

DELLS *US, male vocal group*

Date		Title *Label Number*	Position	Weeks
16 Jul 69		**I CAN SING A RAINBOW - LOVE IS BLUE** (MEDLEY) *Chess CRS 8099*	**15**	9 wks

DELRONS — See *REPARATA and the DELRONS*

Terry DENE *UK, male vocalist*

Date		Title *Label Number*	Position	Weeks
7 Jun 57		**A WHITE SPORT COAT** *Decca F 10895*	**18**	6 wks
19 Jul 57		**START MOVIN'** *Decca F 10914*	**15**	8 wks
26 Jul 57		**A WHITE SPORT COAT** (re-entry) *Decca F 10895*	**30**	1 wk
16 May 58		**STAIRWAY OF LOVE** *Decca F 11016*	**16**	5 wks

Jackie DENNIS *UK, male vocalist*

Date		Title *Label Number*	Position	Weeks
14 Mar 58	●	**LA DEE DAH** *Decca F 10992*	**4**	9 wks
27 Jun 58		**PURPLE PEOPLE EATER** *Decca F 11033*	**29**	1 wk

DENNISONS *UK, male vocal/instrumental group*

Date		Title *Label Number*	Position	Weeks
15 Aug 63		**BE MY GIRL** *Decca F 11691*	**46**	6 wks
7 May 64		**WALKIN' THE DOG** *Decca F 11880*	**36**	7 wks

Richard DENTON and Martin COOK

UK, male orchestral leaders/instrumental duo, guitar and keyboards

Date		Title *Label Number*	Position	Weeks
15 Apr 78		**THEME FROM THE HONG KONG BEAT** *BBC RESL 52*	**25**	7 wks

John DENVER *US, male vocalist*

Date		Title *Label Number*	Position	Weeks
17 Aug 74	★	**ANNIE'S SONG** *RCA APBO 0295*	**1**	13 wks

See also Placido Domingo and John Denver.

Date **Title** *Label Number* **Position**

Karl DENVER *UK, male vocalist*

Date		Title *Label Number*	Position	Weeks
22 Jun 61	●	**MARCHETA** *Decca F 11360*	**8**	20 wks
19 Oct 61	●	**MEXICALI ROSE** *Decca F 11395*	**8**	11 wks
25 Jan 62	●	**WIMOWEH** *Decca F 11420*	**4**	17 wks
22 Feb 62	●	**NEVER GOODBYE** *Decca F 11431*	**9**	18 wks
7 Jun 62		**A LITTLE LOVE A LITTLE KISS** *Decca F 11470*	**19**	10 wks
20 Sep 62		**BLUE WEEKEND** *Decca F 11505*	**33**	5 wks
21 Mar 63		**CAN YOU FORGIVE ME** *Decca F 11608*	**32**	8 wks
13 Jun 63		**INDIAN LOVE CALL** *Decca F 11674*	**32**	8 wks
22 Aug 63		**STILL** *Decca F 11720*	**13**	15 wks
5 Mar 64		**MY WORLD OF BLUE** *Decca F 11828*	**29**	6 wks
4 Jun 64		**LOVE ME WITH ALL YOUR HEART** *Decca F 11905*	**37**	6 wks

DEODATO *US, orchestra*

Date		Title *Label Number*	Position	Weeks
5 May 73	●	**ALSO SPRACH ZARATHUSTRA (2001)** *Creed Taylor CTI 4000*	**7**	9 wks

DEPARTMENT S

UK, male vocal/instrumental group

Date		Title *Label Number*	Position	Weeks
4 Apr 81		**IS VIC THERE?** *Demon D 1003*	**22**	10 wks
11 Jul 81		**GOING LEFT RIGHT** *Stiff BUY 118*	**55**	3 wks

DEPECHE MODE

UK, male vocal/instrumental group

Date		Title *Label Number*	Position	Weeks
4 Apr 81		**DREAMING OF ME** *Mute MUTE 013*	**57**	4 wks
13 Jun 81		**NEW LIFE** *Mute MUTE 014*	**11**	15 wks
19 Sep 81	●	**JUST CAN'T GET ENOUGH** *Mute MUTE 016*	**8**	10 wks
13 Feb 82	●	**SEE YOU** *Mute MUTE 018*	**6**	10 wks
8 May 82		**THE MEANING OF LOVE** *Mute MUTE 022*	**12**	8 wks
28 Aug 82		**LEAVE IN SILENCE** *Mute BONG 1*	**18**	10 wks

DEREK and the DOMINOS

UK/US, male vocal/instrumental group

Date		Title *Label Number*	Position	Weeks
12 Aug 72	●	**LAYLA** *Polydor 2058 130*	**7**	11 wks
6 Mar 82	●	**LAYLA** (re-issue) *RSO 87*	**4**	10 wks

Derek being Eric Clapton under a false name, see also Eric Clapton.

DETROIT EMERALDS *US, male vocal group*

Date		Title *Label Number*	Position	Weeks
10 Feb 73	●	**FEEL THE NEED IN ME** *Janus 6146 020*	**4**	15 wks
5 May 73		**YOU WANT IT YOU GOT IT** *Westbound 6146 103*	**12**	9 wks
11 Aug 73		**I THINK OF YOU** *Westbound 6146 104*	**27**	9 wks
18 Jun 77		**FEEL THE NEED IN ME** *Atlantic K 10945*	**12**	11 wks

The second Feel The Need In Me *was a re-recording*

DETROIT SPINNERS *US, male vocal group*

Date		Title *Label Number*	Position	Weeks
14 Nov 70		**IT'S A SHAME** *Tamla Motown TMG 755*	**20**	11 wks
21 Apr 73		**COULD IT BE I'M FALLING IN LOVE** *Atlantic K 10283*	**11**	11 wks
29 Sep 73	●	**GHETTO CHILD** *Atlantic K 10359*	**7**	10 wks
11 Sep 76		**THE RUBBERBAND MAN** *Atlantic K 10807*	**16**	11 wks
29 Jan 77		**WAKE UP SUSAN** *Atlantic K 10799*	**29**	6 wks
7 May 77		**COULD IT BE I'M FALLING IN LOVE** (EP) *Atlantic K 10935*	**32**	3 wks
23 Feb 80	★	**WORKING MY WAY BACK TO YOU** *Atlantic K 11432*	**1**	14 wks
10 May 80		**BODY LANGUAGE** *Atlantic K 11392*	**40**	7 wks
28 Jun 80	●	**CUPID - I'VE LOVED YOU FOR A LONG TIME** (MEDLEY) *Atlantic K 11498*	**4**	10 wks

See also Dionne Warwicke and the Detroit Spinners. Group is known simply as the Spinners in the US. On It's A Shame *they were called the Motown Spinners in the UK. Tracks on* Could It Be I'm Falling in Love EP: *Could It Be I'm Falling in Love/ You're Throwing a Good Love Away/ Games People Play/ Lazy Susan.*

DETROIT WHEELS — See *Mitch RYDER and the DETROIT WHEELS*

William DEVAUGHN *US, male vocalist*

Date		Title *Label Number*	Position	Weeks
6 Jul 74		**BE THANKFUL FOR WHAT YOU'VE GOT** *Chelsea 2005 002*	**31**	5 wks
20 Sep 80		**BE THANKFUL FOR WHAT YOU'VE GOT** *EMI 5101*	**44**	5 wks

EMI version of hit is a new recording.

Sidney DEVINE *UK, male vocalist*

Date		Title *Label Number*	Position	Weeks
1 Apr 78		**SCOTLAND FOREVER** *Philips SCOT 1*	**48**	1 wk

DEVO *US, male vocal/instrumental group*

Date		Title *Label Number*	Position	Weeks
22 Apr 78		**(I CAN'T ME GET NO) SATISFACTION** *Stiff BOY 1*	**41**	8 wks
13 May 78		**JOCKO HOMO** *Stiff DEV 1*	**62**	3 wks
12 Aug 78		**BE STIFF** *Stiff BOY 2*	**71**	1 wk
2 Sep 78		**COME BACK JONEE** *Virgin VS 223*	**60**	4 wks
22 Nov 80		**WHIP IT** *Virgin VS 383*	**51**	7 wks

Howard DEVOTO — See *BUZZCOCKS*

DEXY'S MIDNIGHT RUNNERS

UK, male vocal/instrumental group

Date		Title *Label Number*	Position	Weeks
19 Jan 80		**DANCE STANCE** *Oddball Productions R 6028*	**40**	6 wks
22 Mar 80	★	**GENO** *Late Night Feelings R 6033*	**1**	14 wks
12 July 80	●	**THERE THERE MY DEAR** *Late Night Feelings R 6038*	**7**	9 wks
21 Mar 81		**PLAN B** *Parlophone R 6046*	**58**	2 wks
11 Jul 81		**SHOW ME** *Mercury DEXYS 6*	**16**	9 wks
20 Mar 82		**THE CELTIC SOUL BROTHERS** *Mercury/Phonogram DEXYS 8*	**45**	4 wks
3 Jul 82	★	**COME ON EILEEN** *Mercury/Phonogram DEXYS 9*	**1**	17 wks
2 Oct 82	●	**JACKIE WILSON SAID** *Mercury/Phonogram DEXYS 10*	**5**	7 wks
4 Dec 82		**LET'S GET THIS STRAIGHT (FROM THE START)/OLD** *Mercury/Phonogram DEXYS 11*	**17**†	4 wks

The Celtic Soul Brothers *and* Come On Eileen *credited to Dexy's Midnight Runners with Emerald Express (female vocal/instrumental group).* Jackie Wilson Said *and* Let's Get This Straight credited to Kevin Rowland and Dexy's Midnight Runners.

Neil DIAMOND *US, male vocalist*

Date		Title *Label Number*	Position	Weeks
7 Nov 70	●	**CRACKLIN' ROSIE** *Uni UN 529*	**3**	17 wks
20 Feb 71	●	**SWEET CAROLINE** *Uni UN 531*	**8**	11 wks
8 May 71	●	**I AM . . . I SAID** *Uni UN 532*	**4**	12 wks
13 May 72		**SONG SUNG BLUE** *Uni UN 538*	**14**	13 wks
14 Aug 76		**IF YOU KNOW WHAT I MEAN** *CBS 4398*	**35**	4 wks
23 Oct 76		**BEAUTIFUL NOISE** *CBS 4601*	**13**	9 wks
24 Dec 77		**DESIREE** *CBS 5869*	**39**	6 wks
3 Mar 79		**FOREVER IN BLUE JEANS** *CBS 7047*	**16**	12 wks

Above **DEPARTMENT S** Lead singer Vaughn Toulouse's greatest influences were Edith Piaf, Marc Bolan and Tom Jones. There is no evidence of this in their hit record! *and right* **DEPECHE MODE** Successfully continued as a three piece when Vince Clarke broke away to form Yazoo

Right **DOLLAR** Three times this duo made position four in the chart with romantic offerings: 'Love's Gotta Hold On Me', 'Mirror Mirror (Mon Amour)' and 'Give Me Back My Heart'.

Date	Title *Label Number*	Position	
15 Nov 80	**LOVE ON THE ROCKS** *Capitol CL 16173*	**17**	12 wks
14 Feb 81	**HELLO AGAIN** *Capitol CL 16176*	**51**	4 wks
20 Nov 82	**HEARTLIGHT** *CBS A 2814*	**47**†	6 wks

See also Barbra and Neil

Gregg DIAMOND BIONIC BOOGIE

US, male/female vocal group

20 Jan 79	**CREAM (ALWAYS RISES TO THE TOP)** *Polydor POSP 18*	**61**	3 wks

DIAMOND HEAD

UK, male vocal/instrumental group

11 Sep 82	**IN THE HEAT OF THE NIGHT** *MCA DHM 102*	**67**	2 wks

DIAMONDS *Canada, male vocal group*

31 May 57	● **LITTLE DARLIN'** *Mercury MT 148*	**3**	17 wks

DICK and DEEDEE *US, male/female vocal duo*

26 Oct 61	**THE MOUNTAIN'S HIGH** *London HLG 9408*	**37**	3 wks

Charles DICKENS *UK, male vocalist*

1 Jul 65	**THAT'S THE WAY LOVE GOES** *Pye 7N 15887*	**37**	8 wks

Neville DICKIE *UK, male instrumentalist, piano*

25 Oct 69	**ROBIN'S RETURN** *Major Minor MM 644*	**33**	7 wks
20 Dec 69	**ROBIN'S RETURN** (re-entry) *Major Minor MM 644*	**43**	3 wks

DICKIES *US, male vocal/instrumental group*

16 Dec 78	**SILENT NIGHT** *A & M AMS 7403*	**47**	4 wks
21 Apr 79	● **BANANA SPLITS (TRA LA LA SONG)** *A & M AMS 7431*	**7**	8 wks
21 Jul 79	**PARANOID** *A & M AMS 7368*	**45**	6 wks
15 Sep 79	**NIGHTS IN WHITE SATIN** *A & M AMS 7469*	**39**	5 wks
16 Feb 80	**FAN MAIL** *A & M AMS 7504*	**57**	3 wks
19 Jul 80	**GIGANTOR** *A and M AMS 7544*	**72**	2 wks

Barbara DICKSON *UK, female vocalist*

17 Jan 76	● **ANSWER ME** *RSO 2090 174*	**9**	7 wks
26 Feb 77	**ANOTHER SUITCASE IN ANOTHER HALL** *MCA 266*	**18**	7 wks
19 Jan 80	**CARAVAN SONG** *Epic EPC 8103*	**41**	7 wks
15 Mar 80	**JANUARY FEBRUARY** *Epic EPC 8115*	**11**	10 wks
14 Jun 80	**IN THE NIGHT** *Epic EPC 8593*	**48**	2 wks

DICTATORS *US, male vocal/instrumental group*

17 Sep 77	**SEARCH AND DESTROY** *Asylum K 13091*	**49**	1 wk
1 Oct 77	**SEARCH AND DESTROY** (re-entry) *Asylum K 13091*	**50**	1 wk

Bo DIDDLEY

US, male vocalist/instrumentalist - guitar

10 Oct 63	**PRETTY THING** *Pye International 7N 25217*	**34**	6 wks
18 Mar 65	**HEY GOOD LOOKIN'** *Chess 8000*	**39**	4 wks

Mark DINNING *US, male vocalist*

10 Mar 60	**TEEN ANGEL** *MGM 1053*	**37**	3 wks
7 Apr 60	**TEEN ANGEL** (re-entry) *MGM 1053*	**42**	1 wk

DINOSAURS — See *Terry DACTYL and the DINOSAURS*

DION *US, male vocalist*

19 Jan 61	**LONELY TEENAGER** *Top Rank JAR 521*	**47**	1 wk
2 Nov 61	**RUNAROUND SUE** *Top Rank JAR 586*	**11**	9 wks
15 Feb 62	● **THE WANDERER** *HMV POP 971*	**10**	12 wks
22 May 76	**THE WANDERER** (re-issue) *Philips 6146 700*	**16**	9 wks

See also Dion and the Belmonts.

DION and the BELMONTS

US, male vocal group

26 Jun 59	**A TEENAGER IN LOVE** *London HLU 8874*	**28**	2 wks

See also Dion.

DIPSTICKS — See *Laurie LINGO and the DIPSTICKS*

DIRE STRAITS *UK, male vocal/instrumental group*

10 Mar 79	● **SULTANS OF SWING** *Vertigo 6059 206*	**8**	11 wks
28 Jul 79	**LADY WRITER** *Vertigo 6059 230*	**51**	6 wks
17 Jan 81	**ROMEO AND JULIET** *Vertigo MOVIE 1*	**11**	11 wks
4 Apr 81	**SKATEAWAY** *Vertigo MOVIE 2*	**37**	5 wks
10 Oct 81	**TUNNEL OF LOVE** *Vertigo MUSIC 3*	**54**	3 wks
4 Sep 82	● **PRIVATE INVESTIGATIONS** *Vertigo/Phonogram DSTR 1*	**2**	8 wks

DISCHARGE *UK, male vocal/instrumental group*

24 Oct 81	**NEVER AGAIN** *Clay CLAY 6*	**64**	3 wks

DISCO TEX and the SEX-O-LETTES

US, male vocalist/female vocal group

23 Nov 74	● **GET DANCING** *Chelsea 2005 013*	**8**	12 wks
26 Apr 75	● **I WANNA DANCE WIT CHOO** *Chelsea 2005 024*	**6**	10 wks

Second hit has credit "featuring Sir Monti Rock III" - the lead vocalist.

Sacha DISTEL *France, male vocalist*

10 Jan 70	**RAINDROPS KEEP FALLING ON MY HEAD** *Warner Bros. WB 7345*	**50**	1 wk
24 Jan 70	● **RAINDROPS KEEP FALLING ON MY HEAD** (re-entry) *Warner Bros. WB 7345*	**10**	20 wks
27 Jun 70	**RAINDROPS KEEP FALLING ON MY HEAD** (2nd re-entry) *Warner Bros. WB 7345*	**43**	4 wks
1 Aug 70	**RAINDROPS KEEP FALLING ON MY HEAD** (3rd re-entry) *Warner Bros. WB 7345*	**47**	1 wk
15 Aug 70	**RAINDROPS KEEP FALLING ON MY HEAD** (4th re-entry) *Warner Bros. WB 7345*	**44**	1 wk

DIVERSIONS

UK, male/female vocal/instrumental group

Date	Title *Label Number*	Position	
20 Sep 75	**FATTIE BUM BUM** *Gull GULS 18*	**34**	3 wks

DIXIE CUPS *US, female vocal group*

Date	Title *Label Number*	Position	
18 Jun 64	**CHAPEL OF LOVE** *Pye International 7N 25245*	**22**	8 wks
13 May 65	**IKO IKO** *Red Bird RB 10024*	**23**	8 wks

DIZZY HEIGHTS

UK, male vocal/instrumental group

Date	Title *Label Number*	Position	
18 Dec 82	**CHRISTMAS RAPPING** *Polydor WRAP 1*	**49**†	2 wks

Carl DOBKINS JR. *US, male vocalist*

Date	Title *Label Number*	Position	
31 Mar 60	**LUCKY DEVIL** *Brunswick 05817*	**44**	1 wk

DR. FEELGOOD

UK, male vocal/instrumental group

Date	Title *Label Number*	Position	
11 Jun 77	**SNEAKIN' SUSPICION** *United Artists UP 36255*	**47**	3 wks
24 Sep 77	**SHE'S A WIND UP** *United Artists UP 36304*	**34**	5 wks
30 Sep 78	**DOWN AT THE DOCTOR'S** *United Artists UP 36444*	**48**	5 wks
20 Jan 79	● **MILK AND ALCOHOL** *United Artists UP 36468*	**9**	9 wks
5 May 79	**AS LONG AS THE PRICE IS RIGHT** *United Artists YUP 36506*	**40**	6 wks
8 Dec 79	**PUT HIM OUT OF YOUR MIND** *United Artists BP 306*	**73**	1 wk

DR. HOOK *US, male vocal/instrumental group*

Date	Title *Label Number*	Position	
24 Jun 72	● **SYLVIA'S MOTHER** *CBS 7929*	**2**	13 wks
26 Jun 76	● **A LITTLE BIT MORE** *Capitol CL 15871*	**2**	14 wks
30 Oct 76	● **IF NOT YOU** *Capitol CL 15885*	**5**	10 wks
25 Mar 78	**MORE LIKE THE MOVIES** *Capitol CL 15967*	**14**	10 wks
22 Sep 79	★ **WHEN YOU'RE IN LOVE WITH A BEAUTIFUL WOMAN** *Capitol CL 16039*	**1**	17 wks
5 Jan 80	● **BETTER LOVE NEXT TIME** *Capitol CL 16112*	**8**	8 wks
29 Mar 80	● **SEXY EYES** *Capitol CL 16127*	**4**	9 wks
23 Aug 80	**YEARS FROM NOW** *Capitol CL 16154*	**47**	6 wks
8 Nov 80	**SHARING THE NIGHT TOGETHER** *Capitol CL 16171*	**43**	4 wks
22 Nov 80	**GIRLS CAN GET IT** *Mercury MER 51*	**40**	5 wks

Group billed as Dr. Hook And The Medicine Show on CBS.

Ken DODD *UK, male vocalist*

Date	Title *Label Number*	Position	
7 Jul 60	● **LOVE IS LIKE A VIOLIN** *Decca F 11248*	**8**	18 wks
15 Jun 61	**ONCE IN EVERY LIFETIME** *Decca F 11355*	**28**	7 wks
10 Aug 61	**ONCE IN EVERY LIFETIME** (re-entry) *Decca F 11355*	**47**	1 wk
24 Aug 61	**ONCE IN EVERY LIFETIME** (2nd re-entry) *Decca F 11355*	**31**	10 wks
1 Feb 62	**PIANISSIMO** *Decca F 11422*	**21**	15 wks
29 Aug 63	**STILL** *Columbia DB 7094*	**35**	10 wks
6 Feb 64	**EIGHT BY TEN** *Columbia DB 7191*	**22**	11 wks
23 Jul 64	**HAPPINESS** *Columbia DB 7325*	**31**	13 wks
26 Nov 64	**SO DEEP IS THE NIGHT** *Columbia DB 7398*	**31**	7 wks
2 Sep 65	★ **TEARS** *Columbia DB 7659*	**1**	24 wks
18 Nov 65	● **THE RIVER (LE COLLINE SONO IN FIORO)** *Columbia DB 7750*	**3**	14 wks
12 May 66	● **PROMISES** *Columbia DB 7914*	**6**	14 wks
4 Aug 66	**MORE THAN LOVE** *Columbia DB 7976*	**14**	11 wks
27 Oct 66	**IT'S LOVE** *Columbia DB 8031*	**36**	7 wks
19 Jan 67	**LET ME CRY ON YOUR SHOULDER** *Columbia DB 8101*	**11**	10 wks
30 Jul 69	**TEARS WON'T WASH AWAY MY HEARTACHE** *Columbia DB 8600*	**22**	11 wks
5 Dec 70	**BROKEN HEARTED** *Columbia DB 8725*	**15**	9 wks
13 Feb 71	**BROKEN HEARTED** (re-entry) *Columbia DB 8725*	**38**	1 wk
10 Jul 71	**WHEN LOVE COMES ROUND AGAIN (L'ARCA DI NOE)** *Columbia DB 8796*	**19**	16 wks
18 Nov 72	**JUST OUT OF REACH (OF MY TWO EMPTY ARMS)** *Columbia DB 8947*	**29**	11 wks
29 Nov 75	**(THINK OF ME) WHEREVER YOU ARE** *EMI 2342*	**21**	8 wks
26 Dec 81	**HOLD MY HAND** *Images IMGS 0002*	**44**	5 wks

Joe DOLAN *Ireland, male vocalist*

Date	Title *Label Number*	Position	
25 Jun 69	● **MAKE ME AN ISLAND** *Pye 7N 17731*	**3**	18 wks
1 Nov 69	**TERESA** *Pye 7N 17833*	**20**	7 wks
8 Nov 69	**MAKE ME AN ISLAND** (re-entry) *Pye 7N 17731*	**48**	1 wk
28 Feb 70	**YOU'RE SUCH A GOOD LOOKING WOMAN** *Pye 7N 17891*	**17**	13 wks
17 Sep 77	**I NEED YOU** *Pye 7N 45702*	**43**	1 wk

Thomas DOLBY *UK, male vocalist/instrumentalist*

Date	Title *Label Number*	Position	
3 Oct 81	**EUROPA AND THE PIRATE TWINS** *Parlophone R 6051*	**48**	3 wks
14 Aug 82	**WINDPOWER** *Venice In Peril VIPS 103*	**31**	8 wks
6 Nov 82	**SHE BLINDED ME WITH SCIENCE** *Venice In Peril VIPS 104*	**49**	4 wks

Joe DOLCE MUSIC THEATRE

US, male vocalist

Date	Title *Label Number*	Position	
7 Feb 81	★ **SHADDAP YOU FACE** *Epic EPC 9518*	**1**	10 wks

DOLL *UK, male/female vocal/instrumental group*

Date	Title *Label Number*	Position	
13 Jan 79	**DESIRE ME** *Beggars Banquet BEG 11*	**28**	8 wks

DOLLAR *UK, male/female vocal duo*

Date	Title *Label Number*	Position	
11 Nov 78	**SHOOTING STAR** *EMI 2871*	**14**	12 wks
19 May 79	**WHO WERE YOU WITH IN THE MOONLIGHT** *Carrere CAR 110*	**14**	12 wks
18 Aug 79	● **LOVE'S GOTTA HOLD ON ME** *Carrere CAR 122*	**4**	13 wks
24 Nov 79	● **I WANNA HOLD YOUR HAND** *Carrere CAR 131*	**9**	14 wks
25 Oct 80	**TAKIN' A CHANCE ON YOU** *WEA K 18353*	**62**	3 wks
15 Aug 81	**HAND HELD IN BLACK AND WHITE** *WEA BUCK 1*	**19**	12 wks
14 Nov 81	● **MIRROR MIRROR (MON AMOUR)** *WEA BUCK 2*	**4**	17 wks
20 Mar 82	**RING RING** *Carrere CAR 225*	**61**	2 wks
27 Mar 82	● **GIVE ME BACK MY HEART** *WEA BUCK 3*	**4**	9 wks
19 Jun 82	**VIDEOTHEQUE** *WEA BUCK 4*	**17**	10 wks
18 Sep 82	**GIVE ME SOME KINDA MAGIC** *WEA BUCK 5*	**34**	6 wks

Placido DOMINGO with John DENVER

Spain, male vocalist with US, male vocalist/instrumentalist

Date	Title *Label Number*	Position	
12 Dec 81	**PERHAPS LOVE** *CBS A 1905*	**46**	9 wks

see also John Denver.

Fats DOMINO

US, male vocalist/instrumentalist, piano

Date	Title *Label Number*	Position	
27 Jul 56	**I'M IN LOVE AGAIN** *London HLU 8280*	**28**	1 wk
17 Aug 56	**I'M IN LOVE AGAIN** (re-entry) *London HLU 8280*	**12**	13 wks
30 Nov 56	**BLUEBERRY HILL** *London HLU 8330*	**26**	1 wk
21 Dec 56	● **BLUEBERRY HILL** (re-entry) *London HLU 8330*	**6**	14 wks
25 Jan 57	**AIN'T THAT A SHAME** *London HLU 8173*	**23**	2 wks
1 Feb 57	**HONEY CHILE** *London HLU 8356*	**29**	1 wk
29 Mar 57	**BLUE MONDAY** *London HLP 8377*	**23**	1 wk
19 Apr 57	**BLUE MONDAY** (re-entry) *London HLP 8377*	**30**	1 wk
19 Apr 57	**I'M WALKIN'** *London HLP 8407*	**19**	7 wks
19 Jul 57	**VALLEY OF TEARS** *London HLP 8449*	**25**	1 wk
28 Mar 58	**THE BIG BEAT** *London HLP 8575*	**20**	4 wks
4 Jul 58	**SICK AND TIRED** *London HLP 8628*	**26**	1 wk
22 May 59	**MARGIE** *London HLP 8865*	**18**	5 wks
16 Oct 59	**I WANT TO WALK YOU HOME** *London HLP 8942*	**14**	5 wks
18 Dec 59	**BE MY GUEST** *London HLP 9005*	**11**	8 wks
19 Feb 60	**BE MY GUEST** (re-entry) *London HLP 9005*	**19**	4 wks
17 Mar 60	**COUNTRY BOY** *London HLP 9073*	**19**	11 wks
21 Jul 60	**WALKING TO NEW ORLEANS** *London HLP 9163*	**19**	10 wks
10 Nov 60	**THREE NIGHTS A WEEK** *London HLP 9198*	**45**	2 wks
5 Jan 61	**MY GIRL JOSEPHINE** *London HLP 9244*	**32**	4 wks
27 Jul 61	**IT KEEPS RAININ'** *London HLP 9374*	**49**	1 wk
30 Nov 61	**WHAT A PARTY** *London HLP 9456*	**43**	1 wk
29 Mar 62	**JAMBALAYA** *London HLP 9520*	**41**	1 wk
31 Oct 63	**RED SAILS IN THE SUNSET** *HMV POP 1219*	**34**	6 wks
24 Apr 76	**BLUEBERRY HILL** (re-issue) *United Artists UP 35797*	**41**	5 wks

DOMINOS — See *Derek and the DOMINOS*

Lonnie DONEGAN *UK, male vocalist*

Date	Title *Label Number*	Position	
6 Jan 56	● **ROCK ISLAND LINE** *Decca F 10647*	**8**	13 wks
13 Apr 56	**ROCK ISLAND LINE** (re-entry) *Decca F 10647*	**16**	3 wks
20 Apr 56	**STEWBALL** *Pye Nixa N 15036*	**27**	1 wk
27 Apr 56	● **LOST JOHN/ STEWBALL** *Pye Nixa N 15036*	**2**	17 wks
11 May 56	**ROCK ISLAND LINE** (2nd re-entry) *Decca F 10647*	**19**	6 wks
6 Jul 56	**SKIFFLE SESSION** (EP) *Pye Nixa NJE 1017*	**20**	2 wks
7 Sep 56	● **BRING A LITTLE WATER SYLVIE/ DEAD OR ALIVE** *Pye Nixa N 15071*	**7**	12 wks
21 Dec 56	**LONNIE DONEGAN SHOWCASE** (LP) *Pye Nixa NPT 19012*	**26**	3 wks
11 Jan 57	**BRING A LITTLE WATER SYLVIE/ DEAD OR ALIVE** (re-entry) *Pye Nixa N 15071*	**30**	1 wk
18 Jan 57	● **DON'T YOU ROCK ME DADDY-O** *Pye Nixa N 15080*	**4**	17 wks
5 Apr 57	★ **CUMBERLAND GAP** *Pye Nixa B 15087*	**1**	12 wks
7 Jun 57	★ **GAMBLIN' MAN/ PUTTING ON THE STYLE** *Pye Nixa N 15093*	**1**	19 wks
11 Oct 57	● **MY DIXIE DARLING** *Pye Nixa N 15108*	**10**	15 wks
20 Dec 57	**JACK O' DIAMONDS** *Pye Nixa N 15116*	**14**	7 wks
11 Apr 58	● **GRAND COOLIE DAM** *Pye Nixa N 15129*	**6**	15 wks
11 Jul 58	**SALLY DON'T YOU GRIEVE/ BETTY BETTY BETTY** *Pye Nixa N 15148*	**11**	7 wks
26 Sep 58	**LONESOME TRAVELLER** *Pye Nixa N 15158*	**28**	1 wk
14 Nov 58	**LONNIE'S SKIFFLE PARTY** *Pye Nixa N 15165*	**23**	5 wks
21 Nov 58	● **TOM DOOLEY** *Pye Nixa 7N 15172*	**3**	14 wks
6 Feb 59	● **DOES YOUR CHEWING GUM LOSE ITS FLAVOUR** *Pye Nixa 7N 15181*	**3**	12 wks
1 May 59	**FORT WORTH JAIL** *Pye Nixa 7N 15198*	**14**	5 wks
26 Jun 59	● **BATTLE OF NEW ORLEANS** *Pye 7N 15206*	**2**	16 wks
11 Sep 59	**SAL'S GOT A SUGAR LIP** *Pye 7N 15223*	**13**	4 wks
4 Dec 59	**SAN MIGUEL** *Pye 7N 15237*	**19**	4 wks
24 Mar 60	★ **MY OLD MAN'S A DUSTMAN** *Pye 7N 15256*	**1**	13 wks
26 May 60	● **I WANNA GO HOME** *Pye 7N 15267*	**5**	17 wks
25 Aug 60	● **LORELEI** *Pye 7N 15275*	**10**	8 wks
24 Nov 60	**LIVELY** *Pye 7N 15312*	**13**	9 wks
8 Dec 60	**VIRGIN MARY** *Pye 7N 15315*	**27**	5 wks
11 May 61	● **HAVE A DRINK ON ME** *Pye 7N 15354*	**8**	15 wks
31 Aug 61	● **MICHAEL ROW THE BOAT/ LUMBERED** *Pye 7N 15371*	**6**	11 wks
18 Jan 62	**THE COMANCHEROS** *Pye 7N 15410*	**14**	10 wks
5 Apr 62	● **THE PARTY'S OVER** *Pye 7N 15424*	**9**	12 wks
16 Aug 62	**PICK A BALE OF COTTON** *Pye 7N 15455*	**11**	10 wks

Stewball *had one week on the chart by itself on 20 Apr 56. Lost John, the other side, replaced it on 27 Apr 56 but* Stewball *was given co-billing with* Lost John *for the weeks of 11, 18 and 25 May 56 only, during* Lost John's *17-week run.* Dead Or Alive *was not listed for the week 7 Sep 56 with* Bring A Little Water Sylvie. Putting On The Style *was not listed for the weeks of 7 & 14 June 56 with* Gamblin' Man. *Tracks on* Skiffle Session *EP: Railroad Bill/ Stackalee/ Ballad of Jesse James/ Ol' Riley. Tracks on* Lonnie Donegan Showcase *LP: Wabash Cannonball/ How Long How Long Blues/ Nobody's Child/ I Shall Not Be Moved/ I'm Alabammy Bound/ I'm A Rambling Man/ Wreck Of The Old '97/ Frankie And Johnny.* Lonnie's Skiffle Party *was a medley as follows: Little Liza Jane/ Putting' On The Style/ Camptown Races/ Knees Up Mother Brown/ So Long/ On Top Of Old Smokey/ Down In The Valley/ So Long. Yes, there are two versions of So Long on this disc.*

DONNA — See *ALTHEA and DONNA*

Ral DONNER *US, male vocalist*

Date	Title *Label Number*	Position	
21 Sep 61	**YOU DON'T KNOW WHAT YOU'VE GOT** *Parlophone R 4820*	**25**	10 wks

DONOVAN *UK, male vocalist*

Date	Title *Label Number*	Position	
25 Mar 65	● **CATCH THE WIND** *Pye 7N 15801*	**4**	13 wks
3 Jun 65	● **COLOURS** *Pye 7N 15866*	**4**	12 wks
11 Nov 65	**TURQUOISE** *Pye 7N 15984*	**30**	6 wks
8 Dec 66	● **SUNSHINE SUPERMAN** *Pye 7N 17241*	**3**	11 wks
9 Feb 67	● **MELLOW YELLOW** *Pye 7N 17267*	**8**	8 wks
25 Oct 67	● **THERE IS A MOUNTAIN** *Pye 7N 17403*	**8**	11 wks
21 Feb 68	● **JENNIFER JUNIPER** *Pye 7N 17457*	**5**	11 wks
29 May 68	● **HURDY GURDY MAN** *Pye 7N 17537*	**4**	10 wks
4 Dec 68	**ATLANTIS** *Pye 7N 17660*	**23**	8 wks

See also Donovan with The Jeff Beck Group.

DONOVAN with the Jeff BECK GROUP

UK, male vocalist/instrumental group

Date	Title *Label Number*	Position	
9 Jul 69	**GOO GOO BARABAJAGAL (LOVE IS HOT)** *Pye 7N 17778*	**12**	9 wks

See also Donovan, Jeff Beck, Jeff Beck and Rod Stewart.

DOOBIE BROTHERS

US, male vocal/instrumental group

Date	Title *Label Number*	Position	
9 Mar 74	**LISTEN TO THE MUSIC** *Warner Bros. K 16208*	**29**	7 wks
7 Jun 75	**TAKE ME IN YOUR ARMS** *Warner Bros. K 16559*	**29**	5 wks
17 Feb 79	**WHAT A FOOL BELIEVES** *Warner Bros. K 17314*	**31**	10 wks
14 Jul 79	**MINUTE BY MINUTE** *Warner Bros. K 17411*	**47**	4 wks
5 May 79	**WHAT A FOOL BELIEVES** (re-entry) *Warner Bros. k17314*	**72**	1 wk

DOOLEYS *UK, male/female vocal/instrumental group*

Date	Title *Label Number*	Position	
13 Aug 77	**THINK I'M GONNA FALL IN LOVE WITH YOU** *GTO GT 95*	**13**	10 wks
12 Nov 77	● **LOVE OF MY LIFE** *GTO GT 110*	**9**	11 wks
13 May 78	**DON'T TAKE IT LYIN' DOWN** *GTO GT 220*	**60**	3 wks
2 Sep 78	**A ROSE HAS TO DIE** *GTO GT 229*	**11**	11 wks
10 Feb 79	**HONEY I'M LOST** *GTO GT 242*	**24**	9 wks
16 Jun 79	● **WANTED** *GTO GT 249*	**3**	14 wks
22 Sep 79	● **THE CHOSEN FEW** *GTO GT 258*	**7**	11 wks
8 Mar 80	**LOVE PATROL** *GTO GT 260*	**29**	7 wks
6 Sep 80	**BODY LANGUAGE** *GTO GT 276*	**46**	4 wks
10 Oct 81	**AND I WISH** *GTO GT 300*	**52**	3 wks

Val DOONICAN *Ireland, male vocalist*

Date	Title *Label Number*	Position	
15 Oct 64	● **WALK TALL** *Decca F 11982*	**3**	21 wks
21 Jan 65	● **THE SPECIAL YEARS** *Decca F 12049*	**7**	12 wks
22 Apr 65	**THE SPECIAL YEARS** (re-entry) *Decca F 12049*	**49**	1 wk
8 Apr 65	**I'M GONNA GET THERE SOMEHOW** *Decca F 12118*	**25**	5 wks
17 Mar 66	● **ELUSIVE BUTTERFLY** *Decca F 12358*	**5**	12 wks
3 Nov 66	● **WHAT WOULD I BE** *Decca F 12505*	**2**	17 wks
23 Feb 67	**MEMORIES ARE MADE OF THIS** *Decca F 12566*	**11**	12 wks
25 May 67	**TWO STREETS** *Decca F 12608*	**39**	4 wks
18 Oct 67	● **IF THE WHOLE WORLD STOPPED LOVING** *Pye 7N 17396*	**3**	19 wks
21 Feb 68	**YOU'RE THE ONLY ONE** *Pye 7N 17465*	**37**	4 wks
12 Jun 68	**NOW** *Pye 7N 17534*	**43**	2 wks
23 Oct 68	**IF I KNEW THEN WHAT I KNOW NOW** *Pye 7N 17616*	**14**	13 wks
23 Apr 69	**RING OF BRIGHT WATER** *Pye 7N 17713*	**48**	1 wk
4 Dec 71	**MORNING** *Philips 6006 177*	**12**	13 wks
10 Mar 73	**HEAVEN IS MY WOMAN'S LOVE** *Philips 6028 031*	**34**	6 wks
28 Apr 73	**HEAVEN IS MY WOMAN'S LOVE** (re-entry) *Philips 6028 031*	**47**	1 wk

DOORS *US, male vocal/instrumental group*

Date	Title *Label Number*	Position	
16 Aug 67	**LIGHT MY FIRE** *Elektra EKSN 45014*	**49**	1 wk
28 Aug 68	**HELLO I LOVE YOU** *Elektra EKSN 45037*	**15**	12 wks
16 Oct 71	**RIDERS ON THE STORM** *Elektra K 12021*	**50**	1 wk
30 Oct 71	**RIDERS ON THE STORM** (re-entry) *Elektra K 12021*	**22**	10 wks
20 Mar 76	**RIDERS ON THE STORM** (re-issue) *Elektra K 12203*	**33**	5 wks
3 Feb 79	**HELLO I LOVE YOU** (re-issue) *Elektra K 12215*	**71**	2 wks

Charlie DORE *UK, female vocalist*

Date	Title *Label Number*	Position	
17 Nov 79	**PILOT OF THE AIRWAVES** *Island WIP 6526*	**66**	2 wks

Lee DORSEY *US, male vocalist*

Date	Title *Label Number*	Position	
3 Feb 66	**GET OUT OF MY LIFE WOMAN** *Stateside SS 485*	**22**	7 wks
5 May 66	**CONFUSION** *Stateside SS 506*	**38**	6 wks
11 Aug 66	● **WORKING IN THE COALMINE** *Stateside SS 528*	**8**	11 wks
27 Oct 66	● **HOLY COW** *Stateside SS 552*	**6**	12 wks

Tommy DORSEY ORCHESTRA starring Warren COVINGTON

US, orchestra, Warren Covington, male, leader

Date	Title *Label Number*	Position	
17 Oct 58	● **TEA FOR TWO CHA CHA** *Brunswick 05757*	**3**	19 wks

Carl DOUGLAS *UK, male vocalist*

Date	Title *Label Number*	Position	
17 Aug 74	★ **KUNG FU FIGHTING** *Pye 7N 45377*	**1**	13 wks
30 Nov 74	**DANCE THE KUNG FU** *Pye 7N 45418*	**35**	5 wks
3 Dec 77	**RUN BACK** *Pye 7N 46018*	**25**	10 wks

Carol DOUGLAS *US, female vocalist*

Date	Title *Label Number*	Position	
22 Jul 78	**NIGHT FEVER** *Gull GULS 61*	**66**	4 wks

Craig DOUGLAS *UK, male vocalist*

Date	Title *Label Number*	Position	
12 Jun 59	**A TEENAGER IN LOVE** *Top Rank JAR 133*	**13**	11 wks
7 Aug 59	★ **ONLY SIXTEEN** *Top Rank JAR 159*	**1**	15 wks
22 Jan 60	● **PRETTY BLUE EYES** *Top Rank JAR 268*	**4**	14 wks
28 Apr 60	● **THE HEART OF A TEENAGE GIRL** *Top Rank JAR 340*	**10**	9 wks
11 Aug 60	**OH! WHAT A DAY** *Top Rank JAR 406*	**43**	1 wk
20 Apr 61	● **A HUNDRED POUNDS OF CLAY** *Top Rank JAR 555*	**9**	9 wks
29 Jul 61	● **TIME** *Top Rank JAR 569*	**9**	14 wks
22 Mar 62	● **WHEN MY LITTLE GIRL IS SMILING** *Top Rank JAR 610*	**9**	13 wks
28 Jun 62	● **OUR FAVOURITE MELODIES** *Columbia DB 4854*	**9**	10 wks
18 Oct 62	**OH LONESOME ME** *Decca F 11523*	**15**	12 wks
28 Feb 63	**TOWN CRIER** *Decca F 11575*	**36**	4 wks

DOWLANDS *UK, male vocal duo*

Date	Title *Label Number*	Position	
9 Jan 64	**ALL MY LOVING** *Oriole CB 1897*	**33**	7 wks

Don DOWNING *US, male vocalist*

Date	Title *Label Number*	Position	
10 Nov 73	**LONELY DAYS, LONELY NIGHTS** *People PEO 102*	**32**	10 wks

Lamont DOZIER — See *HOLLAND-DOZIER*

DOZY — See *Dave DEE, DOZY, BEAKY, MICK and TICH*

Date	Title *Label Number*	Position	

Charlie DRAKE *UK, male vocalist*

8 Aug 58	● **SPLISH SPLASH** *Parlophone R 4461*	**7**	11 wks
24 Oct 58	**VOLARE** *Parlophone R 4478*	**28**	2 wks
27 Oct 60	**MR. CUSTER** *Parlophone R 4699*	**12**	12 wks
5 Oct 61	**MY BOOMERANG WON'T COME BACK** *Parlophone R 4824*	**14**	11 wks
1 Jan 72	**PUCKWUDGIE** *Columbia DB 8829*	**47**	1 wk

DRAMATIS *UK, male vocal/instrumental group*

13 Nov 82	**I CAN SEE HER NOW** *Rocket/Phonogram XPRES 83*	**57**	1 wk

See also Gary Numan.

Rusty DRAPER *US, male vocalist*

11 Aug 60	**MULE SKINNER BLUES** *Mercury AMT 1101*	**39**	4 wks

DREAMERS — See *FREDDIE and the DREAMERS*

DREAMWEAVERS *US, male/female vocal group*

10 Feb 56	★ **IT'S ALMOST TOMORROW** *Brunswick 05515*	**1**	18 wks

DRELLS — See *Archie BELL and the DRELLS*

Eddie DRENNON and B. B. S. UNLIMITED *US, male vocal/instrumental group*

28 Feb 76	**LET'S DO THE LATIN HUSTLE** *Pye International 7N 25702*	**20**	6 wks

Alan DREW *UK, male vocalist*

26 Sep 63	**ALWAYS THE LONELY ONE** *Columbia DB 7090*	**48**	2 wks

DRIFTERS *US, male vocal group*

8 Jan 60	**DANCE WITH ME** *London HLE 8988*	**17**	4 wks
10 Mar 60	**DANCE WITH ME** (re-entry) *London HLE 8988*	**35**	1 wk
3 Nov 60	● **SAVE THE LAST DANCE FOR ME** *London HLK 9201*	**2**	18 wks
16 Mar 61	**I COUNT THE TEARS** *London HLK 9287*	**28**	6 wks
5 Apr 62	**WHEN MY LITTLE GIRL IS SMILING** *London HLK 9522*	**31**	3 wks
10 Oct 63	**I'LL TAKE YOU HOME** *London HLK 9785*	**37**	5 wks
24 Sep 64	**UNDER THE BOARDWALK** *Atlantic AT 4001*	**45**	4 wks
8 Apr 65	**AT THE CLUB** *Atlantic AT 4019*	**35**	7 wks
29 Apr 65	**COME ON OVER TO MY PLACE** *Atlantic AT 4023*	**40**	5 wks
2 Feb 67	**BABY WHAT I MEAN** *Atlantic 584 065*	**49**	1 wk
25 Mar 72	**AT THE CLUB** (re-issue) *Atlantic K 10148*	**39**	1 wk
8 Apr 72	● **AT THE CLUB/ SATURDAY NIGHT AT THE MOVIES** (re-entry of re-issue) *Atlantic K 10148*	**3**	19 wks
26 Aug 72	● **COME ON OVER TO MY PLACE** (re-issue) *Atlantic K 10216*	**9**	11 wks
4 Aug 73	● **LIKE SISTER AND BROTHER** *Bell 1313*	**7**	13 wks
15 Jun 74	● **KISSIN' IN THE BACK ROW OF THE MOVIES** *Bell 1358*	**2**	13 wks
12 Oct 74	● **DOWN ON THE BEACH TONIGHT** *Bell 1381*	**7**	9 wks
8 Feb 75	**LOVE GAMES** *Bell 1396*	**33**	6 wks
6 Sep 75	● **THERE GOES MY FIRST LOVE** *Bell 1433*	**3**	12 wks
29 Nov 75	● **CAN I TAKE YOU HOME LITTLE GIRL** *Bell 1462*	**10**	10 wks
13 Mar 76	**HELLO HAPPINESS** *Bell 1469*	**12**	8 wks
11 Sep 76	**EVERY NITE'S A SATURDAY NIGHT WITH YOU** *Bell 1491*	**29**	7 wks
18 Dec 76	● **YOU'RE MORE THAN A NUMBER IN MY LITTLE RED BOOK** *Arista 78*	**5**	12 wks
14 Apr 79	**SAVE THE LAST DANCE FOR ME/ WHEN MY LITTLE GIRL IS SMILING** (re-issue) *Lightning LIG 9014*	**69**	2 wks

Saturday Night At The Movies *only received chart credit with* At The Club *after the re-issue's return to the chart on 8 Apr 72.*

Julie DRISCOLL, Brian AUGER and the TRINITY *UK, female vocalist/male instrumental group*

17 Apr 68	● **THIS WHEEL'S ON FIRE** *Marmalade 598 006*	**5**	16 wks

DRIVER 67 *UK, male vocalist/instrumentalist*

23 Dec 78	● **CAR 67** *Logo GO 336*	**7**	12 wks

Driver 67 is Paul Phillips.

Frank D'RONE *US, male vocalist*

22 Dec 60	**STRAWBERRY BLONDE** *Mercury AMT 1123*	**24**	6 wks

DRUPI *Italy, male vocalist*

1 Dec 73	**VADO VIA** *A & M AMS 7083*	**17**	12 wks

John DU CANN *UK, male vocalist*

22 Sep 79	**DON'T BE A DUMMY** *Vertigo 6059 241*	**33**	6 wks

DUBLINERS *Ireland, male vocal/instrumental group*

30 Mar 67	● **SEVEN DRUNKEN NIGHTS** *Major Minor MM 506*	**7**	17 wks
30 Aug 67	**BLACK VELVET BAND** *Major Minor MM 530*	**15**	15 wks
20 Dec 67	**NEVER WED AN OLD MAN** *Major Minor MM 551*	**43**	3 wks

DUFFO *Australia, male vocalist*

24 Mar 79	**GIVE ME BACK ME BRAIN** *Beggars Banquet BEG 15*	**60**	2 wks

George DUKE *US, male vocal/instrumentalist*

12 Jul 80	**BRAZILIAN LOVE AFFAIR** *Epic EPC 8751*	**36**	6 wks

DUKES *UK, male vocal duo*

17 Oct 81	**MYSTERY GIRL** *WEA K 18867*	**47**	7 wks
1 May 82	**THANK YOU FOR THE PARTY** *WEA K 19136*	**53**	6 wks

John DUMMER and Helen APRIL *UK, male/female vocal duo*

28 Aug 82	**BLUE SKIES** *Speed SPEED 8*	**54**	3 wks

Above **DURAN DURAN** They captured the hearts of British girls and topped most of the polls in 1982 *Left* **LEE DORSEY** 4 hits in one year for ex-boxer Lee Dorsey but two of them didn't take the count of ten. Chartwise, he'd suffered a technical knockout by 1967 *Below* **DUBLINERS** Shamrock and Roll *Bottom left* **DRIFTERS** The Drifters 1953–1983 and still going! The 1965 line-up (l–rt) Gene Pearson, Johnny Terry, Charles Thomas, Johnny Moore and seated Billy Davis. Previous lead singers had included Clyde McPhatter, Ben E. King and Rudy Lewis *Below right* **DOORS** opened Aug 67 – closed Feb 79

Johnny DUNCAN and the BLUE GRASS BOYS *US, male vocal/instrumental group*

Date	Title *Label Number*	Position	
26 Jul 57	● **LAST TRAIN TO SAN FERNANDO** *Columbia DB 3959*	**2**	17 wks
25 Oct 57	**BLUE BLUE HEARTACHES** *Columbia DB 3996*	**27**	1 wk
29 Nov 57	**FOOTPRINTS IN THE SNOW** *Columbia DB 4029*	**27**	1 wk
3 Jan 58	**FOOTPRINTS IN THE SNOW** (re-entry) *Columbia DB 4029*	**28**	1 wk

David DUNDAS *UK, male vocalist*

Date	Title *Label Number*	Position	
24 Jul 76	● **JEANS ON** *Air CHS 2094*	**3**	9 wks
9 Apr 77	**ANOTHER FUNNY HONEYMOON** *Air CHS 2136*	**29**	5 wks

Erroll DUNKLEY *Jamaica, male vocalist*

Date	Title *Label Number*	Position	
22 Sep 79	**O.K. FRED** *Scope SC 6*	**11**	11 wks
2 Feb 80	**SIT DOWN AND CRY** *Scope SC 11*	**52**	3 wks

Clive DUNN *UK, male vocalist*

Date	Title *Label Number*	Position	
28 Nov 70	★ **GRANDAD** *Columbia DB 8726*	**1**	27 wks
26 Jun 71	**GRANDAD** (re-entry) *Columbia D8 8726*	**50**	1 wk

Simon DUPREE and The BIG SOUND

UK, male vocal/instrumental group

Date	Title *Label Number*	Position	
22 Nov 67	● **KITES** *Parlophone R 5646*	**9**	13 wks
3 Apr 68	**FOR WHOM THE BELL TOLLS** *Parlophone R 5670*	**43**	3 wks

DURAN DURAN

UK, male vocal/instrumental group

Date	Title *Label Number*	Position	
21 Feb 81	**PLANET EARTH** *EMI 5137*	**12**	11 wks
9 May 81	**CARELESS MEMORIES** *EMI 5168*	**37**	7 wks
25 Jul 81	● **GIRLS ON FILM** *EMI 5206*	**5**	11 wks
28 Nov 81	**MY OWN WAY** *EMI 5254*	**14**	11 wks
15 May 82	● **HUNGRY LIKE THE WOLF** *EMI 5295*	**5**	12 wks
21 Aug 82	● **SAVE A PRAYER** *EMI 5327*	**2**	9 wks
13 Nov 82	● **RIO** *EMI 5346*	**9**†	7 wks

Judith DURHAM *Australia, female vocalist*

Date	Title *Label Number*	Position	
15 Jun 67	**OLIVE TREE** *Columbia DB 8207*	**33**	5 wks

Ian DURY and the BLOCKHEADS

UK, male vocal/instrumental group

Date	Title *Label Number*	Position	
29 Apr 78	● **WHAT A WASTE** *Stiff BUY 27*	**9**	12 wks
9 Dec 78	★ **HIT ME WITH YOUR RHYTHM STICK** *Stiff BUY 38*	**1**	15 wks
4 Aug 79	● **REASONS TO BE CHEERFUL,** PT.3 *Stiff BUY 50*	**3**	8 wks
30 Aug 80	**I WANT TO BE STRAIGHT** *Stiff BUY 90*	**22**	7 wks
15 Nov 80	**SUPERMAN'S BIG SISTER** *Stiff BUY 100*	**51**	3 wks

Hit Me With Your Rhythm Stick *credits Ian and the Blockheads.*

Slim DUSTY *Australia, male vocalist*

Date	Title *Label Number*	Position	
30 Jan 59	● **A PUB WITH NO BEER** *Columbia DB 4212*	**3**	15 wks

DYKE — See *ASHTON, GARDNER and DYKE*

Bob DYLAN *US, male vocalist*

Date	Title *Label Number*	Position	
25 Mar 65	● **TIMES THEY ARE A-CHANGIN'** *CBS 201751*	**9**	11 wks
29 Apr 65	● **SUBTERRANEAN HOMESICK BLUES** *CBS 201753*	**9**	9 wks
17 Jun 65	**MAGGIE'S FARM** *CBS 201781*	**22**	8 wks
19 Aug 65	● **LIKE A ROLLING STONE** *CBS 201811*	**4**	12 wks
28 Oct 65	● **POSITIVELY FOURTH STREET** *CBS 201824*	**8**	12 wks
27 Jan 66	**CAN YOU PLEASE CRAWL OUT YOUR WINDOW** *CBS 201900*	**17**	5 wks
14 Apr 66	**ONE OF US MUST KNOW (SOONER OR LATER)** *CBS 202053*	**33**	5 wks
12 May 66	● **RAINY DAY WOMEN NOS. 12 & 35** *CBS 202307*	**7**	8 wks
21 Jul 66	**I WANT YOU** *CBS 202258*	**16**	9 wks
14 May 69	**I THREW IT ALL AWAY** *CBS 4219*	**30**	6 wks
13 Sep 69	● **LAY LADY LAY** *CBS 4434*	**5**	12 wks
10 Jul 71	**WATCHING THE RIVER FLOW** *CBS 7329*	**24**	9 wks
6 Oct 73	**KNOCKIN' ON HEAVEN'S DOOR** *CBS 1762*	**14**	9 wks
7 Feb 76	**HURRICANE** *CBS 3879*	**43**	4 wks
29 Jul 78	**BABY STOP CRYING** *CBS 6499*	**13**	11 wks
28 Oct 78	**IS YOUR LOVE IN VAIN** *CBS 6718*	**56**	3 wks

DYNASTY *US, male vocal/instrumental group*

Date	Title *Label Number*	Position	
13 Oct 79	**I DON'T WANT TO BE A FREAK** *Solar FB 1694*	**20**	13 wks
9 Aug 80	**I'VE JUST BEGUN TO LOVE YOU** *Solar SO 10*	**51**	4 wks

Ronnie DYSON *US, male vocalist*

Date	Title *Label Number*	Position	
4 Dec 71	**WHEN YOU GET RIGHT DOWN TO IT** *CBS 7449*	**34**	6 wks

E

EAGLES *US, male vocal/instrumental group*

Date	Title *Label Number*	Position	
9 Aug 75	**ONE OF THESE NIGHTS** *Asylum AYM 543*	**23**	7 wks
1 Nov 75	**LYIN' EYES** *Asylum AYM 548*	**23**	7 wks
6 Mar 76	**TAKE IT TO THE LIMIT** *Asylum K 13029*	**12**	7 wks
15 Jan 77	**NEW KID IN TOWN** *Asylum K 13069*	**20**	7 wks
16 Apr 77	● **HOTEL CALIFORNIA** *Asylum K 13079*	**8**	10 wks
16 Dec 78	**PLEASE COME HOME FOR CHRISTMAS** *Asylum K 13145*	**30**	5 wks
13 Oct 79	**HEARTACHE TONIGHT** *Asylum K 12394*	**40**	5 wks
1 Dec 79	**THE LONG RUN** *Elektra K 12404*	**66**	2 wks

EARL — See *BOB and EARL*

Date	Title *Label Number*	Position	

Robert EARL *UK, male vocalist*

25 Apr 58	**I MAY NEVER PASS THIS WAY AGAIN** *Philips PB 805*	**14**	13 wks
24 Oct 58	**MORE THAN EVER (COME PRIMA)** *Philips PB 867*	**26**	2 wks
21 Nov 58	**MORE THAN EVER (COME PRIMA)** (re-entry) *Philips PB 867*	**28**	2 wks
13 Feb 59	**WONDERFUL SECRET OF LOVE** *Philips PB 891*	**17**	10 wks

Charles EARLAND

US, male instrumentalist, keyboards

19 Aug 78	**LET THE MUSIC PLAY** *Mercury 6167 703*	**46**	5 wks

Hit features uncredited male vocalist.

EARLY MUSIC CONSORT, Directed by David Munrow *UK, instrumental group*

3 Apr 71	**MUSIC FROM "THE SIX WIVES OF HENRY VIII"** *BBC RESL 1*	**49**	1 wk

EARTH WIND AND FIRE

US, male vocal/instrumental group

12 Feb 77	**SATURDAY NITE** *CBS 4835*	**17**	9 wks
11 Feb 78	**FANTASY** *CBS 6056*	**14**	10 wks
13 May 78	**JUPITER** *CBS 6267*	**41**	5 wks
29 Jul 78	**MAGIC MIND** *CBS 6490*	**75**	1 wk
12 Aug 78	**MAGIC MIND** (re-entry) *CBS 6490*	**54**	4 wks
7 Oct 78	**GOT TO GET YOU INTO MY LIFE** *CBS 6553*	**33**	7 wks
9 Dec 78	● **SEPTEMBER** *CBS 6922*	**3**	13 wks
28 Jul 79	● **AFTER THE LOVE HAS GONE** *CBS 7721*	**4**	10 wks
6 Oct 79	**STAR** *CBS 7092*	**16**	8 wks
15 Dec 79	**CAN'T LET GO** *CBS 8077*	**46**	7 wks
8 Mar 80	**IN THE STONE** *CBS 8252*	**53**	3 wks
11 Oct 80	**LET ME TALK** *CBS 8982*	**29**	5 wks
20 Dec 80	**BACK ON THE ROAD** *CBS 9377*	**63**	4 wks
7 Nov 81	● **LET'S GROOVE** *CBS A 1679*	**3**	13 wks
6 Feb 82	**IVE HAD ENOUGH** *CBS A 1959*	**29**	6 wks

See also Earth Wind and Fire with the Emotions

EARTH WIND AND FIRE with the EMOTIONS

US, male vocal/instrumental group, female vocal group

12 May 79	● **BOOGIE WONDERLAND** *CBS 7292*	**4**	13 wks

See also Earth Wind and Fire , Emotions.

EAST OF EDEN *UK, male instrumental group*

17 Apr 71	● **JIG A JIG** *Deram DM 297*	**7**	12 wks

Sheena EASTON *UK, female vocalist*

5 Apr 80	**MODERN GIRL** *EMI 5042*	**56**	3 wks
19 Jul 80	● **9 TO 5** *EMI 5066*	**3**	15 wks
9 Aug 80	● **MODERN GIRL** (re-entry) *EMI 5042*	**8**	12 wks
25 Oct 80	**ONE MAN WOMAN** *EMI 5114*	**14**	6 wks
14 Feb 81	**TAKE MY TIME** *EMI 5135*	**44**	5 wks
2 May 81	**WHEN HE SHINES** *EMI 5166*	**12**	8 wks
27 Jun 81	● **FOR YOUR EYES ONLY** *EMI 5195*	**8**	13 wks
12 Sep 81	**JUST ANOTHER BROKEN HEART** *EMI 5232*	**33**	8 wks
4 Dec 81	**YOU COULD HAVE BEEN WITH ME** *EMI 5252*	**54**	3 wks
31 Jul 82	**MACHINERY** *EMI 5326*	**38**	5 wks

EASTSIDE CONNECTION

US, disco aggregation

8 Apr 78	**YOU'RE SO RIGHT FOR ME** *Creole CR 149*	**44**	3 wks

Clint EASTWOOD *US, male vocalist*

7 Feb 70	**I TALK TO THE TREES** *Paramount PARA 3004*	**18**	2 wks

This is the flip of Wand'rin Star *by By Lee Marvin and was listed with Marvin's A-side for 2 weeks only. See also Lee Marvin.*

EASYBEATS

Australia, male vocal/instrumental group

27 Oct 66	● **FRIDAY ON MY MIND** *United Artists UP 1157*	**6**	15 wks
10 Apr 68	**HELLO HOW ARE YOU** *United Artists UP 2209*	**20**	9 wks

ECHO and the BUNNYMEN

UK, male vocal/instrumental group

17 May 80	**RESCUE** *Korova KOW 1*	**62**	1 wk
18 Apr 81	**CROCODILES** *Korova ECHO 1*	**37**	4 wks
18 Jul 81	**A PROMISE** *Korova KOW 15*	**49**	4 wks
29 May 82	**THE BACK OF LOVE** *Korova KOW 24*	**19**	7 wks

Billy ECKSTINE *US, male vocalist*

12 Nov 54	● **NO ONE BUT YOU** *MGM 763*	**3**	17 wks
13 Feb 59	● **GIGI** *Mercury AMT 1018*	**8**	14 wks

See also Billy Eckstine and Sarah Vaughan.

Billy ECKSTINE and Sarah VAUGHAN

US, male/female vocal duo

27 Sep 57	**PASSING STRANGERS** *Mercury MT 164*	**22**	2 wks
12 Mar 69	**PASSING STRANGERS** (re-issue) *Mercury MF 1082*	**20**	15 wks

See also Billy Eckstine, Sarah Vaughan.

EDDIE and the HOTRODS

UK, male vocal/instrumental group

11 Sep 76	**LIVE AT THE MARQUEE** (EP) *Island IEP 2*	**43**	5 wks
13 Nov 76	**TEENAGE DEPRESSION** *Island WIP 6354*	**35**	4 wks
23 Apr 77	**I MIGHT BE LYING** *Island WIP 6388*	**44**	3 wks
13 Aug 77	● **DO ANYTHING YOU WANNA DO** *Island WIP 6401*	**9**	10 wks
21 Jan 78	**QUIT THIS TOWN** *Island WIP 6411*	**36**	4 wks

Do Anything You Wanna Do *credited simply to Rods. Tracks on EP: 96 Tears/ Get out of Denver/ Medley: Gloria/ Satisfaction.*

Top **EASYBEATS** Doctor Zhivago on their minds
Left **SHIRLEY ELLIS** 13 years between claps
Right **ELGINS** Both British hits for the group led by Johnny Dawson had been hits in the States in 1966
Above **BILLY ECKSTINE** No British charts before 1952 means that the seven million sellers between 1945 and 1951, for the man known as 'the fabulous Mr B', fail to make this book

Duane EDDY *US, male instrumentalist, guitar*

Date	Title *Label Number*	Position	Weeks
5 Sep 58	**REBEL ROUSER** *London HL 8669*	**19**	10 wks
2 Jan 59	**CANNONBALL** *London HL 8764*	**22**	4 wks
19 Jun 59	● **PETER GUNN THEME** *London HLW 8879*	**6**	10 wks
24 Jul 59	**YEP!** *London HLW 8879*	**17**	5 wks
4 Sep 59	**FORTY MILES OF BAD ROAD** *London HLW 8929*	**11**	9 wks
11 Sep 59	**PETER GUNN THEME** (re-entry) *London HLW 8879*	**27**	1 wk
18 Dec 59	**SOME KINDA EARTHQUAKE** *London HLW 9007*	**12**	5 wks
19 Feb 60	**BONNIE CAME BACK** *London HLW 9050*	**12**	10 wks
28 Apr 60	● **SHAZAM!** *London HLW 9104*	**4**	13 wks
21 Jul 60	● **BECAUSE THEY'RE YOUNG** *London HLW 9162*	**2**	18 wks
10 Nov 60	**KOMMOTION** *London HLW 9225*	**13**	10 wks
12 Jan 61	● **PEPE** *London HLW 9257*	**2**	14 wks
20 Apr 61	● **THEME FROM DIXIE** *London HLW 9324*	**7**	10 wks
22 Jun 61	**RING OF FIRE** *London HLW 9370*	**17**	10 wks
14 Sep 61	**DRIVIN' HOME** *London HLW 9406*	**30**	4 wks
5 Oct 61	**CARAVAN** *Parlophone R 4826*	**42**	3 wks
24 May 62	**DEEP IN THE HEART OF TEXAS** *RCA 1288*	**19**	8 wks
23 Aug 62	● **BALLAD OF PALADIN** *RCA 1300*	**10**	10 wks
8 Nov 62	● **DANCE WITH THE GUITAR MAN** *RCA 1316*	**4**	16 wks
14 Feb 63	**BOSS GUITAR** *RCA 1329*	**27**	8 wks
30 May 63	**LONELY BOY LONELY GUITAR** *RCA 1344*	**35**	4 wks
29 Aug 63	**YOUR BABY'S GONE SURFIN'** *RCA 1357*	**49**	1 wk
8 Mar 75	● **PLAY ME LIKE YOU PLAY YOUR GUITAR** *GTO GT 11*	**9**	9 wks

The London Hits featured Duane Eddy and the Rebels. Dance With The Guitar Man, Boss Guitar *and* Play Me Like You Play Your Guitar *featured Duane Eddy and the Rebelettes.*

Randy EDELMAN *US, male vocalist*

Date	Title *Label Number*	Position	Weeks
6 Mar 76	**CONCRETE AND CLAY** *20th Century BTC 2261*	**11**	7 wks
18 Sep 76	**UPTOWN UPTEMPO WOMAN** *20th Century BTC 2225*	**25**	7 wks
15 Jan 77	**YOU** *20th Century BTC 2253*	**49**	2 wks

EDISON LIGHTHOUSE

UK, male vocal/instrumental group

Date	Title *Label Number*	Position	Weeks
24 Jan 70	★ **LOVE GROWS (WHERE MY ROSEMARY GOES)** *Bell 1091*	**1**	12 wks
30 Jan 71	**IT'S UP TO YOU PETULA** *Bell 1136*	**49**	1 wk

Dave EDMUNDS

UK, male vocalist/multi-instrumentalist

Date	Title *Label Number*	Position	Weeks
21 Nov 70	★ **I HEAR YOU KNOCKING** *MAM 1*	**1**	14 wks
20 Jan 73	● **BABY I LOVE YOU** *Rockfield ROC 1*	**8**	13 wks
9 Jun 73	● **BORN TO BE WITH YOU** *Rockfield ROC 2*	**5**	12 wks
2 Jul 77	**I KNEW THE BRIDE** *Swan Song SSK 19411*	**26**	8 wks
30 Jun 79	● **GIRLS TALK** *Swan Song SSK 19418*	**4**	11 wks
22 Sep 79	**QUEEN OF HEARTS** *Swansong SSK 19419*	**11**	9 wks
24 Nov 79	**CRAWLING FROM THE WRECKAGE** *Swan Song SSK 19420*	**59**	4 wks
9 Feb 80	**SINGING THE BLUES** *Swan Song SSK 19422*	**28**	8 wks
28 Mar 81	**ALMOST SATURDAY NIGHT** *Swan Song SSK 19424*	**58**	3 wks

See also Dave Edmunds and Stray cats

Dave EDMUNDS and the STRAY CATS

UK, male vocalist/instrumentalists and male vocal/instrumental group

Date	Title *Label Number*	Position	Weeks
20 Jun 81	**THE RACE IS ON** *Swansong SSK 19425*	**34**	6 wks

See also Dave Edmunds, Stray Cats.

Alton EDWARDS *UK, male vocalist*

Date	Title *Label Number*	Position	Weeks
9 Jan 82	**I JUST WANNA (SPEND SOME TIME WITH YOU)** *Streetwave STRA 1897*	**20**	9 wks

Rupie EDWARDS *Jamaica, male vocalist*

Date	Title *Label Number*	Position	Weeks
23 Nov 74	● **IRE FEELINGS (SKANGA)** *Cactus CT 38*	**9**	10 wks
8 Feb 75	**LEGO SKANGA** *Cactus CT 51*	**32**	6 wks

Tommy EDWARDS *US, male vocalist*

Date	Title *Label Number*	Position	Weeks
3 Oct 58	★ **IT'S ALL IN THE GAME** *MGM 989*	**1**	17 wks
7 Aug 59	**MY MELANCHOLY BABY** *MGM 1020*	**29**	1 wk

Donnie ELBERT *US, male vocalist*

Date	Title *Label Number*	Position	Weeks
8 Jan 72	● **WHERE DID OUR LOVE GO?** *London HL 10352*	**8**	10 wks
26 Feb 72	**I CAN'T HELP MYSELF** *Avco 6105 009*	**11**	10 wks
29 Apr 72	**LITTLE PIECE OF LEATHER** *London HL 10370*	**27**	9 wks

ELECTRIC LIGHT ORCHESTRA

UK, male vocal/instrumental group

Date	Title *Label Number*	Position	Weeks
29 Jul 72	● **10538 OVERTURE** *Harvest HAR 5053*	**9**	8 wks
27 Jan 73	● **ROLL OVER BEETHOVEN** *Harvest HAR 5063*	**6**	10 wks
6 Oct 73	**SHOWDOWN** *Harvest HAR 5077*	**12**	10 wks
9 Mar 74	**MA-MA-MA-BELLE** *Warner Bros K 16349*	**22**	8 wks
10 Jan 76	● **EVIL WOMAN** *Jet 764*	**10**	8 wks
3 Jul 76	**STRANGE MAGIC** *Jet 779*	**38**	3 wks
13 Nov 76	● **LIVIN' THING** *Jet UP 36184*	**4**	12 wks
19 Feb 77	● **ROCKARIA!** *Jet UP 36209*	**9**	9 wks
21 May 77	● **TELEPHONE LINE** *Jet UP 36254*	**8**	10 wks
9 Oct 77	**TURN TO STONE** *Jet UP 36313*	**18**	12 wks
8 Jan 78	● **MR. BLUE SKY** *Jet UP 36342*	**6**	11 wks
10 Jun 78	● **WILD WEST HERO** *Jet JET 109*	**6**	14 wks
7 Oct 78	● **SWEET TALKIN' WOMAN** *Jet 121*	**6**	9 wks
9 Dec 78	**ELO EP** (EP) *Jet ELO 1*	**34**	8 wks
19 May 79	● **SHINE A LITTLE LOVE** *Jet 144*	**6**	10 wks
21 Jul 79	● **THE DIARY OF HORACE WIMP** *Jet 150*	**8**	9 wks
1 Sep 79	● **DON'T BRING ME DOWN** *Jet 153*	**3**	9 wks
17 Nov 79	● **CONFUSION/ LAST TRAIN TO LONDON** *Jet 166*	**8**	10 wks
24 May 80	**I'M ALIVE** *Jet 179*	**20**	9 wks
2 Aug 80	**ALL OVER THE WORLD** *Jet 195*	**11**	8 wks
22 Nov 80	**DON'T WALK AWAY** *Jet 7004*	**21**	10 wks
1 Aug 81	● **HOLD ON TIGHT** *Jet 7011*	**4**	12 wks
24 Oct 81	**TWILIGHT** *Jet 7015*	**30**	7 wks
9 Jan 82	**TICKET TO THE MOON/HERE IS THE NEWS** *Jet 7018*	**24**	8 wks

Here Is The News *listed from 16 Jan 82. See also Olivia Newton-John and Electric Light Orchestra.*

Date	Title *Label Number*	Position		Date	Title *Label Number*	Position

ELECTRIC PRUNES

US, male vocal/instrumental group

9 Feb 67 **I HAD TOO MUCH TO DREAM LAST NIGHT** *Reprise RS 20532* **49** 1 wk
11 May 67 **GET ME TO THE WORLD ON TIME** *Reprise RS 20564* **42** 4 wks

ELECTRONICAS

Belgium, male instrumental group

19 Sep 81 **ORIGINAL BIRD DANCE** *Polydor POSP 360* **22** 8 wks

ELEGANTS *US, male vocal group*

26 Sep 58 **LITTLE STAR** *HMV POP 520* **25** 2 wks

ELGINS *US, male/female vocal group*

1 May 71 ● **HEAVEN MUST HAVE SENT YOU** *Tamla Motown TMG 771* **3** 13 wks
9 Oct 71 **PUT YOURSELF IN MY PLACE** *Tamla Motown TMG 787* **28** 7 wks

ELIAS and his ZIGZAG JIVE FLUTES

South Africa, male instrumental group

25 Apr 58 ● **TOM HARK** *Columbia DB 4109* **2** 14 wks

Yvonne ELLIMAN *US, female vocalist*

29 Jan 72 **I DON'T KNOW HOW TO LOVE HIM** *MCA MMKS 5077* **47** 1 wk
6 Nov 76 ● **LOVE ME** *RSO 2090 205* **6** 13 wks
7 May 77 **HELLO STRANGER** *RSO 2090 236* **26** 5 wks
13 Aug 77 **I CAN'T GET YOU OUT OF MY MIND** *RSO 2090 251* **17** 13 wks
6 May 78 ● **IF I CAN'T HAVE YOU** *RSO 2090 266* **4** 12 wks

I Don't Know How To Love Him *was one of 4 tracks on a Maxi-Single, 2 of which were credited during the disc's one week on the chart. The other track credited was* Superstar *by Murray Head. See also Murray Head.*

Duke ELLINGTON *US, orchestra*

5 Mar 54 ● **SKIN DEEP** *Philips PB 243* **7** 4 wks

Ray ELLINGTON *UK, orchestra*

15 Nov 62 **THE MADISON** *Ember S 102* **41** 2 wks
20 Dec 62 **THE MADISON** (re-entry) *Ember S 102* **36** 2 wks

Bern ELLIOTT and the FENMEN

UK, male vocalist, male vocal/instrumental backing group

21 Nov 63 **MONEY** *Decca F 11770* **14** 13 wks
19 Mar 64 **NEW ORLEANS** *Decca F 11852* **24** 9 wks

Shirley ELLIS *US, female vocalist*

6 May 65 ● **THE CLAPPING SONG** *London HLR 9961* **6** 13 wks
8 Jul 78 **THE CLAPPING SONG**(EP) *MCA MCEP 1* **59** 4 wks

Tracks on Clapping Song EP: *The Clapping Song/ Ever See a Diver Kiss His Wife While The Bubbles Bounce Above The Water/ The Name Game/ The Nitty Gritty. The Clapping Song itself qualifies as a re-issue*

Keith EMERSON *UK, male instrumentalist, piano*

10 Apr 76 **HONKY TONK TRAIN BLUES** *Manticore K 13513* **21** 5 wks

See also Emerson, Lake and Palmer.

EMERSON, LAKE AND PALMER

UK, male instrumental group

4 Jun 77 ● **FANFARE FOR THE COMMON MAN** *Atlantic K 10946* **2** 13 wks

See also Keith Emerson, Greg Lake.

Dick EMERY *UK, male vocalist*

26 Feb 69 **IF YOU LOVE HER** *Pye 7N 17644* **32** 4 wks
13 Jan 73 **YOU ARE AWFUL** *Pye 7N 45202* **43** 4 wks

EMOTIONS *US, female vocal group*

10 Sep 77 ● **BEST OF MY LOVE** *CBS 5555* **4** 10 wks
24 Dec 77 **I DON'T WANNA LOSE YOUR LOVE** *CBS 5819* **40** 5 wks

See also Earth Wind and Fire with the Emotions.

ENGLAND DAN and John Ford COLEY

US, male vocal duo

25 Sep 76 **I'D REALLY LOVE TO SEE YOU TONIGHT** *Atlantic K 10810* **26** 7 wks
23 Jun 79 **LOVE IS THE ANSWER** *Big Tree K 11296* **45** 5 wks

ENGLAND SISTERS *UK, female vocal group*

17 Mar 60 **HEARTBEAT** *HMV POP 710* **33** 1 wk

ENGLAND WORLD CUP SQUAD

UK, male football team vocalists

18 Apr 70 ★ **BACK HOME** *Pye 7N 17920* **1** 16 wks
15 Aug 70 **BACK HOME** (re-entry) *Pye 7N 17920* **46** 1 wk
10 Apr 82 ● **THIS TIME (WE'LL GET IT RIGHT)/ENGLAND WE'LL FLY THE FLAG** *England ER 1* **2** 13 wks

Scott ENGLISH *US, male vocalist*

9 Oct 71 **BRANDY** *Horse HOSS 7* **12** 10 wks

ENIGMA *UK, male vocal/instrumental group*

23 May 81 **AIN'T NO STOPPING** *Creole CR 9* **11** 8 wks
8 Aug 81 **I LOVE MUSIC** *Creole CR 14* **25** 7 wks

Date	Title *Label Number*	Position	

EQUALS *UK, male vocal/instrumental group*

Date	Title *Label Number*	Position	
21 Feb 68	**I GET SO EXCITED** *President PT 180*	**44**	4 wks
1 May 68	**BABY COME BACK** *President PT 135*	**50**	1 wk
15 May 68	★ **BABY COME BACK** (re-entry) *President PT 135*	**1**	17 wks
21 Aug 68	**LAUREL & HARDY** *President PT 200*	**35**	5 wks
27 Nov 68	**SOFTLY SOFTLY** *President PT 222*	**48**	3 wks
2 Apr 69	**MICHAEL & THE SLIPPER TREE** *President PT 240*	**24**	7 wks
30 Jul 69	● **VIVA BOBBY JOE** *President PT 260*	**6**	14 wks
27 Dec 69	**RUB A DUB DUB** *President PT 275*	**34**	7 wks
19 Dec 70	● **BLACK SKIN BLUE EYED BOYS** *President PT 325*	**9**	11 wks

EROTIC DRUM BAND

Canada, male/female vocal/instrumental group

Date	Title *Label Number*	Position	
9 Jun 79	**LOVE DISCO STYLE** *Scope SC 1*	**47**	3 wks

ERUPTION

US, male/female vocal/instrumental group

Date	Title *Label Number*	Position	
18 Feb 78	● **I CAN'T STAND THE RAIN** *Atlantic K 11068*	**5**	11 wks
21 Apr 79	● **ONE WAY TICKET** *Atlantic/Hansa K 11266*	**9**	10 wks

I Can't Stand The Rain *has credit Eruption featuring Precious Wilson*

ESCORTS *UK, male vocal/instrumental group*

Date	Title *Label Number*	Position	
2 Jul 64	**THE ONE TO CRY** *Fontana TF 474*	**49**	2 wks

ESQUIRES *US, male vocal group*

Date	Title *Label Number*	Position	
31 Jan 58	**LOVE ME FOREVER** *London HLO 8533*	**23**	2 wks

ESSEX *US, male/female vocal group*

Date	Title *Label Number*	Position	
8 Aug 63	**EASIER SAID THAN DONE** *Columbia DB 7077*	**41**	5 wks

David ESSEX *UK, male vocalist*

Date	Title *Label Number*	Position	
18 Aug 73	● **ROCK ON** *CBS 1693*	**3**	11 wks
10 Nov 73	● **LAMPLIGHT** *CBS 1902*	**7**	15 wks
11 May 74	**AMERICA** *CBS 2176*	**32**	5 wks
12 Oct 74	★ **GONNA MAKE YOU A STAR** *CBS 2492*	**1**	17 wks
14 Dec 74	● **STARDUST** *CBS 2828*	**7**	10 wks
5 Jul 75	● **ROLLIN' STONE** *CBS 3425*	**5**	7 wks
13 Sep 75	★ **HOLD ME CLOSE** *CBS 3572*	**1**	10 wks
6 Dec 75	**IF I COULD** *CBS 3776*	**13**	8 wks
20 Mar 76	**CITY LIGHTS** *CBS 4050*	**24**	4 wks
16 Oct 76	**COMING HOME** *CBS 4486*	**24**	6 wks
17 Sep 77	**COOL OUT TONIGHT** *CBS 5495*	**23**	6 wks
11 Mar 78	**STAY WITH ME BABY** *CBS 6063*	**45**	5 wks
19 Aug 78	● **OH WHAT A CIRCUS** *Mercury 6007 185*	**3**	11 wks
21 Oct 78	**BRAVE NEW WORLD** *CBS 6705*	**55**	3 wks
3 Mar 79	**IMPERIAL WIZARD** *Mercury 6007 202*	**32**	8 wks
5 Apr 80	● **SILVER DREAM MACHINE (PART 1)** *Mercury BIKE 1*	**4**	11 wks
14 Jun 80	**HOT LOVE** *Mercury HOT 11*	**57**	4 wks
26 Jun 82	**ME AND MY GIRL (NIGHT-CLUBBING)** *Mercury/Phonogram MER 107*	**13**	10 wks
11 Dec 82	● **A WINTER'S TALE** *Mercury/Phonogram MER 127*	**7**†	3 wks

Don ESTELLE — See *Windsor DAVIES and Don ESTELLE*

ETHIOPIANS

Jamaica, male vocal/instrumental group

Date	Title *Label Number*	Position	
13 Sep 67	**TRAIN TO SKAVILLE** *Rio RIO 130*	**40**	6 wks

Cleveland ETON *UK, male vocalist*

Date	Title *Label Number*	Position	
23 Sep 78	**BAMA BOOGIE WOOGIE** *Gull GULS 63*	**35**	6 wks

Tony ETORIA *UK, male vocalist*

Date	Title *Label Number*	Position	
4 Jun 77	**I CAN PROVE IT** *GTO GT 89*	**21**	8 wks

EURYTHMICS

UK, male/female vocal/instrumental group.

Date	Title *Label Number*	Position	
4 Jul 81	**NEVER GONNA CRY AGAIN** *RCA 68*	**63**	3 wks
20 Nov 82	**LOVE IS A STRANGER** *RCA DA 1*	**54**	4 wks

EVANGEL TEMPLE CHOIR — See *Johnny CASH*

EVANS — See *ZAGER and EVANS*

Maureen EVANS *UK, female vocalist*

Date	Title *Label Number*	Position	
22 Jan 60	**THE BIG HURT** *Oriole CB 1533*	**26**	2 wks
17 Mar 60	**LOVE KISSES & HEARTACHES** *Oriole CB 1540*	**44**	1 wk
2 Jun 60	**PAPER ROSES** *Oriole CB 1550*	**40**	5 wks
29 Nov 62	● **LIKE I DO** *Oriole CB 1763*	**3**	18 wks
27 Feb 64	**I LOVE HOW YOU LOVE ME** *Oriole CB 1906*	**34**	10 wks
14 May 64	**I LOVE HOW YOU LOVE ME** (re-entry) *Oriole CB 1906*	**50**	1 wk

Paul EVANS *US, male vocalist*

Date	Title *Label Number*	Position	
27 Nov 59	**SEVEN LITTLE GIRLS SITTING IN THE BACK SEAT** *London HLL 8968*	**25**	1 wk
31 Mar 60	**MIDNIGHT SPECIAL** *London HLL 9045*	**41**	1 wk
16 Dec 78	● **HELLO THIS IS JOANIE (THE TELEPHONE ANSWERING MACHINE SONG)** *Spring 2066 932*	**6**	12 wks

Seven Little Girls Sitting in the Back Seat *credits Paul Evans and The Curls, The Curls being a female vocal group.*

EVASIONS

UK, male/female vocal/instrumental group

Date	Title *Label Number*	Position	
13 Jun 81	**WIKKA WRAP** *Groove GP 107*	**20**	8 wks

Betty EVERETT *US, female vocalist*

Date	Title *Label Number*	Position	
14 Jan 65	**GETTING MIGHTY CROWDED** *Fontana TF 520*	**29**	7 wks
30 Oct 68	**IT'S IN HIS KISS** *President PT 215*	**34**	7 wks

Above **EXPLOITED** Exploited – to be utilised or worked for someone else's profit or purpose

Left **KENNY EVERETT** Radio and TV personality, Everett teamed up with ex Manfred Mann man Mike Vickers to produce the title track of Kenny's wacky radio serial of the same name

Below **MARIANNE FAITHFULL** Her first and fifth hits were written by the Rolling Stones and Beatles respectively

Right **DAVID ESSEX** Won favour with one of this book's co-authors by his intelligent choice of lyric for his final hit of 1982.

Date Title *Label Number* Position

Date Title *Label Number* Position

Kenny EVERETT and Mike VICKERS

UK, male vocalist and multi-instrumentalist

Date		Title *Label Number*	Position	Weeks
12 Nov 77		**CAPTAIN KREMMEN (RETRIBUTION)** *DJM DJS 10810*	**32**	4 wks

Phil EVERLY *US, male vocalist*

Date		Title *Label Number*	Position	Weeks
6 Nov 82		**LOUISE** *Capitol CL 266*	**47**	6 wks

See also Everly Brothers

EVERLY BROTHERS *US, male vocal duo*

Date		Title *Label Number*	Position	Weeks
12 Jul 57	●	**BYE BYE LOVE** *London HLA 8440*	**6**	16 wks
8 Nov 57	●	**WAKE UP LITTLE SUSIE** *London HLA 8498*	**2**	13 wks
23 May 58	★	**ALL I HAVE TO DO IS DREAM/ CLAUDETTE** *London HLA 8618*	**1**	21 wks
12 Sep 58	●	**BIRD DOG** *London HLA 8685*	**2**	16 wks
23 Jan 59	●	**PROBLEMS** *London HLA 8781*	**6**	12 wks
22 May 59		**TAKE A MESSAGE TO MARY** *London HLA 8863*	**29**	1 wk
29 May 59		**POOR JENNY** *London HLA 8863*	**14**	11 wks
19 Jun 59		**TAKE A MESSAGE TO MARY** (re-entry) *London HLA 8863*	**27**	1 wk
3 Jul 59		**TAKE A MESSAGE TO MARY** (2nd re-entry) *London HLA 8863*	**20**	8 wks
11 Sep 59	●	**('TIL) I KISSED YOU** *London HLA 8934*	**2**	15 wks
12 Feb 60		**LET IT BE ME** *London HLA 9039*	**13**	5 wks
31 Mar 60		**LET IT BE ME** (re-entry) *London HLA 9039*	**26**	4 wks
14 Apr 60	★	**CATHY'S CLOWN** *Warner Bros. WB 1*	**1**	18 wks
14 Jul 60	●	**WHEN WILL I BE LOVED** *London HLA 9157*	**4**	16 wks
22 Sep 60	●	**LUCILLE/ SO SAD (TO WATCH GOOD LOVE GO BAD)** *Warner Bros. WB 19*	**4**	15 wks
15 Dec 60		**LIKE STRANGERS** *London HLA 9250*	**11**	10 wks
9 Feb 61	★	**WALK RIGHT BACK** *Warner Bros. WB 33*	**1**	16 wks
15 Jun 61	★	**TEMPTATION** *Warner Bros. WB 42*	**1**	15 wks
5 Oct 61		**MUSKRAT** *Warner Bros. WB 50*	**20**	6 wks
18 Jan 62	●	**CRYIN' IN THE RAIN** *Warner Bros. WB 56*	**6**	15 wks
17 May 62		**HOW CAN I MEET HER** *Warner Bros. WB 67*	**12**	10 wks
25 Oct 62		**NO ONE CAN MAKE MY SUNSHINE SMILE** *Warner Bros. WB 79*	**11**	11 wks
21 Mar 63		**SO IT WILL ALWAYS BE** *Warner Bros. WB 94*	**23**	11 wks
13 Jun 63		**IT'S BEEN NICE** *Warner Bros. WB 99*	**26**	5 wks
17 Oct 63		**THE GIRL SANG THE BLUES** *Warner Bros. WB 109*	**25**	9 wks
16 Jul 64		**FERRIS WHEEL** *Warner Bros. WB 135*	**22**	10 wks
3 Dec 64		**GONE GONE GONE** *Warner Bros. WB 146*	**36**	7 wks
6 May 65		**THAT'LL BE THE DAY** *Warner Bros. WB 158*	**30**	4 wks
20 May 65	●	**THE PRICE OF LOVE** *Warner Bros. WB 161*	**2**	14 wks
26 Aug 65		**I'LL NEVER GET OVER YOU** *Warner Bros. WB 5639*	**35**	5 wks
21 Oct 65		**LOVE IS STRANGE** *Warner Bros. WB 5649*	**11**	9 wks
8 May 68		**IT'S MY TIME** *Warner Bros. WB 7192*	**39**	6 wks

All I Have To Do Is Dream *was listed without* Claudette *for its first week on the chart, but from 30 May 58 both sides were charted for 20 more weeks.*

EXCITERS *US, male/female vocal group*

Date		Title *Label Number*	Position	Weeks
21 Feb 63		**TELL HIM** *United Artists UP 1011*	**46**	1 wk
4 Oct 75		**REACHING FOR THE BEST** *20th Century BTC 1005*	**31**	6 wks

EXILE *US, male vocal/instrumental group*

Date		Title *Label Number*	Position	Weeks
19 Aug 78	●	**KISS YOU ALL OVER** *RAK 279*	**6**	12 wks
12 May 79		**HOW COULD THIS GO WRONG** *RAK 293*	**67**	2 wks
12 Sep 81		**HEART AND SOUL** *RAK 333*	**54**	4 wks

EXPLOITED *UK, male vocal/instrumental group*

Date		Title *Label Number*	Position	Weeks
18 Apr 81		**DOGS OF WAR** *Secret SHH 110*	**63**	4 wks
17 Oct 81		**DEAD CITIES** *Secret SHH 120*	**31**	5 wks
8 May 82		**ATTACK** *Secret SHH 130*	**50**	3 wks

see also Exploited and Anti-Pasti

EXPLOITED and ANTI-PASTI

UK, male vocal/instrumental group

Date		Title *Label Number*	Position	Weeks
5 Dec 81		**DON'T LET 'EM GRIND YOU DOWN** *Superville EXP 1003*	**70**	1 wk

see also Exploited

EXPRESSOS

UK, male/female vocal/instrumental group

Date		Title *Label Number*	Position	Weeks
21 Jun 80		**HEY GIRL** *WEA K 18246*	**60**	3 wks
14 Mar 81		**TANGO IN MONO** *WEA K 18431*	**70**	2 wks

F

Shelley FABARES *US, female vocalist*

Date		Title *Label Number*	Position	Weeks
26 Apr 62		**JOHNNY ANGEL** *Pye International 7N 25132*	**41**	4 wks

FABIAN *US, male vocalist*

Date		Title *Label Number*	Position	Weeks
10 Mar 60		**HOUND DOG MAN** *HMV POP 695*	**46**	1 wk

FACES *UK, male vocal/instrumental group*

Date		Title *Label Number*	Position	Weeks
18 Dec 71	●	**STAY WITH ME** *Warner Bros. K 16136*	**6**	14 wks
17 Feb 73	●	**CINDY INCIDENTALLY** *Warner Bros. K 16247*	**2**	9 wks
8 Dec 73	●	**POOL HALL RICHARD/ I WISH IT WOULD RAIN** *Warner Bros. K 16341*	**8**	11 wks
7 Dec 74		**YOU CAN MAKE ME DANCE SING OR ANYTHING** *Warner Bros. K 16494*	**12**	9 wks
4 Jun 77		**THE FACES** (EP) *Riva 8*	**41**	3 wks

Tracks on Faces EP: *Memphis/ You Can Make Me Dance Sing or Anything/ Stay With Me/ Cindy Incidentally.* You Can Make Me Dance Sing or Anything *credited to Rod Stewart and the Faces. See also Rod Stewart, Small Faces.*

Yvonne FAIR *US, female vocalist*

Date		Title *Label Number*	Position	Weeks
24 Jan 76	●	**IT SHOULD HAVE BEEN ME** *Tamla Motown TMG 1013*	**5**	11 wks

FAIR WEATHER

UK, male vocal/instrumental group

Date		Title *Label Number*	Position	Weeks
18 Jul 70	●	**NATURAL SINNER** *RCA 1977*	**6**	12 wks

Date	Title *Label Number*	Position	

Date Title *Label Number* Position

FAIRPORT CONVENTION

UK, male/female vocal/instrumental group

23 Jul 69	**SI TU DOIS PARTIR** *Island WIP 6064*	**21**	8 wks
27 Sep 69	**SI TU DOIS PARTIR** (re-entry) *Island WIP 6064*	**49**	1 wk

Andy FAIRWEATHER-LOW

UK, male vocalist

21 Sep 74	● **REGGAE TUNE** *A & M AMS 7129*	**10**	8 wks
6 Dec 75	● **WIDE EYED AND LEGLESS** *A & M AMS 7202*	**6**	10 wks

Adam FAITH *UK, male vocalist*

20 Nov 59	★ **WHAT DO YOU WANT** *Parlophone R 4591*	**1**	15 wks
22 Jan 60	★ **POOR ME** *Parlophone R 4623*	**1**	17 wks
10 Mar 60	**WHAT DO YOU WANT** (re-entry) *Parlophone R 4591*	**24**	4 wks
14 Apr 60	● **SOMEONE ELSE'S BABY** *Parlophone R 4643*	**2**	13 wks
30 Jun 60	● **WHEN JOHNNY COMES MARCHING HOME/ MADE YOU** *Parlophone R 4665*	**5**	13 wks
15 Sep 60	● **HOW ABOUT THAT** *Parlophone R 4689*	**4**	14 wks
17 Nov 60	● **LONELY PUP (IN A CHRISTMAS SHOP)** *Parlophone R 4708*	**4**	11 wks
9 Feb 61	● **THIS IS IT/ WHO AM I** *Parlophone R 4735*	**5**	14 wks
27 Apr 61	**EASY GOING ME** *Parlophone R 4766*	**12**	10 wks
20 Jul 61	**DON'T YOU KNOW IT** *Parlophone R 4807*	**12**	10 wks
26 Oct 61	● **THE TIME HAS COME** *Parlophone R 4837*	**4**	14 wks
18 Jan 62	**LONESOME** *Parlophone R 4864*	**12**	9 wks
3 May 62	● **AS YOU LIKE IT** *Parlophone R 4896*	**5**	15 wks
30 Aug 62	● **DON'T THAT BEAT ALL** *Parlophone R 4930*	**8**	11 wks
13 Dec 62	**BABY TAKE A BOW** *Parlophone R 4964*	**22**	6 wks
31 Jan 63	**WHAT NOW** *Parlophone R 4990*	**31**	5 wks
11 Jul 63	**WALKIN' TALL** *Parlophone R 5039*	**23**	6 wks
19 Sep 63	● **THE FIRST TIME** *Parlophone R 5061*	**5**	13 wks
12 Dec 63	**WE ARE IN LOVE** *Parlophone R 5091*	**11**	12 wks
12 Mar 64	**IF HE TELLS YOU** *Parlophone R 5109*	**25**	9 wks
28 May 64	**I LOVE BEING IN LOVE WITH YOU** *Parlophone R 5138*	**33**	6 wks
26 Nov 64	**MESSAGE TO MARTHA (KENTUCKY BLUEBIRD)** *Parlophone R 5201*	**12**	11 wks
11 Feb 65	**STOP FEELING SORRY FOR YOURSELF** *Parlophone R 5235*	**23**	6 wks
17 Jun 65	**SOMEONE'S TAKEN MARIA AWAY** *Parlophone R 5289*	**34**	5 wks
20 Oct 66	**CHERYL'S GOIN' HOME** *Parlophone R 5516*	**46**	2 wks

The following hits featured the Roulettes, UK, male vocal/instrumental group, backing Adam Faith: The First Time, We Are In Love, If He Tells You, I Love Being In Love With You.

Horace FAITH *Jamaica, male vocalist*

12 Sep 70	**BLACK PEARL** *Trojan TR 7790*	**13**	10 wks

Percy FAITH *US, orchestra*

10 Mar 60	● **THEME FROM "A SUMMER PLACE"** *Philips PB 989*	**2**	30 wks

FAITH, HOPE and CHARITY

US, male/female vocal group

31 Jan 76	**JUST ONE LOOK** *RCA 2632*	**38**	4 wks

Marianne FAITHFULL *UK, female vocalist*

13 Aug 64	● **AS TEARS GO BY** *Decca F 11923*	**9**	13 wks
18 Feb 65	● **COME AND STAY WITH ME** *Decca F 12075*	**4**	13 wks
6 May 65	● **THIS LITTLE BIRD** *Decca F 12162*	**6**	11 wks
22 Jul 65	● **SUMMER NIGHTS** *Decca F 12193*	**10**	10 wks
4 Nov 65	**YESTERDAY** *Decca F 12268*	**36**	4 wks
9 Mar 67	**IS THIS WHAT I GET FOR LOVING YOU** *Decca F 22524*	**43**	2 wks
24 Nov 79	**THE BALLAD OF LUCY JORDAN** *Island WIP 6491*	**48**	6 wks

FAME and PRICE TOGETHER

UK, male vocal/instrumental duo - piano

10 Apr 71	**ROSETTA** *CBS 7108*	**11**	10 wks

See also Georgie Fame, Alan Price.

Georgie FAME *UK, male vocalist*

17 Dec 64	★ **YEH YEH** *Columbia DB 7428*	**1**	12 wks
4 Mar 65	**IN THE MEANTIME** *Columbia DB 7494*	**22**	8 wks
29 Jul 65	**LIKE WE USED TO BE** *Columbia DB 7633*	**33**	7 wks
28 Oct 65	**SOMETHING** *Columbia DB 7727*	**23**	7 wks
23 Jun 66	★ **GET AWAY** *Columbia DB 7946*	**1**	11 wks
22 Sep 66	**SUNNY** *Columbia DB 8015*	**13**	8 wks
22 Dec 66	**SITTING IN THE PARK** *Columbia DB 8096*	**12**	10 wks
23 Mar 67	**BECAUSE I LOVE YOU** *CBS 202587*	**15**	8 wks
13 Sep 67	**TRY MY WORLD** *CBS 2945*	**37**	5 wks
13 Dec 67	★ **BALLAD OF BONNIE & CLYDE** *CBS 3124*	**1**	13 wks
9 Jul 69	**PEACEFUL** *CBS 4295*	**16**	9 wks
13 Dec 69	**SEVENTH SON** *CBS 4659*	**25**	7 wks

All Columbia hits except Sunny *credit The Blue Flames backing Georgie Fame. See also Fame and Price Together.*

FAMILY *UK, male vocal/instrumental group*

1 Nov 69	**NO MULE'S FOOL** *Reprise RS 27001*	**29**	7 wks
22 Aug 70	**STRANGE BAND** *Reprise RS 27009*	**11**	12 wks
17 Jul 71	● **IN MY OWN TIME** *Reprise K 14090*	**4**	13 wks
23 Sep 72	**BURLESQUE** *Reprise K 14196*	**13**	12 wks

FAMILY COOKIN' — See *LIMMIE and the FAMILY COOKIN'*

FAMILY DOGG *UK, male/female vocal group*

28 May 69	● **WAY OF LIFE** *Bell 1055*	**6**	14 wks

FAMILY STONE — See *SLY and the FAMILY STONE*

FAMOUS FLAMES — See *James BROWN*

FANTASTIC FOUR *US, male vocal group*

24 Feb 79	**B.Y.O.F. (BRING YOUR OWN FUNK)** *Atlantic LV 14*	**62**	4 wks

FANTASTICS *US, male vocal group*

27 Mar 71	● **SOMETHING OLD, SOMETHING NEW** *Bell 1141*	**9**	12 wks

Date **Title** *Label Number* **Position**

Don FARDON *UK, male vocalist*

18 Apr 70 **BELFAST BOY** *Young Blood YB 1010* **32** 5 wks
10 Oct 70 ● **INDIAN RESERVATION** *Young Blood YB 1015* **3** 17 wks

Chris FARLOWE *UK, male vocalist*

27 Jan 66 **THINK** *Immediate IM 023* **49** 1 wk
10 Feb 66 **THINK** (re-entry) *Immediate IM 023* **37** 2 wks
23 Jun 66 ★ **OUT OF TIME** *Immediate IM 035* **1** 13 wks
27 Oct 66 **RIDE ON BABY** *Immediate IM 038* **31** 7 wks
16 Feb 67 **MY WAY OF GIVING IN** *Immediate IM 041* **48** 1 wk
29 Jun 67 **MOANIN'** *Immediate IM 056* **46** 2 wks
13 Dec 67 **HANDBAGS & GLADRAGS** *Immediate IM 065* **33** 6 wks
27 Sep 75 **OUT OF TIME** (re-issue) *Immediate IMS 101* **44** 4 wks

Joe FARRELL *US, male instrumentalist, saxophone*

16 Dec 78 **NIGHT DANCING** *Warner Bros. LV 2* **57** 4 wks

Gene FARROW and G.F. BAND

UK, male vocal/instrumental group

1 Apr 78 **MOVE YOUR BODY** *Magnet MAG 109* **33** 7 wks
5 Aug 78 **DON'T STOP NOW** *Magnet MAG 125* **71** 1 wk
19 Aug 78 **DON'T STOP NOW** (re-entry) *Magnet MAG 125* **74** 1 wk

FASCINATIONS *US, female vocal group*

3 Jul 71 **GIRLS ARE OUT TO GET YOU** *Mojo 2092 004* **32** 6 wks

FASHION *UK, male vocal/instrumental group*

3 Apr 82 **STREETPLAYER (MECHANIK)** *Arista ARIST 456* **46** 5 wks
21 Aug 82 **LOVE SHADOW** *Arista ARIST 483* **51** 5 wks

Susan FASSBENDER

17 Jan 81 **TWILIGHT CAFE** *CBS 9468* **21** 8 wks

FAT LARRY'S BAND

US, male vocal/instrumental group

2 Jul 77 **CENTER CITY** *Atlantic K 10951* **31** 5 wks
18 Aug 79 **LOOKING FOR LOVE TONIGHT** *Fantasy FTC 179* **46** 6 wks
18 Sep 82 ● **ZOOM** *WMOT/Virgin VS 546* **2** 11 wks

See also F.L.B.

FATBACK BAND

US, male vocal/instrumental group

6 Sep 75 **YUM YUM (GIMME SOME)** *Polydor 2066 590* **40** 6 wks
6 Dec 75 **(ARE YOU READY) DO THE BUS STOP** *Polydor 2066 637* **18** 10 wks
21 Feb 76 ● **(DO THE) SPANISH HUSTLE** *Polydor 2066 656* **10** 7 wks
29 May 76 **PARTY TIME** *Polydor 2066 682* **41** 4 wks
14 Aug 76 **NIGHT FEVER** *Spring 2066 706* **38** 4 wks
12 Mar 77 **DOUBLE DUTCH** *Spring 2066 777* **31** 4 wks
9 Aug 80 **BACKSTROKIN'** *Spring POSP 149* **41** 9 wks

Backstrokin' *credited simply to Fatback*

Wilton FELDER *US, male instrumentalist*

1 Nov 80 **INHERIT THE WIND** *MCA 646* **39** 5 wks

Bobby Womack was lead vocalist

José FELICIANO

US, male vocalist/instrumentalist, guitar

18 Sep 68 ● **LIGHT MY FIRE** *RCA 1715* **6** 16 wks
18 Oct 69 **AND THE SUN WILL SHINE** *RCA 1871* **25** 7 wks

Julie FELIX *US, female vocalist*

18 Apr 70 **IF I COULD (EL CONDOR PASA)** *RAK 101* **19** 11 wks
17 Oct 70 **HEAVEN IS HERE** *RAK 105* **22** 8 wks

FENDERMEN

US, male vocal/instrumental duo, guitars

18 Aug 60 **MULE SKINNER BLUES** *Top Rank JAR 395* **50** 1 wk
1 Sep 60 **MULE SKINNER BLUES** (re-entry) *Top Rank JAR 395* **37** 2 wks
29 Sep 60 **MULE SKINNER BLUES** (2nd re-entry) *Top Rank JAR 395* **32** 6 wks

FENMEN — See *Bern ELLIOTT and the FENMEN*

Peter FENTON *UK, male vocalist*

10 Nov 66 **MARBLE BREAKS IRON BENDS** *Fontana TF 748* **46** 3 wks

Shane FENTON and the FENTONES

UK, male vocal/instrumental group

26 Oct 61 **I'M A MOODY GUY** *Parlophone R 4827* **22** 8 wks
1 Feb 62 **WALK AWAY** *Parlophone R 4866* **38** 5 wks
5 Apr 62 **IT'S ALL OVER NOW** *Parlophone R 4883* **29** 7 wks
12 Jul 62 **CINDY'S BIRTHDAY** *Parlophone R 4921* **19** 8 wks

Fenton later became Alvin Stardust - see also Alvin Stardust. See also Fentones.

FENTONES *UK, male instrumental group*

19 Apr 62 **THE MEXICAN** *Parlophone R 4899* **41** 3 wks
27 Sep 62 **THE BREEZE & I** *Parlophone R 4937* **48** 1 wk

See also Shane Fenton and the Fentones.

FERKO STRING BAND

US, male vocal/instrumental group

12 Aug 55 **ALABAMA JUBILEE** *London HL 8140* **20** 2 wks

Luisa FERNANDEZ *Spain, female vocalist*

11 Nov 78 **LAY LOVE ON YOU** *Warner Bros. K 17061* **31** 8 wks

Date	Title *Label Number*	Position		Date	Title *Label Number*	Position

FERRANTE and TEICHER

US, male instrumental duo, pianos

18 Aug 60 **THEME FROM THE APARTMENT** *London HLT 9164* **44** 1 wk
9 Mar 61 ● **THEME FROM EXODUS** *London HLT 9298 and HMV POP 881* **6** 17 wks

Theme From Exodus *available first on London, then on HMV when the American label, United Artists, changed its UK outlet.*

José FERRER *US, male vocalist*

19 Feb 54 ● **WOMAN** *Philips PB 220* **7** 3 wks

Woman *coupled with* Man *by Rosemary Clooney. See Rosemary Clooney.*

Bryan FERRY *UK, male vocalist*

29 Sep 73 ● **A HARD RAIN'S GONNA FALL** *Island WIP 6170* **10** 9 wks
25 May 74 **THE IN CROWD** *Island WIP 6196* **13** 6 wks
31 Aug 74 **SMOKE GETS IN YOUR EYES** *Island WIP 6205* **17** 8 wks
5 Jul 75 **YOU GO TO MY HEAD** *Island WIP 6234* **33** 3 wks
12 Jun 76 ● **LET'S STICK TOGETHER** *Island WIP 6307* **4** 10 wks
7 Aug 76 ● **EXTENDED PLAY** (EP) *Island IEP 1* **7** 9 wks
5 Feb 77 ● **THIS IS TOMORROW** *Polydor 2001 704* **9** 9 wks
14 May 77 **TOKYO JOE** *Polydor 2001 711* **15** 7 wks
13 May 78 **WHAT GOES ON** *Polydor POSP 3* **67** 2 wks
5 Aug 78 **SIGN OF THE TIMES** *Polydor 2001 798* **37** 8 wks

Tracks on EP: Price Of Love/ Shame Shame Shame/ Heart On My Sleeve/ It's Only Love.

Karel FIALKA

UK, male vocalist and multi-instrumentalist

17 May 80 **THE EYES HAVE IT** *Blueprint BLU 2005* **52** 4 wks

FIDDLER'S DRAM

UK, male/female vocal/instrumental group

15 Dec 79 ● **DAY TRIP TO BANGOR (DIDN'T WE HAVE A LOVELY TIME)** *Dingles SID 211* **3** 9 wks

Billy FIELD *Australia, male vocalist*

12 Jun 82 **YOU WEREN'T IN LOVE WITH ME** *CBS A 2344* **67** 3 wks

Ernie FIELDS *US, orchestra*

25 Dec 59 **IN THE MOOD** *London HL 8985* **13** 8 wks

Gracie FIELDS *UK, female vocalist*

31 May 57 ● **AROUND THE WORLD** *Columbia DB 3953* **8** 8 wks
2 Aug 57 **AROUND THE WORLD** (re-entry) *Columbia DB 3953* **24** 1 wk
6 Nov 59 **LITTLE DONKEY** *Columbia DB 4360* **30** 1 wk
20 Nov 59 **LITTLE DONKEY** (re-entry) *Columbia DB 4360* **20** 5 wks

Richard 'Dimples' FIELDS *US, male vocalist*

20 Feb 82 **I'VE GOT TO LEARN TO SAY NO** *Epic EPC A 1918* **56** 4 wks

FIFTH DIMENSION

US, male/female vocal group

23 Apr 69 **AQUARIUS - LET THE SUNSHINE IN** (MEDLEY) *Liberty LBF 15198* **11** 11 wks
17 Jan 70 **WEDDING BELL BLUES** *Liberty LBF 15288* **16** 9 wks

53RD and 3RD

UK, male vocal group plus Jonathan King much in evidence on vocals

20 Sep 75 **CHICK A BOOM (DON'T YA JES LOVE IT)** *UK 2012 002* **36** 4 wks

Hit featured "The Sound Of Shag". See also Shag, Jonathan King.

FIREBALLS *US, male instrumental group*

27 Jul 61 **QUITE A PARTY** *Pye International 7N 25092* **29** 9 wks

See also Jimmy Gilmer and the Fireballs.

FIRM *UK, male vocal/instrumental group*

17 Jul 82 **ARTHUR DALEY ('E'S ALRIGHT)** *Bark/Stiff HID 1* **14** 9 wks

FIRST CHOICE *US, female vocal group*

19 May 73 **ARMED & EXTREMELY DANGEROUS** *Bell 1297* **16** 10 wks
4 Aug 73 ● **SMARTY PANTS** *Bell 1324* **9** 11 wks

FIRST CLASS *UK, male vocal group*

15 Jun 74 **BEACH BABY** *UK 66* **13** 10 wks

FIRST EDITION — See *Kenny ROGERS*

FISCHER-Z *UK, male vocal/instrumental group*

26 May 79 **THE WORKER** *United Artists UP 36509* **53** 5 wks
3 May 80 **SO LONG** *United Artists BP 342* **72** 2 wks

Eddie FISHER *US, male vocalist*

2 Jan 53 ★ **OUTSIDE OF HEAVEN** *HMV B 10362* **1** 16 wks
23 Jan 53 **EVERYTHING I HAVE IS YOURS** *HMV B 10398* **12** 1 wk
6 Feb 53 ● **EVERYTHING I HAVE IS YOURS** (re-entry) *HMV B 10398* **8** 4 wks
1 May 53 **OUTSIDE OF HEAVEN** (re-entry) *HMV B 10362* **12** 1 wk
1 May 53 ● **DOWNHEARTED** *HMV B 10450* **3** 15 wks
22 May 53 ★ **I'M WALKING BEHIND YOU** *HMV B 10489* **1** 18 wks
6 Nov 53 ● **WISH YOU WERE HERE** *HMV B 10564* **8** 9 wks
22 Jan 54 ● **OH MEIN PAPA** *HMV B 10614* **9** 1 wk
5 Feb 54 **OH MEIN PAPA** (re-entry) *HMV B 10614* **11** 1 wk
26 Feb 54 ● **OH MEIN PAPA** (2nd re-entry) *HMV B 10614* **10** 1 wk

Date	Title *Label Number*	Position	
12 Mar 54	**OH MEIN PAPA** (3rd re-entry) *HMV B 10614*	**11**	1 wk
29 Oct 54	**I NEED YOU NOW** *HMV B 10755*	**16**	2 wks
19 Nov 54	**I NEED YOU NOW** (re-entry) *HMV B 10755*	**13**	7 wks
21 Jan 55	**I NEED YOU NOW** (2nd re-entry) *HMV B 10755*	**19**	1 wk
18 Mar 55	● **WEDDING BELLS** *HMV B 10839*	**5**	11 wks
23 Nov 56	● **CINDY OH CINDY** *HMV POP 273*	**5**	16 wks

Toni FISHER *US, female vocalist*

Date	Title *Label Number*	Position	
12 Feb 60	**THE BIG HURT** *Top Rank JAR 261*	**30**	1 wk

Ella FITZGERALD *US, female vocalist*

Date	Title *Label Number*	Position	
23 May 58	**SWINGIN' SHEPHERD BLUES** *HMV POP 486*	**15**	5 wks
16 Oct 59	**BUT NOT FOR ME** *HMV POP 657*	**25**	2 wks
25 Dec 59	**BUT NOT FOR ME** (re-entry) *HMV POP 657*	**29**	1 wk
21 Apr 60	**MACK THE KNIFE** *HMV POP 736*	**19**	9 wks
6 Oct 60	**HOW HIGH THE MOON** *HMV POP 782*	**46**	1 wk
22 Nov 62	**DESAFINADO** *Verve VS 502*	**38**	4 wks
27 Dec 62	**DESAFINADO** (re-entry) *Verve VS 502*	**41**	2 wks
30 Apr 64	**CAN'T BUY ME LOVE** *Verve VS 519*	**34**	5 wks

Scott FITZGERALD and Yvonne KEELY

UK/Holland, male/female vocal duo

Date	Title *Label Number*	Position	
14 Jan 78	● **IF I HAD WORDS** *Pepper UP 36333*	**3**	10 wks

Hit credits St. Thomas Moore School Choir.

FIVE SMITH BROTHERS

UK, male vocal group

Date	Title *Label Number*	Position	
22 Jul 55	**I'M IN FAVOUR OF FRIENDSHIP** *Decca F 10527*	**20**	1 wk

5000 VOLTS

UK, male/female vocal/instrumental group

Date	Title *Label Number*	Position	
6 Sep 75	● **I'M ON FIRE** *Philips 6006 464*	**4**	9 wks
24 Jul 76	● **DR. KISS KISS** *Philips 6006 533*	**8**	9 wks

FIXX *UK, male vocal/instrumental group*

Date	Title *Label Number*	Position	
27 Apr 82	**STAND OR FALL** *MCA FIXX 2*	**54**	4 wks
17 Jul 82	**RED SKIES** *MCA FIXX 3*	**57**	4 wks

Roberta FLACK *US, female vocalist*

Date	Title *Label Number*	Position	
27 May 72	**THE FIRST TIME EVER I SAW YOUR FACE** *Atlantic K 10161*	**14**	14 wks
17 Feb 73	● **KILLING ME SOFTLY WITH HIS SONG** *Atlantic K 10282*	**6**	14 wks
24 Aug 74	**FEEL LIKE MAKING LOVE** *Atlantic K 10467*	**34**	7 wks
30 Aug 80	**DON'T MAKE ME WAIT TOO LONG** *Atlantic K 11555*	**44**	7 wks

See also Roberta Flack and Donny Hathaway.

Roberta FLACK and Donny HATHAWAY *US, female/male vocal duo*

Date	Title *Label Number*	Position	
5 Aug 72	**WHERE IS THE LOVE** *Atlantic K 10202*	**29**	7 wks
6 May 78	**THE CLOSER I GET TO YOU** *Atlantic K 11099*	**42**	4 wks
17 May 80	● **BACK TOGETHER AGAIN** *Atlantic K 11481*	**3**	11 wks

See also Roberta Flack

FLAMINGOS *US, male vocal group*

Date	Title *Label Number*	Position	
4 Jun 69	**BOOGALOO PARTY** *Philips BF 1786*	**26**	5 wks

Michael FLANDERS *UK, male vocalist*

Date	Title *Label Number*	Position	
27 Feb 59	**LITTLE DRUMMER BOY** *Parlophone R 4528*	**20**	2 wks
17 Apr 59	**LITTLE DRUMMER BOY** (re-entry) *Parlophone R 4528*	**24**	1 wk

FLASH AND THE PAN

Australia, male vocal/instrumental group

Date	Title *Label Number*	Position	
23 Sep 78	**AND THE BAND PLAYED ON (DOWN AMONG THE DEAD MEN)** *Ensign ENY 15*	**54**	4 wks

Lester FLATT and Earl SCRUGGS

US, male instrumental duo, banjos

Date	Title *Label Number*	Position	
15 Nov 67	**FOGGY MOUNTAIN BREAKDOWN** *CBS 3038 and Mercury MF 1007*	**39**	6 wks

The versions on the two labels were not the same cuts; CBS had a 1965 recording, Mercury a 1967, the chart did not differentiate and listed both together.

Fogwell FLAX and the ANKLEBITERS from FREEHOLD JUNIOR SCHOOL

UK, male vocalist and school choir.

Date	Title *Label Number*	Position	
26 Dec 81	**ONE NINE FOR SANTA** *EMI 5255*	**68**	1 wk

F.L.B. *US, male vocal/instrumental group*

Date	Title *Label Number*	Position	
10 Mar 79	**BOOGIE TOWN** *Fantasy FTC 168*	**46**	4 wks

See also Fat Larry's Band

FLEE-REKKERS *UK, male instrumental group*

Date	Title *Label Number*	Position	
19 May 60	**GREEN JEANS** *Triumph RGM 1008*	**23**	13 wks

FLEETWOOD MAC

UK/US, male/female vocal/instrumental group

Date	Title *Label Number*	Position	
10 Apr 68	**BLACK MAGIC WOMAN** *Blue Horizon 57 3138*	**37**	7 wks
17 Jul 68	**NEED YOUR LOVE SO BAD** *Blue Horizon 57 3139*	**31**	13 wks
4 Dec 68	★ **ALBATROSS** *Blue Horizon 57 3145*	**1**	20 wks
16 Apr 69	● **MAN OF THE WORLD** *Immediate IM 080*	**2**	14 wks
23 Jul 69	**NEED YOUR LOVE SO BAD** (re-issue) *Blue Horizon 57 3157*	**32**	6 wks

Date	Title *Label Number*	Position	
13 Sep 69	**NEED YOUR LOVE SO BAD** (re-entry of re-issue) *Blue Horizon 57 3157*	**42**	3 wks
4 Oct 69	● **OH WELL** *Reprise RS 27000*	**2**	16 wks
23 May 70	● **THE GREEN MANALISHI (WITH THE TWO-PRONG CROWN)** *Reprise RS 27007*	**10**	12 wks
12 May 73	● **ALBATROSS** (re-issue) *CBS 8306*	**2**	15 wks
13 Nov 76	**SAY YOU LOVE ME** *Reprise K 14447*	**40**	4 wks
19 Feb 77	**GO YOUR OWN WAY** *Warner Bros. K 16872*	**38**	4 wks
30 Apr 77	**DON'T STOP** *Warner Bros. K 16930*	**32**	5 wks
9 Jul 77	**DREAMS** *Warner Bros. K 16969*	**24**	9 wks
22 Oct 77	**YOU MAKE LOVING FUN** *Warner Bros. K 17013*	**45**	2 wks
11 Mar 78	**RHIANNON** *Reprise K 14430*	**46**	3 wks
6 Oct 79	● **TUSK** *Warner Bros K 17468*	**6**	10 wks
22 Dec 79	**SARA** *Warner Bros K 17533*	**37**	8 wks
25 Sep 82	**GYPSY** *Warner Bros. K 17997*	**46**	3 wks
18 Dec 82	**OH DIANE** *Warner Bros. FLEET 1*	**60†**	2 wks

Group were UK and male only up to and including the re-issue of Albatross.

FLEETWOODS *US, male/female vocal group*

Date	Title *Label Number*	Position	
24 Apr 59	● **COME SOFTLY TO ME** *London HL 8841*	**6**	8 wks

Bernie FLINT *UK, male vocalist*

Date	Title *Label Number*	Position	
19 Mar 77	● **I DON'T WANT TO PUT A HOLD ON YOU** *EMI 2599*	**3**	10 wks
23 Jul 77	**SOUTHERN COMFORT** *EMI 2621*	**48**	1 wk

FLINTLOCK *UK, male vocal/instrumental group*

Date	Title *Label Number*	Position	
29 May 76	**DAWN** *Pinnacle P 8419*	**30**	5 wks

F.L.O. — See *Rahni HARRIS and F.L.O.*

FLOATERS *US, male vocal/instrumental group*

Date	Title *Label Number*	Position	
23 Jul 77	★ **FLOAT ON** *ABC 4187*	**1**	11 wks

A FLOCK OF SEAGULLS

UK, male vocal/instrumental group

Date	Title *Label Number*	Position	
27 Mar 82	**I RAN** *Jive JIVE 14*	**43**	6 wks
12 Jun 82	**SPACE AGE LOVE SONG** *Jive JIVE 17*	**34**	6 wks
6 Nov 82	● **WISHING (IF I HAD A PHOTOGRAPH OF YOU)** *Jive JIVE 25*	**10†**	8 wks

FLOWERPOT MEN *UK, male vocal group*

Date	Title *Label Number*	Position	
23 Aug 67	● **LET'S GO TO SAN FRANCISCO** *Deram DM 142*	**4**	12 wks

Eddie FLOYD *US, male vocalist*

Date	Title *Label Number*	Position	
2 Feb 67	**KNOCK ON WOOD** *Atlantic 584 041*	**50**	1 wk
2 Mar 67	**KNOCK ON WOOD** (re-entry) *Atlantic 584 041*	**19**	17 wks
16 Mar 67	**RAISE YOUR HAND** *Stax 601 001*	**42**	3 wks
9 Aug 67	**THINGS GET BETTER** *Stax 601 016*	**31**	8 wks

FLYING LIZARDS

UK, male/female vocal/instrumental group

Date	Title *Label Number*	Position	
4 Aug 79	● **MONEY** *Virgin VS 276*	**5**	10 wks
9 Feb 80	**T.V.** *Virgin VS 325*	**43**	6 wks

FOCUS *Holland, male instrumental group*

Date	Title *Label Number*	Position	
20 Jan 73	**HOCUS POCUS** *Polydor 2001 211*	**20**	10 wks
27 Jan 73	● **SYLVIA** *Polydor 2001 422*	**4**	11 wks

Dan FOGELBERG *US, male vocalist*

Date	Title *Label Number*	Position	
15 Mar 80	**LONGER** *Full Moon/Epic EPC 8230*	**59**	4 wks

Wayne FONTANA *UK, male vocalist*

Date	Title *Label Number*	Position	
9 Dec 65	**IT WAS EASIER TO HURT HER** *Fontana TF 642*	**36**	6 wks
21 Apr 66	**COME ON HOME** *Fontana TF 684*	**16**	12 wks
25 Aug 66	**GOODBYE BLUEBIRD** *Fontana TF 737*	**49**	1 wk
8 Dec 66	**PAMELA PAMELA** *Fontana TF 770*	**11**	12 wks

See also Wayne Fontana and the Mindbenders.

Wayne FONTANA and the MINDBENDERS

UK, male vocalist, male vocal/instrumental backing group

Date	Title *Label Number*	Position	
11 Jul 63	**HELLO JOSEPHINE** *Fontana TF 404*	**46**	2 wks
28 May 64	**STOP LOOK & LISTEN** *Fontana TF 451*	**37**	4 wks
8 Oct 64	● **UM UM UM UM UM UM** *Fontana TF 497*	**5**	15 wks
4 Feb 65	● **GAME OF LOVE** *Fontana TF 535*	**2**	11 wks
17 Jun 65	**JUST A LITTLE BIT TOO LATE** *Fontana TF 579*	**20**	7 wks
30 Sep 65	**SHE NEEDS LOVE** *Fontana TF 611*	**32**	6 wks

See also Wayne Fontana, Mindbenders.

Bill FORBES *UK, male vocalist*

Date	Title *Label Number*	Position	
15 Jan 60	**TOO YOUNG** *Columbia DB 4386*	**29**	1 wk

FORBIDDEN — See *Jet BRONX and the FORBIDDEN*

Clinton FORD *UK, male vocalist*

Date	Title *Label Number*	Position	
23 Oct 59	**OLD SHEP** *Oriole CB 1500*	**27**	1 wk
17 Aug 61	**TOO MANY BEAUTIFUL GIRLS** *Oriole CB 1623*	**48**	1 wk
8 Mar 62	**FANLIGHT FANNY** *Oriole CB 1706*	**22**	10 wks
5 Jan 67	**RUN TO THE DOOR** *Piccadilly 7N 35361*	**25**	13 wks

Emile FORD and the CHECKMATES

UK, male vocal/instrumental group

Date	Title *Label Number*	Position	
30 Oct 59	★ **WHAT DO YOU WANT TO MAKE THOSE EYES AT ME FOR** *Pye 7N 15225*	**1**	26 wks
5 Feb 60	● **ON A SLOW BOAT TO CHINA** *Pye 7N 15245*	**3**	14 wks
26 May 60	**YOU'LL NEVER KNOW WHAT YOU'RE MISSING** *Pye 7N 15268*	**12**	9 wks
1 Sep 60	**THEM THERE EYES** *Pye 7N 15282*	**18**	16 wks
8 Dec 60	● **COUNTING TEARDROPS** *Pye 7N 15314*	**4**	12 wks
2 Mar 61	**WHAT AM I GONNA DO** *Pye 7N 15331*	**33**	6 wks

Date	Title *Label Number*	Position	
18 May 61	**HALF OF MY HEART** *Piccadilly 7N 35003*	**50**	1 wk
22 Jun 61	**HALF OF MY HEART** (re-entry) *Piccadilly 7N 35003*	**42**	3 wks
8 Mar 62	**I WONDER WHO'S KISSING HER NOW** *Piccadilly 7N 35033*	**43**	1 wk

Checkmates not on Them There Eyes *or the two Piccadilly hits.*

Martyn FORD *UK, orchestra*

Date	Title *Label Number*	Position	
14 May 77	**LET YOUR BODY GO DOWNTOWN** *Mountain TOP 26*	**38**	3 wks

Mary FORD — See *Les PAUL and Mary FORD*

Tennessee Ernie FORD *US, male vocalist*

Date	Title *Label Number*	Position	
21 Jan 55	★ **GIVE ME YOUR WORD** *Capitol CL 14005*	**1**	24 wks
6 Jan 56	★ **SIXTEEN TONS** *Capitol CL 14500*	**1**	11 wks
13 Jan 56	● **THE BALLAD OF DAVY CROCKETT** *Capitol CL 14506*	**3**	7 wks

FOREIGNER *UK/US, male vocal/instrumental group*

Date	Title *Label Number*	Position	
6 May 78	**FEELS LIKE THE FIRST TIME** *Atlantic K 11086*	**39**	6 wks
15 July 78	**COLD AS ICE** *Atlantic K 10986*	**24**	10 wks
28 Oct 78	**HOT BLOODED** *Atlantic K 11167*	**42**	3 wks
24 Feb 79	**BLUE MORNING BLUE DAY** *Atlantic K 11236*	**45**	4 wks
29 Aug 81	**URGENT** *Atlantic K 11665*	**54**	4 wks
10 Oct 81	**JUKE BOX HERO** *Atlantic K 11678*	**48**	4 wks
11 Dec 81	● **WAITING FOR A GIRL LIKE YOU** *Atlantic K 11696*	**8**	13 wks
8 May 82	**URGENT** (re-issue) *Atlantic K 11728*	**45**	5 wks

FORMATIONS *US, male vocal group*

Date	Title *Label Number*	Position	
31 Jul 71	**AT THE TOP OF THE STAIRS** *Mojo 2027 001*	**50**	1 wk
14 Aug 71	**AT THE TOP OF THE STAIRS** (re-entry) *Mojo 2027 001*	**28**	10 wks

George FORMBY

UK, male vocalist/instrumentalist, ukelele

Date	Title *Label Number*	Position	
21 Jul 60	**HAPPY GO LUCKY ME/ BANJO BOY** *Pye 7N 15269*	**40**	3 wks

Lance FORTUNE *UK, male vocalist*

Date	Title *Label Number*	Position	
19 Feb 60	● **BE MINE** *Pye 7N 15240*	**4**	12 wks
5 May 60	**THIS LOVE I HAVE FOR YOU** *Pye 7N 15260*	**26**	5 wks

FORTUNES *UK, male vocal/instrumental group*

Date	Title *Label Number*	Position	
8 Jul 65	● **YOU'VE GOT YOUR TROUBLES** *Decca F 12173*	**2**	14 wks
7 Oct 65	● **HERE IT COMES AGAIN** *Decca F 12243*	**4**	14 wks
3 Feb 66	**THIS GOLDEN RING** *Decca F 12321*	**15**	9 wks
11 Sep 71	● **FREEDOM COME FREEDOM GO** *Capitol CL 15693*	**6**	17 wks
29 Jan 72	● **STORM IN A TEACUP** *Capitol CL 15707*	**7**	11 wks

FOSTER and ALLEN *UK, male vocal duo*

Date	Title *Label Number*	Position	
27 Feb 82	**A BUNCH OF THYME** *Ritz RITZ 5*	**18**	11 wks
30 Oct 82	**OLD FLAMES** *Ritz RITZ 028*	**51**	8 wks

FOUNDATIONS

UK, male vocal/instrumental group

Date	Title *Label Number*	Position	
27 Sep 67	★ **BABY NOW THAT I'VE FOUND YOU** *Pye 7N 17366*	**1**	16 wks
24 Jan 68	**BACK ON MY FEET AGAIN** *Pye 7N 17417*	**18**	10 wks
1 May 68	**ANY OLD TIME** *Pye 7N 17503*	**48**	1 wk
15 May 68	**ANY OLD TIME** (re-entry) *Pye 7N 17503*	**50**	1 wk
20 Nov 68	● **BUILD ME UP BUTTERCUP** *Pye 7N 17638*	**2**	15 wks
12 Mar 69	● **IN THE BAD BAD OLD DAYS** *Pye 7N 17702*	**8**	10 wks
13 Sep 69	**BORN TO LIVE AND BORN TO DIE** *Pye 7N 17809*	**46**	3 wks

FOUR ACES *US, male vocal group*

Date	Title *Label Number*	Position	
30 Jul 54	● **THREE COINS IN THE FOUNTAIN** *Brunswick 05308*	**5**	5 wks
22 Oct 54	**THREE COINS IN THE FOUNTAIN** (re-entry) *Brunswick 05308*	**17**	1 wk
7 Jan 55	● **MR. SANDMAN** *Brunswick 05355*	**9**	5 wks
20 May 55	● **STRANGER IN PARADISE** *Brunswick 05418*	**6**	6 wks
18 Nov 55	● **LOVE IS A MANY SPLENDOURED THING** *Brunswick 05480*	**2**	13 wks
19 Oct 56	**WOMAN IN LOVE** *Brunswick 05589*	**19**	3 wks
4 Jan 57	**FRIENDLY PERSUASION** *Brunswick 05623*	**29**	1 wk
23 Jan 59	**THE WORLD OUTSIDE** *Brunswick 05773*	**18**	6 wks

FOUR BUCKETEERS

UK, male/female vocal group

Date	Title *Label Number*	Position	
3 May 80	**BUCKET OF WATER SONG** *CBS 8393*	**26**	6 wks

FOUR KNIGHTS *US, male vocal group*

Date	Title *Label Number*	Position	
4 Jun 54	● **I GET SO LONELY** *Capitol CL 14076*	**5**	7 wks
30 Jul 54	● **I GET SO LONELY** (re-entry) *Capitol CL 14076*	**10**	4 wks

FOUR LADS *US, male vocal group*

Date	Title *Label Number*	Position	
28 Apr 60	**STANDING ON THE CORNER** *Philips PB 1000*	**34**	4 wks

FOUR PENNIES

UK, male vocal/instrumental group

Date	Title *Label Number*	Position	
16 Jan 64	**DO YOU WANT ME TO** *Philips BF 1296*	**47**	1 wk
6 Feb 64	**DO YOU WANT ME TO** (re-entry) *Philips BF 1296*	**49**	1 wk
2 Apr 64	★ **JULIET** *Philips BF 1322*	**1**	15 wks
16 Jul 64	**I FOUND OUT THE HARD WAY** *Philips BF 1349*	**14**	11 wks
29 Oct 64	**BLACK GIRL** *Philips BF 1366*	**20**	12 wks
7 Oct 65	**UNTIL IT'S TIME FOR YOU TO GO** *Philips BF 1435*	**19**	11 wks
17 Feb 66	**TROUBLE IS MY MIDDLE NAME** *Philips BF 1469*	**32**	5 wks

Above **FIFTH DIMENSION** started life as The Versatiles then The Hi-fi's before becoming Fifth Dimension in 1967. Members Marilyn McCoo and Billy Davis Jr. scored again in 1977 as a duo *Top right* **EDDIE FISHER** His chart career went for a Burton in early 1957, his marriage to Liz Taylor in 1962

INEZ & CHARLIE FOXX The Foxx's biggest brush with the charts came with an adaptation of a children's song

FIREBALLS The flame was rekindled in 1963 when their pianist, Jimmy Gilmer, fronted them on 'Sugar Shack'

Date	Title *Label Number*	Position	

FOUR PREPS *US male vocal group*

13 Jun 58	● **BIG MAN** *Capitol CL 14873*	**2**	13 wks
19 Sep 58	**BIG MAN** (re-entry) *Capitol CL 14873*	**22**	1 wk
26 May 60	**GOT A GIRL** *Capitol CL 15128*	**28**	6 wks
14 Jul 60	**GOT A GIRL** (re-entry) *Capitol CL 15128*	**47**	1 wk
2 Nov 61	**MORE MONEY FOR YOU AND ME** (MEDLEY) *Capitol CL 15217*	**39**	2 wks

Tracks of medley: Mr. Blue/ Alley Oop/ Smoke Gets In Your Eyes/ In This Whole Wide World/ A Worried Man/ Tom Dooley/ A Teenager In Love.

FOUR SEASONS *US, male vocal group*

4 Oct 62	● **SHERRY** *Stateside SS 122*	**8**	16 wks
17 Jan 63	**BIG GIRLS DONT CRY** *Stateside SS 145*	**13**	10 wks
28 Mar 63	**WALK LIKE A MAN** *Stateside SS 169*	**12**	12 wks
27 Jun 63	**AIN'T THAT A SHAME** *Stateside SS 194*	**38**	3 wks
27 Aug 64	● **RAG DOLL** *Philips BF 1347*	**2**	13 wks
18 Nov 65	● **LET'S HANG ON** *Philips BF 1439*	**4**	16 wks
31 Mar 66	**WORKIN' MY WAY BACK TO YOU** *Philips BF 1474*	**50**	3 wks
2 Jun 66	**OPUS 17 (DON'T YOU WORRY 'BOUT ME)** *Philips BF 1493*	**20**	9 wks
29 Sep 66	**I'VE GOT YOU UNDER MY SKIN** *Philips BF 1511*	**12**	11 wks
12 Jan 67	**TELL IT TO THE RAIN** *Philips BF 1538*	**37**	5 wks
19 Apr 75	● **NIGHT** *Mowest MW 3024*	**7**	9 wks
20 Sep 75	● **WHO LOVES YOU** *Warner Bros. K 16602*	**6**	9 wks
31 Jan 76	★ **DECEMBER '63 (OH WHAT A NIGHT)** *Warner Bros. K 16688*	**1**	10 wks
24 Apr 76	● **SILVER STAR** *Warner Bros. K 16742*	**3**	9 wks
27 Nov 76	**WE CAN WORK IT OUT** *Warner Bros. K 16845*	**34**	4 wks
18 Jun 77	**RHAPSODY** *Warner Bros. K 16932*	**37**	3 wks
20 Aug 77	**DOWN THE HALL** *Warner Bros. K 16982*	**34**	5 wks

First two Philips hits "with the sound of Frankie Valli", last four Philips hits "with Frankie Valli". Mowest hit "Frankie Valli and the Four Seasons". See also Frankie Valli.

FOUR TOPS *US, male vocal group*

1 Jul 65	**I CAN'T HELP MYSELF** *Tamla Motown TMG 515*	**23**	9 wks
2 Sep 65	**IT'S THE SAME OLD SONG** *Tamla Motown TMG 528*	**34**	8 wks
21 Jul 66	**LOVING YOU IS SWEETER THAN EVER** *Tamla Motown TMG 568*	**21**	12 wks
13 Oct 66	★ **REACH OUT I'LL BE THERE** *Tamla Motown TMG 579*	**1**	16 wks
12 Jan 67	● **STANDING IN THE SHADOWS OF LOVE** *Tamla Motown TMG 589*	**6**	8 wks
30 Mar 67	● **BERNADETTE** *Tamla Motown TMG 601*	**8**	10 wks
15 Jun 67	**SEVEN ROOMS OF GLOOM** *Tamla Motown TMG 612*	**12**	9 wks
11 Oct 67	**YOU KEEP RUNNING AWAY** *Tamla Motown TMG 623*	**26**	7 wks
13 Dec 67	● **WALK AWAY RENEE** *Tamla Motown TMG 634*	**3**	11 wks
13 Mar 68	● **IF I WERE A CARPENTER** *Tamla Motown TMG 647*	**7**	11 wks
21 Aug 68	**YESTERDAY'S DREAMS** *Tamla Motown TMG 665*	**23**	15 wks
13 Nov 68	**I'M IN A DIFFERENT WORLD** *Tamla Motown TMG 675*	**27**	13 wks
28 May 69	**WHAT IS A MAN** *Tamla Motown TMG 698*	**16**	11 wks
27 Sep 69	**DO WHAT YOU GOTTA DO** *Tamla Motown TMG 710*	**11**	11 wks
21 Mar 70	● **I CAN'T HELP MYSELF** (re-issue) *Tamla Motown TMG 732*	**10**	11 wks
30 May 70	● **IT'S ALL IN THE GAME** *Tamla Motown TMG 736*	**5**	14 wks

Date	Title *Label Number*	Position	

12 Sep 70	**IT'S ALL IN THE GAME** (re-entry) *Tamla Motown TMG 736*	**48**	2 wks
3 Oct 70	● **STILL WATER (LOVE)** *Tamla Motown TMG 752*	**10**	10 wks
19 Dec 70	**STILL WATER (LOVE)** (re-entry) *Tamla Motown TMG 752*	**44**	2 wks
1 May 71	**JUST SEVEN NUMBERS (CAN STRAIGHTEN OUT MY LIFE)** *Tamla Motown TMG 770*	**36**	5 wks
25 Sep 71	● **SIMPLE GAME** *Tamla Motown TMG 785*	**3**	11 wks
11 Mar 72	**BERNADETTE** (re-issue) *Tamla Motown TMG 803*	**23**	7 wks
5 Aug 72	**WALK WITH ME TALK WITH ME DARLING** *Tamla Motown TMG 823*	**32**	6 wks
18 Nov 72	**KEEPER OF THE CASTLE** *Probe PRO 575*	**18**	9 wks
10 Nov 73	**SWEET UNDERSTANDING LOVE** *Probe PRO 604*	**29**	10 wks
17 Oct 81	● **WHEN SHE WAS MY GIRL** *Casablanca CAN 1005*	**3**	10 wks
19 Dec 81	**DON'T WALK AWAY** *Casablanca CAN 1006*	**16**	11 wks
6 Mar 82	**TONIGHT I'M GONNA LOVE YOU ALL OVER** *Casablanca/Phonogram CAN 1008*	**43**	4 wks
26 Jun 82	**BACK TO SCHOOL AGAIN** *RSO 89*	**62**	2 wks

See also Supremes and the Four Tops.

FOURMOST *UK, male vocal/instrumental group*

12 Sep 63	● **HELLO LITTLE GIRL** *Parlophone R 5056*	**9**	17 wks
26 Dec 63	**I'M IN LOVE** *Parlophone R 5078*	**17**	12 wks
23 Apr 64	● **A LITTLE LOVING** *Parlophone R 5128*	**6**	13 wks
13 Aug 64	**HOW CAN I TELL HER** *Parlophone R 5157*	**33**	4 wks
26 Nov 64	**BABY I NEED YOUR LOVIN'** *Parlophone R 5194*	**24**	12 wks
9 Dec 65	**GIRLS GIRLS GIRLS** *Parlophone R 5379*	**33**	7 wks

14-18

UK, male vocalist, Peter Waterman, under false group name

1 Nov 75	**GOODBYE-EE** *Magnet MAG 48*	**33**	4 wks

FOX *UK, male/female vocal/instrumental group*

15 Feb 75	● **ONLY YOU CAN** *GTO GT 8*	**3**	11 wks
10 May 75	**IMAGINE ME IMAGINE YOU** *GTO GT 21*	**15**	8 wks
10 Apr 76	● **S-S-S-SINGLE BED** *GTO GT 57*	**4**	10 wks

Noosha FOX *UK, female vocalist*

12 Nov 77	**GEORGINA BAILEY** *GTO GT 106*	**31**	6 wks

Inez FOXX *US, female vocalist*

23 Jul 64	**HURT BY LOVE** *Sue WI 323*	**40**	3 wks

See also Inez & Charlie Foxx.

Inez and Charlie FOXX

US, female/male vocal/instrumental duo, Charlie Foxx guitar

19 Feb 69	**MOCKINGBIRD** *United Artists UP 2269*	**36**	2 wks
19 Mar 69	**MOCKINGBIRD** (re-entry) *United Artists UP 2269*	**34**	3 wks

See also Inez Foxx.

Above **WAYNE FONTANA** The fourth single for Wayne Fontana (Glyn Ellis) and the Mindbenders was a Stateside number one *Top right* **THE FRESHIES** Longest ever chart title by a Manchester group *Right* **JOHN FRED AND THE PLAYBOY BAND** Without disguise but with his guys

Below **FORTUNES** 2 years after their last hit they had financial success through recording the Coca-Cola advert 'It's The Real Thing' *Below right* **FOUNDATIONS** Back on their feet again

Date **Title** *Label Number* **Position**

Date **Title** *Label Number* **Position**

John FOXX *UK male vocalist*

Date	Title *Label Number*	Position	Weeks
26 Jan 80	**UNDERPASS** *Virgin/Metal Beat VS 318*	**31**	8 wks
29 Mar 80	**NO-ONE DRIVING**(DOUBLE SINGLE) *Virgin/Metal Beat VS 338*	**32**	4 wks
19 Jul 80	**BURNING CAR** *Virgin/Metal Beat VS 360*	**35**	7 wks
8 Nov 80	**MILES AWAY** *Virgin/Metal Beat VS 382*	**51**	3 wks
29 Aug 81	**EUROPE - AFTER THE RAIN** *Virgin VS 393*	**40**	5 wks

Tracks on double single: No-One Driving/Glimmer/Mr. No/This City.

Peter FRAMPTON *UK, male vocalist*

Date	Title *Label Number*	Position	Weeks
1 May 76	● **SHOW ME THE WAY** *A & M AMS 7218*	**10**	12 wks
11 Sep 76	**BABY I LOVE YOUR WAY** *A & M AMS 7246*	**43**	5 wks
6 Nov 76	**DO YOU FEEL LIKE WE DO** *A & M AMS 7260*	**39**	4 wks
23 Jul 77	**I'M IN YOU** *A & M AMS 7298*	**41**	3 wks

Connie FRANCIS *US, female vocalist*

Date	Title *Label Number*	Position	Weeks
4 Apr 58	★ **WHO'S SORRY NOW** *MGM 975*	**1**	25 wks
27 Jun 58	**I'M SORRY I MADE YOU CRY** *MGM 982*	**11**	10 wks
22 Aug 58	★ **CAROLINA MOON/ STUPID CUPID** *MGM 985*	**1**	19 wks
31 Oct 58	**I'LL GET BY** *MGM 993*	**19**	6 wks
21 Nov 58	**FALLIN'** *MGM 993*	**20**	5 wks
26 Dec 58	**YOU ALWAYS HURT THE ONE YOU LOVE** *MGM 998*	**13**	7 wks
13 Feb 59	● **MY HAPPINESS** *MGM 1001*	**4**	14 wks
29 May 59	**MY HAPPINESS** (re-entry) *MGM 1001*	**30**	1 wk
3 Jul 59	● **LIPSTICK ON YOUR COLLAR** *MGM 1018*	**3**	16 wks
11 Sep 59	**PLENTY GOOD LOVIN'** *MGM 1036*	**18**	6 wks
4 Dec 59	**AMONG MY SOUVENIRS** *MGM 1046*	**11**	10 wks
17 Mar 60	**VALENTINO** *MGM 1060*	**27**	8 wks
19 May 60	● **MAMA/ ROBOT MAN** *MGM 1076*	**2**	19 wks
18 Aug 60	● **EVERYBODY'S SOMEBODY'S FOOL** *MGM 1086*	**5**	13 wks
3 Nov 60	● **MY HEART HAS A MIND OF ITS OWN** *MGM 1100*	**3**	15 wks
12 Jan 61	**MANY TEARS AGO** *MGM 1111*	**12**	9 wks
16 Mar 61	● **WHERE THE BOYS ARE/ BABY ROO** *MGM 1121*	**5**	14 wks
15 Jun 61	**BREAKIN' IN A BRAND NEW BROKEN HEART** *MGM 1136*	**12**	11 wks
14 Sep 61	● **TOGETHER** *MGM 1138*	**6**	11 wks
14 Dec 61	**BABY'S FIRST CHRISTMAS** *MGM 1145*	**30**	4 wks
26 Apr 62	**DON'T BREAK THE HEART THAT LOVES YOU** *MGM 1157*	**39**	3 wks
2 Aug 62	● **VACATION** *MGM 1165*	**10**	9 wks
20 Dec 62	**I'M GONNA BE WARM THIS WINTER** *MGM 1185*	**48**	1 wk
10 Jun 65	**MY CHILD** *MGM 1271*	**26**	6 wks
20 Jan 66	**JEALOUS HEART** *MGM 1293*	**44**	2 wks

Claude FRANCOIS *France, male vocalist*

Date	Title *Label Number*	Position	Weeks
10 Jan 76	**TEARS ON THE TELEPHONE** *Bradley's BRAD 7528*	**35**	4 wks

Joe FRANK — See *HAMILTON, Joe FRANK and REYNOLDS*

Aretha FRANKLIN *US, female vocalist*

Date	Title *Label Number*	Position	Weeks
8 Jun 67	● **RESPECT** *Atlantic 584 115*	**10**	14 wks
23 Aug 67	**BABY I LOVE YOU** *Atlantic 584 127*	**39**	4 wks
20 Dec 67	**CHAIN OF FOOLS/ SATISFACTION** *Atlantic 584 157*	**43**	2 wks
10 Jan 68	**SATISFACTION** (re-entry) *Atlantic 584 157*	**37**	5 wks
13 Mar 68	**SINCE YOU'VE BEEN GONE** *Atlantic 584 172*	**47**	1 wk
22 May 68	**THINK** *Atlantic 584 186*	**26**	9 wks
7 Aug 68	● **I SAY A LITTLE PRAYER** *Atlantic 584 206*	**4**	14 wks
22 Aug 70	**DON'T PLAY THAT SONG** *Atlantic 2091 027*	**13**	11 wks
2 Oct 71	**SPANISH HARLEM** *Atlantic 2091 138*	**14**	9 wks
8 Sep 73	**ANGEL** *Atlantic K 10346*	**37**	5 wks
16 Feb 74	**UNTIL YOU COME BACK TO ME (THAT'S WHAT I'M GONNA DO).** *Atlantic K 10399*	**26**	8 wks
6 Dec 80	**WHAT A FOOL BELIEVES** *Arista ARIST 377*	**46**	7 wks
4 Sep 82	**JUMP TO IT** *Arista ARIST 479*	**42**	5 wks

Aretha FRANKLIN and George BENSON

US, female vocalist and male vocalist/instrumentalist

Date	Title *Label Number*	Position	Weeks
19 Sep 81	**LOVE ALL THE HURT AWAY** *Arista ARIST 428*	**49**	3 wks

see also Aretha Franklin, George Benson

Rodney FRANKLIN *US, male vocalist/pianist*

Date	Title *Label Number*	Position	Weeks
19 Apr 80	● **THE GROOVE** *CBS 8529*	**7**	9 wks

FRANTIC FIVE — See *Don LANG*

FRANTIQUE *US, female vocal group*

Date	Title *Label Number*	Position	Weeks
11 Aug 79	● **STRUT YOUR FUNKY STUFF** *Philadelphia International PIR 7728*	**10**	12 wks

Stan FREBERG *US, male vocalist*

Date	Title *Label Number*	Position	Weeks
19 Nov 54	**SH-BOOM** *Capitol CL 14187*	**15**	2 wks
27 Jul 56	**ROCK ISLAND LINE/ HEARTBREAK HOTEL** *Capitol CL 14608*	**24**	1 wk
10 Aug 56	**ROCK ISLAND LINE/ HEARTBREAK HOTEL** (re-entry) *Capitol CL 14608*	**29**	1 wk

John FRED and the PLAYBOY BAND

US, male vocal/instrumental group

Date	Title *Label Number*	Position	Weeks
3 Jan 68	● **JUDY IN DISGUISE (WITH GLASSES)** *Pye International 7N 25442*	**3**	12 wks

FREDDIE and the DREAMERS

UK, male vocal/instrumental group

Date	Title *Label Number*	Position	Weeks
9 May 63	● **IF YOU GOTTA MAKE A FOOL OF SOMEBODY** *Columbia DB 7032*	**3**	14 wks
8 Aug 63	● **I'M TELLING YOU NOW** *Columbia DB 7068*	**2**	11 wks
7 Nov 63	● **YOU WERE MADE FOR ME** *Columbia DB 7147*	**3**	15 wks
20 Feb 64	**OVER YOU** *Columbia DB 7214*	**13**	11 wks
14 May 64	**I LOVE YOU BABY** *Columbia DB 7286*	**16**	8 wks
16 Jul 64	**JUST FOR YOU** *Columbia DB 7322*	**41**	3 wks
5 Nov 64	● **I UNDERSTAND** *Columbia DB 7381*	**5**	15 wks
22 Apr 65	**A LITTLE YOU** *Columbia DB 7526*	**26**	5 wks
4 Nov 65	**THOU SHALT NOT STEAL** *Columbia DB 7720*	**44**	3 wks

FREDERICK — See *NINA and FREDERICK*

Date Title *Label Number* Position

FREE *UK, male vocal/instrumental group*

Date	Title *Label Number*	Position	Weeks
6 Jun 70	● **ALL RIGHT NOW** *Island WIP 6082*	**2**	16 wks
1 May 71	● **MY BROTHER JAKE** *Island WIP 6100*	**4**	11 wks
27 May 72	**LITTLE BIT OF LOVE** *Island WIP 6129*	**13**	10 wks
13 Jan 73	● **WISHING WELL** *Island WIP 6146*	**7**	10 wks
21 Jul 73	**ALL RIGHT NOW** (re-entry) *Island WIP 6082*	**15**	9 wks
18 Feb 78	**FREE** EP *Island IEP 6*	**11**	7 wks
23 Oct 82	**FREE** (EP) (re-entry) *Island IEP 6*	**57**	3 wks

Tracks on Free *EP: All Right Now/ My Brother Jake/ Wishing Well*

FREEEZ *UK, male instrumental group*

Date	Title *Label Number*	Position	Weeks
7 Jun 80	**KEEP IN TOUCH** *Calibre CAB 103*	**49**	3 wks
7 Feb 81	● **SOUTHERN FREEEZ BEGGARS BANQUET** *BEG 51*	**8**	11 wks
18 Apr 81	**FLYING HIGH BEGGARS BANQUET** *BEG 55*	**35**	5 wks

FREEHOLD JUNIOR SCHOOL — See *Fogwell FLAX and the ANKLEBITERS from FREEHOLD JUNIOR SCHOOL*

FRESHIES *UK, male vocal/instrumental group*

Date	Title *Label Number*	Position	Weeks
14 Feb 81	**I'M IN LOVE WITH THE GIRL ON A CERTAIN MANCHESTER MEGASTORE CHECKOUT DESK** *MCA 760*	**54**	3 wks

FRIDA *Sweden, female vocalist*

Date	Title *Label Number*	Position	Weeks
21 Aug 82	**I KNOW THERE'S SOMETHING GOING ON** *Epic EPC A2603*	**43**	7 wks

Dean FRIEDMAN *US, male vocalist*

Date	Title *Label Number*	Position	Weeks
3 Jun 78	**WOMAN OF MINE** *Lifesong LS 401*	**52**	5 wks
23 Sep 78	● **LUCKY STARS** *Lifesong LS 402*	**3**	10 wks
18 Nov 78	**LYDIA** *Lifesong LS 403*	**31**	7 wks

FRIENDS — See *DELANEY and BONNIE and FRIENDS*

FRIJID PINK *US male vocal/instrumental group*

Date	Title *Label Number*	Position	Weeks
28 Mar 70	● **HOUSE OF THE RISING SUN** *Deram DM 288*	**4**	16 wks

Jane FROMAN *US, female vocalist*

Date	Title *Label Number*	Position	Weeks
17 Jun 55	**I WONDER** *Capitol CL 14254*	**14**	4 wks

Bobby FULLER FOUR

US, male vocal/instrumental group

Date	Title *Label Number*	Position	Weeks
14 Apr 66	**I FOUGHT THE LAW** *London HL 10030*	**33**	4 wks

FUNBOY THREE

UK, male vocal/instrumental group

Date	Title *Label Number*	Position	Weeks
7 Nov 81	**THE LUNATICS (HAVE TAKEN OVER THE ASYLUM)** *Chrysalis CHS 2563*	**20**	12 wks
8 May 82	**THE TELEPHONE ALWAYS RINGS** *Chrysalis CHS 2609*	**17**	9 wks
31 Jul 82	**SUMMERTIME** *Chrysalis CHS 2629*	**18**	8 wks

see also Funboy Three and Bananarama

FUNBOY THREE and BANANARAMA

UK, male vocal group and female vocal group

Date	Title *Label Number*	Position	Weeks
13 Feb 82	● **IT AIN'T WHAT YOU DO IT'S THE WAY THAT YOU DO IT** *Chrysalis CHS 2570*	**4**	10 wks

see also Funboy Three, Bananarama.

FUNKADELIC *US, male vocal/instrumental group*

Date	Title *Label Number*	Position	Weeks
9 Dec 78	● **ONE NATION UNDER A GROOVE -PART 1** *Warner Bros. K 17246*	**9**	12 wks

FUNKAPOLITAN

UK, male vocal/instrumental group

Date	Title *Label Number*	Position	Weeks
22 Aug 81	**AS TIME GOES BY (VOCALS)** *London LON 001*	**41**	7 wks

FUNKY BOYS — See *LINDA and the FUNKY BOYS*

FUREYS *Ireland, male vocal group*

Date	Title *Label Number*	Position	Weeks
10 Oct 81	**WHEN YOU WERE SWEET SIXTEEN** *Ritz RITZ 003*	**14**	11 wks
3 Apr 82	**I WILL LOVE YOU (EVERY TIME WHEN WE ARE GONE)** *Ritz RITZ 012*	**54**	3 wks

When You Were Sweet Sixteen *credits the Fureys with Davey Arthur*

FURIOUS FIVE — See *GRAND MASTER FLASH and the FURIOUS FIVE*

Billy FURY *UK, male vocalist*

Date	Title *Label Number*	Position	Weeks
27 Feb 59	**MAYBE TOMORROW** *Decca F 11102*	**22**	3 wks
27 Mar 59	**MAYBE TOMORROW** (re-entry) *Decca F 11102*	**18**	6 wks
26 Jun 59	**MARGOT** *Decca F 11128*	**28**	1 wk
10 Mar 60	● **COLETTE** *Decca F 11200*	**9**	10 wks
26 May 60	**THAT'S LOVE** *Decca F 11237*	**19**	11 wks
22 Sep 60	**WONDROUS PLACE** *Decca F 11267*	**25**	9 wks
19 Jan 61	**A THOUSAND STARS** *Decca F 11311*	**14**	10 wks
27 Apr 61	**DON'T WORRY** *Decca F 11334*	**40**	2 wks
11 May 61	● **HALFWAY TO PARADISE** *Decca F 11349*	**3**	23 wks
7 Sep 61	● **JEALOUSY** *Decca F 11384*	**2**	12 wks
14 Dec 61	● **I'D NEVER FIND ANOTHER YOU** *Decca F 11409*	**5**	15 wks
15 Mar 62	**LETTER FULL OF TEARS** *Decca F 11437*	**32**	6 wks
3 May 62	● **LAST NIGHT WAS MADE FOR LOVE** *Decca F 11458*	**4**	16 wks
19 Jul 62	● **ONCE UPON A DREAM** *Decca F 11485*	**7**	13 wks
25 Oct 62	**BECAUSE OF LOVE** *Decca F 11508*	**18**	14 wks
14 Feb 63	● **LIKE I'VE NEVER BEEN GONE** *Decca F11582*	**3**	15 wks
16 May 63	● **WHEN WILL YOU SAY I LOVE YOU** *Decca F 11655*	**3**	12 wks
25 Jul 63	● **IN SUMMER** *Decca F 11701*	**5**	11 wks
3 Oct 63	**SOMEBODY ELSE'S GIRL** *Decca F 11744*	**18**	7 wks
2 Jan 64	**DO YOU REALLY LOVE ME TOO** *Decca F 11792*	**13**	10 wks
30 Apr 64	**I WILL** *Decca F 118888*	**14**	12 wks
23 Jul 64	● **IT'S ONLY MAKE BELIEVE** *Decca F 11939*	**10**	10 wks
14 Jan 65	**I'M LOST WITHOUT YOU** *Decca F 12048*	**16**	10 wks
22 Jul 65	● **IN THOUGHTS OF YOU** *Decca F 12178*	**9**	11 wks
16 Sep 65	**RUN TO MY LOVIN' ARMS** *Decca F 12230*	**25**	7 wks
10 Feb 66	**I'LL NEVER QUITE GET OVER YOU** *Decca F 12325*	**35**	5 wks
4 Aug 66	**GIVE ME YOUR WORD** *Decca F 12459*	**27**	7 wks
4 Sep 82	**LOVE OR MONEY** *Polydor POSP 488*	**57**	5 wks
13 Nov 82	**DEVIL OR ANGEL** *Polydor POSP 528*	**58**	4 wks

Above **BILLY FURY** One of Britain's greatest singers; he died at the end of January 1983. The picture shows Billy at the launch for the *Guinness Book of 500 Number One Hits* at Abbey Road

Left **BOBBY FULLER FOUR** They came from the town that gave Marty Robbins his debut hit and brought their Texas Buddy Holly-style rock 'n' roll to the charts via a song written by Cricket Sonny Curtis

Right **DAVID GARRICK** An operatically trained Liverpudlian, the group that became Badfinger were his backing group at the time of his hits

Date	Title *Label Number*	Position	

Leslie FYSON — See *Michael MEDWIN, Bernard BRESSLAW, Alfie BASS and Leslie FYSON*

G

GBH *UK, male vocal/instrumental group*

Date	Title *Label Number*	Position	
6 Feb 82	**NO SURVIVORS** *Clay CLAY 8*	**63**	2 wks
20 Nov 82	**GIVE ME FIRE** *Clay CLAY 16*	**69**	3 wks

G. F. BAND — See *Gene FARROW and G. F. BAND*

G. Q. *US, male vocal/instrumental group*

Date	Title *Label Number*	Position	
10 Mar 79	**DISCO NIGHTS (ROCK FREAK)** *Arista ARIST 245*	**42**	6 wks

Peter GABRIEL *UK male vocalist*

Date	Title *Label Number*	Position	
9 Apr 77	**SOLSBURY HILL** *Charisma CB 301*	**13**	9 wks
9 Feb 80	● **GAMES WITHOUT FRONTIERS** *Charisma CB 354*	**4**	11 wks
10 May 80	**NO SELF CONTROL** *Charisma CB 360*	**33**	6 wks
23 Aug 80	**BIKO** *Charisma CB 370*	**38**	3 wks
25 Sep 82	**SHOCK THE MONKEY** *Charisma/Phonogram SHOCK 1*	**58**	5 wks

Serge GAINSBOURG — See *Jane BIRKIN and Serge GAINSBOURG*

Serge GAINSBOURG — See *Jane BIRKIN and Serge GAINSBOURG*

GALLAGHER and LYLE

UK, male vocal/instrumental duo

Date	Title *Label Number*	Position	
28 Feb 76	● **I WANNA STAY WITH YOU** *A & M AMS 7211*	**6**	9 wks
22 May 76	● **HEART ON MY SLEEVE** *A & M AMS 7227*	**6**	10 wks
11 Sep 76	**BREAKAWAY** *A & M AMS 7245*	**35**	4 wks
29 Jan 77	**EVERY LITTLE TEARDROP** *A & M AMS 7274*	**32**	4 wks

Patsy GALLANT *Canada, female vocalist*

Date	Title *Label Number*	Position	
10 Sep 77	● **FROM NEW YORK TO L.A.** *EMI 2620*	**6**	9 wks

James GALWAY

Ireland, male instrumentalist, flute

Date	Title *Label Number*	Position	
27 May 78	● **ANNIE'S SONG** *RCA Red Seal RB 5085*	**3**	13 wks

GANG OF FOUR

UK, male vocal/instrumental group

Date	Title *Label Number*	Position	
16 Jun 79	**AT HOME HE'S A TOURIST** *EMI 2956*	**58**	3 wks
22 May 82	**I LOVE A MAN IN UNIFORM** *EMI 5299*	**65**	2 wks

GAP BAND *US, male vocal/instrumental group*

Date	Title *Label Number*	Position	
12 Jul 80	● **OOPS UP SIDE YOUR HEAD** *Mercury MER 22*	**6**	14 wks
27 Sep 80	**PARTY LIGHTS** *Mercury MER 37*	**30**	8 wks
27 Dec 80	**BURN RUBBER ON ME (WHY YOU WANNA HURT ME)** *Mercury MER 52*	**22**	wks
11 Apr 81	**HUMPIN'** *Mercury MER 63*	**36**	6 wks
27 Jun 81	**YEARNING FOR YOUR LOVE** *Mercury MER 73*	**47**	4 wks
5 Jun 82	**EARLY IN THE MORNING** *Mercury/Phonogram MER 97*	**55**	3 wks

Paul GARDINER *UK, male instrumentalist, bass*

Date	Title *Label Number*	Position	
25 Jul 81	**STORMTROOPER IN DRAG** *Beggars Banquet BEG 61*	**49**	4 wks

Featuring Gary Numan on vocals. See also Gary Numan.

GARDNER — See *ASHTON, GARDNER and DYKE*

Boris GARDNER

Jamaica, male instrumentalist, organ

Date	Title *Label Number*	Position	
17 Jan 70	**ELIZABETHAN REGGAE** *Duke DU 39*	**48**	1 wk
31 Jan 70	**ELIZABETHAN REGGAE** (re-entry) *Duke DU 39*	**14**	13 wks

Art GARFUNKEL *US, male vocalist*

Date	Title *Label Number*	Position	
13 Sep 75	★ **I ONLY HAVE EYES FOR YOU** *CBS 3575*	**1**	11 wks
3 Mar 79	★ **BRIGHT EYES** *CBS 6947*	**1**	19 wks
7 Jul 79	**SINCE I DON'T HAVE YOU** *CBS 7371*	**38**	7 wks

See also Simon & Garfunkel.

Judy GARLAND *US, female vocalist*

Date	Title *Label Number*	Position	
10 Jun 55	**THE MAN THAT GOT AWAY** *Philips PB 366*	**18**	2 wks

Lee GARRETT *US, male vocalist*

Date	Title *Label Number*	Position	
29 May 76	**YOU'RE MY EVERYTHING** *Chrysalis CHS 2087*	**15**	7 wks

Leif GARRETT *US, male vocalist*

Date	Title *Label Number*	Position	
20 Jan 79	● **I WAS MADE FOR DANCIN'** *Scotti Brothers K 11202*	**4**	10 wks
14 Apr 79	**FEEL THE NEED** *Scotti Brothers K 11274*	**38**	4 wks

David GARRICK *UK, male vocalist*

Date	Title *Label Number*	Position	
9 Jun 66	**LADY JANE** *Piccadilly 7N 35317*	**28**	7 wks
22 Sep 66	**DEAR MRS. APPLEBEE** *Piccadilly 7N 35335*	**22**	9 wks

GARY'S GANG *US, male vocal/instrumental group*

Date	Title *Label Number*	Position	
24 Feb 79	● **KEEP ON DANCIN'** *CBS 7109*	**8**	10 wks
2 Jun 79	**LET'S LOVE DANCE TONIGHT** *CBS 7328*	**49**	4 wks
6 Nov 82	**KNOCK ME OUT** *Arista ARIST 499*	**45**	4 wks

Barbara GASKIN — See *Dave STEWART with Barbara GASKIN*

Date	Title *Label Number*	Position	

David GATES *US, male vocalist*

Date	Title *Label Number*	Position	
22 Jul 78	**TOOK THE LAST TRAIN** *Elektra K 12307*	50	2 wks

Marvin GAYE *US, male vocalist*

Date	Title *Label Number*	Position	
10 Dec 64	**HOW SWEET IT IS** *Stateside SS 360*	49	1 wk
29 Sep 66	**LITTLE DARLIN'** *Tamla Motown TMG 574*	50	1 wk
12 Feb 69 ★	**I HEARD IT THROUGH THE GRAPEVINE** *Tamla Motown TMG 686*	1	15 wks
23 Jul 69 ●	**TOO BUSY THINKING 'BOUT MY BABY** *Tamla Motown TMG 705*	5	16 wks
9 May 70 ●	**ABRAHAM MARTIN & JOHN** *Tamla Motown TMG 734*	9	14 wks
11 Dec 71	**SAVE THE CHILDREN** *Tamla Motown TMG 796*	41	6 wks
22 Sep 73	**LET'S GET IT ON** *Tamla Motown TMG 868*	31	7 wks
7 May 77 ●	**GOT TO GIVE IT UP** *Motown TMG 1069*	7	10 wks
30 Oct 82 ●	**(SEXUAL) HEALING** *CBS A 2855*	4†	9 wks

See also Diana Ross & Marvin Gaye, Marvin Gaye & Tammi Terrell, Marvin Gaye & Mary Wells, Marvin Gaye & Kim Weston.

Marvin GAYE and Tammi TERRELL

US, male/female vocal duo

Date	Title *Label Number*	Position	
17 Jan 68	**IF I COULD BUILD MY WHOLE WORLD AROUND YOU** *Tamla Motown TMG 635*	41	7 wks
12 Jun 68	**AIN'T NOTHIN' LIKE THE REAL THING** *Tamla Motown TMG 655*	34	7 wks
2 Oct 68	**YOU'RE ALL I NEED TO GET BY** *Tamla Motown TMG 668*	19	19 wks
22 Jan 69	**YOU AIN'T LIVIN' TILL YOU'RE LOVIN'** *Tamla Motown TMG 681*	21	8 wks
4 Jun 69	**GOOD LOVIN' AIN'T EASY TO COME BY** *Tamla Motown TMG 697*	26	7 wks
30 Jul 69	**GOOD LOVIN' AIN'T EASY TO COME BY** (re-entry) *Tamla Motown TMG 697*	48	1 wk
15 Nov 69 ●	**ONION SONG** *Tamla Motown TMG 715*	9	12 wks

See also Marvin Gaye, Marvin Gaye & Diana Ross, Marvin Gaye & Mary Wells, Marvin Gaye & Kim Weston.

Marvin GAYE and Mary WELLS

US, male/female vocal duo

Date	Title *Label Number*	Position	
30 Jul 64	**ONCE UPON A TIME** *Stateside SS 316*	50	1 wk

See also Marvin Gaye, Mary Wells, Marvin Gaye & Diana Ross, Marvin Gaye & Tammi Terrell, Marvin Gaye & Kim Weston.

Marvin GAYE and Kim WESTON

US, male/female vocal duo

Date	Title *Label Number*	Position	
26 Jan 67	**IT TAKES TWO** *Tamla Motown TMG 590*	16	11 wks

See also Marvin Gaye, Marvin Gaye & Diana Ross, Marvin Gaye & Tammi Terrell, Marvin Gaye & Mary Wells.

Crystal GAYLE *US, female vocalist*

Date	Title *Label Number*	Position	
12 Nov 77 ●	**DON'T IT MAKE MY BROWN EYES BLUE** *United Artists UP 36307*	5	14 wks
26 Aug 78	**TALKING IN YOUR SLEEP** *United Artists UP 36422*	11	14 wks

Gloria GAYNOR *US, female vocalist*

Date	Title *Label Number*	Position	
7 Dec 74 ●	**NEVER CAN SAY GOODBYE** *MGM 2006 463*	2	13 wks
8 Mar 75	**REACH OUT I'LL BE THERE** *MGM 2006 499*	14	8 wks
9 Aug 75	**ALL I NEED IS YOUR SWEET LOVIN'** *MGM 2006 531*	44	3 wks
17 Jan 76	**HOW HIGH THE MOON** *MGM 2006 558*	33	4 wks
3 Feb 79 ★	**I WILL SURVIVE** *Polydor 2095 017*	1	15 wks
6 Oct 79	**LET ME KNOW (I HAVE A RIGHT)** *Polydor STEP 5*	32	7 wks

GAZ *US, male vocal/instrumental group*

Date	Title *Label Number*	Position	
24 Feb 79	**SING SING** *Salsoul SSOL 116*	60	4 wks

G-CLEFS *US, male vocal group*

Date	Title *Label Number*	Position	
30 Nov 61	**I UNDERSTAND** *London HLU 9433*	17	12 wks

J. GEILS BAND *US, male vocal/instrumental group*

Date	Title *Label Number*	Position	
9 Jun 79	**ONE LAST KISS** *EMI AMERICA AM 507*	74	1 wk
13 Feb 82 ●	**CENTERFOLD** *EMI AMERICA EA 135*	3	9 wks
10 Apr 82	**FREEZE-FRAME** *EMI AMERICA EA 134*	27	7 wks
26 Jun 82	**ANGEL IN BLUE** *EMI AMERICA EA 138*	55	3 wks

GENERATION X

UK, male vocal/instrumental group

Date	Title *Label Number*	Position	
17 Sep 77	**YOUR GENERATION** *Chrysalis CHS 2165*	36	4 wks
11 Mar 78	**READY STEADY GO** *Chrysalis CHS 2207*	47	3 wks
20 Jan 79	**KING ROCKER** *Chrysalis CHS 2261*	11	9 wks
7 Apr 79	**VALLEY OF THE DOLLS** *Chrysalis CHS 2310*	23	7 wks
30 Jun 79	**FRIDAYS ANGELS** *Chrysalis CHS 2330*	62	2 wks
18 Oct 80	**DANCING WITH MYSELF** *Chrysalis CHS 2444*	62	2 wks
24 Jan 81	**DANCING WITH MYSELF** EP *Chrysalis CHS 2488*	60	4 wks

From Dancing With Myself, *group is billed as Gen X* Dancing With Myself EP *contains the following tracks: Dancing with Myself, Untouchables, Rock On, King Rocker.*

GENESIS *UK, male vocal/instrumental group*

Date	Title *Label Number*	Position	
6 Apr 74	**I KNOW WHAT I LIKE (IN YOUR WARDROBE)** *Charisma CB 224*	21	7 wks
26 Feb 77	**YOUR OWN SPECIAL WAY** *Charisma CB 300*	43	3 wks
28 May 77	**SPOT THE PIGEON** (EP) *Charisma GEN 001*	14	7 wks
11 Mar 78 ●	**FOLLOW YOU FOLLOW ME** *Charisma CB 309*	7	13 wks
8 Jul 78	**MANY TOO MANY** *Charisma CB 315*	43	5 wks
15 Mar 80 ●	**TURN IT ON AGAIN** *Charisma CB 356*	8	10 wks
17 May 80	**DUCHESS** *Charisma CB 363*	46	5 wks
13 Sep 80	**MISUNDERSTANDING** *Charisma CB 369*	42	5 wks
22 Aug 81 ●	**ABACAB** *Charisma CB 388*	9	8 wks
31 Oct 81	**KEEP IT DARK** *Charisma CB 391*	33	4 wks
13 Mar 82	**MAN ON THE CORNER** *Charisma CB 393*	41	5 wks
22 May 82 ●	**3 X 3** (EP) *Charisma/Phonogram GEN 1*	10	8 wks

Tracks on Spot The Pigeon EP: *Match Of The Day/Pigeons/Inside and Out* Tracks on 3 x 3 (EP): *Paper Late, You Might Recall, Me and Virgil.*

GENEVEVE *France, female vocalist*

Date	Title *Label Number*	Position	
5 May 66	**ONCE** *CBS 202061*	43	1 wk

Above **GERRY AND THE PACEMAKERS** 20 years on, they are still the only group to top the chart with their first three singles
Right **BOBBIE GENTRY** Bobbie gets to grips with her Bert Weedon 'play in a day' technique
Below **GOLDIE AND THE GINGERBREADS** Not a gingerbread man in sight

GRAHAM GOULDMAN Only one small solo hit, but many as a member of 10cc and as songwriter on occasions for artists that include the Hollies, the Yardbirds and Herman's Hermits
ADRIAN GURVITZ He first hit the chart with 'Race with the Devil' as a member of Gun, went on to form the Baker-Gurvitz Army with his brother Paul and drummer Ginger Baker and in '82 wrote a Classic

DON GIBSON Successfully gloomy twice

Date	Title *Label Number*	Position	

Bobbie GENTRY *US, female vocalist*

13 Sep 67	**ODE TO BILLY JOE** *Capitol CL 15511*	**13**	11 wks
30 Aug 69 ★	**I'LL NEVER FALL IN LOVE AGAIN** *Capitol CL 15606*	**1**	19 wks
21 Feb 70	**RAINDROPS KEEP FALLIN' ON MY HEAD** *Capitol CL 15626*	**40**	4 wks

See also Bobbie Gentry & Glen Campbell.

Bobbie GENTRY and Glen CAMPBELL

US, female/male vocal duo

6 Dec 69 ●	**ALL I HAVE TO DO IS DREAM** *Capitol CL 15619*	**3**	14 wks

See also Bobbie Gentry, Glen Campbell.

GEORDIE *UK, vocal/instrumental group*

2 Dec 72	**DON'T DO THAT** *Regal Zonophone RZ 3067*	**32**	7 wks
17 Mar 73 ●	**ALL BECAUSE OF YOU** *EMI 2008*	**6**	13 wks
16 Jun 73	**CAN YOU DO IT** *EMI 2031*	**13**	9 wks
25 Aug 73	**ELECTRIC LADY** *EMI 2047*	**32**	6 wks

Danyel GERARD *France, male vocalist*

18 Sep 71	**BUTTERFLY** *CBS 7453*	**11**	12 wks

GERRY and THE PACEMAKERS

UK, male vocal/instrumental group

14 Mar 63 ★	**HOW DO YOU DO IT?** *Columbia DB 4987*	**1**	18 wks
30 May 63 ★	**I LIKE IT** *Columbia DB 7041*	**1**	15 wks
10 Oct 63 ★	**YOU'LL NEVER WALK ALONE** *Columbia DB 7126*	**1**	19 wks
16 Jan 64 ●	**I'M THE ONE** *Columbia DB 7189*	**2**	15 wks
16 Apr 64 ●	**DON'T LET THE SUN CATCH YOU CRYING** *Columbia DB 7268*	**6**	11 wks
3 Sep 64	**IT'S GONNA BE ALL RIGHT** *Columbia DB 7353*	**24**	7 wks
17 Dec 64 ●	**FERRY ACROSS THE MERSEY** *Columbia DB 7437*	**8**	13 wks
25 Mar 65	**I'LL BE THERE** *Columbia DB 7504*	**15**	9 wks
18 Nov 65	**WALK HAND IN HAND** *Columbia DB 7738*	**29**	7 wks

Stan GETZ and Charlie BYRD

US, male instrumental duo, sax and guitar

8 Nov 62	**DESAFINADO** *HMV POP 1061*	**11**	11 wks

See also Stan Getz & Joao Gilberto.

Stan GETZ and Joao GILBERTO

US/Brazil, male instrumentalist, tenor sax/male vocalist

23 Jul 64	**THE GIRL FROM IPANEMA (GAROTA DE IPANEMA)** *Verve VS 520*	**29**	10 wks

See also Stan Getz and Charlie Byrd. Joao Gilberto did not actually appear on this hit. The vocalist is in fact Astrud, his wife.

Andy GIBB *UK, male vocalist*

25 Jun 77	**I JUST WANNA BE YOUR EVERYTHING** *RSO 2090 237*	**26**	7 wks
13 May 78	**SHADOW DANCING** *RSO 001*	**42**	6 wks
12 Aug 78 ●	**AN EVERLASTING LOVE** *RSO 015*	**10**	10 wks
27 Jan 79	**(OUR LOVE) DON'T THROW IT ALL AWAY** *RSO 26*	**32**	7 wks

Barry GIBB — See *Barbra STREISAND and Barry GIBB*

Robin GIBB *UK, male vocalist*

9 Jul 69 ●	**SAVED BY THE BELL** *Polydor 56-337*	**2**	16 wks
15 Nov 69	**SAVED BY THE BELL** (re-entry) *Polydor 56-337*	**49**	1 wk
7 Feb 70	**AUGUST OCTOBER** *Polydor 56-371*	**45**	3 wks

Steve GIBBONS BAND

UK, male vocal/instrumental group

6 Aug 77	**TULANE** *Polydor 2058 889*	**12**	10 wks
13 May 78	**EDDY VORTEX** *Polydor 2059 o17*	**56**	4 wks

Georgia GIBBS *US, female vocalist*

22 Apr 55	**TWEEDLE DEE** *Mercury MB 3196*	**20**	1 wk
13 Jul 56	**KISS ME ANOTHER** *Mercury MT 110*	**24**	1 wk

Don GIBSON *US, male vocalist*

31 Aug 61	**SEA OF HEARTBREAK** *RCA 1243*	**14**	13 wks
1 Feb 62	**LONESOME NUMBER ONE** *RCA 1272*	**47**	3 wks

Wayne GIBSON *UK, male vocalist*

3 Sep 64	**KELLY** *Pye 7N 15680*	**48**	2 wks
23 Nov 74	**UNDER MY THUMB** *Pye Disco Demand DDS 2001*	**17**	11 wks

GIBSON BROTHERS

Martinique, male vocal/instrumental group

10 Mar 79	**CUBA** *Island WIP 6483*	**41**	9 wks
21 Jul 79 ●	**OOH! WHAT A LIFE** *Island WIP 6503*	**10**	12 wks
17 Nov 79 ●	**QUE SERA MI VIDA (IF YOU SHOULD GO)** *Island WIP 6525*	**5**	11 wks
23 Feb 80	**CUBA** (RE-ISSUE) /**BETTER DO IT SALSA** *Island WIP 6561*	**12**	9 wks
12 July 80	**MARIANA** *Island WIP 6617*	**11**	10 wks

GIDEA PARK

UK, male vocal/instrumental group, Adrian Baker under fake group name.

4 Jul 81	**BEACHBOY GOLD** *Stone SON 2162*	**11**	13 wks
12 Sep 81	**SEASONS OF GOLD** *Polo POLO 14*	**28**	6 wks

see also Adrian Baker.

Astrid GILBERTO — See *Stan GETZ and Joao GILBERTO*

Joao GILBERTO — See *Stan GETZ and Joao GILBERTO*

Date	Title *Label Number*	Position	

GILLAN *UK, male vocal/instrumental group*

14 Jun 80	**SLEEPIN' ON THE JOB** *Virgin VS 355*	**55**	3 wks
4 Oct 80	**TROUBLE** *Virgin VS 377*	**14**	6 wks
14 Feb 81	**MUTUALLY ASSURED DESTRUCTION** *Virgin VSK 103*	**32**	5 wks
21 Mar 81	**NEW ORLEANS** *Virgin VS 406*	**17**	10 wks
20 Jun 81	**NO LAUGHING IN HEAVEN** *Virgin VS 425*	**31**	6 wks
10 Oct 81	**NIGHTMARE** *Virgin VS 441*	**36**	6 wks
23 Jan 82	**RESTLESS** *Virgin VS 465*	**25**	7 wks
4 Sep 82	**LIVING FOR THE CITY** *Virgin VS 519*	**50**	3 wks

Stuart GILLIES *UK, male vocalist*

31 Mar 73	**AMANDA** *Philips 6006 293*	**13**	10 wks

Jimmy GILMER and the FIREBALLS

US, male vocalist/instrumental backing group

14 Nov 63	**SUGAR SHACK** *London HLD 9789*	**45**	4 wks
19 Dec 63	**SUGAR SHACK** (re-entry) *London HLD 9789*	**46**	4 wks

See also Fireballs.

James GILREATH *US, male vocalist*

2 May 63	**LITTLE BAND OF GOLD** *Pye International 7N 25190*	**29**	10 wks

Jim GILSTRAP *US, male vocalist*

15 Mar 75	● **SWING YOUR DADDY** *Chelsea 2005 021*	**4**	11 wks

Gordon GILTRAP

UK, male instrumentalist - guitar

14 Jan 78	**HEARTSONG** *Electric WOT 19*	**21**	7 wks
28 Apr 79	**FEAR OF THE DARK** *Electric WOT 29*	**58**	3 wks

Fear Of The Dark *credited to the Gordon Giltrap Band.*

GINGERBREADS — See *GOLDIE and the GINGERBREADS*

GIRL *UK, male vocal/instrumental group*

12 Apr 80	**HOLLYWOOD TEASE** *Jet 176*	**50**	3 wks

GIRLSCHOOL *UK, female vocal/instrumental group*

2 Aug 80	**RACE WITH THE DEVIL** *Bronze BRO 100*	**49**	6 wks
11 Apr 81	**HIT AND RUN** *Bronze BRO 118*	**32**	6 wks
11 Jul 81	**C'MON LET'S GO** *Bronze BRO 126*	**42**	3 wks
3 Apr 82	**DON'T CALL IT LOVE (WILDLIFE EP)** *Bronze BRO 144*	**58**	2 wks

See also Headgirl. Tracks on Wildlife EP: *Don't Call it Love, Wildlife, Don't Stop.*

GLADIATORS — See *NERO and the GLADIATORS*

Mayson GLEN ORCHESTRA — See *Paul HENRY and the Mayson GLEN ORCHESTRA*

Gary GLITTER *UK, male vocalist*

10 Jun 72	● **ROCK & ROLL** (PARTS 1 & 2) *Bell 1216*	**2**	15 wks
23 Sep 72	● **I DIDN'T KNOW I LOVED YOU (TILL I SAW YOU ROCK N ROLL)** *Bell 1259*	**4**	11 wks
20 Jan 73	● **DO YOU WANNA TOUCH ME (OH YEAH)** *Bell 1280*	**2**	11 wks
7 Apr 73	● **HELLO HELLO I'M BACK AGAIN** *Bell 1299*	**2**	14 wks
21 Jul 73	★ **I'M THE LEADER OF THE GANG (I AM!)** *Bell 1321*	**1**	12 wks
17 Nov 73	★ **I LOVE YOU LOVE ME LOVE** *Bell 1337*	**1**	14 wks
30 Mar 74	● **REMEMBER ME THIS WAY** *Bell 1349*	**3**	8 wks
15 Jun 74	★ **ALWAYS YOURS** *Bell 1359*	**1**	9 wks
23 Nov 74	● **OH YES! YOU'RE BEAUTIFUL** *Bell 1391*	**2**	10 wks
3 May 75	● **LOVE LIKE YOU AND ME** *Bell 1423*	**10**	6 wks
21 Jun 75	● **DOING ALRIGHT WITH THE BOYS** *Bell 1429*	**6**	7 wks
8 Nov 75	**PAPA OOM MOW MOW** *Bell 1451*	**38**	5 wks
13 Mar 76	**YOU BELONG TO ME** *Bell 1473*	**40**	5 wks
22 Jan 77	**IT TAKES ALL NIGHT LONG** *Arista 85*	**25**	6 wks
16 Jul 77	**A LITTLE BOOGIE WOOGIE IN THE BACK OF MY MIND** *Arista 112*	**31**	5 wks
20 Sep 80	**GARY GLITTER**(EP) (re-issue) *GTO GT 282*	**57**	3 wks
10 Oct 81	**AND THEN SHE KISSED ME** *Bell BELL 1497*	**39**	5 wks
4 Dec 81	**ALL THAT GLITTERS** *Bell (Eagle) BELL 1498*	**48**	4 wks

Rock & Roll Part not listed with Part 2 for weeks of 10 and 17 Jan 72. Tracks On Gary Glitter EP: *I'm The Leader Of The Gang (I Am)/ Rock And Roll (Part 2) Hello Hello I'm Back Again/ Do You Wanna Touch Me? (Oh Yeah!). (All re-issues of the single hits)*

GLITTER BAND

UK, male vocal/instrumental group

23 Mar 74	● **ANGEL FACE** *Bell 1348*	**4**	10 wks
3 Aug 74	● **JUST FOR YOU** *Bell 1368*	**10**	8 wks
19 Oct 74	● **LET'S GET TOGETHER AGAIN** *Bell 1383*	**8**	8 wks
18 Jan 75	● **GOODBYE MY LOVE** *Bell 1395*	**2**	9 wks
12 Apr 75	● **THE TEARS I CRIED** *Bell 1416*	**8**	8 wks
9 Aug 75	**LOVE IN THE SUN** *Bell 1437*	**15**	8 wks
28 Feb 76	● **PEOPLE LIKE YOU AND PEOPLE LIKE ME** *Bell 1471*	**5**	9 wks

GODIEGO *Japan/US, male vocal/instrumental group*

15 Oct 77	**THE WATER MARGIN** *BBC RESL 50*	**37**	4 wks
16 Feb 80	**GANDHARA** *BBC RESL 66*	**56**	7 wks

The Water Margin *is the English version of the song, which shared chart credit with the Japanese language version by Peter Mac Junior. See also Peter Mac Junior.*

GODLEY and CREME *UK, male audiovisual duo*

12 Sep 81	● **UNDER YOUR THUMB** *Polydor POSP 322*	**3**	11 wks
21 Nov 81	● **WEDDING BELLS** *Polydor POSP 369*	**7**	11 wks

GO-GOS *US, female vocal/instrumental group*

15 May 82	**OUR LIPS ARE SEALED** *I.R.S./A & M GDN 102*	**47**	6 wks

Andrew GOLD

US, male vocalist and instrumentalist, piano

2 Apr 77	**LONELY BOY** *Asylum K 13076*	**11**	9 wks
25 Mar 78	● **NEVER LET HER SLIP AWAY** *Asylum K 13112*	**5**	13 wks
24 Jun 78	**HOW CAN THIS BE LOVE** *Asylum K 13126*	**19**	10 wks
14 Oct 78	**THANK YOU FOR BEING A FRIEND** *Asylum K 13135*	**42**	4 wks

GOLDEN EARRING

Holland, male vocal/instrumental group

8 Dec 73 ● **RADAR LOVE** *Track 2094 116* — **7** 13 wks
8 Oct 77 **RADAR LOVE** *Polydor 2121 335* — **44** 1 wk

These are two different recordings of the same song.

GOLDIE *UK, male vocal/instrumental group*

27 May 78 ● **MAKING UP AGAIN** *Bronze BRO 50* — **7** 11 wks

GOLDIE and the GINGERBREADS

US, female vocal/instrumental group

25 Feb 65 **CAN'T YOU HEAR MY HEART BEAT?** *Decca F 12070* — **25** 5 wks

Bobby GOLDSBORO *US, male vocalist*

17 Apr 68 ● **HONEY** *United Artists UP2215* — **2** 15 wks
4 Aug 73 ● **SUMMER (THE FIRST TIME)** *United Artists UP35558* — **9** 10 wks
3 Aug 74 **HELLO SUMMERTIME** *United Artists UP35705* — **14** 10 wks
29 Mar 75 ● **HONEY** (re-issue) *United Artists UP35633* — **2** 12 wks

Leroy GOMEZ — See *SANTA ESMERALDA and Leroy GOMEZ*

GONZALEZ *UK, male vocal/instrumental group*

31 Mar 79 **HAVEN'T STOPPED DANCING YET** *Sidewalk SID 102* — **15** 11 wks

GOODIES *UK, male vocal group*

7 Dec 74 ● **THE IN BETWEENIES/ FATHER CHRISTMAS DO NOT TOUCH ME** *Bradley's BRAD 7421* — **7** 9 wks
15 Mar 75 ● **FUNKY GIBBON/ SICK MAN BLUES** *Bradley's BRAD 7504* — **4** 10 wks
21 Jun 75 **BLACK PUDDING BERTHA** *Bradley's BRAD 7517* — **19** 7 wks
27 Sep 75 **NAPPY LOVE/ WILD THING** *Bradley's BRAD 7524* — **21** 6 wks
13 Dec 75 **MAKE A DAFT NOISE FOR CHRISTMAS** *Bradley's BRAD 7533* — **20** 6 wks

Ron GOODWIN *UK, orchestra*

15 May 53 ● **LIMELIGHT** *Parlophone R 3686* — **3** 23 wks
28 Oct 55 **BLUE STAR (THE MEDIC THEME)** *Parlophone R 4074* — **20** 1 wk

GOODY GOODY *US, female vocal duo*

2 Dec 78 **NUMBER ONE DEE JAY** *Atlantic LV 3* — **55** 5 wks

GOOMBAY DANCE BAND

Germany/Montserrat, male/female vocal/instrumental group

27 Feb 82 ★ **SEVEN TEARS** *Epic EPC A 1242* — **1** 12 wks
15 May 82 **SUN OF JAMAICA** *Epic EPC A 2345* — **50** 4 wks

GOONS *UK, male vocal group*

29 Jun 56 ● **I'M WALKING BACKWARDS FOR CHRISTMAS/ BLUEBOTTLE BLUES** *Decca F 10756* — **4** 10 wks
4 Sep 56 ● **BLOODNOK'S ROCK N ROLL/ YING TONG SONG** *Decca E 10780* — **3** 10 wks
21 Jul 73 ● **YING TONG SONG** (re-issue) *Decca F 13414* — **9** 10 wks

Bluebottle Blues *only listed from 13 Jul 56.*

GORDON — See *PETER and GORDON*

Lesley GORE *US, female vocalist*

20 Jun 63 ● **IT'S MY PARTY** *Mercury AMT 1205* — **9** 12 wks
24 Sep 64 **MAYBE I KNOW** *Mercury MF 829* — **20** 8 wks

Eydie GORMÉ *US, female vocalist*

24 Jan 58 **LOVE ME FOREVER** *HMV POP 432* — **21** 5 wks
21 Jun 62 ● **YES MY DARLING DAUGHTER** *CBS AAG 105* — **10** 9 wks
31 Jan 63 **BLAME IT ON THE BOSSA NOVA** *CBS AAG 131* — **32** 6 wks

See also Steve and Eydie.

Graham GOULDMAN *UK, male vocalist*

23 Jun 79 **SUNBURN** *Mercury SUNNY 1* — **52** 4 wks

GRACE — See *DALE and GRACE*

Charlie GRACIE *US, male vocalist*

19 Apr 57 **BUTTERFLY** *Parlophone R 4290* — **12** 8 wks
14 Jun 57 ● **FABULOUS** *Parlophone R 4313* — **8** 16 wks
23 Aug 57 **I LOVE YOU SO MUCH IT HURTS/ WANDERIN' EYES** *London HL 8467* — **14** 2 wks
6 Sep 57 **I LOVE YOU SO MUCH IT HURTS** *London HL 8467* — **20** 2 wks
6 Sep 57 ● **WANDERIN' EYES** *London HL 8467* — **6** 12 wks
10 Jan 58 **COOL BABY** *London HLU 8521* — **26** 1 wk

I Love You So Much It Hurts *and* Wanderin' Eyes *were listed together for 2 weeks, then listed separately for a further 2 and 12 weeks respectively.*

Eve GRAHAM — See *NEW SEEKERS*

Larry GRAHAM *US, male vocalist*

3 Jul 82 **SOONER OR LATER** *Warner Bros. K 17925* — **54** 4 wks

Ron GRAINER ORCHESTRA *UK, orchestra*

9 Dec 78 **A TOUCH OF VELVET A STING OF BRASS** *Casino Classics CC 5* — **60** 6 wks

GOOMBAY DANCEBAND Just 89 tears short of ? and the Mysterians but 36 places higher *and left* **GEORGE HARRISON** On the back of this 1965 handout pic, it lists George's likes as smallish blondes, driving, sleeping, television, Segovia, Chet Atkins, egg and chips, Eartha Kitt and Alfred Hitchcock. These days he is an avid gardener and film producer

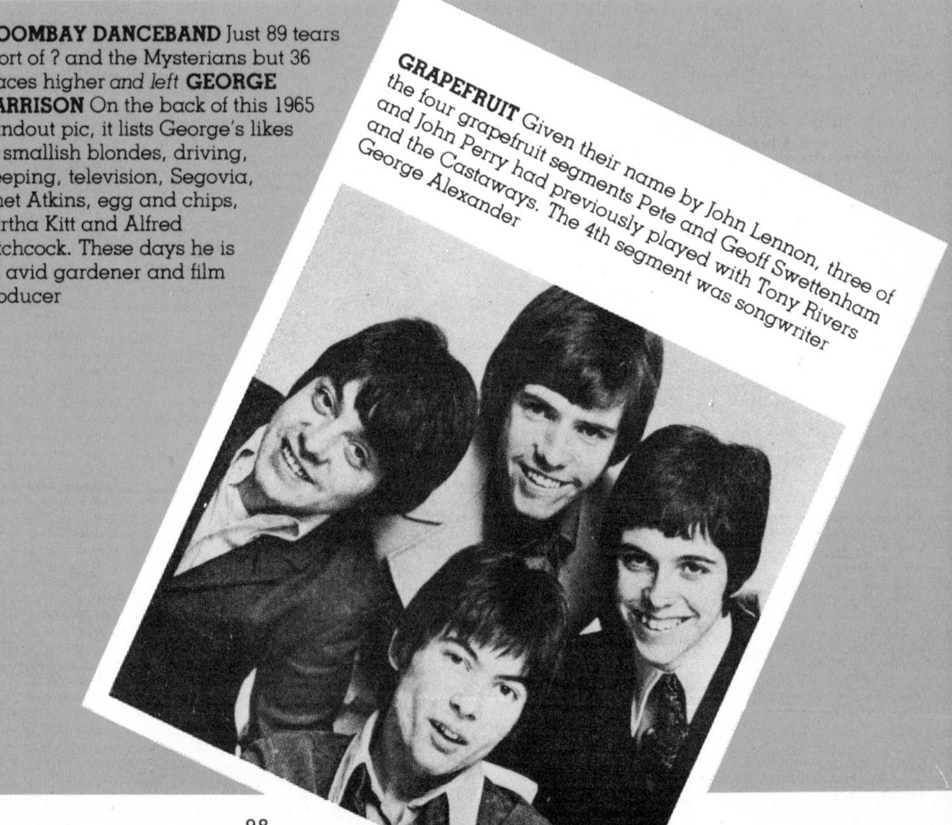

GRAPEFRUIT Given their name by John Lennon, three of the four grapefruit segments Pete and Geoff Swettenham and John Perry had previously played with Tony Rivers and the Castaways. The 4th segment was songwriter George Alexander

Date	Title Label Number	Position		Date	Title Label Number	Position	

GRAND FUNK RAILROAD

US, male vocal/instrumental group

6 Feb 71	**INSIDE LOOKING OUT** *Capitol CL 15668*	**40**	1 wk

GRAND MASTER FLASH and the FURIOUS FIVE

US, male vocalist and male vocal group

28 Aug 82	● **THE MESSAGE** *Sugarhill SHL 117*	**8**	9 wks

GRAND PRIX *UK, male vocal/instrumental group*

27 Feb 82	**KEEP ON BELIEVING** *RCA 162*	**75**	1 wk

Gerri GRANGER *US, female vocalist*

30 Sep 78	**I GO TO PIECES (EVERYTIME)** *Casino Classics CC3*	**50**	3 wks

Boysie GRANT — See *Ezz RECO and the LAUNCHERS with Boysie GRANT*

Eddy GRANT *Guyana, male vocalist/instrumentalist*

2 Jun 79	**LIVING ON THE FRONT LINE** *Ensign ENY 26*	**11**	11 wks
15 Nov 80	● **DO YOU FEEL MY LOVE** *Ensign ENY 45*	**8**	11 wks
4 Apr 81	**CAN'T GET ENOUGH OF YOU** *Ice/Ensign ENY 207*	**13**	10 wks
25 Jul 81	**I LOVE YOU, YES I LOVE YOU** *Ice/Ensign ENY 216*	**37**	6 wks
16 Oct 82	★ **I DON'T WANNA DANCE** *Ice ICE 56*	**1**†	11 wks

Gogi GRANT *US, female vocalist*

29 Jun 56	● **WAYWARD WIND** *London HLB 8282*	**9**	11 wks

Julie GRANT *UK, female vocalist*

3 Jan 63	**UP ON THE ROOF** *Pye 7N 15483*	**33**	3 wks
28 Mar 63	**COUNT ON ME** *Pye 7N 15508*	**24**	9 wks
24 Sep 64	**COME TO ME** *Pye 7N 15684*	**31**	5 wks

Rudy GRANT *Guyana, male vocalist*

14 Feb 81	**LATELY** *Ensign ENY 202*	**58**	3 wks

GRAPEFRUIT *UK, male vocal/instrumental group*

14 Feb 68	**DEAR DELILAH** *RCA 1656*	**21**	9 wks
14 Aug 68	**C'MON MARIANNE** *RCA 1716*	**31**	10 wks

Dobie GRAY *US, male vocalist*

25 Feb 65	**THE IN CROWD** *London HL 9953*	**25**	7 wks
27 Sep 75	**OUT ON THE FLOOR** *Black Magic BM 107*	**42**	4 wks

Dorian GRAY *UK, male vocalist*

27 Mar 68	**I'VE GOT YOU ON MY MIND** *Parlophone R 5667*	**36**	7 wks

Les GRAY *UK, male vocalist*

26 Feb 77	**A GROOVY KIND OF LOVE** *Warner Bros. K 16883*	**32**	5 wks

Barry GRAY ORCHESTRA *UK, orchestra*

11 Jul 81	**THUNDERBIRDS** *PRT 7P 216*	**61**	2 wks

Buddy GRECO *US, male vocalist*

7 Jul 60	**LADY IS A TRAMP** *Fontana H 225*	**26**	8 wks

GREEDIES

Ireland/UK/US, male vocal/instrumental group

15 Dec 79	**A MERRY JINGLE** *Vertigo GREED 1*	**28**	5 wks

GREEK SERENADERS — See *MAKADOPOULOS and his GREEK SERENADERS*

Al GREEN *US, male vocalist*

9 Oct 71	● **TIRED OF BEING ALONE** *London HL 10337*	**4**	13 wks
8 Jan 72	● **LET'S STAY TOGETHER** *London HL 10348*	**7**	12 wks
20 May 72	**LOOK WHAT YOU DONE FOR ME** *London HL 10369*	**44**	4 wks
19 Aug 72	**I'M STILL IN LOVE WITH YOU** *London HL 10382*	**35**	5 wks
16 Nov 74	**SHA-LA-LA (MAKE ME HAPPY)** *London HL 10470*	**20**	11 wks
15 Mar 75	**L. O. V. E.** *London HL 10482*	**24**	8 wks

Jesse GREEN *US, male vocalist*

7 Aug 76	**NICE AND SLOW** *EMI 2492*	**17**	12 wks
18 Dec 76	**FLIP** *EMI 2564*	**26**	8 wks
11 Jun 77	**COME WITH ME** *EMI 2615*	**29**	6 wks

Norman GREENBAUM *US, male vocalist*

21 Mar 70	★ **SPIRIT IN THE SKY** *Reprise RS 20885*	**1**	20 wks

Lorne GREENE *US, male vocalist*

17 Dec 64	**RINGO** *RCA 1428*	**22**	8 wks

Iain GREGORY *UK, male vocalist*

4 Jan 62	**CAN'T YOU HEAR THE BEAT OF A BROKEN HEART** *Pye 7N 15397*	**39**	2 wks

Johnny GREGORY — See *CHAQUITO*

Date	Title Label Number	Position	

GREYHOUND

Jamaica, male vocal/instrumental group

Date	Title Label Number	Position	Weeks
26 Jun 71	● **BLACK AND WHITE** *Trojan TR 7820*	**6**	13 wks
8 Jan 72	**MOON RIVER** *Trojan TR 7848*	**12**	11 wks
25 Mar 72	**I AM WHAT I AM** *Trojan TR 7853*	**20**	9 wks

Zaine GRIFF *NZ, male vocalist*

Date	Title Label Number	Position	Weeks
16 Feb 80	**TONIGHT** *Automatic K 17547*	**54**	3 wks
31 May 80	**ASHES AND DIAMONDS** *Automatic K 17610*	**68**	3 wks

Henry GROSS *US, male vocalist*

Date	Title Label Number	Position	Weeks
28 Aug 76	**SHANNON** *Life Song ELS 45002*	**32**	4 wks

GUESS WHO

Canada, male vocal/instrumental group

Date	Title Label Number	Position	Weeks
16 Feb 67	**HIS GIRL** *King KG 1044*	**45**	1 wk
9 May 70	**AMERICAN WOMAN** *RCA 1943*	**45**	2 wks
30 May 70	**AMERICAN WOMAN** (re-entry) *RCA 1943*	**19**	11 wks

GUN *UK, male vocal/instrumental group*

Date	Title Label Number	Position	Weeks
20 Nov 68	● **RACE WITH THE DEVIL** *CBS 3764*	**8**	11 wks

Adrian GURVITZ *UK, male vocalist*

Date	Title Label Number	Position	Weeks
30 Jan 82	● **CLASSIC** *RAK 339*	**8**	13 wks
12 Jun 82	**YOUR DREAM** *RAK 343*	**61**	3 wks

GUYS and DOLLS *UK, male/female vocal group*

Date	Title Label Number	Position	Weeks
1 Mar 75	● **THERE'S A WHOLE LOT OF LOVING** *Magnet MAG 20*	**2**	11 wks
17 May 75	**HERE I GO AGAIN** *Magnet MAG 30*	**33**	5 wks
21 Feb 76	● **YOU DON'T HAVE TO SAY YOU LOVE ME** *Magnet MAG 50*	**5**	8 wks
6 Nov 76	**STONEY GROUND** *Magnet MAG 76*	**38**	4 wks
13 May 78	**ONLY LOVIN' DOES IT** *Magnet MAG 115*	**42**	5 wks

H

Sammy HAGAR

US, male vocalist/instrumentalist - guitar

Date	Title Label Number	Position	Weeks
15 Dec 79	**THIS PLANET'S ON FIRE/SPACE STATION NO. 5** *Capitol CL 16114*	**52**	5 wks
16 Feb 80	**I'VE DONE EVERYTHING FOR YOU** *Capitol CL 16120*	**36**	5 wks
24 May 80	**HEARTBEAT/ LOVE OR MONEY [B]** *Capitol RED 1*	**67**	2 wks
16 Jan 82	**PIECE OF MY HEART** *Geffen GEFA 1884*	**67**	1 wk
30 Jan 82	**PIECE OF MY HEART** (re-entry) *Geffen GEFA 1884*	**67**	2 wks

HAIRCUT 100 *UK, male vocal/instrumental group*

Date	Title Label Number	Position	Weeks
24 Oct 81	● **FAVOURITE SHIRTS (BOY MEETS GIRL)** *Arista CLIP 1*	**4**	14 wks
30 Jan 82	● **LOVE PLUS ONE** *Arista CLIP 2*	**3**	12 wks
10 Apr 82	● **FANTASTIC DAY** *Arista CLIP 3*	**9**	9 wks
21 Aug 82	● **NOBODY'S FOOL** *Arista CLIP 4*	**9**	7 wks

Bill HALEY and his COMETS

US, male vocalist/guitarist, male vocal/instrumental backing group

Date	Title Label Number	Position	Weeks
17 Dec 54	● **SHAKE RATTLE AND ROLL** *Brunswick 05338*	**4**	14 wks
7 Jan 55	**ROCK AROUND THE CLOCK** *Brunswick 05317*	**17**	2 wks
15 Apr 55	**MAMBO ROCK** *Brunswick 05405*	**14**	2 wks
14 Oct 55	★ **ROCK AROUND THE CLOCK** (re-entry) *Brunswick 05317*	**1**	17 wks
30 Dec 55	● **ROCK-A-BEATIN' BOOGIE** *Brunswick 05509*	**4**	9 wks
2 Mar 56	● **SEE YOU LATER ALLIGATOR** *Brunswick 05530*	**7**	13 wks
25 May 56	● **THE SAINTS ROCK 'N ROLL** *Brunswick 05565*	**5**	24 wks
17 Aug 56	● **ROCKIN' THROUGH THE RYE** *Brunswick 05582*	**3**	18 wks
14 Sep 56	**RAZZLE DAZZLE** *Brunswick 05453*	**13**	8 wks
21 Sep 56	● **ROCK AROUND THE CLOCK** (2nd re-entry) *Brunswick 05317*	**5**	11 wks
21 Sep 56	**SEE YOU LATER ALLIGATOR** (re-entry) *Brunswick 05530*	**12**	8 wks
9 Nov 56	● **RIP IT UP** *Brunswick 05615*	**4**	18 wks
9 Nov 56	**ROCK 'N ROLL STAGE SHOW** (LP) *Brunswick LAT 8139*	**30**	1 wk
23 Nov 56	**RUDY'S ROCK** *Brunswick 05616*	**30**	1 wk
14 Dec 56	**RUDY'S ROCK** (re-entry) *Brunswick 05616*	**26**	4 wks
14 Dec 56	**ROCK AROUND THE CLOCK** (3rd re-entry) *Brunswick 05317*	**24**	2 wks
4 Jan 57	**ROCKIN' THROUGH THE RYE** (re-entry) *Brunswick 05582*	**19**	5 wks
4 Jan 57	**ROCK AROUND THE CLOCK** (4th re-entry) *Brunswick 05317*	**25**	2 wks
25 Jan 57	**ROCK AROUND THE CLOCK** (5th re-entry) *Brunswick 05317*	**22**	2 wks
1 Feb 57	**ROCK THE JOINT** *London HLF 8371*	**20**	4 wks
8 Feb 57	● **DON'T KNOCK THE ROCK** *Brunswick 05640*	**7**	8 wks
3 Apr 68	**ROCK AROUND THE CLOCK** (re-issue) *MCA MU 1013*	**20**	11 wks
16 Mar 74	**ROCK AROUND THE CLOCK** (2nd re-issue) *MCA 128*	**12**	10 wks
25 Apr 81	**HALEY'S GOLDEN MEDLEY** *MCA 694*	**50**	5 wks

Tracks on Rock 'N Roll Stage Show *LP: Calling All Comets/ Rockin' Through The Rye/ A Rockin' Little Tune/ Hide And Seek/ Hey There Now/ Goofin' Around/ Hook Line And Sinker/ Rudy's Rock/ Choo Choo Ch'Boogie/ Blue Comets Rock/ Hot Dog Buddy Buddy/ Tonight's The Night. Occasionally, some of the* Rock Around The Clock *labels billed the song as* (We're Gonna) Rock Around The Clock.

Daryl HALL and John OATES

US, male vocal/instrumental duo

Date	Title Label Number	Position	Weeks
16 Oct 76	**SHE'S GONE** *Atlantic K 10828*	**42**	4 wks
14 Jun 80	**RUNNING FROM PARADISE** *RCA RUN 1*	**41**	6 wks
20 Sep 80	**YOU'VE LOST THAT LOVIN' FEELIN'** *RCA 1*	**55**	3 wks
15 Nov 80	**KISS ON MY LIST** *RCA 15*	**33**	8 wks
23 Jan 82	● **I CAN'T GO FOR THAT (NO CAN DO)** *RCA 172*	**8**	10 wks
10 Apr 82	**PRIVATE EYES** *RCA 134*	**32**	7 wks
30 Oct 82	● **MANEATER** *RCA 290*	**6†**	9 wks

NMExclusive WHAT ELVIS SAID ABOUT FURY!

No. 10
HEY! BABY
BRUCE CHANNEL on Mercury 1171
—A WONDERFUL NEW DISC—
C'EST SI BON
DEAN MARTIN on Reprise 20076
K.P.M. 21 DENMARK STREET, W.C.2 TEM 3856

new MUSICAL EXPRESS
WORLD'S LARGEST CIRCULATION OF ANY MUSIC PAPER —WEEKLY SALES EXCEED 200,000 (MEMBERS OF ABC)

ELVIS
GOOD LUCK CHARM;
Anything that's part of you
45 rpm RCA VICTOR record

THE FANTASTIC NEW SOUND OF

JET HARRIS

BESAME MUCHO CHILLS & FEVER

published by SOUTHERN MUSIC 8 Denmark St. London WC2

recorded on 45 rpm DECCA F 11466

published by BELINDA (LONDON) LTD 17 Savile Row London W1

Above **HAIRCUT 100** Nick Heyward, leader of the group who started in 1982 as everybody's darlings and sadly ended in anonymous disarray *Below* **DARYL HALL AND JOHN OATES** Big daddy would be proud of a hold like this

Above **JET HARRIS** Jet adorns the cover of the NME in May 1962 to advertise his first solo single since leaving the Shadows

Left **BOBBY HEBB** His debut hit was a tribute to John F Kennedy

Right **HEINZ** with the legendary Joe Meek, who as well as working with Heinz, also produced the following acts that appear in this book: Mike Berry, John Leyton, Peter Jay and the Jaywalkers, the Outlaws, the Tornados, Michael Cox, the Flee-Rekkers, Don Charles, the Cryin' Shames, Dowlands, Houston Wells, the Moontrekkers, Iain Gregory and the Honeycombs

Date	Title *Label Number*	Position		Date	Title *Label Number*	Position	

HAMILTON, Joe FRANK and REYNOLDS *US, male vocal group*

13 Sep 75	**FALLIN' IN LOVE** *Pye International 7N 25690*	**33**	6 wks

Russ HAMILTON *UK, male vocalist*

24 May 57	● **WE WILL MAKE LOVE** *Oriole CB 1359*	**2**	20 wks
27 Sep 57	**WEDDING RING** *Oriole CB 1388*	**20**	6 wks

George HAMILTON IV *US, male vocalist*

7 Mar 58	**WHY DON'T THEY UNDERSTAND** *HMV POP 429*	**22**	9 wks
18 Jul 58	**I KNOW WHERE I'M GOING** *HMV POP 505*	**29**	1 wk
8 Aug 58	**I KNOW WHERE I'M GOING** (re-entry) *HMV POP 505*	**23**	3 wks

Marvin HAMLISCH

US, male instrumentalist, piano

30 Mar 74	**THE ENTERTAINER** *MCA 121*	**25**	13 wks

Albert HAMMOND *UK, male vocalist*

30 Jun 73	**FREE ELECTRIC BAND** *Mums 1494*	**19**	11 wks

Herbie HANCOCK

US, male vocalist/instrumentalist - keyboards

26 Aug 78	**I THOUGHT IT WAS YOU** *CBS 6530*	**15**	9 wks
3 Feb 79	**YOU BET YOUR LOVE** *CBS 7010*	**18**	10 wks

HANDLEY FAMILY *UK, male/female vocal group*

7 Apr 73	**WAM BAM** *GL 100*	**30**	7 wks

HANDS OF DR. TELENY — See *Peter STRAKER and the HANDS OF DR. TELENY*

HAPPENINGS *US, male vocal group*

18 May 67	**I GOT RHYTHM** *Stateside SS 2013*	**28**	9 wks
16 Jul 67	**MY MAMMY** *Pye International 7N 25501 and B. T. Puppy BTS 45530*	**34**	5 wks

Pye gave the American B. T. Puppy label its own identification halfway through the success of My Mammy.

Tim HARDIN *US, male vocalist*

5 Jan 67	**HANG ON TO A DREAM** *Verve VS 1504*	**50**	1 wk

Mike HARDING *UK, male vocalist*

2 Aug 75	**ROCHDALE COWBOY** *Rubber ADUB 3*	**22**	8 wks

Francoise HARDY *France, female vocalist*

25 Jun 64	**TOUS LES GARCONS ET LES FILLES** *Pye 7N 15653*	**36**	7 wks
7 Jan 65	**ET MÊME** *Pye 7N 15740*	**31**	4 wks
25 Mar 65	**ALL OVER THE WORLD** *Pye 7N 15802*	**16**	15 wks

HARLEM COMMUNITY CHOIR — See *John LENNON*

Steve HARLEY and COCKNEY REBEL

UK, male vocalist/male vocal/instrumental backing group

11 May 74	● **JUDY TEEN** *EMI 2128*	**5**	11 wks
10 Aug 74	● **MR. SOFT** *EMI 2191*	**8**	9 wks
8 Feb 75	★ **MAKE ME SMILE (COME UP AND SEE ME)** *EMI 2263*	**1**	9 wks
7 Jun 75	**MR. RAFFLES (MAN IT WAS MEAN)** *EMI 2299*	**13**	6 wks
31 Jul 76	● **HERE COMES THE SUN** *EMI 2505*	**10**	7 wks
6 Nov 76	**LOVE'S A PRIMA DONNA** *EMI 2539*	**41**	4 wks
20 Oct 79	**FREEDOM'S PRISONER** *EMI 2994*	**58**	3 wks

First two hits are credited simply to Cockney Rebel, the next two to Steve Harley and Cockney Rebel, the remaining hits to Steve Harley.

HARLEY QUINNE *UK, male vocal group*

14 Oct 72	**NEW ORLEANS** *Bell 1255*	**19**	8 wks

HARMONY GRASS

UK, male vocal/instrumental group

29 Jan 69	**MOVE IN A LITTLE CLOSER** *RCA 1772*	**24**	7 wks

Charlie HARPER *UK, male vocalist*

19 Jul 80	**BARMY LONDON ARMY** *Gem GEMS 35*	**68**	1 wk

HARPERS BIZARRE *US, male vocal group*

30 Mar 67	**59TH STREET BRIDGE SONG (FEELING GROOVY)** *Warner Bros. WB 5890*	**34**	7 wks
4 Oct 67	**ANYTHING GOES** *Warner Bros. WB 7063*	**33**	6 wks

HARPO *Sweden, male vocalist*

17 Apr 76	**MOVIE STAR** *DJM DJS 400*	**24**	6 wks

T. HARRINGTON — See *Rahni HARRIS and F.L.O.*

Anita HARRIS *UK, female vocalist*

29 Jun 67	● **JUST LOVING YOU** *CBS 2724*	**6**	30 wks
11 Oct 67	**PLAYGROUND** *CBS 2991*	**46**	3 wks
24 Jan 68	**ANNIVERSARY WALTZ** *CBS 3211*	**21**	9 wks
14 Aug 68	**DREAM A LITTLE DREAM OF ME** *CBS 3637*	**33**	8 wks

Emmylou HARRIS *US, female vocalist*

6 Mar 76	**HERE THERE AND EVERYWHERE** *Reprise K 14415*	**30**	6 wks

Date	Title *Label Number*	Position	

Jet HARRIS *UK, male instrumentalist, bass guitar*

24 May 62	**BESAME MUCHO** *Decca F 11466*	**22**	7 wks
16 Aug 62	**MAIN TITLE THEME FROM MAN WITH THE GOLDEN ARM** *Decca F 11488*	**12**	11 wks

See also Jet Harris and Tony Meehan.

Jet HARRIS and Tony MEEHAN

UK, male instrumental duo, bass guitar and drums

10 Jan 63	★ **DIAMONDS** *Decca F 11563*	**1**	12 wks
25 Apr 63	● **SCARLETT O'HARA** *Decca F 11644*	**2**	13 wks
5 Sep 63	● **APPLEJACK** *Decca F 11710*	**4**	13 wks

See also Jet Harris, Tony Meehan.

Keith HARRIS and ORVILLE

UK, male ventriloquist vocalist with feathered dummy.

18 Dec 82	**ORVILLE'S SONG** *BBC RESL 124*	**33**†	2 wks

Major HARRIS *US, male vocalist*

9 Aug 75	**LOVE WON'T LET ME WAIT** *Atlantic K 10585*	**37**	7 wks

Max HARRIS *UK, orchestra*

1 Dec 60	**GURNEY SLADE** *Fontana H 282*	**11**	10 wks

Rahni HARRIS and F.L.O.

US, male instrumental group

16 Dec 78	**SIX MILLION STEPS (WEST RUNS SOUTH)** *Mercury 6007 198*	**43**	7 wks

Hit has credit 'Vocals by T.Harrington and O. Rasbury'

Richard HARRIS *Ireland, male vocalist*

26 Jun 68	● **MACARTHUR PARK** *RCA 1699*	**4**	12 wks
8 Jul 72	**MACARTHUR PARK** (re-issue) *Probe GFF 101*	**38**	6 wks

Rolf HARRIS *Australia, male vocalist*

21 Jul 60	● **TIE ME KANGAROO DOWN SPORT** *Columbia DB 4483*	**9**	13 wks
25 Oct 62	● **SUN ARISE** *Columbia DB 4888*	**3**	16 wks
28 Feb 63	**JOHNNY DAY** *Columbia DB 4979*	**44**	2 wks
16 Apr 69	**BLUER THAN BLUE** *Columbia DB 8553*	**30**	8 wks
22 Nov 69	★ **TWO LITTLE BOYS** *Columbia DB 8630*	**1**	24 wks
20 Jun 70	**TWO LITTLE BOYS** (re-entry) *Columbia DB 8630*	**50**	1 wk

Ronnie HARRIS *UK, male vocalist*

24 Sep 54	**STORY OF TINA** *Columbia DB 3499*	**12**	3 wks

George HARRISON *UK, male vocalist*

23 Jan 71	★ **MY SWEET LORD** *Apple R 5884*	**1**	17 wks
14 Aug 71	● **BANGLA DESH** *Apple R 5912*	**10**	9 wks
2 Jun 73	● **GIVE ME LOVE (GIVE ME PEACE ON EARTH)** *Apple R 5988*	**8**	10 wks
21 Dec 74	**DING DONG** *Apple R 6002*	**38**	5 wks
11 Oct 75	**YOU** *Apple R 6007*	**38**	5 wks
10 Mar 79	**BLOW AWAY** *Dark Horse K 17327*	**51**	5 wks
23 May 81	**ALL THOSE YEARS AGO** *Dark Horse 3 K 17807*	**13**	7 wks

Noel HARRISON *UK, male vocalist*

26 Feb 69	● **WINDMILLS OF YOUR MIND** *Reprise RS 20758*	**8**	14 wks

HARRY — See *ALFI and HARRY*

Debbie HARRY *US, female vocalist*

1 Aug 81	**BACKFIRED** *Chrysalis CHS 2526*	**32**	6 wks

HARRY J. ALL STARS

Jamaica, male instrumental group

25 Oct 69	● **LIQUIDATOR** *Trojan TR 675*	**9**	20 wks
29 Mar 80	**LIQUIDATOR** (re-issue) *Trojan TRO 9063*	**42**	5 wks

Re-issue of Liquidator *coupled with re-issue of* Long Shot Kick De Bucket *by The Pioneers.*
See also The Pioneers

Dan HARTMAN *US, male vocalist*

21 Oct 78	● **INSTANT REPLAY** *Sky 6706*	**8**	15 wks
13 Jan 79	**THIS IS IT** *Blue Sky SKY 6999*	**17**	8 wks

Sensational Alex HARVEY BAND

UK, male vocal/instrumental group

26 Jul 75	● **DELILAH** *Vertigo ALEX 001*	**7**	7 wks
22 Nov 75	**GAMBLIN' BAR ROOM BLUES** *Vertigo ALEX 002*	**38**	8 wks
19 Jun 76	**THE BOSTON TEA PARTY** *Mountain TOP 12*	**13**	10 wks

Tony HATCH *UK, orchestra*

4 Oct 62	**OUT OF THIS WORLD** *Pye 7N 15460*	**50**	1 wk

Donny HATHAWAY — See *Roberta FLACK and Donny HATHAWAY*

Edwin HAWKINS SINGERS

US, male/female vocal group

21 May 69	● **OH HAPPY DAY** *Buddah 201 048*	**2**	12 wks
23 Aug 69	**OH HAPPY DAY** (re-entry) *Buddah 201 048*	**43**	1 wk

Hit credits soloist : Dorothy Combs Morrison

HAWKWIND

UK, male vocal/instrumental group with female dancer

1 Jul 72	● **SILVER MACHINE** *United Artists UP 35381*	**3**	15 wks
11 Aug 73	**URBAN GUERRILLA** *United Artists UP 35566*	**39**	3 wks
21 Oct 78	**SILVER MACHINE** (re-entry) *United Artists UP 35381*	**34**	5 wks
19 Jul 80	**SHOT DOWN IN THE NIGHT** *Bronze BRO 98*	**59**	3 wks

Date	Title *Label Number*	Position	

Bill HAYES *US, male vocalist*

6 Jan 56	● **BALLAD OF DAVY CROCKETT** *London HLA 8220*	2	9 wks

Isaac HAYES

US, male vocalist/multi-instrumentalist

4 Dec 71	● **THEME FROM "SHAFT"** *Stax 2025 069*	4	12 wks
3 Apr 76	● **DISCO CONNECTION** *ABC 4100*	10	9 wks

Billed as Isaac Hayes Movement on Disco Connection.

HAYSI FANTAYZEE *UK, male/female vocal duo*

24 Jul 82	**JOHN WAYNE IS BIG LEGGY** *Regard RG 100*	11	10 wks
13 Nov 82	**HOLY JOE** *Regard RG 104*	51	3 wks

Justin HAYWARD *UK, male vocalist*

8 Jul 78	● **FOREVER AUTUMN** *CBS 6368*	5	13 wks

See also Justin Hayward and John Lodge.

Justin HAYWARD and John LODGE

UK, male vocal/instrumental duo

25 Oct 75	● **BLUE GUITAR** *Threshold TH 21*	8	7 wks

see also Justin Hayward

Leon HAYWOOD *US, male vocalist*

15 Mar 80	**DON'T PUSH IT, DON'T FORCE IT** *20th Century Fox TC 2443*	12	11 wks

Lee HAZELWOOD — See *NANCY and LEE*

Murray HEAD *UK, male vocalist*

29 Jan 72	**SUPERSTAR** *MCA MMKS 5077*	47	1 wk

Superstar *was one of 4 tracks on a maxi-single, 2 of which were credited during the disc's one week on the chart. The other track credited was* I Don't Know How To Love Him *by Yvonne Elliman. See also Yvonne Elliman.*

Roy HEAD *US, male vocalist*

4 Nov 65	**TREAT HER RIGHT** *Vocalion V-P 9248*	30	5 wks

HEADBANGERS

UK, male vocal/instrumental group

10 Oct 81	**STATUS ROCK** *Magnet MAG 206*	60	3 wks

HEADBOYS *UK, male vocal/instrumental group*

22 Sep 79	**THE SHAPE OF THINGS TO COME** *RSO 40*	45	8 wks

HEADGIRL

UK, male/female vocal/instrumental group

21 Feb 81	● **ST. VALENTINE'S DAY MASSACRE** (EP) *Bronze BRO 116*	5	8 wks

Headgirl is Motorhead and Girlschool together. See Motorhead, Girlschool. Tracks on St. Valentine's Day Massacre EP *Please Don't Touch, Emergency, Bomber*

HEARTBREAKERS — See *Tom PETTY and the HEARTBREAKERS*

Ted HEATH *UK, orchestra*

16 Jan 53	**VANESSA** *Decca F 9983*	11	1 wk
3 Jul 53	● **HOT TODDY** *Decca F 10093*	6	11 wks
23 Oct 53	**DRAGNET** *Decca F 10176*	12	1 wk
27 Nov 53	● **DRAGNET** (re-entry) *Decca F 10176*	9	1 wk
11 Dec 53	**DRAGNET** (2nd re-entry) *Decca F 10176*	11	1 wk
15 Jan 54	**DRAGNET** (3rd re-entry) *Decca F 10176*	11	1 wk
5 Feb 54	**DRAGNET** (4th re-entry) *Decca F 10176*	12	1 wk
12 Feb 54	● **SKIN DEEP** *Decca F 10246*	9	3 wks
6 Jul 56	**THE FAITHFUL HUSSAR** *Decca F 10746*	18	9 wks
14 Mar 58	● **SWINGIN' SHEPHERD BLUES** *Decca F 11000*	3	14 wks
11 Apr 58	**TEQUILA** *Decca F 11003*	21	6 wks
4 Jul 58	**TOM HARK** *Decca F 11025*	24	2 wks
5 Oct 61	**SUCU SUCU** *Decca F 11392*	36	4 wks
9 Nov 61	**SUCU SUCU** (re-entry) *Decca F 11392*	47	1 wk

HEATWAVE

UK/US, male vocal and instrumental group

22 Jan 77	● **BOOGIE NIGHTS** *GTO GT 77*	2	14 wks
7 May 77	**TOO HOT TO HANDLE/SLIP YOUR DISC TO THIS** *GTO GT 91*	15	11 wks
14 Jan 78	**THE GROOVE LINE** *GTO GT 115*	12	8 wks
3 Jun 78	**MIND BLOWING DECISIONS** *GTO GT 226*	12	11 wks
4 Nov 78	● **ALWAYS AND FOREVER/MIND BLOWING DECISIONS** *GTO GT 236*	9	14 wks
26 May 79	**RAZZLE DAZZLE** *GTO GT 248*	43	5 wks
17 Jan 81	**GANGSTERS OF THE GROOVE** *GTO GT 285*	19	8 wks
21 Mar 81	**JITTERBUGGIN'** *GTO GT 290*	34	7 wks

Mind Blowing Decisions *on GT 236 is an extended remixed version of GT 226.*

HEAVEN 17 *UK, male vocal/instrumental group*

21 Mar 81	**(WE DON'T NEED THIS) FASCIST GROOVE THING** *Virgin VS 400*	45	5 wks
5 Sep 81	**PLAY TO WIN** *Virgin VS 433*	46	7 wks
14 Nov 81	**PENTHOUSE AND PAVEMENT** *Virgin VS 455*	57	3 wks
30 Oct 82	**LET ME GO** *B.E.F./Virgin VS 532*	41	6 wks

Bobby HEBB *US, male vocalist*

8 Sep 66	**SUNNY** *Philips BF 1503*	12	9 wks
19 Aug 72	**LOVE LOVE LOVE** *Philips 6051 023*	32	6 wks

HEDGEHOPPERS ANONYMOUS

UK, male vocal/instrumental group

30 Sep 65	● **IT'S GOOD NEWS WEEK** *Decca F 12241*	5	12 wks

Den HEGARTY *UK, male vocalist*

31 Mar 79	**VOODOO VOODOO** *Magnet MAG 143*	73	2 wks

Date	Title *Label Number*	Position	

HEINZ *UK, male vocalist*

8 Aug 63	● **JUST LIKE EDDIE** *Decca F 11693*	**5**	15 wks
28 Nov 63	**COUNTRY BOY** *Decca F 11768*	**26**	9 wks
27 Feb 64	**YOU WERE THERE** *Decca F 11831*	**26**	8 wks
15 Oct 64	**QUESTIONS I CAN'T ANSWER** *Columbia DB 7374*	**39**	2 wks
18 Mar 65	**DIGGIN' MY POTATOES** *Columbia DB 7482*	**49**	1 wk

HELLO *UK, male vocal/instrumental group*

9 Nov 74	● **TELL HIM** *Bell 1377*	**6**	12 wks
18 Oct 75	● **NEW YORK GROOVE** *Bell 1438*	**9**	9 wks

Bobby HELMS *US, male vocalist*

29 Nov 57	**MY SPECIAL ANGEL** *Brunswick 05721*	**22**	3 wks
21 Feb 58	**NO OTHER BABY** *Brunswick 05730*	**30**	1 wk
1 Aug 58	**JACQUELINE** *Brunswick 05748*	**20**	3 wks

Jimmy HELMS *UK, male vocalist*

24 Feb 73	● **GONNA MAKE YOU AN OFFER YOU CAN'T REFUSE** *Cube BUG 27*	**8**	10 wks

Eddie HENDERSON

US, male vocalist/instrumentalist, trumpet

28 Oct 78	**PRANCE ON** *Capitol CL 16015*	**44**	6 wks

Joe "Mr. Piano" HENDERSON

UK, male instrumentalist, piano

3 Jun 55	**SING IT WITH JOE** *Polygon P 1167*	**14**	4 wks
2 Sep 55	**SING IT AGAIN WITH JOE** *Polygon P 1184*	**18**	3 wks
25 Jul 58	**TRUDIE** *Pye Nixa N 15147*	**14**	12 wks
24 Oct 58	**TRUDIE** (re-entry) *Pye Nixa N 15147*	**23**	2 wks
23 Oct 59	**TREBLE CHANCE** *Pye 7N 15224*	**28**	1 wk
24 Mar 60	**OOH LA LA** *Pye 7N 15257*	**46**	1 wk

First two hits are medleys as follows: Sing It With Joe : *Margie/ I'm Nobody's Sweetheart Now/ Somebody Stole My Gal/ Moonlight Bay/ By The Light Of The Silvery Moon/ Cuddle Up A Little Closer.* Sing It Again With Joe: *Put Your Arms Around Me Honey/ Ain't She Sweet/ When You're Smiling/ Shine On Harvest Moon/ My Blue Heaven/ Show Me The Way To Go Home.*

Wayne HENDERSON — See *Roy AYERS and WAYNE HENDERSON*

Jimi HENDRIX EXPERIENCE

US/UK, male vocal/instrumental group, Jimi Hendrix, vocals and guitar

5 Jan 67	● **HEY JOE** *Polydor 56 139*	**6**	10 wks
23 Mar 67	● **PURPLE HAZE** *Track 604 001*	**3**	14 wks
11 May 67	● **THE WIND CRIES MARY** *Track 604 004*	**6**	11 wks
30 Aug 67	**BURNING OF THE MIDNIGHT LAMP** *Track 604 007*	**18**	9 wks
23 Oct 68	● **ALL ALONG THE WATCHTOWER** *Track 604 025*	**5**	11 wks
16 Apr 69	**CROSSTOWN TRAFFIC** *Track 604 029*	**37**	3 wks
7 Nov 70	★ **VOODOO CHILE** *Track 2095 001*	**1**	13 wks
30 Oct 71	**GYPSY EYES/ REMEMBER** *Track 2094 010*	**35**	5 wks
12 Feb 72	**JOHNNY B. GOODE** *Polydor 2001 277*	**35**	5 wks

On Polydor the act is simply billed as Jimi Hendrix.

Clarence "Frogman" HENRY

US, male vocalist

4 May 61	● **BUT I DO** *Pye International 7N 25078*	**3**	19 wks
13 Jul 61	● **YOU ALWAYS HURT THE ONE YOU LOVE** *Pye International 7N 25089*	**6**	12 wks
21 Sep 61	**LONELY STREET/ WHY CAN'T YOU** *Pye International 7N 25108*	**42**	2 wks

Paul HENRY and the Mayson GLEN ORCHESTRA *UK, male vocalist/orchestra*

14 Jan 78	**BENNY'S THEME** *Pye 7N 46027*	**39**	2 wks

HERB — See *PEACHES and HERB*

HERD *UK, male vocal/instrumental group*

13 Sep 67	● **FROM THE UNDERWORLD** *Fontana TF 856*	**6**	13 wks
20 Dec 67	**PARADISE LOST** *Fontana TF 887*	**15**	9 wks
10 Apr 68	● **I DON'T WANT OUR LOVING TO DIE** *Fontana TF 925*	**5**	13 wks

HERMAN'S HERMITS

UK, male vocal/instrumental group

20 Aug 64	★ **I'M INTO SOMETHING GOOD** *Columbia DB 7338*	**1**	15 wks
19 Nov 64	**SHOW ME GIRL** *Columbia DB 7408*	**19**	9 wks
18 Feb 65	● **SILHOUETTES** *Columbia DB 7475*	**3**	12 wks
29 Apr 65	● **WONDERFUL WORLD** *Columbia DB 7546*	**7**	9 wks
2 Sep 65	**JUST A LITTLE BIT BETTER** *Columbia DB 7670*	**15**	9 wks
23 Dec 65	● **A MUST TO AVOID** *Columbia DB 7791*	**6**	11 wks
24 Mar 66	**YOU WON'T BE LEAVING** *Columbia DB 7861*	**20**	7 wks
23 Jun 66	**THIS DOOR SWINGS BOTH WAYS** *Columbia DB 7947*	**18**	7 wks
6 Oct 66	● **NO MILK TODAY** *Columbia DB 8012*	**7**	11 wks
1 Dec 66	**EAST WEST** *Columbia DB 8076*	**37**	7 wks
9 Feb 67	● **THERE'S A KIND OF HUSH** *Columbia DB 8123*	**7**	11 wks
17 Jan 68	**I CAN TAKE OR LEAVE YOUR LOVING** *Columbia DB 8327*	**11**	9 wks
1 May 68	**SLEEPY JOE** *Columbia DB 8404*	**12**	10 wks
17 Jul 68	● **SUNSHINE GIRL** *Columbia DB 8446*	**8**	14 wks
18 Dec 68	● **SOMETHING'S HAPPENING** *Columbia DB 8504*	**6**	15 wks
23 Apr 69	● **MY SENTIMENTAL FRIEND** *Columbia DB 8563*	**2**	12 wks
8 Nov 69	**HERE COMES THE STAR** *Columbia DB 8626*	**33**	9 wks
7 Feb 70	● **YEARS MAY COME, YEARS MAY GO** *Columbia DB 8656*	**7**	11 wks
2 May 70	**YEARS MAY COME YEARS MAY GO** (re-entry) *Columbia DB 8656*	**45**	1 wk
23 May 70	**BET YER LIFE I DO** *RAK 102*	**22**	10 wks
14 Nov 70	**LADY BARBARA** *RAK 106*	**13**	12 wks

On Lady Barbara *billed as Peter Noone & Herman's Hermits. See also Peter Noone.*

Patrick HERNANDEZ *Germany, male vocalist*

16 Jun 79	● **BORN TO BE ALIVE** *Gem/Aquarius GEM 4*	**10**	14 wks

HI GLOSS *UK, disco aggregation*

8 Aug 81	**YOU'LL NEVER KNOW** *Epic EPC A 1387*	**12**	13 wks

Date **Title** *Label Number* **Position**

HI TENSION *UK, male vocal/instrumental group*

6 May 78 **HI TENSION** *Island WIP 6422* **13** 12 wks
12 Aug 78 ● **BRITISH HUSTLE/PEACE ON EARTH** *Island WIP 6446* **8** 11 wks

Peace On Earth *credited with* British Hustle *from 2 Sep 78 to end of record's chart run.*

Al HIBBLER *US, male vocalist*

13 May 55 ● **UNCHAINED MELODY** *Brunswick 05420* **2** 17 wks

Bertie HIGGINS *US, male vocalist*

5 Jun 82 **KEY LARGO** *Epic EPC A 2168* **60** 4 wks

HIGH NUMBERS

UK, male vocal/instrumental group

5 Apr 80 **I'M THE FACE** *Back Door DOOR 4* **49** 4 wks

The High Numbers are the Who before they became The Who. See also The Who.

HIGH SOCIETY

UK, male vocal/instrumental group

15 Nov 80 **I NEVER GO OUT IN THE RAIN** *Eagle ERS 002* **53** 4 wks

HIGHLY LIKELY

UK, male vocal/instrumental group

21 Apr 73 **WHATEVER HAPPENED TO YOU (LIKELY LADS THEME)** *BBC RESL 10* **35** 4 wks

HIGHWAYMEN *US, male vocal group*

7 Sep 61 ★ **MICHAEL** *HMV POP 910* **1** 14 wks
7 Dec 61 **GYPSY ROVER** *HMV POP 948* **41** 3 wks
11 Jan 62 **GYPSY ROVER** (re-entry) *HMV POP 948* **43** 1 wk

Benny HILL *UK, male vocalist*

16 Feb 61 **GATHER IN THE MUSHROOMS** *Pye 7N 15327* **12** 8 wks
1 Jun 61 **TRANSISTOR RADIO** *Pye 7N 15359* **24** 6 wks
16 May 63 **HARVEST OF LOVE** *Pye 7N 15520* **20** 8 wks
13 Nov 71 ★ **ERNIE (THE FASTEST MILKMAN IN THE WEST)** *Columbia DB 8833* **1** 17 wks

Chris HILL

UK, male vocalist plus extracts from other hit records

6 Dec 75 ● **RENTA SANTA** *Philips 6006 491* **10** 7 wks
4 Dec 76 ● **BIONIC SANTA** *Philips 6006 551* **10** 7 wks

Date **Title** *Label Number* **Position**

Dan HILL *Canada, male vocalist*

18 Feb 78 **SOMETIMES WHEN WE TOUCH** *20th Century BTC 2355* **46** 1 wk
4 Mar 78 **SOMETIMES WHEN WE TOUCH** (re-entry) *20th Century BTC 2355* **13** 12 wks

Roni HILL *US, female vocalist*

7 May 77 **YOU KEEP ME HANGIN' ON - STOP IN THE NAME OF LOVE** (MEDLEY) *Creole CR 138* **36** 4 wks

Vince HILL *UK, male vocalist*

7 Jun 62 **THE RIVER'S RUN DRY** *Piccadilly 7N 35043* **49** 1 wk
28 Jun 62 **THE RIVER'S RUN DRY** (re-entry) *Piccadilly 7N 35043* **41** 1 wk
6 Jan 66 **TAKE ME TO YOUR HEART AGAIN** *Columbia DB 7781* **13** 11 wks
17 Mar 66 **HEARTACHES** *Columbia DB 7852* **28** 5 wks
2 Jun 66 **MERCI CHERI** *Columbia DB 7924* **36** 6 wks
9 Feb 67 ● **EDELWEISS** *Columbia DB 8127* **2** 17 wks
11 May 67 **ROSES OF PICARDY** *Columbia DB 8185* **13** 11 wks
27 Sep 67 **LOVE LETTERS IN THE SAND** *Columbia DB 8268* **23** 9 wks
26 Jun 68 **IMPORTANCE OF YOUR LOVE** *Columbia DB 8414* **32** 12 wks
12 Feb 69 **DOESN'T ANYBODY KNOW MY NAME?** *Columbia DB 8515* **50** 1 wk
25 Oct 69 **LITTLE BLUE BIRD** *Columbia DB 8616* **42** 1 wk
25 Sep 71 **LOOK AROUND** *Columbia DB 8804* **12** 16 wks

HILLTOPPERS *US, male vocal group*

27 Jan 56 ● **ONLY YOU** *London HLD 8221* **3** 22 wks
10 Aug 56 **ONLY YOU** (re-entry) *London HLD 8221* **24** 1 wk
14 Sep 56 **TRYIN'** *London HLD 8298* **30** 1 wk
5 Apr 57 **MARIANNE** *London HLD 8381* **20** 2 wks
26 Apr 57 **MARIANNE** (re-entry) *London HLD 8381* **23** 4 wks

Ronnie HILTON *UK, male vocalist*

26 Nov 54 ● **I STILL BELIEVE** *HMV B 10785* **3** 14 wks
10 Dec 54 **VENI VIDI VICI** *HMV B 10785* **12** 8 wks
11 Mar 55 ● **A BLOSSOM FELL** *HMV B 10808* **10** 5 wks
26 Aug 55 **STARS SHINE IN YOUR EYES** *HMV B 10901* **13** 7 wks
11 Nov 55 **YELLOW ROSE OF TEXAS** *HMV B 10924* **15** 2 wks
10 Feb 56 **YOUNG AND FOOLISH** *HMV POP 154* **17** 1 wk
24 Feb 56 **YOUNG AND FOOLISH** (re-entry) *HMV POP 154* **20** 1 wk
9 Mar 56 **YOUNG AND FOOLISH** (2nd re-entry) *HMV POP 154* **19** 1 wk
20 Apr 56 ★ **NO OTHER LOVE** *HMV POP 198* **1** 14 wks
29 Jun 56 ● **WHO ARE WE** *HMV POP 221* **6** 12 wks
21 Sep 56 **WOMAN IN LOVE** *HMV POP 248* **30** 1 wk
9 Nov 56 **TWO DIFFERENT WORLDS** *HMV POP 274* **13** 13 wks
24 May 57 ● **AROUND THE WORLD** *HMV POP 338* **4** 18 wks
2 Aug 57 **WONDERFUL WONDERFUL** *HMV POP 364* **27** 2 wks
21 Feb 58 **MAGIC MOMENTS** *HMV POP 446* **22** 2 wks
18 Apr 58 **I MAY NEVER PASS THIS WAY AGAIN** *HMV POP 468* **30** 1 wk
2 May 58 **I MAY NEVER PASS THIS WAY AGAIN** (re-entry) *HMV POP 468* **30** 1 wk
6 Jun 58 **I MAY NEVER PASS THIS WAY AGAIN** (2nd re-entry) *HMV POP 468* **27** 1 wk
9 Jan 59 **THE WORLD OUTSIDE** *HMV POP 559* **18** 6 wks

Date	Title *Label Number*	Position	
21 Aug 59	**THE WONDER OF YOU** *HMV POP 638*	**22**	3 wks
21 May 64	**DON'T LET THE RAIN COME DOWN** *HMV POP 1291*	**21**	10 wks
11 Feb 65	**A WINDMILL IN OLD AMSTERDAM** *HMV POP 1378*	**23**	13 wks

Edmund HOCKRIDGE *Canada, male vocalist*

Date	Title *Label Number*	Position	
17 Feb 56	● **YOUNG AND FOOLISH** *Nixa N 15039*	**10**	7 wks
13 Apr 56	**YOUNG AND FOOLISH** (re-entry) *Nixa N 15039*	**28**	1 wk
4 May 56	**YOUNG AND FOOLISH** (2nd re-entry) *Nixa N 15039*	**26**	1 wk
11 May 56	**NO OTHER LOVE** *Nixa N 15046*	**24**	2 wks
1 Jun 56	**NO OTHER LOVE** (re-entry) *Nixa N 15046*	**29**	1 wk
15 Jun 56	**NO OTHER LOVE** (2nd re-entry) *Nixa N 15046*	**30**	1 wk
31 Aug 56	**BY THE FOUNTAINS OF ROME** *Pye Nixa N 15063*	**17**	5 wks

Eddie HODGES *US, male vocalist*

Date	Title *Label Number*	Position	
28 Sep 61	**I'M GONNA KNOCK ON YOUR DOOR** *London HLA 9369*	**37**	6 wks
9 Aug 62	**MADE TO LOVE (GIRLS GIRLS GIRLS)** *London HLA 9576*	**37**	4 wks

HOLLAND-DOZIER *US, male vocal duo*

Date	Title *Label Number*	Position	
28 Oct 72	**WHY CAN'T WE BE LOVERS** *Invictus INV 525*	**29**	5 wks

Hit has credit "featuring Lamont Dozier"

Jennifer HOLLIDAY *US, female vocalist*

Date	Title *Label Number*	Position	
4 Sep 82	**AND I'M TELLING YOU I'M NOT GOING** *Geffen GEF A 2644*	**32**	6 wks

Michael HOLLIDAY *UK, male vocalist*

Date	Title *Label Number*	Position	
30 Mar 56	**NOTHIN' TO DO** *Columbia DB 3746*	**20**	1 wk
27 Apr 56	**NOTHIN' TO DO** (re-entry) *Columbia DB 3746*	**23**	2 wks
15 Jun 56	**GAL WITH THE YALLER SHOES** *Columbia DB 3783*	**13**	3 wks
22 Jun 56	**HOT DIGGITY** *Columbia DB 3783*	**14**	5 wks
3 Aug 56	**HOT DIGGITY/ GAL WITH THE YALLER SHOES** (re-entry) *Columbia DB 3783*	**17**	3 wks
5 Oct 56	**TEN THOUSAND MILES** *Columbia DB 3813*	**24**	3 wks
17 Jan 58	★ **THE STORY OF MY LIFE** *Columbia DB 4058*	**1**	15 wks
14 Mar 58	**IN LOVE** *Columbia DB 4087*	**26**	3 wks
16 May 58	● **STAIRWAY OF LOVE** *Columbia DB 4121*	**3**	13 wks
11 Jul 58	**I'LL ALWAYS BE IN LOVE WITH YOU** *Columbia DB 4155*	**27**	1 wk
1 Jan 60	★ **STARRY EYED** *Columbia DB 4378*	**1**	12 wks
14 Apr 60	**SKYLARK** *Columbia DB 4437*	**39**	3 wks
1 Sep 60	**LITTLE BOY LOST** *Columbia DB 4475*	**50**	1 wk

When Hot Diggity/ Gal With The Yaller Shoes *re-entered the chart on 3 Aug 56,* Hot Diggity *was listed by itself on 3 Aug and 10 Aug. Both sides were listed on 17 Aug.*

HOLLIES *UK, male vocal/instrumental group*

Date	Title *Label Number*	Position	
30 May 63	**JUST LIKE ME** *Parlophone R 5030*	**25**	10 wks
29 Aug 63	**SEARCHIN'** *Parlophone R 5052*	**12**	14 wks
21 Nov 63	● **STAY** *Parlophone R 5077*	**8**	16 wks
27 Feb 64	● **JUST ONE LOOK** *Parlophone R 5104*	**2**	13 wks
21 May 64	● **HERE I GO AGAIN** *Parlophone R 5137*	**4**	12 wks
17 Sep 64	● **WE'RE THROUGH** *Parlophone R 5178*	**7**	11 wks
28 Jan 65	● **YES I WILL** *Parlophone R 5232*	**9**	13 wks
27 May 65	★ **I'M ALIVE** *Parlophone R 5287*	**1**	14 wks
2 Sep 65	● **LOOK THROUGH ANY WINDOW** *Parlophone R 5322*	**4**	11 wks
9 Dec 65	**IF I NEEDED SOMEONE** *Parlophone R 5392*	**20**	9 wks
24 Feb 66	● **I CAN'T LET GO** *Parlophone R 5409*	**2**	10 wks
23 Jun 66	● **BUS STOP** *Parlophone R 5469*	**5**	9 wks
13 Oct 66	● **STOP STOP STOP** *Parlophone R 5508*	**2**	12 wks
16 Feb 67	● **ON A CAROUSEL** *Parlophone R 5562*	**4**	11 wks
1 Jun 67	● **CARRIE-ANNE** *Parlophone R 5602*	**3**	11 wks
27 Sep 67	**KING MIDAS IN REVERSE** *Parlophone R 5637*	**18**	8 wks
27 Mar 68	● **JENNIFER ECCLES** *Parlophone R 5680*	**7**	11 wks
2 Oct 68	**LISTEN TO ME** *Parlophone R 5733*	**11**	11 wks
5 Mar 69	● **SORRY SUZANNE** *Parlophone R 5765*	**3**	12 wks
4 Oct 69	● **HE AIN'T HEAVY HE'S MY BROTHER** *Parlophone R 5806*	**3**	15 wks
18 Apr 70	● **I CAN'T TELL THE BOTTOM FROM THE TOP** *Parlophone R 5837*	**7**	10 wks
3 Oct 70	**GASOLINE ALLEY BRED** *Parlophone R 5862*	**14**	7 wks
22 May 71	**HEY WILLY** *Parlophone R 5905*	**22**	7 wks
26 Feb 72	**THE BABY** *Polydor 2058 199*	**26**	6 wks
2 Sep 72	**LONG COOL WOMAN IN A BLACK DRESS** *Parlophone R 5939*	**32**	8 wks
13 Oct 73	**THE DAY THAT CURLY BILLY SHOT CRAZY SAM MCGHEE** *Polydor 2058 403*	**24**	6 wks
9 Feb 74	● **THE AIR THAT I BREATHE** *Polydor 2058 435*	**2**	13 wks
14 Jun 80	**SOLDIER'S SONG** *Polydor 2059 246*	**58**	3 wks
29 Aug 81	**HOLLIEDAZE (A MEDLEY)** *EMI 5229*	**28**	7 wks

HOLLY and the IVY'S

UK, male/female vocal/instrumental group

Date	Title *Label Number*	Position	
19 Dec 81	**CHRISTMAS ON 45** *Decca SANTA 1*	**40**	4 wks

Buddy HOLLY *US, male vocalist*

Date	Title *Label Number*	Position	
6 Dec 57	● **PEGGY SUE** *Coral Q 72293*	**6**	17 wks
14 Mar 58	**LISTEN TO ME** *Coral Q 72288*	**16**	2 wks
20 Jun 58	● **RAVE ON** *Coral Q 72325*	**5**	14 wks
29 Aug 58	**EARLY IN THE MORNING** *Coral Q 72333*	**17**	4 wks
16 Jan 59	**HEARTBEAT** *Coral Q 72346*	**30**	1 wk
27 Feb 59	★ **IT DOESN'T MATTER ANYMORE** *Coral Q 72360*	**1**	21 wks
31 Jul 59	**MIDNIGHT SHIFT** *Brunswick 05800*	**26**	3 wks
11 Sep 59	**PEGGY SUE GOT MARRIED** *Coral Q 72376*	**13**	10 wks
28 Apr 60	**HEARTBEAT** (re-issue) *Coral Q 72392*	**30**	3 wks
26 May 60	**TRUE LOVE WAYS** *Coral Q 72397*	**25**	7 wks
20 Oct 60	**LEARNIN' THE GAME** *Coral Q 72411*	**36**	3 wks
26 Jan 61	**WHAT TO DO** *Coral Q 72419*	**34**	6 wks
6 Jul 61	**BABY I DON'T CARE/ VALLEY OF TEARS** *Coral Q 72432*	**12**	14 wks
15 Mar 62	**LISTEN TO ME** (re-issue) *Coral Q 72449*	**48**	1 wk
13 Sep 62	**REMINISCING** *Coral Q 72455*	**17**	11 wks
14 Mar 63	● **BROWN-EYED HANDSOME MAN** *Coral Q 72459*	**3**	17 wks
6 Jun 63	● **BO DIDDLEY** *Coral Q 72463*	**4**	12 wks
5 Sep 63	● **WISHING** *Coral Q 72466*	**10**	11 wks
19 Dec 63	**WHAT TO DO** (re-issue) *Coral Q 72469*	**27**	8 wks
14 May 64	**YOU'VE GOT LOVE** *Coral Q 72472*	**40**	6 wks
10 Sep 64	**LOVE'S MADE A FOOL OF YOU** *Coral Q 72475*	**39**	6 wks
3 Apr 68	**PEGGY SUE/ RAVE ON** (re-issue) *MCA MU 1012*	**32**	9 wks

Buddy Holly's version of Love's Made A Fool Of You *is not the same version as the Crickets' hit of 1959, on which Holly did not appear.* You've Got Love *was released with credit to Buddy Holly and The Crickets.* Valley Of Tears *was not listed together with* Baby I Don't Care *until 13 Jul 61. See also Crickets.*

HOLLYWOOD ARGYLES *US, male vocal group*

Date	Title *Label Number*	Position	
21 Jul 60	**ALLEY OOP** *London HLU 9146*	**24**	10 wks

Left **IRON MAIDEN** Their name and third hit is maybe a pointer to a latent obsession with our first lady premier *and below* **IVY LEAGUE** Perry Ford (Brian Pugh), Ken Lewis (James Hawker) and John Carter (John Shakespeare) – they sang backing vocals on The Who's first two hits

Inset **MICHAEL HOLLIDAY** The story of his life ended three years after his last hit *Right* **BUDDY HOLLY** 24 years since his death artists are still having success with songs he made famous *Centre right* **HONEYBUS** As the theme for the Nimble Bread TV commercial, their one hit continued to make money for group leader/songwriter Pete Dello long after it had fallen out of the chart

Bottom right **IMAGINATION** Ashley, Leee and Errol – leaving little to the imagination

Eddie HOLMAN *US, male vocalist*

Date		Title *Label Number*	Position	Weeks
19 Oct 74	●	**(HEY THERE) LONELY GIRL** *ABC 4012*	**4**	13 wks

Rupert HOLMES *US, male vocalist*

Date		Title *Label Number*	Position	Weeks
12 Jan 80		**ESCAPE (THE PINA COLADA SONG)** *Infinity INF 120*	**23**	7 wks
22 Mar 80		**HIM** *MCA 565*	**31**	7 wks

John HOLT *Jamaica, male vocalist*

Date		Title *Label Number*	Position	Weeks
14 Dec 74	●	**HELP ME MAKE IT THROUGH THE NIGHT** *Trojan TR 7909*	**6**	14 wks

HONEYBUS *UK, male vocal/instrumental group*

Date		Title *Label Number*	Position	Weeks
20 Mar 68	●	**I CAN'T LET MAGGIE GO** *Deram DM 182*	**8**	12 wks

HONEYCOMBS

UK, male/female vocal/instrumental group

Date		Title *Label Number*	Position	Weeks
23 Jul 64	★	**HAVE I THE RIGHT** *Pye 7N 15664*	**1**	15 wks
22 Oct 64		**IS IT BECAUSE** *Pye 7N 15705*	**38**	6 wks
29 Apr 65		**SOMETHING BETTER BEGINNING** *Pye 7N 15827*	**39**	4 wks
5 Aug 65		**THAT'S THE WAY** *Pye 7N 15890*	**12**	14 wks

HONKY *UK, male vocal/instrumental group*

Date		Title *Label Number*	Position	Weeks
28 May 77		**JOIN THE PARTY** *Creole CR 137*	**28**	5 wks

Frank HOOKER and POSITIVE PEOPLE

US, male vocal/instrumental group

Date		Title *Label Number*	Position	Weeks
5 Jul 80		**THIS FEELIN'** *DJM DJS 10947*	**48**	4 wks

John Lee HOOKER *US, male vocalist*

Date		Title *Label Number*	Position	Weeks
11 Jun 64		**DIMPLES** *Stateside SS 297*	**23**	10 wks

Mary HOPKIN *UK, female vocalist*

Date		Title *Label Number*	Position	Weeks
4 Sep 68	★	**THOSE WERE THE DAYS** *Apple 2*	**1**	21 wks
2 Apr 69	●	**GOODBYE** *Apple 10*	**2**	14 wks
31 Jan 70	●	**TEMMA HARBOUR** *Apple 22*	**6**	11 wks
28 Mar 70	●	**KNOCK KNOCK WHO'S THERE** *Apple 26*	**2**	14 wks
31 Oct 70		**THINK ABOUT YOUR CHILDREN** *Apple 30*	**19**	7 wks
2 Jan 71		**THINK ABOUT YOUR CHILDREN** (re-entry) *Apple 30*	**46**	2 wks
31 Jul 71		**LET MY NAME BE SORROW** *Apple 34*	**46**	1 wk
20 Mar 76		**IF YOU LOVE ME** *Good Earth GD 2*	**32**	4 wks

Johnny HORTON *US, male vocalist*

Date		Title *Label Number*	Position	Weeks
26 Jun 59		**BATTLE OF NEW ORLEANS** *Philips PB 932*	**16**	4 wks
19 Jan 61		**NORTH TO ALASKA** *Philips PB 1062*	**23**	11 wks

HOT BLOOD *France, male instrumental group*

Date		Title *Label Number*	Position	Weeks
9 Oct 76		**SOUL DRACULA** *Creole CR 132*	**32**	5 wks

HOT BUTTER *US, male instrumental group*

Date		Title *Label Number*	Position	Weeks
22 Jul 72	●	**POPCORN** *Pye International 7N 25583*	**5**	16 wks
23 Dec 72		**POPCORN** (re-entry) *Pye International 7N 25583*	**50**	3 wks

HOT CHOCOLATE

UK, male vocal/instrumental group

Date		Title *Label Number*	Position	Weeks
15 Aug 70	●	**LOVE IS LIFE** *RAK 103*	**6**	12 wks
6 Mar 71		**YOU COULD HAVE BEEN A LADY** *RAK 110*	**22**	9 wks
28 Aug 71	●	**I BELIEVE (IN LOVE)** *RAK 118*	**8**	11 wks
28 Oct 72		**YOU'LL ALWAYS BE A FRIEND** *RAK 139*	**23**	8 wks
14 Apr 73	●	**BROTHER LOUIE** *RAK 149*	**7**	10 wks
18 Aug 73		**RUMOURS** *RAK 157*	**44**	3 wks
16 Mar 74	●	**EMMA** *RAK 168*	**3**	10 wks
30 Nov 74		**CHERI BABE** *RAK 188*	**31**	9 wks
24 May 75		**DISCO QUEEN** *RAK 202*	**11**	7 wks
9 Aug 75	●	**A CHILD'S PRAYER** *RAK 212*	**7**	10 wks
8 Nov 75	●	**YOU SEXY THING** *RAK 221*	**2**	12 wks
20 Mar 76		**DON'T STOP IT NOW** *RAK 230*	**11**	8 wks
26 Jun 76		**MAN TO MAN** *RAK 238*	**14**	8 wks
21 Aug 76		**HEAVEN IS IN THE BACK SEAT OF MY CADILLIAC** *RAK 240*	**25**	8 wks
18 Jun 77	★	**SO YOU WIN AGAIN** *RAK 259*	**1**	11 wks
26 Nov 77	●	**PUT YOUR LOVE IN ME** *RAK 266*	**10**	9 wks
4 Mar 78		**EVERY 1'S A WINNER** *RAK 270*	**12**	11 wks
2 Dec 78		**I'LL PUT YOU TOGETHER AGAIN** *RAK 286*	**13**	11 wks
19 May 79		**MINDLESS BOOGIE** *RAK 292*	**46**	5 wks
28 Jul 79		**GOING THROUGH THE MOTIONS** *RAK 296*	**53**	4 wks
3 May 80	●	**NO DOUBT ABOUT IT** *RAK 310*	**2**	11 wks
19 Jul 80		**ARE YOU GETTING ENOUGH OF WHAT MAKES YOU HAPPY** *RAK 318*	**17**	7 wks
13 Dec 80		**LOVE ME TO SLEEP** *RAK 324*	**50**	5 wks
30 May 81		**YOU'LL NEVER BE SO WRONG** *RAK 331*	**52**	4 wks
17 Apr 82	●	**GIRL CRAZY** *RAK 341*	**7**	11 wks
10 Jul 82	●	**IT STARTED WITH A KISS** *RAK 344*	**5**	12 wks
25 Sep 82		**CHANCES** *RAK 350*	**32**	5 wks

HOT GOSSIP — See *Sarah BRIGHTMAN*

HOTLEGS *UK, male vocal/instrumental group*

Date		Title *Label Number*	Position	Weeks
4 Jul 70	●	**NEANDERTHAL MAN** *Fontana 6007 019*	**2**	14 wks

HOTRODS — See *EDDIE and the HOTRODS*

HOTSHOTS *UK, male vocal group*

Date		Title *Label Number*	Position	Weeks
2 Jun 73	●	**SNOOPY VS. THE RED BARON** *Mooncrest MOON 5*	**4**	15 wks

Thelma HOUSTON *US, female vocalist*

Date		Title *Label Number*	Position	Weeks
5 Feb 77		**DON'T LEAVE ME THIS WAY** *Motown TMG 1060*	**13**	8 wks
27 Jun 81		**IF YOU FEEL IT** *RCA 77*	**48**	4 wks

Billy HOWARD *UK, male vocalist*

Date		Title *Label Number*	Position	Weeks
13 Dec 75	●	**KING OF THE COPS** *Penny Farthing PEN 892*	**6**	12 wks

HOWLIN' WOLF *US, male vocalist*

Date		Title *Label Number*	Position	Weeks
4 Jun 64		**SMOKESTACK LIGHTNIN'** *Pye International 7N 25244*	**42**	5 wks

Date	Title *Label Number*	Position	

Al HUDSON and the PARTNERS

US, male/female vocal/instrumental group

9 Sep 78	**DANCE, GET DOWN/ HOW DO YOU DO** *ABC 4229*	57	5 wks
15 Sep 79	**YOU CAN DO IT** *MCA 511*	15	10 wks

First hit credited to Al Hudson - US, male Vocalist. See also One Way featuring Al Hudson.

HUDSON-FORD *UK, male vocal/instrumental duo*

18 Aug 73	● **PICK UP THE PIECES** *A & M AMS 7078*	8	9 wks
16 Feb 74	**BURN BABY BURN** *A & M AMS 7096*	15	9 wks
29 Jun 74	**FLOATING IN THE WIND** *A & M AMS 7116*	35	2 wks

See also Monks.

HUES CORPORATION

US, male/female vocal group

27 Jul 74	● **ROCK THE BOAT** *RCA APBO 0232*	6	10 wks
19 Oct 74	**ROCKIN' SOUL** *RCA PB 10066*	24	6 wks

David HUGHES *UK, male vocalist*

21 Sep 56	**BY THE FOUNTAINS OF ROME** *Philips PB 606*	27	1 wk

HUGO and LUIGI *US, male vocal duo*

24 Jul 59	**LA PLUME DE MA TANTE** *RCA 1127*	29	2 wks

HUMAN LEAGUE

UK, male/female vocal/instrumental group

3 May 80	**HOLIDAY 80 (DOUBLE SINGLE)** *Virgin SV 105*	56	5 wks
21 Jun 80	**EMPIRE STATE HUMAN** *Virgin VS 351*	62	2 wks
28 Feb 81	**BOYS AND GIRLS** *Virgin VS 395*	48	4 wks
2 May 81	**THE SOUND OF THE CROWD** *Virgin VS 416*	12	10 wks
8 Aug 81	● **LOVE ACTION (I BELIEVE IN LOVE)** *Virgin VS 435*	3	13 wks
10 Oct 81	● **OPEN YOUR HEART** *Virgin VS 453*	6	9 wks
5 Dec 81	★ **DON'T YOU WANT ME** *Virgin VS 466*	1	13 wks
9 Jan 82	● **BEING BOILED** *EMI FAST 4*	6	9 wks
6 Feb 82	**HOLIDAY 80** (DOUBLE SINGLE) (re-entry) *Virgin SV 105*	46	5 wks
20 Nov 82	● **MIRROR MAN** *Virgin VS 522*	2†	6 wks

Tracks on double single: Being Boiled; Marianne; Rock And Roll - Nightclubbing; Dancevision

HUMBLE PIE *UK, male vocal/instrumental group*

23 Aug 69	● **NATURAL BORN BUGIE** *Immediate IM 082*	4	10 wks

Engelbert HUMPERDINCK *UK, male vocalist*

26 Jan 67	★ **RELEASE ME** *Decca F 12541*	1	56 wks
25 May 67	● **THERE GOES MY EVERYTHING** *Decca F 12610*	2	29 wks
23 Aug 67	★ **THE LAST WALTZ** *Decca F 12655*	1	27 wks
10 Jan 68	● **AM I THAT EASY TO FORGET** *Decca F 12722*	3	13 wks
24 Apr 68	● **A MAN WITHOUT LOVE** *Decca F 12770*	2	15 wks
25 Sep 68	● **LES BICYCLETTES DE BELSIZE** *Decca F 12834*	5	15 wks
5 Feb 69	● **THE WAY IT USED TO BE** *Decca F 12879*	3	14 wks
9 Aug 69	**I'M A BETTER MAN** *Decca F 12957*	15	13 wks
15 Nov 69	● **WINTER WORLD OF LOVE** *Decca F 12980*	7	13 wks
30 May 70	**MY MARIE** *Decca F 13032*	31	7 wks
12 Sep 70	**SWEETHEART** *Decca F 13068*	22	6 wks
31 Oct 70	**SWEETHEART** (re-entry) *Decca F 13068*	50	1 wk
11 Sep 71	**ANOTHER TIME ANOTHER PLACE** *Decca F 13212*	13	12 wks
4 Mar 72	**TOO BEAUTIFUL TO LAST** *Decca F 13281*	14	10 wks
20 Oct 73	**LOVE IS ALL** *Decca F 13443*	44	3 wks
17 Nov 73	**LOVE IS ALL** (re-entry) *Decca F 13443*	45	1 wk

Geraldine HUNT *Canada, female vocalist*

25 Oct 80	**CAN'T FAKE THE FEELING** *Champagne FIZZ 5001*	44	5 wks

Marsha HUNT *US, female vocalist*

21 May 69	**WALK ON GILDED SPLINTERS** *Track 604 030*	46	2 wks
2 May 70	**KEEP THE CUSTOMER SATISFIED** *Track 604 037*	41	1 wk

Tommy HUNT *US, male vocalist*

11 Oct 75	**CRACKIN' UP** *Spark SRL 1132*	39	5 wks
21 Aug 76	**LOVING ON THE LOSING SIDE** *Spark SRL 1146*	28	9 wks
4 Dec 76	**ONE FINE MORNING** *Spark SRL 1148*	44	3 wks

Ian HUNTER *UK, male vocalist*

3 May 75	**ONCE BITTEN TWICE SHY** *CBS 3194*	14	10 wks

Tab HUNTER *US, male vocalist*

8 Feb 57	★ **YOUNG LOVE** *London HLD 8380*	1	18 wks
12 Apr 57	● **99 WAYS** *London HLD 8410*	5	11 wks
5 Jul 57	**99 WAYS** (re-entry) *London HLD 8410*	29	1 wk

HURRICANES — See *JOHNNY and the HURRICANES*

Phil HURTT *US, male vocalist*

11 Nov 78	**GIVING IT BACK** *Fantasy FTC 161*	36	5 wks

Willie HUTCH *US, male vocalist*

4 Dec 82	**IN AND OUT** *Motown TMG 1285*	51†	4 wks

June HUTTON *US, female vocalist*

7 Aug 53	● **SAY YOU'RE MINE AGAIN** *Capitol CL 13918*	10	3 wks
4 Sep 53	● **SAY YOU'RE MINE AGAIN** (re-entry) *Capitol CL 13918*	6	4 wks

Brian HYLAND *US, male vocalist*

7 Jul 60	● **ITSY BITSY TEENY WEENY YELLOW POLKA DOT BIKINI** *London HLR 9161*	8	13 wks
20 Oct 60	**FOUR LITTLE HEELS** *London HLR 9203*	29	6 wks
10 May 62	● **GINNY COME LATELY** *HMV POP 1013*	5	15 wks
2 Aug 62	● **SEALED WITH A KISS** *HMV POP 1051*	3	15 wks
8 Nov 62	**WARMED OVER KISSES** *HMV POP 1079*	28	6 wks

Date	Title *Label Number*	Position	
27 Mar 71	**GYPSY WOMAN** *Uni UN 530*	**45**	1 wk
10 Apr 71	**GYPSY WOMAN** (re-entry) *Uni UN 530*	**42**	5 wks
28 Jun 75	● **SEALED WITH A KISS** (re-issue) *ABC 4059*	**7**	11 wks

Sheila HYLTON *Jamaica, female vocalist*

Date	Title *Label Number*	Position	
15 Sep 79	**BREAKFAST IN BED** *United Artists BP 304*	**57**	5 wks
17 Jan 81	**THE BED'S TOO BIG WITHOUT YOU** *Island WIP 6671*	**35**	7 wks

Phyllis HYMAN *US, female vocalist*

Date	Title *Label Number*	Position	
16 Feb 80	**YOU KNOW HOW TO LOVE ME** *Arista ARIST 323*	**47**	6 wks
12 Sep 81	**YOU SURE LOOK GOOD TO ME** *Arista ARIST 424*	**56**	3 wks

Dick HYMAN TRIO

US, male instrumental group, Dick Hyman keyboards

Date	Title *Label Number*	Position	
16 Mar 56	● **THEME FROM THE THREEPENNY OPERA** *MGM 890*	**9**	10 wks

HYSTERICS *UK, male vocal/instrumental group*

Date	Title *Label Number*	Position	
12 Dec 81	**JINGLE BELLS LAUGHING ALL THE WAY** *Record Delivery KA 5*	**44**	5 wks

I

Janis IAN *US, female vocalist*

Date	Title *Label Number*	Position	
17 Nov 79	**FLY TOO HIGH** *CBS 7936*	**44**	7 wks
28 Jun 80	**THE OTHER SIDE OF THE SUN** *CBS 8611*	**44**	3 wks

IAN AND THE BLOCKHEADS — See *Ian DURY*

IDES OF MARCH

US, male vocal/instrumental group

Date	Title *Label Number*	Position	
6 Jun 70	**VEHICLE** *Warner Bros. WB 7378*	**31**	9 wks

Billy IDOL *UK, male vocalist*

Date	Title *Label Number*	Position	
11 Sep 82	**HOT IN THE CITY** *Chrysalis CHS 2625*	**58**	4 wks

Frank IFIELD *UK, male vocalist*

Date	Title *Label Number*	Position	
19 Feb 60	**LUCKY DEVIL** *Columbia DB 4399*	**22**	2 wks
7 Apr 60	**LUCKY DEVIL** (re-entry) *Columbia DB 4399*	**33**	2 wks
29 Sep 60	**GOTTA GET A DATE** *Columbia DB 4496*	**49**	1 wk
5 Jul 62	★ **I REMEMBER YOU** *Columbia DB 4856*	**1**	28 wks
25 Oct 62	★ **LOVESICK BLUES** *Columbia DB 4913*	**1**	17 wks
24 Jan 63	★ **WAYWARD WIND** *Columbia DB 4960*	**1**	13 wks
11 Apr 63	● **NOBODY'S DARLIN' BUT MINE** *Columbia DB 7007*	**4**	16 wks
27 Jun 63	★ **CONFESSIN'** *Columbia DB 7062*	**1**	16 wks
17 Oct 63	**MULE TRAIN** *Columbia DB 7131*	**22**	6 wks
9 Jan 64	● **DON'T BLAME ME** *Columbia DB 7184*	**8**	13 wks
23 Apr 64	**ANGRY AT THE BIG OAK TREE** *Columbia DB 7263*	**25**	8 wks
23 Jul 64	**I SHOULD CARE** *Columbia DB 7319*	**33**	3 wks
1 Oct 64	**SUMMER IS OVER** *Columbia DB 7355*	**25**	6 wks
19 Aug 65	**PARADISE** *Columbia DB 7655*	**26**	9 wks
23 Jun 66	**NO ONE WILL EVER KNOW** *Columbia DB 7940*	**25**	4 wks
8 Dec 66	**CALL HER YOUR SWEETHEART** *Columbia DB 8078*	**24**	11 wks

Julio IGLESIAS *Spain, male vocalist*

Date	Title *Label Number*	Position	
24 Oct 81	★ **BEGIN THE BEGUINE (VOLVER A EMPEZAR)** *CBS A 1612*	**1**	14 wks
6 Mar 82	● **QUIEREME MUCHO (YOURS)** *CBS A 1939*	**3**	9 wks
9 Oct 82	**AMOR** *CBS A 2801*	**32**	7 wks

IMAGINATION *UK, male/female vocal group*

Date	Title *Label Number*	Position	
16 May 81	● **BODY TALK** *R & B RBS 201*	**4**	18 wks
5 Sep 81	**IN AND OUT OF LOVE** *R & B RBS 202*	**16**	9 wks
14 Nov 81	**FLASHBACK** *R & B RBS 206*	**16**	13 wks
6 Mar 82	● **JUST AN ILLUSION** *R & B RBS 208*	**2**	11 wks
26 Jun 82	● **MUSIC AND LIGHTS** *R & B RBS 210*	**5**	9 wks
25 Sep 82	**IN THE HEAT OF THE NIGHT** *R & B RBS 211*	**22**	8 wks
11 Dec 82	**CHANGES** *R & B RBS 213*	**43**†	3 wks

IMPALAS *US, male vocal group*

Date	Title *Label Number*	Position	
21 Aug 59	**SORRY (I RAN ALL THE WAY HOME)** *MGM 1015*	**28**	1 wk

IMPERIALS *US, male vocal group*

Date	Title *Label Number*	Position	
24 Dec 77	**WHO'S GONNA LOVE ME** *Power Exchange PX 266*	**17**	9 wks

See also Little Anthony and the Imperials

IMPRESSIONS *US, male vocal group*

Date	Title *Label Number*	Position	
22 Nov 75	**FIRST IMPRESSIONS** *Curtom K 16638*	**16**	10 wks

IN CROWD *UK, male vocal/instrumental group*

Date	Title *Label Number*	Position	
20 May 65	**THAT'S HOW STRONG MY LOVE IS** *Parlophone R 5276*	**48**	1 wk

INCANTATION *UK, male instrumental group*

Date	Title *Label Number*	Position	
4 Dec 82	**CACHARPAYA (ANDES PUMPSA DAESI)** *Beggars Banquet BEG 84*	**28**†	4 wks

INCOGNITO *France, male instrumental group*

Date	Title *Label Number*	Position	
15 Nov 80	**PARISIENNE GIRL** *Ensign ENY 44*	**73**	2 wks

INDIOS TABAJARAS

Brazil, male instrumental duo, guitars

Date	Title *Label Number*	Position	
31 Oct 63	● **MARIA ELENA** *RCA 1365*	**5**	17 wks

Date **Title** *Label Number* **Position**

INK SPOTS *US, male vocal group*

Date	Title *Label Number*	Position	
29 Apr 55	● **MELODY OF LOVE** *Parlophone MSP 6152*	**10**	4 wks

John INMAN *UK, male vocalist*

Date	Title *Label Number*	Position	
25 Oct 75	**ARE YOU BEING SERVED SIR** *DJM DJS 602*	**39**	6 wks

INMATES *UK, male vocal/instrumental group*

Date	Title *Label Number*	Position	
8 Dec 79	**THE WALK** *Radar ADA 47*	**36**	9 wks

INNER CIRCLE

Jamaica, male vocal/instrumental group

Date	Title *Label Number*	Position	
24 Feb 79	**EVERYTHING IS GREAT** *Island WIP 6472*	**37**	8 wks
12 May 79	**STOP BREAKING MY HEART** *Island WIP 6488*	**50**	3 wks

INSTANT FUNK

US, male vocal/instrumental group

Date	Title *Label Number*	Position	
20 Jan 79	**GOT MY MIND MADE UP** *Salsoul SSOL 114*	**46**	5 wks

INTRUDERS *US, male vocal group*

Date	Title *Label Number*	Position	
13 Apr 74	**I'LL ALWAYS LOVE MY MAMA** *Philadelphia International PIR 2147*	**32**	7 wks
6 Jul 74	**(WIN PLACE OR SHOW) SHE'S A WINNER** *Philadelphia International PIR 2212*	**14**	9 wks

INVISIBLE GIRLS — See *Pauline MURRAY and the INVISIBLE GIRLS*

IRON MAIDEN *UK, male vocal/instrumental group*

Date	Title *Label Number*	Position	
23 Feb 80	**RUNNING FREE** *EMI 5032*	**34**	5 wks
7 Jun 80	**SANCTUARY** *EMI 5065*	**29**	5 wks
8 Nov 80	**WOMEN IN UNIFORM** *EMI 5105*	**35**	4 wks
14 Mar 81	**TWILIGHT ZONE/WRATH CHILD** *EMI 5145*	**31**	5 wks
27 Jun 81	**PURGATORY** *EMI 5184*	**52**	3 wks
26 Sep 81	**MAIDEN JAPAN** *EMI 5219*	**43**	4 wks
20 Feb 82	● **RUN TO THE HILLS** *EMI 5263*	**7**	10 wks
15 May 82	**THE NUMBER OF THE BEAST** *EMI 5287*	**18**	8 wks

IRONHORSE

Canada, male vocal/instrumental group

Date	Title *Label Number*	Position	
5 May 79	**SWEET LUI-LOUISE** *Scotti Brothers K 11271*	**60**	3 wks

Big Dee IRWIN *US, male vocalist*

Date	Title *Label Number*	Position	
21 Nov 63	● **SWINGING ON A STAR** *Colpix PX 11010*	**7**	17 wks

This hit was in fact a vocal duet by Big Dee Irwin and Little Eva, though Little Eva was not credited. See also Little Eva.

ISLEY BROTHERS

US, male vocal/instrumental group

Date	Title *Label Number*	Position	
25 Jul 63	**TWIST AND SHOUT** *Stateside SS 112*	**42**	1 wk
28 Apr 66	**THIS OLD HEART OF MINE** *Tamla Motown TMG 555*	**47**	1 wk
1 Sep 66	**I GUESS I'LL ALWAYS LOVE YOU** *Tamla Motown TMG 572*	**45**	2 wks
23 Oct 68	● **THIS OLD HEART OF MINE** (re-entry) *Tamla Motown TMG 555*	**3**	16 wks
15 Jan 69	**I GUESS I'LL ALWAYS LOVE YOU** (re-issue) *Tamla Motown TMG 683*	**11**	9 wks
16 Apr 69	● **BEHIND A PAINTED SMILE** *Tamla Motown TMG 693*	**5**	12 wks
25 Jun 69	**IT'S YOUR THING** *Major Minor MM 621*	**30**	5 wks
30 Aug 69	**PUT YOURSELF IN MY PLACE** *Tamla Motown TMG 708*	**13**	11 wks
22 Sep 73	**THAT LADY** *Epic EPC 1704*	**14**	9 wks
19 Jan 74	**HIGHWAY OF MY LIFE** *Epic EPC 1980*	**25**	8 wks
25 May 74	**SUMMER BREEZE** *Epic EPC 2244*	**16**	8 wks
10 Jul 76	● **HARVEST FOR THE WORLD** *Epic EPC 4369*	**10**	8 wks
13 May 78	**TAKE ME TO THE NEXT PHASE** *Epic EPC 6292*	**50**	4 wks
3 Nov 79	**IT'S A DISCO NIGHT (ROCK DON'T STOP)** *Epic EPC 7911*	**14**	11 wks

Burl IVES *US, male vocalist*

Date	Title *Label Number*	Position	
25 Jan 62	● **A LITTLE BITTY TEAR** *Brunswick 05863*	**9**	15 wks
17 May 62	**FUNNY WAY OF LAUGHIN'** *Brunswick 05868*	**29**	10 wks

IVY LEAGUE *UK, male vocal group*

Date	Title *Label Number*	Position	
4 Feb 65	● **FUNNY HOW LOVE CAN BE** *Piccadilly 7N 35222*	**8**	9 wks
6 May 65	**THAT'S WHY I'M CRYING** *Piccadilly 7N 35228*	**22**	8 wks
24 Jun 65	● **TOSSING AND TURNING** *Piccadilly 7N 35251*	**3**	13 wks
14 Jul 66	**WILLOW TREE** *Piccadilly 7N 35326*	**50**	1 wk

IVY'S — See *HOLLY and the IVY'S*

J

J. A. L. N. BAND

UK/Jamaica, male vocal/instrumental group

Date	Title *Label Number*	Position	
11 Sep 76	**DISCO MUSIC /I LIKE IT** *Magnet MAG 73*	**21**	9 wks
27 Aug 77	**I GOT TO SING** *Magnet MAG 97*	**40**	4 wks
1 Jul 78	**GET UP** *Magnet MAG 118*	**53**	4 wks

Terry JACKS *Canada, male vocalist*

Date	Title *Label Number*	Position	
23 Mar 74	★ **SEASONS IN THE SUN** *Bell 1344*	**1**	12 wks
29 Jun 74	● **IF YOU GO AWAY** *Bell 1362*	**8**	9 wks

Dee D. JACKSON *UK, female vocalist*

Date	Title *Label Number*	Position	
22 Apr 78	● **AUTOMATIC LOVER** *Mercury 6007 171*	**4**	9 wks
2 Sep 78	**METEOR MAN** *Mercury 6007 182*	**48**	5 wks

Jermaine JACKSON *US, male vocalist*

Date	Title *Label Number*	Position	
10 May 80	● **LET'S GET SERIOUS** *Motown TMG 1183*	**8**	11 wks
26 Jul 80	**BURNIN' HOT** *Motown TMG 1194*	**32**	6 wks
30 May 81	**YOU LIKE ME DON'T YOU** *Motown TMG 1222*	**41**	5 wks

See also Jackson Five but not the Jacksons.

Joe JACKSON *UK, male vocalist*

Date	Title *Label Number*	Position	
4 Aug 79	**IS SHE REALLY GOING OUT WITH HIM?** *A & M AMS 7459*	**13**	9 wks
12 Jan 80	● **IT'S DIFFERENT FOR GIRLS** *A & M AMS 7493*	**5**	9 wks
4 Jul 81	**JUMPIN' JIVE** *A & M AMS 8145*	**43**	5 wks

Jumpin' Jive *credited to Joe Jackson's Jumpin' Jive*

Michael JACKSON *US, male vocalist*

Date	Title *Label Number*	Position	
12 Feb 72	● **GOT TO BE THERE** *Tamla Motown TMG 797*	**5**	11 wks
20 May 72	● **ROCKIN' ROBIN** *Tamla Motown TMG 816*	**3**	14 wks
19 Aug 72	● **AIN'T NO SUNSHINE** *Tamla Motown TMG 826*	**8**	11 wks
25 Nov 72	● **BEN** *Tamla Motown TMG 834*	**7**	14 wks
15 Sep 79	● **DON'T STOP TILL YOU GET ENOUGH** *Epic EPC 7763*	**3**	12 wks
24 Nov 79	● **OFF THE WALL** *Epic EPC 8045*	**7**	10 wks
9 Feb 80	● **ROCK WITH YOU** *Epic EPC 8206*	**7**	9 wks
3 May 80	● **SHE'S OUT OF MY LIFE** *Epic EPC 8384*	**3**	9 wks
26 Jul 80	**GIRLFRIEND** *Epic EPC 8782*	**41**	5 wks
23 May 81	★ **ONE DAY IN YOUR LIFE** *Motown TMG 976*	**1**	14 wks
1 Aug 81	**WE'RE ALMOST THERE** *Motown TMG 977*	**46**	4 wks

See also Jackson Five, Jacksons, Diana Ross and Michael Jackson, Michael Jackson and Paul McCartney

Michael JACKSON and Paul McCARTNEY *US/UK, male vocal duo*

Date	Title *Label Number*	Position	
6 Nov 82	● **THE GIRL IS MINE** *Epic EPC A2729*	**8**†	8 wks

See also Michael Jackson, Jackson Five, Jacksons, Diana Ross and Michael Jackson, Paul McCartney, Paul McCartney with Stevie Wonder, Wings.

Mick JACKSON *UK, male vocalist*

Date	Title *Label Number*	Position	
30 Sep 78	**BLAME IT ON THE BOOGIE** *Atlantic K 11102*	**15**	8 wks
3 Feb 79	**WEEKEND** *Atlantic K 11224*	**38**	8 wks

Millie JACKSON *US, female vocalist*

Date	Title *Label Number*	Position	
18 Nov 72	**MY MAN A SWEET MAN** *Mojo 2093 022*	**50**	1 wk

Stonewall JACKSON *US, male vocalist*

Date	Title *Label Number*	Position	
17 Jul 59	**WATERLOO** *Philips PB 941*	**24**	2 wks

Tony JACKSON and the VIBRATIONS *UK, male vocal/instrumental group*

Date	Title *Label Number*	Position	
8 Oct 64	**BYE BYE BABY** *Pye 7N 15685*	**38**	3 wks

Wanda JACKSON *US, female vocalist*

Date	Title *Label Number*	Position	
1 Sep 60	**LET'S HAVE A PARTY** *Capitol CL 15147*	**32**	8 wks
26 Jan 61	**MEAN MEAN MAN** *Capitol CL 15176*	**46**	1 wk
9 Feb 61	**MEAN MEAN MAN** (re-entry) *Capitol CL 15176*	**40**	2 wks

JACKSON FIVE *US, male vocal group*

Date	Title *Label Number*	Position	
31 Jan 70	● **I WANT YOU BACK** *Tamla Motown TMG 724*	**2**	13 wks
16 May 70	● **ABC** *Tamla Motown TMG 738*	**8**	11 wks
1 Aug 70	● **THE LOVE YOU SAVE** *Tamla Motown TMG 746*	**7**	9 wks
21 Nov 70	● **I'LL BE THERE** *Tamla Motown TMG 758*	**4**	16 wks
10 Apr 71	**MAMA'S PEARL** *Tamla Motown TMG 769*	**25**	7 wks
17 Jul 71	**NEVER CAN SAY GOODBYE** *Tamla Motown TMG 778*	**33**	7 wks
11 Nov 72	● **LOOKIN' THROUGH THE WINDOWS** *Tamla Motown TMG 833*	**9**	11 wks
23 Dec 72	**SANTA CLAUS IS COMING TO TOWN** *Tamla Motown TMG 837*	**43**	3 wks
17 Feb 73	● **DOCTOR MY EYES** *Tamla Motown TMG 842*	**9**	10 wks
9 Jun 73	**HALLELUJAH DAY** *Tamla Motown TMG 856*	**20**	9 wks
8 Sep 73	**SKYWRITER** *Tamla Motown TMG 865*	**25**	8 wks

80 per cent of the group became part of the Jacksons and moved to Epic records. See also Jacksons, Michael Jackson.

JACKSONS *US, male vocal group*

Date	Title *Label Number*	Position	
9 Apr 77	**ENJOY YOURSELF** *Epic EPC 5063*	**42**	4 wks
4 Jun 77	★ **SHOW YOU THE WAY TO GO** *Epic EPC 5266*	**1**	10 wks
13 Aug 77	**DREAMER** *Epic EPC 5458*	**22**	9 wks
5 Nov 77	**GOIN' PLACES** *Epic EPC 5732*	**26**	7 wks
11 Feb 78	**EVEN THOUGH YOU'VE GONE** *Epic EPC 5919*	**31**	4 wks
23 Sep 78	● **BLAME IT ON THE BOOGIE** *Epic EPC 6683*	**8**	12 wks
3 Feb 79	**DESTINY** *Epic EPC 6983*	**39**	6 wks
24 Mar 79	● **SHAKE YOUR BODY (DOWN TO THE GROUND)** *Epic EPC 7181*	**4**	12 wks
25 Oct 80	**LOVELY ONE** *Epic EPC 9302*	**29**	6 wks
13 Dec 80	**HEARTBREAK HOTEL** *Epic EPC 9391*	**44**	6 wks
28 Feb 81	● **CAN YOU FEEL IT** *Epic EPC 9554*	**6**	15 wks
4 Jul 81	● **WALK RIGHT NOW** *Epic EPC A 1294*	**7**	11 wks

The Jacksons are the Jackson Five minus Jermaine, plus other relatives too young to perform in Jackson Five days. See also Jackson Five, Michael Jackson.

JACKY *UK, female vocalist*

Date	Title *Label Number*	Position	
10 Apr 68	● **WHITE HORSES** *Philips BF 1674*	**10**	14 wks

Jacky is Jackie Lee. See also Jackie Lee.

Mick JAGGER *UK, male vocalist*

Date	Title *Label Number*	Position	
14 Nov 70	**MEMO FROM TURNER** *Decca F 13067*	**32**	5 wks

JAGS *UK, male vocal/instrumental group*

Date	Title *Label Number*	Position	
8 Sep 79	**BACK OF MY HAND** *Island WIP 6501*	**17**	10 wks
2 Feb 80	**WOMAN'S WORLD** *Island WIP 6531*	**75**	1 wk

JAM *UK, male vocal/instrumental group*

Date	Title *Label Number*	Position	
7 May 77	**IN THE CITY** *Polydor 2058 866*	**40**	6 wks
23 Jul 77	**ALL AROUND THE WORLD** *Polydor 2058 903*	**13**	8 wks
5 Nov 77	**THE MODERN WORLD** *Polydor 2058 945*	**36**	4 wks
11 Mar 78	**NEWS OF THE WORLD** *Polydor 2058 995*	**27**	5 wks

Date		Title *Label Number*	Position	
26 Aug 78		**DAVID WATTS/'A' BOMB IN WARDOUR STREET** *Polydor 2059 054*	**25**	8 wks
21 Oct 78		**DOWN IN THE TUBE STATION AT MIDNIGHT** *Polydor POSP 8*	**15**	7 wks
17 Mar 79		**STRANGE TOWN** *Polydor POSP 34*	**15**	9 wks
25 Aug 79		**WHEN YOU'RE YOUNG** *Polydor POSP 69*	**17**	7 wks
3 Nov 79	●	**THE ETON RIFLES** *Polydor POSP 83*	**3**	12 wks
22 Mar 80	★	**GOING UNDERGROUND/THE DREAMS OF CHILDREN** *Polydor POSP 113*	**1**	9 wks
26 Apr 80		**STRANGE TOWN** (re-entry) *Polydor POSP 34*	**44**	4 wks
26 Apr 80		**ALL AROUND THE WORLD** (re-entry) *Polydor 2058 903*	**43**	3 wks
26 Apr 80		**THE MODERN WORLD** (re-entry) *Polydor 2058 945*	**52**	3 wks
26 Apr 80		**NEWS OF THE WORLD** (re-entry) *Polydor 2058 995*	**53**	3 wks
26 Apr 80		**DAVID WATTS** (re-entry) *Polydor 2059 054*	**54**	3 wks
23 Aug 80	★	**START** *Polydor 2059 266*	**1**	8 wks
26 Apr 80		**IN THE CITY** (re-entry) *Polydor 2058 866*	**40**	4 wks
7 Feb 81		**THAT'S ENTERTAINMENT** *Metronome 0030 364*	**21**	7 wks
6 Jun 81	●	**FUNERAL PYRE** *Polydor POSP 257*	**4**	6 wks
24 Oct 81	●	**ABSOLUTE BEGINNERS** *Polydor POSP 350*	**4**	6 wks
13 Feb 82	★	**TOWN CALLED MALICE/PRECIOUS** *Polydor POSP 400*	**1**	8 wks
3 Jul 82	●	**JUST WHO IS THE FIVE O'CLOCK HERO** *Polydor 2059 504*	**8**	5 wks
18 Sep 82	●	**THE BITTEREST PILL (I EVER HAD TO SWALLOW)** *Polydor POSP 505*	**2**	7 wks
4 Dec 82	★	**BEAT SURRENDER** *Polydor POSP 540*	**1**†	4 wks

JAMES — See *BELL and JAMES*

Dick JAMES *UK, male vocalist*

Date		Title *Label Number*	Position	
20 Jan 56		**ROBIN HOOD** *Parlophone R 4117*	**14**	8 wks
18 May 56		**ROBIN HOOD/ BALLAD OF DAVY CROCKETT** (re-entry) *Parlophone R 4117*	**29**	1 wk
11 Jan 57		**GARDEN OF EDEN** *Parlophone R 4255*	**18**	4 wks

Freddie JAMES *US, male vocalist*

Date		Title *Label Number*	Position	
24 Nov 79		**GET UP AND BOOGIE** *Warner Bros. K 17478*	**54**	3 wks

Jimmy JAMES and the VAGABONDS

UK, male vocal/instrumental group

Date		Title *Label Number*	Position	
11 Sep 68		**RED RED WINE** *Pye 7N 17579*	**36**	8 wks
24 Apr 76		**I'LL GO WHERE YOUR MUSIC TAKES ME** *Pye 7N 45585*	**23**	8 wks
17 Jul 76	●	**NOW IS THE TIME** *Pye 7N 45606*	**5**	9 wks

Joni JAMES *US, female vocalist*

Date		Title *Label Number*	Position	
6 Mar 53		**WHY DON'T YOU BELIEVE ME** *MGM 582*	**11**	1 wk
30 Jan 59		**THERE MUST BE A WAY** *MGM 1002*	**24**	1 wk

Rick JAMES *US, male vocalist*

Date		Title *Label Number*	Position	
8 Jul 78		**YOU AND I** *Motown TMG 1110*	**46**	7 wks
6 Sep 80		**BIG TIME** *Motown TMG 1198*	**41**	6 wks
4 Jul 81		**GIVE IT TO ME BABY** *Motown TMG 1229*	**47**	3 wks
3 Jul 82		**DANCE WIT' ME** *Motown TMG 1266*	**53**	3 wks

See also Teena Marie.

Sonny JAMES *US, male vocalist*

Date		Title *Label Number*	Position	
30 Nov 56		**THE CAT CAME BACK** *Capitol CL 14635*	**30**	1 wk
8 Feb 57		**YOUNG LOVE** *Capitol CL 14683*	**11**	7 wks

Tommy JAMES and the SHONDELLS

US, male vocal/instrumental group

Date		Title *Label Number*	Position	
21 Jul 66		**HANKY PANKY** *Roulette RK 7000*	**38**	7 wks
5 Jun 68	★	**MONY MONY** *Major Minor MM 567*	**1**	18 wks

JAMES BOYS *UK, male vocal duo*

Date		Title *Label Number*	Position	
19 May 73		**OVER AND OVER** *Penny Farthing PEN 806*	**39**	6 wks

JAN and DEAN *US, male vocal duo*

Date		Title *Label Number*	Position	
24 Aug 61		**HEART AND SOUL** *London HLH 9395*	**24**	8 wks
15 Aug 63		**SURF CITY** *Liberty LIB 55580*	**26**	10 wks

JAN and KJELD *Denmark, male vocal duo*

Date		Title *Label Number*	Position	
21 Jul 60		**BANJO BOY** *Ember S 101*	**36**	4 wks

Horst JANKOWSKI

Germany, male instrumentalist, piano

Date		Title *Label Number*	Position	
29 Jul 65	●	**A WALK IN THE BLACK FOREST** *Mercury MF 861*	**3**	18 wks

Philip JAP *UK, male vocalist*

Date		Title *Label Number*	Position	
31 Jul 82		**SAVE US** *A & M AMS 8217*	**53**	4 wks
25 Sep 82		**TOTAL ERASURE** *A & M JAP 1*	**41**	4 wks

JAPAN *UK, male vocal/instrumental group*

Date		Title *Label Number*	Position	
18 Oct 80		**GENTLEMEN TAKE POLAROIDS** *Virgin VS 379*	**60**	2 wks
9 May 81		**THE ART OF PARTIES** *Virgin VS 409*	**48**	5 wks
19 Sep 81		**QUIET LIFE** *Hansa HANSA 6*	**19**	9 wks
7 Nov 81		**VISIONS OF CHINA** *Virgin VS 436*	**32**	12 wks
23 Jan 82		**EUROPEAN SON** *Hansa/Ariola HANSA 10*	**31**	6 wks
20 Mar 82	●	**GHOSTS** *Virgin VS 472*	**5**	8 wks
22 May 82		**CANTONESE BOY** *Virgin VS 502*	**24**	6 wks
3 Jul 82	●	**I SECOND THAT EMOTION** *Hansa HANSA 12*	**9**	11 wks
9 Oct 82		**LIFE IN TOKYO** *Hansa HANSA 17*	**28**	6 wks
20 Nov 82		**NIGHT PORTER** *Virgin VS 554*	**29**†	6 wks

Jean-Michel JARRE

France, male instrumentalist/producer

Date		Title *Label Number*	Position	
27 Aug 77	●	**OXYGENE PART IV** *Polydor 2001 721*	**4**	9 wks
20 Jan 79		**EQUINOXE PART 5** *Polydor POSP 20*	**45**	5 wks

Al JARREAU *US, male vocalist*

Date		Title *Label Number*	Position	
26 Sep 81		**WE'RE IN THIS LOVE TOGETHER** *Warner Bros. K 17849*	**55**	4 wks

Date	Title *Label Number*	Position	

JAVELLS featuring Nosmo KING

UK, male/female vocal group

9 Nov 74	**GOODBYE NOTHING TO SAY** *Pye Disco Demand DDS 2003*	**26**	8 wks

Peter JAY and the JAYWALKERS

UK, male instrumental group, Peter Jay, drums

8 Nov 62	**CAN CAN 62** *Decca F 11531*	**31**	11 wks

JAYWALKERS — See *Peter JAY and the JAYWALKERS*

JEFFERSON *UK, male vocalist*

9 Apr 69	**COLOUR OF MY LOVE** *Pye 7N 17706*	**22**	8 wks

JEFFERSON STARSHIP

US, male vocal/instrumental group

26 Jan 80	**JANE** *Grunt FB 1750*	**21**	9 wks

JETHRO TULL *UK, male vocal/instrumental group*

1 Jan 69	**LOVE STORY** *Island WIP 6048*	**29**	8 wks
14 May 69	● **LIVING IN THE PAST** *Island WIP 6056*	**3**	14 wks
1 Nov 69	● **SWEET DREAM** *Chrysalis WIP 6070*	**7**	11 wks
24 Jan 70	● **THE WITCH'S PROMISE/ TEACHER** *Chrysalis WIP 6077*	**4**	9 wks
18 Sep 71	**LIFE IS A LONG SONG/UP THE POOL** *Chrysalis WIP 6106*	**11**	8 wks
11 Dec 76	**RING OUT SOLSTICE BELLS** (EP) *Chrysalis CXP 2*	**28**	6 wks

Tracks on EP: Ring Out Solstice Bells/ March the Mad Scientist/ The Christmas Song/ Pan Dance.

JETS *UK, male vocal/instrumental group*

22 Aug 81	**SUGAR DOLL** *EMI 5211*	**55**	3 wks
31 Oct 81	**YES TONIGHT JOSEPHINE** *EMI 5247*	**25**	11 wks
6 Feb 82	**LOVE MAKES THE WORLD GO ROUND** *EMI 5262*	**21**	9 wks
24 Apr 82	**THE HONEYDRIPPER** *EMI 5289*	**58**	3 wks
9 Oct 82	**SOMEBODY TO LOVE** *EMI 5342*	**56**	3 wks

Joan JETT and the BLACKHEARTS

US, female vocalist with male vocal/instrumental group

24 Apr 82	● **I LOVE ROCK 'N' ROLL** *Epic EPC A 2087*	**4**	10 wks
10 Jul 82	**CRIMSON AND CLOVER** *Epic EPC A 2485*	**60**	3 wks

JIGSAW *UK, male vocal/instrumental group*

1 Nov 75	● **SKY HIGH** *Splash CPI 1*	**9**	11 wks
6 Aug 77	**IF I HAVE TO GO AWAY** *Splash CP 11*	**36**	5 wks

JILTED JOHN *UK, male vocalist*

12 Aug 78	● **JILTED JOHN** *EMI International INT 567*	**4**	12 wks

JKD BAND *UK, male vocal/instrumental group*

1 Jul 78	**DRAGON POWER** *Satril SAT 132*	**58**	4 wks

JO JO GUNNE *US, male vocal/instrumental group*

25 Mar 72	● **RUN RUN RUN** *Asylum AYM 501*	**6**	12 wks

John Paul JOANS *UK, male vocalist*

19 Dec 70	**MAN FROM NAZARETH** *RAK 107*	**41**	3 wks
16 Jan 71	**MAN FROM NAZARETH** (re-entry) *RAK 107*	**25**	4 wks

JOCKO *US, male vocalist*

23 Feb 80	**RHYTHM TALK** *Philadelphia International PIR 8222*	**56**	3 wks

Billy JOEL *US, male vocalist*

11 Feb 78	**JUST THE WAY YOU ARE** *CBS 5872*	**19**	9 wks
24 Jun 78	**MOVIN' OUT (ANTHONY'S SONG)** *CBS 6412*	**35**	6 wks
2 Dec 78	**MY LIFE** *CBS 6821*	**12**	15 wks
28 Apr 79	**UNTIL THE NIGHT** *CBS 7242*	**50**	3 wks
12 Apr 80	**ALL FOR LEYNA** *CBS 8325*	**40**	4 wks
9 Aug 80	**IT'S STILL ROCK AND ROLL TO ME** *CBS 8753*	**14**	11 wks

Elton JOHN

UK, male vocalist/instrumentalist - piano

23 Jan 71	● **YOUR SONG** *DJM DJS 233*	**7**	12 wks
22 Apr 72	● **ROCKET MAN** *DJM DJX 501*	**2**	13 wks
9 Sep 72	**HONKY CAT** *DJM DJS 269*	**31**	6 wks
4 Nov 72	● **CROCODILE ROCK** *DJM DJS 271*	**5**	14 wks
20 Jan 73	● **DANIEL** *DJM DJS 275*	**4**	10 wks
7 Jul 73	● **SATURDAY NIGHT'S ALRIGHT FOR FIGHTING** *DJM DJX 502*	**7**	9 wks
29 Sep 73	● **GOODBYE YELLOW BRICK ROAD** *DJM DJS 285*	**6**	16 wks
8 Dec 73	**STEP INTO CHRISTMAS** *DJM DJS 290*	**24**	7 wks
2 Mar 74	**CANDLE IN THE WIND** *DJM DJS 297*	**11**	9 wks
1 Jun 74	**DON'T LET THE SUN GO DOWN ON ME** *DJM DJS 302*	**16**	8 wks
14 Sep 74	**THE BITCH IS BACK** *DJM DJS 322*	**15**	7 wks
23 Nov 74	● **LUCY IN THE SKY WITH DIAMONDS** *DJM DJS 340*	**10**	10 wks
8 Mar 75	**PHILADELPHIA FREEDOM** *DJM DJS 354*	**12**	9 wks
28 Jun 75	**SOMEONE SAVED MY LIFE TONIGHT** *DJM DJS 385*	**22**	5 wks
4 Oct 75	**ISLAND GIRL** *DJM DJS 610*	**14**	8 wks
20 Mar 76	● **PINBALL WIZARD** *DJM DJS 652*	**7**	7 wks
25 Sep 76	**BENNIE AND THE JETS** *DJM DJS 10705*	**37**	5 wks
13 Nov 76	**SORRY SEEMS TO BE THE HARDEST WORD** *Rocket ROKN 517*	**11**	10 wks
26 Feb 77	**CRAZY WATER** *Rocket ROKN 521*	**27**	6 wks
11 Jun 77	**BITE YOUR LIP (GET UP AND DANCE)** *Rocket ROKN 526*	**28**	4 wks
15 Apr 78	**EGO** *Rocket ROKN 539*	**34**	6 wks
21 Oct 78	**PART TIME LOVE** *Rocket XPRES 1*	**15**	13 wks
16 Dec 78	● **SONG FOR GUY** *Rocket XPRES 5*	**4**	10 wks
12 May 79	**ARE YOU READY FOR LOVE** *Rocket XPRES 13*	**42**	6 wks
24 May 80	**LITTLE JEANNIE** *Rocket XPRES 32*	**33**	7 wks
23 Aug 80	**SARTORIAL ELOQUENCE** *Rocket XPRES 41*	**44**	5 wks

Date	Title *Label Number*	Position	
23 May 81	**NOBODY WINS** *Rocket XPRES 54*	**42**	5 wks
27 Mar 82	● **BLUE EYES** *Rocket XPRES 71*	**8**	10 wks
12 Jun 82	**EMPTY GARDEN** *Rocket/Phonogram XPRES 77*	**51**	4 wks

See also Elton John and Kiki Dee. Philadelphia Freedom *credits The Elton John Band.* Bite Your Lip (Get Up and Dance) *was one side of a double-sided chart entry, the other being* Chicago *by Kiki Dee. See also Kiki Dee, Elton John Band featuring John Lennon and the Muscle Shoals Horns.*

Elton JOHN and Kiki DEE *UK, male/female vocal duo*

Date	Title *Label Number*	Position	
3 Jul 76	★ **DON'T GO BREAKING MY HEART** *Rocket ROKN 512*	**1**	14 wks

See also Elton John, Kiki Dee.

Robert JOHN *US, male vocalist*

Date	Title *Label Number*	Position	
17 Jul 68	**IF YOU DON'T WANT MY LOVE** *CBS 3436*	**42**	5 wks

Robert JOHN *US, male vocalist*

Date	Title *Label Number*	Position	
20 Oct 79	**SAD EYES** *EMI American EA 101*	**31**	8 wks

Elton JOHN BAND featuring John LENNON and the MUSCLE SHOALS HORNS *UK, male vocalists/instrumentalists with US, male instrumental group*

Date	Title *Label Number*	Position	
21 Mar 81	**I SAW HER STANDING THERE** *DJM DJS 10965*	**40**	4 wks

See also Elton John, Elton John and Kiki Dee, John Lennon

JOHNNY — See *SANTO and JOHNNY*

JOHNNY and CHARLEY *Spain, male vocal duo*

Date	Title *Label Number*	Position	
14 Oct 65	**LA YENKA** *Pye International 7N 25326*	**49**	1 wk

JOHNNY and the HURRICANES *US, male instrumental group*

Date	Title *Label Number*	Position	
9 Oct 59	● **RED RIVER ROCK** *London HL 8948*	**3**	16 wks
25 Dec 59	**REVEILLE ROCK** *London HL 9017*	**14**	5 wks
17 Mar 60	● **BEATNIK FLY** *London HLI 9072*	**8**	19 wks
16 Jun 60	● **DOWN YONDER** *London HLX 9134*	**8**	11 wks
29 Sep 60	● **ROCKING GOOSE** *London HLX 9190*	**3**	20 wks
2 Mar 61	**JA-DA** *London HLX 9289*	**14**	9 wks
6 Jul 61	**OLD SMOKEY/ HIGH VOLTAGE** *London HLX 9378*	**24**	8 wks

Bryan JOHNSON *UK, male vocalist*

Date	Title *Label Number*	Position	
10 Mar 60	**LOOKING HIGH HIGH HIGH** *Decca F 11213*	**20**	11 wks

Howard JOHNSON *US, male vocalist*

Date	Title *Label Number*	Position	
4 Sep 82	**KEEPIN' LOVE NEW/SO FINE** *A & M USA 1221*	**45**	6 wks

Keepin' Love New listed 4 Sep only.

Johnny JOHNSON and the BANDWAGON *US, male vocal group*

Date	Title *Label Number*	Position	
16 Oct 68	● **BREAKIN' DOWN THE WALLS OF HEARTACHE** *Direction 58-3670*	**4**	15 wks
5 Feb 69	**YOU** *Direction 58-3923*	**34**	4 wks
28 May 69	**LET'S HANG ON** *Direction 58-4180*	**36**	6 wks
25 Jul 70	● **SWEET INSPIRATION** *Bell 1111*	**10**	12 wks
24 Oct 70	**SWEET INSPIRATION** (re-entry) *Bell 1111*	**46**	1 wk
28 Nov 70	● **BLAME IT ON THE PONY EXPRESS** *Bell 1128*	**7**	12 wks

Listed as Bandwagon on Direction hits.

Kevin JOHNSON *Australia, male vocalist*

Date	Title *Label Number*	Position	
11 Jan 75	**ROCK 'N ROLL (I GAVE YOU THE BEST YEARS OF MY LIFE)** *UK UKR 84*	**23**	6 wks

L. J. JOHNSON *US, male vocalist*

Date	Title *Label Number*	Position	
7 Feb 76	**YOUR MAGIC PUT A SPELL ON ME** *Philips 6006 492*	**27**	6 wks

Laurie JOHNSON *UK, orchestra*

Date	Title *Label Number*	Position	
28 Sep 61	● **SUCU SUCU** *Pye 7N 15383*	**9**	12 wks

Lou JOHNSON *US, male vocalist*

Date	Title *Label Number*	Position	
26 Nov 64	**MESSAGE TO MARTHA** *London HL 9929*	**36**	2 wks

Marv JOHNSON *US, male vocalist*

Date	Title *Label Number*	Position	
12 Feb 60	● **YOU GOT WHAT IT TAKES** *London HLT 9013*	**5**	16 wks
5 May 60	**I LOVE THE WAY YOU LOVE** *London HLT 9109*	**35**	3 wks
11 Aug 60	**AIN'T GONNA BE THAT WAY** *London HLT 9156*	**50**	1 wk
22 Jan 69	● **I'LL PICK A ROSE FOR MY ROSE** *Tamla Motown TMG 680*	**10**	11 wks
25 Oct 69	**I MISS YOU BABY** *Tamla Motown TMG 713*	**25**	8 wks

Teddy JOHNSON — See *Pearl CARR and Teddy JOHNSON*

Bruce JOHNSTON *US, male instrumentalist/producer*

Date	Title *Label Number*	Position	
27 Aug 77	**PIPELINE** *CBS 5514*	**33**	4 wks

JOHNSTON BROTHERS *UK, male vocal group*

Date	Title *Label Number*	Position	
3 Apr 53	● **OH HAPPY DAY** *Decca F 10071*	**4**	8 wks
7 Oct 55	★ **HERNANDO'S HIDEAWAY** *Decca F 10608*	**1**	13 wks
30 Dec 55	● **JOIN IN AND SING AGAIN** *Decca F 10636*	**9**	1 wk
13 Apr 56	**NO OTHER LOVE** *Decca F 10721*	**22**	1 wk
30 Nov 56	**IN THE MIDDLE OF THE HOUSE** *Decca F 10781*	**27**	1 wk

Date	Title *Label Number*	Position	
7 Dec 56	**JOIN IN AND SING (NO. 3)** *Decca F 10814*	**30**	1 wk
28 Dec 56	**JOIN IN AND SING (NO. 3)** (re-entry) *Decca F 10814*	**24**	1 wk
8 Feb 57	**GIVE HER MY LOVE** *Decca F 10828*	**27**	1 wk
19 Apr 57	**HEART** *Decca F 10860*	**23**	3 wks

The following two hits were medleys - Join In And Sing Again: Sheik of Araby/ Yes Sir That's My Baby/ California Here I Come/ Some Of These Days/ Charleston/ Margie. Join In And Sing (No. 3): Coal Black Morning/ When You're Smiling/ Alexander's Ragtime Band/ Sweet Sue Just You/ When You Wore A Tulip/ If You Were The Only Girl In The World. See also Joan Regan & the Johnston Brothers, Various Artists - All Star Hit Parade No. 2.

JOLLY BROTHERS

Jamaica, male vocal/instrumental group

28 Jul 79	**CONSCIOUS MAN** *United Artists UP 36415*	**46**	7 wks

JON and VANGELIS

UK, male vocalist/Greece, male multi-instrumentalist

5 Jan 80	● **I HEAR YOU NOW** *Polydor POSP 96*	**8**	11 wks
12 Dec 81	● **I'LL FIND MY WAY HOME** *Polydor JV 1*	**6**	13 wks

See also Vangelis

JONATHAN — See *DAVID and JONATHAN*

Barbara JONES *Jamaica, female vocalist*

31 Jan 81	**JUST WHEN I NEEDED YOU MOST** *Sonet SON 2221*	**31**	7 wks

Grace JONES *US, female vocalist*

26 Jul 80	**PRIVATE LIFE** *Island WIP 6629*	**17**	8 wks
20 Jun 81	**PULL UP TO THE BUMPER** *Island WIP 6696*	**53**	4 wks
30 Oct 82	**THE APPLE STRETCHING/NIPPLE TO THE BOTTLE** *Island WIP 6779*	**50**	4 wks

Janie JONES *UK, female vocalist*

27 Jan 66	**WITCHES' BREW** *HMV POP 1495*	**46**	3 wks

Jimmy JONES *US, male vocalist*

17 Mar 60	● **HANDY MAN** *MGM 1051*	**3**	21 wks
16 Jun 60	★ **GOOD TIMIN'** *MGM 1078*	**1**	15 wks
18 Aug 60	**HANDY MAN** (re-entry) *MGM 1051*	**32**	3 wks
8 Sep 60	**I JUST GO FOR YOU** *MGM 1091*	**35**	4 wks
17 Nov 60	**READY FOR LOVE** *MGM 1103*	**46**	1 wk
30 Mar 61	**I TOLD YOU SO** *MGM 1123*	**33**	3 wks

Juggy JONES *US, male multi-instrumentalist*

7 Feb 76	**INSIDE AMERICA** *Contempo CS 2080*	**39**	4 wks

Paul JONES *UK, male vocalist*

6 Oct 66	● **HIGH TIME** *HMV POP 1554*	**4**	15 wks
19 Jan 67	● **I'VE BEEN A BAD BAD BOY** *HMV POP 1576*	**5**	9 wks
23 Aug 67	**THINKIN' AIN'T FOR ME** *HMV POP 1602*	**47**	1 wk
13 Sep 67	**THINKIN' AIN'T FOR ME** (re-entry) *HMV POP 1602*	**32**	7 wks
5 Feb 69	**AQUARIUS** *Columbia DB 8514*	**45**	2 wks

See also Manfred Mann.

Quincy JONES

US, male arranger/instrumentalist, keyboards

29 Jul 78	**STUFF LIKE THAT** *A & M AMS 7367*	**34**	9 wks
11 Apr 81	**AI NO CORRIDA (I-NO-KO-REE-DA)** *A & M AMS 8109*	**14**	10 wks
20 Jun 81	**RAZZAMATAZZ** *A & M AMS 8140*	**11**	9 wks
5 Sep 81	**BETCHA' WOULDN'T HURT ME** *A & M AMS 8157*	**52**	3 wks

Uncredited lead Singer on Razzamatazz *is Patti Austin.*

Rickie Lee JONES *US, female vocalist*

23 Jun 79	**CHUCK E.'S IN LOVE** *Warner Bros. K 17390*	**18**	9 wks

Shirley JONES — See *(a) PARTRIDGE FAMILY starring Shirley JONES featuring David CASSIDY (b) VARIOUS ARTISTS (Carousel Soundtrack)*

Tammy JONES *UK, female vocalist*

26 Apr 75	● **LET ME TRY AGAIN** *Epic EPC 3211*	**5**	10 wks

Tom JONES *UK, male vocalist*

11 Feb 65	★ **IT'S NOT UNUSUAL** *Decca F 12062*	**1**	14 wks
6 May 65	**ONCE UPON A TIME** *Decca F 12121*	**32**	4 wks
8 Jul 65	**WITH THESE HANDS** *Decca F 12191*	**13**	11 wks
12 Aug 65	**WHAT'S NEW PUSSYCAT** *Decca F 12203*	**11**	10 wks
13 Jan 66	**THUNDERBALL** *Decca F 12292*	**35**	4 wks
19 May 66	**ONCE THERE WAS A TIME/ NOT RESPONSIBLE** *Decca F 12390*	**18**	9 wks
18 Aug 66	**THIS AND THAT** *Decca F 12461*	**44**	3 wks
10 Nov 66	★ **GREEN GREEN GRASS OF HOME** *Decca F 22511*	**1**	22 wks
16 Feb 67	● **DETROIT CITY** *Decca F 22555*	**8**	10 wks
13 Apr 67	● **FUNNY FAMILIAR FORGOTTEN FEELINGS** *Decca F 12599*	**7**	15 wks
26 Jul 67	● **I'LL NEVER FALL IN LOVE AGAIN** *Decca F 12639*	**2**	25 wks
22 Nov 67	● **I'M COMING HOME** *Decca F 12693*	**2**	16 wks
28 Feb 68	● **DELILAH** *Decca F 12747*	**2**	17 wks
17 Jul 68	● **HELP YOURSELF** *Decca F 12812*	**5**	26 wks
27 Nov 68	**A MINUTE OF YOUR TIME** *Decca F 12854*	**14**	15 wks
14 May 69	● **LOVE ME TONIGHT** *Decca F 12924*	**9**	12 wks
13 Dec 69	● **WITHOUT LOVE** *Decca F 12990*	**10**	11 wks
14 Mar 70	**WITHOUT LOVE** (re-entry) *Decca F 12990*	**49**	1 wk
18 Apr 70	● **DAUGHTER OF DARKNESS** *Decca F 13013*	**5**	15 wks
15 Aug 70	**I (WHO HAVE NOTHING)** *Decca F 13061*	**16**	8 wks
17 Oct 70	**I (WHO HAVE NOTHING)** (re-entry) *Decca F 13061*	**47**	3 wks
16 Jan 71	**SHE'S A LADY** *Decca F 13113*	**13**	9 wks
27 Mar 71	**SHE'S A LADY** (re-entry) *Decca F 13113*	**47**	1 wk
5 Jun 71	**PUPPET MAN** *Decca F 13183*	**49**	1 wk
19 Jun 71	**PUPPET MAN** (re-entry) *Decca F 13183*	**50**	1 wk
23 Oct 71	● **TILL** *Decca F 13236*	**2**	15 wks
1 Apr 72	● **THE YOUNG NEW MEXICAN PUPPETEER** *Decca F 13298*	**6**	12 wks
14 Apr 73	**LETTER TO LUCILLE** *Decca F 13393*	**31**	8 wks
7 Sep 74	**SOMETHING 'BOUT YOU BABY I LIKE** *Decca F 13550*	**36**	5 wks
16 Apr 77	**SAY YOU'LL STAY UNTIL TOMORROW** *EMI 2583*	**40**	3 wks

Sue JONES-DAVIES — See *Julie COVINGTON, Rula LENSKA Charlotte CORNWELL and Sue JONES-DAVIES*

Date	Title *Label Number*	Position		Date	Title *Label Number*	Position	

Dick JORDAN *UK, male vocalist*

17 Mar 60	**HALLELUJAH I LOVE HER SO** *Oriole CB 1534*	**47**	1 wk
9 Jun 60	**LITTLE CHRISTINE** *Oriole CB 1548*	**39**	3 wks

JOURNEY *US, male vocal/instrumental group*

27 Feb 82	**DON'T STOP BELIEVIN'** *CBS A 1728*	**62**	4 wks
11 Sep 82	**WHO'S CRYING NOW** *CBS A 2725*	**46**	5 wks

JOY DIVISION *UK, male vocal/instrumental group*

28 Jun 80	**LOVE WILL TEAR US APART** *Factory FAC 23*	**13**	9 wks

JOY STRINGS

UK, male/female vocal/instrumental group

27 Feb 64	**IT'S AN OPEN SECRET** *Regal-Zonophone RZ 501*	**32**	7 wks
17 Dec 64	**A STARRY NIGHT** *Regal-Zonophone RZ 504*	**35**	4 wks

JUDAS PRIEST

UK, male vocal/instrumental group

20 Jan 79	**TAKE ON THE WORLD** *CBS 6915*	**14**	10 wks
12 May 79	**EVENING STAR** *CBS 7312*	**53**	4 wks
29 Mar 80	**LIVING AFTER MIDNIGHT** *CBS 8379*	**12**	7 wks
7 Jun 80	**BREAKING THE LAW** *CBS 8644*	**12**	6 wks
23 Aug 80	**UNITED** *CBS 8897*	**26**	8 wks
21 Feb 81	**DON'T GO** *CBS 9520*	**51**	3 wks
25 Apr 81	**HOT ROCKIN'** *CBS 1153*	**60**	3 wks
21 Aug 82	**YOU'VE GOT ANOTHER THING COMIN'** *CBS A 2611*	**66**	2 wks

JUDGE DREAD *UK, male vocalist*

26 Aug 72	**BIG SIX** *Big Shot BI 608*	**11**	27 wks
9 Dec 72	● **BIG SEVEN** *Big Shot BI 613*	**8**	18 wks
21 Apr 73	**BIG EIGHT** *Big Shot BI 619*	**14**	10 wks
5 Jul 75	● **JE T'AIME (MOI NON PLUS)** *Cactus CT 65*	**9**	9 wks
27 Sep 75	**BIG TEN** *Cactus CT 77*	**14**	7 wks
6 Dec 75	**CHRISTMAS IN DREADLAND/ COME OUTSIDE** *Cactus CT 80*	**14**	7 wks
8 May 76	**THE WINKLE MAN** *Cactus CT 90*	**35**	4 wks
28 Aug 76	**Y VIVA SUSPENDERS** *Cactus CT 99*	**27**	4 wks
2 Apr 77	**5TH ANNIVERSARY** (EP) *Cactus Ct 98*	**31**	4 wks
14 Jan 78	**UP WITH THE COCK/BIG PUNK** *Cactus CT 110*	**49**	1 wk
16 Dec 78	**HOKEY COKEY/JINGLE BELLS** *EMI 2881*	**59**	4 wks

Tracks On 5th Anniversary EP: *Jamaica Jerk (off)/Bring Back The Skins/End Of The World/Big Everything.*

JUICY LUCY *UK, male vocal/instrumental group*

7 Mar 70	**WHO DO YOU LOVE** *Vertigo V 1*	**14**	12 wks
10 Oct 70	**PRETTY WOMAN** *Vertigo 6059 015*	**45**	2 wks
31 Oct 70	**PRETTY WOMAN** (re-entry) *Vertigo 6059 015*	**44**	3 wks

JUMPING JACKS — See *Danny PEPPERMINT and the JUMPING JACKS*

Rosemary JUNE *US, female vocalist*

23 Jan 59	**APPLE BLOSSOM TIME** *Pye International 7N 25005*	**14**	9 wks

JUNIOR *UK, male vocalist*

24 Apr 82	● **MAMA USED TO SAY (AMERICAN REMIX)** *Mercury/Phonogram MER 98*	**7**	13 wks
10 Jul 82	**TOO LATE** *Mercury/Phonogram MER 112*	**20**	9 wks
25 Sep 82	**LET ME KNOW/I CANT HELP IT** *Mercury/Phonogram MER 116*	**53**	53 wks

JUNIORS — See *DANNY and the JUNIORS*

Jimmy JUSTICE *UK, male vocalist*

29 Mar 62	● **WHEN MY LITTLE GIRL IS SMILING** *Pye 7N 15421*	**9**	13 wks
14 Jun 62	● **AIN'T THAT FUNNY** *Pye 7N 15443*	**8**	10 wks
23 Aug 62	**SPANISH HARLEM** *Pye 7N 15457*	**20**	11 wks

Bill JUSTIS *US, male instrumentalist, alto sax*

10 Jan 58	**RAUNCHY** *London HLS 8517*	**24**	2 wks
31 Jan 58	**RAUNCHY** (re-entry) *London HLS 8517*	**11**	6 wks

Patrick JUVET *France, male vocalist*

2 Sep 78	**GOT A FEELING** *Casablanca CAN 127*	**34**	7 wks
4 Nov 78	**I LOVE AMERICA** *Casablanca CAN 132*	**12**	12 wks

K

Bert KAEMPFERT *Germany, orchestra*

23 Dec 65	**BYE BYE BLUES** *Polydor BM 56 504*	**24**	10 wks

KALIN TWINS *US, male vocal duo*

18 Jul 58	★ **WHEN** *Brunswick 05751*	**1**	18 wks

Kitty KALLEN *US, female vocalist*

2 Jul 54	★ **LITTLE THINGS MEAN A LOT** *Brunswick 05287*	**1**	23 wks

Gunther KALLMAN CHOIR

Germany, male/female vocal group

24 Dec 64	**ELISABETH SERENADE** *Polydor NH 24678*	**45**	3 wks

KANDIDATE *UK, male vocal/instrumental group*

19 Aug 78	**DON'T WANNA SAY GOODNIGHT** *RAK 280*	**47**	6 wks
17 Mar 79	**I DON'T WANNA LOSE YOU** *RAK 289*	**11**	12 wks
4 Aug 79	**GIRLS GIRLS GIRLS** *RAK 295*	**34**	7 wks
22 Mar 80	**LET ME ROCK YOU** *RAK 306*	**58**	3 wks

ELTON JOHN Right about the talent, wrong about the year

HEAR THE GREATEST PERFORMANCE ON A 'FIRST' DISC
ELTON JOHN
'I'VE BEEN LOVING YOU'
A "THIS" PRODUCTION
Produced by CALEB
Released on PHILIPS BF 1643
Published by DICK JAMES MUSIC
You have been warned! ELTON JOHN is 1968's great new talent

Left **JONATHAN KING** Singing – some would say good reason for everyone to go to the moon

Left **KRAFTWERK** in 1977 – (l-rt) Karl Bartos, Ralf Hutter, Florian Schneider and Wolfgang Flur *Below centre* **KINGSMEN** Without all the King's horses *Below* **KEITH KELLY** Rhythm guitarist and harmonica player with the John Barry Seven, he went solo in March 1959 and was discovered at London's famous 2I's coffee bar

KEITH In 1967 life for Keith was just a bowl of strawberries

Right **KANDIDATE** Four RAK hits from 1978–80

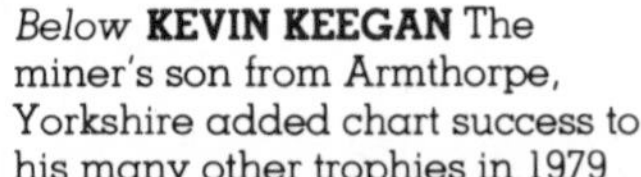

Below **KEVIN KEEGAN** The miner's son from Armthorpe, Yorkshire added chart success to his many other trophies in 1979

Date	Title *Label Number*	Position	

Date Title *Label Number* Position

Eden KANE *UK, male vocalist*

1 Jun 61	★ **WELL I ASK YOU** *Decca F 11353*	**1**	21 wks
14 Sep 61	● **GET LOST** *Decca F 11381*	**10**	11 wks
18 Jan 62	● **FORGET ME NOT** *Decca F 11418*	**3**	14 wks
10 May 62	● **I DON'T KNOW WHY** *Decca F 11460*	**7**	14 wks
30 Jan 64	● **BOYS CRY** *Fontana TF 438*	**8**	14 wks

KANSAS *US, male vocal/instrumental group*

1 Jul 78	**CARRY ON WAYWARD SON** *Kirshner KIR 4932*	**51**	7 wks

KASENETZ-KATZ SINGING ORCHESTRAL CIRCUS

US, male vocal/instrumental group

20 Nov 68	**QUICK JOEY SMALL (RUN JOEY RUN)** *Buddah 201 022*	**19**	15 wks

Janet KAY *UK, female vocalist*

9 Jun 79	● **SILLY GAMES** *Scope SC 2*	**2**	14 wks

Danny KAYE *US, male vocalist*

27 Feb 53	● **WONDERFUL COPENHAGEN** *Brunswick 05023*	**5**	10 wks

KAYE SISTERS *UK, female vocal group*

3 Jan 58	**SHAKE ME I RATTLE/ ALONE** *Philips PB 752*	**27**	1 wk
7 Jul 60	● **PAPER ROSES** *Philips PB 1024*	**7**	19 wks

See also Frankie Vaughan & The Kaye Sisters, Three Kayes.

KC and THE SUNSHINE BAND

US, male vocal/instrumental group

17 Aug 74	● **QUEEN OF CLUBS** *Jayboy BOY 88*	**7**	12 wks
23 Nov 74	**SOUND YOUR FUNKY HORN** *Jayboy BOY 83*	**17**	9 wks
29 Mar 75	**GET DOWN TONIGHT** *Jayboy BOY 93*	**21**	9 wks
2 Aug 75	● **THAT'S THE WAY (I LIKE IT)** *Jayboy BOY 99*	**4**	10 wks
22 Nov 75	**I'M SO CRAZY** *Jayboy BOY 101*	**34**	3 wks
17 Jul 76	**(SHAKE SHAKE SHAKE) SHAKE YOUR BOOTY** *Jayboy BOY 110*	**22**	8 wks
11 Dec 76	**KEEP IT COMIN' LOVE** *Jayboy BOY 112*	**31**	8 wks
30 Apr 77	**I'M YOUR BOOGIE MAN** *TK XB 2167*	**41**	4 wks
6 May 78	**BOOGIE SHOES** *TK TKR 6025*	**34**	5 wks
22 Jul 78	**IT'S THE SAME OLD SONG** *TK TKR 6037*	**49**	5 wks
8 Dec 79	● **PLEASE DON'T GO** *TK TKR 7558*	**3**	12 wks

Ernie K-DOE *US, male vocalist*

11 May 61	**MOTHER-IN-LAW** *London HLU 9330*	**29**	7 wks

Johnny KEATING *UK, orchestra*

1 Mar 62	● **THEME FROM Z CARS** *Piccadilly 7N 35032*	**8**	14 wks

Kevin KEEGAN *UK, male vocalist*

9 Jun 79	**HEAD OVER HEELS IN LOVE** *EMI 2965*	**31**	6 wks

Yvonne KEELY — See *Scott FITZGERALD and Yvonne KEELY*

Nelson KEENE *UK, male vocalist*

25 Aug 60	**IMAGE OF A GIRL** *HMV POP 771*	**37**	4 wks
29 Sep 60	**IMAGE OF A GIRL** (re-entry) *HMV POP 771*	**45**	1 wk

KEITH *US, male vocalist*

26 Jan 67	**98.6.** *Mercury MF 955*	**24**	7 wks
16 Mar 67	**TELL ME TO MY FACE** *Mercury MF 968*	**50**	1 wk

Jerry KELLER *US, male vocalist*

28 Aug 59	★ **HERE COMES SUMMER** *London HLR 8890*	**1**	14 wks

Grace KELLY — See *Bing CROSBY and Grace KELLY*

Keith KELLY *UK, male vocalist*

5 May 60	**TEASE ME** *Parlophone R 4640*	**46**	1 wk
19 May 60	**TEASE ME** (re-entry) *Parlophone R 4640*	**27**	3 wks
18 Aug 60	**LISTEN LITTLE GIRL** *Parlophone R 4676*	**47**	1 wk

Roberta KELLY *US, female vocalist*

21 Jan 78	**ZODIACS** *Oasis/Hansa 3*	**48**	1 wk
4 Feb 78	**ZODIACS** (re-entry) *Oasis/Hansa 3*	**44**	2 wks

Eddie KENDRICKS *US, male vocalist*

3 Nov 73	**KEEP ON TRUCKIN'** *Tamla Motown TMG 873*	**18**	14 wks
16 Mar 74	**BOOGIE DOWN** *Tamla Motown TMG 888*	**39**	4 wks

Jane KENNAWAY and STRANGE BEHAVIOUR

UK, female vocalist, male instrumental group

24 Jan 81	**I.O.U.** *Deram DM 436*	**65**	3 wks

KENNY *Ireland, male vocalist*

3 Mar 73	**HEART OF STONE** *RAK 144*	**11**	13 wks
30 Jun 73	**GIVE IT TO ME NOW** *RAK 153*	**38**	3 wks

KENNY *UK, male vocal/instrumental group*

7 Dec 74	● **THE BUMP** *RAK 186*	**3**	15 wks
8 Mar 75	● **FANCY PANTS** *RAK 196*	**4**	9 wks
7 Jun 75	**BABY I LOVE YOU OK** *RAK 207*	**12**	7 wks
16 Aug 75	● **JULIE ANN** *RAK 214*	**10**	8 wks

Gerard KENNY *US, male vocalist/instrumentalist*

9 Dec 78	**NEW YORK, NEW YORK** *RCA PB 5117*	**43**	8 wks
21 Jun 80	**FANTASY** *RCA PB 5256*	**65**	1 wk
5 Jul 80	**FANTASY** (re-entry) *RCA PB 5256*	**34**	5 wks

Date	Title *Label Number*	Position	

Klark KENT *US, male vocalist/multi-instrumentalist*

26 Aug 78	**DON'T CARE** *A & M AMS 7376*	**48**	4 wks

Chaka KHAN *US, female vocalist*

2 Dec 78	**I'M EVERY WOMAN** *Warner Bros. K 17269*	**11**	13 wks

K.I.D. *Antilles, male/female vocal/instrumental group*

28 Feb 81	**DON'T STOP** *EMI 5143*	**49**	4 wks

Johnny KIDD and the PIRATES *UK, male vocal/instrumental group*

12 Jun 59	**PLEASE DON'T TOUCH** *HMV POP 615*	**26**	3 wks
17 Jul 59	**PLEASE DON'T TOUCH** (re-entry) *HMV POP 615*	**25**	2 wks
12 Feb 60	**YOU GOT WHAT IT TAKES** *HMV POP 698*	**25**	3 wks
16 Jun 60 ★	**SHAKIN' ALL OVER** *HMV POP 753*	**1**	19 wks
6 Oct 60	**RESTLESS** *HMV POP 790*	**22**	7 wks
13 Apr 61	**LINDA LU** *HMV POP 853*	**47**	1 wk
10 Jan 63	**SHOT OF RHYTHM & BLUES** *HMV POP 1088*	**48**	1 wk
25 Jul 63 ●	**I'LL NEVER GET OVER YOU** *HMV POP 1173*	**4**	15 wks
28 Nov 63	**HUNGRY FOR LOVE** *HMV POP 1228*	**20**	10 wks
30 Apr 64	**ALWAYS AND EVER** *HMV POP 1269*	**46**	1 wk

Please Don't Touch *without the Pirates.*

KIDS FROM 'FAME' *US, male/female vocal group*

14 Aug 82 ●	**HI-FIDELITY** *RCA 254*	**5**	10 wks
2 Oct 82 ●	**STARMAKER** *RCA 280*	**3**	10 wks
11 Dec 82	**MANNEQUIN** *RCA 299*	**50†**	3 wks

Hi-Fidelity is 'featuring Valerie Landsberg'. Mannequin is 'featuring Gene Anthony Ray'.

KILLING JOKE *UK, male vocal/instrumental group*

23 May 81	**FOLLOW THE LEADERS** *Malicious Damage/Polydor EGMDS 101*	**55**	5 wks
20 Mar 82	**EMPIRE SONG** *Malicious Damage/Polydor EGO 4*	**43**	4 wks
30 Oct 82	**BIRDS OF A FEATHER** *E.G./Polydor EGO 10*	**64**	2 wks

Andy KIM *Canada, male vocalist*

24 Aug 74 ●	**ROCK ME GENTLY** *Capitol CL 15787*	**2**	12 wks

Ben E. KING *US, male vocalist*

2 Feb 61	**FIRST TASTE OF LOVE** *London HLK 9258*	**27**	11 wks
22 Jun 61	**STAND BY ME** *London HLK 9358*	**50**	1 wk
6 Jul 61	**STAND BY ME** (re-entry) *London HLK 9358*	**27**	6 wks
5 Oct 61	**AMOR' AMOR** *London HLK 9416*	**38**	4 wks

Carole KING *US, female vocalist*

20 Sep 62 ●	**IT MIGHT AS WELL RAIN UNTIL SEPTEMBER** *London HLU 9591*	**3**	13 wks
7 Aug 71 ●	**IT'S TOO LATE** *A & M AMS 849*	**6**	12 wks
28 Oct 72	**IT MIGHT AS WELL RAIN UNTIL SEPTEMBER** (re-issue) *London HL 10391*	**43**	4 wks

Dave KING *Canada, male vocalist*

17 Feb 56 ●	**MEMORIES ARE MADE OF THIS** *Decca F 10684*	**5**	15 wks
13 Apr 56	**YOU CAN'T BE TRUE TO TWO** *Decca F 10720*	**11**	9 wks
21 Dec 56	**CHRISTMAS AND YOU** *Decca F 10791*	**23**	2 wks
24 Jan 58	**THE STORY OF MY LIFE** *Decca F 10973*	**20**	3 wks

See also Various Artists - All Star Hit Parade.

Evelyn KING *US, female vocalist*

13 May 78	**SHAME** *RCA PC 1122*	**39**	23 wks
3 Feb 79	**I DON'T KNOW IF IT'S RIGHT** *RCA PB 1386*	**67**	2 wks
27 Jun 81	**I'M IN LOVE** *RCA 95*	**27**	11 wks
26 Sep 81	**IF YOU WANT MY LOVIN'** *RCA 131*	**43**	6 wks
28 Aug 82 ●	**LOVE COME DOWN** *RCA 249*	**7**	13 wks
20 Nov 82	**BACK TO LOVE** *RCA 287*	**40**	4 wks

Act billed as Evelyn Champagne King for first two hits.

Jonathan KING *UK, male vocalist*

29 Jul 65 ●	**EVERYONE'S GONE TO THE MOON** *Decca F 12187*	**4**	11 wks
10 Jan 70	**LET IT ALL HANG OUT** *Decca F 12988*	**26**	7 wks
29 May 71	**LAZY BONES** *Decca F 13177*	**23**	8 wks
20 Nov 71	**HOOKED ON A FEELING** *Decca F 13241*	**23**	10 wks
5 Feb 72	**FLIRT** *Decca F 13276*	**22**	9 wks
6 Sep 75 ●	**UNA PALOMA BLANCA** *UK 105*	**5**	11 wks
7 Oct 78	**ONE FOR YOU ONE FOR ME** *GTO GT 237*	**29**	6 wks
16 Jun 79	**YOU'RE THE GREATEST LOVER** *UK International INT 586*	**67**	2 wks
3 Nov 79	**GLORIA** *Ariola ARO 198*	**65**	3 wks

See also Bubblerock, 53rd & 3rd, Sakkarin, Shag, 100 Ton & A Feather, Weathermen, Sound 9418, Father Abraphart and the Smurps.

Nosmo KING — See *JAVELLS with Nosmo KING*

Solomon KING *US, male vocalist*

3 Jan 68 ●	**SHE WEARS MY RING** *Columbia DB 8325*	**3**	18 wks
1 May 68	**WHEN WE WERE YOUNG** *Columbia DB 8402*	**21**	10 wks

KING BROTHERS *UK, male vocal/instrumental group*

31 May 57 ●	**A WHITE SPORT COAT** *Parlophone R 4310*	**6**	14 wks
9 Aug 57	**IN THE MIDDLE OF AN ISLAND** *Parlophone R 4338*	**19**	13 wks
6 Dec 57	**WAKE UP LITTLE SUSIE** *Parlophone R 4367*	**22**	3 wks
31 Jan 58	**PUT A LIGHT IN THE WINDOW** *Parlophone R 4389*	**29**	1 wk
14 Feb 58	**PUT A LIGHT IN THE WINDOW** (re-entry) *Parlophone R 4389*	**28**	1 wk
28 Feb 58	**PUT A LIGHT IN THE WINDOW** (2nd re-entry) *Parlophone R 4389*	**25**	2 wks
14 Apr 60 ●	**STANDING ON THE CORNER** *Parlophone R 4639*	**4**	11 wks
28 Jul 60	**MAIS OUI** *Parlophone R 4672*	**16**	10 wks
12 Jan 61	**DOLL HOUSE** *Parlophone R 4715*	**21**	8 wks
2 Mar 61	**76 TROMBONES** *Parlophone R 4737*	**19**	11 wks

KING TRIGGER *UK, male/female vocal/instrumental group*

14 Aug 82	**THE RIVER** *Chrysalis CHS 2623*	**57**	4 wks

Date	Title *Label Number*	Position	

KINGS OF SWING ORCHESTRA

Australia, orchestra

1 May 82 **SWITCHED ON SWING** *Philips (Phonogram) Swing 1* **48** 5 wks

KINGSMEN *US, male vocal/instrumental group*

30 Jan 64 **LOUIE LOUIE** *Pye International 7N 25231* **26** 7 wks

KINGSTON TRIO

US, male vocal/instrumental group

21 Nov 58 ● **TOM DOOLEY** *Capitol CL 14951* **5** 14 wks
4 Dec 59 **SAN MIGUEL** *Capitol CL 15073* **29** 1 wk

KINKS *UK, male vocal/instrumental group*

13 Aug 64 ★ **YOU REALLY GOT ME** *Pye 7N 15673* **1** 12 wks
29 Oct 64 ● **ALL DAY AND ALL OF THE NIGHT** *Pye 7N 15714* **2** 14 wks
21 Jan 65 ★ **TIRED OF WAITING FOR YOU** *Pye 7N 15759* **1** 10 wks
25 Mar 65 **EVERYBODY'S GONNA BE HAPPY** *Pye 7N 15813* **17** 8 wks
27 May 65 ● **SET ME FREE** *Pye 7N 15854* **9** 11 wks
5 Aug 65 ● **SEE MY FRIEND** *Pye 7N 15919* **10** 9 wks
2 Dec 65 ● **TILL THE END OF THE DAY** *Pye 7N 15981* **8** 12 wks
3 Mar 66 ● **DEDICATED FOLLOWER OF FASHION** *Pye 7N 17064* **4** 11 wks
9 Jun 66 ★ **SUNNY AFTERNOON** *Pye 7N 17125* **1** 13 wks
24 Nov 66 ● **DEAD END STREET** *Pye 7N 17222* **5** 11 wks
11 May 67 ● **WATERLOO SUNSET** *Pye 7N 17321* **2** 11 wks
18 Oct 67 ● **AUTUMN ALMANAC** *Pye 7N 17400* **3** 11 wks
17 Apr 68 **WONDERBOY** *Pye 7N 17468* **36** 5 wks
17 Jul 68 **DAYS** *Pye 7N 17573* **12** 10 wks
16 Apr 69 **PLASTIC MAN** *Pye 7N 17724* **31** 4 wks
10 Jan 70 **VICTORIA** *Pye 7N 17865* **33** 4 wks
4 Jul 70 ● **LOLA** *Pye 7N 17961* **2** 14 wks
12 Dec 70 ● **APEMAN** *Pye 7N 45016* **5** 14 wks
27 May 72 **SUPERSONIC ROCKET SHIP** *RCA 2211* **16** 8 wks
27 Jun 81 **BETTER THINGS** *Arista ARIST 415* **46** 5 wks

Fern KINNEY *US, female vocalist*

16 Feb 80 ★ **TOGETHER WE ARE BEAUTIFUL** *WEA K 79111* **1** 11 wks

KINSHASA BAND — See *Johnny WAKELIN*

Kathy KIRBY *UK, female vocalist*

15 Aug 63 **DANCE ON** *Decca F 11682* **11** 13 wks
7 Nov 63 ● **SECRET LOVE** *Decca F 11759* **4** 18 wks
20 Feb 64 ● **LET ME GO LOVER** *Decca F 11832* **10** 11 wks
7 May 64 **YOU'RE THE ONE** *Decca F 11892* **17** 9 wks
4 Mar 65 **I BELONG** *Decca F 12087* **36** 3 wks

Bo KIRKLAND and Ruth DAVIS

US, male/female vocal duo

4 Jun 77 **YOU'RE GONNA GET NEXT TO ME** *EMI International INT 532* **12** 9 wks

KISS *US, male vocal/instrumental group*

30 Jun 79 **I WAS MADE FOR LOVIN' YOU** *Casablanca CAN 152* **50** 7 wks
20 Feb 82 **A WORLD WITHOUT HEROES** *Casablanca/Phonogram KISS 002* **55** 3 wks

Mac and Katie KISSOON

UK, male/female vocal duo

19 Jun 71 **CHIRPY CHIRPY CHEEP CHEEP** *Young Blood YB 1026* **41** 1 wk
18 Jan 75 ● **SUGAR CANDY KISSES** *Polydor 2058 531* **3** 10 wks
3 May 75 ● **DON'T DO IT BABY** *State STAT 4* **9** 8 wks
30 Aug 75 **LIKE A BUTTERFLY** *State STAT 9* **18** 9 wks
15 May 76 **THE TWO OF US** *State STAT 21* **46** 5 wks

Eartha KITT *US, female vocalist*

1 Apr 55 ● **UNDER THE BRIDGES OF PARIS** *HMV B 10647* **7** 9 wks
10 Jun 55 **UNDER THE BRIDGES OF PARIS** (re-entry) *HMV B 10647* **20** 1 wk

KJELD — See *JAN and KJELD*

KLEEER *US, male/female vocal/instrumental group*

17 Mar 79 **KEEP YOUR BODY WORKING** *Atlantic LV 21* **51** 6 wks
14 Mar 81 **GET TOUGH** *Atlantic 11560* **49** 4 wks

KNACK *US, male vocal/instrumental group*

30 Jun 79 ● **MY SHARONA** *Capitol CL 16087* **6** 10 wks
13 Oct 79 **GOOD GIRLS DON'T** *Capitol CL 16097* **66** 2 wks

Frederick KNIGHT *US, male vocalist*

10 Jun 72 **I'VE BEEN LONELY SO LONG** *Stax 2025 098* **22** 10 wks

Gladys KNIGHT and the PIPS

US, female vocalist/male vocal backing group

8 Jun 67 **TAKE ME IN YOUR ARMS & LOVE ME** *Tamla Motown TMG 604* **13** 15 wks
27 Dec 67 **I HEARD IT THROUGH THE GRAPEVINE** *Tamla Motown TMG 629* **47** 1 wk
17 Jun 72 **JUST WALK IN MY SHOES** *Tamla Motown TMG 813* **35** 8 wks
25 Nov 72 **HELP ME MAKE IT THROUGH THE NIGHT** *Tamla Motown TMG 830* **11** 17 wks
3 Mar 73 **LOOK OF LOVE** *Tamla Motown TMG 844* **21** 9 wks
26 May 73 **NEITHER ONE OF US** *Tamla Motown TMG 855* **31** 7 wks
5 Apr 75 ● **THE WAY WE WERE/TRY TO REMEMBER** (MEDLEY) *Buddah BDS 428* **4** 15 wks
2 Aug 75 ● **BEST THING THAT EVER HAPPENED TO ME** *Buddah BDS 432* **7** 10 wks
15 Nov 75 **PART TIME LOVE** *Buddah BDS 438* **30** 5 wks
8 May 76 ● **MIDNIGHT TRAIN TO GEORGIA** *Buddah BDS 444* **10** 9 wks
21 Aug 76 **MAKE YOURS A HAPPY HOME** *Buddah BDS 447* **35** 4 wks
6 Nov 76 **SO SAD THE SONG** *Buddah BDS 448* **20** 9 wks
15 Jan 77 **NOBODY BUT YOU** *Buddah BDS 451* **34** 2 wks

Date	Title *Label Number*	Position	
28 May 77	● **BABY DON'T CHANGE YOUR MIND** *Buddah BDS 458*	**4**	12 wks
24 Sep 77	**HOME IS WHERE THE HEART IS** *Buddah BDS 460*	**35**	4 wks
8 Apr 78	**THE ONE AND ONLY** *Buddah BDS 470*	**32**	6 wks
24 Jun 78	**COME BACK AND FINISH WHAT YOU STARTED** *Buddah BDS 473*	**15**	13 wks
30 Sep 78	**IT'S A BETTER THAN GOOD TIME** *Buddah BDS 478*	**59**	4 wks
30 Aug 80	**TASTE OF BITTER LOVE** *CBS 8890*	**35**	6 wks
8 Nov 80	**BOURGIE BOURGIE** *CBS 9081*	**32**	6 wks

See also Johnny Mathis and Gladys Knight.

Robert KNIGHT *US, male vocalist*

Date	Title *Label Number*	Position	
24 Nov 73	● **LOVE ON A MOUNTAIN TOP** *Monument MNT 1875*	**10**	16 wks
9 Mar 74	**EVERLASTING LOVE** *Monument MNT 2106*	**19**	8 wks

Buddy KNOX *US, male vocalist*

Date	Title *Label Number*	Position	
10 May 57	**PARTY DOLL** *Columbia DB 3914*	**29**	3 wks
6 Aug 62	**SHE'S GONE** *Liberty LIB 55473*	**45**	2 wks

Moe KOFFMAN QUARTETTE

Canada, male instrumental group, Moe Koffman flute

Date	Title *Label Number*	Position	
28 Mar 58	**SWINGIN' SHEPHERD BLUES** *London HLJ 8549*	**23**	2 wks

KOKOMO *US, male instrumentalist, pianist*

Date	Title *Label Number*	Position	
13 Apr 61	**ASIA MINOR** *London HLU 9305*	**35**	7 wks

KOKOMO *UK, male/female vocal/instrumental group*

Date	Title *Label Number*	Position	
29 May 82	**A LITTLE BIT FURTHER AWAY** *CBS A 2064*	**45**	3 wks

John KONGOS

South Africa, male vocalist/multi-instrumentalist

Date	Title *Label Number*	Position	
22 May 71	● **HE'S GONNA STEP ON YOU AGAIN** *Fly BUG 8*	**4**	14 wks
20 Nov 71	● **TOKOLOSHE MAN** *Fly BUG 14*	**4**	11 wks

KOOL and the GANG

US, male vocal/instrumental group

Date	Title *Label Number*	Position	
27 Oct 79	● **LADIES NIGHT** *Mercury KOOL 7*	**9**	12 wks
19 Jan 80	**TOO HOT** *Mercury KOOL 8*	**23**	8 wks
12 Jul 80	**HANGIN' OUT** *De-Lite KOOL 9*	**52**	4 wks
1 Nov 80	● **CELEBRATION** *De-Lite KOOL 10*	**7**	13 wks
21 Feb 81	**JONES VS JONES/SUMMER MADNESS/FUNKY STUFF/HOLLYWOOD SWINGING** *De-Lite KOOL 112, KOOL 11, Gang 11*	**17**	11 wks
30 May 81	**TAKE IT TO THE TOP** *De-Lite DE 2*	**15**	9 wks
31 Oct 81	**STEPPIN' OUT** *De-Lite DE 4*	**12**	13 wks
19 Dec 81	● **GET DOWN ON IT** *De-Lite DE 5*	**3**	12 wks
6 Mar 82	**TAKE MY HEART (YOU CAN HAVE IT IF YOU WANT IT)** *De-Lite/Phonogram DE 6*	**29**	7 wks
7 Aug 82	**BIG FUN** *De-Lite/Phonogram DE 7*	**14**	8 wks
16 Oct 82	● **OOH LA LA LA (LET'S GO DANCIN')** *De-Lite/Phonogram DE 9*	**6**	9 wks
4 Dec 82	**HI DE HI, HI DE HO** *De-Lite/Phonogram DE 14*	**29**†	4 wks

Jones vs Jones/Summer Madness *was issued in three versions, a 7-inch single, a 12-inch single and an EP sales of which were combined for chart purposes. The 7-inch single De-Lite KOOL 11, does not contain* Funky Stuff *or* Hollywood Swinging.

KORGIS *UK, male vocal/instrumental duo*

Date	Title *Label Number*	Position	
23 Jun 79	**IF I HAD YOU** *Rialto TREB 103*	**13**	12 wks
24 May 80	● **EVERYBODY'S GOT TO LEARN SOMETIME** *Rialto TREB 115*	**5**	12 wks
30 Aug 80	**IF IT'S ALRIGHT WITH YOU BABY** *Rialto TREB 118*	**56**	3 wks

KRAFTWERK

Germany, male instrumental/vocal group

Date	Title *Label Number*	Position	
10 May 75	**AUTOBAHN** *Vertigo 6147 012*	**11**	9 wks
28 Oct 78	**NEON LIGHTS** *Capitol CL 15998*	**53**	3 wks
9 May 81	**POCKET CALCULATOR** *EMI 5175*	**39**	6 wks
11 Jul 81	**COMPUTER LOVE/THE MODEL** *EMI 5207*	**36**	8 wks
25 Dec 81	★ **COMPUTER LOVE/THE MODEL** (re-entry) *EMI 5207*	**1**	13 wks
20 Feb 82	**SHOWROOM DUMMIES** *EMI 5272*	**25**	5 wks

Billy J. KRAMER and the DAKOTAS

UK, male vocalist/male instrumental backing group

Date	Title *Label Number*	Position	
2 May 63	● **DO YOU WANT TO KNOW A SECRET?** *Parlophone R 5023*	**2**	15 wks
1 Aug 63	★ **BAD TO ME** *Parlophone R 5049*	**1**	14 wks
7 Nov 63	● **I'LL KEEP YOU SATISFIED** *Parlophone R 5073*	**4**	13 wks
27 Feb 64	★ **LITTLE CHILDREN** *Parlophone R 5105*	**1**	13 wks
23 Jul 64	● **FROM A WINDOW** *Parlophone R 5156*	**10**	8 wks
20 May 65	**TRAINS AND BOATS AND PLANES** *Parlophone R 5285*	**12**	8 wks

See also Dakotas.

KRANKIES *UK, male/female vocal duo*

Date	Title *Label Number*	Position	
7 Feb 81	**FAN'DABI'DOZI** *Monarch MON 21*	**71**	1 wk
7 Mar 81	**FAN'DABI'DOZI** (re-entry) *Monarch MON 21*	**46**	5 wks

KREW-KATS *UK, male instrumental group*

Date	Title *Label Number*	Position	
9 Mar 61	**TRAMBONE** *HMV POP 840*	**33**	9 wks
18 May 61	**TRAMBONE** (re-entry) *HMV POP 840*	**49**	1 wk

KROKUS

Switzerland/Malta, male vocal/instrumental group

Date	Title *Label Number*	Position	
16 May 81	**INDUSTRIAL STRENGTH** EP *Ariola ARO 258*	**62**	2 wks

Tracks on Industrial Strength EP:

Charlie KUNZ *US, male instrumentalist, piano*

Date	Title *Label Number*	Position	
17 Dec 54	**PIANO MEDLEY NO. 114** *Decca F 10419*	**20**	3 wks
14 Jan 55	**PIANO MEDLEY NO. 114** (re-entry) *Decca F 10419*	**16**	1 wk

Medley titles: There Must Be A Reason/ Hold My Hand/ If I Give My Heart To You/ Little Things Mean A Lot/ Make Her Mine/ My Son My Son.

Above **LANDSCAPE** Albert Einstein never lived to see his name in the chart – he died just 26 years too soon

Centre **MAJOR LANCE** Signing for fans at a Chicago record shop

Right **GARY LEWIS** The son of Jerry Lewis had many American hits in the 60s – one of which became a northern soul classic in the 70s

Below **LABELLE** Honest! we got them off the peg at Dorothy Perkins

KURSAAL FLYERS

UK, male vocal/instrumental group

Date	Title *Label Number*	Position	Wks
20 Nov 76	**LITTLE DOES SHE KNOW** *CBS 4689*	**14**	10 wks

Danny LA RUE *UK, male vocalist*

Date	Title *Label Number*	Position	Wks
18 Dec 68	**ON MOTHER KELLY'S DOORSTEP** *Page One POF 108*	**33**	9 wks

LABELLE *US, female vocal group*

Date	Title *Label Number*	Position	Wks
22 Mar 75	**LADY MARMALADE (VOULEZ-VOUS COUCHER AVEC MOI CE SOIR?)** *Epic EPC 2852*	**17**	9 wks

Cleo LAINE *UK, female vocalist*

Date	Title *Label Number*	Position	Wks
29 Dec 60	**LET'S SLIP AWAY** *Fontana H 269*	**42**	1 wk
14 Sep 61	● **YOU'LL ANSWER TO ME** *Fontana H 326*	**5**	13 wks

Frankie LAINE *US, male vocalist*

Date	Title *Label Number*	Position	Wks
14 Nov 52	● **HIGH NOON** *Columbia DB 3113*	**7**	7 wks
20 Mar 53	**GIRL IN THE WOOD** *Columbia DB 2907*	**11**	1 wk
3 Apr 53	★ **I BELIEVE** *Philips PB 117*	**1**	36 wks
4 Sep 53	● **WHERE THE WIND BLOWS** *Philips PB 167*	**2**	12 wks
16 Oct 53	★ **HEY JOE** *Philips PB 172*	**1**	8 wks
30 Oct 53	★ **ANSWER ME** *Philips PB 196*	**1**	17 wks
8 Jan 54	● **BLOWING WILD** *Philips PB 207*	**2**	12 wks
26 Mar 54	● **GRANADA** *Philips PB 242*	**10**	1 wk
9 Apr 54	● **GRANADA** (re-entry) *Philips PB 242*	**9**	1 wk
16 Apr 54	● **THE KID'S LAST FIGHT** *Philips PB 258*	**3**	10 wks
13 Aug 54	● **MY FRIEND** *Philips PB 316*	**3**	15 wks
8 Oct 54	● **THERE MUST BE A REASON** *Philips PB 306*	**9**	9 wks
22 Oct 54	● **RAIN RAIN RAIN** *Philips PB 311*	**8**	16 wks
11 Mar 55	**IN THE BEGINNING** *Philips PB 311*	**20**	1 wk
24 Jun 55	● **COOL WATER** *Philips PB 465*	**2**	22 wks
15 Jul 55	● **STRANGE LADY IN TOWN** *Philips PB 478*	**6**	13 wks
11 Nov 55	**HUMMING BIRD** *Philips PB 498*	**16**	1 wk
25 Nov 55	● **HAWKEYE** *Philips PB 519*	**7**	8 wks
20 Jan 56	● **SIXTEEN TONS** *Philips PB 539*	**10**	3 wks
4 May 56	**HELL HATH NO FURY** *Philips PB 585*	**28**	1 wk
7 Sep 56	★ **A WOMAN IN LOVE** *Philips PB 617*	**1**	21 wks
28 Dec 56	**MOONLIGHT GAMBLER** *Philips PB 638*	**13**	12 wks
29 Mar 57	**MOONLIGHT GAMBLER** (re-entry) *Philips PB 638*	**28**	1 wk
26 Apr 57	**LOVE IS A GOLDEN RING** *Philips PB 676*	**19**	5 wks
13 Nov 59	● **RAWHIDE** *Philips PB 965*	**6**	17 wks
31 Mar 60	**RAWHIDE** (re-entry) *Philips PB 965*	**41**	2 wks
11 May 61	**GUNSLINGER** *Philips PB 1135*	**50**	1 wk

See also Frankie Laine & Jimmy Boyd, Frankie Laine & Johnnie Ray, Doris Day & Frankie Laine.

Frankie LAINE and Jimmy BOYD

US, male vocal duo

Date	Title *Label Number*	Position	Wks
8 May 53	● **TELL ME A STORY** *Philips PB 126*	**5**	15 wks
11 Sep 53	**TELL ME A STORY** (re-entry) *Philips PB 126*	**12**	1 wk

See also Frankie Laine, Jimmy Boyd, Frankie Laine & Johnnie Ray, Doris Day & Frankie Laine.

Frankie LAINE and Johnnie RAY

US, male vocal duo

Date	Title *Label Number*	Position	Wks
4 Oct 57	**GOOD EVENING FRIENDS/ UP ABOVE MY HEAD** *Philips PB 708*	**25**	4 wks

See also Frankie Laine, Johnnie Ray, Frankie Laine & Jimmy Boyd, Doris Day & Frankie Laine, Doris Day & Johnnie Ray.

Greg LAKE *UK, male vocalist*

Date	Title *Label Number*	Position	Wks
6 Dec 75	● **I BELIEVE IN FATHER CHRISTMAS** *Manticore K 13511*	**2**	7 wks
25 Dec 82	**I BELIEVE IN FATHER CHRISTMAS** (re-entry) *Manticore K 13511*	**72**†	1 wk

See also Emerson, Lake and Palmer.

LAMBRETTAS *UK, male vocal/instrumental group*

Date	Title *Label Number*	Position	Wks
1 Mar 80	● **POISON IVY** *Rocket Xpress 25*	**7**	12 wks
24 May 80	**D-A-A-ANCE** *Rocket Xpress 33*	**12**	8 wks
23 Aug 80	**ANOTHER DAY (ANOTHER GIRL)** *Rocket XPRES 36*	**49**	4 wks

LANCASTRIANS

UK, male vocal/instrumental group

Date	Title *Label Number*	Position	Wks
24 Dec 64	**WE'LL SING IN THE SUNSHINE** *Pye 7N 15732*	**47**	2 wks

Major LANCE *US, male vocalist*

Date	Title *Label Number*	Position	Wks
13 Feb 64	**UM UM UM UM UM UM** *Columbia DB 7205*	**40**	2 wks

LANDSCAPE *UK, male vocal/instrumental group*

Date	Title *Label Number*	Position	Wks
28 Feb 81	● **EINSTEIN A GO-GO** *RCA 22*	**5**	13 wks
23 May 81	**NORMAN BATES** *RCA 60*	**40**	7 wks

Ronnie LANE *UK, male vocalist*

Date	Title *Label Number*	Position	Wks
12 Jan 74	**HOW COME** *GM GMS 011*	**11**	8 wks
15 Jun 74	**THE POACHER** *GM GMS 024*	**36**	4 wks

Both hits have the credit "accompanied by the band Slim Chance".

Don LANG *UK, male vocalist*

Date	Title *Label Number*	Position	Wks
4 Nov 55	**CLOUDBURST** *HMV POP 115*	**16**	2 wks
2 Dec 55	**CLOUDBURST** (re-entry) *HMV POP 115*	**18**	1 wk
13 Jan 56	**CLOUDBURST** (2nd re-entry) *HMV POP 115*	**20**	1 wk
5 Jul 57	**SCHOOL DAY** *HMV POP 350*	**26**	2 wks
23 May 58	● **WITCH DOCTOR** *HMV POP 488*	**5**	11 wks
10 Mar 60	**SINK THE BISMARCK** *HMV POP 714*	**43**	1 wk

School Day *and* Witch Doctor *credit Don Lang and his Frantic Five.*

Date **Title** *Label Number* **Position**

Mario LANZA *US, male vocalist*

Date	Title *Label Number*	Position	
14 Nov 52	● **BECAUSE YOU'RE MINE** *HMV DA 2017*	**3**	24 wks
4 Feb 55	**DRINKING SONG** *HMV DA 2065*	**13**	1 wk
18 Feb 55	**I'LL WALK WITH GOD** *HMV DA 2062*	**18**	1 wk
22 Apr 55	**SERENADE** *HMV DA 2065*	**19**	1 wk
6 May 55	**SERENADE** (re-entry) *HMV DA 2065*	**15**	2 wks
6 May 55	**I'LL WALK WITH GOD** (re-entry) *HMV DA 2062*	**20**	1 wk
14 Sep 56	**SERENADE** *HMV DA 2085*	**25**	1 wk
12 oct 56	**SERENADE** (re-entry) *HMV DA 2085*	**29**	1 wk

DA 2065 and DA 2085 are two different songs.

Julius LAROSA *US, male vocalist*

Date	Title *Label Number*	Position	
4 Jul 58	**TORERO** *RCA 1063*	**15**	9 wks

James LAST BAND

Germany, male instrumental group

Date	Title *Label Number*	Position	
3 May 80	**THE SEDUCTION (LOVE THEME)** *Polydor PD 2071*	**48**	4 wks

The LATE SHOW

UK, male vocal/instrumental group

Date	Title *Label Number*	Position	
3 Mar 79	**BRISTOL STOMP** *Decca F 13822*	**40**	6 wks

Stacy LATTISAW *US, female vocalist*

Date	Title *Label Number*	Position	
14 Jun 80	● **JUMP TO THE BEAT** *Atlantic/Cotillion K 11496*	**3**	11 wks
30 Aug 80	**DYNAMITE** *Atlantic K 11554*	**51**	3 wks

LAUNCHERS — See *Ezz RECO and the LAUNCHERS with Boysie GRANT*

LAUREL and HARDY with the AVALON BOYS *UK/US male vocal duo, male vocal group*

Date	Title *Label Number*	Position	
22 Nov 75	● **THE TRAIL OF THE LONESOME PINE** *United Artists UP 36026*	**2**	10 wks

Has credit: featuring Chill Wills.

Lee LAWRENCE *UK, male vocalist*

Date	Title *Label Number*	Position	
20 Nov 53	**CRYING IN THE CHAPEL** *Decca F 10177*	**11**	1 wk
11 Dec 53	● **CRYING IN THE CHAPEL** (re-entry) *Decca F 10177*	**7**	5 wks
2 Dec 55	**SUDDENLY THERE'S A VALLEY** *Columbia DB 3681*	**19**	1 wk
16 Dec 55	**SUDDENLY THERE'S A VALLEY** (re-entry) *Columbia DB 3681*	**14**	3 wks

Steve LAWRENCE *US, male vocalist*

Date	Title *Label Number*	Position	
21 Apr 60	● **FOOTSTEPS** *HMV POP 726*	**4**	13 wks
18 Aug 60	**GIRLS GIRLS GIRLS** *London HLT 9166*	**49**	1 wk

See also Steve and Eydie.

Vicky LEANDROS *Greece, female vocalist*

Date	Title *Label Number*	Position	
8 Apr 72	● **COME WHAT MAY** *Philips 6000 049*	**2**	16 wks
23 Dec 72	**THE LOVE IN YOUR EYES** *Philips 6000 081*	**48**	3 wks
20 Jan 73	**THE LOVE IN YOUR EYES** (re-entry) *Philips 6000 081*	**40**	4 wks
7 Apr 73	**THE LOVE IN YOUR EYES** (2nd re-entry) *Philips 6000 081*	**46**	1 wk
7 Jul 73	**WHEN BOUZOUKIS PLAYED** *Philips 6000 111*	**44**	2 wks
28 Jul 73	**WHEN BOUZOUKIS PLAYED** (re-entry) *Philips 6000 111*	**45**	3 wks

LEE — See *PETERS and LEE*

Brenda LEE *US, female vocalist*

Date	Title *Label Number*	Position	
17 Mar 60	**SWEET NUTHINS** *Brunswick 05819*	**45**	1 wk
7 Apr 60	● **SWEET NUTHINS** (re-entry) *Brunswick 05819*	**4**	18 wks
30 Jun 60	**I'M SORRY** *Brunswick 05833*	**12**	16 wks
20 Oct 60	**I WANT TO BE WANTED** *Brunswick 05839*	**31**	6 wks
19 Jan 61	**LET'S JUMP THE BROOMSTICK** *Brunswick 05823*	**12**	15 wks
6 Apr 61	**EMOTIONS** *Brunswick 05847*	**45**	1 wk
20 Jul 61	**DUM DUM** *Brunswick 05854*	**22**	8 wks
16 Nov 61	**FOOL NUMBER ONE** *Brunswick 05860*	**38**	3 wks
8 Feb 62	**BREAK IT TO ME GENTLY** *Brunswick 05864*	**46**	2 wks
5 Apr 62	● **SPEAK TO ME PRETTY** *Brunswick 05867*	**3**	12 wks
21 Jun 62	● **HERE COMES THAT FEELING** *Brunswick 05871*	**5**	12 wks
13 Sep 62	**IT STARTED ALL OVER AGAIN** *Brunswick 05876*	**15**	11 wks
29 Nov 62	● **ROCKIN' AROUND THE CHRISTMAS TREE** *Brunswick 05880*	**6**	7 wks
17 Jan 63	● **ALL ALONE AM I** *Brunswick 05882*	**7**	17 wks
28 Mar 63	● **LOSING YOU** *Brunswick 05886*	**10**	16 wks
18 Jul 63	**I WONDER** *Brunswick 05891*	**14**	9 wks
31 Oct 63	**SWEET IMPOSSIBLE YOU** *Brunswick 05896*	**28**	6 wks
9 Jan 64	● **AS USUAL** *Brunswick 05899*	**5**	15 wks
9 Apr 64	**THINK** *Brunswick 05903*	**26**	8 wks
10 Sep 64	**IS IT TRUE** *Brunswick 05915*	**17**	8 wks
10 Dec 64	**CHRISTMAS WILL BE JUST ANOTHER LONELY DAY** *Brunswick 05921*	**29**	5 wks
4 Feb 65	**THANKS A LOT** *Brunswick 05927*	**41**	2 wks
29 Jul 65	**TOO MANY RIVERS** *Brunswick 05936*	**22**	12 wks

Curtis LEE *US, male vocalist*

Date	Title *Label Number*	Position	
31 Aug 61	**PRETTY LITTLE ANGEL EYES** *London HLX 9397*	**47**	1 wk
14 Sep 61	**PRETTY LITTLE ANGEL EYES** (re-entry) *London HLX 9397*	**48**	1 wk

Jackie LEE *UK, female vocalist*

Date	Title *Label Number*	Position	
2 Jan 71	**RUPERT** *Pye 7N 45003*	**14**	17 wks

See also Jacky.

Leapy LEE *UK, male vocalist*

Date	Title *Label Number*	Position	
21 Aug 68	● **LITTLE ARROWS** *MCA MU 1028*	**2**	21 wks
20 Dec 69	**GOOD MORNING** *MCA MK 5021*	**47**	1 wk
10 Jan 70	**GOOD MORNING** (re-entry) *MCA MK 5021*	**29**	6 wks

Below **LOVE SCULPTURE** Bob Jones, Dave Edmunds and John Williams had one hit with their Kachaturian melody before Dave Edmunds found even more success as a solo artist and *Right* **LIGHT OF THE WORLD** An 80s version of the Magic Lanterns

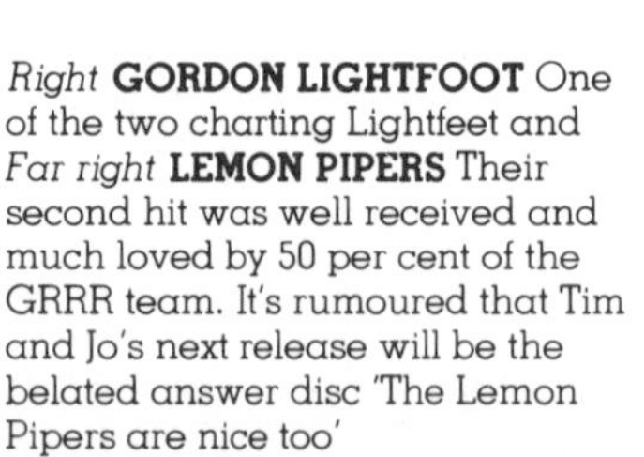

Right **GORDON LIGHTFOOT** One of the two charting Lightfeet and *Far right* **LEMON PIPERS** Their second hit was well received and much loved by 50 per cent of the GRRR team. It's rumoured that Tim and Jo's next release will be the belated answer disc 'The Lemon Pipers are nice too'

LETTERMEN
3 US males

Date	Title *Label Number*	Position	

Peggy LEE *US, female vocalist*

Date	Title *Label Number*	Position	
24 May 57	● **MR. WONDERFUL** *Brunswick 05671*	**5**	13 wks
15 Aug 58	● **FEVER** *Capitol CL 14902*	**5**	11 wks
23 Mar 61	**TILL THERE WAS YOU** *Capitol CL 15184*	**40**	1 wk
6 Apr 61	**TILL THERE WAS YOU** (re-entry) *Capitol CL 15184*	**30**	3 wks

LEEDS UNITED FC

UK, male football team vocalists

Date	Title *Label Number*	Position	
29 Apr 72	● **LEEDS UNITED** *Chapter One SCH 168*	**10**	10 wks

Raymond LEFEVRE *France, orchestra*

Date	Title *Label Number*	Position	
15 May 68	**SOUL COAXING** *Major Minor MM 559*	**46**	2 wks

LEMON PIPERS

US, male vocal/instrumental group

Date	Title *Label Number*	Position	
7 Feb 68	● **GREEN TAMBOURINE** *Pye International 7N 25444*	**7**	11 wks
1 May 68	**RICE IS NICE** *Pye International 7N 25454*	**41**	5 wks

John LENNON *UK, male vocalist*

Date	Title *Label Number*	Position	
9 Jul 69	● **GIVE PEACE A CHANCE** *Apple 13*	**2**	13 wks
1 Nov 69	**COLD TURKEY** *Apple APPLES 1001*	**14**	8 wks
21 Feb 70	● **INSTANT KARMA** *Apple APPLES 1003*	**5**	9 wks
20 Mar 71	● **POWER TO THE PEOPLE** *Apple R 5892*	**7**	9 wks
9 Dec 72	● **HAPPY XMAS (WAR IS OVER)** *Apple R 5970*	**4**	8 wks
24 Nov 73	**MIND GAMES** *Apple R 5994*	**26**	9 wks
19 Oct 74	**WHATEVER GETS YOU THROUGH THE NIGHT** *Apple R 5998*	**36**	4 wks
4 Jan 75	**HAPPY XMAS (WAR IS OVER)** (re-entry) *Apple R 5970*	**48**	1 wk
8 Feb 75	*Apple R 6003*	**23**	8 wks
3 May 75	**STAND BY ME** *Apple R 6005*	**30**	7 wks
1 Nov 75	● **IMAGINE** *Apple R 6009*	**6**	11 wks
8 Nov 80	★ **(JUST LIKE) STARTING OVER** *Geffen K 79186*	**1**	15 wks
20 Dec 80	● **HAPPY XMAS (WAR IS OVER)** (2nd re-entry) *Apple R 5970*	**2**	wks
27 Dec 80	★ **IMAGINE** (re-entry) *Apple R 6009*	**1**	wks
24 Jan 81	★ **WOMAN** *Geffen K 79195*	**1**	11 wks
24 Jan 81	*Give Peace A Chance Apple*	**13**	33 wks
4 Apr 81	**WATCHING THE WHEELS** *Geffen K 79207*	**30**	6 wks
19 Dec 81	**HAPPY XMAS (WAR IS OVER)** (3rd re-entry) *Apple R 5970*	**28**	5 wks
20 Nov 82	**LOVE** *Parlophone R 6059*	**41**†	6 wks
25 Dec 82	**HAPPY XMAS (WAR IS OVER)** (4th re-entry) *Apple R 5970*	**56**†	1 wk

Instant Karma *is by Lennon, Ono and the Plastic Ono Band,* Power To The People *by John Lennon/ Plastic Ono Band,* Happy Xmas War Is Over *by John & Yoko/ Plastic Ono Band with The Harlem Community Choir,* Whatever Gets You Through The Night *by John Lennon with The Plastic Ono Nuclear Band, and the others simply John Lennon. The Yoko and the Ono in these credits refer to Yoko Ono, Japanese female vocalist. See also Elton John Band featuring John Lennon and the Muscle Shoals Horns*

Rula LENSKA — See *Julie COVINGTON, Rula LENSKA, Charlotte CORNWELL and Sue JONES-DAVIES*

Ketty LESTER *US, female vocalist*

Date	Title *Label Number*	Position	
19 Apr 62	● **LOVE LETTERS** *London HLN 9527*	**4**	12 wks
19 Jul 62	**BUT NOT FOR ME** *London HLN 9574*	**45**	4 wks

LETTERMEN *US, male vocal group*

Date	Title *Label Number*	Position	
23 Nov 61	**THE WAY YOU LOOK TONIGHT** *Capitol CL 15222*	**36**	3 wks

LEVEL 42 *UK/France, male vocal/instrumental group*

Date	Title *Label Number*	Position	
30 Aug 80	**LOVE MEETING LOVE** *Polydor POSP 170*	**61**	4 wks
18 Apr 81	**LOVE GAMES** *Polydor POSP 234*	**39**	6 wks
8 Aug 81	**TURN IT ON** *Polydor POSP 286*	**57**	6 wks
14 Nov 81	**STARCHILD** *Polydor POSP 343*	**47**	4 wks
8 May 82	**ARE YOU HEARING (WHAT I HEAR)?** *Polydor POSP 396*	**49**	5 wks
2 Oct 82	**WEAVE YOUR SPELL** *Polydor POSP 500*	**43**	4 wks

Hank LEVINE *US, orchestra*

Date	Title *Label Number*	Position	
21 Dec 61	**IMAGE** *HMV POP 947*	**45**	4 wks

Jona LEWIE *UK, male vocalist*

Date	Title *Label Number*	Position	
10 May 80	**YOU'LL ALWAYS FIND ME IN THE KITCHEN AT PARTIES** *Stiff BUY 73*	**16**	9 wks
29 Nov 80	● **STOP THE CAVALRY** *Stiff BUY 104*	**3**	11 wks

On some copies first title was simply Kitchen At Parties.

Gary LEWIS and the PLAYBOYS

US, male vocal/instrumental group, Gary Lewis lead vocals and drums

Date	Title *Label Number*	Position	
8 Feb 75	**MY HEART'S SYMPHONY** *United Artists UP 35780*	**36**	7 wks

Jerry LEWIS *US, male vocalist*

Date	Title *Label Number*	Position	
8 Feb 57	**ROCK-A-BYE YOUR BABY (WITH A DIXIE MELODY)** *Brunswick 05636*	**12**	7 wks
5 Apr 57	**ROCK-A-BYE YOUR BABY (WITH A DIXIE MELODY)** (re-entry) *Brunswick 05636*	**22**	1 wk

Jerry Lee LEWIS

US, male vocalist/instrumentalist, piano

Date	Title *Label Number*	Position	
27 Sep 57	● **WHOLE LOTTA SHAKIN' GOIN' ON** *London HLS 8457*	**8**	10 wks
20 Dec 57	★ **GREAT BALLS OF FIRE** *London HLS 8529*	**1**	12 wks
27 Dec 57	**WHOLE LOTTA SHAKIN' GOIN' ON** (re-entry) *London HLS 8457*	**26**	1 wk
11 Apr 58	● **BREATHLESS** *London HLS 8592*	**8**	7 wks
23 Jan 59	**HIGH SCHOOL CONFIDENTIAL** *London HLS 8780*	**12**	6 wks
1 May 59	**LOVIN' UP A STORM** *London HLS 8840*	**28**	1 wk
9 Jun 60	**BABY BABY BYE BYE** *London HLS 9131*	**47**	1 wk
4 May 61	● **WHAT'D I SAY** *London HLS 9335*	**10**	12 wks
3 Aug 61	**WHAT'D I SAY** (re-entry) *London HLS 9335*	**49**	2 wks

Date	Title *Label Number*	Position	
6 Sep 62	**SWEET LITTLE SIXTEEN** *London HLS 9584*	**38**	5 wks
14 Mar 63	**GOOD GOLLY MISS MOLLY** *London HLS 9688*	**31**	6 wks
6 May 72	**CHANTILLY LACE** *Mercury 6052 141*	**33**	5 wks

Linda LEWIS *UK, female vocalist*

2 Jun 73	**ROCK-A-DOODLE-DOO** *Raft RA 18502*	**15**	11 wks
12 Jul 75	● **IT'S IN HIS KISS** *Arista 17*	**6**	8 wks
17 Apr 76	**BABY I'M YOURS** *Arista 43*	**33**	6 wks
2 Jun 79	**I'D BE SURPRISINGLY GOOD FOR YOU** *Ariola ARO 166*	**40**	5 wks

Ramsey LEWIS *US, male instrumentalist, piano*

15 Apr 72	**WADE IN THE WATER** *Chess 6145 004*	**31**	8 wks

John LEYTON *UK, male vocalist*

3 Aug 61	★ **JOHNNY REMEMBER ME** *Top Rank JAR 577*	**1**	15 wks
5 Oct 61	● **WILD WIND** *Top Rank JAR 585*	**2**	10 wks
28 Dec 61	**SON THIS IS SHE** *HMV POP 956*	**15**	10 wks
15 Mar 62	**LONE RIDER** *HMV POP 992*	**40**	5 wks
3 May 62	**LONELY CITY** *HMV POP 1014*	**14**	11 wks
23 Aug 62	**DOWN THE RIVER NILE** *HMV POP 1054*	**42**	3 wks
21 Feb 63	**CUPBOARD LOVE** *HMV POP 1122*	**22**	12 wks
18 Jul 63	**I'LL CUT YOUR TAIL OFF** *HMV POP 1175*	**50**	1 wk
8 Aug 63	**I'LL CUT YOUR TAIL OFF** (re-entry) *HMV POP 1175*	**36**	2 wks
20 Feb 64	**MAKE LOVE TO ME** *HMV POP 1264*	**49**	1 wk

LEYTON BUZZARDS

UK, male vocal/instrumental group

3 Mar 79	**SATURDAY NIGHT (BENEATH THE PLASTIC PALM TREES)** *Chrysalis CHS 2288*	**53**	5 wks

LIBERACE *US, male instrumentalist, piano*

17 Jun 55	**UNCHAINED MELODY** *Philips PB 430*	**20**	1 wk
19 Oct 56	**I DON'T CARE** *Columbia DB 3834*	**28**	1 wk

I Don't Care *featured Liberace as vocalist too.*

LIEUTENANT PIGEON

UK, male/female instrumental group

16 Sep 72	★ **MOULDY OLD DOUGH** *Decca F 13278*	**1**	19 wks
16 Dec 72	**DESPERATE DAN** *Decca F 13365*	**17**	10 wks

LIGHT OF THE WORLD

UK, male vocal/instrumental group

14 Apr 79	**SWINGIN'** *Ensign ENY 22*	**45**	5 wks
14 Jul 79	**MIDNIGHT GROOVIN'** *Ensign ENY 29*	**72**	1 wk
18 Oct 80	**LONDON TOWN** *Ensign ENY 43*	**41**	5 wks
17 Jan 81	**I SHOT THE SHERIFF** *Ensign ENY 46*	**40**	5 wks
28 Mar 81	**I'M SO HAPPY** *Mercury/Ensign MER 64*	**35**	6 wks
21 Nov 81	**RIDE THE LOVE TRAIN** *EMI 5242*	**49**	3 wks

Gordon LIGHTFOOT *Canada, male vocalist*

19 Jun 71	**IF YOU COULD READ MY MIND** *Reprise RS 20974*	**30**	9 wks
3 Aug 74	**SUNDOWN** *Reprise K 14327*	**33**	7 wks
15 Jan 77	**THE WRECK OF THE EDMUND FITZGERALD** *Reprise K 14451*	**40**	4 wks
16 Sep 78	**DAYLIGHT KATY** *Warner Bros. K 17214*	**41**	6 wks

Terry LIGHTFOOT and his NEW ORLEANS JAZZMEN

UK, male vocal/instrumental group, Terry Lightfoot clarinet and vocals

7 Sep 61	**TRUE LOVE** *Columbia DB 4696*	**33**	4 wks
23 Nov 61	**KING KONG** *Columbia SCD 2165*	**29**	12 wks
3 May 62	**TAVERN IN THE TOWN** *Columbia DB 4822*	**49**	1 wk

LIMMIE and the FAMILY COOKIN'

US, male/female vocal group

21 Jul 73	● **YOU CAN DO MAGIC** *Avco 6105 019*	**3**	13 wks
20 Oct 73	**DREAMBOAT** *Avco 6105 025*	**31**	5 wks
6 Apr 74	● **A WALKIN' MIRACLE** *Avco 6105 027*	**6**	10 wks

Bob LIND *US, male vocalist*

10 Mar 66	● **ELUSIVE BUTTERFLY** *Fontana TF 670*	**5**	9 wks
26 May 66	**REMEMBER THE RAIN** *Fontana TF 702*	**46**	1 wk

LINDA and the FUNKY BOYS

US, female vocalist, male vocal/instrumental backing group

5 Jun 76	**SOLD MY SOUL FOR ROCK 'N ROLL** *Spark SRL 1139*	**36**	4 wks

Linda is Linda Carr. See also Linda Carr and the Love Squad.

LINDISFARNE *UK, male vocal/instrumental group*

26 Feb 72	● **MEET ME ON THE CORNER** *Charisma CB 173*	**5**	11 wks
13 May 72	● **LADY ELEANOR** *Charisma CB 153*	**3**	11 wks
23 Sep 72	**ALL FALL DOWN** *Charisma CB 191*	**34**	5 wks
3 Jun 78	● **RUN FOR HOME** *Mercury 6007 177*	**10**	15 wks
7 Oct 78	**JUKE BOX GYPSY** *Mercury 6007 187*	**56**	4 wks

LINER *UK, male vocal/instrumental group*

10 Mar 79	**KEEP REACHING OUT FOR LOVE** *Atlantic K 11235*	**49**	3 wks
26 May 79	**YOU AND ME** *Atlantic K 11285*	**44**	3 wks

Laurie LINGO and the DIPSTICKS

UK, male vocal duo, disc jockeys Dave Lee Travis and Paul Burnett

17 Apr 76	● **CONVOY G. B.** *State STAT 23*	**4**	7 wks

LINX *UK, male vocal/instrumental group*

Date	Title *Label Number*	Position	Wks
20 Sep 80	**YOU'RE LYING** *Chrysalis CHS 2461*	**15**	10 wks
7 Mar 81	● **INTUITION** *Chrysalis CHS 2500*	**7**	11 wks
13 Jun 81	**THROW AWAY THE KEY** *Chrysalis CHS 2519*	**21**	9 wks
5 Sep 81	**SO THIS IS ROMANCE** *Chrysalis CHS 2546*	**15**	9 wks
21 Nov 81	**CAN'T HELP MYSELF** *Chrysalis CHS 2565*	**55**	3 wks
10 Jul 82	**PLAYTHING** *Chrysalis CHS 2621*	**48**	3 wks

LIPPS INC.

US, male/female vocal/instrumental group

Date	Title *Label Number*	Position	Wks
17 May 80	● **FUNKYTOWN** *Casablanca CAN 194*	**2**	13 wks

LIQUID GOLD

UK, male/female vocal/instrumental group

Date	Title *Label Number*	Position	Wks
2 Dec 78	**ANYWAY YOU DO IT** *Creole CR 159*	**41**	7 wks
23 Feb 80	● **DANCE YOURSELF DIZZY** *Polo 1*	**2**	14 wks
31 May 80	● **SUBSTITUTE** *Polo POLO 4*	**8**	9 wks
1 Nov 80	**THE NIGHT THE WINE AND THE ROSES** *POLO 6*	**32**	7 wks
28 Mar 81	**DON'T PANIC** *Polo POLO 8*	**42**	5 wks
21 Aug 82	**WHERE DID WE GO WRONG** *Polo POLO 23*	**56**	4 wks

De Etta LITTLE and Nelson PIGFORD

US, female/male vocal duo

Date	Title *Label Number*	Position	Wks
13 Aug 77	**YOU TAKE MY HEART AWAY** *United Artists UP 36257*	**35**	5 wks

LITTLE ANTHONY and the IMPERIALS

US, male vocal group

Date	Title *Label Number*	Position	Wks
31 Jul 76	**BETTER USE YOUR HEAD** *United Artists UP 36118*	**42**	4 wks

See also Imperials

LITTLE EVA *US, female vocalist*

Date	Title *Label Number*	Position	Wks
6 Sep 62	● **THE LOCO-MOTION** *London HL 9581*	**2**	17 wks
3 Jan 63	**KEEP YOUR HANDS OFF MY BABY** *London HLU 9633*	**30**	4 wks
7 Mar 63	**LET'S TURKEY TROT** *London HLU 9687*	**13**	12 wks
29 Jul 72	**THE LOCO-MOTION** (re-entry) *London HL 9581*	**11**	11 wks

See also Big Dee Irwin.

LITTLE RICHARD *US, male vocalist*

Date	Title *Label Number*	Position	Wks
14 Dec 56	**RIP IT UP** *London HLO 8336*	**30**	1 wk
8 Feb 57	● **LONG TALL SALLY** *London HLO 8366*	**3**	16 wks
22 Feb 57	**TUTTI FRUTTI** *London HLO 8366*	**29**	1 wk
8 Mar 57	**SHE'S GOT IT** *London HLO 8382*	**15**	7 wks
15 Mar 57	● **THE GIRL CAN'T HELP IT** *London HLO 8382*	**9**	11 wks
24 May 57	**SHE'S GOT IT** (re-entry) *London HLO 8382*	**28**	2 wks
28 Jun 57	● **LUCILLE** *London HLO 8446*	**10**	9 wks
13 Sep 57	**JENNY JENNY** *London HLO 8470*	**11**	5 wks
29 Nov 57	**KEEP A KNOCKIN'** *London HLO 8509*	**21**	7 wks
28 Feb 58	● **GOOD GOLLY MISS MOLLY** *London HLU 8560*	**8**	9 wks
11 Jul 58	**OOH MY SOUL** *London HLO 8647*	**30**	1 wk
25 Jul 58	**OOH MY SOUL** (re-entry) *London HLO 8647*	**22**	3 wks
2 Jan 59	● **BABY FACE** *London HLU 8770*	**2**	15 wks
3 Apr 59	**BY THE LIGHT OF THE SILVERY MOON** *London HLU 8831*	**17**	5 wks
5 Jun 59	**KANSAS CITY** *London HLU 8868*	**26**	5 wks
11 Oct 62	**HE GOT WHAT HE WANTED** *Mercury AMT 1189*	**38**	4 wks
4 Jun 64	**BAMA LAMA BAMA LOO** *London HL 9896*	**20**	7 wks
2 Jul 77	**GOOD GOLLY MISS MOLLY/RIP IT UP** *Creole CR 140*	**37**	4 wks

The versions of Good Golly Miss Molly *and* Rip It Up *on Creole are re-recordings*

LITTLE TONY *Italy, male vocalist*

Date	Title *Label Number*	Position	Wks
15 Jan 60	**TOO GOOD** *Decca F 11190*	**19**	3 wks

LIVERPOOL EXPRESS

UK, male vocal/instrumental group

Date	Title *Label Number*	Position	Wks
26 Jun 76	**YOU ARE MY LOVE** *Warner Bros. K 16743*	**11**	9 wks
16 Oct 76	**HOLD TIGHT** *Warner Bros. K 16799*	**46**	2 wks
18 Dec 76	**EVERY MAN MUST HAVE A DREAM** *Warner Bros. K 16854*	**17**	11 wks
4 Jun 77	**DREAMIN'** *Warner Bros. K 16933*	**40**	4 wks

LIVERPOOL FOOTBALL TEAM

UK, male football team vocalists

Date	Title *Label Number*	Position	Wks
28 May 77	**WE CAN DO IT** (EP) *State STAT 50*	**15**	4 wks

Tracks on We Can Do It EP: *We Can Do It/ Liverpool Lou/ We Shall Not Be Moved/ You'll Never Walk Alone.*

Dandy LIVINGSTONE *Jamaica, male vocalist*

Date	Title *Label Number*	Position	Wks
2 Sep 72	**SUZANNE BEWARE OF THE DEVIL** *Horse HOSS 16*	**14**	11 wks
13 Jan 73	**BIG CITY/ THINK ABOUT THAT** *Horse HOSS 25*	**26**	8 wks

LOBO *US, male vocalist*

Date	Title *Label Number*	Position	Wks
19 Jun 71	● **ME AND YOU AND A DOG NAMED BOO** *Philips 6073 801*	**4**	14 wks
8 Jun 74	● **I'D LOVE YOU TO WANT ME** *UK 68*	**5**	11 wks

LOBO *Holland, male vocalist*

Date	Title *Label Number*	Position	Wks
25 Jul 81	● **THE CARIBBEAN DISCO SHOW** *Polydor POSP 302*	**8**	11 wks

Hank LOCKLIN *US, male vocalist*

Date	Title *Label Number*	Position	Wks
11 Aug 60	● **PLEASE HELP ME I'M FALLING** *RCA 1188*	**9**	19 wks
15 Feb 62	**FROM HERE TO THERE TO YOU** *RCA 1273*	**44**	3 wks
15 Nov 62	**WE'RE GONNA GO FISHIN'** *RCA 1305*	**18**	11 wks
5 May 66	**I FEEL A CRY COMING ON** *RCA 1510*	**28**	8 wks

LOCKSMITH *US, male vocal/instrumental group*

Date	Title *Label Number*	Position	Wks
23 Aug 80	**UNLOCK THE FUNK** *Arista ARIST 364*	**42**	6 wks

LOCOMOTIVE *UK, male vocal/instrumental group*

Date	Title *Label Number*	Position	Wks
16 Oct 68	**RUDI'S IN LOVE** *Parlophone R 5718*	**25**	8 wks

Date	Title *Label Number*	Position	

John LODGE — See *Justin HAYWARD and John LODGE*

Johnny LOGAN *Australia, male vocalist*

3 May 80 ★	**WHAT'S ANOTHER YEAR** *Epic EPC 8572*	**1**	8 wks

Johnny Logan, although Australian, represented Ireland in the 1980 Eurovision Song Contest

Julie LONDON *US, female vocalist*

5 Apr 57	**CRY ME A RIVER** *London HLU 8240*	**22**	3 wks

Laurie LONDON *UK, male vocalist*

8 Nov 57	**HE'S GOT THE WHOLE WORLD IN HIS HANDS** *Parlophone R 4359*	**12**	12 wks

LONDON STRING CHORALE

UK, orchestra/choir

15 Dec 73	**GALLOPING HOME** *Polydor 2058 280*	**49**	3 wks
19 Jan 74	**GALLOPING HOME** (re-entry) *Polydor 2058 280*	**31**	10 wks

LONDON SYMPHONY ORCHESTRA

UK, orchestra

6 Jan 79	**THEME FROM SUPERMAN** (MAIN TITLE) *Warner Bros. K 17292*	**32**	5 wks

Orchestra conducted by John Williams.

Shorty LONG *US, male vocalist*

17 Jul 68	**HERE COMES THE JUDGE** *Tamla Motown TMG 663*	**30**	7 wks

LONG AND THE SHORT

UK, male vocal/instrumental group

10 Sep 64	**THE LETTER** *Decca F 11959*	**30**	5 wks
24 Dec 64	**CHOC ICE** *Decca F 12043*	**49**	3 wks

LOOK *UK, male vocal/instrumental group*

20 Dec 80 ●	**I AM THE BEAT** *MCA 647*	**6**	wks
29 Aug 81	**FEEDING TIME** *MCA 736*	**50**	3 wks

Trini LOPEZ *US, male vocalist*

12 Sep 63 ●	**IF I HAD A HAMMER** *Reprise R 20198*	**4**	17 wks
12 Dec 63	**KANSAS CITY** *Reprise R 20236*	**35**	5 wks
12 May 66	**I'M COMING HOME CINDY** *Reprise R 20455*	**28**	5 wks
6 Apr 67	**GONNA GET ALONG WITHOUT YA NOW** *Reprise R 20547*	**41**	5 wks
19 Dec 81	**TRINI TRACKS** *RCA 154*	**59**	5 wks

Jerry LORDAN *UK, male vocalist*

8 Jan 60	**I'LL STAY SINGLE** *Parlophone R 4588*	**26**	2 wks
26 Feb 60	**WHO COULD BE BLUER** *Parlophone R 4627*	**17**	9 wks
10 Mar 60	**I'LL STAY SINGLE** (re-entry) *Parlophone R 4588*	**41**	1 wk
19 May 60	**WHO COULD BE BLUER** (re-entry) *Parlophone R 4627*	**45**	1 wk
2 Jun 60	**SING LIKE AN ANGEL** *Parlophone R 4653*	**36**	2 wks

Sophia LOREN — See *Peter SELLERS and Sophia LOREN*

LORI and the CHAMELEONS

UK, male/female vocal/instrumental group

8 Dec 79	**TOUCH** *Sire SIR 4025*	**70**	1 wk

Joe LOSS *UK, orchestra*

29 Jun 61	**WHEELS CHA CHA** *HMV POP 880*	**21**	21 wks
19 Oct 61	**SUCU SUCU** *HMV POP 937*	**48**	1 wk
29 Mar 62	**THE MAIGRET THEME** *HMV POP 995*	**20**	10 wks
1 Nov 62	**MUST BE MADISON** *HMV POP 1075*	**20**	13 wks
5 Nov 64	**MARCH OF THE MODS** *HMV POP 1351*	**35**	4 wks
24 Dec 64	**MARCH OF THE MODS** (re-entry) *HMV POP 1351*	**31**	4 wks

Bonnie LOU *US, female vocalist*

5 Feb 54 ●	**TENNESSEE WIG WALK** *Parlophone R 3730*	**4**	10 wks

John D. LOUDERMILK *US, male vocalist*

4 Jan 62	**THE LANGUAGE OF LOVE** *RCA 1269*	**13**	10 wks

Geoff LOVE — See *MANUEL and his MUSIC OF THE MOUNTAINS*

LOVE AFFAIR *UK, male vocal/instrumental group*

3 Jan 68 ★	**EVERLASTING LOVE** *CBS 3125*	**1**	12 wks
17 Apr 68 ●	**RAINBOW VALLEY** *CBS 3366*	**5**	13 wks
11 Sep 68 ●	**A DAY WITHOUT LOVE** *CBS 3674*	**6**	12 wks
19 Feb 69	**ONE ROAD** *CBS 3994*	**16**	9 wks
16 Jul 69 ●	**BRINGING ON BACK THE GOOD TIMES** *CBS 4300*	**9**	10 wks

LOVE SCULPTURE *UK, instrumental group*

27 Nov 68 ●	**SABRE DANCE** *Parlophone R 5744*	**5**	14 wks

LOVE SQUAD — See *Linda CARR and the LOVE SQUAD*

LOVE UNLIMITED *US, female vocal group*

17 Jun 72	**WALKIN' IN THE RAIN WITH THE ONE I LOVE** *Uni UN 539*	**14**	10 wks
25 Jan 75	**IT MAY BE WINTER OUTSIDE (BUT IN MY HEART ITS SPRING)** *20th Century BTC 2149*	**11**	9 wks

LOVE UNLIMITED ORCHESTRA

US, orchestra

2 Feb 74 ●	**LOVE'S THEME** *Pye International 7N 25635*	**10**	10 wks

Date	Title Label Number	Position	

Bill LOVELADY *UK, male vocalist*

18 Aug 79	**REGGAE FOR IT NOW** *Charisma CB 337*	**12**	10 wks

Lene LOVICH *US, female vocalist*

17 Feb 79	● **LUCKY NUMBER** *Stiff BUY 42*	**3**	11 wks
12 May 79	**SAY WHEN** *Stiff BUY 46*	**19**	10 wks
20 Oct 79	**BIRD SONG** *Stiff BUY 53*	**39**	7 wks
29 Mar 80	**WHAT WILL I DO WITHOUT YOU** *Stiff BUY 69*	**58**	3 wks
14 Mar 81	**NEW TOY** *Stiff BUY 97*	**53**	5 wks
27 Nov 82	**IT'S YOU, ONLY YOU (MEIN SCHMERZ)** *Stiff BUY 164*	**68**	2 wks

LOVIN' SPOONFUL

Canada, male vocal/instrumental group

14 Apr 66	● **DAYDREAM** *Pye International 7N 25361*	**2**	13 wks
14 Jul 66	● **SUMMER IN THE CITY** *Kama Sutra KAS 200*	**8**	11 wks
5 Jan 67	**NASHVILLE CATS** *Kama Sutra KAS 204*	**26**	7 wks
9 Mar 67	**DARLING BE HOME SOON** *Kama Sutra KAS 207*	**44**	2 wks

Jim LOWE *US, male vocalist*

26 Oct 56	● **THE GREEN DOOR** *London HLD 8317*	**8**	9 wks

Nick LOWE *UK, male vocalist*

11 Mar 78	● **I LOVE THE SOUND OF BREAKING GLASS** *Radar ADA 1*	**7**	8 wks
9 Jun 79	**CRACKIN' UP** *Radar ADA 34*	**34**	5 wks
25 Aug 79	**CRUEL TO BE KIND** *Radar ADA 43*	**12**	11 wks

LOWRELL *US, male vocalist*

24 Nov 79	**MELLOW MELLOW RIGHT ON** *AVI AVIS 108*	**37**	9 wks

L.T.D. *US, male vocal/instrumental group*

9 Sep 78	**HOLDING ON** *A & M AMS 7378*	**70**	3 wks

Carrie LUCAS *US, female vocalist*

16 Jun 79	**DANCE WITH YOU** *Solar FB 1482*	**40**	6 wks

LUIGI — See *HUGO and LUIGI*

Robin LUKE *US, male vocalist*

17 Oct 58	**SUSIE DARLIN'** *London HLD 8676*	**24**	3 wks
21 Nov 58	**SUSIE DARLIN'** (re-entry) *London HLD 8676*	**23**	1 wk
5 Dec 58	**SUSIE DARLIN'** (2nd re-entry) *London HLD 8676*	**23**	2 wks

LULU *UK, female vocalist*

14 May 64	● **SHOUT** *Decca F 11884*	**7**	13 wks
12 Nov 64	**HERE COMES THE NIGHT** *Decca F 12017*	**50**	1 wk
17 Jun 65	● **LEAVE A LITTLE LOVE** *Decca F 12169*	**8**	11 wks
2 Sep 65	**TRY TO UNDERSTAND** *Decca F 12214*	**25**	8 wks
13 Apr 67	● **THE BOAT THAT I ROW** *Columbia DB 8169*	**6**	11 wks
29 Jun 67	**LET'S PRETEND** *Columbia DB 8221*	**11**	11 wks
8 Nov 67	**LOVE LOVES TO LOVE LOVE** *Columbia DB 8295*	**32**	6 wks
28 Feb 68	● **ME THE PEACEFUL HEART** *Columbia DB 8358*	**9**	9 wks
5 Jun 68	**BOY** *Columbia DB 8425*	**15**	7 wks
6 Nov 68	● **I'M A TIGER** *Columbia DB 8500*	**9**	13 wks
12 Mar 69	● **BOOM BANG-A-BANG** *Columbia DB 8550*	**2**	13 wks
22 Nov 69	**OH ME OH MY (I'M A FOOL FOR YOU BABY)** *Atco 226 008*	**47**	2 wks
26 Jan 74	● **THE MAN WHO SOLD THE WORLD** *Polydor 2001 490*	**3**	9 wks
19 Apr 75	**TAKE YOUR MAMA FOR A RIDE** *Chelsea 2005 022*	**37**	4 wks
12 Dec 81	**I COULD NEVER MISS YOU (MORE THAN I DO)** *Alfa ALFA 1700*	**62**	3 wks
16 Jan 82	**I COULD NEVER MISS YOU (MORE THAN I DO)** (re-entry) *Alfa ALFA 1700*	**63**	1 wk

Shout *credited to Lulu & The Luvvers.*

Bob LUMAN *US, male vocalist*

8 Sep 60	● **LET'S THINK ABOUT LIVING** *Warner Bros. WB 18*	**6**	18 wks
15 Dec 60	**WHY WHY BYE BYE** *Warner Bros. WB 28*	**46**	1 wk
4 May 61	**THE GREAT SNOWMAN** *Warner Bros. WB 37*	**49**	2 wks

LURKERS *UK, male vocal/instrumental group*

3 Jun 78	**AIN'T GOT A CLUE** *Beggars Banquet BEG 6*	**45**	3 wks
5 Aug 78	**I DON'T NEED TO TELL HER** *Beggars Banquet BEG 9*	**49**	4 wks
3 Feb 79	**JUST THIRTEEN** *Beggars Banquet BEG 14*	**66**	2 wks
9 Jun 79	**OUT IN THE DARK/CYANIDE** *Beggars Banquet BEG 19*	**72**	1 wk
17 Nov 79	**NEW GUITAR IN TOWN** *Beggars Banquet BEG 28*	**72**	1 wk

LUVVERS — See *LULU*

LYLE — See *GALLAGHER and LYLE*

Frankie LYMON and the TEENAGERS

US, male vocal group

29 Jun 56	★ **WHY DO FOOLS FALL IN LOVE** *Columbia DB 3772*	**1**	16 wks
29 Mar 57	**I'M NOT A JUVENILE DELINQUENT** *Columbia DB 3878*	**12**	7 wks
12 Apr 57	● **BABY BABY** *Columbia DB 3878*	**4**	12 wks
20 Sep 57	**GOODY GOODY** *Columbia DB 3983*	**24**	3 wks

First hit billed the group as 'The Teenagers Featuring Frankie Lymon'.

Kenny LYNCH *UK, male vocalist*

30 Jun 60	**MOUNTAIN OF LOVE** *HMV POP 751*	**33**	3 wks
13 Sep 62	**PUFF** *HMV POP 1057*	**33**	5 wks
25 Oct 62	**PUFF** (re-entry) *HMV POP 1057*	**46**	1 wk
6 Dec 62	● **UP ON THE ROOF** *HMV POP 1090*	**10**	12 wks
20 Jun 63	● **YOU CAN NEVER STOP ME LOVING YOU** *HMV POP 1165*	**10**	14 wks
16 Apr 64	**STAND BY ME** *HMV POP 1280*	**39**	7 wks
27 Aug 64	**WHAT AM I TO DO** *HMV POP 1321*	**37**	4 wks
1 Oct 64	**WHAT AM I TO DO** (re-entry) *HMV POP 1321*	**44**	2 wks
17 Jun 65	**I'LL STAY BY YOU** *HMV POP 1430*	**29**	7 wks

Date	Title *Label Number*	Position	

Patti LYNN *UK, female vocalist*

10 May 62	**JOHNNY ANGEL** *Fontana H 391*	**37**	5 wks

Tami LYNN *US, female vocalist*

22 May 71	● **I'M GONNA RUN AWAY FROM YOU** *Mojo 2092 001*	**4**	14 wks
3 May 75	**I'M GONNA RUN AWAY FROM YOU** (re-issue) *Contempo Raries CS 9026*	**36**	6 wks

Vera LYNN *UK, female vocalist*

14 Nov 52	● **HOMING WALTZ** *Decca F 9959*	**9**	3 wks
14 Nov 52	● **AUF WIEDERSEHEN** *Decca F 9927*	**10**	1 wk
14 Nov 52	● **FORGET ME NOT** *Decca F 9985*	**7**	1 wk
28 Nov 52	● **FORGET ME NOT** (re-entry) *Decca F 9985*	**5**	5 wks
5 Jun 53	**WINDSOR WALTZ** *Decca F 10092*	**11**	1 wk
15 Oct 54	★ **MY SON MY SON** *Decca F 10372*	**1**	14 wks
8 Jun 56	**WHO ARE WE** *Decca F 10715*	**30**	1 wk
26 Oct 56	**A HOUSE WITH LOVE IN IT** *Decca F 10799*	**17**	13 wks
15 Mar 57	**THE FAITHFUL HUSSAR (DON'T CRY MY LOVE)** *Decca F 10846*	**29**	2 wks
21 Jun 57	**TRAVELLIN' HOME** *Decca F 10903*	**20**	5 wks

Philip LYNOTT *Ireland, male vocalist*

5 Apr 80	**DEAR MISS LONELY HEARTS** *Vertigo SOLO 1*	**32**	6 wks
21 Jun 80	**KING'S CALL** *Vertigo SOLO 2*	**35**	6 wks
21 Mar 81	**YELLOW PEARL** *Vertigo SOLO 3*	**56**	3 wks
25 Dec 81	**YELLOW PEARL** (re-entry) *Vertigo SOLO 3*	**14**	9 wks

LYNYRD SKYNYRD

US, male vocal/instrumental group

11 Sep 76	**FREE BIRD** EP *MCA 251*	**31**	4 wks
22 Dec 79	**FREE BIRD** EP (re-entry) *MCA 251*	**43**	8 wks
19 Jun 82	**FREE BIRD** (EP) (2nd re-entry) *MCA 251*	**21**	9 wks

Tracks on EP: Free Bird/ Sweet Home Alabama/ Double Trouble

Barbara LYON *US, female vocalist*

24 Jun 55	**STOWAWAY** *Columbia DB 3619*	**12**	8 wks
21 Dec 56	**LETTER TO A SOLDIER** *Columbia DB 3685*	**27**	4 wks

Humphrey LYTTELTON BAND

UK, male instrumental group, Humphrey Lyttelton, trumpet

13 Jul 56	**BAD PENNY BLUES** *Parlophone R 4184*	**19**	6 wks

M

M *UK, male vocalist/multi-instrumentalist*

7 Apr 79	● **POP MUZIK** *MCA 413*	**2**	14 wks
8 Dec 79	**MOONLIGHT AND MUZAK** *MCA 541*	**33**	9 wks
15 Mar 80	**THAT'S THE WAY THE MONEY GOES** *MCA 570*	**45**	5 wks
22 Nov 80	**OFFICIAL SECRETS** *MCA 650*	**64**	2 wks

M is Robin Scott.

M and O BAND *US, male vocal/instrumental group*

28 Feb 76	**LET'S DO THE LATIN HUSTLE** *Creole CR 120*	**16**	6 wks

Lorin MAAZEL — See *PHILHARMONIA ORCHESTRA, conductor Lorin MAAZEL*

Neil MacARTHUR *UK, male vocalist*

5 Feb 69	**SHE'S NOT THERE** *Deram DM 225*	**34**	5 wks

Neil MacArthur is Colin Blunstone under a false name. See also Colin Blunstone.

David MacBETH *UK, male vocalist*

30 Oct 59	**MR. BLUE** *Pye 7N 15231*	**18**	4 wks

Frankie McBRIDE *Ireland, male vocalist*

9 Aug 67	**FIVE LITTLE FINGERS** *Emerald MD 1081*	**19**	15 wks

Dan McCAFFERTY *UK, male vocalist*

13 Sep 75	**OUT OF TIME** *Mountain TOP 1*	**41**	3 wks

C. W. McCALL *US, male vocalist*

14 Feb 76	● **CONVOY** *MGM 2006 560*	**2**	10 wks

David McCALLUM *UK, male vocalist*

14 Apr 66	**COMMUNICATION** *Capitol CL 15439*	**32**	4 wks

Linda McCARTNEY — See *Paul McCARTNEY*

Paul McCARTNEY *UK, male vocalist*

27 Feb 71	● **ANOTHER DAY** *Apple R 5889*	**2**	12 wks
28 Aug 71	**BACK SEAT OF MY CAR** *Apple R 5914*	**39**	5 wks
1 Dec 79	● **WONDERFUL CHRISTMASTIME** *Parlophone R 6029*	**6**	8 wks
19 Apr 80	● **COMING UP** *Parlophone R 6035*	**2**	9 wks
21 Jun 80	● **WATERFALLS** *Parlophone R 6037*	**9**	8 wks
3 Jul 82	**TAKE IT AWAY** *Parlophone R 6056*	**15**	10 wks
9 Oct 82	**TUG OF WAR** *Parlophone R 6057*	**53**	3 wks

See also Paul McCartney with Stevie Wonder, Michael Jackson and Paul McCartney, Wings. Back Seat Of My Car *credited to Paul and Linda McCartney.*

PAUL McCARTNEY and MICHAEL JACKSON 'The Girl Is Mine' was the first hit featuring Paul McCartney since the Beatles' 'Something' that he neither wrote nor produced
Top right **PAUL McCARTNEY** About to drop the Apple in 74

SCOTT MCKENZIE The longest title ever for a number one record

JOHN D. LOUDERMILK
Under the guise of the Rock-olas, Mike Read's version of John D Loudermilk's hit failed to trouble the scorers when released in 1982

KIRSTY MacCOLL Daughter of folk singers Ewan MacColl and Peggy Seeger

Date	Title *Label Number*	Position	

Paul McCARTNEY with Stevie WONDER *UK/US male vocal duo*

10 Apr 82	★ **EBONY AND IVORY** *Panophone R 6054*	**1**	10 wks

See also Paul McCartney Beatles, Wings, Michael Jackson and Paul McCartney. Stevie Wonder, Diana Ross Marvin Gaye Smokey Robinson and Stevie Wonder

Kirsty McCOLL *UK, female vocalist*

13 Jun 81	**THERE'S A GUY WORKS DOWN THE CHIPSHOP SWEARS HE'S ELVIS** *Polydor POSP 250*	**14**	9 wks

Marilyn McCOO and Billy DAVIS JR. *US, female/male vocal duo*

19 Mar 77	● **YOU DON'T HAVE TO BE A STAR (TO BE IN MY SHOW)** *ABC 4147*	**7**	9 wks

Van McCOY *US, orchestra*

31 May 75	● **THE HUSTLE** *Avco 6105 037*	**3**	12 wks
1 Nov 75	**CHANGE WITH THE TIMES** *Avco 6105 042*	**36**	4 wks
12 Feb 77	**SOUL CHA CHA** *H & L 6105 065*	**34**	6 wks
9 Apr 77	● **THE SHUFFLE** *H & L 6105 076*	**4**	14 wks

First hit featured the Soul City Symphony.

McCOYS *US, male vocal/instrumental group*

2 Sep 65	● **HANG ON SLOOPY** *Immediate IM 001*	**5**	13 wks
16 Dec 65	**FEVER** *Immediate IM 021*	**44**	4 wks

George McCRAE *US, male vocalist*

29 Jun 74	★ **ROCK YOUR BABY** *Jayboy BOY 85*	**1**	14 wks
5 Oct 74	● **I CAN'T LEAVE YOU ALONE** *Jayboy BOY 90*	**9**	9 wks
14 Dec 74	**YOU CAN HAVE IT ALL** *Jayboy BOY 92*	**23**	9 wks
22 Mar 75	**SING A HAPPY SONG** *Jayboy BOY 95*	**38**	4 wks
19 Jul 75	● **IT'S BEEN SO LONG** *Jayboy BOY 100*	**4**	11 wks
18 Oct 75	**I AIN'T LYIN'** *Jayboy BOY 105*	**12**	7 wks
24 Jan 76	**HONEY I** *Jayboy BOY 107*	**33**	4 wks

McCRARYS *US, male vocal/instrumental group*

31 Jul 82	**LOVE ON A SUMMER NIGHT** *Capitol CL 251*	**52**	4 wks

Gene McDANIELS *US, male vocalist*

16 Nov 61	**TOWER OF STRENGTH** *London HLG 9448*	**49**	1 wk
30 Nov 61	**TOWER OF STRENGTH** (re-entry) *London HLG 9448*	**49**	1 wk

Charles McDEVITT SKIFFLE GROUP featuring Nancy WHISKEY *UK, male/female vocal/instrumental group*

12 Apr 57	● **FREIGHT TRAIN** *Oriole CB 1352*	**5**	17 wks
14 Jun 57	**GREENBACK DOLLAR** *Oriole CB 1371*	**28**	1 wk
5 Jul 57	**GREENBACK DOLLAR** (re-entry) *Oriole CB 1371*	**30**	1 wk
20 Sep 57	**FREIGHT TRAIN** (re-entry) *Oriole CB 1352*	**27**	1 wk

McFADDEN and WHITEHEAD *US, male vocal duo*

19 May 79	● **AIN'T NO STOPPIN' US NOW** *Philadelphia International PIR 7365*	**5**	10 wks

Mike McGEAR *UK, male vocalist*

5 Oct 74	**LEAVE IT** *Warner Bros. K 16446*	**36**	4 wks

Maureen McGOVERN *US, female vocalist*

5 Jun 76	**THE CONTINENTAL** *20th Century BTC 2222*	**16**	8 wks

Mary MacGREGOR *US, female vocalist*

19 Feb 77	● **TORN BETWEEN TWO LOVERS** *Ariola America AA 111*	**4**	10 wks

McGUINNESS FLINT *UK, male vocal/instrumental group*

21 Nov 70	● **WHEN I'M DEAD AND GONE** *Capitol CL 15662*	**2**	14 wks
1 May 71	● **MALT AND BARLEY BLUES** *Capitol CL 15682*	**5**	12 wks

Barry McGUIRE *US, male vocalist*

9 Sep 65	● **EVE OF DESTRUCTION** *RCA 1469*	**3**	12 wks

McGUIRE SISTERS *US, female vocal group*

1 Apr 55	**NO MORE** *Vogue Coral Q 72050*	**20**	1 wk
15 Jul 55	**SINCERELY** *Vogue Coral Q 72050*	**14**	4 wks
1 Jun 56	**DELILAH JONES** *Vogue Coral Q 72161*	**24**	2 wks
14 Feb 58	**SUGARTIME** *Coral Q 72305*	**14**	6 wks
1 May 59	**MAY YOU ALWAYS** *Coral Q 72356*	**15**	10 wks
17 Jul 59	**MAY YOU ALWAYS** (re-entry) *Coral Q 72356*	**28**	1 wk

Peter MacJUNIOR *US, male vocalist*

15 Oct 77	**THE WATER MARGIN** *BBC RESL 50*	**37**	4 wks

This is the Japanese version of the song which shared chart credit with the English language version by Godiego. See also Godiego

Lonnie MACK *US, male instrumentalist, guitar*

14 Apr 79	**MEMPHIS** *Lightning LIG 9011*	**47**	3 wks

Memphis *was coupled with* Let's Dance *by Chris Montez as a double A-side. See also Chris Montez.*

Kenneth McKELLAR *UK, male vocalist*

10 Mar 66	**A MAN WITHOUT LOVE** *Decca F 12341*	**30**	4 wks

Date	Title *Label Number*	Position		Date	Title *Label Number*	Position	

Gisele McKENZIE *Canada, female vocalist*

17 Jul 53	**SEVEN LONELY DAYS** *Capitol CL 13920*	**12**	1 wk
31 Jul 53	**SEVEN LONELY DAYS** (re-entry) *Capitol CL 13920*	**11**	1 wk
21 Aug 53	● **SEVEN LONELY DAYS** (2nd re-entry) *Capitol CL 13920*	**6**	4 wks

Scott McKENZIE *US, male vocalist*

12 Jul 67	★ **SAN FRANCISCO (BE SURE TO WEAR FLOWERS IN YOUR HAIR)** *CBS 2816*	**1**	17 wks
1 Nov 67	**LIKE AN OLD TIME MOVIE** *CBS 3009*	**50**	1 wk

Second hit credited to The Voice Of Scott McKenzie

Ken MACKINTOSH *UK, orchestra*

15 Jan 54	**THE CREEP** *HMV BD 1295*	**12**	1 wk
29 Jan 54	● **THE CREEP** (re-entry) *HMV BD 1295*	**10**	1 wk
7 Feb 58	**RAUNCHY** *HMV POP 426*	**19**	6 wks
10 Mar 60	**NO HIDING PLACE** *HMV POP 713*	**45**	1 wk

Tommy McLAIN *US, male vocalist*

8 Sep 66	**SWEET DREAMS** *London HL 10065*	**49**	1 wk

McLAIN — See *PRATT and McLAIN with BROTHERLOVE*

Malcolm McLAREN and the WORLD'S FAMOUS SUPREME TEAM

UK, male vocalist and US/UK male/female vocal group

4 Dec 82	**BUFFALO GALS** *Charisma/Phonogram MALC 1*	**18**†	4 wks

Don McLEAN *US, male vocalist*

22 Jan 72	● **AMERICAN PIE** *United Artists UP 35325*	**2**	16 wks
13 May 72	★ **VINCENT** *United Artists UP 35359*	**1**	15 wks
14 Apr 73	**EVERYDAY** *United Artists UP 35519*	**38**	5 wks
10 May 80	★ **CRYING** *EMI 5051*	**1**	14 wks
17 Apr 82	**CASTLES IN THE AIR** *EMI 5258*	**47**	8 wks

Phil McLEAN *US, male vocalist*

18 Jan 62	**SMALL SAD SAM** *Top Rank JAR 597*	**34**	4 wks

Jackie McLEAN

US, male instrumentalist — alto sax, with male/female vocal backing group

7 Jul 79	**DR. JACKYLL AND MISTER FUNK** *RCA PB 1575*	**53**	4 wks

MACNEAL — See *MOUTH and MACNEAL*

Clyde McPHATTER *US, male vocalist*

24 Aug 56	**TREASURE OF LOVE** *London HLE 8293*	**27**	1 wk

Carmen McRAE — See *Sammy DAVIS JR. and Carmen McRAE*

Gordon MACRAE — See *VARIOUS ARTISTS (Carousel Soundtrack)*

Ralph McTELL *UK, male vocalist*

7 Dec 74	● **STREETS OF LONDON** *Reprise K 14380*	**2**	12 wks
20 Dec 75	**DREAMS OF YOU** *Warner Bros K 16648*	**36**	6 wks

MADNESS *UK, male vocal/instrumental group*

1 Sep 79	**THE PRINCE** *2-Tone TT 3*	**16**	11 wks
10 Nov 79	● **ONE STEP BEYOND** *Stiff BUY 56*	**7**	14 wks
5 Jan 80	● **MY GIRL** *Stiff BUY 62*	**3**	10 wks
5 Apr 80	● **WORK REST AND PLAY** EP *Stiff BUY 71*	**6**	8 wks
13 Sep 80	● **BAGGY TROUSERS** *Stiff BUY 84*	**3**	20 wks
22 Nov 80	● **EMBARRASSMENT** *Stiff BUY 102*	**4**	6 wks
24 Jan 81	● **THE RETURN OF THE LOS PALMAS SEVEN** *Stiff BUY 108*	**7**	11 wks
25 Apr 81	● **GREY DAY** *Stiff BUY 112*	**4**	10 wks
26 Sep 81	● **SHUT UP** *Stiff BUY 126*	**7**	9 wks
5 Dec 81	● **IT MUST BE LOVE** *Stiff BUY 134*	**4**	12 wks
20 Feb 82	**CARDIAC ARREST** *Stiff BUY 140*	**14**	10 wks
22 May 82	★ **HOUSE OF FUN** *Stiff BUY 146*	**1**	9 wks
24 Jul 82	● **DRIVING IN MY CAR** *Stiff BUY 153*	**4**	8 wks
27 Nov 82	● **OUR HOUSE** *Stiff BUY 163*	**5**†	5 wks

Tracks on Work Rest and Play EP: *Night Boat to Cairo/Deceives The Eye/The Young And The Old/Don't Quote Me On That*

MAGAZINE *UK, male vocal/instrumental group*

11 Feb 78	**SHOT BY BOTH SIDES** *Virgin VS 200*	**41**	4 wks
26 Jul 80	**SWEET HEART CONTRACT** *Virgin VS 368*	**54**	3 wks

MAGIC LANTERNS

UK, male vocal/instrumental group

7 Jul 66	**EXCUSE ME BABY** *CBS 202094*	**46**	1 wk
28 Jul 66	**EXCUSE ME BABY** (re-entry) *CBS 202094*	**44**	1 wk
11 Aug 66	**EXCUSE ME BABY** (2nd re-entry) *CBS 202094*	**46**	1 wk

MAGNUM *UK, male vocal/instrumental group*

22 Mar 80	**MAGNUM** (DOUBLE SINGLE) *Jet 175*	**47**	6 wks

Tracks on double single: Invasion/ Kingdom of Madness/ All of My Life/ Great Adventure.

MAIN INGREDIENT *US, male vocal group*

29 Jun 74	**JUST DON'T WANT TO BE LONELY** *RCA APBO 0205*	**27**	7 wks

MAISONETTES *UK, male/female vocal group*

11 Dec 82	**HEARTACHE AVENUE** *Ready Steady Go! RSG 1*	**39**†	3 wks

MAKADOPULOS and his GREEK SERENADERS

Greece, male vocal/instrumental group

20 Oct 60	**NEVER ON SUNDAY** *Palette PG 9005*	**36**	14 wks

Date	Title *Label Number*	Position	

Carl MALCOLM *Jamaica, male vocalist*

13 Sep 75	● **FATTIE BUM BUM** *UK 108*	**8**	8 wks

MAMAS and the PAPAS

US, female/male vocal group

28 Apr 66	**CALIFORNIA DREAMIN'** *RCA 1503*	**23**	9 wks
12 May 66	● **MONDAY MONDAY** *RCA 1516*	**3**	13 wks
28 Jul 66	**I SAW HER AGAIN** *RCA 1533*	**11**	11 wks
9 Feb 67	**WORDS OF LOVE** *RCA 1564*	**47**	3 wks
6 Apr 67	● **DEDICATED TO THE ONE I LOVE** *RCA 1576*	**2**	17 wks
26 Jul 67	● **CREEQUE ALLEY** *RCA 1613*	**9**	11 wks

MANCHESTER UNITED FOOTBALL CLUB *UK, male football team vocalists*

8 May 76	**MANCHESTER UNITED** *Decca F 13633*	**50**	1 wk

Henry MANCINI *US, orchestra/chorus*

7 Dec 61	**MOON RIVER** *RCA 1256*	**46**	2 wks
28 Dec 61	**MOON RIVER** (re-entry) *RCA 1256*	**44**	1 wk
24 Sep 64	● **HOW SOON** *RCA 1414*	**10**	12 wks
25 Mar 72	**THEME FROM CADE'S COUNTY** *RCA 2182*	**42**	1 wk

Steve MANDELL — See *DELIVERANCE SOUNDTRACK*

MANFRED MANN

South Africa/UK, male vocal/instrumental group

23 Jan 64	● **5-4-3-2-1** *HMV POP 1252*	**5**	13 wks
16 Apr 64	**HUBBLE BUBBLE TOIL AND TROUBLE** *HMV POP 1282*	**11**	8 wks
16 Jul 64	★ **DO WAH DIDDY DIDDY** *HMV POP 1320*	**1**	14 wks
15 Oct 64	● **SHA LA LA** *HMV POP 1346*	**3**	12 wks
14 Jan 65	● **COME TOMORROW** *HMV POP 1381*	**4**	9 wks
15 Apr 65	**OH NO NOT MY BABY** *HMV POP 1413*	**11**	10 wks
16 Sep 65	● **IF YOU GOTTA GO GO NOW** *HMV POP 1466*	**2**	12 wks
21 Apr 66	★ **PRETTY FLAMINGO** *HMV POP 1523*	**1**	12 wks
7 Jul 66	**YOU GAVE ME SOMEBODY TO LOVE** *HMV POP 1541*	**36**	4 wks
4 Aug 66	● **JUST LIKE A WOMAN** *Fontana TF 730*	**10**	10 wks
27 Oct 66	● **SEMI-DETACHED SUBURBAN MR. JAMES** *Fontana TF 757*	**2**	12 wks
30 Mar 67	● **HA HA SAID THE CLOWN** *Fontana TF 812*	**4**	11 wks
25 May 67	**SWEET PEA** *Fontana TF 828*	**36**	4 wks
24 Jan 68	★ **MIGHTY QUINN** *Fontana TF 897*	**1**	11 wks
12 Jun 68	● **MY NAME IS JACK** *Fontana TF 943*	**8**	11 wks
18 Dec 68	● **FOX ON THE RUN** *Fontana TF 985*	**5**	12 wks
30 May 69	● **RAGAMUFFIN MAN** *Fontana TF 1013*	**8**	11 wks

The HMV hits featured Paul Jones as lead vocalist and the Fontana hits Mike d'Abo, except for Sweet Pea, *an instrumental disc. See also Paul Jones.*

MANHATTAN TRANSFER

US, male/female vocal group

7 Feb 76	**TUXEDO JUNCTION** *Atlantic K 10670*	**24**	6 wks
5 Feb 77	★ **CHANSON D'AMOUR** *Atlantic K 10886*	**1**	13 wks
28 May 77	**DON'T LET GO** *Atlantic K 10930*	**32**	6 wks
18 Feb 78	**WALK IN LOVE** *Atlantic K 11075*	**48**	1 wk
4 Mar 78	**WALK IN LOVE** (re-entry) *Atlantic K 11075*	**12**	11 wks
20 May 78	**ON A LITTLE STREET IN SINGAPORE** *Atlantic K 11136*	**20**	9 wks
16 Sep 78	**WHERE DID OUR LOVE GO/JE VOULAIS TE DIRE (QUE JE T'ATTENDS)** *Atlantic K 11182*	**40**	4 wks
23 Dec 78	**WHO WHAT WHEN WHERE WHY** *Atlantic K 11233*	**49**	6 wks
17 May 80	**TWILIGHT ZONE-TWILIGHT TONE** (MEDLEY) *Atlantic K 11476*	**25**	8 wks

MANHATTANS *US, male vocal group*

19 Jun 76	● **KISS AND SAY GOODBYE** *CBS 4317*	**4**	11 wks
2 Oct 76	● **HURT** *CBS 4562*	**4**	11 wks
23 Apr 77	**IT'S YOU** *CBS 5093*	**43**	3 wks
26 Jul 80	**SHINING STAR** *CBS 8624*	**45**	4 wks

Barry MANILOW *US, male vocalist*

22 Feb 75	**MANDY** *Arista 1*	**11**	9 wks
6 May 78	**CAN'T SMILE WITHOUT YOU** *Arista 176*	**43**	7 wks
29 Jul 78	**SOMEWHERE IN THE NIGHT/COPACABANA (AT THE COPA)** *Arista 196*	**42**	10 wks
23 Dec 78	**COULD IT BE MAGIC** *Arista ARIST 229*	**25**	10 wks
8 Nov 80	**LONELY TOGETHER** *Arista ARIST 373*	**21**	wks
7 Feb 81	**I MADE IT THROUGH THE RAIN** *Arista ARIST 384*	**37**	6 wks
11 Apr 81	**BERMUDA TRIANGLE** *Arista ARIST 406*	**15**	9 wks
26 Sep 81	**LET'S HANG ON** *Arista ARIST 429*	**12**	11 wks
12 Dec 81	**THE OLD SONGS** *Arista ARIST 443*	**48**	8 wks
20 Feb 82	**IF I SHOULD LOVE AGAIN** *Arista ARIST 453*	**66**	2 wks
17 Apr 82	**STAY (LIVE)** *Arista ARIST 464*	**23**	8 wks
16 Oct 82	● **I WANNA DO IT WITH YOU** *Arista ARIST 495*	**8**	8 wks
4 Dec 82	**I'M GONNA SIT RIGHT DOWN AND WRITE MYSELF A LETTER** *Arista ARIST 503*	**36**†	4 wks

MANKIND *UK, male instrumental group*

25 Nov 78	**DR. WHO** *Pinnacle PIN 71*	**25**	12 wks

Johnny MANN SINGERS

US, male/female vocal group

12 Jul 67	● **UP, UP AND AWAY** *Liberty LIB 55972*	**6**	13 wks

Manfred MANN'S EARTH BAND

South Africa/UK, male vocal/instrumental group

8 Sep 73	● **JOYBRINGER** *Vertigo 6059 083*	**9**	10 wks
28 Aug 76	● **BLINDED BY THE LIGHT** *Bronze BRO 29*	**6**	10 wks
20 May 78	● **DAVY'S ON THE ROAD AGAIN** *Bronze BRO 52*	**6**	12 wks
17 Mar 79	**YOU ANGEL YOU** *Bronze BRO 68*	**54**	5 wks
7 Jul 79	**DON'T KILL IT CAROL** *Bronze Bro 77*	**45**	4 wks

See also Manfred Mann

MANTOVANI *UK, orchestra*

19 Dec 52	● **WHITE CHRISTMAS** *Decca F 10017*	**6**	3 wks
29 May 53	★ **MOULIN ROUGE** *Decca F 10094*	**1**	21 wks
23 Oct 53	● **SWEDISH RHAPSODY** *Decca F 10168*	**2**	17 wks
13 Nov 53	● **MOULIN ROUGE** (re-entry) *Decca F 10094*	**10**	1 wk
4 Dec 53	**MOULIN ROUGE** (2nd re-entry) *Decca F 10094*	**12**	1 wk
26 Feb 54	**SWEDISH RHAPSODY** (re-entry) *Decca F 10168*	**12**	1 wk

Above **MARVELETTES** Great favourites of the Beatles in their formative years

Right **CLYDE McPHATTER** The great lead voice of the early Drifters recordings also gave its owner a reasonably rewarding solo career (mainly in the US) in the late fifties and early sixties, but all came to a sad end with his death in 1962

Above **HENRY MANCINI** Henry whose 'Peter Gunn' album was the first ever million seller of a TV soundtrack swaps ideas with Paul McCartney
Right **WINK MARTINDALE** He played solo until 1973 when Max Bygraves cribbed his snappy deck of cards and whisted no time in having a hit with it; mind you the song did shuffle in and out of the chart a good deal
Far right **MAGIC LANTERNS** After three attempts finally excused themselves in August 1966

Date	Title *Label Number*	Position	
11 Feb 55	**LONELY BALLERINA** *Decca F 10395*	**16**	3 wks
18 Mar 55	**LONELY BALLERINA** (re-entry) *Decca F 10395*	**18**	1 wk
31 May 57	**AROUND THE WORLD** *Decca F 10888*	**20**	4 wks

MANUEL and his MUSIC OF THE MOUNTAINS *UK, orchestra, leader Geoff Love*

28 Aug 59	**THEME FROM HONEYMOON** *Columbia DB 4323*	**29**	2 wks
25 Sep 59	**THEME FROM HONEYMOON** (re-entry) *Columbia DB 4323*	**22**	5 wks
6 Nov 59	**THEME FROM HONEYMOON** (2nd re-entry) *Columbia DB 4323*	**27**	2 wks
13 Oct 60	**NEVER ON SUNDAY** *Columbia DB 4515*	**29**	10 wks
13 Oct 66	**SOMEWHERE MY LOVE** *Columbia DB 7969*	**42**	2 wks
31 Jan 76 ●	**RODRIGO'S GUITAR CONCERTO DE ARANJUEZ (THEME FROM 2ND MOVEMENT)** *EMI 2383*	**3**	10 wks

MARAUDERS *UK, male vocal/instrumental group*

8 Aug 63	**THAT'S WANT I WANT** *Decca F 11695*	**48**	1 wk
22 Aug 63	**THAT'S WHAT I WANT** (re-entry) *Decca F 11695*	**43**	3 wks

MARBLES *UK, male vocal duo*

25 Sep 68 ●	**ONLY ONE WOMAN** *Polydor 56 272*	**5**	12 wks
26 Mar 69	**THE WALLS FELL DOWN** *Polydor 56 310*	**28**	6 wks

MARCELS *US, male vocal group*

13 Apr 61 ★	**BLUE MOON** *Pye International 7N 25073*	**1**	13 wks
8 Jun 61	**SUMMERTIME** *Pye International 7N 25083*	**46**	4 wks

Little Peggy MARCH *US, female vocalist*

12 Sep 63	**HELLO HEARTACHE GOODBYE LOVE** *RCA 1362*	**29**	7 wks

MARCIA — See *BOB and MARCIA*

MARDI GRAS *UK, male vocal/instrumental group*

5 Aug 72	**TOO BUSY THINKING 'BOUT MY BABY** *Bell 1226*	**19**	9 wks

Kelly MARIE *UK, female vocalist*

2 Aug 80 ★	**FEELS LIKE I'M IN LOVE** *Calibre PLUS 1*	**1**	16 wks
18 Oct 80	**LOVING JUST FOR FUN** *Calibre PLUS 4*	**21**	7 wks
7 Feb 81	**HOT LOVE** *Calibre PLUS 5*	**22**	10 wks
30 May 81	**TRIAL** *Calibre PLUS 7*	**51**	3 wks

Teena MARIE *US, female vocalist*

7 Jul 79	**I'M A SUCKER FOR YOUR LOVE** *Motown TMG 1146*	**43**	8 wks
31 May 80 ●	**BEHIND THE GROOVE** *Motown TMG 1185*	**6**	10 wks
11 Oct 80	**I NEED YOUR LOVIN'** *Motown TMG 1203*	**28**	6 wks

First hit has credit "Co-lead vocals: Rick James". See also Rick James.

MARILLION *UK, male vocal/instrumental group*

20 Nov 82	**MARKET SQUARE HEROES** *EMI 5351*	**60**	2 wks

Marino MARINI *Italy, male vocalist*

3 Oct 58	**VOLARE** *Durium DC 16632*	**13**	7 wks
10 Oct 58 ●	**COME PRIMA** *Durium DC 16632*	**2**	14 wks
20 Mar 59	**CIAO CIAO BAMBINA** *Durium DC 16636*	**25**	1 wk
3 Apr 59	**CIAO CIAO BAMBINA** (re-entry) *Durium DC 16636*	**24**	1 wk

Pigmeat MARKHAM *US, male vocalist*

17 Jul 68	**HERE COMES THE JUDGE** *Chess CRS 8077*	**19**	8 wks

Yannis MARKOPOULOS *Greece, orchestra*

17 Dec 77	**WHO PAYS THE FERRYMAN** *BBC RESL 51*	**11**	8 wks

Guy MARKS *Australia, male vocalist*

13 May 78	**LOVING YOU HAS MADE ME BANANAS** *ABC 4211*	**25**	8 wks

Bob MARLEY and the WAILERS *Jamaica, male vocal/instrumental group*

27 Sep 75	**NO WOMAN NO CRY** *Island WIP 6244*	**22**	7 wks
25 Jun 77	**EXODUS** *Island WIP 6390*	**14**	9 wks
10 Sep 77	**WAITING IN VAIN** *Island WIP 6402*	**27**	6 wks
10 Dec 77 ●	**JAMMING/PUNKY REGGAE PARTY** *Island WIP 6410*	**9**	12 wks
25 Feb 78 ●	**IS THIS LOVE** *Island WIP 6420*	**9**	9 wks
10 Jun 78	**SATISFY MY SOUL** *Island WIP 6440*	**21**	10 wks
20 Oct 79	**SO MUCH TROUBLE IN THE WORLD** *Island WIP 6510*	**56**	4 wks
21 Jun 80 ●	**COULD YOU BE LOVED** *Island WIP 6610*	**5**	12 wks
13 Sep 80	**THREE LITTLE BIRDS** *Island WIP 6641*	**17**	9 wks
13 Jun 81 ●	**NO WOMAN, NO CRY** (re-entry) *Island WIP 6244*	**8**	11 wks

MARMALADE *UK, male vocal group*

22 May 68 ●	**LOVIN' THINGS** *CBS 3412*	**6**	13 wks
23 Oct 68	**WAIT FOR ME MARIANNE** *CBS 3708*	**30**	5 wks
4 Dec 68 ★	**OB-LA-DI OB-LA-DA** *CBS 3892*	**1**	20 wks
11 Jun 69 ●	**BABY MAKE IT SOON** *CBS 4287*	**9**	13 wks
20 Dec 69 ●	**REFLECTIONS OF MY LIFE** *Decca F 12982*	**3**	12 wks
18 Jul 70 ●	**RAINBOW** *Decca F 13035*	**3**	14 wks
27 Mar 71	**MY LITTLE ONE** *Decca F 13135*	**15**	11 wks
4 Sep 71 ●	**COUSIN NORMAN** *Decca F 13214*	**6**	11 wks
27 Nov 71	**BACK ON THE ROAD** *Decca F 13251*	**35**	7 wks
22 Jan 72	**BACK ON THE ROAD** (re-entry) *Decca F 13251*	**50**	1 wk
1 Apr 72 ●	**RADANCER** *Decca F 13297*	**6**	12 wks
21 Feb 76 ●	**FALLING APART AT THE SEAMS** *Target TGT 105*	**9**	11 wks

Stevie MARSH *UK, female vocalist*

4 Dec 59	**THE ONLY BOY IN THE WORLD** *Decca F 11181*	**29**	2 wks
25 Dec 59	**THE ONLY BOY IN THE WORLD** (re-entry) *Decca F 11181*	**24**	2 wks

Date	Title *Label Number*	Position	

Joy MARSHALL *UK, female vocalist*

Date	Title *Label Number*	Position	
23 Jun 66	**THE MORE I SEE YOU** *Decca F 12422*	**34**	2 wks

Keith MARSHALL *UK, male vocalist*

Date	Title *Label Number*	Position	
4 Apr 81	**ONLY CRYING** *Arrival PIK 2*	**12**	10 wks

MARSHALL HAIN

UK, male/female vocal/instrumental duo

Date	Title *Label Number*	Position	
3 Jun 78	● **DANCING IN THE CITY** *Harvest HAR 5157*	**3**	15 wks
14 Oct 78	**COMING HOME** *Harvest HAR 5168*	**39**	4 wks

Lena MARTELL *UK, female vocalist*

Date	Title *Label Number*	Position	
29 Sep 79	★ **ONE DAY AT A TIME** *Pye 7N 46021*	**1**	18 wks

MARTHA and the MUFFINS

Canada, male/female vocal/instrumental group

Date	Title *Label Number*	Position	
1 Mar 80	● **ECHO BEACH** *Dindisc DIN 9*	**10**	10 wks

Dean MARTIN *US, male vocalist*

Date	Title *Label Number*	Position	
18 Sep 53	● **KISS** *Capitol CL 13893*	**9**	1 wk
2 Oct 53	● **KISS** (re-entry) *Capitol CL 13893*	**5**	7 wks
22 Jan 54	● **THAT'S AMORE** *Capitol CL 14008*	**2**	11 wks
1 Oct 54	● **SWAY** *Capitol CL 14138*	**6**	7 wks
22 Oct 54	**HOW DO YOU SPEAK TO AN ANGEL** *Capitol CL 14150*	**15**	2 wks
19 Nov 54	**HOW DO YOU SPEAK TO AN ANGEL** (re-entry) *Capitol CL 14150*	**17**	4 wks
28 Jan 55	● **NAUGHTY LADY OF SHADY LANE** *Capitol CL 14226*	**5**	10 wks
4 Feb 55	**MAMBO ITALIANO** *Capitol CL 14227*	**14**	2 wks
25 Feb 55	● **LET ME GO LOVER** *Capitol CL 14226*	**3**	9 wks
1 Apr 55	● **UNDER THE BRIDGES OF PARIS** *Capitol CL 14255*	**6**	8 wks
10 Feb 56	★ **MEMORIES ARE MADE OF THIS** *Capitol CL 14523*	**1**	16 wks
2 Mar 56	**YOUNG AND FOOLISH** *Capitol CL 14519*	**20**	1 wk
27 Apr 56	**INNAMORATA** *Capitol CL 14507*	**21**	3 wks
22 Mar 57	**THE MAN WHO PLAYS THE MANDOLINO** *Capitol CL 14690*	**21**	2 wks
13 Jun 58	● **RETURN TO ME** *Capitol CL 14844*	**2**	22 wks
29 Aug 58	● **VOLARE** *Capitol CL 14910*	**2**	14 wks
27 Aug 64	**EVERYBODY LOVES SOMEBODY** *Reprise R 20281*	**11**	13 wks
12 Nov 64	**THE DOOR IS STILL OPEN TO MY HEART** *Reprise R 20307*	**42**	4 wks
5 Feb 69	● **GENTLE ON MY MIND** *Reprise RS 23343*	**2**	23 wks
30 Aug 69	**GENTLE ON MY MIND** (re-entry) *Reprise RS 23343*	**49**	1 wk

Ray MARTIN *UK, orchestra*

Date	Title *Label Number*	Position	
14 Nov 52	● **BLUE TANGO** *Columbia DB 3051*	**8**	1 wk
28 Nov 52	● **BLUE TANGO** (re-entry) *Columbia DB 3051*	**10**	3 wks
4 Dec 53	● **SWEDISH RHAPSODY** *Columbia DB 3346*	**10**	1 wk
18 Dec 53	● **SWEDISH RHAPSODY** (re-entry) *Columbia DB 3346*	**4**	3 wks
15 Jun 56	**CAROUSEL WALTZ** *Columbia DB 3771*	**28**	1 wk
3 Aug 56	**CAROUSEL WALTZ** (re-entry) *Columbia DB 3771*	**24**	2 wks

Tony MARTIN *US, male vocalist*

Date	Title *Label Number*	Position	
22 Apr 55	● **STRANGER IN PARADISE** *HMV B 10849*	**6**	13 wks
13 Jul 56	● **WALK HAND IN HAND** *HMV POP 222*	**2**	15 wks

Vince MARTIN *US, male vocalist*

Date	Title *Label Number*	Position	
14 Dec 56	**CINDY OH CINDY** *London HLN 8340*	**26**	1 wk

Wink MARTINDALE *US, male vocalist*

Date	Title *Label Number*	Position	
4 Dec 59	**DECK OF CARDS** *London HLD 8962*	**18**	5 wks
15 Jan 60	**DECK OF CARDS** (re-entry) *London HLD 8962*	**28**	2 wks
31 Mar 60	**DECK OF CARDS** (2nd re-entry) *London HLD 8962*	**45**	1 wk
18 Apr 63	● **DECK OF CARDS** (3rd re-entry) *London HLD 8962*	**5**	21 wks
20 Oct 73	**DECK OF CARDS** (re-issue) *Dot DOT 109*	**22**	12 wks

Al MARTINO *US, male vocalist*

Date	Title *Label Number*	Position	
14 Nov 52	★ **HERE IN MY HEART** *Capitol CL 13779*	**1**	18 wks
21 Nov 52	● **TAKE MY HEART** *Capitol CL 13769*	**9**	1 wk
30 Jan 53	● **NOW** *Capitol CL 13835*	**3**	12 wks
10 Jul 53	● **RACHEL** *Capitol CL 13879*	**10**	4 wks
11 Sep 53	**RACHEL** (re-entry) *Capitol CL 13879*	**12**	1 wk
4 Jun 54	**WANTED** *Capitol CL 14128*	**12**	1 wk
18 Jun 54	● **WANTED** (re-entry) *Capitol CL 14128*	**4**	14 wks
1 Oct 54	**WANTED** (2nd re-entry) *Capitol CL 14128*	**17**	1 wk
1 Oct 54	● **THE STORY OF TINA** *Capitol CL 14163*	**10**	8 wks
23 Sep 55	**THE MAN FROM LARAMIE** *Capitol CL 14347*	**19**	2 wks
28 Oct 55	**THE MAN FROM LARAMIE** (re-entry) *Capitol CL 14347*	**20**	1 wk
31 Mar 60	**SUMMERTIME** *Top Rank JAR 312*	**49**	1 wk
29 Aug 63	**I LOVE YOU BECAUSE** *Capitol CL 15300*	**48**	1 wk
22 Aug 70	**SPANISH EYES** *Capitol CL 15430*	**49**	1 wk
14 Jul 73	● **SPANISH EYES** (re-entry) *Capitol CL 15430*	**5**	21 wks

MARVELETTES *US, female vocal group*

Date	Title *Label Number*	Position	
15 Jun 67	**WHEN YOU'RE YOUNG AND IN LOVE** *Tamla Motown TMG 609*	**13**	10 wks

MARVIN *UK, Robot*

Date	Title *Label Number*	Position	
16 May 81	**MARVIN THE PARANOID ANDROID** *Polydor POSP 261*	**53**	4 wks

Hank MARVIN

UK, male vocalist/instrumentalist-guitar

Date	Title *Label Number*	Position	
6 Mar 82	**DONT TALK** *Polydor POSP 420*	**49**	4 wks

See also Cliff Richard

Lee MARVIN *US, male vocalist*

Date	Title *Label Number*	Position	
7 Feb 70	★ **WAND'RIN' STAR** *Paramount PARA 3004*	**1**	18 wks
20 Jun 70	**WAND'RIN' STAR** (re-entry) *Paramount PARA 3004*	**42**	3 wks
15 Aug 70	**WAND'RIN' STAR** (2nd re-entry) *Paramount PARA 3004*	**47**	2 wks

I Talk To The Trees, *by Clint Eastwood, the flip side of* Wand'rin' Star, *was listed with* Wand'rin' Star *for 7 Feb and 14 Feb 70 only. See also Clint Eastwood.*

MARY — See *PETER, PAUL and MARY*

Date	Title *Label Number*	Position	

Carolyne MAS *US, female vocalist*

2 Feb 80	**QUOTE GOODBYE QUOTE** *Mercury 6167 873*	**71**	2 wks

MASH *US, male vocal/instrumental group*

10 May 80 ★	**THEME FROM M*A*S*H* (SUICIDE IS PAINLESS)** *CBS 8536*	**1**	12 wks

Glen MASON *UK, male vocalist*

28 Sep 56	**GLENDORA** *Parlophone R 4203*	**28**	2 wks
16 Nov 56	**GREEN DOOR** *Parlophone R 4244*	**24**	5 wks

Mary MASON *UK, female vocalist*

8 Oct 77	**ANGEL OF THE MORNING - ANY WAY THAT YOU WANT ME** (MEDLEY) *Epic EPC 5552*	**27**	6 wks

MASS PRODUCTION

US, male vocal and instrumental group

12 Mar 77	**WELCOME TO OUR WORLD (OF MERRY MUSIC)** *Atlantic K 10898*	**44**	3 wks
17 May 80	**SHANTE** *Atlantic/Cotillion K 11475*	**59**	4 wks

MASSIEL *Spain, female vocalist*

24 Apr 68	**LA LA LA** *Philips BF 1667*	**35**	4 wks

MASTER SINGERS *UK, male vocal group*

14 Apr 66	**HIGHWAY CODE** *Parlophone R 5428*	**25**	6 wks
17 Nov 66	**WEATHER FORECAST** *Parlophone R 5523*	**50**	1 wk

Sammy MASTERS *US, male vocalist*

9 Jun 60	**ROCKIN' RED WING** *Warner Bros. WB 10*	**36**	5 wks

MATCH *UK, male vocal/instrumental group*

16 Jun 79	**BOOGIE MAN** *Flamingo FM 2*	**48**	3 wks

MATCHBOX *UK, male vocal/instrumental group*

3 Nov 79	**ROCKABILLY REBEL** *Magnet MAG 155*	**18**	12 wks
19 Jan 80	**BUZZ BUZZ A DIDDLE IT** *Magnet MAG 157*	**22**	8 wks
10 May 80	**MIDNITE DYNAMOS** *Magnet MAG 169*	**14**	12 wks
27 Sep 80 ●	**WHEN YOU ASK ABOUT LOVE** *Magnet MAG 191*	**4**	12 wks
29 Nov 80	**OVER THE RAINBOW - YOU BELONG TO ME** (MEDLEY) *Magnet MAG 192*	**15**	11 wks
4 Apr 81	**BABES IN THE WOOD** *Magnet MAG 193*	**46**	6 wks
1 Aug 81	**LOVE'S MADE A FOOL OF YOU** *Magnet MAG 194*	**63**	3 wks
29 May 82	**ONE MORE SATURDAY NIGHT** *Magnet MAG 223*	**63**	2 wks

Mireille MATHIEU *France, female vocalist*

13 Dec 67	**LA DERNIERE VALSE** *Columbia DB 8323*	**26**	7 wks

Johnny MATHIS *US, male vocalist*

23 May 58	**TEACHER TEACHER** *Fontana H 130*	**27**	5 wks
26 Sep 58 ●	**A CERTAIN SMILE** *Fontana H 142*	**4**	16 wks
19 Dec 58	**WINTER WONDERLAND** *Fontana H 165*	**17**	3 wks
7 Aug 59 ●	**SOMEONE** *Fontana H 199*	**6**	15 wks
27 Nov 59	**THE BEST OF EVERYTHING** *Fontana H 218*	**30**	1 wk
29 Jan 60	**MISTY** *Fontana H 219*	**12**	13 wks
24 Mar 60	**YOU ARE BEAUTIFUL** *Fontana H 234*	**38**	8 wks
26 May 60	**YOU ARE BEAUTIFUL** (re-entry) *Fontana H 234*	**46**	1 wk
28 Jul 60	**STARBRIGHT** *Fontana H 254*	**47**	2 wks
6 Oct 60 ●	**MY LOVE FOR YOU** *Fontana H 267*	**9**	18 wks
4 Apr 63	**WHAT WILL MY MARY SAY** *CBS AAG 127*	**49**	1 wk
25 Jan 75 ●	**I'M STONE IN LOVE WITH YOU** *CBS 2653*	**10**	12 wks
13 Nov 76 ★	**WHEN A CHILD IS BORN (SOLEADO)** *CBS 4599*	**1**	12 wks
11 Aug 79	**GONE GONE GONE** *CBS 7730*	**15**	10 wks

See also Johnny Mathis and Deniece Williams, Johnny Mathis and Gladys Knight.

Johnny MATHIS and Gladys KNIGHT

US, male/female vocal duo

26 Dec 81	**WHEN A CHILD IS BORN** *CBS S 1758*	**74**	1 wk

See also Johnny Mathis, Gladys Knight and the Pips, Johnny Mathis and Deniece Williams.

Johnny MATHIS and Deniece WILLIAMS *US, male/female vocal duo*

25 Mar 78 ●	**TOO MUCH TOO LITTLE TOO LATE** *CBS 6164*	**3**	14 wks
29 Jul 78	**YOU'RE ALL I NEED TO GET BY** *CBS 6483*	**45**	6 wks

See also Johnny Mathis, Deniece Williams, Johnny Mathis and Gladys Knight.

Al MATTHEWS *US, male vocalist*

23 Aug 75	**FOOL** *CBS 3429*	**16**	8 wks

MATTHEWS SOUTHERN COMFORT

UK, male vocal/instrumental group

26 Sep 70 ★	**WOODSTOCK** *Uni UNS 526*	**1**	18 wks

MATUMBI *UK, male vocal/instrumental group*

29 Sep 79	**POINT OF VIEW** *Matumbi RIC 101*	**35**	7 wks

Susan MAUGHAN *UK, female vocalist*

11 Oct 62 ●	**BOBBY'S GIRL** *Philips 326544 BF*	**3**	19 wks
14 Feb 63	**HAND A HANDKERCHIEF TO HELEN** *Philips 326562 BF*	**41**	3 wks
9 May 63	**SHE'S NEW TO YOU** *Philips 326586 BF*	**45**	3 wks

MAUREEN — See *VERNONS GIRLS*

Paul MAURIAT *France, orchestra*

21 Feb 68	**LOVE IS BLUE (L'AMOUR EST BLEU)** *Philips BF 1637*	**12**	14 wks

Date	Title *Label Number*	Position	

Billy MAY *US, orchestra*

27 Apr 56	● **MAIN TITLE THEME FROM MAN WITH THE GOLDEN ARM** *Capitol CL 14551*	**9**	10 wks

Mary MAY *UK, female vocalist*

27 Feb 64	**ANYONE WHO HAD A HEART** *Fontana TF 440*	**49**	1 wk

Simon MAY *UK, male vocalist*

9 Oct 76	● **SUMMER OF MY LIFE** *Pye 7N 45627*	**7**	8 wks
21 May 77	**WE'LL GATHER LILACS-ALL MY LOVING** (MEDLEY) *Pye 7n 45688*	**49**	1 wk
4 Jun 77	**WE'LL GATHER LILACS-ALL MY LOVING** (MEDLEY) (re-entry) *Pye 7n 45688*	**50**	1 wk

Curtis MAYFIELD *US, male vocalist*

31 Jul 71	**MOVE ON UP** *Buddah 2011 080*	**12**	10 wks
2 Dec 78	**NO GOODBYES** *Atlantic LV 1*	**65**	3 wks

MAYTALS *Jamaica, male vocal/instrumental group*

25 Apr 70	**MONKEY MAN** *Trojan TR 7711*	**50**	1 wk
9 May 70	**MONKEY MAN** (re-entry) *Trojan TR 7711*	**47**	3 wks

ME AND YOU *Jamaica/UK, male/female vocal duo*

28 Jul 79	**YOU NEVER KNOW WHAT YOU'VE GOT** *Laser LAS 8*	**31**	9 wks

Has credit: featuring ***We The People Band.***

MEAT LOAF *US, male vocalist*

20 May 78	**YOU TOOK THE WORDS RIGHT OUT OF MY MOUTH** *Epic EPC 5980*	**33**	8 wks
19 Aug 78	**TWO OUT OF THREE AIN'T BAD** *Epic EPC 6281*	**32**	8 wks
10 Feb 79	**BAT OUT OF HELL** *Epic EPC 7018*	**15**	7 wks
26 Sep 81	**I'M GONNA LOVE HER FOR BOTH OF US** *Epic EPCA 1580*	**62**	3 wks
28 Nov 81	● **DEAD RINGER FOR LOVE** *Epic EPCA 1697*	**5**	17 wks

Dead Ringer For Love *features Cher as uncredited co-vocalist. See Cher, Sonny and Cher.*

MECO *US, Orchestra*

1 Oct 77	● **STAR WARS THEME-CANTINA BAND** *RCA XB 1028*	**7**	9 wks

MEDICINE HEAD

UK, male vocal/instrumental duo

26 Jun 71	**(AND THE) PICTURES IN THE SKY** *Dandelion DAN 7003*	**22**	8 wks
5 May 73	● **ONE AND ONE IS ONE** *Polydor 2001 432*	**3**	13 wks
4 Aug 73	**RISING SUN** *Polydor 2058 389*	**11**	9 wks
9 Feb 74	**SLIP AND SLIDE** *Polydor 2058 436*	**22**	7 wks

MEDICINE SHOW — See *DR. HOOK*

Michael MEDWIN, Bernard BRESSLAW, Alfie BASS and Leslie FYSON *UK, male vocal group*

30 May 58	● **THE SIGNATURE TUNE OF THE ARMY GAME** *HMV POP 490*	**5**	9 wks

See also Bernard Bresslaw.

Tony MEEHAN COMBO

UK, male instrumentalist, drums

16 Jan 64	**SONG OF MEXICO** *Decca F 11801*	**39**	4 wks

See also Jet Harris and Tony Meehan.

MELACHRINO ORCHESTRA

UK, orchestra, conductor George Melachrino

12 Oct 56	**AUTUMN CONCERTO** *HMV B 10958*	**18**	9 wks

MELANIE *US, female vocalist*

26 Sep 70	● **RUBY TUESDAY** *Buddah 2011 038*	**9**	14 wks
9 Jan 71	**RUBY TUESDAY** (re-entry) *Buddah 2011 038*	**43**	1 wk
16 Jan 71	**WHAT HAVE THEY DONE TO MY SONG MA** *Buddah 2011 038*	**39**	1 wk
1 Jan 72	● **BRAND NEW KEY** *Buddah 2011 105*	**4**	12 wks
16 Feb 74	**WILL YOU LOVE ME TOMORROW** *Neighbourhood NBH 9*	**37**	5 wks

MELODIANS

Jamaica, male vocal/instrumental group

10 Jan 70	**SWEET SENSATION** *Trojan TR 695*	**41**	1 wk

Harold MELVIN and the BLUENOTES

US, male vocal group

13 Jan 73	● **IF YOU DON'T KNOW ME BY NOW** *CBS 8496*	**9**	9 wks
12 Jan 74	**THE LOVE I LOST** *Philadelphia International PIR 1879*	**21**	8 wks
13 Apr 74	**SATISFACTION GUARANTEED (OR TAKE YOUR LOVE BACK)** *Philadelphia International PIR 2187*	**32**	6 wks
31 May 75	**GET OUT** *Route RT 06*	**35**	5 wks
28 Feb 76	**WAKE UP EVERYBODY** *Philadelphia PIR 3866*	**23**	7 wks
22 Jan 77	● **DON'T LEAVE ME THIS WAY** *Philadelphia International PIR 4909*	**5**	10 wks
2 Apr 77	**REACHING FOR THE WORLD** *ABC 4161*	**48**	1 wk

MEMBERS *UK, male vocal/instrumental group*

3 Feb 79	**THE SOUND OF THE SUBURBS** *Virgin VS 242*	**12**	9 wks
7 Apr 79	**OFFSHORE BANKING BUSINESS** *Virgin VS 248*	**31**	5 wks

Date	Title *Label Number*	Position	

MEN AT WORK

Australia, male vocal/instrumental group

30 Oct 82	**WHO CAN IT BE NOW?** *Epic EPC A 2392*	**45**	5 wks

Tony MERRICK *UK, male vocalist*

2 Jun 66	**LADY JANE** *Columbia DB 7913*	**49**	1 wk

MERSEYBEATS

UK, male vocal/instrumental group

12 Sep 63	**IT'S LOVE THAT REALLY COUNTS** *Fontana TF 412*	**24**	12 wks
16 Jan 64	● **I THINK OF YOU** *Fontana TF 431*	**5**	17 wks
16 Apr 64	**DON'T TURN AROUND** *Fontana TF 459*	**13**	11 wks
9 Jul 64	**WISHIN' AND HOPIN'** *Fontana TF 482*	**13**	10 wks
5 Nov 64	**LAST NIGHT** *Fontana TF 504*	**40**	3 wks
14 Oct 65	**I LOVE YOU, YES I DO** *Fontana TF 607*	**22**	8 wks
20 Jan 66	**I STAND ACCUSED** *Fontana TF 645*	**38**	3 wks

MERSEYS *UK, male vocal duo*

28 Apr 66	● **SORROW** *Fontana TF 694*	**4**	13 wks

MERTON PARKAS

UK, male vocal/instrumental group

4 Aug 79	**YOU NEED WHEELS** *Beggars Banquet BEG 22*	**40**	6 wks

MFSB *US, orchestra*

27 Apr 74	**TSOP (THE SOUND OF PHILADELPHIA)** *Philadelphia International PIR 2289*	**22**	9 wks
26 Jul 75	**SEXY** *Philadelphia International PIR 3381*	**37**	5 wks
31 Jan 81	**MYSTERIES OF THE WORLD** *The Sound of Philadelphia PIR 9501*	**41**	4 wks

TSOP *billed as MFSB featuring the Three Degrees. See also Three Degrees.*

M.G.'S — See *BOOKER T. and the M.G.'s*

Keith MICHELL *Australia, male vocalist*

27 Mar 71	**I'LL GIVE YOU THE EARTH (TOUS LES BATEAUX, TOUS LES OISEAUX)** *Spark SRL 1046*	**43**	1 wk
17 Apr 71	**I'LL GIVE YOU THE EARTH (TOUS LES BATEAUX, TOUS LES OISEAUX)** (re-entry) *Spark SRL 1046*	**30**	10 wks
26 Jan 80	● **CAPTAIN BEAKY/WILFRED THE WEASEL** *Polydor POSP 106*	**5**	10 wks

See also Keith Michell, Captain Beaky and his Band.

Keith MICHELL, CAPTAIN BEAKY and his BAND

Australia, male vocalist/UK, instrumental group

29 Mar 80	**THE TRIAL OF HISSING SID** *Polydor HISS 1*	**53**	4 wks

see also Keith Michell.

Lloyd MICHELS — See *MISTURA with Lloyd MICHELS*

MICK — See *Dave DEE, DOZY, BEAKY, MICK and TICH*

MICROBE *UK, male vocalist*

14 May 69	**GROOVY BABY** *CBS 4158*	**29**	7 wks

MIDDLE OF THE ROAD

UK, male/female vocal/instrumental group

5 Jun 71	★ **CHIRPY CHIRPY CHEEP CHEEP** *RCA 2047*	**1**	34 wks
4 Sep 71	● **TWEEDLE DEE TWEEDLE DUM** *RCA 2110*	**2**	17 wks
11 Dec 71	● **SOLEY SOLEY** *RCA 2151*	**5**	12 wks
25 Mar 72	**SACRAMENTO** *RCA 2184*	**49**	1 wk
8 Apr 72	**SACRAMENTO** (re-entry) *RCA 2184*	**23**	6 wks
29 Jul 72	**SAMSON & DELILAH** *RCA 2237*	**26**	6 wks

MIDNIGHT BAND — See *Tony RALLO and the MIDNIGHT BAND*

MIDNIGHT COWBOY SOUNDTRACK

US, orchestra

8 Nov 80	**MIDNIGHT COWBOY** *United Artists UP 634*	**47**	4 wks

MIGHTY AVENGERS

UK, male vocal/instrumental group

26 Nov 64	**SO MUCH IN LOVE** *Decca F 11962*	**46**	2 wks

MIGHTY AVONS — See *Larry CUNNINGHAM and the MIGHTY AVONS*

MIGIL FIVE *UK, male vocal/instrumental group*

19 Mar 64	● **MOCKINGBIRD HILL** *Pye 7N 15597*	**10**	13 wks
4 Jun 64	**NEAR YOU** *Pye 7N 15645*	**31**	7 wks

MIKI and GRIFF *UK, male/female vocal duo*

2 Oct 59	**HOLD BACK TOMORROW** *Pye 7N 15213*	**26**	2 wks
13 Oct 60	**ROCKIN' ALONE** *Pye 7N 15296*	**44**	3 wks
1 Feb 62	**LITTLE BITTY TEAR** *Pye 7N 15412*	**16**	13 wks
22 Aug 63	**I WANNA STAY HERE** *Pye 7N 15555*	**23**	7 wks

John MILES *UK, male vocalist/multi-instrumentalist*

18 Oct 75	**HIGH FLY** *Decca F 13595*	**17**	6 wks
20 Mar 76	● **MUSIC** *Decca F 13627*	**3**	9 wks
16 Oct 76	**REMEMBER YESTERDAY** *Decca F 13667*	**32**	5 wks
18 Jun 77	● **SLOW DOWN** *Decca F 13709*	**10**	10 wks

MILK AND HONEY

Israel, male/female vocal/instrumental group

14 Apr 79	● **HALLELUJAH** *Polydor 2001 870*	**5**	8 wks

Hit has credit "featuring Gali Atari", Israeli female vocalist.

MILL GIRLS — See *Billy COTTON and his BAND*

Date	Title *Label Number*	Position	

Frankie MILLER *UK, male vocalist*

4 Jun 77	**BE GOOD TO YOURSELF** *Chrysalis CHS 2147*	**27**	6 wks
14 Oct 78	● **DARLIN'** *Chrysalis CHS 2255*	**6**	15 wks
20 Jan 79	**WHEN I'M AWAY FROM YOU** *Chrysalis CHS 2276*	**42**	5 wks

Gary MILLER *UK, male vocalist*

21 Oct 55	**YELLOW ROSE OF TEXAS** *Nixa N 15004*	**13**	5 wks
13 Jan 56	● **ROBIN HOOD** *Nixa N 15020*	**10**	6 wks
11 Jan 57	**GARDEN OF EDEN** *Pye Nixa N 15070*	**14**	6 wks
1 Mar 57	**GARDEN OF EDEN** (re-entry) *Pye Nixa N 15070*	**27**	1 wk
19 Jul 57	**WONDERFUL WONDERFUL** *Pye Nixa N 15094*	**29**	1 wk
17 Jan 58	**STORY OF MY LIFE** *Pye Nixa N 15120*	**14**	6 wks
21 Dec 61	**THERE GOES THAT SONG AGAIN/ THE NIGHT IS YOUNG** *Pye 7N 15404*	**29**	9 wks
1 Mar 62	**THERE GOES THAT SONG AGAIN** (re-entry) *Pye 7N 15404*	**48**	1 wk

The Night Is Young *only listed with* There Goes That Song Again *for weeks 21 and 28 Dec 61 and 4 Jan 62.*

Glenn MILLER

US Orchestra, Glenn Miller trombone

12 Mar 54	**MOONLIGHT SERENADE** *HMV BD 5942*	**12**	1 wk
24 Jan 76	**MOONLIGHT SERENADE/ LITTLE BROWN JUG/ IN THE MOOD** (re-issue) *RCA 2644*	**13**	8 wks

Jody MILLER *US, female vocalist*

21 Oct 65	**HOME OF THE BRAVE** *Capitol CL 15415*	**49**	1 wk

Mitch MILLER *US, orchestra and chorus*

7 Oct 55	● **YELLOW ROSE OF TEXAS** *Philips PB 505*	**2**	13 wks

Ned MILLER *US, male vocalist*

14 Feb 63	● **FROM A JACK TO A KING** *London HL 9648*	**2**	21 wks
18 Feb 65	**DO WHAT YOU DO DO WELL** *London HL 9937*	**48**	1 wk

Roger MILLER *US, male vocalist*

18 Mar 65	★ **KING OF THE ROAD** *Philips BF 1397*	**1**	15 wks
3 Jun 65	**ENGINE ENGINE NO. 9** *Philips BF 1416*	**33**	5 wks
21 Oct 65	**KANSAS CITY STAR** *Philips BF 1437*	**48**	1 wk
16 Dec 65	**ENGLAND SWINGS** *Philips BF 1456*	**45**	1 wk
6 Jan 66	**ENGLAND SWINGS** (re-entry) *Philips BF 1456*	**13**	7 wks
27 Mar 68	**LITTLE GREEN APPLES** *Mercury MF 1021*	**19**	10 wks
2 Apr 69	**LITTLE GREEN APPLES** (re-entry) *Mercury MF 1021*	**48**	1 wk
7 May 69	**LITTLE GREEN APPLES** (2nd re-entry) *Mercury MF 1021*	**39**	2 wks

Suzi MILLER *UK, female vocalist*

21 Jan 55	**HAPPY DAYS & LONELY NIGHTS** *Decca F 10389*	**14**	2 wks

Steve MILLER BAND

US, male vocal/instrumental group

23 Oct 76	**ROCK'N ME** *Mercury 6078 804*	**11**	9 wks
19 Jun 82	● **ABRACADABRA** *Mercury/Phonogram STEVE 3*	**2**	11 wks
4 Sep 82	**KEEPS ME WONDERING WHY** *Mercury/Phonogram STEVE 4*	**52**	3 wks

MILLICAN and NESBITT *UK, male vocal duo*

1 Dec 73	**VAYA CON DIOS** *Pye 7N 45310*	**20**	11 wks
18 May 74	**FOR OLD TIME'S SAKE** *Pye 7N 45357*	**38**	3 wks

MILLIE *Jamaica, female vocalist*

12 Mar 64	● **MY BOY LOLLIPOP** *Fontana TF 449*	**2**	18 wks
25 Jun 64	**SWEET WILLIAM** *Fontana TF 479*	**30**	9 wks
11 Nov 65	**BLOODSHOT EYES** *Fontana TF 617*	**48**	1 wk

Garry MILLS *UK, male vocalist*

7 Jul 60	● **LOOK FOR A STAR** *Top Rank JAR 336*	**7**	14 wks
20 Oct 60	**TOP TEEN BABY** *Top Rank JAR 500*	**24**	12 wks
22 Jun 61	**I'LL STEP DOWN** *Decca F 11358*	**39**	5 wks

Hayley MILLS *UK, female vocalist*

19 Oct 61	**LET'S GET TOGETHER** *Decca F 21396*	**17**	11 wks

Mrs. MILLS *UK, female instrumentalist, piano*

14 Dec 61	**MRS MILLS' MEDLEY** *Parlophone R 4856*	**18**	5 wks

Mrs Mills' Medley consisted of the following tunes: I Want To Be Happy/ Sheik Of Araby/ Baby Face/ Somebody Stole My Gal/ Ma (He's Making Eyes At Me)/ Swanee/ Ain't She Sweet/ California Here I Come.

Stephanie MILLS *female vocalist*

18 Oct 80	● **NEVER KNEW LOVE LIKE THIS BEFORE** *20th Century TC 2460*	**4**	14 wks
23 May 81	**TWO HEARTS** *20th Century TC 2492*	**49**	5 wks

Two Hearts *is 'featuring Teddy Pendergrass'. See Teddy Pendergrass.*

MILLS BROTHERS *US, male vocal group*

30 Jan 53	● **GLOW WORM** *Brunswick 05007*	**10**	1 wk

Garnet MIMMS and TRUCKIN' CO.

US, male vocalist and male instrumental group

25 Jun 77	**WHAT IT IS** *Arista 109*	**44**	1 wk

MINDBENDERS

UK, male vocal/instrumental group

13 Jan 66	● **A GROOVY KIND OF LOVE** *Fontana TF 644*	**2**	14 wks
5 May 66	**CAN'T LIVE WITH YOU (CAN'T LIVE WITHOUT YOU)** *Fontana TF 697*	**28**	7 wks
25 Aug 66	**ASHES TO ASHES** *Fontana TF 731*	**14**	9 wks
20 Sep 67	**THE LETTER** *Fontana TF 869*	**42**	4 wks

See also Wayne Fontana & The Mindbenders.

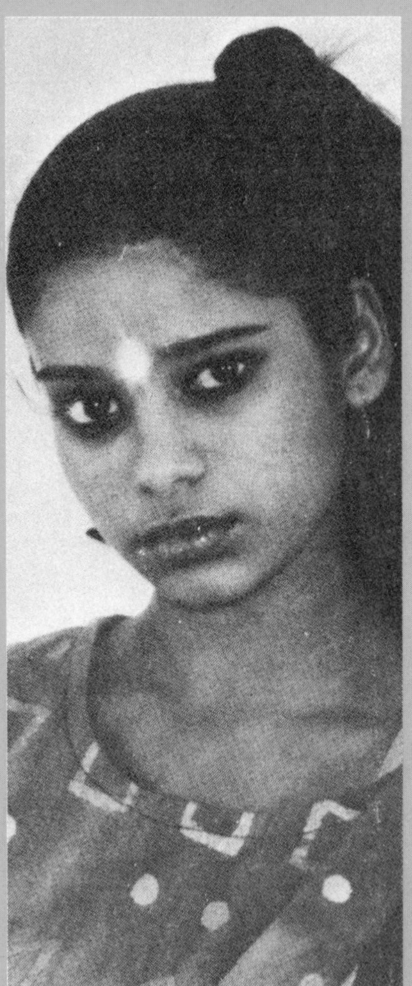

Left **MONSOON** A brief reign in 82 *Below* **MINK DEVILLE** Willy relaxes after his 9 week stroll (Willy's the one on the right) *Below right* **MICKIE MOST** Following his time as a top pop singer in S Africa, Mickie has enjoyed incredible success over the last two decades as a top producer, a career which started with The Animals' 'Baby Let Me Take You Home' in the Spring of '64

Left **THE MINDBENDERS** Bob Lang, Eric Stewart and Ric Rothwell. Eric Stewart went on to even greater things as a member of 10CC and *Below* **CHRIS MONTEZ** The classic 'Let's Dance' was a hit three times for Chris Montez and nearly once for co-author M Read (once again under the guise of the Rockolas) when his bid for chart stardom came to an abrupt halt at No. 91 – just 16 places short of a place in musical history!

Sal MINEO *US, male vocalist*

Date	Title *Label Number*	Position	
12 Jul 57	**START MOVIN'** *Philips PB 707*	**16**	11 wks

Marcello MINERBI *Italy, orchestra*

Date	Title *Label Number*	Position	
22 Jul 65	● **ZORBA'S DANCE** *Durium DRS 54001*	**6**	16 wks

MINK DE VILLE

US, male vocal/instrumental group

Date	Title *Label Number*	Position	
6 Aug 77	**SPANISH STROLL** *Capitol CLX 103*	**20**	9 wks

Sugar MINOTT *male vocalist*

Date	Title *Label Number*	Position	
28 Mar 81	● **GOOD THING GOING (WE'VE GOT A GOOD THING GOING)** *RCA 58*	**4**	12 wks
17 Oct 81	**NEVER MY LOVE** *RCA 138*	**52**	4 wks

MIRACLES *US, male vocal group*

Date	Title *Label Number*	Position	
10 Jan 76	● **LOVE MACHINE** *Tamla Motown TMG 1015*	**3**	10 wks

See also Smokey Robinson and the Miracles.

Danny MIRROR *Holland, male vocalist*

Date	Title *Label Number*	Position	
17 Sep 77	● **I REMEMBER ELVIS PRESLEY (THE KING IS DEAD)** *Sonet SON 2121*	**4**	9 wks

MR. BIG *UK, male vocal and instrumental group*

Date	Title *Label Number*	Position	
12 Feb 77	● **ROMEO** *EMI 2567*	**4**	10 wks
21 May 77	**FEEL LIKE CALLING HOME** *EMI 2610*	**35**	4 wks

MR BLOE *UK, male instrumentalist, harmonica*

Date	Title *Label Number*	Position	
9 May 70	● **GROOVIN' WITH MR. BLOE** *DJM DJS 216*	**2**	18 wks

MISTURA *US, male instrumental group,*

Date	Title *Label Number*	Position	
15 May 76	**THE FLASHER** *Route RT 30*	**23**	10 wks

Has credit: Featuring Lloyd Michels trumpet.

Cameron MITCHELL — See *VARIOUS ARTISTS (Carousel Soundtrack)*

Guy MITCHELL *US, male vocalist*

Date	Title *Label Number*	Position	
14 Nov 52	● **FEET UP** *Columbia DB 3151*	**2**	10 wks
13 Feb 53	★ **SHE WEARS RED FEATHERS** *Columbia DB 3238*	**1**	15 wks
24 Apr 53	● **PRETTY LITTLE BLACK EYED SUSIE** *Columbia DB 3255*	**2**	11 wks
12 Jun 53	**SHE WEARS RED FEATHERS** (re-entry) *Columbia DB 3238*	**12**	1 wk
28 Aug 53	★ **LOOK AT THAT GIRL** *Philips PB 162*	**1**	14 wks
6 Nov 53	● **CHICKA BOOM** *Philips PB 178*	**5**	9 wks
18 Dec 53	● **CLOUD LUCKY SEVEN** *Philips PB 210*	**2**	16 wks
15 Jan 54	● **CHICKA BOOM** (re-entry) *Philips PB 178*	**4**	6 wks
19 Feb 54	● **CUFF OF MY SHIRT** *Philips PB 225*	**9**	1 wk
26 Feb 54	**SIPPIN' SODA** *Philips PB 210*	**11**	1 wk
19 Mar 54	**CUFF OF MY SHIRT** (re-entry) *Philips PB 225*	**12**	1 wk
2 Apr 54	**CUFF OF MY SHIRT** (2nd re-entry) *Philips PB 225*	**11**	1 wk
30 Apr 54	● **DIME AND A DOLLAR** *Philips PB 248*	**8**	1 wk
14 May 54	● **DIME AND A DOLLAR** (re-entry) *Philips PB 248*	**8**	4 wks
7 Dec 56	★ **SINGING THE BLUES** *Philips PB 650*	**1**	22 wks
15 Feb 57	● **KNEE DEEP IN THE BLUES** *Philips PB 669*	**3**	12 wks
26 Apr 57	★ **ROCK-A-BILLY** *Philips PB 685*	**1**	14 wks
26 Jul 57	**IN THE MIDDLE OF A DARK DARK NIGHT/ SWEET STUFF** *Philips PB 712*	**27**	2 wks
23 Aug 57	**IN THE MIDDLE OF A DARK DARK NIGHT/ SWEET STUFF** (re-entry) *Philips PB 712*	**25**	2 wks
11 Oct 57	**CALL ROSIE ON THE PHONE** *Philips PB 743*	**17**	6 wks
27 Nov 59	**HEARTACHES BY THE NUMBER** *Philips PB 964*	**26**	2 wks
18 Dec 59	● **HEARTACHES BY THE NUMBER** (re-entry) *Philips PB 964*	**5**	13 wks

Joni MITCHELL *Canada, female vocalist*

Date	Title *Label Number*	Position	
13 Jun 70	**BIG YELLOW TAXI** *Reprise RS 20906*	**11**	15 wks

Willie MITCHELL *US, male instrumentalist, guitar*

Date	Title *Label Number*	Position	
24 Apr 68	**SOUL SERENADE** *London HLU 10186*	**43**	1 wk
11 Dec 76	**THE CHAMPION** *London HL 10545*	**47**	2 wks

MIXTURES *Australia, male vocal/instrumental group*

Date	Title *Label Number*	Position	
16 Jan 71	● **THE PUSHBIKE SONG** *Polydor 2058 083*	**2**	21 wks

Hank MIZELL *US, male vocalist*

Date	Title *Label Number*	Position	
20 Mar 76	● **JUNGLE ROCK** *Charley CS 1005*	**3**	13 wks

MOBILES *UK, male/female vocal/instrumental group*

Date	Title *Label Number*	Position	
9 Jan 82	● **DROWNING IN BERLIN** *Rialto RIA 3*	**9**	10 wks
27 Mar 82	**AMOUR AMOUR** *Rialto RIA 5*	**45**	4 wks

MODERN LOVERS

US, male vocal/instrumental group

Date	Title *Label Number*	Position	
21 Jan 78	**MORNING OF OUR LIVES** *Beserkley BZZ 7*	**29**	4 wks

See also Jonathan Richman and the Modern Lovers

MODERN ROMANCE

UK, male vocal/instrumental group

Date	Title *Label Number*	Position	
15 Aug 81	**EVERYBODY SALSA** *WEA K 18815*	**12**	10 wks
7 Nov 81	● **AY AY AY AY MOOSEY** *WEA K 18883*	**10**	12 wks
30 Jan 82	**QUEEN OF THE RAPPING SCENE (NOTHING EVER GOES THE WAY YOU PLAN)** *WEA K 18928*	**37**	8 wks
14 Aug 82	**CHERRY PINK AND APPLE BLOSSOM WHITE** *WEA K 19245*	**15**	8 wks
13 Nov 82	● **BEST YEARS OF OUR LIVES** *WEA ROM 1*	**8**†	7 wks

Cherry Pink and Apple Blossom White is 'featuring John du Prez'.

MODETTES *UK, female vocal/instrumental group*

Date	Title *Label Number*	Position	
12 Jul 80	**PAINT IT BLACK** *Deram DET-R 1*	**42**	5 wks
18 Jul 81	**TONIGHT** *Deram DET 3*	**68**	1 wk

Date	Title *Label Number*	Position	

Domenico MODUGNO *Italy, male vocalist*

5 Sep 58	● **VOLARE** *Oriole CB 5000*	**10**	12 wks
27 Mar 59	**CIAO CIAO BAMBINA** *Oriole CB 1489*	**29**	1 wk

MOJO *UK, male instrumental group*

22 Aug 81	**DANCE ON** *Creole CR 17*	**70**	3 wks

The MOJOS *UK, male vocal/instrumental group*

26 Mar 64	● **EVERYTHING'S ALRIGHT** *Decca F 11853*	**9**	11 wks
11 Jun 64	**WHY NOT TONIGHT** *Decca F 11918*	**25**	10 wks
10 Sep 64	**SEVEN DAFFODILS** *Decca F 11959*	**30**	5 wks

MOMENTS *US, male vocal group*

19 Jul 75	● **DOLLY MY LOVE** *All Platinum 6146 306*	**10**	9 wks
25 Oct 75	**LOOK AT ME (I'M IN LOVE)** *All Platinum 6146 309*	**42**	4 wks
22 Jan 77	● **JACK IN THE BOX** *All Platinum 6146 318*	**7**	9 wks

See also Moments and Whatnauts.

MOMENTS and WHATNAUTS

US, male vocal group, male instrumental group

8 Mar 75	● **GIRLS** *All Platinum 6146 302*	**3**	10 wks

See also Moments.

Zoot MONEY and the BIG ROLL BAND

UK, male vocalist/instrumentalist - keyboards, male instrumental backing group

18 Aug 66	**BIG TIME OPERATOR** *Columbia DB 7975*	**25**	8 wks

T S MONK

US male/female vocal/instrumental group

7 Mar 81	**BON BON VIE** *Mirage K 11653*	**63**	2 wks
25 Apr 81	**CANDIDATE FOR LOVE** *Mirage K 11648*	**58**	4 wks

MONKEES *US/UK, male vocal/instrumental group*

5 Jan 67	★ **I'M A BELIEVER** *RCA 1560*	**1**	17 wks
26 Jan 67	**LAST TRAIN TO CLARKSVILLE** *RCA 1547*	**23**	7 wks
6 Apr 67	● **A LITTLE BIT ME A LITTLE BIT YOU** *RCA 1580*	**3**	12 wks
22 Jun 67	● **ALTERNATE TITLE** *RCA 1604*	**2**	12 wks
16 Aug 67	**PLEASANT VALLEY SUNDAY** *RCA 1620*	**11**	8 wks
15 Nov 67	● **DAYDREAM BELIEVER** *RCA 1645*	**5**	17 wks
27 Mar 68	**VALLERI** *RCA 1679*	**12**	8 wks
26 Jun 68	**D. W. WASHBURN** *RCA 1706*	**17**	6 wks
26 Mar 69	**TEARDROP CITY** *RCA 1802*	**46**	1 wk
25 Jun 69	**SOMEDAY MAN** *RCA 1824*	**47**	1 wk
15 Mar 80	**THE MONKEES EP** (RE-ISSUE OF 4 HITS) *ARISTA ARIST 326*	**33**	9 wks

Tracks on EP: I'm a Believer/Daydream Believer/Last Train to Clarksville/A Little Bit Me A Little Bit You

MONKS *UK, male vocal/instrumental group*

21 Apr 79	**NICE LEGS SHAME ABOUT HER FACE** *Carrere CAR 104*	**19**	9 wks

The Monks are Hudson-Ford under new name. See also Hudson-Ford

Matt MONRO *UK, male vocalist*

15 Dec 60	● **PORTRAIT OF MY LOVE** *Parlophone R 4714*	**3**	16 wks
9 Mar 61	● **MY KIND OF GIRL** *Parlophone R 4755*	**5**	12 wks
18 May 61	**WHY NOT NOW/ CAN THIS BE LOVE** *Parlophone R 4775*	**24**	9 wks
28 Sep 61	**GONNA BUILD A MOUNTAIN** *Parlophone R 4819*	**44**	3 wks
8 Feb 62	● **SOFTLY AS I LEAVE YOU** *Parlophone R 4868*	**10**	18 wks
14 Jun 62	**WHEN LOVE COMES ALONG** *Parlophone R 4911*	**46**	3 wks
8 Nov 62	**MY LOVE AND DEVOTION** *Parlophone R 4954*	**29**	5 wks
14 Nov 63	**FROM RUSSIA WITH LOVE** *Parlophone R 5068*	**20**	13 wks
17 Sep 64	● **WALK AWAY** *Parlophone R 5171*	**4**	20 wks
24 Dec 64	**FOR MAMA** *Parlophone R 5215*	**36**	4 wks
25 Mar 65	**WITHOUT YOU** *Parlophone R 5251*	**37**	4 wks
21 Oct 65	● **YESTERDAY** *Parlophone R 5348*	**8**	12 wks
24 Nov 73	**AND YOU SMILED** *EMI 2091*	**28**	8 wks

Gerry MONROE *UK, male vocalist*

23 May 70	● **SALLY** *Chapter One CH 122*	**4**	20 wks
19 Sep 70	**CRY** *Chapter One CH 128*	**38**	5 wks
14 Nov 70	● **MY PRAYER** *Chapter One CH 132*	**9**	12 wks
17 Apr 71	**IT'S A SIN TO TELL A LIE** *Chapter One CH 144*	**13**	12 wks
21 Aug 71	**LITTLE DROPS OF SILVER** *Chapter One CH 152*	**37**	6 wks
12 Feb 72	**GIRL OF MY DREAMS** *Chapter One CH 159*	**43**	2 wks

MONSOON

UK, male/female vocal/instrumental group

3 Apr 82	**EVER SO LONELY** *Phonogram CORP 2*	**12**	9 wks
5 Jun 82	**SHAKTI (THE MEANING OF WITHIN)** *Mobile Suit Corp/Phonogram CORP 4*	**41**	3 wks

MONSTER ORCHESTRA — See *John DAVIS and the MONSTER ORCHESTRA*

Hugo MONTENEGRO *US, orchestra*

11 Sep 68	★ **THE GOOD THE BAD & THE UGLY** *RCA 1727*	**1**	24 wks
8 Jan 69	**HANG 'EM HIGH** *RCA 1771*	**50**	1 wk
19 Mar 69	**THE GOOD THE BAD & THE UGLY** (re-entry) *RCA 1727*	**48**	1 wk

Chris MONTEZ *US, male vocalist*

4 Oct 62	● **LET'S DANCE** *London HLU 9596*	**2**	18 wks
17 Jan 63	● **SOME KINDA FUN** *London HLU 9650*	**10**	9 wks
30 Jun 66	● **THE MORE I SEE YOU** *Pye International 7N 25369*	**3**	13 wks

Date	Title *Label Number*	Position	
22 Sep 66	**THERE WILL NEVER BE ANOTHER YOU** *Pye International 7N 25381*	**37**	4 wks
14 Oct 72 ●	**LET'S DANCE** (re-issue) *London HL 10205*	**9**	14 wks
14 Apr 79	**LET'S DANCE** (2nd re-issue) *Lightning LIG 9011*	**47**	3 wks

The second re-issue of Let's Dance *on Lightning was coupled with* Memphis *by Lonnie Mack as a double A-side. See also Lonnie Mack.*

MONTROSE *US, male vocal/instrumental group*

28 Jun 80	**SPACE STATION NO. 5/GOOD ROCKIN' TONIGHT** *WB HM 9*	**71**	2 wks

MOOD *UK, male vocalal/instrumental group*

6 Feb 82	**DON'T STOP** *RCA 171*	**59**	4 wks
22 May 82	**PARIS IS ONE DAY AWAY** *RCA 211*	**42**	5 wks
30 Oct 82	**PASSION IN DARK ROOMS** *RCA 276*	**74**	1 wk

MOODY BLUES

UK, male vocal/instrumental group

10 Dec 64 ★	**GO NOW** *Decca F 12022*	**1**	14 wks
4 Mar 65	**I DON'T WANT TO GO ON WITHOUT YOU** *Decca F 12095*	**33**	9 wks
10 Jun 65	**FROM THE BOTTOM OF MY HEART** *Decca F 12166*	**22**	9 wks
18 Nov 65	**EVERYDAY** *Decca F 12266*	**44**	2 wks
27 Dec 67	**NIGHTS IN WHITE SATIN** *Deram DM 161*	**19**	11 wks
7 Aug 68	**VOICES IN THE SKY** *Deram DM 196*	**27**	10 wks
4 Dec 68	**RIDE MY SEE-SAW** *Deram DM 213*	**42**	1 wk
2 May 70 ●	**QUESTION** *Threshold TH 4*	**2**	12 wks
6 May 72	**ISN'T LIFE STRANGE** *Threshold TH9*	**13**	10 wks
2 Dec 72 ●	**NIGHTS IN WHITE SATIN** (re-entry) *Deram DM 161*	**9**	11 wks
10 Feb 73	**I'M JUST A SINGER (IN A ROCK 'N ROLL BAND)** *Threshold TH13*	**36**	4 wks
10 Nov 79	**NIGHTS IN WHITE SATIN** (2nd re-entry) *Deram DM 161*	**14**	12 wks

MOONTREKKERS *UK, male instrumental group*

2 Nov 61	**NIGHT OF THE VAMPIRE** *Parlophone R 4814*	**50**	1 wk

Dorothy MOORE *US, female vocalist*

19 Jun 76 ●	**MISTY BLUE** *Contempo CS 2087*	**5**	12 wks
16 Oct 76	**FUNNY HOW TIME SLIPS AWAY** *Contempo CS 2092*	**38**	3 wks
15 Oct 77	**I BELIEVE YOU** *Epic EPC 5573*	**20**	9 wks

Dudley MOORE — See *Peter COOK and Dudley MOORE*

Gary MOORE *UK, male Instrumentalist guitar*

21 Apr 79 ●	**PARISIENNE WALKWAYS** *MCA 419*	**8**	11 wks

Jackie MOORE *US, female vocalist*

15 Sep 79	**THIS TIME BABY** *CBS 7722*	**49**	5 wks

Melba MOORE *US, female vocalist*

15 May 76 ●	**THIS IS IT** *Buddah BDS 443*	**9**	8 wks
26 May 79	**PICK ME UP I'LL DANCE** *Epic EPC 7234*	**48**	5 wks
9 Oct 82	**LOVE'S COMIN' AT YA** *EMI America EA 146*	**15**	8 wks

Mike MORAN — See *Lynsey DE PAUL and Mike MORAN*

MORE *UK, male vocal/instrumental group*

14 Mar 81	**WE ARE THE BAND** *Atlantic K 11561*	**59**	2 wks

Derrick MORGAN *Jamaica, male vocalist*

17 Jan 70	**MOON HOP** *Crab 32*	**49**	1 wk

Jane MORGAN *US, female vocalist*

5 Dec 58 ★	**THE DAY THE RAINS CAME** *London HLR 8751*	**1**	15 wks
22 May 59	**IF ONLY I COULD LIVE MY LIFE AGAIN** *London HLR 8810*	**27**	1 wk
21 Jul 60	**ROMANTICA** *London HLR 9120*	**39**	5 wks

Ray MORGAN *UK, male vocalist*

25 Jul 70	**THE LONG AND WINDING ROAD** *B & C CB 128*	**32**	6 wks

Giorgio MORODER

Italy, male instrumentalist - keyboard synthesisers

24 Sep 77	**FROM HERE TO ETERNITY** *Oasis 1*	**16**	10 wks
17 Mar 79	**CHASE** *Casablanca CAN 144*	**48**	6 wks

First hit credited simply to Giorgio.

Ennio MORRICONE *Italy, orchestra*

11 Apr 81 ●	**CHI MAI** (THEME FROM THE TV SERIES THE LIFE AND TIMES OF DAVID LLOYD GEORGE) *BBC RESL 92*	**2**	12 wks

Van MORRISON *UK, male vocalist*

20 Oct 79	**BRIGHT SIDE OF THE ROAD** *Mercury 6001 121*	**63**	3 wks

Buddy MORROW *US, orchestra*

20 Mar 53	**NIGHT TRAIN** *HMV B 10347*	**12**	1 wk

Mickie MOST *UK, male vocalist*

25 Jul 63	**MISTER PORTER** *Decca F 11664*	**45**	1 wk

MOTELS

US/UK, male/female vocal/instrumental group

11 Oct 80	**WHOSE PROBLEM?** *Capitol CL 16162*	**42**	4 wks
10 Jan 81	**DAYS ARE O.K.** *Capitol CL 16149*	**41**	3 wks

MOTORHEAD *UK, male vocal/instrumental group*

Date		Title *Label Number*	Position	
16 Sep 78		**LOUIE LOUIE** *Bronze BRO 60*	**75**	1 wk
30 Sep 78		**LOUIE LOUIE** (re-entry) *Bronze BRO 60*	**68**	1 wk
10 Mar 79		**OVERKILL** *Bronze BRO 67*	**39**	4 wks
14 Apr 79		**OVERKILL** (re-entry) *Bronze BRO 67*	**57**	3 wks
30 Jun 79		**NO CLASS** *Bronze BRO 78*	**61**	4 wks
1 Dec 79		**BOMBER** *Bronze BRO 85*	**34**	7 wks
3 May 80	●	**THE GOLDEN YEARS** (EP) *Bronze BRO 92*	**8**	7 wks
1 Nov 80		**ACE OF SPADES** *Bronze BRO 106*	**15**	12 wks
22 Nov 80		**BEER DRINKERS AND HELL RAISERS** *Big Beat SWT 61*	**43**	4 wks
11 Jul 81	●	**MOTORHEAD LIVE** *Bronze BRO 124*	**6**	7 wks
3 Apr 82		**IRON FIST** *Bronze BRO 146*	**29**	5 wks

Tracks on EP: Dead Men Tell No Tales/Too Late Too Late/Leaving Here/Stone Dead Forever. See also Headgirl, Young and Moody Band.

MOTORS *UK, male vocal/instrumental group*

Date		Title *Label Number*	Position	
24 Sep 77		**DANCING THE NIGHT AWAY** *Virgin VS 186*	**42**	4 wks
10 Jun 78	●	**AIRPORT** *Virgin VS 219*	**4**	13 wks
19 Aug 78		**FORGET ABOUT YOU** *Virgin VS 222*	**13**	9 wks
12 Apr 80		**LOVE AND LONELINESS** *Virgin VS 263*	**58**	3 wks

MOTOWN SPINNERS — See *DETROIT SPINNERS*

MOTT THE HOOPLE

UK, male vocal/instrumental group

Date		Title *Label Number*	Position	
12 Aug 72	●	**ALL THE YOUNG DUDES** *CBS 8271*	**3**	11 wks
16 Jun 73		**HONALOOCHIE BOOGIE** *CBS 1530*	**12**	9 wks
8 Sep 73	●	**ALL THE WAY FROM MEMPHIS** *CBS 1764*	**10**	8 wks
24 Nov 73	●	**ROLL AWAY THE STONE** *CBS 1895*	**8**	12 wks
30 Mar 74		**GOLDEN AGE OF ROCK AND ROLL** *CBS 2177*	**16**	7 wks
22 Jun 74		**FOXY FOXY** *CBS 2439*	**33**	5 wks
2 Nov 74		**SATURDAY GIG** *CBS 2754*	**41**	3 wks

MOUTH and MACNEAL

Holland, male/female vocal duo

Date		Title *Label Number*	Position	
4 May 74	●	**I SEE A STAR** *Decca F 13504*	**8**	10 wks

MOVE *UK, male vocal/instrumental group*

Date		Title *Label Number*	Position	
5 Jan 67	●	**NIGHT OF FEAR** *Deram DM 109*	**2**	10 wks
6 Apr 67	●	**I CAN HEAR THE GRASS GROW** *Deram DM 117*	**5**	10 wks
6 Sep 67	●	**FLOWERS IN THE RAIN** *Regal Zonophone RZ3001*	**2**	13 wks
7 Feb 68	●	**FIRE BRIGADE** *Regal Zonophone RZ3005*	**3**	11 wks
25 Dec 68	★	**BLACKBERRY WAY** *Regal Zonophone RZ3015*	**1**	12 wks
23 Jul 69		**CURLY** *Regal Zonophone RZ3021*	**12**	12 wks
25 Apr 70	●	**BRONTOSAURUS** *Regal Zonophone RZ3026*	**7**	10 wks
3 Jul 71		**TONIGHT** *Harvest HAR 5038*	**11**	10 wks
23 Oct 71		**CHINATOWN** *Harvest HAR 5043*	**23**	8 wks
13 May 72	●	**CALIFORNIA MAN** *Harvest HAR 5050*	**7**	14 wks

MUD *UK, male vocal/instrumental group*

Date		Title *Label Number*	Position	
10 Mar 73		**CRAZY** *RAK 146*	**12**	12 wks
23 Jun 73		**HYPNOSIS** *RAK 152*	**16**	13 wks
27 Oct 73	●	**DYNA-MITE** *RAK 159*	**4**	12 wks
19 Jan 74	★	**TIGER FEET** *RAK 166*	**1**	11 wks
13 Apr 74	●	**THE CAT CREPT IN** *RAK 170*	**2**	9 wks
27 Jul 74	●	**ROCKET** *RAK 178*	**6**	9 wks
30 Nov 74	★	**LONELY THIS CHRISTMAS** *RAK 187*	**1**	10 wks
15 Feb 75	●	**THE SECRETS THAT YOU KEEP** *RAK 194*	**3**	9 wks
26 Apr 75	★	**OH BOY** *RAK 201*	**1**	9 wks
21 Jun 75	●	**MOONSHINE SALLY** *RAK 208*	**10**	7 wks
2 Aug 75		**ONE NIGHT** *RAK 213*	**32**	4 wks
4 Oct 75	●	**L-L-LUCY** *Private Stock PVT 41*	**10**	6 wks
29 Nov 75	●	**SHOW ME YOU'RE A WOMAN** *Private Stock PVT 45*	**8**	8 wks
15 May 76		**SHAKE IT DOWN** *Private Stock PVT 65*	**12**	8 wks
27 Nov 76	●	**LEAN ON ME** *Private Stock PVT 85*	**7**	9 wks

MUDLARKS *UK, male/female vocal group*

Date		Title *Label Number*	Position	
2 May 58	●	**LOLLIPOP** *Columbia DB 4099*	**2**	9 wks
6 Jun 58	●	**BOOK OF LOVE** *Columbia DB 4133*	**8**	9 wks
27 Feb 59		**THE LOVE GAME** *Columbia DB 4250*	**30**	1 wk

MUFFINS — See *MARTHA and the MUFFINS*

Idris MUHAMMAD *US, male vocalist*

Date		Title *Label Number*	Position	
17 Sep 77		**COULD HEAVEN EVER BE LIKE THIS** *Kudu 935*	**42**	3 wks

Maria MULDAUR *US, female vocalist*

Date		Title *Label Number*	Position	
29 Jul 74		**MIDNIGHT AT THE OASIS** *Reprise K 14331*	**21**	8 wks

Arthur MULLARD — See *Hilda BAKER and Arthur MULLARD*

MUNGO JERRY

UK, male vocal/instrumental group

Date		Title *Label Number*	Position	
6 Jun 70	★	**IN THE SUMMERTIME** *Dawn DNX 2502*	**1**	20 wks
6 Feb 71		**BABY JUMP** *Dawn DNX 2505*	**32**	1 wk
20 Feb 71	★	**BABY JUMP** (re-entry) *Dawn DNX 2505*	**1**	12 wks
29 May 71	●	**LADY ROSE** *Dawn DNX 2510*	**5**	12 wks
18 Sep 71		**YOU DON'T HAVE TO BE IN THE ARMY TO FIGHT IN THE WAR** *Dawn DNX 2513*	**13**	8 wks
22 Apr 72		**OPEN UP** *Dawn DNX 2514*	**21**	8 wks
7 Jul 73	●	**ALRIGHT ALRIGHT ALRIGHT** *Dawn DNS 1037*	**3**	12 wks
10 Nov 73		**WILD LOVE** *Dawn DNS 1051*	**32**	5 wks
6 Apr 74		**LONGLEGGED WOMAN DRESSED IN BLACK** *Dawn DNS 1061*	**13**	9 wks

MUNICH MACHINE

Germany, male instrumental group

Date		Title *Label Number*	Position	
10 Dec 77		**GET ON THE FUNK TRAIN** *Oasis 2*	**41**	4 wks
4 Nov 78		**A WHITER SHADE OF PALE** *Oasis/Hansa OASIS 5*	**42**	4 wks

A Whiter Shade Of Pale *billed as Munich Machine introducing Chris Bennett.*

David MUNROW — See *EARLY MUSIC CONSORT*

MUPPETS *US, puppets*

Date		Title *Label Number*	Position	
28 May 77	●	**HALFWAY DOWN THE STAIRS** *Pye 7N 45698*	**7**	8 wks
17 Dec 77		**THE MUPPET SHOW MUSIC HALL** EP *PYE 7NX 8004*	**19**	7 wks

Halfway Down the Stairs *is sung by Jerry Nelson as Kermit the Frog's nephew, Robin. Tracks of EP: Don't Dilly Dally On The Way/Waiting At The Church/The Boy In The Gallery/Wotcher (Knocked 'Em In The Old Kent Road.)*

Date	Title *Label Number*	Position	

Walter MURPHY and the BIG APPLE BAND *US, orchestra*

10 Jul 76	**A FIFTH OF BEETHOVEN** *Private Stock PVT 59*	**28**	9 wks

Anne MURRAY *Canada, female vocalist*

24 Oct 70	**SNOWBIRD** *Capitol CL 15654*	**23**	17 wks
21 Oct 72	**DESTINY** *Capitol CL 15734*	**41**	4 wks
9 Dec 78	**YOU NEEDED ME** *Capitol CL 16011*	**22**	14 wks
21 Apr 79	**I JUST FALL IN LOVE AGAIN** *Capitol CL 16069*	**58**	2 wks
19 Apr 80	**DAYDREAM BELIEVER** *Capitol CL 16123*	**61**	3 wks

Pauline MURRAY and the INVISIBLE GIRLS

UK, female vocalist with male (really) vocal/instrumental group

2 Aug 80	**DREAM SEQUENCE (ONE)** *Illusive IVE 1*	**67**	2 wks

Ruby MURRAY *Ireland, female vocalist*

3 Dec 54	● **HEARTBEAT** *Columbia DB 3542*	**3**	16 wks
28 Jan 55	★ **SOFTLY SOFTLY** *Columbia DB 3558*	**1**	22 wks
4 Feb 55	● **HAPPY DAYS & LONELY NIGHTS** *Columbia DB 3577*	**6**	8 wks
4 Mar 55	● **LET ME GO LOVER** *Columbia DB 3577*	**5**	7 wks
18 Mar 55	● **IF ANYONE FINDS THIS I LOVE YOU** *Columbia DB 3580*	**4**	11 wks
1 Jul 55	● **EVERMORE** *Columbia DB 3617*	**3**	17 wks
8 Jul 55	**SOFTLY SOFTLY** (re-entry) *Columbia DB 3558*	**20**	1 wk
14 Oct 55	● **I'LL COME WHEN YOU CALL** *Columbia DB 3643*	**6**	7 wks
31 Aug 56	**YOU ARE MY FIRST LOVE** *Columbia DB 3770*	**16**	4 wks
5 Oct 56	**YOU ARE MY FIRST LOVE** (re-entry) *Columbia DB 3770*	**21**	1 wk
12 Dec 58	**REAL LOVE** *Columbia DB 4192*	**18**	6 wks
5 Jun 59	● **GOODBYE JIMMY GOODBYE** *Columbia DB 4305*	**10**	13 wks

Junior MURVIN *Jamaica, male vocalist*

3 May 80	**POLICE AND THIEVES** *Island WIP 6539*	**23**	9 wks

MUSICAL YOUTH

UK, male vocal/instrumental group

25 Sep 82	★ **PASS THE DUTCHIE** *MCA YOU 1*	**1**	12 wks
20 Nov 82	**YOUTH OF TODAY** *MCA YOU 2*	**13**†	6 wks

MUSIQUE *US, female vocal group*

18 Nov 78	**IN THE BUSH** *CBS 6791*	**16**	12 wks

MUSTAFAS — See *STAIFFI and his MUSTAFAS*

Richard MYHILL *UK, male vocalist*

1 Apr 78	**IT TAKES TWO TO TANGO** *Mercury TANGO 1*	**17**	9 wks

Marie MYRIAM *France, female vocalist*

28 May 77	**L'OISEAU ET L'ENFANT** *Polydor 2056 634*	**42**	4 wks

MYSTERIANS — See *?(QUESTION MARK) and the MYSTERIANS*

MYSTI — See *CAMOUFLAGE featuring MYSTI*

MYSTIC MERLIN

US, male vocal/instrumental and magic group

26 Apr 80	**JUST CAN'T GIVE YOU UP** *Capitol CL 16133*	**20**	9 wks

N

NAPOLEON XIV *US, male vocalist*

4 Aug 66	● **THEY'RE COMING TO TAKE ME AWAY HA-HAAA!** *Warner Bros. WB 5831*	**4**	10 wks

NASH — See *CROSBY, STILLS and NASH*

Johnny NASH *US, male vocalist*

7 Aug 68	● **HOLD ME TIGHT** *Regal Zonophone RZ 3010*	**5**	16 wks
8 Jan 69	● **YOU GOT SOUL** *Major Minor MM 586*	**6**	12 wks
2 Apr 69	● **CUPID** *Major Minor MM 603*	**6**	11 wks
25 Jun 69	**CUPID** (re-entry) *Major Minor MM 603*	**50**	1 wk
1 Apr 72	**STIR IT UP** *CBS 7800*	**13**	12 wks
24 Jun 72	● **I CAN SEE CLEARLY NOW** *CBS 8113*	**5**	15 wks
7 Oct 72	● **THERE ARE MORE QUESTIONS THAN ANSWERS** *CBS 8351*	**9**	9 wks
14 Jun 75	★ **TEARS ON MY PILLOW** *CBS 3220*	**1**	11 wks
11 Oct 75	**LET'S BE FRIENDS** *CBS 3597*	**42**	3 wks
12 Jun 76	**(WHAT A) WONDERFUL WORLD** *Epic EPC 4294*	**25**	7 wks

NASHVILLE TEENS

UK, male vocal/instrumental group

9 Jul 64	● **TOBACCO ROAD** *Decca F 11930*	**6**	13 wks
22 Oct 64	● **GOOGLE EYE** *Decca F 12000*	**10**	11 wks
4 Mar 65	**FIND MY WAY BACK HOME** *Decca F 12089*	**34**	6 wks
20 May 65	**THIS LITTLE BIRD** *Decca F 12143*	**38**	4 wks
3 Feb 66	**THE HARD WAY** *Decca F 12316*	**45**	2 wks
24 Feb 66	**THE HARD WAY** (re-entry) *Decca F 12316*	**48**	1 wk

NATASHA *UK, female vocalist*

5 Jun 82	● **IKO IKO** *Towerbell TOW 22*	**10**	11 wks
4 Sep 82	**THE BOOM BOOM ROOM** *Towerbell TOW 25*	**44**	5 wks

NATURALS *UK, male vocal/instrumental group*

20 Aug 64	**I SHOULD HAVE KNOWN BETTER** *Parlophone R 5165*	**24**	9 wks

Date	Title *Label Number*	Position	

David NAUGHTON *US, male vocalist*

Date	Title *Label Number*	Position	
25 Aug 79	**MAKIN' IT** *RSO 32*	**44**	6 wks

NAZARETH *UK, male vocal/instrumental group*

Date	Title *Label Number*	Position	
5 May 73	● **BROKEN DOWN ANGEL** *Mooncrest MOON 1*	**9**	10 wks
21 Jul 73	● **BAD BAD BOY** *Mooncrest MOON 9*	**10**	9 wks
13 Oct 73	**THIS FLIGHT TONIGHT** *Mooncrest MOON 14*	**11**	13 wks
23 Mar 74	**SHANGHAI'D IN SHANGHAI** *Mooncrest MOON 22*	**41**	4 wks
14 Jun 75	**MY WHITE BICYCLE** *Mooncrest MOON 47*	**14**	8 wks
15 Nov 75	**HOLY ROLLER** *Mountain TOP 3*	**36**	4 wks
24 Sep 77	**HOT TRACKS** (EP) *Mountain NAZ 1*	**15**	11 wks
18 Feb 78	**GONE DEAD TRAIN** *Mountain NAZ 002*	**49**	2 wks
13 May 78	**PLACE IN YOUR HEART** *Mountain TOP 37*	**70**	1 wk
27 May 78	**PLACE IN YOUR HEART** (re-entry) *Mountain TOP 37*	**74**	1 wk
27 Jan 79	**MAY THE SUN SHINE** *Mountain NAZ 003*	**22**	8 wks
28 Jul 79	**STAR** *Mountain TOP 45*	**54**	3 wks

Tracks on Hot Tracks EP: *Love Hurts/This Flight Tonight/Broken Down Angel/Hair of the Dog.*

NEIL — See *BARBARA and NEIL*

Bill NELSON *UK, male vocal/instrumental group*

Date	Title *Label Number*	Position	
24 Feb 79	**FURNITURE MUSIC** *Harvest HAR 5176*	**59**	3 wks
5 May 79	**REVOLT INTO STYLE** *Harvest HAR 5183*	**69**	2 wks
5 Jul 80	**DO YOU DREAM IN COLOUR?** *Cocteau COQ 1*	**52**	4 wks
13 Jun 81	**YOUTH OF NATION ON FIRE** *Mercury WILL 2*	**73**	3 wks

Furniture Music *and* Revolt into style *credited to Bill Nelson's Red Noise*

Rick NELSON *US, male vocalist*

Date	Title *Label Number*	Position	
21 Feb 58	**STOOD UP** *London HLP 8542*	**27**	1 wk
7 Mar 58	**STOOD UP** (re-entry) *London HLP 8542*	**29**	1 wk
22 Aug 58	● **POOR LITTLE FOOL** *London HLP 8670*	**4**	13 wks
7 Nov 58	● **SOMEDAY** *London HLP 8732*	**9**	13 wks
21 Nov 58	**I GOT A FEELING** *London HLP 8732*	**27**	1 wk
28 Nov 58	**POOR LITTLE FOOL** (re-entry) *London HLP 8670*	**28**	1 wk
17 Apr 59	● **IT'S LATE** *London HLP 8817*	**3**	20 wks
15 May 59	**NEVER BE ANYONE ELSE BUT YOU** *London HLP 8817*	**19**	1 wk
5 Jun 59	**NEVER BE ANYONE ELSE BUT YOU** (re-entry) *London HLP 8817*	**14**	9 wks
4 Sep 59	**SWEETER THAN YOU** *London HLP 8927*	**19**	3 wks
11 Sep 59	**JUST A LITTLE TOO MUCH** *London HLP 8927*	**11**	8 wks
15 Jan 60	**I WANNA BE LOVED** *London HLP 9021*	**30**	1 wk
7 Jul 60	**YOUNG EMOTIONS** *London HLP 9121*	**48**	1 wk
1 Jun 61	● **HELLO MARY LOU/ TRAVELLIN' MAN** *London HLP 9347*	**2**	18 wks
16 Nov 61	**EVERLOVIN'** *London HLP 9440*	**23**	5 wks
29 Mar 62	**YOUNG WORLD** *London HLP 9524*	**19**	13 wks
30 Aug 62	**TEENAGE IDOL** *London HLP 9583*	**39**	4 wks
17 Jan 63	**IT'S UP TO YOU** *London HLP 9648*	**22**	9 wks
17 Oct 63	**FOOLS RUSH IN** *Brunswick 05895*	**12**	9 wks
30 Jan 64	**FOR YOU** *Brunswick 05900*	**14**	10 wks
21 Oct 72	**GARDEN PARTY** *MCA MU 1165*	**41**	4 wks

Billed as Ricky Nelson on all the hits up to and including Hello Mary Lou/ Travellin' Man.

Sandy NELSON *US, male instrumentalist, drums*

Date	Title *Label Number*	Position	
6 Nov 59	● **TEEN BEAT** *Top Rank JAR 197*	**9**	11 wks
5 Feb 60	**TEEN BEAT** (re-entry) *Top Rank JAR 197*	**25**	1 wk
14 Dec 61	● **LET THERE BE DRUMS** *London HLP 9466*	**3**	16 wks
22 Mar 62	**DRUMS ARE MY BEAT** *London HLP 9521*	**30**	6 wks
7 Jun 62	**DRUMMIN' UP A STORM** *London HLP 9558*	**39**	8 wks

Willie NELSON *US, male vocalist*

Date	Title *Label Number*	Position	
31 Jul 82	**ALWAYS ON MY MIND** *CBS A 2511*	**49**	3 wks

NERO and the GLADIATORS

UK, male instrumental group

Date	Title *Label Number*	Position	
23 Mar 61	**ENTRY OF THE GLADIATORS** *Decca F 11329*	**50**	1 wk
6 Apr 61	**ENTRY OF THE GLADIATORS** (re-entry) *Decca F 11329*	**37**	4 wks
27 Jul 61	**IN THE HALL OF THE MOUNTAIN KING** *Decca F 11367*	**48**	1 wk

NESBITT — See *MILLICAN and NESBITT*

Michael NESMITH *US male vocalist*

Date	Title *Label Number*	Position	
26 Mar 77	**RIO** *Island WIP 6373*	**28**	6 wks

NEW GENERATION

UK, male vocal/instrumental group

Date	Title *Label Number*	Position	
26 Jun 68	**SMOKEY BLUES AWAY** *Spark SRL 1007*	**38**	5 wks

NEW MUSIK *UK, male vocal/instrumental group*

Date	Title *Label Number*	Position	
6 Oct 79	**STRAIGHT LINES** *GTO GT 255*	**53**	5 wks
19 Jan 80	**LIVING BY NUMBERS** *GTO GT 261*	**13**	8 wks
26 Apr 80	**THIS WORLD OF WATER** *GTO GT 268*	**31**	7 wks
12 Jul 80	**SANCTUARY** *GTO GT 275*	**31**	7 wks

NEW ORDER *UK, male vocal/instrumental group*

Date	Title *Label Number*	Position	
14 Mar 81	**CEREMONY** *Factory FAC 33*	**34**	5 wks
3 Oct 81	**PROCESSION/EVERYTHING'S GONE GREEN** *Factory FAC 53*	**38**	5 wks
22 May 82	**TEMPTATION** *Factory FAC 63*	**29**	7 wks

NEW ORLEANS JAZZMEN — See *Terry LIGHTFOOT and his NEW ORLEANS JAZZMEN*

NEW SEEKERS

UK, male/female vocal/instrumental group

Date	Title *Label Number*	Position	
17 Oct 70	**WHAT HAVE THEY DONE TO MY SONG MA** *Philips 6006 027*	**48**	1 wk
31 Oct 70	**WHAT HAVE THEY DONE TO MY SONG MA** (re-entry) *Philips 6006 027*	**44**	1 wk
10 Jul 71	● **NEVER ENDING SONG OF LOVE** *Philips 6006 125*	**2**	19 wks
18 Dec 71	★ **I'D LIKE TO TEACH THE WORLD TO SING** *Polydor 2058 184*	**1**	21 wks
4 Mar 72	● **BEG STEAL OR BORROW** *Polydro 2058 201*	**2**	13 wks
10 Jun 72	● **CIRCLES** *Polydor 2058 242*	**4**	16 wks
2 Dec 72	**COME SOFTLY TO ME** *Polydor 2058 313*	**20**	11 wks

Date	Title *Label Number*	Position	
24 Feb 73	**PINBALL WIZARD - SEE ME FEEL ME** (MEDLEY) *Polydor 2058 338*	**16**	8 wks
7 Apr 73	**NEVERTHELESS** *Polydor 2068 340*	**34**	5 wks
16 Jun 73	**GOODBYE IS JUST ANOTHER WORD** *Polydor 2058 368*	**36**	5 wks
24 Nov 73 ★	**YOU WON'T FIND ANOTHER FOOL LIKE ME** *Polydor 2058 421*	**1**	16 wks
9 Mar 74 ●	**I GET A LITTLE SENTIMENTAL OVER YOU** *Polydor 2058 439*	**5**	9 wks
14 Aug 76	**IT'S SO NICE (TO HAVE YOU HOME)** *CBS 4391*	**44**	4 wks
29 Jan 77	**I WANNA GO BACK** *CBS 4786*	**25**	4 wks
15 Jul 78	**ANTHEM (ONE DAY IN EVERY WEEK)** *CBS 6413*	**21**	10 wks

Come Softly To Me *has credit "featuring Marty Kristian".* Nevertheless *billed as by Eve Graham and the New Seekers.*

NEW VAUDEVILLE BAND

UK, male vocal/instrumental group

Date	Title *Label Number*	Position	
8 Sep 66 ●	**WINCHESTER CATHEDRAL** *Fontana TF 741*	**4**	19 wks
26 Jan 67 ●	**PEEK-A-BOO** *Fontana TF 784*	**7**	11 wks
11 May 67	**FINCHLEY CENTRAL** *Fontana TF 824*	**11**	9 wks
2 Aug 67	**GREEN STREET GREEN** *Fontana TF 853*	**37**	4 wks

Peek-A-Boo *has credit: Featuring Tristram.*

NEW WORLD

Australia, male vocal/instrumental group

Date	Title *Label Number*	Position	
27 Feb 71	**ROSE GARDEN** *RAK 111*	**15**	11 wks
3 Jul 71 ●	**TOM TOM TURNAROUND** *RAK 117*	**6**	15 wks
4 Dec 71	**KARA KARA** *RAK 123*	**17**	13 wks
13 May 72 ●	**SISTER JANE** *RAK 130*	**9**	13 wks
12 May 73	**ROOF TOP SINGING** *RAK 148*	**50**	1 wk

NEW YORK CITY *US, male vocal group*

Date	Title *Label Number*	Position	
21 Jul 73	**I'M DOING FINE NOW** *RCA 2351*	**20**	11 wks

NEW YORK SKYY

US, male/female vocal/instrumental group

Date	Title *Label Number*	Position	
16 Jan 82	**LET'S CELEBRATE** *Epic EPC A 1898*	**71**	1 wk
30 Jan 82	**LET'S CELEBRATE** (re-entry) *Epic EPC A 1898*	**67**	1 wk

NEWBEATS *US, male vocal group*

Date	Title *Label Number*	Position	
10 Sep 64	**BREAD AND BUTTER** *Hickory 1269*	**15**	9 wks
23 Oct 71 ●	**RUN BABY RUN** *London HL 10341*	**10**	13 wks

Mickey NEWBURY *US, male vocalist*

Date	Title *Label Number*	Position	
1 Jul 72	**AMERICAN TRILOGY** *Elektra K 12047*	**42**	5 wks

Anthony NEWLEY *UK, male vocalist*

Date	Title *Label Number*	Position	
1 May 59 ●	**I'VE WAITED SO LONG** *Decca F 11127*	**3**	15 wks
8 May 59	**IDLE ON PARADE** (EP) *Decca DFE 6566*	**13**	4 wks
12 Jun 59 ●	**PERSONALITY** *Decca F 11142*	**6**	12 wks
15 Jan 60 ★	**WHY** *Decca F 11194*	**1**	17 wks
24 Mar 60 ★	**DO YOU MIND** *Decca F 11220*	**1**	15 wks
14 Jul 60 ●	**IF SHE SHOULD COME TO YOU** *Decca F 11254*	**6**	15 wks
24 Nov 60 ●	**STRAWBERRY FAIR** *Decca F 11295*	**3**	11 wks
16 Mar 61 ●	**AND THE HEAVENS CRIED** *Decca F 11331*	**6**	12 wks
15 Jun 61	**POP GOES THE WEASEL/ BEE BOM** *Decca F 11362*	**12**	9 wks
3 Aug 61	**WHAT KIND OF FOOL AM I?** *Decca F 11376*	**36**	8 wks
25 Jan 62	**D-DARLING** *Decca F 11419*	**25**	6 wks
26 Jul 62	**THAT NOISE** *Decca F 11486*	**34**	4 wks

Bee Bom *only listed together with* Pop Goes The Weasel *for weeks of 15 and 22 June 61. Tracks on* Idle On Parade EP: *I've Waited So Long/ Idle Rock-A-Boogie/ Idle On Parade/ Saturday Night Rock-A-Boogie.*

Alfred NEWMAN — See *VARIOUS ARTISTS (Carousel Soundtrack)*

Brad NEWMAN *UK, male vocalist*

Date	Title *Label Number*	Position	
22 Feb 62	**SOMEBODY TO LOVE** *Fontana H 357*	**47**	1 wk

Dave NEWMAN *UK, male vocalist*

Date	Title *Label Number*	Position	
15 Apr 72	**THE LION SLEEPS TONIGHT** *Pye 7N 45134*	**48**	1 wk
29 Apr 72	**THE LION SLEEPS TONIGHT** (re-entry) *Pye 7N 45134*	**34**	5 wks

NEWS *US, male vocal/instrumental group*

Date	Title *Label Number*	Position	
29 Aug 81	**AUDIO VIDEO** *George GEORGE 1*	**52**	3 wks

Juice NEWTON *US, female vocalist*

Date	Title *Label Number*	Position	
2 May 81	**ANGEL OF THE MORNING** *Capitol CL 16189*	**43**	6 wks

Olivia NEWTON-JOHN *UK, female vocalist*

Date	Title *Label Number*	Position	
20 Mar 71 ●	**IF NOT FOR YOU** *Pye International 7N 25543*	**7**	11 wks
23 Oct 71 ●	**BANKS OF THE OHIO** *Pye International 7N 25568*	**6**	17 wks
11 Mar 72	**WHAT IS LIFE** *Pye International 7N 25575*	**16**	8 wks
13 Jan 73	**TAKE ME HOME COUNTRY ROADS** *Pye International 7N 25599*	**15**	13 wks
16 Mar 74	**LONG LIVE LOVE** *Pye International 7N 25638*	**11**	8 wks
12 Oct 74	**I HONESTLY LOVE YOU** *EMI 2216*	**22**	6 wks
11 Jun 77 ●	**SAM** *EMI 2616*	**6**	11 wks
4 Nov 78 ●	**HOPELESSLY DEVOTED TO YOU** *RSO 17*	**2**	11 wks
16 Dec 78 ●	**A LITTLE MORE LOVE** *EMI 2879*	**4**	12 wks
30 Jun 79	**DEEPER THAN THE NIGHT** *EMI 2954*	**64**	3 wks
23 Aug 80	**MAGIC** *Jet 196*	**32**	7 wks
10 Oct 81 ●	**PHYSICAL** *EMI 5234*	**7**	16 wks
16 Jan 82	**LANDSLIDE** *EMI 5257*	**18**	9 wks
17 Apr 82	**MAKE A MOVE ON ME** *EMI 5291*	**43**	3 wks
23 Oct 82	**HEART ATTACK** *EMI 5347*	**46**	4 wks

See also Olivia Newton-John and Electric Light Orchestra, Olivia Newton John and Cliff Richard, John Travolta and Olivia Newton-John

Olivia NEWTON-JOHN and ELECTRIC LIGHT ORCHESTRA

UK, female vocalist, male vocal/instrumental group

Date	Title *Label Number*	Position	
21 Jun 80 ★	**XANADU** *Jet 185*	**1**	11 wks

See also Olivia Newton-John, John Travolta & Olivia Newton-John, Olivia Newton-John and Cliff Richard, Electric Light Orchestra.

Date Title *Label Number* Position

Date Title *Label Number* Position

Olivia NEWTON-JOHN and Cliff RICHARD *UK, female/male vocal duo*

Date		Title *Label Number*	Position	Weeks
25 Oct 80		**SUDDENLY** *Jet 7002*	**15**	7 wks

See also Olivia Newton-John, Cliff Richard, Olivia Newton-John & Electric Light Orchestra, John Travolta and Olivia Newton-John

NICE *UK, male instrumental group*

Date		Title *Label Number*	Position	Weeks
10 Jul 68		**AMERICA** *Immediate IM 068*	**21**	15 wks

Paul NICHOLAS *UK, male vocalist*

Date		Title *Label Number*	Position	Weeks
17 Apr 76		**REGGAE LIKE IT USED TO BE** *RSO 2090 185*	**17**	8 wks
9 Oct 76	●	**DANCING WITH THE CAPTAIN** *RSO 2090 206*	**8**	9 wks
4 Dec 76	●	**GRANDMA'S PARTY** *RSO 2090 216*	**9**	11 wks
9 Jul 77		**HEAVEN ON THE 7TH FLOOR** *RSO 2090 249*	**40**	3 wks

Sue NICHOLS *UK, female vocalist*

Date		Title *Label Number*	Position	Weeks
3 Jul 68		**WHERE WILL YOU BE** *Pye 7N 17565*	**17**	8 wks

Stevie NICKS with Tom PETTY and the HEARTBREAKERS

US, female vocalist with male vocal/instrumental group.

Date		Title *Label Number*	Position	Weeks
15 Aug 81		**STOP DRAGGIN' MY HEART AROUND** *WEA K 79231*	**50**	4 wks

See also Tom Petty and the Heartbreakers

NICOLE *Germany, female vocalist*

Date		Title *Label Number*	Position	Weeks
8 May 82	★	**A LITTLE PEACE** *CBS A 2365*	**1**	9 wks
21 Aug 32		**GIVE ME MORE TIME** *CBS A 2467*	**75**	1 wk

Maxine NIGHTINGALE *UK, female vocalist*

Date		Title *Label Number*	Position	Weeks
1 Nov 75	●	**RIGHT BACK WHERE WE STARTED FROM** *United Artists UP 36015*	**8**	8 wks
12 Mar 77		**LOVE HIT ME** *United Artists UP 36215*	**11**	8 wks

NILSSON *US, male vocalist*

Date		Title *Label Number*	Position	Weeks
27 Sep 69		**EVERYBODY'S TALKIN'** *RCA 1876*	**50**	1 wk
11 Oct 69		**EVERYBODY'S TALKIN'** (re-entry) *RCA 1876*	**23**	9 wks
14 Mar 70		**EVERYBODY'S TALKIN'** (2nd re-entry) *RCA 1876*	**39**	5 wks
5 Feb 72	★	**WITHOUT YOU** *RCA 2165*	**1**	20 wks
3 Jun 72		**COCONUT** *RCA 2214*	**42**	5 wks
16 Oct 76		**WITHOUT YOU** (re-issue) *RCA 2733*	**22**	8 wks
20 Aug 77		**ALL I THINK ABOUT IS YOU** *RCA PB 9104*	**43**	3 wks

NINA and FREDERICK

Denmark, male/female vocal duo

Date		Title *Label Number*	Position	Weeks
18 Dec 59		**MARY'S BOY CHILD** *Columbia DB 4375*	**26**	1 wk
10 Mar 60		**LISTEN TO THE OCEAN** *Columbia DB 4332*	**47**	1 wk
7 Apr 60		**LISTEN TO THE OCEAN** (re-entry) *Columbia DB 4332*	**46**	1 wk
17 Nov 60	●	**LITTLE DONKEY** *Columbia DB 4536*	**3**	10 wks
28 Sep 61		**LONGTIME BOY** *Columbia DB 4703*	**43**	3 wks
5 Oct 61		**SUCU SUCU** *Columbia DB 4632*	**23**	13 wks

999 *UK, male vocal/instrumental group*

Date		Title *Label Number*	Position	Weeks
25 Nov 78		**HOMICIDE** *United Artists UP 36467*	**40**	3 wks
16 May 81		**OBSESSED** *Albion ION 1011*	**71**	1 wk
18 Jul 81		**LIL RED RIDING HOOD** *Albion ION 1017*	**59**	3 wks
14 Nov 81		**INDIAN RESERVATION** *Albion ION 1023*	**51**	4 wks

1910 FRUITGUM CO.

US, male vocal/instrumental group

Date		Title *Label Number*	Position	Weeks
20 Mar 68	●	**SIMON SAYS** *Pye International 7N 25447*	**2**	16 wks

NIRVANA *UK, male vocal/instrumental duo*

Date		Title *Label Number*	Position	Weeks
15 May 68		**RAINBOW CHASER** *Island WIP 6029*	**34**	6 wks

NO DICE *UK, male vocal/instrumental group*

Date		Title *Label Number*	Position	Weeks
5 May 79		**COME DANCING** *EMI 2927*	**65**	2 wks

NOLANS *Ireland, female vocal group*

Date		Title *Label Number*	Position	Weeks
6 Oct 79		**SPIRIT BODY AND SOUL** *Epic EPC 7796*	**34**	6 wks
22 Dec 79	●	**I'M IN THE MOOD FOR DANCING** *Epic EDC 8068*	**3**	15 wks
12 Apr 80		**DON'T MAKE WAVES** *Epic EPC 8349*	**12**	11 wks
13 Sep 80	●	**GOTTA PULL MYSELF TOGETHER** *Epic EPC 8878*	**9**	13 wks
6 Dec 80		**WHO'S GONNA ROCK YOU** *Epic EPC 9325*	**12**	11 wks
14 Mar 81	●	**ATTENTION TO ME** *Epic EPC 9571*	**9**	13 wks
15 Aug 81		**CHEMISTRY** *Epic EPC A1485*	**15**	8 wks
20 Feb 82		**DON'T LOVE ME TOO HARD** *Epic EPC A 1927*	**14**	12 wks

First hit billed as Nolan Sisters. See also Young and Moody Band

Peter NOONE *UK, male vocalist*

Date		Title *Label Number*	Position	Weeks
22 May 71		**OH YOU PRETTY THING** *RAK 114*	**12**	9 wks

See also Herman's Hermits.

Freddie NOTES and the RUDIES

Jamaica, male vocal/instrumental group

Date		Title *Label Number*	Position	Weeks
10 Oct 70		**MONTEGO BAY** *Trojan TR 7791*	**45**	2 wks

Left **NICOLE** German schoolgirl Nicole, whose 1982 Eurovision Winner 'A Little Peace' was the 500th single to top the British charts

Far left **NIRVANA** Multi instrumentalist Patrick Campbell – Lyons and Alex Spyropoulos made a string of great singles in the late 60s including 'Pentecost Hotel', 'Tony Goddess' and their only hit 'Rainbow Chaser'

Centre **1910 FRUITGUM CO** Formed at a New Jersey High School they played under a variety of names – 'Jekell & Hyde', 'The Odyssey' and the 'Lower Road' before rhythm guitarist Frank Jekell discovered '1910 Fruitgum Co' on an old bubblegum wrapper

Below **HAZEL O'CONNOR** The eighth day came round 9 times for her first hit

Left **NEW VAUDEVILLE BAND** Enticed the entire populace of geographical locations to buy their records by singing about them. Maybe a song about the whole of London would have resulted in a No. 1

NOTTINGHAM FOREST F.C. and PAPER LACE

UK, football team vocalists and UK, male vocal/instrumental group

Date	Title *Label Number*	Position	
4 Mar 78	**WE'VE GOT THE WHOLE WORLD IN OUR HANDS** *Warner Bros. K 17710*	**24**	6 wks

See also Paper Lace

Nancy NOVA *US, female vocalist*

Date	Title *Label Number*	Position	
4 Sep 82	**NO NO NO** *EMI 5328*	**63**	2 wks

Gary NUMAN *UK, male vocalist*

Date	Title *Label Number*	Position	
19 May 79	★ **ARE FRIENDS ELECTRIC** *Beggars Banquet BEG 18*	**1**	16 wks
1 Sep 79	★ **CARS** *Beggars Banquet BEG 23*	**1**	11 wks
24 Nov 79	● **COMPLEX** *Beggars Banquet BEG 29*	**6**	9 wks
24 May 80	● **WE ARE GLASS** *Beggars Banquet BEG 35*	**5**	7 wks
30 Aug 80	● **I DIE: YOU DIE** *Beggars Banquet BEG 46*	**6**	7 wks
20 Dec 80	**THIS WRECKAGE** *Beggars Banquet BEG 50*	**20**	7 wks
29 Aug 81	● **SHE'S GOT CLAWS** *Beggars Banquet BEG 62*	**6**	6 wks
5 Dec 81	**LOVE NEEDS NO DISGUISE** *Beggars Banquet BEG 68*	**33**	7 wks
6 Mar 82	**MUSC FOR CHAMELEONS** *Beggars Banquet BEG 70*	**19**	7 wks
19 Jun 82	● **WE TAKE MYSTERY** *Beggars Banquet BEG 77*	**9**	4 wks
28 Aug 82	**WHITE BOYS AND HEROS** *Beggars Banquet BEG 81*	**20**	4 wks

Are Friends Electric *by Gary Numan under the group name Tubeway Army.* Love Needs No Disguise *credited to Gary Numan and Dramatis. Other hits credited to* Gary Numan. *See also Dramatis.*

O

John OATES — See *Daryl HALL and John OATES*

OBERNKIRCHEN CHILDREN'S CHOIR

Germany, children's choir

Date	Title *Label Number*	Position	
22 Jan 54	● **HAPPY WANDERER** *Parlophone R 3799*	**2**	23 wks
9 Jul 54	● **HAPPY WANDERER** (re-entry) *Parlophone R 3799*	**8**	3 wks

Dermot O'BRIEN *Ireland, male vocalist*

Date	Title *Label Number*	Position	
20 Oct 66	**THE MERRY PLOUGHBOY** *Envoy ENV 016*	**46**	1 wk
3 Nov 66	**THE MERRY PLOUGHBOY** (re-entry) *Envoy ENV 016*	**50**	1 wk

Billy OCEAN *UK, male vocalist*

Date	Title *Label Number*	Position	
21 Feb 76	● **LOVE REALLY HURTS WITHOUT YOU** *GTO GT 52*	**2**	10 wks
10 Jul 76	**L.O.D. (LOVE ON DELIVERY)** *GTO GT 62*	**19**	8 wks
13 Nov 76	**STOP ME (IF YOU'VE HEARD IT ALL BEFORE)** *GTO GT 72*	**12**	11 wks
19 Mar 77	● **RED LIGHT SPELLS DANGER** *GTO GT 85*	**2**	10 wks
1 Sep 79	**AMERICAN HEARTS** *GTO GT 244*	**54**	5 wks
19 Jan 80	**ARE YOU READY** *GTO GT 259*	**42**	7 wks

Des O'CONNOR *UK, male vocalist*

Date	Title *Label Number*	Position	
1 Nov 67	● **CARELESS HANDS** *Columbia DB 8275*	**6**	15 wks
8 May 68	★ **I PRETEND** *Columbia DB 8397*	**1**	36 wks
20 Nov 68	● **1-2-3 O'LEARY** *Columbia DB 8492*	**4**	11 wks
7 May 69	**DICK-A-DUM-DUM (KING'S ROAD)** *Columbia DB 8566*	**14**	10 wks
29 Nov 69	**LONELINESS** *Columbia DB 8632*	**18**	11 wks
14 Mar 70	**I'LL GO ON HOPING** *Columbia DB 8661*	**30**	7 wks
26 Sep 70	**THE TIPS OF MY FINGERS** *Columbia DB 8713*	**15**	15 wks

Hazel O'CONNOR *UK, female vocalist*

Date	Title *Label Number*	Position	
16 Aug 80	● **EIGHTH DAY** *A & M AMS 7553*	**5**	11 wks
25 Oct 80	**GIVE ME AN INCH** *A & M AMS 7569*	**41**	4 wks
21 Mar 81	● **D-DAYS** *Albion ION 1009*	**10**	9 wks
23 May 81	● **WILL YOU** *A & M AMS 8131*	**8**	10 wks
1 Aug 81	**(COVER PLUS) WE'RE ALL GROWN UP** *Albion ION 1018*	**41**	6 wks
3 Oct 81	**HANGING AROUND** *Albion ION 1022*	**45**	3 wks
23 Jan 82	**CALLS THE TUNE** *A & M AMS 8203*	**60**	3 wks

Alan O'DAY *US, male vocalist*

Date	Title *Label Number*	Position	
2 Jul 77	**UNDERCOVER ANGEL** *Atlantic K 10926*	**43**	3 wks

ODETTA — See *Harry BELAFONTE and ODETTA*

ODYSSEY *US, male/female vocal group*

Date	Title *Label Number*	Position	
24 Dec 77	● **NATIVE NEW YORKER** *RCA PC 1129*	**5**	11 wks
21 Jun 80	★ **USE IT UP AND WEAR IT OUT** *RCA PB 1962*	**1**	12 wks
13 Sep 80	● **IF YOU'RE LOOKIN' FOR A WAY OUT** *RCA 5*	**6**	15 wks
17 Jan 81	**HANG TOGETHER** *RCA 23*	**36**	7 wks
30 May 81	● **GOING BACK TO MY ROOTS** *RCA 85*	**4**	12 wks
19 Sep 81	**IT WILL BE ALRIGHT** *RCA 128*	**43**	5 wks
12 Jun 82	● **INSIDE OUT** *RCA 226*	**3**	11 wks
11 Sep 82	**MAGIC TOUCH** *RCA 275*	**41**	5 wks

Esther and Abi OFARIM

Israel, male/female vocal duo

Date	Title *Label Number*	Position	
14 Feb 68	★ **CINDERELLA ROCKEFELLA** *Philips BF 1640*	**1**	13 wks
19 Jun 68	**ONE MORE DANCE** *Philips BF 1678*	**13**	9 wks

OHIO EXPRESS

US, male vocal/instrumental group

Date	Title *Label Number*	Position	
5 Jun 68	● **YUMMY YUMMY YUMMY** *Pye International 7N 25459*	**5**	15 wks

OHIO PLAYERS

US, male vocal/instrumental group

Date	Title *Label Number*	Position	
10 Jul 76	**WHO'D SHE COO** *Mercury PLAY 001*	**43**	4 wks

Left **ESTHER AND ABI OFARIM** The only British No. 1 by an act from Israel

Right **DONNY OSMOND** Three number one hits in two years including *Puppy Love* which charted for him on 3 separate occasions

Below **MIKE OLDFIELD** His imaginative multi-instrumental success was not surprisingly greater in the album charts although he has more than once come close to a number one single

Date	Title *Label Number*	Position	

O'JAYS *US, male vocal group*

Date		Title *Label Number*	Pos	Wks
23 Sep 72		**BACK STABBERS** *CBS 8270*	**14**	9 wks
3 Mar 73	●	**LOVE TRAIN** *CBS 1181*	**9**	13 wks
31 Jan 76		**I LOVE MUSIC** *Philadelphia International PIR 3879*	**13**	9 wks
12 Feb 77		**DARLIN' DARLIN' BABY (SWEET, TENDER, LOVE)** *Philadelphia International PIR 4834*	**24**	6 wks
8 Apr 78		**I LOVE MUSIC** (re-issue) *Philadelphia International PIR 6093*	**36**	3 wks
17 Jun 78		**USED TA BE MY GIRL** *Philadelphia International PIR 6332*	**12**	12 wks
30 Sep 78		**BRANDY** *Philadelphia International PIR 6658*	**21**	9 wks
29 Sep 79		**SING A HAPPY SONG** *Philadelphia International PIR 7825*	**39**	6 wks

Mike OLDFIELD

UK, male multi-instrumentalist/vocalist

Date		Title *Label Number*	Pos	Wks
13 Jul 74		**MIKE OLDFIELD'S SINGLE (THEME FROM TUBULAR BELLS)** *Virgin VS 101*	**31**	6 wks
20 Dec 75	●	**IN DULCE JUBILO/ ON HORSEBACK** *Virgin VS 131*	**4**	10 wks
27 Nov 76	●	**PORTSMOUTH** *Virgin VS 163*	**3**	12 wks
23 Dec 78		**TAKE 4** (EP) *Virgin VS 238*	**72**	3 wks
21 Apr 79		**GUILTY** *Virgin VS 245*	**22**	8 wks
8 Dec 79		**BLUE PETER** *Virgin VS 317*	**19**	9 wks
20 Mar 82		**FIVE MILES OUT** *Virgin VS 464*	**43**	5 wks
12 Jun 82		**FAMILY MAN** *Virgin VS 489*	**45**	6 wks

Tracks on Take 4 *EP: Portsmouth/ In Dulci Jubilo/ Wrekorder Wrondo/ Sailors Hornpipe*

Sally OLDFIELD *UK, female vocalist*

Date		Title *Label Number*	Pos	Wks
9 Dec 78		**MIRRORS** *Bronze BRO 66*	**19**	13 wks

OLIVER *US, male vocalist*

Date		Title *Label Number*	Pos	Wks
9 Aug 69	●	**GOOD MORNING STARSHINE** *CBS 4435*	**6**	16 wks
27 Dec 69		**GOOD MORNING STARSHINE** (re-entry) *CBS 4435*	**39**	2 wks

OLYMPIC RUNNERS

UK, male vocal/instrumental group

Date		Title *Label Number*	Pos	Wks
13 May 78		**WHATEVER IT TAKES** *RCA PC 5078*	**61**	2 wks
14 Oct 78		**GET IT WHILE YOU CAN** *Polydor RUN 7*	**35**	6 wks
20 Jan 79		**SIR DANCEALOT** *Polydor POSP 17*	**35**	6 wks
28 Jul 79		**THE BITCH** *Polydor POSP 63*	**37**	7 wks

OLYMPICS *US, male vocal group*

Date		Title *Label Number*	Pos	Wks
3 Oct 58		**WESTERN MOVIES** *HMV POP 528*	**12**	8 wks
19 Jan 61		**I WISH I COULD SHIMMY LIKE MY SISTER KATE** *Vogue V 9174*	**45**	1 wk

ONE HUNDRED TON AND A FEATHER

UK, male vocalist, Jonathan King, under false name

Date		Title *Label Number*	Pos	Wks
26 Jun 76	●	**IT ONLY TAKES A MINUTE** *UK 135*	**9**	9 wks

See also Jonathan King.

ONE WAY featuring Al HUDSON

US, male/female vocal/instrumental group

Date		Title *Label Number*	Pos	Wks
8 Dec 79		**MUSIC** *MCA 542*	**56**	6 wks

See also Al Hudson and the Partners.

Yoko ONO — See *John LENNON*

Yoko ONO *Japan, female vocalist*

Date		Title *Label Number*	Pos	Wks
28 Feb 81		**WALKING ON THIN ICE** *Geffen K 79202*	**35**	5 wks

See also John Lennon

ORANGE JUICE

UK, male vocal/instrumental group

Date		Title *Label Number*	Pos	Wks
7 Nov 81		**L.O.V.E...LOVE** *Polydor POSP 357*	**65**	2 wks
30 Jan 82		**FELICITY** *Polydor POSP 386*	**63**	3 wks
21 Aug 82		**TWO HEARTS TOGETHER/HOKOYO** *Polydor POSP 470*	**60**	2 wks
23 Oct 82		**I CANT HELP MYSELF** *Polydor POSP 522*	**42**	3 wks

Roy ORBISON *US, male vocalist*

Date		Title *Label Number*	Pos	Wks
28 Jul 60		**ONLY THE LONELY** *London HLU 9149*	**36**	1 wk
11 Aug 60	★	**ONLY THE LONELY** (re-entry) *London HLU 9149*	**1**	23 wks
27 Oct 60		**BLUE ANGEL** *London HLU 9207*	**11**	16 wks
25 May 61	●	**RUNNING SCARED** *London HLU 9342*	**9**	15 wks
21 Sep 61		**CRYIN'** *London HLU 9405*	**25**	9 wks
8 Mar 62	●	**DREAM BABY** *London HLU 9511*	**2**	14 wks
28 Jun 62		**THE CROWD** *London HLU 9561*	**40**	4 wks
8 Nov 62		**WORKIN' FOR THE MAN** *London HLU 9607*	**50**	1 wk
28 Feb 63	●	**IN DREAMS** *London HLU 9676*	**6**	23 wks
30 May 63	●	**FALLING** *London HLU 9727*	**9**	11 wks
19 Sep 63	●	**BLUE BAYOU/ MEAN WOMAN BLUES** *London HLU 9777*	**3**	19 wks
20 Feb 64		**BORNE ON THE WIND** *London HLU 9845*	**15**	10 wks
30 Apr 64	★	**IT'S OVER** *London HLU 9882*	**1**	18 wks
10 Sep 64	★	**OH PRETTY WOMAN** *London HLU 9919*	**1**	18 wks
19 Nov 64	●	**PRETTY PAPER** *London HLU 9930*	**6**	11 wks
11 Feb 65		**GOODNIGHT** *London HLU 9951*	**14**	9 wks
22 Jul 65		**(SAY) YOU'RE MY GIRL** *London HLU 9978*	**23**	8 wks
9 Sep 65		**RIDE AWAY** *London HLU 9986*	**34**	6 wks
4 Nov 65		**CRAWLIN' BACK** *London HLU 10000*	**19**	9 wks
27 Jan 66		**BREAKIN' UP IS BREAKIN' MY HEART** *London HL 10015*	**22**	6 wks
7 Apr 66		**TWINKLE TOES** *London HLU 10034*	**29**	5 wks
16 Jun 66		**LANA** *London HL 10051*	**15**	9 wks
18 Aug 66	●	**TOO SOON TO KNOW** *London HLU 10067*	**3**	17 wks
1 Dec 66		**THERE WON'T BE MANY COMING HOME** *London HL 10096*	**18**	9 wks
23 Feb 67		**SO GOOD** *London HL 10113*	**32**	6 wks
24 Jul 68		**WALK ON** *London HLU 10206*	**39**	10 wks
25 Sep 68		**HEARTACHE** *London HLU 10222*	**44**	4 wks
30 May 69		**MY FRIEND** *London HL 10261*	**35**	4 wks
13 Sep 69		**PENNY ARCADE** *London HL 10285*	**40**	3 wks
11 Oct 69		**PENNY ARCADE** (re-entry) *London HL 10285*	**27**	11 wks

ORCHESTRAL MANOEUVRES in the DARK *UK, male vocal/instrumental duo*

Date		Title *Label Number*	Pos	Wks
9 Feb 80		**RED FRAME WHITE LIGHT** *Dindisc DIN 6*	**67**	2 wks
7 May 80		**MESSAGES** *Dindisc DIN 15*	**13**	11 wks
4 Oct 80	●	**ENOLA GAY** *Dindisc DIN 22*	**8**	15 wks

Date	Title *Label Number*	Position	
29 Aug 81	● **SOUVENIR** *Dindisc DIN 24*	**3**	12 wks
24 Oct 81	● **JOAN OF ARC** *Dindisc DIN 36*	**5**	14 wks
23 Jan 82	● **MAID OF ORLEANS (THE WALTZ JOAN OF ARC)** *Dindisc DIN 40*	**4**	10 wks

Tony ORLANDO *US, male vocalist*

5 Oct 61	● **BLESS YOU** *Fontana H 330*	**5**	11 wks

See also Dawn.

Tony ORLANDO — See *DAWN*

ORLONS *US, female/male vocal group*

27 Dec 62	**DON'T HANG UP** *Cameo Parkway C 231*	**50**	1 wk
10 Jan 63	**DON'T HANG UP** (re-entry) *Cameo Parkway C 231*	**39**	2 wks

Tony OSBORNE SOUND *UK, orchestra*

23 Feb 61	**MAN FROM MADRID** *HMV POP 827*	**50**	1 wk
3 Feb 73	**THE SHEPHERD'S SONG** *Philips 6006 266*	**46**	2 wks

Hit has credit featuring Joanne Brown, UK female vocalist.

Ozzy OSBOURNE BLIZZARD OF OZZ

UK, male vocal/instrumental group

13 Sep 80	**CRAZY TRAIN** *Jet 197*	**49**	4 wks
15 Nov 80	**MR. CROWLEY** *Jet 7003*	**46**	3 wks

OSIBISA

Ghana/Nigeria, male vocal/instrumental group

17 Jan 76	**SUNSHINE DAY** *Bronze BRO 20*	**17**	6 wks
5 Jun 76	**DANCE THE BODY MUSIC** *Bronze BRO 26*	**31**	6 wks

Donny OSMOND *US, male vocalist*

17 Jun 72	★ **PUPPY LOVE** *MGM 2006 104*	**1**	19 wks
16 Sep 72	● **TOO YOUNG** *MGM 2006 113*	**5**	12 wks
11 Nov 72	● **WHY** *MGM 2006 119*	**3**	20 wks
23 Dec 72	**PUPPY LOVE** (re-entry) *MGM 2006 104*	**46**	3 wks
23 Dec 72	**TOO YOUNG** (re-entry) *MGM 2006 113*	**47**	3 wks
27 Jan 73	**PUPPY LOVE** (2nd re-entry) *MGM 2006 104*	**48**	1 wk
10 Mar 73	★ **THE TWELFTH OF NEVER** *MGM 2006 199*	**1**	14 wks
18 Aug 73	★ **YOUNG LOVE** *MGM 2006 300*	**1**	10 wks
10 Nov 73	● **WHEN I FALL IN LOVE** *MGM 2006 365*	**4**	13 wks
9 Nov 74	**WHERE DID ALL THE GOOD TIMES GO** *MGM 2006 468*	**18**	10 wks

See also Donny & Marie Osmond, the Osmonds.

Donny and Marie OSMOND

US, male/female vocal duo

3 Aug 74	● **I'M LEAVING IT (ALL) UP TO YOU** *MGM 2006 446*	**2**	12 wks
14 Dec 74	● **MORNING SIDE OF THE MOUNTAIN** *MGM 2006 474*	**5**	12 wks
21 Jun 75	**MAKE THE WORLD GO AWAY** *MGM 2006 523*	**18**	6 wks
17 Jan 76	**DEEP PURPLE** *MGM 2006 561*	**25**	7 wks

See also Donny Osmond, Marie Osmond, the Osmonds.

Little Jimmy OSMOND *US, male vocalist*

25 Nov 72	★ **LONG HAIRED LOVER FROM LIVERPOOL** *MGM 2006 109*	**1**	24 wks
31 Mar 73	● **TWEEDLE DEE** *MGM 2006*	**4**	13 wks
19 May 73	**LONG HAIRED LOVER FROM LIVERPOOL** (re-entry) *MGM 2006 109*	**41**	3 wks
23 Mar 74	**I'M GONNA KNOCK ON YOUR DOOR** *MGM 2006 389*	**11**	10 wks

Marie OSMOND *US, female vocalist*

17 Nov 73	● **PAPER ROSES** *MGM 2006 315*	**2**	15 wks

See also Donny & Marie Osmond.

OSMONDS *US, male vocal/instrumental group*

25 Mar 72	**DOWN BY THE LAZY RIVER** *MGM 2006 096*	**40**	5 wks
11 Nov 72	● **CRAZY HORSES** *MGM 2006 142*	**2**	18 wks
14 Jul 73	● **GOING HOME** *MGM 2006 288*	**4**	10 wks
27 Oct 73	● **LET ME IN** *MGM 2006 321*	**2**	14 wks
20 Apr 74	**I CAN'T STOP** *MCA 129*	**12**	10 wks
24 Aug 74	★ **LOVE ME FOR A REASON** *MGM 2006 458*	**1**	9 wks
1 Mar 75	**HAVING A PARTY** *MGM 2006 492*	**28**	8 wks
24 May 75	● **THE PROUD ONE** *MGM 2006 520*	**5**	8 wks
15 Nov 75	**I'M STILL GONNA NEED YOU** *MGM 2006 551*	**32**	4 wks
30 Oct 76	**I CAN'T LIVE A DREAM** *Polydor 2391 236*	**37**	5 wks

See also Donny Osmond, Donny and Marie Osmond.

Gilbert O'SULLIVAN *UK, male vocalist*

28 Nov 70	● **NOTHING RHYMED** *MAM 3*	**8**	11 wks
3 Apr 71	**UNDERNEATH THE BLANKET GO** *MAM 13*	**40**	1 wk
17 Apr 71	**UNDERNEATH THE BLANKET GO** (re-entry) *MAM 13*	**42**	3 wks
24 Jul 71	**WE WILL** *MAM 30*	**16**	11 wks
27 Nov 71	● **NO MATTER HOW I TRY** *MAM 53*	**5**	15 wks
4 Mar 72	● **ALONE AGAIN (NATURALLY)** *MAM 66*	**3**	12 wks
17 Jun 72	● **OOH-WAKKA-DOO-WAKKA-DAY** *MAM 78*	**8**	11 wks
21 Oct 72	★ **CLAIR** *MAM 84*	**1**	14 wks
17 Mar 73	★ **GET DOWN** *MAM 96*	**1**	13 wks
15 Sep 73	**OOH BABY** *MAM 107*	**18**	7 wks
10 Nov 73	● **WHY OH WHY OH WHY** *MAM 111*	**6**	14 wks
9 Feb 74	**HAPPINESS IS ME AND YOU** *MAM 114*	**19**	7 wks
24 Aug 74	**A WOMAN'S PLACE** *MAM 122*	**42**	3 wks
14 Dec 74	**CHRISTMAS SONG** *MAM 124*	**12**	6 wks
14 Jun 75	**I DON'T LOVE YOU BUT I THINK I LIKE YOU** *MAM 130*	**14**	6 wks
27 Sep 80	**WHAT'S IN A KISS?** *CBS 8929*	**19**	9 wks

Johnny OTIS SHOW *US, orchestra and chorus*

22 Nov 57	● **MA HE'S MAKING EYES AT ME** *Capitol CL 14794*	**2**	15 wks
10 Jan 58	**BYE BYE BABY** *Capitol CL 14817*	**20**	7 wks

Ma He's Making Eyes At Me *credits Johnny Otis and his orchestra with Marie Adams and the Three Tons of Joy.* Bye Bye Baby *features vocals by Marie Adams and Johnny Otis.*

OTTAWAN *France, male/female vocal duo*

13 Sep 80	● **D.I.S.C.O.** *Carrere CAR 161*	**2**	18 wks
13 Dec 80	**YOU'RE O.K.** *Carrere CAR 168*	**56**	6 wks
29 Aug 81	● **HANDS UP (GIVE ME YOUR HEART)** *Carrere CAR 183*	**3**	15 wks
5 Dec 81	**HELP, GET ME SOME HELP!** *Carrere CAR 215*	**49**	6 wks

Date	Title *Label Number*	Position	

John OTWAY and Wild Willy BARRETT

UK, male vocal/instrumental duo

3 Dec 77	**REALLY FREE** *Polydor 2058 951*	**27**	8 wks
5 Jul 80	**DK 50-80** *Polydor 2059 250*	**45**	4 wks

DK 50-80 *Credited simply to Otway and Barrett*

OUR DAUGHTER'S WEDDING

US, male vocal/instrumental group

1 Aug 81	**LAWNCHAIRS** *EMI America EA 124*	**49**	6 wks

OUR KID *UK, male vocal group*

29 May 76	● **YOU JUST MIGHT SEE ME CRY** *Polydor 2058 729*	**2**	11 wks

OUTLAWS *UK, male instrumental group*

13 Apr 61	**SWINGIN' LOW** *HMV POP 844*	**46**	2 wks
8 Jun 61	**AMBUSH** *HMV POP 877*	**43**	2 wks

See also Mike Berry with the Outlaws.

OVERLANDERS

UK, male vocal/instrumental group

13 Jan 66	★ **MICHELLE** *Pye 7N 17034*	**1**	10 wks

Reg OWEN *UK, orchestra*

27 Feb 59	**MANHATTAN SPIRITUAL** *Pye International 7N 25009*	**20**	8 wks
27 Oct 60	**OBSESSION** *Palette PG 9004*	**43**	2 wks

P

Thom PACE *US, male vocalist*

19 May 79	**MAYBE** *RSO 34*	**14**	15 wks

PACEMAKERS — See *GERRY and the PACEMAKERS*

PACKABEATS *UK, male instrumental group*

23 Feb 61	**GYPSY BEAT** *Parlophone R 4729*	**49**	1 wk

Hal PAGE and the WHALERS

US, male vocal/instrumental group

25 Aug 60	**GOING BACK TO MY HOME TOWN** *Melodisc MEL 1553*	**50**	1 wk

Patti PAGE *US, female vocalist*

27 Mar 53	● **(HOW MUCH IS) THAT DOGGIE IN THE WINDOW** *Oriole CB 1156*	**9**	5 wks

PAGLIARO *Canada, male vocalist*

19 Feb 72	**LOVING YOU AIN'T EASY** *Pye 7N 45111*	**31**	6 wks

Elaine PAIGE *UK, female vocalist*

21 Oct 78	**DON'T WALK AWAY TILL I TOUCH YOU** *EMI 2862*	**46**	5 wks
6 Jun 81	● **MEMORY** *Polydor POSP 279*	**6**	12 wks
30 Jan 82	**MEMORY** (re-entry) *Polydor POSP 279*	**67**	3 wks

PALE FOUNTAINS

UK, male vocal/instrumental group

27 Nov 82	**THANK YOU** *Virgin VS 557*	**48**†	5 wks

PALMER — See *EMERSON, LAKE and PALMER*

Robert PALMER *UK, male vocalist*

20 May 78	**EVERY KINDA PEOPLE** *Island WIP 6425*	**53**	4 wks
7 Jul 79	**BAD CASE OF LOVIN' YOU (DOCTOR DOCTOR)** *Island WIP 6481*	**61**	2 wks
6 Sep 80	**JOHNNY AND MARY** *Island WIP 6638*	**44**	8 wks
22 Nov 80	**LOOKING FOR CLUES** *Island WIP 6651*	**33**	9 wks
13 Feb 82	**SOME GUYS HAVE ALL THE LUCK** *Island WIP 6754*	**16**	8 wks

PAPER DOLLS *UK, female vocal group*

13 Mar 68	**SOMETHING HERE IN MY HEART (KEEPS A-TELLIN' ME NO)** *Pye 7N 17456*	**11**	13 wks

PAPER LACE *UK, male vocal/instrumental group*

23 Feb 74	★ **BILLY DON'T BE A HERO** *Bus Stop BUS 1014*	**1**	14 wks
4 May 74	● **THE NIGHT CHICAGO DIED** *Bus Stop BUS 1016*	**3**	11 wks
24 Aug 74	**THE BLACK EYED BOYS** *Bus Stop BUS 1019*	**11**	10 wks

See also Nottingham Forest F.C. with Paper Lace

Norrie PARAMOR *UK, orchestra*

17 Mar 60	**THEME FROM A SUMMER PLACE** *Columbia DB 4419*	**36**	2 wks
22 Mar 62	**THEME FROM Z CARS** *Columbia DB 4789*	**33**	6 wks

PARAMOUNT JAZZ BAND — See *Mr. Acker BILK*

PARAMOUNTS

UK, male vocal/instrumental group

16 Jan 64	**POISON IVY** *Parlophone R 5093*	**35**	7 wks

Top line: left **PEDDLERS** Peddled their jazz orientated blues into the chart for 14 weeks; Trevor Morais, Roy Phillips and Tab Martin *Centre* **PAPER DOLLS** Practising their origami *Right* **PASSIONS** After a brief flirtation with a German film star the passion soon passed *Lower left* **MARIE OSMOND** A fresh bunch 13 years after Anita Bryant, Maureen Evans and the Kaye Sisters *Centre* **DERMOT O'BRIEN** He ploughed two single furrows in the chart *Right* **DON PARTRIDGE** He was discovered while busking theatre queues in London's Leicester Square

Date	Title *Label Number*	Position	

PARCHMENT

UK, male/female vocal/instrumental group

16 Sep 72	**LIGHT UP THE FIRE** *Pye 7N 45178*	**31**	5 wks

PARIS *UK, male/female vocal group*

19 Jun 82	**NO GETTING OVER YOU** *RCA 222*	**49**	4 wks

Simon PARK *UK, orchestra*

25 Nov 72	**EYE LEVEL** *Columbia DB 8946*	**41**	2 wks
15 Sep 73	★ **EYE LEVEL** (re-entry) *Columbia DB 8946*	**1**	14 wks
5 Jan 74	**EYE LEVEL** (2nd re-entry) *Columbia DB 8946*	**31**	6 wks

Graham PARKER *UK, male vocalist*

20 Mar 82	**TEMPORARY BEAUTY** *RCA PARK 100*	**50**	4 wks

See also Graham Parker and the Rumour

Graham PARKER and the RUMOUR

UK, male vocal and instrumental group

19 Mar 77	**THE PINK PARKER** (EP) *Vertigo PARK 001*	**24**	5 wks
22 Apr 78	**HEY LORD DON'T ASK ME QUESTIONS** *Vertigo PARK 002*	**32**	7 wks

Tracks on The Pink Parker EP: *Hold Back The Night/ (Let Me Get) Sweet On You/ White Honey/ Soul Shoes.*

Robert PARKER *US, male vocalist*

4 Aug 66	**BAREFOOTIN'** *Island WI 286*	**24**	8 wks

Jimmy PARKINSON *Australia, male vocalist*

2 Mar 56	● **THE GREAT PRETENDER** *Columbia DB 3729*	**9**	13 wks
17 Aug 56	**WALK HAND IN HAND** *Columbia DB 3775*	**30**	1 wk
5 Oct 56	**WALK HAND IN HAND** (re-entry) *Columbia DB 3775*	**26**	1 wk
9 Nov 56	**IN THE MIDDLE OF THE HOUSE** *Columbia DB 3833*	**26**	2 wks
30 Nov 56	**IN THE MIDDLE OF THE HOUSE** (re-entry) *Columbia DB 3833*	**20**	2 wks

Dean PARRISH *US, male vocalist*

8 Feb 75	**I'M ON MY WAY** *UK USA 2*	**38**	5 wks

Bill PARSONS *US, male vocalist*

10 Apr 59	**ALL AMERICAN BOY** *London HL 8798*	**22**	2 wks

PARTNERS — See *Al HUDSON and the PARTNERS*

David PARTON *UK male vocalist*

15 Jan 77	● **ISN'T SHE LOVELY** *Pye 7N 45663*	**4**	9 wks

Dolly PARTON *US, female vocalist*

15 May 76	● **JOLENE** *RCA 2675*	**7**	10 wks
21 Feb 81	**9 TO 5** *RCA 25*	**47**	5 wks

Stella PARTON *US, female vocalist*

22 Oct 77	**THE DANGER OF A STRANGER** *Elektra K 12272*	**35**	4 wks

Don PARTRIDGE *UK, male vocalist*

7 Feb 68	● **ROSIE** *Columbia DB 8330*	**4**	12 wks
29 May 68	● **BLUE EYES** *Columbia DB 8416*	**3**	13 wks
19 Feb 69	**BREAKFAST ON PLUTO** *Columbia DB 8538*	**26**	7 wks

PARTRIDGE FAMILY starring Shirley JONES featuring David CASSIDY

US, male/female vocal group

13 Feb 71	**I THINK I LOVE YOU** *Bell 1130*	**18**	9 wks
26 Feb 72	**IT'S ONE OF THOSE NIGHTS (YES LOVE)** *Bell 1203*	**11**	11 wks
8 Jul 72	● **BREAKING UP IS HARD TO DO** *Bell MABEL 1*	**3**	13 wks
3 Feb 73	● **LOOKING THROUGH THE EYES OF LOVE** *Bell 1278*	**9**	9 wks
19 May 73	● **WALKING IN THE RAIN** *Bell 1293*	**10**	11 wks

See also David Cassidy, Various Artists - Carousel Soundtrack, on which Shirley Jones appears. Last two hits are simply "starring David Cassidy" - no Shirley Jones credit.

PASSIONS

UK, male/female vocal/instrumental group

31 Jan 81	**I'M IN LOVE WITH A GERMAN FILM STAR** *Polydor POSP 222*	**25**	8 wks

PATIENCE and PRUDENCE

US, female vocal duo

2 Nov 56	**TONIGHT YOU BELONG TO ME** *London HLU 8321*	**28**	3 wks
1 Mar 57	**GONNA GET ALONG WITHOUT YA NOW** *London HLU 8369*	**22**	4 wks
12 Apr 57	**GONNA GET ALONG WITHOUT YA NOW** (re-entry) *London HLU 8369*	**24**	1 wk

Kellee PATTERSON *US, female vocalist*

18 Feb 78	**IF IT DON'T FIT DON'T FORCE IT** *EMI International INT 558*	**44**	7 wks

PAUL — See *PETER, PAUL and MARY*

PAUL and PAULA *US, male/female vocal duo*

14 Feb 63	● **HEY PAULA** *Philips 304012 BF*	**8**	12 wks
18 Apr 63	● **YOUNG LOVERS** *Philips 304016 BF*	**9**	14 wks
16 May 63	**HEY PAULA** (re-entry) *Philips 304012 BF*	**37**	5 wks

Billy PAUL *US, male vocalist*

Date	Title Label Number	Position	Weeks
13 Jan 73	**ME & MRS JONES** *Epic EPC 1055*	**12**	9 wks
12 Jan 74	**THANKS FOR SAVING MY LIFE** *Philadelphia International PIR 1928*	**33**	6 wks
22 May 76	**LET'S MAKE A BABY** *Philadelphia International PIR 4144*	**30**	5 wks
30 Apr 77	**LET 'EM IN** *Philadelphia International PIR 5143*	**26**	5 wks
16 Jul 77	**YOUR SONG** *Philadelphia International PIR 5391*	**37**	7 wks
19 Nov 77	**ONLY THE STRONG SURVIVE** *Philadelphia International PIR 5699*	**33**	7 wks
14 Jul 79	**BRING THE FAMILY BACK** *Philadelphia International PIR 7456*	**51**	5 wks

See also Philadelphia International All-Stars.

Les PAUL and Mary FORD

US, male instrumentalist - guitar, and female vocalist

Date	Title Label Number	Position	Weeks
20 Nov 53	● **VAYA CON DIOS** *Capitol CL 13943*	**7**	4 wks

Lyn PAUL *UK, female vocalist*

Date	Title Label Number	Position	Weeks
28 Jun 75	**IT OUGHTA SELL A MILLION** *Polydor 2058 602*	**37**	6 wks

PAULA — See *PAUL and PAULA*

Rita PAVONE *Italy, female vocalist*

Date	Title Label Number	Position	Weeks
1 Dec 66	**HEART** *RCA 1553*	**27**	12 wks
19 Jan 67	**YOU ONLY YOU** *RCA 1561*	**21**	7 wks

Freda PAYNE *US, female vocalist*

Date	Title Label Number	Position	Weeks
5 Sep 70	★ **BAND OF GOLD** *Invictus INV 502*	**1**	19 wks
21 Nov 70	**DEEPER & DEEPER** *Invictus INV 505*	**33**	9 wks
27 Mar 71	**CHERISH WHAT IS DEAR TO YOU** *Invictus INV 509*	**46**	2 wks

PEACHES and HERB

US, female/male vocal duo

Date	Title Label Number	Position	Weeks
20 Jan 79	**SHAKE YOUR GROOVE THING** *Polydor 2066 992*	**26**	10 wks
21 Apr 79	● **REUNITED** *Polydor POSP 43*	**4**	13 wks

PEARLS *UK, female vocal duo*

Date	Title Label Number	Position	Weeks
27 May 72	**THIRD FINGER, LEFT HAND** *Bell 1217*	**31**	6 wks
23 Sep 72	**YOU CAME YOU SAW YOU CONQUERED** *Bell 1254*	**32**	5 wks
24 Mar 73	**YOU ARE EVERYTHING** *Bell 1284*	**41**	3 wks
1 Jun 74	● **GUILTY** *Bell 1352*	**10**	10 wks

Johnny PEARSON

UK, orchestra, Johnny Pearson featured pianist

Date	Title Label Number	Position	Weeks
18 Dec 71	● **SLEEPY SHORES** *Penny Farthing PEN 778*	**8**	15 wks

PEDDLERS *UK, male vocal/instrumental group*

Date	Title Label Number	Position	Weeks
7 Jan 65	**LET THE SUNSHINE IN** *Philips BF 1375*	**50**	1 wk
23 Aug 69	**BIRTH** *CBS 4449*	**17**	9 wks
31 Jan 70	**GIRLIE** *CBS 4720*	**34**	4 wks

Ann PEEBLES *US, female vocalist*

Date	Title Label Number	Position	Weeks
20 Apr 74	**I CAN'T STAND THE RAIN** *London HL 10428*	**50**	1 wk
4 May 74	**I CAN'T STAND THE RAIN** (re-entry) *London HL 10428*	**41**	2 wks

PEECH BOYS *UK, male vocal/instrumental group*

Date	Title Label Number	Position	Weeks
30 Oct 82	**DON'T MAKE ME WAIT** *TMT TMT 7001*	**49**	3 wks

Donald PEERS *UK, male vocalist*

Date	Title Label Number	Position	Weeks
18 Dec 68	● **PLEASE DON'T GO** *Columbia DB 8502*	**3**	18 wks
30 Apr 69	**PLEASE DON'T GO** (re-entry) *Columbia DB 8502*	**38**	3 wks
24 Jun 72	**GIVE ME ONE MORE CHANCE** *Decca F 13302*	**36**	6 wks

Teddy PENDERGRASS *US, male vocalist*

Date	Title Label Number	Position	Weeks
21 May 77	**THE WHOLE TOWN'S LAUGHING AT ME** *Philadelphia International PIR 5116*	**44**	3 wks
28 Oct 78	**ONLY YOU/ CLOSE THE DOOR [A]** *Philadelphia International S PIR 6713*	**41**	6 wks

See also Philadelphia International All-Stars.

PENTANGLE

UK, male/female vocal/instrumental group

Date	Title Label Number	Position	Weeks
28 May 69	**ONCE I HAD A SWEETHEART** *Big T BIG 124*	**46**	1 wk
14 Feb 70	**LIGHT FLIGHT** *Big T BIG 128*	**43**	1 wk
28 Feb 70	**LIGHT FLIGHT** (re-entry) *Big T BIG 128*	**45**	2 wks

PEOPLES — See *YARBROUGH and PEOPLES*

PEOPLE'S CHOICE

US, male vocal/instrumental group

Date	Title Label Number	Position	Weeks
20 Sep 75	**DO IT ANYWAY YOU WANNA** *Philadelphia International PIR 3500*	**36**	5 wks
21 Jan 78	**JAM JAM JAM** *Philadelphia International PIR 5891*	**40**	4 wks

Danny PEPPERMINT and the JUMPING JACKS

US, male vocal/instrumental group

Date	Title Label Number	Position	Weeks
18 Jan 62	**PEPPERMINT TWIST** *London HLL 9478*	**26**	8 wks

PEPPERS *France, male instrumental group*

Date	Title Label Number	Position	Weeks
26 Oct 74	● **PEPPER BOX** *Spark SRL 1100*	**6**	12 wks

Date	Title *Label Number*	Position	

Lance PERCIVAL *UK, male vocalist*

28 Oct 65	**SHAME AND SCANDAL IN THE FAMILY** *Parlophone R 5335*	**37**	3 wks

Emilio PERICOLI *Italy, male vocalist*

28 Jun 62	**AL DI LA** *Warner Bros. WB 69*	**30**	14 wks

Carl PERKINS *US, male vocalist*

18 May 56	● **BLUE SUEDE SHOES** *London HLU 8271*	**10**	8 wks

Steve PERRY *UK, male vocalist*

4 Aug 60	**STEP BY STEP** *HMV POP 745*	**41**	1 wk

Jon PERTWEE *UK, male Vocalist*

1 Mar 80	**WORZEL'S SONG** *Decca F 13885*	**33**	7 wks

PETER and GORDON *UK, male vocal duo*

12 Mar 64	★ **A WORLD WITHOUT LOVE** *Columbia DB 7225*	**1**	14 wks
4 Jun 64	● **NOBODY I KNOW** *Columbia DB 7292*	**10**	11 wks
8 Apr 65	● **TRUE LOVE WAYS** *Columbia DB 7524*	**2**	15 wks
24 Jun 65	● **TO KNOW YOU IS TO LOVE YOU** *Columbia DB 7617*	**5**	10 wks
21 Oct 65	**BABY I'M YOURS** *Columbia DB 7729*	**19**	9 wks
24 Feb 66	**WOMAN** *Columbia DB 7834*	**28**	7 wks
22 Sep 66	**LADY GODIVA** *Columbia DB 8003*	**16**	11 wks

PETER, PAUL and MARY

US, male/female vocal/instrumental group

10 Oct 63	**BLOWING IN THE WIND** *Warner Bros. WB 104*	**13**	16 wks
16 Apr 64	**TELL IT ON THE MOUNTAIN** *Warner Bros. WB 127*	**33**	4 wks
15 Oct 64	**THE TIMES THEY ARE A-CHANGIN'** *Warner Bros. WB 142*	**44**	2 wks
17 Jan 70	● **LEAVIN' ON A JET PLANE** *Warner Bros. WB 7340*	**2**	16 wks

PETERS and LEE *UK, male/female vocal duo*

26 May 73	★ **WELCOME HOME** *Philips 6006 307*	**1**	24 wks
3 Nov 73	**BY YOUR SIDE** *Philips 6006 339*	**39**	4 wks
20 Apr 74	● **DON'T STAY AWAY TOO LONG** *Philips 6006 388*	**3**	15 wks
17 Aug 74	**RAINBOW** *Philips 6006 406*	**17**	7 wks
6 Mar 76	**HEY MR. MUSIC MAN** *Philips 6006 502*	**16**	7 wks

Ray PETERSON *US, male vocalist*

4 Sep 59	**THE WONDER OF YOU** *RCA 1131*	**23**	1 wk
24 Mar 60	**ANSWER ME** *RCA 1175*	**47**	1 wk
19 Jan 61	**CORRINE, CORRINA** *London HLX 9246*	**48**	1 wk
2 Feb 61	**CORRINE, CORRINA** (re-entry) *London HLX 9246*	**41**	6 wks

Tom PETTY and the HEARTBREAKERS

US, male vocal/instrumental group

25 Jun 77	**ANYTHING THAT'S ROCK 'N' ROLL** *Shelter WIP 6396*	**36**	3 wks
13 Aug 77	**AMERICAN GIRL** *Shelter WIP 6403*	**40**	5 wks

See also Stevie Nicks with Tom Petty and the Heartbreakers.

PHARAOHS — See *SAM THE SHAM and the PHARAOHS*

PhD *UK, male vocal/instrumental duo*

3 Apr 82	● **I WON'T LET YOU DOWN** *WEA K 79209*	**3**	14 wks

PHILADELPHIA INTERNATIONAL ALL-STARS *US, amalgamation of various acts*

13 Aug 77	**LET'S CLEAN UP THE GHETTO** *Philadelphia International PIR 5451*	**34**	8 wks

The All-Stars include Archie Bell, Dee Dee Sharp Gamble, O'Jays, Billy Paul, Teddy Pendergrass and Lou Rawls. See also the separate hit lists of each of these artists. Dee Dee Sharp Gamble, see Dee Dee Sharp. Archie Bell, see Archie Bell and the Drells.

PHILHARMONIA ORCHESTRA, conductor Lorin MAAZEL

UK, orchestra (conductor American)

30 Jul 69	**THUS SPAKE ZARATHUSTRA** *Columbia DB 8607*	**33**	7 wks

Esther PHILLIPS *US, female vocalist*

4 Oct 75	● **WHAT A DIFFERENCE A DAY MADE** *Kudu 925*	**6**	8 wks

Paul PHILLIPS — See *DRIVER 67*

Paul PHOENIX *UK, male vocalist*

3 Nov 79	**NUNC DIMITTIS** *Different HAVE 20*	**56**	4 wks

Full artist credit on hit as follows: Paul Phoenix (treble) with Instrumental Ensemble-James Watson (trumpet) John Scott (organ) conducted by Barry Rose.

PHOTOS *UK, male/female vocal/instrumental group*

17 May 80	**IRENE** *Epic EPC 8517*	**56**	4 wks

Edith PIAF *France, female vocalist*

12 May 60	**MILORD** *Columbia DC 754*	**41**	4 wks
3 Nov 60	**MILORD** (re-entry) *Columbia DC 754*	**24**	11 wks

Bobby 'Boris' PICKETT and the CRYPT-KICKERS

US, male vocalist, male vocal/instrumental backing group

1 Sep 73	● **MONSTER MASH** *London HL 10320*	**3**	13 wks

Date	Title *Label Number*	Position	

Wilson PICKETT *US, male vocalist*

23 Sep 65	**IN THE MIDNIGHT HOUR** *Atlantic AT 4036*	**12**	11 wks
25 Nov 65	**DON'T FIGHT IT** *Atlantic AT 4052*	**29**	8 wks
10 Mar 66	**634-5789** *Atlantic AT 4072*	**36**	5 wks
1 Sep 66	**LAND OF 1000 DANCES** *Atlantic 584-039*	**22**	9 wks
15 Dec 66	**MUSTANG SALLY** *Atlantic 584-066*	**28**	7 wks
27 Sep 67	**FUNKY BROADWAY** *Atlantic 584-130*	**43**	3 wks
11 Sep 68	**IN THE MIDNIGHT HOUR** (re-issue) *Atlantic 584-203*	**38**	6 wks
8 Jan 69	**HEY JUDE** *Atlantic 584-236*	**16**	9 wks

PICKETTYWITCH

UK, male/female vocal/instrumental group

28 Feb 70	● **THAT SAME OLD FEELING** *Pye 7N 17887*	**5**	14 wks
4 Jul 70	**(IT'S LIKE A) SAD OLD KINDA MOVIE** *Pye 7N 17951*	**16**	10 wks
7 Nov 70	**BABY I WON'T LET YOU DOWN** *Pye 7N 45002*	**27**	10 wks

PIG BAG *UK, male instrumental group*

7 Nov 81	**SUNNY DAY** *Y RECORDS Y 12*	**53**	3 wks
27 Feb 82	**GETTING UP** *Y RECORDS Y 16*	**61**	3 wks
3 Apr 82	● **PAPA'S GOT A BRAND NEW PIGBAG** *Y RECORDS Y 10*	**3**	11 wks
10 Jul 82	**THE BIG BEAN** *Y RECORDS Y 24*	**40**	3 wks

Nelson PIGFORD — See *De Etta LITTLE and Nelson PIGFORD*

PIGLETS *UK, female vocal group*

6 Nov 71	● **JOHNNY REGGAE** *Bell 1180*	**3**	12 wks

PILOT *UK, male vocal/instrumental group*

2 Nov 74	**MAGIC** *EMI 2217*	**11**	11 wks
18 Jan 75	★ **JANUARY** *EMI 2255*	**1**	10 wks
19 Apr 75	**CALL ME ROUND** *EMI 2287*	**34**	4 wks
27 Sep 75	**JUST A SMILE** *EMI 2338*	**31**	4 wks

PILTDOWN MEN *US, male instrumental group*

8 Sep 60	**MACDONALD'S CAVE** *Capitol CL 15149*	**14**	18 wks
12 Jan 61	**PILTDOWN RIDES AGAIN** *Capitol CL 15175*	**14**	10 wks
9 Mar 61	**GOODNIGHT MRS. FLINTSTONE** *Capitol CL 15186*	**18**	8 wks

PING PING and Al VERLAINE

Belgium, male vocal duo

28 Sep 61	**SUCU SUCU** *Oriole CB 1589*	**41**	4 wks

PINK FLOYD *UK, male vocal/instrumental group*

30 Mar 67	**ARNOLD LAYNE** *Columbia DB 8156*	**20**	8 wks
22 Jun 67	● **SEE EMILY PLAY** *Columbia DB 8214*	**6**	12 wks
1 Dec 79	★ **ANOTHER BRICK IN THE WALL** (PART II) *Harvest HAR 5194*	**1**	12 wks
7 Aug 82	**WHEN THE TIGERS BROKE FREE** *Harvest HAR 5222*	**39**	5 wks

PINKEES *UK, male vocal/instrumental group*

18 Sep 82	● **DANGER GAMES** *Creole CR 39*	**8**	9 wks

PINKERTON'S ASSORTED COLOURS

UK, male vocal/instrumental group

13 Jan 66	● **MIRROR MIRROR** *Decca F 12307*	**9**	11 wks
21 Apr 66	**DON'T STOP LOVIN' ME BABY** *Decca F 12377*	**50**	1 wk

PIONEERS *Jamaica, male vocal/instrumental group*

18 Oct 69	**LONG SHOT KICK DE BUCKET** *Trojan TR 672*	**21**	10 wks
10 Jan 70	**LONG SHOT KICK DE BUCKET** (re-entry) *Trojan TR 672*	**40**	1 wk
31 Jul 71	● **LET YOUR YEAH BE YEAH** *Trojan TR 7824*	**5**	12 wks
15 Jan 72	**GIVE AND TAKE** *Trojan TR 7846*	**35**	6 wks
29 Mar 80	**LONG SHOT KICK DE BUCKET** (re-issue) *Trojan TRO 9063*	**42**	5 wks

Re-issue of Long Shot Kick De Bucket *coupled with re-issue of* Liquidator *by Harry J. All Stars. See also Harry J. All Stars.*

PIPKINS *UK, male vocal duo*

28 Mar 70	● **GIMME DAT DING** *Columbia DB 8662*	**6**	10 wks

PIPS — See *Gladys KNIGHT and the PIPS*

PIRANHAS *UK, male vocal/instrumental group*

2 Aug 80	● **TOM HARK** *Sire/Hansa SIR 4044*	**6**	12 wks
16 Oct 82	**ZAMBESI** *Dakota DAK 6*	**17**	9 wks

Zambezi is 'featuring Boring Bob Grover'.

PIRATES — See *Johnny KIDD and the PIRATES*

Gene PITNEY *US, male vocalist*

23 Mar 61	**I WANNA LOVE MY LIFE AWAY** *London HL 9270*	**26**	11 wks
8 Mar 62	**TOWN WITHOUT PITY** *HMV POP 952*	**32**	6 wks
5 Dec 63	● **TWENTY FOUR HOURS FROM TULSA** *United Artists UP 1035*	**5**	19 wks
5 Mar 64	● **THAT GIRL BELONGS TO YESTERDAY** *United Artists UP 1045*	**7**	12 wks
15 Oct 64	**IT HURTS TO BE IN LOVE** *United Artists UP 1063*	**36**	4 wks
12 Nov 64	● **I'M GONNA BE STRONG** *Stateside SS 358*	**2**	14 wks
18 Feb 65	● **I MUST BE SEEING THINGS** *Stateside SS 390*	**6**	10 wks
10 Jun 65	● **LOOKING THROUGH THE EYES OF LOVE** *Stateside SS 420*	**3**	12 wks
4 Nov 65	● **PRINCESS IN RAGS** *Stateside SS 471*	**9**	12 wks
17 Feb 66	● **BACKSTAGE** *Stateside SS 490*	**4**	10 wks
9 Jun 66	● **NOBODY NEEDS YOUR LOVE** *Stateside SS 518*	**2**	13 wks
10 Nov 66	● **JUST ONE SMILE** *Stateside SS 558*	**8**	12 wks
23 Feb 67	**COLD LIGHT OF DAY** *Stateside SS 597*	**38**	6 wks
15 Nov 67	● **SOMETHING'S GOTTEN HOLD OF MY HEART** *Stateside SS 2060*	**5**	13 wks
3 Apr 68	**SOMEWHERE IN THE COUNTRY** *Stateside SS 2013*	**19**	9 wks
27 Nov 68	**YOURS UNTIL TOMORROW** *Stateside SS 2131*	**34**	7 wks
5 Mar 69	**MARIA ELENA** *Stateside SS 2142*	**25**	6 wks
14 Mar 70	**A STREET CALLED HOPE** *Stateside SS 2164*	**37**	5 wks

Far left **ELVIS PRESLEY** In this picture looking not a little unlike actor Robert Horton

Left **Ph.D** A degree of success for, *circled above*, Jim Diamond and, *below*, Tony Hymas

Below **PINKEES** Brought a Beatley sound to 1982 chart

Bottom **PICKETTYWITCH** They included Polly Brown (front) who four years later charted twice more as soloist and as half of Sweet Dreams

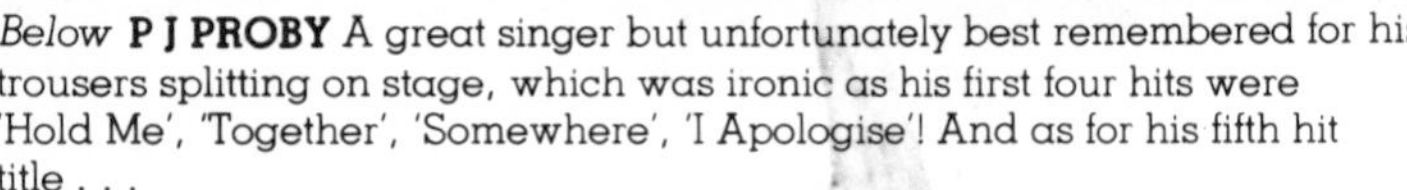

Below **P J PROBY** A great singer but unfortunately best remembered for his trousers splitting on stage, which was ironic as his first four hits were 'Hold Me', 'Together', 'Somewhere', 'I Apologise'! And as for his fifth hit title . . .

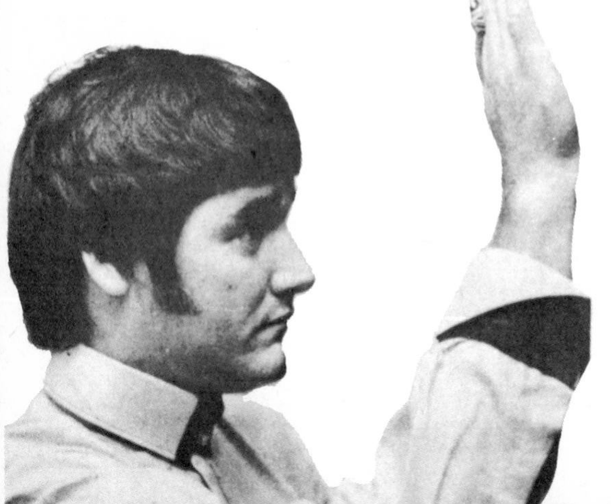

Date	Title *Label Number*	Position	
3 Oct 70	**SHADY LADY** *Stateside SS 2177*	**29**	8 wks
28 Apr 73	**24 SYCAMORE** *Pye International 7N 25606*	**34**	7 wks
2 Nov 74	**BLUE ANGEL** *Bronze BRO 11*	**49**	1 wk
16 Nov 74	**BLUE ANGEL** (re-entry) *Bronze BRO 11*	**39**	3 wks

PLANETS *UK, male vocal/instrumental group*

18 Aug 79	**LINES** *Rialto TREB 104*	**36**	6 wks
25 Oct 80	**DON'T LOOK DOWN** *Rialto TREB 116*	**66**	2 wks

Robert PLANT *UK, male vocalist*

9 Oct 82	**BURNING DOWN ONE SIDE** *Swansong SSK 19429*	**73**	1 wk

PLASMATICS

UK, female/male vocal/instrumental group

26 Jul 80	**BUTCHER BABY** *Stiff BUY 76*	**55**	4 wks

PLASTIC BERTRAND *Belgium, male vocalist*

13 May 78	● **CA PLANE POUR MOI** *Sire 6078 616*	**8**	12 wks
5 Aug 78	**SHA LA LA LA LEE** *Vertigo 6059 209*	**39**	5 wks

PLASTIC ONO BAND — See *John LENNON*

PLASTIC ONO NUCLEAR BAND — See *John LENNON*

PLASTIC PENNY

UK, male vocal/instrumental group

3 Jan 68	● **EVERYTHING I AM** *Page One POF 051*	**6**	10 wks

PLATINUM HOOK

US, male vocal/instrumental group

2 Sep 78	**STANDING ON THE VERGE (OF GETTING IT ON)** *Motown TMG 1115*	**72**	1 wk

PLATTERS *US, male/female vocal group*

7 Sep 56	● **THE GREAT PRETENDER/ ONLY YOU** *Mercury MT 117*	**5**	12 wks
2 Nov 56	● **MY PRAYER** *Mercury MT 120*	**4**	10 wks
7 Dec 56	**THE GREAT PRETENDER/ ONLY YOU** (re-entry) *Mercury MT 117*	**21**	1 wk
18 Jan 57	**MY PRAYER** (re-entry) *Mercury MT 120*	**28**	2 wks
25 Jan 57	**YOU'LL NEVER NEVER KNOW/ IT ISN'T RIGHT** *Mercury MT 130*	**23**	1 wk
8 Feb 57	**YOU'LL NEVER NEVER KNOW/ IT ISN'T RIGHT** (re-entry) *Mercury MT 130*	**29**	1 wk
29 Mar 57	**ONLY YOU** (2nd re-entry) *Mercury MT 117*	**18**	3 wks
29 Mar 57	**MY PRAYER** (2nd re-entry) *Mercury MT 120*	**22**	1 wk
12 Apr 57	**YOU'LL NEVER NEVER KNOW/ IT ISN'T RIGHT** (2nd re-entry) *Mercury MT 130*	**29**	1 wk
17 May 57	**I'M SORRY** *Mercury MT 145*	**18**	6 wks
5 Jul 57	**I'M SORRY** (re-entry) *Mercury MT 145*	**23**	1 wk
19 Jul 57	**I'M SORRY** (2nd re-entry) *Mercury MT 145*	**22**	1 wk
16 May 58	● **TWILIGHT TIME** *Mercury MT 214*	**3**	18 wks
16 Jan 59	★ **SMOKE GETS IN YOUR EYES** *Mercury AMT 1016*	**1**	20 wks
28 Aug 59	**REMEMBER WHEN** *Mercury AMT 1053*	**25**	2 wks
29 Jan 60	**HARBOUR LIGHTS** *Mercury AMT 1081*	**11**	11 wks

PLAYBOY BAND — See *John FRED and the PLAYBOY BAND*

PLAYBOYS — See *Gary LEWIS and the PLAYBOYS*

PLAYER *US/UK, male vocal/instrumental group*

25 Feb 78	**BABY COME BACK** *RSO 2090 254*	**32**	7 wks

PLAYERS ASSOCIATION

US, male/female vocal/instrumental group

10 Mar 79	● **TURN THE MUSIC UP** *Vanguard VS 5011*	**8**	9 wks
5 May 79	**RIDE THE GROOVE** *Vanguard VS 5012*	**42**	5 wks
9 Feb 80	**WE GOT THE GROOVE** *Vanaguard VS 5016*	**61**	3 wks

POETS *UK, male vocal/instrumental group*

29 Oct 64	**NOW WE'RE THRU** *Decca F 11995*	**31**	5 wks

POINTER SISTERS *US, female vocal group*

3 Feb 79	**EVERYBODY IS A STAR** *Planet K 12324*	**61**	3 wks
17 Mar 79	**FIRE** *Planet K 12339*	**34**	8 wks
22 Aug 81	● **SLOWHAND** *Planet K 12530*	**10**	11 wks
4 Dec 81	**SHOULD I DO IT?** *Reprise K 12578*	**50**	4 wks

POLECATS *UK, male vocal/instrumental group*

7 Mar 81	**JOHN I'M ONLY DANCING/BIG GREEN CAR** *Mercury POLE 1*	**35**	8 wks
16 May 81	**ROCKABILLY GUY** *Mercury POLE 2*	**35**	6 wks
22 Aug 81	**JEEPSTER/MARIE CELESTE** *Mercury POLE 3*	**53**	4 wks

POLICE *UK, male vocal/instrumental group*

7 Oct 78	**CAN'T STAND LOSING YOU** *A & M AMS 7381*	**42**	5 wks
28 Apr 79	**ROXANNE** *A & M AMS 7348*	**12**	9 wks
7 Jul 79	● **CAN'T STAND LOSING YOU** (re-entry) *A & M AMS 7381*	**2**	11 wks
22 Sep 79	★ **MESSAGE IN A BOTTLE** *A & M AMS 7474*	**1**	11 wks
17 Nov 79	**FALL OUT** *Illegal IL 001*	**47**	4 wks
1 Dec 79	★ **WALKING ON THE MOON** *A & M AMS 7494*	**1**	10 wks
16 Feb 80	● **SO LONELY** *A & M AMS 7402*	**6**	10 wks
14 Jun 80	**SIX PACK** *A & M AMPP 6001*	**17**	4 wks
27 Sep 80	★ **DON'T STAND SO CLOSE TO ME** *A & M AMS 7564*	**1**	10 wks
13 Dec 80	● **DE DO DO DO, DE DA DA DA** *A & M AMS 7578*	**5**	8 wks
26 Sep 81	● **INVISIBLE SUN** *A & M AMS 8164*	**2**	8 wks
24 Oct 81	★ **EVERY LITTLE THING SHE DOES IS MAGIC** *A & M AMS 8174*	**1**	13 wks
12 Dec 81	**SPIRITS IN THE MATERIAL WORLD** *A & M AMS 8194*	**12**	8 wks

Six Pack *consists of six separate Police singles as follows: The Bed's Too Big Without You; Roxanne; Message in a Bottle; Walking on the Moon; So Lonely; Can't Stand Losing You. The last five titles were re-issues.*

PONI-TAILS *US, female vocal group*

19 Sep 58	● **BORN TOO LATE** *HMV POP 516*	**5**	11 wks
10 Apr 59	**EARLY TO BED** *HMV POP 596*	**26**	3 wks

Date	Title *Label Number*	Position		Date	Title *Label Number*	Position	

Brian POOLE and the TREMELOES

UK, male vocalist, male vocal/instrumental backing group

Date		Title *Label Number*	Position	Weeks
4 Jul 63	●	**TWIST AND SHOUT** *Decca F 11694*	**4**	14 wks
12 Sep 63	★	**DO YOU LOVE ME** *Decca F 11739*	**1**	14 wks
28 Nov 63		**I CAN DANCE** *Decca F 11771*	**31**	8 wks
30 Jan 64	●	**CANDY MAN** *Decca F 11823*	**6**	13 wks
7 May 64	●	**SOMEONE SOMEONE** *Decca F 11893*	**2**	17 wks
20 Aug 64		**TWELVE STEPS TO LOVE** *Decca F 11951*	**32**	7 wks
7 Jan 65		**THREE BELLS** *Decca F 12037*	**17**	9 wks
22 Jul 65		**I WANT CANDY** *Decca F 12197*	**25**	8 wks

See also Tremeloes.

Glyn POOLE *UK, male vocalist*

Date		Title *Label Number*	Position	Weeks
20 Oct 73		**MILLY MOLLY MANDY** *York SYK 565*	**35**	8 wks

POP TOPS *Spain, male vocal group*

Date		Title *Label Number*	Position	Weeks
9 Oct 71		**MAMY BLUE** *A & M AMS 859*	**34**	6 wks

POPPY FAMILY

Canada, male/female vocal/instrumental group

Date		Title *Label Number*	Position	Weeks
15 Aug 70	●	**WHICH WAY YOU GOIN' BILLY** *Decca F 22976*	**7**	14 wks

PORTSMOUTH SINFONIA *UK, orchestra*

Date		Title *Label Number*	Position	Weeks
12 Sep 81		**CLASSICAL MUDDLEY** *Springtime/Island WIP 6736*	**38**	4 wks

Sandy POSEY *US, female vocalist*

Date		Title *Label Number*	Position	Weeks
15 Sep 66		**BORN A WOMAN** *MGM 1321*	**24**	11 wks
5 Jan 67		**SINGLE GIRL** *MGM 1330*	**15**	13 wks
13 Apr 67		**WHAT A WOMAN IN LOVE WON'T DO** *MGM 1335*	**48**	3 wks
6 Sep 75		**SINGLE GIRL** (re-issue) *MGM 2006 533*	**35**	5 wks

POSITIVE FORCE *US, female vocal duo*

Date		Title *Label Number*	Position	Weeks
22 Dec 79		**WE GOT THE FUNK** *Sugarhill SHL 102*	**18**	9 wks

POSITIVE PEOPLE — See *Frank HOOKER and POSITIVE PEOPLE*

Mike POST featuring Larry CARLTON

US

Date		Title *Label Number*	Position	Weeks
16 Jan 82		**THEME FROM HILL STREET BLUES** *Elektron K 12576*	**25**	11 wks

See also Mike Post Coalition

Mike POST COALITION *US, orchestra*

Date		Title *Label Number*	Position	Weeks
9 Aug 75		**AFTERNOON OF THE RHINO** *Warner Bros. K 16588*	**48**	1 wk
23 Aug 75		**AFTERNOON OF THE RHINO** (re-entry) *Warner Bros. K 16588*	**47**	1 wk

POTTERS *UK, male vocal group*

Date		Title *Label Number*	Position	Weeks
1 Apr 72		**WE'LL BE WITH YOU** *Pye JT 100*	**34**	2 wks

Cozy POWELL *UK, male instrumentalist - drums*

Date		Title *Label Number*	Position	Weeks
8 Dec 73	●	**DANCE WITH THE DEVIL** *RAK 165*	**3**	15 wks
25 Mar 74		**THE MAN IN BLACK** *RAK 173*	**18**	8 wks
10 Aug 74	●	**NA NA NA** *RAK 180*	**10**	10 wks
10 Nov 79		**THEME ONE** *Ariola ARO 189*	**62**	2 wks

Perez PRADO *US, orchestra*

Date		Title *Label Number*	Position	Weeks
25 Mar 55	★	**CHERRY PINK & APPLE BLOSSOM WHITE** *HMV B 10833*	**1**	17 wks
25 Jul 58	●	**PATRICIA** *RCA 1067*	**8**	16 wks

Billed on first hit as Perez 'Prez' Prado and His Orchestra, The King of the Mambo.

PRATT and McLAIN with BROTHERLOVE

US, male vocal duo, male instrumental group

Date		Title *Label Number*	Position	Weeks
1 Oct 77		**HAPPY DAYS** *Reprise K 14435*	**31**	6 wks

PRAYING MANTIS

UK, male vocal/instrumental group

Date		Title *Label Number*	Position	Weeks
31 Jan 81		**CHEATED** *Arista ARIST 378*	**69**	2 wks

PRELUDE *UK, male/female vocal group*

Date		Title *Label Number*	Position	Weeks
26 Jan 74		**AFTER THE GOLDRUSH** *Dawn DNS 1052*	**21**	9 wks
26 Apr 80		**PLATINUM BLONDE** *EMI 5046*	**45**	7 wks
22 May 82		**AFTER THE GOLDRUSH** (re-issue) *After Hours AFT 02*	**28**	7 wks
31 Jul 82		**ONLY THE LONELY** *After Hours AFT 06*	**55**	3 wks

Elvis PRESLEY *US, male vocalist*

Date		Title *Label Number*	Position	Weeks
11 May 56	●	**HEARTBREAK HOTEL** *HMV POP 182*	**2**	21 wks
25 May 56	●	**BLUE SUEDE SHOES** *HMV POP 213*	**9**	8 wks
13 Jul 56		**I WANT YOU I NEED YOU I LOVE YOU** *HMV POP 235*	**25**	2 wks
3 Aug 56		**I WANT YOU I NEED YOU I LOVE YOU** (re-entry) *HMV POP 235*	**14**	9 wks
17 Aug 56		**BLUE SUEDE SHOES** (re-entry) *HMV POP 213*	**26**	2 wks
21 Sep 56	●	**HOUND DOG** *HMV POP 249*	**2**	23 wks
26 Oct 56		**HEARTBREAK HOTEL** (re-entry) *HMV POP 182*	**23**	1 wk
16 Nov 56	●	**BLUE MOON** *HMV POP 272*	**9**	11 wks
23 Nov 56		**I DON'T CARE IF THE SUN DON'T SHINE** *HMV POP 272*	**29**	1 wk
7 Dec 56		**LOVE ME TENDER** *HMV POP 253*	**11**	9 wks
21 Dec 56		**I DON'T CARE IF THE SUN DON'T SHINE** (re-entry) *HMV POP 272*	**23**	3 wks
15 Feb 57		**MYSTERY TRAIN** *HMV POP 295*	**25**	5 wks
8 Mar 57		**RIP IT UP** *HMV POP 305*	**27**	1 wk
10 May 57	●	**TOO MUCH** *HMV POP 330*	**6**	8 wks
14 Jun 57		**ALL SHOOK UP** *HMV POP 359*	**24**	1 wk
28 Jun 57	★	**ALL SHOOK UP** (re-entry) *HMV POP 359*	**1**	20 wks
12 Jul 57		**TOO MUCH** (re-entry) *HMV POP 330*	**26**	1 wk
12 Jul 57	●	**TEDDY BEAR** *RCA 1013*	**3**	19 wks
30 Aug 57	●	**PARALYSED** *HMV POP 378*	**8**	10 wks
4 Oct 57	●	**PARTY** *RCA 1020*	**2**	15 wks

Date	Title *Label Number*	Position	
18 Oct 57	**GOT A LOT O' LIVIN' TO DO** *RCA 1020*	**17**	4 wks
1 Nov 57	**LOVING YOU** *RCA 1013*	**24**	2 wks
1 Nov 57	**TRYING TO GET TO YOU** *HMV POP 408*	**16**	4 wks
8 Nov 57	**LAWDY MISS CLAWDY** *HMV POP 408*	**15**	5 wks
15 Nov 57	● **SANTA BRING MY BABY BACK TO ME** *RCA 1025*	**7**	8 wks
17 Jan 58	**I'M LEFT YOU'RE RIGHT SHE'S GONE** *HMV POP 428*	**21**	2 wks
24 Jan 58	★ **JAILHOUSE ROCK** *RCA 1028*	**1**	14 wks
31 Jan 58	**JAILHOUSE ROCK** (EP) *RCA RCX 106*	**18**	5 wks
7 Feb 58	**I'M LEFT YOU'RE RIGHT SHE'S GONE** (re-entry) *HMV POP 428*	**29**	1 wk
28 Feb 58	● **DON'T** *RCA 1043*	**2**	11 wks
2 May 58	● **WEAR MY RING AROUND YOUR NECK** *RCA 1058*	**3**	10 wks
25 Jul 58	● **HARD HEADED WOMAN** *RCA 1070*	**2**	11 wks
3 Oct 58	● **KING CREOLE** *RCA 1081*	**2**	15 wks
23 Jan 59	★ **ONE NIGHT/ I GOT STUNG** *RCA 1100*	**1**	12 wks
24 Apr 59	★ **A FOOL SUCH AS I/ I NEED YOUR LOVE TONIGHT** *RCA 1113*	**1**	15 wks
24 Jul 59	● **A BIG HUNK O' LOVE** *RCA 1136*	**4**	9 wks
12 Feb 60	**STRICTLY ELVIS** (EP) *RCA RCX 175*	**26**	1 wk
7 Apr 60	● **STUCK ON YOU** *RCA 1187*	**3**	14 wks
28 Jul 60	● **A MESS OF BLUES** *RCA 1194*	**2**	18 wks
3 Nov 60	★ **IT'S NOW OR NEVER** *RCA 1207*	**1**	19 wks
19 Jan 61	★ **ARE YOU LONESOME TONIGHT** *RCA 1216*	**1**	15 wks
4 Mar 61	★ **WOODEN HEART** *RCA 1226*	**1**	27 wks
20 May 61	★ **SURRENDER** *RCA 1227*	**1**	15 wks
7 Sep 61	● **WILD IN THE COUNTRY/ I FEEL SO BAD** *RCA 1244*	**4**	12 wks
2 Nov 61	★ **HIS LATEST FLAME/ LITTLE SISTER** *RCA 1258*	**1**	13 wks
1 Feb 62	★ **ROCK A HULA BABY/ CAN'T HELP FALLING IN LOVE** *RCA 1270*	**1**	20 wks
10 May 62	★ **GOOD LUCK CHARM** *RCA 1280*	**1**	17 wks
21 Jun 62	**FOLLOW THAT DREAM** (EP) *RCA RCX 211*	**34**	2 wks
30 Aug 62	★ **SHE'S NOT YOU** *RCA 1303*	**1**	14 wks
29 Nov 62	★ **RETURN TO SENDER** *RCA 1320*	**1**	14 wks
28 Feb 63	**ONE BROKEN HEART FOR SALE** *RCA 1337*	**12**	9 wks
4 Jun 63	★ **DEVIL IN DISGUISE** *RCA 1355*	**1**	12 wks
24 Oct 63	**BOSSA NOVA BABY** *RCA 1374*	**13**	8 wks
19 Dec 63	**KISS ME QUICK** *RCA 1375*	**14**	10 wks
12 Mar 64	**VIVA LAS VEGAS** *RCA 1390*	**17**	12 wks
25 Jun 64	● **KISSIN' COUSINS** *RCA 1404*	**10**	11 wks
20 Aug 64	**SUCH A NIGHT** *RCA 1411*	**13**	10 wks
29 Oct 64	**AIN'T THAT LOVIN' YOU BABY** *RCA 1422*	**15**	8 wks
3 Dec 64	**BLUE CHRISTMAS** *RCA 1430*	**11**	7 wks
11 Mar 65	**DO THE CLAM** *RCA 1443*	**19**	8 wks
27 May 65	★ **CRYING IN THE CHAPEL** *RCA 1455*	**1**	15 wks
11 Nov 65	**TELL ME WHY** *RCA 1489*	**15**	10 wks
24 Feb 66	**BLUE RIVER** *RCA 1504*	**22**	7 wks
7 Apr 66	**FRANKIE AND JOHNNY** *RCA 1509*	**21**	9 wks
7 Jul 66	● **LOVE LETTERS** *RCA 1526*	**6**	10 wks
13 Oct 66	**ALL THAT I AM** *RCA 1545*	**18**	8 wks
1 Dec 66	**IF EVERY DAY WAS LIKE CHRISTMAS** *RCA 1557*	**13**	7 wks
9 Feb 67	**INDESCRIBABLY BLUE** *RCA 1565*	**21**	5 wks
11 May 67	**YOU GOTTA STOP/ LOVE MACHINE** *RCA 1593*	**38**	5 wks
16 Aug 67	**LONG LEGGED GIRL** *RCA Victor RCA 1616*	**49**	2 wks
21 Feb 68	**GUITAR MAN** *RCA 1663*	**19**	9 wks
15 May 68	**U. S. MALE** *RCA 1673*	**15**	8 wks
17 Jul 68	**YOUR TIME HASN'T COME YET BABY** *RCA 1714*	**22**	11 wks
16 Oct 68	**YOU'LL NEVER WALK ALONE** *RCA 1747*	**44**	3 wks
26 Feb 69	**IF I CAN DREAM** *RCA 1795*	**11**	10 wks
11 Jun 69	● **IN THE GHETTO** *RCA 1831*	**2**	16 wks
6 Sep 69	● **CLEAN UP YOUR OWN BACK YARD** *RCA 1869*	**2**	7 wks
18 Oct 69	**IN THE GHETTO** (re-entry) *RCA 1831*	**50**	1 wk
29 Nov 69	● **SUSPICIOUS MINDS** *RCA 1900*	**2**	14 wks
28 Feb 70	● **DON'T CRY DADDY** *RCA 1916*	**8**	11 wks
16 May 70	**KENTUCKY RAIN** *RCA 1949*	**21**	11 wks
11 Jul 70	★ **THE WONDER OF YOU** *RCA 1974*	**1**	20 wks
8 Aug 70	**KENTUCKY RAIN** (re-entry) *RCA 1949*	**46**	1 wk
14 Nov 70	● **I'VE LOST YOU** *RCA 1999*	**9**	12 wks
9 Jan 71	● **YOU DON'T HAVE TO SAY YOU LOVE ME** *RCA 2046*	**9**	7 wks
23 Jan 71	**THE WONDER OF YOU** (re-entry) *RCA 1974*	**47**	1 wk
6 Mar 71	**YOU DON'T HAVE TO SAY YOU LOVE ME** (re-entry) *RCA 2046*	**35**	3 wks
20 Mar 71	● **THERE GOES MY EVERYTHING** *RCA 2060*	**6**	11 wks
15 May 71	● **RAGS TO RICHES** *RCA 2084*	**9**	11 wks
17 Jul 71	● **HEARTBREAK HOTEL/ HOUND DOG** (re-issue) *RCA Maximillion 2104*	**10**	12 wks
2 Oct 71	**I'M LEAVIN'** *RCA 2125*	**23**	9 wks
4 Dec 71	● **I JUST CAN'T HELP BELIEVING** *RCA 2158*	**6**	16 wks
11 Dec 71	**JAILHOUSE ROCK** (re-issue) *RCA Maximillion 2153*	**42**	5 wks
1 Apr 72	● **UNTIL IT'S TIME FOR YOU TO GO** *RCA 2188*	**5**	9 wks
17 Jun 72	● **AMERICAN TRILOGY** *RCA 2229*	**8**	11 wks
30 Sep 72	● **BURNING LOVE** *RCA 2267*	**7**	9 wks
16 Dec 72	● **ALWAYS ON MY MIND** *RCA 2304*	**9**	13 wks
26 May 73	**POLK SALAD ANNIE** *RCA 2359*	**23**	7 wks
11 Aug 73	**FOOL** *RCA 2393*	**15**	10 wks
24 Nov 73	**RAISED ON ROCK** *RCA 2435*	**36**	7 wks
16 Mar 74	**I'VE GOT A THING ABOUT YOU BABY** *RCA APBO 0196*	**33**	5 wks
13 Jul 74	**IF YOU TALK IN YOUR SLEEP** *RCA APBO 0280*	**40**	3 wks
16 Nov 74	● **MY BOY** *RCA 2458*	**5**	13 wks
18 Jan 75	● **PROMISED LAND** *RCA PB 10074*	**9**	8 wks
24 May 75	**T. R. O. U. B. L. E.** *RCA 2562*	**31**	4 wks
29 Nov 75	**GREEN GREEN GRASS OF HOME** *RCA 2635*	**29**	7 wks
1 May 76	**HURT** *RCA 2674*	**37**	5 wks
4 Sep 76	● **GIRL OF MY BEST FRIEND** *RCA 2729*	**9**	12 wks
25 Dec 76	● **SUSPICION** *RCA 2768*	**9**	12 wks
5 Mar 77	● **MOODY BLUE** *RCA PB 0857*	**6**	9 wks
13 Aug 77	★ **WAY DOWN** *RCA PB 0998*	**1**	13 wks
3 Sep 77	**IT'S NOW OR NEVER** (re-issue) *RCA PB 2698*	**39**	2 wks
3 Sep 77	**ALL SHOOK UP** (re-issue) *RCA PB 2694*	**41**	2 wks
3 Sep 77	**CRYING IN THE CHAPEL** (re-issue) *RCA PB 2708*	**43**	2 wks
3 Sep 77	**JAILHOUSE ROCK** (2nd re-issue) *RCA PB 2695*	**44**	2 wks
3 Sep 77	**ARE YOU LONESOME TONIGHT** (re-issue) *RCA PB 2699*	**46**	1 wk
3 Sep 77	**THE WONDER OF YOU** (re-issue) *RCA PB 2709*	**48**	1 wk
3 Sep 77	**WOODEN HEART** (re-issue) *RCA PB 2700*	**49**	1 wk
3 Sep 77	**RETURN TO SENDER** (re-issue) *RCA PB 2706*	**42**	3 wks
10 Dec 77	● **MY WAY** *RCA PB 1165*	**9**	8 wks
24 Jun 78	**DON'T BE CRUEL** *RCA PB 9265*	**24**	12 wks
15 Dec 79	**IT WON'T SEEM LIKE CHRISTMAS (WITHOUT YOU)** *RCA PB 9464*	**13**	6 wks
30 Aug 80	● **IT'S ONLY LOVE/ BEYOND THE REEF** *RCA 4*	**3**	10 wks
6 Dec 80	**SANTA CLAUS IS BACK IN TOWN** *RCA 16*	**41**	wks
14 Feb 81	**GUITAR MAN** *RCA 43*	**43**	4 wks
18 Apr 81	**LOVING ARMS** *RCA 48*	**47**	6 wks
13 Mar 82	**ARE YOU LONESOME TONIGHT** *RCA 196*	**25**	7 wks
26 Jun 82	**THE SOUND OF YOUR CRY** *RCA 232*	**59**	2 wks

Tracks on Jailhouse Rock *EP: Jailhouse Rock/ Young And Beautiful/ I Want To Be Free/ Don't Leave Me Now/ Baby I Don't Care.* On Strictly Elvis *EP: Old Shep/ Any Place Is Paradise/ Paralysed/ Is It So Strange.* On Follow That Dream *EP: Follow That Dream/ Angel/ What A Wonderful Life/ I'm Not The Marrying Kind. On 5 July 62 a note on the Top 50 for that week stated "Due to difficulties in assessing returns of* Follow That Dream *EP, it has been decided not to include it in Britain's Top 50. It is of course No. 1 in the EP charts". Therefore this EP only had a 2 week run on the chart when its sales would certainly have justified a much longer one.* Beyond The Reef *listed only 30 Aug to 13 Sep 80.* Are You Lonesome Tonight *on RCA 196 is a live version.*

Billy PRESTON

US, male vocalist/instrumentalist, keyboards

Date	Title *Label Number*	Position	
2 Jul 69	**THAT'S THE WAY GOD PLANNED IT** *Apple 12*	**11**	10 wks
16 Sep 72	**OUTA SPACE** *A & M AMS 7007*	**44**	3 wks

See also Beatles, Billy Preston and Syreeta.

Billy PRESTON and SYREETA

US, male/female vocal duo

Date	Title *Label Number*	Position	
15 Dec 79	● **WITH YOU I'M BORN AGAIN** *Motown TMG 1159*	**2**	11 wks
8 Mar 80	**IT WILL COME IN TIME** *Motown TMG 1175*	**47**	4 wks

See also Billy Preston, Syreeta, Beatles.

Johnny PRESTON *US, male vocalist*

Date	Title *Label Number*	Position	
12 Feb 60	★ **RUNNING BEAR** *Mercury AMT 1079*	**1**	14 wks
21 Apr 60	● **CRADLE OF LOVE** *Mercury AMT 1092*	**2**	16 wks
2 Jun 60	**RUNNING BEAR** (re-entry) *Mercury AMT 1079*	**41**	1 wk
28 Jul 60	**I'M STARTING TO GO STEADY** *Mercury AMT 1104*	**49**	1 wk
11 Aug 60	**FEEL SO FINE** *Mercury AMT 1104*	**18**	10 wks
8 Dec 60	**CHARMING BILLY** *Mercury AMT 1114*	**34**	1 wk
22 Dec 60	**CHARMING BILLY** (re-entry) *Mercury AMT 1114*	**42**	2 wks

Mike PRESTON *UK, male vocalist*

Date	Title *Label Number*	Position	
30 Oct 59	**MR. BLUE** *Decca F 11167*	**12**	8 wks
25 Aug 60	**I'D DO ANYTHING** *Decca F 11255*	**23**	10 wks
23 Dec 60	**TOGETHERNESS** *Decca F 11287*	**41**	5 wks
9 Mar 61	**MARRY ME** *Decca F 11335*	**14**	10 wks

PRETENDERS

UK/US, male/female vocal/instrumental group

Date	Title *Label Number*	Position	
10 Feb 79	**STOP YOUR SOBBING** *Real ARE 6*	**34**	9 wks
14 Jul 79	**KID** *Real ARE 9*	**33**	7 wks
17 Nov 79	★ **BRASS IN POCKET** *Real ARE 11*	**1**	17 wks
5 Apr 80	● **TALK OF THE TOWN** *Real ARE 12*	**8**	8 wks
14 Feb 81	**MESSAGE OF LOVE** *Real ARE 15*	**11**	7 wks
12 Sep 81	**DAY AFTER DAY** *Real ARE 17*	**45**	4 wks
12 Sep 81	● **I GO TO SLEEP** *Real ARE 18*	**7**	10 wks
12 Sep 81	**BACK ON THE CHAIN GANG** *Real ARE 19*	**17**	9 wks

PRETTY THINGS

UK, male vocal/instrumental group

Date	Title *Label Number*	Position	
18 Jun 64	**ROSALYN** *Fontana TF 469*	**41**	5 wks
22 Oct 64	● **DON'T BRING ME DOWN** *Fontana TF 503*	**10**	11 wks
25 Feb 65	**HONEY I NEED** *Fontana TF 537*	**13**	10 wks
15 Jul 65	**CRY TO ME** *Fontana TF 585*	**28**	7 wks
20 Jan 66	**MIDNIGHT TO SIX MAN** *Fontana TF 647*	**46**	1 wk
5 May 66	**COME SEE ME** *Fontana TF 688*	**43**	5 wks
21 Jul 66	**A HOUSE IN THE COUNTRY** *Fontana TF 722*	**50**	1 wk
4 Aug 66	**A HOUSE IN THE COUNTRY** (re-entry) *Fontana TF 722*	**50**	1 wk

Alan PRICE

UK, male vocalist/instrumentalist, keyboards

Date	Title *Label Number*	Position	
31 Mar 66	● **I PUT A SPELL ON YOU** *Decca F 12367*	**9**	10 wks
14 Jul 66	**HI LILI HI LO** *Decca F 12442*	**11**	12 wks
2 Mar 67	● **SIMON SMITH & HIS AMAZING DANCING BEAR** *Decca F 12570*	**4**	12 wks
2 Aug 67	● **THE HOUSE THAT JACK BUILT** *Decca F 12641*	**4**	10 wks
15 Nov 67	**SHAME** *Decca F 12691*	**45**	2 wks
31 Jan 68	**DON'T STOP THE CARNIVAL** *Decca F 12731*	**13**	8 wks
25 May 74	● **JARROW SONG** *Warner Bros K 16372*	**6**	9 wks
29 Apr 78	**JUST FOR YOU** *Jet UP 36358*	**43**	8 wks
17 Feb 79	**BABY OF MINE/JUST FOR YOU** (RE-ISSUE) *Jet 135*	**32**	3 wks

The Decca hits are credited to the Alan Price Set. See also Fame and Price Together.

Lloyd PRICE *US, male vocalist*

Date	Title *Label Number*	Position	
13 Feb 59	● **STAGGER LEE** *HMV POP 580*	**7**	14 wks
15 May 59	**WHERE WERE YOU** *HMV POP 598*	**15**	6 wks
12 Jun 59	● **PERSONALITY** *HMV POP 626*	**9**	8 wks
14 Aug 59	**PERSONALITY** (re-entry) *HMV POP 626*	**25**	2 wks
11 Sep 59	**I'M GONNA GET MARRIED** *HMV POP 650*	**23**	5 wks
21 Apr 60	**LADY LUCK** *HMV POP 712*	**45**	1 wk

Dickie PRIDE *UK, male vocalist*

Date	Title *Label Number*	Position	
30 Oct 59	**PRIMROSE LANE** *Columbia DB 4340*	**28**	1 wk

Louis PRIMA *US, male vocalist*

Date	Title *Label Number*	Position	
21 Feb 58	**BUONA SERA** *Capitol CL 14841*	**25**	1 wk

PRIMA DONNA *UK, male/female vocal group*

Date	Title *Label Number*	Position	
26 Apr 80	**LOVE ENOUGH FOR TWO** *Ariola ARO 221*	**48**	4 wks

PRINCE *US, male vocalist*

Date	Title *Label Number*	Position	
19 Jan 80	**I WANNA BE YOUR LOVER** *Warner Bros. K 17537*	**41**	3 wks

P. J. PROBY *US, male vocalist*

Date	Title *Label Number*	Position	
28 May 64	● **HOLD ME** *Decca F 11904*	**3**	15 wks
3 Sep 64	● **TOGETHER** *Decca F 11967*	**8**	11 wks
10 Dec 64	● **SOMEWHERE** *Liberty LIB 10182*	**6**	12 wks
25 Feb 65	**I APOLOGISE** *Liberty LIB 10188*	**11**	8 wks
8 Jul 65	**LET THE WATER RUN DOWN** *Liberty LIB 10206*	**19**	8 wks
30 Sep 65	**THAT MEANS A LOT** *Liberty LIB 10215*	**30**	6 wks
25 Nov 65	● **MARIA** *Liberty LIB 10218*	**8**	9 wks
10 Feb 66	**YOU'VE COME BACK** *Liberty LIB 10223*	**25**	7 wks
16 Jun 66	**TO MAKE A BIG MAN CRY** *Liberty LIB 10236*	**34**	3 wks
27 Oct 66	**I CAN'T MAKE IT ALONE** *Liberty LIB 10250*	**37**	5 wks
6 Mar 68	**IT'S YOUR DAY TODAY** *Liberty LBF 15046*	**32**	5 wks

Date **Title** *Label Number* **Position**

PROCOL HARUM

UK, male vocal/instrumental group

Date		Title *Label Number*	Position	Weeks
25 May 67	★	**A WHITER SHADE OF PALE** *Deram DM 126*	**1**	15 wks
4 Oct 67	●	**HOMBURG** *Regal Zonophone RZ 3003*	**6**	10 wks
24 Apr 68		**QUITE RIGHTLY SO** *Regal Zonophone RZ 3007*	**50**	1 wk
18 Jun 69		**SALTY DOG** *Regal Zonophone RZ 3019*	**44**	1 wk
2 Jul 69		**SALTY DOG** (re-entry) *Regal Zonophone RZ 3019*	**44**	1 wk
16 Jul 69		**SALTY DOG** (2nd re-entry) *Regal Zonophone RZ 3019*	**44**	1 wk
22 Apr 72		**A WHITER SHADE OF PALE** (re-issue) *Magnifly Echo 10*	**49**	1 wk
6 May 72		**A WHITER SHADE OF PALE** (re-entry of re-issue) *Magnifly Echo 10*	**13**	11 wks
5 Aug 72		**CONQUISTADOR** *Chrysalis CHS 2003*	**22**	7 wks
23 Aug 75		**PANDORA'S BOX** *Chrysalis CHS 2073*	**16**	7 wks

PROFESSIONALS

UK, male vocal/instrumental group

Date		Title *Label Number*	Position	Weeks
11 Oct 80		**1-2-3** *Virgin VS 376*	**43**	4 wks

Brian PROTHEROE *UK, male vocalist*

Date		Title *Label Number*	Position	Weeks
7 Sep 74		**PINBALL** *Chrysalis CHS 2043*	**22**	6 wks

Dorothy PROVINE *US, female vocalist*

Date		Title *Label Number*	Position	Weeks
7 Dec 61		**DON'T BRING LULU** *Warner Bros. WB 53*	**17**	12 wks
28 Jun 62		**CRAZY WORDS CRAZY TUNE** *Warner Bros. WB 70*	**45**	3 wks

PRUDENCE — See *PATIENCE and PRUDENCE*

PSYCHEDELIC FURS

UK, male vocal/instrumental group

Date		Title *Label Number*	Position	Weeks
2 May 81		**DUMB WAITERS** *CBS 1166*	**59**	2 wks
27 Jun 81		**PRETTY IN PINK** *CBS A 1327*	**43**	5 wks
31 Jul 82		**LOVE MY WAY** *CBS A 2549*	**42**	6 wks

PUBLIC IMAGE LTD.

UK, male vocal/instrumental group

Date		Title *Label Number*	Position	Weeks
21 Oct 78	●	**PUBLIC IMAGE** *Virgin VS 228*	**9**	8 wks
7 Jul 79		**DEATH DISCO** (PARTS 1 & 2) *Virgin VS 274*	**20**	7 wks
20 Oct 79		**MEMORIES** *Virgin VS 299*	**60**	2 wks
4 Apr 81		**FLOWERS OF ROMANCE** *Virgin VS 397*	**24**	7 wks

Gary PUCKETT and the UNION GAP

US, male vocalist, male vocal/instrumental backing group

Date		Title *Label Number*	Position	Weeks
17 Apr 68	★	**YOUNG GIRL** *CBS 3365*	**1**	17 wks
7 Aug 68	●	**LADY WILLPOWER** *CBS 3551*	**5**	16 wks
28 Aug 68		**WOMAN WOMAN** *CBS 3100*	**48**	1 wk
15 Jun 74	●	**YOUNG GIRL** (re-issue) *CBS 8202*	**6**	13 wks

Billed as The Union Gap featuring Gary Puckett on the original issue of Young Girl *and* Lady Willpower.

James and Bobby PURIFY

US, male vocal duo

Date		Title *Label Number*	Position	Weeks
24 Apr 76		**I'M YOUR PUPPET** *Mercury 6167 324*	**12**	10 wks
7 Aug 76		**MORNING GLORY** *Mercury 6167 380*	**27**	6 wks

PURPLE HEARTS

UK, male vocal/instrumental group

Date		Title *Label Number*	Position	Weeks
22 Sep 79		**MILLIONS LIKE US** *Fiction FICS 003*	**57**	3 wks
8 Mar 80		**JIMMY** *Fiction FICS 9*	**60**	2 wks

PUSSYCAT

Holland, male/female vocal/instrumental group

Date		Title *Label Number*	Position	Weeks
28 Aug 76	★	**MISSISSIPPI** *Sonet SON 2077*	**1**	22 wks
25 Dec 76		**SMILE** *Sonet SON 2096*	**24**	8 wks

PYRAMIDS *Jamaica, male vocal/instrumental group*

Date		Title *Label Number*	Position	Weeks
22 Nov 67		**TRAIN TOUR TO RAINBOW CITY** *President PT 161*	**35**	4 wks

PYTHON LEE JACKSON

UK, male vocal/instrumental group

Date		Title *Label Number*	Position	Weeks
30 Sep 72	●	**IN A BROKEN DREAM** *Youngblood YB 1002*	**3**	12 wks

Q

QUADS *UK, male vocal/instrumental group*

Date		Title *Label Number*	Position	Weeks
22 Sep 79		**THERE MUST BE THOUSANDS** *Big Bear BB 23*	**66**	2 wks

QUANTUM JUMP

UK, male vocal/instrumental group

Date		Title *Label Number*	Position	Weeks
2 Jun 79	●	**THE LONE RANGER** *Electric WOT 33*	**5**	10 wks

QUATERFLASH

US, male/female vocal/instrumental group

Date		Title *Label Number*	Position	Weeks
27 Feb 82		**HARDEN MY HEART** *Geffen GEF A 1838*	**49**	5 wks

Suzi QUATRO

US, female vocalist/instrumentalist - guitar

Date		Title *Label Number*	Position	Weeks
19 May 73	★	**CAN THE CAN** *RAK 150*	**1**	14 wks
28 Jul 73	●	**48 CRASH** *RAK 158*	**3**	9 wks
27 Oct 73		**DAYTONA DEMON** *RAK 161*	**14**	13 wks
9 Feb 74	★	**DEVIL GATE DRIVE** *RAK 167*	**1**	11 wks
29 Jun 74		**TOO BIG** *RAK 175*	**14**	6 wks

Date	Title *Label Number*	Position	
9 Nov 74	● **THE WILD ONE** *RAK 185*	**7**	10 wks
8 Feb 75	**YOUR MAMMA WON'T LIKE ME** *RAK 191*	**31**	5 wks
5 Mar 77	**TEAR ME APART** *RAK 248*	**27**	6 wks
18 Mar 78	● **IF YOU CAN'T GIVE ME LOVE** *RAK 271*	**4**	13 wks
22 Jul 78	**THE RACE IS ON** *RAK 278*	**43**	5 wks
20 Oct 79	**SHE'S IN LOVE WITH YOU** *RAK 299*	**11**	9 wks
19 Jan 80	**MAMA'S BOY** *RAK 303*	**34**	5 wks
5 Apr 80	**I'VE NEVER BEEN IN LOVE** *RAK 307*	**56**	3 wks
25 Oct 80	**ROCK HARD** *Dreamland DLSP 6*	**68**	2 wks
13 Nov 82	**HEART OF STONE** *Polydor POSP 477*	**60**	3 wks

See Suzi Quatro and Chris Norman

Suzi QUATRO and Suzi NORMAN

UK/US, female/male vocal duo

Date	Title *Label Number*	Position	
11 Nov 78	**STUMBLIN' IN** *Rak RAK 285*	**41**	8 wks

See also Suzi Quatro

QUEEN *UK, male vocal/instrumental group*

Date	Title *Label Number*	Position	
9 Mar 74	● **SEVEN SEAS OF RHYE** *EMI 2121*	**10**	10 wks
26 Oct 74	● **KILLER QUEEN** *EMI 2229*	**2**	12 wks
25 Jan 75	**NOW I'M HERE** *EMI 2256*	**11**	7 wks
8 Nov 75	★ **BOHEMIAN RHAPSODY** *EMI 2375*	**1**	17 wks
3 Jul 76	● **YOU'RE MY BEST FRIEND** *EMI 2494*	**7**	8 wks
27 Nov 76	● **SOMEBODY TO LOVE** *EMI 2565*	**2**	9 wks
19 Mar 77	**TIE YOUR MOTHER DOWN** *EMI 2593*	**31**	4 wks
4 Jun 77	**QUEENS FIRST EP** (EP) *EMI 2623*	**17**	10 wks
22 Oct 77	● **WE ARE THE CHAMPIONS** *EMI 2708*	**2**	11 wks
25 Feb 78	**SPREAD YOUR WINGS** *EMI 2757*	**34**	4 wks
28 Oct 78	**BICYCLE RACE/FAT BOTTOMED GIRLS** *EMI 2870*	**11**	12 wks
10 Feb 79	● **DON'T STOP ME NOW** *EMI 2910*	**9**	12 wks
14 Jul 79	**LOVE OF MY LIFE** *EMI 2959*	**63**	2 wks
20 Oct 79	● **CRAZY LITTLE THING CALLED LOVE** *EMI 5001*	**2**	14 wks
2 Feb 80	**SAVE ME** *EMI 5022*	**11**	6 wks
14 Jun 80	**PLAY THE GAME** *EMI 5076*	**14**	8 wks
6 Sep 80	● **ANOTHER ONE BITES THE DUST** *EMI 5102*	**7**	9 wks
6 Dec 80	● **FLASH** *EMI 5126*	**10**	13 wks
1 May 82	**BODY LANGUAGE** *EMI 5293*	**25**	6 wks
12 Jun 82	**LAS PALABRAS DE AMOR** *EMI 5316*	**17**	8 wks
21 Aug 82	**BACKCHAT** *EMI 5325*	**40**	4 wks

See also Queen and David Bowie. *Tracks on Queen's First EP: Good Old Fashioned Lover Boy/Death On Two Legs (Dedicated To...)/Tenement Funster/White Queen (As it Began).*

QUEEN and David BOWIE

UK, male vocal/instrumental group and male vocalist

Date	Title *Label Number*	Position	
14 Nov 81	★ **UNDER PRESSURE** *EMI 5250*	**1**	11 wks

See also Queen, David Bowie, David Bowie and Bing Crosby.

? (QUESTION MARK) and the MYSTERIANS *US, male vocal/instrumental group*

Date	Title *Label Number*	Position	
17 Nov 66	**96 TEARS** *Cameo Parkway C428*	**37**	4 wks

QUICK *UK, male vocal/instrumental group*

Date	Title *Label Number*	Position	
15 May 82	**RHYTHM OF THE JUNGLE** *Epic EPC A 2013*	**41**	7 wks

Tommy QUICKLY *UK, male vocalist*

Date	Title *Label Number*	Position	
22 Oct 64	**WILD SIDE OF LIFE** *Pye 7N 15708*	**33**	8 wks

QUIET FIVE *UK, male vocal/instrumental group*

Date	Title *Label Number*	Position	
13 May 65	**WHEN THE MORNING SUN DRIES THE DEW** *Parlophone R 5273*	**45**	1 wk
21 Apr 66	**HOMEWARD BOUND** *Parlophone R 5421*	**44**	2 wks

QUIVER — See *SUTHERLAND BROTHERS*

R

Eddie RABBITT *US, male vocalist*

Date	Title *Label Number*	Position	
27 Jan 79	**EVERY WHICH WAY BUT LOOSE** *Elektra K 12331*	**41**	9 wks
28 Feb 81	**I LOVE A RAINY NIGHT** *Elektra K 12498*	**53**	5 wks

Steve RACE *UK, male instrumentalist, piano*

Date	Title *Label Number*	Position	
28 Feb 63	**PIED PIPER (THE BEEJE)** *Parlophone R 4981*	**29**	9 wks

RACEY *UK, male vocal/instrumental group*

Date	Title *Label Number*	Position	
25 Nov 78	● **LAY YOUR LOVE ON ME** *Rak RAK 284*	**3**	14 wks
31 Mar 79	● **SOME GIRLS** *RAK 291*	**2**	11 wks
18 Aug 79	**BOY OH BOY** *RAK 297*	**22**	9 wks
20 Dec 80	**RUNAROUND SUE** *RAK 325*	**13**	10 wks

RACING CARS *UK, male vocal/instrumental group*

Date	Title *Label Number*	Position	
12 Feb 77	**THEY SHOOT HORSES DON'T THEY** *Chrysalis CHS 2129*	**14**	7 wks

Jimmy RADCLIFFE *US, male vocalist*

Date	Title *Label Number*	Position	
4 Feb 65	**LONG AFTER TONIGHT IS ALL OVER** *Stateside SS 374*	**40**	2 wks

RADHA KRISHNA TEMPLE

Oxford Street, male/female vocal/instrumental group

Date	Title *Label Number*	Position	
13 Sep 69	**HARE KRISHNA MANTRA** *Apple 15*	**12**	9 wks
28 Mar 70	**GOVINDA** *Apple 25*	**23**	8 wks

RADIO REVELLERS — See *Anthony STEEL and the RADIO REVELLERS*

RADIO STARS *UK, male vocal/instrumental group*

Date	Title *Label Number*	Position	
4 Feb 78	**NERVOUS WRECK** *Chiswick NS 23*	**39**	3 wks

Gerry RAFFERTY *UK, male vocalist*

Date	Title *Label Number*	Position	
18 Feb 78	● **BAKER STREET** *United Artists UP 36346*	**3**	15 wks
26 May 79	● **NIGHT OWL** *United Artists UP 36512*	**5**	13 wks
18 Aug 79	**GET IT RIGHT NEXT TIME** *United Artists BP 301*	**30**	9 wks
22 Mar 80	**BRING IT ALL HOME** *United Artists BP 340*	**54**	4 wks
21 Jun 80	**ROYAL MILE** *United Artists BP 354*	**67**	2 wks

DEBBIE REYNOLDS Strictly for the birds – the song gets to grips with whippoorwills, owls and doves

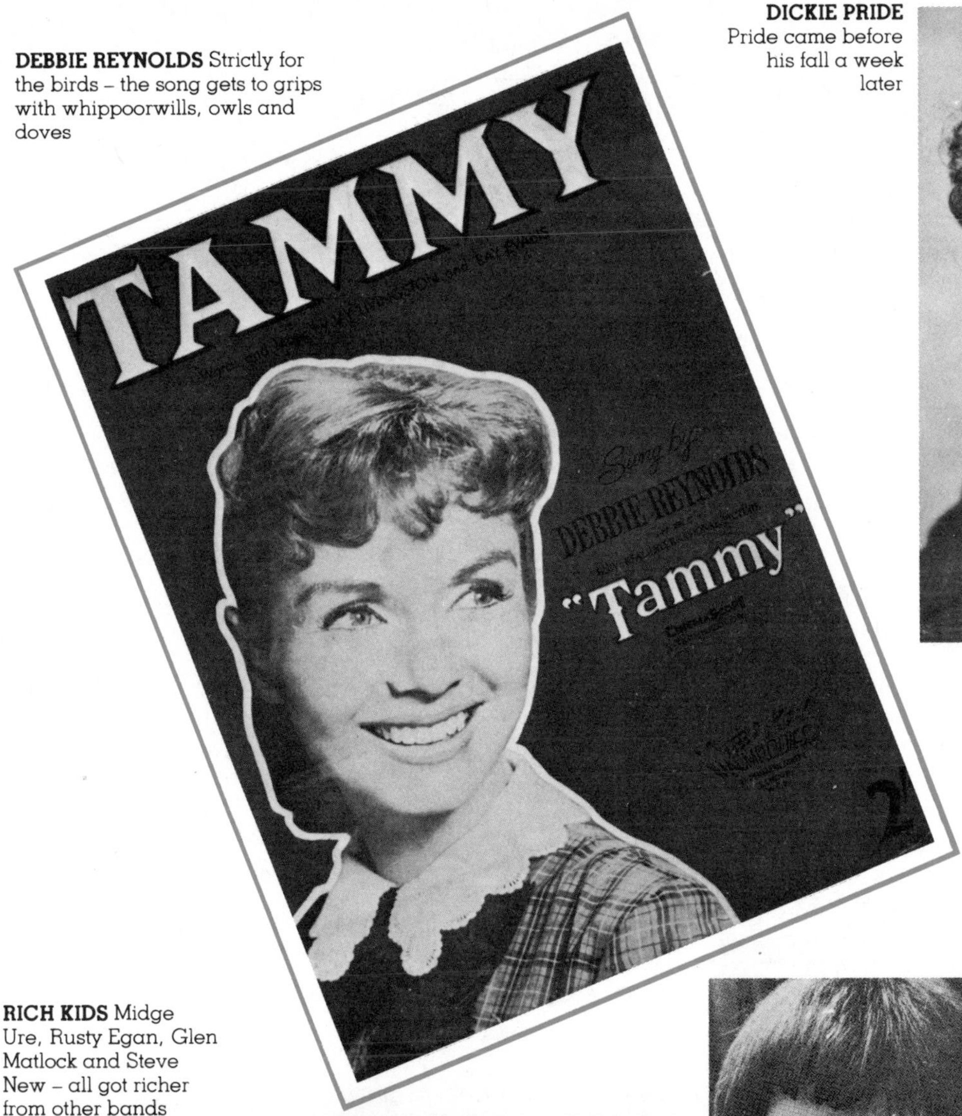

DICKIE PRIDE Pride came before his fall a week later

JOHNNY PRESTON The guy who was discovered and produced by The Big Bopper (J P Richardson) tries out a typically English pub during his visit to this country the year he charted five titles

RICH KIDS Midge Ure, Rusty Egan, Glen Matlock and Steve New – all got richer from other bands

Left **TOMMY ROE** He first made 'Sheila' with his high school band The Satins in 1960 but it was a re-recording two years later that gave him his first British hit

TEX RITTER The legendary cowboy gets anglicised by Peter and Gordon in a Nashville Studio

Date	Title *Label Number*	Position	

Date Title *Label Number* Position

RAGTIMERS *UK, male instrumental group*

16 Mar 74	**THE STING** *Pye 7N 45323*	**46**	1 wk
30 Mar 74	**THE STING** (re-entry) *Pye 7N 45323*	**31**	7 wks

RAH BAND *UK, instrumental group*

9 Jul 77	● **THE CRUNCH** *Good Earth GD 7*	**6**	12 wks
1 Nov 80	**FALCON** *DJM DJS 10954*	**35**	7 wks
7 Feb 81	**SLIDE** *DJM DJS 10964*	**50**	7 wks
1 May 82	**PERFUMED GARDEN** *KR KR 5*	**45**	7 wks

RAIN — See *Stephanie DE SYKES*

RAINBOW *UK, male vocal/instrumental group*

17 Sep 77	**KILL THE KING** *Polydor 2066 845*	**44**	3 wks
8 Apr 78	**LONG LIVE ROCK 'N' ROLL** *Polydor 2066 913*	**33**	3 wks
30 Sep 78	**L. A. CONNECTION** *Polydor 2066 968*	**40**	4 wks
15 Sep 79	● **SINCE YOU'VE BEEN GONE** *Polydor POSP 70*	**6**	10 wks
16 Feb 80	● **ALL NIGHT LONG** *Polydor POSP 104*	**5**	11 wks
31 Jan 81	● **I SURRENDER** *Polydor POSP 221*	**3**	10 wks
20 Jun 81	**CAN'T HAPPEN HERE** *Polydor POSP 251*	**20**	8 wks
11 Jul 81	**KILL THE KING** (re-issue) *Polydor POSP 274*	**41**	4 wks
3 Apr 82	**STONE COLD** *Polydor POSP 421*	**34**	4 wks

RAINBOW COTTAGE

UK, male vocal/instrumental group

6 Mar 76	**SEAGULL** *Penny Farthing PEN 906*	**33**	4 wks

Marvin RAINWATER *US, male vocalist*

7 Mar 58	★ **WHOLE LOTTA WOMAN** *MGM 974*	**1**	15 wks
6 Jun 58	**I DIG YOU BABY** *MGM 980*	**19**	7 wks

Tony RALLO and the MIDNIGHT BAND

France, guitarist with US male vocal/instrumental group

23 Feb 80	**HOLDIN' ON** *Calibre CAB 1*	**34**	8 wks

RAM JAM *US, male vocal/instrumental group*

10 Sep 77	● **BLACK BETTY** *Epic EPC 5492*	**7**	12 wks

RAM JAM BAND — See *Geno WASHINGTON and the RAM JAM BAND*

RAMBLERS (from the Abbey Hey Junior School) *UK, children's choir*

13 Oct 79	**THE SPARROW** *Decca F 13860*	**11**	15 wks

RAMONES *US, male vocal/instrumental group*

21 May 77	**SHEENA IS A PUNK ROCKER** *Sire RAM 001*	**22**	7 wks
6 Aug 77	**SWALLOW MY PRIDE** *Sire 6078 607*	**36**	3 wks
30 Sep 78	**DON'T COME CLOSE** *Sire SRE 1031*	**39**	5 wks
8 Sep 79	**ROCK 'N' ROLL HIGH SCHOOL** *Sire SIR 4021*	**67**	2 wks
26 Jan 80	● **BABY I LOVE YOU** *Sire SIR 4031*	**8**	9 wks
19 Apr 80	**DO YOU REMEMBER ROCK'N'ROLL RADIO** *Sire SIR 4037*	**54**	3 wks

RAMRODS *US, male/female instrumental group*

23 Feb 61	● **RIDERS IN THE SKY** *London HLU 9282*	**8**	12 wks

RARE BIRD *UK, male vocal/instrumental group*

14 Feb 70	**SYMPATHY** *Charisma CB 120*	**27**	8 wks

O. RASBURY — See *Rahni HARRIS and F.L.O.*

RATTLES *Germany, male vocal/instrumental group*

3 Oct 70	● **THE WITCH** *Decca F 23058*	**8**	15 wks

RAW SILK *US, female vocal group*

16 Oct 82	**DO IT TO THE MUSIC** *KR KR 14*	**18**	9 wks

Lou RAWLS *US, male vocalist*

31 Jul 76	● **YOU'LL NEVER FIND ANOTHER LOVE LIKE MINE** *Philadelphia International PIR 4372*	**10**	10 wks

See also Philadelphia International All-Stars.

Johnnie RAY *US, male vocalist*

14 Nov 52	**WALKING MY BABY BACK HOME** *Columbia DB 3060*	**12**	1 wk
19 Dec 52	● **FAITH CAN MOVE MOUNTAINS** *Columbia DB 3154*	**7**	2 wks
9 Jan 53	● **FAITH CAN MOVE MOUNTAINS** (re-entry) *Columbia DB 3154*	**9**	1 wk
10 Apr 53	● **SOMEBODY STOLE MY GAL** *Philips PB 123*	**6**	1 wk
24 Apr 53	● **SOMEBODY STOLE MY GAL** (re-entry) *Philips PB 123*	**6**	4 wks
29 May 53	**SOMEBODY STOLE MY GAL** (2nd re-entry) *Philips PB 123*	**12**	1 wk
7 Aug 53	**SOMEBODY STOLE MY GAL** (3rd re-entry) *Philips PB 123*	**11**	1 wk
9 Apr 54	★ **SUCH A NIGHT** *Philips PB 244*	**1**	18 wks
8 Apr 55	**IF YOU BELIEVE** *Philips PB 379*	**15**	1 wk
13 May 55	● **IF YOU BELIEVE** (re-entry) *Philips PB 379*	**7**	10 wks
20 May 55	**PATHS OF PARADISE** *Philips PB 441*	**20**	1 wk
7 Oct 55	**HERNANDO'S HIDEAWAY** *Philips PB 495*	**11**	5 wks
14 Oct 55	● **HEY THERE** *Philips PB 495*	**5**	9 wks
28 Oct 55	● **SONG OF THE DREAMER** *Philips PB 516*	**10**	5 wks
17 Feb 56	**WHO'S SORRY NOW** *Philips PB 546*	**17**	2 wks
20 Apr 56	**AIN'T MISBEHAVIN'** *Philips PB 580*	**17**	6 wks
8 Jun 56	**AIN'T MISBEHAVIN'** (re-entry) *Philips PB 580*	**24**	1 wk
12 Oct 56	★ **JUST WALKIN' IN THE RAIN** *Philips PB 624*	**1**	19 wks
18 Jan 57	**YOU DON'T OWE ME A THING** *Philips PB 655*	**12**	15 wks
8 Feb 57	● **LOOK HOMEWARD ANGEL** *Philips PB 655*	**7**	16 wks
10 May 57	★ **YES TONIGHT JOSEPHINE** *Philips PB 686*	**1**	16 wks
6 Sep 57	**BUILD YOUR LOVE** *Philips PB 721*	**17**	7 wks

Date **Title** *Label Number* **Position**

4 Dec 59 **I'LL NEVER FALL IN LOVE AGAIN** *Philips PB 952* **26** 4 wks
8 Jan 60 **I'LL NEVER FALL IN LOVE AGAIN** (re-entry) *Philips PB 952* **26** 1 wk
5 Feb 60 **I'LL NEVER FALL IN LOVE AGAIN** (2nd re-entry) *Philips PB 952* **28** 1 wk

See also Doris Day & Johnnie Ray, Frankie Laine & Johnnie Ray. The chart history of You Don't Owe Me A Thing/ Look Homeward Angel *is complicated, as follows;* You Don't Owe Me A Thing *entered the chart by itself on 18 Jan 57. On 8 & 15 Feb 57* Look Homeward Angel *was coupled with* You Don't Owe Me A Thing *but from 22 Feb 57 the two sides went their individual ways on the chart and were listed separately,* You Don't Owe Me A Thing *for a further 10 weeks and* Look Homeward Angel *for a further 14.*

RAYDIO *US, male/female vocal/instrumental group*

8 Apr 78 **JACK AND JILL** *Arista 161* **11** 12 wks
8 Jul 78 **IS THIS A LOVE THING** *Arista 193* **27** 9 wks

Chris REA *UK, male vocalist*

7 Oct 78 **FOOL (IF YOU THINK IT'S OVER)** *Magnet MAG 111* **30** 7 wks
21 Apr 79 **DIAMONDS** *Magnet MAG 144* **44** 3 wks
27 Mar 82 **LOVING YOU** *Magnet MAG 215* **65** 3 wks

Eileen READ — See *CADETS*

REAL THING *UK, male vocal/instrumental group*

5 Jun 76 ★ **YOU TO ME ARE EVERYTHING** *Pye International 7N 25709* **1** 11 wks
4 Sep 76 ● **CAN'T GET BY WITHOUT YOU** *Pye 7N 45618* **2** 10 wks
12 Feb 77 **YOU'LL NEVER KNOW WHAT YOU'RE MISSING** *Pye 7N 45662* **16** 9 wks
30 Jul 77 **LOVE'S SUCH A WONDERFUL THING** *Pye 7N 45701* **33** 5 wks
4 Mar 78 **WHENEVER YOU WANT MY LOVE** *Pye 7N 46045* **18** 9 wks
3 Jun 78 **LET'S GO DISCO** *Pye 7N 46078* **39** 7 wks
12 Aug 78 **RAININ' THROUGH MY SUNSHINE** *Pye 7N 46113* **40** 8 wks
17 Feb 79 ● **CAN YOU FEEL THE FORCE** *Pye 7N 46147* **5** 11 wks
21 Jul 79 **BOOGIE DOWN** *Pye 7P 109* **33** 6 wks
22 Nov 80 **SHE'S A GROOVY FREAK** *Calibre CAB 105* **52** 4 wks

REBEL ROUSERS — See *CLIFF BENNETT and the REBEL ROUSERS*

REBELETTES — See *Duane EDDY*

REBELS — See *Duane EDDY*

Ezz RECO and the LAUNCHERS with Boysie GRANT

Jamaica, male vocal/instrumental group

5 Mar 64 **KING OF KINGS** *Columbia DB 7217* **44** 4 wks

REDBONE *US, male vocal/instrumental group*

25 Sep 71 ● **WITCH QUEEN OF NEW ORLEANS** *Epic EPC 7351* **2** 12 wks

Date **Title** *Label Number* **Position**

Sharon REDD *US, female vocalist*

28 Feb 81 **CAN YOU HANDLE IT** *Epic EPC 9572* **31** 8 wks
2 Oct 82 **NEVER GIVE YOU UP** *Prelude PRL A2755* **20** 9 wks

Otis REDDING *US, male vocalist*

25 Nov 65 **MY GIRL** *Atlantic AT 4050* **11** 16 wks
7 Apr 66 **SATISFACTION** *Atlantic AT 4080* **33** 4 wks
14 Jul 66 **MY LOVER'S PRAYER** *Atlantic 584 019* **37** 6 wks
25 Aug 66 **I CAN'T TURN YOU LOOSE** *Atlantic 584 030* **29** 8 wks
24 Nov 66 **FA FA FA FA FA (SAD SONG)** *Atlantic 584 049* **23** 9 wks
26 Jan 67 **TRY A LITTLE TENDERNESS** *Atlantic 584 070* **46** 4 wks
23 Mar 67 **DAY TRIPPER** *Stax 601 005* **43** 6 wks
4 May 67 **LET ME COME ON HOME** *Stax 601 007* **48** 1 wk
15 Jun 67 **SHAKE** *Stax 601 011* **28** 10 wks
14 Feb 68 **MY GIRL** (re-issue) *Atlantic 584 092* **36** 9 wks
21 Feb 68 ● **(SITTIN' ON) THE DOCK OF THE BAY** *Stax 601 031* **3** 15 wks
29 May 68 **HAPPY SONG** *Stax 601 040* **24** 5 wks
31 Jul 68 **HARD TO HANDLE** *Atlantic 584 199* **15** 12 wks
9 Jul 69 **LOVE MAN** *Atco 226 001* **43** 3 wks

See also Otis Redding & Carla Thomas.

Otis REDDING and Carla THOMAS

US, male/female vocal duo

19 Jul 67 **TRAMP** *Stax 601 012* **18** 11 wks
1 Oct 67 **KNOCK ON WOOD** *Stax 601 021* **35** 5 wks

See also Otis Redding.

Helen REDDY *Australia, female vocalist*

18 Jan 75 ● **ANGIE BABY** *Capitol CL 15799* **5** 10 wks
28 Nov 81 **I CAN'T SAY GOODBYE TO YOU** *MCA 744* **43** 8 wks

Jimmy REED *US, male vocalist*

10 Sep 64 **SHAME SHAME SHAME** *Stateside SS 330* **45** 2 wks

Lou REED *US, male vocalist*

12 May 73 ● **WALK ON THE WILD SIDE** *RCA 2303* **10** 9 wks

Tony REES and the COTTAGERS

UK, male vocal group

10 May 75 **VIVA EL FULHAM** *Sonet SON 2059* **46** 1 wk

Jim REEVES *US, male vocalist*

24 Mar 60 **HE'LL HAVE TO GO** *RCA 1168* **36** 1 wk
7 Apr 60 **HE'LL HAVE TO GO** (re-entry) *RCA 1168* **12** 30 wks
16 Mar 61 **WHISPERING HOPE** *RCA 1223* **50** 1 wk
23 Nov 61 **YOU'RE THE ONLY GOOD THING** *RCA 1261* **17** 19 wks
28 Jun 62 **ADIOS AMIGO** *RCA 1293* **23** 21 wks
22 Nov 62 **I'M GONNA CHANGE EVERYTHING** *RCA 1317* **42** 2 wks
13 Jun 63 ● **WELCOME TO MY WORLD** *RCA 1342* **6** 15 wks
17 Oct 63 **GUILTY** *RCA 1364* **29** 7 wks
20 Feb 64 ● **I LOVE YOU BECAUSE** *RCA 1385* **5** 39 wks
18 Jun 64 ● **I WON'T FORGET YOU** *RCA 1400* **3** 25 wks

Date	Title *Label Number*	Position	
5 Nov 64	● **THERE'S A HEARTACHE FOLLOWING ME** *RCA 1423*	**6**	13 wks
7 Jan 65	**I WON'T FORGET YOU** (re-entry) *RCA 1400*	**47**	1 wk
4 Feb 65	● **IT HURTS SO MUCH** *RCA 1437*	**8**	10 wks
15 Apr 65	**NOT UNTIL THE NEXT TIME** *RCA 1446*	**13**	12 wks
6 May 65	**HOW LONG HAS IT BEEN** *RCA 1445*	**45**	5 wks
15 Jul 65	**THIS WORLD IS NOT MY HOME** *RCA 1412*	**22**	9 wks
11 Nov 65	**IS IT REALLY OVER** *RCA 1488*	**17**	9 wks
18 Aug 66	★ **DISTANT DRUMS** *RCA 1537*	**1**	25 wks
2 Feb 67	**I WON'T COME IN WHILE HE'S THERE** *RCA 1563*	**12**	11 wks
26 Jul 67	**TRYING TO FORGET** *RCA 1611*	**33**	5 wks
22 Nov 67	**I HEARD A HEART BREAK LAST NIGHT** *RCA 1643*	**38**	6 wks
27 Mar 68	**PRETTY BROWN EYES** *RCA 1672*	**33**	5 wks
25 Jun 69	**WHEN TWO WORLDS COLLIDE** *RCA 1830*	**17**	17 wks
6 Dec 69	**BUT YOU LOVE ME DADDY** *RCA 1899*	**15**	16 wks
21 Mar 70	**NOBODY'S FOOL** *RCA 1915*	**32**	5 wks
12 Sep 70	**ANGELS DON'T LIE** *RCA 1997*	**44**	1 wk
26 Sep 70	**ANGELS DON'T LIE** (re-entry) *RCA 1997*	**32**	2 wks
26 Jun 71	**I LOVE YOU BECAUSE** (RE-ISSUE)/ **HE'LL HAVE TO GO** (RE-ISSUE)/ **MOONLIGHT & ROSES** *RCA Maximillion 2092*	**34**	8 wks
19 Feb 72	**YOU'RE FREE TO GO** *RCA 2174*	**48**	2 wks

Martha REEVES and the VANDELLAS

US, female vocal group

Date	Title *Label Number*	Position	
29 Oct 64	**DANCING IN THE STREET** *Stateside SS 345*	**28**	8 wks
1 Apr 65	**NOWHERE TO RUN** *Tamla Motown TMG 502*	**26**	8 wks
1 Dec 66	**I'M READY FOR LOVE** *Tamla Motown TMG 582*	**29**	8 wks
30 Mar 67	**JIMMY MACK** *Tamla Motown TMG 599*	**21**	9 wks
17 Jan 68	**HONEY CHILE** *Tamla Motown TMG 636*	**30**	9 wks
15 Jan 69	● **DANCING IN THE STREET** (re-issue) *Tamla Motown TMG 684*	**4**	12 wks
16 Apr 69	**NOWHERE TO RUN** (re-issue) *Tamla Motown TMG 694*	**42**	3 wks
29 Aug 70	**JIMMY MACK** (re-entry) *Tamla Motown TMG 599*	**21**	12 wks
13 Feb 71	**FORGET ME NOT** *Tamla Motown TMG 762*	**11**	8 wks
8 Jan 72	**BLESS YOU** *Tamla Motown TMG 794*	**33**	5 wks

The group is billed as Martha and the Vandellas - no Reeves - for Dancing In The Street *on Stateside,* Nowhere to run *on Tamla Motown TMG 502,* I'm Ready For Love *and* Jimmy Mack.

Joan REGAN *UK, female vocalist*

Date	Title *Label Number*	Position	
11 Dec 53	● **RICOCHET** *Decca F 10193*	**8**	1 wk
8 Jan 54	● **RICOCHET** (re-entry) *Decca F 10193*	**9**	4 wks
14 May 54	● **SOMEONE ELSE'S ROSES** *Decca F 10257*	**5**	8 wks
1 Oct 54	**IF I GIVE MY HEART TO YOU** *Decca F 10373*	**20**	1 wk
29 Oct 54	● **IF I GIVE MY HEART TO YOU** (re-entry) *Decca F 10373*	**3**	10 wks
25 Mar 55	● **PRIZE OF GOLD** *Decca F 10432*	**6**	8 wks
6 May 55	**OPEN UP YOUR HEART** *Decca F 10474*	**19**	1 wk
1 May 59	● **MAY YOU ALWAYS** *HMV POP 593*	**9**	16 wks
5 Feb 60	**HAPPY ANNIVERSARY** *Pye 7N 15238*	**29**	1 wk
19 Feb 60	**HAPPY ANNIVERSARY** (re-entry) *Pye 7N 15238*	**29**	1 wk
28 Jul 60	**PAPA LOVES MAMA** *Pye 7N 15278*	**29**	8 wks
24 Nov 60	**ONE OF THE LUCKY ONES** *Pye 7N 15310*	**47**	1 wk
5 Jan 61	**MUST BE SANTA** *Pye 7N 15303*	**42**	1 wk

Ricochet *credited to Joan Regan with the Squadronaires. See also Joan Regan & The Johnston Brothers, Various Artists - All Star Hit Parade.*

Joan REGAN and the JOHNSTON BROTHERS *UK, female vocalist, male vocal group*

Date	Title *Label Number*	Position	
5 Nov 54	**WAIT FOR ME** *Decca F 10362*	**18**	1 wk

See also Joan Regan, Johnston Brothers, Various Artists - All Star Hit Parade & All Star Hit Parade No. 2.

REGENTS *UK, male/female vocal/instrumental group*

Date	Title *Label Number*	Position	
22 Dec 79	**7 TEEN** *Rialto TREB 111*	**11**	12 wks
7 Jun 80	**SEE YOU LATER** *Arista ARIST 350*	**55**	2 wks

Mike REID *UK, male vocalist*

Date	Title *Label Number*	Position	
22 Mar 75	● **THE UGLY DUCKLING** *Pye 7N 45434*	**10**	8 wks

Nothing to do with any of this book's co-authors.

Neil REID *UK, male vocalist*

Date	Title *Label Number*	Position	
1 Jan 72	● **MOTHER OF MINE** *Decca F 13264*	**2**	20 wks
8 Apr 72	**THAT'S WHAT I WANT TO BE** *Decca F 13300*	**49**	1 wk
22 Apr 72	**THAT'S WHAT I WANT TO BE** (re-entry) *Decca F 13300*	**45**	5 wks

Keith RELF *UK, male vocalist*

Date	Title *Label Number*	Position	
26 May 66	**MR. ZERO** *Columbia DB 7920*	**50**	1 wk

RENAISSANCE

UK, male/female vocal/instrumental group

Date	Title *Label Number*	Position	
15 Jul 78	● **NORTHERN LIGHTS** *Warner Bros. K 17177*	**10**	11 wks

RENATO — See *RENEE and RENATO*

RENÉE and RENATO

UK/Italy female/male vocal duo

Date	Title *Label Number*	Position	
30 Oct 82	★ **SAVE YOUR LOVE** *Hollywood HWD 003*	**1**†	9 wks

REO SPEEDWAGON

US, male vocal/instrumental group

Date	Title *Label Number*	Position	
11 Apr 81	● **KEEP ON LOVING YOU** *Epic EPC 9544*	**7**	14 wks
27 Jun 81	**TAKE IT ON THE RUN** *Epic EPC A 1207*	**19**	14 wks

REPARATA *US, female vocalist*

Date	Title *Label Number*	Position	
18 Oct 75	**SHOES** *Dart 2066 562*	**43**	2 wks

See also Reparata and the Delrons.

REPARATA and the DELRONS

US, female vocal group

Date	Title *Label Number*	Position	
20 Mar 68	**CAPTAIN OF YOUR SHIP** *Bell 1002*	**13**	10 wks

See also Reparata.

Date Title *Label Number* Position

Date Title *Label Number* Position

REUNION *US, male vocal group*

21 Sep 74 **LIFE IS A ROCK (BUT THE RADIO ROLLED ME)** *RCA PB 10056* **33** 4 wks

REYNOLDS — See *HAMILTON, Joe FRANK and REYNOLDS*

Debbie REYNOLDS *US, female vocalist*

30 Aug 57 ● **TAMMY** *Vogue-Coral Q 72274* **2** 17 wks

Jody REYNOLDS *US, male vocalist*

14 Apr 79 **ENDLESS SLEEP** *Lightning LIG 9015* **66** 1 wk

Endless Sleep was coupled with To Know Him Is To Love Him *by the Teddy Bears as a double A-side. See also the Teddy Bears.*

REZILLOS

UK, male/female vocal/instrumental group

12 Aug 78 **TOP OF THE POPS** *Sire SIR 4001* **17** 9 wks
25 Nov 78 **DESTINATION VENUS** *Sire SIR 4008* **43** 4 wks
18 Aug 79 **I WANNA BE YOUR MAN/I CAN'T STAND MY BABY** *Sensible SAB 1* **71** 1 wk
1 Sep 79 **I WONNA BE YOUR MAN/I CAN'T STAND MY BABY** (re-entry) *Sensible SAB 1* **75** 1 wk
26 Jan 80 **MOTORBIKE BEAT** *Dindisc DIN 5* **45** 6 wks

Motorbike Beat *credited to the Revillos.*

RHODA with the SPECIAL A.K.A.

UK, female vocalist with male vocal/instrumental group

23 Jan 82 **THE BOILER** *2-Tone CHSTT 18* **35** 5 wks

See also Specials.

Charlie RICH *US, male vocalist*

16 Feb 74 ● **THE MOST BEAUTIFUL GIRL** *CBS 1897* **2** 14 wks
13 Apr 74 **BEHIND CLOSED DOORS** *Epic EPC 1539* **16** 10 wks
1 Feb 75 **WE LOVE EACH OTHER** *Epic EPC 2868* **37** 5 wks

RICH KIDS *UK, male vocal/instrumental group*

28 Jan 78 **RICH KIDS** *EMI 2738* **24** 5 wks

Cliff RICHARD *UK, male vocalist*

12 Sep 58 ● **MOVE IT** *Columbia DB 4178* **2** 17 wks
21 Nov 58 ● **HIGH CLASS BABY** *Columbia DB 4203* **7** 10 wks
30 Jan 59 **LIVIN' LOVIN' DOLL** *Columbia DB 4249* **20** 6 wks
8 May 59 ● **MEAN STREAK** *Columbia DB 4290* **10** 9 wks
15 May 59 **NEVER MIND** *Columbia DB 4290* **21** 2 wks
10 Jul 59 ★ **LIVING DOLL** *Columbia DB 4306* **1** 21 wks
9 Oct 59 ★ **TRAVELLIN' LIGHT** *Columbia DB 4351* **1** 17 wks
9 Oct 59 **DYNAMITE** *Columbia DB 4351* **16** 2 wks
30 Oct 59 **DYNAMITE** (re-entry) *Columbia DB 4351* **21** 2 wks
11 Dec 59 **LIVING DOLL** (re-entry) *Columbia DB 4306* **26** 1 wk
1 Jan 60 **LIVING DOLL** (2nd re-entry) *Columbia DB 4306* **28** 1 wk
15 Jan 60 **EXPRESSO BONGO** (EP) *Columbia SEG 7971* **14** 7 wks
22 Jan 60 ● **VOICE IN THE WILDERNESS** *Columbia DB 4398* **2** 13 wks
24 Mar 60 ● **FALL IN LOVE WITH YOU** *Columbia DB 4431* **2** 15 wks
5 May 60 **VOICE IN THE WILDERNESS** (re-entry) *Columbia DB 4398* **36** 2 wks
30 Jun 60 ★ **PLEASE DON'T TEASE** *Columbia DB 4479* **1** 18 wks
22 Sep 60 ● **NINE TIMES OUT OF TEN** *Columbia DB 4506* **3** 12 wks
1 Dec 60 ★ **I LOVE YOU** *Columbia DB 4547* **1** 16 wks
2 Mar 61 ● **THEME FOR A DREAM** *Columbia DB 4593* **3** 14 wks
30 Mar 61 ● **GEE WHIZ IT'S YOU** *Columbia DC 756* **4** 14 wks
22 Jun 61 ● **A GIRL LIKE YOU** *Columbia DB 4667* **3** 14 wks
19 Oct 61 ● **WHEN THE GIRL IN YOUR ARMS IS THE GIRL IN YOUR HEART** *Columbia DB 4716* **3** 15 wks
11 Jan 62 ★ **THE YOUNG ONES** *Columbia DB 4761* **1** 21 wks
10 May 62 ● **I'M LOOKING OUT THE WINDOW/ DO YOU WANNA DANCE** *Columbia DB 4828* **2** 17 wks
6 Sep 62 ● **IT'LL BE ME** *Columbia DB 4886* **2** 12 wks
6 Dec 62 ★ **THE NEXT TIME/ BACHELOR BOY** *Columbia DB 4950* **1** 17 wks
21 Feb 63 ★ **SUMMER HOLIDAY** *Columbia DB 4977* **1** 18 wks
9 May 63 ● **LUCKY LIPS** *Columbia DB 7034* **4** 15 wks
22 Aug 63 ● **IT'S ALL IN THE GAME** *Columbia DB 7089* **2** 13 wks
7 Nov 63 ● **DON'T TALK TO HIM** *Columbia DB 7150* **2** 13 wks
6 Feb 64 ● **I'M THE LONELY ONE** *Columbia DB 7203* **8** 10 wks
13 Feb 64 **DON'T TALK TO HIM** (re-entry) *Columbia DB 7150* **50** 1 wk
30 Apr 64 ● **CONSTANTLY** *Columbia DB 7272* **4** 13 wks
2 Jul 64 ● **ON THE BEACH** *Columbia DB 7305* **7** 13 wks
8 Oct 64 ● **THE TWELFTH OF NEVER** *Columbia DB 7372* **8** 11 wks
10 Dec 64 ● **I COULD EASILY FALL** *Columbia DB 7420* **9** 11 wks
11 Mar 65 ★ **THE MINUTE YOU'RE GONE** *Columbia DB 7496* **1** 14 wks
10 Jun 65 **ON MY WORD** *Columbia DB 7596* **12** 10 wks
19 Aug 65 **THE TIME IN BETWEEN** *Columbia DB 7660* **22** 8 wks
4 Nov 65 ● **WIND ME UP (LET ME GO)** *Columbia DB 7745* **2** 16 wks
24 Mar 66 **BLUE TURNS TO GREY** *Columbia DB 7866* **15** 9 wks
21 Jul 66 ● **VISIONS** *Columbia DB 7968* **7** 12 wks
13 Oct 66 ● **TIME DRAGS BY** *Columbia DB 8017* **10** 12 wks
15 Dec 66 ● **IN THE COUNTRY** *Columbia DB 8094* **6** 10 wks
16 Mar 67 ● **IT'S ALL OVER** *Columbia DB 8150* **9** 10 wks
8 Jun 67 **I'LL COME RUNNING** *Columbia DB 8210* **26** 8 wks
16 Aug 67 ● **THE DAY I MET MARIE** *Columbia DB 8245* **10** 14 wks
15 Nov 67 ● **ALL MY LOVE** *Columbia DB 8293* **6** 12 wks
20 Mar 68 ★ **CONGRATULATIONS** *Columbia DB 8376* **1** 13 wks
26 Jun 68 **I'LL LOVE YOU FOREVER TODAY** *Columbia DB 8437* **27** 6 wks
25 Sep 68 **MARIANNE** *Columbia DB 8476* **22** 8 wks
27 Nov 68 **DON'T FORGET TO CATCH ME** *Columbia DB 8503* **21** 10 wks
26 Feb 69 **GOOD TIMES (BETTER TIMES)** *Columbia DB 8548* **12** 11 wks
28 May 69 ● **BIG SHIP** *Columbia DB 8581* **8** 10 wks
13 Sep 69 ● **THROW DOWN A LINE** *Columbia DB 8615* **7** 9 wks
6 Dec 69 **WITH THE EYES OF A CHILD** *Columbia DB 8641* **20** 11 wks
21 Feb 70 **JOY OF LIVING** *Columbia DB 8657* **25** 8 wks
6 Jun 70 ● **GOODBYE SAM HELLO SAMANTHA** *Columbia DB 8685* **6** 15 wks
5 Sep 70 **I AIN'T GOT TIME ANYMORE** *Columbia DB 8708* **21** 7 wks
23 Jan 71 **SUNNY HONEY GIRL** *Columbia DB 8747* **19** 8 wks
10 Apr 71 **SILVERY RAIN** *Columbia DB 8774* **27** 6 wks
17 Jul 71 **FLYING MACHINE** *Columbia DB 8797* **37** 7 wks
13 Nov 71 **SING A SONG OF FREEDOM** *Columbia DB 8836* **13** 12 wks
11 Mar 72 **JESUS** *Columbia DB 8864* **35** 3 wks
26 Aug 72 **LIVING IN HARMONY** *Columbia DB 8917* **12** 10 wks
17 Mar 73 ● **POWER TO ALL OUR FRIENDS** *EMI 2012* **4** 12 wks
12 May 73 **HELP IT ALONG/ TOMORROW RISING** *EMI 2022* **29** 6 wks
1 Dec 73 **TAKE ME HIGH** *EMI 2088* **27** 12 wks
18 May 74 **(YOU KEEP ME) HANGIN' ON** *EMI 2150* **13** 9 wks
7 Feb 76 **MISS YOU NIGHTS** *EMI 2376* **15** 10 wks
8 May 76 ● **DEVIL WOMAN** *EMI 2458* **9** 8 wks
21 Aug 76 **I CAN'T ASK FOR ANYMORE THAN YOU** *EMI 2499* **17** 8 wks

Date	Title *Label Number*	Position	
4 Dec 76	**HEY MR. DREAM MAKER** *EMI 2559*	**31**	5 wks
5 Mar 77	**MY KINDA LIFE** *EMI 2584*	**15**	8 wks
16 Jul 77	**WHEN TWO WORLDS DRIFT APART** *EMI 2633*	**46**	3 wks
31 Mar 79	**GREEN LIGHT** *EMI 2920*	**57**	3 wks
21 Jul 79	★ **WE DON'T TALK ANYMORE** *EMI 2975*	**1**	14 wks
3 Nov 79	**HOT SHOT** *EMI 5003*	**46**	5 wks
2 Feb 80	● **CARRIE** *EMI 5006*	**4**	10 wks
16 Aug 80	● **DREAMIN'** *EMI 5095*	**8**	10 wks
24 Jan 81	**A LITTLE IN LOVE** *EMI 5123*	**15**	8 wks
29 Aug 81	● **WIRED FOR SOUND** *EMI 5221*	**4**	9 wks
21 Nov 81	● **DADDY'S HOME** *EMI 5251*	**2**	12 wks
17 Jul 82	● **THE ONLY WAY OUT** *EMI 5318*	**10**	9 wks
25 Sep 82	**WHERE DO WE GO FROM HERE** *EMI 5341*	**60**	3 wks
4 Dec 82	**LITTLE TOWN** *EMI 5348*	**11†**	4 wks

The Shadows appear on all Cliff's hits from Move It *to* A Girl Like You. *After that they are on the following hits:* The Young Ones, Do You Wanna Dance, It'll Be Me, The Next Time, Bachelor Boy, Summer Holiday, Lucky Lips, Don't Talk To Him, I'm The Lonely One, On The Beach, I Could Easily Fall, The Time In Between, Blue Turns To Grey, Time Drags By, In The Country *and* Don't Forget To Catch Me. Throw Down A Line *and* Joy Of Living *are credited to 'Cliff and Hank', Hank being Hank B. Marvin of the Shadows, who played guitar on these two hits. The tracks on the* Expresso Bongo *EP: Love/ A Voice in The Wilderness/ The Shrine On The Second Floor/ Bongo Blues. Bongo Blues features only the Shadows. The Shadows were the Drifters on Cliff's hits before* Living Doll. *See also the Shadows. See also Olivia Newton-John and Cliff Richard.*

Wendy RICHARD — See *Mike SARNE*

Lionel RICHIE *US, male vocalist*

20 Nov 82	● **TRULY** *Motown TMG 1284*	**6†**	6 wks

see also Diana Ross and Lionel Richie

Jonathan RICHMAN and the MODERN LOVERS *US, male vocal/instrumental group*

16 Jul 77	**ROADRUNNER** *Beserkley BZZ 1*	**11**	9 wks
29 Oct 77	● **EGYPTIAN REGGAE** *Beserkley BZZ 3*	**5**	14 wks

See also Modern Lovers

RICO — See *SPECIALS (featuring Rico)*

RIGHTEOUS BROTHERS *US, male vocal duo*

14 Jan 65	★ **YOU'VE LOST THAT LOVIN' FEELIN'** *London HLU 9943*	**1**	10 wks
12 Aug 65	**UNCHAINED MELODY** *London HL 9975*	**14**	12 wks
13 Jan 66	**EBB TIDE** *London HL 10011*	**48**	2 wks
14 Apr 66	**(YOU'RE MY) SOUL AND INSPIRATION** *Verve VS 535*	**15**	10 wks
10 Nov 66	**WHITE CLIFFS OF DOVER** *London HL 10086*	**21**	9 wks
22 Dec 66	**ISLAND IN THE SUN** *Verve VS 547*	**36**	5 wks
12 Feb 69	● **YOU'VE LOST THAT LOVIN' FEELIN'** (re-issue) *London HL 10241*	**10**	11 wks
19 Nov 77	**YOU'VE LOST THAT LOVIN' FEELIN'** (2nd re-issue) *Phil Spector International 2010 022*	**42**	4 wks

Jeannie C. RILEY *US, female vocalist*

16 Oct 68	**HARPER VALLEY P. T. A.** *Polydor 56 148*	**12**	15 wks

RIMSHOTS *US, male instrumental/vocal group*

19 Jul 75	**7-6-5-4-3-2-1 (BLOW YOUR WHISTLE)** *All Platinum 6146 304*	**26**	5 wks

Miguel RIOS *Spain, male vocalist*

11 Jul 70	**SONG OF JOY** *A & M AMS 790*	**16**	16 wks

Waldo de los RIOS *Argentina, orchestra*

10 Apr 71	● **MOZART SYMPHONY NO.40 IN G MINOR K550 1ST MOVEMENT (ALLEGRO MOLTO).** *A & M AMS 836*	**5**	16 wks

Minnie RIPERTON *US, female vocalist*

12 Apr 75	● **LOVING YOU** *Epic EPC 3121*	**2**	10 wks

RITCHIE FAMILY *US, female vocal group*

23 Aug 75	**BRAZIL** *Polydor 2058 625*	**41**	4 wks
18 Sep 76	● **THE BEST DISCO IN TOWN** *Polydor 2058 777*	**10**	9 wks
17 Feb 79	**AMERICAN GENERATION** *Mercury 6007 199*	**49**	6 wks

Tex RITTER *US, male vocalist*

22 Jun 56	● **WAYWARD WIND** *Capitol CL 14581*	**8**	14 wks

Danny RIVERS *UK, male vocalist*

12 Jan 61	**CAN'T YOU HEAR MY HEART** *Decca F 11294*	**36**	3 wks

Kate ROBBINS *UK, female vocalist*

30 May 81	● **MORE THAN IN LOVE** *RCA 69*	**2**	10 wks

Marty ROBBINS *US, male vocalist*

29 Jan 60	**EL PASO** *Fontana H 233*	**19**	7 wks
7 Apr 60	**EL PASO** (re-entry) *Fontana H 233*	**44**	1 wk
26 May 60	**BIG IRON** *Fontana H 229*	**48**	1 wk
27 Sep 62	● **DEVIL WOMAN** *CBS AAG 114*	**5**	17 wks
17 Jan 63	**RUBY ANN** *CBS AAG 128*	**24**	6 wks

Austin ROBERTS *US, male vocalist*

25 Oct 75	**ROCKY** *Private Stock PVT 33*	**22**	7 wks

Malcolm ROBERTS *UK, male vocalist*

11 May 67	**TIME ALONE WILL TELL** *RCA 1578*	**45**	2 wks
30 Oct 68	● **MAY I HAVE THE NEXT DREAM WITH YOU** *Major Minor MM 581*	**8**	14 wks
12 Feb 69	**MAY I HAVE THE NEXT DREAM WITH YOU** (re-entry) *Major Minor MM 581*	**45**	1 wk
22 Nov 69	**LOVE IS ALL** *Major Minor MM 637*	**12**	12 wks

B.A. ROBERTSON *UK, male vocalist*

28 Jul 79	● **BANG BANG** *Asylum K 13152*	**2**	12 wks
27 Oct 79	● **KNOCKED IT OFF** *Asylum K 12396*	**8**	12 wks
1 Mar 80	**KOOL IN THE KAFTAN** *Asylum K 12427*	**17**	12 wks
31 May 80	● **TO BE OR NOT TO BE** *Asylum K 12449*	**9**	11 wks

Far left **CLIFF RICHARD** In a white sports coat and a pink carnation

Left **MITCH RYDER** Mitch takes a ride on the octopus at Battersea fun fair

Below **MARTY ROBBINS** Backstage at the Grand Ol' Opry in 1956

Right **ROLLING STONES** The Rolling Stones on 'Ready Steady Go' back in 1966

JULIE ROGERS Her 'child' arrived on the scene 9 months after her 'wedding'

Date	Title *Label Number*	Position	

B.A. ROBERTSON and Maggie BELL

UK, male/female vocal duo

17 Oct 81	**HOLD ME** *Swansong BAM 1*	**11**	8 wks

see also B.A. Robertson, Maggie Bell.

Don ROBERTSON

US, male instrumentalist, piano, and whistler

11 May 56	● **THE HAPPY WHISTLER** *Capitol CL 14575*	**8**	9 wks

Ivo ROBIC *Germany, male vocalist*

6 Nov 59	**MORGEN** *Polydor 23 923*	**23**	1 wk

Floyd ROBINSON *US, male vocalist*

16 Oct 59	● **MAKIN' LOVE** *RCA 1146*	**9**	9 wks

Smokey ROBINSON *US, male vocalist*

23 Feb 74	**JUST MY SOUL RESPONDING** *Tamla Motown TMG 883*	**35**	6 wks
9 May 81	★ **BEING WITH YOU** *Motown TMG 1223*	**1**	13 wks
13 Mar 82	**TELL ME TOMORROW** *Motown TMG 1255*	**51**	4 wks

See also Smokey Robinson and the Miracles; Diana Ross, Marvin Gaye, Smokey Robinson and Stevie Wonder.

Smokey ROBINSON and the MIRACLES *US, male vocal group*

24 Feb 66	**GOING TO A GO-GO** *Tamla Motown TMG 547*	**44**	5 wks
22 Dec 66	**(COME 'ROUND HERE) I'M THE ONE YOU NEED** *Tamla Motown TMG 584*	**45**	2 wks
27 Dec 67	**I SECOND THAT EMOTION** *Tamla Motown TMG 631*	**27**	11 wks
3 Apr 68	**IF YOU CAN WANT** *Tamla Motown TMG 648*	**50**	1 wk
7 May 69	● **TRACKS OF MY TEARS** *Tamla Motown TMG 696*	**9**	13 wks
1 Aug 70	★ **TEARS OF A CLOWN** *Tamla Motown TMG 745*	**1**	14 wks
30 Jan 71	**(COME 'ROUND HERE) I'M THE ONE YOU NEED** (re-issue) *Tamla Motown TMG 761*	**13**	9 wks
5 Jun 71	**I DON'T BLAME YOU AT ALL** *Tamla Motown TMG 774*	**11**	10 wks
2 Oct 76	**TEARS OF A CLOWN** (re-issue) *Tamla Motown TMG 1048*	**34**	6 wks

See also Miracles; Smokey Robinson; Diana Ross, Marvin Gaye, Smokey Robinson and Stevie Wonder.

Tom ROBINSON BAND

UK, male vocal/instrumental group

22 Oct 77	● **2-4-6-8 MOTORWAY** *EMI 2715*	**5**	9 wks
18 Feb 78	**DON'T TAKE NO FOR AN ANSWER** *EMI 2749*	**18**	6 wks
13 May 78	**UP AGAINST THE WALL** *EMI 2787*	**33**	6 wks
17 Mar 79	**BULLY FOR YOU** *EMI 2916*	**68**	2 wks

ROCK CANDY *UK, male vocal/instrumental group*

11 Sep 71	**REMEMBER** *MCA MK 5069*	**32**	6 wks

Sir Monti ROCK III — See *DISCO TEX and the SEX-O-LETTES*

ROCKER'S REVENGE

US, male/female vocal/instrumental group

14 Aug 82	● **WALKING ON SUNSHINE** *London LON 11*	**4**	13 wks

ROCKETS — See *Tony CROMBIE and his ROCKETS*

ROCKIN' BERRIES

UK, male vocal/instrumental group

1 Oct 64	**I DIDN'T MEAN TO HURT YOU** *Piccadilly 7N 35197*	**43**	1 wk
15 Oct 64	● **HE'S IN TOWN** *Piccadilly 7N 35203*	**3**	13 wks
21 Jan 65	**WHAT IN THE WORLD'S COME OVER YOU** *Piccadilly 7N 35217*	**23**	7 wks
13 May 65	● **POOR MAN'S SON** *Piccadilly 7N 35236*	**5**	11 wks
26 Aug 65	**YOU'RE MY GIRL** *Piccadilly 7N 35254*	**40**	7 wks
6 Jan 66	**THE WATER IS OVER MY HEAD** *Piccadilly 7N 35270*	**43**	1 wk
20 Jan 66	**THE WATER IS OVER MY HEAD** (re-entry) *Piccadilly 7N 35270*	**50**	1 wk

Lord ROCKINGHAM'S XI

UK, male instrumental group

24 Oct 58	★ **HOOTS MON** *Decca F 11059*	**1**	17 wks
6 Feb 59	**WEE TOM** *Decca F 11104*	**16**	3 wks

Both of the group's hits contain a little spoken Scottish.

ROCKNEY — See *CHAS and DAVE*

Clodagh RODGERS *Ireland, female vocalist*

26 Apr 69	● **COME BACK AND SHAKE ME** *RCA 1792*	**3**	14 wks
9 Jul 69	● **GOODNIGHT MIDNIGHT** *RCA 1852*	**4**	11 wks
4 Oct 69	**GOODNIGHT MIDNIGHT** (re-entry) *RCA 1852*	**48**	1 wk
8 Nov 69	**BILJO** *RCA 1891*	**22**	9 wks
4 Apr 70	**EVERYBODY GO HOME THE PARTY'S OVER** *RCA 1930*	**47**	2 wks
20 Mar 71	● **JACK IN THE BOX** *RCA 2066*	**4**	10 wks
9 Oct 71	**LADY LOVE BUG** *RCA 2117*	**28**	12 wks

Jimmie RODGERS *US, male vocalist*

1 Nov 57	**HONEYCOMB** *Columbia DB 3986*	**30**	1 wk
20 Dec 57	● **KISSES SWEETER THAN WINE** *Columbia DB 4052*	**7**	11 wks
28 Mar 58	**OH OH, I'M FALLING IN LOVE AGAIN** *Columbia DB 4078*	**18**	6 wks
19 Dec 58	**WOMAN FROM LIBERIA** *Columbia DB 4206*	**18**	6 wks
14 Jun 62	● **ENGLISH COUNTRY GARDEN** *Columbia DB 4847*	**5**	13 wks

Tommy ROE *US, male vocalist*

6 Sep 62	● **SHEILA** *HMV POP 1060*	**3**	14 wks
6 Dec 62	**SUSIE DARLIN'** *HMV POP 1092*	**37**	5 wks
21 Mar 63	● **THE FOLK SINGER** *HMV POP 1138*	**4**	13 wks
26 Sep 63	● **EVERYBODY** *HMV POP 1207*	**9**	11 wks
19 Dec 63	**EVERYBODY** (re-entry) *HMV POP 1207*	**49**	3 wks
16 Apr 69	★ **DIZZY** *Stateside SS 2143*	**1**	19 wks
23 Jul 69	**HEATHER HONEY** *Stateside SS 2152*	**24**	9 wks

Date	Title *Label Number*	Position	

Julie ROGERS *UK, female vocalist*

13 Aug 64	● **THE WEDDING** *Mercury MF 820*	**3**	23 wks
10 Dec 64	**LIKE A CHILD** *Mercury MF 838*	**21**	9 wks
25 Mar 65	**HAWAIIAN WEDDING SONG** *Mercury MF 849*	**31**	6 wks

Kenny ROGERS *US, male vocalist*

18 Oct 69	● **RUBY DON'T TAKE YOUR LOVE TO TOWN** *Reprise RS 20829*	**2**	23 wks
7 Feb 70	● **SOMETHING'S BURNING** *Reprise RS 20888*	**8**	14 wks
30 Apr 77	★ **LUCILLE** *United Artists UP 36242*	**1**	14 wks
17 Sep 77	**DAYTIME FRIENDS** *United Artists UP 36289*	**39**	4 wks
2 Jun 79	**SHE BELIEVES IN ME** *United Artists UP 36533*	**42**	7 wks
26 Jan 80	★ **COWARD OF THE COUNTY** *United Artists UP 614*	**1**	12 wks
15 Nov 80	**LADY** *United Artists UP 635*	**12**	12 wks

First two hits credit Kenny Rogers and the First Edition, his male/female vocal/instrumental backing group, also US.

ROKOTTO *UK, male vocal/instrumental group*

22 Oct 77	**BOOGIE ON UP** *State STAT 62*	**40**	4 wks
10 Jun 78	**FUNK THEORY** *State STAT 80*	**49**	6 wks

ROLLING STONES

UK, male vocal/instrumental group

25 Jul 63	**COME ON** *Decca F 11675*	**21**	14 wks
14 Nov 63	**I WANNA BE YOUR MAN** *Decca F 11764*	**12**	16 wks
27 Feb 64	● **NOT FADE AWAY** *Decca F 11845*	**3**	15 wks
2 Jul 64	★ **IT'S ALL OVER NOW** *Decca F 11934*	**1**	15 wks
19 Nov 64	★ **LITTLE RED ROOSTER** *Decca F 12014*	**1**	12 wks
4 Mar 65	★ **THE LAST TIME** *Decca F 12104*	**1**	13 wks
26 Aug 65	★ **(I CAN'T GET NO) SATISFACTION** *Decca F 12220*	**1**	12 wks
28 Oct 65	★ **GET OFF OF MY CLOUD** *Decca F 12263*	**1**	12 wks
10 Feb 66	● **NINETEENTH NERVOUS BREAKDOWN** *Decca F 12331*	**2**	8 wks
19 May 66	★ **PAINT IT BLACK** *Decca F 12395*	**1**	10 wks
29 Sep 66	● **HAVE YOU SEEN YOUR MOTHER BABY STANDING IN THE SHADOW** *Decca F 12497*	**5**	8 wks
19 Jan 67	● **LET'S SPEND THE NIGHT TOGETHER/ RUBY TUESDAY** *Decca F 12546*	**3**	10 wks
23 Aug 67	● **WE LOVE YOU/ DANDELION** *Decca F 12654*	**8**	8 wks
29 May 68	★ **JUMPING JACK FLASH** *Decca F 12782*	**1**	11 wks
9 Jul 69	★ **HONKY TONK WOMEN** *Decca F 12952*	**1**	17 wks
24 Apr 71	● **BROWN SUGAR/ BITCH/ LET IT ROCK** *Rolling Stones RS 19100*	**2**	13 wks
3 Jul 71	**STREET FIGHTING MAN** *Decca F 13195*	**21**	8 wks
29 Apr 72	● **TUMBLING DICE** *Rolling Stones RS 19103*	**5**	8 wks
1 Sep 73	● **ANGIE** *Rolling Stones RS 19105*	**5**	10 wks
3 Aug 74	● **IT'S ONLY ROCK AND ROLL** *Rolling Stones RS 19114*	**10**	7 wks
20 Sep 75	**OUT OF TIME** *Decca F 13597*	**45**	2 wks
1 May 76	● **FOOL TO CRY** *Rolling Stones RS 19131*	**6**	10 wks
3 Jun 78	● **MISS YOU/ FAR AWAY EYES** *Rolling Stones EMI 2802*	**3**	13 wks
30 Sep 78	**RESPECTABLE** *Rolling Stones EMI 2861*	**23**	9 wks
5 Jul 80	● **EMOTIONAL RESCUE** *Rolling Stones RSR 105*	**9**	8 wks
4 Oct 80	**SHE'S SO COLD** *Rolling Stones RSR 106*	**33**	6 wks
29 Aug 81	● **START ME UP** *Rolling Stones RSR 108*	**7**	9 wks
11 Dec 81	**WAITING ON A FRIEND** *Rolling Stones RSR 109*	**50**	6 wks
12 Jun 82	**GOING TO A GO GO** *Rolling Stones RSR 110*	**26**	6 wks
2 Oct 82	**TIME IS ON MY SIDE** *Rolling Stones RSR 111*	**62**	2 wks

Far Away Eyes *credited from 15 Jul 78 until end of record's run.*

ROMANTICS — See *RUBY and the ROMANTICS*

Max ROMEO *Jamaica, male vocalist*

28 May 69	● **WET DREAM** *Unity UN 503*	**10**	24 wks
29 Nov 69	**WET DREAM** (re-entry) *Unity UN 503*	**50**	1 wk

RONETTES *US, female vocal group*

17 Oct 63	● **BE MY BABY** *London HLU 9793*	**4**	13 wks
9 Jan 64	**BABY I LOVE YOU** *London HLU 9826*	**11**	14 wks
27 Aug 64	**THE BEST PART OF BREAKING UP** *London HLU 9905*	**43**	3 wks
8 Oct 64	**DO I LOVE YOU** *London HLU 9922*	**35**	4 wks

Linda RONSTADT *US, female vocalist*

8 May 76	**TRACKS OF MY TEARS** *Asylum K 13034*	**42**	3 wks
28 Jan 78	**BLUE BAYOU** *Asylum K 13106*	**35**	4 wks
26 May 79	**ALISON** *Asylum K 13149*	**66**	2 wks

ROOFTOP SINGERS

US, male/female vocal group

31 Jan 63	● **WALK RIGHT IN** *Fontana TF 271700*	**10**	12 wks

ROSE OF ROMANCE ORCHESTRA

UK, orchestra

9 Jan 82	**TARA'S THEME FROM GONE WITH THE WIND** *BBC RESL 108*	**71**	1 wk

ROSE ROYCE

US, male/female vocal/instrumental group

25 Dec 76	● **CAR WASH** *MCA 267*	**9**	12 wks
22 Jan 77	**PUT YOUR MONEY WHERE YOUR MOUTH IS** *MCA 259*	**44**	5 wks
2 Apr 77	**I WANNA GET NEXT TO YOU** *MCA 278*	**14**	8 wks
24 Sep 77	**DO YOUR DANCE** *Whitfield K 17006*	**30**	6 wks
14 Jan 78	● **WISHING ON A STAR** *Warner Bros. K 17060*	**3**	14 wks
6 May 78	**IT MAKES YOU FEEL LIKE DANCIN'** *Warner Bros. K 17148*	**16**	10 wks
16 Sep 78	● **LOVE DON'T LIVE HERE ANYMORE** *Whitfield K 17236*	**2**	10 wks
3 Feb 79	**I'M IN LOVE (AND I LOVE THE FEELING)** *Whitfield K 17291*	**51**	4 wks
17 Nov 79	**IS IT LOVE YOU'RE AFTER** *Whitfield K 17456*	**13**	13 wks
8 Mar 80	**OOH BOY** *Whitfield K 17575*	**46**	7 wks
21 Nov 81	**EXPRESS** *Warner Bros. K 17875*	**52**	3 wks

ROSE TATTOO

Australia, male vocal/instrumental group

11 Jul 81	**ROCK'N'ROLL OUTLAW** *Carrere CAR 200*	**60**	4 wks

Diana ROSS *US, female vocalist*

Date	Title *Label Number*	Position	Weeks
18 Jul 70	**REACH OUT AND TOUCH** *Tamla Motown TMG 743*	**33**	5 wks
12 Sep 70	● **AIN'T NO MOUNTAIN HIGH ENOUGH** *Tamla Motown TMG 751*	**6**	12 wks
3 Apr 71	● **REMEMBER ME** *Tamla Motown TMG 768*	**7**	12 wks
31 Jul 71	★ **I'M STILL WAITING** *Tamla Motown TMG 781*	**1**	14 wks
30 Oct 71	● **SURRENDER** *Tamla Motown TMG 792*	**10**	11 wks
13 May 72	**DOOBEDOOD'NDOOBE DOOBEDOOD'NDOOBE** *Tamla Motown TMG 812*	**12**	9 wks
14 Jul 73	● **TOUCH ME IN THE MORNING** *Tamla Motown TMG 861*	**9**	12 wks
13 Oct 73	**TOUCH ME IN THE MORNING** (re-entry) *Tamla Motown TMG 861*	**50**	1 wk
5 Jan 74	● **ALL OF MY LIFE** *Tamla Motown TMG 880*	**9**	13 wks
4 May 74	**LAST TIME I SAW HIM** *Tamla Motown TMG 893*	**35**	4 wks
28 Sep 74	**LOVE ME** *Tamla Motown TMG 917*	**38**	5 wks
29 Mar 75	**SORRY DOESN'T ALWAYS MAKE IT RIGHT** *Tamla Motown TMG 941*	**23**	9 wks
3 Apr 76	● **THEME FROM MAHOGANY (DO YOU KNOW WHERE YOU'RE GOING TO)** *Tamla Motown TMG 1010*	**5**	8 wks
24 Apr 76	● **LOVE HANGOVER** *Tamla Motown TMG 1024*	**10**	10 wks
10 Jul 76	**I THOUGHT IT TOOK A LITTLE TIME** *Tamla Motown TMG 1032*	**32**	5 wks
16 Oct 76	**I'M STILL WAITING** (re-issue) *Tamla Motown TMG 1041*	**41**	4 wks
19 Nov 77	**GETTIN' READY FOR LOVE** *Motown TMG 1090*	**23**	7 wks
22 Jul 78	**LOVIN' LIVIN' AND GIVIN'** *Motown TMG 1112*	**54**	6 wks
21 Jul 79	**THE BOSS** *Motown TMG 1150*	**40**	7 wks
6 Oct 79	**NO-ONE GETS THE PRIZE** *Motown TMG 1160*	**59**	3 wks
24 Nov 79	**IT'S MY HOUSE** *Motown TMG 1169*	**32**	10 wks
19 Jul 80	● **UPSIDE DOWN** *Motown TMG 1195*	**2**	12 wks
20 Sep 80	● **MY OLD PIANO** *Motown TMG 1202*	**5**	9 wks
15 Nov 80	**I'M COMING OUT** *Motown TMG 1210*	**13**	10 wks
17 Jan 81	**IT'S MY TURN** *Motown TMG 1217*	**16**	8 wks
28 Mar 81	**ONE MORE CHANCE** *Motown TMG 1227*	**49**	5 wks
13 Jun 81	**CRYIN' MY HEART OUT FOR YOU** *Motown TMG 1233*	**58**	3 wks
7 Nov 81	● **WHY DO FOOLS FALL IN LOVE** *Capitol CL 226*	**4**	12 wks
23 Jan 82	**TENDERNESS** *Motown TMG 1248*	**73**	1 wk
30 Jan 82	**MIRROR MIRROR** *Capitol CL 234*	**36**	5 wks
6 Feb 82	**TENDERNESS** (re-entry) *Motown TMG 1248*	**75**	1 wk
29 May 82	● **WORK THAT BODY** *Capitol CL 241*	**7**	11 wks
7 Aug 82	**IT'S NEVER TOO LATE** *Capitol CL 256*	**41**	4 wks
23 Oct 82	**MUSCLES** *Capitol CL 268*	**15**	9 wks

See also Supremes, Diana Ross and Michael Jackson, Diana Ross and the Supremes and the Temptations, Marvin Gaye and Diana Ross, Diana Ross, Marvin Gaye, Smokey Robinson and Stevie Wonder and also Diana Ross and Lionel Richie

Diana ROSS and Marvin GAYE

US, male/female vocal duo

Date	Title *Label Number*	Position	Weeks
23 Mar 74	● **YOU ARE EVERYTHING** *Tamla Motown TMG 890*	**5**	12 wks
20 Jul 74	**STOP LOOK LISTEN (TO YOUR HEART)** *Tamla Motown TMG 906*	**25**	8 wks

See also Marvin Gaye, Diana Ross, Marvin Gaye & Tammi Terrell, Marvin Gaye & Mary Wells, Marvin Gaye & Kim Weston, Diana Ross and the Supremes and the Temptations.

Diana ROSS, Marvin GAYE, Smokey ROBINSON and Stevie WONDER

US, female/male vocal group

Date	Title *Label Number*	Position	Weeks
24 Feb 79	**POPS, WE LOVE YOU** *Motown TMG 1136*	**66**	5 wks

See also Diana Ross, Supremes, Diana Ross and Michael Jackson, Diana Ross and Marvin Gaye Marvin Gaye and Tammi Terrell, Miracles, Stevie Wonder, Smokey Robinson, Smokey Robinson and the Miracles.

Diana ROSS and Michael JACKSON

US, female/male vocal duo

Date	Title *Label Number*	Position	Weeks
18 Nov 78	**EASE ON DOWN THE ROAD** *MCA 396*	**45**	4 wks

See also Diana Ross, Supremes, Diana Ross and Marvin Gaye, Michael Jackson, Jackson Five, Jacksons; Diana Ross, Marvin Gaye, Smokey Robinson and Stevie Wonder.

Diana ROSS and Lionel RICHIE

US, female/male vocal duo

Date	Title *Label Number*	Position	Weeks
12 Sep 81	● **ENDLESS LOVE** *Motown TMG 1240*	**7**	12 wks

See also Lionel Richie, Diana Ross, Supremes, Diana Ross and Michael Jackson, Diana Ross and The Supremes and the Temptations, Diana Ross and Marvin Gaye, Diana Ross, Marvin Gaye, Smokey Robinson and Stevie Wonder.

Diana ROSS and the SUPREMES and the TEMPTATIONS

US, female and male vocal groups

Date	Title *Label Number*	Position	Weeks
29 Jan 69	● **I'M GONNA MAKE YOU LOVE ME** *Tamla Motown TMG 685*	**3**	11 wks
23 Apr 69	**I'M GONNA MAKE YOU LOVE ME** (re-entry) *Tamla Motown TMG 685*	**49**	1 wk
20 Sep 69	**I SECOND THAT EMOTION** *Tamla Motown TMG 709*	**18**	8 wks

See also Diana Ross, Supremes, Diana Ross and Marvin Gaye, Supremes and the Temptations, Supremes and the Four Tops, Diana Ross, Marvin Gaye, Smokey Robinson and Stevie Wonder, Diana Ross and Michael Jackson, Diana Ross and Lionel Richie.

Laurent ROSSI — See *BIMBO JET*

Nini ROSSO *Italy, male instrumentalist, trumpet*

Date	Title *Label Number*	Position	Weeks
26 Aug 65	● **IL SILENZIO** *Durium DRS 54000*	**8**	14 wks

ROULETTES — See *Adam FAITH*

Robert ROUNSEVILLE — See *VARIOUS ARTISTS (Carousel Soundtrack)*

Demis ROUSSOS *Greece, male vocalist*

Date	Title *Label Number*	Position	Weeks
22 Nov 75	● **HAPPY TO BE ON AN ISLAND IN THE SUN** *Philips 6042 033*	**5**	10 wks
28 Feb 76	**CAN'T SAY HOW MUCH I LOVE YOU** *Philips 6042 114*	**35**	5 wks
26 Jun 76	★ **THE ROUSSOS PHENOMENON** (EP) *Philips DEMIS 001*	**1**	12 wks

Date	Title *Label Number*	Position	
2 Oct 76	● **WHEN FOREVER HAS GONE** *Philips 6042 186*	**2**	10 wks
19 Mar 77	**BECAUSE** *Philips 6042 245*	**39**	4 wks
18 Jun 77	**KYRILA (EP)** *Philips Demis 002*	**33**	3 wks

Tracks on The Roussos Phenomenon *EP: Forever And Ever/ Sing An Ode To Love/ So Dreamy/ My Friend The Wind.* Tracks on Kyrila EP: *Kyrila/ I'm Gonna Fall in Love/ I Dig You/ Sister Emilyne*

ROUTERS *US, male instrumental group*

Date	Title	Position	
27 Dec 62	**LET'S GO** *Warner Bros. WB 77*	**32**	7 wks

John ROWLES *NZ, male vocalist*

Date	Title	Position	
13 Mar 68	● **IF I ONLY HAD TIME** *MCA MU 1000*	**3**	18 wks
19 Jun 68	**HUSH NOT A WORD TO MARY** *MCA MU 1023*	**12**	10 wks

ROXY MUSIC *UK, male vocal/instrumental group*

Date	Title	Position	
19 Aug 72	● **VIRGINIA PLAIN** *Island WIP 6144*	**4**	12 wks
10 Mar 73	● **PYJAMARAMA** *Island WIP 6159*	**10**	12 wks
17 Nov 73	● **STREET LIFE** *Island WIP 6173*	**9**	12 wks
12 Oct 74	**ALL I WANT IS YOU** *Island WIP 6208*	**12**	8 wks
11 Oct 75	● **LOVE IS THE DRUG** *Island WIP 6248*	**2**	10 wks
27 Dec 75	**BOTH ENDS BURNING** *Island WIP 6262*	**25**	7 wks
22 Oct 77	**VIRGINIA PLAIN** (re-issue) *Polydor 2001 739*	**11**	6 wks
3 Mar 79	**TRASH** *Polydor POSP 32*	**40**	6 wks
28 Apr 79	● **DANCE AWAY** *Polydor POSP 44*	**2**	14 wks
11 Aug 79	● **ANGEL EYES** *Polydor POSP 67*	**4**	11 wks
17 May 80	● **OVER YOU** *Polydor POSP 93*	**5**	9 wks
2 Aug 80	● **OH YEAH (ON THE RADIO)** *Polydor 2001 972*	**5**	8 wks
8 Nov 80	**THE SAME OLD SCENE** *Polydor ROXY 1*	**12**	7 wks
21 Feb 81	★ **JEALOUS GUY** *Polydor/E.G. ROXY 2*	**1**	11 wks
3 Apr 82	● **MORE THAN THIS** *EG/Polydor ROXY 3*	**6**	8 wks
19 Jun 82	**AVALON** *EG/Polydor ROXY 4*	**13**	6 wks
25 Sep 82	**TAKE A CHANCE WITH ME** *EG/Polydor ROXY 5*	**26**	6 wks

ROY 'C' *US, male vocalist*

Date	Title	Position	
21 Apr 66	● **SHOTGUN WEDDING** *Island WI 273*	**6**	11 wks
25 Nov 72	● **SHOTGUN WEDDING** (re-issue) *UK 19*	**8**	13 wks

Billy Joe ROYAL *US, male vocalist*

Date	Title	Position	
7 Oct 65	**DOWN IN THE BOONDOCKS** *CBS 201802*	**38**	4 wks

The Central Band of the ROYAL AIR FORCE, Conductor W/CDR. A.E. SIMS O.B.E. *UK, military band*

Date	Title	Position	
21 Oct 55	**THE DAMBUSTERS MARCH** *HMV B 10877*	**18**	1 wk

ROYAL GUARDSMEN *US, male vocal/instrumental group*

Date	Title	Position	
19 Jan 67	● **SNOOPY VS. THE RED BARON** *Stateside SS 574*	**8**	13 wks
6 Apr 67	**RETURN OF THE RED BARON** *Stateside SS 2010*	**37**	4 wks

ROYAL PHILHARMONIC ORCHESTRA arranged and conducted by Louis CLARK *UK, Orchestra and conductor*

Date	Title	Position	
25 Jul 81	● **HOOKED ON CLASSICS** *RCA 109*	**2**	11 wks
24 Oct 81	**HOOKED ON CAN-CAN** *RCA 151*	**47**	3 wks
10 Jul 82	**BBC WORLD CUP GRANDSTAND** *BBC RESL 116*	**61**	3 wks
7 Aug 82	**IF YOU KNEW SOUSA (AND FRIENDS)** *RCA 256*	**71**	2 wks

See also Elvis Costello.

The Pipes and Drums and Military Band of the ROYAL SCOTS DRAGOON GUARDS *UK, military band*

Date	Title	Position	
1 Apr 72	★ **AMAZING GRACE** *RCA 2191*	**1**	24 wks
19 Aug 72	**HEYKENS SERENADE/ THE DAY IS OVER** *RCA 2251*	**30**	7 wks
2 Dec 72	**LITTLE DRUMMER BOY** *RCA 2301*	**13**	9 wks
23 Dec 72	**AMAZING GRACE** (re-entry) *RCA 2191*	**42**	3 wks

Lita ROZA *UK, female vocalist*

Date	Title	Position	
13 Mar 53	★ **(HOW MUCH IS) THAT DOGGIE IN THE WINDOW** *Decca F 10070*	**1**	11 wks
7 Oct 55	**HEY THERE** *Decca F 10611*	**17**	2 wks
23 Mar 56	**JIMMY UNKNOWN** *Decca F 10679*	**15**	5 wks

See also Various Artists - All Star Hit Parade.

RUBETTES *UK, male vocal/instrumental group*

Date	Title	Position	
4 May 74	★ **SUGAR BABY LOVE** *Polydor 2058 442*	**1**	10 wks
13 Jul 74	**TONIGHT** *Polydor 2058 499*	**12**	9 wks
16 Nov 74	● **JUKE BOX JIVE** *Polydor 2058 529*	**3**	12 wks
8 Mar 75	● **I CAN DO IT** *State STAT 1*	**7**	9 wks
21 Jun 75	**FOE-DEE-O-DEE** *State STAT 7*	**15**	6 wks
22 Nov 75	**LITTLE DARLING** *State STAT 13*	**30**	5 wks
1 May 76	**YOU'RE THE REASON WHY** *State STAT 20*	**28**	4 wks
25 Sep 76	**UNDER ONE ROOF** *State STAT 27*	**40**	3 wks
12 Feb 77	● **BABY I KNOW** *State STAT 37*	**10**	10 wks

RUBY and the ROMANTICS *US, female vocalist, male vocal backing group*

Date	Title	Position	
28 Mar 63	**OUR DAY WILL COME** *London HLR 9679*	**38**	6 wks

RUDIES — See *Freddie NOTES and the RUDIES*

Bruce RUFFIN *Jamaica, male vocalist*

Date	Title	Position	
1 May 71	**RAIN** *Trojan TR 7814*	**19**	11 wks
24 Jun 72	● **MAD ABOUT YOU** *Rhino RNO 101*	**9**	12 wks

David RUFFIN *US, male vocalist*

Date	Title	Position	
17 Jan 76	● **WALK AWAY FROM LOVE** *Tamla Motown TMG 1017*	**10**	8 wks

Date	Title *Label Number*	Position	

Jimmy RUFFIN *US, male vocalist*

Date	Title *Label Number*	Position	
27 Oct 66	● **WHAT BECOMES OF THE BROKEN HEARTED** *Tamla Motown TMG 577*	**10**	15 wks
9 Feb 67	**I'VE PASSED THIS WAY BEFORE** *Tamla Motown TMG 593*	**29**	7 wks
20 Apr 67	**GONNA GIVE HER ALL THE LOVE I'VE GOT** *Tamla Motown TMG 603*	**26**	6 wks
9 Aug 69	**I'VE PASSED THIS WAY BEFORE** (re-issue) *Tamla Motown TMG 703*	**33**	6 wks
28 Feb 70	● **FAREWELL IS A LONELY SOUND** *Tamla Motown TMG 726*	**8**	16 wks
4 Jul 70	● **I'LL SAY FOREVER MY LOVE** *Tamla Motown TMG 740*	**7**	12 wks
17 Oct 70	● **IT'S WONDERFUL** *Tamla Motown TMG 753*	**6**	14 wks
27 Jul 74	● **WHAT BECOMES OF THE BROKEN HEARTED** (re-issue) *Tamla Motown TMG 911*	**4**	12 wks
2 Nov 74	**FAREWELL IS A LONELY SOUND** (re-issue) *Tamla Motown TMG 922*	**30**	5 wks
16 Nov 74	**TELL ME WHAT YOU WANT** *Polydor 2058 433*	**39**	4 wks
3 May 80	● **HOLD ON TO MY LOVE** *RSO 57*	**7**	8 wks

Barbara RUICK — See *VARIOUS ARTISTS (Carousel Soundtrack)*

RUMOUR — See *Graham PARKER and the RUMOUR*

Todd RUNDGREN *US, male vocalist*

Date	Title *Label Number*	Position	
30 Jun 73	**I SAW THE LIGHT** *Bearsville K 15506*	**36**	6 wks

RUSH *Canada, male vocal/instrumental group*

Date	Title *Label Number*	Position	
11 Feb 78	**CLOSER TO THE HEART** *Mercury RUSH 7*	**36**	3 wks
15 Mar 80	**SPIRIT OF RADIO** *Mercury RADIO 7*	**13**	7 wks
28 Mar 81	**VITAL SIGNS/A PASSAGE TO BANGKOK** *Mercury VITAL 7*	**41**	4 wks
31 Oct 81	**TOM SAWYER** *Exit EXIT 7*	**25**	6 wks
4 Sep 82	**NEW WORLD MAN** *Mercury/Phonogram RUSH 8*	**42**	3 wks
30 Oct 82	**SUBDIVISIONS** *Mercury/Phonogram RUSH 9*	**53**	2 wks

Patrice RUSHEN *US, female vocalist*

Date	Title *Label Number*	Position	
1 Mar 80	**HAVEN'T YOU HEARD** *Elektra K 12414*	**62**	3 wks
24 Jan 81	**NEVER GONNA GIVE YOU UP (WON'T LET YOU BE)** *Elektra K 12494*	**66**	3 wks
24 Apr 82	● **FORGET ME NOTS** *Elektra K 13173*	**8**	11 wks
10 Jul 82	**I WAS TIRED OF BEING ALONE** *Elektra K 13184*	**39**	5 wks

Brenda RUSSELL *US, female vocalist*

Date	Title *Label Number*	Position	
19 Apr 80	**SO GOOD SO RIGHT/IN THE THICK OF IT** *A & M AMS 7515*	**51**	5 wks

RUTLES *UK, male vocal group*

Date	Title *Label Number*	Position	
15 Apr 78	**I MUST BE IN LOVE** *Warner Bros. K 17125*	**39**	5 wks

RUTS *UK, male vocal/instrumental group*

Date	Title *Label Number*	Position	
16 Jun 79	● **BABYLON'S BURNING** *Virgin VS 271*	**7**	11 wks
8 Sep 79	**SOMETHING THAT I SAID** *Virgin VS 285*	**29**	5 wks
19 Apr 80	**STARING AT THE RUDE BOYS** *Virgin VS 327*	**22**	8 wks
30 Aug 80	**WEST ONE (SHINE ON ME)** *Virgin VS 370*	**43**	4 wks

Barry RYAN *UK, male vocalist*

Date	Title *Label Number*	Position	
23 Oct 68	● **ELOISE** *MGM 1442*	**2**	12 wks
19 Feb 69	**LOVE IS LOVE** *MGM 1464*	**25**	4 wks
4 Oct 69	**HUNT** *Polydor 56 348*	**34**	5 wks
21 Feb 70	**MAGICAL SPIEL** *Polydor 56 370*	**49**	1 wk
16 May 70	**KITSCH** *Polydor 2001 035*	**37**	6 wks
15 Jan 72	**CAN'T LET YOU GO** *Polydor 2001 256*	**32**	5 wks

See also Paul and Barry Ryan.

Marion RYAN *UK, female vocalist*

Date	Title *Label Number*	Position	
24 Jan 58	● **LOVE ME FOREVER** *Pye Nixa N 15121*	**5**	11 wks

Paul and Barry RYAN *UK, male vocal duo*

Date	Title *Label Number*	Position	
11 Nov 65	**DON'T BRING ME YOUR HEARTACHES** *Decca F 12260*	**13**	9 wks
3 Feb 66	**HAVE PITY ON THE BOY** *Decca F 12319*	**18**	6 wks
12 May 66	**I LOVE HER** *Decca F 12391*	**17**	8 wks
14 Jul 66	**I LOVE HOW YOU LOVE ME** *Decca F 12445*	**21**	7 wks
29 Sep 66	**HAVE YOU EVER LOVED SOMEBODY** *Decca F 12494*	**49**	1 wk
8 Dec 66	**MISSY MISSY** *Decca F 12520*	**43**	4 wks
2 Mar 67	**KEEP IT OUT OF SIGHT** *Decca F 12567*	**30**	6 wks
29 Jun 67	**CLAIRE** *Decca F 12633*	**47**	2 wks

See also Barry Ryan.

Bobby RYDELL *US, male vocalist*

Date	Title *Label Number*	Position	
10 Mar 60	● **WILD ONE** *Columbia DB 4429*	**7**	14 wks
30 Jun 60	**SWINGING SCHOOL** *Columbia DB 4471*	**44**	1 wk
1 Sep 60	**VOLARE** *Columbia DB 4495*	**46**	1 wk
15 Sep 60	**VOLARE** (re-entry) *Columbia DB 4495*	**22**	5 wks
15 Dec 60	**SWAY** *Columbia DB 4545*	**12**	13 wks
23 Mar 61	**GOOD TIME BABY** *Columbia DB 4600*	**42**	7 wks
23 May 63	**FORGET HIM** *Cameo Parkway C 108*	**13**	14 wks

See also Chubby Checker & Bobby Rydell.

Mitch RYDER and the DETROIT WHEELS

US, male vocalist, male vocal/instrumental backing group

Date	Title *Label Number*	Position	
10 Feb 66	**JENNY TAKE A RIDE** *Stateside SS 481*	**44**	1 wk
24 Feb 66	**JENNY TAKE A RIDE** (re-entry) *Stateside SS 481*	**33**	4 wks

S

SABRES — See *Denny SEYTON and the SABRES*

SAD CAFÉ *UK, male vocal/instrumental group*

Date	Title *Label Number*	Position	
22 Sep 79	● **EVERY DAY HURTS** *RCA PB 5180*	**3**	12 wks
19 Jan 80	**STRANGE LITTLEGIRL** *RCA PB 5202*	**32**	5 wks
15 Mar 80	**MY OH MY** *RCA SAD 3*	**14**	11 wks
21 Jun 80	**NOTHING LEFT TOULOUSE** *RCA SAD 4*	**62**	4 wks
27 Sep 80	**LA-DI-DA** *RCA SAD 5*	**41**	6 wks
20 Dec 80	**I'M IN LOVE AGAIN** *RCA SAD 6*	**40**	wks

Date	Title *Label Number*	Position		Date	Title *Label Number*	Position	

Staff Sergeant Barry SADLER *US, male vocalist*

Date	Title *Label Number*	Position	
24 Mar 66	**BALLAD OF THE GREEN BERETS** *RCA 1506*	**24**	8 wks

Mike SAGAR *UK, male vocalist*

Date	Title *Label Number*	Position	
8 Dec 60	**DEEP FEELING** *HMV POP 819*	**44**	5 wks

Carole Bayer SAGER *US, female vocalist*

Date	Title *Label Number*	Position	
28 May 77	● **YOU'RE MOVING OUT TODAY** *Elektra K 12257*	**6**	9 wks

SAILOR *UK, male vocal/instrumental group*

Date	Title *Label Number*	Position	
6 Dec 75	● **GLASS OF CHAMPAGNE** *Epic EPC 3770*	**2**	12 wks
27 Mar 76	● **GIRLS GIRLS GIRLS** *Epic EPC 3858*	**7**	8 wks
19 Feb 77	**ONE DRINK TOO MANY** *Epic EPC 4804*	**35**	4 wks

ST. ANDREWS CHORALE *UK, church choir*

Date	Title *Label Number*	Position	
14 Feb 76	**CLOUD 99** *Decca F 13617*	**31**	5 wks

ST. CECILIA *UK, male vocal/instrumental group*

Date	Title *Label Number*	Position	
19 Jun 71	**LEAP UP AND DOWN (WAVE YOUR KNICKERS IN THE AIR)** *Polydor 2058 104*	**12**	17 wks

Barry ST. JOHN *UK, female vocalist*

Date	Title *Label Number*	Position	
9 Dec 65	**COME AWAY MELINDA** *Columbia DB 7783*	**47**	1 wk

ST. LOUIS UNION *UK, male vocal/instrumental group*

Date	Title *Label Number*	Position	
13 Jan 66	**GIRL** *Decca F 12318*	**11**	10 wks

Crispian ST. PETERS *UK, male vocalist*

Date	Title *Label Number*	Position	
6 Jan 66	● **YOU WERE ON MY MIND** *Decca F 12287*	**2**	14 wks
31 Mar 66	● **PIED PIPER** *Decca F 12359*	**5**	13 wks
15 Sep 66	**CHANGES** *Decca F 12480*	**49**	1 wk
29 Sep 66	**CHANGES** (re-entry) *Decca F 12480*	**47**	3 wks

ST. WINIFRED'S SCHOOL CHOIR *UK, school choir*

Date	Title *Label Number*	Position	
22 Nov 80	★ **NO ONE QUITE LIKE GRANDMA** *MFP FP 900*	**1**	11 wks

Buffy SAINTE-MARIE *US, female vocalist*

Date	Title *Label Number*	Position	
17 Jul 71	● **SOLDIER BLUE** *RCA 2081*	**7**	18 wks
18 Mar 72	**I'M GONNA BE A COUNTRY GIRL AGAIN** *Vanguard VRS 35143*	**34**	5 wks

SAINTS *Australia, male vocal/instrumental group*

Date	Title *Label Number*	Position	
16 Jul 77	**THIS PERFECT DAY** *Harvest HAR 5130*	**34**	4 wks

Kyu SAKAMOTO *Japan, male vocalist*

Date	Title *Label Number*	Position	
27 Jun 63	● **SUKIYAKI** *HMV POP 1171*	**6**	13 wks

SAKKARIN *UK, Jonathan King under a false name*

Date	Title *Label Number*	Position	
3 Apr 71	**SUGAR SUGAR** *RCA 2064*	**12**	14 wks

See also Jonathan King.

SALFORD JETS *UK, male vocal/instrumental group*

Date	Title *Label Number*	Position	
31 May 80	**WHO YOU LOOKING AT** *RCA PB 5239*	**72**	2 wks

SALSOUL ORCHESTRA — See *CHARO and the SALSOUL ORCHESTRA*

SAM and DAVE *US, male vocal duo*

Date	Title *Label Number*	Position	
16 Mar 67	**SOOTHE ME** *Stax 601 004*	**48**	2 wks
1 Nov 67	**SOUL MAN** *Stax 601 023*	**24**	14 wks
13 Mar 68	**I THANK YOU** *Stax 601 030*	**34**	9 wks
29 Jan 69	**SOUL SISTER BROWN SUGAR** *Atlantic 584 237*	**15**	8 wks

SAM THE SHAM and the PHARAOHS *US, male vocal/instrumental group*

Date	Title *Label Number*	Position	
24 Jun 65	**WOOLY BULLY** *MGM 1269*	**11**	15 wks
4 Aug 66	**LIL' RED RIDING HOOD** *MGM 1315*	**48**	1 wk
18 Aug 66	**LIL' RED RIDING HOOD** (re-entry) *MGM 1315*	**46**	2 wks

Mike SAMMES SINGERS *UK, male/female vocal group*

Date	Title *Label Number*	Position	
15 Sep 66	**SOMEWHERE MY LOVE** *HMV POP 1546*	**22**	19 wks
12 Jul 67	**SOMEWHERE MY LOVE** (re-entry) *HMV POP 1546*	**14**	19 wks

Dave SAMPSON *UK, male vocalist*

Date	Title *Label Number*	Position	
19 May 60	**SWEET DREAMS** *Columbia DB 4449*	**48**	1 wk
21 Jun 60	**SWEET DREAMS** (re-entry) *Columbia DB 4449*	**29**	5 wks

SAMSON *UK, male vocal/instrumental group*

Date	Title *Label Number*	Position	
4 Jul 81	**RIDING WITH THE ANGELS** *RCA 67*	**55**	3 wks
24 Jul 82	**LOSING MY GRIP** *Polydor POSP 471*	**63**	2 wks

SAN JOSE *UK, male instrumental group*

Date	Title *Label Number*	Position	
17 Jun 78	**ARGENTINE MELODY (CANCION DE ARGENTINA)** *MCA 369*	**14**	8 wks

Hit has credit 'featuring Rodriguez Argentina'.

SAN REMO STRINGS *US, orchestra*

Date	Title *Label Number*	Position	
18 Dec 71	**FESTIVAL TIME** *Tamla Motown TMG 795*	**39**	8 wks

Date	Title *Label Number*	Position	Date	Title *Label Number*	Position

Chris SANDFORD *UK, male vocalist*

12 Dec 63 **NOT TOO LITTLE NOT TOO MUCH** *Decca F 11778* **17** 9 wks

SANDPIPERS *US, vocal group*

15 Sep 66 ● **GUANTANAMERA** *Pye International 7N 25380* **7** 17 wks
5 Jun 68 **QUANDO M'INNAMORO (A MAN WITHOUT LOVE)** *A & M AMS 723* **33** 6 wks
26 Mar 69 **KUMBAYA** *A & M AMS 744* **39** 1 wk
9 Apr 69 **KUMBAYA** (re-entry) *A & M AMS 744* **49** 1 wk
27 Nov 76 **HANG ON SLOOPY** *Satril SAT 114* **32** 8 wks

Jodie SANDS *US, female vocalist*

17 Oct 58 **SOMEDAY** *HMV POP 533* **14** 10 wks

Tommy SANDS *US, male vocalist*

4 Aug 60 **OLD OAKEN BUCKET** *Capitol CL 15143* **25** 7 wks

Samantha SANG *Australia, female vocalist*

4 Feb 78 **EMOTIONS** *Private stock PVT 128* **11** 13 wks

SANTA CLAUS and the CHRISTMAS TREES *UK, male vocal/instrumental group*

11 Dec 82 **SINGALONG-A-SANTA** *Polydor IVY 1* **19†** 3 wks

SANTA ESMERALDA and Leroy GOMEZ

US/France, male/female vocal/instrumental group

12 Nov 77 **DON'T LET ME BE MISUNDERSTOOD** *Philips 6042 3* **41** 5 wks

SANTANA *US, male vocal/instrumental group*

28 Sep 74 **SAMBA PA TI** *CBS 2561* **27** 7 wks
15 Oct 77 **SHE'S NOT THERE** *CBS 5671* **11** 12 wks
25 Nov 78 **WELL ALL RIGHT** *CBS 6755* **53** 3 wks
22 Mar 80 **ALL I EVER WANTED** *CBS 8160* **57** 3 wks

SANTO and JOHNNY

US, male instrumental duo, steel and electric guitars

16 Oct 59 **SLEEP WALK** *Pye International 7N 25037* **22** 4 wks
31 Mar 60 **TEARDROP** *Parlophone R 4619* **50** 1 wk

Mike SARNE *UK, male vocalist*

10 May 62 ★ **COME OUTSIDE** *Parlophone R 4902* **1** 19 wks
30 Aug 62 **WILL I WHAT** *Parlophone R 4932* **18** 10 wks
10 Jan 63 **JUST FOR KICKS** *Parlophone R 4974* **22** 7 wks
28 Mar 63 **CODE OF LOVE** *Parlophone R 5010* **29** 7 wks

Come Outside - *Mike Sarne with Wendy Richard;* Will I What *with Billie Davis. See also Billie Davis.*

Joy SARNEY *UK, female vocalist*

7 May 77 **NAUGHTY NAUGHTY NAUGHTY** *Alaska ALA 2005* **26** 6 wks

SARR BAND

Italy, female vocalist; England/France, male instrumental group.

16 Sep 78 **MAGIC MANDRAKE** *Calendar Day 115* **68** 1 wk

Peter SARSTEDT *UK, male vocalist*

5 Feb 69 ★ **WHERE DO YOU GO TO MY LOVELY** *United Artists UP 2262* **1** 16 wks
4 Jun 69 ● **FROZEN ORANGE JUICE** *United Artists UP 35021* **10** 9 wks

Robin SARSTEDT *UK, male vocalist*

8 May 76 ● **MY RESISTANCE IS LOW** *Decca F 13624* **3** 9 wks

SATURDAY NIGHT BAND

US, male vocal/instrumental group

1 Jul 78 **COME ON DANCE DANCE** *CBS 6367* **16** 9 wks

Edna SAVAGE *UK, female vocalist*

13 Jan 56 **ARRIVEDERCI DARLING** *Parlophone R 4097* **19** 1 wk

Telly SAVALAS *US, male vocalist*

22 Feb 75 ★ **IF** *MCA 174* **1** 9 wks
31 May 75 **YOU'VE LOST THAT LOVIN' FEELING** *MCA 189* **47** 3 wks

SAVANNAH

US, male vocalist/instrumentalist-guitar

10 Oct 81 **I CAN'T TURN AWAY** *R & B RBS 203* **61** 4 wks

SAXON *UK, male vocal/instrumental group*

22 Mar 80 **WHEELS OF STEEL** *Carrere CAR 143* **20** 11 wks
21 Jun 80 **747 (STRANGERS IN THE NIGHT)** *Carrere CAR 151* **13** 9 wks
28 Jun 80 **BIG TEASER/RAINBOW THEME** *Carrere HM 5* **66** 2 wks
28 Jun 80 **BACKS TO THE WALL** *Carrere HM 6* **64** 2 wks
29 Nov 80 **STRONG ARM OF THE LAW** *Carrere CAR 170* **63** 3 wks
11 Apr 81 **AND THE BANDS PLAYED ON** *Carrere CAR 180* **12** 8 wks
18 Jul 81 **NEVER SURRENDER** *Carrere CAR 204* **18** 6 wks
31 Oct 81 **PRINCESS OF THE NIGHT** *Carrere CAR 208* **57** 3 wks

Al SAXON *UK, male vocalist*

Date	Title *Label Number*	Position	Weeks
16 Jan 59	**YOU'RE THE TOP CHA** *Fontana H 164*	**17**	4 wks
28 Aug 59	**ONLY SIXTEEN** *Fontana H 205*	**24**	3 wks
22 Dec 60	**BLUE-EYED BOY** *Fontana H 278*	**39**	2 wks
7 Sep 61	**THERE I'VE SAID IT AGAIN** *Piccadilly 7N 35011*	**48**	1 wk

Leo SAYER *UK, male vocalist*

Date	Title *Label Number*	Position	Weeks
15 Dec 73	● **THE SHOW MUST GO ON** *Chrysalis CHS 2023*	**2**	13 wks
15 Jun 74	● **ONE MAN BAND** *Chrysalis CHS 2045*	**6**	9 wks
14 Sep 74	● **LONG TALL GLASSES** *Chrysalis CHS 2052*	**4**	9 wks
30 Aug 75	● **MOONLIGHTING** *Chrysalis CHS 2076*	**2**	8 wks
30 Oct 76	● **YOU MAKE ME FEEL LIKE DANCING** *Chrysalis CHS 2119*	**2**	12 wks
29 Jan 77	★ **WHEN I NEED YOU** *Chrysalis CHS 2127*	**1**	13 wks
9 Apr 77	● **HOW MUCH LOVE** *Chrysalis CHS 2140*	**10**	8 wks
10 Sep 77	**THUNDER IN MY HEART** *Chrysalis CHS 2163*	**22**	8 wks
16 Sep 78	● **I CAN'T STOP LOVIN' YOU** *Chrysalis CHS 2240*	**6**	11 wks
25 Nov 78	**RAINING IN MY HEART** *Chryalis CHS 2277*	**21**	10 wks
5 Jul 80	● **MORE THAN I CAN SAY** *Chrysalis CHS 2442*	**2**	11 wks
13 Mar 82	● **HAVE YOU EVER BEEN IN LOVE** *Chrysalis CHS 2596*	**10**	9 wks
19 Jun 82	**HEART (STOP BEATING IN TIME)** *Chrysalis CHS 2616*	**22**	10 wks

SCAFFOLD *UK, male vocal group*

Date	Title *Label Number*	Position	Weeks
22 Nov 67	● **THANK U VERY MUCH** *Parlophone R 5643*	**4**	12 wks
27 Mar 68	**DO YOU REMEMBER** *Parlophone R 5679*	**34**	5 wks
6 Nov 68	★ **LILY THE PINK** *Parlophone R 5734*	**1**	24 wks
1 Nov 69	**GIN GAN GOOLIE** *Parlophone R 5812*	**38**	11 wks
24 Jan 70	**GIN GAN GOOLIE** (re-entry) *Parlophone R 5812*	**50**	1 wk
1 Jun 74	● **LIVERPOOL LOU** *Warner Bros. K 16400*	**7**	9 wks

Boz SCAGGS *US, male vocalist*

Date	Title *Label Number*	Position	Weeks
30 Oct 76	**LOWDOWN** *CBS 4563*	**28**	4 wks
22 Jan 77	● **WHAT CAN I SAY** *CBS 4869*	**10**	10 wks
14 May 77	**LIDO SHUFFLE** *CBS 5136*	**13**	9 wks
10 Dec 77	**HOLLYWOOD** *CBS 5836*	**33**	8 wks

SCARLET PARTY

UK, male vocal/instrumental group

Date	Title *Label Number*	Position	Weeks
16 Oct 82	**101 DAM-NATIONS** *Parlaphone R 6058*	**44**	5 wks

Michael SCHENKER GROUP

Germany/UK, male vocal/instrumental group

Date	Title *Label Number*	Position	Weeks
13 Sep 80	**ARMED AND READY** *Chrysalis CHS 2455*	**53**	3 wks
8 Nov 80	**CRY FOR THE NATIONS** *Chrysalis CHS 2471*	**56**	3 wks
11 Sep 82	**DANCER** *Chrysalis CHS 2636*	**52**	3 wks

Lalo SCHIFRIN *US, orchestra*

Date	Title *Label Number*	Position	Weeks
9 Oct 76	**JAWS** *CTI CTSP 005*	**14**	9 wks

SCORPIONS

Germany, male vocal/instrumental group

Date	Title *Label Number*	Position	Weeks
26 May 79	**IS THERE ANYBODY THERE/ANOTHER PIECE OF MEAT** *Harvest HAR 5185*	**39**	4 wks
25 Aug 79	**LOVEDRIVE** *Harvest HAR 5188*	**69**	2 wks
31 May 80	**MAKE IT REAL** *Harvest HAR 5206*	**72**	2 wks
20 Sep 80	**THE ZOO** *Harvest HAR 5212*	**75**	1 wk
3 Apr 82	**NO ONE LIKE YOU** *Harvest HAR 5219*	**65**	3 wks
1 May 82	**NO ONE LIKE YOU** (re-entry) *Harvest HAR 5219*	**64**	1 wk
17 Jul 82	**CAN'T LIVE WITHOUT YOU** *Harvest HAR 5221*	**63**	2 wks

SCOTLAND WORLD CUP SQUAD

UK, male football team vocalists

Date	Title *Label Number*	Position	Weeks
22 Jun 74	**EASY EASY** *Polydor 2058 452*	**20**	4 wks
1 May 82	● **WE HAVE A DREAM** *WEA K 19145*	**5**	9 wks

Jack SCOTT *Canada, male vocalist*

Date	Title *Label Number*	Position	Weeks
10 Oct 58	● **MY TRUE LOVE** *London HLU 8626*	**9**	10 wks
25 Sep 59	**THE WAY I WALK** *London HLL 8912*	**30**	1 wk
10 Mar 60	**WHAT IN THE WORLD'S COME OVER YOU** *Top Rank JAR 280*	**11**	15 wks
2 Jun 60	**BURNING BRIDGES** *Top Rank JAR 375*	**32**	2 wks

Linda SCOTT *US, female vocalist*

Date	Title *Label Number*	Position	Weeks
18 May 61	● **I'VE TOLD EVERY LITTLE STAR** *Columbia DB 4638*	**7**	13 wks
14 Sep 61	**DON'T BET MONEY HONEY** *Columbia DB 4692*	**50**	1 wk

Simon SCOTT *UK, male vocalist*

Date	Title *Label Number*	Position	Weeks
13 Aug 64	**MOVE IT BABY** *Parlophone R 5164*	**37**	8 wks

SCRITTI POLITTI

UK, male vocal/instrumental group

Date	Title *Label Number*	Position	Weeks
21 Nov 81	**THE SWEETEST GIRL** *Rough Trade RT 091*	**64**	3 wks
22 May 82	**FAITHLESS** *Rough Trade RT 101*	**56**	4 wks
7 Aug 82	**ASYLUMS IN JERUSALEM/JACQUES DERRIDA** *Rough Trade RT 111*	**43**	5 wks

Earl SCRUGGS — See *Lester FLATT and Earl SCRUGGS*

SEA LEVEL *US, male instrumental group*

Date	Title *Label Number*	Position	Weeks
17 Feb 79	**FIFTY-FOUR** *Capricorn POSP 28*	**63**	4 wks

SEARCHERS *UK, male vocal/instrumental group*

Date	Title *Label Number*	Position	Weeks
27 Jun 63	★ **SWEETS FOR MY SWEET** *Pye 7N 15533*	**1**	16 wks
10 Oct 63	**SWEET NOTHINS** *Philips BF 1274*	**48**	2 wks
24 Oct 63	● **SUGAR AND SPICE** *Pye 7N 15566*	**2**	13 wks
16 Jan 64	★ **NEEDLES AND PINS** *Pye 7N 15594*	**1**	15 wks
16 Apr 64	★ **DON'T THROW YOUR LOVE AWAY** *Pye 7N 15630*	**1**	11 wks
16 Jul 64	**SOMEDAY WE'RE GONNA LOVE AGAIN** *Pye 7N 15670*	**11**	8 wks

Date	Title *Label Number*	Position	
17 Sep 64	● **WHEN YOU WALK IN THE ROOM** *Pye 7N 15694*	**3**	12 wks
3 Dec 64	**WHAT HAVE THEY DONE TO THE RAIN** *Pye 7N 15739*	**13**	11 wks
4 Mar 65	● **GOODBYE MY LOVE** *Pye 7N 15794*	**4**	11 wks
8 Jul 65	**HE'S GOT NO LOVE** *Pye 7N 15878*	**12**	10 wks
14 Oct 65	**WHEN I GET HOME** *Pye 7N 15950*	**35**	3 wks
16 Dec 65	**TAKE ME FOR WHAT I'M WORTH** *Pye 7N 15992*	**20**	8 wks
21 Apr 66	**TAKE IT OR LEAVE IT** *Pye 7N 17094*	**31**	6 wks
13 Oct 66	**HAVE YOU EVER LOVED SOMEBODY** *Pye 7N 17170*	**48**	2 wks

SEASHELLS *UK, female vocal group*

Date	Title *Label Number*	Position	
9 Sep 72	**MAYBE I KNOW** *CBS 8218*	**32**	5 wks

Harry SECOMBE *UK, male vocalist*

Date	Title *Label Number*	Position	
9 Dec 55	**ON WITH THE MOTLEY** *Philips PB 523*	**16**	3 wks
3 Oct 63	**IF I RULED THE WORLD** *Philips BF 1261*	**44**	2 wks
21 Nov 63	**IF I RULED THE WORLD** (re-entry) *Philips BF 1261*	**18**	15 wks
23 Feb 67	● **THIS IS MY SONG** *Philips BF 1539*	**2**	15 wks

SECOND CITY SOUND *UK, instrumental group*

Date	Title *Label Number*	Position	
20 Jan 66	**TCHAIKOVSKY ONE** *Decca F 12310*	**22**	7 wks
2 Apr 69	**DREAM OF OLWEN** *Major Minor MM 600*	**43**	1 wk

SECOND IMAGE

UK, male vocal/instrumental group

Date	Title *Label Number*	Position	
24 Jul 82	**STAR** *Polydor POSP 457*	**60**	2 wks

SECRET AFFAIR

UK, male vocal/instrumental group

Date	Title *Label Number*	Position	
1 Sep 79	**TIME FOR ACTION** *I-Spy SEE 1*	**13**	10 wks
10 Nov 79	**LET YOUR HEART DANCE** *I-Spy SEE 3*	**32**	6 wks
8 Mar 80	**MY WORLD** *I-Spy SEE 5*	**16**	9 wks
23 Aug 80	**SOUND OF CONFUSION** *I-Spy SEE 8*	**45**	5 wks
17 Oct 81	**DO YOU KNOW** *I-Spy SEE 10*	**57**	4 wks

Neil SEDAKA *US, male vocalist*

Date	Title *Label Number*	Position	
24 Apr 59	● **I GO APE** *RCA 1115*	**9**	13 wks
13 Nov 59	● **OH CAROL** *RCA 1152*	**3**	17 wks
14 Apr 60	● **STAIRWAY TO HEAVEN** *RCA 1178*	**8**	15 wks
1 Sep 60	**YOU MEAN EVERYTHING TO ME** *RCA 1198*	**45**	3 wks
2 Feb 61	● **CALENDAR GIRL** *RCA 1220*	**8**	14 wks
18 May 61	● **LITTLE DEVIL** *RCA 1236*	**9**	12 wks
21 Dec 61	● **HAPPY BIRTHDAY SWEET SIXTEEN** *RCA 1266*	**3**	18 wks
19 Apr 62	**KING OF CLOWNS** *RCA 1282*	**23**	10 wks
19 Jul 62	● **BREAKING UP IS HARD TO DO** *RCA 1298*	**7**	16 wks
22 Nov 62	**NEXT DOOR TO AN ANGEL** *RCA 1319*	**29**	4 wks
30 May 63	**LET'S GO STEADY AGAIN** *RCA 1343*	**42**	1 wk
13 Jun 63	**LET'S GO STEADY AGAIN** (re-entry) *RCA 1343*	**43**	2 wks
7 Oct 72	**OH CAROL/ BREAKING UP IS HARD TO DO/ LITTLE DEVIL** (re-issue) *RCA Maximillion 2259*	**19**	14 wks
4 Nov 72	**BEAUTIFUL YOU** *RCA 2269*	**43**	3 wks
24 Feb 73	**THAT'S WHEN THE MUSIC TAKES ME** *RCA 2310*	**18**	10 wks
2 Jun 73	**STANDING ON THE INSIDE** *MGM 2006 267*	**26**	9 wks
25 Aug 73	**OUR LAST SONG TOGETHER** *MGM 2006 307*	**31**	8 wks
9 Feb 74	**A LITTLE LOVIN'** *Polydor 2058 434*	**34**	6 wks
22 Jun 74	**LAUGHTER IN THE RAIN** *Polydor 2058 494*	**15**	9 wks
22 Mar 75	**THE QUEEN OF 1964** *Polydor 2058 546*	**35**	5 wks

SEEKERS *Australia, male/female vocal group*

Date	Title *Label Number*	Position	
7 Jan 65	★ **I'LL NEVER FIND ANOTHER YOU** *Columbia DB 7431*	**1**	23 wks
15 Apr 65	● **A WORLD OF OUR OWN** *Columbia DB 7532*	**3**	18 wks
28 Oct 65	★ **THE CARNIVAL IS OVER** *Columbia DB 7711*	**1**	17 wks
24 Mar 66	**SOMEDAY ONE DAY** *Columbia DB 7867*	**11**	11 wks
8 Sep 66	● **WALK WITH ME** *Columbia DB 8000*	**10**	12 wks
24 Nov 66	● **MORNINGTOWN RIDE** *Columbia DB 8060*	**2**	15 wks
23 Feb 67	● **GEORGY GIRL** *Columbia DB 8134*	**3**	11 wks
20 Sep 67	**WHEN WILL THE GOOD APPLES FALL** *Columbia DB 8273*	**11**	12 wks
13 Dec 67	**EMERALD CITY** *Columbia DB 8313*	**50**	1 wk

Bob SEGER AND THE SILVER BULLET BAND *US, male vocal/instrumental group*

Date	Title *Label Number*	Position	
30 Sep 78	**HOLLYWOOD NIGHTS** *Capitol CL 16004*	**42**	6 wks
3 Feb 79	**WE'VE GOT TONITE** *Capitol CL 16028*	**41**	6 wks
24 Oct 81	**HOLLYWOOD NIGHTS** (re-issue) *Capitol CL 223*	**49**	3 wks
6 Feb 82	**WE'VE GOT TONITE** (re-entry) *Capitol CL 235*	**60**	4 wks

The SELECTER

UK, male/female vocal/instrumental group

Date	Title *Label Number*	Position	
13 Oct 79	● **ON MY RADIO** *2 Tone CHSTT 4*	**8**	9 wks
2 Feb 80	**THREE MINUTE HERO** *2 Tone CHS TT 8*	**16**	6 wks
29 Mar 80	**MISSING WORDS** *2 Tone CHS TT 10*	**23**	8 wks
23 Aug 80	**THE WHISPER** *Chrysalis CHSS 1*	**36**	5 wks

Peter SELLERS *UK, male vocalist*

Date	Title *Label Number*	Position	
2 Aug 57	**ANY OLD IRON** *Parlophone R 4337*	**21**	3 wks
6 Sep 57	**ANY OLD IRON** (re-entry) *Parlophone R 4337*	**17**	8 wks
23 Dec 65	**A HARD DAY'S NIGHT** *Parlophone R 5393*	**14**	7 wks

See also Peter Sellers And Sophia Loren.

Peter SELLERS and Sophia LOREN

UK/Italy, male/female vocal duo

Date	Title *Label Number*	Position	
10 Nov 60	● **GOODNESS GRACIOUS ME** *Parlophone R 4702*	**4**	14 wks
12 Jan 61	**BANGERS AND MASH** *Parlophone R 4724*	**22**	4 wks

See also Peter Sellers.

SEMPRINI *UK, orchestra*

Date	Title *Label Number*	Position	
16 Mar 61	**THEME FROM EXODUS** *HMV POP 842*	**25**	8 wks

The SETTLERS

UK, male/female vocal/instrumental group

Date	Title *Label Number*	Position	
16 Oct 71	**THE LIGHTNING TREE** *York SYK 505*	**36**	5 wks

Date	Title *Label Number*	Position	

SEVERINE *France, female vocalist*

Date	Title *Label Number*	Position	
24 Apr 71	● **UN BANC, UN ARBRE, UNE RUE** *Philips 6009 135*	**9**	11 wks

David SEVILLE *US, male vocalist*

Date	Title *Label Number*	Position	
23 May 58	**WITCH DOCTOR** *London HLU 8619*	**11**	6 wks

See also Chipmunks, Alfi and Harry.

SEX PISTOLS *UK, male vocal/instrumental group*

Date	Title *Label Number*	Position	
11 Dec 76	**ANARCHY IN THE U. K.** *EMI 2566*	**38**	4 wks
4 Jun 77	● **GOD SAVE THE QUEEN** *Virgin VS 181*	**2**	9 wks
9 Jul 77	● **PRETTY VACANT** *Virgin VS 184*	**6**	8 wks
22 Oct 77	● **HOLIDAYS IN THE SUN** *Virgin VS 191*	**8**	6 wks
8 Jul 78	● **NO ONE IS INNOCENT/MY WAY** *Virgin VS 220*	**7**	10 wks
3 Mar 79	● **SOMETHING ELSE/FRIGGIN' IN THE RIGGIN'** *Virgin VS 240*	**3**	12 wks
7 Apr 79	● **SILLY THING/WHO KILLED BAMBI** *Virgin VS 256*	**6**	8 wks
30 Jun 79	● **C'MON EVERYBODY** *Virgin VS 272*	**3**	9 wks
13 Oct 79	**THE GREAT ROCK'N'ROLL SWINDLE/ROCK AROUND THE CLOCK** *Virgin VS 290*	**21**	6 wks
14 Jun 80	**(I'M NOT YOUR) STEPPING STONE** *Virgin VS 339*	**21**	8 wks

Rock Around The Clock. *and* Who Killed Bambi *credited to Ten Pole Tudor* No One Is Innocent *is described as a 'Punk Prayer By Ronald Biggs'. See also Ten Pole Tudor*

SEX-O-LETTES — See *DISCO TEX and the SEX-O-LETTES*

Denny SEYTON and the SABRES

UK, male vocal/instrumental group

Date	Title *Label Number*	Position	
17 Sep 64	**THE WAY YOU LOOK TONIGHT** *Mercury MF 824*	**48**	1 wk

SHADOWS *UK, male instrumental/vocal group*

Date	Title *Label Number*	Position	
21 Jul 60	★ **APACHE** *Columbia DB 4484*	**1**	21 wks
10 Nov 60	● **MAN OF MYSTERY/ THE STRANGER** *Columbia DB 4530*	**5**	15 wks
9 Feb 61	● **F. B. I.** *Columbia DB 4580*	**6**	19 wks
11 May 61	● **FRIGHTENED CITY** *Columbia DB 4637*	**3**	20 wks
7 Sep 61	★ **KON-TIKI** *Columbia DB 4698*	**1**	10 wks
23 Nov 61	**KON TIKI** (re-entry) *Columbia DB 4698*	**37**	2 wks
16 Nov 61	● **THE SAVAGE** *Columbia DB 4726*	**10**	8 wks
1 Mar 62	★ **WONDERFUL LAND** *Columbia DB 4790*	**1**	19 wks
2 Aug 62	● **GUITAR TANGO** *Columbia DB 4870*	**4**	15 wks
13 Dec 62	★ **DANCE ON!** *Columbia DB 4948*	**1**	15 wks
7 Mar 63	★ **FOOT TAPPER** *Columbia DB 4984*	**1**	16 wks
6 Jun 63	● **ATLANTIS** *Columbia DB 7047*	**2**	17 wks
19 Sep 63	● **SHINDIG** *Columbia DB 7106*	**6**	12 wks
5 Dec 63	**GERONIMO** *Columbia DB 7163*	**11**	12 wks
5 Mar 64	**THEME FOR YOUNG LOVERS** *Columbia DB 7231*	**12**	10 wks
7 May 64	● **THE RISE & FALL OF FLINGEL BUNT** *Columbia DB 7261*	**5**	14 wks
3 Sep 64	**RHYTHM & GREENS** *Columbia DB 7342*	**22**	7 wks
3 Dec 64	**GENIE WITH THE LIGHT BROWN LAMP** *Columbia DB 7416*	**17**	10 wks
11 Feb 65	**MARY ANNE** *Columbia DB 7476*	**17**	10 wks
10 Jun 65	**STINGRAY** *Columbia DB 7588*	**19**	7 wks
5 Aug 65	● **DON'T MAKE MY BABY BLUE** *Columbia DB 7650*	**10**	10 wks
25 Nov 65	**WAR LORD** *Columbia DB 7769*	**18**	9 wks
17 Mar 66	**I MET A GIRL** *Columbia DB 7853*	**22**	5 wks
7 Jul 66	**A PLACE IN THE SUN** *Columbia DB 7952*	**24**	6 wks
3 Nov 66	**THE DREAMS I DREAM** *Columbia DB 8034*	**42**	6 wks
13 Apr 67	**MAROC 7** *Columbia DB 8170*	**24**	8 wks
8 Mar 75	**LET ME BE THE ONE** *EMI 2269*	**12**	9 wks
16 Dec 78	● **DON'T CRY FOR ME ARGENTINA** *EMI 2890*	**5**	14 wks
28 Apr 79	● **THEME FROM THE DEER HUNTER (CAVATINA)** *EMI 2939*	**9**	14 wks
26 Jan 80	**RIDERS IN THE SKY** *EMI 5027*	**12**	12 wks
23 Aug 80	**EQUINOXE (PART V)** *Polydor POSP 148*	**50**	3 wks
2 May 82	**THE THIRD MAN** *Polydor POSP 255*	**44**	4 wks

See also Cliff Richard. All the above hits were instrumentals except for Mary Anne, Don't Make My Baby Blue, I Met A Girl, The Dreams I Dream *and* Let Me Be The One.

SHAG

UK, male vocalist, Jonathan King, under a false name

Date	Title *Label Number*	Position	
14 Oct 72	● **LOOP DI LOVE** *UK 7*	**4**	13 wks

See also Jonathan King, 53rd & 3rd.

SHAKATAK

UK, male/female vocal/instrumental group

Date	Title *Label Number*	Position	
8 Nov 80	**FEELS LIKE THE RIGHT TIME** *Polydor POSP 188*	**41**	5 wks
7 Mar 81	**LIVING IN THE U.K.** *Polydor POSP 230*	**52**	4 wks
25 Jul 81	**BRAZILIAN DAWN** *Polydor POSP 282*	**48**	3 wks
21 Nov 81	**EASIER SAID THAN DONE** *Polydor POSP 375*	**12**	17 wks
3 Apr 82	● **NIGHT BIRDS** *Polydor POSP 407*	**9**	8 wks
19 Jun 82	**STREETWALKIN'** *Polydor POSP 452*	**38**	6 wks
4 Sep 82	**INVITATIONS** *Polydor POSP 502*	**24**	7 wks
6 Nov 82	**STRANGER** *Polydor POSP 530*	**43**	3 wks

SHALAMAR

US, male/female vocal/instrumental group

Date	Title *Label Number*	Position	
14 May 77	**UPTOWN FESTIVAL** *Soul Train FB 0885*	**30**	5 wks
9 Dec 78	**TAKE THAT TO THE BANK** *RCA FB 1379*	**20**	12 wks
24 Nov 79	**THE SECOND TIME AROUND** *Solar FB 1709*	**45**	9 wks
9 Feb 80	**RIGHT IN THE SOCKET** *Solar SO2*	**44**	6 wks
30 Aug 80	**I OWE YOU ONE** *Solar SO 11*	**13**	10 wks
28 Mar 81	**MAKE THAT MOVE** *Solar SO 17*	**30**	10 wks
27 Mar 82	● **I CAN MAKE YOU FEEL GOOD** *Solar K 12599*	**7**	11 wks
12 Jun 82	● **A NIGHT TO REMEMBER** *Solar K 13162*	**5**	12 wks
4 Sep 82	● **THERE IT IS** *Solar K 13194*	**5**	10 wks
27 Nov 82	**FRIENDS** *Solar CHUM 1*	**12**†	5 wks

SHAM 69 *UK, male vocal/instrumental group*

Date	Title *Label Number*	Position	
13 May 78	**ANGELS WITH DIRTY FACES** *Polydor 2059 023*	**19**	10 wks
29 Jul 78	● **IF THE KIDS ARE UNITED** *Polydor 2059 050*	**9**	9 wks
14 Oct 78	● **HURRY UP HARRY** *Polydor POSP 7*	**10**	8 wks
24 Mar 79	**QUESTIONS AND ANSWERS** *Polydor POSP 27*	**18**	9 wks
4 Aug 79	● **HERSHAM BOYS** *Polydor POSP 64*	**6**	9 wks
27 Oct 79	**YOU'RE A BETTER MAN THAN I** *Polydor POSP 82*	**49**	5 wks
12 Apr 80	**TELL THE CHILDREN** *Polydor POSP 136*	**45**	3 wks

Jimmy SHAND *UK, male dance band*

Date	Title *Label Number*	Position	
23 Dec 55	**BLUEBELL POLKA** *Parlophone F 3436*	**20**	2 wks

Left **DEL SHANNON** As Charles Westover started playing guitar when he was a radio operator attached to the Field Artillery Unit of the US 7th Army stationed at Stuttgart in Germany

Below **SHADOWS** 1983 The Shadows Silver Jubilee Year

Above **DEE DEE SHARP** Despite several hits in the States like 'Mashed Potato Time', 'Gravy', 'Ride' and 'Do The Bird' only the latter charted here for the girl who was born Dione La Rue. She briefly hit the British Chart again as one of the Philadelphia International All-Stars *Above right* **SAXON** As the song was set in a Boeing 747, it can be argued Saxon's 'Strangers in the Night' got higher than Frank and Nancy Sinatra's chart topper of the same name

Above **SCRITTI POLITTI** The fourth member doesn't look too well

PERCY SLEDGE All set to wrap someone in his warm and tender love

Date	Title *Label Number*	Position	

Paul SHANE and the YELLOWCOATS

UK, male vocalist with male/female vocal group

16 May 81	**HI DE HI (HOLIDAY ROCK)** *EMI 5180*	**36**	5 wks

SHANGRI-LAS *US, female vocal group*

8 Oct 64	**REMEMBER (WALKIN' IN THE SAND)** *Red Bird RB 10008*	**14**	13 wks
14 Jan 65	**LEADER OF THE PACK** *Red Bird RB 10014*	**11**	9 wks
14 Oct 72	● **LEADER OF THE PACK** (re-issue) *Kama Sutra 2013 024*	**3**	14 wks
5 Jun 76	● **LEADER OF THE PACK** (2nd re-issue) *Charley CS 1009*	**7**	11 wks
12 Jun 76	● **LEADER OF THE PACK** (3rd re-issue) *Contempo CS 9032*	**7**	10 wks

From 19 Jun 76 until 14 Aug 76, the last week of the disc's chart run, the Charley and Contempo releases of Leader Of The Pack *were bracketed together on the chart.*

Del SHANNON *US, male vocalist*

27 Apr 61	★ **RUNAWAY** *London HLX 9317*	**1**	22 wks
14 Sep 61	● **HATS OFF TO LARRY** *London HLX 9402*	**6**	12 wks
7 Dec 61	● **SO LONG BABY** *London HLX 9462*	**10**	11 wks
15 Mar 62	● **HEY LITTLE GIRL** *London HLX 9515*	**2**	15 wks
6 Sep 62	**CRY MYSELF TO SLEEP** *London HLX 9587*	**29**	6 wks
11 Oct 62	● **SWISS MAID** *London HLX 9609*	**2**	17 wks
17 Jan 63	● **LITTLE TOWN FLIRT** *London HLX 9653*	**4**	13 wks
25 Apr 63	● **TWO KINDS OF TEARDROPS** *London HLX 9710*	**5**	13 wks
22 Aug 63	**TWO SILHOUETTES** *London HLX 9761*	**23**	8 wks
24 Oct 63	**SUE'S GONNA BE MINE** *London HLU 9800*	**21**	8 wks
12 Mar 64	**MARY JANE** *Stateside SS 269*	**35**	5 wks
30 Jul 64	**HANDY MAN** *Stateside SS 317*	**36**	4 wks
14 Jan 65	● **KEEP SEARCHIN' (WE'LL FOLLOW THE SUN)** *Stateside SS 368*	**3**	11 wks
18 Mar 65	**STRANGER IN TOWN** *Stateside SS 395*	**40**	2 wks

Helen SHAPIRO *UK, female vocalist*

23 Mar 61	● **DON'T TREAT ME LIKE A CHILD** *Columbia DB 4589*	**3**	20 wks
29 Jul 61	★ **YOU DON'T KNOW** *Columbia DB 4670*	**1**	23 wks
28 Sep 61	★ **WALKIN' BACK TO HAPPINESS** *Columbia DB 4715*	**1**	19 wks
15 Feb 62	● **TELL ME WHAT HE SAID** *Columbia DB 4782*	**2**	15 wks
3 May 62	**LET'S TALK ABOUT LOVE** *Columbia DB 4824*	**23**	7 wks
12 Jul 62	● **LITTLE MISS LONELY** *Columbia DB 4869*	**8**	11 wks
18 Oct 62	**KEEP AWAY FROM OTHER GIRLS** *Columbia DB 4908*	**40**	6 wks
7 Feb 63	**QUEEN FOR TONIGHT** *Columbia DB 4966*	**33**	5 wks
25 Apr 63	**WOE IS ME** *Columbia DB 7026*	**35**	6 wks
24 Oct 63	**LOOK WHO IT IS** *Columbia DB 7130*	**47**	3 wks
23 Jan 64	**FEVER** *Columbia DB 7190*	**38**	4 wks

SHARONETTES *UK, female vocal group*

26 Apr 75	**PAPA OOM MOW MOW** *Black Magic BM 102*	**26**	5 wks
12 Jul 75	**GOING TO A GO-GO** *Black Magic BM 104*	**46**	3 wks

Dee Dee SHARP *US, female vocalist*

25 Apr 63	**DO THE BIRD** *Cameo Parkway C 244*	**46**	2 wks

See also Philadelphia All-Stars.

Rockey SHARPE and the REPLAYS

UK, male/female vocal group

16 Dec 78	**RAMA LAMA DING DONG** *Chiswick CHIS 104*	**17**	10 wks
24 Mar 79	**IMAGINATION** *Chiswick CHIS 110*	**39**	6 wks
25 Aug 79	**LOVE WILL MAKE YOU FAIL IN SCHOOL** *Chiswick CHIS 114*	**60**	4 wks
9 Feb 80	**MARTIAN HOP** *Chiswick CHIS 121*	**55**	4 wks
17 Apr 82	**SHOUT SHOUT (KNOCK YOURSELF OUT)** *Chiswick DKE 3*	**19**	9 wks
7 Aug 82	**CLAP YOUR HANDS** *RAK 345*	**54**	3 wks

Third and fourth hits feature the Top Liners.

Sandie SHAW *UK, female vocalist*

8 Oct 64	★ **(THERE'S) ALWAYS SOMETHING THERE TO REMIND ME** *Pye 7N 15704*	**1**	11 wks
10 Dec 64	● **GIRL DON'T COME** *Pye 7N 15743*	**3**	12 wks
18 Feb 65	● **I'LL STOP AT NOTHING** *Pye 7N 15783*	**4**	11 wks
13 May 65	★ **LONG LIVE LOVE** *Pye 7N 15841*	**1**	14 wks
23 Sep 65	● **MESSAGE UNDERSTOOD** *Pye 7N 15940*	**6**	10 wks
18 Nov 65	**HOW CAN YOU TELL** *Pye 7N 15987*	**21**	9 wks
27 Jan 66	● **TOMORROW** *Pye 7N 17036*	**9**	9 wks
19 May 66	**NOTHING COMES EASY** *Pye 7N 17086*	**14**	9 wks
8 Sep 66	**RUN** *Pye 7N 17163*	**32**	5 wks
24 Nov 66	**THINK SOMETIMES ABOUT ME** *Pye 7N 17212*	**32**	4 wks
19 Jan 67	**I DON'T NEED ANYTHING** *Pye 7N 17239*	**50**	1 wk
16 Mar 67	★ **PUPPET ON A STRING** *Pye 7N 17272*	**1**	18 wks
12 Jul 67	**TONIGHT IN TOKYO** *Pye 7N 17346*	**21**	6 wks
4 Oct 67	**YOU'VE NOT CHANGED** *Pye 7N 17378*	**18**	12 wks
7 Feb 68	**TODAY** *Pye 7N 17441*	**27**	7 wks
12 Feb 69	● **MONSIEUR DUPONT** *Pye 7N 17615*	**6**	15 wks
14 May 69	**THINK IT ALL OVER** *Pye 7N 17726*	**42**	4 wks

Winifred SHAW *US, female vocalist*

14 Aug 76	**LULLABY OF BROADWAY** *United Artists UP 36131*	**42**	4 wks

George SHEARING

UK, male instrumentalist, piano

4 Oct 62	**BAUBLES BANGLES & BEADS** *Capitol CL 15269*	**49**	1 wk

See also Nat King Cole.

Gary SHEARSTON *Australia, male vocalist*

5 Oct 74	● **I GET A KICK OUT OF YOU** *Charisma CB 234*	**7**	8 wks

SHEER ELEGANCE *UK, male vocal group*

20 Dec 75	**MILKY WAY** *Pye International 7N 25697*	**18**	10 wks
3 Apr 76	● **LIFE IS TOO SHORT GIRL** *Pye International 7N 25703*	**9**	9 wks
24 Jul 76	**IT'S TEMPTATION** *Pye International 7N 25715*	**41**	4 wks

Date **Title** *Label Number* **Position**

SHEILA and B. DEVOTION *France/US/Jamaica, female vocalist and male vocal/instrumental group*

11 Mar 78 **SINGIN' IN THE RAIN** PART 1 *Carrere EMI 2751* **11** 13 wks
22 Jul 78 **YOU LIGHT MY FIRE** *Carrere EMI 2828* **44** 6 wks
24 Nov 79 **SPACER** *Carrere CAR 128* **18** 14 wks

First two hits have no "and" in the act's name.

Doug SHELDON *UK, male vocalist*

9 Nov 61 **RUNAROUND SUE** *Decca F 11398* **36** 3 wks
4 Jan 62 **YOUR MA SAID YOU CRIED IN YOUR SLEEP LAST NIGHT** *Decca F 11416* **29** 6 wks
7 Feb 63 **I SAW LINDA YESTERDAY** *Decca F 11564* **36** 6 wks

Peter SHELLEY *UK, male vocalist*

14 Sep 74 ● **GEE BABY** *Magnet MAG 12* **4** 10 wks
22 Mar 75 ● **LOVE ME LOVE MY DOG** *Magnet MAG 22* **3** 10 wks

Anne SHELTON *UK, female vocalist*

16 Dec 55 **ARRIVEDERCI DARLING** *HMV POP 146* **17** 4 wks
13 Apr 56 **SEVEN DAYS** *Philips PB 567* **20** 4 wks
24 Aug 56 ★ **LAY DOWN YOUR ARMS** *Philips PB 616* **1** 14 wks
20 Nov 59 **VILLAGE OF ST. BERNADETTE** *Philips PB 969* **27** 1 wk
26 Jan 61 ● **SAILOR** *Philips PB 1096* **10** 8 wks

SHEPHERD SISTERS *US, female vocal group*

15 Nov 57 **ALONE** *HMV POP 411* **14** 5 wks
3 Jan 58 **ALONE** (re-entry) *HMV POP 411* **22** 1 wk

SHERBET *Australia, male vocal/instrumental group*

25 Sep 76 ● **HOWZAT** *Epic EPC 4574* **4** 10 wks

Tony SHERIDAN and the BEATLES *UK, male vocalist, male instrumental backing group*

6 Jul 63 **MY BONNIE** *Polydor NH 66833* **48** 1 wk

See also Beatles.

Allan SHERMAN *US, male vocalist*

12 Sep 63 **HELLO MUDDAH HELLO FADDAH** *Warner Bros. WB 106* **14** 10 wks

Bobby SHERMAN *US, male vocalist*

31 Oct 70 **JULIE DO YA LOVE ME** *CBS 5144* **28** 4 wks

Pluto SHERVINGTON *Jamaica, male vocalist*

7 Feb 76 ● **DAT** *Opal PAL 5* **6** 8 wks
10 Apr 76 **RAM GOAT LIVER** *Trojan TR 7978* **43** 4 wks
6 Mar 82 **YOUR HONOUR** *KR KR 4* **19** 8 wks

Your Honour *credited to Pluto*

Holly SHERWOOD *US, female vocalist*

5 Feb 72 **DAY BY DAY** *Bell 1182* **29** 7 wks

Tony SHEVETON *UK, male vocalist*

13 Feb 64 **MILLION DRUMS** *Oriole CB 1895* **49** 1 wk

SHIRELLES *US, female vocal group*

9 Feb 61 ● **WILL YOU LOVE ME TOMORROW** *Top Rank JAR 540* **4** 15 wks
31 May 62 **SOLDIER BOY** *HMV POP 1019* **23** 9 wks
23 May 63 **FOOLISH LITTLE GIRL** *Stateside SS 181* **38** 5 wks

SHIRLEY and COMPANY *US, female vocalist/male vocal/instrumental backing group*

8 Feb 75 ● **SHAME SHAME SHAME** *All Platinum 6146 301* **6** 9 wks

SHO NUFF *US, male vocal/instrumental group*

24 May 80 **IT'S ALRIGHT** *Ensign ENY 37* **53** 4 wks

SHOCKING BLUE *Holland, male/female vocal/instrumental group*

17 Jan 70 ● **VENUS** *Penny Farthing PEN 702* **8** 11 wks
25 Apr 70 **MIGHTY JOE** *Penny Farthing PEN 713* **43** 3 wks

Troy SHONDELL *US, male vocalist*

2 Nov 61 **THIS TIME** *London HLG 9432* **22** 11 wks

SHONDELLS — See *Tommy JAMES and the SHONDELLS*

SHOWADDYWADDY *UK, male vocal/instrumental group*

18 May 74 ● **HEY ROCK AND ROLL** *Bell 1357* **2** 14 wks
17 Aug 74 **ROCK 'N' ROLL LADY** *Bell 1374* **15** 9 wks
30 Nov 74 **HEY MR. CHRISTMAS** *Bell 1387* **13** 8 wks
22 Feb 75 **SWEET MUSIC** *Bell 1403* **14** 9 wks
17 May 75 ● **THREE STEPS TO HEAVEN** *Bell 1426* **2** 11 wks
6 Sep 75 ● **HEARTBEAT** *Bell 1450* **7** 7 wks
15 Nov 75 **HEAVENLY** *Bell 1460* **34** 6 wks
29 May 76 **TROCADERO** *Bell 1476* **32** 3 wks
6 Nov 76 ★ **UNDER THE MOON OF LOVE** *Bell 1495* **1** 15 wks
5 Mar 77 ● **WHEN** *Arista 91* **3** 11 wks
23 Jul 77 ● **YOU GOT WHAT IT TAKES** *Arista 126* **2** 10 wks
5 Nov 77 ● **DANCIN' PARTY** *Arista 149* **4** 11 wks
25 Mar 78 ● **I WONDER WHY** *Arista 174* **2** 11 wks
24 Jun 78 ● **A LITTLE BIT OF SOAP** *Arista 191* **5** 12 wks
4 Nov 78 ● **PRETTY LITTLE ANGEL EYES** *Arista ARIST 222* **5** 12 wks
31 Mar 79 **REMEMBER THEN** *Arista 247* **17** 8 wks
28 Jul 79 **SWEET LITTLE ROCK 'N' ROLLER** *Arista 278* **15** 9 wks
10 Nov 79 **A NIGHT AT DADDY GEE'S** *Arista 314* **39** 5 wks
27 Sep 80 **WHY DO LOVERS BREAK EACH OTHER'S HEARTS** *Arista ARIST 359* **22** 10 wks

Date Title *Label Number* Position

Date	Title *Label Number*	Position	
29 Nov 80	**BLUE MOON** *Arista ARIST 379*	**32**	9 wks
13 Jun 81	**MULTIPLICATION** *Arista ARIST 416*	**39**	4 wks
28 Nov 81	**FOOTSTEPS** *Bell BELL 1499*	**31**	9 wks
28 Aug 82	**WHO PUT THE BOMP (IN THE BOMP-A-BOMP-A-BOMP)** *RCA 236*	**37**	6 wks

SHOWDOWN *US, male vocal/instrumental group*

Date	Title *Label Number*	Position	
17 Dec 77	**KEEP DOIN' IT** *State STAT 63*	**41**	3 wks

SHOWSTOPPERS *US, male vocal group*

Date	Title *Label Number*	Position	
13 Mar 68	**AIN'T NOTHING BUT A HOUSEPARTY** *Beacon 3-100*	**11**	15 wks
13 Nov 68	**EENY MEENY** *MGM 1346*	**33**	7 wks
30 Jan 71	**AIN'T NOTHING BUT A HOUSEPARTY** (re-issue) *Beacon BEA 100*	**43**	1 wk
13 Feb 71	**AIN'T NOTHING BUT A HOUSEPARTY** (re-entry of re-issue) *Beacon BEA 100*	**33**	1 wk
27 Feb 71	**AIN'T NOTHING BUT A HOUSEPARTY** (2nd re-entry of re-issue) *Beacon BEA 100*	**36**	1 wk

SHY *UK, male vocal/instrumental group*

Date	Title *Label Number*	Position	
19 Apr 80	**GIRL (IT'S ALL I HAVE)** *Gallery GA 1*	**60**	3 wks

Labi SIFFRE *UK, male vocalist*

Date	Title *Label Number*	Position	
27 Nov 71	**IT MUST BE LOVE** *Pye International 7N 25572*	**14**	12 wks
25 Mar 72	**CRYING LAUGHING LOVING LYING** *Pye International 7N 25576*	**11**	9 wks
29 Jul 72	**WATCH ME** *Pye International 7N 25586*	**29**	6 wks

SILKIE *UK, male/female vocal/instrumental group*

Date	Title *Label Number*	Position	
23 Sep 65	**YOU'VE GOT TO HIDE YOUR LOVE AWAY** *Fontana TF 603*	**28**	6 wks

SILVER BULLET BAND — See *Bob SEGER and the SILVER BULLET BAND*

SILVER CONVENTION *Germany/US, female vocal group*

Date	Title *Label Number*	Position	
5 Apr 75	**SAVE ME** *Magnet MAG 26*	**30**	7 wks
15 Nov 75	**FLY ROBIN FLY** *Magnet MAG 43*	**28**	8 wks
3 Apr 76	● **GET UP & BOOGIE** *Magnet MAG 55*	**7**	11 wks
19 Jun 76	**TIGER BABY/ NO NO JOE** *Magnet MAG 69*	**41**	4 wks
29 Jan 77	**EVERYBODY'S TALKIN' 'BOUT LOVE** *Magnet MAG 81*	**25**	5 wks

Dooley SILVERSPOON *US, male vocalist*

Date	Title *Label Number*	Position	
31 Jan 76	**LET ME BE THE NUMBER ONE** *Seville SEV 1020*	**44**	3 wks

Harry SIMEONE CHORALE *US, choir*

Date	Title *Label Number*	Position	
13 Feb 59	**LITTLE DRUMMER BOY** *Top Rank JAR 101*	**13**	7 wks
22 Dec 60	**ONWARD CHRISTIAN SOLDIERS** *Ember EMBS 118*	**35**	1 wk
5 Jan 61	**ONWARD CHRISTIAN SOLDIERS** (re-entry) *Ember EMBS 118*	**38**	1 wk
21 Dec 61	**ONWARD CHRISTIAN SOLDIERS** (2nd re-entry) *Ember EMBS 118*	**36**	3 wks
20 Dec 62	**ONWARD CHRISTIAN SOLDIERS** (re-issue) *Ember EMBS 144*	**38**	2 wks

Gene SIMMONS *US, male vocalist*

Date	Title *Label Number*	Position	
27 Jan 79	**RADIOACTIVE** *Casablanca CAN 134*	**41**	4 wks

SIMON and GARFUNKEL *US, male vocal duo*

Date	Title *Label Number*	Position	
24 Mar 66	● **HOMEWARD BOUND** *CBS 202045*	**9**	12 wks
16 Jun 66	**I AM A ROCK** *CBS 202303*	**17**	10 wks
10 Jul 68	● **MRS. ROBINSON** *CBS 3443*	**4**	12 wks
8 Jan 69	● **MRS. ROBINSON** (EP) *CBS EP 6400*	**9**	5 wks
30 May 69	● **THE BOXER** *CBS 4162*	**6**	14 wks
21 Feb 70	★ **BRIDGE OVER TROUBLED WATER** *CBS 4790*	**1**	19 wks
15 Aug 70	**BRIDGE OVER TROUBLED WATER** (re-entry) *CBS 4790*	**45**	1 wk
7 Oct 72	**AMERICA** *CBS 8336*	**25**	7 wks

See also Paul Simon, Art Garfunkel. Titles on Mrs. Robinson *EP: Mrs. Robinson/ Scarborough Fair-Canticle/ Sounds Of Silence/ April Come She Will. This EP would have stayed more than 5 weeks on chart had a decision to exclude EP's from the chart not been taken in February 69.*

Carly SIMON *US, female vocalist*

Date	Title *Label Number*	Position	
16 Dec 72	● **YOU'RE SO VAIN** *Elektra K 12077*	**3**	15 wks
31 Mar 73	**THE RIGHT THING TO DO** *Elektra K 12095*	**17**	9 wks
6 Aug 77	● **NOBODY DOES IT BETTER** *Elektra K 12261*	**7**	12 wks
21 Aug 82	● **WHY** *WEA K 79300*	**10**	13 wks

See also Carly Simon and James Taylor.

Carly SIMON and James TAYLOR *US, female/male vocal duo*

Date	Title *Label Number*	Position	
16 Mar 74	**MOCKINGBIRD** *Elektra K 12134*	**34**	5 wks

See also Carly Simon, James Taylor.

Joe SIMON *US, male vocalist*

Date	Title *Label Number*	Position	
16 Jun 73	**STEP BY STEP** *Mojo 2093 030*	**14**	10 wks

Paul SIMON *US, male vocalist*

Date	Title *Label Number*	Position	
19 Feb 72	● **MOTHER & CHILD REUNION** *CBS 7793*	**5**	12 wks
29 Apr 72	**ME & JULIO DOWN BY THE SCHOOLYARD** *CBS 7964*	**15**	9 wks
16 Jun 73	● **TAKE ME TO THE MARDI GRAS** *CBS 1578*	**7**	11 wks
22 Sep 73	**LOVES ME LIKE A ROCK** *CBS 1700*	**39**	5 wks
10 Jan 76	**50 WAYS TO LEAVE YOUR LOVER** *CBS 3887*	**23**	6 wks
3 Dec 77	**SLIP SLIDIN' AWAY** *CBS 5770*	**36**	5 wks
6 Sep 80	**LATE IN THE EVENING** *Warner Bros. K 17666*	**58**	4 wks

See also Simon and Garfunkel.

Tito SIMON *Jamaica, male vocalist*

Date	Title *Label Number*	Position	Weeks
8 Feb 75	**THIS MONDAY MORNING FEELING** *Horse HOSS 57*	**45**	4 wks

Nina SIMONE *US, female vocalist*

Date	Title *Label Number*	Position	Weeks
5 Aug 65	**I PUT A SPELL ON YOU** *Philips BF 1415*	**49**	1 wk
16 Oct 68 ●	**AIN'T GOT NO - I GOT LIFE/ DO WHAT YOU GOTTA DO** *RCA 1743*	**2**	18 wks
15 Jan 69 ●	**TO LOVE SOMEBODY** *RCA 1779*	**5**	9 wks
15 Jan 69	**I PUT A SPELL ON YOU** (re-issue) *Philips BF 1736*	**28**	4 wks

Do What You Gotta Do *was only credited on the charts for 8 weeks of the 18, its highest position being 7.*

SIMPLE MINDS

UK, male vocal/instrumental group

Date	Title *Label Number*	Position	Weeks
12 May 79	**LIFE IN A DAY** *Zoom ZUM 10*	**62**	2 wks
23 May 81	**THE AMERICAN** *Virgin VS 410*	**59**	3 wks
15 Aug 81	**LOVE SONG** *Virgin VS 434*	**47**	4 wks
7 Nov 81	**SWEAT IN BULLET** *Virgin VS 451*	**52**	3 wks
10 Apr 82	**PROMISED YOU A MIRACLE** *Virgin VS 488*	**13**	11 wks
28 Aug 82	**GLITTERING PRIZE** *Virgin VS 511*	**16**	11 wks
13 Nov 82	**SOMEONE SOMEWHERE (IN SUMMERTIME)** *Virgin VS 538*	**36**	5 wks

SIMPSON — See *ASHFORD and SIMPSON*

W/CDR. A. E. SIMS — See *Central Band of the ROYAL AIR FORCE, conductor W/CDR. A. E. SIMS, OBE*

Frank SINATRA *US, male vocalist*

Date	Title *Label Number*	Position	Weeks
9 Jul 54	**YOUNG AT HEART** *Capitol CL 14064*	**12**	1 wk
16 Jul 54 ★	**THREE COINS IN THE FOUNTAIN** *Capitol CL 14120*	**1**	19 wks
10 Jun 55	**YOU MY LOVE** *Capitol CL 14240*	**13**	3 wks
22 Jul 55	**YOU MY LOVE** (re-entry) *Capitol CL 14240*	**17**	2 wks
5 Aug 55 ●	**LEARNIN' THE BLUES** *Capitol CL 14296*	**2**	13 wks
12 Aug 55	**YOU MY LOVE** (2nd re-entry) *Capitol CL 14240*	**17**	2 wks
2 Sep 55	**NOT AS A STRANGER** *Capitol CL 14326*	**18**	1 wk
13 Jan 56 ●	**LOVE AND MARRIAGE** *Capitol CL 14503*	**3**	8 wks
20 Jan 56 ●	**THE TENDER TRAP** *Capitol CL 14511*	**2**	9 wks
15 Jun 56	**SONGS FOR SWINGING LOVERS** (LP) *Capitol LCT 6106*	**12**	8 wks
22 Nov 57	**ALL THE WAY** *Capitol CL 14800*	**29**	1 wk
29 Nov 57	**CHICAGO** *Capitol CL 14800*	**25**	1 wk
6 Dec 57	**ALL THE WAY/ CHICAGO** *Capitol CL 14800*	**21**	1 wk
13 Dec 57 ●	**ALL THE WAY** *Capitol CL 14800*	**3**	17 wks
7 Feb 58	**WITCHCRAFT** *Capitol CL 14819*	**12**	8 wks
14 Nov 58	**MR. SUCCESS** *Capitol CL 14956*	**29**	1 wk
12 Dec 58	**MR. SUCCESS** (re-entry) *Capitol CL 14956*	**25**	2 wks
2 Jan 59	**MR. SUCCESS** (2nd re-entry) *Capitol CL 14956*	**26**	1 wk
10 Apr 59	**FRENCH FOREIGN LEGION** *Capitol CL 14997*	**18**	5 wks
15 May 59	**COME DANCE WITH ME** (LP) *Capitol LCT 6179*	**30**	1 wk
28 Aug 59	**HIGH HOPES** *Capitol CL 15052*	**28**	1 wk
11 Sep 59 ●	**HIGH HOPES** (re-entry) *Capitol CL 15052*	**6**	13 wks
10 Mar 60	**HIGH HOPES** (2nd re-entry) *Capitol CL 15052*	**42**	1 wk
7 Apr 60	**IT'S NICE TO GO TRAV'LING** *Capitol CL 15116*	**48**	2 wks
16 Jun 60	**RIVER STAY 'WAY FROM MY DOOR** *Capitol CL 15135*	**18**	9 wks
8 Sep 60	**NICE 'N EASY** *Capitol CL 15150*	**15**	12 wks
24 Nov 60	**OL' MACDONALD** *Capitol CL 15168*	**11**	8 wks
20 Apr 61	**MY BLUE HEAVEN** *Capitol CL 15193*	**33**	7 wks
28 Sep 61	**GRANADA** *Reprise R 20010*	**15**	8 wks
23 Nov 61	**THE COFFEE SONG** *Reprise R 20035*	**39**	3 wks
5 Apr 62	**EVERYBODY'S TWISTING** *Reprise R 20063*	**22**	12 wks
7 Mar 63	**MY KIND OF GIRL** *Reprise R 20148*	**35**	6 wks
24 Sep 64	**HELLO DOLLY** *Reprise R 20351*	**47**	1 wk
12 May 66 ★	**STRANGERS IN THE NIGHT** *Reprise R 23052*	**1**	20 wks
29 Sep 66	**SUMMER WIND** *Reprise RS 20509*	**36**	5 wks
15 Dec 66	**THAT'S LIFE** *Reprise RS 20531*	**46**	5 wks
23 Aug 67	**THE WORLD WE KNEW** *Reprise RS 20610*	**33**	11 wks
2 Apr 69 ●	**MY WAY** *Reprise RS 20817*	**5**	42 wks
4 Oct 69 ●	**LOVE'S BEEN GOOD TO ME** *Reprise RS 20852*	**8**	18 wks
31 Jan 70	**MY WAY** (re-entry) *Reprise RS 20817*	**49**	1 wk
28 Feb 70	**MY WAY** (2nd re-entry) *Reprise RS 20817*	**30**	5 wks
11 Apr 70	**MY WAY** (3rd re-entry) *Reprise RS 20817*	**33**	9 wks
27 Jun 70	**MY WAY** (4th re-entry) *Reprise RS 20817*	**28**	21 wks
28 Nov 70	**MY WAY** (5th re-entry) *Reprise RS 20817*	**18**	16 wks
6 Mar 71	**I WILL DRINK THE WINE** *Reprise RS 23487*	**16**	12 wks
27 Mar 71	**MY WAY** (6th re-entry) *Reprise RS 20817*	**22**	19 wks
4 Sep 71	**MY WAY** (7th re-entry) *Reprise RS 20817*	**39**	8 wks
1 Jan 72	**MY WAY** (8th re-entry) *Reprise RS 20817*	**50**	1 wk
20 Dec 75	**I BELIEVE I'M GONNA LOVE YOU** *Reprise K 14400*	**34**	7 wks
9 Aug 80	**THEME FROM NEW YORK, NEW YORK** *Reprise K 14502*	**59**	4 wks

See also Frank Sinatra and Sammy Davis Jr., Nancy Sinatra and Frank Sinatra. My Kind Of Girl *and* Hello Dolly *with Count Basie. Tracks on* Songs For Swinging Lovers *LP: You Make Me Feel So Young/ It Happened In Monterey/ You're Getting To Be A Habit With Me/ You Bought A New Kind Of Love To Me/ Too Marvellous For Words/ Old Devil Moon/ Pennies From Heaven/ Love Is Here To Stay/ I've Got You Under My Skin/ I Thought About You/ We'll Be Together Again/ Making Whoopee/ Swingin' Down The Lane/ Anything Goes/ How About You. On* Come Dance With Me *LP: Something's Gotta Give/ Just In Time/ Dancing In The Dark/ Too Close For Comfort/ I Could Have Danced All Night/ Saturday Night Is The Loneliest Night Of The Week/ Day In Day Out/ Cheek To Cheek/ Baubles Bangles And Beads/ The Song Is You/ The Last Dance.* All The Way *and* Chicago, *Capitol CL 14800, were at first billed separately, then together for one week, then* All The Way *on its own.*

Frank SINATRA and Sammy DAVIS JR. *US, male vocal duo*

Date	Title *Label Number*	Position	Weeks
13 Dec 62	**ME AND MY SHADOW** *Reprise R 20128*	**20**	7 wks
7 Feb 63	**ME AND MY SHADOW** (re-entry) *Reprise R 20128*	**47**	2 wks

See also Frank Sinatra, Sammy Davis Jr., Nancy Sinatra and Frank Sinatra, Sammy Davis Jr. and Carmen McRae.

Nancy SINATRA *US, female vocalist*

Date	Title *Label Number*	Position	Weeks
27 Jan 66 ★	**THESE BOOTS ARE MADE FOR WALKIN'** *Reprise R 20432*	**1**	14 wks
28 Apr 66	**HOW DOES THAT GRAB YOU DARLIN'** *Reprise R 20461*	**19**	8 wks
19 Jan 67 ●	**SUGAR TOWN** *Reprise RS 20527*	**8**	10 wks
5 Jul 67	**YOU ONLY LIVE TWICE/ JACKSON** *Reprise RS 20595*	**11**	19 wks
29 Nov 69	**HIGHWAY SONG** *Reprise RS 20869*	**21**	10 wks

See also Nancy Sinatra and Frank Sinatra, Nancy Sinatra and Lee Hazelwood. Jackson *was billed together with* You Only Live Twice *from 12 Jul 67.* Jackson *is by Nancy Sinatra and Lee Hazelwood.*

Nancy SINATRA and Lee HAZELWOOD *US, male/female vocal duo*

Date	Title *Label Number*	Position	Weeks
8 Nov 67	**LADYBIRD** *Reprise RS 20629*	**47**	1 wk
21 Aug 71 ●	**DID YOU EVER** *Reprise K 14093*	**2**	19 wks

See also Nancy Sinatra, Nancy Sinatra and Frank Sinatra. Did You Ever *bills the duo simply as Nancy and Lee.*

Nancy SINATRA and Frank SINATRA

US, female/male vocal duo

23 Mar 67 ★ **SOMETHIN' STUPID** *Reprise RS 23166* **1** 18 wks

See also Nancy Sinatra, Nancy Sinatra and Lee Hazelwood, Frank Sinatra, Frank Sinatra and Sammy Davis Jr.

SINE *US, Disco aggregation*

10 Jun 78 **JUST LET ME DO MY THING** *CBS 6351* **33** 9 wks

SINGING DOGS *US, canine vocal group*

25 Nov 55 **THE SINGING DOGS** (MEDLEY) *Nixa N 15009* **13** 4 wks

Medley Songs: Pat-a-cake/ Three Blind Mice/ Jingle Bells/ Oh Susanna.

SINGING NUN (Soeur Sourire)

Belgium, female vocalist

5 Dec 63 ● **DOMINIQUE** *Philips BF 1293* **7** 13 wks

SINGING SHEEP *UK, computerised sheep noises*

18 Dec 82 **BAA BAA BLACK SHEEP** *Sheep/Virgin BAA 1* **42**† 2 wks

SIOUXSIE and the BANSHEES

UK, male/female vocal/instrumental group

26 Aug 78 ● **HONG KONG GARDEN** *Polydor 2059 052* **7** 10 wks
31 Mar 79 **THE STAIRCASE (MYSTERY)** *Polydor POSP 9* **24** 8 wks
7 Jul 79 **PLAYGROUND TWIST** *Polydor POSP 59* **28** 6 wks
29 Sep 79 **MITTAGEISEN (METAL POSTCARD)** *Polydor 2059 151* **47** 3 wks
15 Mar 80 **HAPPY HOUSE** *Polydor POSP 117* **17** 8 wks
7 Jun 80 **CHRISTINE** *Polydor 2059 249* **24** 8 wks
6 Dec 80 **ISRAEL** *Polydor POSP 205* **41** 8 wks
30 May 81 **SPELLBOUND** *Polydor POSP 273* **22** 8 wks
1 Aug 81 **ARABIAN KNIGHTS** *Polydor POSP 309* **32** 7 wks
29 May 82 **FIRE WORKS** *Polydor POSPG 450* **22** 6 wks
9 Oct 82 **SLOWDRIVE** *Polydor POSP 510* **41** 4 wks
4 Dec 82 **MELT/IL EST NE LE DIVIN ENFANT** *Polydor POSP 539* **49**† 4 wks

See also Creatures

SIR DOUGLAS QUINTET

US, male vocal/instrumental group

17 Jun 65 **SHE'S ABOUT A MOVER** *London HLU 9964* **15** 10 wks

SISTER SLEDGE *US, female vocal group*

21 Jun 75 **MAMA NEVER TOLD ME** *Atlantic K 10619* **20** 6 wks
17 Mar 79 ● **HE'S THE GREATEST DANCER** *Atlantic/Cotillion K 11257* **6** 11 wks
26 May 79 ● **WE ARE FAMILY** *Atlantic/Cotillion K 11293* **8** 10 wks
11 Aug 79 **LOST IN MUSIC** *Atlantic/Cotillion K 11337* **17** 10 wks
19 Jan 80 **GOT TO LOVE SOMEBODY** *Atlantic/Cotillion K 11404* **34** 4 wks
28 Feb 81 **ALL AMERICAN GIRLS** *Atlantic K 11656* **41** 5 wks

SKATALITES *Jamaica, male instrumental group*

20 Apr 67 **GUNS OF NAVARONE** *Island WI 168* **36** 6 wks

Peter SKELLERN *UK, male vocalist*

23 Sep 72 ● **YOU'RE A LADY** *Decca F 13333* **3** 11 wks
29 Mar 75 **HOLD ON TO LOVE** *Decca F 13568* **14** 9 wks
28 Oct 78 **LOVE IS THE SWEETEST THING** *Mercury 6008 603* **60** 4 wks

Last hit has credit: Featuring Grimethorpe Colliery Band.

SKIDS *UK, male vocal/instrumental group*

23 Sep 78 **SWEET SUBURBIA** *Virgin VS 227* **70** 1 wk
7 Oct 78 **SWEET SUBURBIA** (re-entry) *Virgin VS 227* **71** 2 wks
4 Nov 78 **THE SAINTS ARE COMING** *Virgin VS 232* **48** 3 wks
17 Feb 79 ● **INTO THE VALLEY** *Virgin VS 241* **10** 11 wks
26 May 79 **MASQUERADE** *Virgin VS 262* **14** 9 wks
29 Sep 79 **CHARADE** *Virgin VS 288* **31** 6 wks
24 Nov 79 **WORKING FOR THE YANKEE DOLLAR** *Virgin VS 306* **20** 11 wks
1 Mar 80 **ANIMATION** *Virgin VS 323* **56** 3 wks
16 Aug 80 **CIRCUS GAMES** *Virgin VS 359* **32** 7 wks
18 Oct 80 **GOODBYE CIVILIAN** *Virgin VS 373* **52** 4 wks
6 Dec 80 **WOMEN IN WINTER** *Virgin VSK 101* **49** 3 wks

SKY *UK/Australia, male instrumental group*

5 Apr 80 ● **TOCCATA** *Ariola ARO 300* **5** 11 wks

SKYHOOKS

Australia, male vocal/instrumental group

9 Jun 79 **WOMEN IN UNIFORM** *United Artists UP 36508* **73** 1 wk

SLADE *UK, male vocal/instrumental group*

19 Jun 71 **GET DOWN AND GET WITH IT** *Polydor 2058 112* **16** 14 wks
30 Oct 71 ★ **COZ I LUV YOU** *Polydor 2058 155* **1** 15 wks
5 Feb 72 ● **LOOK WOT YOU DUN** *Polydor 2058 195* **4** 10 wks
3 Jun 72 ★ **TAKE ME BAK 'OME** *Polydor 2058 231* **1** 13 wks
2 Sep 72 ★ **MAMA WEER ALL CRAZEE NOW** *Polydor 2058 274* **1** 10 wks
25 Nov 72 ● **GUDBUY T'JANE** *Polydor 2058 312* **2** 12 wks
3 Mar 73 ★ **CUM ON FEEL THE NOIZE** *Polydor 2058 339* **1** 12 wks
30 Jun 73 ★ **SKWEEZE ME PLEEZE ME** *Polydor 2058 377* **1** 10 wks
6 Oct 73 ● **MY FREND STAN** *Polydor 2058 407* **2** 8 wks
15 Dec 73 ★ **MERRY XMAS EVERYBODY** *Polydor 2058 422* **1** 9 wks
6 Apr 74 ● **EVERYDAY** *Polydor 2058 453* **3** 7 wks
6 Jul 74 ● **BANGIN' MAN** *Polydor 2058 492* **3** 7 wks
19 Oct 74 ● **FAR FAR AWAY** *Polydor 2058 522* **2** 6 wks
15 Feb 75 **HOW DOES IT FEEL** *Polydor 2058 547* **15** 7 wks
17 May 75 ● **THANKS FOR THE MEMORY (WHAM BAM THANK YOU MAM)** *Polydor 2058 585* **7** 7 wks
22 Nov 75 **IN FOR A PENNY** *Polydor 2058 663* **11** 8 wks
7 Feb 76 **LET'S CALL IT QUITS** *Polydor 2058 690* **11** 7 wks
5 Feb 77 **GYPSY ROAD HOG** *Barn 2014 105* **48** 2 wks
29 Oct 77 **MY BABY LEFT ME-THAT'S ALL RIGHT** (MEDLEY) *Barn 2014 114* **32** 4 wks
18 Oct 80 **SLADE ALIVE AT READING '80** (EP) *Cheapskate CHEAP 5* **44** 5 wks
27 Dec 80 **MERRY XMAS EVERYBODY** *Cheapskate CHEAP 11* **70** 2 wks

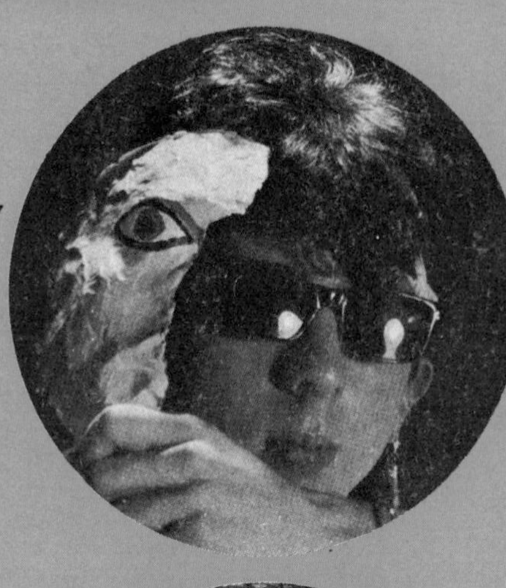

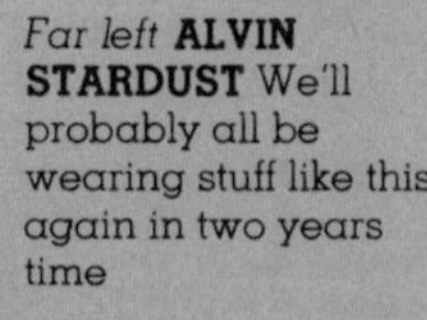

Far left **ALVIN STARDUST** We'll probably all be wearing stuff like this again in two years time

Left **SOFT CELL** In 1982 Soft Cell became the first ever duo to spend more weeks on the chart in one year than any other act

Right **HURRICANE SMITH** Norman Hurricane Smith – Beatles engineer Pink Floyd's producer solo hitmaker

Right **DON SPENCER** XL-ed for 12 weeks with the theme from the TV puppet show

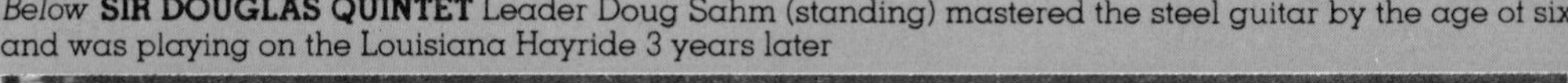

Left **STRAY CATS** The 'Cats' fronted by Brian Setzer. They brought 80s style rockabilly to the chart until they strayed musically

Below **SIR DOUGLAS QUINTET** Leader Doug Sahm (standing) mastered the steel guitar by the age of six and was playing on the Louisiana Hayride 3 years later

Date	Title *Label Number*	Position	
31 Jan 81	● **WE'LL BRING THE HOUSE DOWN** *Cheapskate CHEAP 16*	**10**	9 wks
4 Apr 81	**WHEELS AIN'T COMING DOWN** *Cheapskate CHEAP 21*	**60**	3 wks
4 Apr 81	**LOCK UP YOUR DAUGHTERS** *RCA 124*	**29**	8 wks
19 Dec 81	**MERRY XMAS EVERYBODY** (re-entry) *Polydor 2058 422*	**32**	4 wks
27 Mar 82	**RUBY RED** *RCA 191*	**51**	3 wks
27 Nov 82	**(AND NOW - THE WALTZ) C'EST LA VIE** *RCA 291*	**50**†	5 wks
25 Dec 82	**MERRY XMAS EVERYBODY** (2nd re-entry) *Polydor 2058 422*	**67**†	1 wk

Tracks on Slade Alive at Reading '80 EP: *When I'm Dancin' I Ain't Fightin'; Born To Be Wild; Somethin' Else; Pistol Packin' Mama; Keep A Rollin'.* Merry Xmas Everybody *on Cheapskate is credited to Slade and the Reading Choir and is a re-recording.*

SLAVE *US, male vocal/instrumental group*

Date	Title *Label Number*	Position	
8 Mar 80	**JUST A TOUCH OF LOVE** *Atlantic/Cotillion K 11442*	**64**	3 wks

Percy SLEDGE *US, male vocalist*

Date	Title *Label Number*	Position	
12 May 66	● **WHEN A MAN LOVES A WOMAN** *Atlantic 584 001*	**4**	17 wks
4 Aug 66	**WARM & TENDER LOVE** *Atlantic 584 034*	**34**	7 wks

SLICK *US, male/female vocal/instrumental group*

Date	Title *Label Number*	Position	
16 Jun 79	**SPACE BASS** *Fantasy FTC 176*	**16**	10 wks
15 Sep 79	**SEXY CREAM** *Fantasy FTC 182*	**47**	5 wks

Grace SLICK *US, female vocalist*

Date	Title *Label Number*	Position	
24 May 80	**DREAMS** *RCA PB 9534*	**50**	4 wks

SLIK *UK, male vocal/instrumental group*

Date	Title *Label Number*	Position	
17 Jan 76	★ **FOREVER & EVER** *Bell 1464*	**1**	9 wks
8 May 76	**REQUIEM** *Bell 1478*	**24**	9 wks

SLIM CHANCE — See *Ronnie LANE*

SLITS *UK, female vocal/instrumental group*

Date	Title *Label Number*	Position	
13 Oct 79	**TYPICAL GIRLS/I HEARD IT THROUGH THE GRAPEVINE** *Island WIP 6505*	**60**	3 wks

P. F. SLOAN *US, male vocalist*

Date	Title *Label Number*	Position	
4 Nov 65	**SINS OF THE FAMILY** *RCA 1482*	**38**	3 wks

SLY and the FAMILY STONE

US, male/female vocal/instrumental group. Sly Stone, vocals and keyboards

Date	Title *Label Number*	Position	
10 Jul 68	● **DANCE TO THE MUSIC** *Direction 58 3568*	**7**	14 wks
2 Oct 68	**M'LADY** *Direction 58 3707*	**32**	7 wks
19 Mar 69	**EVERYDAY PEOPLE** *Direction 58 3938*	**36**	1 wk
9 Apr 69	**EVERYDAY PEOPLE** (re-entry) *Direction 58 3938*	**37**	4 wks
8 Jan 72	**FAMILY AFFAIR** *Epic EPC 7632*	**15**	8 wks
15 Apr 72	**RUNNIN' AWAY** *Epic EPC 7810*	**17**	8 wks

Date Title *Label Number* Position

SMALL ADS *UK, male vocal/instrumental group*

Date	Title *Label Number*	Position	
18 Apr 81	**SMALL ADS** *Bronze BRO 115*	**63**	3 wks

SMALL FACES *UK, male vocal/instrumental group*

Date	Title *Label Number*	Position	
2 Sep 65	**WHATCHA GONNA DO ABOUT IT?** *Decca F 12208*	**14**	12 wks
10 Feb 66	● **SHA LA LA LA LEE** *Decca F 12317*	**3**	11 wks
12 May 66	● **HEY GIRL** *Decca F 12393*	**10**	9 wks
11 Aug 66	★ **ALL OR NOTHING** *Decca F 12470*	**1**	12 wks
17 Nov 66	● **MY MIND'S EYE** *Decca F 12500*	**4**	11 wks
9 Mar 67	**I CAN'T MAKE IT** *Decca F 12565*	**26**	7 wks
8 Jun 67	**HERE COMES THE NICE** *Immediate IM 050*	**12**	10 wks
9 Aug 67	● **ITCHYCOO PARK** *Immediate IM 057*	**3**	14 wks
6 Dec 67	● **TIN SOLDIER** *Immediate IM 062*	**9**	12 wks
17 Apr 68	● **LAZY SUNDAY** *Immediate IM 064*	**2**	11 wks
10 Jul 68	**UNIVERSAL** *Immediate IM 069*	**16**	11 wks
19 Mar 69	**AFTERGLOW OF YOUR LOVE** *Immediate IM 077*	**36**	1 wk
13 Dec 75	● **ITCHYCOO PARK** (re-issue) *Immediate IMS 102*	**9**	11 wks
20 Mar 76	**LAZY SUNDAY** (re-issue) *Immediate IMS 106*	**39**	5 wks

See also Faces

Hurricane SMITH *UK, male vocalist*

Date	Title *Label Number*	Position	
12 Jun 71	● **DON'T LET IT DIE** *Columbia DB 8785*	**2**	12 wks
29 Apr 72	● **OH BABE WHAT WOULD YOU SAY?** *Columbia DB 8878*	**4**	16 wks
2 Sep 72	**WHO WAS IT** *Columbia DB 8916*	**23**	7 wks

Jimmy SMITH *US, male instrumentalist, organ*

Date	Title *Label Number*	Position	
28 Apr 66	**GOT MY MOJO WORKING** *Verve VS 536*	**48**	2 wks
19 May 66	**GOT MY MOJO WORKING** (re-entry) *Verve VS 536*	**48**	1 wk

Keely SMITH *US, female vocalist*

Date	Title *Label Number*	Position	
18 Mar 65	**YOU'RE BREAKIN' MY HEART** *Reprise R 20346*	**14**	10 wks

Muriel SMITH *UK, female vocalist*

Date	Title *Label Number*	Position	
15 May 53	● **HOLD ME THRILL ME KISS ME** *Philips PB 122*	**3**	17 wks

O. C. SMITH *US, male vocalist*

Date	Title *Label Number*	Position	
29 May 68	● **SON OF HICKORY HOLLER'S TRAMP** *CBS 3343*	**2**	15 wks
26 Mar 77	**TOGETHER** *Caribou CRB 4910*	**25**	8 wks

Rex SMITH and Rachel SWEET

US, male/female vocal duo

Date	Title *Label Number*	Position	
22 Aug 81	**EVERLASTING LOVE** *CBS A 1405*	**35**	7 wks

see also Rachel Sweet

Whistling Jack SMITH *UK, male whistler*

Date	Title *Label Number*	Position	
2 Mar 67	● **I WAS KAISER BILL'S BATMAN** *Deram DM 112*	**5**	12 wks

Date **Title** *Label Number* **Position**

Date **Title** *Label Number* **Position**

Patti SMITH GROUP

US, female vocalist, male instrumental backing group

29 Apr 78 ● **BECAUSE THE NIGHT** *Arista 181* **5** 12 wks
19 Aug 78 **PRIVILEGE (SET ME FREE)** *Arista 197* **72** 1 wk
2 Jun 79 **FREDERICK** *Arista 264* **63** 3 wks

SMOKE *UK, male vocal/instrumental group*

9 Mar 67 **MY FRIEND JACK** *Columbia DB 8115* **45** 3 wks

SMOKIE *UK, male vocal/instrumental group*

19 Jul 75 ● **IF YOU THINK YOU KNOW HOW TO LOVE ME** *RAK 206* **3** 9 wks
4 Oct 75 ● **DON'T PLAY YOUR ROCK'N ROLL TO ME** *RAK 217* **8** 7 wks
31 Jan 76 **SOMETHING'S BEEN MAKING ME BLUE** *RAK 227* **17** 8 wks
25 Sep 76 **I'LL MEET YOU AT MIDNIGHT** *RAK 241* **11** 9 wks
4 Dec 76 ● **LIVING NEXT DOOR TO ALICE** *RAK 244* **5** 11 wks
19 Mar 77 **LAY BACK IN THE ARMS OF SOMEONE** *RAK 251* **12** 9 wks
16 Jul 77 ● **IT'S YOUR LIFE** *RAK 260* **5** 9 wks
15 Oct 77 ● **NEEDLES AND PINS** *RAK 263* **10** 9 wks
28 Jan 78 **FOR A FEW DOLLARS MORE** *RAK 267* **17** 6 wks
20 May 78 ● **OH CAROL** *RAK 276* **5** 13 wks
23 Sep 78 **MEXICAN GIRL** *RAK 283* **19** 9 wks
19 Apr 80 **TAKE GOOD CARE OF MY BABY** *RAK 309* **34** 7 wks

Group were spelled Smokey for first two hits.

SMURFS — See *Father ABRAHAM and the SMURFS*

SMURPS — See *Father ABRAPHART and the SMURPS*

SNIFF 'N' THE TEARS

UK, male vocal/instrumental group

23 Jun 79 **DRIVER'S SEAT** *Chiswick CHIS 105* **42** 5 wks

Phoebe SNOW *US, female vocalist*

6 Jan 79 **EVERY NIGHT** *CBS 6842* **37** 7 wks

SNOWMEN *UK, male vocal/instrumental group*

12 Dec 81 **HOKEY COKEY** *Stiff ODB 1* **18** 8 wks
18 Dec 82 **XMAS PARTY** *Solid STOP 006* **44**† 2 wks

Gino SOCCIO

Canada, male instrumentalist - keyboards

28 Apr 79 **DANCER** *Warner Bros. LV23/K 17357* **46** 5 wks

SOFT CELL *UK, male vocal/instrumental duo*

1 Aug 81 ★ **TAINTED LOVE** *Some Bizzarre BZS 2* **1** 16 wks
14 Nov 81 ● **BED SITTER** *Some Bizzarre BZS 6* **4** 12 wks
9 Jan 82 **TAINTED LOVE** (re-entry) *Some Bizzarre BZS 2* **43** 10 wks
6 Feb 82 ● **SAY HELLO WAVE GOODBYE** *Some Bizzarre BZS 7* **3** 9 wks
29 May 82 ● **TORCH** *Some Bizzarre BZS 9* **2** 9 wks
24 Jul 82 **TAINTED LOVE** (2nd re-entry) *Some Bizzarre BZS 2* **50** 4 wks
21 Aug 82 ● **WHAT** *Some Bizzarre BZS 11* **3** 8 wks
4 Dec 82 **WHERE THE HEART IS** *Some Bizzarre BZS 16* **21**† 4 wks

SONNY *US, male vocalist*

19 Aug 65 ● **LAUGH AT ME** *Atlantic AT 4038* **9** 11 wks

See also Sonny and Cher.

SONNY and CHER *US, male/female vocal duo*

12 Aug 65 ★ **I GOT YOU BABE** *Atlantic AT 4035* **1** 12 wks
16 Sep 65 **BABY DON'T GO** *Reprise R 20309* **11** 9 wks
21 Oct 65 **BUT YOU'RE MINE** *Atlantic AT 4047* **17** 8 wks
17 Feb 66 **WHAT NOW MY LOVE** *Atlantic AT 4069* **13** 11 wks
30 Jun 66 **HAVE I STAYED TOO LONG** *Atlantic 584 018* **42** 3 wks
8 Sep 66 ● **LITTLE MAN** *Atlantic 584 040* **4** 10 wks
17 Nov 66 **LIVING FOR YOU** *Atlantic 584 057* **44** 4 wks
2 Feb 67 **THE BEAT GOES ON** *Atlantic 584 078* **29** 8 wks
15 Jan 72 ● **ALL I EVER NEED IS YOU** *MCA MU 1145* **8** 12 wks

See also Sonny, Cher.

SORROWS *UK, male vocal/instrumental group*

16 Sep 65 **TAKE A HEART** *Piccadilly 7N 35260* **21** 8 wks

S.O.S. BAND

US, male/female vocal/instrumental group

19 Jul 80 **TAKE YOUR TIME (DO IT RIGHT) PART 1** *Tabu TBU 8564* **51** 4 wks

David SOUL *US, male vocalist*

18 Dec 76 ★ **DON'T GIVE UP ON US** *Private Stock PVT 84* **1** 16 wks
26 Mar 77 ● **GOING IN WITH MY EYES OPEN** *Private Stock PVT 99* **2** 8 wks
27 Aug 77 ★ **SILVER LADY** *Private Stock PVT 115* **1** 14 wks
17 Dec 77 ● **LET'S HAVE A QUIET NIGHT IN** *Private Stock PVT 130* **8** 9 wks
27 May 78 **IT SURE BRINGS OUT THE LOVE IN YOUR EYES** *Private Stock PVT 137* **12** 9 wks

Jimmy SOUL *US, male vocalist*

11 Jul 63 **IF YOU WANNA BE HAPPY** *Stateside SS 178* **39** 2 wks

SOUL BROTHERS

UK, male vocal/instrumental group

22 Apr 65 **I KEEP RINGING MY BABY** *Decca F 12116* **42** 3 wks

SOUL SONIC FORCE — See *AFRICA BAMBAATA and the SOUL SONIC FORCE*

SOUND 9418 *Jonathan King again*

7 Feb 76 **IN THE MOOD** *UK 121* **46** 3 wks

See also Jonathan King

Date	Title *Label Number*	Position	

SOUNDS INCORPORATED

UK, male instrumental group

Date	Title *Label Number*	Position	
23 Apr 64	**THE SPARTANS** *Columbia DB 7239*	**30**	6 wks
30 Jul 64	**SPANISH HARLEM** *Columbia DB 7321*	**35**	5 wks

SOUNDS NICE *UK, male instrumental group*

Date	Title *Label Number*	Position	
6 Sep 69	**LOVE AT FIRST SIGHT (JE T'AIME ... MOI NON PLUS) PARLOPHONE** *R 5797*	**18**	11 wks

Has credit: Tim Mycroft on organ.

SOUNDS ORCHESTRAL *UK, orchestra*

Date	Title *Label Number*	Position	
3 Dec 64	● **CAST YOUR FATE TO THE WIND** *Piccadilly 7N 35206*	**5**	16 wks
8 Jul 65	**MOONGLOW** *Piccadilly 7N 35248*	**43**	2 wks

Joe SOUTH *US, male vocalist*

Date	Title *Label Number*	Position	
5 Mar 69	● **GAMES PEOPLE PLAY** *Capitol CL 15579*	**6**	11 wks

Jeri SOUTHERN *US, female vocalist*

Date	Title *Label Number*	Position	
21 Jun 57	**FIRE DOWN BELOW** *Brunswick 05665*	**22**	3 wks

SOUTHLANDERS *UK, male vocal group*

Date	Title *Label Number*	Position	
22 Nov 57	**ALONE** *Decca F 10946*	**17**	10 wks

SOVEREIGN COLLECTION *UK, orchestra*

Date	Title *Label Number*	Position	
3 Apr 71	**MOZART 40** *Capitol CL 15676*	**27**	6 wks

Red SOVINE *US male vocalist*

Date	Title *Label Number*	Position	
13 Jun 81	● **TEDDY BEAR** *Starday SD 142*	**4**	8 wks

Bob B SOXX and the BLUE JEANS

US, male/female vocal group

Date	Title *Label Number*	Position	
31 Jan 63	**ZIP-A-DEE-DOO-DAH** *London HLU 9646*	**45**	2 wks

SPACE *France, male instrumental group*

Date	Title *Label Number*	Position	
13 Aug 77	● **MAGIC FLY** *Pye International 7N 25746*	**2**	12 wks

SPANDAU BALLET

UK, male vocal/instrumental group

Date	Title *Label Number*	Position	
15 Nov 80	● **TO CUT A LONG STORY SHORT** *Reformation/Chrysalis CHS 2473*	**5**	11 wks
24 Jan 81	**THE FREEZE** *Reformation/Chrysalis CHS 2486*	**17**	8 wks
4 Apr 81	● **MUSCLEBOUND/GLOW** *Reformation/Chrysalis CHS 2509*	**10**	10 wks
18 Jul 81	● **CHANT NO.1 (I DON'T NEED THIS PRESSURE ON)** *Reformation/Chrysalis CHS 2528*	**3**	10 wks
14 Nov 81	**PAINT ME DOWN** *Chrysalis CHS 2560*	**30**	5 wks
30 Jan 82	**SHE LOVED LIKE DIAMOND** *Chrysalis CHS 2585*	**49**	4 wks
10 Apr 82	● **INSTINCTION** *Chrysalis CHS 2602*	**10**	11 wks
2 Oct 82	● **LIFELINE** *Chrysalis CHS 2642*	**7**	9 wks

SPARKS *US/UK, male vocal/instrumental group*

Date	Title *Label Number*	Position	
4 May 74	● **THIS TOWN AIN'T BIG ENOUGH FOR BOTH OF US** *Island WIP 6193*	**2**	10 wks
20 Jul 74	● **AMATEUR HOUR** *Island WIP 6203*	**7**	9 wks
19 Oct 74	**NEVER TURN YOUR BACK ON MOTHER EARTH** *Island WIP 6211*	**13**	7 wks
18 Jan 75	**SOMETHING FOR THE GIRL WITH EVERYTHING** *Island WIP 6221*	**17**	7 wks
19 Jul 75	**GET IN THE SWING** *Island WIP 6236*	**27**	7 wks
4 Oct 75	**LOOKS LOOKS LOOKS** *Island WIP 6249*	**26**	4 wks
21 Apr 79	**THE NUMBER ONE SONG IN HEAVEN** *Virgin VS 244*	**14**	12 wks
21 Jul 79	● **BEAT THE CLOCK** *Virgin VS 270*	**10**	9 wks
27 Oct 79	**TRYOUTS FOR THE HUMAN RACE** *Virgin VS 289*	**45**	5 wks

Billie Jo SPEARS *US, female vocalist*

Date	Title *Label Number*	Position	
12 Jul 75	● **BLANKET ON THE GROUND** *United Artists UP 35805*	**6**	13 wks
17 Jul 76	● **WHAT I'VE GOT IN MIND** *United Artists UP 36118*	**4**	13 wks
11 Dec 76	**SING ME AN OLD FASHIONED SONG** *United Artists UP 36179*	**34**	9 wks
21 Jul 79	**I WILL SURVIVE** *United Artists UP 601*	**47**	5 wks

The SPECIALS *UK, male vocal/instrumental group*

Date	Title *Label Number*	Position	
28 Jul 79	● **GANGSTERS** *2 Tone TT 1*	**6**	12 wks
27 Oct 79	● **A MESSAGE TO YOU RUDY/NITE CLUB** *2 TONE CHS TT5*	**10**	14 wks
26 Jan 80	★ **TOO MUCH TOO YOUNG** (EP) *2 Tone CHS TT 7*	**1**	10 wks
24 May 80	● **RAT RACE/RUDE BUOYS OUTA JAIL** *2 Tone CHS TT 11*	**5**	9 wks
20 Sep 80	● **STEREOTYPE/INTERNATIONAL JET SET** *2 Tone CHS TT 13*	**6**	8 wks
13 Dec 80	● **DO NOTHING/MAGGIE'S FARM** *2 Tone CHS TT 16*	**4**	11 wks
20 Jun 81	★ **GHOST TOWN** *2 Tone CHS TT 17*	**1**	14 wks

Gangsters *credited to the Special A.K.A. second hit billed as The Specials (featuring Rico &). Tracks on* Too Much Too Young (EP)*: Too Much Too Young/Guns of Navarone/Long Shot Kick de Bucket/Liquidator/Skinhead Moonstomp Farm listed from 10 Jan 81 only*

Chris SPEDDING

UK, male vocalist/instrumentalist, guitar

Date	Title *Label Number*	Position	
23 Aug 75	**MOTOR BIKING** *RAK 210*	**14**	8 wks

Johnny SPENCE *UK, orchestra*

Date	Title *Label Number*	Position	
1 Mar 62	**THEME FROM DR. KILDARE** *Parlophone R 4872*	**15**	15 wks

Don SPENCER *UK, male vocalist*

Date	Title *Label Number*	Position	
21 Mar 63	**FIREBALL** *HMV POP 1087*	**32**	11 wks
13 Jun 63	**FIREBALL** (re-entry) *HMV POP 1087*	**49**	1 wk

SPINNERS — See *DETROIT SPINNERS*

Date	Title *Label Number*	Position		Date	Title *Label Number*	Position	

SPLINTER *UK, male vocal/instrumental duo*

Date	Title *Label Number*	Position	Wks
2 Nov 74	**COSTAFINE TOWN** *Dark Horse AMS 7135*	**17**	10 wks

SPLIT ENZ *NZ/UK male vocal/instrumental group*

Date	Title *Label Number*	Position	Wks
16 Aug 80	**I GOT YOU** *A&M AMS 7546*	**12**	11 wks
23 May 81	**HISTORY NEVER REPEATS** *A & M AMS 8128*	**63**	4 wks

SPLODGENESSABOUNDS

UK, male vocal/instrumental group

Date	Title *Label Number*	Position	Wks
14 Jun 80	● **SIMON TEMPLAR/TWO PINTS OF LAGER** *Deram BUM 1*	**7**	8 wks
6 Sep 80	**TWO LITTLE BOYS/HORSE** *Deram ROLF 1*	**26**	7 wks
13 Jun 81	**COWPUNK MEDIUM** *Deram BUM 3*	**69**	2 wks

SPOTNICKS *Sweden, male instrumental group*

Date	Title *Label Number*	Position	Wks
14 Jun 62	**ORANGE BLOSSOM SPECIAL** *Oriole CB 1724*	**29**	10 wks
6 Sep 62	**ROCKET MAN** *Oriole CB 1755*	**38**	9 wks
31 Jan 63	**HAVA NAGILA** *Oriole CB 1790*	**13**	12 wks
25 Apr 63	**JUST LISTEN TO MY HEART** *Oriole CB 1818*	**36**	6 wks

Dusty SPRINGFIELD *UK, female vocalist*

Date	Title *Label Number*	Position	Wks
21 Nov 63	● **I ONLY WANT TO BE WITH YOU** *Philips BF 1292*	**4**	18 wks
20 Feb 64	**STAY AWHILE** *Philips BF 1311*	**13**	10 wks
2 Jul 64	● **I JUST DON'T KNOW WHAT TO DO WITH MYSELF** *Philips BF 1348*	**3**	12 wks
22 Oct 64	● **LOSING YOU** *Philips BF 1369*	**9**	13 wks
18 Feb 65	**YOUR HURTIN' KIND OF LOVE** *Philips BF 1396*	**37**	4 wks
1 Jul 65	● **IN THE MIDDLE OF NOWHERE** *Philips BF 1418*	**8**	10 wks
16 Sep 65	● **SOME OF YOUR LOVIN'** *Philips BF 1430*	**8**	12 wks
27 Jan 66	**LITTLE BY LITTLE** *Philips BF 1466*	**17**	9 wks
31 Mar 66	★ **YOU DON'T HAVE TO SAY YOU LOVE ME** *Philips BF 1482*	**1**	13 wks
7 Jul 66	● **GOING BACK** *Philips BF 1502*	**10**	10 wks
15 Sep 66	● **ALL I SEE IS YOU** *Philips BF 1510*	**9**	12 wks
23 Feb 67	**I'LL TRY ANYTHING** *Philips BF 1553*	**13**	9 wks
25 May 67	**GIVE ME TIME** *Philips BF 1577*	**24**	6 wks
10 Jul 68	● **I CLOSE MY EYES AND COUNT TO TEN** *Philips BF 1682*	**4**	12 wks
4 Dec 68	● **SON OF A PREACHER MAN** *Philips BF 1730*	**9**	9 wks
20 Sep 69	**AM I THE SAME GIRL** *Philips BF 1811*	**43**	3 wks
18 Oct 69	**AM I THE SAME GIRL** (re-entry) *Philips BF 1811*	**46**	1 wk
19 Sep 70	**HOW CAN I BE SURE** *Philips 6006 045*	**36**	4 wks
20 Oct 79	**BABY BLUE** *Mercury DUSTY 4*	**61**	5 wks

See also Springfields.

SPRINGFIELDS

UK, male/female vocal/instrumental group

Date	Title *Label Number*	Position	Wks
31 Aug 61	**BREAKAWAY** *Philips BF 1168*	**31**	8 wks
16 Nov 61	**BAMBINO** *Philips BF 1178*	**16**	11 wks
13 Dec 62	● **ISLAND OF DREAMS** *Philips 326557 BF*	**5**	26 wks
28 Mar 63	● **SAY I WON'T BE THERE** *Philips 326577 BF*	**5**	15 wks
25 Jul 63	**COME ON HOME** *Philips BF 1263*	**31**	6 wks

See also Dusty Springfield.

Bruce SPRINGSTEEN *US, male vocalist*

Date	Title *Label Number*	Position	Wks
22 Nov 80	**HUNGRY HEART** *CBS 9309*	**44**	4 wks
13 Jun 81	**THE RIVER** *CBS A 1179*	**35**	6 wks

SPRINGWATER

UK, male instrumentalist (Phil Cordell)

Date	Title *Label Number*	Position	Wks
23 Oct 71	● **I WILL RETURN** *Polydor 2058 141*	**5**	12 wks

SPYRO GYRA *US, male instrumental group*

Date	Title *Label Number*	Position	Wks
21 Jul 79	**MORNING DANCE** *Infinity INF 111*	**17**	10 wks

SQUADRONAIRES — See *Joan REGAN*

SQUEEZE *UK, male vocal/instrumental group*

Date	Title *Label Number*	Position	Wks
8 Apr 78	**TAKE ME I'M YOURS** *A & M AMS 7335*	**19**	9 wks
10 Jun 78	**BANG BANG** *A & M AMS 7360*	**49**	5 wks
18 Nov 78	**GOODBYE GIRL** *A & M AMS 7398*	**63**	2 wks
24 Mar 79	● **COOL FOR CATS** *A & M AMS 7426*	**2**	11 wks
2 Jun 79	● **UP THE JUNCTION** *A & M AMS 7444*	**2**	11 wks
8 Sep 79	**SLAP AND TICKLE** *A & M AMS 7466*	**24**	8 wks
1 Mar 80	**ANOTHER NAIL IN MY HEART** *A & M AMS 7507*	**17**	9 wks
10 May 80	**PULLING MUSSELS (FROM THE SHELL)** *A & M AMS 7523*	**44**	6 wks
16 May 81	**IS THAT LOVE** *A & M AMS 8129*	**35**	8 wks
25 Jul 81	**TEMPTED** *A & M AMS 8147*	**41**	5 wks
10 Oct 81	● **LABELLED WITH LOVE** *A & M AMS 8166*	**4**	10 wks
24 Apr 82	**BLACK COFFEE IN BED** *A & M AMS 8219*	**51**	4 wks
23 Oct 82	**ANNIE GET YOUR GUN** *A & M AMS 8259*	**43**	4 wks

Billy SQUIER *US, male vocalist*

Date	Title *Label Number*	Position	Wks
3 Oct 81	**THE STROKE** *Capitol CL 214*	**52**	3 wks

Dorothy SQUIRES *UK, female vocalist*

Date	Title *Label Number*	Position	Wks
5 Jun 53	**I'M WALKING BEHIND YOU** *Polygon P 1068*	**12**	1 wk
20 Sep 69	**FOR ONCE IN MY LIFE** *President PT 267*	**24**	10 wks
20 Dec 69	**FOR ONCE IN MY LIFE** (re-entry) *President PT 267*	**48**	1 wk
21 Feb 70	**TILL** *President PT 281*	**25**	10 wks
9 May 70	**TILL** (re-entry) *President PT 281*	**48**	1 wk
8 Aug 70	**MY WAY** *President PT 305*	**40**	5 wks
19 Sep 70	**MY WAY** (re-entry) *President PT 305*	**34**	8 wks
28 Nov 70	**MY WAY** (2nd re-entry) *President PT 305*	**25**	10 wks

See also Dorothy Squires & Russ Conway.

Dorothy SQUIRES and Russ CONWAY

UK, female vocalist, male instrumentalist, piano

Date	Title *Label Number*	Position	Wks
24 Aug 61	**SAY IT WITH FLOWERS** *Columbia DB 4665*	**23**	10 wks

See also Dorothy Squires, Russ Conway.

Jim STAFFORD *US, male vocalist*

Date	Title *Label Number*	Position	Wks
27 Apr 74	**SPIDERS & SNAKES** *MGM 2006 374*	**14**	8 wks
6 Jul 74	**MY GIRL BILL** *MGM 2006 423*	**20**	8 wks

Date **Title** *Label Number* **Position**

Date **Title** *Label Number* **Position**

Jo STAFFORD *US, female vocalist*

Date		Title *Label Number*	Position	
14 Nov 52	★	**YOU BELONG TO ME** *Columbia DB 3152*	**1**	19 wks
19 Dec 52		**JAMBALAYA** *Columbia DB 3169*	**11**	2 wks
7 May 54	●	**MAKE LOVE TO ME** *Philips PB 233*	**8**	1 wk
9 Dec 55		**SUDDENLY THERE'S A VALLEY** *Philips PB 509*	**12**	5 wks
3 Feb 56		**SUDDENLY THERE'S A VALLEY** (re-entry) *Philips PB 509*	**19**	1 wk

Terry STAFFORD *US, male vocalist*

Date		Title *Label Number*	Position	
7 May 64		**SUSPICION** *London HLU 9871*	**31**	9 wks

STAIFFI and his MUSTAFAS

France, male vocal/instrumental group

Date		Title *Label Number*	Position	
28 Jul 60		**MUSTAFA** *Pye International 7N 25057*	**43**	1 wk

STAMFORD BRIDGE *UK, male vocal group*

Date		Title *Label Number*	Position	
16 May 70		**CHELSEA** *Penny Farthing PEN 715*	**47**	1 wk

STAPLE SINGERS *US, male/female vocal group*

Date		Title *Label Number*	Position	
10 Jun 72		**I'LL TAKE YOU THERE** *Stax 2025 110*	**30**	8 wks
8 Jun 74		**IF YOU'RE READY (COME GO WITH ME)** *Stax 2025 224*	**34**	6 wks

Cyril STAPLETON *UK, orchestra*

Date		Title *Label Number*	Position	
27 May 55		**ELEPHANT TANGO** *Decca F 10488*	**20**	2 wks
1 Jul 55		**ELEPHANT TANGO** (re-entry) *Decca F 10488*	**20**	1 wk
22 Jul 55		**ELEPHANT TANGO** (2nd re-entry) *Decca F 10488*	**19**	1 wk
23 Sep 55	●	**BLUE STAR** *Decca F 10559*	**2**	12 wks
6 Apr 56		**THE ITALIAN THEME** *Decca F 10703*	**18**	2 wks
1 Jun 56		**THE HAPPY WHISTLER** *Decca F 10735*	**22**	4 wks
19 Jul 57		**FORGOTTEN DREAMS** *Decca F 10912*	**27**	5 wks

STARDUST

Sweden, male/female vocal/instrumental group

Date		Title *Label Number*	Position	
8 Oct 77		**ARIANA** *Satril SAT 120*	**42**	3 wks

Alvin STARDUST *UK, male vocalist*

Date		Title *Label Number*	Position	
3 Nov 73	●	**MY COO-CA-CHOO** *Magnet MAG 1*	**2**	21 wks
16 Feb 74	★	**JEALOUS MIND** *Magnet MAG 5*	**1**	11 wks
4 May 74	●	**RED DRESS** *Magnet MAG 8*	**7**	8 wks
31 Aug 74	●	**YOU YOU YOU** *Magnet MAG 13*	**6**	10 wks
30 Nov 74		**TELL ME WHY** *Magnet MAG 19*	**16**	8 wks
1 Feb 75		**GOOD LOVE CAN NEVER DIE** *Magnet MAG 21*	**11**	9 wks
12 Jul 75		**SWEET CHEATIN' RITA** *Magnet MAG 32*	**37**	4 wks
5 Sep 81	●	**PRETEND** *Stiff BUY 124*	**4**	10 wks
21 Nov 81		**A WONDERFUL TIME UP THERE** *Stiff BUY 132*	**56**	8 wks

Alvin started his career as Shane Fenton. See also Shane Fenton and the Fentones.

STARGARD *US, female vocal group*

Date		Title *Label Number*	Position	
28 Jan 78		**THEME FROM 'WHICH WAY IS UP'** *MCA 346*	**19**	7 wks
15 Apr 78		**LOVE IS SO EASY** *MCA 354*	**45**	1 wk
9 Sep 78		**WHAT YOU WAITING FOR** *MCA 382*	**39**	6 wks

STARGAZERS *UK, male/female vocal group*

Date		Title *Label Number*	Position	
13 Feb 53		**BROKEN WINGS** *Decca F 10047*	**11**	1 wk
27 Feb 53	★	**BROKEN WINGS** (re-entry) *Decca F 10047*	**1**	11 wks
19 Feb 54	★	**I SEE THE MOON** *Decca F 10213*	**1**	15 wks
9 Apr 54		**HAPPY WANDERER** *Decca F 10259*	**12**	1 wk
4 Mar 55		**SOMEBODY** *Decca F 10437*	**20**	1 wk
3 Jun 55		**CRAZY OTTO RAG** *Decca F 10523*	**18**	3 wks
9 Sep 55	●	**CLOSE THE DOOR** *Decca F 10594*	**6**	9 wks
11 Nov 55	●	**TWENTY TINY FINGERS** *Decca F 10626*	**4**	11 wks
22 Jun 56		**HOT DIGGITY** *Decca F 10731*	**28**	1 wk

STARGAZERS *UK, male vocal/instrumental group*

Date		Title *Label Number*	Position	
6 Feb 82		**GROOVE BABY GROOVE** (EP) *Epic EPC A 1924*	**56**	3 wks

Tracks on Groove Baby Groove EP:

STARJETS *UK, male vocal/instrumental group*

Date		Title *Label Number*	Position	
8 Sep 79		**WAR STORIES** *Epic EPC 7770*	**51**	5 wks

STARLAND VOCAL BAND

US, male/female vocal group

Date		Title *Label Number*	Position	
7 Aug 76		**AFTERNOON DELIGHT** *RCA 2716*	**18**	10 wks

STARLITERS — See *Joey DEE and the STARLITERS*

Edwin STARR *US, male vocalist*

Date		Title *Label Number*	Position	
12 May 66		**STOP HER ON SIGHT (SOS)** *Polydor BM 56 702*	**35**	8 wks
18 Aug 66		**HEADLINE NEWS** *Polydor 56 717*	**39**	3 wks
11 Dec 68		**STOP HER ON SIGHT (SOS)/ HEADLINE NEWS** (re-issue) *Polydor 56 153*	**11**	11 wks
13 Sep 69		**25 MILES** *Tamla Motown TMG 672*	**36**	6 wks
24 Oct 70	●	**WAR** *Tamla Motown TMG 754*	**3**	12 wks
20 Feb 71		**STOP THE WAR NOW** *Tamla Motown TMG 764*	**33**	1 wk
27 Jan 79	●	**CONTACT** *20th Century BTC 2396*	**6**	12 wks
26 May 79	●	**H.A.P.P.Y. RADIO** *RCA TC 2408*	**9**	11 wks

Headline News *not listed with* SOS *from 22 Jan 69 to 19 Feb 69.*

Freddie STARR *UK, male vocalist*

Date		Title *Label Number*	Position	
23 Feb 74	●	**IT'S YOU** *Tiffany 6121 501*	**9**	10 wks
20 Dec 75		**WHITE CHRISTMAS** *Thunderbird THE 102*	**41**	4 wks

Kay STARR *US, female vocalist*

Date		Title *Label Number*	Position	
5 Dec 52	★	**COMES A-LONG A-LOVE** *Capitol CL 13808*	**1**	16 wks
24 Apr 53	●	**SIDE BY SIDE** *Capitol CL 13876*	**7**	4 wks
19 Mar 54	●	**CHANGING PARTNERS** *Capitol CL 14050*	**4**	14 wks

Date	Title Label Number	Position	
15 Oct 54	**AM I A TOY OR A TREASURE** *Capitol CL 14151*	**17**	3 wks
12 Nov 54	**AM I A TOY OR A TREASURE** (re-entry) *Capitol CL 14151*	**20**	1 wk
17 Feb 56	★ **ROCK AND ROLL WALTZ** *HMV POP 168*	**1**	20 wks

Ringo STARR *UK, male vocalist*

Date	Title Label Number	Position	
17 Apr 71	● **IT DON'T COME EASY** *Apple R 5898*	**4**	11 wks
1 Apr 72	● **BACK OFF BOOGALOO** *Apple R 5944*	**2**	10 wks
27 Oct 73	● **PHOTOGRAPH** *Apple R 5992*	**8**	13 wks
23 Feb 74	● **YOU'RE SIXTEEN** *Apple R 5995*	**4**	10 wks
30 Nov 74	**ONLY YOU** *Apple R 6000*	**28**	11 wks

STARSHIP TROOPERS — See *Sarah BRIGHTMAN*

STARSOUND

Holland, producer Jaap Eggermont with male/female session singers

Date	Title Label Number	Position	
18 Apr 81	● **STARS ON 45** *CBS 1102*	**2**	14 wks
4 Jul 81	● **STARS ON 45 VOL.2** *CBS A 1407*	**2**	10 wks
19 Sep 81	**STARS ON 45 VOL.3** *CBS A 1521*	**17**	6 wks
27 Feb 82	**STARS ON STEVIE** *CBS A 2041*	**14**	7 wks

STARTRAK *UK, male/female session group.*

Date	Title Label Number	Position	
1 Aug 81	**STARTRAX CLUB DISCO** *Picksy KSY 1001*	**18**	8 wks

STARTURN ON 45 (PINTS)

UK, male vocal group

Date	Title Label Number	Position	
24 Oct 81	**STARTURN ON 45 (PINTS)** *V Tone V TONE 003*	**45**	4 wks

STATLER BROTHERS *US, male vocal group*

Date	Title Label Number	Position	
24 Feb 66	**FLOWERS ON THE WALL** *CBS 201976*	**38**	4 wks

Candi STATON *US, female vocalist*

Date	Title Label Number	Position	
29 May 76	● **YOUNG HEARTS RUN FREE** *Warner Bros. K 16730*	**2**	13 wks
18 Sep 76	**DESTINY** *Warner Bros K 16806*	**41**	3 wks
23 Jul 77	● **NIGHTS ON BROADWAY** *Warner Bros. K 16972*	**6**	12 wks
3 Jun 78	**HONEST I DO LOVE YOU** *Warner Bros. K 17164*	**48**	5 wks
24 Apr 82	**SUSPICIOUS MINDS** *Sugarhill SH 112*	**31**	9 wks

STATUS QUO *UK, male vocal/instrumental group*

Date	Title Label Number	Position	
24 Jan 68	● **PICTURES OF MATCHSTICK MEN** *Pye 7N 17449*	**7**	12 wks
21 Aug 68	● **ICE IN THE SUN** *Pye 7N 17581*	**8**	12 wks
28 May 69	**ARE YOU GROWING TIRED OF MY LOVE** *Pye 7N 17728*	**46**	2 wks
18 Jun 69	**ARE YOU GROWING TIRED OF MY LOVE** (re-entry) *Pye 7N 17728*	**50**	1 wk
2 May 70	**DOWN THE DUSTPIPE** *Pye 7N 17907*	**12**	17 wks
7 Nov 70	**IN MY CHAIR** *Pye 7N 17998*	**21**	14 wks
13 Jan 73	● **PAPER PLANE** *Vertigo 6059 071*	**8**	11 wks
14 Apr 73	**MEAN GIRL** *Pye 7N 45229*	**20**	11 wks
8 Sep 73	● **CAROLINE** *Vertigo 6059 085*	**5**	13 wks
4 May 74	● **BREAK THE RULES** *Vertigo 6059 101*	**8**	8 wks
7 Dec 74	★ **DOWN DOWN** *Vertigo 6059 114*	**1**	11 wks
17 May 75	● **ROLL OVER LAY DOWN** *Vertigo QUO 13*	**9**	8 wks
14 Feb 76	● **RAIN** *Vertigo 6059 133*	**7**	7 wks
10 Jul 76	**MYSTERY SONG** *Vertigo 6059 146*	**11**	9 wks
11 Dec 76	● **WILD SIDE OF LIFE** *Vertigo 6059 153*	**9**	12 wks
8 Oct 77	● **ROCKIN' ALL OVER THE WORLD** *Vertigo 6059 184*	**3**	16 wks
2 Sep 78	**AGAIN AND AGAIN** *Vertigo QUO 1*	**13**	9 wks
25 Nov 78	**ACCIDENT PRONE** *Vertigo QUO 2*	**36**	8 wks
22 Sep 79	● **WHATEVER YOU WANT** *Vertigo 6059 242*	**4**	9 wks
24 Nov 79	**LIVING ON AN ISLAND** *Vertigo 6059 248*	**16**	10 wks
11 Oct 80	● **WHAT YOU'RE PROPOSING** *Vertigo QUO 3*	**2**	11 wks
6 Dec 80	**LIES/DON'T DRIVE MY CAR** *Vertigo QUO 4*	**11**	10 wks
28 Feb 81	● **SOMETHING 'BOUT YOU BABY I LIKE** *Vertigo QUO 5*	**9**	7 wks
28 Feb 81	● **ROCK'N'ROLL** *Vertigo QUO 6*	**8**	11 wks
27 Mar 82	● **DEAR JOHN** *Vertigo/Phonogram QUO 7*	**10**	8 wks
12 Jun 82	**SHE DONT FOOL ME** *Vertigo/Phonogram QUO 8*	**36**	5 wks
30 Oct 82	**CAROLINE (LIVE AT THE N.E.C.)** *Vertigo/Phonogram QUO 10*	**13**	7 wks

Don't Drive My Car *listed from 20 Dec 80 only.*

STEALER'S WHEEL

UK, male vocal/instrumental group

Date	Title Label Number	Position	
26 May 73	● **STUCK IN THE MIDDLE WITH YOU** *A & M AMS 7036*	**8**	10 wks
1 Sep 73	**EVERYTHING'L TURN OUT FINE** *A & M AMS 7079*	**33**	6 wks
26 Jan 74	**STAR** *A & M AMS 7094*	**25**	6 wks

STEAM *US, male vocal/instrumental group*

Date	Title Label Number	Position	
31 Jan 70	● **NA NA HEY HEY KISS HIM GOODBYE** *Fontana TF 1058*	**9**	14 wks

Anthony STEEL and the RADIO REVELLERS

UK, male vocalist/male instrumental group

Date	Title Label Number	Position	
10 Sep 54	**WEST OF ZANZIBAR** *Polygon P 1114*	**11**	6 wks

STEEL PULSE *UK, male vocal/instrumental group*

Date	Title Label Number	Position	
1 Apr 78	**KU KLUX KLAN** *Island WIP 6428*	**41**	4 wks
8 May 78	**PRODIGAL SON** *Island WIP 6449*	**35**	6 wks
23 Jun 79	**SOUND SYSTEM** *Island WIP 6490*	**71**	2 wks

Tommy STEELE *UK, male vocalist*

Date	Title Label Number	Position	
26 Oct 56	**ROCK WITH THE CAVEMAN** *Decca F 10795*	**13**	4 wks
30 Nov 56	**ROCK WITH THE CAVEMAN** (re-entry) *Decca F 10795*	**23**	1 wk
14 Dec 56	★ **SINGING THE BLUES** *Decca F 10819*	**1**	13 wks
15 Feb 57	**KNEE DEEP IN THE BLUES** *Decca F 10849*	**15**	9 wks
19 Apr 57	**SINGING THE BLUES** (re-entry) *Decca F 10819*	**24**	1 wk
3 May 57	**BUTTERFINGERS** *Decca F 10877*	**25**	1 wk
17 May 57	● **BUTTERFINGERS** (re-entry) *Decca F 10877*	**8**	17 wks
17 May 57	**SINGING THE BLUES** (2nd re-entry) *Decca F 10849*	**29**	1 wk
16 Aug 57	● **WATER WATER/ HANDFUL OF SONGS** *Decca F 10923*	**5**	16 wks
30 Aug 57	**SHIRALEE** *Decca F 10896*	**11**	4 wks

Date	Title *Label Number*	Position	
22 Nov 57	**HEY YOU** *Decca F 10941*	**28**	1 wk
13 Dec 57	**WATER WATER/ HANDFUL OF SONGS** (re-entry) *Decca F 10923*	**28**	1 wk
7 Mar 58	● **NAIROBI** *Decca F 10991*	**3**	11 wks
25 Apr 58	**HAPPY GUITAR** *Decca F 10976*	**20**	5 wks
18 Jul 58	**THE ONLY MAN ON THE ISLAND** *Decca F 11041*	**16**	8 wks
14 Nov 58	● **COME ON LET'S GO** *Decca F 11072*	**10**	13 wks
14 Aug 59	**TALLAHASSEE LASSIE** *Decca F 11152*	**16**	4 wks
28 Aug 59	**GIVE GIVE GIVE** *Decca F 11152*	**28**	2 wks
25 Sep 59	**TALLAHASSEE LASSIE** (re-entry) *Decca F 11152*	**25**	1 wk
4 Dec 59	● **LITTLE WHITE BULL** *Decca F 11177*	**6**	12 wks
10 Mar 60	**LITTLE WHITE BULL** (re-entry) *Decca F 11177*	**30**	5 wks
23 Jun 60	● **WHAT A MOUTH** *Decca F 11245*	**5**	11 wks
29 Dec 60	**MUST BE SANTA** *Decca F 11299*	**40**	1 wk
17 Aug 61	**WRITING ON THE WALL** *Decca F 11372*	**30**	5 wks

Handful Of Songs *listed together with* Water Water *from week of 23 Aug 57. See also Various Artists - All Star Hit Parade No. 2.*

STEELEYE SPAN

UK, male/female vocal/instrumental group

Date	Title *Label Number*	Position	
8 Dec 73	**GAUDETE** *Chrysalis CHS 2007*	**14**	9 wks
15 Nov 75	● **ALL AROUND MY HAT** *Chrysalis CHS 2078*	**5**	9 wks

STEELY DAN *US, male vocal/instrumental group*

Date	Title *Label Number*	Position	
30 Aug 75	**DO IT AGAIN** *ABC 4075*	**39**	4 wks
11 Dec 76	**HAITIAN DIVORCE** *ABC 4152*	**17**	9 wks
29 Jul 78	**FM (NO STATIC AT ALL)** *MCA 374*	**49**	4 wks
26 Aug 78	**FM (NO STATIC AT ALL)** (re-entry) *MCA 374*	**75**	1 wk
10 Mar 79	**RIKKI DON'T LOSE THAT NUMBER** *ABC 4241*	**58**	3 wks

Jim STEINMAN *US, male vocalist*

Date	Title *Label Number*	Position	
4 Jul 81	**ROCK'N'ROLL DREAMS COME THROUGH** *Epic/Cleveland EPC A 1236*	**52**	7 wks

Mike STEIPHENSON — See *BURUNDI STEIPHENSON BLACK*

Doreen STEPHENS — See *Billy COTTON and his BAND*

STEPPENWOLF

US, male vocal/instrumental group

Date	Title *Label Number*	Position	
11 Jun 69	**BORN TO BE WILD** *Stateside SS 8017*	**30**	7 wks
9 Aug 69	**BORN TO BE WILD** (re-entry) *Stateside SS 8017*	**50**	2 wks

STEVE and EYDIE *US, male/female vocal duo*

Date	Title *Label Number*	Position	
22 Aug 63	● **I WANT TO STAY HERE** *CBS AAG 163*	**3**	13 wks

See also Steve Lawrence, Eydie Gormé.

April STEVENS — See *Nino TEMPO and April STEVENS*

Cat STEVENS *UK, male vocalist*

Date	Title *Label Number*	Position	
20 Oct 66	**I LOVE MY DOG** *Deram DM 102*	**28**	7 wks
12 Jan 67	● **MATTHEW AND SON** *Deram DM 110*	**2**	10 wks
30 Mar 67	● **I'M GONNA GET ME A GUN** *Deram DM 118*	**6**	10 wks
2 Aug 67	**A BAD NIGHT** *Deram DM 140*	**20**	8 wks
20 Dec 67	**KITTY** *Deram DM 156*	**47**	1 wk

Date Title *Label Number* Position

Date	Title *Label Number*	Position	
27 Jun 70	● **LADY D'ARBANVILLE** *Island WIP 6086*	**8**	13 wks
28 Aug 71	**MOON SHADOW** *Island WIP 6092*	**22**	11 wks
1 Jan 72	● **MORNING HAS BROKEN** *Island WIP 6121*	**9**	13 wks
9 Dec 72	**CAN'T KEEP IT IN** *Island WIP 6152*	**13**	12 wks
24 Aug 74	**ANOTHER SATURDAY NIGHT** *Island WIP 6206*	**19**	8 wks
2 Jul 77	**(REMEMBER THE DAYS OF THE) OLD SCHOOL YARD** *Island WIP 6387*	**44**	3 wks

Connie STEVENS *US, female vocalist*

Date	Title *Label Number*	Position	
5 May 60	● **SIXTEEN REASONS** *Warner Bros. WB 3*	**9**	11 wks
4 Aug 60	**SIXTEEN REASONS** (re-entry) *Warner Bros. WB 3*	**45**	1 wk

See also Edward Byrnes and Connie Stevens.

Ray STEVENS *US, male vocalist*

Date	Title *Label Number*	Position	
16 May 70	● **EVERYTHING IS BEAUTIFUL** *CBS 4953*	**6**	16 wks
13 Mar 71	● **BRIDGET THE MIDGET (THE QUEEN OF THE BLUES)** *CBS 7070*	**2**	14 wks
25 Mar 72	**TURN YOUR RADIO ON** *CBS 7634*	**33**	4 wks
25 May 74	★ **THE STREAK** *Janus 6146 201*	**1**	12 wks
21 Jun 75	● **MISTY** *Janus 6146 204*	**2**	10 wks
27 Sep 75	**INDIAN LOVE CALL** *Janus 6146 205*	**34**	4 wks
5 Mar 77	**IN THE MOOD** *Warner Bros. K 16875*	**31**	4 wks

In the Mood *does not feature Ray Stevens as a conventional vocalist, but as a group of chickens.In the US, he billed himself on this record as Henhouse Five Plus Two*

Ricky STEVENS *UK, male vocalist*

Date	Title *Label Number*	Position	
14 Dec 61	**I CRIED FOR YOU** *Columbia DB 4739*	**34**	7 wks

Shakin' STEVENS *UK, male vocalist*

Date	Title *Label Number*	Position	
16 Feb 80	**HOT DOG** *Epic EPC 8090*	**24**	9 wks
16 Aug 80	**MARIE MARIE** *Epic EPC 8725*	**19**	10 wks
28 Feb 81	★ **THIS OLE HOUSE** *Epic EPC 9555*	**1**	17 wks
2 May 81	● **YOU DRIVE ME CRAZY** *Epic A1165*	**2**	12 wks
25 Jul 81	★ **GREEN DOOR** *Epic A1354*	**1**	12 wks
10 Oct 81	● **IT'S RAINING** *Epic A1643*	**10**	9 wks
16 Jan 82	★ **OH JULIE** *Epic EPC A1742*	**1**	10 wks
24 Apr 82	● **SHIRLEY** *Epic EPC A2087*	**6**	6 wks
21 Aug 82	**GIVE ME YOUR HEART TONIGHT** *Epic EPC A2656*	**11**	10 wks
16 Oct 82	● **I'LL BE SATISFIED** *Epic EPC A2846*	**10**	8 wks
11 Dec 82	● **THE SHAKIN' STEVENS EP** *Epic SHAKY 1*	**2**†	3 wks

Tracks on The Shakin' Stevens EP: *Blue Christmas, Que Sera Sera, Josephine, Lawdy Miss Clawdy.*

STEVENSON'S ROCKET

UK, male vocal/instrumental group

Date	Title *Label Number*	Position	
29 Nov 75	**ALRIGHT BABY** *Magnet MAG 47*	**37**	2 wks
20 Dec 75	**ALRIGHT BABY** (re-entry) *Magnet MAG 47*	**45**	3 wks

AL STEWART *UK, male vocalist*

Date	Title *Label Number*	Position	
29 Jan 77	**YEAR OF THE CAT** *RCA 2771*	**31**	6 wks

Amii STEWART *US, female vocalist*

Date	Title *Label Number*	Position	
7 Apr 79	● **KNOCK ON WOOD** *Atlantic/Hansa K 11214*	**6**	12 wks
16 Jun 79	● **LIGHT MY FIRE/137 DISCO HEAVEN** (MEDLEY) *Atlantic/Hansa K 11278*	**5**	11 wks
3 Nov 79	**JEALOUSY** *Atlantic/Hansa K 11386*	**58**	3 wks
19 Jan 80	**PARADISE BIRD/THE LETTER** *Atlantic/Hansa K 11424*	**39**	4 wks

Amii STEWART and Johnny BRISTOL

US, male/female vocal duo

Date	Title *Label Number*	Position	
19 Jul 80	**MY GUY - MY GIRL** (MEDLEY) *Atlantic/Hansa K 11550*	**39**	5 wks

See also Amii Stewart, Johnny Bristol.

Andy STEWART *UK, male vocalist*

Date	Title *Label Number*	Position	
15 Dec 60	**DONALD WHERE'S YOUR TROOSERS** *Top Rank JAR 427*	**37**	1 wk
12 Jan 61	**A SCOTTISH SOLDIER** *Top Rank JAR 512*	**19**	38 wks
1 Jun 61	**THE BATTLE'S O'ER** *Top Rank JAR 565*	**28**	13 wks
12 Oct 61	**A SCOTTISH SOLDIER** (re-entry) *Top Rank JAR 512*	**43**	2 wks
12 Aug 65	**DR. FINLAY** *HMV POP 1454*	**50**	1 wk
26 Aug 65	**DR. FINLAY** (re-entry) *HMV POP 1454*	**43**	4 wks

Billy STEWART *US, male vocalist*

Date	Title *Label Number*	Position	
8 Sep 66	**SUMMERTIME** *Chess CRS 8040*	**39**	2 wks

Dave STEWART

Date	Title *Label Number*	Position	
14 Mar 81	**WHAT BECOMES OF THE BROKENHEARTED?** *Stiff BROKEN 1*	**13**	10 wks

Guest vocals: Colin Blunstone. See also Colin Blunstone, Neil MacArthur, Dave Stewart with Barbara Gaskin

Dave STEWART with Barbara GASKIN

UK, male instrumentalist-keyboards-with female vocalist

Date	Title *Label Number*	Position	
19 Sep 81	★ **IT'S MY PARTY** *Stiff/Broken BROKEN 2*	**1**	13 wks

see also Dave Stewart with Colin Blunstone

John STEWART *US, male vocalist*

Date	Title *Label Number*	Position	
30 Jun 79	**GOLD** *RSO 35*	**43**	6 wks

Rod STEWART *UK, male vocalist*

Date	Title *Label Number*	Position	
4 Sep 71	**REASON TO BELIEVE** *Mercury 6052 097*	**19**	2 wks
18 Sep 71	★ **MAGGIE MAY** *Mercury 6052 097*	**1**	19 wks
12 Aug 72	★ **YOU WEAR IT WELL** *Mercury 6052 171*	**1**	12 wks
18 Nov 72	● **ANGEL/ WHAT MADE MILWAUKEE FAMOUS (HAS MADE A LOSER OUT OF ME)** *Mercury 6052 198*	**4**	11 wks
8 Sep 73	● **OH NO NOT MY BABY** *Mercury 6052 371*	**6**	9 wks
5 Oct 74	● **FAREWELL/ BRING IT ON HOME TO ME/ YOU SEND ME** *Mercury 6167 033*	**7**	7 wks
16 Aug 75	★ **SAILING** *Warner Bros. K 16600*	**1**	11 wks
15 Nov 75	● **THIS OLD HEART OF MINE** *Riva 1*	**4**	9 wks
5 Jun 76	● **TONIGHT'S THE NIGHT** *Riva 3*	**5**	9 wks
21 Aug 76	● **THE KILLING OF GEORGIE** *Riva 4*	**2**	10 wks
4 Sep 76	● **SAILING** (re-entry) *Warner Bros. K 16600*	**3**	20 wks
20 Nov 76	**GET BACK** *Riva 6*	**11**	9 wks
4 Dec 76	**MAGGIE MAY** (re-issue) *Mercury 6160 006*	**31**	7 wks
23 Apr 77	★ **I DON'T WANT TO TALK ABOUT IT/FIRST CUT IS THE DEEPEST** *Riva 7*	**1**	13 wks
15 Oct 77	● **YOU'RE IN MY HEART** *Riva 11*	**3**	10 wks
28 Jan 78	● **HOTLEGS/I WAS ONLY JOKING** *Riva 10*	**5**	8 wks
27 May 78	● **OLE OLA (MUHLER BRASILEIRA)** *Riva 15*	**4**	6 wks
18 Nov 78	★ **DA YA THINK I'M SEXY?** *Riva 17*	**1**	13 wks
3 Feb 79	**AIN'T LOVE A BITCH** *Riva 18*	**11**	8 wks
5 May 79	**BLONDES (HAVE MORE FUN)** *Riva 19*	**63**	3 wks
31 May 80	**IF LOVING YOU IS WRONG (I DON'T WANT TO BE RIGHT)** *Riva 23*	**23**	9 wks
8 Nov 80	**PASSION** *Riva 26*	**17**	10 wks
20 Dec 80	**MY GIRL** *Riva 28*	**32**	wks
17 Oct 81	● **TONIGHT I'M YOURS (DON'T HURT ME)** *Riva 33*	**8**	13 wks
11 Dec 81	**YOUNG TURKS** *Riva 34*	**11**	9 wks
27 Feb 82	**HOW LONG** *Riva 35*	**41**	4 wks

See also Faces, Jeff Beck and Rod Stewart. Ole Ola *also features the Scottish World Cup Football Squad.*

STIFF LITTLE FINGERS

UK, male vocal/instrumental group

Date	Title *Label Number*	Position	
29 Sep 79	**STRAW DOGS** *Chrysalis CHS 2368*	**44**	4 wks
16 Feb 80	**AT THE EDGE** *Chrysalis CHS 2406*	**15**	9 wks
24 May 80	**NOBODY'S HERO/TIN SOLDIERS** *Chrysalis CHS 2424*	**36**	5 wks
2 Aug 80	**BACK TO FRONT** *Chrysalis CHS 2447*	**49**	4 wks
28 Mar 81	**JUST FADE AWAY** *Chrysalis CHS 2510*	**47**	6 wks
30 May 81	**SILVER LINING** *Chrysalis CHS 2517*	**68**	3 wks
23 Jan 82	**LISTEN** (EP) *Chrysalis CHS 2580*	**33**	6 wks
18 Sep 82	**BITS OF KIDS** *Chrysalis CHS 2637*	**73**	2 wks

Tracks on Listen EP: *That's When Your Blood Bumps, Two Guitars Clash, Listen, Sad-Eyed People.*

Stephen STILLS *US, male vocalist*

Date	Title *Label Number*	Position	
13 Mar 71	**LOVE THE ONE YOU'RE WITH** *Atlantic 2091 046*	**37**	4 wks

See also Crosby Stills and Nash.

STING *UK, male vocalist*

Date	Title *Label Number*	Position	
14 Aug 82	**SPREAD A LITTLE HAPPINESS** *A & M AMS 8217*	**16**	8 wks

STINGERS — See *B. BUMBLE and the STINGERS*

Rhet STOLLER *UK, male instrumentalist, guitar*

Date	Title *Label Number*	Position	
12 Jan 61	**CHARIOT** *Decca F 11302*	**26**	8 wks

Morris STOLOFF *US, orchestra*

Date	Title *Label Number*	Position	
1 Jun 56	● **MOONGLOW/ THEME FROM PICNIC** *Brunswick 05553*	**7**	11 wks

R & J STONE *UK, male/female vocal duo*

Date	Title *Label Number*	Position	
10 Jan 76	● **WE DO IT** *RCA 2616*	**5**	9 wks

STONEBRIDGE McGUINNESS

UK, male vocal/instrumental duo

Date	Title *Label Number*	Position	Weeks
14 Jul 79	**OO-EEH BABY** *RCA PB 5163*	**54**	2 wks

STORM *UK, male/female vocal/instrumental group*

Date	Title *Label Number*	Position	Weeks
17 Nov 79	**IT'S MY HOUSE** *Scope SC 10*	**36**	10 wks

Danny STORM *UK, male vocalist*

Date	Title *Label Number*	Position	Weeks
12 Apr 62	**HONEST I DO** *Piccadilly 7N 35025*	**42**	4 wks

STORYVILLE JAZZ BAND — See *Bob WALLIS and his STORYVILLE JAZZ BAND*

Peter STRAKER and the HANDS OF DR. TELENY

UK, male vocalist, male vocal/instrumental group

Date	Title *Label Number*	Position	Weeks
19 Feb 72	**THE SPIRIT IS WILLING** *RCA 2163*	**40**	4 wks

Nick STRAKER BAND

UK, male vocal/instrumental group

Date	Title *Label Number*	Position	Weeks
2 Aug 80	**A WALK IN THE PARK** *CBS 8525*	**20**	12 wks
15 Nov 80	**LEAVING ON THE MIDNIGHT TRAIN** *CBS 9088*	**61**	3 wks

STRANGE BEHAVIOUR — See *Jane KENNAWAY and STRANGE BEHAVIOUR*

STRANGLERS *UK, male Vocal/instrumental group*

Date	Title *Label Number*	Position	Weeks
19 Feb 77	**(GET A) GRIP (ON YOURSELF)** *United Artists UP 36211*	**44**	4 wks
21 May 77	● **PEACHES/ GO BUDDY GO** *United Artists Up 36248*	**8**	14 wks
30 Jul 77	● **SOMETHING BETTER CHANGE/STRAIGHTEN OUT** *United Artists Up 36277*	**9**	8 wks
24 Sep 77	● **NO MORE HEROES** *United Artists Up 36300*	**8**	9 wks
4 Feb 78	**FIVE MINUTES** *United Artists UP 36350*	**11**	9 wks
6 May 78	**NICE 'N SLEAZY** *United Artists UP 36379*	**18**	8 wks
12 Aug 78	**WALK ON BY** *United Artists UP 36429*	**21**	8 wks
18 Aug 79	**DUCHESS** *United Artists BP 308*	**14**	9 wks
20 Oct 79	**NUCLEAR DEVICE (THE WIZARD OF AUS)** *United Artists BP 318*	**36**	4 wks
1 Dec 79	**DON'T BRING HARRY** (EP) *United Artists STR 1*	**41**	3 wks
22 Mar 80	**BEAR CAGE** *United Artists BP 344*	**36**	5 wks
7 Jun 80	**WHO WANTS THE WORLD** *United Artists BPX 355*	**39**	4 wks
31 Jan 81	**THROWN AWAY** *Liberty BP 383*	**42**	4 wks
14 Nov 81	**LET ME INTRODUCE YOU TO THE FAMILY** *United Artists BP 405*	**42**	3 wks
9 Jan 82	● **GOLDEN BROWN** *Liberty BP 407*	**2**	12 wks
24 Apr 82	**LA FOLIE** *Liberty BP 410*	**47**	3 wks
24 Jul 82	● **STRANGE LITTLE GIRL** *Liberty BP 412*	**7**	9 wks

Go Buddy Go *credited with* Peaches *from 11 Jun 77.* Straighten Out *credited with* Something Better Change *from 13 Aug 77. Tracks on* Don't Bring Harry EP: *Don't Bring Harry / Wired / Crabs (live) / In the Shadows (live)/*

STRAWBS *UK, male vocal/instrumental group*

Date	Title *Label Number*	Position	Weeks
28 Oct 72	**LAY DOWN** *A & M AMS 7035*	**12**	13 wks
27 Jan 73	● **PART OF THE UNION** *A & M AMS 7047*	**2**	11 wks
6 Oct 73	**SHINE ON SILVER SUN** *A & M AMS 7082*	**34**	3 wks

STRAY CATS *US, male vocal/instrumental group*

Date	Title *Label Number*	Position	Weeks
29 Nov 80	● **RUNAWAY BOYS** *Arista SCAT 1*	**9**	10 wks
7 Feb 81	● **ROCK THIS TOWN** *Arista SCAT 2*	**9**	8 wks
25 Apr 81	**STRAY CAT STRUT** *Arista SCAT 3*	**11**	10 wks
7 Nov 81	**YOU DON'T BELIEVE ME** *Arista SCAT 4*	**57**	3 wks

See also Dave Edmunds and Stray Cats.

STREETBAND *UK, male vocal/instrumental group*

Date	Title *Label Number*	Position	Weeks
4 Nov 78	**TOAST/ HOLD ON** *Logo GO 325*	**18**	6 wks

Barbra STREISAND *US, female vocalist*

Date	Title *Label Number*	Position	Weeks
20 Jan 66	**SECOND HAND ROSE** *CBS 202025*	**14**	13 wks
30 Jan 71	**STONEY END** *CBS 5321*	**46**	1 wk
13 Feb 71	**STONEY END** (re-entry) *CBS 5321*	**27**	10 wks
30 Mar 74	**THE WAY WE WERE** *CBS 1915*	**31**	6 wks
9 Apr 77	● **LOVE THEME FROM A STAR IS BORN (EVERGREEN)** *CBS 4855*	**3**	19 wks
4 Oct 80	★ **WOMAN IN LOVE** *CBS 8966*	**1**	13 wks
30 Jan 82	**COMIN' IN AND OUT OF YOUR LIFE** *CBS A 1789*	**66**	3 wks
20 Mar 82	**MEMORY** *CBS A 1903*	**34**	6 wks

See also Barbra Streisand and Barry Gibb, Barbra and Neil, Donna Summer and Barbra Streisand.

Barbra STREISAND and Barry GIBB

US/UK, female/male vocal duo

Date	Title *Label Number*	Position	Weeks
6 Dec 80	**GUILTY** *CBS 9315*	**34**	wks

See also Barbra Streisand, Donna Summer and Barbra Streisand, Barbra and Neil

STRETCH *UK, male vocal/instrumental group*

Date	Title *Label Number*	Position	Weeks
8 Nov 75	**WHY DID YOU DO IT** *Anchor ANC 1021*	**16**	9 wks

STRIKERS *US, male vocal/instrumental group*

Date	Title *Label Number*	Position	Weeks
6 Jun 81	**BODY MUSIC** *Epic EPC A 1290*	**45**	5 wks

STRING-A-LONGS *US, male instrumental group*

Date	Title *Label Number*	Position	Weeks
23 Feb 61	● **WHEELS** *London HLU 9278*	**8**	16 wks

Chad STUART and Jeremy CLYDE

UK, male vocal duo

Date	Title *Label Number*	Position	Weeks
28 Nov 63	**YESTERDAY'S GONE** *Ember EMB S 180*	**37**	7 wks

Date	Title *Label Number*	Position	

Date Title *Label Number* Position

STUTZ BEARCATS and the Dennis KING ORCHESTRA

UK, male/female vocal group with orchestra

24 Apr 82	**THE SONG THAT I SING (THEME FROM 'WE'LL MEET AGAIN'** *Multi-Media Tapes MMT 6*	**36**	6 wks

See also King Brothers.

STYLISTICS *US, male vocal group*

24 Jun 72	**BETCHA BY GOLLY WOW** *Avco 6105 011*	**13**	12 wks
4 Nov 72 ●	**I'M STONE IN LOVE WITH YOU** *Avco 6105 015*	**9**	10 wks
17 Mar 73	**BREAK UP TO MAKE UP** *Avco 6105 020*	**34**	5 wks
30 Jun 73	**PEEK-A-BOO** *Avco 6105 023*	**35**	6 wks
19 Jan 74 ●	**ROCKIN' ROLL BABY** *Avco 6105 026*	**6**	9 wks
13 Jul 74 ●	**YOU MAKE ME FEEL BRAND NEW** *Avco 6105 028*	**2**	14 wks
19 Oct 74 ●	**LET'S PUT IT ALL TOGETHER** *Avco 6105 032*	**9**	9 wks
25 Jan 75	**STAR ON A TV SHOW** *Avco 6105 035*	**12**	8 wks
10 May 75 ●	**SING BABY SING** *Avco 6105 036*	**3**	10 wks
26 Jul 75 ★	**CAN'T GIVE YOU ANYTHING (BUT MY LOVE)** *Avco 6105 039*	**1**	11 wks
15 Nov 75 ●	**NA NA IS THE SADDEST WORD** *Avco 6105 041*	**5**	10 wks
14 Feb 76 ●	**FUNKY WEEKEND** *Avco 6105 044*	**10**	7 wks
24 Apr 76 ●	**CAN'T HELP FALLING IN LOVE** *Avco 6105 050*	**4**	7 wks
7 Aug 76 ●	**16 BARS** *H & L 6105 059*	**7**	9 wks
27 Nov 76	**YOU'LL NEVER GET TO HEAVEN** (EP) *H & L STYL 001*	**24**	9 wks
26 Mar 77	**7000 DOLLARS AND YOU** *H&L 6105 073*	**24**	7 wks

Tracks on You'll Never Get To Heaven EP: *You'll Never Get To Heaven/ Country Living/ You Are Beautiful/ The Miracle.*

STYX *US, male vocal/instrumental group*

5 Jan 80 ●	**BABE** *A & M AMS 7489*	**6**	10 wks
24 Jan 81	**THE BEST OF TIMES** *A & M AMS 8102*	**42**	5 wks

SUGAR CANE *US, male/female vocal group*

30 Sep 78	**MONTEGO BAY** *Ariola Hansa AHA 524*	**54**	5 wks

SUGARHILL GANG *US, male spoken word group*

1 Dec 79 ●	**RAPPER'S DELIGHT** *Sugarhill SHL 101*	**3**	11 wks
11 Sep 82	**THE LOVER IN YOU** *Sugar Hill SH 116*	**54**	3 wks

Donna SUMMER *US, female vocalist*

17 Jan 76 ●	**LOVE TO LOVE YOU BABY** *GTO GT 17*	**4**	9 wks
29 May 76	**COULD IT BE MAGIC** *GTO GT 60*	**40**	7 wks
25 Dec 76	**WINTER MELODY** *GTO GT 76*	**27**	6 wks
9 Jul 77 ★	**I FEEL LOVE** *GTO GT 100*	**1**	11 wks
20 Aug 77 ●	**DOWN DEEP INSIDE (THEME FROM 'THE DEEP')** *Casablanca CAN 111*	**5**	10 wks
24 Sep 77	**I REMEMBER YESTERDAY** *GTO GT 107*	**14**	7 wks
3 Dec 77 ●	**LOVE'S UNKIND** *GTO GT 113*	**3**	13 wks
10 Dec 77 ●	**I LOVE YOU** *Casablanca CAN 114*	**10**	9 wks
25 Feb 78	**RUMOUR HAS IT** *Casablanca CAN 122*	**19**	8 wks
22 Apr 78	**BACK IN LOVE AGAIN** *GTO GT 117*	**29**	7 wks
10 Jun 78	**LAST DANCE** *Casablanca TGIF 2*	**70**	1 wk
24 Jun 78	**LAST DANCE** (re-entry) *Casablanca TGIF 2*	**51**	8 wks
14 Oct 78 ●	**MACARTHUR PARK** *Casablanca CAN 131*	**5**	10 wks
17 Feb 79	**HEAVEN KNOWS** *Casablanca CAN 141*	**34**	8 wks
12 May 79	**HOT STUFF** *Casablanca CAN 151*	**11**	10 wks
7 Jul 79	**BAD GIRLS** *Casablanca CAN 155*	**14**	10 wks
1 Sep 79	**DIM ALL THE LIGHTS** *Casablanca CAN 162*	**29**	9 wks
16 Feb 80	**ON THE RADIO** *Casablanca NB 2236*	**32**	6 wks
21 Jun 80	**SUNSET PEOPLE** *Casablanca CAN 198*	**46**	5 wks
27 Sep 80	**THE WANDERER** *Warner Bros./Geffen K 79180*	**48**	6 wks
17 Jan 81	**COLD LOVE** *Geffen K 79193*	**44**	3 wks
10 Jul 82	**LOVE IS IN CONTROL (FINGER ON THE TRIGGER)** *Warner Bros. K 79302*	**18**	11 wks
6 Nov 82	**STATE OF INDEPENDENCE** *Warner Bros. K 79344*	**14**†	8 wks
4 Dec 82	**I FEEL LOVE** *Casablanca/Phonogram FEEL 7*	**22**†	4 wks

I Feel Love *on Casablanca/Phonogram FEEL 7 is a re-mixed version of GTO GT 100. See also Donna Summer and Barbra Streisand.*

Donna SUMMER and Barbra STREISAND *US, female vocal duo*

3 Nov 79 ●	**NO MORE TEARS (ENOUGH IS ENOUGH)** *Casablanca/CBS CAN 174 and CBS 8000*	**3**	13 wks

See also Donna Summer, Barbra Streisand, Barbra and Neil. This hit was released simultaneously on two different labels, 7 inch single on Casablanca and 12 inch single on CBS.

SUN DRAGON *UK, male vocal/instrumental duo*

21 Feb 68	**GREEN TAMBOURINE** *MGM 1380*	**50**	1 wk

SUNNY *UK, female vocalist*

30 Mar 74 ●	**DOCTOR'S ORDERS** *CBS 2068*	**7**	10 wks

SUNSHINE BAND — See *K. C. and the SUNSHINE BAND*

SUPERTRAMP

UK/US, male vocal/instrumental group

15 Feb 75	**DREAMER** *A & M AMS 7152*	**13**	10 wks
25 Jun 77	**GIVE A LITTLE BIT** *A & M AMS 7293*	**29**	7 wks
31 Mar 79 ●	**THE LOGICAL SONG** *A & M AMS 7427*	**7**	11 wks
30 Jun 79 ●	**BREAKFAST IN AMERICA** *A & M AMS 7451*	**9**	10 wks
27 Oct 79	**GOODBYE STRANGER** *A & M AMS 7481*	**57**	3 wks
30 Oct 82	**IT'S RAINING AGAIN** *A & M AMS 8255*	**26**†	9 wks

It's Raining Again is 'featuring vocals by Roger Hudson'.

SUPREMES *US, female vocal group*

3 Sep 64 ●	**WHERE DID OUR LOVE GO** *Stateside SS 327*	**3**	14 wks
22 Oct 64 ★	**BABY LOVE** *Stateside SS 350*	**1**	15 wks
21 Jan 65	**COME SEE ABOUT ME** *Stateside SS 376*	**27**	6 wks
25 Mar 65 ●	**STOP IN THE NAME OF LOVE** *Tamla Motown TMG 501*	**7**	12 wks
10 Jun 65	**BACK IN MY ARMS AGAIN** *Tamla Motown TMG 516*	**40**	5 wks
9 Dec 65	**I HEAR A SYMPHONY** *Tamla Motown TMG 543*	**50**	1 wk
23 Dec 65	**I HEAR A SYMPHONY** (re-entry) *Tamla Motown TMG 543*	**39**	4 wks
8 Sep 66 ●	**YOU CAN'T HURRY LOVE** *Tamla Motown TMG 575*	**3**	12 wks
1 Dec 66 ●	**YOU KEEP ME HANGIN' ON** *Tamla Motown TMG 585*	**8**	10 wks
2 Mar 67	**LOVE IS HERE AND NOW YOU'RE GONE** *Tamla Motown TMG 597*	**17**	10 wks

Date	Title *Label Number*	Position	
11 May 67	● **THE HAPPENING** *Tamla Motown TMG 607*	**6**	12 wks
30 Aug 67	● **REFLECTIONS** *Tamla Motown TMG 616*	**5**	14 wks
29 Nov 67	**IN AND OUT OF LOVE** *Tamla Motown TMG 632*	**13**	13 wks
10 Apr 68	**FOREVER CAME TODAY** *Tamla Motown TMG 650*	**28**	8 wks
3 Jul 68	**SOME THINGS YOU NEVER GET USED TO** *Tamla Motown TMG 662*	**34**	6 wks
20 Nov 68	**LOVE CHILD** *Tamla Motown TMG 677*	**15**	14 wks
23 Apr 69	**I'M LIVING IN SHAME** *Tamla Motown TMG 695*	**14**	9 wks
2 Jul 69	**I'M LIVING IN SHAME** (re-entry) *Tamla Motown TMG 695*	**50**	1 wk
16 Jul 69	**NO MATTER WHAT SIGN YOU ARE** *Tamla Motown TMG 704*	**37**	7 wks
13 Dec 69	**SOMEDAY WE'LL BE TOGETHER** *Tamla Motown TMG 721*	**13**	13 wks
2 May 70	● **UP THE LADDER TO THE ROOF** *Tamla Motown TMG 735*	**6**	15 wks
16 Jan 71	● **STONED LOVE** *Tamla Motown TMG 760*	**3**	13 wks
21 Aug 71	● **NATHAN JONES** *Tamla Motown TMG 782*	**5**	11 wks
4 Mar 72	● **FLOY JOY** *Tamla Motown TMG 804*	**9**	10 wks
15 Jul 72	● **AUTOMATICALLY SUNSHINE** *Tamla Motown TMG 821*	**10**	9 wks
21 Apr 73	**BAD WEATHER** *Tamla Motown TMG 847*	**37**	4 wks
24 Aug 74	**BABY LOVE** (re-issue) *Tamla Motown TMG 915*	**12**	10 wks

Diana Ross is lead singer on all the hits up to and including Someday We'll Be Together, *and on the re-issue of* Baby Love. *From* Reflections *up to and including* Someday We'll Be Together, *and on the re-issue of* Baby Love, *the group is billed as Diana Ross and the Supremes. See also Diana Ross, Marvin Gaye and Diana Ross, Supremes and the Four Tops, Supremes and the Temptations, Diana Ross and the Supremes and the Temptations.*

SUPREMES and the FOUR TOPS

US, female and male vocal groups

Date	Title *Label Number*	Position	
26 Jun 71	**RIVER DEEP MOUNTAIN HIGH** *Tamla Motown TMG 777*	**11**	10 wks
20 Nov 71	**YOU GOTTA HAVE LOVE IN YOUR HEART** *Tamla Motown TMG 793*	**25**	10 wks

See also Supremes, Four Tops, Supremes and the Temptations.

SUPREMES and the TEMPTATIONS

US, female and male vocal groups

Date	Title *Label Number*	Position	
21 Mar 70	**WHY (MUST WE FALL IN LOVE)** *Tamla Motown TMG 730*	**31**	7 wks

See also Supremes, Temptations, Diana Ross and the Supremes and the Temptations, Supremes and the Four Tops.

SURFACE NOISE *UK, male instrumental group*

Date	Title *Label Number*	Position	
31 May 80	**THE SCRATCH** *WEA K 18291*	**26**	8 wks
30 Aug 80	**DANCIN' ON A WIRE** *Groove GP102*	**59**	3 wks

SURFARIS *US, male instrumental group*

Date	Title *Label Number*	Position	
25 Jul 63	● **WIPE OUT** *London HLD 9751*	**5**	14 wks

SURPRISE SISTERS *UK, female vocal group*

Date	Title *Label Number*	Position	
13 Mar 76	**LA BOOGA ROOGA** *Good Earth GD 1*	**38**	3 wks

SURVIVOR *US, male vocal/instrumental group*

Date	Title *Label Number*	Position	
31 Jul 82	★ **EYE OF THE TIGER** *Scotti Brothers SCT A 2411*	**1**	15 wks

SUTHERLAND BROTHERS

UK, male vocal/instrumental duo

Date	Title *Label Number*	Position	
3 Apr 76	● **ARMS OF MARY** *CBS 4001*	**5**	12 wks
20 Nov 76	**SECRETS** *CBS 4668*	**35**	4 wks
2 Jun 79	**EASY COME EASY GO** *CBS 7121*	**50**	4 wks

First two hits credited to Sutherland Brothers and Quiver.

Pat SUZUKI *US, female vocalist*

Date	Title *Label Number*	Position	
14 Apr 60	**I ENJOY BEING A GIRL** *RCA 1171*	**49**	1 wk

Billy SWAN *US, male vocalist*

Date	Title *Label Number*	Position	
14 Dec 74	● **I CAN HELP** *Monument MNT 2752*	**6**	9 wks
24 May 75	**DON'T BE CRUEL** *Monument MNT 3244*	**42**	4 wks

SWEET *UK, male vocal/instrumental group*

Date	Title *Label Number*	Position	
13 Mar 71	**FUNNY FUNNY** *RCA 2051*	**13**	14 wks
12 Jun 71	● **CO-CO** *RCA 2087*	**2**	15 wks
16 Oct 71	**ALEXANDER GRAHAM BELL** *RCA 2121*	**33**	5 wks
5 Feb 72	**POPPA JOE** *RCA 2164*	**11**	12 wks
10 Jun 72	● **LITTLE WILLY** *RCA 2225*	**4**	14 wks
9 Sep 72	● **WIG-WAM BAM** *RCA 2260*	**4**	13 wks
13 Jan 73	★ **BLOCKBUSTER** *RCA 2305*	**1**	15 wks
5 May 73	● **HELL RAISER** *RCA 2357*	**2**	11 wks
22 Sep 73	● **BALLROOM BLITZ** *RCA 2403*	**2**	9 wks
19 Jan 74	● **TEENAGE RAMPAGE** *RCA LPBO 5004*	**2**	8 wks
13 Jul 74	**THE SIX TEENS** *RCA LPBO 5037*	**41**	2 wks
9 Nov 74	**TURN IT DOWN** *RCA 2480*	**41**	2 wks
15 Mar 75	● **FOX ON THE RUN** *RCA 2524*	**2**	10 wks
12 Jul 75	**ACTION** *RCA 2578*	**15**	6 wks
24 Jan 76	**LIES IN YOUR EYES** *RCA 2641*	**35**	4 wks
28 Jan 78	● **LOVE IS LIKE OXYGEN** *Polydor POSP 1*	**9**	9 wks

Rachel SWEET *US, female vocalist*

Date	Title *Label Number*	Position	
9 Dec 78	**B-A-B-Y** *Stiff BUY 39*	**35**	8 wks

See also Rex Smith and Rachel Sweet.

SWEET DREAMS *UK, male/female vocal duo*

Date	Title *Label Number*	Position	
20 Jul 74	● **HONEY HONEY** *Bradley's BRAD 7408*	**10**	12 wks

SWEET PEOPLE

France, male instrumental feathered vocal group

Date	Title *Label Number*	Position	
4 Oct 80	● **ET LES OISEAUX CHANTAIENT (AND THE BIRDS WERE SINGING)** *Polydor POSP 179*	**4**	8 wks

SWEET SENSATION *UK, male vocal group*

Date	Title *Label Number*	Position	
14 Sep 74	★ **SAD SWEET DREAMER** *Pye 7N 45385*	**1**	10 wks
18 Jan 75	**PURELY BY COINCIDENCE** *Pye 7N 45421*	**11**	7 wks

Above left **SUNDRAGON** Rob Freeman was originally in Hampton Grammar School R & B group The Others before joining the Sands from where he went on to join fellow member Anthony James before transmogrifying into Sundragon. They finally scored as a duo with a cover of the Lemon Pipers hit

Above **SYMBOLS** Their hits were covers of The Four Seasons and the Marvellettes. 'Bye Bye Baby' became a No. 1 for the BCRs in 1975
Left **ANDY STEWART** Scottish Soldier spent the 7th greatest number of consecutive weeks on the chart

Below **SWINGING BLUE JEANS** The 1959–64 line up (left to right) Les Braid, Norman Kuhlke, Ray Ennis, Ralph Ellis, who hit the high spot with their version of Chan Romero's 'Hippy Hippy Shake'

Date	Title *Label Number*	Position	

SWINGING BLUE JEANS

UK, male vocal/instrumental group

Date	Title *Label Number*	Position	
20 Jun 63	**IT'S TOO LATE NOW** *HMV POP 1170*	**30**	6 wks
8 Aug 63	**IT'S TOO LATE NOW** (re-entry) *HMV POP 1170*	**46**	3 wks
12 Dec 63	● **HIPPY HIPPY SHAKE** *HMV POP 1242*	**2**	17 wks
19 Mar 64	**GOOD GOLLY MISS MOLLY** *HMV POP 1273*	**11**	10 wks
4 Jun 64	● **YOU'RE NO GOOD** *HMV POP 1304*	**3**	13 wks
20 Jan 66	**DON'T MAKE ME OVER** *HMV POP 1501*	**31**	8 wks

SYLVESTER *US, male vocalist*

Date	Title *Label Number*	Position	
19 Aug 78	● **YOU MAKE ME FEEL (MIGHTY REAL)** *Fantasy FTC 160*	**8**	15 wks
18 Nov 78	**DANCE (DISCO HEAT)** *Fantasy FTC 163*	**29**	12 wks
31 Mar 79	**I (WHO HAVE NOTHING)** *Fantasy FTC 171*	**46**	5 wks
7 Jul 79	**STARS** *Fantasy FTC 177*	**47**	3 wks

SYLVESTER with Patrick COWLEY

UK, male vocal duo

Date	Title *Label Number*	Position	
11 Sep 82	**DO YA WANNA FUNK** *London LON 13*	**32**	8 wks

SYLVIA *US, female vocalist*

Date	Title *Label Number*	Position	
23 Jun 73	**PILLOW TALK** *London HL 10415*	**14**	11 wks

SYLVIA *Sweden, female vocalist*

Date	Title *Label Number*	Position	
10 Aug 74	● **Y VIVA ESPANA** *Sonet SON 2037*	**4**	19 wks
4 Jan 75	**Y VIVA ESPANA** (re-entry) *Sonet SON 2037*	**35**	9 wks
26 Apr 75	**HASTA LA VISTA** *Sonet SON 2005*	**38**	5 wks

SYLVIAN SAKAMOTO

UK/Japan, male vocal/instrumental duo

Date	Title *Label Number*	Position	
7 Aug 82	**BAMBOO HOUSES/BAMBOO MUSIC** *Virgin VS 510*	**30**	4 wks

SYMARIP *UK, male vocal/instrumental group*

Date	Title *Label Number*	Position	
2 Feb 80	**SKINHEAD MOONSTOMP** *Trojan TRO 9062*	**54**	3 wks

SYMBOLS *UK, male vocal/instrumental group*

Date	Title *Label Number*	Position	
2 Aug 67	**BYE BYE BABY** *President PT 144*	**44**	3 wks
3 Jan 68	**BEST PART OF BREAKING UP** *President PT 173*	**25**	12 wks

SYREETA *US, female vocalist*

Date	Title *Label Number*	Position	
21 Sep 74	**SPINNIN' & SPINNIN'** *Tamla Motown TMG 912*	**49**	3 wks
1 Feb 75	**YOUR KISS IS SWEET** *Tamla Motown TMG 933*	**12**	8 wks
12 Jul 75	**HARMOUR LOVE** *Tamla Motown TMG 954*	**32**	4 wks

See also Billy Preston and Syreeta.

T. REX *UK, male vocal/instrumental group*

Date	Title *Label Number*	Position	
8 May 68	**DEBORA** *Regal Zonophone RZ 3008*	**34**	7 wks
4 Sep 68	**ONE INCH ROCK** *Regal Zonophone RZ 3011*	**28**	7 wks
9 Aug 69	**KING OF THE RUMBLING SPIRES** *Regal Zonophone RZ 3022*	**44**	1 wk
24 Oct 70	● **RIDE A WHITE SWAN** *Fly BUG 1*	**2**	20 wks
27 Feb 71	★ **HOT LOVE** *Fly BUG 6*	**1**	17 wks
10 Jul 71	★ **GET IT ON** *Fly BUG 10*	**1**	13 wks
13 Nov 71	● **JEEPSTER** *Fly BUG 16*	**2**	15 wks
29 Jan 72	★ **TELEGRAM SAM** *T. Rex 101*	**1**	12 wks
1 Apr 72	● **DEBORA/ ONE INCH ROCK** (re-issue) *Magnifly Echo 102*	**7**	10 wks
13 May 72	★ **METAL GURU** *EMI MARC 1*	**1**	14 wks
16 Sep 72	● **CHILDREN OF THE REVOLUTION** *EMI MARC 2*	**2**	10 wks
9 Dec 72	● **SOLID GOLD EASY ACTION** *EMI MARC 3*	**2**	11 wks
10 Mar 73	● **20TH CENTURY BOY** *EMI MARC 4*	**3**	9 wks
16 Jun 73	● **THE GROOVER** *EMI MARC 5*	**4**	9 wks
24 Nov 73	**TRUCK ON (TYKE)** *EMI MARC 6*	**12**	11 wks
9 Feb 74	**TEENAGE DREAM** *EMI MARC 7*	**13**	5 wks
13 Jul 74	**LIGHT OF LOVE** *EMI MARC 8*	**22**	5 wks
16 Nov 74	**ZIP GUN BOOGIE** *EMI MARC 9*	**41**	3 wks
12 Jul 75	**NEW YORK CITY** *EMI MARC 10*	**15**	8 wks
11 Oct 75	**DREAMY LADY** *EMI MARC 11*	**30**	5 wks
6 Mar 76	**LONDON BOYS** *EMI MARC 13*	**40**	3 wks
19 Jun 76	**I LOVE TO BOOGIE** *EMI MARC 14*	**13**	9 wks
2 Oct 76	**LASER LOVE** *EMI MARC 15*	**41**	4 wks
2 Apr 77	**THE SOUL OF MY SUIT** *EMI MARC 16*	**42**	3 wks
27 Mar 82	**TELEGRAM SAM** (re-entry) *T. Rex 101*	**69**	2 wks

Regal Zonophone and Magnifly hits bill the group as Tyrannosaurus Rex. Teenage Dream *is by Marc Bolan and T. Rex.* Dreamy Lady *is by T. Rex Disco Party.*

TALK TALK *UK, male vocal/instrumental group*

Date	Title *Label Number*	Position	
24 Apr 82	**TALK TALK** *EMI 5284*	**52**	4 wks
24 Jul 82	**TODAY** *EMI 5314*	**14**	13 wks
13 Nov 82	**TALK TALK** *EMI 5352*	**23**†	7 wks

EMI 5352 is a remixed version of EMI 5284.

TALKING HEADS

UK, male vocal/instrumental group

Date	Title *Label Number*	Position	
7 Feb 81	**ONCE IN A LIFETIME** *Sire SIR 4048*	**14**	10 wks
9 May 81	**HOUSES IN MOTION** *Sire SIR 4050*	**50**	3 wks

TAMS *US, male vocal group*

Date	Title *Label Number*	Position	
14 Feb 70	**BE YOUNG BE FOOLISH BE HAPPY** *Stateside SS 2123*	**32**	7 wks
31 Jul 71	★ **HEY GIRL DON'T BOTHER ME** *Probe PRO 532*	**1**	17 wks

Norma TANEGA *US, female vocalist*

Date	Title *Label Number*	Position	
7 Apr 66	**WALKING MY CAT NAMED DOG**	**22**	8 wks

Date	Title *Label Number*	Position	

The Children of TANSLEY SCHOOL

UK, children's choir

28 Mar 81	**MY MUM IS ONE IN A MILLION** *EMI 5151*	**27**	4 wks

TARRIERS *US, male vocal/instrumental group*

1 Mar 57	**BANANA BOAT SONG** *Columbia DB 3891*	**15**	5 wks

A TASTE OF HONEY *US, female vocal duo*

17 Jun 78	● **BOOGIE OOGIE OOGIE** *Capitol CL 15988*	**3**	16 wks

TAVARES *US, male vocal group*

10 Jul 76	● **HEAVEN MUST BE MISSING AN ANGEL** *Capitol CL 15876*	**4**	11 wks
9 Oct 76	● **DON'T TAKE AWAY THE MUSIC** *Capitol CL 15886*	**4**	10 wks
5 Feb 77	**MIGHTY POWER OF LOVE** *Capitol CL 15905*	**25**	6 wks
9 Apr 77	● **WHODUNIT** *Capitol CL 15914*	**5**	10 wks
2 Jul 77	**ONE STEP AWAY** *Capitol CL 15930*	**16**	7 wks
18 Mar 78	**THE GHOST OF LOVE** *Capitol CL 15968*	**29**	6 wks
6 May 78	● **MORE THAN A WOMAN** *Capitol CL 15977*	**7**	11 wks
12 Aug 78	**SLOW TRAIN TO PARADISE** *Capitol CL 15996*	**62**	3 wks

Felice TAYLOR *US, female vocalist*

25 Oct 67	**I FEEL LOVE COMIN' ON** *President PT 155*	**11**	13 wks

James TAYLOR *US, male vocalist*

21 Nov 70	**FIRE AND RAIN** *Warner Bros. WB 6104*	**42**	3 wks
28 Aug 71	● **YOU'VE GOT A FRIEND** *Warner Bros. WB 16085*	**4**	15 wks

See also Carly Simon and James Taylor.

Johnny TAYLOR *US, male vocalist*

24 Apr 76	**DISCO LADY** *CBS 4044*	**25**	7 wks

R. Dean TAYLOR *US, male vocalist*

19 Jun 68	**GOTTA SEE JANE** *Tamla Motown TMG 656*	**17**	12 wks
3 Apr 71	● **INDIANA WANTS ME** *Tamla Motown TMG 763*	**2**	15 wks
11 May 74	● **THERE'S A GHOST IN MY HOUSE** *Tamla Motown TMG 896*	**3**	12 wks
31 Aug 74	**WINDOW SHOPPING** *Polydor 2058 502*	**36**	5 wks
21 Sep 74	**GOTTA SEE JANE** (re-issue) *Tamla Motown TMG 918*	**41**	4 wks

Roger TAYLOR *UK, male vocalist*

18 Apr 81	**FUTURE MANAGEMENT** *EMI 5157*	**49**	4 wks

T-CONNECTION

US, male vocal/instrumental group

18 Jun 77	**DO WHAT YOU WANNA DO** *TK XC 9109*	**11**	8 wks
14 Jan 78	**ON FIRE** *TK TKR 6006*	**16**	5 wks
10 Jun 78	**LET YOURSELF GO** *TK TKR 6024*	**52**	3 wks
24 Feb 79	**AT MIDNIGHT** *TK TKR 7517*	**53**	5 wks
5 May 79	**SATURDAY NIGHT** *TK TKR 7536*	**41**	6 wks

TEACH-IN

Holland, male/female vocal/instrumental group

12 Apr 75	**DING-A-DONG** *Polydor 2058 570*	**13**	7 wks

TEARDROP EXPLODES

UK, male vocal/instrumental group

27 Sep 80	**WHEN I DREAM** *Mercury TEAR 1*	**47**	6 wks
31 Jan 81	● **REWARD** *Vertigo TEAR 2*	**6**	13 wks
2 May 81	**TREASON (IT'S JUST A STORY)** *Mercury TEAR 3*	**18**	8 wks
29 Aug 81	**PASSIONATE FRIEND** *Zoo TEAR 5*	**25**	10 wks
21 Nov 81	**COLOURS FLY AWAY** *Mercury TEAR 6*	**54**	3 wks
19 Jun 82	**TINY CHILDREN** *Mercury/Phonogram TEAR 7*	**44**	7 wks

TEARS — See *SNIFF 'N' The TEARS*

TEARS FOR FEARS

UK, male vocal/instrumental duo

2 Oct 82	● **MAD WORLD** *Mercury/Phonogram IDEA 3*	**3**†	13 wks

TECHNO TWINS *US, male/female vocal duo*

16 Jan 82	**FALLING IN LOVE AGAIN** *PRT 7P 224*	**75**	1 wk
30 Jan 82	**FALLING IN LOVE AGAIN** (re-entry) *PRT 7P 224*	**70**	1 wk

TEDDY BEARS *US, male/female vocal group*

19 Dec 58	● **TO KNOW HIM IS TO LOVE HIM** *London HL 8733*	**2**	16 wks
14 Apr 79	**TO KNOW HIM IS TO LOVE HIM** (re-issue) *Lightning LIG 9015*	**66**	1 wk

To Know Him Is To Love Him *re-issue was coupled with* Endless Sleep *by Jody Reynolds as a double A-side. See also Jody Reynolds.*

TEENAGERS — See *Frankie Lymon and the Teenagers*

TEICHER — See *FERRANTE and TEICHER*

TELEVISION *US, male vocal/instrumental group*

16 Apr 77	**MARQUEE MOON** *Elektra K 12252*	**30**	4 wks
30 Jul 77	**PROVE IT** *Elektra K 12262*	**25**	4 wks
22 Apr 78	**FOXHOLE** *Elektra K 12287*	**36**	2 wks

TELEX *Belgium, male vocal/instrumental duo*

21 Jul 79	**ROCK AROUND THE CLOCK** *Sire SIR 4020*	**34**	7 wks

Date	Title *Label Number*	Position	

TEMPERANCE SEVEN

UK, male vocal/instrumental band

30 Mar 61 ★	**YOU'RE DRIVING ME CRAZY** *Parlophone R 4757*	**1**	16 wks
15 Jun 61 ●	**PASADENA** *Parlophone R 4781*	**4**	17 wks
28 Sep 61	**HARD HEARTED HANNAH/ CHILI BOM BOM** *Parlophone R 4823*	**28**	4 wks
7 Dec 61	**CHARLESTON** *Parlophone R 4851*	**22**	8 wks

Chili Bom Bom *only listed with* Hard Hearted Hannah *for the weeks of 12 and 19 Oct 61.*

Nino TEMPO and April STEVENS

US, male/female vocal duo

7 Nov 63	**DEEP PURPLE** *London HLK 9785*	**17**	11 wks
16 Jan 64	**WHISPERING** *London HLK 9829*	**20**	8 wks

TEMPTATIONS *US, male vocal group*

18 Mar 65	**MY GIRL** *Stateside SS 395*	**43**	1 wk
1 Apr 65	**IT'S GROWING** *Tamla Motown TMG 504*	**49**	1 wk
15 Apr 65	**IT'S GROWING** (re-entry) *Tamla Motown TMG 504*	**45**	1 wk
14 Jul 66	**AIN'T TOO PROUD TO BEG** *Tamla Motown TMG 565*	**21**	11 wks
6 Oct 66	**BEAUTY IS ONLY SKIN DEEP** *Tamla Motown TMG 578*	**18**	10 wks
15 Dec 66	**(I KNOW) I'M LOSING YOU** *Tamla Motown TMG 587*	**19**	9 wks
6 Sep 67	**YOU'RE MY EVERYTHING** *Tamla Motown TMG 620*	**26**	15 wks
6 Mar 68	**I WISH IT WOULD RAIN** *Tamla Motown TMG 641*	**45**	1 wk
12 Jun 68	**I COULD NEVER LOVE ANOTHER** *Tamla Motown TMG 658*	**47**	1 wk
5 Mar 69 ●	**GET READY** *Tamla Motown TMG 688*	**10**	9 wks
23 Aug 69	**CLOUD NINE** *Tamla Motown TMG 707*	**15**	10 wks
17 Jan 70	**I CAN'T GET NEXT TO YOU** *Tamla Motown TMG 722*	**13**	9 wks
13 Jun 70	**PSYCHEDELIC SHACK** *Tamla Motown TMG 741*	**33**	7 wks
19 Sep 70 ●	**BALL OF CONFUSION** *Tamla Motown TMG 749*	**7**	12 wks
19 Dec 70	**BALL OF CONFUSION** (re-entry) *Tamla Motown TMG 749*	**48**	3 wks
22 May 71 ●	**JUST MY IMAGINATION (RUNNING AWAY WITH ME)** *Tamla Motown TMG 773*	**8**	16 wks
5 Feb 72	**SUPERSTAR (REMEMBER HOW YOU GOT WHERE YOU ARE)** *Tamla Motown TMG 800*	**32**	5 wks
15 Apr 72	**TAKE A LOOK AROUND** *Tamla Motown TMG 808*	**13**	10 wks
13 Jan 73	**PAPA WAS A ROLLIN' STONE** *Tamla Motown TMG 839*	**14**	8 wks
29 Sep 73	**LAW OF THE LAND** *Tamla Motown TMG 866*	**41**	4 wks
12 Jun 82	**STANDING ON THE TOP (PART 1)** *Motown TMG 1263*	**53**	3 wks

See also Supremes and the Temptations, Diana Ross and the Supremes and the Temptations. Standing On The Top *is 'featuring Rick James'. See Rick James, Teena Marie*

10 C. C. *UK, male vocal/instrumental group*

23 Sep 72 ●	**DONNA** *UK 6*	**2**	13 wks
19 May 73 ★	**RUBBER BULLETS** *UK 36*	**1**	15 wks
25 Aug 73 ●	**THE DEAN AND I** *UK 48*	**10**	8 wks
15 Jun 74 ●	**WALL STREET SHUFFLE** *UK 69*	**10**	10 wks
14 Sep 74	**SILLY LOVE** *UK 77*	**24**	7 wks
5 Apr 75 ●	**LIFE IS A MINESTRONE** *Mercury 6008 010*	**7**	8 wks
31 May 75 ★	**I'M NOT IN LOVE** *Mercury 6008 014*	**1**	11 wks
29 Nov 75 ●	**ART FOR ART'S SAKE** *Mercury 6008 017*	**5**	10 wks
20 Mar 76 ●	**I'M MANDY FLY ME** *Mercury 6008 019*	**6**	9 wks
11 Dec 76 ●	**THINGS WE DO FOR LOVE** *Mercury 6008 022*	**6**	11 wks
16 Apr 77 ●	**GOOD MORNING JUDGE** *Mercury 6008 025*	**5**	12 wks
12 Aug 78 ★	**DREADLOCK HOLIDAY** *Mercury 6008 035*	**1**	13 wks
7 Aug 82	**RUN AWAY** *Mercury/Phonogram MER 113*	**50**	4 wks

From Dreadlock Holiday, *10 C.C. are a male vocal/instrumental duo.*

TEN POLE TUDOR

UK, male vocal/instrumental group

25 Apr 81 ●	**SWORDS OF A THOUSAND MEN** *Stiff BUY 109*	**6**	12 wks
1 Aug 81	**WUNDERBAR** *Stiff BUY 120*	**16**	9 wks
14 Nov 81	**THROWING MY BABY OUT WITH THE BATHWATER** *Stiff BUY 129*	**49**	5 wks

see also Sex Pistols.

TEN YEARS AFTER

UK, male vocal/instrumental group

6 Jun 70 ●	**LOVE LIKE A MAN** *Deram DM 299*	**10**	18 wks

TENNESSEE THREE — See *Johnny CASH*

TENNILLE — See *CAPTAIN and TENNILLE*

Tammi TERRELL — See *Marvin GAYE and Tammi TERRELL*

Joe TEX *US, male vocalist*

23 Apr 77 ●	**AIN'T GONNA BUMP NO MORE (WITH NO BIG FAT WOMAN)** *Epic EPC 5035*	**2**	11 wks

THE *UK, male vocalist/instrumentalist*

4 Dec 82	**UNCERTAIN SMILE** *Epic EPC A 2787*	**68**	3 wks

THEATRE OF HATE

UK, male vocal/instrumental group

23 Jan 82	**DO YOU BELIEVE IN THE WESTWORLD** *Burning Rome BRR 2*	**40**	7 wks
29 May 82	**THE HOP** *Burning Rome BRR 3*	**70**	2 wks

THEM *UK male vocal/instrumental group*

7 Jan 65 ●	**BABY PLEASE DON'T GO** *Decca F 12018*	**10**	9 wks
25 Mar 65 ●	**HERE COMES THE NIGHT** *Decca F 12094*	**2**	12 wks

THIN LIZZY *Ireland, male vocal/instrumental group*

20 Jan 73 ●	**WHISKY IN THE JAR** *Decca F 13355*	**6**	12 wks
29 May 76 ●	**THE BOYS ARE BACK IN TOWN** *Vertigo 6059 139*	**8**	10 wks
14 Aug 76	**JAILBREAK** *Vertigo 6059 150*	**31**	4 wks
15 Jan 77	**DON'T BELIEVE A WORD** *Vertigo Lizzy 001*	**12**	7 wks
13 Aug 77	**DANCIN' IN THE MOONLIGHT (IT'S CAUGHT ME IN THE SPOTLIGHT)** *Vertigo 6059 177*	**14**	8 wks
13 May 78	**ROSALIE - COWGIRLS' SONG** (MEDLEY) *Vertigo LIZZY 2*	**20**	13 wks

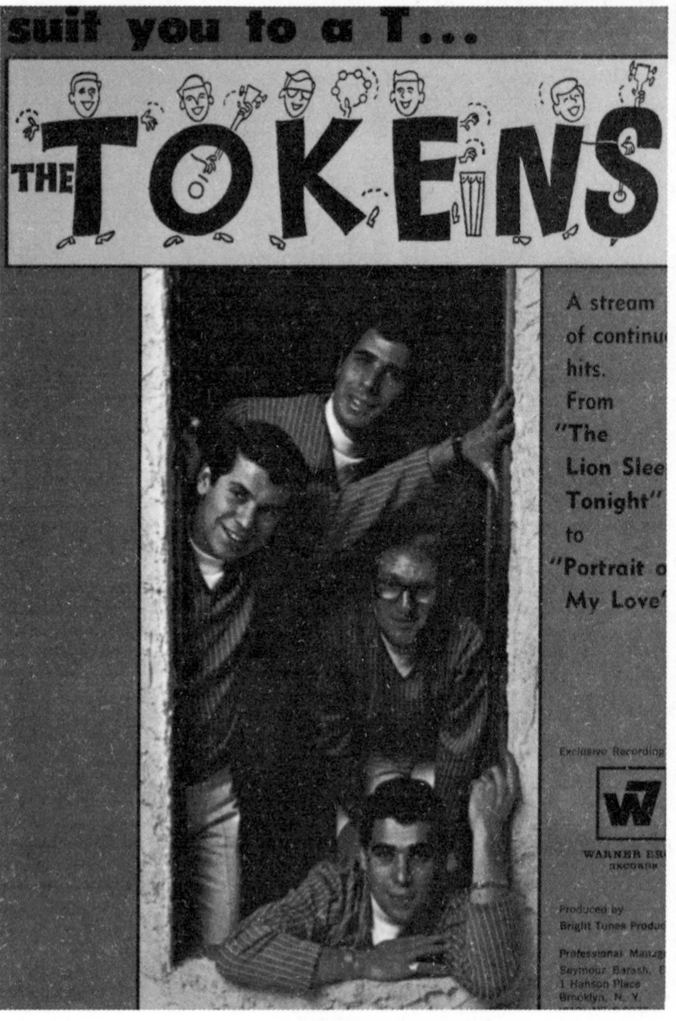

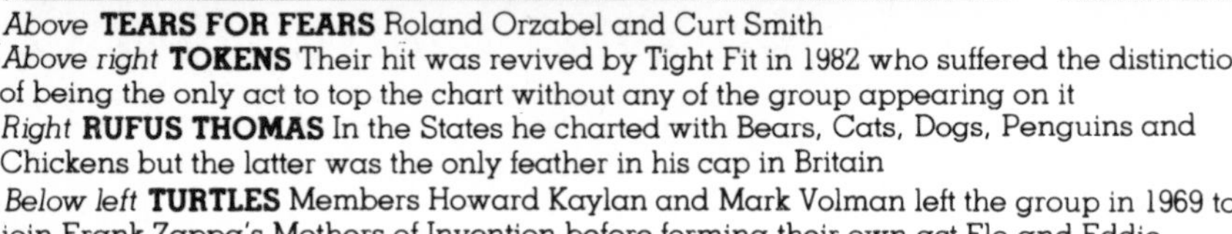

Above **TEARS FOR FEARS** Roland Orzabel and Curt Smith
Above right **TOKENS** Their hit was revived by Tight Fit in 1982 who suffered the distinction of being the only act to top the chart without any of the group appearing on it
Right **RUFUS THOMAS** In the States he charted with Bears, Cats, Dogs, Penguins and Chickens but the latter was the only feather in his cap in Britain
Below left **TURTLES** Members Howard Kaylan and Mark Volman left the group in 1969 to join Frank Zappa's Mothers of Invention before forming their own act Flo and Eddie

Date	Title *Label Number*	Position	
3 Mar 79	● **WAITING FOR AN ALIBI** *Vertigo LIZZY 003*	**9**	8 wks
16 Jun 79	**DO ANYTHING YOU WANT TO** *Vertigo LIZZY 004*	**14**	9 wks
20 Oct 79	**SARAH** *Vertigo LIZZY 5*	**24**	13 wks
24 May 80	**CHINATOWN** *Vertigo LIZZY 6*	**21**	9 wks
27 Sep 80	● **KILLER ON THE LOOSE** *Vertigo LIZZY 7*	**10**	7 wks
2 May 81	**KILLERS LIVE (EP)** *Vertigo LIZZY 8*	**19**	7 wks
8 Aug 81	**TROUBLE BOYS** *Vertigo LIZZY 9*	**53**	4 wks
6 Mar 82	**HOLLYWOOD (DOWN ON YOUR LUCK)** *Vertigo/Phonogram LIZZY 10*	**53**	3 wks

Tracks on Killers Live EP: *Bad Reputation, Are You Ready, Dear Miss Lonely hearts.*

THIRD WORLD

Jamaica, male vocal/instrumental group

Date	Title *Label Number*	Position	
23 Sep 78	● **NOW THAT WE'VE FOUND LOVE** *Island WIP 6457*	**10**	9 wks
6 Jan 79	**COOL MEDITATION** *Island WIP 6469*	**17**	10 wks
16 Jun 79	**TALK TO ME** *Island WIP 6496*	**56**	5 wks
6 Jun 81	● **DANCING ON THE FLOOR (HOOKED ON LOVE)** *CBS A 1214*	**10**	15 wks
17 Apr 82	**TRY JAH LOVE** *CBS A 2063*	**47**	6 wks

THIS YEAR'S BLONDE

UK, male/female vocal/instrumental group

Date	Title *Label Number*	Position	
10 Oct 81	**PLATINUM POP** *Creole CR 19*	**46**	5 wks

B. J. THOMAS *US, male vocalist*

Date	Title *Label Number*	Position	
21 Feb 70	**RAINDROPS KEEP FALLING ON MY HEAD** *Wand WN1*	**38**	3 wks
2 May 70	**RAINDROPS KEEP FALLING ON MY HEAD** (re-entry) *Wand WN1*	**49**	1 wk

Carla THOMAS — See *Otis REDDING and Carla THOMAS*

Evelyn THOMAS *US, female vocalist*

Date	Title *Label Number*	Position	
24 Jan 76	**WEAK SPOT** *20th Century BTC 1014*	**26**	7 wks
17 Apr 76	**DOOMSDAY** *20th Century BTC 1019*	**41**	1 wk
1 May 76	**DOOMSDAY** (re-entry) *20th Century BTC 1019*	**45**	1 wk

Jamo THOMAS *US, male vocalist*

Date	Title *Label Number*	Position	
26 Feb 69	**I SPY FOR THE FBI** *Polydor 56755*	**48**	1 wk
12 Mar 69	**I SPY FOR THE FBI** (re-entry) *Polydor 56755*	**44**	1 wk

Nicky THOMAS *Jamaica, male vocalist*

Date	Title *Label Number*	Position	
13 Jun 70	● **LOVE OF THE COMMON PEOPLE** *Trojan TR 7750*	**9**	14 wks

Rufus THOMAS *US, male vocalist*

Date	Title *Label Number*	Position	
11 Apr 70	**DO THE FUNKY CHICKEN** *Stax 144*	**18**	12 wks

Tasha THOMAS *US, female vocalist*

Date	Title *Label Number*	Position	
20 Jan 79	**SHOOT ME (WITH YOUR LOVE)** *Atlantic LV 4*	**59**	3 wks

Timmy THOMAS *US, male vocalist*

Date	Title *Label Number*	Position	
24 Feb 73	**WHY CAN'T WE LIVE TOGETHER** *Mojo 2027 012*	**12**	11 wks

Chris THOMPSON *UK, male vocalist*

Date	Title *Label Number*	Position	
27 Oct 79	**IF YOU REMEMBER ME** *Planet K 12389*	**42**	5 wks

Sue THOMPSON *US, female vocalist*

Date	Title *Label Number*	Position	
2 Nov 61	**SAD MOVIES** *Polydor NH 66967*	**46**	1 wk
16 Nov 61	**SAD MOVIES** (re-entry) *Polydor NH 66967*	**48**	1 wk
21 Jan 65	**PAPER TIGER** *Hickory 1284*	**50**	1 wk
11 Feb 65	**PAPER TIGER** (re-entry) *Hickory 1284*	**30**	6 wks

THOMPSON TWINS

UK, male/female vocal/instrumental group

Date	Title *Label Number*	Position	
6 Nov 82	**LIES** *Arista ARIST 486*	**67**	3 wks

David THORNE *US, male vocalist*

Date	Title *Label Number*	Position	
24 Jan 63	**ALLEY CAT SONG** *Stateside SS 141*	**21**	8 wks

Ken THORNE *UK, orchestra*

Date	Title *Label Number*	Position	
18 Jul 63	● **THEME FROM THE FILM THE LEGION'S LAST PATROL** *HMV POP 1176*	**4**	15 wks

THREE DEGREES *US, female vocal group*

Date	Title *Label Number*	Position	
13 Apr 74	**YEAR OF DECISION** *Philadelphia International PIR 2073*	**13**	10 wks
13 Jul 74	★ **WHEN WILL I SEE YOU AGAIN** *Philadelphia International PIR 2155*	**1**	16 wks
2 Nov 74	**GET YOUR LOVE BACK** *Philadelphia International PIR 2737*	**34**	4 wks
12 Apr 75	● **TAKE GOOD CARE OF YOURSELF** *Philadelphia International PIR 3177*	**9**	9 wks
5 Jul 75	**LONG LOST LOVER** *Philadelphia International PIR 3352*	**40**	4 wks
1 May 76	**TOAST OF LOVE** *Epic EPC 4215*	**36**	4 wks
7 Oct 78	**GIVIN' UP GIVIN' IN** *Ariola ARO 130*	**12**	10 wks
13 Jan 79	● **WOMAN IN LOVE** *Ariola ARO 141*	**3**	11 wks
24 Mar 79	● **THE RUNNER** *Ariola ARO 154*	**10**	10 wks
23 Jun 79	**THE GOLDEN LADY** *Ariola ARO 170*	**56**	3 wks
29 Sep 79	**JUMP THE GUN** *Ariola ARO 183*	**48**	5 wks
24 Nov 79	● **MY SIMPLE HEART** *Ariola ARO 202*	**9**	11 wks

See also MFSB

THREE DOG NIGHT

US, male vocal/instrumental group

Date	Title *Label Number*	Position	
8 Aug 70	● **MAMA TOLD ME NOT TO COME** *Stateside SS 8052*	**3**	14 wks
29 May 71	**JOY TO THE WORLD** *Probe PRO 523*	**24**	9 wks

THREE GOOD REASONS

UK, male vocal/instrumental group

Date	Title *Label Number*	Position	
10 Mar 66	**NOWHERE MAN** *Mercury MF 899*	**47**	3 wks

Date	Title *Label Number*	Position	

THREE KAYES *UK, female vocal group*

Date	Title *Label Number*	Position	
25 May 56	**IVORY TOWER** *HMV POP 209*	**20**	5 wks

The Three Kayes became The Kaye Sisters. See also Kaye Sisters, Frankie Vaughan and the Kaye Sisters.

THREE TONS OF JOY — See *Johnny OTIS Show*

Harry THUMANN *Germany, male instrumentalist*

Date	Title *Label Number*	Position	
21 Feb 81	**UNDERWATER** *Decca F 13901*	**41**	6 wks

THUNDERCLAP NEWMAN *UK, male vocal/instrumental group*

Date	Title *Label Number*	Position	
11 Jun 69	★ **SOMETHING IN THE AIR** *Track 604-031*	**1**	12 wks
27 Jun 70	**ACCIDENTS** *Track 2094 001*	**46**	1 wk

THUNDERTHIGHS *UK, female vocal group*

Date	Title *Label Number*	Position	
22 Jun 74	**CENTRAL PARK ARREST** *Philips 6006 386*	**30**	5 wks

Bobby THURSTON *US, male vocalist*

Date	Title *Label Number*	Position	
29 Mar 80	● **CHECK OUT THE GROOVE** *Epic EPC 8348*	**10**	10 wks

TICH — See *Dave DEE, DOZY, BEAKY, MICK and TICH*

TIGHT FIT *UK, male/female vocal group.*

Date	Title *Label Number*	Position	
18 Jul 81	● **BACK TO THE SIXTIES** *Jive JIVE 002*	**8**	11 wks
26 Sep 81	**BACK TO THE SIXTIES PART 2** *Jive JIVE 005*	**33**	5 wks
23 Jan 82	★ **THE LION SLEEPS TONIGHT** *Jive JIVE 9*	**1**	15 wks
1 May 82	● **FANTASY ISLAND** *Jive JIVE 13*	**5**	12 wks
31 Jul 82	**SECRET HEART** *Jive JIVE 20*	**41**	6 wks

TIJUANA BRASS — See *Herb ALPERT and the TIJUANA BRASS*

Johnny TILLOTSON *US, male vocalist*

Date	Title *Label Number*	Position	
1 Dec 60	★ **POETRY IN MOTION** *London HLA 9231*	**1**	15 wks
2 Feb 61	**JIMMY'S GIRL** *London HLA 9275*	**50**	1 wk
16 Feb 61	**JIMMY'S GIRL** (re-entry) *London HLA 9275*	**43**	1 wk
12 Jul 62	**IT KEEPS RIGHT ON A HURTIN'** *London HLA 9550*	**31**	10 wks
4 Oct 62	**SEND ME THE PILLOW YOU DREAM ON** *London HLA 9598*	**21**	10 wks
27 Dec 62	**I CAN'T HELP IT** *London HLA 9642*	**42**	1 wk
10 Jan 63	**I CAN'T HELP IT** (re-entry) *London HLA 9642*	**47**	1 wk
24 Jan 63	**I CAN'T HELP IT** (2nd re-entry) *London HLA 9642*	**41**	4 wks
9 May 63	**OUT OF MY MIND** *London HLA 9695*	**34**	5 wks
14 Apr 79	**POETRY IN MOTION** (re-issue) /**PRINCESS PRINCESS** *Lightning LIG 9016*	**67**	2 wks

TIMEBOX *UK, male vocal/instrumental group*

Date	Title *Label Number*	Position	
24 Jul 68	**BEGGIN'** *Deram DM 194*	**38**	4 wks

TINY TIM *US, male vocalist*

Date	Title *Label Number*	Position	
5 Feb 69	**GREAT BALLS OF FIRE** *Reprise RS 20802*	**45**	1 wk

TITANIC *Holland, male instrumental group*

Date	Title *Label Number*	Position	
25 Sep 71	● **SULTANA** *CBS 5365*	**5**	12 wks

Art and Dotty TODD *US, male/female vocal duo*

Date	Title *Label Number*	Position	
13 Feb 53	● **BROKEN WINGS** *HMV B 10399*	**6**	7 wks

TOKENS *US, male vocal group*

Date	Title *Label Number*	Position	
21 Dec 61	**THE LION SLEEPS TONIGHT** *RCA 1263*	**11**	12 wks

TOM TOM CLUB *US, female/male vocal/instrumental group*

Date	Title *Label Number*	Position	
20 Jun 81	● **WORDY RAPPINGHOOD** *Island WIP 6694*	**7**	9 wks
10 Oct 81	**GENIUS OF LOVE** *Island WIP 6735*	**65**	2 wks
7 Aug 82	**UNDER THE BOARDWALK** *Island WIP 6762*	**22**	9 wks

TONIGHT *UK, male vocal/instrumental group*

Date	Title *Label Number*	Position	
28 Jan 78	**DRUMMER MAN** *Target TDS 1*	**14**	8 wks
20 May 78	**MONEY THAT'S YOUR PROBLEM** *Target TDS 2*	**66**	2 wks

TOPOL *Israel, male vocalist*

Date	Title *Label Number*	Position	
20 Apr 67	● **IF I WERE A RICH MAN** *CBS 202651*	**9**	20 wks

Mel TORME *US, male vocalist*

Date	Title *Label Number*	Position	
27 Apr 56	**MOUNTAIN GREENERY** *Vogue/ Coral Q 72150*	**15**	11 wks
27 Jul 56	● **MOUNTAIN GREENERY** (re-entry) *Vogue/ Coral Q 72150*	**4**	13 wks
3 Jan 63	**COMING HOME BABY** *London HLK 9643*	**13**	8 wks

TORNADOS *UK, male instrumental group*

Date	Title *Label Number*	Position	
30 Aug 62	★ **TELSTAR** *Decca F 11494*	**1**	25 wks
10 Jan 63	● **GLOBETROTTER** *Decca F 11562*	**5**	11 wks
21 Mar 63	**ROBOT** *Decca F 11606*	**17**	12 wks
6 Jun 63	**THE ICE CREAM MAN** *Decca F 11662*	**18**	9 wks
10 Oct 63	**DRAGONFLY** *Decca F 11745*	**41**	2 wks

Mitchell TOROK *US, male vocalist*

Date	Title *Label Number*	Position	
28 Sep 56	● **WHEN MEXICO GAVE UP THE RUMBA** *Brunswick 05586*	**6**	17 wks
11 Jan 57	**RED LIGHT GREEN LIGHT** *Brunswick 05626*	**29**	1 wk
1 Feb 57	**WHEN MEXICO GAVE UP THE RUMBA** (re-entry) *Brunswick 05586*	**30**	1 wk

Peter TOSH *Jamaica, male vocalist*

Date	Title *Label Number*	Position	
21 Oct 78	**(YOU GOTTA WALK) DON'T LOOK BACK** *EMI 2859*	**43**	7 wks

TOTO *US, male vocal/instrumental group*

Date	Title *Label Number*	Position	
10 Feb 79	**HOLD THE LINE** *CBS 6784*	**14**	11 wks

Above **TYRANNOSAURUS REX** Steve Peregrine Took and Marc Bolan were Tyrannosaurus Rex and under that name charted with 'Debora', 'One Inch Rock' and 'King Of The Rumbling Spires'. Before 'Ride a White Swan'. Took took off to form a group called the Pink Fairies and was replaced by Mickey Finn from Blues group Hapshash And The Coloured Coat *Left* **NINO TEMPO AND APRIL STEVENS** Years ahead of their time. The first duo to sing about a heavy metal band *Below* **TAMS** Had their first American hit 'Untie Me' 8 years before their British debut

Date	Title *Label Number*	Position	

TOTO COELO *UK, female vocal group*

7 Aug 82	● **I EAT CANNIBALS PART 1** *Radialchoice/Virgin TIC 10*	**8**	10 wks
13 Nov 82	**DRACULA'S TANGO/MUCHO MACHO** *Radialchoice/Virgin TIC 11*	**54**	4 wks

TOTTENHAM HOTSPUR F.A. CUP FINAL SQUAD *UK, male football team vocalists*

9 May 81	● **OSSIE'S DREAM (SPURS ARE ON THEIR WAY TO WEMBLEY)** *Rockney SHELF 1*	**5**	8 wks
1 May 82	**TOTTENHAM TOTTENHAM** *Rockney SHELF 2*	**19**	7 wks

Both hits feature the uncredited vocal and instrumental talents of Chas and Dave. See Chas and Dave.

TOURISTS

UK male/female vocal/instrumental group

9 Jun 79	**BLIND AMONG THE FLOWERS** *Logo GO 350*	**52**	5 wks
8 Sep 79	**THE LONELIEST MAN IN THE WORLD** *Logo GO 360*	**32**	7 wks
10 Nov 79	● **I ONLY WANT TO BE WITH YOU** *Logo GO 370*	**4**	14 wks
9 Feb 80	● **SO GOOD TO BE BACK HOME AGAIN** *Logo TOUR 1*	**8**	9 wks
18 Oct 80	**DON'T SAY I TOLD YOU SO** *RCA TOUR 2*	**40**	5 wks

Pete TOWNSHEND *UK, male vocalist*

5 Apr 80	**ROUGH BOYS** *Atco K 11460*	**39**	6 wks
21 Aug 82	**UNIFORMS (CORPS D'ESPRIT)** *Atco K 11751*	**48**	5 wks

TOYAH *UK, female vocalist*

14 Feb 81	● **FOUR FROM TOYAH (EP)** *Safari TOY 1*	**4**	14 wks
16 May 81	● **I WANT TO BE FREE** *Safari SAFE 34*	**8**	11 wks
3 Oct 81	● **THUNDER IN THE MOUNTAINS** *Safari SAFE 38*	**4**	9 wks
28 Nov 81	**FOUR MORE FROM TOYAH** (EP) *Safari TOY 2*	**14**	9 wks
22 May 82	**BRAVE NEW WORLD** *Safari SAFE 45*	**21**	8 wks
17 Jul 82	**IEYA** *Safari SAFE 28*	**48**	5 wks
9 Oct 82	**BE LOUD BE PROUD (BE HEARD)** *Safari SAFE 52*	**30**	7 wks

Tracks on Four from Toyah EP: *It's A Mystery, Revelations, War Boys, Angels and Demons. Tracks on* Four More From Toyah EP: *Good Morning Universe, Urban Tribesman, In The Fairground, The Furious Futures.*

TOYS *US, female vocal group*

4 Nov 65	● **A LOVER'S CONCERTO** *Stateside SS 460*	**5**	13 wks
27 Jan 66	**ATTACK** *Stateside SS 483*	**36**	4 wks

TRAFFIC *UK, male vocal/instrumental group*

1 Jun 67	● **PAPER SUN** *Island WIP 6002*	**5**	10 wks
6 Sep 67	● **HOLE IN MY SHOE** *Island WIP 6017*	**2**	14 wks
29 Nov 67	● **HERE WE GO ROUND THE MULBERRY BUSH** *Island WIP 6025*	**8**	12 wks
6 Mar 68	**NO FACE, NO NAME, NO NUMBER** *Island WIP 6030*	**40**	4 wks

TRAMMPS *US, male vocal group*

23 Nov 74	**ZING WENT THE STRINGS OF MY HEART** *Buddah BDS 405*	**29**	10 wks
1 Feb 75	**SIXTY MINUTE MAN** *Buddah BDS 415*	**40**	4 wks
11 Oct 75	● **HOLD BACK THE NIGHT** *Buddah BDS 437*	**5**	8 wks
13 Mar 76	**THAT'S WHERE THE HAPPY PEOPLE GO** *Atlantic K 10703*	**35**	8 wks
24 Jul 76	**SOUL SEARCHIN' TIME** *Atlantic K 10797*	**42**	3 wks
14 May 77	**DISCO INFERNO** *Atlantic K 10914*	**16**	7 wks
24 Jun 78	**DISCO INFERNO** (re-issue) *Atlantic K 11135*	**47**	10 wks

TRASH *UK, male vocal/instrumental group*

25 Oct 69	**GOLDEN SLUMBERS - CARRY THAT WEIGHT** (MEDLEY) *Apple 17*	**35**	3 wks

John TRAVOLTA *US, male vocalist*

7 Oct 78	● **SANDY** *Polydor POSP 6*	**2**	15 wks
2 Dec 78	**GREASED LIGHTNIN'** *Polydor/Midsong POSP 14*	**11**	9 wks

See also John Travolta and Olivia Newton-John.

John TRAVOLTA and Olivia NEWTON-JOHN *US/UK, male/female vocal duo*

20 May 78	★ **YOU'RE THE ONE THAT I WANT** *RSO 006*	**1**	26 wks
16 Sep 78	★ **SUMMER NIGHTS** *RSO 18*	**1**	19 wks

See also John Travolta, Olivia Newton-John, Olivia Newton-John and Electric Light Orchestra, Olivia Newton-John and Cliff Richard. Second hit has credit: and cast.

TREMELOES *UK, male vocal/instrumental group*

2 Feb 67	● **HERE COMES MY BABY** *CBS 202519*	**4**	11 wks
27 Apr 67	★ **SILENCE IS GOLDEN** *CBS 2723*	**1**	15 wks
2 Aug 67	● **EVEN THE BAD TIMES ARE GOOD** *CBS 2930*	**4**	13 wks
8 Nov 67	**BE MINE** *CBS 3043*	**39**	2 wks
17 Jan 68	● **SUDDENLY YOU LOVE ME** *CBS 3234*	**6**	11 wks
8 May 68	**HELULE HELULE** *CBS 2889*	**14**	9 wks
18 Sep 68	● **MY LITTLE LADY** *CBS 3443*	**6**	12 wks
11 Dec 68	**I SHALL BE RELEASED** *CBS 3873*	**29**	5 wks
19 Mar 69	**HELLO WORLD** *CBS 4065*	**14**	8 wks
1 Nov 69	● **(CALL ME) NUMBER ONE** *CBS 4582*	**2**	14 wks
21 Mar 70	**BY THE WAY** *CBS 4815*	**35**	6 wks
12 Sep 70	● **ME AND MY LIFE** *CBS 5139*	**4**	18 wks
10 Jul 71	**HELLO BUDDY** *CBS 7294*	**32**	7 wks

See also Brian Poole and the Tremeloes.

Jackie TRENT *UK, female vocalist*

22 Apr 65	★ **WHERE ARE YOU NOW (MY LOVE)** *Pye 7N 15776*	**1**	11 wks
1 Jul 65	**WHEN THE SUMMERTIME IS OVER** *Pye 7N 15865*	**39**	2 wks
2 Apr 69	**I'LL BE THERE** *Pye 7N 17693*	**38**	4 wks

Tony TRIBE *Jamaica, male vocalist*

16 Jul 69	**RED RED WINE** *Downtown DT 419*	**50**	1 wk
9 Aug 69	**RED RED WINE** (re-entry) *Downtown DT 419*	**46**	1 wk

Date	Title *Label Number*	Position		Date	Title *Label Number*	Position	

TRINIDAD OIL COMPANY

Trinidad, male/female vocal/instrumental group

21 May 77 **THE CALENDAR SONG** *Harvest HAR 5122* **34** 5 wks

TRINITY — See *Julie DRISCOLL, Brian AUGER and the TRINITY*

TRIO *Germany, male vocal/instrumental group*

3 Jul 82 ● **DA DA DA** *Mobile Suit Corporation/Phonogram CORP 5* **2** 10 wks

TRIUMPH *Canada, male vocal/instrumental group*

22 Nov 80 **I LIVE FOR THE WEEKEND** *RCA 13* **59** 2 wks

TROGGS *UK, male vocal/instrumental group*

5 May 66 ● **WILD THING** *Fontana TF 689* **2** 12 wks
14 Jul 66 ★ **WITH A GIRL LIKE YOU** *Fontana TF 717* **1** 12 wks
29 Sep 66 ● **I CAN'T CONTROL MYSELF** *Page One POF 001* **2** 14 wks
15 Dec 66 ● **ANY WAY THAT YOU WANT ME** *Page One POF 010* **8** 10 wks
16 Feb 67 **GIVE IT TO ME** *Page One POF 015* **12** 10 wks
1 Jun 67 **NIGHT OF THE LONG GRASS** *Page One POF 022* **17** 6 wks
26 Jul 67 **HI HI HAZEL** *Page One POF 030* **42** 3 wks
18 Oct 67 ● **LOVE IS ALL AROUND** *Page One POF 040* **5** 14 wks
28 Feb 68 **LITTLE GIRL** *Page One POF 056* **37** 4 wks

TROUBADOURS DU ROI BAUDOUIN

Zaire, male/female vocal group

19 Mar 69 **SANCTUS (MISSA LUBA)** *Philips BF 1732* **28** 6 wks
7 May 69 **SANCTUS (MISSA LUBA)** (re-entry) *Philips BF 1732* **37** 5 wks

Doris TROY *US, female vocalist*

19 Nov 64 **WHATCHA GONNA DO ABOUT IT** *Atlantic AT 4011* **37** 7 wks
21 Jan 65 **WHATCHA GONNA DO ABOUT IT** (re-entry) *Atlantic AT 4011* **38** 5 wks

TRUCKIN' CO. — See *Garnet MIMMS and TRUCKIN' CO.*

Andrea TRUE CONNECTION

US, female vocalist, male instrumental backing group

17 Apr 76 ● **MORE MORE MORE** *Buddah BDS 442* **5** 10 wks
4 Mar 78 **WHAT'S YOUR NAME WHAT'S YOUR NUMBER** *Buddah BDS 467* **34** 6 wks

TRUSSEL *US, male vocal/instrumental group*

8 Mar 80 **LOVE INJECTION** *Elektra K 12412* **43** 4 wks

TRUTH *UK, male vocal duo*

3 Feb 66 **GIRL** *Pye 7N 17035* **27** 6 wks

TUBES *US, male vocal/instrumental group*

19 Nov 77 **WHITE PUNKS ON DOPE** *A & M AMS 7323* **28** 4 wks
28 Apr 79 **PRIME TIME** *A & M AMS 7423* **34** 10 wks
12 Sep 81 **DON'T WANT TO WAIT ANYMORE** *Capitol CL 208* **60** 4 wks

TUBEWAY ARMY — See *Gary NUMAN*

Tommy TUCKER *US, male vocalist*

26 Mar 64 **HI-HEEL SNEAKERS** *Pye 7N 25238* **23** 10 wks

Claramae TURNER — See *VARIOUS ARTISTS (Carousel Soundtrack)*

Ike and Tina TURNER

US, male instrumentalist - guitar, and female vocalist

9 Jun 66 ● **RIVER DEEP MOUNTAIN HIGH** *London HL 10046* **3** 13 wks
28 Jul 66 **TELL HER I'M NOT HOME** *Warner Bros. WB 5753* **48** 1 wk
27 Oct 66 **A LOVE LIKE YOURS** *London HL 10083* **16** 10 wks
12 Feb 69 **RIVER DEEP MOUNTAIN HIGH** (re-issue) *London HLU 10242* **33** 7 wks
8 Sep 73 ● **NUTBUSH CITY LIMITS** *United Artists UP 35582* **4** 13 wks

Sammy TURNER *US, male vocalist*

13 Nov 59 **ALWAYS** *London HLX 8963* **26** 2 wks

TURTLES *US, male vocal/instrumental group*

23 Mar 67 **HAPPY TOGETHER** *London HL 10115* **12** 12 wks
15 Jun 67 ● **SHE'D RATHER BE WITH ME** *London HLU 10135* **4** 15 wks
30 Oct 68 ● **ELENORE** *London HL 10223* **7** 12 wks

TUXEDOS — See *Bobby ANGELO and the TUXEDOS*

TWEETS *UK, male instrumental group*

12 Sep 81 ● **THE BIRDIE SONG (BIRDIE DANCE)** *PRT 7P 219* **2** 23 wks
4 Dec 81 **LETS ALL SING LIKE THE BIRDIES SING** *PRT 7P 226* **44** 6 wks
18 Dec 82 **THE BIRDIE SONG (BIRDIE DANCE)** (re-entry) *PRT 7P 219* **55** 2 wks

TWICE AS MUCH *UK, male vocal duo*

16 Jun 66 **SITTIN' ON A FENCE** *Immediate IM 033* **25** 9 wks

TWIGGY *UK, female vocalist*

14 Aug 76 **HERE I GO AGAIN** *Mercury 6007 100* **17** 10 wks

TWINKLE *UK, female vocalist*

26 Nov 64 ● **TERRY** *Decca F 12013* **4** 15 wks
25 Feb 65 **GOLDEN LIGHTS** *Decca F 12076* **21** 5 wks

Conway TWITTY *US, male vocalist*

Date	Title *Label Number*	Position	
14 Nov 58	★ **IT'S ONLY MAKE BELIEVE** *MGM 992*	**1**	15 wks
27 Mar 59	**STORY OF MY LOVE** *MGM 1003*	**30**	1 wk
21 Aug 59	● **MONA LISA** *MGM 1029*	**5**	14 wks
21 Jul 60	**IS A BLUE BIRD BLUE** *MGM 1082*	**43**	3 wks
23 Feb 61	**C'EST SI BON** *MGM 1118*	**40**	3 wks

TWO MAN SOUND

Belgium, male vocal/instrumental group

Date	Title *Label Number*	Position	
20 Jan 79	**QUE TAL AMERICA** *Miracle M 1*	**46**	7 wks

TYGERS OF PAN TANG

UK, male vocal/instrumental group

Date	Title *Label Number*	Position	
14 Feb 81	**HELLBOUND** *MCA 672*	**48**	3 wks
27 Mar 82	**LOVE POTION NO. 9** *MCA 769*	**45**	6 wks
10 Jul 82	**RENDEZVOUS** *MCA 777*	**49**	4 wks
11 Sep 82	**PARIS BY AIR** *MCA 790*	**63**	2 wks

Bonnie TYLER *UK, female vocalist*

Date	Title *Label Number*	Position	
30 Oct 76	● **LOST IN FRANCE** *RCA 2734*	**9**	10 wks
19 Mar 77	**MORE THAN A LOVER** *RCA PB 5008*	**27**	6 wks
3 Dec 77	● **IT'S A HEARTACHE** *RCA PB 5057*	**4**	12 wks
30 Jun 79	**MARRIED MEN** *RCA PB 5164*	**35**	6 wks

TYMES *US, male vocal group*

Date	Title *Label Number*	Position	
25 Jul 63	**SO MUCH IN LOVE** *Cameo Parkway P 871*	**21**	8 wks
15 Jan 69	**PEOPLE** *Direction 58 3903*	**16**	10 wks
21 Feb 74	**YOU LITTLE TRUST MAKER** *RCA 2456*	**18**	9 wks
21 Dec 74	★ **MS GRACE** *RCA 2493*	**1**	11 wks
17 Jan 76	**GOD'S GONNA PUNISH YOU** *RCA 2626*	**41**	3 wks

TYPICALLY TROPICAL

UK, male vocal/instrumental duo

Date	Title *Label Number*	Position	
5 Jul 75	★ **BARBADOS** *Gull GULS 14*	**1**	11 wks

Judie TZUKE *UK, female vocalist*

Date	Title *Label Number*	Position	
14 Jul 79	**STAY WITH ME TILL DAWN** *Rocket XPRES 17*	**16**	10 wks

U

U. K. *UK, male vocal/instrumental group*

Date	Title *Label Number*	Position	
30 Jun 79	**NOTHING TO LOSE** *Polydor POSP 55*	**67**	2 wks

U2 *Ireland, male vocal/instrumental group*

Date	Title *Label Number*	Position	
8 Aug 81	**FIRE** *Island WIP 6679*	**35**	6 wks
17 Oct 81	**GLORIA** *Island WIP 6733*	**55**	4 wks
3 Apr 82	**A CELEBRATION** *Island WIP 6770*	**47**	4 wks

U.B.40 *UK, male vocal/instrumental group*

Date	Title *Label Number*	Position	
8 Mar 80	● **KING/FOOD FOR THOUGHT** *Graduate GRAD 6*	**4**	13 wks
14 Jun 80	● **MY WAY OF THINKING/I THINK IT'S GOING TO RAIN** *Graduate GRAD 8*	**6**	10 wks
1 Nov 80	● **THE EARTH DIES SCREAMING/DREAM A LIE** *Graduate GRAD 10*	**10**	12 wks
23 May 81	**DON'T LET IT PASS YOU BY/DON'T SLOW DOWN** *Dep International DEP 1*	**16**	9 wks
8 Aug 81	● **ONE IN TEN** *Dep International DEP 2*	**7**	10 wks
13 Feb 82	**I WONT CLOSE MY EYES** *Dep International DEP 3*	**32**	6 wks
15 May 82	**LOVE IS ALL IS ALRIGHT** *Dep International DEP 4*	**29**	7 wks
28 Aug 82	**SO HERE I AM** *Dep International DEP 5*	**25**	9 wks

UFO *UK, male vocal/instrumental group*

Date	Title *Label Number*	Position	
5 Aug 78	**ONLY YOU CAN ROCK ME** *Chrysalis CHS 2241*	**50**	4 wks
27 Jan 79	**DOCTOR DOCTOR** *Chrysalis CHS 2287*	**35**	6 wks
31 Mar 79	**SHOOT SHOOT** *Chrysalis CHS 2318*	**48**	5 wks
12 Jan 80	**YOUNG BLOOD** *Chrysalis CHS 2399*	**36**	5 wks
17 Jan 81	**LONELY HEART** *Chrysalis CHS 2482*	**41**	5 wks
30 Jan 82	**LET IT RAIN** *Chrysalis CHS 2576*	**62**	3 wks

U.K. SUBS *UK, male vocal/instrumental group*

Date	Title *Label Number*	Position	
23 Jun 79	**STRANGLEHOLD** *Gem GEMS 5*	**26**	8 wks
8 Sep 79	**TOMORROW'S GIRLS** *Gem GEMS 10*	**28**	6 wks
1 Dec 79	**SHE'S NOT THERE/KICKS** (EP) *Gem GEMS 14*	**36**	7 wks
8 Mar 80	**WARHEAD** *Gem GEMS 23*	**30**	4 wks
17 May 80	**TEENAGE** *Gem GEMS 30*	**32**	5 wks
25 Oct 80	**PARTY IN PARIS** *Gem GEMS 42*	**37**	4 wks
18 Apr 81	**KEEP ON RUNNIN' (TILL YOU BURN)** *Gem GEMS 45*	**41**	5 wks

Tracks on EP: She's Not There/ Kicks/ Victim/ The Same Thing.

ULTRAVOX *UK, male vocal and instrumental group*

Date	Title *Label Number*	Position	
5 Jul 80	**SLEEPWALK** *Chrysalis CHS 2441*	**29**	11 wks
18 Oct 80	**PASSING STRANGERS** *Chrysalis CHS 2457*	**57**	4 wks
17 Jan 81	● **VIENNA** *Chrysalis CHS 2481*	**2**	14 wks
28 Mar 81	**SLOW MOTION** *Island WIP 6691*	**33**	4 wks
6 Jun 81	● **ALL STOOD STILL** *Chrysalis CHS 2522*	**8**	10 wks
2 Aug 81	**THE THIN WALL** *Chrysalis CHS 2540*	**14**	8 wks
7 Nov 81	**THE VOICE** *Chrysalis CHS 2559*	**16**	12 wks
25 Sep 82	**REAP THE WILD WIND** *Chrysalis CHS 2639*	**12**	9 wks
27 Nov 82	**HYMN** *Chrysalis CHS 2657*	**13**†	5 wks

Piero UMILIANI *Italy, orchestra and chorus*

Date	Title *Label Number*	Position	
30 Apr 77	● **MAH NA MAH NA** *EMI International INT 530*	**8**	8 wks

UNDERTAKERS

UK, male vocal/instrumental group

Date	Title *Label Number*	Position	
9 Apr 64	**JUST A LITTLE BIT** *Pye 7N 15607*	**49**	1 wk

UNDERTONES *UK, male vocal/instrumental group*

Date	Title *Label Number*	Position	
21 Oct 78	**TEENAGE KICKS** *Sire SIR 4007*	**31**	6 wks
3 Feb 79	**GET OVER YOU** *Sire SIR 4010*	**57**	4 wks
28 Apr 79	**JIMMY JIMMY** *Sire SIR 4015*	**16**	10 wks

Date	Title *Label Number*	Position	
21 Jul 79	**HERE COMES THE SUMMER** *Sire SIR 4022*	**34**	6 wks
20 Oct 79	**YOU'VE GOT MY NUMBER (WHY DON'T YOU USE IT?)** *Sire SIR 5024*	**32**	6 wks
5 Apr 80	● **MY PERFECT COUSIN** *Sire SIR 4038*	**9**	10 wks
5 Jul 80	**WEDNESDAY WEEK** *Sire SIR 4042*	**11**	9 wks
2 May 81	**IT'S GOING TO HAPPEN!** *Ardeck AROS 8*	**18**	9 wks
25 Jul 81	**JULIE OCEAN** *Ardeck ARDS 9*	**41**	5 wks

UNDISPUTED TRUTH

US, male vocal and instrumental group

Date	Title *Label Number*	Position	
22 Jan 77	**YOU + ME = LOVE** *Warner Bros. K 16804*	**43**	4 wks

UNION GAP — See *Gary PUCKETT and the UNION GAP*

UNIT FOUR PLUS TWO

UK, male vocal/instrumental group

Date	Title *Label Number*	Position	
13 Feb 64	**GREEN FIELDS** *Decca F 11821*	**48**	2 wks
25 Feb 65	★ **CONCRETE AND CLAY** *Decca F 12071*	**1**	15 wks
13 May 65	**YOU'VE NEVER BEEN IN LOVE LIKE THIS BEFORE** *Decca F 12144*	**14**	11 wks
17 Mar 66	**BABY NEVER SAY GOODBYE** *Decca F 12333*	**49**	1 wk

UNITONE — See *Laurel AITKEN and the UNITONE*

Phil UPCHURCH COMBO

US, male instrumental group, Phil Upchurch bass guitar

Date	Title *Label Number*	Position	
5 May 66	**YOU CAN'T SIT DOWN** *Sue WI 4005*	**39**	2 wks

UPSETTERS *Jamaica, male instrumental group*

Date	Title *Label Number*	Position	
4 Oct 69	● **RETURN OF DJANGO/ DOLLAR IN THE TEETH** *Upsetter US 301*	**5**	15 wks

Midge URE *UK, male vocalist*

Date	Title *Label Number*	Position	
12 Jun 82	● **NO REGRETS** *Chrysalis CHS 2618*	**9**	10 wks

V

VAGABONDS — See *Jimmy JAMES and the VAGABONDS*

Ricky VALANCE *UK, male vocalist*

Date	Title *Label Number*	Position	
25 Aug 60	★ **TELL LAURA I LOVE HER** *Columbia DB 4493*	**1**	16 wks

Ritchie VALENS *US, male vocalist*

Date	Title *Label Number*	Position	
6 Mar 59	**DONNA** *London HL 8803*	**29**	1 wk

Caterina VALENTE *France, female vocalist*

Date	Title *Label Number*	Position	
19 Aug 55	● **THE BREEZE AND I** *Polydor BM 6002*	**5**	14 wks

Dickie VALENTINE *UK, male vocalist*

Date	Title *Label Number*	Position	
20 Feb 53	**BROKEN WINGS** *Decca F 9954*	**12**	1 wk
13 Mar 53	● **ALL THE TIME AND EVERYWHERE** *Decca F 10038*	**9**	3 wks
5 Jun 53	● **IN A GOLDEN COACH** *Decca F 10098*	**7**	1 wk
5 Nov 54	**ENDLESS** *Decca F 10346*	**19**	1 wk
17 Dec 54	★ **FINGER OF SUSPICION** *Decca F 10394*	**1**	15 wks
17 Dec 54	● **MR. SANDMAN** *Decca F 10415*	**5**	12 wks
18 Feb 55	● **A BLOSSOM FELL** *Decca F 10430*	**9**	9 wks
29 Apr 55	**A BLOSSOM FELL** (re-entry) *Decca F 10430*	**18**	1 wk
3 Jun 55	● **I WONDER** *Decca F 10493*	**4**	15 wks
25 Nov 55	★ **CHRISTMAS ALPHABET** *Decca F 10628*	**1**	7 wks
16 Dec 55	**OLD PIANNA RAG** *Decca F 10645*	**15**	5 wks
7 Dec 56	● **CHRISTMAS ISLAND** *Decca F 10798*	**8**	5 wks
27 Dec 57	**SNOWBOUND FOR CHRISTMAS** *Decca F 10950*	**28**	1 wk
13 Mar 59	**VENUS** *Pye Nixa 7N 15192*	**28**	1 wk
3 Apr 59	**VENUS** (re-entry) *Pye Nixa 7N 15192*	**25**	1 wk
17 Apr 59	**VENUS** (2nd re-entry) *Pye Nixa 7N 15192*	**20**	4 wks
22 May 59	**VENUS** (3rd re-entry) *Pye Nixa 7N 15192*	**25**	1 wk
19 Jun 59	**VENUS** (4th re-entry) *Pye Nixa 7N 15192*	**28**	1 wk
23 Oct 59	**ONE MORE SUNRISE (MORGEN)** *Pye 7N 15221*	**14**	8 wks

See also Various Artists - All Star Hit Parade.

Joe VALINO *US, male vocalist*

Date	Title *Label Number*	Position	
18 Jan 57	**GARDEN OF EDEN** *HMV POP 283*	**23**	2 wks

Frankie VALLI *US, male vocalist*

Date	Title *Label Number*	Position	
12 Dec 70	**YOU'RE READY NOW** *Philips 320226*	**11**	13 wks
1 Feb 75	● **MY EYES ADORED YOU** *Private Stock PVT 1*	**5**	11 wks
21 Jun 75	**SWEARIN' TO GOD** *Private Stock PVT 21*	**31**	5 wks
17 Apr 76	**FALLEN ANGEL** *Private Stock PVT 51*	**11**	7 wks
26 Aug 78	● **GREASE** *RSO 012*	**3**	14 wks

See also Four Seasons.

Leroy VAN DYKE *US, male vocalist*

Date	Title *Label Number*	Position	
4 Jan 62	● **WALK ON BY** *Mercury AMT 1166*	**5**	17 wks
26 Apr 62	**BIG MAN IN A BIG HOUSE** *Mercury AMT 1173*	**34**	3 wks

VAN HALEN

US/Holland, male vocal/instrumental group

Date	Title *Label Number*	Position	
28 Jun 80	**RUNNIN' WITH THE DEVIL** *Warner Bros. HM 10*	**52**	3 wks

VANDELLAS — See *Martha REEVES and the VANDELLAS*

VANGELIS *Greece, male instrumentalist, keyboards*

Date	Title *Label Number*	Position	
9 May 81	**CHARIOTS OF FIRE - TITLES** *Polydor POSP 246*	**12**	10 wks
11 Jul 81	**HEAVEN AND HELL, THIRD MOVEMENT (THEME FROM THE BBC-TV SERIES, THE COSMOS)** *BBC 1*	**48**	6 wks
24 Apr 82	**CHARIOTS OF FIRE - TITLES** (re-entry) *Polydor POSP 246*	**41**	7 wks

see also Jon and Vangelis

Left **VISAGE** On safari in Carshalton

Lower left **VELVELETTES** Why two of their classic tracks 'He Was Really Saying Something' and 'Needle In A Haystack' failed to chart in Britain still remains a mystery

Below **UNDERTONES** The lads from Derry were relatively successful with their 6th hit

Below **MIDGE URE** Not only has he made the chart with Slik, Rich Kids, Visage and Ultravox but in 1982 charted as an artist in his own right with a cover of the Walker Bros. 1976 hit

Left **VENTURES** Jointly led by Don Wilson and Bob Boyle they'd been featuring 'Walk Don't Run' in their act for two years before deciding to record it

Date	Title *Label Number*	Position	

VANILLA FUDGE

US, male vocal/instrumental group

Date	Title *Label Number*	Position	
9 Aug 67	**YOU KEEP ME HANGIN' ON** *Atlantic 584 123*	**18**	11 wks

VANITY FARE *UK, male vocal/instrumental group*

Date	Title *Label Number*	Position	
28 Aug 68	**I LIVE FOR THE SUN** *Page One POF 075*	**20**	9 wks
23 Jul 69	● **EARLY IN THE MORNING** *Page One POF 142*	**8**	12 wks
27 Dec 69	**HITCHIN' A RIDE** *Page One POF 158*	**16**	13 wks

Randy VANWARMER *US, male vocalist*

Date	Title *Label Number*	Position	
4 Aug 79	● **JUST WHEN I NEEDED YOU MOST** *Bearsville WIP 6516*	**8**	11 wks

VAPORS *UK, male vocal/instrumental group*

Date	Title *Label Number*	Position	
9 Feb 80	● **TURNING JAPANESE** *United Artists BP 334*	**3**	13 wks
5 Jul 80	**NEWS AT TEN** *United Artists BP 345*	**44**	4 wks
11 Jul 81	**JIMMIE JONES** *Liberty BP 401*	**44**	6 wks

VARDIS *UK, male vocal/instrumental group*

Date	Title *Label Number*	Position	
27 Sep 80	**LET'S GO** *Logo VAR 1*	**59**	4 wks

VARIOUS ARTISTS

Date	Title *Label Number*	Position	
15 Jun 56	● **ALL STAR HIT PARADE** *Decca F 10752*	**2**	9 wks
15 Jun 56	**CAROUSEL - ORIGINAL SOUNDTRACK** (LP) *Capitol LCT 6105*	**27**	1 wk
6 Jul 56	**CAROUSEL - ORIGINAL SOUNDTRACK** (LP) (re-entry) *Capitol LCT 6105*	**26**	1 wk
26 Jul 57	**ALL STAR HIT PARADE NO. 2** *Decca F 10915*	**15**	7 wks

All Star Hit Parade *on Decca F 10752 featured the following artists with the following songs: Winifred Atwell* - Theme From The Threepenny Opera; *Dave King* - No Other Love; *Joan Regan* - My September Love; *Lita Roza* - A Tear Fell; *Dickie Valentine* - Out Of Town; *David Whitfield* - It's Almost Tomorrow. *See also the separate hit lists of each of these artists. Tracks and artists on* Carousel *are as follows:* Carousel Waltz - *Orchestra conducted by Alfred Newman;* You're A Queer One Julie Jordan - *Barbara Ruick & Shirley Jones;* Mister Snow - *Barbara Ruick;* If I Loved You - *Shirley Jones & Gordon MacRae;* June Is Busting Out All Over - *Claramae Turner;* Soliloquy - *Gordon MacRae;* Blow High Blow Low - *Cameron Mitchell;* When The Children Are Asleep - *Robert Rounseville & Barbara Ruick;* This Was A Real Nice Clambake - *Barbara Ruick, Claramae Turner, Robert Rounseville & Cameron Mitchell;* Stonecutters Cut It On Stone (There's Nothing So Bad For A Woman) - *Cameron Mitchell;* What's The Use Of Wonderin' - *Shirley Jones;* You'll Never Walk Alone - *Claramae Turner;* If I Loved You - *Gordon MacRae;* You'll Never Walk Alone - *Shirley Jones. The cast are American and the sex of each performer should be obvious. See also Partridge Family starring Shirley Jones.* All Star Hit Parade 2 *featured the following artists with the following songs: Johnston Brothers* - Around The World; *Billy Cotton* - Puttin' On The Style; *Jimmy Young* - When I Fall In Love; *Max Bygraves* - A White Sport Coat; *Beverley Sisters* - Freight Train; *Tommy Steele* - Butterfly. *See also the separate hit lists of each of these artists.*

Frankie VAUGHAN *UK, male vocalist*

Date	Title *Label Number*	Position	
29 Jan 54	**ISTANBUL** *HMV B 10599*	**11**	1 wk
28 Jan 55	**HAPPY DAYS & LONELY NIGHTS** *HMV B 10783*	**12**	3 wks
22 Apr 55	**TWEEDLE DEE** *Philips PB 423*	**17**	1 wk
2 Dec 55	**SEVENTEEN** *Philips PB 511*	**18**	3 wks
3 Feb 56	**MY BOY FLAT TOP** *Philips PB 544*	**20**	2 wks
9 Nov 56	● **GREEN DOOR** *Philips PB 640*	**2**	15 wks
11 Jan 57	★ **GARDEN OF EDEN** *Philips PB 660*	**1**	13 wks
4 Oct 57	● **MAN ON FIRE/ WANDERIN' EYES** *Philips PB 729*	**6**	12 wks
20 Dec 57	● **KISSES SWEETER THAN WINE** *Philips PB 775*	**8**	11 wks
7 Mar 58	**CAN'T GET ALONG WITHOUT YOU/ WE'RE NOT ALONE** *Philips PB 793*	**11**	6 wks
9 May 58	● **KEWPIE DOLL** *Philips PB 825*	**10**	12 wks
1 Aug 58	**WONDERFUL THINGS** *Philips PB 834*	**22**	3 wks
12 Sep 58	**WONDERFUL THINGS** (re-entry) *Philips PB 834*	**27**	3 wks
10 Oct 58	**AM I WASTING MY TIME ON YOU** *Philips PB 865*	**25**	2 wks
9 Jan 59	**AM I WASTING MY TIME ON YOU** (re-entry) *Philips PB 865*	**27**	2 wks
30 Jan 59	**THAT'S MY DOLL** *Philips PB 895*	**28**	2 wks
24 Jul 59	● **THE HEART OF MAN** *Philips PB 930*	**5**	14 wks
18 Sep 59	**WALKIN' TALL** *Philips PB 931*	**28**	1 wk
2 Oct 59	**WALKIN' TALL** (re-entry) *Philips PB 931*	**29**	1 wk
29 Jan 60	**WHAT MORE DO YOU WANT** *Philips PB 985*	**25**	2 wks
22 Sep 60	**KOOKIE LITTLE PARADISE** *Philips PB 1054*	**31**	5 wks
27 Oct 60	**MILORD** *Philips PB 1066*	**34**	6 wks
9 Nov 61	★ **TOWER OF STRENGTH** *Philips PB 1195*	**1**	13 wks
1 Feb 62	**DON'T STOP TWIST** *Philips 1219*	**22**	7 wks
27 Sep 62	**HERCULES** *Philips 326542 BF*	**42**	4 wks
24 Jan 63	● **LOOP-DE-LOOP** *Philips 326566 BF*	**5**	12 wks
20 Jun 63	**HEY MAMA** *Philips BF 1254*	**21**	9 wks
4 Jun 64	**HELLO DOLLY** *Philips BF 1339*	**18**	11 wks
11 Mar 65	**SOMEONE MUST HAVE HURT YOU A LOT** *Philips BF 1394*	**46**	1 wk
28 Feb 67	**NEVERTHELESS** *Columbia DB 8354*	**29**	5 wks
23 Aug 67	● **THERE MUST BE A WAY** *Columbia DB 8248*	**7**	21 wks
15 Nov 67	**SO TIRED** *Columbia DB 8298*	**21**	9 wks

See also Frankie Vaughan & the Kaye Sisters.

Frankie VAUGHAN & The KAYE SISTERS *UK, male vocalist, female vocal group*

Date	Title *Label Number*	Position	
1 Nov 57	● **GOTTA HAVE SOMETHING IN THE BANK FRANK** *Philips PB 751*	**8**	11 wks
1 May 59	● **COME SOFTLY TO ME** *Philips PB 913*	**9**	9 wks

See also Frankie Vaughan, Kaye Sisters, Three Kayes.

Malcolm VAUGHAN *UK, male vocalist*

Date	Title *Label Number*	Position	
1 Jul 55	● **EVERY DAY OF MY LIFE** *HMV B 10874*	**5**	16 wks
27 Jan 56	**WITH YOUR LOVE** *HMV POP 130*	**20**	1 wk
10 Feb 56	**WITH YOUR LOVE** (re-entry) *HMV POP 130*	**18**	1 wk
2 Mar 56	**WITH YOUR LOVE** (2nd re-entry) *HMV POP 130*	**20**	1 wk
26 Oct 56	**ST. THERESE OF THE ROSES** *HMV POP 250*	**27**	1 wk
16 Nov 56	● **ST. THERESE OF THE ROSES** (re-entry) *HMV POP 250*	**3**	19 wks
12 Apr 57	**THE WORLD IS MINE** *HMV POP 303*	**30**	1 wk
3 May 57	**THE WORLD IS MINE** (re-entry) *HMV POP 303*	**29**	2 wks
10 May 57	**CHAPEL OF THE ROSES** *HMV POP 325*	**13**	8 wks
31 May 57	**THE WORLD IS MINE** (2nd re-entry) *HMV POP 303*	**26**	1 wk
29 Nov 57	● **MY SPECIAL ANGEL** *HMV POP 419*	**3**	14 wks
21 Mar 58	**TO BE LOVED** *HMV POP 459*	**14**	12 wks
17 Oct 58	● **MORE THAN EVER (COME PRIMA)** *HMV POP 538*	**5**	14 wks
27 Feb 59	**WAIT FOR ME/ WILLINGLY** *HMV POP 590*	**28**	1 wk
13 Mar 59	**WAIT FOR ME** (re-entry) *HMV POP 590*	**13**	14 wks

Norman VAUGHAN *UK, male vocalist*

Date	Title *Label Number*	Position	
17 May 62	**SWINGING IN THE RAIN** *Pye 7N 15438*	**34**	5 wks

Date	Title *Label Number*	Position	

Sarah VAUGHAN *US, female vocalist*

11 Sep 59	● **BROKEN HEARTED MELODY** *Mercury AMT 1057*	**7**	13 wks
29 Dec 60	**LET'S/ SERENATA** *Columbia DB 4542*	**37**	3 wks
2 Feb 61	**LET'S/ SERENATA** (re-entry) *Columbia DB 4542*	**47**	1 wk

See also Billy Eckstine and Sarah Vaughan.

Billy VAUGHN *US, orchestra and chorus*

27 Jan 56	**SHIFTING WHISPERING SANDS** *London HLD 8205*	**20**	1 wk
23 Mar 56	**THEME FROM THE THREEPENNY OPERA** *London HLD 8238*	**12**	7 wks

Bobby VEE *US, male vocalist*

19 Jan 61	● **RUBBER BALL** *London HLG 9255*	**4**	11 wks
13 Apr 61	● **MORE THAN I CAN SAY** *London HLG 9316*	**4**	16 wks
3 Aug 61	● **HOW MANY TEARS** *London HLG 9389*	**10**	13 wks
26 Oct 61	● **TAKE GOOD CARE OF MY BABY** *London HLG 9438*	**3**	16 wks
21 Dec 61	● **RUN TO HIM** *London HLG 9470*	**6**	15 wks
8 Mar 62	**PLEASE DON'T ASK ABOUT BARBARA** *Liberty LIB 55419*	**29**	9 wks
7 Jun 62	● **SHARING YOU** *Liberty LIB 55451*	**10**	13 wks
27 Sep 62	**A FOREVER KIND OF LOVE** *Liberty LIB 10046*	**13**	19 wks
7 Feb 63	● **THE NIGHT HAS A THOUSAND EYES** *Liberty LIB 10069*	**3**	12 wks
20 Jun 63	**BOBBY TOMORROW** *Liberty LIB 55530*	**21**	10 wks

Tata VEGA *US, female vocalist*

26 May 79	**GET IT UP FOR LOVE/I JUST KEEP THINKING ABOUT YOU BABY** *Motown TMG 1140*	**52**	4 wks

VELVELETTES *US, female vocal group*

31 Jul 71	**THESE THINGS WILL KEEP ME LOVING YOU** *Tamla Motown TMG 780*	**34**	7 wks

VELVETS *US, male vocal group*

11 May 61	**THAT LUCKY OLD SUN** *London HLU 9328*	**46**	1 wk
17 Aug 61	**TONIGHT (COULD BE THE NIGHT)** *London HLU 9372*	**50**	1 wk

VENTURES *US, male instrumental group*

3 Sep 60	● **WALK DON'T RUN** *Top Rank JAR 417*	**8**	13 wks
1 Dec 60	● **PERFIDIA** *London HLG 9232*	**4**	13 wks
9 Mar 61	**RAM-BUNK-SHUSH** *London HLG 9292*	**45**	1 wk
11 May 61	**LULLABY OF THE LEAVES** *London HLG 9344*	**43**	4 wks

Al VERLANE — See *PING PING and Al VERLANE*

VERNONS GIRLS *UK, female vocal group*

17 May 62	**LOVER PLEASE** *Decca F 11450*	**16**	9 wks
23 Aug 62	**LOVER PLEASE/ YOU KNOW WHAT I MEAN** (re-entry) *Decca F 11450*	**39**	7 wks
6 Sep 62	**LOCO-MOTION** *Decca F 11495*	**47**	1 wk
18 Oct 62	**YOU KNOW WHAT I MEAN** (re-entry) *Decca F 11450*	**37**	3 wks
15 Nov 62	**YOU KNOW WHAT I MEAN** (2nd re-entry) *Decca F 11450*	**50**	1 wk
3 Jan 63	**FUNNY ALL OVER** *Decca F 11549*	**31**	8 wks
18 Apr 63	**DO THE BIRD** *Decca F 11629*	**50**	1 wk
2 May 63	**DO THE BIRD** (re-entry) *Decca F 11629*	**44**	1 wk

You Know What I Mean *was not coupled with* Lover Please *on the chart of 23 Aug 62, but both sides of this record were listed for the following 6 weeks.*

VIBRATIONS — See *Tony JACKSON and the VIBRATIONS*

VIBRATORS *UK, male vocal/instrumental group*

18 Mar 78	**AUTOMATIC LOVER** *Epic EPC 6137*	**35**	5 wks
17 Jun 78	**JUDY SAYS (KNOCK YOU IN THE HEAD)** *Epic EPC 6393*	**70**	3 wks

VICE SQUAD

UK, male/female vocal/instrumental group

13 Feb 82	**OUT OF REACH** *Zonophone Z 26*	**68**	1 wk

Mike VICKERS — See *Kenny EVERETT and Mike VICKERS*

VIDEO SYMPHONIC *UK, orchestra*

24 Oct 81	**THE FLAME TREES OF THIKA** *EMI EMI 5222*	**42**	3 wks

VIENNA PHILHARMONIC ORCHESTRA *Austria, orchestra*

18 Dec 71	**THEME FROM THE ONEDIN LINE** *Decca F 13259*	**15**	14 wks

VILLAGE PEOPLE

US, male vocal/instrumental group

3 Dec 77	**SAN FRANCISCO (YOU'VE GOT ME)** *DJM DJS 10817*	**45**	5 wks
25 Nov 78	★ **Y.M.C.A.** *Mercury 6007 192*	**1**	16 wks
17 Mar 79	● **IN THE NAVY** *Mercury 6007 209*	**2**	9 wks
16 Jun 79	**GO WEST** *Mercury 6007 221*	**15**	8 wks
9 Aug 80	**CAN'T STOP THE MUSIC** *Mercury MER 16*	**11**	11 wks

Gene VINCENT *US, male vocalist*

13 Jul 56	**BE BOP A LULA** *Capitol CL 14599*	**30**	2 wks
24 Aug 56	**BE BOP A LULA** (re-entry) *Capitol CL 14599*	**16**	3 wks
28 Sep 56	**BE BOP A LULA** (2nd re-entry) *Capitol CL 14599*	**23**	2 wks
12 Oct 56	**RACE WITH THE DEVIL** *Capitol CL 14628*	**28**	1 wk
19 Oct 56	**BLUE JEAN BOP** *Capitol CL 14637*	**16**	5 wks
8 Jan 60	**WILD CAT** *Capitol CL 15099*	**21**	3 wks
10 Mar 60	**WILD CAT** (re-entry) *Capitol CL 15099*	**39**	3 wks
10 Mar 60	**MY HEART** *Capitol CL 15115*	**16**	6 wks
28 Apr 60	**MY HEART** (re-entry) *Capitol CL 15115*	**47**	1 wk
16 Jun 60	**PISTOL PACKIN' MAMA** *Capitol CL 15136*	**15**	9 wks
1 Jun 61	**SHE SHE LITTLE SHEILA** *Capitol CL 15202*	**22**	10 wks
17 Aug 61	**SHE SHE LITTLE SHEILA** (re-entry) *Capitol CL 15202*	**44**	1 wk
31 Aug 61	**I'M GOING HOME** *Capitol CL 15215*	**36**	4 wks

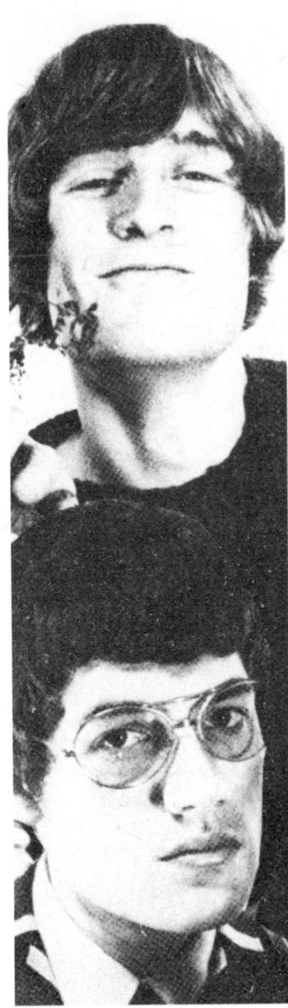

Above **WARM SOUNDS** Barry Younghusband and Denver Gerrard sang about 'Birds and Bees' but different from those of Jewel Akens

Right **WALKER BROS** Scott, Gary and John, an enigmatic trio who had more success here than back home in the States

Right **JUNIOR WALKER AND THE ALL STARS** Junior Walker (real name Aubrey de Walt) was discovered by Johnny Busta in 1961

Below **WAY OF THE WEST** White boys and legless

Date	Title *Label Number*	Position	

Bobby VINTON *US, male vocalist*

2 Aug 62	**ROSES ARE RED** *Columbia DB 4878*	**15**	8 wks
19 Dec 63	**THERE I'VE SAID IT AGAIN** *Columbia DB 7179*	**34**	10 wks

VIOLINSKI *UK, male instrumental group*

17 Feb 79	**CLOG DANCE** *Jet 136*	**17**	9 wks

VIPERS SKIFFLE GROUP

UK, male vocal/instrumental group

25 Jan 57	● **DON'T YOU ROCK ME DADDY-O** *Parlophone R 4261*	**10**	9 wks
22 Mar 57	● **CUMBERLAND GAP** *Parlophone R 4289*	**10**	6 wks
31 May 57	**STREAMLINE TRAIN** *Parlophone R 4308*	**23**	3 wks

V.I.P.S *UK, male vocal/instrumental group*

6 Sep 80	**THE QUARTER MOON** *Gem GEMS 39*	**55**	4 wks

VISAGE *UK, male vocal/instrumental group*

20 Dec 80	● **FADE TO GREY** *Polydor POSP 194*	**8**	wks
14 Mar 81	**MIND OF A TOY** *Polydor POSP 236*	**13**	8 wks
11 Jul 81	**VISAGE** *Polydor POSP 293*	**21**	7 wks
13 Mar 82	**DAMNED DON'T CRY** *Polydor POSP 390*	**11**	8 wks
26 Jun 82	**NIGHT TRAIN** *Polydor POSP 441*	**12**	10 wks
13 Nov 82	**PLEASURE BOYS** *Polydor POSP 523*	**44**	3 wks

VISCOUNTS *UK, male vocal group*

13 Oct 60	**SHORT'NIN' BREAD** *Pye 7N 15287*	**16**	8 wks
14 Sep 61	**WHO PUT THE BOMP** *Pye 7N 15379*	**21**	10 wks

VOGGUE *Canada, female vocalist duo*

18 Jul 81	**DANCIN' THE NIGHT AWAY** *Mercury MER 76*	**39**	6 wks

VOYAGE *UK/France, disco aggregation*

17 Jun 78	**FROM EAST TO WEST/SCOTS MACHINE** *GTO/Hansa GT 224*	**13**	13 wks
25 Nov 78	**SOUVENIRS** *GTO GT 241*	**56**	7 wks
24 Mar 79	**LET'S FLY AWAY** *GTO/Hansa GT 245*	**38**	7 wks

'Scots Machine' *credited from 24 Jun 78 until end of record's chart run.*

VOYAGER *UK, male vocal/instrumental group*

26 May 79	**HALFWAY HOTEL** *Mountain VOY 001*	**33**	8 wks

W

Adam WADE *US, male vocalist*

8 Jun 61	**TAKE GOOD CARE OF HER** *HMV POP 843*	**38**	1 wk
22 Jun 61	**TAKE GOOD CARE OF HER** (re-entry) *HMV POP 843*	**38**	5 wks

WAH! *UK, male/female vocal/instrumental group*

25 Dec 82	**THE STORY OF THE BLUES** *Eternal JF 1*	**59**†	1 wk

WAIKIKIS *US, male instrumental group*

11 Mar 65	**HAWAIIAN TATTOO** *Palette PG 9025*	**41**	2 wks

WAILERS — See *Bob MARLEY and the WAILERS*

WAITRESSES *UK, female vocal group*

18 Dec 82	**CHRISTMAS WRAPPING** *Ze/Island WIP 6821*	**45**†	2 wks

Johnny WAKELIN *UK, male vocalist*

18 Jan 75	● **BLACK SUPERMAN (MUHAMMAD ALI)** *Pye 7N 45420*	**7**	10 wks
24 Jul 76	● **IN ZAIRE** *Pye 7N 45595*	**4**	10 wks

Black Superman *by Johnny Wakelin and the Kinshasa Band.*

Nirada Michael WALDEN

US, male vocalist/Instrumentalist-drums

23 feb 80	**TONIGHT I'M ALL RIGHT** *Atlantic K 11437*	**34**	9 wks
26 Apr 80	● **I SHOULDA LOVEDYA** *Atlantic K 11413*	**8**	9 wks

Gary WALKER *US, male vocalist*

24 Feb 66	**YOU DON'T LOVE ME** *CBS 202036*	**26**	6 wks
26 May 66	**TWINKIE LEE** *CBS 202081*	**26**	6 wks

See also Walker Brothers.

John WALKER *US, male vocalist*

5 Jul 67	**ANNABELLA** *Philips BF 1593*	**48**	1 wk
19 Jul 67	**ANNABELLA** (re-entry) *Philips BF 1593*	**24**	5 wks

See also Walker Brothers.

Junior WALKER and the ALL-STARS

US, male instrumental/vocal group, Junior Walker tenor sax

18 Aug 66	**HOW SWEET IT IS** *Tamla Motown TMG 571*	**22**	10 wks
2 Apr 69	**(I'M A) ROAD RUNNER** *Tamla Motown TMG 691*	**12**	12 wks
18 Oct 69	**WHAT DOES IT TAKE (TO WIN YOUR LOVE)** *Tamla Motown TMG 712*	**13**	12 wks

Date	Title *Label Number*	Position	
26 Aug 72	**WALK IN THE NIGHT** *Tamla Motown TMG 824*	**16**	11 wks
27 Jan 73	**TAKE ME GIRL I'M READY** *Tamla Motown TMG 840*	**16**	9 wks
30 Jun 73	**WAY BACK HOME** *Tamla Motown TMG 857*	**35**	5 wks

Scott WALKER *US, male vocalist*

Date	Title *Label Number*	Position	
6 Dec 67	**JACKIE** *Philips BF 1628*	**22**	9 wks
1 May 68	● **JOANNA** *Philips BF 1662*	**7**	11 wks
11 Jun 69	**LIGHTS OF CINCINATTI** *Philips BF 1793*	**13**	10 wks

See also Walker Brothers.

WALKER BROTHERS *US, male vocal group*

Date	Title *Label Number*	Position	
29 Apr 65	**LOVE HER** *Philips BF 1409*	**20**	13 wks
19 Aug 65	★ **MAKE IT EASY ON YOURSELF** *Philips BF 1428*	**1**	14 wks
2 Dec 65	● **MY SHIP IS COMING IN** *Philips BF 1454*	**3**	12 wks
3 Mar 66	★ **THE SUN AIN'T GONNA SHINE ANYMORE** *Philips BF 1473*	**1**	11 wks
14 Jul 66	**(BABY) YOU DON'T HAVE TO TELL ME** *Philips BF 1497*	**13**	8 wks
22 Sep 66	**ANOTHER TEAR FALLS** *Philips BF 1514*	**12**	8 wks
15 Dec 66	**DEADLIER THAN THE MALE** *Philips BF 1537*	**34**	6 wks
9 Feb 67	**STAY WITH ME BABY** *Philips BF 1548*	**26**	6 wks
18 May 67	**WALKING IN THE RAIN** *Philips BF 1576*	**26**	6 wks
17 Jan 76	● **NO REGRETS** *GTO GT 42*	**7**	9 wks

See also Gary Walker, John Walker, Scott Walker.

Jerry WALLACE *US, male vocalist*

Date	Title *Label Number*	Position	
23 Jun 60	**YOU'RE SINGING OUR LOVE SONG TO SOMEBODY ELSE** *London HLH 9110*	**46**	1 wk

Bob WALLIS and his STORYVILLE JAZZ BAND *UK, male jazz band, Bob Wallis trumpet*

Date	Title *Label Number*	Position	
6 Jul 61	**I'M SHY MARY ELLEN I'M SHY** *Pye Jazz 7NJ 2043*	**44**	2 wks
4 Jan 62	**COME ALONG PLEASE** *Pye Jazz 7NJ 2048*	**33**	5 wks

Joe WALSH *US, male vocalist*

Date	Title *Label Number*	Position	
16 Jul 77	**ROCKY MOUNTAIN WAY** (EP) *ABC ABE 12002*	**39**	4 wks
8 Jul 78	**LIFE'S BEEN GOOD** *Asylum K 13129*	**14**	11 wks

Tracks on Rocky Mountain Way EP: Rocky Mountain Way/Turn To Stone/Meadows/Walk Away.

Trevor WALTERS *UK, male vocalist*

Date	Title *Label Number*	Position	
24 Oct 81	**LOVE ME TONIGHT** *Magnet MAG 198*	**27**	8 wks

Dexter WANSELL *US, male instrumentalist, keyboards*

Date	Title *Label Number*	Position	
20 May 78	**ALL NIGHT LONG** *Philadelphia International PIR 6255*	**59**	3 wks

WAR *US, male vocal/instrumental group*

Date	Title *Label Number*	Position	
24 Jan 76	**LOW RIDER** *Island WIP 6267*	**12**	7 wks
26 Jun 76	**ME AND BABY BROTHER** *Island WIP 6303*	**21**	7 wks
14 Jan 78	**GALAXY** *MCA 339*	**14**	7 wks
15 Apr 78	**HEY SENORITA** *MCA 359*	**40**	2 wks
10 Apr 82	**YOU GOT THE POWER** *RCA 201*	**58**	4 wks

Anita WARD *US, female vocalist*

Date	Title *Label Number*	Position	
2 Jun 79	★ **RING MY BELL** *TK TKR 7543*	**1**	11 wks

Billy WARD *US, male vocalist*

Date	Title *Label Number*	Position	
13 Sep 57	**STARDUST** *London HLU 8465*	**13**	11 wks
29 Nov 57	**DEEP PURPLE** *London HLU 8502*	**30**	1 wk
3 Jan 58	**STARDUST** (re-entry) *London HLU 8465*	**26**	1 wk

Clifford T. WARD *UK, male vocalist*

Date	Title *Label Number*	Position	
30 Jun 73	● **GAYE** *Charisma CB 205*	**8**	11 wks
26 Jan 74	**SCULLERY** *Charisma CB 221*	**37**	5 wks

Michael WARD *UK, male vocalist*

Date	Title *Label Number*	Position	
29 Sep 73	**LET THERE BE PEACE ON EARTH (LET IT BEGIN WITH ME)** *Philips 6006 340*	**15**	10 wks
15 Dec 73	**LET THERE BE PEACE ON EARTH (LET IT BEGIN WITH ME)** (re-entry) *Philips 6006 340*	**50**	3 wks

WARM SOUNDS *UK, male vocal duo*

Date	Title *Label Number*	Position	
4 May 67	**BIRDS AND BEES** *Deram DM 120*	**27**	6 wks

Dionne WARWICK *US, female vocalist*

Date	Title *Label Number*	Position	
13 Feb 64	**ANYONE WHO HAD A HEART** *Pye International 7N 25234*	**42**	3 wks
16 Apr 64	● **WALK ON BY** *Pye International 7N 25241*	**9**	14 wks
30 Jul 64	**YOU'LL NEVER GET TO HEAVEN** *Pye International 7N 25256*	**20**	8 wks
8 Oct 64	**REACH OUT FOR ME** *Pye International 7N 25265*	**23**	7 wks
1 Apr 65	**YOU CAN HAVE HIM** *Pye International 7N 25290*	**37**	5 wks
13 Mar 68	**VALLEY OF THE DOLLS** *Pye International 7N 25445*	**28**	8 wks
15 May 68	● **DO YOU KNOW THE WAY TO SAN JOSE** *Pye International 7N 25457*	**8**	10 wks
23 Oct 82	● **HEARTBREAKER** *Arista ARIST 496*	**2**†	10 wks
11 Dec 82	**ALL THE LOVE IN THE WORLD** *Arista ARIST 507*	**14**†	3 wks

See also Dionne Warwicke and the Detroit Spinners. Warwick had no final 'e' at the time of the first seven hits above.

Dionne WARWICKE and the DETROIT SPINNERS *US, female vocalist, male vocal group*

Date	Title *Label Number*	Position	
19 Oct 74	**THEN CAME YOU** *Atlantic K 10495*	**29**	6 wks

See also Dionne Warwick, Detroit Spinners.

Date	Title *Label Number*	Position	

Dinah WASHINGTON *US, female vocalist*

Date	Title *Label Number*	Position	
30 Nov 61	**SEPTEMBER IN THE RAIN** *Mercury AMT 1162*	**35**	3 wks
18 Jan 62	**SEPTEMBER IN THE RAIN** (re-entry) *Mercury AMT 1162*	**49**	1 wk

Geno WASHINGTON and the RAM JAM BAND

UK, male vocalist, male instrumental backing group

Date	Title *Label Number*	Position	
19 May 66	**WATER** *Piccadilly 7N 35312*	**39**	8 wks
21 Jul 66	**HI HI HAZEL** *Piccadilly 7N 35329*	**45**	3 wks
25 Aug 66	**HI HI HAZEL** (re-entry) *Piccadilly 7N 35329*	**48**	1 wk
6 Oct 66	**QUE SERA SERA** *Piccadilly 7N 35346*	**43**	3 wks
2 Feb 67	**MICHAEL** *Piccadilly 7N 35359*	**39**	5 wks

Grover WASHINGTON JR. *US, male vocalist*

Date	Title *Label Number*	Position	
16 May 81	**JUST THE TWO OF US** *Elektra K 12514*	**34**	7 wks

Dennis WATERMAN with the DENNIS WATERMAN BAND

UK, male vocalist/male instrumental group

Date	Title *Label Number*	Position	
25 Oct 80	● **I COULD BE SO GOOD FOR YOU** *EMI 5009*	**3**	12 wks

Peter WATERMAN — See *14-18*

Johnny 'Guitar' WATSON

US, male vocalist, instrumentalist - guitar

Date	Title *Label Number*	Position	
28 Aug 76	**I NEED IT** *DJM DJS 20694*	**35**	5 wks
23 Apr 77	**A REAL MOTHER FOR YA** *DJM DJT 10762*	**44**	3 wks

WAVELENGTH *UK, male vocal group*

Date	Title *Label Number*	Position	
10 Jul 82	**HURRY HOME** *Ariola ARO 281*	**17**	12 wks

WAY OF THE WEST

UK, male vocal/instrumental group

Date	Title *Label Number*	Position	
25 Apr 81	**DON'T SAY THAT'S JUST FOR WHITE BOYS** *Mercury MER 66*	**54**	5 wks

Jeff WAYNE *US/UK, orchestra*

Date	Title *Label Number*	Position	
10 Jul 82	**MATADOR** *CBS A 2493*	**57**	3 wks

See also Jeff Wayne's War Of The World's

Jeff WAYNE'S WAR OF THE WORLDS

US/UK,male/female vocal/instrumental cast

Date	Title *Label Number*	Position	
9 Sep 78	**EVE OF THE WAR** *CBS 6496*	**36**	8 wks

Date	Title *Label Number*	Position	

WEATHERMEN

UK, Jonathan King, male vocalist, under false name

Date	Title *Label Number*	Position	
16 Jan 71	**IT'S THE SAME OLD SONG** *B and C CB 139*	**19**	9 wks

See also Jonathan King.

Marti WEBB *UK, female vocalist*

Date	Title *Label Number*	Position	
9 Feb 80	● **TAKE THAT LOOK OFF YOUR FACE** *Polydor POSP 100*	**3**	12 wks
9 Apr 80	**TELL ME ON A SUNDAY** *Polydor POSP 111*	**67**	2 wks
20 Sep 80	**YOUR EARS SHOULD BE BURNING NOW** *Polydor POSP 166*	**61**	4 wks

Joan WEBER *US, female vocalist*

Date	Title *Label Number*	Position	
18 Feb 55	**LET ME GO LOVER** *Philips PB 389*	**16**	1 wk

Max WEBSTER

Canada, male vocal/instrumental group

Date	Title *Label Number*	Position	
19 May 79	**PARADISE SKIES** *Capitol CL 16079*	**43**	3 wks

Fred WEDLOCK *UK, male vocalist*

Date	Title *Label Number*	Position	
31 Jan 81	● **OLDEST SWINGER IN TOWN** *Rocket XPRES 46*	**6**	10 wks

Bert WEEDON *UK, male instrumentalist, guitar*

Date	Title *Label Number*	Position	
15 May 59	● **GUITAR BOOGIE SHUFFLE** *Top Rank JAR 117*	**10**	9 wks
20 Nov 59	**NASHVILLE BOOGIE** *Top Rank JAR 221*	**29**	2 wks
10 Mar 60	**BIG BEAT BOOGIE** *Top Rank JAR 300*	**37**	3 wks
7 Apr 60	**BIG BEAT BOOGIE** (re-entry) *Top Rank JAR 300*	**49**	1 wk
9 Jun 60	**TWELFTH STREET RAG** *Top Rank JAR 360*	**47**	2 wks
28 Jul 60	**APACHE** *Top Rank JAR 415*	**44**	1 wk
11 Aug 60	**APACHE** (re-entry) *Top Rank JAR 415*	**24**	3 wks
27 Oct 60	**SORRY ROBBIE** *Top Rank JAR 517*	**28**	11 wks
2 Feb 61	**GINCHY** *Top Rank JAR 537*	**35**	5 wks
4 May 61	**MR. GUITAR** *Top Rank JAR 559*	**47**	1 wk

Frank WEIR *UK, orchestra*

Date	Title *Label Number*	Position	
15 Sep 60	**CARIBBEAN HONEYMOON** *Oriole CB 1559*	**42**	4 wks

Eric WEISSBERG — See *DELIVERANCE SOUNDTRACK*

Brandi WELLS *US, female vocalist*

Date	Title *Label Number*	Position	
20 Feb 82	**WATCH OUT** *Virgin VS 479*	**74**	1 wk

Houston WELLS *UK, male vocalist*

Date	Title *Label Number*	Position	
1 Aug 63	**ONLY THE HEARTACHES** *Parlophone R 5031*	**22**	10 wks

Mary WELLS *US, female vocalist*

Date	Title *Label Number*	Position	
21 May 64	● **MY GUY** *Stateside SS 288*	**5**	14 wks
8 Jul 72	**MY GUY** (re-issue) *Tamla Motown TMG 820*	**14**	10 wks

See also Marvin Gaye and Mary Wells.

Date	Title *Label Number*	Position	

Alex WELSH *UK, male instrumentalist, trumpet*

Date	Title *Label Number*	Position	
10 Aug 61	**TANSY** *Columbia DB 4686*	**45**	4 wks

Dodie WEST *UK, female vocalist*

Date	Title *Label Number*	Position	
14 Jan 65	**GOING OUT OF MY HEAD** *Decca F 12046*	**39**	4 wks

Keith WEST *UK, male vocalist*

Date	Title *Label Number*	Position	
9 Aug 67	● **EXCERPT FROM A TEENAGE OPERA** *Parlophone R 5623*	**2**	15 wks
22 Nov 67	**SAM** *Parlophone R 5651*	**38**	3 wks

WEST HAM UNITED CUP SQUAD

UK, male football team vocalists

Date	Title *Label Number*	Position	
10 May 75	**I'M FOREVER BLOWING BUBBLES** *Pye 7N 45470*	**31**	2 wks

Kim WESTON — See *Marvin GAYE and Kim WESTON*

WHALERS — See *Hal PAGE and the WHALERS*

WHAM! *UK, male/female vocal/instrumental group*

Date	Title *Label Number*	Position	
16 Oct 82	● **YOUNG GUNS (GO FOR IT)** *Innervision IVL A2766*	**3**†	11 wks

WHATNAUTS — See *MOMENTS and WHATNAUTS*

Nancy WHISKEY — See *Charles McDEVITT Skiffle Group featuring Nancy WHISKEY*

WHISPERS *US, male vocal group*

Date	Title *Label Number*	Position	
2 Feb 80	● **AND THE BEAT GOES ON** *Solar SO 1*	**2**	12 wks
10 May 80	**LADY** *Solar SO 4*	**55**	3 wks
12 Jul 80	**MY GIRL** *Solar SO 8*	**26**	6 wks
14 Mar 81	● **IT'S A LOVE THING** *Solar SO 16*	**9**	11 wks
13 Jun 81	**I CAN MAKE IT BETTER** *Solar SO 19*	**44**	5 wks

WHITE and TORCH

UK, male vocal/instrumental duo

Date	Title *Label Number*	Position	
2 Oct 82	**PARADE** *Chrysalis CHS 2641*	**54**	4 wks

Barry WHITE *US, male vocalist*

Date	Title *Label Number*	Position	
9 Jun 73	**I'M GONNA LOVE YOU JUST A LITTLE BIT MORE BABY** *Pye International 7N 25610*	**23**	7 wks
26 Jan 74	**NEVER NEVER GONNA GIVE YA UP** *Pye International 7N 25633*	**14**	11 wks
17 Aug 74	● **CAN'T GET ENOUGH OF YOUR LOVE BABE** *Pye International 7N 25661*	**8**	12 wks
2 Nov 74	★ **YOU'RE THE FIRST THE LAST MY EVERYTHING** *20th Century BTC 2133*	**1**	14 wks
8 Mar 75	● **WHAT AM I GONNA DO WITH YOU** *20th Century BTC 2177*	**5**	8 wks
24 May 75	**I'LL DO ANYTHING YOU WANT ME TO** *20th Century BTC 2208*	**20**	6 wks
27 Dec 75	● **LET THE MUSIC PLAY** *20th Century BTC 2265*	**9**	8 wks
6 Mar 76	● **YOU SEE THE TROUBLE WITH ME** *20th Century BTC 2277*	**2**	10 wks
21 Aug 76	**BABY WE BETTER TRY AND GET IT TOGETHER** *20th Century BTC 2298*	**15**	7 wks
13 Nov 76	**DON'T MAKE ME WAIT TOO LONG** *20th Century BTC 2309*	**17**	8 wks
5 Mar 77	**I'M QUALIFIED TO SATISFY** *20th Century BTC 2328*	**37**	5 wks
15 Oct 77	**IT'S ECSTASY WHEN YOU LAY DOWN NEXT TO ME** *20th Century BTC 2350*	**40**	3 wks
16 Dec 78	**JUST THE WAY YOU ARE** *20th Century BTC 2380*	**12**	12 wks
24 Mar 79	**SHA LA LA MEANS I LOVE YOU** *20th Century BTC 1041*	**55**	6 wks

Chris WHITE *UK, male vocalist*

Date	Title *Label Number*	Position	
20 Mar 76	**SPANISH WINE** *Charisma CB 272*	**37**	4 wks

Tam WHITE *UK, male vocalist*

Date	Title *Label Number*	Position	
15 Mar 75	**WHAT IN THE WORLD'S COME OVER YOU** *RAK 193*	**36**	4 wks

Tony Joe WHITE *US, male vocalist*

Date	Title *Label Number*	Position	
6 Jun 70	**GROUPIE GIRL** *Monument MON 1043*	**22**	10 wks

WHITE PLAINS *UK, male vocal group*

Date	Title *Label Number*	Position	
7 Feb 70	● **MY BABY LOVES LOVIN'** *Deram DM 280*	**9**	11 wks
18 Apr 70	**I'VE GOT YOU ON MY MIND** *Deram DM 291*	**17**	11 wks
24 Oct 70	● **JULIE DO YA LOVE ME** *Deram DM 315*	**8**	14 wks
12 Jun 71	**WHEN YOU ARE A KING** *Deram DM 333*	**13**	11 wks
17 Feb 73	**STEP INTO A DREAM** *Deram DM 371*	**21**	9 wks

WHITEHEAD — See *McFADDEN and WHITEHEAD*

WHITESNAKE *UK, male vocal/instrumental group*

Date	Title *Label Number*	Position	
24 Jun 78	**SNAKE BITE** (EP) *EMI International INEP 751*	**61**	3 wks
10 Nov 79	**LONG WAY FROM HOME** *United Artists BP 324*	**55**	2 wks
26 Apr 80	**FOOL FOR YOUR LOVING** *United Artists BP 352*	**13**	9 wks
12 Jul 80	**READY AN' WILLING (SWEET SATISFACTION)** *United Artists BP 363*	**43**	4 wks
22 Nov 80	**AIN'T NO LOVE IN THE HEART OF THE CITY** *Sunburst/Liberty BP 381*	**51**	4 wks
11 Apr 81	**DON'T BREAK MY HEART AGAIN** *Liberty BP 395*	**17**	9 wks
6 Jun 81	**WOULD I LIE TO YOU** *Liberty BP 399*	**37**	6 wks
6 Nov 82	**HERE I GO AGAIN/BLOODY LUXURY** *Liberty BP 416*	**34**†	8 wks

Tracks on Snake Bite EP: *Bloody Mary/Steal Away/Ain't No Love In The Heart Of The City/Come On. This EP and* Long Way From Home *were credited to David Coverdale's Whitesnake.*

David WHITFIELD *UK, male vocalist*

Date	Title *Label Number*	Position	
2 Oct 53	● **BRIDGE OF SIGHS** *Decca F 10129*	**9**	1 wk
16 Oct 53	★ **ANSWER ME** *Decca F 10192*	**1**	13 wks
11 Dec 53	**RAGS TO RICHES** *Decca F 10207*	**12**	1 wk
8 Jan 54	● **RAGS TO RICHES** (re-entry) *Decca F 10207*	**3**	10 wks
29 Jan 54	**ANSWER ME** (re-entry) *Decca F 10192*	**12**	1 wk
19 Feb 54	● **THE BOOK** *Decca F 10242*	**5**	12 wks
28 May 54	● **THE BOOK** (re-entry) *Decca F 10242*	**10**	3 wks
18 Jun 54	★ **CARA MIA** *Decca F 10327*	**1**	25 wks

Date	Title *Label Number*	Position	
12 Nov 54	● **SANTO NATALE** *Decca F 10399*	**2**	10 wks
11 Feb 55	● **BEYOND THE STARS** *Decca F 10458*	**8**	9 wks
27 May 55	**MAMA** *Decca F 10515*	**20**	1 wk
24 Jun 55	**MAMA** (re-entry) *Decca F 10515*	**19**	2 wks
8 Jul 55	● **EV'RYWHERE** *Decca F 10515*	**3**	20 wks
29 Jul 55	**MAMA** (2nd re-entry) *Decca F 10515*	**12**	8 wks
25 Nov 55	● **WHEN YOU LOSE THE ONE YOU LOVE** *Decca F 10627*	**7**	11 wks
2 Mar 56	**MY SEPTEMBER LOVE** *Decca F 10690*	**19**	2 wks
23 Mar 56	**MY SEPTEMBER LOVE** (re-entry) *Decca F 10690*	**18**	1 wk
6 Apr 56	● **MY SEPTEMBER LOVE** (2nd re-entry) *Decca F 10690*	**3**	20 wks
24 Aug 56	**MY SON JOHN** *Decca F 10769*	**22**	4 wks
31 Aug 56	**MY UNFINISHED SYMPHONY** *Decca F 10769*	**29**	1 wk
7 Sep 56	**MY SEPTEMBER LOVE** (3rd re-entry) *Decca F 10690*	**25**	1 wk
25 Jan 57	● **ADORATION WALTZ** *Decca F 10833*	**9**	11 wks
5 Apr 57	**I'LL FIND YOU** *Decca F 10864*	**28**	2 wks
7 Jun 57	**I'LL FIND YOU** (re-entry) *Decca F 10864*	**27**	2 wks
14 Feb 58	**CRY MY HEART** *Decca F 10978*	**22**	3 wks
16 May 58	**ON THE STREET WHERE YOU LIVE** *Decca F 11018*	**16**	14 wks
8 Aug 58	**THE RIGHT TO LOVE** *Decca F 11039*	**30**	1 wk
24 Nov 60	**I BELIEVE** *Decca F 11289*	**49**	1 wk

Slim WHITMAN *US, male vocalist*

Date	Title	Position	
15 Jul 55	★ **ROSE MARIE** *London HL 8061*	**1**	19 wks
29 Jul 55	● **INDIAN LOVE CALL** *London L 1149*	**7**	12 wks
23 Sep 55	**CHINA DOLL** *London L 1149*	**15**	2 wks
9 Mar 56	**TUMBLING TUMBLEWEEDS** *London HLU 8230*	**19**	2 wks
13 Apr 56	**I'M A FOOL** *London HLU 8252*	**16**	3 wks
11 May 56	**I'M A FOOL** (re-entry) *London HLU 8252*	**29**	1 wk
22 Jun 56	**SERENADE** *London HLU 8287*	**24**	3 wks
27 Jul 56	● **SERENADE** (re-entry) *London HLU 8287*	**8**	12 wks
12 Apr 57	● **I'LL TAKE YOU HOME AGAIN KATHLEEN** *London HLP 8403*	**7**	13 wks
5 Oct 74	**HAPPY ANNIVERSARY** *United Artists UP 35728*	**14**	10 wks

Roger WHITTAKER *South Africa, male vocalist*

Date	Title	Position	
8 Nov 69	**DURHAM TOWN (THE LEAVIN')** *Columbia DB 8613*	**12**	18 wks
11 Apr 70	● **I DON'T BELIEVE IN IF ANYMORE** *Columbia DB 8664*	**8**	18 wks
10 Oct 70	**NEW WORLD IN THE MORNING** *Columbia DB 8718*	**17**	14 wks
3 Apr 71	**WHY** *Columbia DB 8752*	**47**	1 wk
2 Oct 71	**MAMY BLUE** *Columbia DB 8822*	**31**	10 wks
26 Jul 75	● **THE LAST FAREWELL** *EMI 2294*	**2**	14 wks

WHO *UK, male vocal/instrumental group*

Date	Title	Position	
18 Feb 65	● **I CAN'T EXPLAIN** *Brunswick 05926*	**8**	13 wks
27 May 65	● **ANYWAY ANYHOW ANYWHERE** *Brunswick 05935*	**10**	12 wks
4 Nov 65	● **MY GENERATION** *Brunswick 05944*	**2**	13 wks
10 Mar 66	● **SUBSTITUTE** *Reaction 591 001*	**5**	13 wks
24 Mar 66	**A LEGAL MATTER** *Brunswick 05956*	**32**	6 wks
1 Sep 66	● **I'M A BOY** *Reaction 591 004*	**2**	13 wks
1 Sep 66	**THE KIDS ARE ALRIGHT** *Brunswick 05965*	**41**	2 wks
22 Sep 66	**THE KIDS ARE ALRIGHT** (re-entry) *Brunswick 05965*	**48**	1 wk
15 Dec 66	● **HAPPY JACK** *Reaction 591 010*	**3**	11 wks
27 Apr 67	● **PICTURES OF LILY** *Track 604 002*	**4**	10 wks
26 Jul 67	**THE LAST TIME/ UNDER MY THUMB** *Track 604 006*	**44**	3 wks
18 Oct 67	● **I CAN SEE FOR MILES** *Track 604 011*	**10**	12 wks
19 Jun 68	**DOGS** *Track 604 023*	**25**	5 wks
23 Oct 68	**MAGIC BUS** *Track 604 024*	**26**	6 wks
19 Mar 69	● **PINBALL WIZARD** *Track 604 027*	**4**	13 wks
4 Apr 70	**THE SEEKER** *Track 604 036*	**19**	11 wks
8 Aug 70	**SUMMERTIME BLUES** *Track 2094 002*	**38**	4 wks
10 Jul 71	● **WON'T GET FOOLED AGAIN** *Track 2094 009*	**9**	12 wks
23 Oct 71	**LET'S SEE ACTION** *Track 2094 012*	**16**	12 wks
24 Jun 72	● **JOIN TOGETHER** *Track 2094 102*	**9**	9 wks
13 Jan 73	**RELAY** *Track 2094 106*	**21**	5 wks
13 Oct 73	**5:15** *Track 2094 115*	**20**	6 wks
24 Jan 76	● **SQUEEZE BOX** *Polydor 2121 275*	**10**	9 wks
30 Oct 76	● **SUBSTITUTE** (re-issue) *Polydor 2058 803*	**7**	7 wks
22 Jul 78	**WHO ARE YOU** *Polydor WHO 1*	**18**	12 wks
28 Apr 79	**LONG LIVE ROCK** *Polydor WHO 2*	**48**	5 wks
7 Mar 81	● **YOU BETTER YOU BET** *Polydor WHO 004*	**9**	8 wks
9 May 81	**DON'T LET GO THE COAT** *Polydor WHO 005*	**47**	4 wks
2 Oct 82	**ATHENA** *Polydor WHO 6*	**40**	4 wks

See also High Numbers.

WHODINI *US/UK, male vocal/instrumental group*

Date	Title	Position	
25 Dec 82	**MAGIC'S WAND** *Jive JIVE 28*	**73**†	1 wk

WIGAN'S CHOSEN FEW

US, instrumental track plus UK crowd vocal

Date	Title	Position	
18 Jan 75	● **FOOTSEE** *Pye Disco Demand DDS 111*	**9**	11 wks

WIGAN'S OVATION

UK, male vocal/instrumental group

Date	Title	Position	
15 Mar 75	**SKIING IN THE SNOW** *Spark SRL 1122*	**12**	10 wks
28 Jun 75	**PER-SO-NAL-LY** *Spark SRL 1129*	**38**	6 wks
29 Nov 75	**SUPER LOVE** *Spark SRL 1133*	**41**	3 wks

Jack WILD *UK, male vocalist*

Date	Title	Position	
2 May 70	**SOMETHING BEAUTIFUL** *Capitol CL 15635*	**46**	2 wks

WILD CHERRY *US, male vocal/instrumental group*

Date	Title	Position	
9 Oct 76	● **PLAY THAT FUNKY MUSIC** *Epic EPC 4593*	**7**	11 wks

Kim WILDE *UK, female vocalist*

Date	Title	Position	
21 Feb 81	● **KIDS IN AMERICA** *RAK 327*	**2**	13 wks
9 May 81	● **CHEQUERED LOVE** *RAK 330*	**4**	9 wks
1 Aug 81	**WATER ON GLASS/BOYS** *RAK 334*	**11**	8 wks
14 Nov 81	**CAMBODIA** *RAK 336*	**12**	12 wks
17 Apr 82	**VIEW FROM A BRIDGE** *RAK 342*	**16**	7 wks
16 Oct 82	**CHILD COME AWAY** *RAK 352*	**43**	4 wks

Marty WILDE *UK, male vocalist*

Date	Title	Position	
11 Jul 58	● **ENDLESS SLEEP** *Philips PB 835*	**4**	14 wks
6 Mar 59	● **DONNA** *Philips PB 902*	**3**	16 wks
5 Jun 59	● **A TEENAGER IN LOVE** *Philips PB 926*	**2**	17 wks
3 Jul 59	**DONNA** (re-entry) *Philips PB 902*	**25**	2 wks
25 Sep 59	● **SEA OF LOVE** *Philips PB 959*	**3**	12 wks
11 Dec 59	● **BAD BOY** *Philips PB 972*	**7**	8 wks
10 Mar 60	**JOHNNY ROCCO** *Philips PB 1002*	**30**	4 wks
19 May 60	**THE FIGHT** *Philips PB 1022*	**47**	1 wk
22 Dec 60	**LITTLE GIRL** *Philips PB 1078*	**16**	9 wks
26 Jan 61	● **RUBBER BALL** *Philips PB 1101*	**9**	9 wks

Above **MAURICE WILLIAMS AND THE ZODIACS** Orginally the Gladiolas, Maurice Williams penned their 1957 American hit 'Little Darlin', a smash here for the cover version by Canadian group the Diamonds. The Gladiolas became the Zodiacs in 1959

Right **MARI WILSON** 'Miss Beehive' The Queen of Neasden

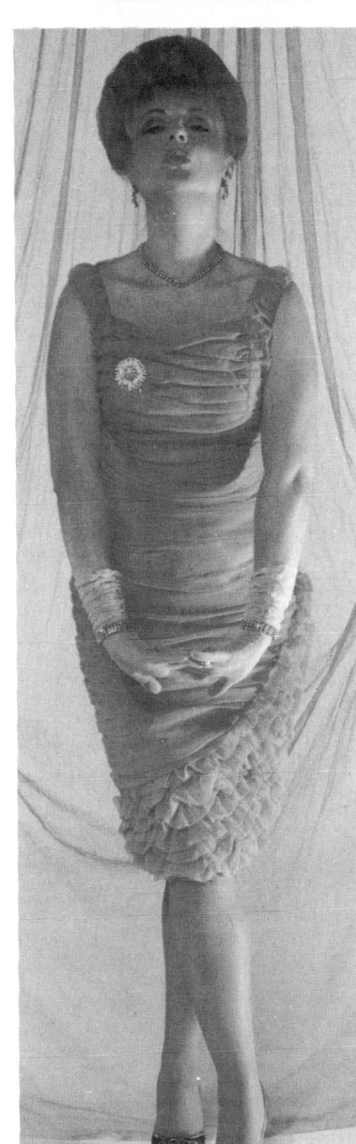

Above **BERT WEEDON** 'Mr Guitar' – His first guitar cost 15/– from a street barrow in London's Petticoat Lane

BRENTON WOOD Alfred Smith – feeling a little flash in 1967

Below **DIONNE WARWICK** Suddenly, in 1982, it was like she'd never been away

Date	Title *Label Number*	Position	
27 Jul 61	**HIDE AND SEEK** *Philips PB 1161*	**47**	2 wks
9 Nov 61	**TOMORROW'S CLOWN** *Philips PB 1191*	**33**	5 wks
24 May 62	**JEZEBEL** *Philips PB 1240*	**19**	12 wks
25 Oct 62	**EVER SINCE YOU SAID GOODBYE** *Philips 326546 BF*	**31**	7 wks

Sue WILKINSON *UK, female vocalist*

Date	Title *Label Number*	Position	
2 Aug 80	**YOU GOTTA BE A HUSTLER IF YOU WANNA GET ON** *Cheapskate CHEAP 2*	**25**	8 wks

Andy WILLIAMS *US, male vocalist*

Date	Title *Label Number*	Position	
19 Apr 57 ★	**BUTTERFLY** *London HLA 8399*	**1**	15 wks
21 Jun 57	**I LIKE YOUR KIND OF LOVE** *London HLA 8437*	**16**	10 wks
30 Aug 57	**BUTTERFLY** (re-entry) *London HLA 8399*	**29**	1 wk
14 Jun 62	**STRANGER ON THE SHORE** *CBS AAG 103*	**30**	10 wks
21 Mar 63 ●	**CAN'T GET USED TO LOSING YOU** *CBS AAG 138*	**2**	18 wks
27 Feb 64	**A FOOL NEVER LEARNS** *CBS AAG 182*	**40**	4 wks
16 Sep 65 ●	**ALMOST THERE** *CBS 201813*	**2**	17 wks
24 Feb 66	**MAY EACH DAY** *CBS 202042*	**19**	8 wks
22 Sep 66	**IN THE ARMS OF LOVE** *CBS 202300*	**33**	7 wks
4 May 67	**MUSIC TO WATCH GIRLS BY** *CBS 2675*	**33**	6 wks
2 Aug 67	**MORE AND MORE** *CBS 2886*	**45**	1 wk
13 Mar 68 ●	**CAN'T TAKE MY EYES OFF YOU** *CBS 3928*	**5**	18 wks
7 May 69	**HAPPY HEART** *CBS 4062*	**47**	1 wk
21 May 69	**HAPPY HEART** (re-entry) *CBS 4062*	**19**	9 wks
14 Mar 70 ●	**CAN'T HELP FALLING IN LOVE** *CBS 4818*	**3**	17 wks
1 Aug 70	**IT'S SO EASY** *CBS 5113*	**13**	13 wks
7 Nov 70	**IT'S SO EASY** (re-entry) *CBS 5113*	**49**	1 wk
21 Nov 70 ●	**HOME LOVIN' MAN** *CBS 5267*	**7**	12 wks
20 Mar 71 ●	**(WHERE DO I BEGIN) LOVE STORY** *CBS 7020*	**4**	17 wks
24 Jul 71	**(WHERE DO I BEGIN) LOVE STORY** (re-entry) *CBS 7020*	**49**	1 wk
5 Aug 72	**LOVE THEME FROM THE GODFATHER** *CBS 8166*	**50**	1 wk
2 Sep 72	**LOVE THEME FROM THE GODFATHER** (re-entry) *CBS 8166*	**44**	3 wks
30 Sep 72	**LOVE THEME FROM THE GODFATHER** (2nd re-entry) *CBS 8166*	**42**	5 wks
8 Dec 73 ●	**SOLITAIRE** *CBS 1824*	**4**	18 wks
18 May 74	**GETTING OVER YOU** *CBS 2181*	**35**	5 wks
31 May 75	**YOU LAY SO EASY ON MY MIND** *CBS 3167*	**32**	7 wks
6 Mar 76	**THE OTHER SIDE OF ME** *CBS 3903*	**42**	3 wks

Andy and David WILLIAMS

US, male vocal duo

Date	Title *Label Number*	Position	
24 Mar 73	**I DON'T KNOW WHY** *MCA MUS 1183*	**37**	5 wks

Do not see Andy Williams. This Andy and the other Andy are not the same, although they are related.

Billy WILLIAMS *US, male vocalist*

Date	Title *Label Number*	Position	
2 Aug 57	**I'M GONNA SIT RIGHT DOWN AND WRITE MYSELF A LETTER** *Vogue Coral Q 72266*	**22**	8 wks
18 Oct 57	**I'M GONNA SIT RIGHT DOWN AND WRITE MYSELF A LETTER** (re-entry) *Vogue Coral Q 72266*	**28**	1 wk

Danny WILLIAMS *UK, male vocalist*

Date	Title *Label Number*	Position	
25 May 61	**WE WILL NEVER BE AS YOUNG AS THIS AGAIN** *HMV POP 839*	**44**	3 wks
6 Jul 61	**THE MIRACLE OF YOU** *HMV POP 885*	**41**	8 wks
2 Nov 61 ★	**MOON RIVER** *HMV POP 932*	**1**	19 wks
18 Jan 62	**JEANNIE** *HMV POP 968*	**14**	14 wks
12 Apr 62 ●	**WONDERFUL WORLD OF THE YOUNG** *HMV POP 1002*	**8**	13 wks
5 Jul 62	**TEARS** *HMV POP 1035*	**22**	7 wks
28 Feb 63	**MY OWN TRUE LOVE** *HMV POP 1112*	**45**	3 wks
30 Jul 77	**DANCIN' EASY** *Ensign ENY 3*	**30**	7 wks

Deniece WILLIAMS *US, female vocalist*

Date	Title *Label Number*	Position	
2 Apr 77 ★	**FREE** *CBS 4978*	**1**	10 wks
30 Jul 77 ●	**THAT'S WHAT FRIENDS ARE FOR** *CBS 5432*	**8**	11 wks
12 Nov 77	**BABY BABY MY LOVE'S ALL FOR YOU** *CBS 5779*	**32**	5 wks

See also Johnny Mathis and Deniece Williams

Diana WILLIAMS *US, female vocalist*

Date	Title *Label Number*	Position	
25 Jul 81	**TEDDY BEAR'S LAST RIDE** *Capitol CL 207*	**54**	3 wks

Don WILLIAMS *US, male vocalist*

Date	Title *Label Number*	Position	
19 Jun 76	**I RECALL A GYPSY WOMAN** *ABC 4098*	**13**	10 wks
23 Oct 76	**YOU'RE MY BEST FRIEND** *ABC 4144*	**35**	6 wks

Iris WILLIAMS *UK, female vocalist*

Date	Title *Label Number*	Position	
27 Oct 79	**HE WAS BEAUTIFUL (CAVATINA) (THE THEME FROM THE DEER HUNTER)** *Columbia DB 9070*	**18**	8 wks

John WILLIAMS *UK, male instrumentalist - guitar*

Date	Title *Label Number*	Position	
19 May 79	**CAVATINA** *Cube BUG 80*	**13**	11 wks

John WILLIAMS

US, orchestra leader with UK/US orchestra

Date	Title *Label Number*	Position	
18 Dec 82	**THEME FROM 'E.T.' (THE EXTRA-TERRESTRIAL)** *MCA 800*	**34**†	2 wks

Theme from 'E.T.' is by Williams Conducting US Orchestra.

Kenny WILLIAMS *US, male vocalist*

Date	Title *Label Number*	Position	
19 Nov 77	**(YOU'RE) FABULOUS BABE** *Decca FR 13731*	**35**	7 wks

Larry WILLIAMS *US, male vocalist*

Date	Title *Label Number*	Position	
20 Sep 57	**SHORT FAT FANNY** *London HLN 8472*	**21**	8 wks
17 Jan 58	**BONY MORONIE** *London HLU 8532*	**11**	10 wks

Lenny WILLIAMS *US, male vocalist*

Date	Title *Label Number*	Position	
5 Nov 77	**SHOO DOO FU FU OOH!** *ABC 4194*	**38**	4 wks
16 Sep 78	**YOU GOT ME BURNING** *ABC 4228*	**67**	3 wks

Date	Title *Label Number*	Position	

Mason WILLIAMS

US, male instrumentalist, guitar

28 Aug 68	● **CLASSICAL GAS** *Warner Bros. WB 7190*	**9**	13 wks

Maurice WILLIAMS and the ZODIACS

US, male vocal group

5 Jan 61	**STAY** *Top Rank JAR 526*	**14**	9 wks

Viola WILLS *US, female vocalist*

6 Oct 79	● **GONNA GET ALONG WITHOUT YOU NOW** *Ariola/Hansa AHA 546*	**8**	10 wks

Al WILSON *US, male vocalist*

23 Aug 75	**THE SNAKE** *Bell 1436*	**41**	5 wks

Dooley WILSON *US, male vocalist*

3 Dec 77	**AS TIME GOES BY** *United Artists UP 36331*	**15**	9 wks

Disc has credit 'with the voices of Humphrey Bogart and Ingrid Bergman'

Jackie WILSON *US, male vocalist*

15 Nov 57	● **REET PETITE** *Coral Q 72290*	**6**	14 wks
14 Mar 58	**TO BE LOVED** *Coral Q 72306*	**27**	1 wk
28 Mar 58	**TO BE LOVED** (re-entry) *Coral Q 72306*	**23**	6 wks
16 May 58	**TO BE LOVED** (2nd re-entry) *Coral Q 72306*	**23**	1 wk
15 Sep 60	**ALL MY LOVE** *Coral Q 72407*	**33**	6 wks
3 Nov 60	**ALL MY LOVE** (re-entry) *Coral Q 72407*	**47**	1 wk
22 Dec 60	**ALONE AT LAST** *Coral Q 72412*	**50**	1 wk
14 May 69	**(YOUR LOVE KEEPS LIFTING ME) HIGHER AND HIGHER** *MCA BAG 2*	**11**	11 wks
29 Jul 72	● **I GET THE SWEETEST FEELING** *MCA MU 1160*	**9**	13 wks
3 May 75	**I GET THE SWEETEST FEELING/ HIGHER AND HIGHER** (re-issue) *Brunswick BR 18*	**25**	8 wks

Higher and Higher *was not listed together with* I Get The Sweetest Feeling *on Brunswick until 17 May 75.*

Mari WILSON *UK, female vocalist*

6 Mar 82	**BEAT THE BEAT** *Compact PINK 2*	**59**	3 wks
8 May 82	**BABY IT'S TRUE** *Compact PINK 3*	**42**	6 wks
11 Sep 82	● **JUST WHAT I ALWAYS WANTED** *Compact PINK 4*	**8**	10 wks
13 Nov 82	**(BEWARE) BOYFRIEND** *Compact/London PINK 5*	**51**	4 wks

Meri WILSON *US, female vocalist*

27 Aug 77	● **TELEPHONE MAN** *Pye International 7N 25747*	**6**	10 wks

WING AND A PRAYER Fife and Drum Corps *US, male/female vocal/instrumental group*

24 Jan 76	**BABY FACE** *Atlantic K 10705*	**12**	7 wks

Pete WINGFIELD *UK, male vocalist*

28 Jun 75	● **EIGHTEEN WITH A BULLET** *Island WIP 6231*	**7**	7 wks

WINGS

UK/US, male/female vocal/instrumental group.

26 Feb 72	**GIVE IRELAND BACK TO THE IRISH** *Apple R 5936*	**16**	8 wks
27 May 72	● **MARY HAD A LITTLE LAMB** *Apple R 5949*	**9**	11 wks
9 Dec 72	● **HI HI HI/ C MOON** *Apple R 5973*	**5**	13 wks
7 Apr 73	● **MY LOVE** *Apple R 5985*	**9**	11 wks
9 Jun 73	● **LIVE AND LET DIE** *Apple R 5987*	**9**	13 wks
15 Sep 73	**LIVE AND LET DIE** (re-entry) *Apple R 5987*	**49**	1 wk
3 Nov 73	**HELEN WHEELS** *Apple R 5993*	**12**	12 wks
2 Mar 74	● **JET** *Apple R 5996*	**7**	9 wks
6 Jul 74	● **BAND ON THE RUN** *Apple R 5997*	**3**	11 wks
9 Nov 74	**JUNIOR'S FARM** *Apple R 5999*	**16**	10 wks
31 May 75	● **LISTEN TO WHAT THE MAN SAID** *Capitol R 6006*	**6**	8 wks
18 Oct 75	**LETTING GO** *Capitol R 6008*	**41**	3 wks
15 May 76	● **SILLY LOVE SONGS** *Parlophone R 6014*	**2**	11 wks
7 Aug 76	● **LET 'EM IN** *Parlophone R 6015*	**2**	10 wks
19 Feb 77	**MAYBE I'M AMAZED** *Parlophone R 6017*	**28**	5 wks
19 Nov 77	★ **MULL OF KINTYRE/GIRL'S SCHOOL** *Capitol R 6018*	**1**	17 wks
1 Apr 78	● **WITH A LITTLE LUCK** *Parlophone R 6019*	**5**	9 wks
1 Jul 78	**I'VE HAD ENOUGH** *Parlophone R 6020*	**42**	7 wks
9 Sep 78	**LONDON TOWN** *Parlophone R 6021*	**60**	4 wks
7 Apr 79	● **GOODNIGHT TONIGHT** *Parlophone R 6023*	**5**	10 wks
16 Jun 79	**OLD SIAM SIR** *MPL R 6026*	**35**	6 wks
1 Sep 79	**GETTING CLOSER/BABY'S REQUEST** *- R 6027*	**60**	3 wks

My Love, Helen Wheels, Jet, Band On The Run *and* Junior's Farm: *are credited to Paul McCartney and Wings. R 6027 credited no label at all, although the number is a Parlophone one. See also Paul McCartney.*

Edgar WINTER GROUP

US, male instrumental group

26 May 73	**FRANKENSTEIN** *Epic EPC 1440*	**18**	9 wks

Ruby WINTERS *US, female vocalist*

5 Nov 77	● **I WILL** *Creole CR 141*	**4**	13 wks
29 Apr 78	**COME TO ME** *Creole CR 153*	**11**	12 wks
26 Aug 78	**I WON'T MENTION IT AGAIN** *Creole CR 160*	**45**	5 wks
16 Jun 79	**BABY LAY DOWN** *Creole CR 171*	**43**	5 wks

Steve WINWOOD

UK, male vocalist/instrumentalist

17 Jan 81	**WHILE YOU SEE A CHANCE** *Island WIP 6655*	**45**	5 wks
9 Oct 82	**VALERIE** *Island WIP 6818*	**51**	4 wks

WIRE *UK, male vocal/instrumental group*

27 Jan 79	**OUTDOOR MINER** *Harvest HAR 5172*	**51**	3 wks

Norman WISDOM *UK, male vocalist*

19 Feb 54	● **DON'T LAUGH AT ME** *Columbia DB 3133*	**3**	15 wks
15 Mar 57	**WISDOM OF A FOOL** *Columbia DB 3903*	**13**	5 wks

Bill WITHERS *US, male vocalist*

Date	Title *Label Number*	Position	
12 Aug 72	**LEAN ON ME** *A & M AMS 7004*	**18**	9 wks
14 Jan 78	● **LOVELY DAY** *CBS 5773*	**7**	8 wks

WIZZARD *UK, male vocal/instrumental group*

Date	Title *Label Number*	Position	
9 Dec 72	● **BALL PARK INCIDENT** *Harvest HAR 5062*	**6**	12 wks
21 Apr 73	★ **SEE MY BABY JIVE** *Harvest HAR 5070*	**1**	17 wks
1 Sep 73	★ **ANGEL FINGERS** *Harvest HAR 5076*	**1**	10 wks
8 Dec 73	● **I WISH IT COULD BE CHRISTMAS EVERYDAY** *Harvest HAR 5079*	**4**	9 wks
27 Apr 74	● **ROCK 'N ROLL WINTER** *Warner Bros. K 16357*	**6**	7 wks
10 Aug 74	**THIS IS THE STORY OF MY LOVE (BABY)** *Warner Bros. K 16434*	**34**	4 wks
21 Dec 74	● **ARE YOU READY TO ROCK** *Warner Bros. K 16497*	**8**	10 wks
19 Dec 81	**I WISH IT COULD BE CHRISTMAS EVERY DAY** (re-issue) *Harvest HAR 5173*	**41**	4 wks

I Wish It Could Be Christmas Everyday *features vocal backing by the Suedettes plus the Stockland Green Bilateral School First Year Choir with additional noises Miss Snob and Class 3C.*

Terry WOGAN *Ireland, male vocalist*

Date	Title *Label Number*	Position	
7 Jan 78	**FLORAL DANCE** *Philips 6006 592*	**21**	5 wks

WOMBLES

UK, Mike Batt, male vocalist, arranger and producer under group name

Date	Title *Label Number*	Position	
26 Jan 74	● **THE WOMBLING SONG** *CBS 1794*	**4**	23 wks
6 Apr 74	● **REMEMBER YOU'RE A WOMBLE** *CBS 2241*	**3**	16 wks
22 Jun 74	● **BANANA ROCK** *CBS 2465*	**9**	13 wks
12 Oct 74	**MINUETTO ALLEGRETTO** *CBS 2710*	**16**	9 wks
7 Dec 74	● **WOMBLING MERRY CHRISTMAS** *CBS 2842*	**2**	8 wks
10 May 75	**WOMBLING WHITE TIE AND TAILS** *CBS 3266*	**22**	7 wks
9 Aug 75	**SUPER WOMBLE** *CBS 3480*	**20**	6 wks
13 Dec 75	**LET'S WOMBLE TO THE PARTY TONIGHT** *CBS 3794*	**34**	5 wks

See also Mike Batt.

Stevie WONDER

US, male vocalist/instrumentalist, mainly keyboards & harmonica

Date	Title *Label Number*	Position	
3 Feb 66	**UPTIGHT** *Tamla Motown TMG 545*	**14**	10 wks
18 Aug 66	**BLOWIN' IN THE WIND** *Tamla Motown TMG 570*	**36**	5 wks
5 Jan 67	**A PLACE IN THE SUN** *Tamla Motown TMG 588*	**20**	5 wks
26 Jul 67	● **I WAS MADE TO LOVE HER** *Tamla Motown TMG 613*	**5**	15 wks
25 Oct 67	**I'M WONDERING** *Tamla Motown TMG 626*	**22**	8 wks
8 May 68	**SHOO BE DOO BE DOO DA DAY** *Tamla Motown TMG 653*	**46**	4 wks
18 Dec 68	● **FOR ONCE IN MY LIFE** *Tamla Motown TMG 679*	**3**	13 wks
19 Mar 69	**I DON'T KNOW WHY** *Tamla Motown TMG 690*	**14**	10 wks
9 Jul 69	**I DON'T KNOW WHY** (re-entry) *Tamla Motown TMG 690*	**43**	1 wk
16 Jul 69	● **MY CHERIE AMOUR** *Tamla Motown TMG 690*	**4**	16 wks
15 Nov 69	● **YESTER-ME YESTER-YOU YESTERDAY** *Tamla Motown TMG 717*	**2**	13 wks
28 Mar 70	● **NEVER HAD A DREAM COME TRUE** *Tamla Motown TMG 731*	**6**	12 wks
18 Jul 70	**SIGNED SEALED DELIVERED I'M YOURS** *Tamla Motown TMG 744*	**15**	9 wks
26 Sep 70	**SIGNED SEALED DELIVERED I'M YOURS** (re-entry) *Tamla Motown TMG 744*	**49**	1 wk
21 Nov 70	**HEAVEN HELP US ALL** *Tamla Motown TMG 757*	**29**	11 wks
15 May 71	**WE CAN WORK IT OUT** *Tamla Motown TMG 772*	**27**	7 wks
22 Jan 72	**IF YOU REALLY LOVE ME** *Tamla Motown TMG 798*	**20**	7 wks
3 Feb 73	**SUPERSTITION** *Tamla Motown TMG 841*	**11**	9 wks
19 May 73	● **YOU ARE THE SUNSHINE OF MY LIFE** *Tamla Motown TMG 852*	**7**	11 wks
13 Oct 73	**HIGHER GROUND** *Tamla Motown TMG 869*	**29**	5 wks
12 Jan 74	**LIVING FOR THE CITY** *Tamla Motown TMG 881*	**15**	9 wks
13 Apr 74	● **HE'S MISSTRA KNOW IT ALL** *Tamla Motown TMG 892*	**10**	9 wks
19 Oct 74	**YOU HAVEN'T DONE NOTHIN'** *Tamla Motown TMG 921*	**30**	5 wks
11 Jan 75	**BOOGIE ON REGGAE WOMAN** *Tamla Motown TMG 928*	**12**	8 wks
18 Dec 76	● **I WISH** *Tamla Motown TMG 1054*	**5**	10 wks
9 Apr 77	● **SIR DUKE** *Motown TMG 1068*	**2**	9 wks
10 Sep 77	**ANOTHER STAR** *Motown TMG 1083*	**29**	5 wks
24 Nov 79	**SEND ONE YOUR LOVE** *Motown TMG 1149*	**52**	3 wks
26 Jan 80	**BLACK ORCHID** *Motown TMG 1173*	**63**	3 wks
29 Mar 80	**OUTSIDE MY WINDOW** *Motown TMG 1179*	**52**	4 wks
13 Sep 80	● **MASTERBLASTER (JAMMIN')** *Motown TMG 1204*	**2**	10 wks
27 Dec 80	● **I AIN'T GONNA STAND FOR IT** *Motown TMG 1215*	**10**	10 wks
27 Dec 80	● **LATELY** *Motown TMG 1226*	**3**	13 wks
27 Dec 80	● **HAPPY BIRTHDAY** *Motown TMG 1235*	**2**	11 wks
23 Jan 82	**THAT GIRL** *Motown TMG 1254*	**39**	6 wks
5 Jun 82	● **DO I DO** *Motown TMG 1269*	**10**	7 wks
25 Sep 82	**RIBBON IN THE SKY** *Motown TMG 1280*	**45**	4 wks

See also Diana Ross, Marvin Gaye, Smokey Robinson and Stevie Wonder, Paul McCartney with Stevie Wonder and also Jackson Five. You Havn't Done Nothing *has credit: DooDoo Wopsss by the Jackson Five.*

WONDER DOGS *UK, canine vocal group*

Date	Title *Label Number*	Position	
21 Aug 82	**RUFF MIX** *Flip FLIP 001*	**31**	7 wks

Brenton WOOD *US, male vocalist*

Date	Title *Label Number*	Position	
27 Dec 67	● **GIMME LITTLE SIGN** *Liberty LBF 15021*	**8**	14 wks

Roy WOOD *UK, male vocalist/multi-instrumentalist*

Date	Title *Label Number*	Position	
11 Aug 73	**DEAR ELAINE** *Harvest HAR 5074*	**18**	8 wks
1 Dec 73	● **FOREVER** *Harvest HAR 5078*	**8**	13 wks
15 Jun 74	**GOING DOWN THE ROAD** *Harvest HAR 5083*	**13**	7 wks
31 May 75	**OH WHAT A SHAME** *Jet 754*	**13**	7 wks

Edward WOODWARD *UK, male vocalist*

Date	Title *Label Number*	Position	
16 Jan 71	**THE WAY YOU LOOK TONIGHT** *DJM DJS 232*	**50**	1 wk
30 Jan 71	**THE WAY YOU LOOK TONIGHT** (re-entry) *DJM DJS 232*	**42**	1 wk

Date	Title *Label Number*	Position	

Sheb WOOLEY *US, male vocalist*

20 Jun 58	**PURPLE PEOPLE EATER** *MGM 981*	**12**	8 wks

WORLD'S FAMOUS SUPREME TEAM — See *Malcolm McLAREN and the WORLD'S FAMOUS SUPREME TEAM*

Betty WRIGHT *US, female vocalist*

25 Jan 75	**SHOORAH SHOORAH** *RCA 2491*	**27**	7 wks
19 Apr 75	**WHERE IS THE LOVE** *RCA 2548*	**25**	7 wks

Ruby WRIGHT *UK, female vocalist*

16 Apr 54 ●	**BIMBO** *Parlophone R 3816*	**7**	4 wks
21 May 54	**BIMBO** (re-entry) *Parlophone R 3816*	**12**	1 wk
22 May 59	**THREE STARS** *Parlophone R 4556*	**19**	10 wks

WURZELS *UK, male vocal/instrumental group*

15 May 76 ★	**COMBINE HARVESTER (BRAND NEW KEY)** *EMI 2450*	**1**	13 wks
11 Sep 76 ●	**I AM A CIDER DRINKER (PALOMA BLANCA)** *EMI 2520*	**3**	9 wks
25 Jun 77	**FARMER BILL'S COWMAN (I WAS KAISER BILL'S BATMAN)** *EMI 2637*	**32**	5 wks

See also Adge Cutler and the Wurzels.

Robert WYATT *UK, male vocalist*

28 Sep 74	**I'M A BELIEVER** *Virgin VS 114*	**29**	5 wks

Bill WYMAN *UK, male vocalist*

25 Jul 81	**(SI SI) JE SUIS UN ROCK STAR** *A & M AMS 8144*	**14**	9 wks
20 Mar 82	**A NEW FASHION** *A & M AMS 8209*	**37**	4 wks

Jane WYMAN — See *Bing CROSBY and Jane WYMAN*

Tammy WYNETTE *US, female vocalist*

26 Apr 75 ★	**STAND BY YOUR MAN** *Epic EPC 7137*	**1**	12 wks
28 Jun 75	**D. I. V. O. R. C. E.** *Epic EPC 3361*	**12**	7 wks
12 Jun 76	**I DON'T WANNA PLAY HOUSE** *Epic EPC 4091*	**37**	4 wks

Mark WYNTER *UK, male vocalist*

25 Aug 60	**IMAGE OF A GIRL** *Decca F 11263*	**11**	10 wks
10 Nov 60	**KICKING UP THE LEAVES** *Decca F 11279*	**24**	10 wks
9 Mar 61	**DREAM GIRL** *Decca F 11323*	**27**	5 wks
8 Jun 61	**EXCLUSIVELY YOURS** *Decca F 11354*	**32**	7 wks
4 Oct 62 ●	**VENUS IN BLUE JEANS** *Pye 7N 15466*	**4**	15 wks
13 Dec 62 ●	**GO AWAY LITTLE GIRL** *Pye 7N 15482*	**6**	11 wks
6 Jun 63	**SHY GIRL** *Pye 7N 15525*	**28**	6 wks
14 Nov 63	**IT'S ALMOST TOMORROW** *Pye 7N 15577*	**12**	12 wks
9 Apr 64	**ONLY YOU** *Pye 7N 15626*	**38**	4 wks

X

Miss X *UK, female vocalist*

1 Aug 63	**CHRISTINE** *Ember S 175*	**37**	6 wks

Miss X was Joyce Blair.

XAVIER *US, male vocal/instrumental group*

20 Mar 82	**WORK THAT SUCKER TO DEATH** *Liberty UP 651*	**53**	3 wks

X-RAY SPEX

UK, male/female vocal/instrumental group

29 Apr 78	**THE DAY THE WORLD TURNED DAY-GLOW** *EMI International INT 533*	**23**	7 wks
22 Jul 78	**IDENTITY** *EMI International INT 563*	**24**	10 wks
4 Nov 78	**GERM-FREE ADOLESCENCE** *EMI International INT 573*	**19**	11 wks
21 Apr 79	**HIGHLY INFLAMMABLE** *EMI International INT 583*	**45**	4 wks

XTC *UK, male vocal/instrumental group*

12 May 79	**LIFE BEGINS AT THE HOP** *Virgin VS 259*	**54**	4 wks
22 Sep 79	**MAKING PLANS FOR NIGEL** *Virgin VS 282*	**17**	11 wks
6 Sep 80	**GENERALS AND MAJORS/DON'T LOOSE YOUR TEMPER** *Virgin VS 365*	**32**	8 wks
18 Oct 80	**TOWERS OF LONDON** *Virgin VS 372*	**31**	5 wks
24 Jan 81	**SGT ROCK (IS GOING TO HELP ME)** *Virgin VS 384*	**16**	9 wks
23 Jan 82 ●	**SENSES WORKING OVERTIME** *Virgin VS 462*	**10**	9 wks
27 Mar 82	**BALL AND CHAIN** *Virgin VS 482*	**58**	4 wks

Y

YAN — See *YIN and YAN*

YARBROUGH and PEOPLES

US, male/female vocal/instrumental duo

27 Dec 80 ●	**DON'T STOP THE MUSIC** *Mercury MER 53*	**7**	12 wks

YARDBIRDS *UK, male vocal/instrumental group*

12 Nov 64	**GOOD MORNING LITTLE SCHOOLGIRL** *Columbia DB 7391*	**44**	4 wks
18 Mar 65 ●	**FOR YOUR LOVE** *Columbia DB 7499*	**3**	12 wks
17 Jul 65 ●	**HEART FULL OF SOUL** *Columbia DB 7594*	**2**	13 wks
14 Oct 65 ●	**EVIL HEARTED YOU/ STILL I'M SAD**	**3**	10 wks

Date	Title *Label Number*	Position	
3 Mar 66	● **SHAPES OF THINGS** *Columbia DB 7848*	**3**	9 wks
2 Jun 66	● **OVER UNDER SIDEWAYS DOWN** *Columbia DB 7928*	**10**	9 wks
27 Oct 66	**HAPPENINGS TEN YEARS TIME AGO** *Columbia DB 8024*	**43**	5 wks

YAZOO *UK, female/male vocal/instrumental duo*

Date	Title *Label Number*	Position	
17 Apr 82	● **ONLY YOU** *Mute MUTE 020*	**2**	14 wks
17 Jul 82	● **DON'T GO** *Mute YAZ 001*	**3**	11 wks
20 Nov 82	**THE OTHER SIDE OF LOVE** *Mute YAZ 002*	**13**†	6 wks

YELLOW DOG

US/UK, male vocal/instrumental group

Date	Title *Label Number*	Position	
4 Feb 78	● **JUST ONE MORE NIGHT** *Virgin VS 195*	**8**	9 wks
22 Jul 78	**WAIT UNTIL MIDNIGHT** *Virgin VS 217*	**54**	4 wks

YELLOW MAGIC ORCHESTRA

Japan, male instrumental group

Date	Title *Label Number*	Position	
14 Jun 80	**COMPUTER GAME (THEME FROM THE INVADERS)** *A & M AMS 7502*	**17**	11 wks

YELLOWCOATS — See *Paul SHANE and the YELLOWCOATS*

YES *UK, male vocal/instrumental group*

Date	Title *Label Number*	Position	
17 Sep 77	● **WONDEROUS STORIES** *Atlantic K 10999*	**7**	9 wks
26 Nov 77	**GOING FOR THE ONE** *Atlantic K 11047*	**24**	4 wks
9 Sep 78	**DON'T KILL THE WHALE** *Atlantic K 11184*	**36**	4 wks

YIN and YAN *UK, male vocal duo*

Date	Title *Label Number*	Position	
29 Mar 75	**IF** *EMI 2282*	**25**	5 wks

YOUNG and COMPANY

US, male/female vocal/instrumental group

Date	Title *Label Number*	Position	
1 Nov 80	**I LIKE (WHAT YOU'RE DOING TO ME)** *Excalibur EXC 501*	**20**	12 wks

Faron YOUNG *US, male vocalist*

Date	Title *Label Number*	Position	
15 Jul 72	● **IT'S FOUR IN THE MORNING** *Mercury 6052 140*	**3**	23 wks

Jimmy YOUNG *UK, male vocalist*

Date	Title *Label Number*	Position	
9 Jan 53	**FAITH CAN MOVE MOUNTAINS** *Decca F 9986*	**11**	1 wk
21 Aug 53	● **ETERNALLY** *Decca F 10130*	**8**	9 wks
6 May 55	★ **UNCHAINED MELODY** *Decca F 10502*	**1**	19 wks
16 Sep 55	★ **THE MAN FROM LARAMIE** *Decca F 10597*	**1**	12 wks
23 Dec 55	**SOMEONE ON YOUR MIND** *Decca F 10640*	**13**	5 wks
16 Mar 56	● **CHAIN GANG** *Decca F 10694*	**9**	6 wks
8 Jun 56	**WAYWARD WIND** *Decca F 10736*	**27**	1 wk
22 Jun 56	**RICH MAN POOR MAN** *Decca F 10736*	**25**	1 wk
28 Sep 56	● **MORE** *Decca F 10774*	**4**	17 wks
3 May 57	**ROUND AND ROUND** *Decca F 10875*	**30**	1 wk
10 Oct 63	**MISS YOU** *Columbia DB 7119*	**15**	13 wks
26 Mar 64	**UNCHAINED MELODY** *Columbia DB 7234*	**43**	3 wks

The versions of Unchained Melody *on Decca and on Columbia are different recordings of the same song.*

John Paul YOUNG *Australia, male vocalist*

Date	Title *Label Number*	Position	
29 Apr 78	● **LOVE IS IN THE AIR** *Ariola ARO 117*	**5**	13 wks

Karen YOUNG *UK, female vocalist*

Date	Title *Label Number*	Position	
6 Sep 69	● **NOBODY'S CHILD** *Major Minor MM 625*	**6**	21 wks

Karen YOUNG *US, Female vocalist*

Date	Title *Label Number*	Position	
19 Aug 78	**HOT SHOT** *Atlantic K 11180*	**34**	7 wks
24 Feb 79	**HOT SHOT** (re-issue) *Atlantic LV 8*	**75**	1 wk

Neil YOUNG *Canada, male vocalist*

Date	Title *Label Number*	Position	
11 Mar 72	● **HEART OF GOLD** *Reprise K 14140*	**10**	11 wks
6 Jan 79	**FOUR STRONG WINDS** *Reprise K 14493*	**57**	4 wks

Retta YOUNG *US, female vocalist*

Date	Title *Label Number*	Position	
24 May 75	**SENDING OUT AN S. O. S.** *All Platinum 6146 305*	**28**	7 wks

YOUNG AND MOODY BAND

UK, male/female vocal/instrumental group

Date	Title *Label Number*	Position	
10 Oct 81	**DONT DO THAT** *Bronze BRO 130*	**63**	4 wks

Young and Moody Band comprises Motorhead and the Nolans. See Motorhead, Nolans.

YOUNG IDEA *UK, male vocal duo*

Date	Title *Label Number*	Position	
29 Jun 67	● **WITH A LITTLE HELP FROM MY FRIENDS** *Columbia DB 8205*	**10**	6 wks

YOUNG RASCALS

US, male vocal/instrumental group

Date	Title *Label Number*	Position	
25 May 67	● **GROOVIN'** *Atlantic 584 111*	**8**	13 wks
16 Aug 67	**A GIRL LIKE YOU** *Atlantic 584 128*	**37**	4 wks

YOUNG STEVE and the AFTERNOON BOYS

UK, male vocalist (Steve Wright) and male vocal/instrumental group

Date	Title *Label Number*	Position	
27 Nov 82	**I'M ALRIGHT** *RCA 296*	**40**†	5 wks

Leon YOUNG STRING CHORALE — See *Mr Acker BILK*

YAZOO Vincent Clarke (Vince) and Genevieve Alison Moyet (Alf)
Inset **LENA ZAVARONI** Despite only two hits she continues to be an established TV and Radio performer

YOUNG RASCALS The original stage clothes included plus-fours and knickerbockers which they dropped along with the first half of their name in the latter part of 1967

BILL WYMAN – Toujours un Rock Star
TAMMY WYNETTE In the words of the Mojos hit 'Wynette Tonight'

Date	Title *Label Number*	Position	

Z

Helmut ZACHARIAS *Germany, orchestra*

29 Oct 64	● **TOKYO MELODY** *Polydor YNH 52341*	**9**	11 wks

ZAGER and EVANS *US, male vocal duo*

9 Aug 69	★ **IN THE YEAR 2525 (EXORDIUM AND TERMINUS)** *RCA 1860*	**1**	13 wks

Michael ZAGER BAND

US, male/female vocal/instrumental group

1 Apr 78	● **LET'S ALL CHANT** *Private Stock PVT 143*	**8**	12 wks

Georghe ZAMFIR

Romania, male instrumentalist, pipes

21 Aug 76	● **(LIGHT OF EXPERIENCE) DOINA DE JALE** *Epic EPC 4480*	**6**	13 wks

Tommy ZANG *US, male vocalist*

16 Feb 61	**HEY GOOD LOOKING** *Polydor NH 66957*	**45**	1 wk

Lena ZAVARONI *UK, female vocalist*

9 Feb 74	● **MA HE'S MAKING EYES AT ME** *Philips 6006 367*	**10**	11 wks
1 Jun 74	**PERSONALITY** *Philips 6006 391*	**33**	3 wks

ZEPHYRS *UK, male vocal/instrumental group*

18 Mar 65	**SHE'S LOST YOU** *Columbia DB 7481*	**48**	1 wk

ZIGZAG JIVE FLUTES — See *ELIAS and his ZIGZAG JIVE FLUTES*

ZODIACS — See *Maurice WILLIAMS and the ZODIACS*

ZOMBIES *UK, male vocal/instrumental group*

13 Aug 64	**SHE'S NOT THERE** *Decca F 11940*	**12**	11 wks
11 Feb 65	**TELL HER NO** *Decca F 12072*	**42**	5 wks

PART 2

The British Hit Singles: Alphabetically by Title

Different songs/tunes with the same title (e.g. IT'S ALL OVER NOW which has been a hit title for both the Rolling Stones and for Shane Fenton and The Fentones) are indicated by (A), (B), etc. Where there is no letter in brackets after the title, all hit recordings are of just one number. Individual titles of songs or tunes on L.P.'s, E.P.'s or medley singles which made the singles chart are not included here, with the obvious exception of titles that are actually part of the overall title of the hit L.P., E.P. or medley single.

The recording act named alongside each song title is not necessarily exactly the same act that is billed on the record, but is the act under whose name all the information about the title can be found in Part 1 of this book. The year of chart entry column contains the year in which each disc made its very first appearance on the chart. Subsequent appearances are only listed here if they signify a period of success totally separate from the disc's first impact.

Title — Act (Position)	Year of Chart Entry
— **Classix Nouveaux** (0)	82
— John **Lennon** (13)	81
A BA NI BI — Izhar **Cohen and Alphabeta** (20)	78
'A' BOMB IN WARDOUR STREET — **Jam** (25)	78
ABACAB — **Genesis** (9)	81
ABC — **Jackson Five** (8)	70
ABRACADABRA — Steve **Miller Band** (2)	82
ABRAHAM MARTIN & JOHN — Marvin **Gaye** (9)	70
ABSOLUTE BEGINNERS — **Jam** (4)	81
ACAPULCO 1922 — Kenny **Ball and his Jazzmen** (27)	63
ACCIDENT PRONE — **Status Quo** (36)	78
ACCIDENTS — **Thunderclap Newman** (46)	70
ACCIDENTS WILL HAPPEN — Elvis **Costello and the Attractions** (28)	79
ACE OF SPADES — **Motorhead** (15)	80
ACTION — **Sweet** (15)	75
ADIOS AMIGO — Jim **Reeves** (23)	62
ADORATION WALTZ — David **Whitfield** (9)	57
ADVENTURES OF THE LOVE CRUSADER, THE — Sarah **Brightman** (53)	79
AFFAIR TO REMEMBER, AN — Vic **Damone** (29)	57
AFRICAN AND WHITE — **China Crisis** (45)	82
AFRICAN WALTZ — Johnny **Dankworth** (9)	61
AFTER THE GOLDRUSH — **Prelude** (21)	74,82
AFTER THE LOVE HAS GONE — **Earth Wind and Fire** (4)	79
AFTER YOU'VE GONE — Alice **Babs** (43)	63
AFTERGLOW OF YOUR LOVE — **Small Faces** (36)	69
AFTERNOON DELIGHT — **Starland Vocal Band** (18)	76
AFTERNOON OF THE RHINO — Mike **Post Coalition** (47)	75
AGAIN AND AGAIN — **Status Quo** (13)	78
AI NO CORRIDA (I-NO-KO-REE-DA) — Quincy **Jones** (14)	81
AIN'T DOIN' NOTHIN' — Jet **Bronx and the Forbidden** (49)	77
AIN'T GONNA BE THAT WAY — Marv **Johnson** (50)	60
AIN'T GONNA BUMP NO MORE (WITH NO BIG FAT WOMAN) — Joe **Tex** (2)	77
AIN'T GONNA WASH FOR A WEEK — **Brook Brothers** (13)	61
AIN'T GOT A CLUE — **Lurkers** (45)	78
AIN'T GOT NO - I GOT LIFE — Nina **Simone** (2)	68
AIN'T LOVE A BITCH — Rod **Stewart** (11)	79
AIN'T MISBEHAVIN' — Tommy **Bruce** (3)	60
AIN'T MISBEHAVIN' — Johnnie **Ray** (17)	56
AIN'T NO LOVE IN THE HEART OF THE CITY — **Whitesnake** (51)	80
AIN'T NO MOUNTAIN HIGH ENOUGH — **Boystown Gang** (46)	81
AIN'T NO MOUNTAIN HIGH ENOUGH — Diana **Ross** (6)	70
AIN'T NO PLEASING YOU — **Chas and Dave** (2)	82
AIN'T NO STOPPIN' US NOW — **McFadden and Whitehead** (5)	79
AIN'T NO STOPPING — **Enigma** (11)	81
AIN'T NO SUNSHINE — Michael **Jackson** (8)	72
AIN'T NOTHIN' LIKE THE REAL THING — Marvin **Gaye and Tammi Terrell** (34)	68
AIN'T NOTHING BUT A HOUSEPARTY — **Showstoppers** (11)	68,71
AIN'T SHE SWEET — **Beatles** (29)	64
AIN'T THAT A SHAME — Pat **Boone** (7)	55,57
AIN'T THAT A SHAME — Fats **Domino** (23)	57
AIN'T THAT A SHAME — **Four Seasons** (38)	63
AIN'T THAT ENOUGH FOR YOU — John **Davis and the Monster Orchestra** (70)	79
AIN'T THAT FUNNY — Jimmy **Justice** (8)	62
AIN'T THAT LOVIN' YOU BABY — Elvis **Presley** (15)	64
AIN'T TOO PROUD TO BEG — **Temptations** (21)	66
AIN'T WE FUNKIN' NOW — **Brothers Johnson** (43)	78
AIR THAT I BREATHE, THE — **Hollies** (2)	74
AIRPORT — **Motors** (4)	78
AL CAPONE — Prince **Buster** (18)	67
AL DI LA — Emilio **Pericoli** (30)	62
ALABAMA JUBILEE — **Ferko String Band** (20)	55
ALABAMA SONG — David **Bowie** (23)	80
ALBATROSS — **Fleetwood Mac** (1)	68,73
ALEXANDER GRAHAM BELL — **Sweet** (33)	71
ALFIE — Cilla **Black** (9)	66
ALISON — Linda **Ronstadt** (66)	79
ALL ALONE AM I — Brenda **Lee** (7)	63
ALL ALONG THE WATCHTOWER — Jimi **Hendrix Experience** (5)	68
ALL AMERICAN BOY — Bill **Parsons** (22)	59
ALL AMERICAN GIRLS — **Sister Sledge** (41)	81
ALL AROUND MY HAT — **Steeleye Span** (5)	75
ALL AROUND THE WORLD — **Jam** (13)	77,80
ALL BECAUSE OF YOU — **Geordie** (6)	73
ALL BY MYSELF — Eric **Carmen** (12)	76
ALL DAY AND ALL OF THE NIGHT — **Kinks** (2)	64
ALL FALL DOWN — **Lindisfarne** (34)	72
ALL FOR LEYNA — Billy **Joel** (40)	80
ALL I EVER NEED IS YOU — **Sonny and Cher** (8)	72
ALL I EVER WANTED — **Santana** (57)	80
ALL I HAVE TO DO IS DREAM — **Everly Brothers** (1)	58
ALL I HAVE TO DO IS DREAM — Bobbie **Gentry and Glen Campbell** (3)	69
ALL I NEED IS YOUR SWEET LOVIN' — Gloria **Gaynor** (44)	75
ALL I REALLY WANT TO DO — **Byrds** (4)	65
ALL I REALLY WANT TO DO — **Cher** (9)	65
ALL I SEE IS YOU — Dusty **Springfield** (9)	66
ALL I THINK ABOUT IS YOU — **Nilsson** (43)	77
ALL I WANT FOR CHRISTMAS IS A BEATLE — Dora **Bryan** (20)	63
ALL I WANT IS YOU — **Roxy Music** (12)	74
ALL KINDS OF EVERYTHING — **Dana** (1)	70
ALL MY LOVE — Jackie **Wilson** (33)	60
ALL MY LOVE [B] — Cliff **Richard** (6)	67
ALL MY LOVING — **Dowlands** (33)	64
ALL NIGHT LONG — **Cloud** (72)	81
ALL NIGHT LONG [A] — **Rainbow** (5)	80
ALL NIGHT LONG [B] — Dexter **Wansell** (59)	78
(ALL OF A SUDDEN) MY HEART SINGS — Paul **Anka** (10)	59
ALL OF ME LOVES ALL OF YOU — **Bay City Rollers** (4)	74
ALL OF MY HEART — **ABC** (5)	82
ALL OF MY LIFE — Diana **Ross** (9)	74
ALL OF YOU — Sammy **Davis Jr.** (28)	56
ALL OR NOTHING — **Small Faces** (1)	66
ALL OUT OF LOVE — **Air Supply** (11)	80
ALL OUT TO GET YOU — The **Beat** (22)	81
ALL OVER THE WORLD [A] — **Electric Light Orchestra** (11)	80
ALL OVER THE WORLD [B] — Francoise **Hardy** (16)	65
ALL RIGHT NOW — **Free** (2)	70,73
ALL SHOOK UP — Elvis **Presley** (1)	57,77
ALL STAR HIT PARADE — **Various Artists** (2)	56
ALL STAR HIT PARADE NO. 2 — **Various Artists** (15)	57
ALL STOOD STILL — **Ultravox** (8)	81
ALL THAT GLITTERS — Gary **Glitter** (48)	81
ALL THAT I AM — Elvis **Presley** (18)	66
ALL THE LOVE IN THE WORLD [A] — **Consortium** (22)	69
ALL THE LOVE IN THE WORLD [B] — Dionne **Warwick** (14)	82
ALL THE TIME AND EVERYWHERE — Dickie **Valentine** (9)	53
ALL THE WAY — Frank **Sinatra** (3)	57
ALL THE WAY FROM AMERICA — Joan **Armatrading** (54)	80
ALL THE WAY FROM MEMPHIS — **Mott The Hoople** (10)	73
ALL THE YOUNG DUDES — **Mott The Hoople** (3)	72
ALL THOSE YEARS AGO — George **Harrison** (13)	81
ALL YOU NEED IS LOVE — **Beatles** (1)	67
ALLEY CAT SONG — David **Thorne** (21)	63
ALLEY OOP — **Hollywood Argyles** (24)	60
ALLY'S TARTAN ARMY — Andy **Cameron** (6)	78
ALMOST SATURDAY NIGHT — Dave **Edmunds** (58)	81
ALMOST THERE — Andy **Williams** (2)	65
ALONE — Petula **Clark** (8)	57
ALONE — **Kaye Sisters** (27)	58
ALONE — **Shepherd Sisters** (14)	57
ALONE — **Southlanders** (17)	57
ALONE AGAIN (NATURALLY) — Gilbert **O'Sullivan** (3)	72
ALONE AT LAST — Jackie **Wilson** (50)	60
ALONG CAME CAROLINE — Michael **Cox** (41)	60
ALRIGHT ALRIGHT ALRIGHT — **Mungo Jerry** (3)	73
ALRIGHT BABY — **Stevenson's Rocket** (37)	75
ALSO SPRACH ZARATHUSTRA (2001) — **Deodato** (7)	73
ALTERNATE TITLE — **Monkees** (2)	67
ALWAYS — Sammy **Turner** (26)	59
ALWAYS AND EVER — Johnny **Kidd and the Pirates** (46)	64
ALWAYS AND FOREVER — **Heatwave** (9)	78
ALWAYS ON MY MIND — Willie **Nelson** (49)	82
ALWAYS ON MY MIND — Elvis **Presley** (9)	72
ALWAYS THE LONELY ONE — Alan **Drew** (48)	63
ALWAYS YOU AND ME — Russ **Conway** (33)	62
ALWAYS YOURS — Gary **Glitter** (1)	74
AM I A TOY OR A TREASURE — Kay **Starr** (17)	54
AM I THAT EASY TO FORGET — Engelbert **Humperdinck** (3)	68
AM I THE SAME GIRL — Dusty **Springfield** (43)	69
AM I WASTING MY TIME ON YOU — Frankie **Vaughan** (25)	58
AMANDA — Stuart **Gillies** (13)	73
AMATEUR HOUR — **Sparks** (7)	74
AMAZING GRACE — Judy **Collins** (5)	70
AMAZING GRACE — The Pipes and Drums and Military Band of the **Royal Scots Dragoon Guards** (1)	72
AMBUSH — **Outlaws** (43)	61
AMERICA [A] — David **Essex** (32)	74
AMERICA [B] — **Nice** (21)	68
AMERICA [C] — **Simon and Garfunkel** (25)	72
AMERICAN GENERATION — **Ritchie Family** (49)	79
AMERICAN GIRL — Tom **Petty and the Heartbreakers** (40)	77
AMERICAN HEARTS — Billy **Ocean** (54)	79
AMERICAN PIE — Don **McLean** (2)	72
AMERICAN, THE — **Simple Minds** (59)	81
AMERICAN TRILOGY — Mickey **Newbury** (42)	72
AMERICAN TRILOGY — Elvis **Presley** (8)	72
AMERICAN WOMAN — **Guess Who** (19)	70
AMIGO — **Black Slate** (9)	80
AMONG MY SOUVENIRS — Connie **Francis** (11)	59
AMOR — Julio **Iglesias** (32)	82
AMOR' AMOR — Ben E. **King** (38)	61
AMOUR AMOUR — **Mobiles** (45)	82
AMOUREUSE — Kiki **Dee** (13)	73
AMOUREUSE (RE-ISSUE OF AMOUREUSE) — Kiki **Dee** (13)	76
ANARCHY IN THE U. K. — **Sex Pistols** (38)	76
AND I LOVE YOU SO — Perry **Como** (3)	73
AND I WISH — **Dooleys** (52)	81
AND I'M TELLING YOU I'M NOT GOING — Jennifer **Holliday** (32)	82
(AND NOW - THE WALTZ) C'EST LA VIE — **Slade** (50)	82
AND THE BAND PLAYED ON (DOWN AMONG THE DEAD MEN) — **Flash and the Pan** (54)	78
AND THE BANDS PLAYED ON — **Saxon** (12)	81
AND THE BEAT GOES ON — **Whispers** (2)	80
AND THE HEAVENS CRIED — Anthony **Newley** (6)	61
(AND THE) PICTURES IN THE SKY — **Medicine Head** (22)	71
AND THE SUN WILL SHINE — José **Feliciano** (25)	69
AND THEN SHE KISSED ME — Gary **Glitter** (39)	81
AND YOU SMILED — Matt **Monro** (28)	73
ANGEL [A] — Rod **Stewart** (4)	72
ANGEL [B] — Aretha **Franklin** (37)	73
ANGEL EYES — **Roxy Music** (4)	79
ANGEL FACE — **Glitter Band** (4)	74
ANGEL FINGERS — **Wizzard** (1)	73
ANGEL IN BLUE — J. **Geils Band** (55)	82
ANGEL OF THE MORNING — P. P. **Arnold** (29)	68
ANGEL OF THE MORNING — Juice **Newton** (43)	81
ANGEL OF THE MORNING - ANY WAY THAT YOU WANT ME (MEDLEY) — Mary **Mason** (27)	77
ANGELA JONES — Michael **Cox** (7)	60
ANGELEYES — **Abba** (3)	79
ANGELO — **Brotherhood Of Man** (1)	77
ANGELS DON'T LIE — Jim **Reeves** (32)	70
ANGELS WITH DIRTY FACES — **Sham 69** (19)	78
ANGIE — **Rolling Stones** (5)	73
ANGIE BABY — Helen **Reddy** (5)	75
ANGRY AT THE BIG OAK TREE — Frank **Ifield** (25)	64
ANIMATION — **Skids** (56)	80
ANNABELLA — John **Walker** (24)	67
ANNIE GET YOUR GUN — **Squeeze** (43)	82
ANNIE I'M NOT YOUR DADDY — Kid **Creole and the Coconuts** (2)	82
ANNIE'S SONG — John **Denver** (1)	74
ANNIE'S SONG — James **Galway** (3)	78
ANNIVERSARY WALTZ — Anita **Harris** (21)	68
ANOTHER BRICK IN THE WALL (PART II) — **Pink Floyd** (1)	79
ANOTHER DAY — Paul **McCartney** (2)	71
ANOTHER DAY (ANOTHER GIRL) — **Lambrettas** (49)	80
ANOTHER FUNNY HONEYMOON — David **Dundas** (29)	77
ANOTHER NAIL IN MY HEART — **Squeeze** (17)	80
ANOTHER ONE BITES THE DUST — **Queen** (7)	80
ANOTHER PIECE OF MEAT — **Scorpions** (39)	79
ANOTHER SATURDAY NIGHT — Sam **Cooke** (23)	63
ANOTHER SATURDAY NIGHT — Cat **Stevens** (19)	74
ANOTHER SLEEPLESS NIGHT — Jimmy **Clanton** (50)	60
ANOTHER STAR — Stevie **Wonder** (29)	77

Title — Act (Position)	Year of Chart Entry
ANOTHER SUITCASE IN ANOTHER HALL — Barbara Dickson (18)	77
ANOTHER TEAR FALLS — Walker Brothers (12)	66
ANOTHER TIME ANOTHER PLACE — Engelbert Humperdinck (13)	71
ANSWER ME — Barbara Dickson (9)	76
ANSWER ME — Frankie Laine (1)	53
ANSWER ME — Ray Peterson (47)	60
ANSWER ME — David Whitfield (1)	53
ANT RAP — Adam and The Ants (3)	81
ANTHEM (ONE DAY IN EVERY WEEK) — New Seekers (21)	78
ANTMUSIC — Adam and The Ants (2)	80
ANTMUSIC EP (THE B-SIDES), THE — Adam and The Ants (46)	82
ANY OLD IRON — Peter Sellers (17)	57
ANY OLD TIME — Foundations (48)	68
ANY WAY THAT YOU WANT ME — Troggs (8)	66
ANYONE FOR TENNIS (THE SAVAGE SEVEN THEME) — Cream (40)	68
ANYONE WHO HAD A HEART — Cilla Black (1)	64
ANYONE WHO HAD A HEART — Mary May (49)	64
ANYONE WHO HAD A HEART — Dionne Warwick (42)	64
ANYTHING GOES — Harpers Bizarre (33)	67
ANYTHING THAT'S ROCK 'N' ROLL — Tom Petty and the Heartbreakers (36)	77
ANYWAY ANYHOW ANYWHERE — Who (10)	65
ANYWAY YOU DO IT — Liquid Gold (41)	78
ANYWAY YOU WANT IT — Dave Clark Five (25)	64
APACHE — Shadows (1)	60
APACHE — Bert Weedon (24)	60
APACHE DROPOUT — Edgar Broughton Band (33)	71
APARTMENT, THEME FROM THE — Ferrante and Teicher (44)	60
APEMAN — Kinks (5)	70
APPLE BLOSSOM TIME — Rosemary June (14)	59
APPLE STRETCHING, THE — Grace Jones (50)	82
APPLEJACK — Jet Harris and Tony Meehan (4)	63
APRIL LOVE — Pat Boone (7)	57
AQUARIUS — Paul Jones (45)	69
AQUARIUS - LET THE SUNSHINE IN (MEDLEY) — Fifth Dimension (11)	69
ARABIAN KNIGHTS — Siouxsie and the Banshees (32)	81
ARE EVERYTHING — Buzzcocks (61)	80
ARE FRIENDS ELECTRIC — Gary Numan (1)	79
ARE YOU BEING SERVED SIR — John Inman (39)	75
ARE YOU GETTING ENOUGH OF WHAT MAKES YOU HAPPY — Hot Chocolate (17)	80
ARE YOU GROWING TIRED OF MY LOVE — Status Quo (46)	69
ARE YOU HEARING (WHAT I HEAR)? — Level 42 (49)	82
ARE YOU LONESOME TONIGHT — Elvis Presley (1)	61,77,82
ARE YOU READY — Billy Ocean (42)	80
(ARE YOU READY) DO THE BUS STOP — Fatback Band (18)	75
ARE YOU READY FOR LOVE — Elton John (42)	79
ARE YOU READY TO ROCK — Wizzard (8)	74
ARE YOU SURE — Allisons (2)	61
ARGENTINE MELODY (CANCION DE ARGENTINA) — San Jose (14)	78
ARIA — Mr. Acker Bilk (5)	76
ARIANA — Stardust (42)	77
ARMED & EXTREMELY DANGEROUS — First Choice (16)	73
ARMED AND READY — Michael Schenker Group (53)	80
ARMS OF MARY — Sutherland Brothers (5)	76
ARMY DREAMERS — Kate Bush (16)	80
ARNOLD LAYNE — Pink Floyd (20)	67
AROUND THE WORLD — Bing Crosby (5)	57
AROUND THE WORLD — Gracie Fields (8)	57
AROUND THE WORLD — Ronnie Hilton (4)	57
AROUND THE WORLD — Mantovani (20)	57
ARRIVEDERCI DARLING — Edna Savage (19)	56
ARRIVEDERCI DARLING — Anne Shelton (17)	55
ART FOR ART'S SAKE — 10 C. C. (5)	75
ART OF PARTIES, THE — Japan (48)	81
ARTHUR DALEY ('E'S ALRIGHT) — Firm (14)	82
ARTHUR'S THEME (BEST THAT YOU CAN DO) — Christopher Cross (56)	81
ARTHUR'S THEME (THE BEST YOU CAN DO) — Christopher Cross (7)	82
AS I LOVE YOU — Shirley Bassey (1)	58
AS LONG AS HE NEEDS ME — Shirley Bassey (2)	60
AS LONG AS THE PRICE IS RIGHT — Dr. Feelgood (40)	79
AS TEARS GO BY — Marianne Faithfull (9)	64
AS TIME GOES BY — Richard Allan (44)	60
AS TIME GOES BY — Dooley Wilson (15)	77
AS TIME GOES BY (VOCALS) — Funkapolitan (41)	81
AS USUAL — Brenda Lee (5)	64
AS YOU LIKE IT — Adam Faith (5)	62
ASHES AND DIAMONDS — Zaine Griff (68)	80
ASHES TO ASHES [A] — David Bowie (1)	80
ASHES TO ASHES [B] — Mindbenders (14)	66
ASIA MINOR — Kokomo (35)	61
ASYLUMS IN JERUSALEM — Scritti Politti (43)	82
AT HOME HE'S A TOURIST — Gang Of Four (58)	79
AT MIDNIGHT — T-Connection (53)	79
AT THE CLUB — Drifters (3)	65,72
AT THE EDGE — Stiff Little Fingers (15)	80
AT THE HOP — Danny and the Juniors (3)	58,76
AT THE PALACE (PARTS 1 & 2) — Wilfred Brambell and Harry H. Corbett (25)	63
AT THE TOP OF THE STAIRS — Formations (28)	71
ATHENA — Who (40)	82
ATLANTIS [A] — Shadows (2)	63
ATLANTIS [B] — Donovan (23)	68
ATOMIC — Blondie (1)	80
ATTACK [A] — Exploited (50)	82
ATTACK [A] — Toys (36)	66
ATTENTION TO ME — Nolans (9)	81
AUDIO VIDEO — News (52)	81
AUF WIEDERSEHEN — Vera Lynn (10)	52
AUGUST OCTOBER — Robin Gibb (45)	70
AUTOBAHN — Kraftwerk (11)	75
AUTOMATIC LOVER [A] — Dee D. Jackson (4)	78
AUTOMATIC LOVER [B] — Vibrators (35)	78
AUTOMATICALLY SUNSHINE — Supremes (10)	72
AUTUMN ALMANAC — Kinks (3)	67
AUTUMN CONCERTO — Melachrino Orchestra (18)	56
AVALON — Roxy Music (13)	82
AVE MARIA — Shirley Bassey (34)	62
AVENUES AND ALLEYWAYS — Tony Christie (37)	73
AY AY AY AY MOOSEY — Modern Romance (10)	81
BAA BAA BLACK SHEEP — Singing Sheep (42)	82
BAAL'S HYMN (EP) — David Bowie (29)	82
BABE — Styx (6)	80
BABES IN THE WOOD — Matchbox (46)	81
BABETTE — Tommy Bruce (50)	62
BABOOSHKA — Kate Bush (5)	80
B-A-B-Y — Rachel Sweet (35)	78
BABY BABY — Frankie Lymon and the Teenagers (4)	57
BABY BABY BYE BYE — Jerry Lee Lewis (47)	60
BABY BABY MY LOVE'S ALL FOR YOU — Deniece Williams (32)	77
BABY BLUE — Dusty Springfield (61)	79
BABY COME BACK [A] — Equals (1)	68
BABY COME BACK [B] — Player (32)	78
BABY DON'T CHANGE YOUR MIND — Gladys Knight and the Pips (4)	77
BABY DON'T GET HOOKED ON ME — Mac Davis (29)	72
BABY DON'T GO — Sonny and Cher (11)	65
BABY FACE — Bobby Darin (40)	62
BABY FACE — Little Richard (2)	59
BABY FACE — Wing And A Prayer Fife and Drum Corps (12)	76
BABY I DON'T CARE — Buddy Holly (12)	61
BABY I KNOW — Rubettes (10)	77
BABY I LOVE YOU [A] — Dave Edmunds (8)	73
BABY I LOVE YOU [A] — Ramones (8)	80
BABY I LOVE YOU [A] — Ronettes (11)	64
BABY I LOVE YOU [B] — Aretha Franklin (39)	67
BABY I LOVE YOU OK — Kenny (12)	75
BABY I LOVE YOUR WAY — Peter Frampton (43)	76
BABY I NEED YOUR LOVIN' — Fourmost (24)	64
BABY I WON'T LET YOU DOWN — Pickettywitch (27)	70
BABY I'M A WANT YOU — Bread (14)	72
BABY I'M YOURS — Linda Lewis (33)	76
BABY I'M YOURS — Peter and Gordon (19)	65
BABY IT'S TRUE — Mari Wilson (42)	82
BABY IT'S YOU — Dave Berry (24)	64
BABY JUMP — Mungo Jerry (1)	71
BABY LAY DOWN — Ruby Winters (43)	79
BABY LET ME TAKE YOU HOME — Animals (21)	64
BABY LOVE — Honey Bane (58)	81
BABY LOVE — Supremes (1)	64,74
BABY LOVER — Petula Clark (12)	58
BABY MAKE IT SOON — Marmalade (9)	69
BABY MY HEART — Crickets (33)	60
BABY NEVER SAY GOODBYE — Unit Four Plus Two (49)	66
BABY NOW THAT I'VE FOUND YOU — Foundations (1)	67
BABY OF MINE — Alan Price (32)	79
BABY PLEASE DON'T GO — Them (10)	65
BABY ROO — Connie Francis (5)	61
BABY SITTIN' — Bobby Angelo and the Tuxedos (30)	61
BABY SITTIN' BOOGIE — Buzz Clifford (17)	61
BABY STOP CRYING — Bob Dylan (13)	78
BABY TAKE A BOW — Adam Faith (22)	62
BABY, THE — Hollies (26)	72
BABY WE BETTER TRY AND GET IT TOGETHER — Barry White (15)	76
BABY WE CAN'T GO WRONG — Cilla Black (36)	74
BABY WHAT A BIG SURPRISE — Chicago (41)	77
BABY WHAT I MEAN — Drifters (49)	67
(BABY) YOU DON'T HAVE TO TELL ME — Walker Brothers (13)	66
BABYLON'S BURNING — Ruts (7)	79
BABY'S FIRST CHRISTMAS — Connie Francis (30)	61
BABY'S REQUEST — Wings (60)	79
BACHELOR BOY — Cliff Richard (1)	62
BACK HOME — England World Cup Squad (1)	70
BACK IN LOVE AGAIN — Donna Summer (29)	78
BACK IN MY ARMS AGAIN — Supremes (40)	65
BACK IN THE U. S. S. R. — Beatles (19)	76
BACK OF LOVE, THE — Echo and the Bunnymen (19)	82
BACK OF MY HAND — Jags (17)	79
BACK OFF BOOGALOO — Ringo Starr (2)	72
BACK ON MY FEET AGAIN — Foundations (18)	68
BACK ON THE CHAIN GANG — Pretenders (17)	81
BACK ON THE ROAD — Marmalade (35)	72,71
BACK ON THE ROAD [B] — Earth Wind and Fire (63)	80
BACK SEAT OF MY CAR — Paul McCartney (39)	71
BACK STABBERS — O'Jays (14)	72
BACK STREET LUV — Curved Air (4)	71
BACK TO FRONT — Stiff Little Fingers (49)	80
BACK TO LOVE — Evelyn King (40)	82
BACK TO SCHOOL AGAIN — Four Tops (62)	82
BACK TO THE SIXTIES — Tight Fit (8)	81
BACK TO THE SIXTIES PART 2 — Tight Fit (33)	81
BACK TOGETHER AGAIN — Roberta Flack and Donny Hathaway (3)	80
BACKCHAT — Queen (40)	82
BACKFIRED — Debbie Harry (32)	81
BACKS TO THE WALL — Saxon (64)	80
BACKSTAGE — Gene Pitney (4)	66
BACKSTROKIN' — Fatback Band (41)	80
BAD BAD BOY — Nazareth (10)	73
BAD BOY — Marty Wilde (7)	59
BAD CASE OF LOVIN' YOU (DOCTOR DOCTOR) — Robert Palmer (61)	79
BAD GIRLS — Donna Summer (14)	79
BAD MOON RISING — Creedence Clearwater Revival (1)	69
BAD NIGHT, A — Cat Stevens (20)	67
BAD OLD DAYS — Co-Co (13)	78
BAD PENNY BLUES — Humphrey Lyttelton Band (19)	56
BAD TO ME — Billy J. Kramer and the Dakotas (1)	63
BAD WEATHER — Supremes (37)	73
BADGE — Cream (18)	69,72
BADMAN — Cockney Rejects (65)	80
BAGGY TROUSERS — Madness (3)	80
BAKER STREET — Gerry Rafferty (3)	78
BALL AND CHAIN — XTC (58)	82
BALL OF CONFUSION — Temptations (7)	70
BALL PARK INCIDENT — Wizzard (6)	72
BALLAD OF BONNIE & CLYDE — Georgie Fame (1)	67
BALLAD OF DAVY CROCKETT — Max Bygraves (20)	56
BALLAD OF DAVY CROCKETT — Bill Hayes (2)	56
BALLAD OF DAVY CROCKETT — Dick James (29)	56
BALLAD OF DAVY CROCKETT, THE — Tennessee Ernie Ford (3)	56
BALLAD OF JOHN AND YOKO — Beatles (1)	69
BALLAD OF LUCY JORDAN, THE — Marianne Faithfull (48)	79
BALLAD OF PALADIN — Duane Eddy (10)	62
BALLAD OF SPOTTY MULDOON, THE — Peter Cook (34)	65
BALLAD OF THE GREEN BERETS — Staff Sergeant Barry Sadler (24)	66
BALLROOM BLITZ — Sweet (2)	73
BAMA BOOGIE WOOGIE — Cleveland Eton (35)	78
BAMA LAMA BAMA LOO — Little Richard (20)	64

Title — Act (Position)	Year of Chart Entry
BAMBINO — **Springfields** (16)	**61**
BAMBOO HOUSES — **Sylvian Sakamoto** (30)	**82**
BAMBOO MUSIC — **Sylvian Sakamoto** (30)	**82**
BANANA BOAT SONG — Shirley **Bassey** (8)	**57**
BANANA BOAT SONG — Harry **Belafonte** (2)	**57**
BANANA BOAT SONG — **Tarriers** (15)	**57**
BANANA REPUBLIC — **Boomtown Rats** (3)	**80**
BANANA ROCK — **Wombles** (9)	**74**
BANANA SPLITS (TRA LA LA SONG) — **Dickies** (7)	**79**
BAND OF GOLD [A] — Don **Cherry** (6)	**56**
BAND OF GOLD [B] — Freda **Payne** (1)	**70**
BAND ON THE RUN — **Wings** (3)	**74**
BAND PLAYED THE BOOGIE — **C. C. S.** (36)	**73**
BANG BANG [A] — **Squeeze** (49)	**78**
BANG BANG [B] — B.A. **Robertson** (2)	**79**
BANG BANG (MY BABY SHOT ME DOWN) — **Cher** (3)	**66**
BANGERS AND MASH — Peter **Sellers and Sophia Loren** (22)	**61**
BANGIN' MAN — **Slade** (3)	**74**
BANGLA DESH — George **Harrison** (10)	**71**
BANJO BOY — George **Formby** (40)	**60**
BANJO BOY — **Jan and Kjeld** (36)	**60**
BANJO'S BACK IN TOWN — Alma **Cogan** (17)	**55**
BANKROBBER — **Clash** (12)	**80**
BANKS OF THE OHIO — Olivia **Newton-John** (6)	**71**
BANNER MAN — **Blue Mink** (3)	**71**
BARBADOS — **Typically Tropical** (1)	**75**
BARBARA ANN — **Beach Boys** (3)	**66**
BAREFOOTIN' — Robert **Parker** (24)	**66**
BARMY LONDON ARMY — Charlie **Harper** (68)	**80**
BAT OUT OF HELL — **Meat Loaf** (15)	**79**
BATTLE OF NEW ORLEANS — Lonnie **Donegan** (2)	**59**
BATTLE OF NEW ORLEANS — Johnny **Horton** (16)	**59**
BATTLE'S O'ER, THE — Andy **Stewart** (28)	**61**
BAUBLES BANGLES & BEADS — George **Shearing** (49)	**62**
BBC WORLD CUP GRANDSTAND — **Royal Philharmonic Orchestra arranged and conducted by Louis Clark** (61)	**82**
BE BOP A LULA — Gene **Vincent** (16)	**56**
BE GOOD TO YOURSELF — Frankie **Miller** (27)	**77**
BE LOUD BE PROUD (BE HEARD) — **Toyah** (30)	**82**
BE MINE [A] — Lance **Fortune** (4)	**60**
BE MINE [B] — **Tremeloes** (39)	**67**
BE MY BABY — **Ronettes** (4)	**63**
BE MY GIRL [A] — Jim **Dale** (2)	**57**
BE MY GIRL [B] — **Dennisons** (46)	**63**
BE MY GUEST — Fats **Domino** (11)	**59**
BE STIFF — **Devo** (71)	**78**
BE THANKFUL FOR WHAT YOU'VE GOT — William **DeVaughn** (31)	**74,80**
BE YOUNG BE FOOLISH BE HAPPY — **Tams** (32)	**70**
BEACH BABY — **First Class** (13)	**74**
BEACH BOYS MEDLEY — **Beach Boys** (47)	**81**
BEACHBOY GOLD — **Gidea Park** (11)	**81**
BEAR CAGE — **Stranglers** (36)	**80**
BEAT FOR BEATNIKS — John **Barry** (40)	**60**
BEAT GOES ON, THE — **Sonny and Cher** (29)	**67**
BEAT SURRENDER — **Jam** (1)	**82**
BEAT THE BEAT — Mari **Wilson** (59)	**82**
BEAT THE CLOCK — **Sparks** (10)	**79**
BEATLES MOVIE MEDLEY — **Beatles** (10)	**82**
BEATNIK FLY — **Johnny and the Hurricanes** (8)	**60**
BEAUTIFUL LOVER — **Brotherhood Of Man** (15)	**78**
BEAUTIFUL NOISE — Neil **Diamond** (13)	**76**
BEAUTIFUL SUNDAY — Daniel **Boone** (21)	**72**
BEAUTIFUL YOU — Neil **Sedaka** (43)	**72**
BEAUTY AND THE BEAST — David **Bowie** (39)	**78**
BEAUTY IS ONLY SKIN DEEP — **Temptations** (18)	**66**
BECAUSE — Demis **Roussos** (39)	**77**
BECAUSE I LOVE YOU — Georgie **Fame** (15)	**67**
BECAUSE OF LOVE — Billy **Fury** (18)	**62**
BECAUSE THE NIGHT — **Patti Smith Group** (5)	**78**
BECAUSE THEY'RE YOUNG — James **Darren** (29)	**60**
BECAUSE THEY'RE YOUNG — Duane **Eddy** (2)	**60**
BECAUSE YOU'RE MINE — Nat "King" **Cole** (6)	**52**
BECAUSE YOU'RE MINE — Mario **Lanza** (3)	**52**
BECAUSE YOU'RE YOUNG — **Classix Nouveaux** (43)	**82**
BED SITTER — **Soft Cell** (4)	**81**
BED'S TOO BIG WITHOUT YOU, THE — Sheila **Hylton** (35)	**81**
BEE BOM — Anthony **Newley** (12)	**61**
BEE STING — **Camouflage featuring Mysti** (48)	**77**
BEER DRINKERS AND HELL RAISERS — **Motorhead** (43)	**80**
BEG STEAL OR BORROW — **New Seekers** (2)	**72**
BEGGIN' — **Timebox** (38)	**68**

Title — Act (Position)	Year of Chart Entry
BEGIN THE BEGUINE (VOLVER A EMPEZAR) — Julio **Iglesias** (1)	**81**
BEHIND A PAINTED SMILE — **Isley Brothers** (5)	**69**
BEHIND CLOSED DOORS — Charlie **Rich** (16)	**74**
BEHIND THE GROOVE — Teena **Marie** (6)	**80**
BEING BOILED — **Human League** (6)	**82**
BEING WITH YOU — Smokey **Robinson** (1)	**81**
BELFAST — **Boney M** (8)	**77**
BELFAST BOY — Don **Fardon** (32)	**70**
BELL BOTTOM BLUES — Alma **Cogan** (4)	**54**
BELLS OF AVIGNON — Max **Bygraves** (36)	**61**
BEN — Michael **Jackson** (7)	**72**
BEND IT — Dave **Dee, Dozy, Beaky, Mick and Tich** (2)	**66**
BEND ME SHAPE ME — **Amen Corner** (3)	**68**
BEND ME SHAPE ME — **American Breed** (24)	**68**
BENNIE AND THE JETS — Elton **John** (37)	**76**
BENNY'S THEME — Paul **Henry and the Mayson Glen Orchestra** (39)	**78**
BERMUDA TRIANGLE — Barry **Manilow** (15)	**81**
BERNADETTE — **Four Tops** (8)	**67,72**
BESAME MUCHO — Jet **Harris** (22)	**62**
BEST DISCO IN TOWN, THE — **Ritchie Family** (10)	**76**
BEST FRIEND — The **Beat** (22)	**80**
BEST OF EVERYTHING, THE — Johnny **Mathis** (30)	**59**
BEST OF MY LOVE — **Emotions** (4)	**77**
BEST OF TIMES, THE — **Styx** (42)	**81**
BEST PART OF BREAKING UP — **Symbols** (25)	**68**
BEST PART OF BREAKING UP, THE — **Ronettes** (43)	**64**
BEST THING THAT EVER HAPPENED TO ME — Gladys **Knight and the Pips** (7)	**75**
BEST YEARS OF OUR LIVES — **Modern Romance** (8)	**82**
BET YER LIFE I DO — **Herman's Hermits** (22)	**70**
BETCHA BY GOLLY WOW — **Stylistics** (13)	**72**
BETCHA' WOULDN'T HURT ME — Quincy **Jones** (52)	**81**
BETTE DAVIS EYES — Kim **Carnes** (10)	**81**
BETTER DO IT SALSA — **Gibson Brothers** (12)	**80**
BETTER LOVE NEXT TIME — **Dr. Hook** (8)	**80**
BETTER THINGS — **Kinks** (46)	**81**
BETTER USE YOUR HEAD — **Little Anthony and the Imperials** (42)	**76**
BETTY BETTY BETTY — Lonnie **Donegan** (11)	**58**
(BEWARE) BOYFRIEND — Mari **Wilson** (51)	**82**
BEYOND THE REEF — Elvis **Presley** (3)	**80**
BEYOND THE STARS — David **Whitfield** (8)	**55**
BICYCLE RACE — **Queen** (11)	**78**
BIG BAD JOHN — Jimmy **Dean** (2)	**61**
BIG BEAN, THE — **Pig Bag** (40)	**82**
BIG BEAT BOOGIE — Bert **Weedon** (37)	**60**
BIG BEAT, THE — Fats **Domino** (20)	**58**
BIG CITY — Dandy **Livingstone** (26)	**73**
BIG EIGHT — **Judge Dread** (14)	**73**
BIG FUN — **Kool and the Gang** (14)	**82**
BIG GIRLS DONT CRY — **Four Seasons** (13)	**63**
BIG GREEN CAR — **Polecats** (35)	**81**
BIG HUNK O' LOVE, A — Elvis **Presley** (4)	**59**
BIG HURT, THE — Maureen **Evans** (26)	**60**
BIG HURT, THE — Toni **Fisher** (30)	**60**
BIG IRON — Marty **Robbins** (48)	**60**
BIG MAN — **Four Preps** (2)	**58**
BIG MAN IN A BIG HOUSE — Leroy **Van Dyke** (34)	**62**
BIG PUNK — **Judge Dread** (49)	**78**
BIG SEVEN — **Judge Dread** (8)	**72**
BIG SHIP — Cliff **Richard** (8)	**69**
BIG SIX — **Judge Dread** (11)	**72**
BIG SPENDER — Shirley **Bassey** (21)	**67**
BIG TEASER — **Saxon** (66)	**80**
BIG TEN — **Judge Dread** (14)	**75**
BIG TIME — Rick **James** (41)	**80**
BIG TIME OPERATOR — Zoot **Money and the Big Roll Band** (25)	**66**
BIG YELLOW TAXI — Joni **Mitchell** (11)	**70**
BIKO — Peter **Gabriel** (38)	**80**
BILJO — Clodagh **Rodgers** (22)	**69**
BILL BAILEY — Bobby **Darin** (34)	**60**
BILLY BOY — Dick **Charlesworth and his City Gents** (43)	**61**
BILLY DON'T BE A HERO — **Paper Lace** (1)	**74**
BIMBO — Ruby **Wright** (7)	**54**
BIONIC SANTA — Chris **Hill** (10)	**76**
BIRD DOG — **Everly Brothers** (2)	**58**
BIRD SONG — Lene **Lovich** (39)	**79**
BIRDIE SONG (BIRDIE DANCE), THE — **Tweets** (2)	**81**
BIRDS AND BEES — **Warm Sounds** (27)	**67**
BIRDS AND THE BEES [A] — Alma **Cogan** (25)	**56**
BIRDS AND THE BEES [B] — Jewel **Akens** (29)	**65**
BIRDS OF A FEATHER — **Killing Joke** (64)	**82**

Title — Act (Position)	Year of Chart Entry
BIRTH — **Peddlers** (17)	**69**
BITCH — **Rolling Stones** (2)	**71**
BITCH IS BACK, THE — Elton **John** (15)	**74**
BITCH, THE — **Olympic Runners** (37)	**79**
BITE YOUR LIP (GET UP AND DANCE) — Elton **John** (28)	**77**
BITS AND PIECES — Dave **Clark Five** (2)	**64**
BITS OF KIDS — **Stiff Little Fingers** (73)	**82**
BITTEREST PILL (I EVER HAD TO SWALLOW), THE — **Jam** (2)	**82**
BLACK AND WHITE — **Greyhound** (6)	**71**
BLACK BEAR — Frank **Cordell** (44)	**61**
BLACK BETTY — **Ram Jam** (7)	**77**
BLACK COFFEE IN BED — **Squeeze** (51)	**82**
BLACK EYED BOYS, THE — **Paper Lace** (11)	**74**
BLACK GIRL — **Four Pennies** (20)	**64**
BLACK HILLS OF DAKOTA — Doris **Day** (7)	**54**
BLACK IS BLACK — La **Belle Epoque** (2)	**77**
BLACK IS BLACK — **Bravos** (2)	**66**
BLACK MAGIC WOMAN — **Fleetwood Mac** (37)	**68**
BLACK NIGHT — **Deep Purple** (2)	**70,80**
BLACK ORCHID — Stevie **Wonder** (63)	**80**
BLACK PEARL — Horace **Faith** (13)	**70**
BLACK PUDDING BERTHA — **Goodies** (19)	**75**
BLACK SKIN BLUE EYED BOYS — **Equals** (9)	**70**
BLACK STOCKINGS — John **Barry** (27)	**60**
BLACK SUPERMAN (MUHAMMAD ALI) — Johnny **Wakelin** (7)	**75**
BLACK VELVET BAND — **Dubliners** (15)	**67**
BLACKBERRY WAY — **Move** (1)	**68**
BLACKBOARD JUMBLE — **Barron Knights** (52)	**81**
BLAME IT ON THE BOOGIE — Mick **Jackson** (15)	**78**
BLAME IT ON THE BOOGIE — **Jacksons** (8)	**78**
BLAME IT ON THE BOSSA NOVA — Eydie **Gormé** (32)	**63**
BLAME IT ON THE PONY EXPRESS — Johnny **Johnson and the Bandwagon** (7)	**70**
BLANKET ON THE GROUND — Billie Jo **Spears** (6)	**75**
BLESS YOU [A] — Tony **Orlando** (5)	**61**
BLESS YOU [B] — Martha **Reeves and the Vandellas** (33)	**72**
BLIND AMONG THE FLOWERS — **Tourists** (52)	**79**
BLINDED BY THE LIGHT — Manfred **Mann's Earth Band** (6)	**76**
BLOCKBUSTER — **Sweet** (1)	**73**
BLONDES (HAVE MORE FUN) — Rod **Stewart** (63)	**79**
BLOODNOK'S ROCK N ROLL — **Goons** (3)	**56**
BLOODSHOT EYES — **Millie** (48)	**65**
BLOODY LUXURY — **Whitesnake** (34)	**82**
BLOSSOM FELL, A — Nat "King" **Cole** (3)	**55**
BLOSSOM FELL, A — Ronnie **Hilton** (10)	**55**
BLOSSOM FELL, A — Dickie **Valentine** (9)	**55**
BLOW AWAY — George **Harrison** (51)	**79**
BLOWIN' IN THE WIND — Stevie **Wonder** (36)	**66**
BLOWING IN THE WIND — **Peter, Paul and Mary** (13)	**63**
BLOWING WILD — Frankie **Laine** (2)	**54**
BLUE ANGEL — Gene **Pitney** (39)	**74**
BLUE ANGEL [A] — Roy **Orbison** (11)	**60**
BLUE ANGEL [B] — Gene **Pitney** (49)	**74**
BLUE BAYOU — Roy **Orbison** (3)	**63**
BLUE BAYOU — Linda **Ronstadt** (35)	**78**
BLUE BLUE HEARTACHES — Johnny **Duncan and the Blue Grass Boys** (27)	**57**
BLUE CHRISTMAS — Elvis **Presley** (11)	**64**
BLUE EYES [A] — Don **Partridge** (3)	**68**
BLUE EYES [A] — Elton **John** (8)	**82**
BLUE GIRL — **Bruisers** (31)	**63**
BLUE GUITAR — **Justin Hayward and John Lodge** (8)	**75**
BLUE IS THE COLOUR — **Chelsea F.C.** (5)	**72**
BLUE JEAN BOP — Gene **Vincent** (16)	**56**
BLUE MONDAY — Fats **Domino** (23)	**57**
BLUE MOON — **Marcels** (1)	**61**
BLUE MOON — Elvis **Presley** (9)	**56**
BLUE MOON — **Showaddywaddy** (32)	**80**
BLUE MORNING BLUE DAY — **Foreigner** (45)	**79**
BLUE PETER — Mike **Oldfield** (19)	**79**
BLUE RIVER — Elvis **Presley** (22)	**66**
BLUE SKIES — **John Dummer and Helen April** (54)	**82**
BLUE STAR — Cyril **Stapleton** (2)	**55**
BLUE STAR (THE MEDIC THEME) — Charlie **Applewhite** (20)	**55**
BLUE STAR (THE MEDIC THEME) — Ron **Goodwin** (20)	**55**
BLUE SUEDE SHOES — Carl **Perkins** (10)	**56**
BLUE SUEDE SHOES — Elvis **Presley** (9)	**56**
BLUE TANGO — Ray **Martin** (8)	**52**
BLUE TURNS TO GREY — Cliff **Richard** (15)	**66**
BLUE WEEKEND — Karl **Denver** (33)	**62**

Title — Act (Position)	Year of Chart Entry
BLUEBELL POLKA — Jimmy **Shand** (20)	**55**
BLUEBERRY HILL — John **Barry** (34)	**60**
BLUEBERRY HILL — Fats **Domino** (6)	**56,76**
BLUEBIRDS OVER THE MOUNTAIN — **Beach Boys** (33)	**68**
BLUEBOTTLE BLUES — **Goons** (4)	**56**
BLUE-EYED BOY — Al **Saxon** (39)	**60**
BLUER THAN BLUE — Rolf **Harris** (30)	**69**
BLUES BAND (EP) — **Blues Band** (68)	**80**
BO DIDDLEY — Buddy **Holly** (4)	**63**
BOAT THAT I ROW, THE — **Lulu** (6)	**67**
BOBBY TOMORROW — Bobby **Vee** (21)	**63**
BOBBY'S GIRL — Susan **Maughan** (3)	**62**
BODY HEAT — James **Brown** (36)	**77**
BODY LANGUAGE [A] — **Detroit Spinners** (40)	**80**
BODY LANGUAGE [A] — **Dooleys** (46)	**80**
BODY LANGUAGE [B] — **Queen** (25)	**82**
BODY MUSIC — **Strikers** (45)	**81**
BODY TALK — **Imagination** (4)	**81**
BOHEMIAN RHAPSODY — **Queen** (1)	**75**
BOILER, THE — **Rhoda with the Special A.K.A.** (35)	**82**
BOLL WEEVIL SONG — Brook **Benton** (30)	**61**
BOMBER — **Motorhead** (34)	**79**
BON BON VIE — T S **Monk** (63)	**81**
BONNIE CAME BACK — Duane **Eddy** (12)	**60**
BONY MORONIE — Larry **Williams** (11)	**58**
BOOGALOO PARTY — **Flamingos** (26)	**69**
BOOGIE DOWN [A] — Eddie **Kendricks** (39)	**74**
BOOGIE DOWN [B] — **Real Thing** (33)	**79**
BOOGIE MAN — **MATCH** (48)	**79**
BOOGIE NIGHTS — **Heatwave** (2)	**77**
BOOGIE ON REGGAE WOMAN — Stevie **Wonder** (12)	**75**
BOOGIE ON UP — **Rokotto** (40)	**77**
BOOGIE OOGIE OOGIE — **A Taste Of Honey** (3)	**78**
BOOGIE SHOES — **KC and The Sunshine Band** (34)	**78**
BOOGIE TOWN — **F.L.B.** (46)	**79**
BOOGIE WONDERLAND — **Earth Wind and Fire with the Emotions** (4)	**79**
BOOK OF LOVE — **Mudlarks** (8)	**58**
BOOK, THE — David **Whitfield** (5)	**54**
BOOM BANG-A-BANG — **Lulu** (2)	**69**
BOOM BOOM — **Black Slate** (51)	**80**
BOOM BOOM ROOM, THE — **Natasha** (44)	**82**
BOOTZILLA — **Bootsy's Rubber Band** (43)	**78**
BORN A WOMAN — Sandy **Posey** (24)	**66**
BORN TO BE ALIVE — Patrick **Hernandez** (10)	**79**
BORN TO BE WILD — **Steppenwolf** (30)	**69**
BORN TO BE WITH YOU — **Chordettes** (8)	**56**
BORN TO BE WITH YOU — Dave **Edmunds** (5)	**73**
BORN TO LIVE AND BORN TO DIE — **Foundations** (46)	**69**
BORN TOO LATE — **Poni-Tails** (5)	**58**
BORN WITH A SMILE ON MY FACE — Stephanie **De Sykes** (2)	**74**
BORNE ON THE WIND — Roy **Orbison** (15)	**64**
BORSALINO — Bobby **Crush** (37)	**72**
BOSS GUITAR — Duane **Eddy** (27)	**63**
BOSS, THE — Diana **Ross** (40)	**79**
BOSSA NOVA BABY — Elvis **Presley** (13)	**63**
BOSTON TEA PARTY, THE — Sensational Alex **Harvey Band** (13)	**76**
BOTH ENDS BURNING — **Roxy Music** (25)	**75**
BOTH SIDES NOW — Judy **Collins** (14)	**70**
BOURGIE BOURGIE — Gladys **Knight and the Pips** (32)	**80**
BOXER, THE — **Simon and Garfunkel** (6)	**69**
BOY — **Lulu** (15)	**68**
BOY FROM NEW YORK CITY — **Darts** (2)	**78**
BOY NAMED SUE, A — Johnny **Cash** (4)	**69**
BOY OH BOY — **Racey** (22)	**79**
BOYS — Kim **Wilde** (11)	**81**
BOYS AND GIRLS — **Human League** (48)	**81**
BOYS ARE BACK IN TOWN, THE — **Thin Lizzy** (8)	**76**
BOYS CRY — Eden **Kane** (8)	**64**
BOYS KEEP SWINGING — David **Bowie** (7)	**79**
BRAND NEW KEY — **Melanie** (4)	**72**
BRANDY [A] — Scott **English** (12)	**71**
BRANDY [B] — **O'Jays** (21)	**78**
BRAS ON 45 (FAMILY VERSION) — Ivor **Biggun** (50)	**81**
BRASS IN POCKET — **Pretenders** (1)	**79**
BRAVE NEW WORLD [A] — David **Essex** (55)	**78**
BRAVE NEW WORLD [B] — **Toyah** (21)	**82**
BRAZIL — **Crispy And Company** (26)	**75**
BRAZIL — **Ritchie Family** (41)	**75**
BRAZILIAN DAWN — **Shakatak** (48)	**81**
BRAZILIAN LOVE AFFAIR — George **Duke** (36)	**80**
BRAZILIAN LOVE SONG — Nat "King" **Cole** (34)	**62**
BREAD AND BUTTER — **Newbeats** (15)	**64**
BREAK AWAY — **Beach Boys** (6)	**69**
BREAK IT TO ME GENTLY — Brenda **Lee** (46)	**62**
BREAK THE RULES — **Status Quo** (8)	**74**
BREAK UP TO MAKE UP — **Stylistics** (34)	**73**
BREAKAWAY [A] — **Springfields** (31)	**61**
BREAKAWAY [B] — **Gallagher and Lyle** (35)	**76**
BREAKFAST IN AMERICA — **Supertramp** (9)	**79**
BREAKFAST IN BED — Sheila **Hylton** (57)	**79**
BREAKFAST ON PLUTO — Don **Partridge** (26)	**69**
BREAKIN' DOWN THE WALLS OF HEARTACHE — Johnny **Johnson and the Bandwagon** (4)	**68**
BREAKIN' IN A BRAND NEW BROKEN HEART — Connie **Francis** (12)	**61**
BREAKIN' UP IS BREAKIN' MY HEART — Roy **Orbison** (22)	**66**
BREAKING GLASS(EP) — David **Bowie** (54)	**78**
BREAKING THE LAW [A] — **Judas Priest** (12)	**80**
BREAKING UP IS HARD TO DO — **Partridge Family starring Shirley Jones Cassidy** (3)	**72**
BREAKING UP IS HARD TO DO — Neil **Sedaka** (7)	**62,72**
BREAKS, THE — Kurtis **Blow** (47)	**80**
BREATHING — Kate **Bush** (16)	**80**
BREATHLESS — Jerry Lee **Lewis** (8)	**58**
BREEZE & I, THE — **Fentones** (48)	**62**
BREEZE AND I, THE — Caterina **Valente** (5)	**55**
BRICK HOUSE — **Commodores** (32)	**77**
BRIDESHEAD THEME — Geoffrey **Burgon** (48)	**81**
BRIDGE OF SIGHS — David **Whitfield** (9)	**53**
BRIDGE OVER TROUBLED WATER — Linda **Clifford** (28)	**79**
BRIDGE OVER TROUBLED WATER — **Simon and Garfunkel** (1)	**70**
BRIDGET THE MIDGET (THE QUEEN OF THE BLUES) — Ray **Stevens** (2)	**71**
BRIGHT EYES — Art **Garfunkel** (1)	**79**
BRIGHT SIDE OF THE ROAD — Van **Morrison** (63)	**79**
BRING A LITTLE WATER SYLVIE — Lonnie **Donegan** (7)	**56**
BRING IT ALL HOME — Gerry **Rafferty** (54)	**80**
BRING IT ON HOME TO ME — **Animals** (7)	**65**
BRING IT ON HOME TO ME — Rod **Stewart** (7)	**74**
BRING THE FAMILY BACK — Billy **Paul** (51)	**79**
BRINGING ON BACK THE GOOD TIMES — **Love Affair** (9)	**69**
BRISTOL STOMP — The **Late Show** (40)	**79**
BRITANNIA RAG — Winifred **Atwell** (5)	**52**
BRITISH HUSTLE — **Hi Tension** (8)	**78**
BRITISH WAY OF LIFE, THE — **Chords** (54)	**80**
BROKEN DOLL — Tommy **Bruce** (36)	**60**
BROKEN DOWN ANGEL — **Nazareth** (9)	**73**
BROKEN HEARTED — Ken **Dodd** (15)	**70**
BROKEN HEARTED MELODY — Sarah **Vaughan** (7)	**59**
BROKEN WINGS — **Stargazers** (1)	**53**
BROKEN WINGS — Art and Dotty **Todd** (6)	**53**
BROKEN WINGS — Dickie **Valentine** (12)	**53**
BRONTOSAURUS — **Move** (7)	**70**
BROTHER — **C. C. S.** (25)	**72**
BROTHER LOUIE — **Hot Chocolate** (7)	**73**
BROWN GIRL IN THE RING — **Boney M** (1)	**78**
BROWN SUGAR — **Rolling Stones** (2)	**71**
BROWN-EYED HANDSOME MAN — Buddy **Holly** (3)	**63**
BUCKET OF WATER SONG — **Four Bucketeers** (26)	**80**
BUFFALO GALS — Malcolm **Mclaren and the World's Famour Supreme Team** (18)	**82**
BUILD ME UP BUTTERCUP — **Foundations** (2)	**68**
BUILD YOUR LOVE — Johnnie **Ray** (17)	**57**
BULLY FOR YOU — Tom **Robinson Band** (68)	**79**
BUMP, THE — **Kenny** (3)	**74**
BUNCH OF THYME, A — **Foster and Allen** (18)	**82**
BUONA SERA — **Bad Manners** (34)	**81**
BUONA SERA — Mr. Acker **Bilk** (7)	**60**
BUONA SERA — Louis **Prima** (25)	**58**
BURLESQUE — **Family** (13)	**72**
BURN BABY BURN — **Hudson-Ford** (15)	**74**
BURN RUBBER ON ME (WHY YOU WANNA HURT ME) — **Gap Band** (22)	**80**
BURNIN' HOT — Jermaine **Jackson** (32)	**80**
BURNING BRIDGES — Jack **Scott** (32)	**60**
BURNING CAR — John **Foxx** (35)	**80**
BURNING DOWN ONE SIDE — Robert **Plant** (73)	**82**
BURNING LOVE — Elvis **Presley** (7)	**72**
BURNING OF THE MIDNIGHT LAMP — Jimi **Hendrix Experience** (18)	**67**
BURUNDI BLACK — **Burundi Steiphenson Black** (31)	**71**
BUS STOP — **Hollies** (5)	**66**
BUSHEL AND A PECK — Vivian **Blaine** (12)	**53**
BUSTED — Ray **Charles** (21)	**63**
BUT I DO — Clarence "Frogman" **Henry** (3)	**61**
BUT NOT FOR ME — Ella **Fitzgerald** (25)	**59**
BUT NOT FOR ME — Ketty **Lester** (45)	**62**
BUT YOU LOVE ME DADDY — Jim **Reeves** (15)	**69**
BUT YOU'RE MINE — **Sonny and Cher** (17)	**65**
BUTCHER BABY — **Plasmatics** (55)	**80**
BUTTERFINGERS — Tommy **Steele** (8)	**57**
BUTTERFLY — Andy **Williams** (29)	**57**
BUTTERFLY [A] — Charlie **Gracie** (12)	**57**
BUTTERFLY [A] — Andy **Williams** (1)	**57**
BUTTERFLY [B] — Danyel **Gerard** (11)	**71**
BUZZ BUZZ A DIDDLE IT — **Matchbox** (22)	**80**
BY THE DEVIL — **Blue Mink** (26)	**73**
BY THE FOUNTAINS OF ROME — Edmund **Hockridge** (17)	**56**
BY THE FOUNTAINS OF ROME — David **Hughes** (27)	**56**
BY THE LIGHT OF THE SILVERY MOON — **Little Richard** (17)	**59**
BY THE WAY [A] — **Big Three** (22)	**63**
BY THE WAY [B] — **Tremeloes** (35)	**70**
BY YOUR SIDE — **Peters and Lee** (39)	**73**
BYE BYE BABY [A] — **Bay City Rollers** (1)	**75**
BYE BYE BABY [A] — **Symbols** (44)	**67**
BYE BYE BABY [B] — Tony **Jackson and the Vibrations** (38)	**64**
BYE BYE BABY [C] — Johnny **Otis Show** (20)	**58**
BYE BYE BLUES — Bert **Kaempfert** (24)	**65**
BYE BYE LOVE — **Everly Brothers** (6)	**57**
B.Y.O.F. (BRING YOUR OWN FUNK) — **Fantastic Four** (62)	**79**
C MOON — **Wings** (5)	**72**
C30, C60, C90, GO — **Bow Wow Wow** (34)	**80**
CA PLANE POUR MOI — **Plastic Bertrand** (8)	**78**
CABARET — Louis **Armstrong** (1)	**68**
CACHARPAYA (ANDES PUMPSA DAESI) — **Incantation** (28)	**82**
CADE'S COUNTY, THEME FROM — Henry **Mancini** (42)	**72**
CALENDAR GIRL — Neil **Sedaka** (8)	**61**
CALENDAR SONG, THE — **Trinidad Oil Company** (34)	**77**
CALIBRE CUTS — **Calibre Cuts** (75)	**80**
CALIFORNIA DREAMIN' — **Colorado** (45)	**78**
CALIFORNIA DREAMIN' — **Mamas and the Papas** (23)	**66**
CALIFORNIA GIRLS — **Beach Boys** (26)	**65**
CALIFORNIA HERE I COME — Freddy **Cannon** (33)	**60**
CALIFORNIA MAN — **Move** (7)	**72**
CALIFORNIA SAGA - CALIFORNIA — **Beach Boys** (37)	**73**
CALL HER YOUR SWEETHEART — Frank **Ifield** (24)	**66**
CALL ME — **Blondie** (1)	**80**
(CALL ME) NUMBER ONE — **Tremeloes** (2)	**69**
CALL ME ROUND — **Pilot** (34)	**75**
CALL ROSIE ON THE PHONE — Guy **Mitchell** (17)	**57**
CALL UP, THE — **Clash** (40)	**80**
CALL UP THE GROUPS — **Barron Knights** (3)	**64**
CALLING OCCUPANTS OF INTERPLANETARY CRAFT (THE RECOGNIZED ANTHEM OF WORLD CONTACT DAY) — **Carpenters** (9)	**77**
CALLS THE TUNE — Hazel **O'Connor** (60)	**82**
CAMBODIA — Kim **Wilde** (12)	**81**
CAN CAN — **Bad Manners** (3)	**81**
CAN CAN 62 — Peter **Jay and the Jaywalkers** (31)	**62**
CAN I TAKE YOU HOME LITTLE GIRL — **Drifters** (10)	**75**
CAN I TRUST YOU — **Bachelors** (26)	**66**
CAN THE CAN — Suzi **Quatro** (1)	**73**
CAN THIS BE LOVE — Matt **Monro** (24)	**61**
CAN YOU DO IT — **Geordie** (13)	**73**
CAN YOU FEEL IT — **Jacksons** (6)	**81**
CAN YOU FEEL THE FORCE — **Real Thing** (5)	**79**
CAN YOU FORGIVE ME — Karl **Denver** (32)	**63**
CAN YOU HANDLE IT — Sharon **Redd** (31)	**81**
CAN YOU PLEASE CRAWL OUT YOUR WINDOW — Bob **Dylan** (17)	**66**
CANDIDA — **Dawn** (9)	**71**
CANDIDATE FOR LOVE — T S **Monk** (58)	**81**
CANDLE IN THE WIND — Elton **John** (11)	**74**
CANDY MAN — Brian **Poole and the Tremeloes** (6)	**64**
CANNONBALL — Duane **Eddy** (22)	**59**
CAN'T BUY ME LOVE — **Beatles** (1)	**64**
CAN'T BUY ME LOVE — Ella **Fitzgerald** (34)	**64**
CAN'T FAKE THE FEELING — Geraldine **Hunt** (44)	**80**
CAN'T GET ALONG WITHOUT YOU — Frankie **Vaughan** (11)	**58**
CAN'T GET BY WITHOUT YOU — **Real Thing** (2)	**76**
CAN'T GET ENOUGH — **Bad Company** (15)	**74**

Title — Act (Position)	Year of Chart Entry
CAN'T GET ENOUGH OF YOU — Eddy **Grant** (13)	**81**
CAN'T GET ENOUGH OF YOUR LOVE — **Darts** (43)	**79**
CAN'T GET ENOUGH OF YOUR LOVE BABE — Barry **White** (8)	**74**
CAN'T GET USED TO LOSING YOU — Andy **Williams** (2)	**63**
CAN'T GIVE YOU ANYTHING (BUT MY LOVE) — **Stylistics** (1)	**75**
CAN'T HAPPEN HERE — **Rainbow** (20)	**81**
CAN'T HELP FALLING IN LOVE — Elvis **Presley** (1)	**62**
CAN'T HELP FALLING IN LOVE — **Stylistics** (4)	**76**
CAN'T HELP FALLING IN LOVE — Andy **Williams** (3)	**70**
CAN'T HELP MYSELF — **Linx** (55)	**81**
CAN'T I? — Nat "King" **Cole** (6)	**53**
CAN'T KEEP IT IN — Cat **Stevens** (13)	**72**
CAN'T LET GO — **Earth Wind and Fire** (46)	**79**
CAN'T LET YOU GO — Barry **Ryan** (32)	**72**
CAN'T LIVE WITH YOU (CAN'T LIVE WITHOUT YOU) — **Mindbenders** (28)	**66**
CAN'T LIVE WITHOUT YOU — **Scorpions** (63)	**82**
CAN'T SAY HOW MUCH I LOVE YOU — Demis **Roussos** (35)	**76**
CAN'T SMILE WITHOUT YOU — Barry **Manilow** (43)	**78**
CAN'T STAND LOSING YOU — **Police** (2)	**78**
CAN'T STOP THE MUSIC — **Village People** (11)	**80**
CAN'T TAKE MY EYES OFF YOU — **Boystown Gang** (4)	**82**
CAN'T TAKE MY EYES OFF YOU — Andy **Williams** (5)	**68**
CAN'T YOU HEAR MY HEART — Danny **Rivers** (36)	**61**
CAN'T YOU HEAR MY HEART BEAT? — **Goldie and the Gingerbreads** (25)	**65**
CAN'T YOU HEAR THE BEAT OF A BROKEN HEART — Iain **Gregory** (39)	**62**
CAN'T YOU SEE THAT SHE'S MINE — **Dave Clark Five** (10)	**64**
CANTONESE BOY — **Japan** (24)	**82**
CAPSTICK COMES HOME — Tony **Capstick and the Carlton Main/Frickley Colliery Band** (3)	**81**
CAPTAIN BEAKY — Keith **Michell** (5)	**80**
CAPTAIN KREMMEN (RETRIBUTION) — Kenny **Everett and Mike Vickers** (32)	**77**
CAPTAIN OF YOUR SHIP — **Reparata and the Delrons** (13)	**68**
CAR 67 — **Driver 67** (7)	**78**
CAR TROUBLE — **Adam and The Ants** (33)	**81**
CAR WASH — **Rose Royce** (9)	**76**
CARA MIA — David **Whitfield** (1)	**54**
CARAVAN — Duane **Eddy** (42)	**61**
CARAVAN SONG — Barbara **Dickson** (41)	**80**
CARDIAC ARREST — **Madness** (14)	**82**
CARELESS HANDS — Des **O'Connor** (6)	**67**
CARELESS MEMORIES — **Duran Duran** (37)	**81**
CARIBBEAN DISCO SHOW, THE — **Lobo** (8)	**81**
CARIBBEAN HONEYMOON — Frank **Weir** (42)	**60**
CARNIVAL IS OVER, THE — **Seekers** (1)	**65**
CAROLINA MOON — Connie **Francis** (1)	**58**
CAROLINE — **Status Quo** (5)	**73**
CAROLINE (LIVE AT THE N.E.C.) — **Status Quo** (13)	**82**
CAROUSEL - ORIGINAL SOUNDTRACK (LP) — **Various Artists** (26)	**56**
CAROUSEL WALTZ — Ray **Martin** (24)	**56**
CARRIE — Cliff **Richard** (4)	**80**
CARRIE-ANNE — **Hollies** (3)	**67**
CARRY ON WAYWARD SON — **Kansas** (51)	**78**
CARS — Gary **Numan** (1)	**79**
CASABLANCA — Kenny **Ball and his Jazzmen** (21)	**63**
CASANOVA [A] — Petula **Clark** (39)	**63**
CASANOVA [B] — **Coffee** (13)	**80**
CASINO ROYALE — Herb **Alpert** (27)	**67**
CAST YOUR FATE TO THE WIND — **Sounds Orchestral** (5)	**64**
CASTLES IN THE AIR — Don **McLean** (47)	**82**
CAT CAME BACK, THE — Sonny **James** (30)	**56**
CAT CREPT IN, THE — **Mud** (2)	**74**
CAT PEOPLE (PUTTING OUT FIRE) — David **Bowie** (26)	**82**
CATCH A FALLING STAR — Perry **Como** (9)	**58**
CATCH THE WIND — **Donovan** (4)	**65**
CATCH US IF YOU CAN — **Dave Clark Five** (5)	**65**
CATERINA — Perry **Como** (37)	**62**
CATHY'S CLOWN — **Everly Brothers** (1)	**60**
CAVATINA — John **Williams** (13)	**79**
CELEBRATION — **Kool and the Gang** (7)	**80**
CELEBRATION, A — **U2** (47)	**82**
CELTIC SOUL BROTHERS, THE — **Dexy's Midnight Runners** (45)	**82**
CENTER CITY — **Fat Larry's Band** (31)	**77**
CENTERFOLD — **J. Geils Band** (3)	**82**
CENTRAL PARK ARREST — **Thunderthighs** (30)	**74**
CEREMONY — **New Order** (34)	**81**
CERTAIN SMILE, A — Johnny **Mathis** (4)	**58**
C'EST SI BON — Conway **Twitty** (40)	**61**
CHAIN GANG [A] — Jimmy **Young** (9)	**56**
CHAIN GANG [B] — Sam **Cooke** (9)	**60**
CHAIN OF FOOLS — Aretha **Franklin** (43)	**67**
CHAINS — **Cookies** (50)	**63**
CHAIRMAN OF THE BOARD — **Chairmen Of The Board** (48)	**71**
CHALK DUST - THE UMPIRE STRIKES BACK — **Brat** (19)	**82**
CHAMPION, THE — Willie **Mitchell** (47)	**76**
CHANCES — **Hot Chocolate** (32)	**82**
CHANGE WITH THE TIMES — Van **McCoy** (36)	**75**
CHANGES — Crispian **St. Peters** (47)	**66**
CHANGES [A] — **Imagination** (43)	**82**
CHANGES [B] — Crispian **St. Peters** (49)	**66**
CHANGING PARTNERS — Bing **Crosby** (9)	**54**
CHANGING PARTNERS — Kay **Starr** (4)	**54**
CHANSON D'AMOUR — **Manhattan Transfer** (1)	**77**
CHANT NO.1 (I DON'T NEED THIS PRESSURE ON) — **Spandau Ballet** (3)	**81**
CHANTILLY LACE — **Big Bopper** (12)	**58**
CHANTILLY LACE — Jerry Lee **Lewis** (33)	**72**
CHAPEL OF LOVE — **Dixie Cups** (22)	**64**
CHAPEL OF THE ROSES — Malcolm **Vaughan** (13)	**57**
CHARADE — **Skids** (31)	**79**
CHARIOT [A] — Rhet **Stoller** (26)	**61**
CHARIOT [B] — Petula **Clark** (39)	**63**
CHARIOTS OF FIRE - TITLES — **Vangelis** (12)	**81**
CHARLESTON — **Temperance Seven** (22)	**61**
CHARLIE BROWN — **Coasters** (6)	**59**
CHARLOTTE SOMETIMES — **Cure** (44)	**81**
CHARMAINE — **Bachelors** (6)	**63**
CHARMING BILLY — Johnny **Preston** (34)	**60**
CHASE — Giorgio **Moroder** (48)	**79**
CHEATED — **Praying Mantis** (69)	**81**
CHECK OUT THE GROOVE — Bobby **Thurston** (10)	**80**
CHEERS THEN — **Bananarama** (45)	**82**
CHELSEA — **Stamford Bridge** (47)	**70**
CHEMISTRY — **Nolans** (15)	**81**
CHEQUERED LOVE — Kim **Wilde** (4)	**81**
CHERI BABE — **Hot Chocolate** (31)	**74**
CHERISH WHAT IS DEAR TO YOU — Freda **Payne** (46)	**71**
CHERRY PIE — Jess **Conrad** (39)	**60**
CHERRY PINK & APPLE BLOSSOM WHITE — Eddie **Calvert** (1)	**55**
CHERRY PINK & APPLE BLOSSOM WHITE — Perez **Prado** (1)	**55**
CHERRY PINK AND APPLE BLOSSOM WHITE — **Modern Romance** (15)	**82**
CHERYL'S GOIN' HOME — Adam **Faith** (46)	**66**
CHESTNUT MARE — **Byrds** (19)	**71**
CHI MAI (THEME FROM THE TV SERIES THE LIFE AND TIMES OF DAVID LLOYD GEORGE) — Ennio **Morricone** (2)	**81**
CHICAGO — Frank **Sinatra** (21)	**57**
CHICAGO [A] — Kiki **Dee** (28)	**77**
CHICAGO [B] — Frank **Sinatra** (25)	**57**
CHICK A BOOM (DON'T YA JES LOVE IT) — **53RD and 3RD** (36)	**75**
CHICKA BOOM — Guy **Mitchell** (4)	**53**
CHIHUAHUA — **Bow Wow Wow** (51)	**81**
CHILD COME AWAY — Kim **Wilde** (43)	**82**
CHILDREN OF PARADISE — **Boney M** (66)	**81**
CHILDREN OF THE REVOLUTION — **T. Rex** (2)	**72**
CHILD'S PRAYER, A — **Hot Chocolate** (7)	**75**
CHILI BOM BOM — **Temperance Seven** (28)	**61**
CHINA DOLL — Slim **Whitman** (15)	**55**
CHINA TEA — Russ **Conway** (5)	**59**
CHINATOWN [A] — **Move** (23)	**71**
CHINATOWN [B] — **Thin Lizzy** (21)	**80**
CHIQUITITA — **Abba** (2)	**79**
CHIRPY CHIRPY CHEEP CHEEP — Mac and Katie **Kissoon** (41)	**71**
CHIRPY CHIRPY CHEEP CHEEP — **Middle Of The Road** (1)	**71**
CHOC ICE — **Long And The Short** (49)	**64**
CHOSEN FEW, THE — **Dooleys** (7)	**79**
CHRISTINE [A] — **Siouxsie and the Banshees** (24)	**80**
CHRISTINE [B] — Miss **X** (37)	**63**
CHRISTMAS ALPHABET — Dickie **Valentine** (1)	**55**
CHRISTMAS AND YOU — Dave **King** (23)	**56**
CHRISTMAS IN DREADLAND — **Judge Dread** (14)	**75**
CHRISTMAS IN SMURFLAND — Father **Abraham and the Smurfs** (19)	**78**
CHRISTMAS ISLAND — Dickie **Valentine** (8)	**56**
CHRISTMAS ON 45 — **Holly and the Ivy's** (40)	**81**
CHRISTMAS RAPPIN' — Kurtis **Blow** (30)	**79**
CHRISTMAS RAPPING — **Dizzy Heights** (49)	**82**
CHRISTMAS SONG — Gilbert **O'Sullivan** (12)	**74**
CHRISTMAS WILL BE JUST ANOTHER LONELY DAY — Brenda **Lee** (29)	**64**
CHRISTMAS WRAPPING — **Waitresses** (45)	**82**
CHUCK E.'S IN LOVE — Rickie Lee **Jones** (18)	**79**
CIAO CIAO BAMBINA — Marino **Marini** (24)	**59**
CIAO CIAO BAMBINA — Domenico **Modugno** (29)	**59**
CINDERELLA ROCKEFELLA — Esther and Abi **Ofarim** (1)	**68**
CINDY INCIDENTALLY — **Faces** (2)	**73**
CINDY OH CINDY — Tony **Brent** (16)	**56**
CINDY OH CINDY — Eddie **Fisher** (5)	**56**
CINDY OH CINDY — Vince **Martin** (26)	**56**
CINDY'S BIRTHDAY — Shane **Fenton and the Fentones** (19)	**62**
CIRCLES — **New Seekers** (4)	**72**
CIRCUS GAMES — **Skids** (32)	**80**
CITY LIGHTS — David **Essex** (24)	**76**
CLAIR — Gilbert **O'Sullivan** (1)	**72**
CLAIRE — Paul and Barry **Ryan** (47)	**67**
CLAP YOUR HANDS — Rockey **Sharpe and the Replays** (54)	**82**
CLAPPING SONG, THE — **Belle Stars** (11)	**82**
CLAPPING SONG, THE — Shirley **Ellis** (6)	**65**
CLAPPING SONG(EP), THE — Shirley **Ellis** (59)	**78**
CLASH CITY ROCKERS — **Clash** (35)	**78**
CLASSIC — Adrian **Gurvitz** (8)	**82**
CLASSICAL GAS — Mason **Williams** (9)	**68**
CLASSICAL MUDDLEY — **Portsmouth Sinfonia** (38)	**81**
CLAUDETTE — **Everly Brothers** (1)	**58**
CLEAN CLEAN — **Buggles** (38)	**80**
CLEAN UP YOUR OWN BACK YARD — Elvis **Presley** (2)	**69**
CLEMENTINE — Bobby **Darin** (8)	**60**
CLIMB EV'RY MOUNTAIN — Shirley **Bassey** (1)	**61**
CLOG DANCE — **Violinski** (17)	**79**
CLOSE THE DOOR [A] — Teddy **Pendergrass** (41)	**78**
CLOSE THE DOOR [B] — **Stargazers** (6)	**55**
CLOSE YOUR EYES — Tony **Bennett** (18)	**55**
CLOSER I GET TO YOU, THE — Roberta **Flack and Donny Hathaway** (42)	**78**
CLOSER TO THE HEART — **Rush** (36)	**78**
CLOUD LUCKY SEVEN — Guy **Mitchell** (2)	**53**
CLOUD NINE — **Temptations** (15)	**69**
CLOUD 99 — **St. Andrews Chorale** (31)	**76**
CLOUDBURST — Don **Lang** (16)	**55**
CLOUDS WILL SOON ROLL BY, THE — Tony **Brent** (20)	**58**
CLOWN SHOES — Johnny **Burnette** (35)	**62**
CLUB COUNTRY — **Associates** (13)	**82**
CLUBLAND — Elvis **Costello and the Attractions** (60)	**80**
C'MON EVERYBODY — Eddie **Cochran** (6)	**59**
C'MON EVERYBODY — **Sex Pistols** (3)	**79**
C'MON LET'S GO — **Girlschool** (42)	**81**
C'MON MARIANNE — **Grapefruit** (31)	**68**
CO-CO — **Sweet** (2)	**71**
COCOMOTION — **El Coco** (31)	**78**
COCONUT — **Nilsson** (42)	**72**
CODE OF LOVE — Mike **Sarne** (29)	**63**
COFFEE SONG, THE — Frank **Sinatra** (39)	**61**
COLD AS ICE — **Foreigner** (24)	**78**
COLD LIGHT OF DAY — Gene **Pitney** (38)	**67**
COLD LOVE — Donna **Summer** (44)	**81**
COLD TURKEY — John **Lennon** (14)	**69**
COLETTE — Billy **Fury** (9)	**60**
COLOUR OF MY LOVE — **Jefferson** (22)	**69**
COLOURS — **Donovan** (4)	**65**
COLOURS FLY AWAY — **Teardrop Explodes** (54)	**81**
COMANCHEROS, THE — Lonnie **Donegan** (14)	**62**
COMBINE HARVESTER (BRAND NEW KEY) — **Wurzels** (1)	**76**
COME ALONG PLEASE — Bob **Wallis and his Storyville Jazz Band** (33)	**62**
COME AND GET IT — **Badfinger** (4)	**70**
COME AND STAY WITH ME — Marianne **Faithfull** (4)	**65**
COME AWAY MELINDA — Barry **St. John** (47)	**65**
COME BACK AND FINISH WHAT YOU STARTED — Gladys **Knight and the Pips** (15)	**78**
COME BACK AND SHAKE ME — Clodagh **Rodgers** (3)	**69**
COME BACK JONEE — **Devo** (60)	**78**
COME BACK MY LOVE — **Darts** (2)	**78**
COME DANCE WITH ME (LP) — Frank **Sinatra** (30)	**59**
COME DANCING — **No Dice** (65)	**79**
COME HOME — **Dave Clark Five** (16)	**65**
COME NEXT SPRING — Tony **Bennett** (29)	**56**

Title — Act (Position)	Year of Chart Entry
COME ON — **Rolling Stones** (21)	**63**
COME ON DANCE DANCE — **Saturday Night Band** (16)	**78**
COME ON EILEEN — **Dexy's Midnight Runners** (1)	**82**
COME ON HOME [A] — Wayne **Fontana** (16)	**66**
COME ON HOME [B] — **Springfields** (31)	**63**
COME ON LET'S GO — Tommy **Steele** (10)	**58**
COME ON OVER TO MY PLACE — **Drifters** (9)	**65,72**
COME OUTSIDE — **Judge Dread** (14)	**75**
COME OUTSIDE — Mike **Sarne** (1)	**62**
COME PRIMA — Marino **Marini** (2)	**58**
(COME 'ROUND HERE) I'M THE ONE YOU NEED — Smokey **Robinson and the Miracles** (13)	**66,71**
COME SEE ABOUT ME — **Supremes** (27)	**65**
COME SEE ME — **Pretty Things** (43)	**66**
COME SEPTEMBER — Bobby **Darin** (50)	**61**
COME SOFTLY TO ME — **Fleetwoods** (6)	**59**
COME SOFTLY TO ME — **New Seekers** (20)	**72**
COME SOFTLY TO ME — Frankie **Vaughan & The Kaye Sisters** (9)	**59**
COME TO ME [A] — Julie **Grant** (31)	**64**
COME TO ME [B] — Ruby **Winters** (11)	**78**
COME TO THE DANCE — **Barron Knights** (42)	**64**
COME TOGETHER — **Beatles** (4)	**69**
COME TOMORROW — **Manfred Mann** (4)	**65**
COME WHAT MAY — Vicky **Leandros** (2)	**72**
COME WITH ME — Jesse **Green** (29)	**77**
COMES A-LONG A-LOVE — Kay **Starr** (1)	**52**
COMIN' HOME — **Delaney and Bonnie Friends featuring Eric Clapton** (16)	**69**
COMIN' IN AND OUT OF YOUR LIFE — Barbra **Streisand** (66)	**82**
COMING HOME [A] — David **Essex** (24)	**76**
COMING HOME [B] — **Marshall Hain** (39)	**78**
COMING HOME BABY — Mel **Torme** (13)	**63**
COMING UP — Paul **McCartney** (2)	**80**
COMMUNICATION — David **McCallum** (32)	**66**
COMPLETE CONTROL — **Clash** (28)	**77**
COMPLEX — Gary **Numan** (6)	**79**
COMPUTER GAME (THEME FROM THE INVADERS) — **Yellow Magic Orchestra** (17)	**80**
COMPUTER LOVE — **Kraftwerk** (1)	**81**
CONCRETE AND CLAY — Randy **Edelman** (11)	**76**
CONCRETE AND CLAY — **Unit Four Plus Two** (1)	**65**
CONFESSIN' — Frank **Ifield** (1)	**63**
CONFUSION [A] — Lee **Dorsey** (38)	**66**
CONFUSION [B] — **Electric Light Orchestra** (8)	**79**
CONGRATULATIONS — Cliff **Richard** (1)	**68**
CONQUISTADOR — **Procol Harum** (22)	**72**
CONSCIENCE — James **Darren** (30)	**62**
CONSCIOUS MAN — **Jolly Brothers** (46)	**79**
CONSIDER YOURSELF — Max **Bygraves** (50)	**60**
CONSTANTLY — Cliff **Richard** (4)	**64**
CONTACT — Edwin **Starr** (6)	**79**
CONTINENTAL, THE — Maureen **McGovern** (16)	**76**
CONVERSATIONS — Cilla **Black** (7)	**69**
CONVOY — C. W. **McCall** (2)	**76**
CONVOY G. B. — Laurie **Lingo and the Dipsticks** (4)	**76**
COOL BABY — Charlie **Gracie** (26)	**58**
COOL FOR CATS — **Squeeze** (2)	**79**
COOL MEDITATION — **Third World** (17)	**79**
COOL OUT TONIGHT — David **Essex** (23)	**77**
COOL WATER — Frankie **Laine** (2)	**55**
COPACABANA (AT THE COPA) — Barry **Manilow** (42)	**78**
CORONATION RAG — Winifred **Atwell** (5)	**53**
CORRINE, CORRINA — Ray **Peterson** (41)	**61**
COST OF LIVING (EP), THE — **Clash** (22)	**79**
COSTAFINE TOWN — **Splinter** (17)	**74**
COTTONFIELDS — **Beach Boys** (5)	**70**
COULD HEAVEN EVER BE LIKE THIS — Idris **Muhammad** (42)	**77**
COULD IT BE FOREVER — David **Cassidy** (2)	**72**
COULD IT BE I'M FALLING IN LOVE — **Detroit Spinners** (11)	**73**
COULD IT BE I'M FALLING IN LOVE (EP) — **Detroit Spinners** (32)	**77**
COULD IT BE MAGIC — Barry **Manilow** (25)	**78**
COULD IT BE MAGIC — Donna **Summer** (40)	**76**
COULD YOU BE LOVED — Bob **Marley and the Wailers** (5)	**80**
COULDN'T GET IT RIGHT — **Climax Blues Band** (10)	**76**
COUNT ON ME — Julie **Grant** (24)	**63**
COUNT YOUR BLESSINGS — Bing **Crosby** (11)	**55**
COUNTING TEARDROPS — Emile **Ford and the Checkmates** (4)	**60**
COUNTRY BOY [A] — Fats **Domino** (19)	**60**
COUNTRY BOY [B] — **Heinz** (26)	**63**
COUSIN NORMAN — **Marmalade** (6)	**71**
(COVER PLUS) WE'RE ALL GROWN UP — Hazel **O'Connor** (41)	**81**
COWARD OF THE COUNTY — Kenny **Rogers** (1)	**80**
COWBOY JIMMY JOE — Alma **Cogan** (37)	**61**
COWPUNCHER'S CANTATA — Max **Bygraves** (6)	**52**
COWPUNK MEDIUM — **Splodgenessabounds** (69)	**81**
COZ I LUV YOU — **Slade** (1)	**71**
CRACKIN' UP [A] — Tommy **Hunt** (39)	**75**
CRACKIN' UP [B] — Nick **Lowe** (34)	**79**
CRACKLIN' ROSIE — Neil **Diamond** (3)	**70**
CRADLE OF LOVE — Johnny **Preston** (2)	**60**
CRAWLIN' BACK — Roy **Orbison** (19)	**65**
CRAWLING FROM THE WRECKAGE — Dave **Edmunds** (59)	**79**
CRAZY — **Mud** (12)	**73**
CRAZY DREAM — Jim **Dale** (24)	**58**
CRAZY HORSES — **Osmonds** (2)	**72**
CRAZY LITTLE THING CALLED LOVE — **Queen** (2)	**79**
CRAZY LOVE — Paul **Anka** (26)	**58**
CRAZY OTTO RAG — **Stargazers** (18)	**55**
CRAZY TRAIN — Ozzy **Osbourne Blizzard Of Ozz** (49)	**80**
CRAZY WATER — Elton **John** (27)	**77**
CRAZY WORDS CRAZY TUNE — Dorothy **Provine** (45)	**62**
CREAM (ALWAYS RISES TO THE TOP) — Gregg **Diamond Bionic Boogie** (61)	**79**
CREEP, THE — Ken **Mackintosh** (10)	**54**
CREEQUE ALLEY — **Mamas and the Papas** (9)	**67**
CREOLE JAZZ — Mr. Acker **Bilk** (22)	**61**
CRIMSON AND CLOVER — Joan **Jett and the Blackhearts** (60)	**82**
CROCODILE ROCK — Elton **John** (5)	**72**
CROCODILES — **Echo and the Bunnymen** (37)	**81**
CROSSTOWN TRAFFIC — Jimi **Hendrix Experience** (37)	**69**
CROWD, THE — Roy **Orbison** (40)	**62**
CRUEL SEA, THE — **Dakotas** (18)	**63**
CRUEL TO BE KIND — Nick **Lowe** (12)	**79**
CRUNCH, THE — **Rah Band** (6)	**77**
CRY — Gerry **Monroe** (38)	**70**
CRY BOY CRY — **Blue Zoo** (13)	**82**
CRY FOR THE NATIONS — Michael **Schenker Group** (56)	**80**
CRY LIKE A BABY — **Box Tops** (15)	**68**
CRY ME A RIVER — Julie **London** (22)	**57**
CRY MY HEART — David **Whitfield** (22)	**58**
CRY MYSELF TO SLEEP — Del **Shannon** (29)	**62**
CRY TO ME — **Pretty Things** (28)	**65**
CRYIN' — Roy **Orbison** (25)	**61**
CRYIN' IN THE RAIN — **Everly Brothers** (6)	**62**
CRYIN' MY HEART OUT FOR YOU — Diana **Ross** (58)	**81**
CRYIN' TIME — Ray **Charles** (50)	**66**
CRYING — Don **McLean** (1)	**80**
CRYING GAME, THE — Dave **Berry** (5)	**64**
CRYING IN THE CHAPEL — Lee **Lawrence** (7)	**53**
CRYING IN THE CHAPEL — Elvis **Presley** (1)	**65,77**
CRYING LAUGHING LOVING LYING — Labi **Siffre** (11)	**72**
CRYING OVER YOU — Ken **Boothe** (11)	**74**
CUBA — **Gibson Brothers** (41)	**79**
CUBA (RE-ISSUE) — **Gibson Brothers** (12)	**80**
CUFF OF MY SHIRT — Guy **Mitchell** (9)	**54**
CUM ON FEEL THE NOIZE — **Slade** (1)	**73**
CUMBERLAND GAP — Lonnie **Donegan** (1)	**57**
CUMBERLAND GAP — **Vipers Skiffle Group** (10)	**57**
CUPBOARD LOVE — John **Leyton** (22)	**63**
CUPID — Sam **Cooke** (7)	**61**
CUPID — Johnny **Nash** (6)	**69**
CUPID - I'VE LOVED YOU FOR A LONG TIME (MEDLEY) — **Detroit Spinners** (4)	**80**
CURLY — **Move** (12)	**69**
CUT THE CAKE — **Average White Band** (31)	**75**
CUTTY SARK — John **Barry** (35)	**62**
CYANIDE — **Lurkers** (72)	**79**
D. W. WASHBURN — **Monkees** (17)	**68**
DA DA DA — **Trio** (2)	**82**
DA DOO RON RON — **Crystals** (5)	**63,74**
DA YA THINK I'M SEXY? — Rod **Stewart** (1)	**78**
D-A-A-ANCE — **Lambrettas** (12)	**80**
DADDY COOL — **Boney M** (6)	**76**
DADDY COOL - THE GIRL CAN'T HELP IT — **Darts** (6)	**77**
DADDY DON'T YOU WALK SO FAST — Daniel **Boone** (17)	**71**
DADDY'S HOME — Cliff **Richard** (2)	**81**
DAMBUSTERS MARCH, THE — The Central Band of the **Royal Air Force, Conductor W/CDR. A.E. Sims O.B.E.** (18)	**55**
DAMNED DON'T CRY — **Visage** (11)	**82**
DANCE A LITTLE BIT CLOSER — **Charo and the Salsoul Orchestra** (44)	**78**
DANCE AWAY — **Roxy Music** (2)	**79**
DANCE DANCE DANCE — **Beach Boys** (24)	**65**
DANCE DANCE DANCE (YOWSAH YOWSAH YOWSAH) — **Chic** (6)	**77**
DANCE (DISCO HEAT) — **Sylvester** (29)	**78**
DANCE, GET DOWN — Al **Hudson and the Partners** (57)	**78**
DANCE LADY DANCE — **Crown Heights Affair** (44)	**79**
DANCE LITTLE LADY DANCE — Tina **Charles** (6)	**76**
DANCE OF THE CUCKOOS — Band of the **Black Watch** (37)	**75**
DANCE ON [A] — Kathy **Kirby** (11)	**63**
DANCE ON! [A] — **Shadows** (1)	**62**
DANCE ON [B] — **Mojo** (70)	**81**
DANCE STANCE — **Dexy's Midnight Runners** (40)	**80**
DANCE THE BODY MUSIC — **Osibisa** (31)	**76**
DANCE THE KUNG FU — Carl **Douglas** (35)	**74**
DANCE TO THE MUSIC — **Sly and the Family Stone** (7)	**68**
DANCE WIT' ME — Rick **James** (53)	**82**
DANCE WITH ME — **Drifters** (35)	**60**
DANCE WITH ME [A] — Peter **Brown** (57)	**78**
DANCE WITH ME [B] — **Drifters** (17)	**60**
DANCE WITH THE DEVIL — Cozy **Powell** (3)	**73**
DANCE WITH THE GUITAR MAN — Duane **Eddy** (4)	**62**
DANCE WITH YOU — Carrie **Lucas** (40)	**79**
DANCE YOURSELF DIZZY — **Liquid Gold** (2)	**80**
DANCER — Michael **Schenker Group** (52)	**82**
DANCER — Gino **Soccio** (46)	**79**
DANCIN' EASY — Danny **Williams** (30)	**77**
DANCIN' IN THE MOONLIGHT (IT'S CAUGHT ME IN THE SPOTLIGHT) — **Thin Lizzy** (14)	**77**
DANCIN' ON A WIRE — **Surface Noise** (59)	**80**
DANCIN' PARTY — Chubby **Checker** (19)	**62**
DANCIN' PARTY — **Showaddywaddy** (4)	**77**
DANCIN' THE NIGHT AWAY — **Voggue** (39)	**81**
DANCING IN OUTER SPACE — **Atmosfear** (46)	**79**
DANCING IN THE CITY — **Marshall Hain** (3)	**78**
DANCING IN THE STREET — Martha **Reeves and the Vandellas** (4)	**64,69**
(DANCING) ON A SATURDAY NIGHT — Barry **Blue** (2)	**73**
DANCING ON THE FLOOR (HOOKED ON LOVE) — **Third World** (10)	**81**
DANCING QUEEN — **Abba** (1)	**76**
DANCING THE NIGHT AWAY — **Motors** (42)	**77**
DANCING WITH MYSELF — **Generation X** (62)	**80**
DANCING WITH MYSELF EP — **Generation X** (60)	**81**
DANCING WITH THE CAPTAIN — Paul **Nicholas** (8)	**76**
DANDELION — **Rolling Stones** (8)	**67**
DANGER GAMES — **Pinkees** (8)	**82**
DANGER OF A STRANGER, THE — Stella **Parton** (35)	**77**
DANIEL — Elton **John** (4)	**73**
DARK LADY — **Cher** (36)	**74**
DARK MOON — Tony **Brent** (17)	**57**
DARKTOWN STRUTTERS BALL — Joe **Brown** (34)	**60**
DARLIN' [A] — **Beach Boys** (11)	**68**
DARLIN' [A] — David **Cassidy** (16)	**75**
DARLIN' [B] — Frankie **Miller** (6)	**78**
DARLIN' DARLIN' BABY (SWEET, TENDER, LOVE) — **O'Jays** (24)	**77**
DARLING BE HOME SOON — **Lovin' Spoonful** (44)	**67**
DAT — Pluto **Shervington** (6)	**76**
DAUGHTER OF DARKNESS — Tom **Jones** (5)	**70**
DAVID WATTS — **Jam** (25)	**78,80**
DAVID'S SONG (MAIN THEME FROM "KIDNAPPED") — Vladimir **Cosma** (64)	**79**
DAVY'S ON THE ROAD AGAIN — Manfred **Mann's Earth Band** (6)	**78**
DAWN — **Flintlock** (30)	**76**
DAY AFTER DAY [A] — **Badfinger** (10)	**72**
DAY AFTER DAY [B] — **Pretenders** (45)	**81**
DAY BEFORE YOU CAME, THE — **Abba** (32)	**82**
DAY BY DAY — Holly **Sherwood** (29)	**72**
DAY I MET MARIE, THE — Cliff **Richard** (10)	**67**
DAY IN THE LIFE OF VINCE PRINCE, A — Russ **Abbott** (61)	**82**
DAY IS OVER, THE — The Pipes and Drums and Military Band of the **Royal Scots Dragoon Guards** (30)	**72**
DAY THAT CURLY BILLY SHOT CRAZY SAM MCGHEE, THE — **Hollies** (24)	**73**

Title — Act (Position)	Year of Chart Entry
DAY THE EARTH CAUGHT FIRE, THE — City Boy (67)	79
DAY THE RAINS CAME, THE — Jane Morgan (1)	58
DAY THE WORLD TURNED DAY-GLOW, THE — X-Ray Spex (23)	78
DAY TRIP TO BANGOR (DIDN'T WE HAVE A LOVELY TIME) — Fiddler's Dram (3)	79
DAY TRIPPER — Beatles (1)	65
DAY TRIPPER — Otis Redding (43)	67
DAY WITHOUT LOVE, A — Love Affair (6)	68
DAYDREAM — Lovin' Spoonful (2)	66
DAYDREAM BELIEVER — Monkees (5)	67
DAYDREAM BELIEVER — Anne Murray (61)	80
DAYDREAMER — David Cassidy (1)	73
DAYLIGHT KATY — Gordon Lightfoot (41)	78
DAYS — Kinks (12)	68
DAYS ARE O.K. — Motels (41)	81
DAYTIME FRIENDS — Kenny Rogers (39)	77
DAYTONA DEMON — Suzi Quatro (14)	73
DAZZ — Brick (36)	77
D-DARLING — Anthony Newley (25)	62
D-DAYS — Hazel O'Connor (10)	81
DE DO DO DO, DE DA DA DA — Police (5)	80
DEAD CITIES — Exploited (31)	81
DEAD END STREET — Kinks (5)	66
DEAD OR ALIVE — Lonnie Donegan (7)	56
DEAD POP STARS — Altered Images (67)	81
DEAD RINGER FOR LOVE — Meat Loaf (5)	81
DEADLIER THAN THE MALE — Walker Brothers (34)	66
DEAL, THE — Pat Campbell (31)	69
DEAN AND I, THE — 10 C. C. (10)	73
DEAR ADDY — Kid Creole and the Coconuts (29)	82
DEAR DELILAH — Grapefruit (21)	68
DEAR ELAINE — Roy Wood (18)	73
DEAR JOHN — Status Quo (10)	82
DEAR LONELY HEARTS — Nat "King" Cole (37)	62
DEAR MISS LONELY HEARTS — Philip Lynott (32)	80
DEAR MRS. APPLEBEE — David Garrick (22)	66
DEATH DISCO (PARTS 1 & 2) — Public Image Ltd. (20)	79
DEATH OF A CLOWN — Dave Davies (3)	67
DEBORA — T. Rex (7)	68,72
DECEMBER WILL BE MAGIC AGAIN — Kate Bush (29)	80
DECEMBER '63 (OH WHAT A NIGHT) — Four Seasons (1)	76
DECK OF CARDS — Max Bygraves (13)	73
DECK OF CARDS — Wink Martindale (5)	59,63,73
DEDICATED FOLLOWER OF FASHION — Kinks (4)	66
DEDICATED TO THE ONE I LOVE — Mamas and the Papas (2)	67
DEEP FEELING — Mike Sagar (44)	60
DEEP IN THE HEART OF TEXAS — Duane Eddy (19)	62
DEEP PURPLE — Donny and Marie Osmond (25)	76
DEEP PURPLE — Nino Tempo and April Stevens (17)	63
DEEP PURPLE — Billy Ward (30)	57
DEEPER & DEEPER — Freda Payne (33)	70
DEEPER THAN THE NIGHT — Olivia Newton-John (64)	79
THEME FROM THE DEER HUNTER (CAVATINA) — Shadows (9)	79
DELAWARE — Perry Como (3)	60
DELILAH — Sensational Alex Harvey Band (7)	75
DELILAH — Tom Jones (2)	68
DELILAH JONES — McGuire Sisters (24)	56
DELLA AND THE DEALER — Hoyt Axton (48)	80
DELTA LADY — Joe Cocker (10)	69
DENIS — Blondie (2)	78
LA DERNIERE VALSE — Mireille Mathieu (26)	67
DESAFINADO — Ella Fitzgerald (38)	62
DESAFINADO — Stan Getz and Charlie Byrd (11)	62
DESIDERATA — Les Crane (7)	72
DESIRE ME — Doll (28)	79
DESIREE — Neil Diamond (39)	77
DESPERATE BUT NOT SERIOUS — Adam and The Ants (33)	82
DESPERATE DAN — Lieutenant Pigeon (17)	72
DESTINATION VENUS — Rezillos (43)	78
DESTINY [A] — Anne Murray (41)	72
DESTINY [B] — Candi Staton (41)	76
DESTINY [C] — Jacksons (39)	79
DETROIT CITY — Tom Jones (8)	67
DEUTSCHER GIRLS — Adam and The Ants (13)	82
DEVIL GATE DRIVE — Suzi Quatro (1)	74
DEVIL IN DISGUISE — Elvis Presley (1)	63
DEVIL OR ANGEL — Billy Fury (58)	82
DEVIL WENT DOWN TO GEORGIA, THE — Charlie Daniels Band (14)	79
DEVIL WOMAN [A] — Marty Robbins (5)	62
DEVIL WOMAN [B] — Cliff Richard (9)	76
DEVIL'S ANSWER, THE — Atomic Rooster (4)	71
DEVIL'S GUN — C.J.& Co. (43)	77
DIAMOND DOGS — David Bowie (21)	74
DIAMOND SMILES — Boomtown Rats (13)	79
DIAMONDS [A] — Jet Harris and Tony Meehan (1)	63
DIAMONDS [B] — Chris Rea (44)	79
DIAMONDS ARE FOREVER — Shirley Bassey (38)	72
DIANA — Paul Anka (1)	57
DIANE — Bachelors (1)	64
DIARY OF HORACE WIMP, THE — Electric Light Orchestra (8)	79
DICK-A-DUM-DUM (KING'S ROAD) — Des O'Connor (14)	69
DID YOU EVER — Nancy Sinatra and Lee Hazelwood (2)	71
DIDN'T I (BLOW YOUR MIND THIS TIME) — Delfonics (22)	71
DIE YOUNG — Black Sabbath (41)	80
DIGGIN' MY POTATOES — Heinz (49)	65
DIM ALL THE LIGHTS — Donna Summer (29)	79
DIME AND A DOLLAR — Guy Mitchell (8)	54
DIMPLES — John Lee Hooker (23)	64
DING DONG — George Harrison (38)	74
DING-A-DONG — Teach-In (13)	75
DIPPETY DAY — Father Abraham and the Smurfs (13)	78
DIRTY DEEDS DONE DIRT CHEAP — AC/DC (47)	80
D.I.S.C.O. — Ottawan (2)	80
DISCO BEATLEMANIA — D.B.M. (45)	77
DISCO CONNECTION — Isaac Hayes (10)	76
DISCO DUCK — Rick Dees and his Cast Of Idiots (6)	76
DISCO INFERNO — Trammps (16)	77,78
DISCO LADY — Johnny Taylor (25)	76
DISCO MUSIC — J. A. L. N. Band (21)	76
DISCO NIGHTS (ROCK FREAK) — G. Q. (42)	79
DISCO QUEEN — Hot Chocolate (11)	75
DISCO STOMP — Hamilton Bohannon (6)	75
DISTANT DRUMS — Jim Reeves (1)	66
D. I. V. O. R. C. E. [A] — Billy Connolly (1)	75
D. I. V. O. R. C. E. [B] — Tammy Wynette (12)	75
DIZZY — Tommy Roe (1)	69
D.J. — David Bowie (29)	79
DK 50-80 — John Otway and Wild Willy Barrett (45)	80
DO ANYTHING YOU WANNA DO — Eddie and the Hotrods (9)	77
DO ANYTHING YOU WANT TO — Thin Lizzy (14)	79
DO I DO — Stevie Wonder (10)	82
DO I LOVE YOU — Ronettes (35)	64
DO IT AGAIN [A] — Beach Boys (1)	68
DO IT AGAIN [B] — Steely Dan (39)	75
DO IT ANYWAY YOU WANNA — People's Choice (36)	75
DO IT DO IT AGAIN — Raffaella Carra (9)	78
DO IT TO THE MUSIC — Raw Silk (18)	82
DO NOTHING — The Specials (4)	80
DO THAT TO ME ONE MORE TIME — Captain and Tennille (7)	80
DO THE BIRD — Dee Dee Sharp (46)	63
DO THE BIRD — Vernons Girls (44)	63
DO THE CLAM — Elvis Presley (19)	65
DO THE FUNKY CHICKEN — Rufus Thomas (18)	70
(DO) THE HUCKLEBUCK — Coast To Coast (5)	81
(DO THE) SPANISH HUSTLE — Fatback Band (10)	76
DO WAH DIDDY DIDDY — Manfred Mann (1)	64
DO WHAT YOU DO DO WELL — Ned Miller (48)	65
DO WHAT YOU GOTTA DO — Four Tops (11)	69
DO WHAT YOU GOTTA DO — Nina Simone (2)	68
DO WHAT YOU WANNA DO — T-Connection (11)	77
DO YA WANNA FUNK — Sylvester with Patrick Cowley (32)	82
DO YA WANNA GET FUNKY WITH ME — Peter Brown (43)	78
DO YOU BELIEVE IN THE WESTWORLD — Theatre Of Hate (40)	82
DO YOU DREAM IN COLOUR? — Bill Nelson (52)	80
DO YOU FEEL LIKE WE DO — Peter Frampton (39)	76
DO YOU FEEL MY LOVE — Eddy Grant (8)	80
DO YOU KNOW — Secret Affair (57)	81
DO YOU KNOW THE WAY TO SAN JOSE — Dionne Warwick (8)	68
DO YOU LOVE ME — Dave Clark Five (30)	63
DO YOU LOVE ME — Deep Feeling (34)	70
DO YOU LOVE ME — Brian Poole and the Tremeloes (1)	63
DO YOU MIND — Anthony Newley (1)	60
DO YOU REALLY LOVE ME TOO — Billy Fury (13)	64
DO YOU REALLY WANT TO HURT ME — Culture Club (1)	82
DO YOU REMEMBER — Scaffold (34)	68
DO YOU REMEMBER ROCK'N'ROLL RADIO — Ramones (54)	80
DO YOU WANNA DANCE [A] — Cliff Richard (2)	62
DO YOU WANNA DANCE [B] — Barry Blue (7)	73
DO YOU WANNA TOUCH ME (OH YEAH) — Gary Glitter (2)	73
DO YOU WANT ME TO — Four Pennies (47)	64
DO YOU WANT TO KNOW A SECRET? — Billy J. Kramer and the Dakotas (2)	63
DO YOUR DANCE — Rose Royce (30)	77
DOCTOR DOCTOR — UFO (35)	79
DR. FINLAY — Andy Stewart (43)	65
DR. JACKYLL AND MISTER FUNK — Jackie Mclean (53)	79
THEME FROM DR. KILDARE — Johnny Spence (15)	62
DR. KILDARE (THREE STARS WILL SHINE TONIGHT), THEME FROM — Richard Chamberlain (12)	62
DR. KISS KISS — 5000 Volts (8)	76
DR. LOVE — Tina Charles (4)	76
DOCTOR MY EYES — Jackson Five (9)	73
DR. WHO — Mankind (25)	78
DOCTOR'S ORDERS — Sunny (7)	74
DOES IT FEEL GOOD — B. T. Express (52)	80
DOES SHE HAVE A FRIEND — Gene Chandler (28)	80
DOES YOUR CHEWING GUM LOSE ITS FLAVOUR — Lonnie Donegan (3)	59
DOES YOUR MOTHER KNOW — Abba (4)	79
DOESN'T ANYBODY KNOW MY NAME? — Vince Hill (50)	69
DOG EAT DOG — Adam and The Ants (4)	80
DOGS — Who (25)	68
DOGS OF WAR — Exploited (63)	81
DOING ALRIGHT WITH THE BOYS — Gary Glitter (6)	75
DOLL HOUSE — King Brothers (21)	61
DOLLAR IN THE TEETH — Upsetters (5)	69
DOLLY MY LOVE — Moments (10)	75
DOMINIQUE — Singing Nun (Soeur Sourire) (7)	63
DON JUAN — Dave Dee, Dozy, Beaky, Mick and Tich (23)	69
DONALD WHERE'S YOUR TROOSERS — Andy Stewart (37)	60
DONKEY CART — Frank Chacksfield (26)	56
DONNA — Marty Wilde (25)	59
DONNA [A] — Ritchie Valens (29)	59
DONNA [A] — Marty Wilde (3)	59
DONNA [B] — 10 C. C. (2)	72
DON'T — Elvis Presley (2)	58
DON'T ANSWER ME — Cilla Black (6)	66
DON'T BE A DUMMY — John Du Cann (33)	79
DON'T BE CRUEL — Bill Black's Combo (32)	60
DON'T BE CRUEL — Elvis Presley (24)	78
DON'T BE CRUEL — Billy Swan (42)	75
DON'T BELIEVE A WORD — Thin Lizzy (12)	77
DON'T BET MONEY HONEY — Linda Scott (50)	61
DON'T BLAME ME — Frank Ifield (8)	64
DON'T BREAK MY HEART AGAIN — Whitesnake (17)	81
DON'T BREAK THE HEART THAT LOVES YOU — Connie Francis (39)	62
DON'T BRING HARRY (EP) — Stranglers (41)	79
DON'T BRING LULU — Dorothy Provine (17)	61
DON'T BRING ME DOWN [A] — Pretty Things (10)	64
DON'T BRING ME DOWN [B] — Animals (6)	66
DON'T BRING ME DOWN [C] — Electric Light Orchestra (3)	79
DON'T BRING ME YOUR HEARTACHES — Paul and Barry Ryan (13)	65
DON'T CALL IT LOVE (WILDLIFE EP) — Girlschool (58)	82
DON'T CARE — Klark Kent (48)	78
DON'T COME CLOSE — Ramones (39)	78
DON'T CRY DADDY — Elvis Presley (8)	70
DON'T CRY FOR ME ARGENTINA — Julie Covington (1)	76,78
DON'T CRY FOR ME ARGENTINA — Shadows (5)	78
DON'T CRY OUT LOUD — Elkie Brooks (12)	78
DON'T DO IT BABY — Mac and Katie Kissoon (9)	75
DON'T DO THAT — Geordie (32)	72
DONT DO THAT — Young and Moody Band (63)	81
DON'T DRIVE MY CAR — Status Quo (11)	80
DON'T EVER CHANGE — Crickets (5)	62
(DON'T FEAR) THE REAPER — Blue Oyster Cult (16)	78
DON'T FIGHT IT — Wilson Pickett (29)	65
DON'T FORBID ME — Pat Boone (2)	57
DON'T FORGET TO CATCH ME — Cliff Richard (21)	68

Title — Act (Position)	Year of Chart Entry
DON'T FORGET TO REMEMBER — **Bee Gees** (2)	69
DON'T GIVE UP ON US — David **Soul** (1)	76
DON'T GO — **Judas Priest** (51)	81
DON'T GO [B] — **Yazoo** (3)	82
DON'T GO BREAKING MY HEART — Elton **John and Kiki Dee** (1)	76
DON'T HANG UP — **Orlons** (39)	62
DON'T HOLD BACK — **Chanson** (33)	79
DON'T IT MAKE MY BROWN EYES BLUE — Crystal **Gayle** (5)	77
DON'T JUMP OFF THE ROOF DAD — Tommy **Cooper** (40)	61
DON'T KILL IT CAROL — Manfred **Mann's Earth Band** (45)	79
DON'T KILL THE WHALE — **Yes** (36)	78
DON'T KNOCK THE ROCK — Bill **Haley and his Comets** (7)	57
DON'T LAUGH AT ME — Norman **Wisdom** (3)	54
DON'T LEAVE ME THIS WAY — Thelma **Houston** (13)	77
DON'T LEAVE ME THIS WAY — Harold **Melvin and the Bluenotes** (5)	77
DON'T LET 'EM GRIND YOU DOWN — **Exploited and Anti-Pasti** (70)	81
DON'T LET GO — **Manhattan Transfer** (32)	77
DON'T LET GO THE COAT — **Who** (47)	81
DON'T LET HIM TOUCH YOU — **Angelettes** (35)	72
DON'T LET IT DIE — Hurricane **Smith** (2)	71
DON'T LET IT FADE AWAY — **Darts** (18)	78
DON'T LET IT PASS YOU BY — **U.B.40** (16)	81
DON'T LET ME BE MISUNDERSTOOD — **Animals** (3)	65
DON'T LET ME BE MISUNDERSTOOD — **Santa Esmeralda and Leroy Gomez** (41)	77
DON'T LET THE RAIN COME DOWN — Ronnie **Hilton** (21)	64
DON'T LET THE STARS GET IN YOUR EYES — Perry **Como** (1)	53
DON'T LET THE SUN CATCH YOU CRYING — **Gerry and the Pacemakers** (6)	64
DON'T LET THE SUN GO DOWN ON ME — Elton **John** (16)	74
DON'T LOOK BACK — **Boston** (43)	78
DON'T LOOK DOWN — **Planets** (66)	80
DON'T LOOSE YOUR TEMPER — **XTC** (32)	80
DON'T LOVE ME TOO HARD — **Nolans** (14)	82
DON'T MAKE ME — Babbity **Blue** (48)	65
DON'T MAKE ME OVER — **Swinging Blue Jeans** (31)	66
DON'T MAKE ME WAIT — **Peech Boys** (49)	82
DON'T MAKE ME WAIT TOO LONG [A] — Roberta **Flack** (44)	80
DON'T MAKE ME WAIT TOO LONG [B] — Barry **White** (17)	76
DON'T MAKE MY BABY BLUE — **Shadows** (10)	65
DON'T MAKE WAVES — **Nolans** (12)	80
DON'T PANIC — **Liquid Gold** (42)	81
DON'T PAY THE FERRYMAN — Chris **De Burgh** (48)	82
DON'T PLAY THAT SONG — Aretha **Franklin** (13)	70
DON'T PLAY YOUR ROCK'N ROLL TO ME — **Smokie** (8)	75
DON'T PUSH IT, DON'T FORCE IT — Leon **Haywood** (12)	80
DON'T SAY I TOLD YOU SO — **Tourists** (40)	80
DON'T SAY THAT'S JUST FOR WHITE BOYS — **Way Of The West** (54)	81
DON'T SET ME FREE — Ray **Charles** (37)	63
DON'T SLEEP IN THE SUBWAY — Petula **Clark** (12)	67
DON'T SLOW DOWN — **U.B.40** (16)	81
DON'T STAND SO CLOSE TO ME — **Police** (1)	80
DON'T STAY AWAY TOO LONG — **Peters and Lee** (3)	74
DON'T STOP [A] — **Fleetwood Mac** (32)	77
DON'T STOP [C] — **Mood** (59)	82
DON'T STOP [B] — **K.I.D.** (49)	81
DON'T STOP BELIEVIN' — **Journey** (62)	82
DON'T STOP IT NOW — **Hot Chocolate** (11)	76
DON'T STOP LOVIN' ME BABY — **Pinkerton's Assorted Colours** (50)	66
DON'T STOP ME NOW — **Queen** (9)	79
DON'T STOP NOW — Gene **Farrow and G.F. Band** (71)	78
DON'T STOP THE CARNIVAL — Alan **Price** (13)	68
DON'T STOP THE FEELING — Roy **Ayers** (56)	80
DON'T STOP THE MUSIC — **Yarbrough and Peoples** (7)	80
DON'T STOP TILL YOU GET ENOUGH — Michael **Jackson** (3)	79
DON'T STOP TWIST — Frankie **Vaughan** (22)	62
DON'T TAKE AWAY THE MUSIC — **Tavares** (4)	76
DON'T TAKE IT LYIN' DOWN — **Dooleys** (60)	78
DON'T TAKE NO FOR AN ANSWER — Tom **Robinson Band** (18)	78
DONT TALK — Hank **Marvin** (49)	82
DON'T TALK TO HIM — Cliff **Richard** (2)	63
DON'T TELL ME — **Central Line** (55)	82
DON'T THAT BEAT ALL — Adam **Faith** (8)	62
DON'T THROW AWAY ALL THOSE TEARDROPS — Frankie **Avalon** (37)	60
DON'T THROW IT ALL AWAY — Gary **Benson** (20)	75
DON'T THROW YOUR LOVE AWAY — **Searchers** (1)	64
DON'T TREAT ME LIKE A CHILD — Helen **Shapiro** (3)	61
DON'T TRY TO CHANGE ME — **Crickets** (37)	63
DON'T TURN AROUND — **Merseybeats** (13)	64
DON'T WALK AWAY [A] — **Electric Light Orchestra** (21)	80
DON'T WALK AWAY [B] — **Four Tops** (16)	81
DON'T WALK AWAY TILL I TOUCH YOU — Elaine **Paige** (46)	78
DON'T WANNA SAY GOODNIGHT — **Kandidate** (47)	78
DON'T WANT TO WAIT ANYMORE — **Tubes** (60)	81
DON'T WORRY [A] — Johnny **Brandon** (18)	55
DON'T WORRY [B] — Billy **Fury** (40)	61
DON'T YOU KNOW — **Butterscotch** (17)	70
DON'T YOU KNOW IT — Adam **Faith** (12)	61
DON'T YOU ROCK ME DADDY-O — Lonnie **Donegan** (4)	57
DON'T YOU ROCK ME DADDY-O — **Vipers Skiffle Group** (10)	57
DON'T YOU THINK IT'S TIME — **Mike Berry** (6)	63
DON'T YOU WANT ME — **Human League** (1)	81
DOOBEDOOD'NDOOBE DOOBEDOOD'NDOOBE — Diana **Ross** (12)	72
DOOMSDAY — Evelyn **Thomas** (41)	76
DOOR IS STILL OPEN TO MY HEART, THE — Dean **Martin** (42)	64
DOORS OF YOUR HEART — The **Beat** (33)	81
DOUBLE BARREL — Dave and Ansil **Collins** (1)	71
DOUBLE DUTCH — **Fatback Band** (31)	77
DOWN AT THE DOCTOR'S — **Dr. Feelgood** (48)	78
DOWN BY THE LAZY RIVER — **Osmonds** (40)	72
DOWN DEEP INSIDE (THEME FROM 'THE DEEP') — Donna **Summer** (5)	77
DOWN DOWN — **Status Quo** (1)	74
DOWN IN THE BOONDOCKS — Billy Joe **Royal** (38)	65
DOWN IN THE TUBE STATION AT MIDNIGHT — **Jam** (15)	78
DOWN ON THE BEACH TONIGHT — **Drifters** (7)	74
DOWN ON THE CORNER — **Creedence Clearwater Revival** (31)	70
DOWN THE DUSTPIPE — **Status Quo** (12)	70
DOWN THE HALL — **Four Seasons** (34)	77
DOWN THE RIVER NILE — John **Leyton** (42)	62
DOWN YONDER — **Johnny and the Hurricanes** (8)	60
DOWNHEARTED — Eddie **Fisher** (3)	53
DOWNTOWN — Petula **Clark** (2)	64
DRACULA'S TANGO — **Toto Coelo** (54)	82
DRAGNET — Ray **Anthony** (7)	53
DRAGNET — Ted **Heath** (9)	53
DRAGON POWER — **JKD Band** (58)	78
DRAGONFLY — **Tornados** (41)	63
DRAW OF THE CARDS — Kim **Carnes** (49)	81
DREADLOCK HOLIDAY — **10 C. C.** (1)	78
DREAM A LIE — **U.B.40** (10)	80
DREAM A LITTLE DREAM OF ME — Mama **Cass** (11)	68
DREAM A LITTLE DREAM OF ME — Anita **Harris** (33)	68
DREAM BABY — Glen **Campbell** (39)	71
DREAM BABY — Roy **Orbison** (2)	62
DREAM GIRL — Mark **Wynter** (27)	61
DREAM LOVER — Bobby **Darin** (1)	59,79
DREAM OF OLWEN — **Second City Sound** (43)	69
DREAM SEQUENCE (ONE) — Pauline **Murray and the Invisible Girls** (67)	80
DREAMBOAT [A] — Alma **Cogan** (1)	55
DREAMBOAT [B] — **Limmie and the Family Cookin'** (31)	73
DREAMER [A] — **Jacksons** (22)	77
DREAMER [B] — **Supertramp** (13)	75
DREAMIN' [A] — Johnny **Burnette** (5)	60
DREAMIN' [B] — **Liverpool Express** (40)	77
DREAMIN' [C] — Cliff **Richard** (8)	80
DREAMING — **Blondie** (2)	79
DREAMING OF ME — **Depeche Mode** (57)	81
DREAMING, THE — Kate **Bush** (48)	82
DREAMS [A] — **Fleetwood Mac** (24)	77
DREAMS [B] — Grace **Slick** (50)	80
DREAMS CAN TELL A LIE — Nat "King" **Cole** (10)	56
DREAMS I DREAM, THE — **Shadows** (42)	66
DREAMS OF CHILDREN, THE — **Jam** (1)	80
DREAMS OF YOU — Ralph **McTell** (36)	75
DREAMY LADY — **T. Rex** (30)	75
DRINK UP THY ZIDER — Adge **Cutler and the Wurzels** (45)	67
DRINKING SONG — Mario **Lanza** (13)	55
DRIVE SAFELY DARLIN' — Tony **Christie** (35)	76
DRIVE-IN SATURDAY — David **Bowie** (3)	73
DRIVER'S SEAT — **Sniff 'N' The Tears** (42)	79
DRIVIN' HOME — Duane **Eddy** (30)	61
DRIVING IN MY CAR — **Madness** (4)	82
DROWNING — The **Beat** (22)	81
DROWNING IN BERLIN — **Mobiles** (9)	82
DRUMMER MAN — **Tonight** (14)	78
DRUMMIN' UP A STORM — Sandy **Nelson** (39)	62
DRUMS ARE MY BEAT — Sandy **Nelson** (30)	62
DRY COUNTY — **Blackfoot** (43)	82
DUCHESS [A] — **Genesis** (46)	80
DUCHESS [B] — **Stranglers** (14)	79
DUELLING BANJOS — "**Deliverance**" **Soundtrack** (17)	73
DUKE OF EARL — **Darts** (6)	79
DUM DUM — Brenda **Lee** (22)	61
DUMB WAITERS — **Psychedelic Furs** (59)	81
DURHAM TOWN (THE LEAVIN') — Roger **Whittaker** (12)	69
DYNAMITE — Cliff **Richard** (16)	59
DYNA-MITE [B] — **Mud** (4)	73
DYNAMITE [C] — Stacy **Lattisaw** (51)	80
DYNOMITE PART 1. — Tony **Camillo's Bazuka** (28)	75
EARLY IN THE MORNING [A] — Buddy **Holly** (17)	58
EARLY IN THE MORNING [B] — **Vanity Fare** (8)	69
EARLY IN THE MORNING [C] — **Gap Band** (55)	82
EARLY TO BED — **Poni-Tails** (26)	59
EARTH ANGEL — **Crew Cuts** (4)	55
EARTH DIES SCREAMING, THE — **U.B.40** (10)	80
EASE ON DOWN THE ROAD — Diana **Ross and Michael Jackson** (45)	78
EASIER SAID THAN DONE [A] — **Essex** (41)	63
EASIER SAID THAN DONE [B] — **Shakatak** (12)	81
EAST RIVER — **Brecker Brothers** (34)	78
EAST WEST — **Herman's Hermits** (37)	66
EASY — **Commodores** (9)	77
EASY COME EASY GO — **Sutherland Brothers** (50)	79
EASY EASY — **Scotland World Cup Squad** (20)	74
EASY GOING ME — Adam **Faith** (12)	61
EASY LIFE — **Bodysnatchers** (50)	80
EBB TIDE — Frank **Chacksfield** (9)	54
EBB TIDE — **Righteous Brothers** (48)	66
EBONY AND IVORY — Paul **McCartney with Stevie Wonder** (1)	82
ECHO BEACH — **Martha and the Muffins** (10)	80
EDDY VORTEX — Steve **Gibbons Band** (56)	78
EDELWEISS — Vince **Hill** (2)	67
EENY MEENY — **Showstoppers** (33)	68
EGO — Elton **John** (34)	78
EGYPTIAN REGGAE — Jonathan **Richman and the Modern Lovers** (5)	77
EIGHT BY TEN — Ken **Dodd** (22)	64
EIGHT MILES HIGH — **Byrds** (24)	66
18 CARAT LOVE AFFAIR — **Associates** (21)	82
EIGHTEEN WITH A BULLET — Pete **Wingfield** (7)	75
EIGHTEEN YELLOW ROSES — Bobby **Darin** (37)	63
EIGHTH DAY — Hazel **O'Connor** (5)	80
EINSTEIN A GO-GO — **Landscape** (5)	81
EL BIMBO — **Bimbo Jet** (12)	75
EL PASO — Marty **Robbins** (19)	60
ELEANOR RIGBY — **Beatles** (1)	66
ELEANOR RIGBY — Ray **Charles** (36)	68
ELECTED — Alice **Cooper** (4)	72
ELECTRIC LADY — **Geordie** (32)	73
ELENORE — **Turtles** (7)	68
ELEPHANT TANGO — Cyril **Stapleton** (19)	55
ELEPHANT'S GRAVEYARD (GUILTY), THE — **Boomtown Rats** (26)	81
ELISABETH SERENADE — Gunther **Kallman Choir** (45)	64
ELIZABETHAN REGGAE — Boris **Gardner** (14)	70
ELMO JAMES — **Chairmen Of The Board** (21)	72
ELO EP (EP) — **Electric Light Orchestra** (34)	78
ELOISE — Barry **Ryan** (2)	68
ELSTREE — **Buggles** (55)	80
ELUSIVE BUTTERFLY — Val **Doonican** (5)	66
ELUSIVE BUTTERFLY — Bob **Lind** (5)	66
EMBARRASSMENT — **Madness** (4)	80
EMERALD CITY — **Seekers** (50)	67

Title — Act (Position)	Year of Chart Entry
EMMA — Hot Chocolate (3)	74
EMOTIONAL RESCUE — Rolling Stones (9)	80
EMOTIONS — Brenda Lee (45)	61
EMOTIONS — Samantha Sang (11)	78
EMPIRE SONG — Killing Joke (43)	82
EMPIRE STATE HUMAN — Human League (62)	80
EMPTY GARDEN — Elton John (51)	82
END ... OR THE BEGINNING, THE — Classix Nouveaux (60)	82
END OF THE WORLD — Skeeter Davis (18)	63
ENDLESS — Dickie Valentine (19)	54
ENDLESS LOVE — Diana Ross and Lionel Richie (7)	81
ENDLESS SLEEP — Jody Reynolds (66)	79
ENDLESS SLEEP — Marty Wilde (4)	58
ENDLESSLY — Brook Benton (28)	59
ENGINE ENGINE NO. 9 — Roger Miller (33)	65
ENGLAND SWINGS — Roger Miller (13)	65
ENGLAND WE'LL FLY THE FLAG — England World Cup Squad (2)	82
ENGLISH CIVIL WAR (JOHNNY COMES MARCHING HOME) — Clash (25)	79
ENGLISH COUNTRY GARDEN — Jimmie Rodgers (5)	62
ENJOY YOURSELF — Jacksons (42)	77
ENOLA GAY — Orchestral Manoeuvres in the Dark (8)	80
ENTERTAINER, THE — Marvin Hamlisch (25)	74
ENTRY OF THE GLADIATORS — Nero and the Gladiators (37)	61
EQUINOXE (PART V) — Shadows (50)	80
EQUINOXE PART 5 — Jean-Michel Jarre (45)	79
ERNIE (THE FASTEST MILKMAN IN THE WEST) — Benny Hill (1)	71
ESCAPE (THE PINA COLADA SONG) — Rupert Holmes (23)	80
ET LES OISEAUX CHANTAIENT (AND THE BIRDS WERE SINGING) — Sweet People (4)	80
ET MÊME — Francoise Hardy (31)	65
THEME FROM 'E.T.' (THE EXTRA-TERRESTRIAL) — John Williams (34)	82
ETERNALLY — Jimmy Young (8)	53
ETON RIFLES, THE — Jam (3)	79
EUROPA AND THE PIRATE TWINS — Thomas Dolby (48)	81
EUROPE - AFTER THE RUN — John Foxx (40)	81
EUROPEAN SON — Japan (31)	82
EVE OF DESTRUCTION — Barry McGuire (3)	65
EVE OF THE WAR — Jeff Wayne's War Of The Worlds (36)	78
EVEN MORE PARTY POPS — Russ Conway (27)	60
EVEN THE BAD TIMES ARE GOOD — Tremeloes (4)	67
EVEN THE NIGHTS ARE BETTER — Air Supply (44)	82
EVEN THOUGH YOU'VE GONE — Jacksons (31)	78
EVENING STAR — Judas Priest (53)	79
EVER FALLEN IN LOVE (WITH SOMEONE YOU SHOULDN'T'VE HAVE) — Buzzcocks (12)	78
EVER SINCE YOU SAID GOODBYE — Marty Wilde (31)	62
EVER SO LONELY — Monsoon (12)	82
EVERGREEN (LOVE THEME FROM A STAR IS BORN) — Barbra Streisand (3)	77
EVERLASTING LOVE — Robert Knight (19)	74
EVERLASTING LOVE — Love Affair (1)	68
EVERLASTING LOVE — Rex Smith and Rachel Sweet (35)	81
EVERLASTING LOVE, AN — Andy Gibb (10)	78
EVERLOVIN' — Rick Nelson (23)	61
EVERMORE — Ruby Murray (3)	55
EVERY DAY HURTS — Sad Café (3)	79
EVERY DAY OF MY LIFE — Malcolm Vaughan (5)	55
EVERY KINDA PEOPLE — Robert Palmer (53)	78
EVERY LITTLE BIT HURTS — Spencer Davis Group (41)	65
EVERY LITTLE TEARDROP — Gallagher and Lyle (32)	77
EVERY LITTLE THING SHE DOES IS MAGIC — Police (1)	81
EVERY MAN MUST HAVE A DREAM — Liverpool Express (17)	76
EVERY NIGHT — Phoebe Snow (37)	79
EVERY NITE'S A SATURDAY NIGHT WITH YOU — Drifters (29)	76
EVERY WHICH WAY BUT LOOSE — Eddie Rabbitt (41)	79
EVERY 1'S A WINNER — Hot Chocolate (12)	78
EVERYBODY — Tommy Roe (9)	63
EVERYBODY DANCE — Chic (9)	78
(EVERYBODY) GET DANCIN' — Bombers (37)	79
EVERYBODY GET TOGETHER — Dave Clark Five (8)	70
EVERYBODY GO HOME THE PARTY'S OVER — Clodagh Rodgers (47)	70
EVERYBODY HAVE A GOOD TIME — Archie Bell and the Drells (43)	77
EVERYBODY IS A STAR — Pointer Sisters (61)	79
EVERYBODY KNOWS [A] — Dave Clark Five (2)	65,67
EVERYBODY LOVES A LOVER — Doris Day (25)	58
EVERYBODY LOVES SOMEBODY — Dean Martin (11)	64
EVERYBODY SALSA — Modern Romance (12)	81
EVERYBODY'S GONNA BE HAPPY — Kinks (17)	65
EVERYBODY'S GOT TO LEARN SOMETIME — Korgis (5)	80
EVERYBODY'S HAPPY NOWADAYS — Buzzcocks (29)	79
EVERYBODY'S SOMEBODY'S FOOL — Connie Francis (5)	60
EVERYBODY'S TALKIN' — Nilsson (23)	69
EVERYBODY'S TALKIN' 'BOUT LOVE — Silver Convention (25)	77
EVERYBODY'S TWISTING — Frank Sinatra (22)	62
EVERYDAY [A] — Don McLean (38)	73
EVERYDAY [B] — Moody Blues (44)	65
EVERYDAY [C] — Slade (3)	74
EVERYDAY PEOPLE — Sly and the Family Stone (36)	69
EVERYONE'S GONE TO THE MOON — Jonathan King (4)	65
EVERYTHING A MAN COULD EVER NEED — Glen Campbell (32)	70
EVERYTHING I AM — Plastic Penny (6)	68
EVERYTHING I HAVE IS YOURS — Eddie Fisher (8)	53
EVERYTHING I OWN — Ken Boothe (1)	74
EVERYTHING I OWN — Bread (32)	72
EVERYTHING IS BEAUTIFUL — Ray Stevens (6)	70
EVERYTHING IS GREAT — Inner Circle (37)	79
EVERYTHING'L TURN OUT FINE — Stealer's Wheel (33)	73
EVERYTHING'S ALRIGHT — The Mojos (9)	64
EVERYTHING'S GONE GREEN — New Order (38)	81
EVERYTHING'S TUESDAY — Chairmen Of The Board (12)	71
EV'RYWHERE — David Whitfield (3)	55
EVIL HEARTED YOU — Yardbirds (3)	65
EVIL WOMAN — Electric Light Orchestra (10)	76
EXCLUSIVELY YOURS — Mark Wynter (32)	61
EXCUSE ME BABY — Magic Lanterns (44)	66
EXODUS — Bob Marley and the Wailers (14)	77
EXODUS, THEME FROM — Ferrante and Teicher (6)	61
EXODUS, THEME FROM — Semprini (25)	61
EXPERIMENTS WITH MICE — Johnny Dankworth (7)	56
EXPRESS [A] — B. T. Express (34)	75
EXPRESS [B] — Rose Royce (52)	81
EXPRESSO BONGO (EP) — Cliff Richard (14)	60
EXTENDED PLAY (EP) — Bryan Ferry (7)	76
EYE LEVEL — Simon Park (1)	72,73
EYE OF THE TIGER — Survivor (1)	82
EYES HAVE IT, THE — Karel Fialka (52)	80
F. B. I. — Shadows (6)	61
FA FA FA FA FA (SAD SONG) — Otis Redding (23)	66
FABULOUS — Charlie Gracie (8)	57
FACES (EP), THE — Faces (41)	77
FADE TO GREY — Visage (8)	80
FAIRYTALE — Dana (13)	76
FAITH CAN MOVE MOUNTAINS — Nat "King" Cole (10)	53
FAITH CAN MOVE MOUNTAINS — Johnnie Ray (7)	52
FAITH CAN MOVE MOUNTAINS — Jimmy Young (11)	53
FAITHFUL HUSSAR (DON'T CRY MY LOVE), THE — Vera Lynn (29)	57
FAITHFUL HUSSAR, THE — Louis Armstrong (27)	56
FAITHFUL HUSSAR, THE — Ted Heath (18)	56
FAITHLESS — Scritti Politti (56)	82
FALCON — Rah Band (35)	80
FALL IN LOVE WITH YOU — Cliff Richard (2)	60
FALL OUT — Police (47)	79
FALLEN ANGEL — Frankie Valli (11)	76
FALLIN' — Connie Francis (20)	58
FALLIN' IN LOVE — Hamilton, Joe Frank Reynolds (33)	75
FALLING — Roy Orbison (9)	63
FALLING APART AT THE SEAMS — Marmalade (9)	76
FALLING IN LOVE AGAIN — Techno Twins (70)	82
FAME [A] — David Bowie (17)	75
FAME [B] — Irene Cara (1)	82
FAMILY AFFAIR — Sly and the Family Stone (15)	72
FAMILY MAN — Mike Oldfield (45)	82
FAN MAIL — Dickies (57)	80
FANCY PANTS — Kenny (4)	75
FAN'DABI'DOZI — Krankies (46)	81
FANFARE FOR THE COMMON MAN — Emerson, Lake and Palmer (2)	77
FANLIGHT FANNY — Clinton Ford (22)	62
FANTASTIC DAY — Haircut 100 (9)	82
FANTASY [A] — Earth Wind and Fire (14)	78
FANTASY [B] — Gerard Kenny (34)	80
FANTASY ISLAND — Tight Fit (5)	82
FAR AWAY — Shirley Bassey (24)	62
FAR AWAY EYES — Rolling Stones (3)	78
FAR FAR AWAY — Slade (2)	74
FARAWAY PLACES — Bachelors (36)	63
FAREWELL — Rod Stewart (7)	74
FAREWELL ANGELINA — Joan Baez (35)	65
FAREWELL IS A LONELY SOUND — Jimmy Ruffin (8)	70,74
FARMER BILL'S COWMAN (I WAS KAISER BILL'S BATMAN) — Wurzels (32)	77
FASHION — David Bowie (5)	80
FAT BOTTOMED GIRLS — Queen (11)	78
FATHER CHRISTMAS DO NOT TOUCH ME — Goodies (7)	74
FATTIE BUM BUM — Diversions (34)	75
FATTIE BUM BUM — Carl Malcolm (8)	75
FAVOURITE SHIRTS (BOY MEETS GIRL) — Haircut 100 (4)	81
FEAR OF THE DARK — Gordon Giltrap (58)	79
FEEDING TIME — Look (50)	81
FEEL LIKE CALLING HOME — Mr. Big (35)	77
FEEL LIKE MAKIN' LOVE — Bad Company (20)	75
FEEL LIKE MAKING LOVE — Roberta Flack (34)	74
FEEL ME — Blancmange (46)	82
FEEL SO FINE — Johnny Preston (18)	60
FEEL THE NEED — Leif Garrett (38)	79
FEEL THE NEED IN ME — Detroit Emeralds (4)	73,77
FEEL THE REAL — David Bendeth (44)	79
FEELINGS — Morris Albert (4)	75
FEELS LIKE I'M IN LOVE — Kelly Marie (1)	80
FEELS LIKE THE FIRST TIME — Foreigner (39)	78
FEELS LIKE THE RIGHT TIME — Shakatak (41)	80
FEET UP — Guy Mitchell (2)	52
FELICITY — Orange Juice (63)	82
FERNANDO — Abba (1)	76
FERRIS WHEEL — Everly Brothers (22)	64
FERRY ACROSS THE MERSEY — Gerry and the Pacemakers (8)	64
FESTIVAL TIME — San Remo Strings (39)	71
FEVER — Peggy Lee (5)	58
FEVER — McCoys (44)	65
FEVER — Helen Shapiro (38)	64
5TH ANNIVERSARY (EP) — Judge Dread (31)	77
FIFTH OF BEETHOVEN, A — Walter Murphy and the Big Apple Band (28)	76
50 WAYS TO LEAVE YOUR LOVER — Paul Simon (23)	76
59TH STREET BRIDGE SONG (FEELING GROOVY) — Harpers Bizarre (34)	67
FIFTY-FOUR — Sea Level (63)	79
FIGARO — Brotherhood Of Man (1)	78
FIGHT, THE — Marty Wilde (47)	60
FINCHLEY CENTRAL — New Vaudeville Band (11)	67
FIND MY WAY BACK HOME — Nashville Teens (34)	65
FINDERS KEEPERS — Chairmen Of The Board (21)	73
FINGER OF SUSPICION — Dickie Valentine (1)	54
FINGS AIN'T WOT THEY USED T'BE — Max Bygraves (5)	60
FINGS AIN'T WOT THEY USED T'BE — Russ Conway (47)	60
FIRE [A] — Crazy World of Arthur Brown (1)	68
FIRE [B] — Pointer Sisters (34)	79
FIRE AND RAIN — James Taylor (42)	70
FIRE BRIGADE — Move (3)	68
FIRE [C] — U2 (35)	81
FIRE DOWN BELOW — Shirley Bassey (30)	57
FIRE DOWN BELOW — Jeri Southern (22)	57
FIRE WORKS — Siouxsie and the Banshees (22)	82
FIREBALL — Deep Purple (15)	71
FIREBALL — Don Spencer (32)	63
FIRST CUT IS THE DEEPEST — P. P. Arnold (18)	67
FIRST CUT IS THE DEEPEST — Rod Stewart (1)	77
FIRST IMPRESSIONS — Impressions (16)	75
FIRST OF MAY — Bee Gees (6)	69
FIRST TASTE OF LOVE — Ben E. King (27)	61
FIRST THING IN THE MORNING — Kiki Dee (32)	77
FIRST TIME EVER I SAW YOUR FACE, THE — Roberta Flack (14)	72
FIRST TIME, THE — Adam Faith (5)	63
5:15 — Who (20)	73
5-4-3-2-1 — Manfred Mann (5)	64

Title — Act (Position)	Year of Chart Entry
FIVE LITTLE FINGERS — Frankie **McBride** (19)	**67**
FIVE MILES OUT — Mike **Oldfield** (43)	**82**
FIVE MINUTES — **Stranglers** (11)	**78**
5-7-0-5 — **City Boy** (8)	**78**
FLAME TREES OF THIKA, THE — **Video Symphonic** (42)	**81**
FLASH — **Queen** (10)	**80**
FLASHBACK — **Imagination** (16)	**81**
FLASHER, THE — **Mistura** (23)	**76**
FLIP — Jesse **Green** (26)	**76**
FLIRT — Jonathan **King** (22)	**72**
FLIRTATION WALTZ — Winifred **Atwell** (10)	**53**
FLOAT ON — **Floaters** (1)	**77**
FLOATING IN THE WIND — **Hudson-Ford** (35)	**74**
FLORAL DANCE — Terry **Wogan** (21)	**78**
FLORAL DANCE, THE — **Brighouse and Rastrick Brass Band** (2)	**77**
FLOWERS IN THE RAIN — **Move** (2)	**67**
FLOWERS OF ROMANCE — **Public Image Ltd.** (24)	**81**
FLOWERS ON THE WALL — **Statler Brothers** (38)	**66**
FLOY JOY — **Supremes** (9)	**72**
FLY ROBIN FLY — **Silver Convention** (28)	**75**
FLY TOO HIGH — Janis **Ian** (44)	**79**
FLYING HIGH — **Commodores** (37)	**78**
FLYING HIGH BEGGARS BANQUET — **Freeez** (35)	**81**
FLYING MACHINE — Cliff **Richard** (37)	**71**
FM (NO STATIC AT ALL) — **Steely Dan** (49)	**78**
FOE-DEE-O-DEE — **Rubettes** (15)	**75**
FOGGY MOUNTAIN BREAKDOWN — Lester **Flatt and Earl Scruggs** (39)	**67**
FOLK SINGER, THE — Tommy **Roe** (4)	**63**
FOLLOW THAT DREAM (EP) — Elvis **Presley** (34)	**62**
FOLLOW THE LEADERS — **Killing Joke** (55)	**81**
FOLLOW YOU FOLLOW ME — **Genesis** (7)	**78**
FOOD FOR THOUGHT [A] — **Barron Knights** (46)	**79**
FOOD FOR THOUGHT [B] — **U.B.40** (4)	**80**
FOOL [A] — Al **Matthews** (16)	**75**
FOOL [B] — Elvis **Presley** (15)	**73**
FOOL AM I, A — Cilla **Black** (13)	**66**
FOOL FOR YOUR LOVING — **Whitesnake** (13)	**80**
FOOL IF YOU THINK IT'S OVER — Elkie **Brooks** (17)	**82**
FOOL (IF YOU THINK IT'S OVER) — Chris **Rea** (30)	**78**
FOOL NEVER LEARNS, A — Andy **Williams** (40)	**64**
FOOL NUMBER ONE — Brenda **Lee** (38)	**61**
FOOL ON THE HILL, THE — Shirley **Bassey** (48)	**71**
FOOL SUCH AS I, A — Elvis **Presley** (1)	**59**
FOOL TO CRY — **Rolling Stones** (6)	**76**
FOOLED AROUND AND FELL IN LOVE — Elvin **Bishop** (34)	**76**
FOOLISH LITTLE GIRL — **Shirelles** (38)	**63**
FOOLS RUSH IN — Brook **Benton** (50)	**61**
FOOLS RUSH IN — Rick **Nelson** (12)	**63**
FOOT STOMPIN' MUSIC — Hamilton **Bohannon** (23)	**75**
FOOT TAPPER — **Shadows** (1)	**63**
FOOTPRINTS IN THE SNOW — Johnny **Duncan and the Blue Grass Boys** (27)	**57**
FOOTSEE — **Wigan's Chosen Few** (9)	**75**
FOOTSTEPS — Ronnie **Carroll** (36)	**60**
FOOTSTEPS — Steve **Lawrence** (4)	**60**
FOOTSTEPS — **Showaddywaddy** (31)	**81**
FOR A FEW DOLLARS MORE — **Smokie** (17)	**78**
FOR A PENNY — Pat **Boone** (19)	**59**
FOR ALL WE KNOW — Shirley **Bassey** (6)	**71**
FOR ALL WE KNOW — **Carpenters** (18)	**71**
FOR BRITAIN ONLY — Alice **Cooper** (66)	**82**
(FOR GOD'S SAKE) GIVE MORE POWER TO THE PEOPLE — **Chi-Lites** (32)	**71**
FOR MAMA — Matt **Monro** (36)	**64**
FOR OLD TIME'S SAKE — **Millican and Nesbitt** (38)	**74**
FOR ONCE IN MY LIFE — Dorothy **Squires** (24)	**69**
FOR ONCE IN MY LIFE — Stevie **Wonder** (3)	**68**
FOR THE GOOD TIMES — Perry **Como** (7)	**73**
FOR THOSE ABOUT TO ROCK (WE SALUTE YOU) — **AC/DC** (15)	**82**
FOR WHOM THE BELL TOLLS — Simon **Dupree and The Big Sound** (43)	**68**
FOR YOU — Rick **Nelson** (14)	**64**
FOR YOU FOR LOVE — **Average White Band** (46)	**80**
FOR YOUR EYES ONLY — Sheena **Easton** (8)	**81**
FOR YOUR LOVE — **Yardbirds** (3)	**65**
FOREST, A — **Cure** (31)	**80**
FOREVER — Roy **Wood** (8)	**73**
FOREVER & EVER — **Slik** (1)	**76**
FOREVER AUTUMN — Justin **Hayward** (5)	**78**
FOREVER CAME TODAY — **Supremes** (28)	**68**
FOREVER IN BLUE JEANS — Neil **Diamond** (16)	**79**
FOREVER KIND OF LOVE, A — Bobby **Vee** (13)	**62**
FORGET ABOUT YOU — **Motors** (13)	**78**
FORGET HIM — Bobby **Rydell** (13)	**63**
FORGET ME NOT [A] — Vera **Lynn** (5)	**52**

Title — Act (Position)	Year of Chart Entry
FORGET ME NOT [B] — Eden **Kane** (3)	**62**
FORGET ME NOT [C] — Martha **Reeves and the Vandellas** (11)	**71**
FORGET ME NOTS — Patrice **Rushen** (8)	**82**
FORGOTTEN DREAMS — Leroy **Anderson** (24)	**57**
FORGOTTEN DREAMS — Cyril **Stapleton** (27)	**57**
FORT WORTH JAIL — Lonnie **Donegan** (14)	**59**
48 CRASH — Suzi **Quatro** (3)	**73**
FORTY MILES OF BAD ROAD — Duane **Eddy** (11)	**59**
FOUR FROM TOYAH (EP) — **Toyah** (4)	**81**
FOUR LITTLE HEELS — **Avons** (45)	**60**
FOUR LITTLE HEELS — Brian **Hyland** (29)	**60**
FOUR MORE FROM TOYAH (EP) — **Toyah** (14)	**81**
FOUR STRONG WINDS — Neil **Young** (57)	**79**
FOX ON THE RUN [A] — **Manfred Mann** (5)	**68**
FOX ON THE RUN [B] — **Sweet** (2)	**75**
FOXHOLE — **Television** (36)	**78**
FOXY FOXY — **Mott The Hoople** (33)	**74**
FRANKENSTEIN — Edgar **Winter Group** (18)	**73**
FRANKIE AND JOHNNY — Sam **Cooke** (30)	**63**
FRANKIE AND JOHNNY — Elvis **Presley** (21)	**66**
FREDERICK — Patti **Smith Group** (63)	**79**
FREE — Deniece **Williams** (1)	**77**
FREE EP — **Free** (11)	**78**
FREE BIRD EP — **Lynyrd Skynyrd** (31)	**76**
FREE BIRD (EP) — **Lynyrd Skynyrd** (21)	**82**
FREE ELECTRIC BAND — Albert **Hammond** (19)	**73**
FREE (EP) — **Free** (57)	**82**
FREE ME — Roger **Daltrey** (39)	**80**
FREEDOM COME FREEDOM GO — **Fortunes** (6)	**71**
FREEDOM'S PRISONER — Steve **Harley and COCKNEY REBEL** (58)	**79**
FREEZE, THE — **Spandau Ballet** (17)	**81**
FREEZE-FRAME — **J. Geils Band** (27)	**82**
FREIGHT TRAIN — Charles **McDevitt Skiffle Group featuring Nancy Whiskey** (5)	**57**
FRENCH FOREIGN LEGION — Frank **Sinatra** (18)	**59**
FRIDAY ON MY MIND — **Easybeats** (6)	**66**
FRIDAY 13TH (EP) — **Damned** (50)	**81**
FRIDAYS ANGELS — **Generation X** (62)	**79**
FRIEND OR FOE — **Adam and The Ants** (9)	**82**
FRIENDLY PERSUASION — Pat **Boone** (3)	**56**
FRIENDLY PERSUASION — **Four Aces** (29)	**57**
FRIENDS [A] — **Arrival** (8)	**70**
FRIENDS [B] — **Beach Boys** (25)	**68**
FRIENDS [C] — **Shalamar** (12)	**82**
FRIENDS AND NEIGHBOURS — Billy **Cotton and his Band** (3)	**54**
FRIGGIN' IN THE RIGGIN' — **Sex Pistols** (3)	**79**
FRIGHTENED CITY — **Shadows** (3)	**61**
FROM A JACK TO A KING — Ned **Miller** (2)	**63**
FROM A WINDOW — Billy J. **Kramer and the Dakotas** (10)	**64**
FROM EAST TO WEST — **Voyage** (13)	**78**
FROM HEAD TO TOE — Elvis **Costello and the Attractions** (43)	**82**
FROM HERE TO ETERNITY — Giorgio **Moroder** (16)	**77**
FROM HERE TO THERE TO YOU — Hank **Locklin** (44)	**62**
FROM ME TO YOU — **Beatles** (1)	**63**
FROM NEW YORK TO L.A. — Patsy **Gallant** (6)	**77**
FROM RUSSIA WITH LOVE — John **Barry** (39)	**63**
FROM RUSSIA WITH LOVE — Matt **Monro** (20)	**63**
FROM THE BOTTOM OF MY HEART — **Moody Blues** (22)	**65**
FROM THE UNDERWORLD — **Herd** (6)	**67**
FROZEN ORANGE JUICE — Peter **Sarstedt** (10)	**69**
FULL TIME JOB — Doris **Day and Johnnie Ray** (11)	**53**
FUNERAL PYRE — **Jam** (4)	**81**
FUNGI MAMA (BEBOPAFUNKADISCOLYPSO) — Tom **Browne** (58)	**82**
FUNK THEORY — **Rokotto** (49)	**78**
FUNKIN' FOR JAMAICA (N.Y.) — Tom **Browne** (10)	**80**
FUNKY BROADWAY — Wilson **Pickett** (43)	**67**
FUNKY GIBBON — **Goodies** (4)	**75**
FUNKY MOPED — Jasper **Carrott** (5)	**75**
FUNKY NASSAU — **Beginning Of The End** (31)	**74**
FUNKY STREET — Arthur **Conley** (46)	**68**
FUNKY STUFF — **Kool and the Gang** (17)	**81**
FUNKY WEEKEND — **Stylistics** (10)	**76**
FUNKYTOWN — **Lipps Inc.** (2)	**80**
FUNNY ALL OVER — **Vernons Girls** (31)	**63**
FUNNY FAMILIAR FORGOTTEN FEELINGS — Tom **Jones** (7)	**67**
FUNNY FUNNY — **Sweet** (13)	**71**
FUNNY HOW LOVE CAN BE — **Ivy League** (8)	**65**
FUNNY HOW TIME SLIPS AWAY — Dorothy **Moore** (38)	**76**
FUNNY WAY OF LAUGHIN' — Burl **Ives** (29)	**62**
FURNITURE MUSIC — Bill **Nelson** (59)	**79**

Title — Act (Position)	Year of Chart Entry
FUTURE MANAGEMENT — Roger **Taylor** (49)	**81**
GAL WITH THE YALLER SHOES — Michael **Holliday** (13)	**56**
GALAXY — **War** (14)	**78**
GALAXY OF LOVE — **Crown Heights Affair** (24)	**78**
GALLOPING HOME — **London String Chorale** (31)	**73**
GALVESTON — Glen **Campbell** (14)	**69**
GAMBLIN' BAR ROOM BLUES — Sensational Alex **Harvey Band** (38)	**75**
GAMBLIN' MAN — Lonnie **Donegan** (1)	**57**
GAME OF LOVE — Wayne **Fontana and the Mindbenders** (2)	**65**
GAMES PEOPLE PLAY — Joe **South** (6)	**69**
GAMES WITHOUT FRONTIERS — Peter **Gabriel** (4)	**80**
GANDHARA — **Godiego** (56)	**80**
GANGSTERS — The **Specials** (6)	**79**
GANGSTERS OF THE GROOVE — **Heatwave** (19)	**81**
GARDEN OF EDEN — Dick **James** (18)	**57**
GARDEN OF EDEN — Gary **Miller** (14)	**57**
GARDEN OF EDEN — Joe **Valino** (23)	**57**
GARDEN OF EDEN — Frankie **Vaughan** (1)	**57**
GARDEN PARTY — Rick **Nelson** (41)	**72**
GARY GILMORE'S EYES — **Adverts** (18)	**77**
GARY GLITTER(EP) — Gary **Glitter** (57)	**80**
GASOLINE ALLEY BRED — **Hollies** (14)	**70**
GATHER IN THE MUSHROOMS — Benny **Hill** (12)	**61**
GAUDETE — **Steeleye Span** (14)	**73**
GAYE — Clifford T. **Ward** (8)	**73**
GEE BABY — Peter **Shelley** (4)	**74**
GEE BUT IT'S LONELY — Pat **Boone** (30)	**58**
GEE WHIZ IT'S YOU — Cliff **Richard** (4)	**61**
GENERALS AND MAJORS — **XTC** (32)	**80**
GENIE WITH THE LIGHT BROWN LAMP — **Shadows** (17)	**64**
GENIUS OF LOVE — **Tom Tom Club** (65)	**81**
GENO — **Dexy's Midnight Runners** (1)	**80**
GENTLE ON MY MIND — Dean **Martin** (2)	**69**
GENTLEMEN TAKE POLAROIDS — **Japan** (60)	**80**
GEORGIA ON MY MIND — Ray **Charles** (24)	**60**
GEORGINA BAILEY — Noosha **Fox** (31)	**77**
GEORGY GIRL — **Seekers** (3)	**67**
GERM-FREE ADOLESCENCE — **X-Ray Spex** (19)	**78**
GERONIMO — **Shadows** (11)	**63**
GERTCHA — **Chas and Dave** (20)	**79**
(GET A) GRIP (ON YOURSELF) — **Stranglers** (44)	**77**
GET ANOTHER LOVE — Chantal **Curtis** (51)	**79**
GET AWAY — Georgie **Fame** (1)	**66**
GET BACK — **Beatles** (1)	**69,76**
GET BACK — Rod **Stewart** (11)	**76**
GET DANCING — **Disco Tex and the Sex-O-Lettes** (8)	**74**
GET DOWN [A] — Gilbert **O'Sullivan** (1)	**73**
GET DOWN [B] — Gene **Chandler** (11)	**79**
GET DOWN AND GET WITH IT — **Slade** (16)	**71**
GET DOWN ON IT — **Kool and the Gang** (3)	**81**
GET DOWN TONIGHT — **KC and The Sunshine Band** (21)	**75**
GET IN THE SWING — **Sparks** (27)	**75**
GET IT — **Darts** (10)	**79**
GET IT ON — **T. Rex** (1)	**71**
GET IT RIGHT NEXT TIME — Gerry **Rafferty** (30)	**79**
GET IT TOGETHER — **Crispy And Company** (21)	**75**
GET IT UP FOR LOVE — David **Cassidy** (11)	**75**
GET IT UP FOR LOVE — Tata **Vega** (52)	**79**
GET IT WHILE YOU CAN — **Olympic Runners** (35)	**78**
GET LOST — Eden **Kane** (10)	**61**
GET ME TO THE WORLD ON TIME — **Electric Prunes** (42)	**67**
GET OFF OF MY CLOUD — **Rolling Stones** (1)	**65**
GET ON THE FUNK TRAIN — **Munich Machine** (41)	**77**
GET ON UP, GET ON DOWN — Roy **Ayers** (41)	**78**
GET OUT — Harold **Melvin and the Bluenotes** (35)	**75**
GET OUT OF MY LIFE WOMAN — Lee **Dorsey** (22)	**66**
GET OVER YOU — **Undertones** (57)	**79**
GET READY — **Temptations** (10)	**69**
GET TOUGH — **Kleeer** (49)	**81**
GET UP — **J. A. L. N. Band** (53)	**78**
GET UP & BOOGIE [A] — **Silver Convention** (7)	**76**
GET UP AND BOOGIE [B] — Freddie **James** (54)	**79**
GET UP I FEEL LIKE BEING A SEX MACHINE — James **Brown** (32)	**70**
GET UP OFFA THAT THING — James **Brown** (22)	**76**
GET YOUR LOVE BACK — **Three Degrees** (34)	**74**
GETTIN' READY FOR LOVE — Diana **Ross** (23)	**77**
GETTING A DRAG — Lynsey **De Paul** (18)	**72**
GETTING CLOSER — **Wings** (60)	**79**
GETTING MIGHTY CROWDED — Betty **Everett** (29)	**65**
GETTING OVER YOU — Andy **Williams** (35)	**74**
GETTING UP — **Pig Bag** (61)	**82**

Title — Act (Position)	Year of Chart Entry
GHETTO CHILD — **Detroit Spinners** (7)	**73**
GHOST DANCER — **Addrisi Brothers** (57)	**79**
GHOST OF LOVE, THE — **Tavares** (29)	**78**
GHOST TOWN — The **Specials** (1)	**81**
GHOSTS — **Japan** (5)	**82**
GIDDY-UP-A-DING-DONG — Freddie **Bell and the Bellboys** (4)	**56**
GIGANTOR — **Dickies** (72)	**80**
GIGI — Billy **Eckstine** (8)	**59**
GILLY GILLY OSSENFEFFER KATZENELLEN BOGEN BY THE SEA — Max **Bygraves** (7)	**54**
GIMME DAT BANANA — **Black Gorilla** (29)	**77**
GIMME DAT DING — **Pipkins** (6)	**70**
GIMME GIMME GIMME (A MAN AFTER MIDNIGHT) — **Abba** (3)	**79**
GIMME GIMME GOOD LOVIN' — **Crazy Elephant** (12)	**69**
GIMME LITTLE SIGN — Brenton **Wood** (8)	**67**
GIMME SOME — **Brendon** (14)	**77**
GIMME SOME LOVING — Spencer **Davis Group** (2)	**66**
GIMME YOUR LOVIN' — **Atlantic Starr** (66)	**78**
¡GIMMIX! PLAY LOUD — John Cooper **Clarke** (39)	**79**
GIN GAN GOOLIE — **Scaffold** (38)	**69**
GIN HOUSE BLUES — **Amen Corner** (12)	**67**
GINCHY — Bert **Weedon** (35)	**61**
GINGERBREAD — Frankie **Avalon** (30)	**58**
GINNY COME LATELY — Brian **Hyland** (5)	**62**
GIRL — **St. Louis Union** (11)	**66**
GIRL — **Truth** (27)	**66**
GIRL CAN'T HELP IT, THE — **Little Richard** (9)	**57**
GIRL CRAZY — **Hot Chocolate** (7)	**82**
GIRL DON'T COME — Sandie **Shaw** (3)	**64**
GIRL FROM IPANEMA (GAROTA DE IPANEMA), THE — Stan **Getz and Joao Gilberto** (29)	**64**
GIRL IN THE WOOD — Frankie **Laine** (11)	**53**
GIRL IS MINE, THE — Michael **Jackson and Paul McCartney** (8)	**82**
GIRL (IT'S ALL I HAVE) — **Shy** (60)	**80**
GIRL LIKE YOU [A] — Cliff **Richard** (3)	**61**
GIRL LIKE YOU [B] — **Young Rascals** (37)	**67**
GIRL OF MY BEST FRIEND — Elvis **Presley** (9)	**76**
GIRL OF MY DREAMS — Tony **Brent** (16)	**58**
GIRL OF MY DREAMS — Gerry **Monroe** (43)	**72**
GIRL SANG THE BLUES, THE — **Everly Brothers** (25)	**63**
GIRLFRIEND — Michael **Jackson** (41)	**80**
GIRLIE — **Peddlers** (34)	**70**
GIRLS [A] — Johnny **Burnette** (37)	**61**
GIRLS [B] — **Moments and Whatnauts** (3)	**75**
GIRLS ARE OUT TO GET YOU — **Fascinations** (32)	**71**
GIRLS CAN GET IT — **Dr. Hook** (40)	**80**
GIRLS GIRLS GIRLS [A] — **Fourmost** (33)	**65**
GIRLS GIRLS GIRLS [B] — Steve **Lawrence** (49)	**60**
GIRLS GIRLS GIRLS [C] — **Sailor** (7)	**76**
GIRLS GIRLS GIRLS [D] — **Kandidate** (34)	**79**
GIRLS ON FILM — **Duran Duran** (5)	**81**
GIRL'S SCHOOL — **Wings** (1)	**77**
GIRLS TALK — Dave **Edmunds** (4)	**79**
GIVE A LITTLE BIT — **Supertramp** (29)	**77**
GIVE A LITTLE LOVE — **Bay City Rollers** (1)	**75**
GIVE AND TAKE — **Pioneers** (35)	**72**
GIVE GIVE GIVE — Tommy **Steele** (28)	**59**
GIVE HER MY LOVE — **Johnston Brothers** (27)	**57**
GIVE IRELAND BACK TO THE IRISH — **Wings** (16)	**72**
GIVE IT TO ME — **Troggs** (12)	**67**
GIVE IT TO ME BABY — Rick **James** (47)	**81**
GIVE IT TO ME NOW — **Kenny** (38)	**73**
GIVE ME AN INCH — Hazel **O'Connor** (41)	**80**
GIVE ME BACK ME BRAIN — **Duffo** (60)	**79**
GIVE ME BACK MY HEART — **Dollar** (4)	**82**
GIVE ME BACK MY MAN — **B-52's** (61)	**80**
GIVE ME FIRE — **GBH** (69)	**82**
GIVE ME JUST A LITTLE MORE TIME — **Chairmen Of The Board** (3)	**70**
GIVE ME LOVE (GIVE ME PEACE ON EARTH) — George **Harrison** (8)	**73**
GIVE ME MORE TIME — **Nicole** (75)	**82**
GIVE ME ONE MORE CHANCE — Donald **Peers** (36)	**72**
GIVE ME SOME KINDA MAGIC — **Dollar** (34)	**82**
GIVE ME THE NIGHT — George **Benson** (7)	**80**
GIVE ME TIME — Dusty **Springfield** (24)	**67**
GIVE ME YOUR HEART TONIGHT — **Shakin' Stevens** (11)	**82**
GIVE ME YOUR WORD — Tennessee Ernie **Ford** (1)	**55**
GIVE ME YOUR WORD — Billy **Fury** (27)	**66**
GIVE PEACE A CHANCE — John **Lennon** (2)	**69**
GIVE UP THE FUNK (LET'S DANCE) — **B. T. Express** (52)	**80**
GIVIN' UP GIVIN' IN — **Three Degrees** (12)	**78**
GIVING IT ALL AWAY — Roger **Daltrey** (5)	**73**
GIVING IT BACK — Phil **Hurtt** (36)	**78**
GLAD ALL OVER — **Dave Clark Five** (1)	**63**
GLASS OF CHAMPAGNE — **Sailor** (2)	**75**
GLENDORA — Perry **Como** (18)	**56**
GLENDORA — Glen **Mason** (28)	**56**
GLITTERING PRIZE — **Simple Minds** (16)	**82**
GLOBETROTTER — **Tornados** (5)	**63**
GLORIA [A] — Laura **Branigan** (51)	**82**
GLORIA [A] — Jonathan **King** (65)	**79**
GLORIA [B] — **U2** (55)	**81**
GLOW — **Spandau Ballet** (10)	**81**
GLOW OF LOVE — **Change** (14)	**80**
GLOW WORM — **Mills Brothers** (10)	**53**
GO AWAY LITTLE GIRL — Mark **Wynter** (6)	**62**
GO (BEFORE YOU BREAK MY HEART) — Gigliola **Cinquetti** (8)	**74**
GO BUDDY GO — **Stranglers** (8)	**77**
GO GO GO — Chuck **Berry** (38)	**63**
GO NORTH — Richard **Barnes** (38)	**70**
GO NOW — **Moody Blues** (1)	**64**
GO ON BY — Alma **Cogan** (16)	**55**
GO WEST — **Village People** (15)	**79**
GO WILD IN THE COUNTRY — **Bow Wow Wow** (7)	**82**
GO YOUR OWN WAY — **Fleetwood Mac** (38)	**77**
GOD GAVE ROCK & ROLL TO YOU — **Argent** (18)	**73**
GOD ONLY KNOWS — **Beach Boys** (2)	**66**
GOD SAVE THE QUEEN — **Sex Pistols** (2)	**77**
GOD'S GONNA PUNISH YOU — **Tymes** (41)	**76**
GOD'S KITCHEN — **Blancmange** (65)	**82**
GOIN' PLACES — **Jacksons** (26)	**77**
GOING BACK — Dusty **Springfield** (10)	**66**
GOING BACK TO MY HOME TOWN — Hal **Page and the Whalers** (50)	**60**
GOING BACK TO MY ROOTS — **Odyssey** (4)	**81**
GOING DOWN THE ROAD — Roy **Wood** (13)	**74**
GOING FOR THE ONE — **Yes** (24)	**77**
GOING HOME — **Osmonds** (4)	**73**
GOING IN WITH MY EYES OPEN — David **Soul** (2)	**77**
GOING LEFT RIGHT — **Department S** (55)	**81**
GOING OUT OF MY HEAD — Dodie **West** (39)	**65**
GOING THROUGH THE MOTIONS — **Hot Chocolate** (53)	**79**
GOING TO A GO GO — **Rolling Stones** (26)	**82**
GOING TO A GO-GO — Smokey **Robinson and the Miracles** (44)	**66**
GOING TO A GO-GO — **Sharonettes** (46)	**75**
GOING UNDERGROUND — **Jam** (1)	**80**
GOING UP THE COUNTRY — **Canned Heat** (19)	**69**
GOLD — John **STEWART** (43)	**79**
GOLDEN AGE OF ROCK AND ROLL — **Mott The Hoople** (16)	**74**
GOLDEN BROWN — **Stranglers** (2)	**82**
GOLDEN LADY, THE — **Three Degrees** (56)	**79**
GOLDEN LIGHTS — **Twinkle** (21)	**65**
GOLDEN SLUMBERS - CARRY THAT WEIGHT (MEDLEY) — **Trash** (35)	**69**
GOLDEN YEARS — David **Bowie** (8)	**75**
GOLDEN YEARS (EP), THE — **Motorhead** (8)	**80**
GOLDFINGER — Shirley **Bassey** (21)	**64**
GONE — Shirley **Bassey** (36)	**64**
GONE DEAD TRAIN — **Nazareth** (49)	**78**
GONE GONE GONE [A] — **Everly Brothers** (36)	**64**
GONE GONE GONE [B] — Johnny **Mathis** (15)	**79**
GONNA BUILD A MOUNTAIN — Sammy **Davis Jr.** (26)	**62**
GONNA BUILD A MOUNTAIN — Matt **Monro** (44)	**61**
GONNA CAPTURE YOUR HEART — **Blue** (18)	**77**
GONNA GET ALONG WITHOUT YA NOW — Trini **Lopez** (41)	**67**
GONNA GET ALONG WITHOUT YA NOW — **Patience and Prudence** (22)	**57**
GONNA GET ALONG WITHOUT YOU NOW — Viola **Wills** (8)	**79**
GONNA GIVE HER ALL THE LOVE I'VE GOT — Jimmy **Ruffin** (26)	**67**
GONNA MAKE YOU A STAR — David **Essex** (1)	**74**
GONNA MAKE YOU AN OFFER YOU CAN'T REFUSE — Jimmy **Helms** (8)	**73**
GOO GOO BARABAJAGAL (LOVE IS HOT) — **Donovan with the Jeff Beck Group** (12)	**69**
GOOD EVENING FRIENDS — Frankie **Laine and Johnnie Ray** (25)	**57**
GOOD GIRLS DON'T — **KNACK** (66)	**79**
GOOD GOLLY MISS MOLLY — Jerry Lee **Lewis** (31)	**63**
GOOD GOLLY MISS MOLLY — **Little Richard** (8)	**58,77**
GOOD GOLLY MISS MOLLY — **Swinging Blue Jeans** (11)	**64**
GOOD GRIEF CHRISTINA — **Chicory Tip** (17)	**73**
GOOD LIFE, THE — Tony **Bennett** (27)	**63**
GOOD LOVE CAN NEVER DIE — Alvin **Stardust** (11)	**75**
GOOD LOVIN' AIN'T EASY TO COME BY — Marvin **Gaye and Tammi Terrell** (26)	**69**
GOOD LOVIN' GONE BAD — **Bad Company** (31)	**75**
GOOD LUCK CHARM — Elvis **Presley** (1)	**62**
GOOD MORNING — Leapy **Lee** (29)	**69**
GOOD MORNING FREEDOM — **Blue Mink** (10)	**70**
GOOD MORNING JUDGE — **10 C. C.** (5)	**77**
GOOD MORNING LITTLE SCHOOLGIRL — **Yardbirds** (44)	**64**
GOOD MORNING STARSHINE — **Oliver** (6)	**69**
GOOD OLD ARSENAL — **Arsenal F.C. First Team Squad** (16)	**71**
GOOD OLD ROCK 'N ROLL — **Dave Clark Five** (7)	**69**
GOOD ROCKIN' TONIGHT — **Montrose** (71)	**80**
GOOD THE BAD & THE UGLY, THE — Hugo **Montenegro** (1)	**68**
GOOD THING GOING (WE'VE GOT A GOOD THING GOING) — Sugar **Minott** (4)	**81**
GOOD TIME BABY — Bobby **Rydell** (42)	**61**
GOOD TIMES [A] — Eric **Burdon** (20)	**67**
GOOD TIMES [B] — **Chic** (5)	**79**
GOOD TIMES (BETTER TIMES) — Cliff **Richard** (12)	**69**
GOOD TIMIN' — Jimmy **Jones** (1)	**60**
GOOD VIBRATIONS — **Beach Boys** (1)	**66,76**
GOOD YEAR FOR THE ROSES, A — Elvis **Costello and the Attractions** (6)	**81**
GOODBYE — Mary **Hopkin** (2)	**69**
GOODBYE BLUEBIRD — Wayne **Fontana** (49)	**66**
GOODBYE CIVILIAN — **Skids** (52)	**80**
GOODBYE CRUEL WORLD — James **Darren** (28)	**61**
GOODBYE GIRL — **Squeeze** (63)	**78**
GOODBYE IS JUST ANOTHER WORD — **New Seekers** (36)	**73**
GOODBYE JIMMY GOODBYE — Ruby **Murray** (10)	**59**
GOODBYE MY LOVE [A] — **Glitter Band** (2)	**75**
GOODBYE MY LOVE [B] — **Searchers** (4)	**65**
GOODBYE NOTHING TO SAY — **Javells featuring Nosmo King** (26)	**74**
GOODBYE SAM HELLO SAMANTHA — Cliff **Richard** (6)	**70**
GOODBYE STRANGER — **Supertramp** (57)	**79**
GOODBYE TO LOVE — **Carpenters** (9)	**72**
GOODBYE YELLOW BRICK ROAD — Elton **John** (6)	**73**
GOODBYE-EE [A] — **Peter Cook and Dudley Moore** (18)	**65**
GOODBYE-EE [B] — **14-18** (33)	**75**
GOODNESS GRACIOUS ME — Peter **Sellers and Sophia Loren** (4)	**60**
GOODNIGHT — Roy **Orbison** (14)	**65**
GOODNIGHT MIDNIGHT — Clodagh **Rodgers** (4)	**69**
GOODNIGHT MRS. FLINTSTONE — **Piltdown Men** (18)	**61**
GOODNIGHT SWEET PRINCE — Mr. Acker **Bilk** (50)	**60**
GOODNIGHT TONIGHT — **Wings** (5)	**79**
GOODY GOODY — Frankie **Lymon and the Teenagers** (24)	**57**
GOODY TWO SHOES — **Adam and The Ants** (1)	**82**
GOOGLE EYE — **Nashville Teens** (10)	**64**
GOSSIP CALYPSO — Bernard **Cribbins** (25)	**62**
GOT A FEELING — Patrick **Juvet** (34)	**78**
GOT A GIRL — **Four Preps** (28)	**60**
GOT A LOT O' LIVIN' TO DO — Elvis **Presley** (17)	**57**
GOT A MATCH — Russ **Conway** (30)	**58**
GOT MY MIND MADE UP — **Instant Funk** (46)	**79**
GOT MY MOJO WORKING — Jimmy **Smith** (48)	**66**
GOT NO BRAINS — **Bad Manners** (44)	**82**
GOT TO BE THERE — Michael **Jackson** (5)	**72**
GOT TO GET YOU INTO MY LIFE — Cliff **Bennett and the Rebel Rousers** (6)	**66**
GOT TO GET YOU INTO MY LIFE — **Earth Wind and Fire** (33)	**78**
GOT TO GIVE IT UP — Marvin **Gaye** (7)	**77**
GOT TO LOVE SOMEBODY — **Sister Sledge** (34)	**80**
GOT YOU ON MY MIND — Tony **Brent** (12)	**53**
GOTTA GET A DATE — Frank **Ifield** (49)	**60**
GOTTA GO HOME — **Boney M** (12)	**79**
GOTTA HAVE RAIN — Max **Bygraves** (28)	**58**
GOTTA HAVE SOMETHING IN THE BANK FRANK — Frankie **Vaughan & The Kaye Sisters** (8)	**57**
GOTTA PULL MYSELF TOGETHER — **Nolans** (9)	**80**
GOTTA SEE BABY TONIGHT — Mr. Acker **Bilk** (24)	**62**
GOTTA SEE JANE — R. Dean **Taylor** (17)	**68,74**
GOVINDA — **Radha Krishna Temple** (23)	**70**
GRACE — **Band Aka** (41)	**82**
GRANADA — Frankie **Laine** (9)	**54**
GRANADA — Frank **Sinatra** (15)	**61**
GRAND COOLIE DAM — Lonnie **Donegan** (6)	**58**
GRANDAD — Clive **Dunn** (1)	**70**
GRANDMA'S PARTY — Paul **Nicholas** (9)	**76**
GREASE — Frankie **Valli** (3)	**78**

Title — Act (Position)	Year of Chart Entry
GREASED LIGHTNIN' — John **Travolta** (11)	**78**
GREAT BALLS OF FIRE — Jerry Lee **Lewis** (1)	**57**
GREAT BALLS OF FIRE — **Tiny Tim** (45)	**69**
GREAT PRETENDER, THE — Jimmy **Parkinson** (9)	**56**
GREAT PRETENDER, THE — **Platters** (5)	**56**
GREAT ROCK'N'ROLL SWINDLE, THE — **Sex Pistols** (21)	**79**
GREAT SNOWMAN, THE — Bob **Luman** (49)	**61**
GREATEST COCKNEY RIPOFF, THE — **Cockney Rejects** (21)	**80**
GREATEST LOVE OF ALL, THE — George **Benson** (27)	**77**
GREEN DOOR — Glen **Mason** (24)	**56**
GREEN DOOR — Shakin' **Stevens** (1)	**81**
GREEN DOOR — Frankie **Vaughan** (2)	**56**
GREEN DOOR, THE — Jim **Lowe** (8)	**56**
GREEN FIELDS [A] — **Beverley Sisters** (29)	**60**
GREEN FIELDS [B] — **Unit Four Plus Two** (48)	**64**
GREEN GREEN GRASS OF HOME — Tom **Jones** (1)	**66**
GREEN GREEN GRASS OF HOME — Elvis **Presley** (29)	**75**
GREEN JEANS — **Flee-Rekkers** (23)	**60**
GREEN LEAVES OF SUMMER, THE — Kenny **Ball and his Jazzmen** (7)	**62**
GREEN LIGHT — Cliff **Richard** (57)	**79**
GREEN MANALISHI (WITH THE TWO-PRONG CROWN), THE — **Fleetwood Mac** (10)	**70**
GREEN ONIONS — **Booker T. & The M. G.'s** (7)	**79**
GREEN RIVER — **Creedence Clearwater Revival** (19)	**69**
GREEN STREET GREEN — **New Vaudeville Band** (37)	**67**
GREEN TAMBOURINE — **Lemon Pipers** (7)	**68**
GREEN TAMBOURINE — **Sun Dragon** (50)	**68**
GREENBACK DOLLAR — Charles **McDevitt Skiffle Group featuring Nancy Whiskey** (28)	**57**
GREENFIELDS — **Brothers Four** (40)	**60**
GREY DAY — **Madness** (4)	**81**
GROOVE BABY GROOVE (EP) — **Stargazers** (56)	**82**
GROOVE LINE, THE — **Heatwave** (12)	**78**
GROOVE, THE — Rodney **Franklin** (7)	**80**
GROOVER, THE — **T. Rex** (4)	**73**
GROOVIN' — **Young Rascals** (8)	**67**
GROOVIN' WITH MR. BLOE — **Mr Bloe** (2)	**70**
GROOVY — P. P. **Arnold** (41)	**68**
GROOVÝ BABY — **Microbe** (29)	**69**
GROOVY KIND OF LOVE, A — Les **Gray** (32)	**77**
GROOVY KIND OF LOVE, A — **Mindbenders** (2)	**66**
GROUPIE GIRL — Tony Joe **White** (22)	**70**
GUANTANAMERA — **Sandpipers** (7)	**66**
GUDBUY T'JANE — **Slade** (2)	**72**
GUILTY [A] — Jim **Reeves** (29)	**63**
GUILTY [B] — **Pearls** (10)	**74**
GUILTY [C] — Mike **Oldfield** (22)	**79**
GUILTY [D] — Barbra **Streisand and Barry Gibb** (34)	**80**
GUILTY [E] — **Classix Nouveaux** (43)	**81**
GUITAR BOOGIE SHUFFLE — Bert **Weedon** (10)	**59**
GUITAR MAN [A] — Elvis **Presley** (19)	**68,81**
GUITAR MAN [B] — **Bread** (16)	**72**
GUITAR TANGO — **Shadows** (4)	**62**
GUNS OF NAVARONE — **Skatalites** (36)	**67**
GUNSLINGER — Frankie **Laine** (50)	**61**
GURNEY SLADE — Max **Harris** (11)	**60**
GYPSIES TRAMPS AND THIEVES — **Cher** (4)	**71**
GYPSY — **Fleetwood Mac** (46)	**82**
GYPSY BEAT — **Packabeats** (49)	**61**
GYPSY EYES — Jimi **Hendrix Experience** (35)	**71**
GYPSY ROAD HOG — **Slade** (48)	**77**
GYPSY ROVER — **Highwaymen** (41)	**61**
GYPSY WOMAN — Brian **Hyland** (42)	**71**
HA CHA CHA(FUNKTION) — **Brass Construction** (37)	**77**
HA HA SAID THE CLOWN — **Manfred Mann** (4)	**67**
HAITIAN DIVORCE — **Steely Dan** (17)	**76**
HALEY'S GOLDEN MEDLEY — Bill **Haley and his Comets** (50)	**81**
HALF AS MUCH — Rosemary **Clooney** (3)	**52**
HALF OF MY HEART — Emile **Ford and the Checkmates** (42)	**61**
HALFWAY DOWN THE STAIRS — **Muppets** (7)	**77**
HALFWAY HOTEL — **Voyager** (33)	**79**
HALFWAY TO PARADISE — Billy **Fury** (3)	**61**
HALFWAY UP HALFWAY DOWN — Dennis **Brown** (56)	**82**
HALLELUJAH — **Milk and Honey** (5)	**79**
HALLELUJAH DAY — **Jackson Five** (20)	**73**
HALLELUJAH FREEDOM — Junior **Campbell** (10)	**72**
HALLELUJAH I LOVE HER SO — Eddie **Cochran** (22)	**60**
HALLELUJAH I LOVE HER SO — Dick **Jordan** (47)	**60**
HAMMER HORROR — Kate **Bush** (44)	**78**
HAND A HANDKERCHIEF TO HELEN — Susan **Maughan** (41)	**63**
HAND HELD IN BLACK AND WHITE — **Dollar** (19)	**81**
HANDBAGS & GLADRAGS — Chris **Farlowe** (33)	**67**
HANDFUL OF SONGS — Tommy **Steele** (5)	**57**
HANDS OFF - SHE'S MINE — The **Beat** (9)	**80**
HANDS UP (GIVE ME YOUR HEART) — **Ottawan** (3)	**81**
HANDY MAN — Jimmy **Jones** (3)	**60**
HANDY MAN — Del **Shannon** (36)	**64**
HANG 'EM HIGH — Hugo **Montenegro** (50)	**69**
HANG ON IN THERE BABY — Johnny **Bristol** (3)	**74**
HANG ON SLOOPY — **McCoys** (5)	**65**
HANG ON SLOOPY — **Sandpipers** (32)	**76**
HANG ON TO A DREAM — Tim **Hardin** (50)	**67**
HANG TOGETHER — **Odyssey** (36)	**81**
HANGIN' OUT — **Kool and the Gang** (52)	**80**
HANGING AROUND — Hazel **O'Connor** (45)	**81**
HANGING GARDEN — **Cure** (34)	**82**
HANGING ON THE TELEPHONE — **Blondie** (5)	**78**
HANKY PANKY — Tommy **James and the Shondells** (38)	**66**
HAPPENING, THE — **Supremes** (6)	**67**
HAPPENINGS TEN YEARS TIME AGO — **Yardbirds** (43)	**66**
HAPPINESS — Ken **Dodd** (31)	**64**
HAPPINESS IS ME AND YOU — Gilbert **O'Sullivan** (19)	**74**
HAPPY ANNIVERSARY — Joan **Regan** (29)	**60**
HAPPY ANNIVERSARY [B] — Slim **Whitman** (14)	**74**
HAPPY BIRTHDAY [A] — Stevie **Wonder** (2)	**80**
HAPPY BIRTHDAY [B] — **Altered Images** (2)	**81**
HAPPY BIRTHDAY SWEET SIXTEEN — Neil **Sedaka** (3)	**61**
HAPPY DAYS — **Pratt and McLain Brotherlove** (31)	**77**
HAPPY DAYS & LONELY NIGHTS — Suzi **Miller** (14)	**55**
HAPPY DAYS & LONELY NIGHTS — Ruby **Murray** (6)	**55**
HAPPY DAYS & LONELY NIGHTS — Frankie **Vaughan** (12)	**55**
HAPPY FEELING — Hamilton **Bohannon** (49)	**75**
HAPPY GO LUCKY ME — George **Formby** (40)	**60**
HAPPY GUITAR — Tommy **Steele** (20)	**58**
HAPPY HEART — Andy **Williams** (19)	**69**
HAPPY HOUSE — **Siouxsie and the Banshees** (17)	**80**
HAPPY JACK — **Who** (3)	**66**
H.A.P.P.Y. RADIO — Edwin **Starr** (9)	**79**
HAPPY SONG — Otis **Redding** (24)	**68**
HAPPY TALK — **Captain Sensible** (1)	**82**
HAPPY TO BE ON AN ISLAND IN THE SUN — Demis **Roussos** (5)	**75**
HAPPY TO MAKE YOUR ACQUAINTANCE — Sammy **Davis Jr. and Carmen McRae** (46)	**60**
HAPPY TOGETHER — **Turtles** (12)	**67**
HAPPY WANDERER — **Obernkirchen Children's Choir** (2)	**54**
HAPPY WANDERER — **Stargazers** (12)	**54**
HAPPY WHISTLER, THE — Don **Robertson** (8)	**56**
HAPPY WHISTLER, THE — Cyril **Stapleton** (22)	**56**
HAPPY XMAS (WAR IS OVER) — John **Lennon** (2)	**72,75**
HARBOUR LIGHTS — **Platters** (11)	**60**
HARD DAY'S NIGHT, A — **Beatles** (1)	**64**
HARD DAY'S NIGHT, A — Peter **Sellers** (14)	**65**
HARD HEADED WOMAN — Elvis **Presley** (2)	**58**
HARD HEARTED HANNAH — **Temperance Seven** (28)	**61**
HARD RAIN'S GONNA FALL, A — Bryan **Ferry** (10)	**73**
HARD ROAD — **Black Sabbath** (33)	**78**
HARD TO HANDLE — Otis **Redding** (15)	**68**
HARD TO SAY I'M SORRY — **Chicago** (4)	**82**
HARD WAY, THE — **Nashville Teens** (45)	**66**
HARDEN MY HEART — **Quaterflash** (49)	**82**
HARE KRISHNA MANTRA — **Radha Krishna Temple** (12)	**69**
HARLEM SHUFFLE — **Bob and Earl** (7)	**69**
HARMONY IN MY HEAD — **Buzzcocks** (32)	**79**
HARMOUR LOVE — **Syreeta** (32)	**75**
HARPER VALLEY P. T. A. — Jeannie C. **Riley** (12)	**68**
THEME FROM HARRY'S GAME — **Clannad** (5)	**82**
HARVEST FOR THE WORLD — **Isley Brothers** (10)	**76**
HARVEST OF LOVE — Benny **Hill** (20)	**63**
HASTA LA VISTA — **Sylvia** (38)	**75**
HATS OFF TO LARRY — Del **Shannon** (6)	**61**
HAVA NAGILA — **Spotnicks** (13)	**63**
HAVE A DRINK ON ME — Lonnie **Donegan** (8)	**61**
HAVE I STAYED TOO LONG — **Sonny and Cher** (42)	**66**
HAVE I THE RIGHT — **Dead End Kids** (6)	**77**
HAVE I THE RIGHT — **Honeycombs** (1)	**64**
HAVE PITY ON THE BOY — Paul and Barry **Ryan** (18)	**66**
HAVE YOU EVER BEEN IN LOVE — Leo **Sayer** (10)	**82**
HAVE YOU EVER LOVED SOMEBODY — Paul and Barry **Ryan** (49)	**66**
HAVE YOU EVER LOVED SOMEBODY — **Searchers** (48)	**66**
HAVE YOU EVER SEEN THE RAIN — **Creedence Clearwater Revival** (36)	**71**
HAVE YOU SEEN HER — **Chi-Lites** (3)	**72,75**
HAVE YOU SEEN YOUR MOTHER BABY STANDING IN THE SHADOW — **Rolling Stones** (5)	**66**
HAVEN'T STOPPED DANCING YET — **Gonzalez** (15)	**79**
HAVEN'T YOU HEARD — Patrice **Rushen** (62)	**80**
HAVING A PARTY — **Osmonds** (28)	**75**
HAWAIIAN TATTOO — **Waikikis** (41)	**65**
HAWAIIAN WEDDING SONG — Julie **Rogers** (31)	**65**
HAWKEYE — Frankie **Laine** (7)	**55**
HAZELL — Maggie **Bell** (37)	**78**
HE AIN'T HEAVY HE'S MY BROTHER — **Hollies** (3)	**69**
HE GOT WHAT HE WANTED — **Little Richard** (38)	**62**
HE WAS BEAUTIFUL (CAVATINA) (THE THEME FROM THE DEER HUNTER) — Iris **Williams** (18)	**79**
HEAD OVER HEELS — **Abba** (25)	**82**
HEAD OVER HEELS IN LOVE — Kevin **Keegan** (31)	**79**
HEADLINE NEWS — Edwin **Starr** (11)	**66,68**
HEADS DOWN NO NONSENSE MINDLESS BOOGIE — **Alberto Y Lost Trios Paranoias** (47)	**78**
HEART [A] — Max **Bygraves** (14)	**57**
HEART [A] — **Johnston Brothers** (23)	**57**
HEART [B] — Rita **Pavone** (27)	**66**
HEART AND SOUL [A] — **Jan and Dean** (24)	**61**
HEART AND SOUL [B] — **Exile** (54)	**81**
HEART ATTACK — Olivia **Newton-John** (46)	**82**
HEART FULL OF SOUL — **Yardbirds** (2)	**65**
HEART OF A TEENAGE GIRL — George **Chakiris** (49)	**60**
HEART OF A TEENAGE GIRL, THE — Craig **Douglas** (10)	**60**
HEART OF GLASS — **Blondie** (1)	**79**
HEART OF GOLD — Neil **Young** (10)	**72**
HEART OF MAN, THE — Frankie **Vaughan** (5)	**59**
HEART OF MY HEART — Max **Bygraves** (7)	**54**
HEART OF STONE [A] — **Kenny** (11)	**73**
HEART OF STONE [B] — Suzi **Quatro** (60)	**82**
HEART ON MY SLEEVE — **Gallagher and Lyle** (6)	**76**
HEART (STOP BEATING IN TIME) — Leo **Sayer** (22)	**82**
HEARTACHE — Roy **Orbison** (44)	**68**
HEARTACHE AVENUE — **Maisonettes** (39)	**82**
HEARTACHE TONIGHT — **Eagles** (40)	**79**
HEARTACHES — Patsy **Cline** (31)	**62**
HEARTACHES — Vince **Hill** (28)	**66**
HEARTACHES BY THE NUMBER — Guy **Mitchell** (5)	**59**
HEARTBEAT [A] — Ruby **Murray** (3)	**54**
HEARTBEAT [B] — **England Sisters** (33)	**60**
HEARTBEAT [B] — Buddy **Holly** (30)	**59,60**
HEARTBEAT [B] — **Showaddywaddy** (7)	**75**
HEARTBEAT [C] — Sammy **Hagar** (67)	**80**
HEARTBREAK HOTEL — Stan **Freberg** (29)	**56**
HEARTBREAK HOTEL — Elvis **Presley** (10)	**56,71**
HEARTBREAK HOTEL [A] — Stan **Freberg** (24)	**56**
HEARTBREAK HOTEL [A] — Elvis **Presley** (2)	**56**
HEARTBREAK HOTEL [B] — **Jacksons** (44)	**80**
HEARTBREAKER — Dionne **Warwick** (2)	**82**
HEARTLIGHT — Neil **Diamond** (47)	**82**
HEARTSONG — Gordon **Giltrap** (21)	**78**
HEAT OF THE BEAT — Roy **Ayers and Wayne Henderson** (43)	**79**
HEAT OF THE MOMENT — **Asia** (46)	**82**
HEATHER HONEY — Tommy **Roe** (24)	**69**
HEAVEN AND HELL, THIRD MOVEMENT (THEME FROM THE BBC-TV SERIES, THE COSMOS) — **Vangelis** (48)	**81**
HEAVEN HELP US ALL — Stevie **Wonder** (29)	**70**
HEAVEN IS HERE — Julie **Felix** (22)	**70**
HEAVEN IS IN THE BACK SEAT OF MY CADILLIAC — **Hot Chocolate** (25)	**76**
HEAVEN IS MY WOMAN'S LOVE — Val **Doonican** (34)	**73**
HEAVEN KNOWS — Donna **Summer** (34)	**79**
HEAVEN MUST BE MISSING AN ANGEL — **Tavares** (4)	**76**
HEAVEN MUST HAVE SENT YOU — **Elgins** (3)	**71**
HEAVEN ON THE 7TH FLOOR — Paul **Nicholas** (40)	**77**
HEAVENLY — **Showaddywaddy** (34)	**75**
HEAVY MAKES YOU HAPPY — Bobby **Bloom** (31)	**71**
HELEN WHEELS — **Wings** (12)	**73**
HELL HATH NO FURY — Frankie **Laine** (28)	**56**
HE'LL HAVE TO GO — Jim **Reeves** (12)	**60**
HE'LL HAVE TO GO — Jim **Reeves** (34)	**71**

Title — Act (Position)	Year of Chart Entry
HE'LL HAVE TO STAY — Jeanne **Black** (41)	**60**
HELL RAISER — **Sweet** (2)	**73**
HELLBOUND — **Tygers of Pan Tang** (48)	**81**
HELLO AGAIN — Neil **Diamond** (51)	**81**
HELLO AMERICA — **Def Leppard** (45)	**80**
HELLO BUDDY — **Tremeloes** (32)	**71**
HELLO DOLLY — Louis **Armstrong** (4)	**64**
HELLO DOLLY — **Bachelors** (38)	**66**
HELLO DOLLY — Kenny **Ball and his Jazzmen** (30)	**64**
HELLO DOLLY — Frank **Sinatra** (47)	**64**
HELLO DOLLY — Frankie **Vaughan** (18)	**64**
HELLO GOODBYE — **Beatles** (1)	**67**
HELLO HAPPINESS — **Drifters** (12)	**76**
HELLO HEARTACHE GOODBYE LOVE — Little Peggy **March** (29)	**63**
HELLO HELLO I'M BACK AGAIN — Gary **Glitter** (2)	**73**
HELLO HOW ARE YOU — **Easybeats** (20)	**68**
HELLO HURRAY — Alice **Cooper** (6)	**73**
HELLO I AM YOUR HEART — Bette **Bright** (50)	**80**
HELLO I LOVE YOU — **Doors** (15)	**68,79**
HELLO JOSEPHINE — Wayne **Fontana and the Mindbenders** (46)	**63**
HELLO LITTLE GIRL — **Fourmost** (9)	**63**
HELLO MARY LOU — Rick **Nelson** (2)	**61**
HELLO MUDDAH HELLO FADDAH — Allan **Sherman** (14)	**63**
HELLO STRANGER — Yvonne **Elliman** (26)	**77**
HELLO SUMMERTIME — Bobby **Goldsboro** (14)	**74**
HELLO SUZIE — **Amen Corner** (4)	**69**
HELLO THIS IS JOANIE (THE TELEPHONE ANSWERING MACHINE SONG) — Paul **Evans** (6)	**78**
HELLO WORLD — **Tremeloes** (14)	**69**
HELLO YOUNG LOVERS — Paul **Anka** (44)	**60**
HELP! — **Beatles** (1)	**65,76**
HELP, GET ME SOME HELP! — **Ottawan** (49)	**81**
HELP IT ALONG — Cliff **Richard** (29)	**73**
HELP ME GIRL — Eric **Burdon** (14)	**66**
HELP ME MAKE IT THROUGH THE NIGHT — John **Holt** (6)	**74**
HELP ME MAKE IT THROUGH THE NIGHT — Gladys **Knight and the Pips** (11)	**72**
HELP ME RHONDA — **Beach Boys** (27)	**65**
HELP YOURSELF — Tom **Jones** (5)	**68**
HELULE HELULE — **Tremeloes** (14)	**68**
HER ROYAL MAJESTY — James **Darren** (36)	**62**
HERCULES — Frankie **Vaughan** (42)	**62**
HERE COMES MY BABY — **Tremeloes** (4)	**67**
HERE COMES SUMMER — Dave **Clark Five** (44)	**70**
HERE COMES SUMMER — Jerry **Keller** (1)	**59**
HERE COMES THAT FEELING — Brenda **Lee** (5)	**62**
HERE COMES THE JUDGE [A] — Shorty **Long** (30)	**68**
HERE COMES THE JUDGE [B] — Pigmeat **Markham** (19)	**68**
HERE COMES THE NICE — **Small Faces** (12)	**67**
HERE COMES THE NIGHT [A] — **Beach Boys** (37)	**79**
HERE COMES THE NIGHT [B] — **Lulu** (50)	**64**
HERE COMES THE NIGHT [B] — **Them** (2)	**65**
HERE COMES THE STAR — **Herman's Hermits** (33)	**69**
HERE COMES THE SUMMER — **Undertones** (34)	**79**
HERE COMES THE SUN — Steve **Harley and COCKNEY REBEL** (10)	**76**
HERE I GO AGAIN [A] — **Hollies** (4)	**64**
HERE I GO AGAIN [B] — Archie **Bell and the Drells** (11)	**72**
HERE I GO AGAIN [C] — **Guys and Dolls** (33)	**75**
HERE I GO AGAIN [D] — **Twiggy** (17)	**76**
HERE I GO AGAIN [E] — **Whitesnake** (34)	**82**
HERE IN MY HEART — Al **Martino** (1)	**52**
HERE IS THE NEWS — **Electric Light Orchestra** (24)	**82**
HERE IT COMES AGAIN — **Fortunes** (4)	**65**
HERE THERE AND EVERYWHERE — Emmylou **Harris** (30)	**76**
HERE WE GO AGAIN — Ray **Charles** (38)	**67**
HERE WE GO ROUND THE MULBERRY BUSH — **Traffic** (8)	**67**
HERE'S TO LOVE (AULD LANG SYNE) — John **Christie** (24)	**76**
HERNANDO'S HIDEAWAY — **Johnston Brothers** (1)	**55**
HERNANDO'S HIDEAWAY — Johnnie **Ray** (11)	**55**
HEROES — David **Bowie** (24)	**77**
HEROES AND VILLAINS — **Beach Boys** (8)	**67**
HERSHAM BOYS — **Sham 69** (6)	**79**
HE'S A REBEL — **Crystals** (19)	**62**
HE'S GONNA STEP ON YOU AGAIN — John **Kongos** (4)	**71**
HE'S GOT NO LOVE — **Searchers** (12)	**65**
HE'S GOT THE WHOLE WORLD IN HIS HANDS — Laurie **London** (12)	**57**
HE'S IN TOWN — **Rockin' Berries** (3)	**64**
HE'S MISSTRA KNOW IT ALL — Stevie **Wonder** (10)	**74**
HE'S OLD ENOUGH TO KNOW BETTER — **Brook Brothers** (37)	**62**
HE'S SO FINE — **Chiffons** (16)	**63**
HE'S THE GREATEST DANCER — **Sister Sledge** (6)	**79**
HE'S THE ONE — Billie **Davis** (40)	**63**
HEY AMERICA — James **Brown** (47)	**71**
HEY! BABY — Bruce **Channel** (2)	**62**
HEY GIRL [A] — **Small Faces** (10)	**66**
HEY GIRL [B] — **Expressos** (60)	**80**
HEY GIRL DON'T BOTHER ME — **Tams** (1)	**71**
HEY GOOD LOOKIN' — Bo **Diddley** (39)	**65**
HEY GOOD LOOKING — Tommy **Zang** (45)	**61**
HEY JOE [A] — Frankie **Laine** (1)	**53**
HEY JOE [B] — Jimi **Hendrix Experience** (6)	**67**
HEY JUDE — **Beatles** (1)	**68,76**
HEY JUDE — Wilson **Pickett** (16)	**69**
HEY LITTLE GIRL — Del **Shannon** (2)	**62**
HEY LORD DON'T ASK ME QUESTIONS — Graham **Parker and the Rumour** (32)	**78**
HEY MAMA [A] — Frankie **Vaughan** (21)	**63**
HEY MAMA [B] — Joe **Brown** (33)	**73**
HEY MISS PAYNE — **Chequers** (32)	**76**
HEY MR. CHRISTMAS — **Showaddywaddy** (13)	**74**
HEY MR. DREAM MAKER — Cliff **Richard** (31)	**76**
HEY MR. MUSIC MAN — **Peters and Lee** (16)	**76**
HEY PAULA — **Paul and Paula** (8)	**63**
HEY ROCK AND ROLL — **Showaddywaddy** (2)	**74**
HEY SENORITA — **War** (40)	**78**
HEY THERE — Rosemary **Clooney** (4)	**55**
HEY THERE — Sammy **Davis Jr.** (19)	**55**
HEY THERE — Johnnie **Ray** (5)	**55**
HEY THERE — Lita **Roza** (17)	**55**
(HEY THERE) LONELY GIRL — Eddie **Holman** (4)	**74**
HEY WILLY — **Hollies** (22)	**71**
HEY YOU — Tommy **Steele** (28)	**57**
HEYKENS SERENADE — The Pipes and Drums and Military Band of the **Royal Scots Dragoon Guards** (30)	**72**
HI DE HI, HI DE HO — **Kool and the Gang** (29)	**82**
HI DE HI (HOLIDAY ROCK) — Paul **Shane and the Yellowcoats** (36)	**81**
HI FIDELITY — Elvis **Costello and the Attractions** (30)	**80**
HI HI HAZEL — **Troggs** (42)	**67**
HI HI HAZEL — Geno **Washington and the Ram Jam Band** (45)	**66**
HI HI HI — **Wings** (5)	**72**
HI LILI HI LO — Alan **Price** (11)	**66**
HI TENSION — **Hi Tension** (13)	**78**
HIDE AND SEEK — Marty **Wilde** (47)	**61**
HIDEAWAY — **Dave Dee, Dozy, Beaky, Mick and Tich** (10)	**66**
HI-FIDELITY [B] — **Kids From 'Fame'** (5)	**82**
HIGH CLASS BABY — Cliff **Richard** (7)	**58**
HIGH FLY — John **Miles** (17)	**75**
HIGH HOPES — Frank **Sinatra** (6)	**59**
HIGH IN THE SKY — **Amen Corner** (6)	**68**
HIGH NOON — Frankie **Laine** (7)	**52**
HIGH SCHOOL CONFIDENTIAL — Jerry Lee **Lewis** (12)	**59**
HIGH TIME — Paul **Jones** (4)	**66**
HIGH VOLTAGE — **Johnny and the Hurricanes** (24)	**61**
HIGH VOLTAGE (LIVE VERSION) — **AC/DC** (48)	**80**
HIGHER AND HIGHER — Jackie **Wilson** (25)	**75**
HIGHER GROUND — Stevie **Wonder** (29)	**73**
HIGHLY INFLAMMABLE — **X-Ray Spex** (45)	**79**
HIGHWAY CODE — **Master Singers** (25)	**66**
HIGHWAY OF MY LIFE — **Isley Brothers** (25)	**74**
HIGHWAY SONG — Nancy **Sinatra** (21)	**69**
HIGHWAY TO HELL — **AC/DC** (56)	**79**
HIGHWIRE — Linda **Carr and the Love Squad** (15)	**75**
HI-HEEL SNEAKERS — Tommy **Tucker** (23)	**64**
HI-HO SILVER LINING — Jeff **Beck** (14)	**67,72**
HI-LILI HI-LO — Richard **Chamberlain** (20)	**63**
HIM — Rupert **Holmes** (31)	**80**
HIPPY HIPPY SHAKE — **Swinging Blue Jeans** (2)	**63**
HIS GIRL — **Guess Who** (45)	**67**
HIS LATEST FLAME — Elvis **Presley** (1)	**61**
HISTORY NEVER REPEATS — **Split Enz** (63)	**81**
HISTORY OF THE WORLD (PART 1) — **Damned** (51)	**80**
HIT AND MISS — John **Barry** (10)	**60**
HIT AND RUN — **Girlschool** (32)	**81**
HIT IT — The **Beat** (70)	**81**
HIT ME WITH YOUR RHYTHM STICK — Ian **Dury and the Blockheads** (1)	**78**
HIT THE ROAD JACK — Ray **Charles** (6)	**61**
HITCHIN' A RIDE — **Vanity Fare** (16)	**69**
HITSVILLE UK — **Clash** (56)	**81**
HOCUS POCUS — **Focus** (20)	**73**
HOKEY COKEY — **Judge Dread** (59)	**78**
HOKEY COKEY — **Snowmen** (18)	**81**
HOKOYO — **Orange Juice** (60)	**82**
HOLD BACK THE NIGHT — **Trammps** (5)	**75**
HOLD BACK TOMORROW — **Miki and Griff** (26)	**59**
HOLD ME — P. J. **Proby** (3)	**64**
HOLD ME — B.A. **Robertson and Maggie Bell** (11)	**81**
HOLD ME CLOSE — David **Essex** (1)	**75**
HOLD ME THRILL ME KISS ME — Muriel **Smith** (3)	**53**
HOLD ME TIGHT — Johnny **Nash** (5)	**68**
HOLD MY HAND [A] — Don **Cornell** (1)	**54**
HOLD MY HAND [B] — Ken **Dodd** (44)	**81**
HOLD ON — **Streetband** (18)	**78**
HOLD ON TIGHT — **Electric Light Orchestra** (4)	**81**
HOLD ON TO LOVE — Peter **Skellern** (14)	**75**
HOLD ON TO MY LOVE — Jimmy **Ruffin** (7)	**80**
HOLD THE LINE — **Toto** (14)	**79**
HOLD TIGHT [A] — **Dave Dee, Dozy, Beaky, Mick and Tich** (4)	**66**
HOLD TIGHT [B] — **Liverpool Express** (46)	**76**
HOLD YOUR HEAD UP — **Argent** (5)	**72**
HOLD YOUR HORSES BABE — Celi **Bee and the Buzzy Bunch** (72)	**78**
HOLDIN' ON [A] — Tony **Rallo and the Midnight Band** (34)	**80**
HOLDING ON [B] — **L.T.D.** (70)	**78**
HOLE IN MY SHOE — **Traffic** (2)	**67**
HOLE IN THE BUCKET — Harry **Belafonte and Odetta** (32)	**61**
HOLE IN THE GROUND — Bernard **Cribbins** (9)	**62**
HOLIDAY 80 (DOUBLE SINGLE) — **Human League** (56)	**80**
HOLIDAY 80 (DOUBLE SINGLE) — **Human League** (46)	**82**
HOLIDAYS IN THE SUN — **Sex Pistols** (8)	**77**
HOLLIEDAZE (A MEDLEY) — **Hollies** (28)	**81**
HOLLYWOOD — Boz **Scaggs** (33)	**77**
HOLLYWOOD (DOWN ON YOUR LUCK) — **Thin Lizzy** (53)	**82**
HOLLYWOOD NIGHTS — Bob **Seger and the Silver Bullet Band** (42)	**78,81**
HOLLYWOOD SWINGING — **Kool and the Gang** (17)	**81**
HOLLYWOOD TEASE — **Girl** (50)	**80**
HOLY CITY — Moira **Anderson** (43)	**69**
HOLY COW — Lee **Dorsey** (6)	**66**
HOLY JOE — **Haysi Fantayzee** (51)	**82**
HOLY ROLLER — **Nazareth** (36)	**75**
HOMBURG — **Procol Harum** (6)	**67**
HOME IS WHERE THE HEART IS — Gladys **Knight and the Pips** (35)	**77**
HOME LOVIN' MAN — Andy **Williams** (7)	**70**
HOME OF THE BRAVE — Jody **Miller** (49)	**65**
HOMELY GIRL — **Chi-Lites** (5)	**74**
HOMEWARD BOUND — **Quiet Five** (44)	**66**
HOMEWARD BOUND — **Simon and Garfunkel** (9)	**66**
HOMICIDE — **999** (40)	**78**
HOMING WALTZ — Vera **Lynn** (9)	**52**
HONALOOCHIE BOOGIE — **Mott The Hoople** (12)	**73**
HONEST I DO — Danny **Storm** (42)	**62**
HONEST I DO LOVE YOU — Candi **Staton** (48)	**78**
HONEY — Bobby **Goldsboro** (2)	**68,75**
HONEY CHILE [A] — Fats **Domino** (29)	**57**
HONEY CHILE [B] — Martha **Reeves and the Vandellas** (30)	**68**
HONEY COME BACK — Glen **Campbell** (4)	**70**
HONEY HONEY — **Sweet Dreams** (10)	**74**
HONEY I — George **McCrae** (33)	**76**
HONEY I NEED — **Pretty Things** (13)	**65**
HONEY I'M LOST — **Dooleys** (24)	**79**
HONEYCOMB — Jimmie **Rodgers** (30)	**57**
HONEYDRIPPER, THE — **Jets** (58)	**82**
HONEYMOON, THEME FROM — **Manuel and his Music Of The Mountains** (22)	**59**
HONG KONG BEAT, THEME FROM THE — Richard **Denton and Martin Cook** (25)	**78**
HONG KONG GARDEN — **Siouxsie and the Banshees** (7)	**78**
HONKY CAT — Elton **John** (31)	**72**
HONKY TONK TRAIN BLUES — Keith **Emerson** (21)	**76**
HONKY TONK WOMEN — **Rolling Stones** (1)	**69**
HOOKED ON A FEELING — Jonathan **King** (23)	**71**
HOOKED ON CAN-CAN — **Royal Philharmonic Orchestra arranged and conducted by Louis Clark** (47)	**81**
HOOKED ON CLASSICS — **Royal Philharmonic Orchestra arranged and conducted by Louis Clark** (2)	**81**

Title — Act (Position)	Year of Chart Entry
HOORAY! HOORAY! IT'S A HOLI HOLIDAY — **Boney M** (3)	**79**
HOOTS MON — Lord **Rockingham's XI** (1)	**58**
HOP, THE — **Theatre Of Hate** (70)	**82**
HOPELESSLY DEVOTED TO YOU — Olivia **Newton-John** (2)	**78**
HORSE — **Splodgenessabounds** (26)	**80**
HORSE WITH NO NAME — **America** (3)	**71**
HOT BLOODED — **Foreigner** (42)	**78**
HOT DIGGITY — Perry **Como** (4)	**56**
HOT DIGGITY — Michael **Holliday** (14)	**56**
HOT DIGGITY — **Stargazers** (28)	**56**
HOT DOG — Shakin' **Stevens** (24)	**80**
HOT IN THE CITY — Billy **Idol** (58)	**82**
HOT LOVE [A] — David **Essex** (57)	**80**
HOT LOVE [B] — **T. Rex** (1)	**71**
HOT LOVE [C] — Kelly **Marie** (22)	**81**
HOT PEPPER — Floyd **Cramer** (46)	**62**
HOT ROCKIN' — **Judas Priest** (60)	**81**
HOT SHOT [A] — Barry **Blue** (23)	**74**
HOT SHOT [B] — Karen **Young** (34)	**78,79**
HOT SHOT [C] — Cliff **Richard** (46)	**79**
HOT STUFF — Donna **Summer** (11)	**79**
HOT TODDY — Ted **Heath** (6)	**53**
HOT TRACKS (EP) — **Nazareth** (15)	**77**
HOT VALVES (EP) — **Be Bop Deluxe** (36)	**76**
HOTEL CALIFORNIA — **Eagles** (8)	**77**
HOTLEGS — Rod **Stewart** (5)	**78**
HOUND DOG — Elvis **Presley** (2)	**56,71**
HOUND DOG MAN — **Fabian** (46)	**60**
HOUSE IN THE COUNTRY, A — **Pretty Things** (50)	**66**
HOUSE OF FUN — **Madness** (1)	**82**
HOUSE OF THE RISING SUN — **Animals** (1)	**64,72**
HOUSE OF THE RISING SUN — **Frijid Pink** (4)	**70**
HOUSE ON FIRE — **Boomtown Rats** (24)	**82**
HOUSE THAT JACK BUILT, THE — Alan **Price** (4)	**67**
HOUSE WITH LOVE IN IT, A — Vera **Lynn** (17)	**56**
HOUSES IN MOTION — **Talking Heads** (50)	**81**
HOW ABOUT THAT — Adam **Faith** (4)	**60**
HOW 'BOUT US — **Champagne** (5)	**81**
HOW CAN I BE SURE — David **Cassidy** (1)	**72**
HOW CAN I BE SURE — Dusty **Springfield** (36)	**70**
HOW CAN I MEET HER — **Everly Brothers** (12)	**62**
HOW CAN I TELL HER — **Fourmost** (33)	**64**
HOW CAN THIS BE LOVE — Andrew **Gold** (19)	**78**
HOW CAN YOU TELL — Sandie **Shaw** (21)	**65**
HOW COME — Ronnie **Lane** (11)	**74**
HOW COULD THIS GO WRONG — **Exile** (67)	**79**
HOW COULD WE DARE TO BE WRONG — Colin **Blunstone** (45)	**73**
HOW DEEP IS YOUR LOVE — **Bee Gees** (3)	**77**
HOW DO YOU DO — Al **Hudson and the Partners** (57)	**78**
HOW DO YOU DO IT? — **Gerry and the Pacemakers** (1)	**63**
HOW DO YOU KNOW IT'S LOVE — Teresa **Brewer** (21)	**60**
HOW DO YOU SPEAK TO AN ANGEL — Dean **Martin** (15)	**54**
HOW DOES IT FEEL — **Slade** (15)	**75**
HOW DOES THAT GRAB YOU DARLIN' — Nancy **Sinatra** (19)	**66**
HOW HIGH THE MOON — Ella **Fitzgerald** (46)	**60**
HOW HIGH THE MOON — Gloria **Gaynor** (33)	**76**
HOW LONG — **Ace** (20)	**74**
HOW LONG — Rod **Stewart** (41)	**82**
HOW LONG HAS IT BEEN — Jim **Reeves** (45)	**65**
HOW MANY TEARS — Bobby **Vee** (10)	**61**
(HOW MUCH IS) THAT DOGGIE IN THE WINDOW — Patti **Page** (9)	**53**
(HOW MUCH IS) THAT DOGGIE IN THE WINDOW — Lita **Roza** (1)	**53**
HOW MUCH LOVE — Leo **Sayer** (10)	**77**
HOW SOON — Henry **Mancini** (10)	**64**
HOW SWEET IT IS — Marvin **Gaye** (49)	**64**
HOW SWEET IT IS — Junior **Walker and the All-Stars** (22)	**66**
HOW WONDERFUL TO KNOW — **Pearl Carr and Teddy Johnson** (23)	**61**
HOW YOU GONNA SEE ME NOW — Alice **Cooper** (61)	**78**
HOWZAT — **Sherbet** (4)	**76**
HUBBLE BUBBLE TOIL AND TROUBLE — **Manfred Mann** (11)	**64**
HUMMING BIRD — Frankie **Laine** (16)	**55**
HUMPIN' — **Gap Band** (36)	**81**
101 DAM-NATIONS — **Scarlet Party** (44)	**82**
HUNDRED POUNDS OF CLAY, A — Craig **Douglas** (9)	**61**
HUNGRY FOR LOVE — Johnny **Kidd and the Pirates** (20)	**63**
HUNGRY HEART — Bruce **Springsteen** (44)	**80**
HUNGRY LIKE THE WOLF — **Duran Duran** (5)	**82**
HUNT — Barry **Ryan** (34)	**69**
HURDY GURDY MAN — **Donovan** (4)	**68**
HURRICANE — Bob **Dylan** (43)	**76**
HURRY HOME — **Wavelength** (17)	**82**
HURRY UP HARRY — **Sham 69** (10)	**78**
HURT [A] — **Manhattans** (4)	**76**
HURT [B] — Elvis **Presley** (37)	**76**
HURT BY LOVE — Inez **Foxx** (40)	**64**
HURT SO GOOD — Susan **Cadogan** (4)	**75**
HUSH NOT A WORD TO MARY — John **Rowles** (12)	**68**
HUSTLE, THE — Van **McCoy** (3)	**75**
HYMN — **Ultravox** (13)	**82**
HYPNOSIS — **Mud** (16)	**73**
I AIN'T GONNA STAND FOR IT — Stevie **Wonder** (10)	**80**
I AIN'T GOT TIME ANYMORE — Cliff **Richard** (21)	**70**
I AIN'T LYIN' — George **McCrae** (12)	**75**
I ALMOST LOST MY MIND — Pat **Boone** (14)	**56**
I AM . . . I SAID — Neil **Diamond** (4)	**71**
I AM A CIDER DRINKER (PALOMA BLANCA) — **Wurzels** (3)	**76**
I AM A ROCK — **Simon and Garfunkel** (17)	**66**
I AM THE BEAT — **Look** (6)	**80**
I AM WHAT I AM — **Greyhound** (20)	**72**
I APOLOGISE — P. J. **Proby** (11)	**65**
I BELIEVE — **Bachelors** (2)	**64**
I BELIEVE — Frankie **Laine** (1)	**53**
I BELIEVE — David **Whitfield** (49)	**60**
I BELIEVE I'M GONNA LOVE YOU — Frank **Sinatra** (34)	**75**
I BELIEVE IN FATHER CHRISTMAS — Greg **Lake** (2)	**75**
I BELIEVE (IN LOVE) — **Hot Chocolate** (8)	**71**
I BELIEVE YOU — Dorothy **Moore** (20)	**77**
I BELONG — Kathy **Kirby** (36)	**65**
I CAN DANCE — Brian **Poole and the Tremeloes** (31)	**63**
I CAN DO IT — **Rubettes** (7)	**75**
I CAN HEAR MUSIC — **Beach Boys** (10)	**69**
I CAN HEAR THE GRASS GROW — **Move** (5)	**67**
I CAN HELP — Billy **Swan** (6)	**74**
I CAN MAKE IT BETTER — **Whispers** (44)	**81**
I CAN MAKE YOU FEEL GOOD — **Shalamar** (7)	**82**
I CAN PROVE IT — Tony **Etoria** (21)	**77**
I CAN SEE CLEARLY NOW — Johnny **Nash** (5)	**72**
I CAN SEE FOR MILES — **Who** (10)	**67**
I CAN SEE HER NOW — **Dramatis** (57)	**82**
I CAN SING A RAINBOW - LOVE IS BLUE (MEDLEY) — **Dells** (15)	**69**
I CAN TAKE OR LEAVE YOUR LOVING — **Herman's Hermits** (11)	**68**
I CAN'T ASK FOR ANYMORE THAN YOU — Cliff **Richard** (17)	**76**
I CAN'T CONTROL MYSELF — **Troggs** (2)	**66**
I CAN'T EXPLAIN — **Who** (8)	**65**
I CAN'T GET NEXT TO YOU — **Temptations** (13)	**70**
(I CAN'T GET NO) SATISFACTION — **Bubblerock** (29)	**74**
(I CAN'T GET NO) SATISFACTION — **Rolling Stones** (1)	**65**
I CAN'T GET YOU OUT OF MY MIND — Yvonne **Elliman** (17)	**77**
I CAN'T GO FOR THAT (NO CAN DO) — Daryl **Hall and John Oates** (8)	**82**
I CAN'T HELP IT — Johnny **Tillotson** (41)	**63,62**
LET ME KNOW — **Junior** (53)	**82**
I CAN'T HELP MYSELF [A] — Donnie **Elbert** (11)	**72**
I CAN'T HELP MYSELF [A] — **Four Tops** (10)	**65,70**
I CANT HELP MYSELF [B] — **Orange Juice** (42)	**82**
I CAN'T LEAVE YOU ALONE — George **McCrae** (9)	**74**
I CAN'T LET GO — **Hollies** (2)	**66**
I CAN'T LET MAGGIE GO — **Honeybus** (8)	**68**
I CAN'T LIVE A DREAM — **Osmonds** (37)	**76**
I CAN'T MAKE IT — **Small Faces** (26)	**67**
I CAN'T MAKE IT ALONE — P. J. **Proby** (37)	**66**
(I CAN'T ME GET NO) SATISFACTION — **Devo** (41)	**78**
I CAN'T SAY GOODBYE TO YOU — Helen **Reddy** (43)	**81**
I CAN'T STAND IT — Spencer **Davis Group** (47)	**64**
I CAN'T STAND MY BABY — **Rezillos** (71)	**79**
I CAN'T STAND THE RAIN — **Eruption** (5)	**78**
I CAN'T STAND THE RAIN — Ann **Peebles** (41)	**74**
I CAN'T STAND UP FOR FALLING DOWN — Elvis **Costello and the Attractions** (4)	**80**
I CAN'T STOP — **Osmonds** (12)	**74**
I CAN'T STOP LOVIN' YOU [A] — Leo **Sayer** (6)	**78**
I CAN'T STOP LOVING YOU [B] — Ray **Charles** (1)	**62**
I CAN'T TELL A WALTZ FROM A TANGO — Alma **Cogan** (6)	**54**
I CAN'T TELL THE BOTTOM FROM THE TOP — **Hollies** (7)	**70**
I CAN'T TURN AWAY — **Savannah** (61)	**81**
I CAN'T TURN YOU LOOSE — Otis **Redding** (29)	**66**
I CLOSE MY EYES AND COUNT TO TEN — Dusty **Springfield** (4)	**68**
I CONFESS — The **Beat** (54)	**82**
I COULD BE HAPPY — **Altered Images** (7)	**81**
I COULD BE SO GOOD FOR YOU — Dennis **Waterman with the Dennis Waterman Band** (3)	**80**
I COULD EASILY FALL — Cliff **Richard** (9)	**64**
I COULD NEVER LOVE ANOTHER — **Temptations** (47)	**68**
I COULD NEVER MISS YOU (MORE THAN I DO) — **Lulu** (62)	**81**
I COULDN'T LIVE WITHOUT YOUR LOVE — Petula **Clark** (6)	**66**
I COUNT THE TEARS — **Drifters** (28)	**61**
I CRIED FOR YOU — Ricky **Stevens** (34)	**61**
I DID WHAT I DID FOR MARIA — Tony **Christie** (2)	**71**
I DIDN'T KNOW I LOVED YOU (TILL I SAW YOU ROCK N ROLL) — Gary **Glitter** (4)	**72**
I DIDN'T MEAN TO HURT YOU — **Rockin' Berries** (43)	**64**
I DIE: YOU DIE — Gary **Numan** (6)	**80**
I DIG YOU BABY — Marvin **Rainwater** (19)	**58**
I DO I DO I DO I DO I DO — **Abba** (38)	**75**
I DON'T BELIEVE IN IF ANYMORE — Roger **Whittaker** (8)	**70**
I DON'T BELIEVE IN MIRACLES — Colin **Blunstone** (31)	**72**
I DON'T BLAME YOU AT ALL — Smokey **Robinson and the Miracles** (11)	**71**
I DON'T CARE [A] — **Bravos** (16)	**66**
I DON'T CARE [B] — **Liberace** (28)	**56**
I DON'T CARE IF THE SUN DON'T SHINE — Elvis **Presley** (23)	**56**
I DON'T KNOW HOW TO LOVE HIM — Petula **Clark** (47)	**72**
I DON'T KNOW HOW TO LOVE HIM — Yvonne **Elliman** (47)	**72**
I DON'T KNOW IF IT'S RIGHT — Evelyn **King** (67)	**79**
I DON'T KNOW WHY — Stevie **Wonder** (43)	**69**
I DON'T KNOW WHY [A] — Eden **Kane** (7)	**62**
I DON'T KNOW WHY [A] — Andy and David **Williams** (37)	**73**
I DON'T KNOW WHY [B] — Stevie **Wonder** (14)	**69**
I DON'T LIKE MONDAYS — **Boomtown Rats** (1)	**79**
I DON'T LOVE YOU BUT I THINK I LIKE YOU — Gilbert **O'Sullivan** (14)	**75**
I DON'T MIND — **Buzzcocks** (55)	**78**
I DON'T NEED ANYTHING — Sandie **Shaw** (50)	**67**
I DON'T NEED TO TELL HER — **Lurkers** (49)	**78**
I DON'T WANNA DANCE — Eddy **Grant** (1)	**82**
(I DON'T WANNA GO TO) CHELSEA — Elvis **Costello and the Attractions** (16)	**78**
I DON'T WANNA LOSE YOU — **Kandidate** (11)	**79**
I DON'T WANNA LOSE YOUR LOVE — **Emotions** (40)	**77**
I DON'T WANNA PLAY HOUSE — Tammy **Wynette** (37)	**76**
I DON'T WANT OUR LOVING TO DIE — **Herd** (5)	**68**
I DON'T WANT TO BE A FREAK — **Dynasty** (20)	**79**
I DON'T WANT TO GO ON WITHOUT YOU — **Moody Blues** (33)	**65**
I DON'T WANT TO PUT A HOLD ON YOU — Bernie **Flint** (3)	**77**
I DON'T WANT TO TALK ABOUT IT — Rod **Stewart** (1)	**77**
I DREAMED — **Beverley Sisters** (24)	**57**
I EAT CANNIBALS PART 1 — **Toto Coelo** (8)	**82**
I ENJOY BEING A GIRL — Pat **Suzuki** (49)	**60**
I FEEL A CRY COMING ON — Hank **Locklin** (28)	**66**
I FEEL FINE — **Beatles** (1)	**64**
I FEEL FREE — **Cream** (11)	**66**
I FEEL LOVE — Donna **Summer** (1)	**77,82**
I FEEL LOVE COMIN' ON — **Dana** (66)	**82**
I FEEL LOVE COMIN' ON — Felice **Taylor** (11)	**67**
I FEEL SO BAD — Elvis **Presley** (4)	**61**
I FEEL SOMETHING IN THE AIR — **Cher** (43)	**66**
I FOUGHT THE LAW — Bobby **Fuller Four** (33)	**66**
I FOUND OUT THE HARD WAY — **Four Pennies** (14)	**64**
I FOUND SUNSHINE — **Chi-Lites** (35)	**74**
I GET A KICK OUT OF YOU — Gary **Shearston** (7)	**74**

Title — Act (Position)	Year of Chart Entry
I GET A LITTLE SENTIMENTAL OVER YOU — **New Seekers** (5)	**74**
I GET AROUND — **Beach Boys** (7)	**64**
I GET SO EXCITED — **Equals** (44)	**68**
I GET SO LONELY — **Four Knights** (5)	**54**
I GET THE SWEETEST FEELING — Jackie **Wilson** (9)	**72,75**
I GO APE — Neil **Sedaka** (9)	**59**
I GO TO PIECES (EVERYTIME) — Gerri **Granger** (50)	**78**
I GO TO SLEEP — **Pretenders** (7)	**81**
I GOT A FEELING — Rick **Nelson** (27)	**58**
I GOT RHYTHM — **Happenings** (28)	**67**
I GOT STUNG — Elvis **Presley** (1)	**59**
I GOT THE MUSIC IN ME — Kiki **Dee** (19)	**74**
I GOT TO SING — **J. A. L. N. Band** (40)	**77**
I GOT YOU [A] — James **Brown** (29)	**66**
I GOT YOU [B] — **Split Enz** (12)	**80**
I GOT YOU BABE — **Sonny and Cher** (1)	**65**
I GUESS I'LL ALWAYS LOVE YOU — **Isley Brothers** (11)	**66,69**
I HAD TOO MUCH TO DREAM LAST NIGHT — **Electric Prunes** (49)	**67**
I HATE ... PEOPLE — **Anti-Nowhere League** (46)	**82**
I HAVE A DREAM — **Abba** (2)	**79**
I HEAR A SYMPHONY — **Supremes** (39)	**65**
I HEAR YOU KNOCKING — Dave **Edmunds** (1)	**70**
I HEAR YOU NOW — **Jon and Vangelis** (8)	**80**
I HEARD A HEART BREAK LAST NIGHT — Jim **Reeves** (38)	**67**
I HEARD IT THROUGH THE GRAPEVINE — Marvin **Gaye** (1)	**69**
I HEARD IT THROUGH THE GRAPEVINE — Gladys **Knight and the Pips** (47)	**67**
I HEARD IT THROUGH THE GRAPEVINE — **Slits** (60)	**79**
I HONESTLY LOVE YOU — Olivia **Newton-John** (22)	**74**
I JUST CAN'T BE HAPPY TODAY — **Damned** (46)	**79**
I JUST CAN'T HELP BELIEVING — Elvis **Presley** (6)	**71**
I JUST DON'T KNOW WHAT TO DO WITH MYSELF — Dusty **Springfield** (3)	**64**
I JUST FALL IN LOVE AGAIN — Anne **Murray** (58)	**79**
I JUST GO FOR YOU — Jimmy **Jones** (35)	**60**
I JUST KEEP THINKING ABOUT YOU BABY — Tata **Vega** (52)	**79**
I JUST WANNA BE YOUR EVERYTHING — Andy **Gibb** (26)	**77**
I JUST WANNA (SPEND SOME TIME WITH YOU) — Alton **Edwards** (20)	**82**
I KEEP RINGING MY BABY — **Soul Brothers** (42)	**65**
I KNEW THE BRIDE — Dave **Edmunds** (26)	**77**
I KNOW — Perry **Como** (13)	**59**
I KNOW A PLACE — Petula **Clark** (17)	**65**
(I KNOW) I'M LOSING YOU — **Temptations** (19)	**66**
I KNOW THERE'S SOMETHING GOING ON — **Frida** (43)	**82**
I KNOW WHAT I LIKE (IN YOUR WARDROBE) — **Genesis** (21)	**74**
I KNOW WHERE I'M GOING — **Countrymen** (45)	**62**
I KNOW WHERE I'M GOING — George **Hamilton IV** (23)	**58**
I LEFT MY HEART IN SAN FRANCISCO — Tony **Bennett** (25)	**65**
I LIKE IT — **Gerry and the Pacemakers** (1)	**63**
I LIKE IT — **J. A. L. N. Band** (21)	**76**
I LIKE TO ROCK — **April Wine** (41)	**80**
I LIKE (WHAT YOU'RE DOING TO ME) — **Young and Company** (20)	**80**
I LIKE YOUR KIND OF LOVE — Andy **Williams** (16)	**57**
I LIVE FOR THE SUN — **Vanity Fare** (20)	**68**
I LIVE FOR THE WEEKEND — **Triumph** (59)	**80**
I LOST MY HEART TO A STARSHIP TROOPER — Sarah **Brightman** (6)	**78**
I LOVE A MAN IN UNIFORM — **Gang Of Four** (65)	**82**
I LOVE A RAINY NIGHT — Eddie **Rabbitt** (53)	**81**
I LOVE AMERICA — Patrick **Juvet** (12)	**78**
I LOVE BEING IN LOVE WITH YOU — Adam **Faith** (33)	**64**
I LOVE HER — Paul and Barry **Ryan** (17)	**66**
I LOVE HOW YOU LOVE ME — Jimmy **Crawford** (18)	**61**
I LOVE HOW YOU LOVE ME — Maureen **Evans** (34)	**64**
I LOVE HOW YOU LOVE ME — Paul and Barry **Ryan** (21)	**66**
I LOVE MUSIC — **O'Jays** (36)	**78**
I LOVE MUSIC [A] — **Enigma** (25)	**81**
I LOVE MUSIC [B] — **O'Jays** (13)	**76**
I LOVE MY DOG — Cat **Stevens** (28)	**66**
I LOVE ROCK 'N' ROLL — Joan **Jett and the Blackhearts** (4)	**82**
I LOVE THE NIGHT LIFE (DISCO'ROUND) — Alicia **Bridges** (32)	**78**
I LOVE THE SOUND OF BREAKING GLASS — Nick **Lowe** (7)	**78**
I LOVE THE WAY YOU LOVE — Marv **Johnson** (35)	**60**
I LOVE TO BOOGIE — **T. Rex** (13)	**76**
I LOVE TO LOVE (BUT MY BABY LOVES TO DANCE) — Tina **Charles** (1)	**76**
I LOVE YOU [A] — Cliff **Richard** (1)	**60**
I LOVE YOU [B] — Donna **Summer** (10)	**77**
I LOVE YOU BABY — Paul **Anka** (3)	**57**
I LOVE YOU BABY — **Freddie and the Dreamers** (16)	**64**
I LOVE YOU BECAUSE — Al **Martino** (48)	**63**
I LOVE YOU BECAUSE — Jim **Reeves** (5)	**64**
I LOVE YOU BECAUSE — Jim **Reeves** (34)	**71**
I LOVE YOU LOVE ME LOVE — Gary **Glitter** (1)	**73**
I LOVE YOU SO MUCH IT HURTS — Charlie **Gracie** (14)	**57**
I LOVE YOU, YES I DO — **Merseybeats** (22)	**65**
I LOVE YOU, YES I LOVE YOU — Eddy **Grant** (37)	**81**
I MADE IT THROUGH THE RAIN — Barry **Manilow** (37)	**81**
I MAY NEVER PASS THIS WAY AGAIN — Perry **Como** (15)	**58**
I MAY NEVER PASS THIS WAY AGAIN — Robert **Earl** (14)	**58**
I MAY NEVER PASS THIS WAY AGAIN — Ronnie **Hilton** (27)	**58**
I MET A GIRL — **Shadows** (22)	**66**
I MIGHT BE LYING — **Eddie and the Hotrods** (44)	**77**
I MISS YOU BABY — Marv **Johnson** (25)	**69**
I MISSED AGAIN — Phil **Collins** (14)	**81**
I MUST BE IN LOVE — **Rutles** (39)	**78**
I MUST BE SEEING THINGS — Gene **Pitney** (6)	**65**
I NEED IT — Johnny 'Guitar' **Watson** (35)	**76**
I NEED TO BE IN LOVE — **Carpenters** (36)	**76**
I NEED YOU — Joe **Dolan** (43)	**77**
I NEED YOU NOW — Eddie **Fisher** (13)	**54**
I NEED YOUR LOVE TONIGHT — Elvis **Presley** (1)	**59**
I NEED YOUR LOVIN' — Teena **Marie** (28)	**80**
I NEVER GO OUT IN THE RAIN — **High Society** (53)	**80**
I. O. I. O. — **Bee Gees** (49)	**70**
I ONLY HAVE EYES FOR YOU — Art **Garfunkel** (1)	**75**
I ONLY LIVE TO LOVE YOU — Cilla **Black** (26)	**67**
I ONLY WANNA BE WITH YOU — **Bay City Rollers** (4)	**76**
I ONLY WANT TO BE WITH YOU — Dusty **Springfield** (4)	**63**
I ONLY WANT TO BE WITH YOU — **Tourists** (4)	**79**
I OWE YOU ONE — **Shalamar** (13)	**80**
I PRETEND — Des **O'Connor** (1)	**68**
I PUT A SPELL ON YOU — Alan **Price** (9)	**66**
I PUT A SPELL ON YOU — Nina **Simone** (28)	**65,69**
I RAN — **A Flock of Seagulls** (43)	**82**
I RECALL A GYPSY WOMAN — Don **Williams** (13)	**76**
I REMEMBER ELVIS PRESLEY (THE KING IS DEAD) — Danny **Mirror** (4)	**77**
I REMEMBER YESTERDAY — Donna **Summer** (14)	**77**
I REMEMBER YOU — Frank **Ifield** (1)	**62**
I SAW HER AGAIN — **Mamas and the Papas** (11)	**66**
I SAW HER STANDING THERE — Elton **John Band featuring John Lennon Muscle Shoals Horns** (40)	**81**
I SAW LINDA YESTERDAY — Doug **Sheldon** (36)	**63**
I SAW MOMMY KISSING SANTA CLAUS — **Beverley Sisters** (6)	**53**
I SAW MOMMY KISSING SANTA CLAUS — Jimmy **Boyd** (3)	**53**
I SAW MOMMY KISSING SANTA CLAUS — Billy **Cotton and his Band** (11)	**53**
I SAW THE LIGHT — Todd **Rundgren** (36)	**73**
I SAY A LITTLE PRAYER — Aretha **Franklin** (4)	**68**
I SECOND THAT EMOTION — **Japan** (9)	**82**
I SECOND THAT EMOTION — Smokey **Robinson and the Miracles** (27)	**67**
I SECOND THAT EMOTION — Diana **Ross and the Supremes Temptations** (18)	**69**
I SEE A STAR — **Mouth and Macneal** (8)	**74**
I SEE THE MOON — **Stargazers** (1)	**54**
I SHALL BE RELEASED — **Tremeloes** (29)	**68**
I SHOT THE SHERIFF — Eric **Clapton** (9)	**74,82**
I SHOT THE SHERIFF — **Light of the World** (40)	**81**
I SHOULD CARE — Frank **Ifield** (33)	**64**
I SHOULD HAVE KNOWN BETTER — **Naturals** (24)	**64**
I SHOULDA LOVEDYA — Nirada Michael **Walden** (8)	**80**
I SPECIALIZE IN LOVE — Sharon **Brown** (38)	**82**
I SPY FOR THE FBI — Jamo **Thomas** (44)	**69**
I STAND ACCUSED — **Merseybeats** (38)	**66**
I STILL BELIEVE — Ronnie **Hilton** (3)	**54**
I STILL LOVE YOU ALL — Kenny **Ball and his Jazzmen** (24)	**61**
I SURRENDER — **Rainbow** (3)	**81**
I TALK TO THE TREES — Clint **Eastwood** (18)	**70**
I THANK YOU — **Sam and Dave** (34)	**68**
I THINK I LOVE YOU — **Partridge Family starring Shirley Jones Cassidy** (18)	**71**
I THINK IT'S GOING TO RAIN — **U.B.40** (6)	**80**
I THINK OF YOU [A] — Perry **Como** (14)	**71**
I THINK OF YOU [B] — **Detroit Emeralds** (27)	**73**
I THINK OF YOU [C] — **Merseybeats** (5)	**64**
I THOUGHT IT TOOK A LITTLE TIME — Diana **Ross** (32)	**76**
I THOUGHT IT WAS YOU — Herbie **Hancock** (15)	**78**
I THREW IT ALL AWAY — Bob **Dylan** (30)	**69**
I TOLD YOU SO — Jimmy **Jones** (33)	**61**
I UNDERSTAND — **Freddie and the Dreamers** (5)	**64**
I UNDERSTAND — **G-Clefs** (17)	**61**
I WANNA BE A WINNER — **Brown Sauce** (15)	**81**
I WANNA BE LOVED — Rick **Nelson** (30)	**60**
I WANNA BE WITH YOU — **Coffee** (57)	**80**
I WANNA BE YOUR LOVER — **Prince** (41)	**80**
I WANNA BE YOUR MAN — **Rezillos** (71)	**79**
I WANNA BE YOUR MAN — **Rolling Stones** (12)	**63**
I WANNA DANCE WIT CHOO — **Disco Tex and the Sex-O-Lettes** (6)	**75**
I WANNA DO IT WITH YOU — Barry **Manilow** (8)	**82**
I WANNA GET NEXT TO YOU — **Rose Royce** (14)	**77**
I WANNA GO BACK — **New Seekers** (25)	**77**
I WANNA GO HOME — Lonnie **Donegan** (5)	**60**
I WANNA HOLD YOUR HAND — **Dollar** (9)	**79**
I WANNA LOVE MY LIFE AWAY — Gene **Pitney** (26)	**61**
I WANNA STAY HERE — **Miki and Griff** (23)	**63**
I WANNA STAY WITH YOU — **Gallagher and Lyle** (6)	**76**
I WANT CANDY — **Bow Wow Wow** (9)	**82**
I WANT CANDY — Brian **Poole and the Tremeloes** (25)	**65**
I WANT MORE — **Can** (26)	**76**
I WANT TO BE FREE — **Toyah** (8)	**81**
I WANT TO BE STRAIGHT — Ian **Dury and the Blockheads** (22)	**80**
I WANT TO BE WANTED — Brenda **Lee** (31)	**60**
I WANT TO GIVE — Perry **Como** (31)	**74**
I WANT TO GO WITH YOU — Eddy **Arnold** (46)	**66**
I WANT TO HOLD YOUR HAND — **Beatles** (1)	**63**
I WANT TO STAY HERE — **Steve and Eydie** (3)	**63**
I WANT TO WALK YOU HOME — Fats **Domino** (14)	**59**
I WANT YOU — Bob **Dylan** (16)	**66**
I WANT YOU BACK — **Jackson Five** (2)	**70**
I WANT YOU I NEED YOU I LOVE YOU — Elvis **Presley** (14)	**56**
I WANT YOU TO BE MY BABY — Billie **Davis** (33)	**68**
I WANT YOU TO WANT ME — **Cheap Trick** (29)	**79**
I WANT YOUR LOVE — **Chic** (4)	**79**
I WAS KAISER BILL'S BATMAN — Whistling Jack **Smith** (5)	**67**
I WAS MADE FOR DANCIN' — Leif **Garrett** (4)	**79**
I WAS MADE FOR LOVIN' YOU — **Kiss** (50)	**79**
I WAS MADE TO LOVE HER — Stevie **Wonder** (5)	**67**
I WAS ONLY JOKING — Rod **Stewart** (5)	**78**
I WAS TIRED OF BEING ALONE — Patrice **Rushen** (39)	**82**
I (WHO HAVE NOTHING) — Shirley **Bassey** (6)	**63**
I (WHO HAVE NOTHING) — Tom **Jones** (16)	**70**
I (WHO HAVE NOTHING) — **Sylvester** (46)	**79**
I WILL — Billy **Fury** (14)	**64**
I WILL — Ruby **Winters** (4)	**77**
I WILL DRINK THE WINE — Frank **Sinatra** (16)	**71**
I WILL LOVE YOU (EVERY TIME WHEN WE ARE GONE) — **Fureys** (54)	**82**
I WILL RETURN — **Springwater** (5)	**71**
I WILL SURVIVE [A] — **Arrival** (16)	**70**
I WILL SURVIVE [B] — Gloria **Gaynor** (1)	**79**
I WILL SURVIVE [B] — Billie Jo **Spears** (47)	**79**
I WISH — Stevie **Wonder** (5)	**76**
I WISH I COULD SHIMMY LIKE MY SISTER KATE — **Olympics** (45)	**61**
I WISH IT COULD BE CHRISTMAS EVERYDAY — **Wizzard** (4)	**73**
I WISH IT COULD BE CHRISTMAS EVERY DAY — **Wizzard** (41)	**81**
I WISH IT WOULD RAIN — **Faces** (8)	**73**
I WISH IT WOULD RAIN — **Temptations** (45)	**68**
I WONDER [A] — **Crystals** (36)	**64**
I WONDER [B] — Jane **Froman** (14)	**55**
I WONDER [B] — Dickie **Valentine** (4)	**55**
I WONDER [C] — Brenda **Lee** (14)	**63**

Title — Act (Position)	Year of Chart Entry
I WONDER WHO'S KISSING HER NOW — Emile **Ford and the Checkmates** (43)	**62**
I WONDER WHY — **Showaddywaddy** (2)	**78**
I WONNA BE YOUR MAN — **Rezillos** (75)	**79**
I WONT CLOSE MY EYES — **U.B.40** (32)	**82**
I WON'T COME IN WHILE HE'S THERE — Jim **Reeves** (12)	**67**
I WON'T FORGET YOU — Jim **Reeves** (3)	**64**
I WON'T LAST A DAY WITHOUT YOU — **Carpenters** (9)	**72,74**
I WON'T LET YOU DOWN — **PhD** (3)	**82**
I WON'T MENTION IT AGAIN — Ruby **Winters** (45)	**78**
I WOULDN'T TRADE YOU FOR THE WORLD — **Bachelors** (4)	**64**
I WRITE THE SONGS — David **Cassidy** (11)	**75**
ICE CREAM MAN, THE — **Tornados** (18)	**63**
ICE IN THE SUN — **Status Quo** (8)	**68**
I'D BE SURPRISINGLY GOOD FOR YOU — Linda **Lewis** (40)	**79**
I'D DO ANYTHING — Mike **Preston** (23)	**60**
I'D LIKE TO TEACH THE WORLD TO SING — **New Seekers** (1)	**71**
I'D LOVE YOU TO WANT ME — **Lobo** (5)	**74**
I'D NEVER FIND ANOTHER YOU — Billy **Fury** (5)	**61**
I'D RATHER GO BLIND — **Chicken Shack** (14)	**69**
I'D REALLY LOVE TO SEE YOU TONIGHT — **England Dan and John Ford Coley** (26)	**76**
IDENTITY — **X-Ray Spex** (24)	**78**
IDLE GOSSIP — Perry **Como** (3)	**54**
IDLE ON PARADE (EP) — Anthony **Newley** (13)	**59**
IEYA — **Toyah** (48)	**82**
IF — Telly **Savalas** (1)	**75**
IF — **Yin and Yan** (25)	**75**
IF A MAN ANSWERS — Bobby **Darin** (24)	**62**
IF ANYONE FINDS THIS I LOVE YOU — Ruby **Murray** (4)	**55**
IF DREAMS CAME TRUE — Pat **Boone** (16)	**58**
IF EVERY DAY WAS LIKE CHRISTMAS — Elvis **Presley** (13)	**66**
IF HE TELLS YOU — Adam **Faith** (25)	**64**
IF I CAN DREAM — Elvis **Presley** (11)	**69**
IF I CAN'T HAVE YOU — Yvonne **Elliman** (4)	**78**
IF I COULD — David **Essex** (13)	**75**
IF I COULD BUILD MY WHOLE WORLD AROUND YOU — Marvin **Gaye and Tammi Terrell** (41)	**68**
IF I COULD (EL CONDOR PASA) — Julie **Felix** (19)	**70**
IF I COULD ONLY MAKE YOU CARE — Mike **Berry** (37)	**80**
IF I DIDN'T CARE — David **Cassidy** (9)	**74**
IF I GIVE MY HEART TO YOU — Doris **Day** (4)	**54**
IF I GIVE MY HEART TO YOU — Joan **Regan** (3)	**54**
IF I HAD A HAMMER — Trini **Lopez** (4)	**63**
IF I HAD WORDS — Scott **Fitzgerald and Yvonne Keely** (3)	**78**
IF I HAD YOU — **Korgis** (13)	**79**
IF I HAVE TO GO AWAY — **Jigsaw** (36)	**77**
IF I KNEW THEN WHAT I KNOW NOW — Val **Doonican** (14)	**68**
IF I LOVED YOU — Richard **Anthony** (18)	**64**
IF I NEEDED SOMEONE — **Hollies** (20)	**65**
IF I ONLY HAD TIME — John **Rowles** (3)	**68**
IF I RULED THE WORLD — Tony **Bennett** (40)	**65**
IF I RULED THE WORLD — Harry **Secombe** (18)	**63**
IF I SAID YOU HAVE A BEAUTIFUL BODY WOULD YOU HOLD IT AGAINST ME — **Bellamy Brothers** (3)	**79**
IF I SHOULD LOVE AGAIN — Barry **Manilow** (66)	**82**
IF I THOUGHT YOU'D EVER CHANGE YOUR MIND — Cilla **Black** (20)	**69**
IF I WERE A CARPENTER — Bobby **Darin** (9)	**66**
IF I WERE A CARPENTER — **Four Tops** (7)	**68**
IF I WERE A RICH MAN — **Topol** (9)	**67**
IF IT DON'T FIT DON'T FORCE IT — Kellee **Patterson** (44)	**78**
IF IT WASN'T FOR THE REASON THAT I LOVE YOU — Miki **Anthony** (27)	**73**
IF IT'S ALRIGHT WITH YOU BABY — **Korgis** (56)	**80**
IF LEAVING ME IS EASY — Phil **Collins** (17)	**81**
IF LOVING YOU IS WRONG (I DON'T WANT TO BE RIGHT) — Rod **Stewart** (23)	**80**
IF MY FRIENDS COULD SEE ME NOW — Linda **Clifford** (50)	**78**
IF NOT FOR YOU — Olivia **Newton-John** (7)	**71**
IF NOT YOU — **Dr. Hook** (5)	**76**
IF ONLY I COULD LIVE MY LIFE AGAIN — Jane **Morgan** (27)	**59**
IF ONLY TOMORROW — Ronnie **Carroll** (33)	**62**
(IF PARADISE IS) HALF AS NICE — **Amen Corner** (1)	**69,76**
IF SHE SHOULD COME TO YOU — Anthony **Newley** (6)	**60**
IF THE KIDS ARE UNITED — **Sham 69** (9)	**78**
IF THE WHOLE WORLD STOPPED LOVING — Val **Doonican** (3)	**67**
IF YOU BELIEVE — Johnnie **Ray** (7)	**55**
IF YOU CAN WANT — Smokey **Robinson and the Miracles** (50)	**68**
IF YOU CAN'T GIVE ME LOVE — Suzi **Quatro** (4)	**78**
IF YOU CAN'T STAND THE HEAT — **Buck's Fizz** (20)	**82**
IF YOU COULD READ MY MIND — Gordon **Lightfoot** (30)	**71**
IF YOU DON'T KNOW ME BY NOW — Harold **Melvin and the Bluenotes** (9)	**73**
IF YOU DON'T WANT MY LOVE — Robert **John** (42)	**68**
IF YOU FEEL IT — Thelma **Houston** (48)	**81**
IF YOU GO AWAY — Terry **Jacks** (8)	**74**
IF YOU GOTTA GO GO NOW — **Manfred Mann** (2)	**65**
IF YOU GOTTA MAKE A FOOL OF SOMEBODY — **Freddie and the Dreamers** (3)	**63**
IF YOU KNEW SOUSA (AND FRIENDS) — **Royal Philharmonic Orchestra arranged and conducted by Louis Clark** (71)	**82**
IF YOU KNOW WHAT I MEAN — Neil **Diamond** (35)	**76**
IF YOU LEAVE ME NOW — **Chicago** (1)	**76**
IF YOU LOVE HER — Dick **Emery** (32)	**69**
IF YOU LOVE ME — Mary **Hopkin** (32)	**76**
IF YOU REALLY LOVE ME — Stevie **Wonder** (20)	**72**
IF YOU REMEMBER ME — Chris **Thompson** (42)	**79**
IF YOU TALK IN YOUR SLEEP — Elvis **Presley** (40)	**74**
IF YOU THINK YOU KNOW HOW TO LOVE ME — **Smokie** (3)	**75**
IF YOU WANNA BE HAPPY — Jimmy **Soul** (39)	**63**
IF YOU WANT MY LOVE — **Cheap Trick** (57)	**82**
IF YOU WANT MY LOVIN' — Evelyn **King** (43)	**81**
IF YOU WERE MINE MARY — Eddy **Arnold** (49)	**66**
IF YOU'RE LOOKIN' FOR A WAY OUT — **Odyssey** (6)	**80**
IF YOU'RE READY (COME GO WITH ME) — **Staple Singers** (34)	**74**
IKO IKO — **Belle Stars** (35)	**82**
IKO IKO — **Dixie Cups** (23)	**65**
IKO IKO — **Natasha** (10)	**82**
IL EST NE LE DIVIN ENFANT — **Siouxsie and the Banshees** (49)	**82**
IL NOSTRO CONCERTO — Umberto **Bindi** (47)	**60**
IL SILENZIO — Nini **Rosso** (8)	**65**
I'LL ALWAYS BE IN LOVE WITH YOU — Michael **Holliday** (27)	**58**
I'LL ALWAYS LOVE MY MAMA — **Intruders** (32)	**74**
I'LL BE HOME — Pat **Boone** (1)	**56**
I'LL BE SATISFIED — Shakin' **Stevens** (10)	**82**
I'LL BE THERE [A] — **Gerry and the Pacemakers** (15)	**65**
I'LL BE THERE [B] — **Jackson Five** (4)	**70**
I'LL BE THERE [C] — Jackie **Trent** (38)	**69**
I'LL COME RUNNING — Cliff **Richard** (26)	**67**
I'LL COME WHEN YOU CALL — Ruby **Murray** (6)	**55**
I'LL CUT YOUR TAIL OFF — John **Leyton** (36)	**63**
I'LL DO ANYTHING YOU WANT ME TO — Barry **White** (20)	**75**
I'LL FIND MY WAY HOME — **Jon and Vangelis** (6)	**81**
I'LL FIND YOU — David **Whitfield** (27)	**57**
I'LL GET BY — Shirley **Bassey** (10)	**61**
I'LL GET BY — Connie **Francis** (19)	**58**
I'LL GIVE YOU THE EARTH (TOUS LES BATEUX, TOUS LES OISEAUX) — Keith **Michell** (30)	**71**
I'LL GO ON HOPING — Des **O'Connor** (30)	**70**
I'LL GO WHERE YOUR MUSIC TAKES ME — Tina **Charles** (27)	**78**
I'LL GO WHERE YOUR MUSIC TAKES ME — Jimmy **James and the Vagabonds** (23)	**76**
I'LL KEEP YOU SATISFIED — Billy J. **Kramer and the Dakotas** (4)	**63**
I'LL LOVE YOU FOREVER TODAY — Cliff **Richard** (27)	**68**
I'LL MEET YOU AT MIDNIGHT — **Smokie** (11)	**76**
I'LL NEVER FALL IN LOVE AGAIN — Johnnie **Ray** (26)	**60**
I'LL NEVER FALL IN LOVE AGAIN [A] — Bobbie **Gentry** (1)	**69**
I'LL NEVER FALL IN LOVE AGAIN [B] — Tom **Jones** (2)	**67**
I'LL NEVER FALL IN LOVE AGAIN [C] — Johnnie **Ray** (26)	**59**
I'LL NEVER FIND ANOTHER YOU — **Seekers** (1)	**65**
I'LL NEVER GET OVER YOU [A] — **Everly Brothers** (35)	**65**
I'LL NEVER GET OVER YOU [B] — Johnny **Kidd and the Pirates** (4)	**63**
I'LL NEVER QUITE GET OVER YOU — Billy **Fury** (35)	**66**
I'LL NEVER STOP LOVING YOU — Doris **Day** (17)	**55**
I'LL PICK A ROSE FOR MY ROSE — Marv **Johnson** (10)	**69**
I'LL PUT YOU TOGETHER AGAIN — **Hot Chocolate** (13)	**78**
I'LL REMEMBER TONIGHT — Pat **Boone** (18)	**59**
I'LL SAY FOREVER MY LOVE — Jimmy **Ruffin** (7)	**70**
I'LL SEE YOU IN MY DREAMS — Pat **Boone** (27)	**62**
I'LL STAY BY YOU — Kenny **Lynch** (29)	**65**
I'LL STAY SINGLE — Jerry **Lordan** (26)	**60**
I'LL STEP DOWN — Garry **Mills** (39)	**61**
I'LL STOP AT NOTHING — Sandie **Shaw** (4)	**65**
I'LL TAKE YOU HOME — Cliff **Bennett and the Rebel Rousers** (42)	**65**
I'LL TAKE YOU HOME — **Drifters** (37)	**63**
I'LL TAKE YOU HOME AGAIN KATHLEEN — Slim **Whitman** (7)	**57**
I'LL TAKE YOU THERE — **Staple Singers** (30)	**72**
I'LL TRY ANYTHING — Dusty **Springfield** (13)	**67**
I'LL WALK WITH GOD — Mario **Lanza** (18)	**55**
I'M A BELIEVER — **Monkees** (1)	**67**
I'M A BELIEVER — Robert **Wyatt** (29)	**74**
I'M A BETTER MAN — Engelbert **Humperdinck** (15)	**69**
I'M A BOY — **Who** (2)	**66**
I'M A CLOWN — David **Cassidy** (3)	**73**
I'M A FOOL — Slim **Whitman** (16)	**56**
I'M A FOOL TO CARE — Joe **Barry** (49)	**61**
I'M A MAN — **Chicago** (8)	**70**
I'M A MAN — Spencer **Davis Group** (9)	**67**
I'M A MOODY GUY — Shane **Fenton and the Fentones** (22)	**61**
(I'M A) ROAD RUNNER — Junior **Walker and the All-Stars** (12)	**69**
I'M A SUCKER FOR YOUR LOVE — Teena **Marie** (43)	**79**
I'M A TIGER — **Lulu** (9)	**68**
I'M A WONDERFUL THING, BABY — Kid **Creole and the Coconuts** (4)	**82**
I'M ALIVE [A] — **Hollies** (1)	**65**
I'M ALIVE [B] — **Electric Light Orchestra** (20)	**80**
I'M ALRIGHT — **Young Steve and the Afternoon Boys** (40)	**82**
(I'M ALWAYS TOUCHED BY YOUR) PRESENCE DEAR — **Blondie** (10)	**78**
I'M AN UPSTART — **Angelic Upstarts** (31)	**79**
I'M BORN AGAIN — **Boney M** (35)	**79**
I'M COMING HOME — Tom **Jones** (2)	**67**
I'M COMING HOME CINDY — Trini **Lopez** (28)	**66**
I'M COMING OUT — Diana **Ross** (13)	**80**
I'M COUNTING ON YOU — Petula **Clark** (41)	**62**
I'M CRYING — **Animals** (8)	**64**
I'M DOING FINE NOW — **New York City** (20)	**73**
I'M EVERY WOMAN — Chaka **Khan** (11)	**78**
I'M FOREVER BLOWING BUBBLES — **Cockney Rejects** (35)	**80**
I'M FOREVER BLOWING BUBBLES — **West Ham United Cup Squad** (31)	**75**
I'M FREE — Roger **Daltrey** (13)	**73**
I'M GOING HOME — Gene **Vincent** (36)	**61**
I'M GONNA BE A COUNTRY GIRL AGAIN — Buffy **Sainte-Marie** (34)	**72**
I'M GONNA BE STRONG — Gene **Pitney** (2)	**64**
I'M GONNA BE WARM THIS WINTER — Connie **Francis** (48)	**62**
I'M GONNA CHANGE EVERYTHING — Jim **Reeves** (42)	**62**
I'M GONNA GET MARRIED — Lloyd **Price** (23)	**59**
I'M GONNA GET ME A GUN — Cat **Stevens** (6)	**67**
I'M GONNA GET THERE SOMEHOW — Val **Doonican** (25)	**65**
I'M GONNA KNOCK ON YOUR DOOR — Eddie **Hodges** (37)	**61**
I'M GONNA KNOCK ON YOUR DOOR — Little Jimmy **Osmond** (11)	**74**
I'M GONNA LOVE HER FOR BOTH OF US — **Meat Loaf** (62)	**81**
I'M GONNA LOVE YOU FOREVER — **Crown Heights Affair** (47)	**78**
I'M GONNA LOVE YOU JUST A LITTLE BIT MORE BABY — Barry **White** (23)	**73**
I'M GONNA MAKE YOU LOVE ME — Diana **Ross and the Supremes Temptations** (3)	**69**
I'M GONNA MAKE YOU MINE — Lou **Christie** (2)	**69**
I'M GONNA RUN AWAY FROM YOU — Tami **Lynn** (4)	**71,75**
I'M GONNA SIT RIGHT DOWN AND WRITE MYSELF A LETTER — Barry **Manilow** (36)	**82**
I'M GONNA SIT RIGHT DOWN AND WRITE MYSELF A LETTER — Billy **Williams** (22)	**57**
I'M IN A DIFFERENT WORLD — **Four Tops** (27)	**68**

Title — Act (Position)	Year of Chart Entry
I'M IN FAVOUR OF FRIENDSHIP — **Five Smith Brothers** (20)	55
I'M IN LOVE [A] — **Fourmost** (17)	63
I'M IN LOVE [B] — Evelyn **King** (27)	81
I'M IN LOVE AGAIN [A] — Fats **Domino** (12)	56
I'M IN LOVE AGAIN [B] — **Sad Café** (40)	80
I'M IN LOVE (AND I LOVE THE FEELING) — **Rose Royce** (51)	79
I'M IN LOVE WITH A GERMAN FILM STAR — **Passions** (25)	81
I'M IN LOVE WITH THE GIRL ON A CERTAIN MANCHESTER MEGASTORE CHECKOUT DESK — **Freshies** (54)	81
I'M IN THE MOOD FOR DANCING — **Nolans** (3)	79
I'M IN YOU — Peter **Frampton** (41)	77
I'M INTO SOMETHING GOOD — **Herman's Hermits** (1)	64
I'M JUST A BABY — Louise **Cordet** (13)	62
I'M JUST A SINGER (IN A ROCK 'N ROLL BAND) — **Moody Blues** (36)	73
I'M LEAVIN' — Elvis **Presley** (23)	71
I'M LEAVING IT (ALL) UP TO YOU — Donny and Marie **Osmond** (2)	74
I'M LEAVING IT UP TO YOU — **Dale And Grace** (42)	64
I'M LEFT YOU'RE RIGHT SHE'S GONE — Elvis **Presley** (21)	58
I'M LIVING IN SHAME — **Supremes** (14)	69
I'M LOOKING OUT THE WINDOW — Cliff **Richard** (2)	62
I'M LOST WITHOUT YOU — Billy **Fury** (16)	65
I'M LUCKY — Joan **Armatrading** (46)	81
I'M MANDY FLY ME — **10 C. C.** (6)	76
I'M NOT A FOOL — **Cockney Rejects** (65)	79
I'M NOT A JUVENILE DELINQUENT — Frankie **Lymon and the Teenagers** (12)	57
I'M NOT IN LOVE — **10 C. C.** (1)	75
(I'M NOT YOUR) STEPPING STONE — **Sex Pistols** (21)	80
I'M ON FIRE — **5000 Volts** (4)	75
I'M ON MY WAY — Dean **Parrish** (38)	75
I'M ON MY WAY TO A BETTER PLACE — **Chairmen Of The Board** (30)	72
I'M QUALIFIED TO SATISFY — Barry **White** (37)	77
I'M READY FOR LOVE — Martha **Reeves and the Vandellas** (29)	66
I'M SHY MARY ELLEN I'M SHY — Bob **Wallis and his Storyville Jazz Band** (44)	61
I'M SO CRAZY — **KC and The Sunshine Band** (34)	75
I'M SO GLAD I'M STANDING HERE TODAY — **Crusaders** (61)	81
I'M SO HAPPY — **Light of the World** (35)	81
I'M SORRY — **Platters** (22)	57
I'M SORRY [A] — Brenda **Lee** (12)	60
I'M SORRY [B] — **Platters** (18)	57
I'M SORRY I MADE YOU CRY — Connie **Francis** (11)	58
I'M STARTING TO GO STEADY — Johnny **Preston** (49)	60
I'M STILL GONNA NEED YOU — **Osmonds** (32)	75
I'M STILL IN LOVE WITH YOU — Al **Green** (35)	72
I'M STILL WAITING — Diana **Ross** (1)	71,76
I'M STONE IN LOVE WITH YOU — Johnny **Mathis** (10)	75
I'M STONE IN LOVE WITH YOU — **Stylistics** (9)	72
I'M TELLING YOU NOW — **Freddie and the Dreamers** (2)	63
I'M THE FACE — **High Numbers** (49)	80
I'M THE LEADER OF THE GANG (I AM!) — Gary **Glitter** (1)	73
I'M THE LONELY ONE — Cliff **Richard** (8)	64
I'M THE ONE — **Gerry and the Pacemakers** (2)	64
I'M THE URBAN SPACEMAN — **Bonzo Dog Doo-Dah Band** (5)	68
I'M WALKIN' — Fats **Domino** (19)	57
I'M WALKING BACKWARDS FOR CHRISTMAS — **Goons** (4)	56
I'M WALKING BEHIND YOU — Eddie **Fisher** (1)	53
I'M WALKING BEHIND YOU — Dorothy **Squires** (12)	53
I'M WONDERING — Stevie **Wonder** (22)	67
I'M YOUR BOOGIE MAN — **KC and The Sunshine Band** (41)	77
I'M YOUR MAN — **Blue Zoo** (55)	82
I'M YOUR PUPPET — James and Bobby **Purify** (12)	76
I'M YOUR TOY — Elvis **Costello and the Attractions** (51)	82
IMAGE — Hank **Levine** (45)	61
IMAGE OF A GIRL — Nelson **Keene** (37)	60
IMAGE OF A GIRL — Mark **Wynter** (11)	60
IMAGINATION — Rockey **Sharpe and the Replays** (39)	79
IMAGINE — Randy **Crawford** (60)	82
IMAGINE — John **Lennon** (1)	75
IMAGINE ME IMAGINE YOU — **Fox** (15)	75
IMPERIAL WIZARD — David **Essex** (32)	79
IMPORTANCE OF YOUR LOVE — Vince **Hill** (32)	68
IN A BROKEN DREAM — **Python Lee Jackson** (3)	72
IN A GOLDEN COACH — Billy **Cotton and his Band** (3)	53
IN A GOLDEN COACH — Dickie **Valentine** (7)	53
IN A LITTLE SPANISH TOWN — Bing **Crosby** (22)	56
IN A PERSIAN MARKET — Sammy **Davis Jr.** (28)	56
IN AND OUT — Willie **Hutch** (51)	82
IN AND OUT OF LOVE [A] — **Imagination** (16)	81
IN AND OUT OF LOVE [B] — **Supremes** (13)	67
IN BETWEENIES, THE — **Goodies** (7)	74
IN CROWD, THE — Bryan **Ferry** (13)	74
IN CROWD, THE — Dobie **Gray** (25)	65
IN DREAMS — Roy **Orbison** (6)	63
IN DULCE JUBILO — Mike **Oldfield** (4)	75
IN FOR A PENNY — **Slade** (11)	75
IN LOVE — Michael **Holliday** (26)	58
IN MY CHAIR — **Status Quo** (21)	70
IN MY OWN TIME — **Family** (4)	71
IN MY STREET — **Chords** (50)	80
IN OLD LISBON — Frank **Chacksfield** (15)	56
IN SUMMER — Billy **Fury** (5)	63
IN THE AIR TONIGHT — Phil **Collins** (2)	81
IN THE ARMS OF LOVE — Andy **Williams** (33)	66
IN THE BAD BAD OLD DAYS — **Foundations** (8)	69
IN THE BEGINNING — Frankie **Laine** (20)	55
IN THE BROWNIES — Billy **Connolly** (38)	79
IN THE BUSH — **Musique** (16)	78
IN THE CHAPEL IN THE MOONLIGHT — **Bachelors** (27)	65
IN THE CITY — **Jam** (40)	77
IN THE COUNTRY — Cliff **Richard** (6)	66
IN THE FOREST — **Baby O** (46)	80
IN THE GHETTO — Elvis **Presley** (2)	69
IN THE HALL OF THE MOUNTAIN KING — **Nero and the Gladiators** (48)	61
IN THE HEAT OF THE NIGHT [A] — **Diamond Head** (67)	82
IN THE HEAT OF THE NIGHT [B] — **Imagination** (22)	82
IN THE MEANTIME — Georgie **Fame** (22)	65
IN THE MIDDLE OF A DARK DARK NIGHT — Guy **Mitchell** (25)	57
IN THE MIDDLE OF AN ISLAND — **King Brothers** (19)	57
IN THE MIDDLE OF NOWHERE — Dusty **Springfield** (8)	65
IN THE MIDDLE OF THE HOUSE — Alma **Cogan** (20)	56
IN THE MIDDLE OF THE HOUSE — **Johnston Brothers** (27)	56
IN THE MIDDLE OF THE HOUSE — Jimmy **Parkinson** (20)	56
IN THE MIDNIGHT HOUR — Wilson **Pickett** (12)	65,68
IN THE MOOD — Ernie **Fields** (13)	59
IN THE MOOD — Glenn **Miller** (13)	76
IN THE MOOD — **Sound 9418** (46)	76
IN THE MOOD — Ray **Stevens** (31)	77
IN THE NAVY — **Village People** (2)	79
IN THE NIGHT — Barbara **Dickson** (48)	80
IN THE STONE — **Earth Wind and Fire** (53)	80
IN THE SUMMERTIME — **Mungo Jerry** (1)	70
IN THE THICK OF IT — Brenda **Russell** (51)	80
IN THE YEAR 2525 (EXORDIUM AND TERMINUS) — **Zager and Evans** (1)	69
IN THOUGHTS OF YOU — Billy **Fury** (9)	65
IN ZAIRE — Johnny **Wakelin** (4)	76
INDESCRIBABLY BLUE — Elvis **Presley** (21)	67
INDIAN LOVE CALL — Karl **Denver** (32)	63
INDIAN LOVE CALL — Ray **Stevens** (34)	75
INDIAN LOVE CALL — Slim **Whitman** (7)	55
INDIAN RESERVATION — Don **Fardon** (3)	70
INDIAN RESERVATION — **999** (51)	81
INDIANA — Freddy **Cannon** (42)	60
INDIANA WANTS ME — R. Dean **Taylor** (2)	71
INDUSTRIAL STRENGTH EP — **Krokus** (62)	81
INHERIT THE WIND — Wilton **Felder** (39)	80
INNAMORATA — Dean **Martin** (21)	56
INSIDE - LOOKING OUT — **Animals** (12)	66
INSIDE AMERICA — Juggy **Jones** (39)	76
INSIDE LOOKING OUT — **Grand Funk Railroad** (40)	71
INSIDE OUT — **Odyssey** (3)	82
INSIDE OUTSIDE — **Classix Nouveaux** (46)	81
INSTANT KARMA — John **Lennon** (5)	70
INSTANT REPLAY — Dan **Hartman** (8)	78
INSTINCTION — **Spandau Ballet** (10)	82
INTERNATIONAL JET SET — The **Specials** (6)	80
INTO THE VALLEY — **Skids** (10)	79
INTUITION — **Linx** (7)	81
INVISIBLE SUN — **Police** (2)	81
INVITATIONS — **Shakatak** (24)	82
I.O.U. — Jane **Kennaway and Strange Behaviour** (65)	81
IRE FEELINGS (SKANGA) — Rupie **Edwards** (9)	74
IRENE — **Photos** (56)	80
IRON FIST — **Motorhead** (29)	82
IRON HORSE — **Christie** (47)	72
IS A BLUE BIRD BLUE — Conway **Twitty** (43)	60
IS IT A DREAM — **Classix Nouveaux** (11)	82
IS IT BECAUSE — **Honeycombs** (38)	64
IS IT LOVE YOU'RE AFTER — **Rose Royce** (13)	79
IS IT REALLY OVER — Jim **Reeves** (17)	65
IS IT TRUE — Brenda **Lee** (17)	64
IS SHE REALLY GOING OUT WITH HIM? — Joe **Jackson** (13)	79
IS THAT LOVE — **Squeeze** (35)	81
IS THERE ANYBODY THERE — **Scorpions** (39)	79
IS THIS A LOVE THING — **Raydio** (27)	78
IS THIS LOVE — Bob **Marley and the Wailers** (9)	78
IS THIS THE WAY TO AMARILLO — Tony **Christie** (18)	71
IS THIS WHAT I GET FOR LOVING YOU — Marianne **Faithfull** (43)	67
IS VIC THERE? — **Department S** (22)	81
IS YOUR LOVE IN VAIN — Bob **Dylan** (56)	78
ISLAND GIRL — Elton **John** (14)	75
ISLAND IN THE SUN — Harry **Belafonte** (3)	57
ISLAND IN THE SUN — **Righteous Brothers** (36)	66
ISLAND OF DREAMS — **Springfields** (5)	62
ISLAND OF LOST SOULS — **Blondie** (11)	82
ISLE OF INNISFREE — Bing **Crosby** (3)	52
ISN'T IT TIME — **Babys** (45)	78
ISN'T LIFE STRANGE — **Moody Blues** (13)	72
ISN'T SHE LOVELY — David **Parton** (4)	77
ISRAEL — **Siouxsie and the Banshees** (41)	80
ISRAELITES — Desmond **Dekker and the Aces** (1)	69,75
ISTANBUL — Frankie **Vaughan** (11)	54
IT AIN'T ME BABE — Johnny **Cash** (28)	65
IT AIN'T WHAT YOU DO IT'S THE WAY THAT YOU DO IT — **Funboy Three and Bananarama** (4)	82
IT DOESN'T MATTER ANYMORE — Buddy **Holly** (1)	59
IT DON'T COME EASY — Ringo **Starr** (4)	71
IT HURTS SO MUCH — Jim **Reeves** (8)	65
IT HURTS TO BE IN LOVE — Gene **Pitney** (36)	64
IT ISN'T RIGHT — **Platters** (23)	57
IT KEEPS RAININ' — Fats **Domino** (49)	61
IT KEEPS RIGHT ON A HURTIN' — Johnny **Tillotson** (31)	62
IT MAKES YOU FEEL LIKE DANCIN' — **Rose Royce** (16)	78
IT MAY BE WINTER OUTSIDE (BUT IN MY HEART ITS SPRING) — **Love Unlimited** (11)	75
IT MIEK — Desmond **Dekker and the Aces** (7)	69
IT MIGHT AS WELL RAIN UNTIL SEPTEMBER — Carole **King** (3)	62,72
IT MUST BE HIM (SUEL SUR SON ETOILE) — Vikki **Carr** (2)	67
IT MUST BE LOVE — **Madness** (4)	81
IT MUST BE LOVE — Labi **Siffre** (14)	71
IT ONLY TAKES A MINUTE — **One Hundred Ton And A Feather** (9)	76
IT ONLY TOOK A MINUTE — Joe **Brown** (6)	62
IT OUGHTA SELL A MILLION — Lyn **Paul** (37)	75
IT SEEMS TO HANG ON — **Ashford and Simpson** (48)	78
IT SHOULD HAVE BEEN ME — Yvonne **Fair** (5)	76
IT STARTED ALL OVER AGAIN — Brenda **Lee** (15)	62
IT STARTED WITH A KISS — **Hot Chocolate** (5)	82
IT SURE BRINGS OUT THE LOVE IN YOUR EYES — David **Soul** (12)	78
IT TAKES ALL NIGHT LONG — Gary **Glitter** (25)	77
IT TAKES TWO — Marvin **Gaye and Kim Weston** (16)	67
IT TAKES TWO TO TANGO — Richard **Myhill** (17)	78
IT WAS EASIER TO HURT HER — Wayne **Fontana** (36)	65
IT WILL BE ALRIGHT — **Odyssey** (43)	81
IT WILL COME IN TIME — Billy **Preston and Syreeta** (47)	80
IT WON'T SEEM LIKE CHRISTMAS (WITHOUT YOU) — Elvis **Presley** (13)	79
ITALIAN THEME, THE — Cyril **Stapleton** (18)	56
ITCHYCOO PARK — **Small Faces** (3)	67,75

Title — Act (Position)	Year of Chart Entry
IT'LL BE ME — Cliff Richard (2)	62
IT'S A BETTER THAN GOOD TIME — Gladys Knight and the Pips (59)	78
IT'S A DISCO NIGHT (ROCK DON'T STOP) — Isley Brothers (14)	79
IT'S A GAME — Bay City Rollers (16)	77
IT'S A HEARTACHE — Bonnie Tyler (4)	77
IT'S A LONG WAY TO THE TOP (IF YOU WANNA ROCK'N'ROLL) — AC/DC (55)	80
IT'S A LOVE THING — Whispers (9)	81
IT'S A MAN'S MAN'S MAN'S WORLD — James Brown (13)	66
IT'S A RAGGY WALTZ — Dave Brubeck Quartet (36)	62
IT'S A SHAME — Detroit Spinners (20)	70
IT'S A SIN TO TELL A LIE — Gerry Monroe (13)	71
IT'S ALL IN THE GAME — Tommy Edwards (1)	58
IT'S ALL IN THE GAME — Four Tops (5)	70
IT'S ALL IN THE GAME — Cliff Richard (2)	63
IT'S ALL OVER — Cliff Richard (9)	67
IT'S ALL OVER NOW [A] — Shane Fenton and the Fentones (29)	62
IT'S ALL OVER NOW [B] — Rolling Stones (1)	64
IT'S ALL OVER NOW BABY BLUE — Joan Baez (22)	65
IT'S ALL UP TO YOU — Jim Capaldi (27)	74
IT'S ALMOST TOMORROW — Dreamweavers (1)	56
IT'S ALMOST TOMORROW — Mark Wynter (12)	63
IT'S ALRIGHT — Sho Nuff (53)	80
IT'S AN OPEN SECRET — Joy Strings (32)	64
IT'S BEEN NICE — Everly Brothers (26)	63
IT'S BEEN SO LONG — George McCrae (4)	75
IT'S BETTER TO HAVE (AND DON'T NEED) — Don Covay (29)	74
IT'S DIFFERENT FOR GIRLS — Joe Jackson (5)	80
IT'S ECSTASY WHEN YOU LAY DOWN NEXT TO ME — Barry White (40)	77
IT'S FOR YOU — Cilla Black (7)	64
IT'S FOUR IN THE MORNING — Faron Young (3)	72
IT'S GETTING BETTER — Mama Cass (8)	69
IT'S GOING TO HAPPEN! — Undertones (18)	81
IT'S GONNA BE A COLD COLD CHRISTMAS — Dana (4)	75
IT'S GONNA BE ALL RIGHT — Gerry and the Pacemakers (24)	64
IT'S GOOD NEWS WEEK — Hedgehoppers Anonymous (5)	65
IT'S GROWING — Temptations (45)	65
IT'S HARD TO BE HUMBLE — Mac Davis (27)	80
IT'S IMPOSSIBLE — Perry Como (4)	71
IT'S IN HIS KISS — Betty Everett (34)	68
IT'S IN HIS KISS — Linda Lewis (6)	75
IT'S LATE — Rick Nelson (3)	59
(IT'S LIKE A) SAD OLD KINDA MOVIE — Pickettywitch (16)	70
IT'S LOVE — Ken Dodd (36)	66
IT'S LOVE THAT REALLY COUNTS — Merseybeats (24)	63
IT'S MY HOUSE — Diana Ross (32)	79
IT'S MY HOUSE — Storm (36)	79
IT'S MY LIFE — Animals (7)	65
IT'S MY PARTY — Lesley Gore (9)	63
IT'S MY PARTY — Dave Stewart with Barbara Gaskin (1)	81
IT'S MY TIME — Everly Brothers (39)	68
IT'S MY TURN — Diana Ross (16)	81
IT'S NEVER TOO LATE — Diana Ross (41)	82
IT'S NICE TO GO TRAV'LING — Frank Sinatra (48)	60
IT'S NOT UNUSUAL — Tom Jones (1)	65
IT'S NOW OR NEVER — Elvis Presley (1)	60,77
IT'S ONE OF THOSE NIGHTS (YES LOVE) — Partridge Family starring Shirley Jones Cassidy (11)	72
IT'S ONLY LOVE — Gary 'U.S.' Bonds (43)	81
IT'S ONLY LOVE [A] — Elvis Presley (3)	80
IT'S ONLY LOVE [B] — Tony Blackburn (42)	69
IT'S ONLY MAKE BELIEVE — Glen Campbell (4)	70
IT'S ONLY MAKE BELIEVE — Child (10)	78
IT'S ONLY MAKE BELIEVE — Billy Fury (10)	64
IT'S ONLY MAKE BELIEVE — Conway Twitty (1)	58
IT'S ONLY ROCK AND ROLL — Rolling Stones (10)	74
IT'S OVER — Roy Orbison (1)	64
IT'S RAINING [A] — Darts (2)	78
IT'S RAINING [B] — Shakin' Stevens (10)	81
IT'S RAINING AGAIN — Supertramp (26)	82
IT'S SO EASY — Andy Williams (13)	70
IT'S SO NICE (TO HAVE YOU HOME) — New Seekers (44)	76
IT'S STILL ROCK AND ROLL TO ME — Billy Joel (14)	80
IT'S TEMPTATION — Sheer Elegance (41)	76
IT'S THE SAME OLD SONG — Four Tops (34)	65
IT'S THE SAME OLD SONG — KC and The Sunshine Band (49)	78
IT'S THE SAME OLD SONG — Weathermen (19)	71
IT'S TIME FOR LOVE — Chi-Lites (5)	75
IT'S TIME TO CRY — Paul Anka (28)	60
IT'S TOO LATE — Carole King (6)	71
IT'S TOO LATE NOW [A] — Long John Baldry (21)	69
IT'S TOO LATE NOW [B] — Swinging Blue Jeans (30)	63
IT'S TOO SOON TO KNOW — Pat Boone (7)	58
IT'S UP TO YOU — Rick Nelson (22)	63
IT'S UP TO YOU PETULA — Edison Lighthouse (49)	71
IT'S WONDERFUL — Jimmy Ruffin (6)	70
IT'S WRITTEN ON YOUR BODY — Ronnie Bond (52)	80
IT'S YOU [A] — Manhattans (43)	77
IT'S YOU [B] — Freddie Starr (9)	74
IT'S YOU, ONLY YOU (MEIN SCHMERZ) — Lene Lovich (68)	82
IT'S YOUR DAY TODAY — P. J. Proby (32)	68
IT'S YOUR LIFE — Smokie (5)	77
IT'S YOUR THING — Isley Brothers (30)	69
ITSY BITSY TEENY WEENY YELLOW POLKA DOT BIKINI — Brian Hyland (8)	60
I'VE BEEN A BAD BAD BOY — Paul Jones (5)	67
I'VE BEEN DRINKING — Jeff Beck and Rod Stewart (27)	73
I'VE BEEN HURT — Guy Darrell (12)	73
I'VE BEEN LONELY SO LONG — Frederick Knight (22)	72
I'VE BEEN WRONG BEFORE — Cilla Black (17)	65
I'VE DONE EVERYTHING FOR YOU — Sammy Hagar (36)	80
I'VE GOT A THING ABOUT YOU BABY — Elvis Presley (33)	74
I'VE GOT TO LEARN TO SAY NO — Richard 'Dimples' Fields (56)	82
I'VE GOT YOU ON MY MIND — Dorian Gray (36)	68
I'VE GOT YOU ON MY MIND — White Plains (17)	70
I'VE GOT YOU UNDER MY SKIN — Four Seasons (12)	66
I'VE GOTTA GET A MESSAGE TO YOU — Bee Gees (1)	68
IVE HAD ENOUGH [A] — Earth Wind and Fire (29)	82
I'VE HAD ENOUGH [B] — Wings (42)	78
I'VE JUST BEGUN TO LOVE YOU — Dynasty (51)	80
I'VE LOST YOU — Elvis Presley (9)	70
I'VE NEVER BEEN IN LOVE — Suzi Quatro (56)	80
I'VE NEVER BEEN TO ME — Charlene (1)	82
I'VE PASSED THIS WAY BEFORE — Jimmy Ruffin (29)	67,69
I'VE SEEN THE WORD — Blancmange (65)	82
I'VE TOLD EVERY LITTLE STAR — Linda Scott (7)	61
I'VE WAITED SO LONG — Anthony Newley (3)	59
IVORY TOWER — Three Kayes (20)	56
JACK AND DIANE — John Cougar (25)	82
JACK AND JILL — Raydio (11)	78
JACK IN THE BOX [A] — Moments (7)	77
JACK IN THE BOX [B] — Clodagh Rodgers (4)	71
JACK O' DIAMONDS — Lonnie Donegan (14)	57
JACKIE — Scott Walker (22)	67
JACKIE WILSON SAID — Dexy's Midnight Runners (5)	82
JACKSON — Nancy Sinatra (11)	67
JACQUELINE — Bobby Helms (20)	58
JACQUES DERRIDA — Scritti Politti (43)	82
JA-DA — Johnny and the Hurricanes (14)	61
JAILBREAK — Thin Lizzy (31)	76
JAILHOUSE ROCK — Elvis Presley (1)	58,71,77
JAILHOUSE ROCK (EP) — Elvis Presley (18)	58
JAM JAM JAM — People's Choice (40)	78
JAMBALAYA (ON THE BAYOU) — Carpenters (12)	74
JAMBALAYA — Fats Domino (41)	62
JAMBALAYA — Jo Stafford (11)	52
JAMES BOND THEME — John Barry (13)	62
JAMMING — Bob Marley and the Wailers (9)	77
JANE — Jefferson Starship (21)	80
JANUARY — Pilot (1)	75
JANUARY FEBRUARY — Barbara Dickson (11)	80
JAPANESE BOY — Aneka (1)	81
JARROW SONG — Alan Price (6)	74
JAWS — Lalo Schifrin (14)	76
JAZZ CARNIVAL — Azymuth (19)	80
JE SUIS MUSIC — Cerrone (39)	79
JE T'AIME. . . MOI NON PLUS — Jane Birkin and Serge Gainsbourg (1)	69,74
JE T'AIME (MOI NON PLUS) — Judge Dread (9)	75
JE VOULAIS TE DIRE (QUE JE T'ATTENDS) — Manhattan Transfer (40)	78
JEALOUS GUY — Roxy Music (1)	81
JEALOUS HEART — Cadets (42)	65
JEALOUS HEART — Connie Francis (44)	66
JEALOUS MIND — Alvin Stardust (1)	74
JEALOUSY [A] — Billy Fury (2)	61
JEALOUSY [B] — Amii Stewart (58)	79
JEAN GENIE, THE — David Bowie (2)	72
JEANETTE — The Beat (45)	82
JEANNIE — Danny Williams (14)	62
JEANNIE, JEANNIE, JEANNIE — Eddie Cochran (31)	61
JEANS ON — David Dundas (3)	76
JEEPSTER — Polecats (53)	81
JEEPSTER — T. Rex (2)	71
JENNIFER ECCLES — Hollies (7)	68
JENNIFER JUNIPER — Donovan (5)	68
JENNY JENNY — Little Richard (11)	57
JENNY TAKE A RIDE — Mitch Ryder and the Detroit Wheels (33)	66
JERUSALEM — Herb Alpert (42)	70
JESAMINE — Casuals (2)	68
JESUS — Cliff Richard (35)	72
JET — Wings (7)	74
JEZEBEL — Marty Wilde (19)	62
JIG A JIG — East Of Eden (7)	71
JILTED JOHN — Jilted John (4)	78
JIMMIE JONES — Vapors (44)	81
JIMMY — Purple Hearts (60)	80
JIMMY JIMMY — Undertones (16)	79
JIMMY MACK — Martha Reeves and the Vandellas (21)	67,70
JIMMY UNKNOWN — Lita Roza (15)	56
JIMMY'S GIRL — Johnny Tillotson (43)	61
JINGLE BELL ROCK — Max Bygraves (7)	59
JINGLE BELL ROCK — Chubby Checker and Bobby Rydell (40)	62
JINGLE BELLS — Judge Dread (59)	78
JINGLE BELLS LAUGHING ALL THE WAY — Hysterics (44)	81
JINGO — Candido (55)	81
JITTERBUGGIN' — Heatwave (34)	81
JIVE TALKIN' — Bee Gees (5)	75
JOAN OF ARC — Orchestral Manoeuvres in the Dark (5)	81
JOANNA — Scott Walker (7)	68
JOCKO HOMO — Devo (62)	78
JOHN AND JULIE — Eddie Calvert (6)	55
JOHN I'M ONLY DANCING — David Bowie (12)	72
JOHN I'M ONLY DANCING — Polecats (35)	81
JOHN I'M ONLY DANCING (AGAIN) (1975) — David Bowie (12)	79
JOHN I'M ONLY DANCING (1972) — David Bowie (12)	79
JOHN WAYNE IS BIG LEGGY — Haysi Fantayzee (11)	82
JOHNNY AND MARY — Robert Palmer (44)	80
JOHNNY ANGEL — Shelley Fabares (41)	62
JOHNNY ANGEL — Patti Lynn (37)	62
JOHNNY B. GOODE — Jimi Hendrix Experience (35)	72
JOHNNY DAY — Rolf Harris (44)	63
JOHNNY GET ANGRY — Carol Deene (32)	62
JOHNNY REGGAE — Piglets (3)	71
JOHNNY REMEMBER ME — John Leyton (1)	61
JOHNNY ROCCO — Marty Wilde (30)	60
JOHNNY WILL — Pat Boone (4)	61
JOIN IN AND SING AGAIN — Johnston Brothers (9)	55
JOIN IN AND SING (NO. 3) — Johnston Brothers (24)	56
JOIN THE PARTY — Honky (28)	77
JOIN TOGETHER — Who (9)	72
JOKER (THE WIGAN JOKER), THE — Allnight Band (50)	79
JOLE BLON — Gary 'U.S.' Bonds (51)	81
JOLENE — Dolly Parton (7)	76
JONES VS JONES — Kool and the Gang (17)	81
JOURNEY — Duncan Browne (23)	72
JOURNEY TO THE MOON — Biddu (41)	78
JOY OF LIVING — Cliff Richard (25)	70
JOY TO THE WORLD — Three Dog Night (24)	71
JOYBRINGER — Manfred Mann's Earth Band (9)	73
JUDY IN DISGUISE (WITH GLASSES) — John Fred and the Playboy Band (3)	68
JUDY SAYS (KNOCK YOU IN THE HEAD) — Vibrators (70)	78
JUDY TEEN — Steve Harley and COCKNEY REBEL (5)	74
JUKE BOX BABY — Perry Como (22)	56
JUKE BOX GYPSY — Lindisfarne (56)	78
JUKE BOX HERO — Foreigner (48)	81

Title — Act (Position)	Year of Chart Entry
JUKE BOX JIVE — **Rubettes** (3)	74
JULIE ANN — **Kenny** (10)	75
JULIE DO YA LOVE ME — Bobby **Sherman** (28)	70
JULIE DO YA LOVE ME — **White Plains** (8)	70
JULIE OCEAN — **Undertones** (41)	81
JULIET — **Four Pennies** (1)	64
JUMBO — **Bee Gees** (25)	68
JUMP THE GUN — **Three Degrees** (48)	79
JUMP TO IT — Aretha **Franklin** (42)	82
JUMP TO THE BEAT — Stacy **Lattisaw** (3)	80
JUMPIN' JIVE — Joe **Jackson** (43)	81
JUMPING JACK FLASH — **Rolling Stones** (1)	68
JUNGLE FEVER — **Chakachas** (29)	72
JUNGLE ROCK — Hank **Mizell** (3)	76
JUNIOR'S FARM — **Wings** (16)	74
JUPITER — **Earth Wind and Fire** (41)	78
JUST A FEELING — **Bad Manners** (13)	81
JUST A LITTLE BIT — **Undertakers** (49)	64
JUST A LITTLE BIT BETTER — **Herman's Hermits** (15)	65
JUST A LITTLE BIT TOO LATE — Wayne **Fontana and the Mindbenders** (20)	65
JUST A LITTLE MISUNDERSTANDING — **Contours** (31)	70
JUST A LITTLE TOO MUCH — Rick **Nelson** (11)	59
JUST A SMILE — **Pilot** (31)	75
JUST A TOUCH OF LOVE — **Slave** (64)	80
JUST AN ILLUSION — **Imagination** (2)	82
JUST ANOTHER BROKEN HEART — Sheena **Easton** (33)	81
JUST AS MUCH AS EVER — Nat "King" **Cole** (18)	60
JUST BETWEEN YOU AND ME — **April Wine** (52)	81
JUST BORN — Jim **Dale** (27)	58
JUST CAN'T GET ENOUGH — **Depeche Mode** (8)	81
JUST CAN'T GIVE YOU UP — **Mystic Merlin** (20)	80
JUST DON'T WANT TO BE LONELY — **Main Ingredient** (27)	74
JUST FADE AWAY — **Stiff Little Fingers** (47)	81
JUST FOR KICKS — Mike **Sarne** (22)	63
JUST FOR YOU [A] — **Freddie and the Dreamers** (41)	64
JUST FOR YOU [B] — **Glitter Band** (10)	74
JUST FOR YOU [C] — Alan **Price** (43)	78
JUST FOR YOU (RE-ISSUE) — Alan **Price** (32)	79
JUST KEEP IT UP — Dee **Clark** (26)	59
JUST LET ME DO MY THING — **Sine** (33)	78
JUST LIKE A WOMAN — **Manfred Mann** (10)	66
JUST LIKE EDDIE — **Heinz** (5)	63
JUST LIKE ME — **Hollies** (25)	63
(JUST LIKE) STARTING OVER — John **Lennon** (1)	80
JUST LISTEN TO MY HEART — **Spotnicks** (36)	63
JUST LOVING YOU — Anita **Harris** (6)	67
JUST MY IMAGINATION (RUNNING AWAY WITH ME) — **Temptations** (8)	71
JUST MY SOUL RESPONDING — Smokey **Robinson** (35)	74
JUST ONE LOOK — **Faith, Hope and Charity** (38)	76
JUST ONE LOOK — **Hollies** (2)	64
JUST ONE MORE NIGHT — **Yellow Dog** (8)	78
JUST ONE SMILE — Gene **Pitney** (8)	66
JUST OUT OF REACH (OF MY TWO EMPTY ARMS) — Ken **Dodd** (29)	72
JUST SEVEN NUMBERS (CAN STRAIGHTEN OUT MY LIFE) — **Four Tops** (36)	71
JUST THE TWO OF US — Grover **Washington Jr.** (34)	81
JUST THE WAY YOU ARE — Billy **Joel** (19)	78
JUST THE WAY YOU ARE — Barry **White** (12)	78
JUST THIRTEEN — **Lurkers** (66)	79
JUST TO BE CLOSE TO YOU — **Commodores** (62)	78
JUST WALK IN MY SHOES — Gladys **Knight and the Pips** (35)	72
JUST WALKIN' IN THE RAIN — Johnnie **Ray** (1)	56
JUST WHAT I ALWAYS WANTED — Mari **Wilson** (8)	82
JUST WHAT I NEEDED — **Cars** (17)	79
JUST WHEN I NEEDED YOU MOST — Barbara **Jones** (31)	81
JUST WHEN I NEEDED YOU MOST — Randy **Vanwarmer** (8)	79
JUST WHO IS THE FIVE O'CLOCK HERO — **Jam** (8)	82
KANSAS CITY — **Little Richard** (26)	59
KANSAS CITY — Trini **Lopez** (35)	63
KANSAS CITY STAR — Roger **Miller** (48)	65
KARA KARA — **New World** (17)	71
KATE BUSH ON STAGE (EP) — Kate **Bush** (10)	79
KEEP A KNOCKIN' — **Little Richard** (21)	57
KEEP AWAY FROM OTHER GIRLS — Helen **Shapiro** (40)	62
KEEP DOIN' IT — **Showdown** (41)	77
KEEP IN TOUCH — **Freeez** (49)	80
KEEP IT COMIN' LOVE — **KC and The Sunshine Band** (31)	76
KEEP IT DARK — **Genesis** (33)	81
KEEP IT OUT OF SIGHT — Paul and Barry **Ryan** (30)	67
KEEP ON — Bruce **Channel** (12)	68
KEEP ON BELIEVING — **Grand Prix** (75)	82
KEEP ON DANCIN' — **Gary's Gang** (8)	79
KEEP ON DANCING — **Bay City Rollers** (9)	71
KEEP ON LOVING YOU — **REO Speedwagon** (7)	81
KEEP ON RUNNIN' (TILL YOU BURN) — **U.K. Subs** (41)	81
KEEP ON RUNNING — Spencer **Davis Group** (1)	65
KEEP ON TRUCKIN' — Eddie **Kendricks** (18)	73
KEEP REACHING OUT FOR LOVE — **Liner** (49)	79
KEEP SEARCHIN' (WE'LL FOLLOW THE SUN) — Del **Shannon** (3)	65
KEEP THE CUSTOMER SATISFIED — Marsha **Hunt** (41)	70
KEEP YOUR BODY WORKING — **Kleeer** (51)	79
KEEP YOUR HANDS OFF MY BABY — **Little Eva** (30)	63
KEEPER OF THE CASTLE — **Four Tops** (18)	72
KEEPIN' LOVE NEW — Howard **Johnson** (45)	82
KEEPING A RENDEZVOUS — **Budgie** (71)	81
KEEPS ME WONDERING WHY — Steve **Miller Band** (52)	82
KELLY — Wayne **Gibson** (48)	64
KENTUCKY RAIN — Elvis **Presley** (21)	70
KEWPIE DOLL — Perry **Como** (9)	58
KEWPIE DOLL — Frankie **Vaughan** (10)	58
KEY LARGO — Bertie **Higgins** (60)	82
KICK IN THE EYE — **Bauhaus** (59)	81
KICK IN THE EYE (EP) — **Bauhaus** (45)	82
KICKING UP THE LEAVES — Mark **Wynter** (24)	60
KICKS (EP) — **U.K. Subs** (36)	79
KID — **Pretenders** (33)	79
KIDDIO — Brook **Benton** (41)	60
KIDS ARE ALRIGHT, THE — **Who** (41)	66
KIDS IN AMERICA — Kim **Wilde** (2)	81
KID'S LAST FIGHT, THE — Frankie **Laine** (3)	54
KIDS ON THE STREET — **Angelic Upstarts** (57)	81
KILL THE KING — **Rainbow** (41)	77,81
KILL THE POOR — **Dead Kennedys** (49)	80
KILLER ON THE LOOSE — **Thin Lizzy** (10)	80
KILLER QUEEN — **Queen** (2)	74
KILLERS LIVE (EP) — **Thin Lizzy** (19)	81
KILLING ME SOFTLY WITH HIS SONG — Roberta **Flack** (6)	73
KILLING OF GEORGIE, THE — Rod **Stewart** (2)	76
KING — **U.B.40** (4)	80
KING CREOLE — Elvis **Presley** (2)	58
KING KONG — Terry **Lightfoot and his New Orleans Jazzmen** (29)	61
KING MIDAS IN REVERSE — **Hollies** (18)	67
KING OF CLOWNS — Neil **Sedaka** (23)	62
KING OF KINGS — Ezz **Reco and the Launchers Grant** (44)	64
KING OF THE COPS — Billy **Howard** (6)	75
KING OF THE ROAD — Roger **Miller** (1)	65
KING OF THE RUMBLING SPIRES — **T. Rex** (44)	69
KING ROCKER — **Generation X** (11)	79
KING'S CALL — Philip **Lynott** (35)	80
KINGS OF THE WILD FRONTIER — **Adam and The Ants** (2)	80,81
KISS — Dean **Martin** (5)	53
KISS AND SAY GOODBYE — **Manhattans** (4)	76
KISS ME ANOTHER — Georgia **Gibbs** (24)	56
KISS ME GOODBYE — Petula **Clark** (50)	68
KISS ME HONEY HONEY KISS ME — Shirley **Bassey** (3)	58
KISS ME QUICK — Elvis **Presley** (14)	63
KISS ON MY LIST — Daryl **Hall and John Oates** (33)	80
KISS YOU ALL OVER — **Exile** (6)	78
KISSES SWEETER THAN WINE — Jimmie **Rodgers** (7)	57
KISSES SWEETER THAN WINE — Frankie **Vaughan** (8)	57
KISSIN' COUSINS — Elvis **Presley** (10)	64
KISSIN' IN THE BACK ROW OF THE MOVIES — **Drifters** (2)	74
KITES — Simon **Dupree and The Big Sound** (9)	67
KITSCH — Barry **Ryan** (37)	70
KITTY — Cat **Stevens** (47)	67
KLACTOVEESEDSTEIN — **Blue Rondo a la Turk** (50)	82
KNEE DEEP IN THE BLUES — Guy **Mitchell** (3)	57
KNEE DEEP IN THE BLUES — Tommy **Steele** (15)	57
KNOCK KNOCK WHO'S THERE — Mary **Hopkin** (2)	70
KNOCK ME OUT — **Gary's Gang** (45)	82
KNOCK ON WOOD — David **Bowie** (10)	74
KNOCK ON WOOD — Eddie **Floyd** (19)	67
KNOCK ON WOOD — Otis **Redding and Carla Thomas** (35)	67
KNOCK ON WOOD — Amii **Stewart** (6)	79
KNOCK THREE TIMES — **Dawn** (1)	71
KNOCKED IT OFF — B.A. **Robertson** (8)	79
KNOCKIN' ON HEAVEN'S DOOR — Eric **Clapton** (38)	75
KNOCKIN' ON HEAVEN'S DOOR — Bob **Dylan** (14)	73
KNOW YOUR RIGHTS — **Clash** (43)	82
KNOWING ME KNOWING YOU — **Abba** (1)	77
KOMMOTION — Duane **Eddy** (13)	60
KON TIKI — **Shadows** (37)	61
KON-TIKI — **Shadows** (1)	61
KOOKIE KOOKIE (LEND ME YOUR COMB) — Edward **Byrnes and Connie Stevens** (27)	60
KOOKIE LITTLE PARADISE — Frankie **Vaughan** (31)	60
KOOL IN THE KAFTAN — B.A. **Robertson** (17)	80
KU KLUX KLAN — **Steel Pulse** (41)	78
KUMBAYA — **Sandpipers** (39)	69
KUNG FU FIGHTING — Carl **Douglas** (1)	74
KYRILA (EP) — Demis **Roussos** (33)	77
L. A. CONNECTION — **Rainbow** (40)	78
LA BOOGA ROOGA — **Surprise Sisters** (38)	76
LA DEE DAH — Jackie **Dennis** (4)	58
LA FOLIE — **Stranglers** (47)	82
LA LA LA — **Massiel** (35)	68
LA YENKA — **Johnny and Charley** (49)	65
LABELLED WITH LOVE — **Squeeze** (4)	81
LA-DI-DA — **Sad Café** (41)	80
LADIES NIGHT — **Kool and the Gang** (9)	79
LADY [A] — Kenny **Rogers** (12)	80
LADY [B] — **Whispers** (55)	80
LADY BARBARA — **Herman's Hermits** (13)	70
LADY D'ARBANVILLE — Cat **Stevens** (8)	70
LADY ELEANOR — **Lindisfarne** (3)	72
LADY GODIVA — **Peter and Gordon** (16)	66
LADY IS A TRAMP — Buddy **Greco** (26)	60
LADY JANE — David **Garrick** (28)	66
LADY JANE — Tony **Merrick** (49)	66
LADY LOVE BUG — Clodagh **Rodgers** (28)	71
LADY LUCK — Lloyd **Price** (45)	60
LADY LYNDA — **Beach Boys** (6)	79
LADY MADONNA — **Beatles** (1)	68
LADY MARMALADE (VOULEZ-VOUS COUCHER AVEC MOI CE SOIR?) — **Labelle** (17)	75
LADY ROSE — **Mungo Jerry** (5)	71
LADY WILLPOWER — Gary **Puckett and the Union Gap** (5)	68
LADY WRITER — **Dire Straits** (51)	79
LADY (YOU BRING ME UP) — **Commodores** (56)	81
LADYBIRD — Nancy **Sinatra and Lee Hazelwood** (47)	67
LA-LA MEANS I LOVE YOU — **Delfonics** (19)	71
LAMPLIGHT — David **Essex** (7)	73
LANA — Roy **Orbison** (15)	66
LAND OF MAKE BELIEVE, THE — **Buck's Fizz** (1)	81
LAND OF 1000 DANCES — Wilson **Pickett** (22)	66
LANDSLIDE — Olivia **Newton-John** (18)	82
LANGUAGE OF LOVE, THE — John D. **Loudermilk** (13)	62
L.A.RUN, THE — **Carvells** (31)	77
LAS PALABRAS DE AMOR — **Queen** (17)	82
LAS VEGAS — Tony **Christie** (21)	71
LASER LOVE [A] — **T. Rex** (41)	76
LASER LOVE [B] — **After The Fire** (62)	79
LAST DANCE — Donna **Summer** (51)	78
LAST FAREWELL, THE — Ship's Company and Royal Marine band of H.M.S. **Ark Royal** (46)	78
LAST FAREWELL, THE — Roger **Whittaker** (2)	75
LAST NIGHT — **Merseybeats** (40)	64
LAST NIGHT ANOTHER SOLDIER — **Angelic Upstarts** (51)	80
LAST NIGHT AT DANCELAND — Randy **Crawford** (61)	80
LAST NIGHT IN SOHO — Dave **Dee, Dozy, Beaky, Mick and Tich** (8)	68
LAST NIGHT ON THE BACK PORCH — Alma **Cogan** (27)	59
LAST NIGHT WAS MADE FOR LOVE — Billy **Fury** (4)	62
LAST TIME I SAW HIM — Diana **Ross** (35)	74
LAST TIME, THE — **Rolling Stones** (1)	65
LAST TIME, THE — **Who** (44)	67
LAST TRAIN TO CLARKSVILLE — **Monkees** (23)	67
LAST TRAIN TO LONDON — **Electric Light Orchestra** (8)	79

Title — Act (Position)	Year of Chart Entry
LAST TRAIN TO SAN FERNANDO — Johnny **Duncan and the Blue Grass Boys** (2)	57
LAST WALTZ, THE — Engelbert **Humperdinck** (1)	67
LATE IN THE EVENING — Paul **Simon** (58)	80
LATELY — Rudy **Grant** (58)	81
LATELY — Stevie **Wonder** (3)	80
LAUGH AT ME — **Sonny** (9)	65
LAUGHING GNOME, THE — David **Bowie** (6)	73
LAUGHTER IN THE RAIN — Neil **Sedaka** (15)	74
LAUREL & HARDY — **Equals** (35)	68
LAW OF THE LAND — **Temptations** (41)	73
LAWDY MISS CLAWDY — Elvis **Presley** (15)	57
LAWNCHAIRS — **Our Daughter's Wedding** (49)	81
LAY ALL YOUR LOVE ON ME — **Abba** (7)	81
LAY BACK IN THE ARMS OF SOMEONE — **Smokie** (12)	77
LAY DOWN — **Strawbs** (12)	72
LAY DOWN SALLY — Eric **Clapton** (39)	77
LAY DOWN YOUR ARMS — Anne **Shelton** (1)	56
LAY LADY LAY — Bob **Dylan** (5)	69
LAY LOVE ON YOU — Luisa **Fernandez** (31)	78
LAY YOUR LOVE ON ME — **Racey** (3)	78
LAYLA — **Derek and the Dominos** (4)	72,82
LAZY BONES — Jonathan **King** (23)	71
LAZY RIVER — Bobby **Darin** (2)	61
LAZY SUNDAY — **Small Faces** (2)	68,76
LE FREAK — **Chic** (7)	78
LEADER OF THE PACK — **Shangri-Las** (3)	65,72,76
LEAN ON ME — **Mud** (7)	76
LEAN ON ME — Bill **Withers** (18)	72
LEAP UP AND DOWN (WAVE YOUR KNICKERS IN THE AIR) — **St. Cecilia** (12)	71
LEARNIN' THE BLUES — Frank **Sinatra** (2)	55
LEARNIN' THE GAME — Buddy **Holly** (36)	60
LEAVE A LITTLE LOVE — **Lulu** (8)	65
LEAVE IN SILENCE — **Depeche Mode** (18)	82
LEAVE IT — Mike **McGear** (36)	74
LEAVIN' ON A JET PLANE — **Peter, Paul and Mary** (2)	70
LEAVING HERE — **Birds** (45)	65
LEAVING ON THE MIDNIGHT TRAIN — Nick **Straker Band** (61)	80
LEEDS UNITED — **Leeds United FC** (10)	72
LEFT BANK — Winifred **Atwell** (14)	56
LEGAL MATTER, A — **Who** (32)	66
LEGEND OF XANADU — Dave **Dee, Dozy, Beaky, Mick and Tich** (1)	68
LEGO SKANGA — Rupie **Edwards** (32)	75
LES BICYCLETTES DE BELSIZE — Engelbert **Humperdinck** (5)	68
LESSON ONE — Russ **Conway** (21)	62
LESSONS IN LOVE — **Allisons** (30)	62
LET 'EM IN — Billy **Paul** (26)	77
LET 'EM IN — **Wings** (2)	76
LET IT ALL HANG OUT — Jonathan **King** (26)	70
LET IT BE — **Beatles** (2)	70
LET IT BE ME — **Everly Brothers** (13)	60
LET IT RAIN — **UFO** (62)	82
LET IT ROCK — Chuck **Berry** (6)	63
LET IT ROCK — **Rolling Stones** (2)	71
LET ME BE THE NUMBER ONE — Dooley **Silverspoon** (44)	76
LET ME BE THE ONE — **Shadows** (12)	75
LET ME COME ON HOME — Otis **Redding** (48)	67
LET ME CRY ON YOUR SHOULDER — Ken **Dodd** (11)	67
LET ME GO — **Heaven 17** (41)	82
LET ME GO LOVER — Teresa **Brewer** (9)	55
LET ME GO LOVER — Kathy **Kirby** (10)	64
LET ME GO LOVER — Dean **Martin** (3)	55
LET ME GO LOVER — Ruby **Murray** (5)	55
LET ME GO LOVER — Joan **Weber** (16)	55
LET ME IN — **Osmonds** (2)	73
LET ME INTRODUCE YOU TO THE FAMILY — **Stranglers** (42)	81
LET ME KNOW (I HAVE A RIGHT) — Gloria **Gaynor** (32)	79
LET ME ROCK YOU — **Kandidate** (58)	80
LET ME TALK — **Earth Wind and Fire** (29)	80
LET ME TRY AGAIN — Tammy **Jones** (5)	75
LET MY NAME BE SORROW — Mary **Hopkin** (46)	71
LET SOMEBODY LOVE YOU — Keni **Burke** (59)	81
LET THE HEARTACHES BEGIN — Long John **Baldry** (1)	67
LET THE LITTLE GIRL DANCE — Billy **Bland** (15)	60
LET THE MUSIC PLAY [A] — Charles **Earland** (46)	78
LET THE MUSIC PLAY [B] — Barry **White** (9)	75
LET THE SUNSHINE IN — **Peddlers** (50)	65
LET THE WATER RUN DOWN — P. J. **Proby** (19)	65
LET THERE BE DRUMS — Sandy **Nelson** (3)	61
LET THERE BE LOVE — Nat "King" **Cole** (11)	62
LET THERE BE PEACE ON EARTH (LET IT BEGIN WITH ME) — Michael **Ward** (15)	73
LET TRUE LOVE BEGIN — Nat "King" **Cole** (29)	61
LET YOUR BODY GO DOWNTOWN — Martyn **Ford** (38)	77
LET YOUR HEART DANCE — **Secret Affair** (32)	79
LET YOUR LOVE FLOW — **Bellamy Brothers** (7)	76
LET YOUR YEAH BE YEAH — **Pioneers** (5)	71
LET YOURSELF GO — **T-Connection** (52)	78
LET'S — Sarah **Vaughan** (37)	60
LET'S ALL CHANT — Michael **Zager Band** (8)	78
LETS ALL SING LIKE THE BIRDIES SING — **Tweets** (44)	81
LET'S BE FRIENDS — Johnny **Nash** (42)	75
LET'S CALL IT QUITS — **Slade** (11)	76
LET'S CELEBRATE — **New York Skyy** (67)	82
LET'S CLEAN UP THE GHETTO — **Philadelphia International All-stars** (34)	77
LET'S DANCE — **Bombers** (58)	79
LET'S DANCE — Chris **Montez** (2)	62,72,79
LET'S DO ROCK STEADY — **Bodysnatchers** (22)	80
LET'S DO THE LATIN HUSTLE — Eddie **Drennon and B. B. S. Unlimited** (20)	76
LET'S DO THE LATIN HUSTLE — **M and O Band** (16)	76
LET'S FLY AWAY — **Voyage** (38)	79
LET'S FUNK TONIGHT — **Blue Feather** (50)	82
LET'S GET FUNKTIFIED — **Boiling Point** (41)	78
LET'S GET IT ON — Marvin **Gaye** (31)	73
LET'S GET IT UP — **AC/DC** (13)	82
LET'S GET SERIOUS — Jermaine **Jackson** (8)	80
LET'S GET THIS STRAIGHT (FROM THE START) — **Dexy's Midnight Runners** (17)	82
LET'S GET TOGETHER — Hayley **Mills** (17)	61
LET'S GET TOGETHER AGAIN — **Big Ben Banjo Band** (18)	55
LET'S GET TOGETHER AGAIN [B] — **Glitter Band** (8)	74
LET'S GET TOGETHER NO. 1 [A] — **Big Ben Banjo Band** (6)	54
LET'S GO [A] — **Cars** (51)	79
LET'S GO [B] — **Routers** (32)	62
LET'S GO [C] — **Vardis** (59)	80
LET'S GO DISCO — **Real Thing** (39)	78
LET'S GO ROUND AGAIN PT.1 — **Average White Band** (12)	80
LET'S GO STEADY AGAIN — Neil **Sedaka** (42)	63
LET'S GO TO BED — **Cure** (44)	82
LET'S GO TO SAN FRANCISCO — **Flowerpot Men** (4)	67
LET'S GROOVE — **Earth Wind and Fire** (3)	81
LET'S HANG ON — **Darts** (11)	80
LET'S HANG ON — **Four Seasons** (4)	65
LET'S HANG ON — Johnny **Johnson and the Bandwagon** (36)	69
LET'S HANG ON — Barry **Manilow** (12)	81
LET'S HAVE A BALL — Winifred **Atwell** (4)	57
LET'S HAVE A DING DONG — Winifred **Atwell** (3)	55
LET'S HAVE A PARTY [A] — Winifred **Atwell** (2)	53,54
LET'S HAVE A PARTY [B] — Wanda **Jackson** (32)	60
LET'S HAVE A QUIET NIGHT IN — David **Soul** (8)	77
LET'S HAVE ANOTHER PARTY — Winifred **Atwell** (1)	54
LET'S JUMP THE BROOMSTICK — **Coast To Coast** (28)	81
LET'S JUMP THE BROOMSTICK — Brenda **Lee** (12)	61
LET'S LOVE DANCE TONIGHT — **Gary's Gang** (49)	79
LET'S MAKE A BABY — Billy **Paul** (30)	76
LET'S PRETEND — **Lulu** (11)	67
LET'S PUT IT ALL TOGETHER — **Stylistics** (9)	74
LET'S ROCK 'N ROLL — Winifred **Atwell** (24)	57
LET'S SEE ACTION — **Who** (16)	71
LET'S SLIP AWAY — Cleo **Laine** (42)	60
LET'S SPEND THE NIGHT TOGETHER — **Rolling Stones** (3)	67
LET'S START THE DANCE — Hamilton **Bohannon** (56)	78
LET'S START TO DANCE AGAIN — Hamilton **Bohannon** (49)	82
LET'S STAY TOGETHER — Al **Green** (7)	72
LET'S STICK TOGETHER — Bryan **Ferry** (4)	76
LET'S TALK ABOUT LOVE — Helen **Shapiro** (23)	62
LET'S THINK ABOUT LIVING — Bob **Luman** (6)	60
LET'S TURKEY TROT — **Little Eva** (13)	63
LET'S TWIST AGAIN — John **Asher** (14)	75
LET'S TWIST AGAIN — Chubby **Checker** (2)	61,62,75
LET'S WALK THATA-WAY — Doris **Day and Johnnie Ray** (4)	53
LET'S WOMBLE TO THE PARTY TONIGHT — **Wombles** (34)	75
LET'S WORK TOGETHER — **Canned Heat** (2)	70
LETTER [A] — **Box Tops** (5)	67
LETTER [A] — **Long And The Short** (30)	64
LETTER [B] — Joe **Cocker** (39)	70
LETTER [B] — **Mindbenders** (42)	67
LETTER FULL OF TEARS — Billy **Fury** (32)	62
LETTER, THE — Amii **Stewart** (39)	80
LETTER TO A SOLDIER — Barbara **Lyon** (27)	56
LETTER TO LUCILLE — Tom **Jones** (31)	73
LETTING GO — **Wings** (41)	75
LIAR — Graham **Bonnet** (51)	81
LICK A SMURP FOR CHRISTMAS (ALL FALL DOWN) — Father **Abraphart and the Smurps** (58)	78
LIDO SHUFFLE — Boz **Scaggs** (13)	77
LIES [A] — **Status Quo** (11)	80
LIES [B] — **Thompson Twins** (67)	82
LIES IN YOUR EYES — **Sweet** (35)	76
LIFE BEGINS AT THE HOP — **XTC** (54)	79
LIFE IN A DAY — **Simple Minds** (62)	79
LIFE IN TOKYO — **Japan** (28)	82
LIFE IS A LONG SONG — **Jethro Tull** (11)	71
LIFE IS A MINESTRONE — **10 C. C.** (7)	75
LIFE IS A ROCK (BUT THE RADIO ROLLED ME) — **Reunion** (33)	74
LIFE IS FOR LIVING — **Barclay James Harvest** (61)	80
LIFE IS TOO SHORT GIRL — **Sheer Elegance** (9)	76
LIFE ON MARS — David **Bowie** (3)	73
LIFELINE — **Spandau Ballet** (7)	82
LIFE'S BEEN GOOD — Joe **Walsh** (14)	78
LIGHT FLIGHT — **Pentangle** (43)	70
LIGHT MY FIRE — **Doors** (49)	67
LIGHT MY FIRE — José **Feliciano** (6)	68
LIGHT MY FIRE — Amii **Stewart** (5)	79
(LIGHT OF EXPERIENCE) DOINA DE JALE — Georghe **Zamfir** (6)	76
LIGHT OF LOVE — **T. Rex** (22)	74
LIGHT UP THE FIRE — **Parchment** (31)	72
LIGHT UP THE NIGHT — **Brothers Johnson** (47)	80
LIGHTNIN' STRIKES — Lou **Christie** (11)	66
LIGHTNING FLASH — **Brotherhood Of Man** (67)	82
LIGHTNING TREE, THE — The **SETTLERS** (36)	71
LIGHTS OF CINCINATTI — Scott **Walker** (13)	69
LIKE A BABY — Len **Barry** (10)	66
LIKE A BUTTERFLY — Mac and Katie **Kissoon** (18)	75
LIKE A CHILD — Julie **Rogers** (21)	64
LIKE A ROLLING STONE — Bob **Dylan** (4)	65
LIKE AN OLD TIME MOVIE — Scott **McKenzie** (50)	67
LIKE CLOCKWORK — **Boomtown Rats** (6)	78
LIKE DREAMERS DO — **Applejacks** (20)	64
LIKE I DO — Maureen **Evans** (3)	62
LIKE I'VE NEVER BEEN GONE — Billy **Fury** (3)	63
LIKE SISTER AND BROTHER — **Drifters** (7)	73
LIKE STRANGERS — **Everly Brothers** (11)	60
LIKE WE USED TO BE — Georgie **Fame** (33)	65
LIL RED RIDING HOOD — **999** (59)	81
LIL' RED RIDING HOOD — **Sam The Sham and the Pharaohs** (46)	66
LILAC WINE — Elkie **Brooks** (16)	78
LILY THE PINK — **Scaffold** (1)	68
LIMBO ROCK — Chubby **Checker** (32)	62
LIMELIGHT — Frank **Chacksfield** (2)	53
LIMELIGHT — Ron **Goodwin** (3)	53
LINDA LU — Johnny **Kidd and the Pirates** (47)	61
LINES — **Planets** (36)	79
LION SLEEPS TONIGHT, THE — Dave **Newman** (34)	72
LION SLEEPS TONIGHT, THE — **Tight Fit** (1)	82
LION SLEEPS TONIGHT, THE — **Tokens** (11)	61
LIP UP FATTY — **Bad Manners** (15)	80
LIPSMACKIN' ROCK 'N' ROLLIN' — Peter **Blake** (40)	77
LIPSTICK ON YOUR COLLAR — Connie **Francis** (3)	59
LIQUIDATOR — **Harry J. All Stars** (9)	69,80
LISTEN (EP) — **Stiff Little Fingers** (33)	82
LISTEN LITTLE GIRL — Keith **Kelly** (47)	60
LISTEN TO ME [A] — **Hollies** (11)	68
LISTEN TO ME [B] — Buddy **Holly** (16)	58,62
LISTEN TO THE MUSIC — **Doobie Brothers** (29)	74
LISTEN TO THE OCEAN — **Nina and Frederick** (46)	60
LISTEN TO WHAT THE MAN SAID — **Wings** (6)	75
LITTLE ARROWS — Leapy **Lee** (2)	68
LITTLE BAND OF GOLD — James **Gilreath** (29)	63
LITTLE BERNADETTE — Harry **Belafonte** (16)	58
LITTLE BIT FURTHER AWAY, A — **Kokomo** (45)	82
LITTLE BIT ME A LITTLE BIT YOU, A — **Monkees** (3)	67
LITTLE BIT MORE, A — **Dr. Hook** (2)	76
LITTLE BIT OF LOVE — **Free** (13)	72
LITTLE BIT OF SOAP, A — **Showaddywaddy** (5)	78
LITTLE BITTY TEAR — **Miki and Griff** (16)	62
LITTLE BITTY TEAR, A — Burl **Ives** (9)	62
LITTLE BLACK BOOK — Jimmy **Dean** (33)	62

Title — Act (Position)	Year of Chart Entry
LITTLE BLUE BIRD — Vince **Hill** (42)	**69**
LITTLE BOOGIE WOOGIE IN THE BACK OF MY MIND, A — Gary **Glitter** (31)	**77**
LITTLE BOY LOST — Michael **Holliday** (50)	**60**
LITTLE BOY SAD — Johnny **Burnette** (12)	**61**
LITTLE BROWN JUG — Glenn **Miller** (13)	**76**
LITTLE BY LITTLE — Dusty **Springfield** (17)	**66**
LITTLE CHILDREN — Billy J. **Kramer and the Dakotas** (1)	**64**
LITTLE CHRISTINE — Dick **Jordan** (39)	**60**
LITTLE DARLIN' [A] — **Diamonds** (3)	**57**
LITTLE DARLIN' [B] — Marvin **Gaye** (50)	**66**
LITTLE DARLING — **Rubettes** (30)	**75**
LITTLE DEVIL — Neil **Sedaka** (9)	**61,72**
LITTLE DOES SHE KNOW — **Kursaal Flyers** (14)	**76**
LITTLE DONKEY — **Beverley Sisters** (14)	**59**
LITTLE DONKEY — Gracie **Fields** (20)	**59**
LITTLE DONKEY — **Nina and Frederick** (3)	**60**
LITTLE DROPS OF SILVER — Gerry **Monroe** (37)	**71**
LITTLE DRUMMER BOY — **Beverley Sisters** (6)	**59**
LITTLE DRUMMER BOY — Michael **Flanders** (20)	**59**
LITTLE DRUMMER BOY — The Pipes and Drums and Military Band of the **Royal Scots Dragoon Guards** (13)	**72**
LITTLE DRUMMER BOY — Harry **Simeone Chorale** (13)	**59**
LITTLE GIRL [A] — **Banned** (36)	**77**
LITTLE GIRL [B] — **Troggs** (37)	**68**
LITTLE GIRL [C] — Marty **Wilde** (16)	**60**
LITTLE GREEN APPLES — Roger **Miller** (19)	**68,69**
LITTLE IN LOVE, A — Cliff **Richard** (15)	**81**
LITTLE JEANNIE — Elton **John** (33)	**80**
LITTLE LADY — **Aneka** (50)	**81**
LITTLE LOVE A LITTLE KISS, A — Karl **Denver** (19)	**62**
LITTLE LOVE AND UNDERSTANDING, A — Gilbert **Becaud** (10)	**75**
LITTLE LOVIN', A — Neil **Sedaka** (34)	**74**
LITTLE LOVING, A — **Fourmost** (6)	**64**
LITTLE MAN — **Sonny and Cher** (4)	**66**
LITTLE MISS LONELY — Helen **Shapiro** (8)	**62**
LITTLE MORE LOVE, A — Olivia **Newton-John** (4)	**78**
LITTLE PEACE, A — **Nicole** (1)	**82**
LITTLE PIECE OF LEATHER — Donnie **Elbert** (27)	**72**
LITTLE RED MONKEY — Frank **Chacksfield** (10)	**53**
LITTLE RED ROOSTER — **Rolling Stones** (1)	**64**
LITTLE SERENADE — Eddie **Calvert** (28)	**58**
LITTLE SHOEMAKER, THE — Petula **Clark** (7)	**54**
LITTLE SISTER — Elvis **Presley** (1)	**61**
LITTLE STAR — **Elegants** (25)	**58**
LITTLE THINGS — Dave **Berry** (5)	**65**
LITTLE THINGS MEAN A LOT — Alma **Cogan** (11)	**54**
LITTLE THINGS MEAN A LOT — Kitty **Kallen** (1)	**54**
LITTLE TOWN — Cliff **Richard** (11)	**82**
LITTLE TOWN FLIRT — Del **Shannon** (4)	**63**
LITTLE TRAIN — Max **Bygraves** (28)	**58**
LITTLE WHITE BERRY — Roy **Castle** (40)	**60**
LITTLE WHITE BULL — Tommy **Steele** (6)	**59**
LITTLE WILLY — **Sweet** (4)	**72**
LITTLE YOU, A — **Freddie and the Dreamers** (26)	**65**
LIVE AND LET DIE — **Wings** (9)	**73**
LIVE AT THE MARQUEE (EP) — **Eddie and the Hotrods** (43)	**76**
LIVE (EP) — **Barclay James Harvest** (49)	**77**
LIVE IN THE SKY — Dave **Clark Five** (39)	**68**
LIVE IN TROUBLE — **Barron Knights** (7)	**77**
LIVELY — Lonnie **Donegan** (13)	**60**
LIVERPOOL LOU — **Scaffold** (7)	**74**
LIVIN' IT UP (FRIDAY NIGHT) — **Bell and James** (59)	**79**
LIVIN' LOVIN' DOLL — Cliff **Richard** (20)	**59**
LIVIN' THING — **Electric Light Orchestra** (4)	**76**
LIVING AFTER MIDNIGHT — **Judas Priest** (12)	**80**
LIVING BY NUMBERS — **New Musik** (13)	**80**
LIVING DOLL — Cliff **Richard** (1)	**59**
LIVING FOR THE CITY — **Gillan** (50)	**82**
LIVING FOR THE CITY — Stevie **Wonder** (15)	**74**
LIVING FOR YOU — **Sonny and Cher** (44)	**66**
LIVING IN HARMONY — Cliff **Richard** (12)	**72**
LIVING IN THE PAST — **Jethro Tull** (3)	**69**
LIVING IN THE U.K. — **Shakatak** (52)	**81**
LIVING NEXT DOOR TO ALICE — **Smokie** (5)	**76**
LIVING ON AN ISLAND — **Status Quo** (16)	**79**
LIVING ON THE CEILING — **Blancmange** (7)	**82**
LIVING ON THE FRONT LINE — Eddy **Grant** (11)	**79**
L-L-LUCY — **Mud** (10)	**75**
LOCK UP YOUR DAUGHTERS — **Slade** (29)	**81**
LOCO-MOTION — **Vernons Girls** (47)	**62**
LOCO-MOTION, THE — **Little Eva** (2)	**62,72**
L.O.D. (LOVE ON DELIVERY) — Billy **Ocean** (19)	**76**
LOGICAL SONG, THE — **Supertramp** (7)	**79**
LOLA — **Kinks** (2)	**70**

Title — Act (Position)	Year of Chart Entry
LOLLIPOP — **Chordettes** (6)	**58**
LOLLIPOP — **Mudlarks** (2)	**58**
LONDON BOYS — **T. Rex** (40)	**76**
LONDON CALLING — **Clash** (11)	**79**
LONDON TOWN [A] — **Wings** (60)	**78**
LONDON TOWN [B] — **Light of the World** (41)	**80**
LONE RANGER, THE — **Quantum Jump** (5)	**79**
LONE RIDER — John **Leyton** (40)	**62**
LONELIEST MAN IN THE WORLD, THE — **Tourists** (32)	**79**
LONELINESS — Des **O'Connor** (18)	**69**
LONELY [A] — Mr. Acker **Bilk** (14)	**62**
LONELY [B] — Eddie **Cochran** (41)	**60**
LONELY BALLERINA — **Mantovani** (16)	**55**
LONELY BOY [A] — Paul **Anka** (3)	**59**
LONELY BOY [B] — Andrew **Gold** (11)	**77**
LONELY BOY LONELY GUITAR — Duane **Eddy** (35)	**63**
LONELY BULL, THE — Herb **Alpert** (22)	**63**
LONELY CITY — John **Leyton** (14)	**62**
LONELY DAYS — **Bee Gees** (33)	**70**
LONELY DAYS, LONELY NIGHTS — Don **Downing** (32)	**73**
LONELY HEART — **UFO** (41)	**81**
LONELY MAN THEME — Cliff **Adams** (39)	**60**
LONELY PUP (IN A CHRISTMAS SHOP) — Adam **Faith** (4)	**60**
LONELY STREET — Clarence "Frogman" **Henry** (42)	**61**
LONELY TEENAGER — **Dion** (47)	**61**
LONELY THIS CHRISTMAS — **Mud** (1)	**74**
LONELY TOGETHER — Barry **Manilow** (21)	**80**
LONESOME [A] — Chris **Barber's Jazz Band** (27)	**59**
LONESOME [B] — Adam **Faith** (12)	**62**
LONESOME NUMBER ONE — Don **Gibson** (47)	**62**
LONESOME TRAVELLER — Lonnie **Donegan** (28)	**58**
LONG AFTER TONIGHT IS ALL OVER — Jimmy **Radcliffe** (40)	**65**
LONG AND WINDING ROAD, THE — Ray **Morgan** (32)	**70**
LONG AS I CAN SEE THE LIGHT — **Creedence Clearwater Revival** (20)	**70**
LONG COOL WOMAN IN A BLACK DRESS — **Hollies** (32)	**72**
LONG HAIRED LOVER FROM LIVERPOOL — Little Jimmy **Osmond** (1)	**72**
LONG LEGGED GIRL — Elvis **Presley** (49)	**67**
LONG LIVE LOVE [A] — Olivia **Newton-John** (11)	**74**
LONG LIVE LOVE [B] — Sandie **Shaw** (1)	**65**
LONG LIVE ROCK — **Who** (48)	**79**
LONG LIVE ROCK 'N' ROLL — **Rainbow** (33)	**78**
LONG LOST LOVER — **Three Degrees** (40)	**75**
LONG RUN, THE — **Eagles** (66)	**79**
LONG SHOT KICK DE BUCKET — **Pioneers** (21)	**69,80**
LONG TALL GLASSES — Leo **Sayer** (4)	**74**
LONG TALL SALLY — Pat **Boone** (18)	**56**
LONG TALL SALLY — **Little Richard** (3)	**57**
LONG WAY FROM HOME — **Whitesnake** (55)	**79**
LONGER — Dan **Fogelberg** (59)	**80**
LONGLEGGED WOMAN DRESSED IN BLACK — **Mungo Jerry** (13)	**74**
LONGTIME BOY — **Nina and Frederick** (43)	**61**
LONNIE DONEGAN SHOWCASE (LP) — Lonnie **Donegan** (26)	**56**
LONNIE'S SKIFFLE PARTY — Lonnie **Donegan** (23)	**58**
LOO-BE-LOO — **Chucks** (22)	**63**
LOOK AROUND — Vince **Hill** (12)	**71**
LOOK AT ME (I'M IN LOVE) — **Moments** (42)	**75**
LOOK AT THAT GIRL — Guy **Mitchell** (1)	**53**
LOOK BEFORE YOU LEAP — Dave **Clark Five** (50)	**66**
LOOK FOR A STAR — Garry **Mills** (7)	**60**
LOOK HOMEWARD ANGEL — Johnnie **Ray** (7)	**57**
LOOK OF LOVE [A] — Gladys **Knight and the Pips** (21)	**73**
LOOK OF LOVE [B] — **ABC** (4)	**82**
LOOK THROUGH ANY WINDOW — **Hollies** (4)	**65**
LOOK WHAT YOU DONE FOR ME — Al **Green** (44)	**72**
LOOK WHO IT IS — Helen **Shapiro** (47)	**63**
LOOK WOT YOU DUN — **Slade** (4)	**72**
LOOKIN' THROUGH THE WINDOWS — **Jackson Five** (9)	**72**
LOOKING AFTER NO. 1 — **Boomtown Rats** (11)	**77**
LOOKING FOR CLUES — Robert **Palmer** (33)	**80**
LOOKING FOR LOVE TONIGHT — **Fat Larry's Band** (46)	**79**
LOOKING HIGH HIGH HIGH — Bryan **Johnson** (20)	**60**
LOOKING THROUGH THE EYES OF LOVE — **Partridge Family starring Shirley Jones Cassidy** (9)	**73**
LOOKING THROUGH THE EYES OF LOVE — Gene **Pitney** (3)	**65**
LOOKS LOOKS LOOKS — **Sparks** (26)	**75**
LOOP DI LOVE — **Shag** (4)	**72**

Title — Act (Position)	Year of Chart Entry
LOOP-DE-LOOP — Frankie **Vaughan** (5)	**63**
LOOPZILLA — George **Clinton** (57)	**82**
LORELEI — Lonnie **Donegan** (10)	**60**
LORRAINE — **Bad Manners** (21)	**80**
LOSING MY GRIP — **Samson** (63)	**82**
LOSING YOU [A] — Brenda **Lee** (10)	**63**
LOSING YOU [B] — Dusty **Springfield** (9)	**64**
LOST IN FRANCE — Bonnie **Tyler** (9)	**76**
LOST IN MUSIC — **Sister Sledge** (17)	**79**
LOST JOHN — Lonnie **Donegan** (2)	**56**
LOST WITHOUT YOUR LOVE — **Bread** (27)	**76**
LOUIE LOUIE — **Kingsmen** (26)	**64**
LOUIE LOUIE — **Motorhead** (68)	**78**
LOUIS QUATORZE — **Bow Wow Wow** (66)	**82**
LOUISE — Phil **Everly** (47)	**82**
L. O. V. E. — Al **Green** (24)	**75**
LOVE — John **Lennon** (41)	**82**
LOVE ACTION (I BELIEVE IN LOVE) — **Human League** (3)	**81**
LOVE ALL THE HURT AWAY — Aretha **Franklin and George Benson** (49)	**81**
LOVE AND AFFECTION — Joan **Armatrading** (10)	**76**
LOVE AND DESIRE (PART 1) — **Arpeggio** (63)	**79**
LOVE AND LONELINESS — **Motors** (58)	**80**
LOVE AND MARRIAGE — Frank **Sinatra** (3)	**56**
LOVE AT FIRST SIGHT (JE T'AIME ... MOI NON PLUS) PARLOPHONE — **Sounds Nice** (18)	**69**
LOVE BALLAD — George **Benson** (29)	**79**
LOVE BUG-SWEETS FOR MY SWEET (MEDLEY) — Tina **Charles** (26)	**77**
LOVE CHILD — **Supremes** (15)	**68**
LOVE COME DOWN — Evelyn **King** (7)	**82**
LOVE DISCO STYLE — **Erotic Drum Band** (47)	**79**
LOVE DON'T LIVE HERE ANYMORE — **Rose Royce** (2)	**78**
LOVE ENOUGH FOR TWO — **Prima Donna** (48)	**80**
LOVE GAME, THE — **Mudlarks** (30)	**59**
LOVE GAMES [A] — **Drifters** (33)	**75**
LOVE GAMES [B] — **Level 42** (39)	**81**
LOVE GROWS (WHERE MY ROSEMARY GOES) — **Edison Lighthouse** (1)	**70**
LOVE HANGOVER [A] — Diana **Ross** (10)	**76**
LOVE HANGOVER [B] — **Associates** (21)	**82**
LOVE HAS FOUND ITS WAY — Dennis **Brown** (47)	**82**
LOVE HER — **Walker Brothers** (20)	**65**
LOVE HIT ME — Maxine **Nightingale** (11)	**77**
LOVE HURTS — Jim **Capaldi** (4)	**75**
LOVE I LOST, THE — Harold **Melvin and the Bluenotes** (21)	**74**
LOVE IN C MINOR — **Cerrone** (31)	**77**
LOVE IN THE SUN — **Glitter Band** (15)	**75**
LOVE IN YOUR EYES, THE — Vicky **Leandros** (40)	**72**
LOVE INJECTION — **Trussel** (43)	**80**
LOVE IS A GOLDEN RING — Frankie **Laine** (19)	**57**
LOVE IS A MANY SPLENDOURED THING — **Four Aces** (2)	**55**
LOVE IS A STRANGER — **Eurythmics** (54)	**82**
LOVE IS ALL — Engelbert **Humperdinck** (44)	**73**
LOVE IS ALL — Malcolm **Roberts** (12)	**69**
LOVE IS ALL AROUND — **Troggs** (5)	**67**
LOVE IS ALL IS ALRIGHT — **U.B.40** (29)	**82**
LOVE IS BLUE — Jeff **Beck** (23)	**68**
LOVE IS BLUE (L'AMOUR EST BLEU) — Paul **Mauriat** (12)	**68**
LOVE IS HERE AND NOW YOU'RE GONE — **Supremes** (17)	**67**
LOVE IS IN CONTROL (FINGER ON THE TRIGGER) — Donna **Summer** (18)	**82**
LOVE IS IN THE AIR — John Paul **Young** (5)	**78**
LOVE IS LIFE — **Hot Chocolate** (6)	**70**
LOVE IS LIKE A VIOLIN — Ken **Dodd** (8)	**60**
LOVE IS LIKE OXYGEN — **Sweet** (9)	**78**
LOVE IS LOVE — Barry **Ryan** (25)	**69**
LOVE IS SO EASY — **Stargard** (45)	**78**
LOVE IS STRANGE — **Everly Brothers** (11)	**65**
LOVE IS THE ANSWER — **England Dan and John Ford Coley** (45)	**79**
LOVE IS THE DRUG — **Roxy Music** (2)	**75**
LOVE IS THE SWEETEST THING — Peter **Skellern** (60)	**78**
LOVE KISSES & HEARTACHES — Maureen **Evans** (44)	**60**
LOVE LETTERS — Ketty **Lester** (4)	**62**
LOVE LETTERS — Elvis **Presley** (6)	**66**
LOVE LETTERS IN THE SAND — Pat **Boone** (2)	**57**
LOVE LETTERS IN THE SAND — Vince **Hill** (23)	**67**
LOVE LIKE A MAN — **Ten Years After** (10)	**70**
LOVE LIKE YOU AND ME — Gary **Glitter** (10)	**75**
LOVE LIKE YOURS, A — Ike and Tina **Turner** (16)	**66**
LOVE LOVE LOVE — Bobby **Hebb** (32)	**72**

Title — Act (Position)	Year of Chart Entry
LOVE LOVES TO LOVE LOVE — **Lulu** (32)	67
LOVE MACHINE [A] — **Miracles** (3)	76
LOVE MACHINE [B] — Elvis **Presley** (38)	67
LOVE MAKES THE WORLD GO ROUND — Perry **Como** (6)	58
LOVE MAKES THE WORLD GO ROUND — **Jets** (21)	82
LOVE MAN — Otis **Redding** (43)	69
LOVE ME [A] — Yvonne **Elliman** (6)	76
LOVE ME [B] — Diana **Ross** (38)	74
LOVE ME AS IF THERE WERE NO TOMORROW — Nat "King" **Cole** (11)	56
LOVE ME BABY — Susan **Cadogan** (22)	75
LOVE ME DO — **Beatles** (4)	62
LOVE ME FOR A REASON — **Osmonds** (1)	74
LOVE ME FOREVER — **Esquires** (23)	58
LOVE ME FOREVER — Eydie **Gormé** (21)	58
LOVE ME FOREVER — Marion **Ryan** (5)	58
LOVE ME LIKE A LOVER — Tina **Charles** (28)	76
LOVE ME LIKE I LOVE YOU — **Bay City Rollers** (4)	76
LOVE ME LOVE MY DOG — Peter **Shelley** (3)	75
LOVE ME OR LEAVE ME — Sammy **Davis Jr.** (8)	55
LOVE ME OR LEAVE ME — Doris **Day** (20)	55
LOVE ME TENDER — Richard **Chamberlain** (15)	62
LOVE ME TENDER — Elvis **Presley** (11)	56
LOVE ME TO SLEEP — **Hot Chocolate** (50)	80
LOVE ME TONIGHT [A] — Tom **Jones** (9)	69
LOVE ME TONIGHT [B] — Trevor **Walters** (27)	81
LOVE ME WARM AND TENDER — Paul **Anka** (19)	62
LOVE ME WITH ALL YOUR HEART — Karl **Denver** (37)	64
LOVE MEETING LOVE — **Level 42** (61)	80
LOVE MY WAY — **Psychedelic Furs** (42)	82
LOVE NEEDS NO DISGUISE — Gary **Numan** (33)	81
LOVE OF MY LIFE [A] — **Queen** (63)	79
LOVE OF MY LIFE [B] — **Dooleys** (9)	77
LOVE OF THE COMMON PEOPLE — Nicky **Thomas** (9)	70
LOVE OF THE LOVED — Cilla **Black** (35)	63
LOVE ON A MOUNTAIN TOP — Robert **Knight** (10)	73
LOVE ON A SUMMER NIGHT — **McCrarys** (52)	82
LOVE ON THE LINE — **Barclay James Harvest** (63)	80
LOVE ON THE ROCKS — Neil **Diamond** (17)	80
LOVE OR MONEY [A] — **Blackwells** (46)	61
LOVE OR MONEY [A] — Jimmy **Crawford** (49)	61
LOVE OR MONEY [A] — Billy **Fury** (57)	82
LOVE OR MONEY [B] — Sammy **Hagar** (67)	80
LOVE PATROL — **Dooleys** (29)	80
LOVE PLUS ONE — **Haircut 100** (3)	82
LOVE POTION NO. 9 — **Tygers of Pan Tang** (45)	82
LOVE REALLY HURTS WITHOUT YOU — Billy **Ocean** (2)	76
LOVE SHADOW — **Fashion** (51)	82
LOVE SO RIGHT — **Bee Gees** (41)	76
LOVE SONG [A] — **Damned** (20)	79
LOVE SONG [B] — **Simple Minds** (47)	81
LOVE STORY — **Jethro Tull** (29)	69
LOVE THE ONE YOU'RE WITH — Stephen **Stills** (37)	71
LOVE THEME FROM THE GODFATHER — Andy **Williams** (42)	72
LOVE TO LOVE YOU BABY — Donna **Summer** (4)	76
LOVE TRAIN — **O'Jays** (9)	73
LOVE WILL KEEP US TOGETHER — **Captain and Tennille** (32)	75
LOVE WILL MAKE YOU FAIL IN SCHOOL — Rockey **Sharpe and the Replays** (60)	79
LOVE WILL TEAR US APART — **Joy Division** (13)	80
LOVE WON'T LET ME WAIT — Major **Harris** (37)	75
LOVE X LOVE — George **Benson** (10)	80
LOVE YOU INSIDE OUT — **Bee Gees** (13)	79
LOVE YOU MORE — **Buzzcocks** (34)	78
LOVE YOU SAVE, THE — **Jackson Five** (7)	70
LOVEDRIVE — **Scorpions** (69)	79
L.O.V.E...LOVE — **Orange Juice** (65)	81
LOVELY DAY — Bill **Withers** (7)	78
LOVELY MONEY — **Damned** (42)	82
LOVELY ONE — **Jacksons** (29)	80
LOVER IN YOU, THE — **Sugarhill Gang** (54)	82
LOVER PLEASE — **Vernons Girls** (16)	62
LOVER'S CONCERTO, A — **Toys** (5)	65
LOVER'S HOLIDAY, A — **Change** (14)	80
LOVERS OF THE WORLD UNITE — **David and Jonathan** (7)	66
LOVE'S A PRIMA DONNA — Steve **Harley and COCKNEY REBEL** (41)	76
LOVE'S BEEN GOOD TO ME — Frank **Sinatra** (8)	69
LOVE'S COMIN' AT YA — Melba **Moore** (15)	82
LOVE'S GOTTA HOLD ON ME — **Dollar** (4)	79
LOVE'S JUST A BROKEN HEART — Cilla **Black** (5)	66
LOVE'S MADE A FOOL OF YOU — **Crickets** (26)	59
LOVE'S MADE A FOOL OF YOU — Buddy **Holly** (39)	64
LOVE'S MADE A FOOL OF YOU — **Matchbox** (63)	81
LOVES ME LIKE A ROCK — Paul **Simon** (39)	73
LOVE'S SUCH A WONDERFUL THING — **Real Thing** (33)	77
LOVE'S THEME — **Love Unlimited Orchestra** (10)	74
LOVE'S UNKIND — Donna **Summer** (3)	77
LOVESICK BLUES — Frank **Ifield** (1)	62
LOVIN' LIVIN' AND GIVIN' — Diana **Ross** (54)	78
LOVIN' THINGS — **Marmalade** (6)	68
LOVIN' UP A STORM — Jerry Lee **Lewis** (28)	59
LOVING AND FREE — Kiki **Dee** (13)	76
LOVING ARMS — Elvis **Presley** (47)	81
LOVING JUST FOR FUN — Kelly **Marie** (21)	80
LOVING ON THE LOSING SIDE — Tommy **Hunt** (28)	76
LOVING YOU [A] — Elvis **Presley** (24)	57
LOVING YOU [B] — Minnie **Riperton** (2)	75
LOVE HAS COME AROUND — Donald **Byrd** (41)	81
LOVING YOU AIN'T EASY — **Pagliaro** (31)	72
LOVING YOU [C] — Chris **Rea** (65)	82
LOVING YOU HAS MADE ME BANANAS — Guy **Marks** (25)	78
LOVING YOU IS SWEETER THAN EVER — **Four Tops** (21)	66
LOW RIDER — **War** (12)	76
LOWDOWN — Boz **Scaggs** (28)	76
LUCILLE [A] — **Everly Brothers** (4)	60
LUCILLE [A] — **Little Richard** (10)	57
LUCILLE [B] — Kenny **Rogers** (1)	77
LUCKY DEVIL — Carl **Dobkins JR.** (44)	60
LUCKY DEVIL — Frank **Ifield** (22)	60
LUCKY FIVE — Russ **Conway** (14)	60
LUCKY LIPS — Cliff **Richard** (4)	63
LUCKY NUMBER — Lene **Lovich** (3)	79
LUCKY STARS — Dean **Friedman** (3)	78
LUCY IN THE SKY WITH DIAMONDS — Elton **John** (10)	74
LULLABY OF BROADWAY — Winifred **Shaw** (42)	76
LULLABY OF THE LEAVES — **Ventures** (43)	61
LUMBERED — Lonnie **Donegan** (6)	61
LUNATICS (HAVE TAKEN OVER THE ASYLUM), THE — **Funboy Three** (20)	81
EL LUTE — **Boney M** (12)	79
LUTON AIRPORT — **Cats U.K.** (22)	79
LYDIA — Dean **Friedman** (31)	78
LYIN' EYES — **Eagles** (23)	75
MA BAKER — **Boney M** (2)	77
MA HE'S MAKING EYES AT ME — Johnny **Otis Show** (2)	57
MA HE'S MAKING EYES AT ME — Lena **Zavaroni** (10)	74
MA SAYS PA SAYS — Doris **Day and Johnnie Ray** (12)	53
MACARTHUR PARK — Richard **Harris** (4)	68,72
MACARTHUR PARK — Donna **Summer** (5)	78
MACDONALD'S CAVE — **Piltdown Men** (14)	60
MACHINE GUN — **Commodores** (20)	74
MACHINERY — Sheena **Easton** (38)	82
MACK THE KNIFE — Louis **Armstrong** (24)	59
MACK THE KNIFE — Bobby **Darin** (1)	59,79
MACK THE KNIFE — Ella **Fitzgerald** (19)	60
MAD ABOUT YOU — Bruce **Ruffin** (9)	72
MAD EYED SCREAMER — **Creatures** (24)	81
MAD PASSIONATE LOVE — Bernard **Bresslaw** (6)	58
MAD WORLD — **Tears For Fears** (3)	82
MADE TO LOVE (GIRLS GIRLS GIRLS) — Eddie **Hodges** (37)	62
MADE YOU — Adam **Faith** (5)	60
MADISON, THE — Ray **Ellington** (36)	62
MAGGIE MAY — Rod **Stewart** (1)	71,76
MAGGIE'S FARM — Bob **Dylan** (22)	65
MAGGIE'S FARM — The **Specials** (4)	80
MAGIC [A] — Olivia **Newton-John** (32)	80
MAGIC [B] — **Pilot** (11)	74
MAGIC BUS — **Who** (26)	68
MAGIC FLY — **Space** (2)	77
MAGIC MANDRAKE — **Sarr Band** (68)	78
MAGIC MIND — **Earth Wind and Fire** (54)	78
MAGIC MOMENTS — Perry **Como** (1)	58
MAGIC MOMENTS — Ronnie **Hilton** (22)	58
MAGIC ROUNDABOUT — Jasper **Carrott** (5)	75
MAGIC TOUCH — **Odyssey** (41)	82
MAGICAL MYSTERY TOUR (DOUBLE EP) — **Beatles** (2)	67
MAGICAL SPIEL — Barry **Ryan** (49)	70
MAGIC'S WAND — **Whodini** (73)	82
MAGNIFICENT SEVEN [A] — John **Barry** (45)	61
MAGNIFICENT SEVEN [A] — Al **Caiola** (34)	61
MAGNIFICENT SEVEN, THE — John **Barry** (47)	61
MAGNIFICENT SEVEN [B] — **Clash** (34)	81
MAGNUM (DOUBLE SINGLE) — **Magnum** (47)	80
MAH NA MAH NA — Piero **Umiliani** (8)	77
MAHOGANY (DO YOU KNOW WHERE YOU'RE GOING TO), THEME FROM — Diana **Ross** (5)	76
MAID OF ORLEANS (THE WALTZ JOAN OF ARC) — **Orchestral Manoeuvres in the Dark** (4)	82
MAIDEN JAPAN — **Iron Maiden** (43)	81
MAIGRET THEME, THE — Joe **Loss** (20)	62
MAIN ATTRACTION, THE — Pat **Boone** (12)	62
MAIS OUI — **King Brothers** (16)	60
MAJORCA — Petula **Clark** (12)	55
MAKE A DAFT NOISE FOR CHRISTMAS — **Goodies** (20)	75
MAKE A MOVE ON ME — Olivia **Newton-John** (43)	82
MAKE HER MINE — Nat "King" **Cole** (11)	54
MAKE IT A PARTY — Winifred **Atwell** (7)	56
MAKE IT EASY ON YOURSELF — **Walker Brothers** (1)	65
MAKE IT REAL — **Scorpions** (72)	80
MAKE IT SOON — Tony **Brent** (9)	53
MAKE IT WITH YOU — **Bread** (5)	70
MAKE LOVE TO ME — John **Leyton** (49)	64
MAKE LOVE TO ME — Jo **Stafford** (8)	54
MAKE ME AN ISLAND — Joe **Dolan** (3)	69
MAKE ME SMILE (COME UP AND SEE ME) — Steve **Harley and COCKNEY REBEL** (1)	75
MAKE THAT MOVE — **Shalamar** (30)	81
MAKE THE WORLD GO AWAY — Eddy **Arnold** (8)	66
MAKE THE WORLD GO AWAY — Donny and Marie **Osmond** (18)	75
MAKE YOURS A HAPPY HOME — Gladys **Knight and the Pips** (35)	76
MAKIN' IT — David **Naughton** (44)	79
MAKIN' LOVE — Floyd **Robinson** (9)	59
MAKIN' WHOOPEE — Ray **Charles** (42)	65
MAKING PLANS FOR NIGEL — **XTC** (17)	79
MAKING TIME — **Creation** (49)	66
MAKING UP AGAIN — **Goldie** (7)	78
MAKING YOUR MIND UP — **Buck's Fizz** (1)	81
MALT AND BARLEY BLUES — **McGuinness Flint** (5)	71
MAMA — David **Whitfield** (12)	55
MAMA [A] — Dave **Berry** (5)	66
MAMA [B] — Connie **Francis** (2)	60
MAMA [B] — David **Whitfield** (20)	55
MAMA NEVER TOLD ME — **Sister Sledge** (20)	75
MAMA TOLD ME NOT TO COME — **Three Dog Night** (3)	70
MAMA USED TO SAY (AMERICAN REMIX) — **Junior** (7)	82
MAMA WEER ALL CRAZEE NOW — **Slade** (1)	72
MA-MA-MA-BELLE — **Electric Light Orchestra** (22)	74
MAMA'S BOY — Suzi **Quatro** (34)	80
MAMA'S PEARL — **Jackson Five** (25)	71
MAMBO ITALIANO — Rosemary **Clooney** (1)	54
MAMBO ITALIANO — Dean **Martin** (14)	55
MAMBO ROCK — Bill **Haley and his Comets** (14)	55
MAMMA MIA — **Abba** (1)	75
MAMY BLUE — **Pop Tops** (34)	71
MAMY BLUE — Roger **Whittaker** (31)	71
MAN — Rosemary **Clooney** (7)	54
MAN FROM LARAMIE, THE — Al **Martino** (19)	55
MAN FROM LARAMIE, THE — Jimmy **Young** (1)	55
MAN FROM MADRID — Tony **Osborne Sound** (50)	61
MAN FROM NAZARETH — John Paul **Joans** (25)	70
MAN IN BLACK, THE — Cozy **Powell** (18)	74
MAN OF MYSTERY — **Shadows** (5)	60
MAN OF THE WORLD — **Fleetwood Mac** (2)	69
MAN ON FIRE — Frankie **Vaughan** (6)	57
MAN ON THE CORNER — **Genesis** (41)	82
MAN OUT OF TIME — Elvis **Costello and the Attractions** (58)	82
MAN THAT GOT AWAY, THE — Judy **Garland** (18)	55
MAN TO MAN — **Hot Chocolate** (14)	76
MAN WHO PLAYS THE MANDOLINO, THE — Dean **Martin** (21)	57
MAN WHO SOLD THE WORLD, THE — **Lulu** (3)	74
MAN WITH THE CHILD IN HIS EYES — Kate **Bush** (6)	78
MAN WITH THE GOLDEN ARM, MAIN TITLE THEME FROM — Jet **Harris** (12)	62
MAN WITH THE GOLDEN ARM, MAIN TITLE THEME FROM — Billy **May** (9)	56
MAN WITHOUT LOVE [A] — Engelbert **Humperdinck** (2)	68
MAN WITHOUT LOVE [B] — Kenneth **McKellar** (30)	66
MANCHESTER UNITED — **Manchester United Football Club** (50)	76
MANDOLINS IN THE MOONLIGHT — Perry **Como** (13)	58

Title — Act (Position)	Year of Chart Entry
MANDY [A] — Eddie **Calvert** (9)	**58**
MANDY [B] — Barry **Manilow** (11)	**75**
MANEATER — Daryl **Hall and John Oates** (6)	**82**
MANGOS — Rosemary **Clooney** (17)	**57**
MANHATTAN SPIRITUAL — Reg **Owen** (20)	**59**
MANNEQUIN — **Kids From 'Fame'** (50)	**82**
MANY TEARS AGO — Connie **Francis** (12)	**61**
MANY TOO MANY — **Genesis** (43)	**78**
MARBLE BREAKS IRON BENDS — Peter **Fenton** (46)	**66**
MARCH OF THE MODS — Joe **Loss** (31)	**64**
MARCH OF THE SIAMESE CHILDREN — Kenny **Ball and his Jazzmen** (4)	**62**
MARCHETA — Karl **Denver** (8)	**61**
MARGATE — **Chas and Dave** (46)	**82**
MARGIE — Fats **Domino** (18)	**59**
MARGOT — Billy **Fury** (28)	**59**
MARIA — P. J. **Proby** (8)	**65**
MARIA ELENA [A] — **Indios Tabajaras** (5)	**63**
MARIA ELENA [B] — Gene **Pitney** (25)	**69**
MARIANA — **Gibson Brothers** (11)	**80**
MARIANNE — **Hilltoppers** (20)	**57**
MARIANNE [B] — Cliff **Richard** (22)	**68**
MARIE — **Bachelors** (9)	**65**
MARIE CELESTE — **Polecats** (53)	**81**
MARIE MARIE — Shakin' **Stevens** (19)	**80**
MARJORINE — Joe **Cocker** (48)	**68**
MARKET SQUARE HEROES — **Marillion** (60)	**82**
MAROC 7 — **Shadows** (24)	**67**
MARQUEE MOON — **Television** (30)	**77**
MARRAKESH EXPRESS — **Crosby, Stills and Nash** (17)	**69**
MARRIED MEN — Bonnie **Tyler** (35)	**79**
MARRY ME — Mike **Preston** (14)	**61**
MARTA — **Bachelors** (20)	**67**
MARTIAN HOP — Rockey **Sharpe and the Replays** (55)	**80**
MARVIN THE PARANOID ANDROID — **Marvin** (53)	**81**
MARY ANN — **Black Lace** (42)	**79**
MARY ANNE — **Shadows** (17)	**65**
MARY HAD A LITTLE LAMB — **Wings** (9)	**72**
MARY JANE — Del **Shannon** (35)	**64**
MARY OF THE FOURTH FORM — **Boomtown Rats** (15)	**77**
MARY'S BOY CHILD — Harry **Belafonte** (1)	**57,58,59**
MARY'S BOY CHILD — **Nina and Frederick** (26)	**59**
MARY'S BOY CHILD - OH MY LORD — **Boney M** (1)	**78**
MASQUERADE — **Skids** (14)	**79**
MASSACHUSETTS — **Bee Gees** (1)	**67**
MASTERBLASTER (JAMMIN') — Stevie **Wonder** (2)	**80**
MATADOR — **Jeff Wayne** (57)	**82**
MATCHSTALK MEN AND MATCHSTALK CATS AND DOGS — **Brian and Michael** (1)	**78**
MATTHEW AND SON — Cat **Stevens** (2)	**67**
MAY EACH DAY — Andy **Williams** (19)	**66**
MAY I HAVE THE NEXT DREAM WITH YOU — Malcolm **Roberts** (8)	**68**
MAY THE SUN SHINE — **Nazareth** (22)	**79**
MAY YOU ALWAYS — **McGuire Sisters** (15)	**59**
MAY YOU ALWAYS — Joan **Regan** (9)	**59**
MAYBE — Thom **Pace** (14)	**79**
MAYBE BABY — **Crickets** (4)	**58**
MAYBE I KNOW — Lesley **Gore** (20)	**64**
MAYBE I KNOW — **Seashells** (32)	**72**
MAYBE I'M AMAZED — **Wings** (28)	**77**
MAYBE TOMORROW — Billy **Fury** (18)	**59**
MAYBE TOMORROW [A] — **Chords** (40)	**80**
MAYBE TOMORROW [B] — Billy **Fury** (22)	**59**
ME & JULIO DOWN BY THE SCHOOLYARD — Paul **Simon** (15)	**72**
ME & MRS JONES — Billy **Paul** (12)	**73**
ME AND BABY BROTHER — **War** (21)	**76**
ME AND MR SANCHEZ — **Blue Rondo a la Turk** (40)	**81**
ME AND MY GIRL (NIGHT-CLUBBING) — David **Essex** (13)	**82**
ME AND MY LIFE — **Tremeloes** (4)	**70**
ME AND MY SHADOW — Frank **Sinatra and Sammy Davis JR.** (20)	**62**
ME AND YOU AND A DOG NAMED BOO — **Lobo** (4)	**71**
ME MYSELF I — Joan **Armatrading** (21)	**80**
ME NO POP I — Kid **Creole and the Coconuts** (40)	**81**
ME THE PEACEFUL HEART — **Lulu** (9)	**68**
MEAN GIRL — **Status Quo** (20)	**73**
MEAN MEAN MAN — Wanda **Jackson** (40)	**61**
MEAN STREAK — Cliff **Richard** (10)	**59**
MEAN TO ME — Shaye **Cogan** (43)	**60**
MEAN WOMAN BLUES — Roy **Orbison** (3)	**63**
MEANING OF LOVE, THE — **Depeche Mode** (12)	**82**
MECCA — **Cheetahs** (36)	**64**
MEET ME ON THE CORNER [A] — Max **Bygraves** (2)	**55**
MEET ME ON THE CORNER [B] — **Lindisfarne** (5)	**72**
MELLOW MELLOW RIGHT ON — **Lowrell** (37)	**79**
MELLOW YELLOW — **Donovan** (8)	**67**
MELODY OF LOVE — **Ink Spots** (10)	**55**
MELT — **Siouxsie and the Banshees** (49)	**82**
MELTING POT — **Blue Mink** (3)	**69**
MEMO FROM TURNER — Mick **Jagger** (32)	**70**
MEMORIES [A] — Mike **Berry** (55)	**81**
MEMORIES [B] — **Public Image Ltd.** (60)	**79**
MEMORIES ARE MADE OF THIS — Val **Doonican** (11)	**67**
MEMORIES ARE MADE OF THIS — Dave **King** (5)	**56**
MEMORIES ARE MADE OF THIS — Dean **Martin** (1)	**56**
MEMORY — Elaine **Paige** (6)	**81**
MEMORY — Barbra **Streisand** (34)	**82**
MEMPHIS — Lonnie **Mack** (47)	**79**
MEMPHIS TENNESSEE — Chuck **Berry** (6)	**63**
MEMPHIS TENNESSEE — Dave **Berry** (19)	**63**
LA MER (BEYOND THE SEA) — Bobby **Darin** (8)	**60**
MERCI CHERI — Vince **Hill** (36)	**66**
MERRY CHRISTMAS DARLING — **Carpenters** (45)	**72**
MERRY GENTLE POPS — **Barron Knights** (9)	**65**
MERRY JINGLE, A — **Greedies** (28)	**79**
MERRY PLOUGHBOY, THE — Dermot **O'Brien** (46)	**66**
MERRY XMAS EVERYBODY — **Slade** (1)	**73,80**
MESS OF BLUES, A — Elvis **Presley** (2)	**60**
MESSAGE IN A BOTTLE — **Police** (1)	**79**
MESSAGE OF LOVE — **Pretenders** (11)	**81**
MESSAGE, THE — **Grand Master Flash and the Furious Five** (8)	**82**
MESSAGE TO MARTHA — Lou **Johnson** (36)	**64**
MESSAGE TO MARTHA (KENTUCKY BLUEBIRD) — Adam **Faith** (12)	**64**
MESSAGE TO YOU RUDY, A — The **Specials** (10)	**79**
MESSAGE UNDERSTOOD — Sandie **Shaw** (6)	**65**
MESSAGES — **Orchestral Manoeuvres in the Dark** (13)	**80**
METAL GURU — **T. Rex** (1)	**72**
METEOR MAN — Dee D. **Jackson** (48)	**78**
MEXICALI ROSE — Karl **Denver** (8)	**61**
MEXICAN GIRL — **Smokie** (19)	**78**
MEXICAN, THE — **Fentones** (41)	**62**
MEXICO — Long John **Baldry** (15)	**68**
MICHAEL — **Highwaymen** (1)	**61**
MICHAEL — Geno **Washington and the Ram Jam Band** (39)	**67**
MICHAEL & THE SLIPPER TREE — **Equals** (24)	**69**
MICHAEL ROW THE BOAT — Lonnie **Donegan** (6)	**61**
MICHELLE — **David and Jonathan** (11)	**66**
MICHELLE — **Overlanders** (1)	**66**
MICKEY — Toni **Basil** (2)	**82**
MIDDLE OF THE NIGHT — **Brotherhood Of Man** (41)	**78**
MIDNIGHT — Paul **Anka** (26)	**58**
MIDNIGHT AT THE OASIS — Maria **Muldaur** (21)	**74**
MIDNIGHT COWBOY — **Midnight Cowboy Soundtrack** (47)	**80**
MIDNIGHT FLYER — Nat "King" **Cole** (23)	**59**
MIDNIGHT GROOVIN' — **Light of the World** (72)	**79**
MIDNIGHT IN MOSCOW — Kenny **Ball and his Jazzmen** (2)	**61**
MIDNIGHT RIDER — **Paul Davidson** (10)	**75**
MIDNIGHT SHIFT — Buddy **Holly** (26)	**59**
MIDNIGHT SPECIAL — Paul **Evans** (41)	**60**
MIDNIGHT TO SIX MAN — **Pretty Things** (46)	**66**
MIDNIGHT TRAIN TO GEORGIA — Gladys **Knight and the Pips** (10)	**76**
MIDNITE DYNAMOS — **Matchbox** (14)	**80**
MIGHTY JOE — **Shocking Blue** (43)	**70**
MIGHTY POWER OF LOVE — **Tavares** (25)	**77**
MIGHTY QUINN — **Manfred Mann** (1)	**68**
MIKE OLDFIELD'S SINGLE (THEME FROM TUBULAR BELLS) — Mike **Oldfield** (31)	**74**
MILES AWAY — John **Foxx** (51)	**80**
MILK AND ALCOHOL — **Dr. Feelgood** (9)	**79**
MILKY WAY — **Sheer Elegance** (18)	**75**
MILLION DRUMS — Tony **Sheveton** (49)	**64**
MILLIONS LIKE US — **Purple Hearts** (57)	**79**
MILLY MOLLY MANDY — Glyn **Poole** (35)	**73**
MILORD — Edith **Piaf** (24)	**60**
MILORD — Frankie **Vaughan** (34)	**60**
MIND BLOWING DECISIONS — **Heatwave** (12)	**78**
MIND BLOWING DECISIONS (REMIXED) — **Heatwave** (9)	**78**
MIND GAMES — John **Lennon** (26)	**73**
MIND OF A TOY — **Visage** (13)	**81**
MINDLESS BOOGIE — **Hot Chocolate** (46)	**79**
MINUETTO ALLEGRETTO — **Wombles** (16)	**74**
MINUTE BY MINUTE — **Doobie Brothers** (47)	**79**
MINUTE OF YOUR TIME, A — Tom **Jones** (14)	**68**
MINUTE YOU'RE GONE, THE — Cliff **Richard** (1)	**65**
MIRACLE OF YOU, THE — Danny **Williams** (41)	**61**
MIRROR IN THE BATHROOM — The **Beat** (4)	**80**
MIRROR MAN — **Human League** (2)	**82**
MIRROR MIRROR [A] — **Pinkerton's Assorted Colours** (9)	**66**
MIRROR MIRROR [B] — Diana **Ross** (36)	**82**
MIRROR MIRROR (MON AMOUR) — **Dollar** (4)	**81**
MIRRORS — Sally **Oldfield** (19)	**78**
MISS HIT AND RUN — Barry **Blue** (26)	**74**
MISS YOU [A] — **Rolling Stones** (3)	**78**
MISS YOU [B] — Jimmy **Young** (15)	**63**
MISS YOU NIGHTS — Cliff **Richard** (15)	**76**
MISSING WORDS — The **Selecter** (23)	**80**
MISSISSIPPI — **Pussycat** (1)	**76**
MISSY MISSY — Paul and Barry **Ryan** (43)	**66**
MR. BASS MAN — Johnny **Cymbal** (24)	**63**
MR. BLUE — David **MacBeth** (18)	**59**
MR. BLUE — Mike **Preston** (12)	**59**
MR. BLUE SKY — **Electric Light Orchestra** (6)	**78**
MR. CROWLEY — Ozzy **Osbourne Blizzard Of Ozz** (46)	**80**
MR. CUSTER — Charlie **Drake** (12)	**60**
MR. GUDER — **Carpenters** (12)	**74**
MR. GUITAR — Bert **Weedon** (47)	**61**
MISTER PORTER — Mickie **Most** (45)	**63**
MR. PRESIDENT — **D, B, M and T** (33)	**70**
MR. RAFFLES (MAN IT WAS MEAN) — Steve **Harley and COCKNEY REBEL** (13)	**75**
MR. SANDMAN — Max **Bygraves** (16)	**55**
MR. SANDMAN — **Chordettes** (11)	**54**
MR. SANDMAN — **Four Aces** (9)	**55**
MR. SANDMAN — Dickie **Valentine** (5)	**54**
MR. SOFT — Steve **Harley and COCKNEY REBEL** (8)	**74**
MR. SUCCESS — Frank **Sinatra** (25)	**58**
MR. TAMBOURINE MAN — **Byrds** (1)	**65**
MR. WONDERFUL — Peggy **Lee** (5)	**57**
MR. ZERO — Keith **Relf** (50)	**66**
MRS MILLS' MEDLEY — Mrs. **Mills** (18)	**61**
MRS. ROBINSON — **Simon and Garfunkel** (4)	**68**
MRS. ROBINSON (EP) — **Simon and Garfunkel** (9)	**69**
MS GRACE — **Tymes** (1)	**74**
MISTY — Johnny **Mathis** (12)	**60**
MISTY — Ray **Stevens** (2)	**75**
MISTY BLUE — Dorothy **Moore** (5)	**76**
MISUNDERSTANDING — **Genesis** (42)	**80**
MITTAGEISEN (METAL POSTCARD) — **Siouxsie and the Banshees** (47)	**79**
M'LADY — **Sly and the Family Stone** (32)	**68**
MOANIN' — Chris **Farlowe** (46)	**67**
MOB RULES — **Black Sabbath** (46)	**81**
MOBILE — Ray **Burns** (4)	**55**
MOCKINGBIRD — **Belle Stars** (51)	**82**
MOCKINGBIRD — Inez and Charlie **Foxx** (34)	**69**
MOCKINGBIRD — Carly **Simon and James Taylor** (34)	**74**
MOCKINGBIRD HILL — **Migil Five** (10)	**64**
MODEL, THE — **Kraftwerk** (1)	**81**
MODERN GIRL — Sheena **Easton** (8)	**80**
MODERN WORLD, THE — **Jam** (36)	**77,80**
MONA LISA — Conway **Twitty** (5)	**59**
MONDAY MONDAY — **Mamas and the Papas** (3)	**66**
MONEY — Bern **Elliott and the Fenmen** (14)	**63**
MONEY — **Flying Lizards** (5)	**79**
MONEY HONEY — **Bay City Rollers** (3)	**75**
MONEY IN MY POCKET — Dennis **Brown** (14)	**79**
MONEY MONEY MONEY — **Abba** (3)	**76**
MONEY THAT'S YOUR PROBLEM — **Tonight** (66)	**78**
MONKEES EP (RE-ISSUE OF 4 HITS), THE — **Monkees** (33)	**80**
MONKEY CHOP — **Dan-I** (30)	**79**
MONKEY MAN — **Maytals** (47)	**70**
MONKEY SPANNER — Dave and Ansil **Collins** (7)	**71**
MONSIEUR DUPONT — Sandie **Shaw** (6)	**69**
MONSTER MASH — Bobby 'Boris' **Pickett and the Crypt-Kickers** (3)	**73**
MONTEGO BAY — Bobby **Bloom** (3)	**70**
MONTEGO BAY — Freddie **Notes and the Rudies** (45)	**70**
MONTEGO BAY — **Sugar Cane** (54)	**78**
MONY MONY — Tommy **James and the Shondells** (1)	**68**
MOODY BLUE — Elvis **Presley** (6)	**77**
MOODY RIVER — Pat **Boone** (18)	**61**
MOON HOP — Derrick **Morgan** (49)	**70**
MOON RIVER — **Greyhound** (12)	**72**
MOON RIVER — Henry **Mancini** (44)	**61**

Title — Act (Position)	Year of Chart Entry
MOON RIVER — Danny **Williams** (1)	**61**
MOON SHADOW — Cat **Stevens** (22)	**71**
MOON TALK — Perry **Como** (17)	**58**
MOONGLOW — **Sounds Orchestral** (43)	**65**
MOONGLOW — Morris **Stoloff** (7)	**56**
MOONLIGHT & ROSES — Jim **Reeves** (34)	**71**
MOONLIGHT AND MUZAK — **M** (33)	**79**
MOONLIGHT GAMBLER — Frankie **Laine** (13)	**56**
MOONLIGHT SERENADE — Glenn **Miller** (12)	**54,76**
MOONLIGHTING — Leo **Sayer** (2)	**75**
MOONSHINE SALLY — **Mud** (10)	**75**
MORE — Perry **Como** (10)	**56**
MORE — Jimmy **Young** (4)	**56**
MORE AND MORE — Andy **Williams** (45)	**67**
MORE AND MORE PARTY POPS — Russ **Conway** (5)	**59**
MORE GOOD OLD ROCK 'N ROLL — Dave **Clark Five** (34)	**70**
MORE I SEE YOU, THE — Joy **Marshall** (34)	**66**
MORE I SEE YOU, THE — Chris **Montez** (3)	**66**
MORE LIKE THE MOVIES — **Dr. Hook** (14)	**78**
MORE MONEY FOR YOU AND ME (MEDLEY) — **Four Preps** (39)	**61**
MORE MORE MORE — Andrea **True Connection** (5)	**76**
MORE PARTY POPS — Russ **Conway** (10)	**58**
MORE THAN A FEELING — **Boston** (22)	**77**
MORE THAN A LOVER — Bonnie **Tyler** (27)	**77**
MORE THAN A WOMAN — **Tavares** (7)	**78**
MORE THAN EVER (COME PRIMA) — Robert **Earl** (26)	**58**
MORE THAN EVER (COME PRIMA) — Malcolm **Vaughan** (5)	**58**
MORE THAN I CAN SAY — Leo **Sayer** (2)	**80**
MORE THAN I CAN SAY — Bobby **Vee** (4)	**61**
MORE THAN IN LOVE — Kate **Robbins** (2)	**81**
MORE THAN LOVE — Ken **Dodd** (14)	**66**
MORE THAN THIS — **Roxy Music** (6)	**82**
MORGEN — Ivo **Robic** (23)	**59**
MORNING — Val **Doonican** (12)	**71**
MORNING DANCE — **Spyro Gyra** (17)	**79**
MORNING GLORY — James and Bobby **Purify** (27)	**76**
MORNING HAS BROKEN — Cat **Stevens** (9)	**72**
MORNING OF OUR LIVES — **Modern Lovers** (29)	**78**
MORNING SIDE OF THE MOUNTAIN — Donny and Marie **Osmond** (5)	**74**
MORNINGTOWN RIDE — **Seekers** (2)	**66**
MOST BEAUTIFUL GIRL, THE — Charlie **Rich** (2)	**74**
MOTHER & CHILD REUNION — Paul **Simon** (5)	**72**
MOTHER NATURE AND FATHER TIME — Nat "King" **Cole** (7)	**53**
MOTHER OF MINE — Neil **Reid** (2)	**72**
MOTHER-IN-LAW — Ernie **K-Doe** (29)	**61**
MOTOR BIKING — Chris **Spedding** (14)	**75**
MOTORBIKE BEAT — **Rezillos** (45)	**80**
MOTORCYCLE MICHAEL — Jo-Anne **Campbell** (41)	**61**
MOTORHEAD LIVE — **Motorhead** (6)	**81**
MOULDY OLD DOUGH — **Lieutenant Pigeon** (1)	**72**
MOULIN ROUGE — **Mantovani** (1)	**53**
MOUNTAIN GREENERY — Mel **Torme** (4)	**56**
MOUNTAIN OF LOVE — Kenny **Lynch** (33)	**60**
MOUNTAIN'S HIGH, THE — **Dick and Deedee** (37)	**61**
MOVE IN A LITTLE CLOSER — **Harmony Grass** (24)	**69**
MOVE IT — Cliff **Richard** (2)	**58**
MOVE IT BABY — Simon **Scott** (37)	**64**
MOVE ON UP — Curtis **Mayfield** (12)	**71**
MOVE OVER DARLING — Doris **Day** (8)	**64**
MOVE YOUR BODY — Gene **Farrow and G.F. Band** (33)	**78**
MOVIE STAR — **Harpo** (24)	**76**
MOVIN' — **Brass Construction** (23)	**76**
MOVIN' OUT (ANTHONY'S SONG) — Billy **Joel** (35)	**78**
MOZART SYMPHONY NO.40 IN G MINOR K550 1ST MOVEMENT (ALLEGRO MOLTO). — Waldo de los **Rios** (5)	**71**
MOZART 40 — **Sovereign Collection** (27)	**71**
MR. SECOND CLASS — Spencer **Davis Group** (35)	**68**
MUCHO MACHO — **Toto Coelo** (54)	**82**
MULE (CHANT NO.2) — **Beggar and Co** (37)	**81**
MULE SKINNER BLUES — Rusty **Draper** (39)	**60**
MULE SKINNER BLUES — **Fendermen** (32)	**60**
MULE TRAIN — Frank **Ifield** (22)	**63**
MULL OF KINTYRE — **Wings** (1)	**77**
MULTIPLICATION — Bobby **Darin** (5)	**61**
MULTIPLICATION — **Showaddywaddy** (39)	**81**
MUPPET SHOW MUSIC HALL EP, THE — **Muppets** (19)	**77**
MURPHY'S LAW — **Cheri** (13)	**82**
MUSC FOR CHAMELEONS — Gary **Numan** (19)	**82**
MUSCLEBOUND — **Spandau Ballet** (10)	**81**
MUSCLES — Diana **Ross** (15)	**82**
MUSIC [A] — John **Miles** (3)	**76**
MUSIC [B] — **One Way featuring Al Hudson** (56)	**79**
MUSIC AND LIGHTS — **Imagination** (5)	**82**
MUSIC MAKES YOU FEEL LIKE DANCING — **Brass Construction** (39)	**80**
MUSIC TO WATCH GIRLS BY — Andy **Williams** (33)	**67**
MUSKRAT — **Everly Brothers** (20)	**61**
MUSKRAT RAMBLE — Freddy **Cannon** (32)	**61**
MUST BE MADISON — Joe **Loss** (20)	**62**
MUST BE SANTA — Joan **Regan** (42)	**61**
MUST BE SANTA — Tommy **Steele** (40)	**60**
MUST TO AVOID, A — **Herman's Hermits** (6)	**65**
MUSTAFA — **Staiffi and his Mustafas** (43)	**60**
MUSTANG SALLY — Wilson **Pickett** (28)	**66**
MUSTAPHA — Bob **Azzam** (23)	**60**
MUTUALLY ASSURED DESTRUCTION — **Gillan** (32)	**81**
MY BABY LEFT ME — Dave **Berry** (37)	**64**
MY BABY LEFT ME-THAT'S ALL RIGHT (MEDLEY) — **Slade** (32)	**77**
MY BABY LOVES LOVIN' — **White Plains** (9)	**70**
MY BEST FRIEND'S GIRL — **Cars** (3)	**78**
MY BLUE HEAVEN — Frank **Sinatra** (33)	**61**
MY BONNIE — Tony **Sheridan and the Beatles** (48)	**63**
MY BOOMERANG WON'T COME BACK — Charlie **Drake** (14)	**61**
MY BOY — Elvis **Presley** (5)	**74**
MY BOY FLAT TOP — Frankie **Vaughan** (20)	**56**
MY BOY LOLLIPOP — **Millie** (2)	**64**
MY BOYFRIEND'S BACK — **Angels** (50)	**63**
MY BROTHER JAKE — **Free** (4)	**71**
MY CAMERA NEVER LIES — **Buck's Fizz** (1)	**82**
MY CHERIE AMOUR — Stevie **Wonder** (4)	**69**
MY CHILD — Connie **Francis** (26)	**65**
MY COO-CA-CHOO — Alvin **Stardust** (2)	**73**
MY DING-A-LING — Chuck **Berry** (1)	**72**
MY DIXIE DARLING — Lonnie **Donegan** (10)	**57**
MY EYES ADORED YOU — Frankie **Valli** (5)	**75**
MY FEET KEEP DANCING — **Chic** (21)	**79**
MY FORBIDDEN LOVER — **Chic** (15)	**79**
MY FREND STAN — **Slade** (2)	**73**
MY FRIEND [A] — Frankie **Laine** (3)	**54**
MY FRIEND [B] — Roy **Orbison** (35)	**69**
MY FRIEND JACK [A] — **Boney M** (57)	**80**
MY FRIEND JACK [B] — **Smoke** (45)	**67**
MY FRIEND THE SEA — Petula **Clark** (7)	**61**
MY GENERATION — **Who** (2)	**65**
MY GIRL — Otis **Redding** (11)	**65,68**
MY GIRL [A] — **Temptations** (43)	**65**
MY GIRL [A] — **Whispers** (26)	**80**
MY GIRL [B] — Rod **Stewart** (32)	**80**
MY GIRL [C] — **Madness** (3)	**80**
MY GIRL BILL — Jim **Stafford** (20)	**74**
MY GIRL JOSEPHINE — Fats **Domino** (32)	**61**
MY GIRL LOLLIPOP (MY BOY LOLLIPOP) — **Bad Manners** (9)	**82**
MY GUY — Mary **Wells** (5)	**64,72**
MY GUY - MY GIRL (MEDLEY) — Amii **Stewart and Johnny Bristol** (39)	**80**
MY HAPPINESS — Connie **Francis** (4)	**59**
MY HEART — Gene **Vincent** (16)	**60**
MY HEART HAS A MIND OF ITS OWN — Connie **Francis** (3)	**60**
MY HEART'S SYMPHONY — Gary **Lewis and the Playboys** (36)	**75**
MY KIND OF GIRL — Matt **Monro** (5)	**61**
MY KIND OF GIRL — Frank **Sinatra** (35)	**63**
MY KINDA LIFE — Cliff **Richard** (15)	**77**
MY LAST NIGHT WITH YOU — **Arrows** (25)	**75**
MY LIFE — Billy **Joel** (12)	**78**
MY LITTLE BABY — Mike **Berry** (34)	**63**
MY LITTLE CORNER OF THE WORLD — Anita **Bryant** (48)	**60**
MY LITTLE GIRL [A] — **Autumn** (37)	**71**
MY LITTLE GIRL [B] — **Crickets** (17)	**63**
MY LITTLE LADY — **Tremeloes** (6)	**68**
MY LITTLE ONE — **Marmalade** (15)	**71**
MY LOVE [A] — Petula **Clark** (4)	**66**
MY LOVE [B] — **Wings** (9)	**73**
MY LOVE AND DEVOTION — Doris **Day** (10)	**52**
MY LOVE AND DEVOTION — Matt **Monro** (29)	**62**
MY LOVE FOR YOU — Johnny **Mathis** (9)	**60**
MY LOVER'S PRAYER — Otis **Redding** (37)	**66**
MY MAMMY — **Happenings** (34)	**67**
MY MAN A SWEET MAN — Millie **Jackson** (50)	**72**
MY MAN AND ME — Lynsey **De Paul** (40)	**75**
MY MARIE — Engelbert **Humperdinck** (31)	**70**
MY MELANCHOLY BABY — Tommy **Edwards** (29)	**59**
MY MIND'S EYE — **Small Faces** (4)	**66**
MY MUM IS ONE IN A MILLION — The Children of **Tansley School** (27)	**81**
MY NAME IS JACK — **Manfred Mann** (8)	**68**
MY OH MY — **Sad Café** (14)	**80**
MY OLD MAN'S A DUSTMAN — Lonnie **Donegan** (1)	**60**
MY OLD PIANO — Diana **Ross** (5)	**80**
MY ONE SIN — Nat "King" **Cole** (17)	**55**
MY OWN TRUE LOVE — Danny **Williams** (45)	**63**
MY OWN WAY — **Duran Duran** (14)	**81**
MY PERFECT COUSIN — **Undertones** (9)	**80**
MY PERSONAL POSSESSION — Nat "King" **Cole** (21)	**57**
MY PRAYER — Gerry **Monroe** (9)	**70**
MY PRAYER — **Platters** (4)	**56**
MY RESISTANCE IS LOW — Robin **Sarstedt** (3)	**76**
MY SENTIMENTAL FRIEND — **Herman's Hermits** (2)	**69**
MY SEPTEMBER LOVE — David **Whitfield** (3)	**56**
MY SHARONA — **KNACK** (6)	**79**
MY SHIP IS COMING IN — **Walker Brothers** (3)	**65**
MY SIMPLE HEART — **Three Degrees** (9)	**79**
MY SON JOHN — David **Whitfield** (22)	**56**
MY SON MY SON — Vera **Lynn** (1)	**54**
MY SPECIAL ANGEL — Bobby **Helms** (22)	**57**
MY SPECIAL ANGEL — Malcolm **Vaughan** (3)	**57**
MY SPECIAL DREAM — Shirley **Bassey** (32)	**64**
MY SUNDAY BABY — **Dale Sisters** (36)	**61**
MY SWEET LORD — George **Harrison** (1)	**71**
MY SWEET ROSALIE — **Brotherhood Of Man** (30)	**76**
MY TRUE LOVE — Jack **Scott** (9)	**58**
MY UKELELE — Max **Bygraves** (19)	**59**
MY UNFINISHED SYMPHONY — David **Whitfield** (29)	**56**
MY WAY — Frank **Sinatra** (18)	**70**
MY WAY — Dorothy **Squires** (25)	**70**
MY WAY [A] — Eddie **Cochran** (23)	**63**
MY WAY [B] — Elvis **Presley** (9)	**77**
MY WAY [B] — **Sex Pistols** (7)	**78**
MY WAY [B] — Frank **Sinatra** (5)	**69**
MY WAY [B] — Dorothy **Squires** (40)	**70**
MY WAY OF GIVING IN — Chris **Farlowe** (48)	**67**
MY WAY OF THINKING — **U.B.40** (6)	**80**
MY WHITE BICYCLE — **Nazareth** (14)	**75**
MY WOMAN'S MAN — Dave **Dee** (42)	**70**
MY WORLD [A] — **Bee Gees** (16)	**72**
MY WORLD [B] — **Cupid's Inspiration** (33)	**68**
MY WORLD [C] — **Secret Affair** (16)	**80**
MY WORLD OF BLUE — Karl **Denver** (29)	**64**
MYSTERIES OF THE WORLD — **MFSB** (41)	**81**
MYSTERY GIRL [A] — Jess **Conrad** (18)	**61**
MYSTERY GIRL [B] — **Dukes** (47)	**81**
MYSTERY SONG — **Status Quo** (11)	**76**
MYSTERY TRAIN — Elvis **Presley** (25)	**57**
NA NA HEY HEY KISS HIM GOODBYE — **Steam** (9)	**70**
NA NA IS THE SADDEST WORD — **Stylistics** (5)	**75**
NA NA NA — Cozy **Powell** (10)	**74**
NADINE (IS IT YOU) — Chuck **Berry** (27)	**64**
NAIROBI — Tommy **Steele** (3)	**58**
NAME OF THE GAME, THE — **Abba** (1)	**77**
NAPPY LOVE — **Goodies** (21)	**75**
NASHVILLE BOOGIE — Bert **Weedon** (29)	**59**
NASHVILLE CATS — **Lovin' Spoonful** (26)	**67**
NATHAN JONES — **Supremes** (5)	**71**
NATIVE NEW YORKER — **Odyssey** (5)	**77**
NATURAL BORN BUGIE — **Humble Pie** (4)	**69**
NATURAL HIGH — **Bloodstone** (40)	**73**
NATURAL SINNER — **Fair Weather** (6)	**70**
NATURE BOY — George **Benson** (26)	**77**
NATURE BOY — Bobby **Darin** (24)	**61**
NATURE'S TIME FOR LOVE — Joe **Brown** (26)	**63**
NAUGHTY LADY OF SHADY LANE — **Ames Brothers** (6)	**55**
NAUGHTY LADY OF SHADY LANE — Dean **Martin** (5)	**55**
NAUGHTY NAUGHTY NAUGHTY — Joy **Sarney** (26)	**77**
NEANDERTHAL MAN — **Hotlegs** (2)	**70**
NEAR YOU — **Migil Five** (31)	**64**
NEED YOUR LOVE SO BAD — **Fleetwood Mac** (31)	**68,69**
NEEDLES AND PINS — **Searchers** (1)	**64**
NEEDLES AND PINS — **Smokie** (10)	**77**
NEITHER ONE OF US — Gladys **Knight and the Pips** (31)	**73**
NE-NE NA-NA NA-NA NU-NU — **Bad Manners** (28)	**80**
NEON KNIGHTS — **Black Sabbath** (22)	**80**
NEON LIGHTS — **Kraftwerk** (53)	**78**
NERVOUS WRECK — **Radio Stars** (39)	**78**
NEVER 'AD NOTHIN' — **Angelic Upstarts** (52)	**79**
NEVER AGAIN — **Discharge** (64)	**81**

Title — Act (Position)	Year of Chart Entry
NEVER AGAIN (THE DAYS TIME ERASED) — **Classix Nouveaux** (44)	**81**
NEVER BE ANYONE ELSE BUT YOU — Rick **Nelson** (14)	**59**
NEVER BEFORE — **Deep Purple** (35)	**72**
NEVER CAN SAY GOODBYE — Gloria **Gaynor** (2)	**74**
NEVER CAN SAY GOODBYE — **Jackson Five** (33)	**71**
NEVER DO A TANGO WITH AN ESKIMO — Alma **Cogan** (6)	**55**
NEVER ENDING SONG OF LOVE — **New Seekers** (2)	**71**
NEVER GIVE UP ON A GOOD THING — George **Benson** (14)	**82**
NEVER GIVE YOU UP — Sharon **Redd** (20)	**82**
NEVER GONNA CRY AGAIN — **Eurythmics** (63)	**81**
NEVER GONNA FALL IN LOVE AGAIN — **Dana** (31)	**76**
NEVER GONNA GIVE YOU UP (WON'T LET YOU BE) — Patrice **Rushen** (66)	**81**
NEVER GOODBYE — Karl **Denver** (9)	**62**
NEVER HAD A DREAM COME TRUE — Stevie **Wonder** (6)	**70**
NEVER IN A MILLION YEARS — **Boomtown Rats** (62)	**81**
NEVER KNEW LOVE LIKE THIS BEFORE — Stephanie **Mills** (4)	**80**
NEVER LET GO — John **Barry** (49)	**60**
NEVER LET HER SLIP AWAY — Andrew **Gold** (5)	**78**
NEVER MIND — Cliff **Richard** (21)	**59**
NEVER MIND THE PRESENTS — **Barron Knights** (17)	**80**
NEVER MY LOVE — Sugar **Minott** (52)	**81**
NEVER NEVER GONNA GIVE YA UP — Barry **White** (14)	**74**
NEVER NEVER NEVER — Shirley **Bassey** (8)	**73**
NEVER ON SUNDAY — **Chaquito** (50)	**60**
NEVER ON SUNDAY — Lynn **Cornell** (30)	**60**
NEVER ON SUNDAY — Don **Costa** (27)	**60**
NEVER ON SUNDAY — **Makadopulos and his Greek Serenaders** (36)	**60**
NEVER ON SUNDAY — **Manuel and his Music Of The Mountains** (29)	**60**
NEVER SAY DIE — **Black Sabbath** (21)	**78**
NEVER SURRENDER — **Saxon** (18)	**81**
NEVER TURN YOUR BACK ON MOTHER EARTH — **Sparks** (13)	**74**
NEVER WED AN OLD MAN — **Dubliners** (43)	**67**
NEVERTHELESS — **New Seekers** (34)	**73**
NEVERTHELESS — Frankie **Vaughan** (29)	**67**
NEW AMSTERDAM — Elvis **Costello and the Attractions** (36)	**80**
NEW FASHION, A — Bill **Wyman** (37)	**82**
NEW GUITAR IN TOWN — **Lurkers** (72)	**79**
NEW KID IN TOWN — **Eagles** (20)	**77**
NEW LIFE — **Depeche Mode** (11)	**81**
NEW LIVE AND RARE — **Deep Purple** (31)	**77**
NEW LIVE AND RARE II EP — **Deep Purple** (45)	**78**
NEW LIVE AND RARE VOLUME 3 — **Deep Purple** (48)	**80**
NEW ORLEANS — Gary 'U.S.' **Bonds** (16)	**61**
NEW ORLEANS — Bern **Elliott and the Fenmen** (24)	**64**
NEW ORLEANS — **Gillan** (17)	**81**
NEW ORLEANS — **Harley Quinne** (19)	**72**
NEW TOY — Lene **Lovich** (53)	**81**
NEW WORLD IN THE MORNING — Roger **Whittaker** (17)	**70**
NEW WORLD MAN — **Rush** (42)	**82**
NEW YORK CITY — **T. Rex** (15)	**75**
NEW YORK GROOVE — **Hello** (9)	**75**
NEW YORK MINING DISASTER 1941 — **Bee Gees** (12)	**67**
NEW YORK, NEW YORK — Gerard **Kenny** (43)	**78**
THEME FROM NEW YORK, NEW YORK — Frank **Sinatra** (59)	**80**
NEWS AT TEN — **Vapors** (44)	**80**
NEWS OF THE WORLD — **Jam** (27)	**78,80**
NEXT DOOR TO AN ANGEL — Neil **Sedaka** (29)	**62**
NEXT TIME, THE — Cliff **Richard** (1)	**62**
NICE AND SLOW — Jesse **Green** (17)	**76**
NICE LEGS SHAME ABOUT HER FACE — **Monks** (19)	**79**
NICE 'N EASY — Frank **Sinatra** (15)	**60**
NICE 'N SLEAZY — **Stranglers** (18)	**78**
NICE ONE CYRIL — **Cockerel Chorus** (14)	**73**
NIGHT — **Four Seasons** (7)	**75**
NIGHT AT DADDY GEE'S, A — **Showaddywaddy** (39)	**79**
NIGHT BIRDS — **Shakatak** (9)	**82**
NIGHT CHICAGO DIED, THE — **Paper Lace** (3)	**74**
NIGHT DANCING — Joe **Farrell** (57)	**78**
NIGHT FEVER [A] — **Bee Gees** (1)	**78**
NIGHT FEVER [A] — Carol **Douglas** (66)	**78**
NIGHT FEVER [B] — **Fatback Band** (38)	**76**
NIGHT GAMES — Graham **Bonnet** (6)	**81**
NIGHT HAS A THOUSAND EYES, THE — Bobby **Vee** (3)	**63**
NIGHT IS YOUNG, THE — Gary **Miller** (29)	**61**
NIGHT OF FEAR — **Move** (2)	**67**
NIGHT OF THE LONG GRASS — **Troggs** (17)	**67**
NIGHT OF THE VAMPIRE — **Moontrekkers** (50)	**61**
NIGHT OWL — Gerry **Rafferty** (5)	**79**
NIGHT PORTER — **Japan** (29)	**82**
NIGHT THE WINE AND THE ROSES, THE — **Liquid Gold** (32)	**80**
NIGHT THEY DROVE OLD DIXIE DOWN, THE — Joan **Baez** (6)	**71**
NIGHT TO REMEMBER, A — **Shalamar** (5)	**82**
NIGHT TRAIN [A] — Buddy **Morrow** (12)	**53**
NIGHT TRAIN [B] — **Visage** (12)	**82**
NIGHTMARE — **Gillan** (36)	**81**
NIGHTS IN WHITE SATIN — Elkie **Brooks** (33)	**82**
NIGHTS IN WHITE SATIN — **Dickies** (39)	**79**
NIGHTS IN WHITE SATIN — **Moody Blues** (9)	**67,72**
NIGHTS ON BROADWAY — Candi **Staton** (6)	**77**
NINE TIMES OUT OF TEN — Cliff **Richard** (3)	**60**
9 TO 5 [A] — Sheena **Easton** (3)	**80**
9 TO 5 [B] — Dolly **Parton** (47)	**81**
NINETEENTH NERVOUS BREAKDOWN — **Rolling Stones** (2)	**66**
96 TEARS — **? (Question Mark) and the Mysterians** (37)	**66**
98.6 — **Bystanders** (45)	**67**
98.6. — **Keith** (24)	**67**
99 WAYS — Tab **Hunter** (5)	**57**
NIPPLE TO THE BOTTLE — Grace **Jones** (50)	**82**
NITE CLUB — The **Specials** (10)	**79**
NO ARMS CAN EVER HOLD YOU — **Bachelors** (7)	**64**
NO CHANCE (NO CHARGE) — Billy **Connolly** (24)	**76**
NO CHARGE — J. J. **Barrie** (1)	**76**
NO CLASS — **Motorhead** (61)	**79**
NO DOUBT ABOUT IT — **Hot Chocolate** (2)	**80**
NO FACE, NO NAME, NO NUMBER — **Traffic** (40)	**68**
NO GETTING OVER YOU — **Paris** (49)	**82**
NO GOODBYES — Curtis **Mayfield** (65)	**78**
NO HIDING PLACE — Ken **Mackintosh** (45)	**60**
NO HONESTLY — Lynsey **De Paul** (7)	**74**
NO LAUGHING IN HEAVEN — **Gillan** (31)	**81**
NO LOVE — Joan **Armatrading** (50)	**82**
NO MATTER HOW I TRY — Gilbert **O'Sullivan** (5)	**71**
NO MATTER WHAT — **Badfinger** (5)	**71**
NO MATTER WHAT SIGN YOU ARE — **Supremes** (37)	**69**
NO MILK TODAY — **Herman's Hermits** (7)	**66**
NO MORE — **McGuire Sisters** (20)	**55**
NO MORE HEROES — **Stranglers** (8)	**77**
(NO MORE) LOVE AT YOUR CONVENIENCE — Alice **Cooper** (44)	**77**
NO MORE MR. NICE GUY — Alice **Cooper** (10)	**73**
NO MORE TEARS (ENOUGH IS ENOUGH) — Donna **Summer and Barbra Streisand** (3)	**79**
NO MULE'S FOOL — **Family** (29)	**69**
NO NO JOE — **Silver Convention** (41)	**76**
NO NO NO — Nancy **Nova** (63)	**82**
NO ONE — Ray **Charles** (35)	**63**
NO ONE BUT YOU — Billy **Eckstine** (3)	**54**
NO ONE CAN BREAK A HEART LIKE YOU — Dave **Clark Five** (28)	**68**
NO ONE CAN MAKE MY SUNSHINE SMILE — **Everly Brothers** (11)	**62**
NO ONE IS INNOCENT — **Sex Pistols** (7)	**78**
NO ONE LIKE YOU — **Scorpions** (64)	**82**
NO ONE QUITE LIKE GRANDMA — **St. Winifred's School Choir** (1)	**80**
NO ONE WILL EVER KNOW — Frank **Ifield** (25)	**66**
NO OTHER BABY — Bobby **Helms** (30)	**58**
NO OTHER LOVE — Ronnie **Hilton** (1)	**56**
NO OTHER LOVE — Edmund **Hockridge** (24)	**56**
NO OTHER LOVE — **Johnston Brothers** (22)	**56**
NO PARTICULAR PLACE TO GO — Chuck **Berry** (3)	**64**
NO REGRETS [A] — Shirley **Bassey** (39)	**65**
NO REGRETS [B] — Midge **Ure** (9)	**82**
NO REGRETS [B] — **Walker Brothers** (7)	**76**
NO SELF CONTROL — Peter **Gabriel** (33)	**80**
NO SURVIVORS — **GBH** (63)	**82**
NO TIME TO BE 21 — **Adverts** (38)	**78**
NO WOMAN, NO CRY — Bob **Marley and the Wailers** (8)	**75,81**
NOBODY — Toni **Basil** (52)	**82**
NOBODY BUT YOU — Gladys **Knight and the Pips** (34)	**77**
NOBODY DOES IT BETTER — Carly **Simon** (7)	**77**
NOBODY I KNOW — **Peter and Gordon** (10)	**64**
NOBODY NEEDS YOUR LOVE — Gene **Pitney** (2)	**66**
NOBODY WINS — Elton **John** (42)	**81**
NOBODY'S CHILD — Karen **Young** (6)	**69**
NOBODY'S DARLIN' BUT MINE — Frank **Ifield** (4)	**63**
NOBODY'S FOOL [A] — **Haircut 100** (9)	**82**
NOBODY'S FOOL [B] — Jim **Reeves** (32)	**70**
NOBODY'S HERO — **Stiff Little Fingers** (36)	**80**
NON HO L'ETA PER AMARTI — Gigliola **Cinquetti** (17)	**64**
NO-ONE DRIVING(DOUBLE SINGLE) — John **Foxx** (32)	**80**
NO-ONE GETS THE PRIZE — Diana **Ross** (59)	**79**
NO-ONE TO CRY TO — Ray **Charles** (38)	**64**
NORA MALONE — Teresa **Brewer** (26)	**57**
NORMAN — Carol **Deene** (24)	**62**
NORMAN BATES — **Landscape** (40)	**81**
NORTH TO ALASKA — Johnny **Horton** (23)	**61**
NORTHERN LIGHTS — **Renaissance** (10)	**78**
NOT AS A STRANGER — Frank **Sinatra** (18)	**55**
NOT FADE AWAY — **Rolling Stones** (3)	**64**
NOT RESPONSIBLE — Tom **Jones** (18)	**66**
NOT TOO LITTLE NOT TOO MUCH — Chris **Sandford** (17)	**63**
NOT UNTIL THE NEXT TIME — Jim **Reeves** (13)	**65**
NOTHIN' TO DO — Michael **Holliday** (20)	**56**
NOTHING CAN STOP ME — Gene **Chandler** (41)	**68**
NOTHING COMES EASY — Sandie **Shaw** (14)	**66**
NOTHING LEFT TOULOUSE — **Sad Café** (62)	**80**
NOTHING RHYMED — Gilbert **O'Sullivan** (8)	**70**
NOTHING TO LOSE — **U. K.** (67)	**79**
NOW — Val **Doonican** (43)	**68**
NOW — Al **Martino** (3)	**53**
NOW I'M HERE — **Queen** (11)	**75**
NOW IS THE TIME — Jimmy **James and the Vagabonds** (5)	**76**
NOW IT'S GONE — **Chords** (63)	**79**
NOW THAT WE'VE FOUND LOVE — **Third World** (10)	**78**
NOW THOSE DAYS ARE GONE — **Buck's Fizz** (8)	**82**
NOW WE'RE THRU — **Poets** (31)	**64**
NOWHERE GIRL — **B-Movie** (67)	**82**
NOWHERE MAN — **Three Good Reasons** (47)	**66**
NOWHERE TO RUN — Martha **Reeves and the Vandellas** (26)	**65,69**
NUCLEAR DEVICE (THE WIZARD OF AUS) — **Stranglers** (36)	**79**
— John **Lennon** (23)	**75**
NUMBER OF THE BEAST, THE — **Iron Maiden** (18)	**82**
NUMBER ONE DEE JAY — **Goody Goody** (55)	**78**
NUMBER ONE SONG IN HEAVEN, THE — **Sparks** (14)	**79**
NUNC DIMITTIS — Paul **Phoenix** (56)	**79**
NUT ROCKER — B. **Bumble and the Stingers** (1)	**62,72**
NUTBUSH CITY LIMITS — Ike and Tina **Turner** (4)	**73**
007 — Desmond **Dekker and the Aces** (14)	**67**
O SUPERMAN — Laurie **Anderson** (2)	**81**
OB-LA-DI OBLA-DA — **Bedrocks** (20)	**68**
OB-LA-DI OB-LA-DA — **Marmalade** (1)	**68**
OBSESSED — **999** (71)	**81**
OBSESSION — Reg **Owen** (43)	**60**
ODE TO BILLY JOE — Bobbie **Gentry** (13)	**67**
OFF THE WALL — Michael **Jackson** (7)	**79**
OFFICIAL SECRETS — **M** (64)	**80**
OFFSHORE BANKING BUSINESS — **Members** (31)	**79**
OH BABE WHAT WOULD YOU SAY? — Hurricane **Smith** (4)	**72**
OH BOY — **Crickets** (3)	**57**
OH BOY — **Mud** (1)	**75**
OH BOY (THE MOOD I'M IN) — **Brotherhood Of Man** (8)	**77**
OH CAROL [A] — Neil **Sedaka** (3)	**59,72**
OH CAROL [B] — **Smokie** (5)	**78**
OH DIANE — **Fleetwood Mac** (60)	**82**
OH GIRL — **Chi-Lites** (5)	**72,75**
OH HAPPY DAY — Edwin **Hawkins Singers** (2)	**69**
OH HAPPY DAY [B] — **Johnston Brothers** (4)	**53**
OH HOW I MISS YOU — **Bachelors** (30)	**67**
OH JULIE — Shakin' **Stevens** (1)	**82**
OH LONESOME ME — Craig **Douglas** (15)	**62**
OH LORI — **Alessi** (8)	**77**
OH ME OH MY (I'M A FOOL FOR YOU BABY) — **Lulu** (47)	**69**
OH MEIN PAPA — Eddie **Calvert** (1)	**53**
OH MEIN PAPA — Eddie **Fisher** (9)	**54**
OH NO — **Commodores** (44)	**81**

Title — Act (Position)	Year of Chart Entry
OH NO NOT MY BABY — **Manfred Mann** (11)	**65**
OH NO NOT MY BABY — Rod **Stewart** (6)	**73**
OH OH, I'M FALLING IN LOVE AGAIN — Jimmie **Rodgers** (18)	**58**
OH PRETTY WOMAN — Roy **Orbison** (1)	**64**
OH WELL — **Fleetwood Mac** (2)	**69**
OH WHAT A CIRCUS — David **Essex** (3)	**78**
OH! WHAT A DAY — Craig **Douglas** (43)	**60**
OH WHAT A SHAME — Roy **Wood** (13)	**75**
OH YEAH (ON THE RADIO) — **Roxy Music** (5)	**80**
OH YES! YOU'RE BEAUTIFUL — Gary **Glitter** (2)	**74**
OH YOU PRETTY THING — Peter **Noone** (12)	**71**
L'OISEAU ET L'ENFANT — Marie **Myriam** (42)	**77**
O.K? — Julie **Covington, Rula Lenska, Cornwell and Sue Jones-Davies** (10)	**77**
O.K. FRED — Erroll **Dunkley** (11)	**79**
OKAY! — Dave **Dee, Dozy, Beaky, Mick and Tich** (4)	**67**
OL' MACDONALD — Frank **Sinatra** (11)	**60**
OLD — **Dexy's Midnight Runners** (17)	**82**
OLD FASHIONED WAY, THE — Charles **Aznavour** (38)	**73,74**
OLD FLAMES — **Foster and Allen** (51)	**82**
OLD OAKEN BUCKET — Tommy **Sands** (25)	**60**
OLD PIANNA RAG — Dickie **Valentine** (15)	**55**
OLD RIVERS — Walter **Brennan** (38)	**62**
OLD RUGGED CROSS, THE — Ethna **Campbell** (33)	**75**
OLD SHEP — Clinton **Ford** (27)	**59**
OLD SIAM SIR — **Wings** (35)	**79**
OLD SMOKEY — **Johnny and the Hurricanes** (24)	**61**
OLD SONGS, THE — Barry **Manilow** (48)	**81**
OLDEST SWINGER IN TOWN — Fred **Wedlock** (6)	**81**
OLE OLA (MUHLER BRASILEIRA) — Rod **Stewart** (4)	**78**
OLIVE TREE — Judith **Durham** (33)	**67**
OLIVER'S ARMY — Elvis **Costello and the Attractions** (2)	**79**
OLYMPIC RECORD, AN — **Barron Knights** (35)	**68**
ON A CAROUSEL — **Hollies** (4)	**67**
ON A LITTLE STREET IN SINGAPORE — **Manhattan Transfer** (20)	**78**
ON A SATURDAY NIGHT — Terry **Dactyl and the Dinosaurs** (45)	**73**
ON A SLOW BOAT TO CHINA — Emile **Ford and the Checkmates** (3)	**60**
ON FIRE — **T-Connection** (16)	**78**
ON HORSEBACK — Mike **Oldfield** (4)	**75**
ON MOTHER KELLY'S DOORSTEP — Danny **La Rue** (33)	**68**
ON MY RADIO — The **Selecter** (8)	**79**
ON MY WORD — Cliff **Richard** (12)	**65**
ON THE BEACH — Cliff **Richard** (7)	**64**
ON THE BEAT — **B, B, and Q Band** (41)	**81**
ON THE RADIO — Donna **Summer** (32)	**80**
ON THE REBOUND — Floyd **Cramer** (1)	**61**
ON THE ROAD AGAIN — **Canned Heat** (8)	**68**
ON THE STREET WHERE YOU LIVE — Vic **Damone** (1)	**58**
ON THE STREET WHERE YOU LIVE — David **Whitfield** (16)	**58**
ON WITH THE MOTLEY — Harry **Secombe** (16)	**55**
ONCE — **Geneveve** (43)	**66**
ONCE BITTEN TWICE SHY — Ian **Hunter** (14)	**75**
ONCE I HAD A SWEETHEART — **Pentangle** (46)	**69**
ONCE IN A LIFETIME — **Talking Heads** (14)	**81**
ONCE IN EVERY LIFETIME — Ken **Dodd** (28)	**61**
ONCE THERE WAS A TIME — Tom **Jones** (18)	**66**
ONCE UPON A DREAM — Billy **Fury** (7)	**62**
ONCE UPON A TIME [A] — Marvin **Gaye and Mary Wells** (50)	**64**
ONCE UPON A TIME [B] — Tom **Jones** (32)	**65**
ONE AND ONE IS ONE — **Medicine Head** (3)	**73**
ONE AND ONLY, THE — Gladys **Knight and the Pips** (32)	**78**
ONE BROKEN HEART FOR SALE — Elvis **Presley** (12)	**63**
ONE DAY AT A TIME — Lena **Martell** (1)	**79**
ONE DAY I'LL FLY AWAY — Randy **Crawford** (2)	**80**
ONE DAY IN YOUR LIFE — Michael **Jackson** (1)	**81**
ONE DRINK TOO MANY — **Sailor** (35)	**77**
ONE FINE DAY — **Chiffons** (29)	**63**
ONE FINE MORNING — Tommy **Hunt** (44)	**76**
ONE FOR YOU ONE FOR ME — La **Bionda** (54)	**78**
ONE FOR YOU ONE FOR ME — Jonathan **King** (29)	**78**
ONE HEART BETWEEN TWO — Dave **Berry** (41)	**64**
ONE HELLO — Randy **Crawford** (48)	**82**
ONE IN TEN — **U.B.40** (7)	**81**
ONE INCH ROCK — **T. Rex** (7)	**68,72**
ONE LAST KISS — J. **Geils Band** (74)	**79**
ONE MAN BAND — Leo **Sayer** (6)	**74**
ONE MAN WOMAN — Sheena **Easton** (14)	**80**
ONE MORE CHANCE — Diana **Ross** (49)	**81**
ONE MORE DANCE — Esther and Abi **Ofarim** (13)	**68**
ONE MORE SATURDAY NIGHT — **Matchbox** (63)	**82**
ONE MORE SUNRISE (MORGEN) — Dickie **Valentine** (14)	**59**
ONE NATION UNDER A GROOVE -PART 1 — **Funkadelic** (9)	**78**
ONE NIGHT — **Mud** (32)	**75**
ONE NIGHT — Elvis **Presley** (1)	**59**
ONE NINE FOR SANTA — Fogwell **Flax and the Anklebiters Freehold Junior School** (68)	**81**
ONE OF THE LUCKY ONES — Joan **Regan** (47)	**60**
ONE OF THESE NIGHTS — **Eagles** (23)	**75**
ONE OF THOSE NIGHTS — **Buck's Fizz** (20)	**81**
ONE OF US — **Abba** (3)	**81**
ONE OF US MUST KNOW (SOONER OR LATER) — Bob **Dylan** (33)	**66**
ONE PIECE AT A TIME — Johnny **Cash** (32)	**76**
ONE ROAD — **Love Affair** (16)	**69**
ONE RULE FOR YOU — **After The Fire** (40)	**79**
ONE STEP AWAY — **Tavares** (16)	**77**
ONE STEP BEYOND — **Madness** (7)	**79**
ONE STEP FURTHER — **Bardo** (2)	**82**
137 DISCO HEAVEN (MEDLEY) — Amii **Stewart** (5)	**79**
ONE TO CRY, THE — **Escorts** (49)	**64**
1-2-3 [A] — Len **Barry** (3)	**65**
1-2-3 [B] — **Professionals** (43)	**80**
1-2-3 O'LEARY — Des **O'Connor** (4)	**68**
ONE WAY LOVE — Cliff **Bennett and the Rebel Rousers** (9)	**64**
ONE WAY TICKET — **Eruption** (9)	**79**
ONEDIN LINE, THEME FROM THE — **Vienna Philharmonic Orchestra** (15)	**71**
ONION SONG — Marvin **Gaye and Tammi Terrell** (9)	**69**
ONLY BOY IN THE WORLD, THE — Stevie **Marsh** (24)	**59**
ONLY CRYING — Keith **Marshall** (12)	**81**
ONLY LOVE CAN BREAK YOUR HEART — Elkie **Brooks** (43)	**78**
ONLY LOVIN' DOES IT — **Guys and Dolls** (42)	**78**
ONLY MAN ON THE ISLAND, THE — Vic **Damone** (24)	**58**
ONLY MAN ON THE ISLAND, THE — Tommy **Steele** (16)	**58**
ONLY ONE WOMAN — **Marbles** (5)	**68**
ONLY SIXTEEN — Sam **Cooke** (23)	**59**
ONLY SIXTEEN — Craig **Douglas** (1)	**59**
ONLY SIXTEEN — Al **Saxon** (24)	**59**
ONLY THE HEARTACHES — Houston **Wells** (22)	**63**
ONLY THE LONELY — Roy **Orbison** (1)	**60**
ONLY THE LONELY — **Prelude** (55)	**82**
ONLY THE STRONG SURVIVE — Billy **Paul** (33)	**77**
ONLY TIME WILL TELL — **Asia** (54)	**82**
ONLY WAY OUT, THE — Cliff **Richard** (10)	**82**
ONLY WOMEN BLEED — Julie **Covington** (12)	**77**
ONLY YESTERDAY — **Carpenters** (7)	**75**
ONLY YOU — **Platters** (5)	**56**
ONLY YOU [A] — Jeff **Collins** (40)	**72**
ONLY YOU [A] — **Hilltoppers** (3)	**56**
ONLY YOU [A] — **Platters** (5)	**56,57**
ONLY YOU [A] — Ringo **Starr** (28)	**74**
ONLY YOU [A] — Mark **Wynter** (38)	**64**
ONLY YOU [B] — Teddy **Pendergrass** (41)	**78**
ONLY YOU [C] — **Yazoo** (2)	**82**
ONLY YOU (AND YOU ALONE) — **Child** (33)	**79**
ONLY YOU CAN — **Fox** (3)	**75**
ONLY YOU CAN ROCK ME — **UFO** (50)	**78**
ONWARD CHRISTIAN SOLDIERS — Harry **Simeone Chorale** (35)	**60,61,62**
OO-EEH BABY — **Stonebridge Mcguinness** (54)	**79**
OOH BABY — Gilbert **O'Sullivan** (18)	**73**
OOH BOY — **Rose Royce** (46)	**80**
OOH I DO — Lynsey **De Paul** (25)	**74**
OOH LA LA — Joe "Mr. Piano" **Henderson** (46)	**60**
OOH LA LA LA (LET'S GO DANCIN') — **Kool and the Gang** (6)	**82**
OOH MY SOUL — **Little Richard** (22)	**58**
OOH! WHAT A LIFE — **Gibson Brothers** (10)	**79**
OOH-WAKKA-DOO-WAKKA-DAY — Gilbert **O'Sullivan** (8)	**72**
OOPS UP SIDE YOUR HEAD — **Gap Band** (6)	**80**
OPEN UP — **Mungo Jerry** (21)	**72**
OPEN UP YOUR HEART — Joan **Regan** (19)	**55**
OPEN YOUR HEART — **Human League** (6)	**81**
OPUS 17 (DON'T YOU WORRY 'BOUT ME) — **Four Seasons** (20)	**66**
ORANGE BLOSSOM SPECIAL — **Spotnicks** (29)	**62**
ORIGINAL BIRD DANCE — **Electronicas** (22)	**81**
ORVILLE'S SONG — Keith **Harris and Orville** (33)	**82**
OSSIE'S DREAM (SPURS ARE ON THEIR WAY TO WEMBLEY) — **Tottenham Hotspur F.A. Cup Final Squad** (5)	**81**
OTHER MAN'S GRASS, THE — Petula **Clark** (20)	**67**
OTHER SIDE OF LOVE, THE — **Yazoo** (13)	**82**
OTHER SIDE OF ME, THE — Andy **Williams** (42)	**76**
OTHER SIDE OF THE SUN, THE — Janis **Ian** (44)	**80**
OUR DAY WILL COME — **Ruby and the Romantics** (38)	**63**
OUR FAVOURITE MELODIES — Craig **Douglas** (9)	**62**
OUR HOUSE — **Madness** (5)	**82**
OUR LAST SONG TOGETHER — Neil **Sedaka** (31)	**73**
OUR LIPS ARE SEALED — **Go-Gos** (47)	**82**
OUR LOVE — Elkie **Brooks** (43)	**82**
(OUR LOVE) DON'T THROW IT ALL AWAY — Andy **Gibb** (32)	**79**
OUR WORLD — **Blue Mink** (17)	**70**
OUT DEMONS OUT — Edgar **Broughton Band** (39)	**70**
OUT HERE ON MY OWN — Irene **Cara** (58)	**82**
OUT IN THE DARK — **Lurkers** (72)	**79**
OUT OF CONTROL — **Angelic Upstarts** (58)	**80**
OUT OF MY MIND — Johnny **Tillotson** (34)	**63**
OUT OF REACH — **Vice Squad** (68)	**82**
OUT OF THIS WORLD — Tony **Hatch** (50)	**62**
OUT OF TIME — Chris **Farlowe** (1)	**66,75**
OUT OF TIME — Dan **McCafferty** (41)	**75**
OUT OF TIME — **Rolling Stones** (45)	**75**
OUT OF TOWN — Max **Bygraves** (18)	**56**
OUT ON THE FLOOR — Dobie **Gray** (42)	**75**
OUTA SPACE — Billy **Preston** (44)	**72**
OUTDOOR MINER — **Wire** (51)	**79**
OUTSIDE MY WINDOW — Stevie **Wonder** (52)	**80**
OUTSIDE OF HEAVEN — Eddie **Fisher** (1)	**53**
OVER AND OVER [A] — Dave **Clark Five** (45)	**65**
OVER AND OVER [B] — **James Boys** (39)	**73**
OVER THE RAINBOW - YOU BELONG TO ME (MEDLEY) — **Matchbox** (15)	**80**
OVER UNDER SIDEWAYS DOWN — **Yardbirds** (10)	**66**
OVER YOU [A] — **Roxy Music** (5)	**80**
OVER YOU [B] — **Freddie and the Dreamers** (13)	**64**
OVERKILL — **Motorhead** (39)	**79**
OXYGENE PART IV — Jean-Michel **Jarre** (4)	**77**
PABLO — Russ **Conway** (45)	**61**
PACK UP YOUR SORROWS — Joan **Baez** (50)	**66**
PAINT IT BLACK — **Modettes** (42)	**80**
PAINT IT BLACK — **Rolling Stones** (1)	**66**
PAINT ME DOWN — **Spandau Ballet** (30)	**81**
PAINTER MAN — **Boney M** (10)	**79**
PAINTER MAN — **Creation** (36)	**66**
PALISADES PARK — Freddy **Cannon** (20)	**62**
PALOMA BLANCA — George **Baker Selection** (10)	**75**
PAMELA PAMELA — Wayne **Fontana** (11)	**66**
PANDORA'S BOX — **Procol Harum** (16)	**75**
PAPA LOVES MAMA — Joan **Regan** (29)	**60**
PAPA LOVES MAMBO — Perry **Como** (16)	**54**
PAPA OOM MOW MOW — Gary **Glitter** (38)	**75**
PAPA OOM MOW MOW — **Sharonettes** (26)	**75**
PAPA WAS A ROLLIN' STONE — **Temptations** (14)	**73**
PAPA'S GOT A BRAND NEW BAG — James **Brown** (25)	**65**
PAPA'S GOT A BRAND NEW PIGBAG — **Pig Bag** (3)	**82**
PAPER DOLL — Windsor **Davies and Don Estelle** (41)	**75**
PAPER PLANE — **Status Quo** (8)	**73**
PAPER ROSES — Anita **Bryant** (24)	**60**
PAPER ROSES — Maureen **Evans** (40)	**60**
PAPER ROSES — **Kaye Sisters** (7)	**60**
PAPER ROSES — Marie **Osmond** (2)	**73**
PAPER SUN — **Traffic** (5)	**67**
PAPER TIGER — Sue **Thompson** (30)	**65**
PAPERBACK WRITER — **Beatles** (1)	**66,76**
PARADE — **White and Torch** (54)	**82**
PARADISE — Frank **Ifield** (26)	**65**
PARADISE BIRD — Amii **Stewart** (39)	**80**
PARADISE LOST — **Herd** (15)	**67**
PARADISE SKIES — Max **Webster** (43)	**79**
PARALYSED — Elvis **Presley** (8)	**57**
PARANOID — **Black Sabbath** (4)	**70,80**
PARANOID — **Dickies** (45)	**79**
PARIS BY AIR — **Tygers of Pan Tang** (63)	**82**
PARIS IS ONE DAY AWAY — **Mood** (42)	**82**
PARISIENNE GIRL — **Incognito** (73)	**80**
PARISIENNE WALKWAYS — Gary **Moore** (8)	**79**
PART OF THE UNION — **Strawbs** (2)	**73**
PART TIME LOVE [A] — Elton **John** (15)	**78**
PART TIME LOVE [B] — Gladys **Knight and the Pips** (30)	**75**
PARTY — Elvis **Presley** (2)	**57**

Title — Act (Position)	Year of Chart Entry
PARTY DOLL — Buddy **Knox** (29)	57
PARTY FEARS TWO — **Associates** (9)	82
PARTY IN PARIS — **U.K. Subs** (37)	80
PARTY LIGHTS — **Gap Band** (30)	80
PARTY PARTY — Elvis **Costello and the Attractions** (48)	82
PARTY POPS — Russ **Conway** (24)	57
PARTY TIME — **Fatback Band** (41)	76
PARTY'S OVER, THE — Lonnie **Donegan** (9)	62
PASADENA — **Temperance Seven** (4)	61
PASS THE DUTCHIE — **Musical Youth** (1)	82
PASSAGE TO BANGKOK, A — **Rush** (41)	81
PASSING BREEZE — Russ **Conway** (16)	60
PASSING STRANGERS [A] — Billy **Eckstine and Sarah Vaughan** (20)	57,69
PASSING STRANGERS [B] — **Ultravox** (57)	80
PASSION — Rod **Stewart** (17)	80
PASSION IN DARK ROOMS — **Mood** (74)	82
PASSIONATE FRIEND — **Teardrop Explodes** (25)	81
PASSIONS OF LOVERS, THE — **Bauhaus** (51)	81
PATCHES — Clarence **Carter** (2)	70
PATHS OF PARADISE — Johnnie **Ray** (20)	55
PATRICIA — Perez **Prado** (8)	58
PAY OFF, THE — Kenny **Ball and his Jazzmen** (23)	62
PAY TO THE PIPER — **Chairmen Of The Board** (34)	71
PEACE ON EARTH — **Hi Tension** (8)	78
PEACE ON EARTH - LITTLE DRUMMER BOY — David **Bowie and Bing Crosby** (3)	82
PEACEFUL — Georgie **Fame** (16)	69
PEACHES [A] — **Darts** (66)	80
PEACHES [B] — **Stranglers** (8)	77
PEARL'S A SINGER — Elkie **Brooks** (8)	77
PEEK-A-BOO [A] — **New Vaudeville Band** (7)	67
PEEK-A-BOO [B] — **Stylistics** (35)	73
PEGGY SUE — Buddy **Holly** (6)	57,68
PEGGY SUE GOT MARRIED — Buddy **Holly** (13)	59
PENNY ARCADE — Roy **Orbison** (27)	69
PENNY LANE — **Beatles** (2)	67
PENTHOUSE AND PAVEMENT — **Heaven 17** (57)	81
PEOPLE — **Tymes** (16)	69
PEOPLE LIKE YOU AND PEOPLE LIKE ME — **Glitter Band** (5)	76
PEPE — Russ **Conway** (19)	61
PEPE — Duane **Eddy** (2)	61
PEPPER BOX — **Peppers** (6)	74
PEPPERMINT TWIST [A] — Joey **Dee and the Starliters** (33)	62
PEPPERMINT TWIST [B] — Danny **Peppermint and the Jumping Jacks** (26)	62
PERFECT TIMING — Kiki **Dee** (66)	81
PERFIDIA — **Ventures** (4)	60
PERFUMED GARDEN — **Rah Band** (45)	82
PERHAPS LOVE — Placido **Domingo with John Denver** (46)	81
PERSONALITY — Anthony **Newley** (6)	59
PERSONALITY — Lloyd **Price** (9)	59
PERSONALITY — Lena **Zavaroni** (33)	74
PER-SO-NAL-LY — **Wigan's Ovation** (38)	75
PERSUADERS, THE — John **Barry** (13)	71
PETER AND THE WOLF — **Clyde Valley Stompers** (25)	62
PETER GUNN THEME — Duane **Eddy** (6)	59
PETITE FLEUR — Chris **Barber's Jazz Band** (3)	59
PHILADELPHIA FREEDOM — Elton **John** (12)	75
PHOTOGRAPH — Ringo **Starr** (8)	73
PHYSICAL — Olivia **Newton-John** (7)	81
PIANISSIMO — Ken **Dodd** (21)	62
PIANO MEDLEY NO. 114 — Charlie **Kunz** (16)	54
PIANO PARTY — Winifred **Atwell** (10)	59
PICK A BALE OF COTTON — Lonnie **Donegan** (11)	62
PICK ME UP I'LL DANCE — Melba **Moore** (48)	79
PICK UP THE PIECES [A] — **Average White Band** (6)	75
PICK UP THE PIECES [B] — **Hudson-Ford** (8)	73
PICKIN' A CHICKEN — Eve **Boswell** (9)	55
PICKNEY GAL — Desmond **Dekker and the Aces** (42)	70
PICTURE OF YOU, A — Joe **Brown** (2)	62
PICTURE THIS — **Blondie** (12)	78
PICTURES OF LILY — **Who** (4)	67
PICTURES OF MATCHSTICK MEN — **Status Quo** (7)	68
PIECE OF MY HEART — Sammy **Hagar** (67)	82
PIECE OF THE ACTION — **Buck's Fizz** (12)	81
PIED PIPER — **Bob and Marcia** (11)	71
PIED PIPER — Crispian **St. Peters** (5)	66
PIED PIPER (THE BEEJE) — Steve **Race** (29)	63
PILLOW TALK — **Sylvia** (14)	73
PILOT OF THE AIRWAVES — Charlie **Dore** (66)	79
PILTDOWN RIDES AGAIN — **Piltdown Men** (14)	61
PINBALL — Brian **Protheroe** (22)	74
PINBALL WIZARD — Elton **John** (7)	76
PINBALL WIZARD — **Who** (4)	69
PINBALL WIZARD - SEE ME FEEL ME (MEDLEY) — **New Seekers** (16)	73
PINK PARKER (EP), THE — Graham **Parker and the Rumour** (24)	77
PINKY BLUE — **Altered Images** (35)	82
PIPELINE — **Chantays** (16)	63
PIPELINE — Bruce **Johnston** (33)	77
PISTOL PACKIN' MAMA — Gene **Vincent** (15)	60
PLACE IN THE SUN [A] — **Shadows** (24)	66
PLACE IN THE SUN [B] — Stevie **Wonder** (20)	67
PLACE IN YOUR HEART — **Nazareth** (70)	78
PLAN B — **Dexy's Midnight Runners** (58)	81
PLANET EARTH — **Duran Duran** (12)	81
PLANET ROCK — **Africa Bambaata and the Soul Sonic Force** (53)	82
PLASTIC AGE, THE — **Buggles** (16)	80
PLASTIC MAN — **Kinks** (31)	69
PLATINUM BLONDE — **Prelude** (45)	80
PLATINUM POP — **This Year's Blonde** (46)	81
PLAY ME LIKE YOU PLAY YOUR GUITAR — Duane **Eddy** (9)	75
PLAY THAT FUNKY MUSIC — **Wild Cherry** (7)	76
PLAY THE GAME — **Queen** (14)	80
PLAY TO WIN — **Heaven 17** (46)	81
PLAYGROUND — Anita **Harris** (46)	67
PLAYGROUND TWIST — **Siouxsie and the Banshees** (28)	79
PLAYTHING — **Linx** (48)	82
PLEASANT VALLEY SUNDAY — **Monkees** (11)	67
PLEASE COME HOME FOR CHRISTMAS — **Eagles** (30)	78
PLEASE DON'T ASK ABOUT BARBARA — Bobby **Vee** (29)	62
PLEASE DON'T GO — Donald **Peers** (3)	68
PLEASE DON'T GO [B] — **KC and The Sunshine Band** (3)	79
PLEASE DON'T TEASE — Cliff **Richard** (1)	60
PLEASE DON'T TOUCH — Johnny **Kidd and the Pirates** (25)	59
PLEASE HELP ME I'M FALLING — Hank **Locklin** (9)	60
PLEASE MR. POSTMAN — **Carpenters** (2)	75
PLEASE PLEASE ME — **Beatles** (2)	63
PLEASE PLEASE ME — David **Cassidy** (16)	74
PLEASE STAY — **Cryin' Shames** (26)	66
PLEASE TELL HIM THAT I SAID HELLO — **Dana** (8)	75
PLEASURE BOYS — **Visage** (44)	82
PLENTY GOOD LOVIN' — Connie **Francis** (18)	59
LA PLUME DE MA TANTE — **Hugo and Luigi** (29)	59
POACHER, THE — Ronnie **Lane** (36)	74
POCKET CALCULATOR — **Kraftwerk** (39)	81
POETRY IN MOTION — Johnny **Tillotson** (1)	60
POETRY IN MOTION — Johnny **Tillotson** (67)	79
POINT OF VIEW — **Matumbi** (35)	79
POISON ARROW — **ABC** (6)	82
POISON IVY — **Coasters** (15)	59
POISON IVY — **Lambrettas** (7)	80
POISON IVY — **Paramounts** (35)	64
POLICE AND THIEVES — Junior **Murvin** (23)	80
POLK SALAD ANNIE — Elvis **Presley** (23)	73
PONY TIME — Chubby **Checker** (27)	61
POOL HALL RICHARD — **Faces** (8)	73
POOR JENNY — **Everly Brothers** (14)	59
POOR LITTLE FOOL — Rick **Nelson** (4)	58
POOR MAN'S SON — **Rockin' Berries** (5)	65
POOR ME — Adam **Faith** (1)	60
POOR PEOPLE OF PARIS — Winifred **Atwell** (1)	56
POP GO THE WORKERS — **Barron Knights** (5)	65
POP GOES THE WEASEL — Anthony **Newley** (12)	61
POP MUZIK — **M** (2)	79
POPCORN — **Hot Butter** (5)	72
POPPA JOE — **Sweet** (11)	72
POPPA PICCOLINO — Diana **Decker** (2)	53
POPS, WE LOVE YOU — Diana **Ross, Marvin Gaye, Robinson and Stevie Wonder** (66)	79
PORT AU PRINCE — Winifred **Atwell** (18)	56
PORTRAIT OF MY LOVE — Matt **Monro** (3)	60
PORTSMOUTH — Mike **Oldfield** (3)	76
PORTUGUESE WASHERWOMAN — Joe "Fingers" **Carr** (20)	56
POSITIVELY FOURTH STREET — Bob **Dylan** (8)	65
POSTMAN PAT — Ken **Barrie** (44)	82
POWER TO ALL OUR FRIENDS — Cliff **Richard** (4)	73
POWER TO THE PEOPLE — John **Lennon** (7)	71
PRANCE ON — Eddie **Henderson** (44)	78
PRECIOUS — **Jam** (1)	82
PRETEND — Nat "King" **Cole** (2)	53
PRETEND — Alvin **Stardust** (4)	81
PRETTY BLUE EYES — Craig **Douglas** (4)	60
PRETTY BROWN EYES — Jim **Reeves** (33)	68
PRETTY FLAMINGO — **Manfred Mann** (1)	66
PRETTY IN PINK — **Psychedelic Furs** (43)	81
PRETTY JENNY — Jess **Conrad** (50)	62
PRETTY LITTLE ANGEL EYES — Curtis **Lee** (47)	61
PRETTY LITTLE ANGEL EYES — **Showaddywaddy** (5)	78
PRETTY LITTLE BLACK EYED SUSIE — Guy **Mitchell** (2)	53
PRETTY PAPER — Roy **Orbison** (6)	64
PRETTY THING — Bo **Diddley** (34)	63
PRETTY VACANT — **Sex Pistols** (6)	77
PRETTY WOMAN — **Juicy Lucy** (44)	70
PRICE OF LOVE, THE — **Everly Brothers** (2)	65
PRIMARY — **Cure** (43)	81
PRIME TIME — **Tubes** (34)	79
PRIMROSE LANE — Dickie **Pride** (28)	59
PRINCE CHARMING — **Adam and The Ants** (1)	81
PRINCE OF DARKNESS — **Bow Wow Wow** (58)	81
PRINCE, THE — **Madness** (16)	79
PRINCESS IN RAGS — Gene **Pitney** (9)	65
PRINCESS OF THE NIGHT — **Saxon** (57)	81
PRINCESS PRINCESS — Johnny **Tillotson** (67)	79
PRIVATE EYES — Daryl **Hall and John Oates** (32)	82
PRIVATE INVESTIGATIONS — **Dire Straits** (2)	82
PRIVATE LIFE — Grace **Jones** (17)	80
PRIVATE NUMBER — Judy **Clay and William Bell** (8)	68
PRIVILEGE (SET ME FREE) — **Patti Smith Group** (72)	78
PRIZE OF GOLD — Joan **Regan** (6)	55
PROBLEMS — **Everly Brothers** (6)	59
PROCESSION — **New Order** (38)	81
PRODIGAL SON — **Steel Pulse** (35)	78
PROMISE, A — **Echo and the Bunnymen** (49)	81
PROMISED LAND — Chuck **Berry** (26)	65
PROMISED LAND — Elvis **Presley** (9)	75
PROMISED YOU A MIRACLE — **Simple Minds** (13)	82
PROMISES [A] — **Buzzcocks** (20)	78
PROMISES [B] — Eric **Clapton** (37)	78
PROMISES [C] — Ken **Dodd** (6)	66
PROUD MARY — **Checkmates Ltd.** (30)	69
PROUD MARY — **Creedence Clearwater Revival** (8)	69
PROUD ONE, THE — **Osmonds** (5)	75
PROVE IT — **Television** (25)	77
PSYCHEDELIC SHACK — **Temptations** (33)	70
PUB WITH NO BEER, A — Slim **Dusty** (3)	59
PUBLIC IMAGE — **Public Image Ltd.** (9)	78
PUCKWUDGIE — Charlie **Drake** (47)	72
PUFF — Kenny **Lynch** (33)	62
PULL UP TO THE BUMPER — Grace **Jones** (53)	81
PULLING MUSSELS (FROM THE SHELL) — **Squeeze** (44)	80
PUMP IT UP — Elvis **Costello and the Attractions** (24)	78
PUNKY REGGAE PARTY — Bob **Marley and the Wailers** (9)	77
PUPPET MAN — Tom **Jones** (49)	71
PUPPET ON A STRING — Sandie **Shaw** (1)	67
PUPPY LOVE — Paul **Anka** (33)	60
PUPPY LOVE — Donny **Osmond** (1)	72
PUPPY SONG, THE — David **Cassidy** (1)	73
PURELY BY COINCIDENCE — **Sweet Sensation** (11)	75
PURGATORY — **Iron Maiden** (52)	81
PURPLE HAZE — Jimi **Hendrix Experience** (3)	67
PURPLE PEOPLE EATER — Jackie **Dennis** (29)	58
PURPLE PEOPLE EATER — Sheb **Wooley** (12)	58
PUSHBIKE SONG, THE — **Mixtures** (2)	71
PUT A LIGHT IN THE WINDOW — **King Brothers** (25)	58
PUT A LITTLE LOVE IN YOUR HEART — **Dave Clark Five** (31)	69
PUT HIM OUT OF YOUR MIND — **Dr. Feelgood** (73)	79
PUT YOUR HEAD ON MY SHOULDER — Paul **Anka** (7)	59
PUT YOUR LOVE IN ME — **Hot Chocolate** (10)	77
PUT YOUR MONEY WHERE YOUR MOUTH IS — **Rose Royce** (44)	77
PUT YOURSELF IN MY PLACE — **Elgins** (28)	71
PUT YOURSELF IN MY PLACE — **Isley Brothers** (13)	69
PUTTING ON THE STYLE — Lonnie **Donegan** (1)	57
PYJAMARAMA — **Roxy Music** (10)	73
QUANDO M'INNAMORO (A MAN WITHOUT LOVE) — **Sandpipers** (33)	68
QUANDO QUANDO QUANDO — Pat **Boone** (41)	62
QUARTER MOON, THE — **V.I.P.s** (55)	80
QUARTER TO THREE — Gary 'U.S.' **Bonds** (7)	61

Title — Act (Position)	Year of Chart Entry
QUE SERA MI VIDA (IF YOU SHOULD GO) — **Gibson Brothers** (5)	**79**
QUE SERA SERA — Geno **Washington and the Ram Jam Band** (43)	**66**
QUE TAL AMERICA — **Two Man Sound** (46)	**79**
QUEEN FOR TONIGHT — Helen **Shapiro** (33)	**63**
QUEEN OF CLUBS — **KC and The Sunshine Band** (7)	**74**
QUEEN OF HEARTS — Dave **Edmunds** (11)	**79**
QUEEN OF MY SOUL — **Average White Band** (23)	**76**
QUEEN OF THE HOP — Bobby **Darin** (24)	**59**
QUEEN OF THE RAPPING SCENE (NOTHING EVER GOES THE WAY YOU PLAN) — **Modern Romance** (37)	**82**
QUEEN OF 1964, THE — Neil **Sedaka** (35)	**75**
QUEENS FIRST EP (EP) — **Queen** (17)	**77**
QUESTION — **Moody Blues** (2)	**70**
QUESTIONS AND ANSWERS — **Sham 69** (18)	**79**
QUESTIONS I CAN'T ANSWER — **Heinz** (39)	**64**
QUICK JOEY SMALL (RUN JOEY RUN) — **Kasenetz-Katz Singing Orchestral Circus** (19)	**68**
QUIEREME MUCHO (YOURS) — Julio **Iglesias** (3)	**82**
QUIET LIFE — **Japan** (19)	**81**
QUIT THIS TOWN — **Eddie and the Hotrods** (36)	**78**
QUITE A PARTY — **Fireballs** (29)	**61**
QUITE RIGHTLY SO — **Procol Harum** (50)	**68**
QUOTE GOODBYE QUOTE — Carolyne **Mas** (71)	**80**
RABBIT — **Chas and Dave** (8)	**80**
RACE IS ON, THE — Dave **Edmunds and the Stray Cats** (34)	**81**
RACE IS ON, THE — Suzi **Quatro** (43)	**78**
RACE WITH THE DEVIL [A] — **Girlschool** (49)	**80**
RACE WITH THE DEVIL [A] — **Gun** (8)	**68**
RACE WITH THE DEVIL [B] — Gene **Vincent** (28)	**56**
RACHEL — Al **Martino** (10)	**53**
RACHMANINOFF'S 18TH VARIATION ON A THEME BY PAGANINI — Winifred **Atwell** (9)	**54**
RADANCER — **Marmalade** (6)	**72**
RADAR LOVE — **Golden Earring** (7)	**73,77**
RADIO RADIO — Elvis **Costello and the Attractions** (29)	**78**
RADIOACTIVE — Gene **Simmons** (41)	**79**
RAG DOLL — **Four Seasons** (2)	**64**
RAG MAMA RAG — **Band** (16)	**70**
RAGAMUFFIN MAN — **Manfred Mann** (8)	**69**
RAGS TO RICHES — Elvis **Presley** (9)	**71**
RAGS TO RICHES — David **Whitfield** (3)	**53**
RAGTIME COWBOY JOE — **Chipmunks** (11)	**59**
RAIN [A] — Bruce **Ruffin** (19)	**71**
RAIN [B] — **Status Quo** (7)	**76**
RAIN AND TEARS — **Aphrodite's Child** (30)	**68**
RAIN FOREST — **Biddu** (39)	**76**
RAIN RAIN RAIN — Frankie **Laine** (8)	**54**
RAINBOW [A] — **Marmalade** (3)	**70**
RAINBOW [B] — **Peters and Lee** (17)	**74**
RAINBOW CHASER — **Nirvana** (34)	**68**
RAINBOW THEME — **Saxon** (66)	**80**
RAINBOW VALLEY — **Love Affair** (5)	**68**
RAINDROPS KEEP FALLIN' ON MY HEAD — Bobbie **Gentry** (40)	**70**
RAINDROPS KEEP FALLING ON MY HEAD — Sacha **Distel** (10)	**70**
RAINDROPS KEEP FALLING ON MY HEAD — B. J. **Thomas** (38)	**70**
RAININ' THROUGH MY SUNSHINE — **Real Thing** (40)	**78**
RAINING IN MY HEART — Leo **Sayer** (21)	**78**
RAINY DAY WOMEN NOS. 12 & 35 — Bob **Dylan** (7)	**66**
RAINY NIGHT IN GEORGIA — Randy **Crawford** (18)	**81**
RAISE YOUR HAND — Eddie **Floyd** (42)	**67**
RAISED ON ROCK — Elvis **Presley** (36)	**73**
RAM GOAT LIVER — Pluto **Shervington** (43)	**76**
RAMA LAMA DING DONG — Rockey **Sharpe and the Replays** (17)	**78**
RAMBLIN' ROSE — Nat "King" **Cole** (5)	**62**
RAM-BUNK-SHUSH — **Ventures** (45)	**61**
RAMONA — **Bachelors** (4)	**64**
RANDY — **Blue Mink** (9)	**73**
RANKING FULL STOP — The **Beat** (6)	**79**
RAPP PLAYBACK (WHERE IZ MOSES?) — James **Brown** (39)	**81**
RAPPER'S DELIGHT — **Sugarhill Gang** (3)	**79**
RAPTURE — **Blondie** (5)	**81**
RASPUTIN — **Boney M** (2)	**78**
RAT RACE — The **Specials** (5)	**80**
RAT TRAP — **Boomtown Rats** (1)	**78**
RAUNCHY — Bill **Justis** (11)	**58**
RAUNCHY — Ken **Mackintosh** (19)	**58**
RAVE ON — Buddy **Holly** (5)	**58,68**
RAWHIDE — Frankie **Laine** (6)	**59**
RAZZAMATAZZ — Quincy **Jones** (11)	**81**
RAZZLE DAZZLE [A] — Bill **Haley and his Comets** (13)	**56**
RAZZLE DAZZLE [B] — **Heatwave** (43)	**79**
REACH FOR THE STARS — Shirley **Bassey** (1)	**61**
REACH OUT AND TOUCH — Diana **Ross** (33)	**70**
REACH OUT FOR ME — Dionne **Warwick** (23)	**64**
REACH OUT I'LL BE THERE — **Four Tops** (1)	**66**
REACH OUT I'LL BE THERE — Gloria **Gaynor** (14)	**75**
REACHING FOR THE BEST — **Exciters** (31)	**75**
REACHING FOR THE WORLD — Harold **Melvin and the Bluenotes** (48)	**77**
READY AN' WILLING (SWEET SATISFACTION) — **Whitesnake** (43)	**80**
READY FOR LOVE — Jimmy **Jones** (46)	**60**
READY OR NOT HERE I COME — **Delfonics** (41)	**71**
READY STEADY GO — **Generation X** (47)	**78**
READY WILLING AND ABLE — Doris **Day** (7)	**55**
REAL LOVE — Ruby **Murray** (18)	**58**
REAL MOTHER FOR YA, A — Johnny 'Guitar' **Watson** (44)	**77**
REAL THING, THE — **Brothers Johnson** (50)	**81**
REALLY FREE — John **Otway and Wild Willy Barrett** (27)	**77**
REALLY SAYING SOMETHING — **Bananarama** (5)	**82**
REAP THE WILD WIND — **Ultravox** (12)	**82**
REASON TO BELIEVE — Rod **Stewart** (19)	**71**
REASONS TO BE CHEERFUL, PT.3 — Ian **Dury and the Blockheads** (3)	**79**
REBEL REBEL — David **Bowie** (5)	**74**
REBEL ROUSER — Duane **Eddy** (19)	**58**
RECOVERY — Fontella **Bass** (32)	**66**
RED BALLOON — Dave **Clark Five** (7)	**68**
RED DRESS — Alvin **Stardust** (7)	**74**
RED FRAME WHITE LIGHT — **Orchestral Manoeuvres in the Dark** (67)	**80**
RED LIGHT GREEN LIGHT — Mitchell **Torok** (29)	**57**
RED LIGHT SPELLS DANGER — Billy **Ocean** (2)	**77**
RED RED WINE — Jimmy **James and the Vagabonds** (36)	**68**
RED RED WINE — **Tony Tribe** (46)	**69**
RED RIVER ROCK — **Johnny and the Hurricanes** (3)	**59**
RED SAILS IN THE SUNSET — Fats **Domino** (34)	**63**
RED SKIES — **Fixx** (57)	**82**
REELIN' AND ROCKIN' — Chuck **Berry** (18)	**73**
REELIN' AND ROCKIN' — Dave **Clark Five** (24)	**65**
REET PETITE — **Darts** (51)	**79**
REET PETITE — Jackie **Wilson** (6)	**57**
REFLECTIONS — **Supremes** (5)	**67**
REFLECTIONS OF MY LIFE — **Marmalade** (3)	**69**
REGGAE FOR IT NOW — Bill **Lovelady** (12)	**79**
REGGAE LIKE IT USED TO BE — Paul **Nicholas** (17)	**76**
REGGAE TUNE — Andy **Fairweather-Low** (10)	**74**
RELAY — **Who** (21)	**73**
RELEASE ME — Engelbert **Humperdinck** (1)	**67**
REMEMBER [A] — Jimi **Hendrix Experience** (35)	**71**
REMEMBER [B] — **Rock Candy** (32)	**71**
REMEMBER ME — Diana **Ross** (7)	**71**
REMEMBER ME THIS WAY — Gary **Glitter** (3)	**74**
REMEMBER (SHA-LA-LA) — **Bay City Rollers** (6)	**74**
(REMEMBER THE DAYS OF THE) OLD SCHOOL YARD — Cat **Stevens** (44)	**77**
REMEMBER THE RAIN — Bob **Lind** (46)	**66**
REMEMBER THEN — **Showaddywaddy** (17)	**79**
REMEMBER (WALKIN' IN THE SAND) — **Shangri-Las** (14)	**64**
REMEMBER WHEN — **Platters** (25)	**59**
REMEMBER YESTERDAY — John **Miles** (32)	**76**
REMEMBER YOU'RE A WOMBLE — **Wombles** (3)	**74**
REMEMBER YOU'RE MINE — Pat **Boone** (5)	**57**
REMEMBRANCE DAY — **B-Movie** (61)	**81**
REMINISCING — Buddy **Holly** (17)	**62**
RENDEZVOUS [A] — Tina **Charles** (27)	**77**
RENDEZVOUS [B] — **Tygers of Pan Tang** (49)	**82**
RENTA SANTA — Chris **Hill** (10)	**75**
REQUIEM — **Slik** (24)	**76**
RESCUE — **Echo and the Bunnymen** (62)	**80**
RESCUE ME — Fontella **Bass** (11)	**65**
RESPECT — Aretha **Franklin** (10)	**67**
RESPECTABLE — **Rolling Stones** (23)	**78**
RESTLESS [A] — Johnny **Kidd and the Pirates** (22)	**60**
RESTLESS [B] — **Gillan** (25)	**82**
RESURRECTION SHUFFLE — **Ashton, Gardner and Dyke** (3)	**71**
RETURN OF DJANGO — **Upsetters** (5)	**69**
RETURN OF THE ELECTRIC WARRIOR (EP) — Marc **Bolan** (50)	**81**
RETURN OF THE LOS PALMAS SEVEN, THE — **Madness** (7)	**81**
RETURN OF THE RED BARON — **Royal Guardsmen** (37)	**67**
RETURN TO ME — Dean **Martin** (2)	**58**
RETURN TO SENDER — Elvis **Presley** (1)	**62,77**
REUNITED — **Peaches and Herb** (4)	**79**
REVEILLE ROCK — **Johnny and the Hurricanes** (14)	**59**
REVIVAL — Chris **Barber's Jazz Band** (43)	**62**
REVOLT INTO STYLE — Bill **Nelson** (69)	**79**
REWARD — **Teardrop Explodes** (6)	**81**
RHAPSODY — **Four Seasons** (37)	**77**
RHAPSODY IN THE RAIN — Lou **Christie** (37)	**66**
RHIANNON — **Fleetwood Mac** (46)	**78**
RHINESTONE COWBOY — Glen **Campbell** (4)	**75**
RHYTHM & GREENS — **Shadows** (22)	**64**
RHYTHM OF THE JUNGLE — **Quick** (41)	**82**
RHYTHM OF THE RAIN — **Cascades** (5)	**63**
RHYTHM TALK — **Jocko** (56)	**80**
RIBBON IN THE SKY — Stevie **Wonder** (45)	**82**
RICE IS NICE — **Lemon Pipers** (41)	**68**
RICH KIDS — **Rich Kids** (24)	**78**
RICH MAN POOR MAN — Jimmy **Young** (25)	**56**
RICOCHET — Joan **Regan** (8)	**53**
RIDE A WHITE SWAN — **T. Rex** (2)	**70**
RIDE A WILD HORSE — Dee **Clark** (16)	**75**
RIDE AWAY — Roy **Orbison** (34)	**65**
RIDE LIKE THE WIND — Christopher **Cross** (69)	**80**
RIDE MY SEE-SAW — **Moody Blues** (42)	**68**
RIDE ON BABY — Chris **Farlowe** (31)	**66**
RIDE THE GROOVE — **Players Association** (42)	**79**
RIDE THE LOVE TRAIN — **Light of the World** (49)	**81**
RIDE-O-ROCKET — **Brothers Johnson** (50)	**78**
RIDERS IN THE SKY — **Ramrods** (8)	**61**
RIDERS IN THE SKY — **Shadows** (12)	**80**
RIDERS ON THE STORM — **Doors** (22)	**71,76**
RIDING WITH THE ANGELS — **Samson** (55)	**81**
RIGHT BACK WHERE WE STARTED FROM — Maxine **Nightingale** (8)	**75**
RIGHT IN THE SOCKET — **Shalamar** (44)	**80**
RIGHT SAID FRED — Bernard **Cribbins** (10)	**62**
RIGHT THING TO DO, THE — Carly **Simon** (17)	**73**
RIGHT THING TO SAY, THE — Nat "King" **Cole** (42)	**62**
RIGHT TO LOVE, THE — David **Whitfield** (30)	**58**
RIKKI DON'T LOSE THAT NUMBER — **Steely Dan** (58)	**79**
RING A DING GIRL — Ronnie **Carroll** (46)	**62**
RING MY BELL — Anita **Ward** (1)	**79**
RING OF BRIGHT WATER — Val **Doonican** (48)	**69**
RING OF FIRE [A] — Eric **Burdon** (35)	**69**
RING OF FIRE [B] — Duane **Eddy** (17)	**61**
RING OUT SOLSTICE BELLS (EP) — **Jethro Tull** (28)	**76**
RING RING [A] — **Abba** (32)	**74**
RING RING [B] — **Dollar** (61)	**82**
RINGO — Lorne **Greene** (22)	**64**
RIO [A] — **Duran Duran** (9)	**82**
RIO [B] — Michael **Nesmith** (28)	**77**
RIP IT UP — Bill **Haley and his Comets** (4)	**56**
RIP IT UP — **Little Richard** (30)	**56,77**
RIP IT UP — Elvis **Presley** (27)	**57**
RISE — Herb **Alpert** (13)	**79**
RISE & FALL OF FLINGEL BUNT, THE — **Shadows** (5)	**64**
RISING SUN — **Medicine Head** (11)	**73**
RIVER [A] — Bruce **Springsteen** (35)	**81**
RIVER [B] — **King Trigger** (57)	**82**
Four Tops (11)	**71**
RIVER DEEP MOUNTAIN HIGH — Ike and Tina **Turner** (3)	**66,69**
RIVER (LE COLLINE SONO IN FIORO), THE — Ken **Dodd** (3)	**65**
RIVER STAY 'WAY FROM MY DOOR — Frank **Sinatra** (18)	**60**
RIVER DEEP MOUNTAIN HIGH — **Supremes and the**	
RIVERS OF BABYLON — **Boney M** (1)	**78**
RIVER'S RUN DRY, THE — Vince **Hill** (41)	**62**
ROADRUNNER — Jonathan **Richman and the Modern Lovers** (11)	**77**
ROBIN HOOD — Dick **James** (14)	**56**
ROBIN HOOD — Gary **Miller** (10)	**56**
ROBIN'S RETURN — Neville **Dickie** (33)	**69**
ROBOT — **Tornados** (17)	**63**
ROBOT MAN — Connie **Francis** (2)	**60**
ROCHDALE COWBOY — Mike **Harding** (22)	**75**
ROCK A HULA BABY — Elvis **Presley** (1)	**62**
ROCK & ROLL (PARTS 1 & 2) — Gary **Glitter** (2)	**72**
ROCK 'N' ROLL HIGH SCHOOL — **Ramones** (67)	**79**
ROCK 'N' ROLL LADY — **Showaddywaddy** (15)	**74**
ROCK AND ROLL MUSIC — **Beach Boys** (36)	**76**
ROCK AND ROLL SUICIDE — David **Bowie** (22)	**74**
ROCK AND ROLL WALTZ — Kay **Starr** (1)	**56**

Title — Act (Position)	Year of Chart Entry
ROCK AROUND THE CLOCK — Bill **Haley and his Comets** (1)	55,56,68,74
ROCK AROUND THE CLOCK — **Sex Pistols** (21)	79
ROCK AROUND THE CLOCK — **Telex** (34)	79
ROCK BOTTOM — Lynsey **De Paul and Mike Moran** (19)	77
ROCK HARD — Suzi **Quatro** (68)	80
ROCK ISLAND LINE — Lonnie **Donegan** (8)	56
ROCK ISLAND LINE — Stan **Freberg** (24)	56
ROCK LOBSTER — **B-52's** (37)	79
ROCK ME BABY — David **Cassidy** (11)	72
ROCK ME GENTLY — Andy **Kim** (2)	74
ROCK 'N' ROLL AIN'T NOISE POLLUTION — **AC/DC** (15)	80
ROCK 'N' ROLL DAMNATION — **AC/DC** (24)	78
ROCK 'N ROLL (I GAVE YOU THE BEST YEARS OF MY LIFE) — Kevin **Johnson** (23)	75
ROCK 'N ROLL STAGE SHOW (LP) — Bill **Haley and his Comets** (30)	56
ROCK 'N ROLL WINTER — **Wizzard** (6)	74
ROCK ON — David **Essex** (3)	73
ROCK ON BROTHER — **Chequers** (21)	75
ROCK THE BOAT — **Hues Corporation** (6)	74
ROCK THE CASBAH — **Clash** (30)	82
ROCK THE JOINT — Bill **Haley and his Comets** (20)	57
ROCK THIS TOWN — **Stray Cats** (9)	81
ROCK WITH THE CAVEMAN — Tommy **Steele** (13)	56
ROCK WITH YOU — Michael **Jackson** (7)	80
ROCK YOUR BABY — George **McCrae** (1)	74
ROCK-A-BEATIN' BOOGIE — Bill **Haley and his Comets** (4)	55
ROCK-A-BILLY — Guy **Mitchell** (1)	57
ROCKABILLY GUY — **Polecats** (35)	81
ROCKABILLY REBEL — **Matchbox** (18)	79
ROCK-A-BYE YOUR BABY (WITH A DIXIE MELODY) — Jerry **Lewis** (12)	57
ROCK-A-DOODLE-DOO — Linda **Lewis** (15)	73
ROCKARIA! — **Electric Light Orchestra** (9)	77
ROCKET — **Mud** (6)	74
ROCKET MAN [A] — Elton **John** (2)	72
ROCKET MAN [B] — **Spotnicks** (38)	62
ROCKIN' ALL OVER THE WORLD — **Status Quo** (3)	77
ROCKIN' ALONE — **Miki and Griff** (44)	60
ROCKIN' AROUND THE CHRISTMAS TREE — Brenda **Lee** (6)	62
ROCKIN' RED WING — Sammy **Masters** (36)	60
ROCKIN' ROBIN — Bobby **Day** (29)	58
ROCKIN' ROBIN — Michael **Jackson** (3)	72
ROCKIN' ROLL BABY — **Stylistics** (6)	74
ROCKIN' SOUL — **Hues Corporation** (24)	74
ROCKIN' THROUGH THE RYE — Bill **Haley and his Comets** (3)	56
ROCKING GOOSE — **Johnny and the Hurricanes** (3)	60
ROCK'N ME — Steve **Miller Band** (11)	76
ROCK'N'ROLL — **Status Quo** (8)	81
ROCK'N'ROLL DREAMS COME THROUGH — Jim **Steinman** (52)	81
ROCK'N'ROLL OUTLAW — **Rose Tattoo** (60)	81
ROCKY — Austin **Roberts** (22)	75
ROCKY MOUNTAIN WAY (EP) — Joe **Walsh** (39)	77
RODRIGO'S GUITAR CONCERTO DE ARANJUEZ (THEME FROM 2ND MOVEMENT) — **Manuel and his Music Of The Mountains** (3)	76
ROLL AWAY THE STONE — **Mott The Hoople** (8)	73
ROLL ON DOWN THE HIGHWAY — **Bachman-Turner Overdrive** (22)	75
ROLL OVER BEETHOVEN — **Electric Light Orchestra** (6)	73
ROLL OVER LAY DOWN — **Status Quo** (9)	75
ROLLIN' ON — **Cirrus** (62)	78
ROLLIN' STONE — David **Essex** (5)	75
ROMANTICA — Jane **Morgan** (39)	60
ROMEO [A] — **Mr. Big** (4)	77
ROMEO [B] — Petula **Clark** (3)	61
ROMEO AND JULIET — **Dire Straits** (11)	81
RONDO — Kenny **Ball and his Jazzmen** (24)	63
ROOF TOP SINGING — **New World** (50)	73
ROSALIE - COWGIRLS' SONG (MEDLEY) — **Thin Lizzy** (20)	78
ROSALYN — **Pretty Things** (41)	64
ROSE GARDEN — Lynn **Anderson** (3)	71
ROSE GARDEN — **New World** (15)	71
ROSE HAS TO DIE, A — **Dooleys** (11)	78
ROSE MARIE — Slim **Whitman** (1)	55
ROSES ARE RED — Ronnie **Carroll** (3)	62
ROSES ARE RED — Bobby **Vinton** (15)	62
ROSES OF PICARDY — Vince **Hill** (13)	67
ROSETTA — **Fame and Price Together** (11)	71
ROSIE [A] — Don **Partridge** (4)	68
ROSIE [B] — Joan **Armatrading** (49)	80
ROTATION [A] — Herb **Alpert** (46)	80
ROUGH BOYS — Pete **Townshend** (39)	80
ROULETTE — Russ **Conway** (1)	59
ROUND AND ROUND — Jimmy **Young** (30)	57
ROUND EVERY CORNER — Petula **Clark** (43)	65
ROUSSOS PHENOMENON (EP), THE — Demis **Roussos** (1)	76
ROXANNE — **Police** (12)	79
ROYAL EVENT — Russ **Conway** (15)	60
ROYAL MILE — Gerry **Rafferty** (67)	80
RUB A DUB DUB — **Equals** (34)	69
RUBBER BALL — **Avons** (30)	61
RUBBER BALL — Bobby **Vee** (4)	61
RUBBER BALL — Marty **Wilde** (9)	61
RUBBER BULLETS — **10 C. C.** (1)	73
RUBBERBAND MAN, THE — **Detroit Spinners** (16)	76
RUBY ANN — Marty **Robbins** (24)	63
RUBY DON'T TAKE YOUR LOVE TO TOWN — Kenny **Rogers** (2)	69
RUBY RED — **Slade** (51)	82
RUBY TUESDAY — **Melanie** (9)	70
RUBY TUESDAY — **Rolling Stones** (3)	67
RUDE BUOYS OUTA JAIL — The **Specials** (5)	80
RUDI GOT MARRIED — Laurel **Aitken and the Unitone** (60)	80
RUDI'S IN LOVE — **Locomotive** (25)	68
RUDY'S ROCK — Bill **Haley and his Comets** (26)	56
RUFF MIX — **Wonder Dogs** (31)	82
RUMOUR HAS IT — Donna **Summer** (19)	78
RUMOURS — **Hot Chocolate** (44)	73
RUN — Sandie **Shaw** (32)	66
RUN AWAY — **10 C. C.** (50)	82
RUN BABY RUN — **Newbeats** (10)	71
RUN BACK — Carl **Douglas** (25)	77
RUN FOR HOME — **Lindisfarne** (10)	78
RUN RUDOLPH RUN — Chuck **Berry** (36)	63
RUN RUN RUN — **Jo Jo Gunne** (6)	72
RUN TO HIM — Bobby **Vee** (6)	61
RUN TO ME — **Bee Gees** (9)	72
RUN TO MY LOVIN' ARMS — Billy **Fury** (25)	65
RUN TO THE DOOR — Clinton **Ford** (25)	67
RUN TO THE HILLS — **Iron Maiden** (7)	82
RUNAROUND SUE — **Dion** (11)	61
RUNAROUND SUE — **Racey** (13)	80
RUNAROUND SUE — Doug **Sheldon** (36)	61
RUNAWAY — Del **Shannon** (1)	61
RUNAWAY BOYS — **Stray Cats** (9)	80
RUNAWAY, THE — Elkie **Brooks** (50)	79
RUNNER, THE — **Three Degrees** (10)	79
RUNNIN' AWAY — **Sly and the Family Stone** (17)	72
RUNNIN' WITH THE DEVIL — **Van Halen** (52)	80
RUNNING BEAR — Johnny **Preston** (1)	60
RUNNING FREE — **Iron Maiden** (34)	80
RUNNING FROM PARADISE — Daryl **Hall and John Oates** (41)	80
RUNNING SCARED — Roy **Orbison** (9)	61
RUPERT — Jackie **Lee** (14)	71
S. O. S. — **Abba** (6)	75
SABRE DANCE — **Love Sculpture** (5)	68
SACRAMENTO — **Middle Of The Road** (23)	72
SAD EYES — Robert **John** (31)	79
SAD MOVIES — Carol **Deene** (44)	61
SAD MOVIES — Sue **Thompson** (46)	61
SAD SWEET DREAMER — **Sweet Sensation** (1)	74
SADDLE UP — David **Christie** (9)	82
SADIE'S SHAWL — Frank **Cordell** (29)	56
SAIL ON — **Commodores** (8)	79
SAILING — Rod **Stewart** (1)	76,75
SAILING [B] — Christopher **Cross** (48)	81
SAILOR — Petula **Clark** (1)	61
SAILOR — Anne **Shelton** (10)	61
ST. THERESE OF THE ROSES — Malcolm **Vaughan** (3)	56
SAINTS ARE COMING, THE — **Skids** (48)	78
SAINTS ROCK 'N ROLL, THE — Bill **Haley and his Comets** (5)	56
SALLY — Gerry **Monroe** (4)	70
SALLY ANN — Joe **Brown** (28)	63
SALLY DON'T YOU GRIEVE — Lonnie **Donegan** (11)	58
SAL'S GOT A SUGAR LIP — Lonnie **Donegan** (13)	59
SALTY DOG — **Procol Harum** (44)	69
SAM [A] — Olivia **Newton-John** (6)	77
SAM [B] — Keith **West** (38)	67
SAMANTHA — Kenny **Ball and his Jazzmen** (13)	61
SAMBA PA TI — **Santana** (27)	74
SAME OLD SCENE, THE — **Roxy Music** (12)	80
SAMSON & DELILAH [A] — **Middle Of The Road** (26)	72
SAMSON AND DELILAH [B] — **Bad Manners** (58)	82
SAN ANTONIO ROSE — Floyd **Cramer** (36)	61
SAN BERNADINO — **Christie** (7)	70
SAN FRANCISCAN NIGHTS — Eric **Burdon** (7)	67
SAN FRANCISCO (BE SURE TO WEAR FLOWERS IN YOUR HAIR) — Scott **McKenzie** (1)	67
SAN FRANCISCO (YOU'VE GOT ME) — **Village People** (45)	77
SAN MIGUEL — Lonnie **Donegan** (19)	59
SAN MIGUEL — **Kingston Trio** (29)	59
SANCTUARY [A] — **Iron Maiden** (29)	80
SANCTUARY [B] — **New Musik** (31)	80
SANCTUS (MISSA LUBA) — **Troubadours Du Roi Baudouin** (28)	69
SANDY — John **Travolta** (2)	78
SANTA BRING MY BABY BACK TO ME — Elvis **Presley** (7)	57
SANTA CLAUS IS BACK IN TOWN — Elvis **Presley** (41)	80
SANTA CLAUS IS COMIN' TO TOWN — **Carpenters** (37)	75
SANTA CLAUS IS COMING TO TOWN — **Jackson Five** (43)	72
SANTO NATALE — David **Whitfield** (2)	54
SARA — **Fleetwood Mac** (37)	79
SARAH — **Thin Lizzy** (24)	79
SARTORIAL ELOQUENCE — Elton **John** (44)	80
SAT IN YOUR LAP — Kate **Bush** (11)	81
SATIN SHEETS — **Bellamy Brothers** (43)	76
SATISFACTION — Aretha **Franklin** (37)	67
SATISFACTION — Otis **Redding** (33)	66
SATISFACTION GUARANTEED (OR TAKE YOUR LOVE BACK) — Harold **Melvin and the Bluenotes** (32)	74
SATISFY MY SOUL — Bob **Marley and the Wailers** (21)	78
SATURDAY GIG — **Mott The Hoople** (41)	74
SATURDAY NIGHT — **T-Connection** (41)	79
SATURDAY NIGHT AT THE MOVIES — **Drifters** (3)	72
SATURDAY NIGHT (BENEATH THE PLASTIC PALM TREES) — **Leyton Buzzards** (53)	79
SATURDAY NIGHT'S ALRIGHT FOR FIGHTING — Elton **John** (7)	73
SATURDAY NITE — **Earth Wind and Fire** (17)	77
SATURDAY NITE AT THE DUCK POND — **Cougars** (33)	63
SAVAGE, THE — **Shadows** (10)	61
SAVE A PRAYER — **Duran Duran** (2)	82
SAVE IT FOR LATER — The **Beat** (47)	82
SAVE ME [A] — **Dave Dee, Dozy, Beaky, Mick and Tich** (4)	66
SAVE ME [B] — **Silver Convention** (30)	75
SAVE ME [C] — **Queen** (11)	80
SAVE THE CHILDREN — Marvin **Gaye** (41)	71
SAVE THE LAST DANCE FOR ME — **Drifters** (2)	60,79
SAVE US — Philip **Jap** (53)	82
SAVE YOUR KISSES FOR ME — **Brotherhood Of Man** (1)	76
SAVE YOUR LOVE — **Renée and Renato** (1)	82
SAVED BY THE BELL — Robin **Gibb** (2)	69
SAY, HAS ANYBODY SEEN MY SWEET GYPSY ROSE — **Dawn** (12)	73
SAY HELLO WAVE GOODBYE — **Soft Cell** (3)	82
SAY I WON'T BE THERE — **Springfields** (5)	63
SAY IT WITH FLOWERS — Dorothy **Squires and Russ Conway** (23)	61
SAY WHEN — Lene **Lovich** (19)	79
SAY WONDERFUL THINGS — Ronnie **Carroll** (6)	63
SAY YOU DON'T MIND — Colin **Blunstone** (15)	72
SAY YOU LOVE ME — **Fleetwood Mac** (40)	76
SAY YOU'LL STAY UNTIL TOMORROW — Tom **Jones** (40)	77
SAY YOU'RE MINE AGAIN — June **Hutton** (6)	53
(SAY) YOU'RE MY GIRL — Roy **Orbison** (23)	65
SCARLET RIBBONS — Harry **Belafonte** (18)	57
SCARLETT O'HARA — Jet **Harris and Tony Meehan** (2)	63
SCARY MONSTERS (AND SUPER CREEPS) — David **Bowie** (20)	81
SCHOOL DAY — Chuck **Berry** (24)	57
SCHOOL DAY — Don **Lang** (26)	57
SCHOOL LOVE — Barry **Blue** (11)	74
SCHOOL'S OUT — Alice **Cooper** (1)	72
SCOTCH ON THE ROCKS — Band of the **Black Watch** (8)	75
SCOTLAND FOREVER — Sidney **Devine** (48)	78
SCOTS MACHINE — **Voyage** (13)	78
SCOTTISH SOLDIER, A — Andy **Stewart** (19)	61
SCRATCH, THE — **Surface Noise** (26)	80
SCULLERY — Clifford T. **Ward** (37)	74
SEA OF HEARTBREAK — Don **Gibson** (14)	61
SEA OF LOVE — Marty **Wilde** (3)	59

Title — Act (Position)	Year of Chart Entry
SEAGULL — **Rainbow Cottage** (33)	76
SEAGULL'S NAME WAS NELSON, THE — Peter E. **Bennett** (45)	70
SEALED WITH A KISS — Brian **Hyland** (3)	62,75
SEARCH AND DESTROY — **Dictators** (49)	77
SEARCHIN' — **Coasters** (30)	57
SEARCHIN' — **Hollies** (12)	63
SEARCHING — **Change** (11)	80
SEASIDE SHUFFLE — Terry **Dactyl and the Dinosaurs** (2)	72
SEASONS IN THE SUN — Terry **Jacks** (1)	74
SEASONS OF GOLD — **Gidea Park** (28)	81
SECOND HAND ROSE — Barbra **Streisand** (14)	66
SECOND TIME AROUND, THE — **Shalamar** (45)	79
SECRET COMBINATION — Randy **Crawford** (48)	81
SECRET HEART — **Tight Fit** (41)	82
SECRET LOVE — Doris **Day** (1)	54
SECRET LOVE — Kathy **Kirby** (4)	63
SECRETS — **Sutherland Brothers** (35)	76
SECRETS THAT YOU KEEP, THE — **Mud** (3)	75
SEDUCTION (LOVE THEME), THE — James **Last Band** (48)	80
SEE EMILY PLAY — **Pink Floyd** (6)	67
SEE JUNGLE (JUNGLE BOY) TV SAVAGE — **Bow Wow Wow** (45)	82
SEE MY BABY JIVE — **Wizzard** (1)	73
SEE MY FRIEND — **Kinks** (10)	65
SEE THOSE EYES — **Altered Images** (11)	82
SEE YOU — **Depeche Mode** (6)	82
SEE YOU LATER — **Regents** (55)	80
SEE YOU LATER ALLIGATOR — Bill **Haley and his Comets** (7)	56
SEEKER, THE — **Who** (19)	70
SEMI-DETACHED SUBURBAN MR. JAMES — **Manfred Mann** (2)	66
SEND IN THE CLOWNS — Judy **Collins** (6)	75
SEND ME THE PILLOW YOU DREAM ON — Johnny **Tillotson** (21)	62
SEND ONE YOUR LOVE — Stevie **Wonder** (52)	79
SENDING OUT AN S. O. S. — Retta **Young** (28)	75
SENSES WORKING OVERTIME — **XTC** (10)	82
SEPTEMBER — **Earth Wind and Fire** (3)	78
SEPTEMBER IN THE RAIN — Dinah **Washington** (35)	61
SERENADE — Mario **Lanza** (15)	55
SERENADE — Slim **Whitman** (8)	56
SERENADE [A] — Mario **Lanza** (19)	55
SERENADE [B] — Slim **Whitman** (24)	56
SERENADE (RE-RECORDING) — Mario **Lanza** (25)	56
SERENATA — Tony **Bennett** (35)	61
SERENATA — Sarah **Vaughan** (37)	60
SGT. PEPPER'S LONELY HEARTS CLUB BAND - WITH A LITTLE HELP FROM MY FRIENDS — **Beatles** (63)	78
SET ME FREE — **Kinks** (9)	65
SEVEN AND SEVEN IS (LIVE VERSION) — Alice **Cooper** (62)	82
SEVEN DAFFODILS — **Cherokees** (33)	64
SEVEN DAFFODILS — The **Mojos** (30)	64
SEVEN DAYS — Anne **Shelton** (20)	56
SEVEN DRUNKEN NIGHTS — **Dubliners** (7)	67
747 (STRANGERS IN THE NIGHT) — **Saxon** (13)	80
SEVEN LITTLE GIRLS SITTING IN THE BACK SEAT — **Avons** (3)	59
SEVEN LITTLE GIRLS SITTING IN THE BACK SEAT — Paul **Evans** (25)	59
SEVEN LONELY DAYS — Gisele **McKenzie** (6)	53
SEVEN ROOMS OF GLOOM — **Four Tops** (12)	67
SEVEN SEAS OF RHYE — **Queen** (10)	74
7-6-5-4-3-2-1 (BLOW YOUR WHISTLE) — **Rimshots** (26)	75
SEVEN TEARS — **Goombay Dance Band** (1)	82
7 TEEN — **Regents** (11)	79
7000 DOLLARS AND YOU — **Stylistics** (24)	77
SEVENTEEN — Boyd **Bennett** (16)	55
SEVENTEEN — Frankie **Vaughan** (18)	55
SEVENTH SON — Georgie **Fame** (25)	69
76 TROMBONES — **King Brothers** (19)	61
(SEXUAL) HEALING — Marvin **Gaye** (4)	82
SEXY — **MFSB** (37)	75
SEXY CREAM — **Slick** (47)	79
SEXY EYES — **Dr. Hook** (4)	80
SGT ROCK (IS GOING TO HELP ME) — **XTC** (16)	81
SHA LA LA — **Manfred Mann** (3)	64
SHA LA LA LA LEE — **Plastic Bertrand** (39)	78
SHA LA LA LA LEE — **Small Faces** (3)	66
SHA LA LA MEANS I LOVE YOU — Barry **White** (55)	79
SHADDAP YOU FACE — Joe **Dolce Music Theatre** (1)	81
SHADOW DANCING — Andy **Gibb** (42)	78
SHADY LADY — Gene **Pitney** (29)	70
"SHAFT", THEME FROM — Isaac **Hayes** (4)	71
SHAKE — Otis **Redding** (28)	67
SHAKE IT DOWN — **Mud** (12)	76
SHAKE ME I RATTLE — **Kaye Sisters** (27)	58
SHAKE RATTLE AND ROLL — Bill **Haley and his Comets** (4)	54
(SHAKE SHAKE SHAKE) SHAKE YOUR BOOTY — **KC and The Sunshine Band** (22)	76
SHAKE YOUR BODY (DOWN TO THE GROUND) — **Jacksons** (4)	79
SHAKE YOUR GROOVE THING — **Peaches and Herb** (26)	79
SHAKE YOUR RUMP TO THE FUNK — **Bar-Kays** (41)	77
SHAKIN' ALL OVER — Johnny **Kidd and the Pirates** (1)	60
SHAKIN' STEVENS EP, THE — Shakin' **Stevens** (2)	82
SHAKTI (THE MEANING OF WITHIN) — **Monsoon** (41)	82
SHA-LA-LA (MAKE ME HAPPY) — Al **Green** (20)	74
SHAME [A] — Evelyn **King** (39)	78
SHAME [B] — Alan **Price** (45)	67
SHAME AND SCANDAL IN THE FAMILY — Lance **Percival** (37)	65
SHAME SHAME SHAME [A] — Jimmy **Reed** (45)	64
SHAME SHAME SHAME [B] — **Shirley and Company** (6)	75
SHANG-A-LANG — **Bay City Rollers** (2)	74
SHANGHAI'D IN SHANGHAI — **Nazareth** (41)	74
SHANNON — Henry **Gross** (32)	76
SHANTE — **Mass Production** (59)	80
SHAPE OF THINGS TO COME, THE — **Headboys** (45)	79
SHAPES OF THINGS — **Yardbirds** (3)	66
SHARING THE NIGHT TOGETHER — **Dr. Hook** (43)	80
SHARING YOU — Bobby **Vee** (10)	62
SHAZAM! — Duane **Eddy** (4)	60
SH-BOOM — **Crew Cuts** (12)	54
SH-BOOM — Stan **Freberg** (15)	54
SH-BOOM (LIFE COULD BE A DREAM) — **Darts** (48)	80
SHE — Charles **Aznavour** (1)	74
SHE BELIEVES IN ME — Kenny **Rogers** (42)	79
SHE BLINDED ME WITH SCIENCE — Thomas **Dolby** (49)	82
SHE DONT FOOL ME — **Status Quo** (36)	82
SHE LOVED LIKE DIAMOND — **Spandau Ballet** (49)	82
SHE LOVES YOU — **Beatles** (1)	63
SHE NEEDS LOVE — Wayne **Fontana and the Mindbenders** (32)	65
SHE SHE LITTLE SHEILA — Gene **Vincent** (22)	61
SHE SOLD ME MAGIC — Lou **Christie** (25)	69
SHE WEARS MY RING — Solomon **King** (3)	68
SHE WEARS RED FEATHERS — Guy **Mitchell** (1)	53
SHE'D RATHER BE WITH ME — **Turtles** (4)	67
SHEENA IS A PUNK ROCKER — **Ramones** (22)	77
SHEFFIELD GRINDER, THE — Tony **Capstick and the Carlton Main/Frickley Colliery Band** (3)	81
SHEILA — Tommy **Roe** (3)	62
SHEPHERD'S SONG, THE — Tony **Osborne Sound** (46)	73
SHERRY — Adrian **Baker** (10)	75
SHERRY — **Four Seasons** (8)	62
SHE'S A BAD MAMA JAMA (SHE'S BUILT, SHE'S STACKED) — Carl **Carlton** (34)	81
SHE'S A GROOVY FREAK — **Real Thing** (52)	80
SHE'S A LADY — Tom **Jones** (13)	71
SHE'S A WIND UP — **Dr. Feelgood** (34)	77
SHE'S ABOUT A MOVER — **Sir Douglas Quintet** (15)	65
SHE'S GONE [A] — Daryl **Hall and John Oates** (42)	76
SHE'S GONE [B] — Buddy **Knox** (45)	62
SHE'S GONNA WIN — **Bilbo** (42)	78
SHE'S GOT CLAWS — Gary **Numan** (6)	81
SHE'S GOT IT — **Little Richard** (15)	57
SHE'S GOT YOU — Patsy **Cline** (43)	62
SHE'S IN LOVE WITH YOU — Suzi **Quatro** (11)	79
SHE'S LOST YOU — **Zephyrs** (48)	65
SHE'S NEW TO YOU — Susan **Maughan** (45)	63
SHE'S NOT THERE — Neil **MacArthur** (34)	69
SHE'S NOT THERE — **Santana** (11)	77
SHE'S NOT THERE — **Zombies** (12)	64
SHE'S NOT THERE — **U.K. Subs** (36)	79
SHE'S NOT YOU — Elvis **Presley** (1)	62
SHE'S OUT OF MY LIFE — Michael **Jackson** (3)	80
SHE'S SO COLD — **Rolling Stones** (33)	80
SHE'S SO MODERN — **Boomtown Rats** (12)	78
SHIFTING WHISPERING SANDS — Billy **Vaughn** (20)	56
SHIFTING WHISPERING SANDS (PARTS 1 & 2) — Eamonn **Andrews** (18)	56
SHINDIG — **Shadows** (6)	63
SHINE — Joe **Brown** (33)	61
SHINE A LITTLE LOVE — **Electric Light Orchestra** (6)	79
SHINE ON SILVER SUN — **Strawbs** (34)	73
SHINING STAR — **Manhattans** (45)	80
SHIPS IN THE NIGHT — **Be Bop Deluxe** (23)	76
SHIRALEE — Tommy **Steele** (11)	57
SHIRLEY — Shakin' **Stevens** (6)	82
SHOCK THE MONKEY — Peter **Gabriel** (58)	82
SHOES — **Reparata** (43)	75
SHOO BE DOO BE DOO DA DAY — Stevie **Wonder** (46)	68
SHOO DOO FU FU OOH! — Lenny **Williams** (38)	77
SHOORAH SHOORAH — Betty **Wright** (27)	75
SHOOT ME (WITH YOUR LOVE) — Tasha **Thomas** (59)	79
SHOOT SHOOT — **UFO** (48)	79
SHOOTING STAR — **Dollar** (14)	78
SHORT FAT FANNY — Larry **Williams** (21)	57
SHORT'NIN' BREAD — Tony **Crombie and his Rockets** (25)	56
SHORT'NIN' BREAD — **Viscounts** (16)	60
SHOT BY BOTH SIDES — **Magazine** (41)	78
SHOT DOWN IN THE NIGHT — **Hawkwind** (59)	80
SHOT OF RHYTHM & BLUES — Johnny **Kidd and the Pirates** (48)	63
SHOTGUN WEDDING — **Roy 'C'** (6)	66,72
SHOULD I DO IT? — **Pointer Sisters** (50)	81
SHOULD I STAY OR SHOULD I GO — **Clash** (17)	82
SHOUT — **Lulu** (7)	64
SHOUT SHOUT (KNOCK YOURSELF OUT) — Rockey **Sharpe and the Replays** (19)	82
SHOW ME — **Dexy's Midnight Runners** (16)	81
SHOW ME GIRL — **Herman's Hermits** (19)	64
SHOW ME THE WAY — Peter **Frampton** (10)	76
SHOW ME YOU'RE A WOMAN — **Mud** (8)	75
SHOW MUST GO ON, THE — Leo **Sayer** (2)	73
SHOW YOU THE WAY TO GO — **Jacksons** (1)	77
SHOWDOWN — **Electric Light Orchestra** (12)	73
SHOWROOM DUMMIES — **Kraftwerk** (25)	82
SHUFFLE, THE — Van **McCoy** (4)	77
SHUT UP — **Madness** (7)	81
SHY BOY — **Bananarama** (4)	82
SHY GIRL — Mark **Wynter** (28)	63
(SI SI) JE SUIS UN ROCK STAR — Bill **Wyman** (14)	81
SI TU DOIS PARTIR — **Fairport Convention** (21)	69
SICK AND TIRED — Fats **Domino** (26)	58
SICK MAN BLUES — **Goodies** (4)	75
SIDE BY SIDE — Kay **Starr** (7)	53
SIDE SADDLE — Russ **Conway** (1)	59
SIDE SHOW — **Chanter Sisters** (43)	76
SIDEBOARD SONG (GOT MY BEER IN THE SIDEBOARD HERE), THE — **Chas and Dave** (55)	79
SIDESHOW — Barry **Biggs** (3)	76
SIGN OF THE TIMES [A] — Petula **Clark** (49)	66
SIGN OF THE TIMES [B] — Bryan **Ferry** (37)	78
SIGNATURE TUNE OF THE Ü ARMY GAME, THE — Michael **Medwin, Bernard Bresslaw, Bass and Leslie Fyson** (5)	58
SIGNED SEALED DELIVERED (I'M YOURS) — **Boystown Gang** (50)	82
SIGNED SEALED DELIVERED I'M YOURS — Stevie **Wonder** (15)	70
SILENCE IS GOLDEN — **Tremeloes** (1)	67
SILENT NIGHT — Bing **Crosby** (8)	52
SILENT NIGHT — **Dickies** (47)	78
SILHOUETTES — **Herman's Hermits** (3)	65
SILLY GAMES — Janet **Kay** (2)	79
SILLY LOVE — **10 C. C.** (24)	74
SILLY LOVE SONGS — **Wings** (2)	76
SILLY THING — **Sex Pistols** (6)	79
SILVER DREAM MACHINE (PART 1) — David **Essex** (4)	80
SILVER LADY — David **Soul** (1)	77
SILVER LINING — **Stiff Little Fingers** (68)	81
SILVER MACHINE — **Hawkwind** (3)	72,78
SILVER STAR — **Four Seasons** (3)	76
SILVERY RAIN — Cliff **Richard** (27)	71
SIMON SAYS — **1910 Fruitgum Co.** (2)	68
SIMON SMITH & HIS AMAZING DANCING BEAR — Alan **Price** (4)	67
SIMON TEMPLAR — **Splodgenessabounds** (7)	80
SIMPLE GAME — **Four Tops** (3)	71
SINCE I DON'T HAVE YOU — Art **Garfunkel** (38)	79
SINCE YOU'RE GONE — **Cars** (37)	82
SINCE YOU'VE BEEN GONE [A] — Aretha **Franklin** (47)	68
SINCE YOU'VE BEEN GONE [B] — **Rainbow** (6)	79
SINCERELY — **McGuire Sisters** (14)	55

Title — Act (Position)	Year of Chart Entry
SING A HAPPY SONG [A] — George **McCrae** (38)	**75**
SING A HAPPY SONG [B] — **O'Jays** (39)	**79**
SING A LITTLE SONG — Desmond **Dekker and the Aces** (16)	**75**
SING A SONG OF FREEDOM — Cliff **Richard** (13)	**71**
SING BABY SING — **Stylistics** (3)	**75**
SING DON'T SPEAK — **Blackfoot Sue** (36)	**72**
SING IT AGAIN WITH JOE — Joe "Mr. Piano" **Henderson** (18)	**55**
SING IT WITH JOE — Joe "Mr. Piano" **Henderson** (14)	**55**
SING LIKE AN ANGEL — Jerry **Lordan** (36)	**60**
SING LITTLE BIRDIE — Pearl **Carr and Teddy Johnson** (12)	**59**
SING ME — **Brothers** (8)	**77**
SING ME AN OLD FASHIONED SONG — Billie Jo **Spears** (34)	**76**
SING SING — **Gaz** (60)	**79**
SINGALONG-A-SANTA — **Santa Claus and the Christmas Trees** (19)	**82**
SINGER SANG HIS SONG, THE — **Bee Gees** (25)	**68**
SINGIN' IN THE RAIN PART 1 — **Sheila and B. Devotion** (11)	**78**
SINGING DOGS (MEDLEY), THE — **Singing Dogs** (13)	**55**
SINGING THE BLUES — Dave **Edmunds** (28)	**80**
SINGING THE BLUES — Guy **Mitchell** (1)	**56**
SINGING THE BLUES — Tommy **Steele** (1)	**56**
S-S-S-SINGLE BED — **Fox** (4)	**76**
SINGLE GIRL — Sandy **Posey** (15)	**67,75**
SINK THE BISMARCK — Don **Lang** (43)	**60**
SINS OF THE FAMILY — P. F. **Sloan** (38)	**65**
SIPPIN' SODA — Guy **Mitchell** (11)	**54**
SIR DANCEALOT — **Olympic Runners** (35)	**79**
SIR DUKE — Stevie **Wonder** (2)	**77**
SISTER JANE — **New World** (9)	**72**
SIT DOWN AND CRY — Erroll **Dunkley** (52)	**80**
SIT SONG, THE — **Barron Knights** (44)	**80**
SITTIN' ON A FENCE — **Twice As Much** (25)	**66**
(SITTIN' ON) THE DOCK OF THE BAY — Otis **Redding** (3)	**68**
SITTING IN THE PARK — Georgie **Fame** (12)	**66**
SIX MILLION STEPS (WEST RUNS SOUTH) — Rahni **Harris and F.L.O.** (43)	**78**
SIX PACK — **Police** (17)	**80**
SIX TEENS, THE — **Sweet** (41)	**74**
634-5789 — Wilson **Pickett** (36)	**66**
SIX WIVES OF HENRY VIII, THE MUSIC FROM — **Early Music Consort, Directed by David Munrow** (49)	**71**
16 BARS — **Stylistics** (7)	**76**
SIXTEEN REASONS — Connie **Stevens** (9)	**60**
SIXTEEN TONS — Tennessee Ernie **Ford** (1)	**56**
SIXTEEN TONS — Frankie **Laine** (10)	**56**
SIXTY MINUTE MAN — **Trammps** (40)	**75**
SKATEAWAY — **Dire Straits** (37)	**81**
SKIFFLE SESSION (EP) — Lonnie **Donegan** (20)	**56**
SKIING IN THE SNOW — **Wigan's Ovation** (12)	**75**
SKIN DEEP — Duke **Ellington** (7)	**54**
SKIN DEEP — Ted **Heath** (9)	**54**
SKINHEAD MOONSTOMP — **Symarip** (54)	**80**
SKWEEZE ME PLEEZE ME — **Slade** (1)	**73**
SKY BLUE SHIRT AND A RAINBOW TIE, A — Norman **Brooks** (17)	**54**
SKY HIGH — **Jigsaw** (9)	**75**
SKY PILOT — Eric **Burdon** (40)	**68**
SKYLARK — Michael **Holliday** (39)	**60**
SKYWRITER — **Jackson Five** (25)	**73**
SLADE ALIVE AT READING '80 (EP) — **Slade** (44)	**80**
SLAP AND TICKLE — **Squeeze** (24)	**79**
SLEEP WALK — **Santo and Johnny** (22)	**59**
SLEEPIN' ON THE JOB — **Gillan** (55)	**80**
SLEEPWALK — **Ultravox** (29)	**80**
SLEEPY JOE — **Herman's Hermits** (12)	**68**
SLEEPY SHORES — Johnny **Pearson** (8)	**71**
SLIDE — **Rah Band** (50)	**81**
SLIP AND DIP — **Coffee** (57)	**80**
SLIP AND SLIDE — **Medicine Head** (22)	**74**
SLIP SLIDIN' AWAY — Paul **Simon** (36)	**77**
SLIP YOUR DISC TO THIS — **Heatwave** (15)	**77**
SLOOP JOHN B — **Beach Boys** (2)	**66**
SLOW DOWN — John **Miles** (10)	**77**
SLOW MOTION — **Ultravox** (33)	**81**
SLOW TRAIN TO PARADISE — **Tavares** (62)	**78**
SLOW TWISTIN' — Chubby **Checker** (23)	**62**
SLOWDRIVE — **Siouxsie and the Banshees** (41)	**82**
SLOWHAND — **Pointer Sisters** (10)	**81**
SMALL ADS — **Small Ads** (63)	**81**
SMALL SAD SAM — Phil **McLean** (34)	**62**
SMARTY PANTS — **First Choice** (9)	**73**
SMASH IT UP — **Damned** (35)	**79**
SMILE [A] — Nat "King" **Cole** (2)	**54**
SMILE [B] — **Pussycat** (24)	**76**
SMOKE GETS IN YOUR EYES — **Blue Haze** (32)	**72**
SMOKE GETS IN YOUR EYES — Bryan **Ferry** (17)	**74**
SMOKE GETS IN YOUR EYES — **Platters** (1)	**59**
SMOKE ON THE WATER — **Deep Purple** (21)	**77**
SMOKESTACK LIGHTNIN' — **Howlin' Wolf** (42)	**64**
SMOKEY BLUES AWAY — **New Generation** (38)	**68**
SMOKIN' IN THE BOY'S ROOM — **brownsville Station** (27)	**74**
SMURF SONG, THE — Father **Abraham and the Smurfs** (2)	**78**
SMURF, THE — Tyrone **Brunson** (69)	**82**
SNAKE BITE (EP) — **Whitesnake** (61)	**78**
SNAKE IN THE GRASS — Dave **Dee, Dozy, Beaky, Mick and Tich** (23)	**69**
SNAKE, THE — Al **Wilson** (41)	**75**
SNEAKIN' SUSPICION — **Dr. Feelgood** (47)	**77**
SNOOPY VS. THE RED BARON — **Hotshots** (4)	**73**
SNOOPY VS. THE RED BARON — **Royal Guardsmen** (8)	**67**
SNOW COACH — Russ **Conway** (7)	**59**
SNOWBIRD — Anne **Murray** (23)	**70**
SNOWBOUND FOR CHRISTMAS — Dickie **Valentine** (28)	**57**
SO DEEP IS THE NIGHT — Ken **Dodd** (31)	**64**
SO DO I — Kenny **Ball and his Jazzmen** (14)	**62**
SO FINE — Howard **Johnson** (45)	**82**
SO GOOD — Roy **Orbison** (32)	**67**
SO GOOD SO RIGHT — Brenda **Russell** (51)	**80**
SO GOOD TO BE BACK HOME AGAIN — **Tourists** (8)	**80**
SO HERE I AM — **U.B.40** (25)	**82**
SO IN LOVE WITH YOU — Freddy **Breck** (44)	**74**
SO IT WILL ALWAYS BE — **Everly Brothers** (23)	**63**
SO LONELY — **Police** (6)	**80**
SO LONG — **Fischer-Z** (72)	**80**
SO LONG BABY — Del **Shannon** (10)	**61**
SO MUCH IN LOVE [A] — **Mighty Avengers** (46)	**64**
SO MUCH IN LOVE [B] — **Tymes** (21)	**63**
SO MUCH LOVE — Tony **Blackburn** (31)	**68**
SO MUCH TROUBLE IN THE WORLD — Bob **Marley and the Wailers** (56)	**79**
SO SAD THE SONG — Gladys **Knight and the Pips** (20)	**76**
SO SAD (TO WATCH GOOD LOVE GO BAD) — **Everly Brothers** (4)	**60**
SO THIS IS ROMANCE — **Linx** (15)	**81**
SO TIRED — Frankie **Vaughan** (21)	**67**
SO YOU WIN AGAIN — **Hot Chocolate** (1)	**77**
SOFTLY AS I LEAVE YOU — Matt **Monro** (10)	**62**
SOFTLY SOFTLY — Ruby **Murray** (1)	**55**
SOFTLY SOFTLY [A] — **Equals** (48)	**68**
SOFTLY SOFTLY [B] — Ruby **Murray** (20)	**55**
SOFTLY WHISPERING I LOVE YOU — **Congregation** (4)	**71**
SOLD MY SOUL FOR ROCK 'N ROLL — **Linda and the Funky Boys** (36)	**76**
SOLDIER BLUE — Buffy **Sainte-Marie** (7)	**71**
SOLDIER BOY — **Cheetahs** (39)	**65**
SOLDIER BOY — **Shirelles** (23)	**62**
SOLDIER'S SONG — **Hollies** (58)	**80**
SOLEY SOLEY — **Middle Of The Road** (5)	**71**
SOLID GOLD EASY ACTION — **T. Rex** (2)	**72**
SOLITAIRE — **Carpenters** (32)	**75**
SOLITAIRE — Andy **Williams** (4)	**73**
SOLSBURY HILL — Peter **Gabriel** (13)	**77**
SOME GIRLS — **Racey** (2)	**79**
SOME GUYS HAVE ALL THE LUCK — Robert **Palmer** (16)	**82**
SOME KIND OF A SUMMER — David **Cassidy** (3)	**73**
SOME KINDA EARTHQUAKE — Duane **Eddy** (12)	**59**
SOME KINDA FUN — Chris **Montez** (10)	**63**
SOME OF YOUR LOVIN' — Dusty **Springfield** (8)	**65**
SOME OTHER GUY — **Big Three** (37)	**63**
SOME PEOPLE — Carol **Deene** (25)	**62**
SOME THINGS YOU NEVER GET USED TO — **Supremes** (34)	**68**
SOMEBODY — **Stargazers** (20)	**55**
SOMEBODY ELSE'S GIRL — Billy **Fury** (18)	**63**
SOMEBODY HELP ME — Spencer **Davis Group** (1)	**66**
(SOMEBODY) HELP ME OUT — **Beggar and Co** (15)	**81**
SOMEBODY STOLE MY GAL — Johnnie **Ray** (6)	**53**
SOMEBODY TO LOVE [A] — Brad **Newman** (47)	**62**
SOMEBODY TO LOVE [B] — **Queen** (2)	**76**
SOMEBODY TO LOVE [A] — **Jets** (56)	**82**
SOMEDAY [A] — Kenny **Ball and his Jazzmen** (28)	**61**
SOMEDAY [B] — Rick **Nelson** (9)	**58**
SOMEDAY [B] — Jodie **Sands** (14)	**58**
SOMEDAY MAN — **Monkees** (47)	**69**
SOMEDAY ONE DAY — **Seekers** (11)	**66**
SOMEDAY WE'LL BE TOGETHER — **Supremes** (13)	**69**
SOMEDAY WE'RE GONNA LOVE AGAIN — **Searchers** (11)	**64**
SOMEONE — Johnny **Mathis** (6)	**59**
SOMEONE ELSE'S BABY — Adam **Faith** (2)	**60**
SOMEONE ELSE'S ROSES — Joan **Regan** (5)	**54**
SOMEONE MUST HAVE HURT YOU A LOT — Frankie **Vaughan** (46)	**65**
SOMEONE ON YOUR MIND — Jimmy **Young** (13)	**55**
SOMEONE SAVED MY LIFE TONIGHT — Elton **John** (22)	**75**
SOMEONE SOMEONE — Brian **Poole and the Tremeloes** (2)	**64**
SOMEONE SOMEWHERE (IN SUMMERTIME) — **Simple Minds** (36)	**82**
SOMEONE'S LOOKING AT YOU — **Boomtown Rats** (4)	**80**
SOMEONE'S TAKEN MARIA AWAY — Adam **Faith** (34)	**65**
SOMETHIN' ELSE — Eddie **Cochran** (22)	**59**
SOMETHIN' STUPID — Nancy **Sinatra and Frank Sinatra** (1)	**67**
SOMETHING — Shirley **Bassey** (4)	**71,70**
SOMETHING [A] — **Beatles** (4)	**69**
SOMETHING [B] — Georgie **Fame** (23)	**65**
SOMETHING BEAUTIFUL — Jack **Wild** (46)	**70**
SOMETHING BETTER BEGINNING — **Honeycombs** (39)	**65**
SOMETHING BETTER CHANGE — **Stranglers** (9)	**77**
SOMETHING 'BOUT YOU BABY I LIKE — Tom **Jones** (36)	**74**
SOMETHING 'BOUT YOU BABY I LIKE — **Status Quo** (9)	**81**
SOMETHING ELSE — **Sex Pistols** (3)	**79**
SOMETHING FOR THE GIRL WITH EVERYTHING — **Sparks** (17)	**75**
SOMETHING HERE IN MY HEART (KEEPS A-TELLIN' ME NO) — **Paper Dolls** (11)	**68**
SOMETHING IN THE AIR — **Thunderclap Newman** (1)	**69**
SOMETHING MISSING — Petula **Clark** (44)	**61**
SOMETHING OLD, SOMETHING NEW — **Fantastics** (9)	**71**
SOMETHING ON MY MIND — Chris **Andrews** (41)	**66**
SOMETHING TELLS ME (SOMETHING IS GONNA HAPPEN TONIGHT) — Cilla **Black** (3)	**71**
SOMETHING THAT I SAID — **Ruts** (29)	**79**
SOMETHING'S BEEN MAKING ME BLUE — **Smokie** (17)	**76**
SOMETHING'S BURNING — Kenny **Rogers** (8)	**70**
SOMETHING'S COOKIN' IN THE KITCHEN — **Dana** (44)	**79**
SOMETHING'S GOTTA GIVE — Sammy **Davis Jr.** (11)	**55**
SOMETHING'S GOTTEN HOLD OF MY HEART — Gene **Pitney** (5)	**67**
SOMETHING'S HAPPENING — **Herman's Hermits** (6)	**68**
SOMETHING'S MISSING — **Chords** (55)	**80**
SOMETIMES WHEN WE TOUCH — Dan **Hill** (13)	**78**
SOMEWHERE — P. J. **Proby** (6)	**64**
SOMEWHERE ALONG THE WAY — Nat "King" **Cole** (3)	**52**
SOMEWHERE IN THE COUNTRY — Gene **Pitney** (19)	**68**
SOMEWHERE IN THE NIGHT — Barry **Manilow** (42)	**78**
SOMEWHERE MY LOVE — **Manuel and his Music Of The Mountains** (42)	**66**
SOMEWHERE MY LOVE — **Mike Sammes Singers** (14)	**66,67**
SON OF A PREACHER MAN — Dusty **Springfield** (9)	**68**
SON OF HICKORY HOLLER'S TRAMP — O. C. **Smith** (2)	**68**
SON OF MARY — Harry **Belafonte** (18)	**58**
SON OF MY FATHER — **Chicory Tip** (1)	**72**
SON THIS IS SHE — John **Leyton** (15)	**61**
SONG FOR GUY — Elton **John** (4)	**78**
SONG OF JOY — Miguel **Rios** (16)	**70**
SONG OF MEXICO — Tony **Meehan Combo** (39)	**64**
SONG OF MY LIFE, THE — Petula **Clark** (32)	**71**
SONG OF THE DREAMER — Johnnie **Ray** (10)	**55**
SONG SUNG BLUE — **Neil Diamond** (14)	**72**
SONG THAT I SING (THEME FROM 'WE'LL MEET AGAIN', THE — **Stutz Bearcats and the Dennis King Orchestra** (36)	**82**
SONGS FOR SWINGING LOVERS (LP) — Frank **Sinatra** (12)	**56**
SOONER OR LATER — Larry **Graham** (54)	**82**
SOOTHE ME — **Sam and Dave** (48)	**67**

Title — Act (Position)	Year of Chart Entry
SORROW — David **Bowie** (3)	73
SORROW — **Merseys** (4)	66
SORRY DOESN'T ALWAYS MAKE IT RIGHT — Diana **Ross** (23)	75
SORRY (I RAN ALL THE WAY HOME) — **Impalas** (28)	59
SORRY I'M A LADY — **Baccara** (8)	78
SORRY ROBBIE — Bert **Weedon** (28)	60
SORRY SEEMS TO BE THE HARDEST WORD — Elton **John** (11)	76
SORRY SUZANNE — **Hollies** (3)	69
SOUL CHA CHA — Van **McCoy** (34)	77
SOUL CITY WALK — Archie **Bell and the Drells** (13)	76
SOUL CLAP '69 — **Booker T. & The M. G.'s** (35)	69
SOUL COAXING — Raymond **Lefevre** (46)	68
SOUL DEEP — Gary 'U.S.' **Bonds** (59)	82
SOUL DEEP — **Box Tops** (22)	69
SOUL DRACULA — **Hot Blood** (32)	76
SOUL FINGER — **Bar-Kays** (33)	67
SOUL LIMBO — **Booker T. & The M. G.'s** (30)	68
SOUL MAN — **Sam and Dave** (24)	67
SOUL OF MY SUIT, THE — **T. Rex** (42)	77
SOUL SEARCHIN' TIME — **Trammps** (42)	76
SOUL SERENADE — Willie **Mitchell** (43)	68
SOUL SISTER BROWN SUGAR — **Sam and Dave** (15)	69
SOUND AND VISION — David **Bowie** (3)	77
SOUND OF CONFUSION — **Secret Affair** (45)	80
TSOP (THE SOUND OF PHILADELPHIA) — **MFSB** (22)	74
SOUND OF SILENCE, THE — **Bachelors** (3)	66
SOUND OF THE CROWD, THE — **Human League** (12)	81
SOUND OF THE SUBURBS, THE — **Members** (12)	79
SOUND OF YOUR CRY, THE — Elvis **Presley** (59)	82
SOUND SYSTEM — **Steel Pulse** (71)	79
SOUND YOUR FUNKY HORN — **KC and The Sunshine Band** (17)	74
SOUTH AFRICAN MAN — Hamilton **Bohannon** (22)	75
SOUTHERN COMFORT — Bernie **Flint** (48)	77
SOUTHERN FREEEZ BEGGARS BANQUET — **Freeez** (8)	81
SOUTHERN NIGHTS — Glen **Campbell** (28)	77
SOUVENIR — **Orchestral Manoeuvres in the Dark** (3)	81
SOUVENIRS — **Voyage** (56)	78
SPACE AGE LOVE SONG — A **Flock of Seagulls** (34)	82
SPACE BASS — **Slick** (16)	79
SPACE ODDITY — David **Bowie** (1)	69,75
SPACE STATION NO. 5 — Sammy **Hagar** (52)	79
SPACE STATION NO. 5 — **Montrose** (71)	80
SPACER — **Sheila and B. Devotion** (18)	79
SPANISH EYES — Al **Martino** (5)	70,73
SPANISH FLEA — Herb **Alpert** (3)	65
SPANISH HARLEM — Aretha **Franklin** (14)	71
SPANISH HARLEM — Jimmy **Justice** (20)	62
SPANISH HARLEM — **Sounds Incorporated** (35)	64
SPANISH STROLL — **Mink de Ville** (20)	77
SPANISH WINE — Chris **White** (37)	76
SPARROW, THE — **Ramblers (from the Abbey Hey Junior School)** (11)	79
SPARTANS, THE — **Sounds Incorporated** (30)	64
SPEAK TO ME PRETTY — Brenda **Lee** (3)	62
SPECIAL BREW — **Bad Manners** (3)	80
SPECIAL YEARS, THE — Val **Doonican** (7)	65
SPEEDY GONZALES — Pat **Boone** (2)	62
SPELLBOUND — **Siouxsie and the Banshees** (22)	81
SPIDERS & SNAKES — Jim **Stafford** (14)	74
SPINNIN' & SPINNIN' — **Syreeta** (49)	74
SPINNING ROCK BOOGIE — Hank C. **Burnette** (21)	76
SPIRAL SCRATCH (EP) — **Buzzcocks** (31)	79
SPIRIT — **Bauhaus** (42)	82
SPIRIT BODY AND SOUL — **Nolans** (34)	79
SPIRIT IN THE SKY — Norman **Greenbaum** (1)	70
SPIRIT IS WILLING, THE — Peter **Straker and the Hands Of Dr. Teleny** (40)	72
SPIRIT OF RADIO — **Rush** (13)	80
SPIRITS (HAVING FLOWN) — **Bee Gees** (16)	80
SPIRITS IN THE MATERIAL WORLD — **Police** (12)	81
SPLISH SPLASH — Bobby **Darin** (28)	58
SPLISH SPLASH — Charlie **Drake** (7)	58
SPOOKY — **Atlanta Rhythm Section** (48)	79
SPOOKY — **Classics IV** (46)	68
SPOT THE PIGEON (EP) — **Genesis** (14)	77
SPREAD A LITTLE HAPPINESS — **Sting** (16)	82
SPREAD YOUR WINGS — **Queen** (34)	78
SQUEEZE BOX — **Who** (10)	76
ST. VALENTINE'S DAY MASSACRE (EP) — **Headgirl** (5)	81
STACCATOS THEME — Elmer **Bernstein** (4)	59
STAGGER LEE — Lloyd **Price** (7)	59
STAIRCASE (MYSTERY), THE — **Siouxsie and the Banshees** (24)	79
STAIRWAY OF LOVE — Terry **Dene** (16)	58
STAIRWAY OF LOVE — Michael **Holliday** (3)	58
STAIRWAY TO HEAVEN — Neil **Sedaka** (8)	60
STAND AND DELIVER — **Adam and The Ants** (1)	81
STAND BY ME — Ben E. **King** (27)	61
STAND BY ME — John **Lennon** (30)	75
STAND BY ME — Kenny **Lynch** (39)	64
STAND BY YOUR MAN — Tammy **Wynette** (1)	75
STAND DOWN MARGARET (DUB) — The **Beat** (22)	80
STAND OR FALL — **Fixx** (54)	82
STANDING IN THE ROAD — **Blackfoot Sue** (4)	72
STANDING IN THE SHADOWS OF LOVE — **Four Tops** (6)	67
STANDING ON THE CORNER — **Four Lads** (34)	60
STANDING ON THE CORNER — **King Brothers** (4)	60
STANDING ON THE INSIDE — Neil **Sedaka** (26)	73
STANDING ON THE TOP (PART 1) — **Temptations** (53)	82
STANDING ON THE VERGE (OF GETTING IT ON) — **Platinum Hook** (72)	78
STAR [A] — **Stealer's Wheel** (25)	74
STAR [B] — **Earth Wind and Fire** (16)	79
STAR [C] — **Nazareth** (54)	79
STAR [D] — Kiki **Dee** (13)	81
STAR [E] — **Second Image** (60)	82
STAR ON A TV SHOW — **Stylistics** (12)	75
STAR WARS THEME-CANTINA BAND — **Meco** (7)	77
STARBRIGHT — Johnny **Mathis** (47)	60
STARCHILD — **Level 42** (47)	81
STARDUST — Billy **Ward** (26)	58
STARDUST [A] — Nat "King" **Cole** (24)	57
STARDUST [A] — Billy **Ward** (13)	57
STARDUST [B] — David **Essex** (7)	74
STARING AT THE RUDE BOYS — **Ruts** (22)	80
STARMAKER — **Kids From 'Fame'** (3)	82
STARMAN — David **Bowie** (10)	72
STARRY EYED — Michael **Holliday** (1)	60
STARRY NIGHT, A — **Joy Strings** (35)	64
STARS — **Sylvester** (47)	79
STARS AND STRIPES FOREVER — Mr. Acker **Bilk** (22)	61
STARS ON 45 — **Starsound** (2)	81
STARS ON 45 VOL.3 — **Starsound** (17)	81
STARS ON 45 VOL.2 — **Starsound** (2)	81
STARS ON STEVIE — **Starsound** (14)	82
STARS OVER 45 — **Chas and Dave** (21)	81
STARS SHINE IN YOUR EYES — Ronnie **Hilton** (13)	55
START — **Jam** (1)	80
START ME UP — **Rolling Stones** (7)	81
START MOVIN' — Terry **Dene** (15)	57
START MOVIN' — Sal **Mineo** (16)	57
STARTRAX CLUB DISCO — **Startrak** (18)	81
STARTURN ON 45 (PINTS) — **Starturn On 45 (Pints)** (45)	81
STATE OF INDEPENDENCE — Donna **Summer** (14)	82
STATUS ROCK — **Headbangers** (60)	81
STAY — Jackson **Browne** (12)	78
STAY — **Hollies** (8)	63
STAY — Maurice **Williams and the Zodiacs** (14)	61
STAY AWHILE — Dusty **Springfield** (13)	64
STAY (LIVE) — Barry **Manilow** (23)	82
STAY WITH ME [A] — **Blue Mink** (11)	72
STAY WITH ME [B] — **Faces** (6)	71
STAY WITH ME BABY — David **Essex** (45)	78
STAY WITH ME BABY — **Walker Brothers** (26)	67
STAY WITH ME TILL DAWN — Judie **Tzuke** (16)	79
STAYIN' ALIVE — Richard **Ace** (66)	78
STAYIN' ALIVE — **Bee Gees** (4)	78
STEEL GUITAR AND A GLASS OF WINE, A — Paul **Anka** (41)	62
STEP BY STEP [A] — Steve **Perry** (41)	60
STEP BY STEP [B] — Joe **Simon** (14)	73
STEP INSIDE LOVE — Cilla **Black** (8)	68
STEP INTO A DREAM — **White Plains** (21)	73
STEP INTO CHRISTMAS — Elton **John** (24)	73
STEPPIN' OUT — **Kool and the Gang** (12)	81
STEREOTYPE — The **Specials** (6)	80
STEWBALL — Lonnie **Donegan** (2)	56
STILL [A] — **Commodores** (4)	79
STILL [B] — Karl **Denver** (13)	63
STILL [B] — Ken **Dodd** (35)	63
STILL I'M SAD — **Yardbirds** (3)	65
STILL WATER (LOVE) — **Four Tops** (10)	70
STING, THE — **Ragtimers** (31)	74
STINGRAY — **Shadows** (19)	65
STIR IT UP — Johnny **Nash** (13)	72
STOMP — **Brothers Johnson** (6)	80
STONE COLD — **Rainbow** (34)	82
STONED LOVE — **Supremes** (3)	71
STONEY END — Barbra **Streisand** (27)	71
STONEY GROUND — **Guys and Dolls** (38)	76
STOOD UP — Rick **Nelson** (27)	58
STOOL PIDGEON — Kid **Creole and the Coconuts** (7)	82
STOP BREAKING MY HEART — **Inner Circle** (50)	79
STOP DRAGGIN' MY HEART AROUND — Stevie **Nicks with Tom Petty Heartbreakers** (50)	81
STOP FEELING SORRY FOR YOURSELF — Adam **Faith** (23)	65
STOP HER ON SIGHT (SOS) — Edwin **Starr** (11)	66,68
STOP IN THE NAME OF LOVE — **Supremes** (7)	65
STOP LOOK & LISTEN — Wayne **Fontana and the Mindbenders** (37)	64
STOP LOOK LISTEN (TO YOUR HEART) — Diana **Ross and Marvin Gaye** (25)	74
STOP ME (IF YOU'VE HEARD IT ALL BEFORE) — Billy **Ocean** (12)	76
STOP STOP STOP — **Hollies** (2)	66
STOP THAT GIRL — Chris **Andrews** (36)	66
STOP THE CAVALRY — Jona **Lewie** (3)	80
STOP THE WAR NOW — Edwin **Starr** (33)	71
STOP YOUR SOBBING — **Pretenders** (34)	79
STORM IN A TEACUP — **Fortunes** (7)	72
STORMTROOPER IN DRAG — Paul **Gardiner** (49)	81
STORY OF MY LIFE — Gary **Miller** (14)	58
STORY OF MY LIFE, THE — Alma **Cogan** (25)	58
STORY OF MY LIFE, THE — Michael **Holliday** (1)	58
STORY OF MY LIFE, THE — Dave **King** (20)	58
STORY OF MY LOVE — Conway **Twitty** (30)	59
STORY OF THE BLUES, THE — **Wah!** (59)	82
STORY OF TINA — Ronnie **Harris** (12)	54
STORY OF TINA, THE — Al **Martino** (10)	54
STOWAWAY — Barbara **Lyon** (12)	55
STRAIGHT LINES — **New Musik** (53)	79
STRAIGHT TO HELL — **Clash** (17)	82
STRAIGHTEN OUT — **Stranglers** (9)	77
STRANGE BAND — **Family** (11)	70
STRANGE BREW — **Cream** (17)	67
STRANGE KIND OF WOMAN — **Deep Purple** (8)	71
STRANGE LADY IN TOWN — Frankie **Laine** (6)	55
STRANGE LITTLE [A] — **Sad Café** (32)	80
STRANGE LITTLE GIRL [B] — **Stranglers** (7)	82
STRANGE MAGIC — **Electric Light Orchestra** (38)	76
STRANGE TOWN — **Jam** (15)	79,80
STRANGER — **Shakatak** (43)	82
STRANGER IN PARADISE — Tony **Bennett** (1)	55
STRANGER IN PARADISE — Eddie **Calvert** (14)	55
STRANGER IN PARADISE — Don **Cornell** (19)	55
STRANGER IN PARADISE — Bing **Crosby** (17)	55
STRANGER IN PARADISE — **Four Aces** (6)	55
STRANGER IN PARADISE — Tony **Martin** (6)	55
STRANGER IN TOWN — Del **Shannon** (40)	65
STRANGER ON THE SHORE — Mr. Acker **Bilk** (2)	61
STRANGER ON THE SHORE — Andy **Williams** (30)	62
STRANGER, THE — **Shadows** (5)	60
STRANGERS IN THE NIGHT — Frank **Sinatra** (1)	66
STRANGLEHOLD — **U.K. Subs** (26)	79
STRAW DOGS — **Stiff Little Fingers** (44)	79
STRAWBERRY BLONDE — Frank **D'rone** (24)	60
STRAWBERRY FAIR — Anthony **Newley** (3)	60
STRAWBERRY FIELDS FOREVER — **Beatles** (2)	67,76
STRAWBERRY LETTER 23 — **Brothers Johnson** (35)	77
STRAY CAT STRUT — **Stray Cats** (11)	81
STREAK, THE — Ray **Stevens** (1)	74
STREAMLINE TRAIN — **Vipers Skiffle Group** (23)	57
STREET CALLED HOPE, A — Gene **Pitney** (37)	70
STREET FIGHTING MAN — **Rolling Stones** (21)	71
STREET LIFE [A] — **Roxy Music** (9)	73
STREET LIFE [B] — **Crusaders** (5)	79
STREETPLAYER (MECHANIK) — **Fashion** (46)	82
STREETS OF LONDON — **Anti-Nowhere League** (48)	82
STREETS OF LONDON — Ralph **McTell** (2)	74
STREETWALKIN' — **Shakatak** (38)	82
STRETCHIN' OUT — Gayle **Adams** (64)	80
STRICTLY ELVIS (EP) — Elvis **Presley** (26)	60
STROKE, THE — Billy **Squier** (52)	81
STRONG ARM OF THE LAW — **Saxon** (63)	80
STRONG LOVE — Spencer **Davis Group** (44)	65
STRUMMIN' — **Chas and Dave** (52)	78
STRUT YOUR FUNKY STUFF — **Frantique** (10)	79
STUCK IN THE MIDDLE WITH YOU — **Stealer's Wheel** (8)	73
STUCK ON YOU — Elvis **Presley** (3)	60
STUFF LIKE THAT — Quincy **Jones** (34)	78

Title — Act (Position)	Year of Chart Entry
STUMBLIN' IN — Suzi Quatro and Suzi Norman (41)	78
STUPID CUPID — Connie Francis (1)	58
SUBDIVISIONS — Rush (53)	82
SUBSTITUTE [A] — Who (5)	66,76
SUBSTITUTE [B] — Clout (2)	78
SUBSTITUTE [C] — Liquid Gold (8)	80
SUBTERRANEAN HOMESICK BLUES — Bob Dylan (9)	65
SUCH A NIGHT — Elvis Presley (13)	64
SUCH A NIGHT — Johnnie Ray (1)	54
SUCU SUCU — Ted Heath (36)	61
SUCU SUCU — Laurie Johnson (9)	61
SUCU SUCU — Joe Loss (48)	61
SUCU SUCU — Nina and Frederick (23)	61
SUCU SUCU — Ping Ping and Al Verlaine (41)	61
SUDDENLY — Olivia Newton-John and Cliff Richard (15)	80
SUDDENLY THERE'S A VALLEY — Petula Clark (7)	55
SUDDENLY THERE'S A VALLEY — Lee Lawrence (14)	55
SUDDENLY THERE'S A VALLEY — Jo Stafford (12)	56,55
SUDDENLY YOU LOVE ME — Tremeloes (6)	68
SUE'S GONNA BE MINE — Del Shannon (21)	63
SUGAR AND SPICE — Searchers (2)	63
SUGAR BABY LOVE — Rubettes (1)	74
SUGAR BEE — Canned Heat (49)	70
SUGAR CANDY KISSES — Mac and Katie Kissoon (3)	75
SUGAR DOLL — Jets (55)	81
SUGAR ME — Lynsey De Paul (5)	72
SUGAR MOON — Pat Boone (6)	58
SUGAR SHACK — Jimmy Gilmer and the Fireballs (45)	63
SUGAR SUGAR — Archies (1)	69
SUGAR SUGAR — Sakkarin (12)	71
SUGAR TOWN — Nancy Sinatra (8)	67
SUGARBUSH — Doris Day and Frankie Laine (8)	52
SUGARTIME — Alma Cogan (16)	58
SUGARTIME — Jim Dale (25)	58
SUGARTIME — McGuire Sisters (14)	58
SUKIYAKI — Kenny Ball and his Jazzmen (10)	63
SUKIYAKI — Kyu Sakamoto (6)	63
SULTANA — Titanic (5)	71
SULTANS OF SWING — Dire Straits (8)	79
SUMAHAMA — Beach Boys (45)	79
SUMMER BREEZE — Isley Brothers (16)	74
SUMMER FUN — Barracudas (37)	80
SUMMER HOLIDAY — Cliff Richard (1)	63
SUMMER IN THE CITY — Lovin' Spoonful (8)	66
SUMMER IS OVER — Frank Ifield (25)	64
SUMMER MADNESS — Kool and the Gang (17)	81
SUMMER NIGHT CITY — Abba (5)	78
SUMMER NIGHTS [A] — Marianne Faithfull (10)	65
SUMMER NIGHTS [B] — John Travolta and Olivia Newton-John (1)	78
SUMMER OF MY LIFE — Simon May (7)	76
SUMMER OF THE SEVENTEENTH DOLL — Winifred Atwell (24)	59
SUMMER OF '42 — Biddu (14)	75
'SUMMER PLACE', THEME FROM A — Percy Faith (2)	60
SUMMER PLACE, THEME FROM A — Norrie Paramor (36)	60
SUMMER SET — Mr. Acker Bilk (5)	60
SUMMER (THE FIRST TIME) — Bobby Goldsboro (9)	73
SUMMER WIND — Frank Sinatra (36)	66
SUMMERLOVE SENSATION — Bay City Rollers (3)	74
SUMMERTIME — Funboy Three (18)	82
SUMMERTIME — Marcels (46)	61
SUMMERTIME — Al Martino (49)	60
SUMMERTIME — Billy Stewart (39)	66
SUMMERTIME BLUES — Eddie Cochran (18)	58,68
SUMMERTIME BLUES — Who (38)	70
SUMMERTIME CITY — Mike Batt (4)	75
SUN AIN'T GONNA SHINE ANYMORE, THE — Walker Brothers (1)	66
SUN ARISE — Rolf Harris (3)	62
SUN OF JAMAICA — Goombay Dance Band (50)	82
SUNBURN — Graham Gouldman (52)	79
SUNDAY — Buster (49)	76
SUNDAY GIRL — Blondie (1)	79
SUNDOWN — Gordon Lightfoot (33)	74
SUNNY — Boney M (3)	77
SUNNY — Cher (32)	66
SUNNY — Georgie Fame (13)	66
SUNNY — Bobby Hebb (12)	66
SUNNY AFTERNOON — Kinks (1)	66
SUNNY DAY — Pig Bag (53)	81
SUNNY HONEY GIRL — Cliff Richard (19)	71
SUNSET PEOPLE — Donna Summer (46)	80
SUNSHINE AFTER THE RAIN — Elkie Brooks (10)	77
SUNSHINE DAY — Osibisa (17)	76
SUNSHINE GIRL — Herman's Hermits (8)	68
SUNSHINE OF LOVE — Louis Armstrong (41)	68
SUNSHINE OF YOUR LOVE — Cream (25)	68
SUNSHINE OF YOUR SMILE, THE — Mike Berry (9)	80
SUNSHINE SUPERMAN — Donovan (3)	66
SUPER LOVE — Wigan's Ovation (41)	75
SUPER NATURE — Cerrone (8)	78
SUPER TROUPER — Abba (1)	80
SUPER WOMBLE — Wombles (20)	75
SUPERGIRL — Graham Bonney (19)	66
THEME FROM SUPERMAN (MAIN TITLE) — London Symphony Orchestra (32)	79
SUPERMAN'S BIG SISTER — Ian Dury and the Blockheads (51)	80
SUPERSHIP — George Benson (30)	75
SUPERSONIC ROCKET SHIP — Kinks (16)	72
SUPERSTAR [A] — Carpenters (18)	71
SUPERSTAR [B] — Murray Head (47)	72
SUPERSTAR (REMEMBER HOW YOU GOT WHERE YOU ARE) — Temptations (32)	72
SUPERSTITION — Stevie Wonder (11)	73
SURF CITY — Jan and Dean (26)	63
SURFIN' USA — Beach Boys (34)	63
SURRENDER [A] — Elvis Presley (1)	61
SURRENDER [B] — Diana Ross (10)	71
SURROUND YOURSELF WITH SORROW — Cilla Black (3)	69
SUSANNAH'S STILL ALIVE — Dave Davies (20)	67
SUSIE DARLIN' — Robin Luke (23)	58
SUSIE DARLIN' — Tommy Roe (37)	62
SUSPICION — Elvis Presley (9)	76
SUSPICION — Terry Stafford (31)	64
SUSPICIOUS MINDS — Elvis Presley (2)	69
SUSPICIOUS MINDS — Candi Staton (31)	82
SUZANNE BEWARE OF THE DEVIL — Dandy Livingstone (14)	72
SWALLOW MY PRIDE — Ramones (36)	77
SWAN LAKE — Cats (48)	69
SWAY — Dean Martin (6)	54
SWAY — Bobby Rydell (12)	60
SWEARIN' TO GOD — Frankie Valli (31)	75
SWEAT IN BULLET — Simple Minds (52)	81
SWEDISH RHAPSODY — Mantovani (2)	53
SWEDISH RHAPSODY — Ray Martin (4)	53
SWEET CAROLINE — Neil Diamond (8)	71
SWEET CHEATIN' RITA — Alvin Stardust (37)	75
SWEET DANGER — Angelwitch (75)	80
SWEET DREAM — Jethro Tull (7)	69
SWEET DREAMS [A] — Dave Sampson (29)	60
SWEET DREAMS [B] — Roy Buchanan (40)	73
SWEET DREAMS [B] — Elvis Costello and the Attractions (42)	81
SWEET DREAMS [B] — Tommy McLain (49)	66
SWEET HEART CONTRACT — Magazine (54)	80
SWEET HITCH-HIKER — Creedence Clearwater Revival (36)	71
SWEET ILLUSION — Junior Campbell (15)	73
SWEET IMPOSSIBLE YOU — Brenda Lee (28)	63
SWEET INSPIRATION — Johnny Johnson and the Bandwagon (10)	70
SWEET LITTLE ROCK 'N' ROLLER — Showaddywaddy (15)	79
SWEET LITTLE SIXTEEN — Chuck Berry (16)	58
SWEET LITTLE SIXTEEN — Jerry Lee Lewis (38)	62
SWEET LOVE — Commodores (32)	77
SWEET LUI-LOUISE — Ironhorse (60)	79
SWEET MUSIC — Showaddywaddy (14)	75
SWEET NOTHINS — Searchers (48)	63
SWEET NUTHINS — Brenda Lee (4)	60
SWEET OLD-FASHIONED GIRL — Teresa Brewer (3)	56
SWEET PEA — Manfred Mann (36)	67
SWEET SENSATION — Melodians (41)	70
SWEET SOUL MUSIC — Arthur Conley (7)	67
SWEET STUFF — Guy Mitchell (25)	57
SWEET SUBURBIA — Skids (70)	78
SWEET SWEET SMILE — Carpenters (40)	78
SWEET TALKIN' GUY — Chiffons (4)	66,72
SWEET TALKIN' WOMAN — Electric Light Orchestra (6)	78
SWEET UNDERSTANDING LOVE — Four Tops (29)	73
SWEET WILLIAM — Millie (30)	64
SWEETER THAN YOU — Rick Nelson (19)	59
SWEETEST GIRL, THE — Scritti Politti (64)	81
SWEETHEART — Engelbert Humperdinck (22)	70
SWEETIE PIE — Eddie Cochran (38)	60
SWEETS FOR MY SWEET — Searchers (1)	63
SWING LOW SWEET CHARIOT — Eric Clapton (19)	75
SWING THAT HAMMER — Mike Cotton's Jazzmen (36)	63
SWING YOUR DADDY — Jim Gilstrap (4)	75
SWINGIN' — Light of the World (45)	79
SWINGIN' LOW — Outlaws (46)	61
SWINGIN' SHEPHERD BLUES — Ella Fitzgerald (15)	58
SWINGIN' SHEPHERD BLUES — Ted Heath (3)	58
SWINGIN' SHEPHERD BLUES — Moe Koffman Quartette (23)	58
SWINGING IN THE RAIN — Norman Vaughan (34)	62
SWINGING ON A STAR — Big Dee Irwin (7)	63
SWINGING SCHOOL — Bobby Rydell (44)	60
SWISS MAID — Del Shannon (2)	62
SWITCH — Benelux and Nancy Dee (52)	79
SWITCHED ON SWING — Kings Of Swing Orchestra (48)	82
SWORDS OF A THOUSAND MEN — Ten Pole Tudor (6)	81
SYLVIA — Focus (4)	73
SYLVIA'S MOTHER — Dr. Hook (2)	72
SYMPATHY — Rare Bird (27)	70
TAINTED LOVE — Soft Cell (1)	81
TAKE A CHANCE ON ME — Abba (1)	78
TAKE A CHANCE WITH ME — Roxy Music (26)	82
TAKE A HEART — Sorrows (21)	65
TAKE A LOOK AROUND — Temptations (13)	72
TAKE A MESSAGE TO MARY — Everly Brothers (20)	59
TAKE FIVE — Dave Brubeck Quartet (6)	61
TAKE 4 (EP) — Mike Oldfield (72)	78
TAKE GOOD CARE OF HER — Adam Wade (38)	61
TAKE GOOD CARE OF MY BABY — Smokie (34)	80
TAKE GOOD CARE OF MY BABY — Bobby Vee (3)	61
TAKE GOOD CARE OF YOURSELF — Three Degrees (9)	75
TAKE IT AWAY — Paul McCartney (15)	82
TAKE IT ON THE RUN — REO Speedwagon (19)	81
TAKE IT OR LEAVE IT — Searchers (31)	66
TAKE IT SATCH (EP) — Louis Armstrong (29)	56
TAKE IT TO THE LIMIT — Eagles (12)	76
TAKE IT TO THE TOP [A] — Kool and the Gang (15)	81
TAKE IT TO TOP [B] — Cloud (72)	81
TAKE ME BAK 'OME — Slade (1)	72
TAKE ME FOR WHAT I'M WORTH — Searchers (20)	65
TAKE ME GIRL I'M READY — Junior Walker and the All-Stars (16)	73
TAKE ME HIGH — Cliff Richard (27)	73
TAKE ME HOME COUNTRY ROADS — Olivia Newton-John (15)	73
TAKE ME I'M YOURS — Squeeze (19)	78
TAKE ME IN YOUR ARMS — Doobie Brothers (29)	75
TAKE ME IN YOUR ARMS & LOVE ME — Gladys Knight and the Pips (13)	67
TAKE ME TO THE MARDI GRAS — Paul Simon (7)	73
TAKE ME TO THE NEXT PHASE — Isley Brothers (50)	78
TAKE ME TO YOUR HEART AGAIN — Vince Hill (13)	66
TAKE MY HEART — Al Martino (9)	52
TAKE MY HEART (YOU CAN HAVE IT IF YOU WANT IT) — Kool and the Gang (29)	82
TAKE MY TIME — Sheena Easton (44)	81
TAKE ON THE WORLD — Judas Priest (14)	79
TAKE THAT LOOK OFF YOUR FACE — Marti Webb (3)	80
TAKE THAT TO THE BANK — Shalamar (20)	78
TAKE THESE CHAINS FROM MY HEART — Ray Charles (5)	63
TAKE TO THE MOUNTAINS — Richard Barnes (35)	70
TAKE YOUR MAMA FOR A RIDE — Lulu (37)	75
TAKE YOUR TIME (DO IT RIGHT) PART 1 — S.O.S. Band (51)	80
TAKES TWO TO TANGO — Louis Armstrong (6)	52
TAKIN' A CHANCE ON YOU — Dollar (62)	80
TALK OF THE TOWN — Pretenders (8)	80
TALK TALK — Talk Talk (23)	82
TALK TO ME — Third World (56)	79
TALKING IN YOUR SLEEP — Crystal Gayle (11)	78
TALL DARK STRANGER — Rose Brennan (31)	61
TALLAHASSEE LASSIE — Freddy Cannon (17)	59
TALLAHASSEE LASSIE — Tommy Steele (16)	59
TALLYMAN — Jeff Beck (30)	67
TAMMY — Debbie Reynolds (2)	57
TANGO IN MONO — Expressos (70)	81
TANSY — Alex Welsh (45)	61
TAP TURNS ON THE WATER — C. C. S. (5)	71
TARA'S THEME FROM GONE WITH THE WIND — Rose of Romance Orchestra (71)	82
TASTE OF AGGRO, A — Barron Knights (3)	78

Title — Act (Position)	Year of Chart Entry
TASTE OF BITTER LOVE — Gladys Knight and the Pips (35)	80
TASTE OF HONEY, A — Mr. Acker Bilk (16)	63
TAVERN IN THE TOWN — Terry Lightfoot and his New Orleans Jazzmen (49)	62
TCHAIKOVSKY ONE — Second City Sound (22)	66
TEA FOR TWO CHA CHA — Tommy Dorsey Orchestra starring Warren Covington (3)	58
TEACH ME TO TWIST — Chubby Checker and Bobby Rydell (45)	62
TEACH ME TONIGHT — De Castro Sisters (20)	55
TEACH YOU TO ROCK — Tony Crombie and his Rockets (25)	56
TEACHER — Jethro Tull (4)	70
TEACHER TEACHER — Johnny Mathis (27)	58
TEAR FELL, A — Teresa Brewer (2)	56
TEAR ME APART — Suzi Quatro (27)	77
TEARDROP — Santo and Johnny (50)	60
TEARDROP CITY — Monkees (46)	69
TEARS [A] — Ken Dodd (1)	65
TEARS [B] — Danny Williams (22)	62
TEARS ARE NOT ENOUGH — ABC (19)	81
TEARS I CRIED, THE — Glitter Band (8)	75
TEARS IN THE WIND — Chicken Shack (29)	69
TEARS OF A CLOWN — The Beat (6)	79
TEARS OF A CLOWN — Smokey Robinson and the Miracles (1)	70,76
TEARS ON MY PILLOW — Johnny Nash (1)	75
TEARS ON THE TELEPHONE — Claude Francois (35)	76
TEARS WON'T WASH AWAY MY HEARTACHE — Ken Dodd (22)	69
TEASE ME — Keith Kelly (27)	60
TEDDY BEAR [A] — Elvis Presley (3)	57
TEDDY BEAR [B] — Red Sovine (4)	81
TEDDY BEAR'S LAST RIDE — Diana Williams (54)	81
TEEN ANGEL — Mark Dinning (37)	60
TEEN BEAT — Sandy Nelson (9)	59
TEENAGE — U.K. Subs (32)	80
TEENAGE DEPRESSION — Eddie and the Hotrods (35)	76
TEENAGE DREAM — T. Rex (13)	74
TEENAGE IDOL — Rick Nelson (39)	62
TEENAGE KICKS — Undertones (31)	78
TEENAGE LAMENT '74 — Alice Cooper (12)	74
TEENAGE OPERA, EXCERPT FROM A — Keith West (2)	67
TEENAGE RAMPAGE — Sweet (2)	74
TEENAGE WARNING — Angelic Upstarts (29)	79
TEENAGER IN LOVE, A — Dion and the Belmonts (28)	59
TEENAGER IN LOVE, A — Craig Douglas (13)	59
TEENAGER IN LOVE, A — Marty Wilde (2)	59
TEENSVILLE — Chet Atkins (46)	60
TELEGRAM SAM — T. Rex (1)	72
TELEPHONE ALWAYS RINGS, THE — Funboy Three (17)	82
TELEPHONE LINE — Electric Light Orchestra (8)	77
TELEPHONE MAN — Meri Wilson (6)	77
TELL HER I'M NOT HOME — Ike and Tina Turner (48)	66
TELL HER NO — Zombies (42)	65
TELL HIM — Billie Davis (10)	63
TELL HIM — Exciters (46)	63
TELL HIM — Hello (6)	74
TELL IT ON THE MOUNTAIN — Peter, Paul and Mary (33)	64
TELL IT TO THE RAIN — Four Seasons (37)	67
TELL LAURA I LOVE HER — Ricky Valance (1)	60
TELL ME A STORY — Frankie Laine and Jimmy Boyd (5)	53
TELL ME ON A SUNDAY — Marti Webb (67)	80
TELL ME THAT YOU LOVE ME — Paul Anka (25)	57
TELL ME TO MY FACE — Keith (50)	67
TELL ME TOMORROW — Smokey Robinson (51)	82
TELL ME WHAT HE SAID — Helen Shapiro (2)	62
TELL ME WHAT YOU WANT — Jimmy Ruffin (39)	74
TELL ME WHEN — Applejacks (7)	64
TELL ME WHY [A] — Elvis Presley (15)	65
TELL ME WHY [B] — Alvin Stardust (16)	74
TELL THE CHILDREN — Sham 69 (45)	80
TELSTAR — Tornados (1)	62
TEMMA HARBOUR — Mary Hopkin (6)	70
TEMPORARY BEAUTY — Graham Parker (50)	82
TEMPTATION [A] — Everly Brothers (1)	61
TEMPTATION [B] — New Order (29)	82
TEMPTED — Squeeze (41)	81
10538 OVERTURE — Electric Light Orchestra (9)	72
TEN THOUSAND MILES — Michael Holliday (24)	56
TENDER TRAP, THE — Frank Sinatra (2)	56
TENDERLY — Nat "King" Cole (10)	54
TENDERNESS — Diana Ross (73)	82
TENNESSEE WIG WALK — Bonnie Lou (4)	54
TEQUILA — Champs (5)	58
TEQUILA — Ted Heath (21)	58
TERESA — Joe Dolan (20)	69
TERRY — Twinkle (4)	64
THANK U VERY MUCH — Scaffold (4)	67
THANK YOU — Pale Fountains (48)	82
THANK YOU FOR BEING A FRIEND — Andrew Gold (42)	78
THANK YOU FOR THE PARTY — Dukes (53)	82
THANKS A LOT — Brenda Lee (41)	65
THANKS FOR SAVING MY LIFE — Billy Paul (33)	74
THANKS FOR THE MEMORY (WHAM BAM THANK YOU MAM) — Slade (7)	75
THAT GIRL — Stevie Wonder (39)	82
THAT GIRL BELONGS TO YESTERDAY — Gene Pitney (7)	64
THAT LADY — Isley Brothers (14)	73
THAT LUCKY OLD SUN — Velvets (46)	61
THAT MEANS A LOT — P. J. Proby (30)	65
THAT NOISE — Anthony Newley (34)	62
THAT OLD BLACK MAGIC — Sammy Davis Jr. (16)	55
THAT SAME OLD FEELING — Pickettywitch (5)	70
THAT'LL BE THE DAY — Crickets (1)	57
THAT'LL BE THE DAY — Everly Brothers (30)	65
THAT'S AMORE — Dean Martin (2)	54
THAT'S ENTERTAINMENT — Jam (21)	81
THAT'S HOW A LOVE SONG WAS BORN — Ray Burns (14)	55
THAT'S HOW STRONG MY LOVE IS — In Crowd (48)	65
THAT'S LIFE — Frank Sinatra (46)	66
THAT'S LOVE — Billy Fury (19)	60
THAT'S MY DOLL — Frankie Vaughan (28)	59
THAT'S MY HOME — Mr. Acker Bilk (7)	61
THAT'S NICE — Neil Christian (14)	66
THAT'S RIGHT — Deep River Boys (29)	56
THAT'S THE WAY — Honeycombs (12)	65
THAT'S THE WAY GOD PLANNED IT — Billy Preston (11)	69
THAT'S THE WAY (I LIKE IT) — KC and The Sunshine Band (4)	75
THAT'S THE WAY LOVE GOES — Charles Dickens (37)	65
THAT'S THE WAY THE MONEY GOES — M (45)	80
THAT'S WANT I WANT — Marauders (48)	63
THAT'S WHAT FRIENDS ARE FOR — Deniece Williams (8)	77
THAT'S WHAT I WANT — Marauders (43)	63
THAT'S WHAT I WANT TO BE — Neil Reid (45)	72
THAT'S WHAT LIFE IS ALL ABOUT — Bing Crosby (41)	75
THAT'S WHAT LOVE WILL DO — Joe Brown (3)	63
THAT'S WHEN THE MUSIC TAKES ME — Neil Sedaka (18)	73
THAT'S WHERE THE HAPPY PEOPLE GO — Trammps (35)	76
THAT'S WHY I'M CRYING — Ivy League (22)	65
THAT'S YOU — Nat "King" Cole (10)	60
THEM THERE EYES — Emile Ford and the Checkmates (18)	60
THEME FOR A DREAM — Cliff Richard (3)	61
THEME FOR YOUNG LOVERS — Shadows (12)	64
THEME FROM DIXIE — Duane Eddy (7)	61
THEME FROM HILL STREET BLUES — Mike Post featuring Larry Carlton (25)	82
THEME FROM M*A*S*H* (SUICIDE IS PAINLESS) — Mash (1)	80
THEME FROM PICNIC — Morris Stoloff (7)	56
THEME FROM THE FILM THE LEGION'S LAST PATROL — Ken Thorne (4)	63
THEME ONE — Cozy Powell (62)	79
THEN CAME YOU — Dionne Warwicke and the Detroit Spinners (29)	74
THEN HE KISSED ME — Crystals (2)	63
THEN I KISSED HER — Beach Boys (4)	67
THEN YOU CAN TELL ME GOODBYE — Casinos (28)	67
THERE ARE MORE QUESTIONS THAN ANSWERS — Johnny Nash (9)	72
THERE BUT FOR FORTUNE — Joan Baez (8)	65
THERE GOES MY EVERYTHING — Engelbert Humperdinck (2)	67
THERE GOES MY EVERYTHING — Elvis Presley (6)	71
THERE GOES MY FIRST LOVE — Drifters (3)	75
THERE GOES THAT SONG AGAIN — Gary Miller (29)	61
THERE I GO — Vikki Carr (50)	67
THERE IS A MOUNTAIN — Donovan (8)	67
THERE IT IS — Shalamar (5)	82
THERE I'VE SAID IT AGAIN — Al Saxon (48)	61
THERE I'VE SAID IT AGAIN — Bobby Vinton (34)	63
THERE MUST BE A REASON — Frankie Laine (9)	54
THERE MUST BE A WAY — Joni James (24)	59
THERE MUST BE A WAY — Frankie Vaughan (7)	67
THERE MUST BE THOUSANDS — Quads (66)	79
THERE THERE MY DEAR — Dexy's Midnight Runners (7)	80
THERE WILL NEVER BE ANOTHER YOU — Chris Montez (37)	66
THERE WON'T BE MANY COMING HOME — Roy Orbison (18)	66
THERE'S A GHOST IN MY HOUSE — R. Dean Taylor (3)	74
THERE'S A GOLDMINE IN THE SKY — Pat Boone (5)	57
THERE'S A GUY WORKS DOWN THE CHIPSHOP SWEARS HE'S ELVIS — Kirsty Mccoll (14)	81
THERE'S A HEARTACHE FOLLOWING ME — Jim Reeves (6)	64
THERE'S A KIND OF HUSH — Herman's Hermits (7)	67
THERE'S A KIND OF HUSH (ALL OVER THE WORLD) — Carpenters (22)	76
THERE'S A WHOLE LOT OF LOVING — Guys and Dolls (2)	75
(THERE'S) ALWAYS SOMETHING THERE TO REMIND ME — Sandie Shaw (1)	64
THERE'S GONNA BE A SHOWDOWN — Archie Bell and the Drells (36)	73
THESE BOOTS ARE MADE FOR WALKIN' — Nancy Sinatra (1)	66
THESE THINGS WILL KEEP ME LOVING YOU — Velvelettes (34)	71
(THEY CALL HER) LA BAMBA — Crickets (21)	64
(THEY LONG TO BE) CLOSE TO YOU — Carpenters (6)	70
THEY SHOOT HORSES DON'T THEY — Racing Cars (14)	77
THEY'RE COMING TO TAKE ME AWAY HA-HAAA! — Napoleon XIV (4)	66
THIGHS HIGH (GRIP YOUR HIPS AND MOVE) — Tom Browne (45)	80
THIN WALL, THE — Ultravox (14)	81
THING CALLED LOVE, A — Johnny Cash (4)	72
THINGS — Bobby Darin (2)	62
THINGS GET BETTER — Eddie Floyd (31)	67
THINGS WE DO FOR LOVE — 10 C. C. (6)	76
THINK [A] — Chris Farlowe (37)	66
THINK [B] — Aretha Franklin (26)	68
THINK [C] — Brenda Lee (26)	64
THINK ABOUT THAT — Dandy Livingstone (26)	73
THINK ABOUT YOUR CHILDREN — Mary Hopkin (19)	70
THINK I'M GONNA FALL IN LOVE WITH YOU — Dooleys (13)	77
THINK IT ALL OVER — Sandie Shaw (42)	69
THINK IT OVER — Crickets (11)	58
(THINK OF ME) WHEREVER YOU ARE — Ken Dodd (21)	75
THINK SOMETIMES ABOUT ME — Sandie Shaw (32)	66
THINKIN' AIN'T FOR ME — Paul Jones (32)	67
THINKING OF YOU BABY — Dave Clark Five (26)	64
THIRD FINGER, LEFT HAND — Pearls (31)	72
THIRD MAN, THE — Shadows (44)	82
THIS AND THAT — Tom Jones (44)	66
THIS BEAT IS MINE — Vicky D (42)	82
THIS DOOR SWINGS BOTH WAYS — Herman's Hermits (18)	66
THIS FEELIN' — Frank Hooker and Positive People (48)	80
THIS FLIGHT TONIGHT — Nazareth (11)	73
THIS GOLDEN RING — Fortunes (15)	66
THIS GUY'S IN LOVE WITH YOU — Herb Alpert (3)	68,69
THIS IS IT [A] — Adam Faith (5)	61
THIS IS IT [B] — Melba Moore (9)	76
THIS IS IT [C] — Dan Hartman (17)	79
THIS IS MY SONG — Petula Clark (1)	67
THIS IS MY SONG — Harry Secombe (2)	67
THIS IS RADIO CLASH — Clash (47)	81
THIS IS THE STORY OF MY LOVE (BABY) — Wizzard (34)	74
THIS IS TOMORROW — Bryan Ferry (9)	77
THIS LITTLE BIRD — Marianne Faithfull (6)	65
THIS LITTLE BIRD — Nashville Teens (38)	65
THIS LITTLE GIRL — Gary 'U.S.' Bonds (43)	81

Title — Act (Position)	Year of Chart Entry
THIS LOVE I HAVE FOR YOU — Lance **Fortune** (26)	**60**
THIS MONDAY MORNING FEELING — Tito **Simon** (45)	**75**
THIS OLD HEART OF MINE — **Isley Brothers** (3)	**66,68**
THIS OLD HEART OF MINE — Rod **Stewart** (4)	**75**
THIS OLE HOUSE — Billie **Anthony** (4)	**54**
THIS OLE HOUSE — Rosemary **Clooney** (1)	**54**
THIS OLE HOUSE — **Shakin' Stevens** (1)	**81**
THIS PERFECT DAY — **Saints** (34)	**77**
THIS PLANET'S ON FIRE — Sammy **Hagar** (52)	**79**
THIS STRANGE EFFECT — Dave **Berry** (37)	**65**
THIS TIME — Troy **Shondell** (22)	**61**
THIS TIME BABY — Jackie **Moore** (49)	**79**
THIS TIME (WE'LL GET IT RIGHT) — **England World Cup Squad** (2)	**82**
THIS TOWN AIN'T BIG ENOUGH FOR BOTH OF US — **Sparks** (2)	**74**
THIS WHEEL'S ON FIRE — Julie **Driscoll, Brian Auger Trinity** (5)	**68**
THIS WILL BE — Natalie **Cole** (32)	**75**
THIS WORLD IS NOT MY HOME — Jim **Reeves** (22)	**65**
THIS WORLD OF WATER — **New Musik** (31)	**80**
THIS WRECKAGE — Gary **Numan** (20)	**80**
THOSE WERE THE DAYS — Mary **Hopkin** (1)	**68**
THOU SHALT NOT STEAL — **Freddie and the Dreamers** (44)	**65**
THOUSAND STARS, A — Billy **Fury** (14)	**61**
THREE BELLS — Brian **Poole and the Tremeloes** (17)	**65**
THREE BELLS, THE — **Browns** (6)	**59**
THREE BELLS, THE — **Compagnons De La Chanson** (21)	**59**
3 X 3 (EP) — **Genesis** (10)	**82**
THREE COINS IN THE FOUNTAIN — **Four Aces** (5)	**54**
THREE COINS IN THE FOUNTAIN — Frank **Sinatra** (1)	**54**
THREE LITTLE BIRDS — Bob **Marley and the Wailers** (17)	**80**
THREE LITTLE WORDS — **Applejacks** (23)	**64**
THREE MINUTE HERO — The **Selecter** (16)	**80**
THREE NIGHTS A WEEK — Fats **Domino** (45)	**60**
THREE RING CIRCUS — Barry **Biggs** (22)	**77**
THREE STARS — Ruby **Wright** (19)	**59**
THREE STEPS TO HEAVEN — Eddie **Cochran** (1)	**60**
THREE STEPS TO HEAVEN — **Showaddywaddy** (2)	**75**
THREE TIMES A LADY — **Commodores** (1)	**78**
THREEPENNY OPERA, THEME FROM THE — Louis **Armstrong** (8)	**56**
THREEPENNY OPERA, THEME FROM THE — Dick **Hyman Trio** (9)	**56**
THREEPENNY OPERA, THEME FROM THE — Billy **Vaughn** (12)	**56**
THROW AWAY THE KEY — **Linx** (21)	**81**
THROW DOWN A LINE — Cliff **Richard** (7)	**69**
THROWING MY BABY OUT WITH THE BATHWATER — **Ten Pole Tudor** (49)	**81**
THROWN AWAY — **Stranglers** (42)	**81**
THRU' THESE WALLS — Phil **Collins** (56)	**82**
THUNDER IN MY HEART — Leo **Sayer** (22)	**77**
THUNDER IN THE MOUNTAINS — **Toyah** (4)	**81**
THUNDERBALL — Tom **Jones** (35)	**66**
THUNDERBIRDS — Barry **Gray Orchestra** (61)	**81**
THUS SPAKE ZARATHUSTRA — **Philharmonia Orchestra, conductor Lorin Maazel** (33)	**69**
TICKET TO RIDE — **Beatles** (1)	**65**
TICKET TO THE MOON — **Electric Light Orchestra** (24)	**82**
TIDE IS HIGH, THE — **Blondie** (1)	**80**
TIE A YELLOW RIBBON ROUND THE OLD OAK TREE — **Dawn** (1)	**73**
TIE A YELLOW RIBBON ROUND THE OLE OAK TREE — **Dawn** (41)	**74**
TIE ME KANGAROO DOWN SPORT — Rolf **Harris** (9)	**60**
TIE YOUR MOTHER DOWN — **Queen** (31)	**77**
TIGER BABY — **Silver Convention** (41)	**76**
TIGER FEET — **Mud** (1)	**74**
TIJUANA TAXI — Herb **Alpert** (37)	**66**
('TIL) I KISSED YOU — **Everly Brothers** (2)	**59**
TILL — Tony **Bennett** (35)	**61**
TILL — Tom **Jones** (2)	**71**
TILL — Dorothy **Squires** (25)	**70**
TILL THE END OF THE DAY — **Kinks** (8)	**65**
TILL THERE WAS YOU — Peggy **Lee** (30)	**61**
TIME — Craig **Douglas** (9)	**61**
TIME ALONE WILL TELL — Malcolm **Roberts** (45)	**67**
TIME AND THE RIVER — Nat "King" **Cole** (23)	**60**
TIME (CLOCK OF THE HEART) — **Culture Club** (3)	**82**
TIME DRAGS BY — Cliff **Richard** (10)	**66**
TIME FOR ACTION — **Secret Affair** (13)	**79**
TIME FOR LIVING — **Association** (23)	**68**
TIME HAS COME [A] — P. P. **Arnold** (47)	**67**
TIME HAS COME [B] — Adam **Faith** (4)	**61**
TIME IN BETWEEN, THE — Cliff **Richard** (22)	**65**
TIME IS ON MY SIDE — **Rolling Stones** (62)	**82**
TIME IS TIGHT — **Booker T. & The M. G.'s** (4)	**69**
TIME SELLER — Spencer **Davis Group** (30)	**67**
TIMES THEY ARE A-CHANGIN' — Bob **Dylan** (9)	**65**
TIMES THEY ARE A-CHANGIN', THE — Ian **Campbell Folk Group** (42)	**65**
TIMES THEY ARE A-CHANGIN', THE — **Peter, Paul and Mary** (44)	**64**
TIN SOLDIER — **Small Faces** (9)	**67**
TIN SOLDIERS — **Stiff Little Fingers** (36)	**80**
TINA MARIE — Perry **Como** (24)	**55**
TINY CHILDREN — **Teardrop Explodes** (44)	**82**
TIPS OF MY FINGERS, THE — Des **O'Connor** (15)	**70**
TIRED OF BEING ALONE — Al **Green** (4)	**71**
TIRED OF TOEIN' THE LINE — Rocky **Burnette** (58)	**79**
TIRED OF WAITING FOR YOU — **Kinks** (1)	**65**
TO BE LOVED — Malcolm **Vaughan** (14)	**58**
TO BE LOVED — Jackie **Wilson** (23)	**58**
TO BE OR NOT TO BE — B.A. **Robertson** (9)	**80**
TO CUT A LONG STORY SHORT — **Spandau Ballet** (5)	**80**
TO KNOW HIM IS TO LOVE HIM — **Teddy Bears** (2)	**58,79**
TO KNOW YOU IS TO LOVE YOU — **Peter and Gordon** (5)	**65**
TO LOVE SOMEBODY — **Bee Gees** (41)	**67**
TO LOVE SOMEBODY — Nina **Simone** (5)	**69**
TO MAKE A BIG MAN CRY — P. J. **Proby** (34)	**66**
TO WHOM IT CONCERNS — Chris **Andrews** (13)	**65**
TOAST — **Streetband** (18)	**78**
TOAST OF LOVE — **Three Degrees** (36)	**76**
TOBACCO ROAD — **Nashville Teens** (6)	**64**
TOCCATA — **Sky** (5)	**80**
TODAY — Sandie **Shaw** (27)	**68**
TODAY [B] — **Talk Talk** (14)	**82**
TOGETHER [A] — Connie **Francis** (6)	**61**
TOGETHER [A] — P. J. **Proby** (8)	**64**
TOGETHER [B] — O. C. **Smith** (25)	**77**
TOGETHER AGAIN — Ray **Charles** (48)	**66**
TOGETHER WE ARE BEAUTIFUL — Steve **Allan** (67)	**79**
TOGETHER WE ARE BEAUTIFUL — Fern **Kinney** (1)	**80**
TOGETHERNESS — Mike **Preston** (41)	**60**
TOKOLOSHE MAN — John **Kongos** (4)	**71**
TOKYO — **Classix Nouveaux** (67)	**81**
TOKYO JOE — Bryan **Ferry** (15)	**77**
TOKYO MELODY — Helmut **Zacharias** (9)	**64**
TOM DOOLEY — Lonnie **Donegan** (3)	**58**
TOM DOOLEY — **Kingston Trio** (5)	**58**
TOM HARK — **Elias and his Zigzag Jive Flutes** (2)	**58**
TOM HARK — Ted **Heath** (24)	**58**
TOM HARK — **Piranhas** (6)	**80**
TOM PILLIBI — Jacqueline **Boyer** (33)	**60**
TOM SAWYER — **Rush** (25)	**81**
TOM THE PEEPER — **Act One** (40)	**74**
TOM TOM TURNAROUND — **New World** (6)	**71**
TOMBOY — Perry **Como** (10)	**59**
TOMMY GUN — **Clash** (19)	**78**
TOMORROW — Johnny **Brandon** (8)	**55**
TOMORROW [B] — Sandie **Shaw** (9)	**66**
TOMORROW NIGHT — **Atomic Rooster** (11)	**71**
TOMORROW RISING — Cliff **Richard** (29)	**73**
TOMORROW TOMORROW — **Bee Gees** (23)	**69**
TOMORROW'S CLOWN — Marty **Wilde** (33)	**61**
TOMORROW'S GIRLS — **U.K. Subs** (28)	**79**
TONIGHT [A] — Shirley **Bassey** (21)	**62**
TONIGHT [B] — **Move** (11)	**71**
TONIGHT [C] — **Rubettes** (12)	**74**
TONIGHT [D] — Zaine **Griff** (54)	**80**
TONIGHT [E] — **Modettes** (68)	**81**
TONIGHT (COULD BE THE NIGHT) — **Velvets** (50)	**61**
TONIGHT I'M ALL RIGHT — Nirada Michael **Walden** (34)	**80**
TONIGHT I'M GONNA LOVE YOU ALL OVER — **Four Tops** (43)	**82**
TONIGHT I'M YOURS (DON'T HURT ME) — Rod **Stewart** (8)	**81**
TONIGHT IN TOKYO — Sandie **Shaw** (21)	**67**
TONIGHT YOU BELONG TO ME — **Patience and Prudence** (28)	**56**
TONIGHT'S THE NIGHT — Rod **Stewart** (5)	**76**
TOO BEAUTIFUL TO LAST — Engelbert **Humperdinck** (14)	**72**
TOO BIG — Suzi **Quatro** (14)	**74**
TOO BUSY THINKING 'BOUT MY BABY — **Marvin Gaye** (5)	**69**
TOO BUSY THINKING 'BOUT MY BABY — **Mardi Gras** (19)	**72**
TOO DRUNK TO FUCK — **Dead Kennedys** (36)	**81**
TOO GOOD — **Little Tony** (19)	**60**
TOO GOOD TO BE FORGOTTEN — **Chi-Lites** (10)	**74**
TOO HOT — **Kool and the Gang** (23)	**80**
TOO HOT TO HANDLE — **Heatwave** (15)	**77**
TOO HOT TO TROT [A] — **Commodores** (38)	**78**
TOO LATE — **Junior** (20)	**82**
TOO MANY BEAUTIFUL GIRLS — Clinton **Ford** (48)	**61**
TOO MANY RIVERS — Brenda **Lee** (22)	**65**
TOO MUCH — Elvis **Presley** (6)	**57**
TOO MUCH HEAVEN — **Bee Gees** (3)	**78**
TOO MUCH TEQUILA — **Champs** (49)	**60**
TOO MUCH TOO LITTLE TOO LATE — Johnny **Mathis and Deniece Williams** (3)	**78**
TOO MUCH TOO YOUNG (EP) — The **Specials** (1)	**80**
TOO NICE TO TALK TO — The **Beat** (7)	**80**
TOO RISKY — Jim **Davidson** (52)	**80**
TOO SOON TO KNOW — Roy **Orbison** (3)	**66**
TOO YOUNG — Bill **Forbes** (29)	**60**
TOO YOUNG — Donny **Osmond** (5)	**72**
TOO YOUNG TO GO STEADY — Nat "King" **Cole** (8)	**56**
TOOK THE LAST TRAIN — David **Gates** (50)	**78**
TOP OF THE POPS — **Rezillos** (17)	**78**
TOP OF THE WORLD — **Carpenters** (5)	**73**
TOP TEEN BABY — Garry **Mills** (24)	**60**
TOPSY PARTS I AND II — Cozy **Cole** (29)	**58**
TORCH — **Soft Cell** (2)	**82**
TORERO — Julius **Larosa** (15)	**58**
TORERO - CHA CHA CHA — Renato **Carosone and his Sextet** (25)	**58**
TORN BETWEEN TWO LOVERS — Mary **MacGregor** (4)	**77**
TOSSING AND TURNING — **Ivy League** (3)	**65**
TOTAL ERASURE — Philip **Jap** (41)	**82**
TOTTENHAM TOTTENHAM — **Tottenham Hotspur F.A. Cup Final Squad** (19)	**82**
TOUCH — **Lori and the Chameleons** (70)	**79**
TOUCH ME IN THE MORNING — Diana **Ross** (9)	**73**
TOUCH ME TOUCH ME — Dave **Dee, Dozy, Beaky, Mick and Tich** (13)	**67**
TOUCH OF VELVET A STING OF BRASS, A — Ron **Grainer Orchestra** (60)	**78**
TOUCH TOO MUCH [A] — **Arrows** (8)	**74**
TOUCH TOO MUCH [B] — **AC/DC** (29)	**80**
TOUS LES GARCONS ET LES FILLES — Francoise **Hardy** (36)	**64**
TOWER OF STRENGTH — Gene **McDaniels** (49)	**61**
TOWER OF STRENGTH — Frankie **Vaughan** (1)	**61**
TOWERS OF LONDON — **XTC** (31)	**80**
TOWN CALLED MALICE — **Jam** (1)	**82**
TOWN CRIER — Craig **Douglas** (36)	**63**
TOWN WITHOUT PITY — Gene **Pitney** (32)	**62**
TOY — **Casuals** (30)	**68**
TOY BALLOONS — Russ **Conway** (7)	**61**
TRACKS OF MY TEARS — Colin **Blunstone** (60)	**82**
TRACKS OF MY TEARS — Smokey **Robinson and the Miracles** (9)	**69**
TRACKS OF MY TEARS — Linda **Ronstadt** (42)	**76**
TRACY — **Cuff-Links** (4)	**69**
TRAGEDY [A] — **Argent** (34)	**72**
TRAGEDY [B] — **Bee Gees** (1)	**79**
TRAIL OF THE LONESOME PINE, THE — **Laurel and Hardy Avalon Boys** (2)	**75**
TRAIN OF LOVE — Alma **Cogan** (27)	**60**
TRAIN TO SKAVILLE — **Ethiopians** (40)	**67**
TRAIN TOUR TO RAINBOW CITY — **Pyramids** (35)	**67**
TRAINS AND BOATS AND PLANES — Burt **Bacharach** (4)	**65**
TRAINS AND BOATS AND PLANES — Billy J. **Kramer and the Dakotas** (12)	**65**
TRAMBONE — **Krew-Kats** (33)	**61**
TRAMP — Otis **Redding and Carla Thomas** (18)	**67**
TRANSISTOR RADIO — Benny **Hill** (24)	**61**
TRASH — **Roxy Music** (40)	**79**
TRAVELLIN' BAND — **Creedence Clearwater Revival** (8)	**70**
TRAVELLIN' HOME — Vera **Lynn** (20)	**57**
TRAVELLIN' LIGHT — Cliff **Richard** (1)	**59**
TRAVELLIN' MAN — Rick **Nelson** (2)	**61**
TREASON (IT'S JUST A STORY) — **Teardrop Explodes** (18)	**81**
TREASURE OF LOVE — Clyde **McPhatter** (27)	**56**
TREAT HER RIGHT — Roy **Head** (30)	**65**
TREBLE CHANCE — Joe "Mr. Piano" **Henderson** (28)	**59**
TRIAL — Kelly **Marie** (51)	**81**
TRIAL OF HISSING SID, THE — Keith **Michell, Captain Beaky and his Band** (53)	**80**

Title — Act (Position)	Year of Chart Entry
TRIBUTE TO A KING — William **Bell** (31)	**68**
TRIBUTE TO BUDDY HOLLY — Mike **Berry** (24)	**61**
TRIBUTE TO JIM REEVES — Larry **Cunningham and the Mighty Avons** (40)	**64**
TRINI TRACKS — Trini **Lopez** (59)	**81**
TROCADERO — **Showaddywaddy** (32)	**76**
T. R. O. U. B. L. E. — Elvis **Presley** (31)	**75**
TROUBLE [A] — **Gillan** (14)	**80**
TROUBLE [B] — Lindsey **Buckingham** (31)	**82**
TROUBLE BOYS — **Thin Lizzy** (53)	**81**
TROUBLE IS MY MIDDLE NAME — **Brook Brothers** (38)	**63**
TROUBLE IS MY MIDDLE NAME — **Four Pennies** (32)	**66**
TROUBLE WITH HARRY, THE — **Alfi and Harry** (15)	**56**
TRUCK ON (TYKE) — **T. Rex** (12)	**73**
TRUDIE — Joe "Mr. Piano" **Henderson** (14)	**58**
TRUE LOVE — Richard **Chamberlain** (30)	**63**
TRUE LOVE — Bing **Crosby and Grace Kelly** (4)	**56**
TRUE LOVE — Terry **Lightfoot and his New Orleans Jazzmen** (33)	**61**
TRUE LOVE FOR EVER MORE — **Bachelors** (34)	**65**
TRUE LOVE WAYS — Buddy **Holly** (25)	**60**
TRUE LOVE WAYS — **Peter and Gordon** (2)	**65**
TRULY — Lionel **Richie** (6)	**82**
TRY A LITTLE KINDNESS — Glen **Campbell** (45)	**70**
TRY A LITTLE TENDERNESS — Otis **Redding** (46)	**67**
TRY JAH LOVE — **Third World** (47)	**82**
TRY MY WORLD — Georgie **Fame** (37)	**67**
TRY TO REMEMBER (MEDLEY) — Gladys **Knight and the Pips** (4)	**75**
TRY TO UNDERSTAND — **Lulu** (25)	**65**
TRYIN' — **Hilltoppers** (30)	**56**
TRYING TO FORGET — Jim **Reeves** (33)	**67**
TRYING TO GET TO YOU — Elvis **Presley** (16)	**57**
TRYOUTS FOR THE HUMAN RACE — **Sparks** (45)	**79**
TUBULAR BELLS — **Champs Boys** (41)	**76**
TUG OF WAR — Paul **McCartney** (53)	**82**
TULANE — Steve **Gibbons Band** (12)	**77**
TULIPS FROM AMSTERDAM — Max **Bygraves** (3)	**58**
TUMBLING DICE — **Rolling Stones** (5)	**72**
TUMBLING TUMBLEWEEDS — Slim **Whitman** (19)	**56**
TUNNEL OF LOVE — **Dire Straits** (54)	**81**
TURN IT DOWN — **Sweet** (41)	**74**
TURN IT ON — **Level 42** (57)	**81**
TURN IT ON AGAIN — **Genesis** (8)	**80**
TURN ME ON TURN ME OFF — Honey **Bane** (37)	**81**
TURN THE MUSIC UP — **Players Association** (8)	**79**
TURN TO STONE — **Electric Light Orchestra** (18)	**77**
TURN! TURN! TURN! — **Byrds** (26)	**65**
TURN UP THE NIGHT — **Black Sabbath** (37)	**82**
TURN YOUR LOVE AROUND — George **Benson** (29)	**81**
TURN YOUR RADIO ON — Ray **Stevens** (33)	**72**
TURNING JAPANESE — **Vapors** (3)	**80**
TURQUOISE — **Donovan** (30)	**65**
TUSK — **Fleetwood Mac** (6)	**79**
TUTTI FRUTTI — **Little Richard** (29)	**57**
TUXEDO JUNCTION — **Manhattan Transfer** (24)	**76**
T.V. — **Flying Lizards** (43)	**80**
TVC 15 — David **Bowie** (33)	**76**
TWEEDLE DEE — Georgia **Gibbs** (20)	**55**
TWEEDLE DEE — Little Jimmy **Osmond** (4)	**73**
TWEEDLE DEE — Frankie **Vaughan** (17)	**55**
TWEEDLE DEE TWEEDLE DUM — **Middle Of The Road** (2)	**71**
TWELFTH OF NEVER, THE — Donny **Osmond** (1)	**73**
TWELFTH OF NEVER, THE — Cliff **Richard** (8)	**64**
TWELFTH STREET RAG — Bert **Weedon** (47)	**60**
TWELVE STEPS TO LOVE — Brian **Poole and the Tremeloes** (32)	**64**
20TH CENTURY BOY — **T. Rex** (3)	**73**
25 MILES — Edwin **Starr** (36)	**69**
25 OR 6 TO 4 — **Chicago** (7)	**70**
TWENTY FOUR HOURS FROM TULSA — Gene **Pitney** (5)	**63**
24 SYCAMORE — Gene **Pitney** (34)	**73**
TWENTY TINY FINGERS — Alma **Cogan** (17)	**55**
TWENTY TINY FINGERS — **Coronets** (20)	**55**
TWENTY TINY FINGERS — **Stargazers** (4)	**55**
TWILIGHT — **Electric Light Orchestra** (30)	**81**
TWILIGHT CAFE — Susan **Fassbender** (21)	**81**
TWILIGHT TIME — **Platters** (3)	**58**
TWILIGHT ZONE — **Iron Maiden** (31)	**81**
TWILIGHT ZONE-TWILIGHT TONE (MEDLEY) — **Manhattan Transfer** (25)	**80**
TWINKIE LEE — Gary **Walker** (26)	**66**
TWINKLE TOES — Roy **Orbison** (29)	**66**
TWIST AND SHOUT — **Isley Brothers** (42)	**63**
TWIST AND SHOUT — Brian **Poole and the Tremeloes** (4)	**63**
TWIST, THE — Chubby **Checker** (5)	**60,62,75**
TWIST TWIST — **Chakachas** (48)	**62**
TWISTIN' THE NIGHT AWAY — Sam **Cooke** (6)	**62**
'TWIXT TWELVE AND TWENTY — Pat **Boone** (18)	**59**
TWO DIFFERENT WORLDS — Ronnie **Hilton** (13)	**56**
TWO HEARTS — Stephanie **Mills** (49)	**81**
TWO HEARTS TOGETHER — **Orange Juice** (60)	**82**
TWO KINDS OF TEARDROPS — Del **Shannon** (5)	**63**
TWO LITTLE BOYS — Rolf **Harris** (1)	**69**
TWO LITTLE BOYS — **Splodgenessabounds** (26)	**80**
TWO OF US, THE — Mac and Katie **Kissoon** (46)	**76**
TWO OUT OF THREE AIN'T BAD — **Meat Loaf** (32)	**78**
TWO PINTS OF LAGER — **Splodgenessabounds** (7)	**80**
TWO SILHOUETTES — Del **Shannon** (23)	**63**
TWO STREETS — Val **Doonican** (39)	**67**
2-4-6-8 MOTORWAY — Tom **Robinson Band** (5)	**77**
TYPICAL GIRLS — **Slits** (60)	**79**
U. S. MALE — Elvis **Presley** (15)	**68**
UGLY DUCKLING, THE — Mike **Reid** (10)	**75**
UM UM UM UM UM UM — Wayne **Fontana and the Mindbenders** (5)	**64**
UM UM UM UM UM UM — Major **Lance** (40)	**64**
UN BANC, UN ARBRE, UNE RUE — **Severine** (9)	**71**
UNA PALOMA BLANCA — Jonathan **King** (5)	**75**
UNCERTAIN SMILE — **The** (68)	**82**
UNCHAINED MELODY — Les **Baxter** (10)	**55**
UNCHAINED MELODY — Al **Hibbler** (2)	**55**
UNCHAINED MELODY — **Liberace** (20)	**55**
UNCHAINED MELODY — **Righteous Brothers** (14)	**65**
UNCHAINED MELODY — Jimmy **Young** (1)	**55,64**
UNDER ATTACK — **Abba** (26)	**82**
UNDER MY THUMB — Wayne **Gibson** (17)	**74**
UNDER MY THUMB — **Who** (44)	**67**
UNDER MY WHEELS — Alice **Cooper** (66)	**82**
UNDER NEW MANAGEMENT — **Barron Knights** (15)	**66**
UNDER ONE ROOF — **Rubettes** (40)	**76**
UNDER PRESSURE — **Queen and David Bowie** (1)	**81**
UNDER THE BOARDWALK — **Drifters** (45)	**64**
UNDER THE BOARDWALK — **Tom Tom Club** (22)	**82**
UNDER THE BRIDGES OF PARIS — Eartha **Kitt** (7)	**55**
UNDER THE BRIDGES OF PARIS — Dean **Martin** (6)	**55**
UNDER THE MOON OF LOVE — **Showaddywaddy** (1)	**76**
UNDER YOUR THUMB — **Godley and Creme** (3)	**81**
UNDERCOVER ANGEL — Alan **O'Day** (43)	**77**
UNDERNEATH THE BLANKET GO — Gilbert **O'Sullivan** (40)	**71**
UNDERPASS — John **Foxx** (31)	**80**
UNDERWATER — Harry **Thumann** (41)	**81**
UNIFORMS (CORPS D'ESPRIT) — Pete **Townshend** (48)	**82**
UNION CITY BLUE — **Blondie** (13)	**79**
UNITED — **Judas Priest** (26)	**80**
UNITED WE STAND — **Brotherhood Of Man** (10)	**70**
UNIVERSAL — **Small Faces** (16)	**68**
UNLOCK THE FUNK — **Locksmith** (42)	**80**
UNSQUARE DANCE — Dave **Brubeck Quartet** (14)	**62**
UNTIL IT'S TIME FOR YOU TO GO — **Four Pennies** (19)	**65**
UNTIL IT'S TIME FOR YOU TO GO — Elvis **Presley** (5)	**72**
UNTIL THE NIGHT — Billy **Joel** (50)	**79**
UNTIL YOU COME BACK TO ME (THAT'S WHAT I'M GONNA DO). — Aretha **Franklin** (26)	**74**
UP ABOVE MY HEAD — Frankie **Laine and Johnnie Ray** (25)	**57**
UP AGAINST THE WALL — Tom **Robinson Band** (33)	**78**
UP AROUND THE BEND — **Creedence Clearwater Revival** (3)	**70**
UP IN A PUFF OF SMOKE — Polly **Brown** (43)	**74**
UP ON THE ROOF — Julie **Grant** (33)	**63**
UP ON THE ROOF — Kenny **Lynch** (10)	**62**
UP THE JUNCTION — **Squeeze** (2)	**79**
UP THE LADDER TO THE ROOF — **Supremes** (6)	**70**
UP THE POOL — **Jethro Tull** (11)	**71**
UP TOWN TOP RANKING — **Althia and Donna** (1)	**77**
UP, UP AND AWAY — Johnny **MANN SINGERS** (6)	**67**
UP WITH THE COCK — **Judge Dread** (49)	**78**
UPSIDE DOWN — Diana **Ross** (2)	**80**
UPTIGHT — Stevie **Wonder** (14)	**66**
UPTOWN FESTIVAL — **Shalamar** (30)	**77**
UPTOWN UPTEMPO WOMAN — Randy **Edelman** (25)	**76**
URBAN GUERRILLA — **Hawkwind** (39)	**73**
URGE, THE — Freddy **Cannon** (18)	**60**
URGENT — **Foreigner** (45)	**81,82**
USE IT UP AND WEAR IT OUT — **Odyssey** (1)	**80**
USED TA BE MY GIRL — **O'Jays** (12)	**78**
VACATION — Connie **Francis** (10)	**62**
VADO VIA — **Drupi** (17)	**73**
VALENTINO — Connie **Francis** (27)	**60**
VALERIE — Steve **Winwood** (51)	**82**
VALLERI — **Monkees** (12)	**68**
VALLEY OF TEARS — Fats **Domino** (25)	**57**
VALLEY OF TEARS — Buddy **Holly** (12)	**61**
VALLEY OF THE DOLLS [A] — **Generation X** (23)	**79**
VALLEY OF THE DOLLS [B] — Dionne **Warwick** (28)	**68**
VANESSA — Ted **Heath** (11)	**53**
VAYA CON DIOS — **Millican and Nesbitt** (20)	**73**
VAYA CON DIOS — Les **Paul and Mary Ford** (7)	**53**
VEHICLE — **Ides Of March** (31)	**70**
VENI VIDI VICI — Ronnie **Hilton** (12)	**54**
VENTURA HIGHWAY — **America** (43)	**72**
VENUS — Dickie **Valentine** (25)	**59**
VENUS [A] — Frankie **Avalon** (16)	**59**
VENUS [A] — Dickie **Valentine** (20)	**59**
VENUS [B] — **Shocking Blue** (8)	**70**
VENUS IN BLUE JEANS — Mark **Wynter** (4)	**62**
VERY PRECIOUS LOVE, A — Doris **Day** (16)	**58**
VERY THOUGHT OF YOU, THE — Tony **Bennett** (21)	**65**
VICTORIA — **Kinks** (33)	**70**
VIDEO KILLED THE RADIO STAR — **Buggles** (1)	**79**
VIDEOTHEQUE — **Dollar** (17)	**82**
VIENNA — **Ultravox** (2)	**81**
VIETNAM — Jimmy **Cliff** (46)	**70**
VIEW FROM A BRIDGE — Kim **Wilde** (16)	**82**
VILLAGE OF ST. BERNADETTE — Anne **Shelton** (27)	**59**
VINCENT — Don **McLean** (1)	**72**
VIRGIN MARY — Lonnie **Donegan** (27)	**60**
VIRGINIA PLAIN — **Roxy Music** (4)	**72,77**
VISAGE — **Visage** (21)	**81**
VISIONS — Cliff **Richard** (7)	**66**
VISIONS OF CHINA — **Japan** (32)	**81**
VITAL SIGNS — **Rush** (41)	**81**
VIVA BOBBY JOE — **Equals** (6)	**69**
VIVA EL FULHAM — Tony **Rees and the Cottagers** (46)	**75**
VIVA LAS VEGAS — Elvis **Presley** (17)	**64**
VOICE IN THE WILDERNESS — Cliff **Richard** (2)	**60**
VOICE, THE — **Ultravox** (16)	**81**
VOICES IN THE SKY — **Moody Blues** (27)	**68**
VOLARE — Charlie **Drake** (28)	**58**
VOLARE — Marino **Marini** (13)	**58**
VOLARE — Dean **Martin** (2)	**58**
VOLARE — Domenico **Modugno** (10)	**58**
VOLARE — Bobby **Rydell** (22)	**60**
VOODOO CHILE — Jimi **Hendrix Experience** (1)	**70**
VOODOO VOODOO — Den **Hegarty** (73)	**79**
VOULEZ-VOUS — **Abba** (3)	**79**
VOYEUR — Kim **Carnes** (68)	**82**
W. O. L. D. — Harry **Chapin** (34)	**74**
WADE IN THE WATER — Ramsey **Lewis** (31)	**72**
WAIT FOR ME — Joan **Regan and the Johnston Brothers** (18)	**54**
WAIT FOR ME — Malcolm **Vaughan** (13)	**59**
WAIT FOR ME MARIANNE — **Marmalade** (30)	**68**
WAIT UNTIL MIDNIGHT — **Yellow Dog** (54)	**78**
WAITING FOR A GIRL LIKE YOU — **Foreigner** (8)	**81**
WAITING FOR AN ALIBI — **Thin Lizzy** (9)	**79**
WAITING IN VAIN — Bob **Marley and the Wailers** (27)	**77**
WAITING ON A FRIEND — **Rolling Stones** (50)	**81**
WAKE UP EVERYBODY — Harold **Melvin and the Bluenotes** (23)	**76**
WAKE UP LITTLE SUSIE — **Everly Brothers** (2)	**57**
WAKE UP LITTLE SUSIE — **King Brothers** (22)	**57**
WAKE UP SUSAN — **Detroit Spinners** (29)	**77**
WALK AWAY [A] — Shane **Fenton and the Fentones** (38)	**62**
WALK AWAY [B] — Matt **Monro** (4)	**64**
WALK AWAY FROM LOVE — David **Ruffin** (10)	**76**
WALK AWAY RENEE — **Four Tops** (3)	**67**
WALK DON'T RUN — John **Barry** (11)	**60**
WALK DON'T RUN — **Ventures** (8)	**60**
WALK HAND IN HAND — Ronnie **Carroll** (13)	**56**
WALK HAND IN HAND — **Gerry and the Pacemakers** (29)	**65**
WALK HAND IN HAND — Tony **Martin** (2)	**56**
WALK HAND IN HAND — Jimmy **Parkinson** (26)	**56**
WALK IN LOVE — **Manhattan Transfer** (12)	**78**
WALK IN THE BLACK FOREST, A — Horst **Jankowski** (3)	**65**
WALK IN THE NIGHT — Junior **Walker and the All-Stars** (16)	**72**
WALK IN THE PARK, A — Nick **Straker Band** (20)	**80**

Title — Act (Position)	Year of Chart Entry
WALK LIKE A MAN — **Four Seasons** (12)	**63**
WALK ON — Roy **Orbison** (39)	**68**
WALK ON BY [A] — Leroy **Van Dyke** (5)	**62**
WALK ON BY [B] — **Average White Band** (46)	**79**
WALK ON BY [B] — **D Train** (44)	**82**
WALK ON BY [B] — **Stranglers** (21)	**78**
WALK ON BY [B] — Dionne **Warwick** (9)	**64**
WALK ON GILDED SPLINTERS — Marsha **Hunt** (46)	**69**
WALK ON THE WILD SIDE — Lou **Reed** (10)	**73**
WALK RIGHT BACK — Perry **Como** (33)	**73**
WALK RIGHT BACK — **Everly Brothers** (1)	**61**
WALK RIGHT IN — **Rooftop Singers** (10)	**63**
WALK RIGHT NOW — **Jacksons** (7)	**81**
WALK TALL — Val **Doonican** (3)	**64**
WALK, THE — **Inmates** (36)	**79**
WALK WITH FAITH IN YOUR HEART — **Bachelors** (22)	**66**
WALK WITH ME — **Seekers** (10)	**66**
WALK WITH ME MY ANGEL — Don **Charles** (39)	**62**
WALK WITH ME TALK WITH ME DARLING — **Four Tops** (32)	**72**
WALKIN' — **C. C. S.** (7)	**71**
WALKIN' BACK TO HAPPINESS — Helen **Shapiro** (1)	**61**
WALKIN' IN THE RAIN WITH THE ONE I LOVE — **Love Unlimited** (14)	**72**
WALKIN' MIRACLE, A — **Limmie and the Family Cookin'** (6)	**74**
WALKIN' TALL — Frankie **Vaughan** (29)	**59**
WALKIN' TALL [A] — Adam **Faith** (23)	**63**
WALKIN' TALL [B] — Frankie **Vaughan** (28)	**59**
WALKIN' THE DOG — **Dennisons** (36)	**64**
WALKIN' TO MISSOURI — Tony **Brent** (7)	**52**
WALKING ALONE — Richard **Anthony** (37)	**63**
WALKING IN RHYTHM — **Blackbyrds** (23)	**75**
WALKING IN THE RAIN — **Partridge Family starring Shirley Jones Cassidy** (10)	**73**
WALKING IN THE RAIN — **Walker Brothers** (26)	**67**
WALKING IN THE SUNSHINE — **Bad Manners** (10)	**81**
WALKING INTO SUNSHINE — **Central Line** (42)	**81**
WALKING MY BABY BACK HOME — Johnnie **Ray** (12)	**52**
WALKING MY CAT NAMED DOG — Norma **Tanega** (22)	**66**
WALKING ON SUNSHINE — **Rocker's Revenge** (4)	**82**
WALKING ON THE MOON — **Police** (1)	**79**
WALKING ON THIN ICE — Yoko **Ono** (35)	**81**
WALKING THE FLOOR OVER YOU — Pat **Boone** (39)	**60**
WALKING TO NEW ORLEANS — Fats **Domino** (19)	**60**
WALL STREET SHUFFLE — **10 C. C.** (10)	**74**
WALLS FELL DOWN, THE — **Marbles** (28)	**69**
WAM BAM — **Handley Family** (30)	**73**
WANDERER [A] — Donna **Summer** (48)	**80**
WANDERER [B] — **Dion** (10)	**62**
WANDERER, THE — **Dion** (16)	**76**
WANDERIN' EYES — Charlie **Gracie** (6)	**57**
WANDERIN' EYES — Frankie **Vaughan** (6)	**57**
WAND'RIN' STAR — Lee **Marvin** (1)	**70**
WANTED — Perry **Como** (4)	**54**
WANTED [A] — Al **Martino** (4)	**54**
WANTED [B] — **Dooleys** (3)	**79**
WAR — Edwin **Starr** (3)	**70**
WAR CHILD — **Blondie** (39)	**82**
WAR LORD — **Shadows** (18)	**65**
WAR STORIES — **Starjets** (51)	**79**
WARHEAD — **U.K. Subs** (30)	**80**
WARM & TENDER LOVE — Percy **Sledge** (34)	**66**
WARMED OVER KISSES — Brian **Hyland** (28)	**62**
WARPAINT — **Brook Brothers** (5)	**61**
WASTED — **Def Leppard** (61)	**79**
WATCH ME — Labi **Siffre** (29)	**72**
WATCH OUT — Brandi **Wells** (74)	**82**
WATCHING THE DETECTIVES — Elvis **Costello and the Attractions** (15)	**77**
WATCHING THE RIVER FLOW — Bob **Dylan** (24)	**71**
WATCHING THE WHEELS — John **Lennon** (30)	**81**
WATER — Geno **Washington and the Ram Jam Band** (39)	**66**
WATER IS OVER MY HEAD, THE — **Rockin' Berries** (43)	**66**
WATER MARGIN, THE — **Godiego** (37)	**77**
WATER MARGIN, THE — Peter **MacJUNIOR** (37)	**77**
WATER ON GLASS — Kim **Wilde** (11)	**81**
WATER WATER — Tommy **Steele** (5)	**57**
WATERFALLS — Paul **McCartney** (9)	**80**
WATERLOO [A] — **Abba** (1)	**74**
WATERLOO [B] — Stonewall **Jackson** (24)	**59**
WATERLOO SUNSET — **Kinks** (2)	**67**
WAY BACK HOME — Junior **Walker and the All-Stars** (35)	**73**
WAY DOWN — Elvis **Presley** (1)	**77**
WAY DOWN YONDER IN NEW ORLEANS — Freddy **Cannon** (3)	**60**
WAY I WALK, THE — Jack **Scott** (30)	**59**
WAY I WANT TO TOUCH YOU, THE — **Captain and Tennille** (28)	**76**
WAY IT USED TO BE, THE — Engelbert **Humperdinck** (3)	**69**
WAY OF LIFE — **Family Dogg** (6)	**69**
WAY OF THE WORLD — **Cheap Trick** (73)	**80**
WAY WE WERE, THE — Gladys **Knight and the Pips** (4)	**75**
WAY WE WERE, THE — Barbra **Streisand** (31)	**74**
WAY YOU LOOK TONIGHT, THE — **Lettermen** (36)	**61**
WAY YOU LOOK TONIGHT, THE — Denny **Seyton and the Sabres** (48)	**64**
WAY YOU LOOK TONIGHT, THE — Edward **Woodward** (42)	**71**
WAYWARD WIND — Gogi **Grant** (9)	**56**
WAYWARD WIND — Frank **Ifield** (1)	**63**
WAYWARD WIND — Tex **Ritter** (8)	**56**
WAYWARD WIND — Jimmy **Young** (27)	**56**
WE ARE FAMILY — **Sister Sledge** (8)	**79**
WE ARE GLASS — Gary **Numan** (5)	**80**
WE ARE IN LOVE — Adam **Faith** (11)	**63**
WE ARE THE BAND — **More** (59)	**81**
WE ARE THE CHAMPIONS — **Queen** (2)	**77**
WE ARE THE FIRM — **Cockney Rejects** (54)	**80**
WE CAN DO ANYTHING — **Cockney Rejects** (65)	**80**
WE CAN DO IT (EP) — **Liverpool Football Team** (15)	**77**
WE CAN WORK IT OUT — **Beatles** (1)	**65**
WE CAN WORK IT OUT — **Four Seasons** (34)	**76**
WE CAN WORK IT OUT — Stevie **Wonder** (27)	**71**
WE DO IT — **R & J Stone** (5)	**76**
(WE DON'T NEED THIS) FASCIST GROOVE THING — **Heaven 17** (45)	**81**
WE DON'T TALK ANYMORE — Cliff **Richard** (1)	**79**
WE GOT LOVE — Alma **Cogan** (26)	**59**
WE GOT THE FUNK — **Positive Force** (18)	**79**
WE GOT THE GROOVE — **Players Association** (61)	**80**
WE GOTTA GET OUT OF THIS PLACE — **Angelic Upstarts** (65)	**80**
WE HAVE A DREAM — **Scotland World Cup Squad** (5)	**82**
WE KILL THE WORLD (DON'T KILL THE WORLD) — **Boney M** (39)	**81**
WE LOVE EACH OTHER — Charlie **Rich** (37)	**75**
WE LOVE YOU — **Rolling Stones** (8)	**67**
WE SHALL OVERCOME — Joan **Baez** (26)	**65**
WE TAKE MYSTERY — Gary **Numan** (9)	**82**
WE WILL — Gilbert **O'Sullivan** (16)	**71**
WE WILL MAKE LOVE — Russ **Hamilton** (2)	**57**
WE WILL NEVER BE AS YOUNG AS THIS AGAIN — Danny **Williams** (44)	**61**
WEAK SPOT — Evelyn **Thomas** (26)	**76**
WEAR MY RING AROUND YOUR NECK — Elvis **Presley** (3)	**58**
WEATHER FORECAST — **Master Singers** (50)	**66**
WEAVE YOUR SPELL — **Level 42** (43)	**82**
WEDDING BELL BLUES — **Fifth Dimension** (16)	**70**
WEDDING BELLS [A] — Eddie **Fisher** (5)	**55**
WEDDING BELLS [B] — **Godley and Creme** (7)	**81**
WEDDING RING — Russ **Hamilton** (20)	**57**
WEDDING, THE — Julie **Rogers** (3)	**64**
WEDNESDAY WEEK — **Undertones** (11)	**80**
WEE TOM — Lord **Rockingham's XI** (16)	**59**
WEEKEND [A] — Eddie **Cochran** (15)	**61**
WEEKEND [B] — Mick **Jackson** (38)	**79**
WEIGHT, THE — **Band** (21)	**68**
WELCOME HOME — **Peters and Lee** (1)	**73**
WELCOME HOME BABY — **Brook Brothers** (33)	**62**
WELCOME TO MY WORLD — Jim **Reeves** (6)	**63**
WELCOME TO OUR WORLD (OF MERRY MUSIC) — **Mass Production** (44)	**77**
WELL ALL RIGHT — **Santana** (53)	**78**
WE'LL BE WITH YOU — **Potters** (34)	**72**
WE'LL BRING THE HOUSE DOWN — **Slade** (10)	**81**
WE'LL FIND OUR DAY — Stephanie **De Sykes** (17)	**75**
WE'LL GATHER LILACS-ALL MY LOVING (MEDLEY) — Simon **May** (49)	**77**
WELL I ASK YOU — Eden **Kane** (1)	**61**
WE'LL SING IN THE SUNSHINE — **Lancastrians** (47)	**64**
WE'RE ALL ALONE — Rita **Coolidge** (6)	**77**
WE'RE ALMOST THERE — Michael **Jackson** (46)	**81**
WE'RE GONNA GO FISHIN' — Hank **Locklin** (18)	**62**
WE'RE IN THIS LOVE TOGETHER — Al **Jarreau** (55)	**81**
WE'RE NOT ALONE — Frankie **Vaughan** (11)	**58**
WE'RE ONLY YOUNG ONCE — **Avons** (45)	**60**
WE'RE THROUGH — **Hollies** (7)	**64**
WEST OF ZANZIBAR — Anthony **Steel and the Radio Revellers** (11)	**54**
WEST ONE (SHINE ON ME) — **Ruts** (43)	**80**
WESTERN MOVIES — **Olympics** (12)	**58**
WET DREAM — Max **Romeo** (10)	**69**
WE'VE GOT THE WHOLE WORLD IN OUR HANDS — **Nottingham Forest F.C. and Paper Lace** (24)	**78**
WE'VE GOT TONITE — Bob **Seger and the Silver Bullet Band** (41)	**79**
WE'VE GOTTA GET OUT OF THIS PLACE — **Animals** (2)	**65**
WE'VE ONLY JUST BEGUN — **Carpenters** (28)	**71**
WHAT — **Soft Cell** (3)	**82**
WHAT A CRAZY WORLD WE'RE LIVING IN — Joe **Brown** (37)	**62**
WHAT A DIFFERENCE A DAY MADE — Esther **Phillips** (6)	**75**
WHAT A FOOL BELIEVES — **Doobie Brothers** (31)	**79**
WHAT A FOOL BELIEVES — Aretha **Franklin** (46)	**80**
WHAT A MOUTH — Tommy **Steele** (5)	**60**
WHAT A NIGHT — **City Boy** (39)	**78**
WHAT A PARTY — Fats **Domino** (43)	**61**
WHAT A WASTE — Ian **Dury and the Blockheads** (9)	**78**
WHAT A WOMAN IN LOVE WON'T DO — Sandy **Posey** (48)	**67**
WHAT A WONDERFUL WORLD — Louis **Armstrong** (1)	**68**
WHAT AM I GONNA DO — Emile **Ford and the Checkmates** (33)	**61**
WHAT AM I GONNA DO WITH YOU — Barry **White** (5)	**75**
WHAT AM I TO DO — Kenny **Lynch** (37)	**64**
WHAT ARE YOU DOING SUNDAY — **Dawn** (3)	**71**
WHAT BECOMES OF THE BROKEN HEARTED — Jimmy **Ruffin** (4)	**66,74**
WHAT BECOMES OF THE BROKENHEARTED? — Dave **Stewart** (13)	**81**
WHAT CAN I SAY — Boz **Scaggs** (10)	**77**
WHAT DO I GET — **Buzzcocks** (37)	**78**
WHAT DO YA SAY — Chubby **Checker** (37)	**63**
WHAT DO YOU WANT — Adam **Faith** (1)	**59**
WHAT DO YOU WANT TO MAKE THOSE EYES AT ME FOR — Emile **Ford and the Checkmates** (1)	**59**
WHAT DOES IT TAKE (TO WIN YOUR LOVE) — Junior **Walker and the All-Stars** (13)	**69**
WHAT GOES ON — Bryan **Ferry** (67)	**78**
WHAT GOOD AM I — Cilla **Black** (24)	**67**
WHAT HAVE THEY DONE TO MY SONG MA — **Melanie** (39)	**71**
WHAT HAVE THEY DONE TO MY SONG MA — **New Seekers** (44)	**70**
WHAT HAVE THEY DONE TO THE RAIN — **Searchers** (13)	**64**
WHAT IN THE WORLD'S COME OVER YOU [A] — Jack **Scott** (11)	**60**
WHAT IN THE WORLD'S COME OVER YOU [A] — Tam **White** (36)	**75**
WHAT IN THE WORLD'S COME OVER YOU [B] — **Rockin' Berries** (23)	**65**
WHAT IS A MAN — **Four Tops** (16)	**69**
WHAT IS LIFE — Olivia **Newton-John** (16)	**72**
WHAT IS TRUTH — Johnny **Cash** (21)	**70**
WHAT IT IS — Garnet **Mimms and Truckin' Co.** (44)	**77**
WHAT I'VE GOT IN MIND — Billie Jo **Spears** (4)	**76**
WHAT KIND OF FOOL AM I? — Shirley **Bassey** (47)	**63**
WHAT KIND OF FOOL AM I? — Sammy **Davis Jr.** (26)	**62**
WHAT KIND OF FOOL AM I? — Anthony **Newley** (36)	**61**
WHAT MADE MILWAUKEE FAMOUS (HAS MADE A LOSER OUT OF ME) — Rod **Stewart** (4)	**72**
WHAT MORE DO YOU WANT — Frankie **Vaughan** (25)	**60**
WHAT NOW — Adam **Faith** (31)	**63**
WHAT NOW MY LOVE — Shirley **Bassey** (5)	**62**
WHAT NOW MY LOVE — **Sonny and Cher** (13)	**66**
WHAT TO DO — Buddy **Holly** (27)	**61,63**
WHAT WILL I DO WITHOUT YOU — Lene **Lovich** (58)	**80**
WHAT WILL MY MARY SAY — Johnny **Mathis** (49)	**63**
WHAT WOULD I BE — Val **Doonican** (2)	**66**
WHAT YOU WAITING FOR — **Stargard** (39)	**78**
WHAT YOU'RE PROPOSING — **Status Quo** (2)	**80**
WHATCHA GONNA DO ABOUT IT? — **Small Faces** (14)	**65**

Title — Act (Position)	Year of Chart Entry
WHATCHA GONNA DO ABOUT IT — Doris **Troy** (37)	**64**
WHATCHA GONNA DO NOW — Chris **Andrews** (40)	**66**
WHAT'D I SAY — Jerry Lee **Lewis** (10)	**61**
WHATEVER GETS YOU THROUGH THE NIGHT — John **Lennon** (36)	**74**
WHATEVER HAPPENED TO YOU (LIKELY LADS THEME) — **Highly Likely** (35)	**73**
WHATEVER IT TAKES — **Olympic Runners** (61)	**78**
WHATEVER LOLA WANTS — Alma **Cogan** (26)	**57**
WHATEVER WILL BE WILL BE — Doris **Day** (1)	**56**
WHATEVER YOU WANT — **Status Quo** (4)	**79**
WHAT'S ANOTHER YEAR — Johnny **Logan** (1)	**80**
WHAT'S IN A KISS? — Gilbert **O'Sullivan** (19)	**80**
WHAT'S NEW PUSSYCAT — Tom **Jones** (11)	**65**
WHAT'S ON YOUR MIND — George **Benson** (45)	**81**
WHAT'S YOUR NAME — **Chicory Tip** (13)	**72**
WHAT'S YOUR NAME WHAT'S YOUR NUMBER — Andrea **True Connection** (34)	**78**
WHAT'S YOUR SIGN GIRL — Barry **Biggs** (55)	**79**
WHEELS — **String-A-Longs** (8)	**61**
WHEELS AIN'T COMING DOWN — **Slade** (60)	**81**
WHEELS CHA CHA — Joe **Loss** (21)	**61**
WHEELS OF STEEL — **Saxon** (20)	**80**
WHEN — **Kalin Twins** (1)	**58**
WHEN — **Showaddywaddy** (3)	**77**
WHEN A CHILD IS BORN — Johnny **Mathis and Gladys Knight** (74)	**81**
WHEN A CHILD IS BORN (SOLEADO) — Johnny **Mathis** (1)	**76**
WHEN A MAN LOVES A WOMAN — Percy **Sledge** (4)	**66**
WHEN BOUZOUKIS PLAYED — Vicky **Leandros** (44)	**73**
WHEN FOREVER HAS GONE — Demis **Roussos** (2)	**76**
WHEN HE SHINES — Sheena **Easton** (12)	**81**
WHEN I COME HOME — Spencer **Davis Group** (12)	**66**
WHEN I DREAM — **Teardrop Explodes** (47)	**80**
WHEN I FALL IN LOVE — Nat "King" **Cole** (2)	**57**
WHEN I FALL IN LOVE — Donny **Osmond** (4)	**73**
WHEN I GET HOME — **Searchers** (35)	**65**
WHEN I GROW UP (TO BE A MAN) — **Beach Boys** (27)	**64**
WHEN I NEED YOU — Leo **Sayer** (1)	**77**
WHEN I WAS YOUNG — Eric **Burdon** (45)	**67**
WHEN I'M AWAY FROM YOU — Frankie **Miller** (42)	**79**
WHEN I'M DEAD AND GONE — **McGuinness Flint** (2)	**70**
WHEN I'M 64 — Kenny **Ball and his Jazzmen** (43)	**67**
WHEN JOHNNY COMES MARCHING HOME — Adam **Faith** (5)	**60**
WHEN JULIE COMES AROUND — **Cuff-Links** (10)	**70**
WHEN LOVE COMES ALONG — Matt **Monro** (46)	**62**
WHEN LOVE COMES ROUND AGAIN (L'ARCA DI NOE) — Ken **Dodd** (19)	**71**
WHEN MEXICO GAVE UP THE RUMBA — Mitchell **Torok** (6)	**56**
WHEN MY LITTLE GIRL IS SMILING — Craig **Douglas** (9)	**62**
WHEN MY LITTLE GIRL IS SMILING — **Drifters** (31)	**62,79**
WHEN MY LITTLE GIRL IS SMILING — Jimmy **Justice** (9)	**62**
WHEN ROCK 'N ROLL CAME TO TRINIDAD — Nat "King" **Cole** (28)	**57**
WHEN SHE WAS MY GIRL — **Four Tops** (3)	**81**
WHEN THE BOYS TALK ABOUT THE GIRLS — Valerie **Carr** (29)	**58**
WHEN THE GIRL IN YOUR ARMS IS THE GIRL IN YOUR HEART — Cliff **Richard** (3)	**61**
WHEN THE MORNING SUN DRIES THE DEW — **Quiet Five** (45)	**65**
WHEN THE SUMMERTIME IS OVER — Jackie **Trent** (39)	**65**
WHEN THE SUN COMES SHININ' THRU — Long John **Baldry** (29)	**68**
WHEN THE TIGERS BROKE FREE — **Pink Floyd** (39)	**82**
WHEN TWO WORLDS COLLIDE — Jim **Reeves** (17)	**69**
WHEN TWO WORLDS DRIFT APART — Cliff **Richard** (46)	**77**
WHEN WE WERE YOUNG — Solomon **King** (21)	**68**
WHEN WILL I BE LOVED — **Everly Brothers** (4)	**60**
WHEN WILL I SEE YOU AGAIN — **Three Degrees** (1)	**74**
WHEN WILL THE GOOD APPLES FALL — **Seekers** (11)	**67**
WHEN WILL YOU BE MINE — **Average White Band** (49)	**79**
WHEN WILL YOU SAY I LOVE YOU — Billy **Fury** (3)	**63**
WHEN YOU ARE A KING — **White Plains** (13)	**71**
WHEN YOU ASK ABOUT LOVE — **Crickets** (27)	**60**
WHEN YOU ASK ABOUT LOVE — **Matchbox** (4)	**80**
WHEN YOU GET RIGHT DOWN TO IT — Ronnie **Dyson** (34)	**71**
WHEN YOU LOSE THE ONE YOU LOVE — David **Whitfield** (7)	**55**
WHEN YOU WALK IN THE ROOM — **Child** (38)	**78**
WHEN YOU WALK IN THE ROOM — **Searchers** (3)	**64**
WHEN YOU WERE SWEET SIXTEEN — **Fureys** (14)	**81**
WHEN YOU'RE IN LOVE WITH A BEAUTIFUL WOMAN — **Dr. Hook** (1)	**79**
WHEN YOU'RE NUMBER 1 — Gene **Chandler** (43)	**79**
WHEN YOU'RE YOUNG — **Jam** (17)	**79**
WHEN YOU'RE YOUNG AND IN LOVE — **Marvelettes** (13)	**67**
WHENEVER YOU WANT MY LOVE — **Real Thing** (18)	**78**
WHERE ARE YOU GOING TO MY LOVE — **Brotherhood Of Man** (22)	**70**
WHERE ARE YOU NOW (MY LOVE) — Jackie **Trent** (1)	**65**
WHERE DID ALL THE GOOD TIMES GO — Donny **Osmond** (18)	**74**
WHERE DID OUR LOVE GO? — Donnie **Elbert** (8)	**72**
WHERE DID OUR LOVE GO — **Manhattan Transfer** (40)	**78**
WHERE DID OUR LOVE GO — **Supremes** (3)	**64**
WHERE DID WE GO WRONG — **Liquid Gold** (56)	**82**
(WHERE DO I BEGIN) LOVE STORY — Shirley **Bassey** (34)	**71**
(WHERE DO I BEGIN) LOVE STORY — Andy **Williams** (4)	**71**
WHERE DO WE GO FROM HERE — Cliff **Richard** (60)	**82**
WHERE DO YOU GO TO MY LOVELY — Peter **Sarstedt** (1)	**69**
WHERE IS THE LOVE — Roberta **Flack and Donny Hathaway** (29)	**72**
WHERE IS THE LOVE — Betty **Wright** (25)	**75**
WHERE IS THE LOVE (WE USED TO KNOW) — **Delegation** (22)	**77**
WHERE IS TOMORROW — Cilla **Black** (40)	**68**
WHERE THE BOYS ARE — Connie **Francis** (5)	**61**
WHERE THE HEART IS — **Soft Cell** (21)	**82**
WHERE THE WIND BLOWS — Frankie **Laine** (2)	**53**
WHERE WERE YOU — Lloyd **Price** (15)	**59**
WHERE WILL THE BABY'S DIMPLE BE — Rosemary **Clooney** (6)	**55**
WHERE WILL YOU BE — Sue **Nichols** (17)	**68**
WHERE'S ROMEO? — **Ça va Ça va** (49)	**82**
'WHICH WAY IS UP', THEME FROM — **Stargard** (19)	**78**
WHICH WAY YOU GOIN' BILLY — **Poppy Family** (7)	**70**
WHILE I LIVE — Kenny **Damon** (48)	**66**
WHILE YOU SEE A CHANCE — Steve **Winwood** (45)	**81**
WHIP IT — **Devo** (51)	**80**
WHISKY IN THE JAR — **Thin Lizzy** (6)	**73**
WHISPER, THE — The **Selecter** (36)	**80**
WHISPERING — **Bachelors** (18)	**63**
WHISPERING — Nino **Tempo and April Stevens** (20)	**64**
WHISPERING GRASS — Windsor **Davies and Don Estelle** (1)	**75**
WHISPERING HOPE — Jim **Reeves** (50)	**61**
WHITE BOYS AND HEROS — Gary **Numan** (20)	**82**
WHITE CHRISTMAS — Pat **Boone** (29)	**57**
WHITE CHRISTMAS — Bing **Crosby** (5)	**77**
WHITE CHRISTMAS — **Darts** (48)	**80**
WHITE CHRISTMAS — Jim **Davidson** (52)	**80**
WHITE CHRISTMAS — **Mantovani** (6)	**52**
WHITE CHRISTMAS — Freddie **Starr** (41)	**75**
WHITE CLIFFS OF DOVER — Mr. Acker **Bilk** (30)	**60**
WHITE CLIFFS OF DOVER — **Righteous Brothers** (21)	**66**
WHITE HORSES — **Jacky** (10)	**68**
(WHITE MAN) IN HAMMERSMITH PALAIS — **Clash** (32)	**78**
WHITE PUNKS ON DOPE — **Tubes** (28)	**77**
WHITE RIOT — **Clash** (38)	**77**
WHITE ROOM — **Cream** (28)	**69**
WHITE SILVER SANDS — Bill **Black's Combo** (50)	**60**
WHITE SPORT COAT, A — Terry **Dene** (18)	**57**
WHITE SPORT COAT, A — **King Brothers** (6)	**57**
WHITER SHADE OF PALE, A — **Munich Machine** (42)	**78**
WHITER SHADE OF PALE, A — **Procol Harum** (1)	**67,72**
WHO AM I — Adam **Faith** (5)	**61**
WHO ARE WE — Ronnie **Hilton** (6)	**56**
WHO ARE WE — Vera **Lynn** (30)	**56**
WHO ARE YOU — **Who** (18)	**78**
WHO CAN IT BE NOW? — **Men At Work** (45)	**82**
WHO COULD BE BLUER — Jerry **Lordan** (17)	**60**
WHO DO YOU LOVE — **Juicy Lucy** (14)	**70**
WHO DO YOU THINK YOU ARE — **Candlewick Green** (21)	**74**
WHO KILLED BAMBI — **Sex Pistols** (6)	**79**
WHO LOVES YOU — **Four Seasons** (6)	**75**
WHO PAYS THE FERRYMAN — Yannis **Markopoulos** (11)	**77**
WHO PUT THE BOMP — **Viscounts** (21)	**61**
WHO PUT THE BOMP (IN THE BOMP-A-BOMP-A-BOMP) — **Showaddywaddy** (37)	**82**
WHO PUT THE LIGHTS OUT — **Dana** (14)	**71**
WHO WANTS THE WORLD — **Stranglers** (39)	**80**
WHO WAS IT — Hurricane **Smith** (23)	**72**
WHO WERE YOU WITH IN THE MOONLIGHT — **Dollar** (14)	**79**
WHO WHAT WHEN WHERE WHY — **Manhattan Transfer** (49)	**78**
WHO YOU LOOKING AT — **Salford Jets** (72)	**80**
WHO'D SHE COO — **Ohio Players** (43)	**76**
WHODUNIT — **Tavares** (5)	**77**
WHOLE LOTTA LOVE — **C. C. S.** (13)	**70**
WHOLE LOTTA ROSIE — **AC/DC** (36)	**80**
WHOLE LOTTA SHAKIN' GOIN' ON — Jerry Lee **Lewis** (8)	**57**
WHOLE LOTTA WOMAN — Marvin **Rainwater** (1)	**58**
WHOLE TOWN'S LAUGHING AT ME, THE — Teddy **Pendergrass** (44)	**77**
WHO'S CRYING NOW — **Journey** (46)	**82**
WHO'S GONNA LOVE ME — **Imperials** (17)	**77**
WHO'S GONNA ROCK YOU — **Nolans** (12)	**80**
WHO'S IN THE STRAWBERRY PATCH WITH SALLY — **Dawn** (37)	**74**
WHO'S SORRY NOW — Connie **Francis** (1)	**58**
WHO'S SORRY NOW — Johnnie **Ray** (17)	**56**
WHOSE PROBLEM? — **Motels** (42)	**80**
WHY [A] — Frankie **Avalon** (20)	**60**
WHY [A] — Anthony **Newley** (1)	**60**
WHY [A] — Donny **Osmond** (3)	**72**
WHY [B] — Roger **Whittaker** (47)	**71**
WHY [C] — Carly **Simon** (10)	**82**
WHY BABY WHY — Pat **Boone** (17)	**57**
WHY CAN'T WE BE LOVERS — **Holland-Dozier** (29)	**72**
WHY CAN'T WE LIVE TOGETHER — Timmy **Thomas** (12)	**73**
WHY CAN'T YOU — Clarence "Frogman" **Henry** (42)	**61**
WHY DID YOU DO IT — **Stretch** (16)	**75**
WHY DO FOOLS FALL IN LOVE — Alma **Cogan** (22)	**56**
WHY DO FOOLS FALL IN LOVE — Frankie **Lymon and the Teenagers** (1)	**56**
WHY DO FOOLS FALL IN LOVE — Diana **Ross** (4)	**81**
WHY DO LOVERS BREAK EACH OTHER'S HEARTS — **Showaddywaddy** (22)	**80**
WHY DON'T THEY UNDERSTAND — George **Hamilton IV** (22)	**58**
WHY DON'T YOU BELIEVE ME — Joni **James** (11)	**53**
WHY (MUST WE FALL IN LOVE) — **Supremes and the Temptations** (31)	**70**
WHY NOT NOW — Matt **Monro** (24)	**61**
WHY NOT TONIGHT — The **Mojos** (25)	**64**
WHY OH WHY OH WHY — Gilbert **O'Sullivan** (6)	**73**
WHY SHE'S A GIRL FROM THE CHAINSTORE — **Buzzcocks** (61)	**80**
WHY SHOULD I BE LONELY — Tony **Brent** (24)	**59**
WHY WHY BYE BYE — Bob **Luman** (46)	**60**
WICHITA LINEMAN — Glen **Campbell** (7)	**69**
WIDE AWAKE IN A DREAM — Barry **Biggs** (44)	**81**
WIDE EYED AND LEGLESS — Andy **Fairweather-Low** (6)	**75**
WIG-WAM BAM — **Sweet** (4)	**72**
WIKKA WRAP — **Evasions** (20)	**81**
WILD CAT — Gene **Vincent** (21)	**60**
WILD HONEY — **Beach Boys** (29)	**67**
WILD IN THE COUNTRY — Elvis **Presley** (4)	**61**
WILD IS THE WIND — David **Bowie** (24)	**81**
WILD LOVE — **Mungo Jerry** (32)	**73**
WILD ONE — Bobby **Rydell** (7)	**60**
WILD ONE, THE — Suzi **Quatro** (7)	**74**
WILD SIDE OF LIFE [A] — Tommy **Quickly** (33)	**64**
WILD SIDE OF LIFE [A] — **Status Quo** (9)	**76**
WILD THING — **Goodies** (21)	**75**
WILD THING — **Troggs** (2)	**66**
WILD WEST HERO — **Electric Light Orchestra** (6)	**78**
WILD WIND — John **Leyton** (2)	**61**

Title — Act (Position)	Year of Chart Entry
WILD WORLD — Jimmy Cliff (8)	70
WILFRED THE WEASEL — Keith Michell (5)	80
WILL I WHAT — Mike Sarne (18)	62
WILL YOU — Hazel O'Connor (8)	81
WILL YOU LOVE ME TOMORROW — Melanie (37)	74
WILL YOU LOVE ME TOMORROW — Shirelles (4)	61
WILLIE CAN — Beverley Sisters (23)	56
WILLIE CAN — Alma Cogan (13)	56
WILLINGLY — Malcolm Vaughan (28)	59
WILLOW TREE — Ivy League (50)	66
WIMOWEH — Karl Denver (4)	62
(WIN PLACE OR SHOW) SHE'S A WINNER — Intruders (14)	74
WINCHESTER CATHEDRAL — New Vaudeville Band (4)	66
WIND CRIES MARY, THE — Jimi Hendrix Experience (6)	67
WIND ME UP (LET ME GO) — Cliff Richard (2)	65
WINDMILL IN OLD AMSTERDAM, A — Ronnie Hilton (23)	65
WINDMILLS OF YOUR MIND — Noel Harrison (8)	69
WINDOW SHOPPING — R. Dean Taylor (36)	74
WINDPOWER — Thomas Dolby (31)	82
WINDSOR WALTZ — Vera Lynn (11)	53
WINKER'S SONG (MISPRINT) — Ivor Biggun (22)	78
WINKLE MAN, THE — Judge Dread (35)	76
WINNER TAKES IT ALL, THE — Abba (1)	80
WINTER MELODY — Donna Summer (27)	76
WINTER WONDERLAND — Johnny Mathis (17)	58
WINTER WORLD OF LOVE — Engelbert Humperdinck (7)	69
WINTER'S TALE, A — David Essex (7)	82
WIPE OUT — Surfaris (5)	63
WIRED FOR SOUND — Cliff Richard (4)	81
WISDOM OF A FOOL — Norman Wisdom (13)	57
WISDOM OF A FOOL, THE — Ronnie Carroll (20)	57
WISH YOU WERE HERE — Eddie Fisher (8)	53
WISHIN' AND HOPIN' — Merseybeats (13)	64
WISHING — Buddy Holly (10)	63
WISHING (IF I HAD A PHOTOGRAPH OF YOU) — A Flock of Seagulls (10)	82
WISHING ON A STAR — Rose Royce (3)	78
WISHING WELL — Free (7)	73
WITCH DOCTOR — Don Lang (5)	58
WITCH DOCTOR — David Seville (11)	58
WITCH QUEEN OF NEW ORLEANS — Redbone (2)	71
WITCH, THE — Rattles (8)	70
WITCHCRAFT — Frank Sinatra (12)	58
WITCHES' BREW — Janie Jones (46)	66
WITCH'S PROMISE, THE — Jethro Tull (4)	70
WITH A GIRL LIKE YOU — Troggs (1)	66
WITH A LITTLE HELP FROM MY FRIENDS — Joe Brown (32)	67
WITH A LITTLE HELP FROM MY FRIENDS — Joe Cocker (1)	68
WITH A LITTLE HELP FROM MY FRIENDS — Young Idea (10)	67
WITH A LITTLE LUCK — Wings (5)	78
WITH ALL MY HEART — Petula Clark (4)	57
WITH PEN IN HAND — Vikki Carr (40)	69
WITH THE EYES OF A CHILD — Cliff Richard (20)	69
WITH THE WIND AND THE RAIN IN YOUR HAIR — Pat Boone (21)	59
WITH THESE HANDS — Shirley Bassey (31)	60
WITH THESE HANDS — Tom Jones (13)	65
WITH YOU I'M BORN AGAIN — Billy Preston and Syreeta (2)	79
WITH YOUR LOVE — Malcolm Vaughan (18)	56
WITHOUT HER — Herb Alpert (36)	69
WITHOUT LOVE — Tom Jones (10)	69
WITHOUT YOU [A] — Matt Monro (37)	65
WITHOUT YOU [B] — Nilsson (1)	72,76
WITHOUT YOUR LOVE — Roger Daltrey (55)	80
WOE IS ME — Helen Shapiro (35)	63
WOMAN [A] — John Lennon (1)	81
WOMAN [B] — José Ferrer (7)	54
WOMAN [C] — Peter and Gordon (28)	66
WOMAN [D] — Anti-Nowhere League (72)	82
WOMAN FROM LIBERIA — Jimmie Rodgers (18)	58
WOMAN IN LOVE [A] — Four Aces (19)	56
WOMAN IN LOVE [A] — Ronnie Hilton (30)	56
WOMAN IN LOVE [A] — Frankie Laine (1)	56
WOMAN IN LOVE [B] — Barbra Streisand (1)	80
WOMAN IN LOVE [C] — Three Degrees (3)	79
WOMAN OF MINE — Dean Friedman (52)	78
WOMAN WOMAN — Gary Puckett and the Union Gap (48)	68
WOMAN'S PLACE, A — Gilbert O'Sullivan (42)	74
WOMAN'S WORLD — Jags (75)	80
WOMBLING MERRY CHRISTMAS — Wombles (2)	74
WOMBLING SONG, THE — Wombles (4)	74
WOMBLING WHITE TIE AND TAILS — Wombles (22)	75
WOMEN IN UNIFORM — Iron Maiden (35)	80
WOMEN IN UNIFORM — Skyhooks (73)	79
WOMEN IN WINTER — Skids (49)	80
WONDER OF YOU, THE — Ronnie Hilton (22)	59
WONDER OF YOU, THE — Ray Peterson (23)	59
WONDER OF YOU, THE — Elvis Presley (1)	70,77
WONDERBOY — Kinks (36)	68
WONDERFUL CHRISTMASTIME — Paul McCartney (6)	79
WONDERFUL COPENHAGEN — Danny Kaye (5)	53
WONDERFUL DREAM — Anne-Marie David (13)	73
WONDERFUL LAND — Shadows (1)	62
WONDERFUL SECRET OF LOVE — Robert Earl (17)	59
WONDERFUL THINGS — Frankie Vaughan (22)	58
WONDERFUL TIME UP THERE, A — Pat Boone (2)	58
WONDERFUL TIME UP THERE, A — Alvin Stardust (56)	81
WONDERFUL WONDERFUL — Ronnie Hilton (27)	57
WONDERFUL WONDERFUL — Gary Miller (29)	57
WONDERFUL WORLD — Sam Cooke (27)	60
WONDERFUL WORLD — Herman's Hermits (7)	65
WONDERFUL WORLD BEAUTIFUL PEOPLE — Jimmy Cliff (6)	69
WONDERFUL WORLD OF THE YOUNG — Danny Williams (8)	62
WONDERFUL WORLD, (WHAT A) — Johnny Nash (25)	76
WONDERLAND — Commodores (40)	80
WONDEROUS STORIES — Yes (7)	77
WONDROUS PLACE — Billy Fury (25)	60
WON'T GET FOOLED AGAIN — Who (9)	71
WON'T SOMEBODY DANCE WITH ME — Lynsey De Paul (14)	73
WOODEN HEART — Elvis Presley (1)	61,77
WOODSTOCK — Matthews Southern Comfort (1)	70
WOOLY BULLY — Sam The Sham and the Pharaohs (11)	65
WORDS [A] — Allisons (34)	61
WORDS [B] — Bee Gees (8)	68
WORDS [B] — Rita Coolidge (25)	78
WORDS OF LOVE — Mamas and the Papas (47)	67
WORDY RAPPINGHOOD — Tom Tom Club (7)	81
WORK ALL DAY — Barry Biggs (38)	76
W.O.R.K. (N.O. NAH NO! NO! MY DADDY DON'T) — Bow Wow Wow (62)	80
WORK REST AND PLAY EP — Madness (6)	80
WORK THAT BODY — Diana Ross (7)	82
WORK THAT SUCKER TO DEATH — Xavier (53)	82
WORKER, THE — Fischer-Z (53)	79
WORKIN' FOR THE MAN — Roy Orbison (50)	62
WORKIN' MY WAY BACK TO YOU — Four Seasons (50)	66
WORKING FOR THE YANKEE DOLLAR — Skids (20)	79
WORKING IN THE COALMINE — Lee Dorsey (8)	66
WORKING MY WAY BACK TO YOU — Detroit Spinners (1)	80
WORKING ON A BUILDING OF LOVE — Chairmen Of The Board (20)	72
WORLD — Bee Gees (9)	67
WORLD IN MY ARMS, THE — Nat "King" Cole (36)	61
WORLD IS MINE, THE — Malcolm Vaughan (26)	57
WORLD OF BROKEN HEARTS — Amen Corner (26)	67
WORLD OF OUR OWN, A — Seekers (3)	65
WORLD OUTSIDE, THE — Russ Conway (24)	59
WORLD OUTSIDE, THE — Four Aces (18)	59
WORLD OUTSIDE, THE — Ronnie Hilton (18)	59
WORLD WE KNEW, THE — Frank Sinatra (33)	67
WORLD WITHOUT HEROES, A — Kiss (55)	82
WORLD WITHOUT LOVE, A — Peter and Gordon (1)	64
WORZEL'S SONG — Jon Pertwee (33)	80
WOT — Captain Sensible (26)	82
WOULD I LIE TO YOU — Whitesnake (37)	81
WOW — Kate Bush (14)	79
WRAPPING PAPER — Cream (34)	66
WRATH CHILD — Iron Maiden (31)	81
WRECK OF THE ANTOINETTE — Dave Dee, Dozy, Beaky, Mick and Tich (14)	68
WRECK OF THE EDMUND FITZGERALD, THE — Gordon Lightfoot (40)	77
WRITING ON THE WALL — Tommy Steele (30)	61
WRITTEN ON THE WIND — Roger Daltrey (46)	77
WUNDERBAR — Ten Pole Tudor (16)	81
WUTHERING HEIGHTS — Kate Bush (1)	78
XANADU — Olivia Newton-John and Electric Light Orchestra (1)	80
XMAS PARTY — Snowmen (44)	82
Y VIVA ESPANA — Sylvia (4)	74
Y VIVA SUSPENDERS — Judge Dread (27)	76
YA YA TWIST — Petula Clark (14)	62
YAKETY YAK — Coasters (12)	58
YEAR OF DECISION — Three Degrees (13)	74
YEAR OF THE CAT — AL Stewart (31)	77
YEARNING FOR YOUR LOVE — Gap Band (47)	81
YEARS FROM NOW — Dr. Hook (47)	80
YEARS MAY COME, YEARS MAY GO — Herman's Hermits (7)	70
YEARS MAY COME YEARS MAY GO — Herman's Hermits (45)	70
YEH YEH — Georgie Fame (1)	64
YELLOW PEARL — Philip Lynott (14)	81
YELLOW RIVER — Christie (1)	70
YELLOW ROSE OF TEXAS — Ronnie Hilton (15)	55
YELLOW ROSE OF TEXAS — Gary Miller (13)	55
YELLOW ROSE OF TEXAS — Mitch Miller (2)	55
YELLOW SUBMARINE — Beatles (1)	66
YEP! — Duane Eddy (17)	59
YES I WILL — Hollies (9)	65
YES MY DARLING DAUGHTER — Eydie Gormé (10)	62
YES SIR I CAN BOOGIE — Baccara (1)	77
YES TONIGHT JOSEPHINE — Jets (25)	81
YES TONIGHT JOSEPHINE — Johnnie Ray (1)	57
YESTERDAY — Beatles (8)	76
YESTERDAY — Ray Charles (44)	67
YESTERDAY — Marianne Faithfull (36)	65
YESTERDAY — Matt Monro (8)	65
YESTERDAY HAS GONE — Cupid's Inspiration (4)	68
YESTERDAY MAN — Chris Andrews (3)	65
YESTERDAY ONCE MORE — Carpenters (2)	73
YESTERDAY'S DREAMS — Four Tops (23)	68
YESTERDAY'S GONE — Chad Stuart and Jeremy Clyde (37)	63
YESTER-ME YESTER-YOU YESTERDAY — Stevie Wonder (2)	69
YING TONG SONG — Goons (3)	56,73
Y.M.C.A. — Village People (1)	78
YOU [A] — Johnny Johnson and the Bandwagon (34)	69
YOU [B] — George Harrison (38)	75
YOU [C] — Randy Edelman (49)	77
YOU AIN'T GOIN' NOWHERE — Byrds (45)	68
YOU AIN'T LIVIN' TILL YOU'RE LOVIN' — Marvin Gaye and Tammi Terrell (21)	69
YOU AIN'T SEEN NOTHIN' YET — Bachman-Turner Overdrive (2)	74
YOU ALWAYS HURT THE ONE YOU LOVE — Connie Francis (13)	58
YOU ALWAYS HURT THE ONE YOU LOVE — Clarence "Frogman" Henry (6)	61
YOU AND I — Rick James (46)	78
YOU AND ME — Liner (44)	79
YOU ANGEL YOU — Manfred Mann's Earth Band (54)	79
YOU ARE AWFUL — Dick Emery (43)	73
YOU ARE BEAUTIFUL — Johnny Mathis (38)	60
YOU ARE EVERYTHING — Pearls (41)	73
YOU ARE EVERYTHING — Diana Ross and Marvin Gaye (5)	74
YOU ARE MY DESTINY — Paul Anka (6)	58
YOU ARE MY FIRST LOVE — Ruby Murray (16)	56
YOU ARE MY LOVE — Liverpool Express (11)	76
YOU ARE THE SUNSHINE OF MY LIFE — Stevie Wonder (7)	73
YOU BELONG TO ME [A] — Jo Stafford (1)	52
YOU BELONG TO ME [B] — Gary Glitter (40)	76
YOU BET YOUR LOVE — Herbie Hancock (18)	79
YOU BETTER COME HOME — Petula Clark (44)	65
YOU BETTER YOU BET — Who (9)	81
YOU CAME YOU SAW YOU CONQUERED — Pearls (32)	72
YOU CAN DO IT — Al Hudson and the Partners (15)	79
YOU CAN DO MAGIC [A] — Limmie and the Family Cookin' (3)	73
YOU CAN DO MAGIC [B] — America (59)	82
YOU CAN GET IT IF YOU REALLY WANT — Desmond Dekker and the Aces (2)	70
YOU CAN HAVE HIM — Dionne Warwick (37)	65
YOU CAN HAVE IT ALL — George McCrae (23)	74
YOU CAN MAKE ME DANCE SING OR ANYTHING — Faces (12)	74
YOU CAN NEVER STOP ME LOVING YOU — Kenny Lynch (10)	63
YOU CAN'T BE TRUE TO TWO — Dave King (11)	56
YOU CAN'T HURRY LOVE — Phil Collins (6)	82
YOU CAN'T HURRY LOVE — Supremes (3)	66

Title — Act (Position)	Year of Chart Entry
YOU CAN'T SIT DOWN — Phil **Upchurch Combo** (39)	**66**
YOU COULD HAVE BEEN A LADY — **Hot Chocolate** (22)	**71**
YOU COULD HAVE BEEN WITH ME — Sheena **Easton** (54)	**81**
YOU DON'T BELIEVE ME — **Stray Cats** (57)	**81**
YOU DON'T BRING ME FLOWERS — **Barbra and Neil** (5)	**78**
YOU DON'T HAVE TO BE A BABY TO CRY — **Caravelles** (6)	**63**
YOU DON'T HAVE TO BE A STAR (TO BE IN MY SHOW) — Marilyn **McCoo and Billy Davis Jr.** (7)	**77**
YOU DON'T HAVE TO BE IN THE ARMY TO FIGHT IN THE WAR — **Mungo Jerry** (13)	**71**
YOU DON'T HAVE TO GO — **Chi-Lites** (3)	**76**
YOU DON'T HAVE TO SAY YOU LOVE ME — **Guys and Dolls** (5)	**76**
YOU DON'T HAVE TO SAY YOU LOVE ME — Elvis **Presley** (9)	**71**
YOU DON'T HAVE TO SAY YOU LOVE ME — Dusty **Springfield** (1)	**66**
YOU DON'T KNOW — Helen **Shapiro** (1)	**61**
(YOU DONT KNOW) HOW GLAD I AM — Kiki **Dee** (33)	**75**
YOU DON'T KNOW ME — Ray **Charles** (9)	**62**
YOU DON'T KNOW WHAT YOU'VE GOT — Ral **Donner** (25)	**61**
YOU DON'T LOVE ME — Gary **Walker** (26)	**66**
YOU DON'T OWE ME A THING — Johnnie **Ray** (12)	**57**
YOU DRIVE ME CRAZY — Shakin' **Stevens** (2)	**81**
YOU GAVE ME LOVE — **Crown Heights Affair** (10)	**80**
YOU GAVE ME SOMEBODY TO LOVE — **Manfred Mann** (36)	**66**
YOU GO TO MY HEAD — Bryan **Ferry** (33)	**75**
YOU GOT ME BURNING — Lenny **Williams** (67)	**78**
YOU GOT SOUL — Johnny **Nash** (6)	**69**
YOU GOT THE FLOOR — Arthur **Adams** (38)	**81**
YOU GOT THE POWER — **War** (58)	**82**
YOU GOT WHAT IT TAKES — Dave **Clark Five** (28)	**67**
YOU GOT WHAT IT TAKES — Marv **Johnson** (5)	**60**
YOU GOT WHAT IT TAKES — Johnny **Kidd and the Pirates** (25)	**60**
YOU GOT WHAT IT TAKES — **Showaddywaddy** (2)	**77**
YOU GOTTA BE A HUSTLER IF YOU WANNA GET ON — Sue **Wilkinson** (25)	**80**
YOU GOTTA HAVE LOVE IN YOUR HEART — **Supremes and the Four Tops** (25)	**71**
YOU GOTTA STOP — Elvis **Presley** (38)	**67**
(YOU GOTTA WALK) DON'T LOOK BACK — Peter **Tosh** (43)	**78**
YOU HAVEN'T DONE NOTHIN' — Stevie **Wonder** (30)	**74**
YOU JUST MIGHT SEE ME CRY — **Our Kid** (2)	**76**
YOU KEEP ME HANGIN' ON - STOP IN THE NAME OF LOVE (MEDLEY) — Roni **Hill** (36)	**77**
(YOU KEEP ME) HANGIN' ON [A] — Cliff **Richard** (13)	**74**
YOU KEEP ME HANGIN' ON [B] — **Supremes** (8)	**66**
YOU KEEP ME HANGIN' ON [B] — **Vanilla Fudge** (18)	**67**
YOU KEEP RUNNING AWAY — **Four Tops** (26)	**67**
YOU KNOW HOW TO LOVE ME — Phyllis **Hyman** (47)	**80**
YOU KNOW WHAT I MEAN — **Vernons Girls** (37)	**62**
(YOU KNOW) YOU CAN DO IT — **Central Line** (67)	**81**
YOU LAY SO EASY ON MY MIND — Andy **Williams** (32)	**75**
YOU LIGHT MY FIRE — **Sheila and B. Devotion** (44)	**78**
YOU LIGHT UP MY LIFE — Debby **Boone** (48)	**77**
YOU LIKE ME DON'T YOU — Jermaine **Jackson** (41)	**81**
YOU LITTLE FOOL — Elvis **Costello and the Attractions** (52)	**82**
YOU LITTLE TRUST MAKER — **Tymes** (18)	**74**
YOU MADE ME BELIEVE IN MAGIC — **Bay City Rollers** (34)	**77**
YOU MADE ME LOVE YOU — Nat "King" **Cole** (22)	**59**
YOU MAKE IT MOVE — Dave **Dee, Dozy, Beaky, Mick and Tich** (26)	**65**
YOU MAKE LOVING FUN — **Fleetwood Mac** (45)	**77**
YOU MAKE ME FEEL BRAND NEW — **Stylistics** (2)	**74**
YOU MAKE ME FEEL LIKE DANCING — Leo **Sayer** (2)	**76**
YOU MAKE ME FEEL (MIGHTY REAL) — **Sylvester** (8)	**78**
YOU ME AND US — Alma **Cogan** (18)	**57**
YOU MEAN EVERYTHING TO ME — Neil **Sedaka** (45)	**60**
YOU MIGHT NEED SOMEBODY — Randy **Crawford** (11)	**81**
YOU MUST HAVE BEEN A BEAUTIFUL BABY — Bobby **Darin** (10)	**61**
YOU MY LOVE — Frank **Sinatra** (13)	**55**
YOU NEED HANDS — Max **Bygraves** (3)	**58**
YOU NEED WHEELS — **Merton Parkas** (40)	**79**
YOU NEEDED ME — Anne **Murray** (22)	**78**
YOU NEVER CAN TELL — Chuck **Berry** (23)	**64**
YOU NEVER DONE IT LIKE THAT — **Captain and Tennille** (63)	**78**
YOU NEVER KNOW WHAT YOU'VE GOT — **Me And You** (31)	**79**
YOU ONLY LIVE TWICE — Nancy **Sinatra** (11)	**67**
YOU ONLY YOU — Rita **Pavone** (21)	**67**
YOU + ME = LOVE — **Undisputed Truth** (43)	**77**
YOU REALLY GOT ME — **Kinks** (1)	**64**
YOU SCARE ME TO DEATH — Marc **Bolan** (51)	**81**
YOU SEE THE TROUBLE WITH ME — Barry **White** (2)	**76**
YOU SEND ME — Sam **Cooke** (29)	**58**
YOU SEND ME — Rod **Stewart** (7)	**74**
YOU SEXY SUGAR PLUM (BUT I LIKE IT) — Rodger **Collins** (22)	**76**
YOU SEXY THING — **Hot Chocolate** (2)	**75**
YOU SHOOK ME ALL NIGHT LONG — **AC/DC** (38)	**80**
YOU SHOULD BE DANCING — **Bee Gees** (5)	**76**
YOU SURE LOOK GOOD TO ME — Phyllis **Hyman** (56)	**81**
YOU TAKE MY HEART AWAY — De Etta **Little and Nelson Pigford** (35)	**77**
YOU TO ME ARE EVERYTHING — **Real Thing** (1)	**76**
YOU TOOK THE WORDS RIGHT OUT OF MY MOUTH — **Meat Loaf** (33)	**78**
YOU WANT IT YOU GOT IT — **Detroit Emeralds** (12)	**73**
YOU WEAR IT WELL — Rod **Stewart** (1)	**72**
YOU WERE MADE FOR ME — **Freddie and the Dreamers** (3)	**63**
YOU WERE ON MY MIND — Crispian **St. Peters** (2)	**66**
YOU WERE THERE — **Heinz** (26)	**64**
YOU WEREN'T IN LOVE WITH ME — Billy **Field** (67)	**82**
YOU WON'T BE LEAVING — **Herman's Hermits** (20)	**66**
YOU WON'T FIND ANOTHER FOOL LIKE ME — **New Seekers** (1)	**73**
YOU YOU ROMEO — Shirley **Bassey** (29)	**57**
YOU YOU YOU — Alvin **Stardust** (6)	**74**
YOU'LL ALWAYS BE A FRIEND — **Hot Chocolate** (23)	**72**
YOU'LL ALWAYS FIND ME IN THE KITCHEN AT PARTIES — Jona **Lewie** (16)	**80**
YOU'LL ANSWER TO ME — Cleo **Laine** (5)	**61**
YOU'LL NEVER BE SO WRONG — **Hot Chocolate** (52)	**81**
YOU'LL NEVER FIND ANOTHER LOVE LIKE MINE — Lou **Rawls** (10)	**76**
YOU'LL NEVER GET TO HEAVEN (EP) — **Stylistics** (24)	**76**
YOU'LL NEVER GET TO HEAVEN — Dionne **Warwick** (20)	**64**
YOU'LL NEVER KNOW [A] — Shirley **Bassey** (6)	**61**
YOU'LL NEVER KNOW [B] — **Hi Gloss** (12)	**81**
YOU'LL NEVER KNOW WHAT YOU'RE MISSING [A] — Emile **Ford and the Checkmates** (12)	**60**
YOU'LL NEVER KNOW WHAT YOU'RE MISSING [B] — **Real Thing** (16)	**77**
YOU'LL NEVER NEVER KNOW — **Platters** (23)	**57**
YOU'LL NEVER WALK ALONE — **Gerry and the Pacemakers** (1)	**63**
YOU'LL NEVER WALK ALONE — Elvis **Presley** (44)	**68**
YOUNG AMERICANS — David **Bowie** (18)	**75**
YOUNG AND FOOLISH — Ronnie **Hilton** (17)	**56**
YOUNG AND FOOLISH — Edmund **Hockridge** (10)	**56**
YOUNG AND FOOLISH — Dean **Martin** (20)	**56**
YOUNG AT HEART — Frank **Sinatra** (12)	**54**
YOUNG BLOOD — **UFO** (36)	**80**
YOUNG EMOTIONS — Rick **Nelson** (48)	**60**
YOUNG GIFTED AND BLACK — **Bob and Marcia** (5)	**70**
YOUNG GIRL — Gary **Puckett and the Union Gap** (1)	**68,74**
YOUNG GUNS (GO FOR IT) — **Wham!** (3)	**82**
YOUNG HEARTS RUN FREE — Candi **Staton** (2)	**76**
YOUNG LOVE — Tab **Hunter** (1)	**57**
YOUNG LOVE — Sonny **James** (11)	**57**
YOUNG LOVE — Donny **Osmond** (1)	**73**
YOUNG LOVERS — **Paul and Paula** (9)	**63**
YOUNG NEW MEXICAN PUPPETEER, THE — Tom **Jones** (6)	**72**
YOUNG ONES, THE — Cliff **Richard** (1)	**62**
YOUNG PARISIANS — **Adam and The Ants** (9)	**8C**
YOUNG TURKS — Rod **Stewart** (11)	**81**
YOUNG WORLD — Rick **Nelson** (19)	**62**
YOUNGER GIRL — **Critters** (38)	**66**
YOUR BABY AIN'T YOUR BABY ANYMORE — Paul **Da Vinci** (20)	**74**
YOUR BABY'S GONE SURFIN' — Duane **Eddy** (49)	**63**
YOUR CASSETTE PET — **Bow Wow Wow** (58)	**80**
YOUR CHEATING HEART — Ray **Charles** (13)	**62**
YOUR DREAM — Adrian **Gurvitz** (61)	**82**
YOUR EARS SHOULD BE BURNING NOW — Marti **Webb** (61)	**80**
YOUR GENERATION — **Generation X** (36)	**77**
YOUR HONOUR — Pluto **Shervington** (19)	**82**
YOUR HURTIN' KIND OF LOVE — Dusty **Springfield** (37)	**65**
YOUR KISS IS SWEET — **Syreeta** (12)	**75**
(YOUR LOVE HAS LIFTED ME)HIGHER AND HIGHER — Rita **Coolidge** (48)	**77**
(YOUR LOVE KEEPS LIFTING ME) HIGHER AND HIGHER — Jackie **Wilson** (11)	**69**
YOUR MA SAID YOU CRIED IN YOUR SLEEP LAST NIGHT — Doug **Sheldon** (29)	**62**
YOUR MAGIC PUT A SPELL ON ME — L. J. **Johnson** (27)	**76**
YOUR MAMMA WON'T LIKE ME — Suzi **Quatro** (31)	**75**
YOUR OWN SPECIAL WAY — **Genesis** (43)	**77**
YOUR SONG — Elton **John** (7)	**71**
YOUR SONG — Billy **Paul** (37)	**77**
YOUR TENDER LOOK — Joe **Brown** (31)	**62**
YOUR TIME HASN'T COME YET BABY — Elvis **Presley** (22)	**68**
YOU'RE A BETTER MAN THAN I — **Sham 69** (49)	**79**
YOU'RE A LADY — Peter **Skellern** (3)	**72**
YOU'RE A STAR — **Aquarian Dream** (67)	**79**
YOU'RE ALL I NEED TO GET BY — Marvin **Gaye and Tammi Terrell** (19)	**68**
YOU'RE ALL I NEED TO GET BY — Johnny **Mathis and Deniece Williams** (45)	**78**
YOU'RE BREAKIN' MY HEART — Keely **Smith** (14)	**65**
YOU'RE DRIVING ME CRAZY — **Temperance Seven** (1)	**61**
(YOU'RE) FABULOUS BABE — Kenny **Williams** (35)	**77**
YOU'RE FREE TO GO — Jim **Reeves** (48)	**72**
YOU'RE GONNA GET NEXT TO ME — Bo **Kirkland and Ruth Davis** (12)	**77**
(YOU'RE) HAVING MY BABY — Paul **Anka** (6)	**74**
YOU'RE IN MY HEART — Rod **Stewart** (3)	**77**
YOU'RE LYING — **Linx** (15)	**80**
YOU'RE MORE THAN A NUMBER IN MY LITTLE RED BOOK — **Drifters** (5)	**76**
YOU'RE MOVING OUT TODAY — Carole Bayer **Sager** (6)	**77**
YOU'RE MY BEST FRIEND [A] — **Queen** (7)	**76**
YOU'RE MY BEST FRIEND [B] — Don **Williams** (35)	**76**
YOU'RE MY EVERYTHING [A] — Max **Bygraves** (34)	**69**
YOU'RE MY EVERYTHING [B] — Lee **Garrett** (15)	**76**
YOU'RE MY EVERYTHING [C] — **Temptations** (26)	**67**
YOU'RE MY GIRL — **Rockin' Berries** (40)	**65**
YOU'RE MY LIFE — Barry **Biggs** (36)	**77**
(YOU'RE MY) SOUL AND INSPIRATION — **Righteous Brothers** (15)	**66**
YOU'RE MY WORLD — Cilla **Black** (1)	**64**
YOU'RE NO GOOD — **Swinging Blue Jeans** (3)	**64**
YOU'RE O.K. — **Ottawan** (56)	**80**
YOU'RE READY NOW — Frankie **Valli** (11)	**70**
YOU'RE SINGING OUR LOVE SONG TO SOMEBODY ELSE — Jerry **Wallace** (46)	**60**
YOU'RE SIXTEEN — Johnny **Burnette** (3)	**61**
YOU'RE SIXTEEN — Ringo **Starr** (4)	**74**
YOU'RE SO RIGHT FOR ME — **Eastside Connection** (44)	**78**
YOU'RE SO VAIN — Carly **Simon** (3)	**72**
YOU'RE SUCH A GOOD LOOKING WOMAN — Joe **Dolan** (17)	**70**
YOU'RE THE FIRST THE LAST MY EVERYTHING — Barry **White** (1)	**74**
YOU'RE THE GREATEST LOVER — Jonathan **King** (67)	**79**
YOU'RE THE ONE [A] — Petula **Clark** (23)	**65**
YOU'RE THE ONE [B] — Kathy **Kirby** (17)	**64**
YOU'RE THE ONE FOR ME — **D Train** (30)	**82**
YOU'RE THE ONE THAT I WANT — Hilda **Baker and Arthur Mullard** (22)	**78**
YOU'RE THE ONE THAT I WANT — John **Travolta and Olivia Newton-John** (1)	**78**
YOU'RE THE ONLY GOOD THING — Jim **Reeves** (17)	**61**
YOU'RE THE ONLY ONE — Val **Doonican** (37)	**68**

Title — Act (Position)	Year of Chart Entry
YOU'RE THE REASON WHY — **Rubettes** (28)	**76**
YOU'RE THE TOP CHA — Al **Saxon** (17)	**59**
YOURS UNTIL TOMORROW — Gene **Pitney** (34)	**68**
YOUTH OF NATION ON FIRE — Bill **Nelson** (73)	**81**
YOUTH OF TODAY — **Musical Youth** (13)	**82**
YOU'VE BEEN DOING ME WRONG — **Delegation** (49)	**77**
YOU'VE BEEN GONE — **Crown Heights Affair** (44)	**80**
YOU'VE COME BACK — P. J. **Proby** (25)	**66**
YOU'VE GOT A FRIEND — James **Taylor** (4)	**71**
YOU'VE GOT ANOTHER THING COMIN' — **Judas Priest** (66)	**82**
YOU'VE GOT LOVE — Buddy **Holly** (40)	**64**
YOU'VE GOT ME DANGLING ON A STRING — **Chairmen Of The Board** (5)	**70**
YOU'VE GOT MY NUMBER (WHY DON'T YOU USE IT?) — **Undertones** (32)	**79**
YOU'VE GOT TO HIDE YOUR LOVE AWAY — **Silkie** (28)	**65**
YOU'VE GOT YOUR TROUBLES — **Fortunes** (2)	**65**
YOU'VE LOST THAT LOVIN' FEELIN' — Cilla **Black** (2)	**65**
YOU'VE LOST THAT LOVIN' FEELIN' — Daryl **Hall and John Oates** (55)	**80**
YOU'VE LOST THAT LOVIN' FEELIN' — **Righteous Brothers** (1)	**65,69,77**
YOU'VE LOST THAT LOVIN' FEELING — Telly **Savalas** (47)	**75**
YOU'VE MADE ME SO VERY HAPPY — **Blood Sweat And Tears** (35)	**69**
YOU'VE NEVER BEEN IN LOVE LIKE THIS BEFORE — **Unit Four Plus Two** (14)	**65**
YOU'VE NOT CHANGED — Sandie **Shaw** (18)	**67**
YOU'VE SAID ENOUGH — **Central Line** (58)	**82**
YUM YUM (GIMME SOME) — **Fatback Band** (40)	**75**
YUMMY YUMMY YUMMY — **Ohio Express** (5)	**68**
Z CARS, THEME FROM — Johnny **Keating** (8)	**62**
Z CARS, THEME FROM — Norrie **Paramor** (33)	**62**
ZABADAK! — Dave **Dee, Dozy, Beaky, Mick and Tich** (3)	**67**
ZAMBESI — Lou **Busch** (2)	**56**
ZAMBESI — Eddie **Calvert** (13)	**56**
ZAMBESI — **Piranhas** (17)	**82**
ZEROX — **Adam and The Ants** (45)	**81**
ZIGGY STARDUST — **Bauhaus** (15)	**82**
ZING A LITTLE ZONG — Bing **Crosby and Jane Wyman** (10)	**52**
ZING WENT THE STRINGS OF MY HEART — **Trammps** (29)	**74**
ZIP GUN BOOGIE — **T. Rex** (41)	**74**
ZIP-A-DEE-DOO-DAH — Bob B **Soxx and the Blue Jeans** (45)	**63**
ZODIACS — Roberta **Kelly** (44)	**78**
ZOO, THE — **Scorpions** (75)	**80**
ZOO (THE HUMAN ZOO), THE — **Commodores** (44)	**74**
ZOOM [A] — **Commodores** (38)	**78**
ZOOM [B] — **Fat Larry's Band** (2)	**82**
ZORBA'S DANCE — Marcello **Minerbi** (6)	**65**

PART 3

The British Hit Singles: Facts and Feats

This section should not be used as proof that the Shadows are a greater instrumental unit than the Brighouse and Rastrick Brass Band, nor that the Everly Brothers have been a more significant force in popular music than Renee and Renato. All statistics and information cover the period 14 November 1952–31 December 1982 and are as follows:

MOST WEEKS ON CHART

The following table lists all the recording acts that spent 100 weeks or more on the British singles chart from the first chart on 14 November 1952 up to and including the chart for 25 December 1982. It is of course possible for an act to be credited with 2 or more chart weeks in the same week from simultaneous hits. Double-sided hits, EPs, LPs and double singles only count as 1 week each week.

Weeks

ELVIS PRESLEY **1098**
CLIFF RICHARD **861**
(+ 7 wks with Olivia Newton-John)
BEATLES **402**
(+ 1 wk with Tony Sheridan)
FRANK SINATRA **391**
(+ 18 wks with Nancy Sinatra and 9 wks with Sammy Davis Jnr)
SHADOWS **361**
(+ 404 wks backing Cliff Richard)
EVERLY BROTHERS **328**
JIM REEVES **322**
LONNIE DONEGAN **321**
SHIRLEY BASSEY **312**
ROY ORBISON **309**
TOM JONES **306**
HOLLIES **300**
ROLLING STONES **298**
PAT BOONE **296**
PERRY COMO **292**
STEVIE WONDER **285**
(+ 10 wks with Paul McCartney and 5 wks with Diana Ross, Marvin Gaye & Smokey Robinson)
BILLY FURY **277**
DAVID BOWIE **273**
(+ 11 wks with Queen, and 5 with Bing Crosby)
FOUR TOPS **265**
(+ 20 wks with Supremes)
BEE GEES **262**
STATUS QUO **259**
SUPREMES **258**
(+ 27 wks with Temptations, 20 wks with Four Tops)
DIANA ROSS **257**
(+ 196 wks as a Supreme, 20 wks with Supremes & Temptations, 20 with Marvin Gaye, 5 with Marvin Gaye, Smokey Robinson & Stevie Wonder, 4 with Michael Jackson and 12 with Lionel Richie)
BEACH BOYS **253**
FRANKIE LAINE **253**
(+ 16 wks with Jimmy Boyd, 8 wks with Doris Day and 4 wks with Johnnie Ray)
ADAM FAITH **251**
ROD STEWART **248**
(+ 46 wks with Faces and 6 wks with Jeff Beck)
PAUL McCARTNEY/WINGS **247**
(+ 402 wks as a Beatle, 10 wks with Stevie Wonder and 8 wks with Michael Jackson)
CONNIE FRANCIS **241**
ELTON JOHN **241**
(+ 14 wks with Kiki Dee, and 4 wks with John Lennon)
WHO **241**
(+ 4 wks as Hi-Numbers)
ABBA **236**
PETULA CLARK **236**
ENGELBERT HUMPERDINCK **235**
KEN DODD **234**
HOT CHOCOLATE **231**
ANDY WILLIAMS **228**
NAT 'KING' COLE **225**
ELECTRIC LIGHT ORCHESTRA **224**
(+ 11 wks with Olivia Newton-John)
T. REX **213**
FRANKIE VAUGHAN **212**
(+ 20 wks with Kaye Sisters)
HERMAN'S HERMITS **211**
BRENDA LEE **210**
SHOWADDYWADDY **209**
SLADE **208**
JACKSON FIVE/JACKSONS **206**
(104 wks as Jackson Five, 102 weeks as Jacksons)
GENE PITNEY **200**
BILL HALEY **199**
KINKS **197**
CILLA BLACK **192**
NEIL SEDAKA **189**
BACHELORS **187**
DUANE EDDY **187**
BUDDY HOLLY **186**
(+ 47 wks as a Cricket)
QUEEN **186**
(+ 11 wks with David Bowie)
DONNA SUMMER **186**
(+ 13 wks with Barbra Streisand)
DAVID WHITFIELD **181**
(+ 9 wks as one of the artists on All Star Hit Parade)
DRIFTERS **177**
MANFRED MANN **176**
(+ 41 wks as Manfred Mann's Earth Band)
DUSTY SPRINGFIELD **172**
(+ 66 wks as a Springfield)
DAVE CLARK FIVE **171**
ACKER BILK **169**
RUSS CONWAY **168**
(+ 10 wks with Dorothy Squires)
GUY MITCHELL **163**
CARPENTERS **161**
FRANK IFIELD **158**
JOHN LENNON/PLASTIC ONO BAND **158**
(+ 402 wks as a Beatle and 4 wks with Elton John)
SANDIE SHAW **157**
FLEETWOOD MAC **156**
BOBBY DARIN **155**
SWEET **154**
DEAN MARTIN **154**
DAVID ESSEX **154**
ROXY MUSIC **153**
ADAM & THE ANTS **153**
BONEY M **152**
GARY GLITTER **150**
GLADYS KNIGHT & THE PIPS ... **150**
(Gladys Knight 1 wk with Johnny Mathis)
MADNESS **149**
FOUR SEASONS **147**
DEL SHANNON **147**
TEMPTATIONS **146**
(+ 27 wks with Supremes)
TOMMY STEELE **145**
(+ 7 wks as one of the artists on All Star Hit Parade Vol 2)
VAL DOONICAN **143**
NEW SEEKERS **143**
GILBERT O'SULLIVAN **143**
STYLISTICS **143**
JAM **142**
DAVE DEE, DOZY, BEAKY, MICK & TICH **141**
(Dave Dee 4 more wks solo, D,B,M & T 8 more weeks)
BLONDIE **140**
OLIVIA NEWTON-JOHN **139**
(+ 45 wks with John Travolta, 11 wks with ELO, and 7 with Cliff Richard)
SMALL FACES **137**
(excluding 46 wks by Faces)
KENNY BALL & HIS JAZZMEN.... **136**
MUD **136**
BOBBY VEE **134**
BOB DYLAN **133**
PAUL ANKA **132**
RICK NELSON **132**
JOHNNIE RAY **132**
(+ 16 wks with Doris Day, and 4 wks with Frankie Laine)
LEO SAYER **131**
TREMELOES **131**
(+ 90 wks with Brian Poole)
10 CC **131**
MARMALADE **130**

RONNIE HILTON **128**
ANTHONY NEWLEY **128**
SEARCHERS........................... **128**
MAX BYGRAVES...................... **127**
JONATHAN KING **127**
(67 wks as Jonathan King, and 60 more under the following pseudonyms: Bubblerock, 53rd and 3rd, Shag, 100 Ton and a Feather, Weathermen, Father Abraphart and the Smurps, Sakkarin and Sound 9418. His claim to be the Piglets is still unratified)
MATT MONRO **127**
KARL DENVER........................ **124**
RAY CHARLES **123**
LULU **122**
SEEKERS............................... **120**
HELEN SHAPIRO..................... **119**
MARTY WILDE........................ **118**
WINIFRED ATWELL **117**
(+ 9 wks as one of the artists on All Star Hit Parade)
DARTS.................................. **117**
SHANE FENTON/ALVIN STARDUST **117**
(28 wks as Shane Fenton, 89 wks as Alvin Stardust)
JOHNNY MATHIS.................... **117**
(+ 20 wks with Deniece Williams and 1 wk with Gladys Knight)
BARRY WHITE **117**
DORIS DAY **116**
(+ 16 wks with Johnnie Ray, and 8 wks with Frankie Laine)
STRANGLERS......................... **116**
ELVIS COSTELLO.................... **115**
GERRY AND THE PACEMAKERS....................... **114**
SUZI QUATRO **114**
(+ 8 wks with Chris Norman)
THIN LIZZY **114**
BAY CITY ROLLERS................. **113**
MICHAEL JACKSON **113**
(+ 206 wks as a Jackson, 8 wks with Paul McCartney and 4 wks with Diana Ross)
CRAIG DOUGLAS.................... **112**
POLICE................................. **111**
DOLLAR **110**
FATS DOMINO **110**
MOVE................................... **110**
KOOL AND THE GANG........... **110**
ALMA COGAN **109**
DAWN **109**
(Tony Orlando 11 extra wks solo)
RUBY MURRAY...................... **109**
BAD MANNERS...................... **108**
OTIS REDDING **108**
(+ 16 wks with Carla Thomas)
BOOMTOWN RATS **106**

ELVIS PRESLEY The first artist in chart history to achieve the double – 1000 weeks and 100 hits, surveys the competition from his position at the top

	Weeks
SMOKIE	**106**
SHAKIN' STEVENS	**106**
MALCOLM VAUGHAN	**106**
ANIMALS *(+ 29 wks backing Eric Burdon)*	**105**
NEIL DIAMOND *(+ 12 wks with Barbra Streisand)*	**105**
EARTH WIND AND FIRE *(+ 13 wks with Emotions)*	**105**
GEORGIE FAME *(+ 10 wks with Fame and Price Together)*	**105**
EDDIE FISHER	**105**
ISLEY BROTHERS	**105**
BARRY MANILOW	**105**
MOODY BLUES	**105**
DES O'CONNOR	**105**
DONNY OSMOND *(+ 91 wks with Osmonds and 37 with Marie Osmond)*	**105**
JIMMY RUFFIN	**105**
LITTLE RICHARD	**104**
CLASH	**102**

Other performers who have spent more than 100 weeks on the chart in various disguises include:

MARVIN GAYE **177 weeks** (79 solo, 5 with Diana Ross, Stevie Wonder and Smokey Robinson, and 93 with four separate female partners)

ALAN PRICE **161 weeks** (73 solo, 78 with Animals and 10 with Fame and Price Together)

DAVID CASSIDY **147 weeks** (94 solo, 53 with Partridge Family)

CHER **140 weeks** (46 solo, 77 with Sonny & Cher, and 17 uncredited with Meatloaf)

PAUL SIMON **132 weeks** (52 solo, 80 with Simon & Garfunkel)

ERIC CLAPTON **129 weeks** (35 solo, 57 with Cream, 21 with Derek and the Dominoes, 16 weeks with Yardbirds. He also played uncredited on many other hit singles)

SCOTT WALKER **123 weeks** (30 solo, 93 with Walker Brothers)

EDDY GRANT **118 weeks** (49 solo, 69 with Equals)

ART GARFUNKEL **117 weeks** (37 solo, 80 with Simon & Garfunkel)

PHIL COLLINS **112 weeks** (32 solo, 80 with Genesis)

LIONEL RICHIE **109 weeks** (6 solo, 91 with Commodores, 12 with Diana Ross)

BARBRA STREISAND **109 weeks** (74 solo, 13 with Donna Summer, 12 with Neil Diamond and 10 with Barry Gibb)

GARY WALKER **105 weeks** (12 solo, 93 with Walker Brothers)

MIKE NESMITH **104 weeks** (6 solo, 98 with Monkees)

CHUBBY CHECKER **101 weeks** (97 solo, 4 with Bobby Rydell)

Since the first edition of *The Guinness Book Of British Hit Singles*, which included statistics up to the end of 1976, no new act has broken into the Top Ten in the Most Weeks On Chart list. In those 6 years, only four acts have dropped out of the all time top twenty (Supremes, Frankie Laine, Adam Faith and Connie Francis). They have been replaced by Stevie Wonder, David Bowie, the Four Tops and the Bee Gees. In the Top Thirty All Time Acts in the list above, the fastest risers over the past 6 years have been Diana Ross, up 50 places from 73rd to 23rd, Status Quo, up 37 places from 58th to 21st, David Bowie, up 35 places from 53rd to 18th, and Paul McCartney/Wings, up 30 places from 58th to 28th.

It is extremely difficult to list in correct order the individuals who have spent most weeks on the charts under all guises, groups and other pseudonyms. One member of Survivor, for example, used to be in Ides Of March, and who is to say whether one of Renato Carosone's Sextet also played on Marino Marini's hits? The following list ignores session musicians and the uncredited contributions of, for example, Little Eva on Big Dee Irwin's 'Swinging On A Star'.

A Top Ten of the individuals who have spent most weeks on the charts, whether alone, in duos or in groups, looks like this:

ELVIS PRESLEY **1098 weeks**
CLIFF RICHARD **868 weeks**
HANK B. MARVIN **786 weeks**
BRUCE WELCH **765 weeks**
PAUL McCARTNEY **668 weeks**
JOHN LENNON **565 weeks**
DIANA ROSS **514 weeks**
RINGO STARR **457 weeks**
GEORGE HARRISON **456 weeks**
FRANK SINATRA **418 weeks**

Diana Ross has very conveniently chalked up 257 weeks on her own and also 257 weeks in other combinations of groups and duos.

MOST WEEKS ON CHART IN EACH YEAR

(charts began 14 Nov 52)		*Weeks*
1952	Vera Lynn	10
1953	Frankie Laine	66
1954	Frankie Laine	67
1955	Ruby Murray	80
1956	Bill Haley	110
1957	Elvis Presley	108
1958	Elvis Presley	70
1959	Russ Conway	79
1960	Adam Faith	77
1961	Elvis Presley	88
1962	Mr Acker Bilk	71
1963	Beatles	67
	Cliff Richard	67
1964	Jim Reeves	73
1965	Seekers	51
1966	Dave Dee, Dozy, Beaky Mick and Tich	50
1967	Engelbert Humperdinck	96
1968	Engelbert Humperdinck	58
	Tom Jones	58
1969	Frank Sinatra	53
1970	Elvis Presley	59
1971	Elvis Presley	66
1972	T. Rex	58
1973	David Bowie	55
1974	Wombles	65
1975	Mud	45
1976	Rod Stewart	48
1977	Elvis Presley	51
1978	Boney M	54

		Weeks
1979	Abba	43
	Blondie	43
	Chic	43
1980	Madness	46
1981	Adam & The Ants	91
1982	Soft Cell	49

MOST WEEKS ON CHART IN ONE YEAR

Weeks		*Year*
110	Bill Haley	1956
108	Elvis Presley	1957
96	Engelbert Humperdinck	1967
91	Adam & The Ants	1981
88	Elvis Presley	1961
84	Pat Boone	1957
80	Ruby Murray	1955
79	Russ Conway	1959
77	Adam Faith	1960
73	Jim Reeves	1964
	Cliff Richard	1960
72	Beatles	1964
71	Mr Acker Bilk	1962
70	Bachelors	1964
	Chubby Checker	1962
	Elvis Presley	1958

MOST WEEKS ON CHART: 1981

	Weeks
ADAM & THE ANTS	91
JOHN LENNON *(+ 4 with Elton John)*	50
SHAKIN' STEVENS	50
BAD MANNERS	45
MADNESS	44
ULTRAVOX	44
HUMAN LEAGUE	40
TOYAH	39
SHEENA EASTON	37
SPANDAU BALLET	37
KIM WILDE	37

Only three acts, Bad Manners, Madness and Sheena Easton, remain from the Top Ten acts of 1980 (see *Guinness Book Of British Hit Singles, 3rd edition, page 318*). For the first time since 1961, three female vocalists made the Top Ten.

BILL HALEY The 1956 chart champion had the most ever weeks on chart in one year (110 weeks) *London Features International*

MOST WEEKS ON CHART: 1982

	Weeks
SOFT CELL	49
JAPAN	47
KOOL & THE GANG	42
ADAM & THE ANTS	41
MADNESS	40
SHALAMAR	38
DOLLAR	37
IMAGINATION	37
SHAKIN' STEVENS	37
DIANA ROSS	35
SHAKATAK	35

For the first time ever, the top act of the year was a duo. Madness completed a third consecutive year in the Top Ten, becoming the 21st act to achieve this feat, and the first since 1979, when Boney M, Electric Light Orchestra and Donna Summer all spent their third consecutive year among the Top Ten acts of the year. If Madness are one of the top acts of 1983, they will become only the sixth act to stay on top for at least 4 years. The record holder is Cliff Richard, who was one of the Top Ten acts each year from 1959 to 1970, 12 years in all. Lonnie Donegan has managed 5 consecutive years (1956 to 1960) in the Top Ten weeks on chart, while Elvis Presley (from 1956 to 1959 and from 1969 to 1972), Frankie Laine (from 1952 to 1955) and Connie Francis (from 1958 to 1961) have all been one of the Top Ten chart acts for 4 consecutive years.

MOST HITS

Double-sided hits, double singles, EPs and LPs only count as one hit each time. Re-issues and re-entries do not count as new hits, but re-recordings or re-mixes of the same song by the same act do count as two hits. A record is a hit if it makes the chart, even if only for 1 week at number 75.

102 ELVIS PRESLEY
78 CLIFF RICHARD *(+ 1 with Olivia Newton-John)*
33 FRANK SINATRA *(+ 1 with Nancy Sinatra, 1 with Sammy Davis Jr)*
STEVIE WONDER *(+ 1 with Paul McCartney, 1 with Diana Ross, Marvin Gaye and Smokey Robinson)*
31 DAVID BOWIE *(+ 1 with Queen, 1 with Bing Crosby)*
DIANA ROSS *(+ 18 with Supremes, 2 with Supremes and Temptations, 2 with Marvin Gaye, 1 with Michael Jackson, 1 with Lionel Richie and 1 with Marvin Gaye, Stevie Wonder and Smokey Robinson)*
SHADOWS *(+ 30 with Cliff Richard)*
30 LONNIE DONEGAN
ROLLING STONES
29 BEATLES *(+ 1 with Tony Sheridan)*
HOLLIES
ELTON JOHN *(+ 1 with Kiki Dee, 1 with John Lennon)*
FRANKIE VAUGHAN *(+ 2 with Kaye Sisters)*
28 NAT 'KING' COLE
EVERLY BROTHERS
BILLY FURY
ROY ORBISON
27 PETULA CLARK
HOT CHOCOLATE
WHO *(+ 1 as Hi-Numbers)*
26 SHIRLEY BASSEY
BEACH BOYS
PAT BOONE
TOM JONES
SLADE
STATUS QUO
25 FOUR TOPS *(+ 2 with Supremes)*
JIM REEVES
24 ABBA
BEE GEES
ADAM FAITH
ELECTRIC LIGHT ORCHESTRA *(+ 1 with Olivia Newton-John)*
SUPREMES *(+ 3 with Temptations, 2 with Four Tops)*
23 PERRY COMO
CONNIE FRANCIS
JACKSON FIVE/JACKSONS *(11 as Jackson Five, 12 as Jacksons)*
FRANKIE LAINE *(+ 1 with Doris Day, 1 with Jimmy Boyd and 1 with Johnnie Ray)*
SHOWADDYWADDY
ROD STEWART *(+ 5 with Faces, 1 with Jeff Beck and 1, uncredited, with Python Lee Jackson)*
DONNA SUMMER *(+ 1 with Barbra Streisand)*
T. REX
22 DAVE CLARK FIVE
BRENDA LEE
21 DUANE EDDY
GENE PITNEY
QUEEN *(+ 1 with David Bowie)*
ANDY WILLIAMS
WINGS *(Paul McCartney 7 more solo, and 1 with Stevie Wonder, 1 with Michael Jackson)*
20 FATS DOMINO
HERMAN'S HERMITS
KINKS
GLADYS KNIGHT & THE PIPS *(Gladys Knight 1 more with Johnny Mathis)*
19 CILLA BLACK
RUSS CONWAY *(+ 1 with Dorothy Squires)*
DRIFTERS
DAVID ESSEX
TEMPTATIONS *(+ 3 with Supremes)*
18 KEN DODD
BUDDY HOLLY *(+ 4 as a Cricket)*
JAM
NEIL SEDAKA
DUSTY SPRINGFIELD
17 BACHELORS
MAX BYGRAVES *(+ 1 as part of All Star Hit Parade Vol 2)*
CARPENTERS
ALMA COGAN
ELVIS COSTELLO
BOBBY DARIN
FOUR SEASONS
GARY GLITTER
RONNIE HILTON
JONATHAN KING *(9 under his own name, 8 under pseudonyms)*
MANFRED MANN *(+ 5 as Manfred Mann's Earth Band)*
SANDIE SHAW
STRANGLERS
DAVID WHITFIELD *(+ 1 as part of All Star Hit Parade)*
16 RAY CHARLES
CLASH
BOB DYLAN
FLEETWOOD MAC
DEAN MARTIN
ROXY MUSIC
TOMMY STEELE *(+ 1 as part of All Star Hit Parade)*
STYLISTICS
SWEET
15 ADAM & THE ANTS
WINIFRED ATWELL *(+ 1 as part of All Star Hit Parade)*
FRANK IFIELD
LULU
MUD
RICK NELSON
OLIVIA NEWTON-JOHN *(+ 2 with John Travolta, 1 with Electric Light Orchestra and 1 with Cliff Richard)*
GILBERT O'SULLIVAN
SUZI QUATRO *(+ 1 with Chris Norman)*
JOHNNIE RAY *(+ 2 with Doris Day, 1 with Frankie Laine)*

Mention should also be made of the Osmonds who as a family have enjoyed 25 hits: ten by the Osmonds, seven by Donny, four by Donny and Marie, three by Little Jimmy and one by Marie. Marvin Gaye has hit nine times solo and eleven other times with various girls. Eric Burdon has fronted 15 hits, nine as an uncredited member of the Animals and six more under his own name. Otis Redding's 14 solo hits are boosted by two more with Carla Thomas. Three quarters of the Small Faces participated in the five Faces hits as well as the 12 Small Faces successes. The Tremeloes had 13 hits on their own and another eight with Brian Poole. Eric Stewart featured on 13 hits by 10 CC, one by Hotlegs, six by Wayne Fontana and the Mindbenders and four by the Mindbenders after their split from Wayne Fontana.

GARY GLITTER discussing his 11 top ten hits in a row with Tim Rice

HOLLIES Third most top ten hits for a British group

MOST TOP TEN HITS

The same rules apply as for the Most Hits list, except that a disc must have made the Top Ten for at least 1 week to qualify.

55 ELVIS PRESLEY
47 CLIFF RICHARD
25 BEATLES
21 ROLLING STONES
19 ABBA
17 LONNIE DONEGAN
HOLLIES
FRANKIE LAINE *(+ 1 with Jimmy Boyd, 1 with Doris Day)*
16 SHADOWS *(+ 25 with Cliff Richard)*
15 STATUS QUO
ROD STEWART *(+ 3 with Faces, 1 with Python Lee Jackson)*
14 BEE GEES
DAVID BOWIE *(+ 1 with Queen, 1 with Bing Crosby)*
ELECTRIC LIGHT ORCHESTRA *(+ 1 with Olivia Newton-John)*
SLADE
STEVIE WONDER *(+ 1 with Paul McCartney)*
13 NAT 'KING' COLE
EVERLY BROTHERS
TOM JONES
KINKS
MANFRED MANN *(+ 3 as Manfred Mann's Earth Band)*
WHO
12 SHIRLEY BASSEY
BEACH BOYS
MADNESS
GUY MITCHELL
DIANA ROSS *(+ 1 with Marvin Gaye, 1 with Lionel Richie)*
SUPREMES
DAVID WHITFIELD *(+ 1 as part of All Star Hit Parade)*
WINGS *(Paul McCartney 4 more solo, plus 1 with Stevie Wonder, 1 with Michael Jackson)*
11 WINIFRED ATWELL *(+ 1 as part of All Star Hit Parade)*
CILLA BLACK
PAT BOONE
PETULA CLARK
ADAM FAITH
BILLY FURY
GARY GLITTER
JACKSON FIVE/JACKSONS *(6 as Jackson Five, 5 as Jacksons)*
MUD
T. REX
10 CC *(+ one more as Hotlegs, more or less)*
10 BAY CITY ROLLERS
BLONDIE
FOUR TOPS
CONNIE FRANCIS
HERMAN'S HERMITS
HOT CHOCOLATE

10 ELTON JOHN *(+ 1 with Kiki Dee)*
QUEEN *(+ 1 with David Bowie)*
ROXY MUSIC
LEO SAYER
SHOWADDYWADDY
DUSTY SPRINGFIELD *(+ 2 with Springfields)*
STYLISTICS
SWEET

Michael Jackson, apart from his 11 Top Ten hits with the Jacksons, has had nine solo Top Ten hits and one more with Paul McCartney. The Osmond clan have reached the Top Ten 16 times in various combinations. Frank Sinatra has the surprisingly low total of nine Top Ten hits, plus one more with his daughter Nancy. Frankie Vaughan has had nine solo Top Ten hits, plus two more with the Kaye Sisters. Johnnie Ray's nine Top Tenners are augmented by one more in duet with Doris Day, who herself has had seven solo Top Ten hits, two more with Frankie Laine and that one with Johnnie Ray.

MOST HITS WITHOUT A TOP TEN HIT

No act which has had a Top Ten hit has yet needed more than 10 chart hits to reach the Top Ten for the first time. The slowest Top Tenner is Otis Redding, whose 10th hit was his first and only Top Ten hit, Dock Of The Bay.

Two acts have already had more than 10 hits without ever reaching the Top Ten. They are **CLASH** 16 hits and **AC/DC** 11 hits.

Fats Domino had 18 more hits after his only Top Ten hit, Blueberry Hill.

MOST TOP TEN HITS WITHOUT A NUMBER ONE HIT

14 Electric Light Orchestra, Stevie Wonder **13** Nat 'King' Cole, The Who **11** Billy Fury **10** Gene Pitney, Elton John

CLASH Only two acts have had more than ten hits without reaching the Top Ten – AC/DC (11) and Clash (16)

MOST HITS WITHOUT A NUMBER ONE HIT

33 STEVIE WONDER *(who has had 4 number two hits, and a number one hit with Paul McCartney)*
29 ELTON JOHN *(who has had 1 number two hit, and a number one hit with Kiki Dee)*
28 NAT 'KING' COLE *(who has had 3 number two hits)*
BILLY FURY *(who has had 1 number two hit)*
27 WHO *(who have had 2 number two hits)*
24 ELECTRIC LIGHT ORCHESTRA *(who have had 1 number three hit, and a number one hit with Olivia Newton-John)*
22 BRENDA LEE *(who has had 1 number three hit)*
21 DUANE EDDY *(who has had 2 number two hits)*
GENE PITNEY *(who has had 2 number two hits)*
20 FATS DOMINO *(who had only one Top Ten hit, which reached number six)*
GLADYS KNIGHT & THE PIPS *(who have had 2 number four hits)*

STEVIE WONDER As a soloist a record 33 hits without a number one but topped the chart with a one off single with Paul McCartney

THE NUMBER ONE HITS

Date disc hit the top	Title/Artist/Label	Number of weeks at no. 1

1952 (Top Twelve – *N.M.E.* Chart)

14 Nov	HERE IN MY HEART Al Martino (Capitol)	9

1953

16 Jan	YOU BELONG TO ME Jo Stafford (Columbia)	1
23 Jan	COMES A-LONG A-LOVE Kay Starr (Capitol)	1
30 Jan	OUTSIDE OF HEAVEN Eddie Fisher (HMV)	1
6 Feb	DON'T LET THE STARS GET IN YOUR EYES Perry Como (HMV)	5
13 Mar	SHE WEARS RED FEATHERS Guy Mitchell (Columbia)	4
10 Apr	BROKEN WINGS Stargazers (Decca)	1
17 Apr	(HOW MUCH IS) THAT DOGGIE IN THE WINDOW Lita Roza (Decca)	1
24 Apr	I BELIEVE Frankie Laine (Philips)	9
26 Jun	I'M WALKING BEHIND YOU Eddie Fisher (HMV)	1
3 Jul	I BELIEVE Frankie Laine (Philips)	6
14 Aug	MOULIN ROUGE Mantovani (Decca)	1
21 Aug	I BELIEVE Frankie Laine (Philips)	3
11 Sep	LOOK AT THAT GIRL Guy Mitchell (Philips)	6
23 Oct	HEY JOE Frankie Laine (Philips)	2
6 Nov	ANSWER ME David Whitfield (Decca)	1
13 Nov	ANSWER ME Frankie Laine (Philips) (ANSWER ME by David Whitfield returned to number one for one week to share the top spot with Frankie Laine's version on 11 Dec 1953)	8

1954

8 Jan	OH MEIN PAPA Eddie Calvert (Columbia)	9
12 Mar	I SEE THE MOON Stargazers (Decca)	5
16 Apr	SECRET LOVE Doris Day (Philips)	1
23 Apr	I SEE THE MOON Stargazers (Decca)	1
30 Apr	SUCH A NIGHT Johnnie Ray (Philips)	1
7 May	SECRET LOVE Doris Day (Philips)	8
2 Jul	CARA MIA David Whitfield with chorus and Mantovani and his orchestra (Decca)	10
10 Sep	LITTLE THINGS MEAN A LOT Kitty Kallen (Brunswick)	1
17 Sep	THREE COINS IN THE FOUNTAIN Frank Sinatra (Capitol)	3

Top Twenty began 1 Oct 1954

8 Oct	HOLD MY HAND Don Cornell (Vogue)	4
5 Nov	MY SON MY SON Vera Lynn (Decca)	2
19 Nov	HOLD MY HAND Don Cornell (Vogue)	1
26 Nov	THIS OLE HOUSE Rosemary Clooney (Philips)	1
3 Dec	LET'S HAVE ANOTHER PARTY Winifred Atwell (Philips)	5

1955

7 Jan	FINGER OF SUSPICION Dickie Valentine (Decca)	1
14 Jan	MAMBO ITALIANO Rosemary Clooney (Philips)	1
21 Jan	FINGER OF SUSPICION Dickie Valentine (Decca)	2
4 Feb	MAMBO ITALIANO Rosemary Clooney (Philips)	2
18 Feb	SOFTLY SOFTLY Ruby Murray (Columbia)	3
11 Mar	GIVE ME YOUR WORD Tennessee Ernie Ford (Capitol)	7
29 Apr	CHERRY PINK AND APPLE BLOSSOM WHITE Perez Prado (HMV)	2
13 May	STRANGER IN PARADISE Tony Bennett (Philips)	2
27 May	CHERRY PINK AND APPLE BLOSSOM WHITE Eddie Calvert (Columbia)	4
24 Jun	UNCHAINED MELODY Jimmy Young (Decca)	3
15 Jul	DREAMBOAT Alma Cogan (HMV)	2
29 Jul	ROSE MARIE Slim Whitman (London)	11
14 Oct	THE MAN FROM LARAMIE Jimmy Young (Decca)	4
11 Nov	HERNANDO'S HIDEAWAY Johnston Brothers (Decca)	2
25 Nov	ROCK AROUND THE CLOCK Bill Haley and his Comets (Brunswick)	3
16 Dec	CHRISTMAS ALPHABET Dickie Valentine (Decca)	3

On 30 Dec 1955 the chart was extended to 25 records for one week only

1956

6 Jan	ROCK AROUND THE CLOCK Bill Haley and his Comets (Brunswick)	2
20 Jan	SIXTEEN TONS Tennessee Ernie Ford (Capitol)	4
17 Feb	MEMORIES ARE MADE OF THIS Dean Martin (Capitol)	4
16 Mar	IT'S ALMOST TOMORROW Dreamweavers (Brunswick)	2
30 Mar	ROCK AND ROLL WALTZ Kay Starr (HMV)	1
6 Apr	IT'S ALMOST TOMORROW Dreamweavers (Brunswick)	1

Top Thirty began 13 Apr 1956

13 Apr	POOR PEOPLE OF PARIS Winifred Atwell (Decca)	3
4 May	NO OTHER LOVE Ronnie Hilton (HMV)	6
15 Jun	I'LL BE HOME Pat Boone (London)	5
20 Jul	WHY DO FOOLS FALL IN LOVE Teenagers featuring Frankie Lymon (Columbia)	3
10 Aug	WHATEVER WILL BE WILL BE Doris Day (Philips)	6
21 Sep	LAY DOWN YOUR ARMS Anne Shelton (Philips)	4
19 Oct	A WOMAN IN LOVE Frankie Laine (Philips)	4
16 Nov	JUST WALKIN' IN THE RAIN Johnnie Ray (Philips)	7

1957

4 Jan	SINGING THE BLUES Guy Mitchell (Philips)	1
11 Jan	SINGING THE BLUES Tommy Steele (Decca)	1
18 Jan	SINGING THE BLUES Guy Mitchell (Philips)	1
25 Jan	GARDEN OF EDEN Frankie Vaughan (Philips)	4
	(SINGING THE BLUES by Guy Mitchell returned to number one for one week to share the top spot with GARDEN OF EDEN by Frankie Vaughan on 1 Feb 1957)	
22 Feb	YOUNG LOVE Tab Hunter (London)	7
12 Apr	CUMBERLAND GAP Lonnie Donegan (Pye Nixa)	5
17 May	ROCK-A-BILLY Guy Mitchell (Philips)	1
24 May	BUTTERFLY Andy Williams (London)	2
7 Jun	YES TONIGHT JOSEPHINE Johnnie Ray (Philips)	3
28 Jun	GAMBLIN' MAN/PUTTING ON THE STYLE Lonnie Donegan (Pye Nixa)	2
12 Jul	ALL SHOOK UP Elvis Presley (HMV)	7
30 Aug	DIANA Paul Anka (Columbia)	9
1 Nov	THAT'LL BE THE DAY Crickets (Vogue-Coral)	3
22 Nov	MARY'S BOY CHILD Harry Belafonte (RCA)	7

1958

10 Jan	GREAT BALLS OF FIRE Jerry Lee Lewis (London)	2
24 Jan	JAILHOUSE ROCK Elvis Presley (RCA)	3
14 Feb	THE STORY OF MY LIFE Michael Holliday (Columbia)	2
28 Feb	MAGIC MOMENTS Perry Como (RCA)	8
25 Apr	WHOLE LOTTA WOMAN Marvin Rainwater (MGM)	3
16 May	WHO'S SORRY NOW Connie Francis (MGM)	6
27 Jun	ON THE STREET WHERE YOU LIVE Vic Damone (Philips)	2
	(On 4 Jul 1958 ON THE STREET WHERE YOU LIVE by Vic Damone and ALL I HAVE TO DO IS DREAM/CLAUDETTE by the Everly Brothers shared the top spot)	
4 Jul	ALL I HAVE TO DO IS DREAM/CLAUDETTE Everly Brothers (London)	7
22 Aug	WHEN Kalin Twins (Brunswick)	5
26 Sep	CAROLINA MOON/STUPID CUPID Connie Francis (MGM)	6
7 Nov	IT'S ALL IN THE GAME Tommy Edwards (MGM)	3
28 Nov	HOOTS MON Lord Rockingham's XI (Decca)	3
19 Dec	IT'S ONLY MAKE BELIEVE Conway Twitty (MGM)	5

1959

23 Jan	THE DAY THE RAINS CAME Jane Morgan (London)	1
30 Jan	ONE NIGHT/I GOT STUNG Elvis Presley (RCA)	3
20 Feb	AS I LOVE YOU Shirley Bassey (Philips)	4
20 Mar	SMOKE GETS IN YOUR EYES Platters (Mercury)	1
27 Mar	SIDE SADDLE Russ Conway (Columbia)	4
24 Apr	IT DOESN'T MATTER ANYMORE Buddy Holly (Coral)	3
15 May	A FOOL SUCH AS I/I NEED YOUR LOVE TONIGHT Elvis Presley (RCA)	5
19 Jun	ROULETTE Russ Conway (Columbia)	2
3 Jul	DREAM LOVER Bobby Darin (London)	4
31 Jul	LIVING DOLL Cliff Richard and the Drifters (Columbia)	6
11 Sep	ONLY SIXTEEN Craig Douglas (Top Rank)	4
9 Oct	HERE COMES SUMMER Jerry Keller (London)	1
16 Oct	MACK THE KNIFE Bobby Darin (London)	2
30 Oct	TRAVELLIN' LIGHT Cliff Richard and the Shadows (Columbia)	5
4 Dec	WHAT DO YOU WANT Adam Faith (Parlophone)	3
	(On 18 Dec 1959 WHAT DO YOU WANT by Adam Faith and WHAT DO YOU WANT TO MAKE THOSE EYES AT ME FOR by Emile Ford and the Checkmates shared the top spot)	
18 Dec	WHAT DO YOU WANT TO MAKE THOSE EYES AT ME FOR Emile Ford and the Checkmates (Pye)	6

1960

29 Jan	STARRY EYED Michael Holliday (Columbia)	1
5 Feb	WHY Anthony Newley (Decca)	4

***Record Retailer*, now *Music and Video Week*, began publication of a Top Fifty on 10 Mar 1960. From this point on their charts are used. The final *New Musical Express* chart used is that of 26 Feb 1960, as the chart published in *Record Retailer* on 10 Mar 1960 was dated 5 Mar 1960 and clearly corresponded with the *N.M.E.* chart of 4 Mar 1960.**

10 Mar	POOR ME Adam Faith (Parlophone)	1
17 Mar	RUNNING BEAR Johnny Preston (Mercury)	2
31 Mar	MY OLD MAN'S A DUSTMAN Lonnie Donegan (Pye)	4
28 Apr	DO YOU MIND Anthony Newley (Decca)	1
5 May	CATHY'S CLOWN Everly Brothers (Warner Brothers)	7
23 Jun	THREE STEPS TO HEAVEN Eddie Cochran (London)	2
7 Jul	GOOD TIMIN' Jimmy Jones (MGM)	3
28 Jul	PLEASE DON'T TEASE Cliff Richard and the Shadows (Columbia)	1
4 Aug	SHAKIN' ALL OVER Johnny Kidd and the Pirates (HMV)	1
11 Aug	PLEASE DON'T TEASE Cliff Richard and the Shadows (Columbia)	2
25 Aug	APACHE Shadows (Columbia)	5
29 Sep	TELL LAURA I LOVE HER Ricky Valance (Columbia)	3
20 Oct	ONLY THE LONELY Roy Orbison (London)	2
3 Nov	IT'S NOW OR NEVER Elvis Presley (RCA)	8
29 Dec	I LOVE YOU Cliff Richard and the Shadows (Columbia)	2

1961

12 Jan	POETRY IN MOTION Johnny Tillotson (London)	2

26 Jan	ARE YOU LONESOME TONIGHT? Elvis Presley (RCA)	4
23 Feb	SAILOR Petula Clark (Pye)	1
2 Mar	WALK RIGHT BACK Everly Brothers (Warner Brothers)	3
23 Mar	WOODEN HEART Elvis Presley (RCA)	6
4 May	BLUE MOON Marcels (Pye International)	2
18 May	ON THE REBOUND Floyd Cramer (RCA)	1
25 May	YOU'RE DRIVING ME CRAZY Temperance Seven (Parlophone)	1
1 Jun	SURRENDER Elvis Presley (RCA)	4
29 Jun	RUNAWAY Del Shannon (London)	3
20 Jul	TEMPTATION Everly Brothers (Warner Brothers)	2
3 Aug	WELL I ASK YOU Eden Kane (Decca)	1
10 Aug	YOU DON'T KNOW Helen Shapiro (Columbia)	3
31 Aug	JOHNNY REMEMBER ME John Leyton (Top Rank)	3
21 Sep	REACH FOR THE STARS/CLIMB EV'RY MOUNTAIN Shirley Bassey (Columbia)	1
28 Sep	JOHNNY REMEMBER ME John Leyton (Top Rank)	1
5 Oct	KON-TIKI Shadows (Columbia)	1
12 Oct	MICHAEL Highwaymen (HMV)	1
19 Oct	WALKIN' BACK TO HAPPINESS Helen Shapiro (Columbia)	3
9 Nov	LITTLE SISTER/HIS LATEST FLAME Elvis Presley (RCA)	4
7 Dec	TOWER OF STRENGTH Frankie Vaughan (Philips)	3
28 Dec	MOON RIVER Danny Williams (HMV)	2

1962

11 Jan	THE YOUNG ONES Cliff Richard and the Shadows (Columbia)	6
22 Feb	ROCK-A-HULA BABY/CAN'T HELP FALLING IN LOVE Elvis Presley (RCA)	4
22 Mar	WONDERFUL LAND Shadows (Columbia)	8
17 May	NUT ROCKER B. Bumble and the Stingers (Top Rank)	1
24 May	GOOD LUCK CHARM Elvis Presley (RCA)	5
28 Jun	COME OUTSIDE Mike Sarne with Wendy Richard (Parlophone)	2
12 Jul	I CAN'T STOP LOVING YOU Ray Charles (HMV)	2
26 Jul	I REMEMBER YOU Frank Ifield (Columbia)	7
13 Sep	SHE'S NOT YOU Elvis Presley (RCA)	3
4 Oct	TELSTAR Tornados (Decca)	5
8 Nov	LOVESICK BLUES Frank Ifield (Columbia)	5
13 Dec	RETURN TO SENDER Elvis Presley (RCA)	3

1963

3 Jan	THE NEXT TIME/BACHELOR BOY Cliff Richard and the Shadows (Columbia)	3
24 Jan	DANCE ON Shadows (Columbia)	1
31 Jan	DIAMONDS Jet Harris & Tony Meehan (Decca)	3
21 Feb	WAYWARD WIND Frank Ifield (Columbia)	3
14 Mar	SUMMER HOLIDAY Cliff Richard and the Shadows (Columbia)	2
28 Mar	FOOT TAPPER Shadows (Columbia)	1
4 Apr	SUMMER HOLIDAY Cliff Richard and the Shadows (Columbia)	1
11 Apr	HOW DO YOU DO IT? Gerry and the Pacemakers (Columbia)	3
2 May	FROM ME TO YOU Beatles (Parlophone)	7
20 Jun	I LIKE IT Gerry and the Pacemakers (Columbia)	4
18 Jul	CONFESSIN' Frank Ifield (Columbia)	2
1 Aug	(YOU'RE THE) DEVIL IN DISGUISE Elvis Presley (RCA)	1
8 Aug	SWEETS FOR MY SWEET Searchers (Pye)	2
22 Aug	BAD TO ME Billy J. Kramer and the Dakotas (Parlophone)	3
12 Sep	SHE LOVES YOU Beatles (Parlophone)	4
10 Oct	DO YOU LOVE ME Brian Poole and the Tremeloes (Decca)	3
31 Oct	YOU'LL NEVER WALK ALONE Gerry and the Pacemakers (Columbia)	4
28 Nov	SHE LOVES YOU Beatles (Parlophone)	2
12 Dec	I WANT TO HOLD YOUR HAND Beatles (Parlophone)	5

1964

16 Jan	GLAD ALL OVER Dave Clark Five (Columbia)	2
30 Jan	NEEDLES AND PINS Searchers (Pye)	3
20 Feb	DIANE Bachelors (Decca)	1
27 Feb	ANYONE WHO HAD A HEART Cilla Black (Parlophone)	3
19 Mar	LITTLE CHILDREN Billy J. Kramer and the Dakotas (Parlophone)	2
2 Apr	CAN'T BUY ME LOVE Beatles (Parlophone)	3
23 Apr	WORLD WITHOUT LOVE Peter and Gordon (Columbia)	2
7 May	DON'T THROW YOUR LOVE AWAY Searchers (Pye)	2
21 May	JULIET Four Pennies (Philips)	1
28 May	YOU'RE MY WORLD Cilla Black (Parlophone)	4
25 Jun	IT'S OVER Roy Orbison (London)	2
9 Jul	HOUSE OF THE RISING SUN Animals (Columbia)	1
16 Jul	IT'S ALL OVER NOW Rolling Stones (Decca)	1
23 Jul	A HARD DAY'S NIGHT Beatles (Parlophone)	3
13 Aug	DO WAH DIDDY DIDDY Manfred Mann (HMV)	2
27 Aug	HAVE I THE RIGHT Honeycombs (Pye)	2
10 Sep	YOU REALLY GOT ME Kinks (Pye)	2
24 Sep	I'M INTO SOMETHING GOOD Herman's Hermits (Columbia)	2
8 Oct	OH PRETTY WOMAN Roy Orbison (London)	2
22 Oct	(THERE'S) ALWAYS SOMETHING THERE TO REMIND ME Sandie Shaw (Pye)	3
12 Nov	OH PRETTY WOMAN Roy Orbison (London)	1
19 Nov	BABY LOVE Supremes (Stateside)	2
3 Dec	LITTLE RED ROOSTER Rolling Stones (Decca)	1
10 Dec	I FEEL FINE Beatles (Parlophone)	5

1965

14 Jan	YEH YEH Georgie Fame with the Blue Flames (Columbia)	2

28 Jan GO NOW Moody Blues (Decca) 1
4 Feb YOU'VE LOST THAT LOVIN' FEELIN' Righteous Brothers (London) 2
18 Feb TIRED OF WAITING FOR YOU Kinks (Pye) 1
25 Feb I'LL NEVER FIND ANOTHER YOU Seekers (Columbia) 2
11 Mar IT'S NOT UNUSUAL Tom Jones (Decca) 1
18 Mar THE LAST TIME Rolling Stones (Decca) 3
8 Apr CONCRETE AND CLAY Unit Four Plus Two (Decca) 1
15 Apr THE MINUTE YOU'RE GONE Cliff Richard (Columbia) 1
22 Apr TICKET TO RIDE Beatles (Parlophone) 3
13 May KING OF THE ROAD Roger Miller (Philips) 1
20 May WHERE ARE YOU NOW (MY LOVE) Jackie Trent (Pye) 1
27 May LONG LIVE LOVE Sandie Shaw (Pye) 3
17 Jun CRYING IN THE CHAPEL Elvis Presley (RCA) 1
24 Jun I'M ALIVE Hollies (Parlophone) 1
1 Jul CRYING IN THE CHAPEL Elvis Presley (RCA) 1
8 Jul I'M ALIVE Hollies (Parlophone) 2
22 Jul MR. TAMBOURINE MAN Byrds (CBS) 2
5 Aug HELP! Beatles (Parlophone) 3
26 Aug I GOT YOU BABE Sonny and Cher (Atlantic) 2
9 Sep (I CAN'T GET NO) SATISFACTION Rolling Stones (Decca) 2
23 Sep MAKE IT EASY ON YOURSELF Walker Brothers (Philips) 1
30 Sep TEARS Ken Dodd (Columbia) 5
4 Nov GET OFF OF MY CLOUD Rolling Stones (Decca) 3
25 Nov THE CARNIVAL IS OVER Seekers (Columbia) 3
16 Dec DAY TRIPPER/WE CAN WORK IT OUT Beatles (Parlophone) 5

1966

20 Jan KEEP ON RUNNING Spencer Davis Group (Fontana) 1
27 Jan MICHELLE Overlanders (Pye) 3
17 Feb THESE BOOTS ARE MADE FOR WALKIN' Nancy Sinatra (Reprise) 4
17 Mar THE SUN AIN'T GONNA SHINE ANYMORE Walker Brothers (Philips) 4
14 Apr SOMEBODY HELP ME Spencer Davis Group (Fontana) 2
28 Apr YOU DON'T HAVE TO SAY YOU LOVE ME Dusty Springfield (Philips) 1
5 May PRETTY FLAMINGO Manfred Mann (HMV) 3
26 May PAINT IT BLACK Rolling Stones (Decca) 1
2 Jun STRANGERS IN THE NIGHT Frank Sinatra (Reprise) 3
23 Jun PAPERBACK WRITER Beatles (Parlophone) 2
7 Jul SUNNY AFTERNOON Kinks (Pye) 2
21 Jul GET AWAY Georgie Fame with the Blue Flames (Columbia) 1
28 Jul OUT OF TIME Chris Farlowe and the Thunderbirds (Immediate) 1
4 Aug WITH A GIRL LIKE YOU Troggs (Fontana) 2
18 Aug YELLOW SUBMARINE/ELEANOR RIGBY Beatles (Parlophone) 4
15 Sep ALL OR NOTHING Small Faces (Decca) 1
22 Sep DISTANT DRUMS Jim Reeves (RCA) 5
27 Oct REACH OUT I'LL BE THERE Four Tops (Tamla Motown) 3
17 Nov GOOD VIBRATIONS Beach Boys (Capitol) 2
1 Dec GREEN GREEN GRASS OF HOME Tom Jones (Decca) 7

1967

19 Jan I'M A BELIEVER Monkees (RCA) 4
16 Feb THIS IS MY SONG Petula Clark (Pye) 2
2 Mar RELEASE ME Engelbert Humperdinck (Decca) 6
13 Apr SOMETHING STUPID Nancy Sinatra and Frank Sinatra (Reprise) 2
27 Apr PUPPET ON A STRING Sandie Shaw (Pye) 3
18 May SILENCE IS GOLDEN Tremeloes (CBS) 3
8 Jun A WHITER SHADE OF PALE Procol Harum (Deram) 6
19 Jul ALL YOU NEED IS LOVE Beatles (Parlophone) 3
9 Aug SAN FRANCISCO (BE SURE TO WEAR SOME FLOWERS IN YOUR HAIR) Scott McKenzie (CBS) 4
6 Sep THE LAST WALTZ Engelbert Humperdinck (Decca) 5
11 Oct MASSACHUSETTS Bee Gees (Polydor) 4
8 Nov BABY NOW THAT I'VE FOUND YOU Foundations (Pye) 2
22 Nov LET THE HEARTACHES BEGIN Long John Baldry (Pye) 2
6 Dec HELLO GOODBYE Beatles (Parlophone) 7

1968

24 Jan THE BALLAD OF BONNIE AND CLYDE Georgie Fame (CBS) 1
31 Jan EVERLASTING LOVE Love Affair (CBS) 2
14 Feb MIGHTY QUINN Manfred Mann (Fontana) 2
28 Feb CINDERELLA ROCKEFELLA Esther and Abi Ofarim (Philips) 3
20 Mar THE LEGEND OF XANADU Dave Dee, Dozy, Beaky, Mick and Tich (Fontana) 1
27 Mar LADY MADONNA Beatles (Parlophone) 2
10 Apr CONGRATULATIONS Cliff Richard (Columbia) 2
24 Apr WHAT A WONDERFUL WORLD/CABARET Louis Armstrong (HMV) 4
22 May YOUNG GIRL Union Gap featuring Gary Puckett (CBS) 4
19 Jun JUMPING JACK FLASH Rolling Stones (Decca) 2
3 Jul BABY COME BACK Equals (President) 3
24 Jul I PRETEND Des O'Connor (Columbia) 1
31 Jul MONY MONY Tommy James and the Shondells (Major Minor) 2
14 Aug FIRE Crazy World of Arthur Brown (Track) 1
21 Aug MONY MONY Tommy James and the Shondells (Major Minor) 1
28 Aug DO IT AGAIN Beach Boys (Capitol) 1
4 Sep I'VE GOTTA GET A MESSAGE TO YOU Bee Gees (Polydor) 1
11 Sep HEY JUDE Beatles (Apple) 2

25 Sep	THOSE WERE THE DAYS Mary Hopkin (Apple)	6
6 Nov	WITH A LITTLE HELP FROM MY FRIENDS Joe Cocker (Regal-Zonophone)	1
13 Nov	THE GOOD THE BAD AND THE UGLY Hugo Montenegro and his Orchestra and chorus (RCA)	4
11 Dec	LILY THE PINK Scaffold (Parlophone)	3

1969

1 Jan	OB-LA-DI OB-LA-DA Marmalade (CBS)	1
8 Jan	LILY THE PINK Scaffold (Parlophone)	1
15 Jan	OB-LA-DI OB-LA-DA Marmalade (CBS)	2
29 Jan	ALBATROSS Fleetwood Mac (Blue Horizon)	1
5 Feb	BLACKBERRY WAY Move (Regal-Zonophone)	1
12 Feb	(IF PARADISE IS) HALF AS NICE Amen Corner (Immediate)	2
26 Feb	WHERE DO YOU GO TO MY LOVELY Peter Sarstedt (United Artists)	4
26 Mar	I HEARD IT THROUGH THE GRAPEVINE Marvin Gaye (Tamla Motown)	3
16 Apr	THE ISRAELITES Desmond Dekker and the Aces (Pyramid)	1
23 Apr	GET BACK Beatles with Billy Preston (Apple)	6
4 Jun	DIZZY Tommy Roe (Stateside)	1
11 Jun	THE BALLAD OF JOHN AND YOKO Beatles (Apple)	3
2 Jul	SOMETHING IN THE AIR Thunderclap Newman (Track)	3
23 Jul	HONKY TONK WOMEN Rolling Stones (Decca)	5
30 Aug	IN THE YEAR 2525 (EXORDIUM AND TERMINUS) Zager and Evans (RCA)	3
20 Sep	BAD MOON RISING Creedence Clearwater Revival (Liberty)	3
11 Oct	JE T'AIME MOI NON PLUS Jane Birkin and Serge Gainsbourg (Major Minor)	1
18 Oct	I'LL NEVER FALL IN LOVE AGAIN Bobbie Gentry (Capitol)	1
25 Oct	SUGAR SUGAR Archies (RCA)	8
20 Dec	TWO LITTLE BOYS Rolf Harris (Columbia)	6

1970

31 Jan	LOVE GROWS (WHERE MY ROSEMARY GOES) Edison Lighthouse (Bell)	5
7 Mar	WAND'RIN' STAR Lee Marvin (Paramount)	3
28 Mar	BRIDGE OVER TROUBLED WATER Simon and Garfunkel (CBS)	3
18 Apr	ALL KINDS OF EVERYTHING Dana (Rex)	2
2 May	SPIRIT IN THE SKY Norman Greenbaum (Reprise)	2
16 May	BACK HOME England World Cup Squad (Pye)	3
6 Jun	YELLOW RIVER Christie (CBS)	1
13 Jun	IN THE SUMMERTIME Mungo Jerry (Dawn)	7
1 Aug	THE WONDER OF YOU Elvis Presley (RCA)	6
12 Sep	TEARS OF A CLOWN Smokey Robinson and the Miracles (Tamla Motown)	1
19 Sep	BAND OF GOLD Freda Payne (Invictus)	6
31 Oct	WOODSTOCK Matthews' Southern Comfort (Uni)	3
21 Nov	VOODOO CHILE Jimi Hendrix Experience (Track)	1
28 Nov	I HEAR YOU KNOCKIN' Dave Edmunds (MAM)	6

1971

9 Jan	GRANDAD Clive Dunn (Columbia)	3
30 Jan	MY SWEET LORD George Harrison (Apple)	5
6 Mar	BABY JUMP Mungo Jerry (Dawn)	2
20 Mar	HOT LOVE T. Rex (Fly)	6
1 May	DOUBLE BARREL Dave and Ansil Collins (Technique)	2
15 May	KNOCK THREE TIMES Dawn (Bell)	5
19 Jun	CHIRPY CHIRPY CHEEP CHEEP Middle of the Road (RCA)	5
24 Jul	GET IT ON T. Rex (Fly)	4
21 Aug	I'M STILL WAITING Diana Ross (Tamla Motown)	4
18 Sep	HEY GIRL DON'T BOTHER ME Tams (Probe)	3
9 Oct	MAGGIE MAY Rod Stewart (Mercury)	5
13 Nov	COZ I LUV YOU Slade (Polydor)	4
11 Dec	ERNIE (THE FASTEST MILKMAN IN THE WEST) Benny Hill (Columbia)	4

1972

8 Jan	I'D LIKE TO TEACH THE WORLD TO SING New Seekers (Polydor)	4
5 Feb	TELEGRAM SAM T. Rex (T. Rex)	2
19 Feb	SON OF MY FATHER Chicory Tip (CBS)	3
11 Mar	WITHOUT YOU Nilsson (RCA)	5
15 Apr	AMAZING GRACE Pipes and Drums and Military Band of the Royal Scots Dragoon Guards (RCA)	5
20 May	METAL GURU T. Rex (EMI)	4
17 Jun	VINCENT Don McLean (United Artists)	2
1 Jul	TAKE ME BAK 'OME Slade (Polydor)	1
8 Jul	PUPPY LOVE Donny Osmond (MGM)	5
12 Aug	SCHOOL'S OUT Alice Cooper (Warner Brothers)	3
2 Sep	YOU WEAR IT WELL Rod Stewart (Mercury)	1
9 Sep	MAMA WEER ALL CRAZEE NOW Slade (Polydor)	3
30 Sep	HOW CAN I BE SURE David Cassidy (Bell)	2
14 Oct	MOULDY OLD DOUGH Lieutenant Pigeon (Decca)	4
11 Nov	CLAIR Gilbert O'Sullivan (MAM)	2
25 Nov	MY DING-A-LING Chuck Berry (Chess)	4
23 Dec	LONG HAIRED LOVER FROM LIVERPOOL Little Jimmy Osmond (MGM)	5

1973

27 Jan	BLOCKBUSTER Sweet (RCA)	5
3 Mar	CUM ON FEEL THE NOIZE Slade (Polydor)	4
31 Mar	THE TWELFTH OF NEVER Donny Osmond (MGM)	1
7 Apr	GET DOWN Gilbert O'Sullivan (MAM)	2

21 Apr TIE A YELLOW RIBBON ROUND THE OLD OAK TREE Dawn featuring Tony Orlando (Bell) 4
19 May SEE MY BABY JIVE Wizzard (Harvest) 4
16 Jun CAN THE CAN Suzi Quatro (RAK) 1
23 Jun RUBBER BULLETS 10 cc (UK) 1
30 Jun SKWEEZE ME PLEEZE ME Slade (Polydor) 3
21 Jul WELCOME HOME Peters and Lee (Philips) 1
28 Jul I'M THE LEADER OF THE GANG (I AM) Gary Glitter (Bell) 4
25 Aug YOUNG LOVE Donny Osmond (MGM) 4
22 Sep ANGEL FINGERS Wizzard (Harvest) 1
29 Sep EYE LEVEL Simon Park Orchestra (Columbia) 4
27 Oct DAYDREAMER/THE PUPPY SONG David Cassidy (Bell) 3
17 Nov I LOVE YOU LOVE ME LOVE Gary Glitter (Bell) 4
15 Dec MERRY XMAS EVERYBODY Slade (Polydor) 5

1974

19 Jan YOU WON'T FIND ANOTHER FOOL LIKE ME New Seekers (Polydor) 1
26 Jan TIGER FEET Mud (Rak) 4
23 Feb DEVIL GATE DRIVE Suzi Quatro (Rak) 2
9 Mar JEALOUS MIND Alvin Stardust (Magnet) 1
16 Mar BILLY DON'T BE A HERO Paper Lace (Bus Stop) 3
6 Apr SEASONS IN THE SUN Terry Jacks (Bell) 4
4 May WATERLOO Abba (Epic) 2
18 May SUGAR BABY LOVE Rubettes (Polydor) 4
15 Jun THE STREAK Ray Stevens (Janus) 1
22 Jun ALWAYS YOURS Gary Glitter (Bell) 1
29 Jun SHE Charles Aznavour (Barclay) 4
27 Jul ROCK YOUR BABY George McCrae (Jayboy) 3
17 Aug WHEN WILL I SEE YOU AGAIN Three Degrees (Philadelphia International) 2
31 Aug LOVE ME FOR A REASON Osmonds (MGM) 3
21 Sep KUNG FU FIGHTING Carl Douglas (Pye) 3
12 Oct ANNIE'S SONG John Denver (RCA) 1
19 Oct SAD SWEET DREAMER Sweet Sensation (Pye) 1
26 Oct EVERYTHING I OWN Ken Boothe (Trojan) 3
16 Nov GONNA MAKE YOU A STAR David Essex (CBS) 3
7 Dec YOU'RE THE FIRST THE LAST MY EVERYTHING Barry White (20th Century) 2
21 Dec LONELY THIS CHRISTMAS Mud (Rak) 4

1975

18 Jan DOWN DOWN Status Quo (Vertigo) 1
25 Jan MS. GRACE Tymes (RCA) 1
1 Feb JANUARY Pilot (EMI) 3
22 Feb MAKE ME SMILE (COME UP AND SEE ME) Steve Harley and Cockney Rebel (EMI) 2
8 Mar IF Telly Savalas (MCA) 2
22 Mar BYE BYE BABY Bay City Rollers (Bell) 6
3 May OH BOY Mud (Rak) 2
17 May STAND BY YOUR MAN Tammy Wynette (Epic) 3
7 Jun WHISPERING GRASS Windsor Davies and Don Estelle (EMI) 3
28 Jun I'M NOT IN LOVE 10 cc (Mercury) 2
12 Jul TEARS ON MY PILLOW Johnny Nash (CBS) 1
19 Jul GIVE A LITTLE LOVE Bay City Rollers (Bell) 3
9 Aug BARBADOS Typically Tropical (Gull) 1
16 Aug I CAN'T GIVE YOU ANYTHING (BUT MY LOVE) Stylistics (Avco) 3
6 Sep SAILING Rod Stewart (Warner Brothers) 4
4 Oct HOLD ME CLOSE David Essex (CBS) 3
25 Oct I ONLY HAVE EYES FOR YOU Art Garfunkel (CBS) 2
8 Nov SPACE ODDITY David Bowie (RCA) 2
22 Nov D.I.V.O.R.C.E. Billy Connolly (Polydor) 1
29 Nov BOHEMIAN RHAPSODY Queen (EMI) 9

1976

31 Jan MAMMA MIA Abba (Epic) 2
14 Feb FOREVER AND EVER Slik (Bell) 1
21 Feb DECEMBER '63 (OH WHAT A NIGHT) Four Seasons (Warner Brothers) 2
6 Mar I LOVE TO LOVE (BUT MY BABY LOVES TO DANCE) Tina Charles (CBS) 3
27 Mar SAVE YOUR KISSES FOR ME Brotherhood of Man (Pye) 6
8 May FERNANDO Abba (Epic) 4
5 June NO CHARGE J. J. Barrie (Power Exchange) 1
12 Jun COMBINE HARVESTER (BRAND NEW KEY) Wurzels (EMI) 2
26 Jun YOU TO ME ARE EVERYTHING Real Thing (Pye International) 3
17 Jul THE ROUSSOS PHENOMENON (EP) Demis Roussos (Philips) 1
24 Jul DON'T GO BREAKING MY HEART Elton John and Kiki Dee (Rocket) 6
4 Sep DANCING QUEEN Abba (Epic) 6
16 Oct MISSISSIPPI Pussycat (Sonet) 4
13 Nov IF YOU LEAVE ME NOW Chicago (CBS) 3
4 Dec UNDER THE MOON OF LOVE Showaddywaddy (Bell) 3
25 Dec WHEN A CHILD IS BORN (SOLEADO) Johnny Mathis (CBS) 3

1977

15 Jan DON'T GIVE UP ON US David Soul (Private Stock) 4
12 Feb DON'T CRY FOR ME ARGENTINA Julie Covington (MCA) 1
19 Feb WHEN I NEED YOU Leo Sayer (Chrysalis) 3
12 Mar CHANSON D'AMOUR Manhattan Transfer (Atlantic) 3
2 Apr KNOWING ME KNOWING YOU Abba (Epic) 5
7 May FREE Deniece Williams (CBS) 2
21 May I DON'T WANT TO TALK ABOUT IT/FIRST CUT IS THE DEEPEST Rod Stewart (Riva) 4
18 Jun LUCILLE Kenny Rogers (United Artists) 1
25 Jun SHOW YOU THE WAY TO GO Jacksons (Epic) 1
2 Jul SO YOU WIN AGAIN Hot Chocolate (Rak) 3
23 Jul I FEEL LOVE Donna Summer (GTO) 4
20 Aug ANGELO Brotherhood of Man (Pye) 1

27 Aug FLOAT ON Floaters (ABC) 1
3 Sep WAY DOWN Elvis Presley (RCA) 5
8 Oct SILVER LADY David Soul (Private Stock) 3
29 Oct YES SIR I CAN BOOGIE Baccara (RCA) 1
5 Nov NAME OF THE GAME Abba (Epic) 4
3 Dec MULL OF KINTYRE/GIRLS' SCHOOL Wings (Capitol) 9

1978

4 Feb UP TOWN TOP RANKING Althia and Donna (Lightning) 1
11 Feb FIGARO Brotherhood of Man (Pye) 1
18 Feb TAKE A CHANCE ON ME Abba (Epic) 3
11 Mar WUTHERING HEIGHTS Kate Bush (EMI) 4
8 Apr MATCHSTALK MEN AND MATCHSTALK CATS AND DOGS Brian and Michael (Pye) 3
29 Apr NIGHT FEVER Bee Gees (RSO) 2
13 May RIVERS OF BABYLON Boney M. (Atlantic/Hansa) 5
17 Jun YOU'RE THE ONE THAT I WANT John Travolta and Olivia Newton-John (RSO) 9
19 Aug THREE TIMES A LADY Commodores (Motown) 5
23 Sep DREADLOCK HOLIDAY 10 cc (Mercury) 1
30 Sep SUMMER NIGHTS John Travolta and Olivia Newton-John (RSO) 7
18 Nov RAT TRAP Boomtown Rats (Ensign) 2
2 Dec DA YA THINK I'M SEXY Rod Stewart (Riva) 1
9 Dec MARY'S BOY CHILD – OH MY LORD Boney M. (Atlantic/Hansa) 4

1979

6 Jan Y.M.C.A. Village People (Mercury) 3
27 Jan HIT ME WITH YOUR RHYTHM STICK Ian & the Blockheads (Stiff) 1
3 Feb HEART OF GLASS Blondie (Chrysalis) 4
3 Mar TRAGEDY Bee Gees (RSO) 2
17 Mar I WILL SURVIVE Gloria Gaynor (Polydor) 4
14 Apr BRIGHT EYES Art Garfunkel (CBS) 6
26 May SUNDAY GIRL Blondie (Chrysalis) 3
16 Jun RING MY BELL Anita Ward (TK) 2
30 Jan ARE 'FRIENDS' ELECTRIC? Tubeway Army (Beggars Banquet) 4
28 Jul I DON'T LIKE MONDAYS Boomtown Rats (Ensign) 4
25 Aug WE DON'T TALK ANYMORE Cliff Richard (EMI) 4
22 Sep CARS Gary Numan (Beggars Banquet) 1
29 Sep MESSAGE IN A BOTTLE Police (A & M) 3
20 Oct VIDEO KILLED THE RADIO STAR Buggles (Island) 1
27 Oct ONE DAY AT A TIME Lena Martell (Pye) 3
17 Nov WHEN YOU'RE IN LOVE WITH A BEAUTIFUL WOMAN Dr Hook (Capitol) 3
8 Dec WALKING ON THE MOON Police (A & M) 1
15 Dec ANOTHER BRICK IN THE WALL (PART II) Pink Floyd (Harvest) 5

1980

19 Jan BRASS IN POCKET Pretenders (Real) 2
2 Feb THE SPECIAL AKA LIVE (EP) Specials (2 Tone) 2
16 Feb COWARD OF THE COUNTY Kenny Rogers (United Artists) 2
1 Mar ATOMIC Blondie (Chrysalis) 2
15 Mar TOGETHER WE ARE BEAUTIFUL Fern Kinney (WEA) 1
22 Mar GOING UNDERGROUND/DREAMS OF CHILDREN Jam (Polydor) 3
12 Apr WORKING MY WAY BACK TO YOU Detroit Spinners (Atlantic) 2
26 Apr CALL ME Blondie (Chrysalis) 1
3 May GENO Dexy's Midnight Runners (Parlophone) 2
17 May WHAT'S ANOTHER YEAR Johnny Logan (Epic) 2
31 May THEME FROM M*A*S*H (SUICIDE IS PAINLESS) Mash (CBS) 3
21 Jun CRYING Don McLean (EMI) 3
12 Jul XANADU Olivia Newton-John and Electric Light Orchestra (Jet) 2
26 Jul USE IT UP AND WEAR IT OUT Odyssey (RCA) 2
9 Aug THE WINNER TAKES IT ALL Abba (Epic) 2
23 Aug ASHES TO ASHES David Bowie (RCA) 2
6 Sep START Jam (Polydor) 1
13 Sep FEELS LIKE I'M IN LOVE Kelly Marie (Calibre) 2
27 Sep DON'T STAND SO CLOSE TO ME Police (A & M) 4
25 Oct WOMAN IN LOVE Barbra Streisand (CBS) 3
15 Nov THE TIDE IS HIGH Blondie (Chrysalis) 2
29 Nov SUPER TROUPER Abba (Epic) 3
20 Dec (JUST LIKE) STARTING OVER John Lennon (WEA/Geffen) 1
27 Dec THERE'S NO ONE QUITE LIKE GRANDMA St. Winifred's School Choir (MFP) 2

1981

10 Jan IMAGINE John Lennon (Parlophone) 4
7 Feb WOMAN John Lennon (Geffen) 2
21 Feb SHADDUP YOU FACE Joe Dolce (Epic) 3
14 Mar JEALOUS GUY Roxy Music (Polydor/EG) 2
28 Mar THIS OLE HOUSE Shakin' Stevens (Epic) 3
18 Apr MAKING YOUR MIND UP Bucks Fizz (RCA) 3
9 May STAND AND DELIVER Adam & The Ants (CBS) 5
13 Jun BEING WITH YOU Smokey Robinson (Motown) 2
27 Jun ONE DAY IN YOUR LIFE Michael Jackson (Motown) 2
11 Jul GHOST TOWN Specials (2 Tone) 3
1 Aug GREEN DOOR Shakin' Stevens (Epic) 4
29 Aug JAPANESE BOY Aneka (Hansa/Ariola) 1
5 Sep TAINTED LOVE Soft Cell (Some Bizzarre) 2
19 Sep PRINCE CHARMING Adam & The Ants (CBS) 4
17 Oct IT'S MY PARTY Dave Stewart with Barbara Gaskin (Stiff/Broken) 4
14 Nov EVERY LITTLE THING SHE DOES IS MAGIC Police (A & M) 1
21 Nov UNDER PRESSURE Queen and David Bowie (EMI) 2

5 Dec	BEGIN THE BEGUINE (VOLVER A EMPEZAR) Julio Iglesias (CBS)	1
12 Dec	DON'T YOU WANT ME Human League (Virgin)	5

1982

16 Jan	THE LAND OF MAKE BELIEVE Bucks Fizz (RCA)	2
30 Jan	OH JULIE Shakin' Stevens (Epic)	1
6 Feb	THE MODEL/COMPUTER LOVE Kraftwerk (EMI)	1
13 Feb	A TOWN CALLED MALICE/PRECIOUS Jam (Polydor)	3
6 Mar	THE LION SLEEPS TONIGHT Tight Fit (Jive)	3
27 Mar	SEVEN TEARS Goombay Dance Band (Epic)	3
17 Apr	MY CAMERA NEVER LIES Bucks Fizz (RCA)	1
24 Apr	EBONY AND IVORY Paul McCartney with Stevie Wonder (Parlophone)	3
15 May	A LITTLE PEACE Nicole (CBS)	2
29 May	HOUSE OF FUN Madness (Stiff)	2
12 Jun	GOODY TWO SHOES Adam Ant (CBS)	2
26 Jun	I'VE NEVER BEEN TO ME Charlene (Motown)	1
3 Jul	HAPPY TALK Captain Sensible (A & M)	2
17 Jul	FAME Irene Cara (RSO)	3
7 Aug	COME ON EILEEN Dexy's Midnight Runners and Emerald Express (Mercury/Phonogram)	4
4 Sep	EYE OF THE TIGER Survivor (Scotti Brothers)	4
2 Oct	PASS THE DUTCHIE Musical Youth (MCA)	3
23 Oct	DO YOU REALLY WANT TO HURT ME Culture Club (Virgin)	3
13 Nov	I DON'T WANNA DANCE Eddy Grant (Ice)	3
4 Dec	BEAT SURRENDER Jam (Polydor)	2
18 Dec	SAVE YOUR LOVE Renée and Renato (Hollywood)	2

MOST NUMBER ONE HITS

17 BEATLES; ELVIS PRESLEY; **10** CLIFF RICHARD; **9** ABBA; **8** ROLLING STONES; **6** SLADE; **5** BLONDIE, SHADOWS *(+ 7 with Cliff Richard)*, ROD STEWART; **4** BEE GEES, EVERLY BROTHERS, FRANK IFIELD, JAM, FRANKIE LAINE, GUY MITCHELL, POLICE, T REX; **3** ADAM & THE ANTS, BROTHERHOOD OF MAN, BUCKS FIZZ, LONNIE DONEGAN, GEORGIE FAME, GERRY & THE PACEMAKERS, GARY GLITTER, KINKS, JOHN LENNON, MANFRED MANN, MUD, ROY ORBISON, DONNY OSMOND, JOHNNIE RAY, SANDIE SHAW, SEARCHERS, SHAKIN' STEVENS, 10 CC.

Olivia Newton-John has had two number one hits with John Travolta and one with Electric Light Orchestra. Frank Sinatra has had two solo number ones and one with Nancy Sinatra. Art Garfunkel has had two solo number ones and one with Paul Simon. David Bowie has had two solo number ones and one with Queen.

MOST WEEKS AT NUMBER ONE

a) BY ARTIST

73 ELVIS PRESLEY
65 BEATLES *(Paul McCartney 9 more with Wings and 3 more with Stevie Wonder. John Lennon 7 more solo and George Harrison 5 more solo)*
35 CLIFF RICHARD
32 FRANKIE LAINE *(one week top equal)*
31 ABBA
20 SLADE
19 EVERLY BROTHERS *(one week top equal)*
18 ROLLING STONES
17 FRANK IFIELD
16 SHADOWS *(plus 28 wks backing Cliff Richard)*
T REX
JOHN TRAVOLTA & OLIVIA NEWTON-JOHN *(Olivia Newton-John 2 more with Electric Light Orchestra)*
15 DORIS DAY
ROD STEWART
14 GUY MITCHELL *(one week top equal)*
13 EDDIE CALVERT
PERRY COMO
12 BLONDIE
CONNIE FRANCIS
DAVID WHITFIELD *(one week top equal)*
11 ADAM & THE ANTS
LONNIE DONEGAN
TENNESSEE ERNIE FORD
GERRY & THE PACEMAKERS
ENGELBERT HUMPERDINCK
JOHNNIE RAY
SLIM WHITMAN
10 MUD
DONNY OSMOND *(plus 3 weeks with Osmonds)*

Queen have been top for 9 weeks, plus 2 weeks with David Bowie. Art Garfunkel has been at number one for 8 weeks, plus 3 weeks with Simon & Garfunkel. Mantovani has been top for 1 week, plus 10 weeks backing David Whitfield.

b) BY ARTIST IN ONE CALENDAR YEAR

27 FRANKIE LAINE **1953** *(one week top equal)*
18 ELVIS PRESLEY **1961**
16 BEATLES **1963**
JOHN TRAVOLTA & OLIVIA NEWTON-JOHN **1978**
15 ELVIS PRESLEY **1962**
12 CONNIE FRANCIS **1958**
FRANK IFIELD **1962**
BEATLES **1964**
ABBA **1976**

c) BY ONE DISC: IN TOTAL

18 I BELIEVE Frankie Laine (1953)
11 ROSE MARIE Slim Whitman (1955)
10 CARA MIA David Whitfield (1954)
9 HERE IN MY HEART Al Martino (1952/3)
OH MEIN PAPA Eddie Calvert (1954)
SECRET LOVE Doris Dey (1954)
DIANA Paul Anka (1957)

BOHEMIAN RHAPSODY Queen (1975/6)
MULL OF KINTYRE/GIRLS' SCHOOL Wings (1977/8)
YOU'RE THE ONE THAT I WANT John Travolta & Olivia Newton-John (1978)

BY ONE DISC: CONSECUTIVE WEEKS

11 ROSE MARIE Slim Whitman (1955)
10 CARA MIA David Whitfield (1954)
9 HERE IN MY HEART Al Martino (1952/3)
I BELIEVE Frankie Laine (1953)
OH MEIN PAPA Eddie Calvert (1954)
DIANA Paul Anka (1957)
BOHEMIAN RHAPSODY Queen (1975/6)
MULL OF KINTYRE/GIRLS' SCHOOL Wings (1977/8)
YOU'RE THE ONE THAT I WANT John Travolta & Olivia Newton-John (1978)
8 ANSWER ME Frankie Laine (1953/4)*
SECRET LOVE Doris Day (1954)
MAGIC MOMENTS Perry Como (1958)
IT'S NOW OR NEVER Elvis Presley (1960)
WONDERFUL LAND Shadows (1962)
SUGAR SUGAR Archies (1969)

* One week top equal

To the end of 1982, there had been 76 number ones since the last one to stay on top for at least 6 weeks ('Bright Eyes' by Art Garfunkel). This equals the previous longest gap between number ones which lasted 6 weeks on top, from 'From Me To You' which lasted at number one for 7 weeks in mid-1963, to 'Green Green Grass Of Home', which also held the top for 7 weeks at Christmas 1966.

MOST CONSECUTIVE NUMBER ONES

11 in a row: BEATLES
(FROM ME TO YOU through to YELLOW SUBMARINE/ELEANOR RIGBY, 1963 to 1966)

6 in a row: BEATLES
(ALL YOU NEED IS LOVE through to BALLAD OF JOHN AND YOKO, 1967 to 1969)

5 in a row: ELVIS PRESLEY
(HIS LATEST FLAME through to RETURN TO SENDER 1961 to 1962)

5 in a row: ROLLING STONES
(IT'S ALL OVER NOW through to GET OFF OF MY CLOUD, 1964 to 1965)

4 in a row: ELVIS PRESLEY
(IT'S NOW OR NEVER through to SURRENDER, 1960 to 1961). The first number one hat-trick.

4 in a row: T REX
(HOT LOVE through to METAL GURU, 1971 to 1972)

3 in a row: FRANK IFIELD
(I REMEMBER YOU, LOVESICK BLUES and WAYWARD WIND, 1962 to 1963). The first number one hat-trick by a British artist.

3 in a row: GERRY AND THE PACEMAKERS
(HOW DO YOU DO IT, I LIKE IT and YOU'LL NEVER WALK ALONE, 1963). The first and only instance of an act hitting number one with each of their first 3 releases

3 in a row: ABBA
(MAMMA MIA, FERNANDO and DANCING QUEEN, 1975 to 1976)

3 in a row: ABBA
(KNOWING ME KNOWING YOU, NAME OF THE GAME, TAKE A CHANCE ON ME, 1977 to 1978)

3 in a row: POLICE
(MESSAGE IN A BOTTLE, WALKING ON THE MOON, and DON'T STAND SO CLOSE TO ME, 1979 to 1980). The only instance of the third record of the hat-trick coming on to the chart at number one.

POLICE Three consecutive number ones were also their best-selling singles

3 in a row: BLONDIE
(ATOMIC, CALL ME, and THE TIDE IS HIGH, 1980)

3 in a row: JOHN LENNON
(IMAGINE, (JUST LIKE) STARTING OVER and WOMAN, 1980 and 1981). Both the fastest and the slowest hat-trick, depending whether it started when IMAGINE first entered the chart in November 1975, or when (JUST LIKE) STARTING OVER came in late in 1980.

Successive releases for the purposes of this table are successive official single releases. The Beatles' two runs of number ones were each interrupted by irregular releases. An old single with Tony Sheridan reached number 29 in the midst of their 11 number ones, and their double EP 'Magical Mystery Tour' made number two while 'Hello Goodbye' was becoming the second of their six chart-toppers on the trot. An LP track, 'Jeepster', and an old recording 'Debora/One Inch Rock', were released during T. Rex's run of number ones, while the group were changing labels. An EP by Elvis, 'Follow That Dream', pottered about the lower reaches of the charts during Elvis' run of five consecutive number ones. During Police's hat-trick, one single on another label, one old single re-issued and a six-pack of singles hit the chart in an attempt to distract the compilers of this table. John Lennon's 'Imagine' was the first of the three singles of his hat-trick (his last single for 5 years), but the second of the three to reach the top.

Left **THE BEATLES** 11 consecutive number ones from 1963 to 1966. Then 6 between 1967 and 1969 followed by a run of 3 from John Lennon as a solo artist posthumously in 1980 and 1981

Below **JOHNNY MATHIS** The slowest number one

SLOWEST NUMBER ONE (ARTIST)

If an artist is going to have a number one hit, it usually happens within a year or two of the artist's first chart hit. About half of all the 328 acts to have topped the charts did so with their first hit. The acts listed below are the only ones who waited more than ten years after their chart debut to chalk up their first number one hit.

18 years 216 days JOHNNY MATHIS (23 May 1958 to 25 Dec 1976)
15 years 164 days CHUCK BERRY (21 Jun 1957 to 25 Nov 1972)
15 years 127 days LOUIS ARMSTRONG (19 Dec 1952 to 24 Apr 1968)
14 years 279 days BARBRA STREISAND (20 Jan 1966 to 25 Oct 1980)
13 years 140 days FOUR SEASONS (4 Oct 1962 to 21 Feb 1976)
12 years 260 days PINK FLOYD (30 Mar 1967 to 15 Dec 1979)
11 years 183 days TYMES (25 Jul 1963 to 25 Jan 1975)
11 years 164 days JOHN LENNON (9 Jul 1969 to 20 Dec 1980)
10 years 298 days BENNY HILL (16 Feb 1961 to 11 Dec 1971)

It is interesting (slightly) to note that only John Lennon of these acts has had more than one number one hit and that four of the nine acts had the Christmas number one of their year. Chuck Berry missed this distinction by only 2 days, being displaced on 23 Dec 1972 by Little Jimmy Osmond – who was not born when Berry's first hit entered the British charts.

SLOWEST NUMBER ONE HIT: DISC

Only five records have taken longer than 200 days to hit the top after their first appearance on the chart.

6 years 63 days	Space Oddity by David Bowie (6 Sep 1969 to 8 Nov 1975)
5 years 70 days	Imagine by John Lennon (1 Nov 1975 to 10 Jan 1981)
322 days	Rock Around The Clock by Bill Haley (7 Jan 1955 to 25 Nov 1955)
307 days	Eye Level by Simon Park Orchestra (25 Nov 1972 to 29 Sep 1973)
210 days	The Model/Computer Love by Kraftwerk (11 Jul 1981 to 6 Feb 1982)

FASTEST NUMBER ONE HIT

The period of time between an act's first appearance on the chart and its first number one.

0 days	Al Martino (14 Nov 1952)*
7 days	Edison Lighthouse (24 to 31 Jan 1970)
	Mungo Jerry (6 to 13 Jun 1970)
	Dave Edmunds (21 to 28 Nov 1970)
	George Harrison (23 to 30 Jan 1971)
	Queen and David Bowie (14 to 21 Nov 1981)
	Nicole (8 to 15 May 1982)
	Captain Sensible (26 Jun to 3 Jul 1982)
	Musical Youth (25 Sep to 3 Oct 1982)
14 days	22 different acts

* *The first chart of all.*

GAP BETWEEN NUMBER ONE HITS

Of all the acts who have had two or more number one hits, only four acts have suffered through a gap of more than 7 years between consecutive number ones. The Beatles crammed all 17 of their chart toppers into a period of 6 years and 54 days.

11 years 239 days	Frank Sinatra (7 Oct 1954 to 2 Jun 1966)
11 years 124 days	Cliff Richard (23 Apr 1968 to 25 Aug 1979)
9 years 231 days	Bee Gees (10 Sep 1968 to 29 Apr 1978)
7 years 357 days	Don McLean (30 Jun 1972 to 21 Jun 1980)

Right **FRANK SINATRA** 11 years 239 days between number ones

STRAIGHT IN AT NUMBER ONE

Only fourteen records have come straight in to the chart at number one.

14 Nov 52	**HERE IN MY HEART** Al Martino
24 Jan 58	**JAILHOUSE ROCK** Elvis Presley
3 Nov 60	**IT'S NOW OR NEVER** Elvis Presley
11 Jan 62	**THE YOUNG ONES** Cliff Richard & The Shadows
23 Apr 69	**GET BACK** The Beatles with Billy Preston
3 Mar 73	**CUM ON FEEL THE NOIZE** Slade
30 Jun 73	**SKWEEZE ME PLEEZE ME** Slade
17 Nov 73	**I LOVE YOU LOVE ME LOVE** Gary Glitter
15 Dec 73	**MERRY XMAS EVERYBODY** Slade
22 Mar 80	**GOING UNDERGROUND/DREAMS OF CHILDREN** Jam
27 Sep 80	**DON'T STAND SO CLOSE TO ME** Police
9 May 81	**STAND AND DELIVER** Adam & The Ants
13 Feb 82	**A TOWN CALLED MALICE/PRECIOUS** Jam
4 Dec 82	**BEAT SURRENDER** Jam

Slade are the only act to enter the chart at number one with consecutive releases. Jam, Adam and the Ants and Al Martino (in the first chart of all) went straight in at number one with their first number one hit. Jam's BEAT SURRENDER, which remained on top for two weeks, is the only one of the fourteen which did not last at least three weeks at number one.

BIGGEST JUMP TO NUMBER ONE

Apart from the records which hit number one in their first week on the chart, there have been 26 discs that have jumped from outside the top ten straight in to the top spot, as follows:

33 to 1 HAPPY TALK Captain Sensible 3 Jul 82
27 to 1 SURRENDER Elvis Presley 27 May 61
26 to 1 PASS THE DUTCHIE Musical Youth 2 Oct 82
22 to 1 GREEN DOOR Shakin' Stevens 1 Aug 81
21 to 1 HEY JUDE Beatles 11 Sep 68
(JUST LIKE) STARTING OVER John Lennon 20 Dec 80
19 to 1 ARE YOU LONESOME TONIGHT Elvis Presley 21 Jan 61
HALF AS NICE Amen Corner 12 Feb 69
LOVE ME FOR A REASON Osmonds 31 Aug 74
17 to 1 GET OFF OF MY CLOUD Rolling Stones 4 Nov 65
16 to 1 I HEAR YOU KNOCKING Dave Edmunds 28 Nov 70
CHIRPY CHIRPY CHEEP CHEEP Middle Of The Road 19 Jun 71
YOUNG LOVE Donny Osmond 25 Aug 73
DANCING QUEEN Abba 4 Sep 76
15 to 1 I DON'T LIKE MONDAYS Boomtown Rats 28 Jul 79
THE SPECIAL AKA LIVE EP Specials 2 Feb 80
14 to 1 EYE LEVEL Simon Park Orchestra 29 Sep 73
13 to 1 IN THE SUMMERTIME Mungo Jerry 13 Jun 70
12 to 1 LOVE GROWS Edison Lighthouse 31 Jan 70
11 to 1 (THERE'S) ALWAYS SOMETHING THERE TO REMIND ME Sandie Shaw 22 Oct 64
TICKET TO RIDE Beatles 22 Apr 65
MICHELLE Overlanders 27 Jan 66
LADY MADONNA Beatles 20 Mar 68
SUGAR SUGAR Archies 25 Oct 69
SHE Charles Aznavour 29 Jun 74
SUMMER NIGHTS John Travolta & Olivia Newton-John 30 Sep 78

The biggest jump within the chart is a leap of 55 places, from 62 to 7 on 26 April 1980 by Paul McCartney's aptly-titled 'Coming Up'. It never reached number one, peaking at number two. The lowest initial chart entry by a record that eventually reached number one is 73, which is the position at which Charlene's 'I've Never Been To Me' entered the chart on 15 May 1982.

FIRST TWO HITS AT NUMBER ONE

Almost half the acts who have hit the top did so with their first chart hit. Only ten acts have started off with two number ones.

EDDIE CALVERT *(his number one hits were consecutive chart entries but not consecutive releases)*, **ADAM FAITH**, **TENNESSEE ERNIE FORD** *(not consecutive releases)*, **ART GARFUNKEL** *(not consecutive releases)*, **GERRY & THE PACEMAKERS**, **MUNGO JERRY**, **GARY NUMAN/TUBEWAY ARMY**, **STARGAZERS** *(not consecutive releases)*, **ROD STEWART**, **JOHN TRAVOLTA AND OLIVIA NEWTON-JOHN.**

Of these ten acts, only **GERRY & THE PACEMAKERS**, **MUNGO JERRY** and **JOHN TRAVOLTA AND OLIVIA NEWTON-JOHN** hit the top with their first two *releases*.

FIRST THREE HITS AT NUMBER ONE

Only **Gerry and the Pacemakers** have achieved this feat. These were the group's first three releases, and they never had another number one hit.

THE ONE HIT WONDERS

Qualification: One number one hit, and nothing else – ever.

1954 KITTY KALLEN **Little Things Mean A Lot**
1956 DREAMWEAVERS **It's Almost Tomorrow**
1958 KALIN TWINS **When**
1959 JERRY KELLER **Here Comes Summer**
1960 RICKY VALANCE **Tell Laura I Love Her**
1962 B BUMBLE & THE STINGERS **Nut Rocker**
1966 OVERLANDERS **Michelle**
1967 NANCY SINATRA & FRANK SINATRA **Somethin' Stupid**
1968 CRAZY WORLD OF ARTHUR BROWN **Fire**
1969 ZAGER AND EVANS **In The Year 2525**
1969 JANE BIRKIN & SERGE GAINSBOURG **Je T'Aime . . . Moi Non Plus**
1969 ARCHIES **Sugar Sugar**
1970 LEE MARVIN **Wand'rin' Star**
1970 NORMAN GREENBAUM **Spirit In The Sky**
1970 MATTHEWS SOUTHERN COMFORT **Woodstock**
1971 CLIVE DUNN **Grandad**
1973 SIMON PARK ORCHESTRA **Eye Level**
1974 JOHN DENVER **Annie's Song**
1975 TYPICALLY TROPICAL **Barbados**
1976 J J BARRIE **No Charge**
1976 ELTON JOHN & KIKI DEE **Don't Go Breaking My Heart**
1977 FLOATERS **Float On**
1978 ALTHIA & DONNA **Up Town Top Ranking**
1978 BRIAN & MICHAEL **Matchstalk Men And Matchstalk Cats And Dogs**
1979 ANITA WARD **Ring My Bell**
1979 LENA MARTELL **One Day At A Time**
1980 FERN KINNEY **Together We Are Beautiful**
1980 JOHNNY LOGAN **What's Another Year**
1980 MASH **Theme From 'M*A*S*H*'**

Top **JOHN DENVER** with Muppets and *below* 'Grandad' **CLIVE DUNN** with parrot. One entry into the chart each and both with number one singles *BBC*

1980 OLIVIA NEWTON-JOHN & ELECTRIC LIGHT ORCHESTRA **Xanadu**
1980 ST WINIFRED'S SCHOOL CHOIR **There's No One Quite Like Grandma**
1981 JOE DOLCE **Shaddup You Face**
1981 DAVE STEWART WITH BARBARA GASKIN **It's My Party**
1981 QUEEN AND DAVID BOWIE **Under Pressure**
1982 PAUL McCARTNEY WITH STEVIE WONDER **Ebony And Ivory**
1982 CHARLENE **I've Never Been To Me**
1982 SURVIVOR **Eye Of The Tiger**
1982 RENEE AND RENATO **Save Your Love**

Of these performers, David Bowie, Kiki Dee, Electric Light Orchestra, Elton John, Paul McCartney, Olivia Newton-John, Queen, Frank Sinatra, Nancy Sinatra and Stevie Wonder have all had hits as solo acts. John Denver has also had a hit with Placido Domingo and Dave Stewart has had a hit with Colin Blunstone. This means that seven of the 38 one hit wonders have appeared on the charts in another guise.

The least successful of all the one hit wonders is Johnny Logan, whose Eurovision Song Contest winning song stayed on the charts for only 8 weeks, two of which were spent at number one. The longest stay at number one by any one hit wonder is 8 weeks by the Archies. The longest stay in the chart by any one hit wonder is 34 weeks by Jane Birkin and Serge Gainsbourg.

In recent years, the only acts to remove themselves from the one hit wonder list after more than a year as a member of this exclusive club are Art Garfunkel and the England World Cup Squad.

A fuller list of number one hit facts and feats is included in the *Guinness Book Of 500 Number One Hits* (Guinness Superlatives, £5.95).

LAST HIT AT NUMBER ONE

It is not easy to hit number one, but chart history shows that once an act has scored its first number one it is far more likely to hit the top again than to have no more chart hits at all. Disappearing without trace, chart-wise, after a number one hit is comparatively rare, and apart from the one hit wonders, listed separately, only eight acts have failed to follow up a number one.

CHARLES AZNAVOUR, ROLF HARRIS, BENNY HILL, TOMMY JAMES & THE SHONDELLS, SPECIALS, KAY STARR, TAMS, JOHN TRAVOLTA AND OLIVIA NEWTON-JOHN.

To add to their long list of original chart achievements, John Travolta and Olivia Newton-John share with Kay Starr the distinction of being the only acts to hit number one with both their first and their last chart hits.

THE 'UNSUCCESSFUL' NUMBER TWO HITS

No record that climbs to number two can really be described as unsuccessful, but what follows is a list of the records that climbed to number two, but failed to climb that final all-important rung of the ladder to the top. There have been 377 of these 'unsuccessful' number twos to the end of 1982, and we list them in chronological order. Obviously there are time gaps in the list, as records that occupied the number two position on their way up to, or down from number one are not included.

1952

21 Nov	FEET UP Guy Mitchell	1

1953

1 May	PRETTY LITTLE BLACK EYED SUSIE Guy Mitchell	1
8 May	PRETEND Nat 'King' Cole	4
5 Jun	LIMELIGHT Frank Chacksfield Orch	2
19 Jun	PRETEND Nat 'King' Cole	1
3 Jul	LIMELIGHT Frank Chacksfield Orch	3
31 Jul	LIMELIGHT Frank Chacksfield Orch	2
28 Aug	LIMELIGHT Frank Chacksfield Orch	1
2 Oct	WHERE THE WIND BLOWS Frankie Laine	1
4 Dec	SWEDISH RHAPSODY Mantovani	1
11 Dec	POPPA PICCOLINO Diana Decker	1

1954

15 Jan	LET'S HAVE A PARTY Winifred Atwell	1
22 Jan	BLOWING WILD Frankie Laine	3
12 Feb	CLOUD LUCKY SEVEN Guy Mitchell	1
19 Feb	THAT'S AMORE Dean Martin	1
26 Feb	BLOWING WILD Frankie Laine	1
19 Mar	THE HAPPY WANDERER Obernkirchen Choir	5
1 Oct	SMILE Nat 'King' Cole	1
15 Oct	SMILE Nat 'King' Cole	2
3 Dec	SANTO NATALE David Whitfield	5

1955

8 Jul	UNCHAINED MELODY Al Hibbler	2
29 Jul	UNCHAINED MELODY Al Hibbler	2
5 Aug	COOL WATER Frankie Laine	3
26 Aug	LEARNIN' THE BLUES Frank Sinatra	5
30 Sep	COOL WATER Frankie Laine	1
14 Oct	COOL WATER Frankie Laine	1
21 Oct	BLUE STAR Cyril Stapleton	1
28 Oct	YELLOW ROSE OF TEXAS Mitch Miller	1
25 Nov	LOVE IS A MANY SPLENDOURED THING Four Aces	2
30 Dec	MEET ME ON THE CORNER Max Bygraves	1

1956

20 Jan	BALLAD OF DAVY CROCKETT Bill Hayes	3
10 Feb	THE TENDER TRAP Frank Sinatra	1
24 Feb	ZAMBESI Lou Busch	4
25 May	A TEAR FELL Teresa Brewer	1
1 Jun	LOST JOHN/STEWBALL Lonnie Donegan	1
15 Jun	LOST JOHN/STEWBALL Lonnie Donegan	1
22 Jun	HEARTBREAK HOTEL Elvis Presley	2
6 Jul	LOST JOHN/STEWBALL Lonnie Donegan	1
13 Jul	ALL STAR HIT PARADE Various Artists	1
10 Aug	WALK HAND IN HAND Tony Martin	1
26 Oct	HOUND DOG Elvis Presley	3
7 Dec	GREEN DOOR Frankie Vaughan	3

1957

8 Mar	DON'T FORBID ME Pat Boone	5
12 Apr	BANANA BOAT SONG Harry Belafonte	1
26 Apr	BANANA BOAT SONG Harry Belafonte	2
14 June	WHEN I FALL IN LOVE Nat 'King' Cole	1
2 Aug	WE WILL MAKE LOVE Russ Hamilton	1
16 Aug	LOVE LETTERS IN THE SAND Pat Boone	4
13 Sep	LAST TRAIN TO SAN FERNANDO Johnny Duncan	1
20 Sep	LOVE LETTERS IN THE SAND Pat Boone	2
4 Oct	LAST TRAIN TO SAN FERNANDO Johnny Duncan	1
11 Oct	LOVE LETTERS IN THE SAND Pat Boone	1
25 Oct	PARTY Elvis Presley	1
1 Nov	TAMMY Debbie Reynolds	1
8 Nov	PARTY Elvis Presley	3
29 Nov	BE MY GIRL Jim Dale	2
13 Dec	WAKE UP LITTLE SUSIE Everly Brothers	1
20 Dec	MA HE'S MAKING EYES AT ME Johnny Otis Show	2

1958

3 Jan	WAKE UP LITTLE SUSIE Everly Brothers	1
10 Jan	MA HE'S MAKING EYES AT ME Johnny Otis Show	3
28 Mar	DON'T Elvis Presley	1
16 May	A WONDERFUL TIME UP THERE Pat Boone	1
23 May	TOM HARK Elias & his Zig Zag Jive Flutes	4
30 May	LOLLIPOP Mudlarks	1
18 Jul	BIG MAN Four Preps	2
1 Aug	HARD HEADED WOMAN Elvis Presley	2
5 Sep	RETURN TO ME Dean Martin	1
26 Sep	VOLARE Dean Martin	3
10 Oct	KING CREOLE Elvis Presley	1

24 Oct MOVE IT Cliff Richard 1
24 Oct COME PRIMA Marino Marini 3
14 Nov BIRD DOG Everly Brothers 2

1959

23 Jan BABY FACE Little Richard 1
30 Jan TO KNOW HIM IS TO LOVE HIM Teddy Bears 2
10 Jul A TEENAGER IN LOVE Marty Wilde 2
24 Jul BATTLE OF NEW ORLEANS Lonnie Donegan 1
14 Aug BATTLE OF NEW ORLEANS Lonnie Donegan 1
23 Oct 'TIL I KISSED YOU Everly Brothers 1

1960

5 Feb VOICE IN THE WILDERNESS Cliff Richard 3
24 Mar THEME FROM 'A SUMMER PLACE' Percy Faith Orchestra 1
14 Apr FALL IN LOVE WITH YOU Cliff Richard 1
19 May SOMEONE ELSE'S BABY Adam Faith 1
26 May CRADLE OF LOVE Johnny Preston 3
23 Jun MAMA/ROBOT MAN Connie Francis 1
8 Sep BECAUSE THEY'RE YOUNG Duane Eddy 1
15 Sep A MESS OF BLUES Elvis Presley 2
27 Oct AS LONG AS HE NEEDS ME Shirley Bassey 5
1 Dec SAVE THE LAST DANCE FOR ME Drifters 3

1961

5 Jan SAVE THE LAST DANCE FOR ME Drifters 1
2 Feb PEPE Duane Eddy 1
9 Mar ARE YOU SURE Allisons 2
30 Mar ARE YOU SURE Allisons 4
27 Apr LAZY RIVER Bobby Darin 1
6 Jul HELLO MARY LOU/TRAVELLIN' MAN Ricky Nelson 2
5 Oct JEALOUSY Billy Fury 2
26 Oct WILD WIND John Leyton 2
23 Nov BIG BAD JOHN Jimmy Dean 1

1962

4 Jan MIDNIGHT IN MOSCOW Kenny Ball's Jazzmen 1
11 Jan STRANGER ON THE SHORE Acker Bilk 3
1 Feb LET'S TWIST AGAIN Chubby Checker 2
22 Mar TELL ME WHAT HE SAID Helen Shapiro 3
12 Apr DREAM BABY Roy Orbison 2
26 Apr HEY! BABY Bruce Channel 1
3 May HEY LITTLE GIRL Del Shannon 1
31 May I'M LOOKING OUT THE WINDOW/DO YOU WANNA DANCE? Cliff Richard 3
28 Jun A PICTURE OF YOU Joe Brown 2
9 Aug SPEEDY GONZALES Pat Boone 4
6 Sep THINGS Bobby Darin 1
27 Sep IT'LL BE ME Cliff Richard 1
11 Oct THE LOCO-MOTION Little Eva 3
1 Nov LET'S DANCE Chris Montez 4
29 Nov SWISS MAID Del Shannon 1

1963

21 Feb PLEASE PLEASE ME Beatles 2
14 Mar PLEASE PLEASE ME Beatles 1
11 Apr FROM A JACK TO A KING Ned Miller 2
16 May CAN'T GET USED TO LOSING YOU Andy Williams 1
23 May SCARLETT O'HARA Jet Harris & Tony Meehan 1
30 May DO YOU WANT TO KNOW A SECRET? Billy J. Kramer & the Dakotas 2
27 Jun ATLANTIS Shadows 2
29 Aug I'M TELLING YOU NOW Freddie & The Dreamers 2
12 Sep IT'S ALL IN THE GAME Cliff Richard 3
10 Oct THEN HE KISSED ME Crystals 2
14 Nov SUGAR AND SPICE Searchers 1
5 Dec DON'T TALK TO HIM Cliff Richard 1

1964

23 Jan HIPPY HIPPY SHAKE Swinging Blue Jeans 1
6 Feb I'M THE ONE Gerry & the Pacemakers 2
5 Mar BITS AND PIECES Dave Clark Five 3
26 Mar JUST ONE LOOK Hollies 1
7 May I BELIEVE Bachelors 1
21 May MY BOY LOLLIPOP Millie 1
25 Jun SOMEONE, SOMEONE Brian Poole & the Tremeloes 2
24 Sep RAG DOLL Four Seasons 2
19 Nov ALL DAY AND ALL OF THE NIGHT Kinks 2
3 Dec I'M GONNA BE STRONG Gene Pitney 2
17 Dec DOWNTOWN Petula Clark 3

1965

28 Jan YOU'VE LOST THAT LOVIN' FEELING Cilla Black 1
25 Feb THE GAME OF LOVE Wayne Fontana & the Mindbenders 1
22 Apr HERE COMES THE NIGHT Them 1
20 May TRUE LOVE WAYS Peter & Gordon 1
17 Jun THE PRICE OF LOVE Everly Brothers 1
15 Jul HEART FULL OF SOUL Yardbirds 3
12 Aug WE'VE GOTTA GET OUT OF THIS PLACE Animals 1
19 Aug YOU'VE GOT YOUR TROUBLES Fortunes 1
7 Oct IF YOU GOTTA GO, GO NOW Manfred Mann 1
14 Oct ALMOST THERE Andy Williams 3
25 Nov MY GENERATION Who 2
23 Dec WIND ME UP (LET ME GO) Cliff Richard 3

1966

10 Feb YOU WERE ON MY MIND Crispian St Peters 1

17 Feb	NINETEENTH NERVOUS BREAKDOWN Rolling Stones	3
10 Mar	GROOVY KIND OF LOVE Mindbenders	1
17 Mar	I CAN'T LET GO Hollies	3
5 May	DAYDREAM Lovin' Spoonful	2
19 May	SLOOP JOHN B Beach Boys	1
26 May	WILD THING Troggs	1
14 Jul	NOBODY NEEDS YOUR LOVE Gene Pitney	1
28 Jul	BLACK IS BLACK Los Bravos	1
25 Aug	GOD ONLY KNOWS Beach Boys	2
29 Sep	I'M A BOY Who	1
6 Oct	BEND IT Dave Dee, Dozy, Beaky, Mick and Tich	2
27 Oct	I CAN'T CONTROL MYSELF Troggs	1
3 Nov	STOP STOP STOP Hollies	2
17 Nov	SEMI-DETACHED SUBURBAN MR JAMES Manfred Mann	1
24 Nov	GIMME SOME LOVING Spencer Davis Group	1
15 Dec	WHAT WOULD I BE Val Doonican	1
22 Dec	MORNINGTOWN RIDE Seekers	4

1967

26 Jan	NIGHT OF FEAR Move	1
2 Feb	MATTHEW AND SON Cat Stevens	2
2 Mar	PENNY LANE/STRAWBERRY FIELDS FOREVER Beatles	3
23 Mar	EDELWEISS Vince Hill	1
30 Mar	THIS IS MY SONG Harry Secombe	1
18 May	DEDICATED TO THE ONE I LOVE Mamas & Papas	1
25 May	WATERLOO SUNSET Kinks	2
15 Jun	THERE GOES MY EVERYTHING Engelbert Humperdinck	4
26 Jul	ALTERNATE TITLE Monkees	1
2 Aug	IT MUST BE HIM Vikki Carr	1
30 Aug	I'LL NEVER FALL IN LOVE AGAIN Tom Jones	4
27 Sep	EXCERPT FROM A TEENAGE OPERA Keith West	2
11 Oct	FLOWERS IN THE RAIN Move	2
25 Oct	HOLE IN MY SHOE Traffic	1
29 Nov	EVERYBODY KNOWS Dave Clark Five	2
20 Dec	EVERYBODY KNOWS Dave Clark Five	1
27 Dec	I'M COMING HOME Tom Jones	1

1968

3 Jan	MAGICAL MYSTERY TOUR EP Beatles	3
27 Mar	DELILAH Tom Jones	3
1 May	SIMON SAYS 1910 Fruitgum Company	1
8 May	LAZY SUNDAY Small Faces	1
15 May	A MAN WITHOUT LOVE Engelbert Humperdinck	2
29 May	HONEY Bobby Goldsboro	1
5 Jun	A MAN WITHOUT LOVE Engelbert Humperdinck	1
3 Jul	SON OF HICKORY HOLLER'S TRAMP O. C. Smith	3
9 Oct	LITTLE ARROWS Leapy Lee	1
16 Oct	JESAMINE Casuals	1
20 Nov	ELOISE Barry Ryan	2
18 Dec	AIN'T GOT NO – I GOT LIFE Nina Simone	1
25 Dec	BUILD ME UP BUTTERCUP Foundations	1

1969

8 Jan	BUILD ME UP BUTTERCUP Foundations	1
2 Apr	GENTLE ON MY MIND Dean Martin	2
9 Apr	BOOM BANG A BANG Lulu	1
16 Apr	GOODBYE Mary Hopkin	1
30 Apr	GOODBYE Mary Hopkin	2
14 May	MY SENTIMENTAL FRIEND Herman's Hermits	2
28 May	MAN OF THE WORLD Fleetwood Mac	1
18 Jun	OH HAPPY DAY Edwin Hawkins Singers	2
2 Jul	IN THE GHETTO Elvis Presley	3
23 Jul	GIVE PEACE A CHANCE Plastic Ono Band	3
16 Aug	SAVED BY THE BELL Robin Gibb	2
20 Sep	DON'T FORGET TO REMEMBER Bee Gees	1
1 Nov	I'M GONNA MAKE YOU MINE Lou Christie	1
8 Nov	OH WELL Fleetwood Mac	2
22 Nov	(CALL ME) NUMBER ONE Tremeloes	2
29 Nov	YESTER-ME, YESTER-YOU, YESTERDAY Stevie Wonder	1(2=)
13 Dec	RUBY DON'T TAKE YOUR LOVE TO TOWN Kenny Rogers & First Edition	5

1970

17 Jan	SUSPICIOUS MINDS Elvis Presley	1
24 Jan	RUBY DON'T TAKE YOUR LOVE TO TOWN Kenny Rogers & First Edition	1
14 Feb	LEAVIN' ON A JET PLANE Peter Paul & Mary	1
21 Feb	LET'S WORK TOGETHER Canned Heat	1
7 Mar	I WANT YOU BACK Jackson Five	1
14 Mar	LET IT BE Beatles	1
4 Apr	KNOCK KNOCK WHO'S THERE Mary Hopkin	1
30 May	QUESTION Moody Blues	1
27 Jun	GROOVIN' WITH MR BLOE Mr Bloe	1
4 Jul	ALL RIGHT NOW Free	5
8 Aug	LOLA Kinks	1
15 Aug	NEANDERTHAL MAN Hotlegs	2
3 Oct	YOU CAN GET IT IF YOU REALLY WANT Desmond Decker	2
17 Oct	BLACK NIGHT Deep Purple	2
31 Oct	PATCHES Clarence Carter	3
12 Dec	WHEN I'M DEAD AND GONE McGuinness Flint	3

1971

23 Jan	RIDE A WHITE SWAN T. Rex	1
6 Feb	PUSHBIKE SONG Mixtures	4
13 Mar	ANOTHER DAY Paul McCartney	1
27 Mar	ANOTHER DAY Paul McCartney	1
3 Apr	BRIDGET THE MIDGET Ray Stevens	3

15 May	BROWN SUGAR/BITCH/LET IT ROCK Rolling Stones	3
5 Jun	INDIANA WANTS ME R Dean Taylor	1
12 Jun	I DID WHAT I DID FOR MARIA Tony Christie	1
26 Jun	I DID WHAT I DID FOR MARIA Tony Christie	1
3 Jul	DON'T LET IT DIE Hurricane Smith	1
10 Jul	CO-CO Sweet	2
7 Aug	NEVER ENDING SONG OF LOVE New Seekers	5
25 Sep	DID YOU EVER Nancy and Lee	1
16 Oct	TWEEDLE DEE TWEEDLE DUM Middle Of The Road	1
23 Oct	WITCH QUEEN OF NEW ORLEANS Redbone	3
20 Nov	TILL Tom Jones	1
27 Nov	JEEPSTER T. Rex	1
11 Dec	JEEPSTER T. Rex	3

1972

15 Jan	MOTHER OF MINE Neil Reid	3
4 Mar	AMERICAN PIE Don McLean	3
25 Mar	BEG STEAL OR BORROW New Seekers	3
29 Apr	BACK OFF BOOGALOO Ringo Starr	2
13 May	COME WHAT MAY Vicky Leandros	2
27 May	COULD IT BE FOREVER/CHERISH David Cassidy	1
3 Jun	ROCKET MAN Elton John	1
8 Jul	ROCK AND ROLL (PARTS I & II) Gary Glitter	3
29 Jul	SYLVIA'S MOTHER Dr Hook & the Medicine Show	1
12 Aug	SEASIDE SHUFFLE Terry Dactyl & the Dinosaurs	2
23 Sep	CHILDREN OF THE REVOLUTION T Rex	3
21 Oct	DONNA 10 CC	2
25 Nov	CRAZY HORSES Osmonds	3
16 Dec	GUDBUY T'JANE Slade	2

1973

6 Jan	SOLID GOLD EASY ACTION T Rex	1
13 Jan	THE JEAN GENIE David Bowie	1
3 Feb	DO YOU WANNA TOUCH ME (OH YEAH) Gary Glitter	2
17 Feb	PART OF THE UNION Strawbs	3
10 Mar	CINDY INCIDENTALLY Faces	1
21 Apr	HELLO HELLO I'M BACK AGAIN Gary Glitter	3
12 May	HELL RAISER Sweet	3
18 Aug	YESTERDAY ONCE MORE Carpenters	2
1 Sep	DANCING ON A SATURDAY NIGHT Barry Blue	2
22 Sep	BALLROOM BLITZ Sweet	3
13 Oct	MY FREND STAN Slade	1
10 Nov	LET ME IN Osmonds	3
1 Dec	MY COO CA CHOO Alvin Stardust	1
8 Dec	PAPER ROSES Marie Osmond	1

1974

19 Jan	THE SHOW MUST GO ON Leo Sayer	1
26 Jan	TEENAGE RAMPAGE Sweet	3
23 Mar	THE AIR THAT I BREATHE Hollies	1
30 Mar	THE MOST BEAUTIFUL GIRL Charlie Rich	1
20 Apr	THE CAT CREPT IN Mud	1
4 May	THE CAT CREPT IN Mud	1
25 May	SHANG A LANG Bay City Rollers	1
1 Jun	THIS TOWN AIN'T BIG ENOUGH FOR BOTH OF US Sparks	2
15 Jun	HEY ROCK AND ROLL Showaddywaddy	1
6 Jul	KISSIN' IN THE BACK ROW OF THE MOVIES Drifters	3
3 Aug	BORN WITH A SMILE ON MY FACE Stephanie de Sykes & Rain	1
24 Aug	YOU MAKE ME FEEL BRAND NEW Stylistics	1
7 Sep	I'M LEAVING IT UP TO YOU Donny & Marie Osmond	1
12 Oct	ROCK ME GENTLY Andy Kim	1
26 Oct	FAR FAR AWAY Slade	2
16 Nov	KILLER QUEEN Queen	2
14 Dec	OH YES YOU'RE BEAUTIFUL Gary Glitter	1
21 Dec	YOU AIN'T SEEN NOTHIN' YET Bachman Turner Overdrive	2

1975

4 Jan	WOMBLING MERRY CHRISTMAS Wombles	1
11 Jan	STREETS OF LONDON Ralph McTell	2
25 Jan	NEVER CAN SAY GOODBYE Gloria Gaynor	1
8 Feb	GOODBYE MY LOVE Glitter Band	1
15 Feb	PLEASE MR POSTMAN Carpenters	1
29 Mar	THERE'S A WHOLE LOT OF LOVING Guys and Dolls	2
12 Apr	FOX ON THE RUN Sweet	2
26 Apr	HONEY Bobby Goldsboro	1
3 May	LOVING YOU Minnie Riperton	2
14 Jun	THREE STEPS TO HEAVEN Showaddywaddy	1
12 Jul	MISTY Ray Stevens	1
13 Sep	THE LAST FAREWELL Roger Whittaker	1
20 Sep	MOONLIGHTING Leo Sayer	1
8 Nov	LOVE IS THE DRUG Roxy Music	1
29 Nov	YOU SEXY THING Hot Chocolate	3
20 Dec	THE TRAIL OF THE LONESOME PINE Laurel & Hardy	1
27 Dec	I BELIEVE IN FATHER CHRISTMAS Greg Lake	2

1976

10 Jan	THE TRAIL OF THE LONESOME PINE Laurel & Hardy	1
17 Jan	GLASS OF CHAMPAGNE Sailor	2
20 Mar	CONVOY C W McCall	1
27 Mar	LOVE REALLY HURTS WITHOUT YOU Billy Ocean	1
3 Apr	YOU SEE THE TROUBLE WITH ME Barry White	2

12 Jun	SILLY LOVE SONGS Wings	1
3 Jul	YOU JUST MIGHT SEE ME CRY Our Kid	1
10 Jul	YOUNG HEARTS RUN FREE Candi Staton	1
24 Jul	A LITTLE BIT MORE Dr Hook	5
28 Aug	LET 'EM IN Wings	3
18 Sep	THE KILLING OF GEORGIE Rod Stewart	1
25 Sep	CAN'T GET BY WITHOUT YOU Real Thing	2
23 Oct	WHEN FOREVER HAS GONE Demis Roussos	2
20 Nov	YOU MAKE ME FEEL LIKE DANCING Leo Sayer	2
11 Dec	SOMEBODY TO LOVE Queen	1

1977

5 Mar	BOOGIE NIGHTS Heatwave	1
2 Apr	GOING IN WITH MY EYES OPEN David Soul	3
23 Apr	RED LIGHT SPELLS DANGER Billy Ocean	2
7 May	SIR DUKE Stevie Wonder	1
28 May	AIN'T GONNA BUMP NO MORE Joe Tex	1
11 Jun	GOD SAVE THE QUEEN Sex Pistols	1
16 Jul	FANFARE FOR THE COMMON MAN Emerson Lake and Palmer	1
30 Jul	MA BAKER Boney M	1
20 Aug	YOU GOT WHAT IT TAKES Showaddywaddy	1
10 Sep	MAGIC FLY Space	3
15 Oct	BLACK IS BLACK La Belle Epoque	3
19 Nov	WE ARE THE CHAMPIONS Queen	3
10 Dec	FLORAL DANCE Brighouse & Rastrick Brass Band	6

1978

4 Mar	COME BACK MY LOVE Darts	1
25 Mar	DENIS Blondie	3
15 Apr	I WONDER WHY Showaddywaddy	1
3 Jun	BOY FROM NEW YORK CITY Darts	1
24 Jun	THE SMURF SONG Father Abraham & the Smurfs	6
5 Aug	SUBSTITUTE Clout	2
2 Sep	IT'S RAINING Darts	1
7 Oct	LOVE DON'T LIVE HERE ANYMORE Rose Royce	2
21 Oct	RASPUTIN Boney M	2
4 Nov	SANDY John Travolta	1
18 Nov	HOPELESSLY DEVOTED TO YOU Olivia Newton-John	2

1979

10 Feb	CHIQUITITA Abba	2
10 Mar	OLIVER'S ARMY Elvis Costello	3
31 Mar	IN THE NAVY Village People	2
14 Apr	COOL FOR CATS Squeeze	1
21 Apr	SOME GIRLS Racey	3
12 May	POP MUZIK M	2
26 May	DANCE AWAY Roxy Music	3
7 Jul	UP THE JUNCTION Squeeze	1
14 Jul	SILLY GAMES Janet Kay	2
4 Aug	CAN'T STAND LOSING YOU Police	1
8 Sep	BANG BANG B A Robertson	1
6 Oct	DREAMING Blondie	1
24 Nov	CRAZY LITTLE THING CALLED LOVE Queen	2
22 Dec	I HAVE A DREAM Abba	4

1980

19 Jan	WITH YOU I'M BORN AGAIN Billy Preston & Syreeta	2
23 Feb	AND THE BEAT GOES ON Whispers	1
5 Apr	DANCE YOURSELF DIZZY Liquid Gold	2
3 May	COMING UP Paul McCartney	1
24 May	NO DOUBT ABOUT IT Hot Chocolate	3
28 Jun	FUNKY TOWN Lipps Inc	2
2 Aug	MORE THAN I CAN SAY Leo Sayer	1
9 Aug	UPSIDE DOWN Diana Ross	2
20 Sep	ONE DAY I'LL FLY AWAY Randy Crawford	2
4 Oct	MASTERBLASTER (JAMMIN') Stevie Wonder	1
11 Oct	D.I.S.C.O. Ottawan	3
1 Nov	WHAT YOU'RE PROPOSIN' Status Quo	2

1981

10 Jan	HAPPY XMAS (WAR IS OVER) John & Yoko & Plastic Ono Band	1
17 Jan	ANTMUSIC Adam & The Ants	2
7 Feb	IN THE AIR TONIGHT Phil Collins	1
14 Feb	VIENNA Ultravox	4
14 Mar	KINGS OF THE WILD FRONTIER Adam & The Ants	1
28 Mar	KIDS IN AMERICA Kim Wilde	2
25 Apr	CHI MAI (THEME FROM THE BBC-TV SERIES 'LIFE AND TIMES OF DAVID LLOYD GEORGE') Ennio Morricone	2
9 May	STARS ON 45 Starsound	1
16 May	YOU DRIVE ME CRAZY Shakin' Stevens	4
13 Jun	MORE THAN IN LOVE Kate Robbins	1
18 Jul	STARS ON 45 (VOLUME 2) Starsound	2
8 Aug	HAPPY BIRTHDAY Stevie Wonder	1
15 Aug	HOOKED ON CLASSICS Louis Clark and the Royal Philharmonic Orchestra	2
3 Oct	INVISIBLE SUN Police	1
10 Oct	BIRDIE SONG (BIRDIE DANCE) Tweets	2
24 Oct	O SUPERMAN Laurie Anderson	1
31 Oct	HAPPY BIRTHDAY Altered Images	3
12 Dec	DADDY'S HOME Cliff Richard	4

1982

13 Feb	GOLDEN BROWN Stranglers	2
6 Mar	MICKEY Toni Basil	2
3 Apr	JUST AN ILLUSION Imagination	1
17 Apr	AIN'T NO PLEASING YOU Chas and Dave	1
1 May	ONE STEP FURTHER Bardo	1
8 May	THIS TIME WE'LL GET IT RIGHT/WE'LL FLY THE FLAG England World Cup Squad	1

22 May	ONLY YOU Yazoo	1
19 Jun	TORCH Soft Cell	1
10 Jul	ABRACADABRA Steve Miller Band	2
24 Jul	DA DA DA Trio	1
11 Sep	SAVE A PRAYER Duran Duran	1
18 Sep	PRIVATE INVESTIGATIONS Dire Straits	1
25 Sep	THE BITTEREST PILL (I EVER HAD TO SWALLOW) Jam	2
9 Oct	ZOOM Fat Larry's Band	1
30 Oct	ANNIE I'M NOT YOUR DADDY Kid Creole & the Coconuts	1
13 Nov	HEARTBREAKER Dionne Warwick	2
27 Nov	MIRROR MAN Human League	3
25 Dec	SHAKIN' STEVENS EP Shakin' Stevens	1

As will be clear from the dates of these unsuccessful number twos, some records were 2= for one or more weeks.

MOST WEEKS AT NUMBER TWO BY AN 'UNSUCCESSFUL' SINGLE IN TOTAL

8 Theme from 'Limelight' FRANK CHACKSFIELD
7 Love Letters In The Sand PAT BOONE
6 The Smurf Song FATHER ABRAHAM & THE SMURFS
Are You Sure ALLISONS
Floral Dance BRIGHOUSE AND RASTRICK BRASS BAND
Ruby Don't Take Your Love To Town KENNY ROGERS & FIRST EDITION
5 As Long As He Needs Me SHIRLEY BASSEY
Don't Forbid Me PAT BOONE
Pretend NAT 'KING' COLE
All Right Now FREE
A Little Bit More DR HOOK
Cool Water FRANKIE LAINE
Never Ending Song Of Love NEW SEEKERS
The Happy Wanderer OBERNKIRCHEN CHILDREN'S CHOIR
Ma He's Making Eyes At Me JOHNNY OTIS SHOW
Learnin' The Blues FRANK SINATRA
Santo Natale DAVID WHITFIELD

The most consecutive weeks at number two is 6, a record jointly held by 'The Smurf Song' and 'Floral Dance'.

Only one record has ever reached number two on two totally separate occasions. 'Honey' by Bobby Goldsboro reached number two on 29 May 1968 for one week. It returned to number two as a re-issue on 26 April 1975, almost 7 years later. Fleetwood Mac's 'Albatross', a number one hit when originally released, climbed to number two as a re-issue.

MOST 'UNSUCCESSFUL' NUMBER TWOS

9	CLIFF RICHARD	(20 wks)
9	ELVIS PRESLEY	(19 wks)
5	SWEET	(13 wks)
4	PAT BOONE	(17 wks)
4	BEATLES	(10 wks)
4	GARY GLITTER	(9 wks)
4	TOM JONES	(9 wks)
4	T. REX	(9 wks)
4	QUEEN	(8 wks)
4	HOLLIES	(7 wks)
4	DEAN MARTIN	(7 wks)
4	EVERLY BROTHERS	(6 wks)
4	LEO SAYER	(5 wks)
4	SHOWADDYWADDY	(4 wks)
4	STEVIE WONDER	(4 wks)
3	FRANKIE LAINE	(11 wks)
3	NAT 'KING' COLE	(9 wks)
3	KINKS	(5 wks)
3	SLADE	(5 wks)
3	DARTS	(3 wks)
3	GUY MITCHELL	(3 wks)

Paul McCartney has had a further two number twos with Wings and two as a solo act, bringing to eight the number of number two hits he has written and performed on.

MOST WEEKS AT NUMBER TWO BY AN ACT THAT HAS NEVER REACHED NUMBER ONE

The record for being so near yet so far is held by

NAT 'KING' COLE **9 weeks**
FRANK CHACKSFIELD **8 weeks**
DRIFTERS **7 weeks**
FATHER ABRAHAM & THE SMURFS **6 weeks**
ALLISONS **6 weeks**
BRIGHOUSE & RASTRICK BRASS BAND **6 weeks**
FREE **5 weeks**
OBERNKIRCHEN CHILDREN'S CHOIR **5 weeks**
STEVIE WONDER **4 weeks**

DARTS Still waiting for that number one bus?
TOM JONES Three consecutive number twos in 1967/68 for the Welshman who had previously gone straight to the top with his first chart entry

MOST CONSECUTIVE NUMBER TWOS

The hat-trick has been performed three times, as follows

TOM JONES	I'll Never Fall In Love Again, I'm Coming Home, Delilah	1967 to 1968
SWEET	Hell Raiser, Ballroom Blitz, Teenage Rampage	1973 to 1974
DARTS	Come Back My Love, Boy From New York City, It's Raining	1978
	Darts never had a number one hit.	

CONSECUTIVE HITS OF THE SAME SIZE

Number one hat-tricks are comparatively common, the number two hat-trick has been achieved three times, but what of a hat-trick of lower placings? They have been performed as follows

Three consecutive number 3 hits:
CLIFF RICHARD Theme For A Dream, A Girl Like You, When The Girl In Your Arms Is The Girl In Your Heart

Three consecutive number 6 hits:
ELECTRIC LIGHT ORCHESTRA
Mr Blue Sky, Wild West Hero, Sweet Talkin' Woman

Four consecutive number 9 hits:
CRAIG DOUGLAS
A Hundred Pounds Of Clay, Time, When My Little Girl Is Smiling, Our Favourite Melodies

An unofficial release, 'Gee Whiz It's You', reached number 4 for Cliff between 'Theme For A Dream' and 'A Girl Like You'.

Between 'Time' and 'When My Little Girl Is Smiling', Craig Douglas released two singles that never made the chart at all.

No hat-trick of rankings of any other chart position has ever been achieved. Some acts have come very close. Nat 'King' Cole had six consecutive hits whose highest chart positions were 28, 21, 24, 22, 23, 23. Frank Ifield had four consecutive chart entries that peaked at 25, 26, 25, 24. Karl Denver (33, 32, 32), David Essex (24, 24, 23), Jonathan King (23, 23, 22) and Dean Martin (20, 21, 21) came within one position of the elusive hat-trick. Generation X, with successive hits rising to 62, 62, and 60, very nearly achieved the first hat-trick outside the Top Fifty.

LEAST SUCCESSFUL CHART ACTS

During the period from 10 March 1960 to 6 May 1978, when a Top Fifty was published, there were thirteen acts whose entire chart career consisted of one week at number 50. These acts ranged from Chaquito, whose version of 'Never On Sunday' was the fifth most successful of five chart versions of that song, to Tony Hatch, whose success as a writer and producer of hits far outdid his triumphs as a recording artist. The full list of these thirteen acts is given in the second edition of *The Guinness Book of British Hit Singles*, page 314.

Since the inauguration of the Top 75 on 6 May 1978, two acts have enjoyed a chart career consisting of only one week at number 75. These two acts are **ANGELWITCH**, No. 75 with SWEET DANGER (EMI 5064) on 7 June 1980 and **GRAND PRIX**, No. 75 with KEEP ON BELIEVING (RCA 162) on 27 Feb 1982.

Although they have secured for themselves the ignominious title of Least Successful Chart Acts ever, they can take comfort from the fact that some great popular music names – Led Zeppelin, Mothers of Invention and Jerry Butler to name but three – have never had a British Hit Single of any size.

GRAND PRIX The least successful chart act but still more singles success than Led Zeppelin!

MOST WEEKS ON CHART (RECORDINGS)

a) Total Weeks Irrespective of the number of re-issues or re-entries.

Weeks	Separate Chart Runs	
122	9	MY WAY Frank Sinatra
67	8	AMAZING GRACE Judy Collins
57	8	ROCK AROUND THE CLOCK * Bill Haley
56	1	RELEASE ME * Engelbert Humperdinck
55	1	STRANGER ON THE SHORE Acker Bilk
47	2	I LOVE YOU BECAUSE Jim Reeves
44	5	LET'S TWIST AGAIN Chubby Checker
41	5	DECK OF CARDS Wink Martindale
40	1	RIVERS OF BABYLON/BROWN GIRL IN THE RING * Boney M
40	2	TIE A YELLOW RIBBON ROUND THE OLD OAK TREE * Dawn

40	2	A SCOTTISH SOLDIER Andy Stewart
39	3	HE'LL HAVE TO GO Jim Reeves
38	2	SOMEWHERE MY LOVE Mike Sammes Singers
36	1	I BELIEVE * Frankie Laine
36	1	I PRETEND * Des O'Connor
35	2	AND I LOVE YOU SO Perry Como
35	2	ALBATROSS * Fleetwood Mac
35	2	HOUND DOG Elvis Presley
35	4	ALL RIGHT NOW Free
34	1	CHIRPY CHIRPY CHEEP CHEEP * Middle Of The Road
34	3	HEARTBREAK HOTEL Elvis Presley
34	3	JE T'AIME . . . MOI NON PLUS * Jane Birkin & Serge Gainsbourg
34	3	LEADER OF THE PACK Shangri-Las
34	3	NIGHTS IN WHITE SATIN Moody Blues
33	2	SHE LOVES YOU * Beatles
32	2	LET'S DANCE Chris Montez
31	2	SAILING * Rod Stewart
30	1	AS LONG AS HE NEEDS ME Shirley Bassey
30	1	SIDE SADDLE * Russ Conway
30	1	THEME FROM 'A SUMMER PLACE' Percy Faith
30	1	JUST LOVING YOU Anita Harris
30	2	YOUNG GIRL * Gary Puckett & Union Gap
30	2	PARANOID Black Sabbath
30	3	TAINTED LOVE * Soft Cell
30	4	MY BROTHER JAKE Free

* *indicates record was a number one hit.*

ROCK AROUND THE CLOCK enjoyed a further five weeks chart success in 1981 in shortened form as part of HALEY'S GOLDEN MEDLEY.

b) Consecutive weeks

56 RELEASE ME Engelbert Humperdinck
55 STRANGER ON THE SHORE Acker Bilk
42 MY WAY Frank Sinatra
40 RIVERS OF BABYLON/BROWN GIRL IN THE RING Boney M
39 TIE A YELLOW RIBBON ROUND THE OLD OAK TREE Dawn
39 I LOVE YOU BECAUSE Jim Reeves
38 A SCOTTISH SOLDIER Andy Stewart
36 I BELIEVE Frankie Laine
36 I PRETEND Des O'Connor
34 CHIRPY CHIRPY CHEEP CHEEP Middle Of The Road
32 AMAZING GRACE Judy Collins
31 SHE LOVES YOU Beatles
31 AND I LOVE YOU SO Perry Como
30 AS LONG AS HE NEEDS ME Shirley Bassey
30 SIDE SADDLE Russ Conway
30 THEME FROM 'A SUMMER PLACE' Percy Faith
30 JUST LOVING YOU Anita Harris

MOST WEEKS ON CHART BY A SONG IN ALL ITS RECORDED VERSIONS

This list shows the most successful songs chart-wise from 1952 to 1980. Only complete recordings of the songs count – parts of songs in medley discs are disqualified.

Weeks Chart Versions

163 MY WAY **4** all vocal
94 AMAZING GRACE **2** one vocal one instrumental
70 ROCK AROUND THE CLOCK **3** all vocal
67 ONLY YOU **6** all vocal
66 MACK THE KNIFE **6** five vocal, one instrumental
65 STRANGER ON THE SHORE **2** one vocal, one instrumental
61 UNCHAINED MELODY **6** five vocal, one instrumental
56 DECK OF CARDS **2** both vocal
56 RELEASE ME **1** vocal
54 I BELIEVE **3** all vocal
54 JE T'AIME . . . MOI NON PLUS/LOVE AT FIRST SIGHT **3** two vocal, one instrumental
51 IT'S ONLY MAKE BELIEVE **4** all vocal
50 LET'S TWIST AGAIN **2** both vocal.

'It's Only Make Believe' (written by Conway Twitty and Jack Nance) is the only song in British chart history to have been a Top Ten hit in four different versions, at four different times.

Five songs have hit the charts in six different versions. They are: 'Unchained Melody' (written by Alex North and Hy Zaret), 'Mack The Knife' (Theme From *The Threepenny Opera*) (written by Bertholt Brecht and Kurt Weill, English lyrics by Marc Blitzstein), 'Stranger In Paradise' (written by Robert Wright and George Forrest, based on a theme by Aleksandr Borodin), 'White Christmas' (written by Irving Berlin) and 'Only You' (written by Buck Ram and Ande Rande). 'White Christmas' is one of two songs to have been hits in five different years. The other song is '(I Can't Get No) Satisfaction' (written by Mick Jagger and Keith Richard).

Six songs have reached number one in two different versions: 'Answer Me' (Frankie Laine and David Whitfield), 'Cherry Pink And Apple Blossom White' (Perez Prado and Eddie Calvert), 'Singing The Blues' (Guy Mitchell and Tommy Steele), 'Young Love' (Tab Hunter and Donny Osmond), 'Mary's Boy Child' (Harry Belafonte and Boney M) and 'This Ole House' (Rosemary Clooney and Shakin' Stevens).

The most commonly used title for British Hit Singles are 'Guilty', 'Here I Go Again', 'Star', and 'Tonight'. Each of these titles has been used for five completely different hit songs. 'Woman In Love' (Frankie Laine and Barbra Streisand) and 'Forever And Ever' (Demis Roussos and Slik) are the only titles used more than once for different number one hits.

1981

In the past some readers have questioned whether a weeks on chart table is the best way to reflect the relative popularity of pop stars through the years. There is an inevitable occasional distortion, such as in 1969, when the lengthy run of 'My Way' made it appear that Frank Sinatra had had a more successful year than the Beatles, who had scored two number ones. But these quirks tend to even themselves out in time and, even in the course of only a single year, weeks on chart seems a remarkably accurate way of measuring an act's success.

1981 is a perfect example. **Adam and the Ants** dominated the table, and it is certainly true that they ruled the singles scene. They scored two of the year's top three sellers, 'Stand and Deliver' and 'Prince Charming', being beaten to the number one spot only by Soft Cell's 'Tainted Love'. They had three hits from *Kings of the Wild Frontier*, including the title track, a minor entry in the summer of 1980 but a top ten hit during the Antmania of '81. Even

ADAM AND THE ANTS who dominated 1981 with two of the year's three bestsellers

back catalogue material on different labels came into the charts as companies realised there was gold in them thar anthills. The re-issue of Decca's 'Young Parisians' went Top Ten, even though it featured a completely different sound from the double drumming that characterised the 1981 releases. No artist had registered as many weeks on chart in one year since Engelbert Humperdinck in 1967.

One of the great heroes of 1967, **John Lennon**, returned to chart distinction in 1981 under the saddest circumstances. An unprecedented demand for his sole recordings followed his murder in December 1980, and he wound up with the second highest total of weeks on chart in 1981, all achieved posthumously. This sum gave him a dramatic entry in the all-time table, which is found elsewhere in this section.

Lennon achieved the fastest hat-trick of number ones ever when '(Just Like) Starting Over', 'Imagine' and 'Woman' all made it with only **St. Winifred's School Choir** interrupting. When 'Woman' followed 'Imagine' it was the first time an act had replaced itself at number one since the Beatles did it in 1963.

The public can only be obsessed by one or two artists at a time, and in 1981 it was time for the **Police** to relinquish the reputation as automatic number ones to Adam and the Ants. (This assumed position is always inflated; the Police had only actually accumulated three number ones prior to 1981, and the Ants two during it.) The trendily tressed trio managed four hits in the year, but only 1 week at number one. Another firm favourite, the **Specials**, broke up with a bang, leaving the scene with a number one, 'Ghost Town', which seemed an eerily appropriate commentary on the urban disturbances which occurred while the single was a hit. The Specials would unexpectedly issue a more overt and less successful political song, 'War Crimes', in late 1982.

Motown enjoyed its first consecutive number ones in June when **Michael Jackson's** re-activated 'One Day In Your Life' replaced **Smokey Robinson's** 'Being With You'. Other soloists to achieve their first number ones included **Shakin' Stevens** and **Julio Iglesias**. It was likely that the rock revivalist was the globe's leading English-speaking seller of singles in 1981, in spite of being shut out in the American market. Iglesias was reputed to be the most marketed man in the universe, though actual sales figures were never forthcoming.

Technopop, the synthesiser style which threatened to make the electric guitar obsolete, made major inroads, particularly with the big ballad 'Vienna' by **Ultravox**, successes by **Orchestral Manoeuvres in the Dark**, the aforementioned 'Tainted Love', and four hit singles from one album by the **Human League**. The last of the quartet from *Dare*, 'Don't You Want Me', was the Christmas number one, and ultimately achieved 5 weeks on top. That 1981 should have produced six singles which led the list for at least 4 weeks was a healthy sign, indicating the presence of substance in the field. The last year in which this figure had been observed was 1978, a vintage time which had seen a historic level of sales.

1982

No single act paced the pack in 1982 like **Adam and the Ants** had the previous year, least of all the defending champions themselves. Shortly after giving 'Marco Merrick, Terry Lee, Gary Tibbs and yours truly' name checks in 'Ant Rap', Adam gave them their notice, though the exact dynamics of the clash have never been revealed. Only Marco remained when Adam recorded 'Goody Two Shoes' with production assistance from Chris Hughes (a.k.a.Merrick). That Ant should enjoy a number one with his first solo single, and that he should experience his long-awaited US breakthrough with the same disc, was exciting. For chart-watchers it was equally enthralling that Adam became the first artist ever to have four chart records in one year all about himself. No tears should be shed for Chris Hughes: another co-production of his, **Tears For Fears'** 'Mad World', was one of the year's top twenty sellers.

'Come On Eileen' by **Dexy's Midnight Runners and the Emerald Express** outsold the lot. Dexy's return was dramatic for a group whose low profile had become almost subterranean after their 1980 breakthrough. The 'Come On' comeback overshadowed the feats of 'Fame', the year's number two. 'Remember, remember, remember, remember', the chorus chanted on **Irene Cara's** smash. Who could forget when **The Kids From Fame** followed with two Top Ten hits of their own? This was the first occasion in chart history when what could be assumed to be the follow-ups to a number one record were not by the actual artist who made the number one. Cara herself had been stuck without a UK distribution deal for her own discs during the crucial period after she scaled the summit.

With Adam and the Ants unwilling and John Lennon unable to consolidate their 1981 feats, **Soft Cell** assumed the vacant top spot in the weeks on chart table, admittedly with a far less spectacular sum. The distinctive duo made their mark with three new Top Ten hits, a less distinguished year ender, and the continued long run of 1981's national number one, 'Tainted Love'. The latter title was a phenomenon, breaking Marc Almond and David Ball around the world. In the United States 'Tainted Love' stayed on the *Billboard* Hot 100 for 43 consecutive weeks, an all-time record, though the dance favourite still had a way to go to top Bing Crosby's cumulative total of 72 weeks with 'White Christmas'.

Even the act that came in second would find its placing difficult to believe. From the perspective of members of **Japan**, 1982 was a year of increased solo activities preceding a band break-up. From the point of view of their former label, it was a time to take advantage of the success achieved with another company, and Japan material of various vintages flowed. Fans took it all in. 'Saki it to me', they seemed to be saying, going for an old re-make of Smokey Robinson and the Miracles' 'I Second That Emotion' as readily as the trancelike 'Ghosts'.

KEVIN ROWLAND'S DEXY'S MIDNIGHT RUNNERS outsold the lot in 1982

By entering at number one with 'Beat Surrender' the **Jam** tied Slade as the only act to come in on top three times, a glorious goodbye. (It should be pointed out that the Beatles often vaulted to number one in their second week, suggesting that Parlophone marketing men were not attempting to match release dates with the beginning of chart weeks as Polydor's people often did.) The Jam's fourth number one put them joint tenth on the all-time list of Most Number One Hits.

In what cannot be a coincidence, 'Town Called Malice/Precious', their early 1982 topper, was their third straight number one to appear in the Fewest Weeks on Chart By a Number One Disc table, and the fall of 'Beat Surrender' at the end of the year suggested it might follow suit. 'Over and Out' would be an apt title for the story of the Jam's number one hits.

In one of the year's odder developments, one and a half number ones were sung by someone other than the credited artist. **Tight Fit's** 'The Lion Sleeps Tonight' was yodelled by the uncredited Roy Ward, and the Renee on 'Save Your Love' was not the woman featured in the **Renee and Renato** video. She had said *arrivederci* before the record became the Christmas number one.